A HISTORY OF ENGLISH LAW

A HISTORY OF ENGLISH LAW

IN SIXTEEN VOLUMES

For List of Volumes and Scheme of the History, see pp. ix-x

A HISTORY
OF ENGLISH LAW

BY

SIR WILLIAM HOLDSWORTH
O.M., K.C., D.C.L., HON. LL.D.

LATE VINERIAN PROFESSOR OF ENGLISH LAW IN THE UNIVERSITY OF OXFORD; FELLOW
OF ALL SOULS COLLEGE, OXFORD; HON. FELLOW OF ST. JOHN'S COLLEGE,
OXFORD; FOREIGN ASSOCIATE OF THE ROYAL BELGIAN ACADEMY;
FELLOW OF THE BRITISH ACADEMY; BENCHER OF LINCOLN'S INN

VOLUME XIII

EDITED BY

A. L. GOODHART
K.B.E., K.C., D.C.L., LL.D.

AND

H. G. HANBURY
D.C.L.

*To say truth, although it is not necessary for counsel to know what
the history of a point is, but to know how it now stands resolved, yet it is a
wonderful accomplishment, and, without it, a lawyer cannot be accounted
learned in the law.* ROGER NORTH

METHUEN & CO. LTD. LONDON
36 Essex Street, Strand, W.C. 2

First published in 1952
Reprinted 1971

SBN 421 05130 2/10

REPRODUCED AND PRINTED IN GREAT BRITAIN BY
REDWOOD PRESS LIMITED
TROWBRIDGE & LONDON

TO

THE MEMORY OF MY SON

FLIGHT-LIEUTENANT R. W. G. HOLDSWORTH, R.A.F.V.R.

STOWELL FELLOW AND DEAN OF UNIVERSITY COLLEGE, OXFORD

WHO WAS KILLED IN THE WAR TO DEFEND HIS COUNTRY

AND CIVILIZATION FROM THE INNATE AND

INCORRIGIBLE SAVAGERY OF THE GERMAN PEOPLE

THIS AND THE REMAINING VOLUME OF THIS HISTORY

ARE DEDICATED

PREFACE

MORE than a decade has passed since the appearance of volume XII of Holdsworth's great history, and seven years have elapsed since his death. He left his life-work unfinished, but fortunately the entire material for the thirteenth and most of the material for the fourteenth volumes had reached an advanced stage of preparation. On his literary executors has devolved the honourable and congenial task of arranging this mass of material for the press.

Holdsworth's account, in earlier volumes, of certain branches of the law, for instance, conspiracy and maintenance, stretched far into the present century, but in general his final goal for the entire history was the Judicature Act, 1873. The thirteenth volume covers the period from 1793 to the Reform Act, 1832.

The volume is a complete whole, and is all Holdsworth's own, apart from two omissions which his editors have supplied. These are the commentaries on Tidd's *Practice* and Maddock's *Equity*, whose compilation he clearly postponed until too late. His editors have also drawn up a Table of Contents, following, as exactly as possible, the model of earlier volumes.

The subject matter of the volume is a continuation of Part I of Book V, whose title is "the Centuries of Settlement and Reform, 1701-1875 : Sources and General Development." Over the greater part of it broods the figure of Jeremy Bentham. Holdsworth sketches the background from which the ideas of Bentham emerged, and then proceeds to give us a full account of his life, work and influence. He then proceeds to discuss some of the other pioneers of philosophic radicalism, notably James Mill, and their chief opponents, outstanding among whom was Coleridge.

Next comes a study of the Political and Constitutional Background, which is divided into three periods, (*a*) from 1793 to the death of Pitt in 1806, (*b*) 1806-1815, (*c*) from 1815 to the Reform Act, 1832. We are presented with a vivid picture of the chief events, and of the parts played by leading politicians, Pitt himself, Fox, Perceval, Liverpool, and especially Brougham, whose complex character fascinated Holdsworth, and of whom he gives us a prolonged survey.

Then we are introduced to reforms in different branches of the law, and presented with a detailed appraisal of the achievements of such men as Romilly, Mackintosh, Michael Angelo Taylor, C. P. Cooper and Humphreys. This is followed by an exhaustive analysis of contemporary legislation. The study of the professional development of law, equity, and the various subjects of the civilians' practice, with which the volume ends, supplies a vivid reminder of the method which Holdsworth, both as writer and as teacher, persistently employed, of treating legal history as largely dependent on legal biography. A host of names are here passed in review. These belong partly to reporters, partly to writers of text-books, but principally to judges. The greatest judicial figures are, of course, Ellenborough and Tenterden on the common law side, Eldon on the equity side, and Stowell on the civilian side.

Such is, in barest outline, the composition of a volume which will serve to perpetuate the memory of one who was, in life, the greatest exponent of English Law.

The editors are in possession of much, though not, unfortunately, of all the material for the fourteenth volume, which brings the history down to the Judicature Acts, 1873-1875. Part I, on " Sources and General Development " is almost intact : what is missing is the greater portion of Part II, on " The Rules of Law ". The manuscript shows, however, that this portion was not intended to be very protracted. The work of preparing the available material for press is going forward.

The heartiest thanks of the editors are due to Dr. J. B. Jaworczykowski, of University College, Oxford, and Leon Fellow, London University, who shouldered the very arduous task of the compilation of the Indices, and Tables of Cases and Statutes. The labour, moreover, expended by him in checking references was prodigious, whereby he placed the editors yet further in his debt.

A. L. GOODHART
H. G. HANBURY

Oxford, 1952

PLAN OF THE HISTORY

CONTENTS

BOOK V (*Continued*)

PART I

SOURCES AND GENERAL DEVELOPMENT (*Continued*)

CHAPTER IV

FROM SETTLEMENT TO REFORM (1793-1832)

xi

CONTENTS   xix

CONTENTS

CONTENTS

LIST OF CASES

LIST OF STATUTES

BOOK V *(Continued)*
(1701-1875)
THE CENTURIES OF SETTLEMENT AND
REFORM

A HISTORY OF ENGLISH LAW

PART I

SOURCES AND GENERAL DEVELOPMENT

(*Continued*)

CHAPTER IV

FROM SETTLEMENT TO REFORM
(1793-1832)

IN January 1794 one of Bentham's correspondents, writing from Dresden, said : " The French Revolution, notwithstanding its atrocities, has produced a kind of revolution in the human mind in Europe, and mankind think on many points as they never thought before." [1] Forty-five years later Carlyle endorsed this verdict. He said : " The French Revolution is seen . . . as the crowning phenomenon of our Modern Time ; the inevitable stern end of much ; the fearful, but also wonderful, indispensable and sternly beneficent beginning of much. He who would understand the struggling convulsive unrest of European society, in any and every country, at this day, may read it in broad glaring lines there, in that most convulsive phenomenon of the last thousand years." [2] In England, as abroad, the fundamental character of the French Revolution was not immediately recognized. When, taught by Burke, Englishmen began to recognize its true character,[3] the Whig party was split ;[4] and when, in spite of Pitt's efforts, war broke out with France, England definitely ranged herself amongst its opponents. Nevertheless England could not escape its influence. For its influence was due not only to the political and literary pre-eminence of France,[5] but also to the fact that before the Revolution both the intellectual and material foundations of eighteenth-century society were being undermined all over Europe. New political ideas, new ideas as to religion, new economic ideas, and new ideas as to the reforms needed in the law

[1] Bentham, Works x 299.
[2] Chartism, Critical and Miscellaneous Essays vi 137-138.
[3] Vol. x 95 ; below 13, 14.
[4] Vol. x 124 ; below 8, 13, 16, 157, 288.   [5] Vol. x 3, 16.

had made their appearance, and England had felt their impact.[1]
The French Revolution gave a wider currency and an enormously
increased practical importance to these ideas. Their open discussion by advocates and opponents, and the controversies
aroused by attempts to put them into practice or to suppress
them, introduced a new world of thought on all these topics,
which affected England as deeply as it affected all other
European countries.

We have seen that, at the end of the eighteenth century, a
school of radical reformers had arisen in England.[2] The American
War of Independence, and the grant of a large measure of auton-
omy to Ireland had given an impetus to the new political ideas
preached by such writers as Rousseau and Hume and Priestley
and Price, and had led to the advocacy of projects for Parliamentary reform, shorter Parliaments, and a uniform and extended
franchize. The new religious ideas, which were either atheistic or
deistic in character, had made their appearance in England in the
eighteenth century ;[3] and, after the French Revolution, Paine's
Age of Reason had a considerable circulation in spite of the
prosecution of its publisher.[4] But these anti-Christian ideas
never had much influence in England ; for we have seen that the
revolt against social and moral evils, which in France had led to
atheism or deism, in England had led to the religious revival of
the Methodists,[5] and the formation of that " Clapham Sect,"[6]
the leaders of which secured the abolition first of the slave trade
and then of slavery itself, and, in alliance with the followers of
Bentham,[7] did good work in the crusade for humanizing the rules
of English law. The new economic ideas contained in Adam
Smith's *Wealth of Nations* had begun to influence the Legislature.[8] Though modified to some extent by Malthus's *Essay on
Population*,[9] they were generally accepted, and converted by
Ricardo and his followers into a rigid pseudo-scientific system.[10]
The new ideas as to law reform preached by Beccaria[11] and
Helvetius[12] had found in Bentham an advocate who was destined
to leave deep marks on the public and private law of England ;
for, as we shall see, he aimed at creating a new science by the
principles of which all existing legal rules could be tested and new
rules could be evolved.[13] The thinkers who were elaborating these

[1] " It has been easy to ascribe to the contagion of French example political
movements which were already beginning in England and which were modified
rather than materially altered by our share in the great European convulsion,"
Leslie Stephen, The English Utilitarians i 121.

[2] Vol. x 116-118.   [3] Ibid 11 n. 4.   [4] Below 18.

[5] Vol. x 12 ; cp. Sorel, L'Europe et la Revolution Française i 355-356.

[6] For this sect see J. Stephen, Essays in Ecclesiastical Biography ii 287-383 ;
below 183.

[7] Dicey, Law and Opinion 398-404.   [8] Vol. x 121 ; vol. xi 393-394.

[9] Below 27, 31 seqq.   [10] Below 30 seqq.   [11] Vol. xi 575-578.

[12] Below 41, 42.   [13] Below 76, 77, 131.

new ideas as to law and other reforms found a home in Shelburne's house ;[1] and there were then many who, like Pitt [2] and Gibbon,[3] favoured reforms based on some of these ideas, but who later, owing to the fear of the spread in England of French revolutionary ideas, became their opponents.[4]

All these ideas had begun to influence public opinion in England at the end of the eighteenth and the beginning of the nineteenth centuries. Though they had produced little practical effect during the war years,[5] many of them had exerted an increasing influence after 1815,[6] and had produced the reforms in the law needed to give effect to them before 1832.[7] The fact that the Whig victory in 1831 accelerated their reception and more especially the movement for reform in all branches of the law, was due primarily to the Reform Act which gave a greatly increased Parliamentary influence to their supporters.[8] But it was also due in part to the fact that James Mill had reduced the new political economic and legal ideas of Bentham and Ricardo to an ethical and philosophic system.[9] That system which is known as " philosophic radicalism " [10] was a compact body of doctrine which put all these new ideas on a philosophic basis. Its leaders advocated democratic principles, and they justified these principles on grounds which were more rational, though hardly less questionable, than Rousseau's and Paine's theories of natural rights.[11] They reduced the new economic ideas to so rigid and logical a system that the injustices caused by the attempt to apply it rigidly had begun to excite opposition.[12] They advocated wholesale reforms of the legal system by means of the Legislature in order to give effect to the many detailed deductions which Bentham had drawn from his principle of utility.[13] They were definitely non-Christian—though they were careful not to parade this fact ;[14] and they advocated a system of national and secular education.[15]

These new ideas naturally aroused opposition of many different kinds. But in order to combat them new arguments were necessary, and old arguments must be readjusted. The need for these new arguments and for the readjustment of old arguments

---

[1] Vol. x 117 ; Camb. Mod. Hist. viii 755 ; below 274.

[2] Vol. x 117 ; below 101, 157, 158.   [3] Vol. xii 730, 754.   [4] Below 157, 158.

[5] Below 167, 188.   [6] Below 194, 195.   [7] Below 259 seqq.   [8] Below 308.

[9] " Benthamism was a coherent system ; its ethics, its constitutional theories, its jurisprudence, and its political economy were indissolubly linked together, and were indeed different aspects of one and the same theory of life and human nature. The creed owed its power in part to the large element of truth . . . which it contained, in part to its self-consistency and to the clearness and precision of its dogmas, and in part also to the unbounded faith of its adherents," Dicey, Law and Opinion 443.

[10] Below 134 seqq.   [11] Below 10-13, 138.   [12] Below 140, 144 seqq.

[13] Below 138-141.   [14] Below 139.   [15] Below 139.

became pressing after 1815 ; for the cessation of war conditions emphasized the need for reforms, and made it impossible to meet all suggestions for reform by a blank *non possumus.* It is for these reasons that the French Revolution, the new ideas which it let loose and the new political and economic conditions which were emerging, " transformed party." [1] We begin to see a new conservative party emerging from the old Tory party, and a new liberal party emerging from the old Whig party, which will hold an intermediate position between the new conservative party and the party which desired still more radical reforms.

The new alignment of parties, caused by the new conditions and the new ideas, shows us that the reception of these new ideas, and the character of the opposition to them, was determined by the past history of England, by her economic position, by her legal institutions, and by her resulting intellectual outlook.

The new political ideas which advocated the importation of democratic principles into the constitution were suppressed during the Napoleonic wars. [2] As Romilly said, the higher classes were opposed to all reform, and the lower classes advocated impossible changes. [3] After 1815 the democratic principle was advocated by the philosophic radicals, but upon grounds very different from Paine's theory of natural rights. Bentham and his followers poured scorn on the theory of natural rights. [4] They advocated a democratic form of government upon the ground that any other form of government would take account only of the interests of those who had political power, and would neglect the interests of the people. [5] And thus, although the theory of natural rights was not lost sight of, though it still continued to inspire the democratic cause, [6] it was to a considerable extent replaced by this new theory which, as Dicey has pointed out, gives less security against the tyranny of the majority than the theory based on natural rights. [7]

It gradually became apparent that the reform of Parliament was the first step towards a more democratic form of government. Many plans of reform small and large were suggested and discussed during the first two decades of the nineteenth century. [8] The plan adopted in 1831 [9] was to some extent a radical plan ; but it stopped far short of the radical demand for universal suffrage and short Parliaments. Grey wished to save as much of the old order as he could by a timely concession which swept away the rotten boroughs, gave power to the middle classes, and would, he hoped, be a final settlement. [10] His plan was denounced by the Tories who

---

[1] Feiling, The Second Tory Party 184.   [2] Below 221, 249, 250.
[3] Memoirs ii 537, cited vol. x 19 n. 3.   [4] Below 22, 56.
[5] Below 138, 139.   [6] Above 2.   [7] Law and Opinion 308-309.
[8] Below 239-241.   [9] Below 247 seqq.
[10] Below 257 ; Davis, Age of Grey and Peel 227-228.

deplored the predominance which it gave to the middle classes,[1] and foretold, as its result, the destruction of the Monarchy, the Church, and the House of Lords.[2] It was welcomed by the radicals who saw that the uniformity of the franchize introduced by it would lead to successful agitation to lower it, and so introduce a larger and larger measure of democracy. " The Reform Bills," said Place,[3] " are in themselves of little value, but as a commencement of the breaking up of the old rotten system they are invaluable." Grey's hope that his settlement would be final was soon frustrated ; but his plan did save much of the old order, and enabled it to play a changed but considerable part in the new ordering of the constitution which the Reform Act introduced. For some time to come the landowners retained their influence, the King and the House of Lords retained some of their powers, and the Church was not disestablished. It was due to the conservative elements in Grey's plan that it was possible for Dicey to say in 1905 that " democracy in England has to a great extent inherited the traditions of the aristocratic government, of which it is the heir."[4] On the other hand, the Tory view was right in that the Act did mean the diminution of the independent powers of the King and the House of Lords—it did mean the end of the balanced eighteenth-century constitution ; and the radicals were right in that the bill did lead to successive lowerings of the franchize in the century which followed its enactment. The result of the simplification of the political institutions of the state and of the many other reforms which were effected in the nineteenth century, has been the realization in practice of the sovereignty of a Legislature which has come to be the delegate of a pure democracy.[5]

The new deistic or atheistic ideas made for increasing toleration of rival creeds, and even of men with no religious creed. But we have seen that, otherwise, they had little direct influence in England.[6] On the other hand religious differences helped to spread the new political, economic, and legal ideas. We have seen that the disabilities under which the Protestant dissenters still suffered led them to look critically at the existing constitution of the state and the established church.[7] The Protestant dissenters, Price and Priestley, were amongst the advocates of radical reforms[8]—Price's sermon was the immediate occasion of Burke's great book on the French Revolution ;[9] and throughout this period the movement in favour of complete

---

[1] Below 256; for Coleridge's view see R. J. White, Political Thought, S. T. Coleridge 231, cited below 149.
[2] Below 257.   [3] Graham Wallas, Life of Francis Place 326.
[4] Law and Opinion 58.
[5] Vol. x 22 ; Maine, Popular Government 169 ; Dicey, Law and Opinion 309.
[6] Above 4.   [7] Vol. x 116-117.   [8] Ibid 116-117.   [9] Below 13.

religious toleration gathered strength, until its victory in 1829 split the Tory party [1] and gave power to the Whig party, who were prepared to give effect to some of the new political ideas, and to give emphasis and impetus to the influence which the new economic ideas, and the new ideas as to law reform had already begun to exert.   On the other hand the anti-religious character of some of the advocates of these new ideas antagonized Christian feeling, and gained many supporters for the opposition to some or all of them.[2]   That opposition helped to build up the new conservative party which was prepared to defend and to preserve the fundamental principles of the constitution and the established church, and yet was ready to make the reforms required by new social and economic conditions.[3]

The new economic ideas obtained a more complete acceptance than any of the other new ideas.   This was due partly to the fact that Adam Smith's book had familiarized English statesmen with them before the outbreak of the French Revolution, partly to the fact that they met the needs of the leaders of the industrial revolution, and partly to the fact that they harmonized with that old feeling in favour of individual liberty which was emphasized by the philosophic radicals.[4]   Adam Smith's ideas were worked up by his successors into a rigid system,[5] which so exalted the beneficial results of absolute freedom from state interference, that many of its advocates were blind to the evil results of child labour in the factories,[6] that they procured the total repeal of the combination acts,[7] and that they were practically unanimous in urging the repeal of the corn laws,[8] and the establishment of that system of one-sided free trade which undermined the strength of the state, and sapped that leadership of industry which England had acquired during this period.[9]

The new ideas as to law reform which Bentham preached had won the acceptance of both parties in the state before 1832. Their influence was accentuated after 1832, and it is apparent in the course of legislation right down to our own days.   But neither Bentham's political ideas nor his ideas as to law reform were accepted in the same wholesale way as the new economic ideas.   We have seen that the Reform Act was a measure which differed widely from the measure advocated by the philosophic radicals,[10] because its contents were largely determined by the political institutions of the English state, and by the ideals of the political parties in that state.   Similarly, much to Bentham's

---

[1] Below 231, 232.   [2] Below 147 seqq.   [3] Below 148.
[4] Dicey, Law and Opinion (1st ed.) 175.   [5] Below 29 seqq.   [6] Below 36.
[7] Below 341, 346 ; but we shall see that in this case the results were so disastrous that the Legislature was obliged to interfere in the year after the Acts had been repealed, below 348.
[8] Below 357, 358.   [9] Below 356-358.   [10] Above, 6 ; below 257.

disgust,[1] his suggestions for the reform of the law were not accepted in their entirety. They were in many cases preceded by elaborate enquiries made by royal commissions composed of distinguished English lawyers,[2] and they were put into practical shape and worked into the existing fabric of the law by those same lawyers.[3] The result was that the continuity of the development of English law was maintained ; and this fact helped to maintain that law-abiding habit amongst Englishmen which played no small part in saving England from those revolutions which afflicted so many European states in the nineteenth century. Macaulay, speaking in 1852 of the revolutions and counter-revolutions of the year 1848,[4] said : " The madness of 1848 did not subvert the British throne. The reaction which followed has not destroyed British liberty. And why is this ? . . . We owe this singular happiness, under the blessing of God, to a wise and noble constitution, the work of many generations of great men." This History has shown that amongst these great men who have made the constitution and the law abiding habit upon which it rests, the lawyers have played a large part ; and it is inevitable that they should have played this large part for the constitution is part of the common law and rests upon it.

That the many law reforms of the century, before and after 1832, were able thus to be worked into the fabric of the law with these beneficial results, was due largely to the character of the professional development of the law during the latter part of the eighteenth century. Lord Mansfield and his successors had taken a long step towards modernizing the law and fitting it to meet the needs of this new age,[5] with the result that the statutory changes could the more easily be assimilated. This work of assimilation was carried out by a succession of able lawyers during this period and during the following period of extensive law reform.[6] They adapted English law to the needs of a new age ; and so, like the great English lawyers of past ages, they showed that they possessed that capacity for conservative reform which has made English law one of the great legal systems of the world.

This survey of the character of this transition period indicates the main topics which I must discuss in this chapter and the main lines of division. I shall deal with these topics under the following heads : The New Ideas and the Old ; The Political and Constitutional Background ; The Movement for Reforms in the Law ; The Enacted Law ; The Reports ; The Common Law ; Equity ; Some Eminent Civilians.

---

[1] Below 127.   [2] Below 306, 307.   [3] Below 127, 128.
[4] Speech at Edinburgh on his re-election to Parliament.
[5] Vol. xii 560.   [6] Below 127.

I

THE NEW IDEAS AND THE OLD

As in earlier centuries[1] some account of the prevalent ideas upon political, religious, economic, and legal questions must be given, in order that the political environment, and the development of the law which resulted from that environment, may be understood. I shall deal with this topic under the following heads : The New Political and Religious Ideas ; The New Economic Ideas ; Bentham and the New Ideas as to Law Reform ; Philosophic Radicalism ; The Opposition to the New Ideas.

The New Political and Religious Ideas

During the greater part of the eighteenth century Locke's political theory[2] was dominant. According to it, all men have certain fundamental or natural rights ; and the state exists to secure them. Because this theory of the state was the dominant theory, Hobbes's theory of sovereignty [3] failed then to acquire the importance which it deserved and ultimately gained during the later period with which we are now dealing. His sovereign looked too much like an absolute Stuart King, and the reasoning by which his theory was supported attacked the technicalities both of lawyers and divines.[4] Till the latter part of the century the fundamental rights which the state was created to secure were supposed to depend, not on mere expediency or utility, but on the theory of an original contract.[5] As that theory receded into the background,[6] and as the influence of the study of the physical laws of the universe increased,[7] it became possible to take the view that the laws which guaranteed the fundamental rights of men and governed their political and legal relations were, like the laws which governed the physical universe, natural, universal, and discoverable by the human intellect.[8] At the same time the acceptance of Hobbes's theory of sovereignty made it possible to maintain that it was within the competence of the state to reform its institutions and laws so as to give effect to those natural laws which reason, expediency, or utility had suggested.[9]

But what were the contents of those natural laws ? According to Locke, they guaranteed the rights to life, liberty, and property.[10] According to Rousseau, they taught that all men were equal, and

---

[1] Vol. ii 127-144 ; vol. iv 11-54 ; vol. vi 273-299 ; vol. x 3-19.
[2] For his theory see vol. vi 284-289.
[3] For Hobbes's theory see ibid 294-299.
[4] Ibid 298.   [5] Ibid 293.   [6] Ibid 299.   [7] Vol. x 8.
[8] Ibid 8-9.   [9] Vol. vi 299 ; below 131.   [10] Vol. vi 285-287.

that all had equal rights to liberty, property and security, and equal rights to resist oppression and to exercize political power.[1] At the same time Rousseau recognized more clearly than Locke the doctrine of sovereignty. The general will of these equal citizens is sovereign.[2] Thus Rousseau's theory, though it owes some of its ideas to both Locke and Hobbes, differs from both. It differs from Locke's theory in two respects : first, in the emphasis laid on the equality of all citizens for all purposes, and secondly, in its recognition of the sovereign power of these equal citizens. It differs from Hobbes's theory in its postulate of the existence of an ideal state of nature, in its recognition of equal rights possessed by men in this ideal state, and in the idea that the sovereign exists to give effect to these equal rights. But all these political theories were alike in one respect. They were all *a priori* theories, which depended on the view that these natural laws which determined the constitution of, and the balance of powers within, the state, were fixed and universal and discoverable by logic and reason.

Locke's theory was in effect a justification of the results of the Revolution of 1688. It reflected the ideas of the Whig party ; and its fundamental ideas came to be those accepted by all parties during the greater part of the eighteenth century. We have seen that though, from many points of view, those ideas were illogical, they did succeed in establishing and maintaining a constitution in which " dominion and liberty were happily reconciled." [3] That they were able to do so is due to the fact that, though the dominant political theory was of an *a priori* character, the essential defect of a purely *a priori* theory was remedied by the character of the Revolution of 1688. It is the essential defect of such a theory that it neglects the lessons of history, that it looks too critically on institutions and laws which do not square with it, that it is too ready to scrap institutions and laws which work, for the new and untried institutions and laws which square with the logical reasonings of its supporters. But the Revolution of 1688 had been effected with the minimum of change in the law and institutions of England. Both statesmen and lawyers regarded it as being merely the assertion by the Legislature of the better opinion as to certain points of constitutional law ; and, though the dynasty was changed, all the other institutions of government remained unchanged and hardly at all reformed.[4] Thus the main defect in a purely *a priori* theory of government was remedied. The law and institutions of England were the product of the long political and legal experience of the race. They were reverenced, and rightly

---

[1] Vol. x 13. [2] Ibid 13.
[3] Vol. vi 287-289. [4] Ibid 195, 230-242.

reverenced, because they worked on the whole well. At the same time the political theory by which they were justified did admit the possibility of changes and reforms to remedy proved abuses, provided that fundamental laws and institutions were not touched. It was generally recognized that, as Horace Walpole put it, there was " a wide difference between correcting abuses and the removal of landmarks." [1] This was the reason why, as I have pointed out,[2] the statesmen and lawyers of the eighteenth century had some of the characteristics of the schools both of the analytical and of the historical lawyers which arose in the nineteenth century. They were ready to reform, but they were not ready to change fundamental principles merely to satisfy the demands of logic.

This mental attitude is possible so long as conditions remain static. But it is more difficult to maintain when political, social, and economic conditions are changing. It was inevitable that, in a time when these conditions were changing, more weight should be given to those *a priori* principles, based on logic or expediency, which could be used to suggest the reforms which changed conditions were making necessary. At the end of the century Adam Smith had used this method of approval to create a scientific body of principles for the settlement of economic questions,[3] and Bentham had begun his life work of creating a similar body of principles upon which reforms in the law ought to be made.[4] Many thinkers and statesmen were ready to welcome and to attempt to give effect to the reforms suggested by their speculations.[5] The same tendencies are evident in political speculation. The American Declaration of Independence had advertised those rights of men which Rousseau's *Contrat Social* had proclaimed ;[6] and the controversies aroused by the War of Independence and by discontent with the policy of the government had given rise to agitations for economic and Parliamentary reform.[7] Some very democratic proposals for Parliamentary reform had made their appearance in the course of the last thirty years of the eighteenth century ;[8] and writers on political theory had reflected these ideas. Priestley and Price[9] and many others had voiced them, so that, when the French Revolution broke out,

---

[1] Letters (ed. Toynbee) xiii 86, cited vol. xii 729.
[2] Vol. xii 550.   [3] Vol. xi 392-393, 503-518.
[4] Vol. xii 733 ; above 5, 6 ; below 124, 125.
[5] Vol. x 116-117.   [6] Ibid 15 ; vol. xi 129-130.
[7] Vol. x 102, 116-117.   [8] Below 191, 192.
[9] Vol. x 116-117 ; for a more detailed account of their political theories see Leslie Stephen, English Thought in the Eighteenth Century ii 252-259 ; Leslie Stephen says at pp. 252-253, " In their writings we catch for the first time the true revolutionary tone. . . . Priestley, the crude materialist, and Price, the cloudy advocate of an *a priori* philosophy, united in condemning the existing order which would satisfy neither the test of utility nor the test of abstract justice."

there was a body of opinion in England which was ready to welcome those democratic ideas which the Americans had successfully asserted and the French were now making the basis of their new régime.

The French Revolution brought to a head the conflict between those who wished for no change in the fundamental principles in the law and constitution of England, and those who, with the help of the new *a priori* democratic principles, wished to make far-reaching reforms.[1]   We have seen that this conflict split the Whig party.[2]   The New Whigs who sided with Fox welcomed the Revolution—they thought that the French were only doing in 1789 what the Whigs had done in 1688. The Old Whigs who sided with Burke saw with dismay the break up of all the old institutions of church and state—the scrapping of all existing institutions and traditions and experience in favour of new institutions constructed on *a priori* theories which they rightly distrusted. It was this conflict which produced the books which were destined to have an enormous influence on the political ideas of the future.

The immediate cause which produced these epoch making books was a sermon. On November 4 (the anniversary of the Revolution of 1688) Richard Price preached at the Meeting House, Old Jewry, a sermon on " The Love of our Country." In it he maintained the proposition that the English people had three fundamental rights—to choose their own governors, to cashier them for misconduct, and to form a government for themselves. It was these propositions which Burke set out to disprove in his great book on the French Revolution ; and Burke's book called forth, amongst other answers,[3] Mackintosh's *Vindiciæ Gallicæ*, and Thomas Paine's *Rights of Man*. With the latter book must be considered Paine's *Age of Reason*, which is, from some points of view, a supplement to the *Rights of Man*.

Burke's historical sense which led him to regard a political society as a living organism ; his religious temperament which led him to believe that, because a political society was a living organism, there was in it, as in life itself, a mysterious and a divine element ; his reverence for all old and well-established systems of government, and more especially for the British constitution, which had shown themselves capable of mastering the forces of anarchy—all led him to revolt against the individualism which magnified the rights of each separate man, and the *a priori* rationalism which not only discarded all historical experience, but even regarded it as pernicious.[4]   The essential

---

[1] Below 16, 157.   [2] Vol. x 124.
[3] For a list of some of the authors who entered the lists against Burke see G. P. Gooch, Camb. Mod. Hist. viii 758.
[4] For these characteristics of Burke's thought see vol. x 93-97.

correctness of Burke's diagnosis, and therefore the superiority of the historical as compared with the rationalistic and *a priori* approach to the problems of the French Revolution and to other political problems, is proved by the number of his predictions which were fulfilled.[1] It is the manner in which Burke developed this manner of approach which has made his *Reflections on the Revolution in France* " not only the greatest exposition of the philosophic basis of conservatism ever written, but also a declaration of the principles of evolution, continuity, and solidarity, which must hold their place in all sound political thinking."[2] But of these features of Burke's book I shall have more to say when I describe the opposition of the old to the new political ideas.[3] At this point we are concerned with the new political ideas, and with the criticisms which their advocates were able, with some justice, to make to some of Burke's positions.

The three most important books were, as I have said, the *Vindiciæ Gallicæ* and the *Rights of Man* and, in a lesser degree, the *Age of Reason*. The first had some importance in its own day and in the years immediately succeeding : the second has had a larger and a more permanent importance because it fore-shadowed many of those democratic ideas to which the course of nineteenth-century history has given a constantly increasing importance. The third had little direct influence in England ; but, indirectly, it had perhaps some small influence in inducing the Legislature to abolish all disabilities based on theological differences of opinion, and to tolerate even those who disbelieved in all religions.

Mackintosh's *Vindiciæ Gallicæ*, which was published in 1791, is in effect the manifesto of the New Whigs who adhered to Fox. Their predominant feeling was joy at the enormous impetus which the cause of liberty had received, and at the great blow given to despotism. Mackintosh follows the Old Whig tradition when he argues that it is right to try to improve the institutions of a state, and therefore denies Burke's statement that legislators should retain a constitution if it has been found "*tolerably* to answer the common purposes of government."[4] But he states the views of the New Whigs when he maintains that, in this age of political enlightenment, when the principles of government had attained a large measure of certainty, it is right " that Legislators instead of that narrow and dastardly *coasting* which never ventures to lose sight of usage and precedent, should, guided by the *polarity* of reason, hazard a bolder navigation."[5] Like them, he favours an *a priori* approach to the problems of government. He argues that it is reason and not precedent which

[1] Vol. x 96, n. 1.   [2] G. P. Gooch, Camb. Mod. Hist. viii 757.
[3] Below 156.   [4] Vindiciæ 114, 109-116.   [5] Ibid 117.

should guide a nation as to the nature of the reforms which are
necessary ;[1] that men have certain natural rights which a free
state must protect if it is " to preserve its purity, consistency,
and stability " ; [2] and that a due regard to these principles would
in England lead to many reforms, notably a diminution in the
powers of the government to oppress the citizens,[3] and above all a
radical reform of Parliament, based on something like universal
suffrage,[4] which would make it really representative, and the laws
which it enacts a real expression of the general will.[5] The
Revolution of 1688 which Burke so much admired did much. In
fact it helped to pave the way for the American and French
revolutions.[6] But it was limited in its effects. Burke deifies those
limitations which were in fact its great defect.[7] The progress of
political reasoning has enabled us to see more clearly.[8] Partly for
this reason, and partly by reason of the enormous defects of the
French government, it was necessary to make a clean sweep of the
old system—to abolish feudal privileges, and to destroy " the
three great corporations of the Nobility, the Church, and the
Parliaments."[9] It was necessary to give all power to a representative assembly in order to enable it to establish a new
constitution, which should guarantee those rights of man for the
sake of which government exists.[10] To idealize the old French
institutions and to talk of the age of chivalry is mere delusion.[11]

Mackintosh was, as against Burke, clearly right when he
maintained that a clean sweep of the old system was necessary,
and when he criticized the manner in which Burke had idealized
the old system. His weakness, as compared with Burke, was that
he approached his subject simply from the standpoint of a
contemporary writing in the year 1791. He had none of Burke's
insight into the tremendous forces which so great an upheaval had
unloosed, and the dire consequences of an attempt, by means of

---

[1] " They (the lawyers) display their elaborate frivolity, their perfidious friendship
in disgracing freedom with the fantastic honour of a pedigree. . . . A man who
should pretend that the reason why we had right to property is, because our ancestors enjoyed that right 400 years ago, would be justly condemned. Yet so little
is plain sense heard in the mysterious nonsense which is the cloak of political fraud,
that the Cokes, the Blackstones, and Burkes speak as if our right to freedom depended on its possession by our ancestors. . . . It is not because we *have* been
free, but because we have a right to be free, that we ought to demand freedom,"
Vindiciæ 304-306.   [2] Ibid 219, 204-219.
[3] Ibid 338-342 ; a follower of Locke was bound to take this view, vol. vi 286-
287 ; and in fact in the eighteenth century the powers of the government were
dangerously small, vol. xi 277 ; the view that the powers of government ought to
be diminished, inherited from Locke, was repeated by those who advocated radical
reforms on democratic lines, below 27, 40, and by the economists who inherited
the Adam Smith tradition, below 36 ; it was not shared by Bentham in his later
years or by the philosophic radicals, below 35, 92, 138, 139.
[4] Vindiciæ 224-228.   [5] Ibid 337.   [6] Ibid 328-330.
[7] Ibid 331.   [8] Ibid 309, 332, 345.   [9] Ibid 67, 70-73.
[10] Ibid 252-265.   [11] Ibid 194-199.

the unfettered reason of inexperienced men and in an atmosphere of fear and passion and intrigue, to construct from its foundations a new political society. Mackintosh lived to recant his views as to the beneficent effects of the French Revolution.[1] But as Macaulay said,[2] he had an essentially moderate judicial mind.

He never proclaimed doctrines inconsistent with the safety of property and the just authority of governments. He never in the most gloomy times abandoned the causes of peace, of liberty, and of toleration. The opinions in which he at last reposed were a just mean between those which he had defended against Mr. Burke, and those to which he had inclined during the darkest and saddest years in the history of modern Europe.

His *Vindiciæ* helped to keep alive the Whig cause in the days which succeeded the split in the party ; and some of the liberal principles contained in his book, to which he always adhered, helped in later years to revive it, and to enable it to assert its principles as against both the Tories and those radical reformers who would have liked to treat the British constitution as the French revolutionaries had treated the old régime in France.[3] Thus both the book and the principles of its author may be said to have helped to make possible that Whig reform of 1832 which for a season stayed the advent of a purely democratic form of government.[4]

The influence and importance of Paine's books have been very different from Mackintosh's book, and very much greater. I must give first a brief sketch of Paine's career, because the events of his life help us to understand his books. I shall then give an account of the political ideas contained in his *Rights of Man*. Lastly I shall say something of the religious ideas contained in his *Age of Reason*.

Paine's Career.[5]—Paine was born January 29, 1737. On his father's side he came of Quaker stock—with the result, as he says, that he had " a good moral education and a tolerable stock of useful learning."[6] When he was thirteen he was apprenticed to a stay maker, but in 1756 he abandoned his trade and went to sea with a privateer. In 1758 he resumed his trade in London and showed the interest which he retained all his life in natural science by attending lectures on scientific subjects. But his business did not prosper, and in 1760 he abandoned it and became an exciseman. He was dismissed in 1765,[7] but was reinstated in

---

[1] Davis, Age of Grey and Peel, 131.   [2] Essay on Sir James Mackintosh.
[3] Davis, Age of Grey and Peel 131-133 ; below 138.   [4] Below 257.
[5] The best account of Paine's life is by M. D. Conway on which I have mainly relied ; the D.N.B. gives a good short biography.
[6] Conway i 12, citing some reminiscences by Paine.
[7] He was dismissed for indulging in a practice common among excise officers called " stamping," that is " setting down surveys of work on his books, without actually travelling to the traders' premises and examining specimens," ibid i 17.

1767 ; and in 1772 he prepared on behalf of his fellow excisemen an appeal to Parliament for an increase of pay. In 1774 he was again dismissed for absence without leave. But by this time Paine was emerging from obscurity. He had made the acquaintance of Goldsmith and Franklin ; and when he went to America in 1774 Franklin gave him a letter of introduction to his son-in-law.

The American War of Independence made Paine a publicist and introduced him into public life. We have seen that his pamphlet *Common Sense* helped to induce the Americans to declare their independence ; that in it Paine appears as the advocate of the democratic creed ; and that it shows both the merits and the weakness of that creed.[1] Both by this pamphlet, and by his paper *The Crisis*,[2] and other writings, Paine gave valuable help to the Americans, who in 1777 made him secretary of the committee of foreign affairs. But disputes between him and the American commissioners in Paris on the question whether the funds sent by the French government were a loan or a gift led to his resignation in 1779. In the same year he was appointed clerk to the Assembly of Pennsylvania which office he held till, in 1781, he went to Paris with Colonel Laurens to negotiate a loan. They returned with a frigate, military stores and 2,500,000 livres in silver. In 1782 he was given a salary of 800 dollars a year to enable him to write on behalf of the government. In 1784 the State of New York gave him an estate at New Rochelle.

Paine had become a famous man in America ; but at this period his interest in mechanics competed with his interest in politics. He had become interested in an invention for an iron bridge, and in 1787 he returned to England to introduce it and to see his parents. In 1790 he was in Paris, and, as a leading American, Lafayette entrusted to him the key of the Bastille for transmission to Washington. When Burke's book appeared Paine at once set to work to answer him. The first part of his *Rights of Man* appeared in 1791. It contains a narrative of the events in France which Paine had witnessed, so that, apart from its importance as a book of political theory, it is a valuable historical document. It had a very large sale, and it has been suggested that the government were so frightened by it that it attempted to stop the publication of the second part of the book by purchasing the copyright. Whether or not this attempt was made, Paine did not sell, and the book appeared in 1792. The government resolved to prosecute ; but Paine just managed to escape to France, where he was given a great welcome. He had already been made a French citizen and elected as a deputy to the

[1] Vol. xi 116, 130-131.

[2] His famous first *Crisis* beginning with the words " These are the times that try men's souls " was read to the American army before the battle of Trenton, Conway i 86.

Convention by Calais as well as by the other departments. Paine was tried in absence, and was found guilty of publishing a seditious libel, and outlawed, in spite of Erskine's magnificent plea for freedom of discussion[1]—indeed his letter to the Attorney-General in which he reiterated his libel on the English government in the most offensive terms made his conviction certain.[2]

As a French citizen and deputy Paine tried to save the life of Louis XVI. Naturally he became suspect to Robespierre and the Committee of Public Safety. He was imprisoned in December 1793 and narrowly escaped the guillotine. It was just before his arrest that he finished the first part of his *Age of Reason*. The other two parts he wrote in 1795 and 1807. The publisher of this book was prosecuted for blasphemy in 1797 ;[3] and it is significant of the small hold that anti-Christian opinions had taken in England that Erskine, the great upholder of the right of freedom of discussion, appeared for the prosecution. In November 1794 Paine was released by the good offices of Monroe, the American minister in Paris, who took him into his house and cared for him till his health was restored. In 1802 he returned to the United States. But he had attacked Washington in 1796, and so he found that, in spite of his past services to the Americans, both his politics and his theology had made him unpopular. He died June 8, 1809, and was buried on his property at New Rochelle. In 1819 Cobbett exhumed his bones and carried them to England. He contemplated raising over them a monument to his honour. But he found little support for this proposition ; the monument was never raised ; and the bones disappeared.

Paine had many enemies. His political and more especially his religious ideas caused him to be represented as a species of devil incarnate. He was said to be a drunkard, sexually immoral, and an atheist who recanted his heresies on his death bed. These tales have been proved to be fictions.[4] Paine was an honest, clean living man, true to his friends, and respected by those who knew him well. He had had little regular education ; but he was a student of mechanics, and his iron bridge and his study of marine steam engines earned the praise of engineers. His political and religious philosophy was derived mainly from his association with the great events in which he had taken part and the men who had moulded them, and from his reflection on the political and religious phenomena of his day. That knowledge and that reflection had convinced him of the truth of Rousseau's creed which had inspired the men who had made the American

---

[1] R. v. Paine (1792) 22 S.T. 358 ; for Erskine's statement of the principles which should regulate the rules as to freedom of discussion see vol. x 673, 694.

[2] For the letter see 22 S.T. 397-398 ; Erskine was reduced to contending that the letter was a fabrication, ibid 410.

[3] R. v. Williams (1797) 26 S.T. 654.   [4] See Conway ii 388-426.

Revolution and were making the French Revolution. In his *Rights of Man* he preached that creed to the English people ; and in his *Age of Reason* he introduced them to those deistic beliefs, and to the reasons given by the deists for the rejection of the Christian theology, and of the authority of the Bible on which it was based. His experience as a pamphleteer and journalist enabled him to state his political and religious creed so lucidly, and with such epigrammatic force, that his *Rights of Man*, and, to a considerably less extent, his *Age of Reason*, became the bible of English democrats of that and later ages. We must now examine the theories set out in these two books, and estimate their influence.

Paine's Rights of Man.—The book was an answer to Burke ; and it owed part of its popularity to its just criticism of some parts of Burke's book, and to the incisiveness and pungency with which that criticism is expressed. Burke is wrong, he says, in saying that the French rebelled against " a mild and lawful monarch " : " it was not against Louis XVI but against the despotic principles of government, that the Nation revolted." [1] " We see a revolution generated in the rational contemplation of the rights of man, and distinguishing from the beginning between persons and principles." [2] Burke " is not affected by the reality of distress touching his heart, but by the showy resemblance of it striking his imagination. He pities the plumage but forgets the dying bird." [3] " When in countries that are called civilized, we see age going to the workhouse and youth to the gallows, something must be wrong in the system of Government." [4] He makes a good point against Burke, who had said that Paine's book deserved no other refutation than that of criminal justice, when he remarked that " it must be *criminal* justice indeed that should condemn a work as a substitute for not being able to refute it." [5] He is clearly right when he insists that " Government is not a trade which any man, or any body of men, has a right to set up and exercise for his own emolument, but is altogether a trust in right of those by whom the trust is delegated, and by whom it is always resumable. It has of itself no rights ; they are altogether duties." [6]

It is, Paine maintains, the people who have rights—natural rights belonging to each man in right of his existence,[7] which are both indefeasible and hereditary.[8] It is upon these natural rights

---

[1] Rights of Man (Everyman's Library) 18.
[2] Ibid 21.   [3] Ibid 24.   [4] Ibid 221.
[5] Ibid 145-146.   [6] Ibid 186-187.   [7] Ibid 40-43.
[8] " Government founded on a moral theory, on a system of universal peace, on the indefeasible hereditary rights of man, is now revolving from west to east by a stronger impulse than the Government of the sword revolved from east to west," ibid 154.

that a man's civil rights are founded ; and government exists that
these rights may be better secured.[1] All men are equal, and
therefore have the same natural rights—the Mosaic account of the
creation is sufficient to show this.[2] The conception of aristocracy
is contrary to the law of nature, " and Nature herself calls for its
destruction." [3] The French have acted rightly in making the
Nation, and not the King, the sovereign,[4] for " sovereignty, as a
matter of right, appertains to the nation only, and not to any
individual." [5] The Crown is merely " a *metaphor* shown at the
Tower for sixpence or a shilling a piece : so are the lions."[6] By
the revolutions in American and France these principles have been
reasserted,[7] and the following principles—" as universal as truth
and the existence of man, and combining moral with political
happiness and national prosperity " [8]—have been asserted :

I.   Men are born, and always continue, free and equal in respect of
     their rights. Civil distinctions, therefore, can only be founded on
     public utility.
II. The end of all political associations is the preservation of the
     natural and imprescriptible rights of man ; and these rights are
     liberty, property, security, and resistance of oppression.
III. The Nation is essentially the source of all sovereignty ; nor can
     ANY INDIVIDUAL or ANY BODY OF MEN, be entitled to any authority
     which is not expressly derived from it.[9]

It follows that the only legitimate government is one founded, not
as the older governments were founded on superstition or power,
but on " the common interests of society and the common rights
of man." [10] The only rational form of government is, therefore,
" representation ingrafted upon Democracy " ; [11] for that
system " diffuses such a body of knowledge throughout a Nation
on the subject of Government, as to explode ignorance and
preclude imposition." [12] To appeal, as Burke is constantly
appealing, to the precedent of 1688 or indeed to any precedent
is absurd : " The circumstances of the world are continually
changing, and the opinions of men change also ; and as Government is for the living, and not for the dead, it is the living only
that has any right in it."[13]

In fact the sphere in which even the most legitimate government can usefully operate is very limited :

Great part of that order which reigns among mankind is not the effect
of Government. It has its origin in the principles of society and the
natural constitution of man, and would exist if the formality of Government was abolished. . . . Government is no farther necessary than to

---

[1] Rights of Man (Everyman's Library) 44-45.

[2] Ibid 42-43.   [3] Ibid 61.   [4] Ibid 69-70.

[5] Ibid 134.   [6] Ibid 55.   [7] Ibid 72.

[8] Ibid 135.   [9] Ibid.   [10] Ibid 46.

[11] Ibid 177.   [12] Ibid 181.   [13] Ibid 16.

supply the few cases to which society and civilization are not conveniently competent ; and instances are not wanting to show that everything which Government can usefully add thereto has been performed by the common consent of society, without Government. . . . The more perfect civilization is the less occasion has it for government, because the more it does regulate its own affairs and govern itself.[1]

It is clear that in this passage Paine applies to government a principle very similar to that which Adam Smith applied to economics.[2] *Laissez faire*, and the natural instincts of men, unimpeded by the artificial restraints imposed by government, will lead to the best results. On the other hand, in the latter half of the second part of his book he deserts this *laissez faire* principle. He proposes measures designed to relieve poverty and to produce a measure of economic equality. In other words, he ceases to rely entirely on the natural identification of interests if men are left to go their own way, and proposes by legislation to bring about an artificial identification of interests. These measures were to be financed by drastic reductions in the expenses of civil government and of the army and navy, and by the imposition of a progressive property tax, which, on incomes of £23,000 and over, was to be 20s. in the £. From the money so raised there was to be a liberal provision for the poor, free education for their children, old age pensions, marriage allowances, allowances for birth and funeral expenses, and employment for the casual poor of London and Westminster.[3] How all these measures were to be carried out by means of the very slender governmental machinery provided for in his scheme he does not seem to have considered.

The defects of Paine's book are patent. He knows no history, and denies that a nation can derive any profit from its experience in the past.[4] He ascribes all laws and institutions which he dislikes to superstition or fraud.[5] He does not see that the capacity of society to settle many matters for itself without the aid of government[6] was due to the discipline imposed for many centuries by the governments which he denounced as the products of conquest or priest craft.[7] He deduces universal laws from his

---

[1] Rights of Man (Everyman's Library) 157-159.   [2] Vol. xi 392-393.
[3] Rights of Man (Everyman's Library) 240-267.
[4] " Those who have quitted the world, and those who are not yet arrived at it, are as remote from each other as the utmost stretch of mortal imagination can conceive. What possible obligation, then, can exist between them ; what rule or principle can be laid down that of two non-entities, the one out of existence and the other not in, and who can never meet in this world, the one should control the other to the end of time ? ", ibid 13-14.
[5] Ibid 195-196.   [6] Above 11, 12.
[7] As Bentham said, Anarchical Fallacies, Works ii 502, " Whence is it, but from government, that contracts derive their binding force ? Contracts came from government, not government from contracts. It is from the habit of enforcing contracts, and seeing them enforced, that governments are chiefly indebted for whatever disposition they have to observe them."

very limited experience in America and France. Consequently
his prophecies of the future are as foolish as Burke's were acute.[1]
He showed his ignorance of a very fundamental principle of
constitutional law when he said that "that which is called the
judicial power is strictly and properly the executive power of
every country"; [2] he showed his ignorance of the rules of
English law when he supposed that trial by peers extended to
misdemeanours; [3] and he showed his ignorance of the working of
machinery of government when he said that the Crown "signifies
a nominal office of a million sterling a year, the business of which
consists in receiving the money." [4] But the most dangerous and
the most important in practice of his fallacies are his insistence,
first, on the doctrine of the natural rights of all citizens, secondly,
on the equal right of all citizens to take part through their
representatives in the government, and thirdly, on the right of a
government to confiscate a large part of the property of the rich
to provide indiscriminate relief for the poor.

(1) Paine's doctrine of natural rights was submitted to a
devastating criticism by Bentham.[5] In the first place, there
are no such things as natural rights, i.e. rights anterior to the
establishment of government, in contradistinction to legal
rights.[6] "Natural rights is simple nonsense: natural and im-
prescriptible rights, rhetorical nonsense—nonsense upon stilts."[7]
In the second place, any attempt to give effect to these natural
rights leads to mischievous error:

The great enemies of public peace are the selfish and dissocial passions—
necessary as they are—the one to the very existence of each individual,
the other to his security. On the part of these affections, a deficiency in
point of strength is never to be apprehended: all that is to be apprehended in respect of them, is to be apprehended on the side of their
excess. Society is held together only by the sacrifices that man can be
induced to make of the gratifications they demand: to obtain these
sacrifices is the great difficulty, the great task of government. What has
been the object, the perpetual and palpable object, of this declaration
of pretended rights? To add as much force as possible to these passions,
already but too strong—to burst the cords that hold them in—to say to
the selfish passions, there, everywhere is your prey—to the angry
passions, there, everywhere is your enemy.[8]

(2) His doctrine of the equal right of all citizens to take part
in the government assumes the obviously false proposition that
all human beings are equally qualified intellectually to take this

---

[1] " Just emerging from such a barbarous condition, it is too soon to determine
to what extent of improvement Government may yet be carried. For what we
can foresee, all Europe may form but one great Republic; and man be free of the
whole," Rights of Man 211.
    [2] Ibid 199.   [3] Ibid 200 n. 1.   [4] Ibid 234.
    [5] Anarchical Fallacies, being an examination of the Declarations of Rights
issued during the French Revolution, Works ii 491-529.
    [6] Works ii 500.   [7] Ibid 501.   [8] Ibid ii 497.

part.[1] But, in so far as there is an equality amongst human beings, it is in respect, not of their intellectual, but of their physical characteristics ; and it is possible to argue that, for this reason, it is desirable, in the interest of wise government, to emphasize not their equalities but their inequalities. But in fact it is impossible to maintain either of these purely *a priori* arguments ; for as Burke said,[2]

the rights of men are in a sort of *middle*, incapable of definition, but not impossible to be discussed. The rights of men in government are their advantages ; and these are often in balance between differences of good ; and in compromises sometimes between good and evil, and sometimes between evil and evil. Political reason is a computing principle ; adding, subtracting, multiplying, and dividing, morally and not metaphysically or mathematically, true moral denominations.

Some legal rights and powers must be secured to all citizens ; but, as Bentham truly said, in the days before he became a democrat,[3] to give the greatest power to a majority of the least educated is ridiculous.[4] It was the great merit of what Bentham happily called " the chance-medley " of the unreformed constitution[5] that the variety of franchize recognized by the law gave some power to all citizens but most power to the most enlightened. No doubt reform was needed ; but we shall see that the greatest blot upon the reform made was that it substituted for variety a uniformity, which paved the way for the introduction of a purely democratic government.[6]

(3) Paine's proposal to confiscate a large part of the property of the rich to provide indiscriminate relief for the poor was also condemned by Bentham. He would have approved of moderate death duties ; but he held that it was fatal to sacrifice security to equality. " The establishment of perfect equality is a chimera " ; and " if property should be overturned with the direct intention of establishing an equality of possessions, the evil would be irreparable. No more security, no more industry,

[1] Rights of Man 42-44 ; above 20.
[2] French Revolution 92.   [3] Below 104.
[4] " What then shall we say of that system of government, of which the professed object is to call upon the untaught and unlettered multitude . . . to occupy themselves without ceasing upon all questions of government . . . the most general and the most particular, but more especially upon the most important and the most general—that is in other words the most scientific—those that require the greatest measures of science to qualify a man for deciding upon, and in respect of which any want of science and skill are liable to be attended with the most fatal consequences ? What should we have said, if, with a view of collecting the surest grounds for the decision of any of the great questions of chemistry, the French Academy of Sciences (if its members had remained unmurdered) had referred such questions to the Primary Assemblies ? ", Works ii 522.
[5] " How much inferior has the maturest design that could be furnished by the united powers of the whole nation proved, in comparison with the wisdom and felicity of the chance-medley of the British constitution," ibid.
[6] Below 256, 257.

no more abundance.   Society would return to the savage state whence it emerged." [1]

But in spite of, and to some extent because of, these defects in Paine's theories, his book foreshadows the ideas of those principles of democratic socialism which are the dominant influence in modern democratic states.   The ordinary man naturally looks with favour on theories which magnify his rights and promise him easy money ;   he can easily be persuaded to embrace with a religious fervour the simple dogmas of a creed which promises these benefits ;   and he is generally incapable of seeing the fallacies on which these theories and dogmas are founded.   And so, although the democratic creed was justified by Bentham and his followers upon less obviously fallacious premises, [2] Paine's theories and dogmas hold their ground.   As Bryce has said : [3]

These transcendental maxims have in fact done more to commend democracy to mankind than any utilitarian arguments drawn from history, for they appeal to emotion at least as much as to reason.   They are simpler and more direct.   Their very vagueness and the feeling that man is lifted to a higher plane, where Liberty and Equality are proclaimed as indefeasible rights, gave them a magic power.   Rousseau fired a thousand for one whom Benthamism convinced.

Paine's Age of Reason.—Paine was not an atheist.   He was a deist who believed in a wise and good God, [4] whose existence he deduced from the creation of the world and the mechanism of the solar system. [5]   Without knowing it, his views were in line with earlier deists, such as Tindal, Morgan, and Middleton. [6]   What he was concerned to combat was the Christian theory of the fall of man and the scheme of salvation, and the authority of the Old and New Testaments upon which that theory rested.   " He confronts the theories that God dictated the Bible ;   that all the human race has been damned to everlasting fire because Eve ate the apple ;   and that God's wrath against guilty man was satiated by punishing his innocent son." [7]   He comments on the barbaric character of some of the Old Testament stories, and concludes that, when we read such stories, it would be more reasonable to say that the Bible was the work of a demon than the work of God ; [8] and he insists on the incoherencies and inconsistencies contained in the narratives both of the Old and the New Testaments. [9]   His book is

---

[1] Theory of Legislation (ed. by C. K. Ogden) 120 ;   below 74.

[2] Below 104, 138, 142.   [3] Modern Democracies i 51.

[4] " The creation we behold is the real and ever-existing word of God, in which we cannot be deceived.   It proclaimeth his power, it demonstrates his wisdom, it manifests his goodness and beneficence," last page of Part I of the Age of Reason, cited Conway, Life of Paine ii 103.

[5] Letter addressed by Paine to the society of Theophilanthropists, cited Leslie Stephen, English Thought in the Eighteenth Century i 460.

[6] Ibid i 460-461.   [7] Ibid i 460.   [8] Ibid i 461.

[9] Leslie Stephen, English Thought in the Eighteenth Century i 462.

a rough and a brutal book; but it appealed " to genuine moral instincts." [1] It translated the scholarly arguments of the older deists into popular language, and presented them to the people in language which they could understand. As Leslie Stephen says, the book shows that " democracy and infidelity have embraced, and scepticism has flashed out into sudden explosion."[2]

In a sense the book is a supplement to the *Rights of Man*. Reason is to guide men's religious beliefs as it is to guide their politics. The old abusive régime which disregarded reason rested on superstition as much as on illegitimate power. Church and State were close allies, and both must succumb to victorious reason. In fact Paine tells us that he had early foreseen that a revolution in religion would follow upon a revolution in government, and that " man would return to the pure, unmixed, and unadulterated belief of one God and no more."[3] But though in later years the book had some influence in promoting the existing tendencies to secularize politics, and though it had, in consequence, some influence in getting rid of political disabilities founded on religious heterodoxy,[4] it never had the same influence as that exercized by the *Rights of Man*. The prosecution of its publisher was generally applauded; for we have seen that the English as a whole were, unlike the French, profoundly religious.[5] Wilberforce's *Practical View of Christianity*[6] had far more influence than Paine's *Age of Reason*. And it was well for England that this was so. During the nineteenth century the influence of the religions of many different denominations did a great work in abolishing slavery,[7] in humanizing the penal code,[8] and in modifying some of the worst of the social results which followed upon the industrial revolution, and the too literal following of the theories of the classical political economists.[9] Though the Protestant non-conformists, and to a lesser extent the Evangelical party in the church,[10] tended to gravitate to the new liberal party and to adopt more completely the new economic doctrines,[11] and members of the established church to gravitate to the new conservative party which was more critical of some of the results of those doctrines, the leading statesmen on both sides were genuine Christians interested in religion ;[12] and this fact had

[1] Leslie Stephen, English Thought in the Eighteenth Century, i 463.
[2] Ibid i 458.   [3] Cited, Conway, Life of Paine ii 191-192.
[4] Above 14 ; below 116.   [5] Above 4, 7.
[6] A Practical View of the Prevailing Religious System of Professed Christians in the High and Middle Classes of this Country contrasted with Real Christianity (1797) ; by 1824 fifteen editions of the book had appeared, and it had been translated into French, Italian, Spanish, Dutch, and German.
[7] Below 184, 192.   [8] Below 226, 279.   [9] Below 184, 192.
[10] Above 4 ; Dicey, Law and Opinion 398-404.   [11] Below 183.
[12] G. M. Young, Victorian England 5.

considerable influence upon national life and therefore upon politics and legislation.[1]

Dean Inge has said :[2] " We have a deep conviction that the only irreparable mistakes are those which are made by consistent logicians. There is a kind of higher stupidity of which we are seldom guilty." This aphorism hits the weakness of the purely *a priori* political and economic philosophies which set out to solve the problems of this age of change ; and no more striking illustration of its truth can be found than Godwin's *Political Justice*.[3] It is a large and pretentious work—in fact its size and price (three guineas) is said to have saved its author from prosecution, for Pitt thought that such a book could never cause a revolution.[4] It is primarily a treatise on sociology ; and includes ethics, philosophy, religion, and psychology.[5] It is intended to supersede all the old learnings on these topics, and, in the light of the new ideas of this age of change, to substitute new and true doctrines on all these matters.[6]

Its central idea is the sovereignty of pure reason. All men are equal. They are all equally capable of reason, and they cannot help being guided by it as soon as they can be induced to see it. So soon as they can be induced to see it vice will disappear automatically ; for vice is the product of an error of reasoning.[7] It follows that just as the discoveries of science open up prospects of illimitable progress, so the victory of reason will introduce the millennium.[8] As Leslie Stephen says,[9] " The intellect breaking its old fetters and rejoicing in the consciousness of its strength, looked forward to the conquest of the whole physical and moral world."

What then are the lessons which reason teaches us, and what are the practical consequences of these lessons ? Reason teaches us that it is each man's duty to aim at the happiness of all, and it will enable each man by a species of " moral arithmetic " to show him in any given case what his duty is.[10] It is reason alone that must be relied on to solve these problems. There is no place for any such sentiments as gratitude or friendship or family affection, for they merely obscure the calculations of pure reason.[11] On the same principle all political institutions must be abolished because they rely for their authority on means other than reason.[12]

---

[1] Below 186, 187.   [2] A Rustic Moralist 235.
[3] For Godwin and his book see Leslie Stephen, English Thought in the Eighteenth Century ii 264-281 ; Social and Political Ideas of the Revolutionary Era (ed. by Hearnshaw) 141-180—an essay by C. H. Driver ; Halévy, Growth of Philosophic Radicalism 191-203.   [4] Halévy, op. cit. 200.
[5] C. H. Driver, Social and Political Ideas of the Revolutionary Era 152.
[6] Ibid 146.   [7] Ibid 147, 161-162, 168-170.
[8] Ibid 147.
[9] English Thought in the Eighteenth Century ii 269.
[10] Ibid ii 270.   [11] Ibid.   [12] Ibid ii 272-273.

Monarchy and aristocracy are contrary to the fundamental equality of all men ; and even a democratic government cannot be justified because, like any other government, it involves persuasion by coercion instead of by reason.[1] With the disappearance of political institutions and therefore of coercion, law also disappears.[2] We must reason with our criminals, not punish them. Property must disappear because it fosters inequality, and inequality leads to servility, oppression, class wars, and wars between nations.[3] Marriage, like property, must be condemned ; for it too leads to dependence. Like the institution of property, it prevents the rule of reason.[4] Thus in Godwin's ideal state " mankind is a vast collection of incarnate syllogisms." [5] They will live, he suggests, in small communities, in which all temptations to vice will be removed, in which no one will wish to act other than reason dictates.[6] War, crime, and disease will disappear. Each will seek the good of all ; and with the growing power of mind over matter death itself may disappear.[7]

Godwin's book was published in 1793, and there was a second edition in 1794. It was much studied by the young enthusiasts for the French revolutionary ideas ;[8] he influenced the thought of his son-in-law Shelley ;[9] and his views on property influenced some of the early English socialists.[10] But the absurdities of his conclusions, and the course of events in France and England, caused a rapid decline in the influence of his book.[11] But it had one effect which was by no means unimportant. Godwin's dreams of a millennium, in which human life might be indefinitely extended, suggested the objection that, in that event, population would soon increase at such a rate that no means of subsistence would be left. Malthus developed this objection in his famous *Essay on Population* ;[12] and as we shall now see that essay played a large part in shaping the new economic theories which took shape in the classical political economy.

[1] English Thought in the Eighteenth Century ii 273-274 ; Driver, Social and Political Ideas of the Revolutionary Era 164-166, 167-170.
[2] Ibid 166-167.
[3] Ibid 170-171.
[4] Ibid 172-173.
[5] Leslie Stephen, English Thought in the Eighteenth Century ii 278.
[6] Driver, Social and Political Ideas of the Revolutionary Era 175.
[7] Ibid 175-176 ; Leslie Stephen, English Thought in the Eighteenth Century ii 279.
[8] Driver, Social and Political Ideas of the Revolutionary Era 142-143.
[9] Ibid 179.
[10] Ibid ; H. W. C. Davis, Age of Grey and Peel 309 ; below 39, 40.
[11] " The Godwinian teaching, as a system, very soon failed to satisfy ; and by the time of Peterloo had ceased to have intellectual validity for most of the practical reformers of the new age," Driver, op. cit. 179 ; Clapham, An Economic History of Modern Britain i 313-314.
[12] Leslie Stephen, English Thought in the Eighteenth Century ii 279.

The New Economic Ideas

We have seen that the foundations of the new economic ideas, which were generally accepted in this period and up to the end of the nineteenth century, had been laid by Adam Smith in the eighteenth century in his great book on *The Wealth of Nations*.[1] The central idea of that book was the idea that the wealth of a nation is best secured by giving free play to the efforts of the individual to better his condition—" man's self-love is God's providence " ; that the laws of nature if left to themselves will produce the best and most just results ; and therefore that each individual should be left free to conduct his own trade in his own way.[2] But we have seen also that Adam Smith had always maintained close touch with business men and with statesmen such as Turgot and Franklin, and therefore with the facts of business life ; and that he had made some use of his own experience as commissioner of customs.[3] His theories were therefore leavened by a knowledge of practical life at first or second hand, with the result that he never became a slave to them. He was willing to admit that there were circumstances in which it was for the good of the state that men's natural liberty should be restrained—to admit, that is, that the principle that each man's interests are naturally identical with the interests of the state is not always true, and that therefore there must be legislation to secure artificially this identification of interests.[4] As M. Halévy has shown,[5] Adam Smith never really faced the logical difficulty which is raised by such an admission. One reason why he did not face it was the inefficacy and antiquated character of the existing legal restrictions upon trade ;[6] another was the objection felt by many schools of liberal thinkers to all interference by a government constructed on a plan of which they disapproved ;[7] and another was the spread of liberal ideas which was brought about by the American War of Independence :

This, in a sense by force, converted the English public to the new doctrine of commercial liberalism, and showed the possibility of establishing commercial cosmopolitanism in the near future . . . . These liberal ideas implied a principle ; they needed a doctrine and a thinker to arrange them in a system. At a propitious moment Adam Smith gave them a definite and a classical form . . . . Any regulation limiting the freedom of commerce—between two provinces, between a mother-country and its colonies, between two colonies of the same mother-country, between any two nations whatever—when it is not useless is evil, because it contradicts the principle of the identity of interests.[8]

---

[1] Vol. xi 393-394 ; above 4. [2] Vol. xi 393, 517.
[3] Ibid 510, 511, 512. [4] Ibid 514-516.
[5] Philosophic Radicalism 101-102. [6] Vol. xi 466-469, 517.
[7] Above 8; below 111, 118 ; cp. Halévy, Philosophic Radicalism 104 ; Beer, History of British Socialism i 220, says very truly of the Utilitarians that " in practice their libertarian views really meant opposition to a Tory government."
[8] Beer, History of British Socialism i 106-107.

It was because Adam Smith had not realized all the impli-cations which his admission of necessary modifications to his main thesis of the natural identification of interests involved, that he laid himself open to the criticism, which Bentham made in 1787 in his *Defence of Usury*,[1] of his failure to condemn the usury laws. Bentham accepted Adam Smith's central theory; and contended that therefore trade in money should be as free as trade in any other commodity. In the same way, too, he neglected Adam Smith's practical objections to the immediate abolition of all the laws which regulated colonial trade, and to the thesis that colonies were economically useless.[2] In his tract entitled *Emancipate your Colonies* addressed in 1793 to the French National Convention,[3] he reasoned logically from some of Adam Smith's principles. In his *Manual of Political Economy*[4] he recommends a policy of *laissez faire*. He says:[5]

With a view of causing an increase to take place in the national wealth, or with a view to increase the means either of subsistence or enjoyment, without some special reason, the general rule is, that nothing ought to be done or attempted by government. The motto or watchword of government, on these occasions, ought to be—*Be quiet.*

It is true that at the end of his life he somewhat modified his views, both with respect to colonial policy,[6] and with respect to the proper sphere of governmental action;[7] and it is true that in his *Manual of Political Economy* he admitted a longer list of " agenda " by the government than the economists would have approved.[8] But for the most part he continued to maintain his *laissez faire* attitude on economic questions for reasons of which I shall speak later.[9]

This insistence on the logical consequences of Adam Smith's central idea, and its simplification by the omission of the qualifications which Adam Smith's practical knowledge of affairs led him to make, foreshadows the form which economic ideas will ultimately take under the influence of economists who had adopted many of Bentham's principles.[10] These founders of the " classical political economy " created a logical science, on the foundations laid by Adam Smith, which was so rigorously logical and so scientific that it tended to produce social and commercial consequences which were immediately injurious to the health and peace of the state, and ultimately injurious to its wealth and prosperity.[11] We must now examine the causes for the rise of this new school of political economists which for many years had a

[1] Works iii 3-29; vol. xi 515; below 110.
[2] Wealth of Nations (Cannan's ed.) ii 106, 108, 110-111.
[3] Works iv 407-418; cf. his Manual of Political Economy, Works iii 52-57.
[4] Works iii 31-84. [5] Ibid 33. [6] Below 107.
[7] Below 111. [8] Below 36, 111. [9] Below 34, 75, 110, 111. [10] Below 33-36.
[11] Vol. xi 517-518; above 8; below 30, 31, 36.

large influence on the commercial and industrial legislation of the
state.

We have seen that the French school of political economists
—the Physiocrats—aimed at constructing a logical system ; and
that, because, unlike Adam Smith, they pursued this aim without
troubling to bring their system into relation with concrete facts,
they fell into errors which Adam Smith avoided.[1] But they did
succeed in creating a logical system with the result that " about
the year 1800 it was France and not England that owned a
school of economists." [2] Thus J. B. Say, in his *Traité d'Economie
Politique*, which was published in 1803, said of Adam Smith's
book that it was " a confused assembly of the sanest principles of
political economy, supported by luminous examples, and of the
strangest notions of statistics, mingled with instructive reflections ;
but it is a complete treatise, neither of the one nor of the other ;
his book is a vast chaos of sound ideas, jumbled up with positive
knowledge." [3] In fact, as M. Halévy points out,[4] the theoretical
part of Adam Smith's work is merely preliminary to practical
observations upon phenomena of the industrial and commercial
world.   On the other hand the classical economists, such as
Ricardo and James Mill, tended towards the French idea that
political economy should be treated as a system which was above
all logical and scientific. " What for Adam Smith had been a
preliminary became, for Ricardo, the essence of political economy.
Political economy was not a theory detached from practice,
whatever might subsequently be its practical consequences." [5]
Its object is to discover the laws which regulate the distribution of
wealth ;[6] and those laws were to be as certain as the propositions
of Euclid.[7]

But the attempt to construct this rigidly scientific and
severely logical system encountered a serious difficulty. Adam
Smith's principles explained the mechanism of commerce, and
demonstrated that the less the Legislature interfered with it the
more prosperous it was likely to be, and the more quickly would
the wealth of nations be promoted. But we have seen that even
Adam Smith had admitted that there were circumstances in which
the Legislature should sometimes interfere to prevent evils which
flowed from unfettered freedom—his treatment of the usury
laws and the Navigation Acts are two examples.[8] When Ricardo
and his followers and successors attacked the problem of the
distribution of wealth, the incompetence of *laissez faire* to solve
all problems, and the need for legislation to prevent the evils

---

[1] Vol. xi 514.
[2] Halévy, Philosophic Radicalism 268.
[3] Cited ibid 269.
[4] Ibid 266-267.
[5] Ibid 267.
[6] Ibid.
[7] Ibid 494 ; cp. Stephen, H.C.L. iii 211, cited vol. xi 499 n. 1.
[8] Vol. xi 515-516 ; above 29.

which flowed from unfettered freedom, became even more obvious. This fact has been very clearly explained by Leslie Stephen.[1] He says :

To the theory of exchange was to be added a theory which should determine how the wealth acquired by society was to be distributed amongst its different classes, and to what extent the efforts for well being were confined by irremovable limits. The new doctrines of socialism or communism, tending to a regeneration or a disintegration of society, were beginning to stir in men's minds, and the doctrines of the later investigators begin to take a different colour and to centre round more vital problems. It becomes more evident at each step that a mere theory of commerce . . . cannot answer the serious difficulties which are beginning to present themselves to the legislator and the social reformer. The doctrines enunciated by Adam Smith refer chiefly to the superficial phenomena presented by a society of which it has hitherto been the greatest triumph to preserve a decent amount of fair-play between individuals and classes immersed in a blind struggle for existence. Is that struggle always to continue on its present terms ? Is it always to be blind ? Must starvation and misery be always in the immediate background, and selfishness, more or less decently disguised, and more or less equitably regulated, be the one great force by which to determine the conformation of society ? What are the conditions which we can hope to modify by combined effort, and what are the irrevocable conditions imposed upon men by virtue of their position in the planet, by accommodating themselves to which they can minimize the evils of their lot, but of which it is vain to seek the absolute removal ? In the coming years such problems were to assume continually greater prominence. . . . On one side were to range to themselves the Utopians, who hoped for an extemporized regeneration of society ; on the other, the rigid and sometimes cynical observers who proclaimed too unequivocally the impossibility of ever delivering ourselves from the tyranny of our fate.

Towards the solution of such problems as these a *laissez faire* attitude can make no contribution ; for their existence shows that man's interests are not naturally identical, and that therefore the Legislature should take measures to redress the resulting evils. The fact that nature left to itself does not produce ideally the best and most beneficial results was emphasized by Malthus's *Essay on Population* and by his theory of rent. His *Essay on Population* was written in the first instance to show that Godwin's theory[2] that the abolition of government and law, property and marriage, would eventually produce a race of perfect men governed only by reason, was absurd. He demonstrated that nature, if left to itself, ensures that population increases in a geometrical ratio, while means of subsistence increase only in an arithmetical ratio ; and therefore that, unless some checks to the growth of population were imposed on the growth of population, civilized life would soon disappear.[3]

[1] English Thought in the Eighteenth Century ii 326-327.
[2] Above 26, 27 ; his essay combated also the similar theories of Condorcet, see Essay on Population (Everyman's Library) ii 1-22.
[3] Malthus, Essay on Population (Everyman's Library) i 1-11.

His theory of rent was the outcome of his theory of population. As population increases it must have recourse to less fertile land to get subsistence. The food raised from this less fertile land is less in amount than that raised from the more fertile, though the cost of raising it is the same as raising the larger quantity from the more fertile land. There is therefore a larger profit on the more fertile land, and that larger profit is taken by the landlord as rent. The greater the pressure of population the more it is necessary to have recourse to the less fertile land, the more is taken by the landlord of the more fertile land for rent, and the less is left for wages and profit.[1]

It would seem to follow from Malthus's principles that nature, if left to itself, produces results which are the reverse of beneficial to the community. His law of population shows that, unless the natural increase of population can be prevented, there is an end of civilized life : his law of rent shows that the interest of the land-lord is not the same as the interest of those whose wages and profits are diminished by the necessity of paying an increased rent. Moreover, if wages must be determined by free competition only, they were determined by a natural law which " perpetuates the poverty of the labourer," for, according to that law, they are an amount which merely allows the labourer to subsist.[2] But such a natural law was bound to result in conflicts between capital and labour, which, in the interests of the peace of the state and of the well being of its members, ought to be regulated by the state. Having regard to all these considerations, it is clear that the state, in the interests of the greatest happiness of the greatest number, ought to take a hand and regulate the economic life of the nation by artificial rules. In the sphere of law Bentham fully recognized that the state ought to intervene. The whole object of law, civil and criminal, was to secure the greatest happiness of the greatest number by artificial rules. But in the sphere of economics he took the opposite line. He regarded attempts to interfere in economic questions as attempts to enforce either the duty of prudence which could be best left to the individual,[3] or the duty of benevolence which would wither if an attempt were made to enforce it by artificial sanctions ;[4] or as an attempt to secure abundance by artificial means, which were needless and therefore harmful, because natural means sufficed.[5] Hence there is a logical con-tradiction in his thought in these two spheres. As M. Halévy says :[6]

---

[1] Halévy, Philosophic Radicalism 276-280 ; Malthus's Theory of Rent is contained in his Nature and Progress of Rent which he published in 1815.

[2] Halévy, Philosophic Radicalism 331, 338.

[3] Theory of Legislation (Ogden's ed.) 61.

[4] Ibid 65.   [5] Works ix 13-14.   [6] Op. cit. 119.

Exchange is the fundamental idea in political economy, and the postulate implied in the principle of the identity of interests is the idea that exchange is constantly giving labour its recompense, and that the mechanism of exchange is just. But in fact, the laws of exchange are only in conformity with justice in cases when the individuals affected by the exchange are both of them labourers deriving an equal produce from equal labour. If then this condition is not realized, does not the principle of utility prescribe that, when the two notions of *exchange* and *recompense* do not coincide, the notion of *recompense* should be put before the notion of *exchange*, and that legislative artifices should be conceived such that all labour may be guaranteed its recompense, and every need its satisfaction ? Or else, if on the contrary, the principle of the spontaneous identity of interests is true, why should it not be applied in its entirety ? And why, since all constraint is recognized as bad, should not the State be refused the right of intervening by means of penal restraints in the social relations of its citizens ? Why should the idea of criticizing the notion of punishment be considered Utopian, when it logically rests on the same foundation as does the criticism of all intervention by the State in the economic relations of the citizens ?

What then were the reasons why Bentham and his followers— Ricardo and James Mill and the school of political economy which they founded—refused to recognize the logical consequences of the fact that nature does not secure " the spontaneous identity of interests," or, in other words, the greatest happiness of the greatest number ?

The reasons why they refused to recognize this fact, and why they insisted on the *laissez faire* principle, even more rigorously than Adam Smith, were in some respects similar to the reasons which influenced Adam Smith and in some respects different. They can, I think, be summed up as follows :

(1) We have seen that those who supported these new economic ideas, like those who supported the new political ideas, distrusted all state control, partly because they disliked and distrusted the existing political machinery which gave power to a small class, and partly because they believed (with some justice) that the existing laws which controlled industry were obsolete and unsuited in their present form to modern conditions.[1] More especially they disliked the poor law. Malthus would have liked to abolish it altogether [2]—its obvious tendency was " to increase population without increasing subsistence." [3] Workhouses might be permitted for the relief of very hard cases ; but even that relief should only be given in exchange for work done.[4] Ricardo recognized that the introduction of machinery might for the moment bear hardly on the labourer ; but he maintained that, as it made for the wealth of the state, that hardship must be

---

[1] Above 30, 31.   [2] Essay on Population ii 200-209.
[3] Halévy, Philosophic Radicalism 239.
[4] Ibid 239 ; and the references to the 1st ed. of the Essay on Population there cited.

endured.[1] It was impossible to regulate wages by law because the value of labour must depend on supply and demand[2]—he was surprised that the Acts which allowed the magistrates to settle wages in the silk trade[3] should be allowed to remain on the statute book in the year 1823.[4] The state could do nothing to mitigate the hardships resulting from economic crises, and should not attempt to intervene. This " is an evil to which a rich man must submit : and it would not be more reasonable to complain of it than it would be in a rich merchant to lament that his ship was exposed to the dangers of the sea, whilst his poor neighbour's cottage was safe from all such hazard." [5] Ricardo's and Malthus's point of view is, as M. Halévy points out, somewhat different from Adam Smith's optimistic belief that nature if left to itself will produce good results. " It is a fatalism rather than an optimism." [6] And this was the attitude of Bentham who once said that Ricardo was his spiritual grandson.[7] We have seen that in his *Manual of Political Economy* he preached the gospel of " quietism," partly because governmental interference is needless and therefore pernicious—abundance can be best secured by letting nature take its course ;[8] partly because all coercion is an evil, and therefore must not be resorted to unless the resulting benefit will, on balance, produce a larger amount of good ; and partly because the attempt to interfere would be an attempt to enforce duties of prudence or benevolence which cannot usefully be undertaken by the Legislature.[9] Therefore he held that the list of things " non agenda " by a government is very large.[10]

(2) Ricardo was a financier and the son of a financier. He represented the interests of big business, which wished to see all restraints on individual enterprise swept away.[11] If all protective duties could be so far as possible abolished, and, in particular, if the corn laws were repealed, prices would be regulated wholly by those " principles of true political economy which never change."[12] Free trade in corn would diminish the unfair advantage which the increase in the prosperity of the country gave, by the law of rent, to the landlords.[13] The usury laws must be repealed because " they

---

[1] See a speech of his in 1823 9 Hansard (N.S.) 601.
[2] Ibid.   [3] Vol. xi 472.   [4] 9 Hansard (N.S.) 149.
[5] Principles of Political Economy 161, cited Halévy, Philosophic Radicalism 340.
[6] " The theory of economic freedom in Ricardo, is on occasions less like an act of faith in nature than a recognition of man's powerlessness to correct the calamities which assail him. It is a fatalism rather than an optimism. The government must not try to interfere in economic relations ; for possibly the remedies it tried would be worse than the evils to be cured," Philosophic Radicalism 340.
[7] " Of Ricardo Bentham used to say : ' I was the spiritual father of Mill, and Mill was the spiritual father of Ricardo : so that Ricardo was my spiritual grandson.' " Bowring, Works of Bentham x 498.
[8] Above 29.   [9] Above 32.   [10] Works, iii 42-66.
[11] Halévy, Philosophic Radicalism 340-342, 370.
[12] He said this in a speech made in 1823 9 Hansard (N.S.) 381.
[13] Halévy, Philosophic Radicalism 341.

are a dead weight on those seeking to raise money."[1]   The Act
which prohibited the truck system was an obnoxious Act, for in
many cases workmen were benefited by payments in kind.[2]
Proposals to restrict the use of machinery or to fix a minimum
rate of wages must be resisted, because the adoption of those
expedients would enable rivals to outsell us in foreign markets.[3]
These conclusions were fortified partly by that distrust of all
governmental interference which I have already mentioned,[4]
and partly by that prejudice in favour of individual freedom and
freedom of trade which had been fostered by the principles of the
common law.[5]

(3) We have seen that Bentham considered that, though
equality might be desirable, it was impossible to establish it by
legislation, and that any attempt to establish it would be fatal to
that security, which should be the paramount aim of the Legislature.[6]   " Nature has instituted inequality of conditions. . . .
If this inequality were destroyed by force, there could only be
substituted for it either a worse inequality, or universal poverty.
To protect the inequality of fortunes against violence is, according
to the definition which Bentham borrowed from Adam Smith, the
raison d'etre and the justification of government." [7]   It is true
that, so far as possible, fortunes should be equalized. A society in
which the varieties of fortune are graded, so that there is a
numerous and prosperous middle class is most favourable to the
" maximization of happiness." [8]   What should be aimed at
therefore is the encouragement of this class.   We shall see that
James Mill subscribed to this idea when he magnified the virtues
of this class in his *Essay on Government*, and contended that the
democratic form of government which he advocated would
conduce to its predominance ;[9] and that this predominance was
in fact realized by the Reform Act of 1832.[10] But the realization of
this ideal could be best secured, not by governmental inter-
ferences with the regular course of trade or by legislation
designed to help the poorer classes, but by letting each individual
work out his own salvation.

[1] Speech in Parliament in 1821 5 Hansard (N.S.) 178-179.
[2] 7 Hansard (N.S.) 1124 (1822).
[3] 9 Hansard (N.S.) 601 (1823).   [4] Above 33.
[5] Vol. xi 477-484 ; cp. vol. iv 344 n. 6, 350 ; below 339 seqq.   [6] Above 23.
[7] Halévy, Philosophic Radicalism 366 ; Bentham Pannomial Fragments,
Works iii 228-230.
[8] " On consideration of what is stated above, it will be found that the plan of
distribution applied to the matter of wealth, which is most favourable to universality
of subsistence, and thence, in other words, to the maximization of happiness, is
that in which, while the fortune of the richest . . . is greatest, the degrees between
the fortune of the least rich and that of the most rich are most numerous—in other
words, the gradation most regular and insensible," Pannomial Fragments, Works
iii 230.
[9] Below 138, 139.   [10] Below 258.

(4) It followed that the only way in which government could usefully interfere was by the dissemination of knowledge, by rewards given to discoveries of new knowledge, by education, by encouraging prudence and thrift by such means as savings banks and benefit societies, by colonization, by discouraging early marriages, by restricting the number of children to the number which the parents could bring up and educate.[1] In these ways the evils which flowed from Malthus's law of population would be diminished.

By these arguments the economists sought to justify their belief that, since political economy was a system governed by laws of universal validity, it was not only inexpedient and useless, but even dangerous, to interfere with them by legislative action. But the practical consequences of this *laissez faire* attitude were so cruel and so evidently harmful to the state that public opinion was shocked. The evils of child labour, the effect upon the artisans of long hours of work in insanitary factories, the evils of the truck system, the unemployment produced by the introduction of new machinery and by periodical economic crises, the growing hostility between capital and labour resulting in industrial disputes which disturbed the peace of the state—all aroused against the principles of the classical economists an increasing weight of hostility. This hostility was aggravated by the manner in which some of their advocates preached the new Malthusian doctrine of birth control as a means of remedying many economic ills.[2] This doctrine added strength to the feeling that this new political economy was God-less and anti-religious. In 1823 Ricardo said in Parliament that " the words ' political economy ' had of late become terms of ridicule and reproach ";[3] Sydney Smith said that Malthus and Ricardo had made political economy " a school of metaphysics ";[4] and in 1829 Macaulay said[5] that the utilitarians had " made the science of political economy—a science of vast importance to the welfare of nations—an object of disgust to the majority of the community." In these circumstances it is not surprising to find that, beside the new economic ideas of the classical economists, other ideas of a much more radical and revolutionary character were springing up. " If in the

---

[1] Bentham, Manual of Political Economy, Works iii 71 ; Malthus, Essay on Population (Everyman's Library) ii 151-167, 211-215 ; Halévy, Philosophic Radicalism 362-363, 364-365.

[2] Halévy, Philosophic Radicalism 365 ; J. S. Mill, Autobiography 105, says, " This great doctrine (Malthus's population principle), originally brought forward as an argument against the indefinite improvability of human affairs, we took up with ardent zeal in the contrary sense, as indicating the sole means of realizing that improvability by securing full employment and high wages to the whole labouring population through a voluntary restriction of the increase of their numbers."

[3] 9 Hansard (N.S.) 816.   [4] Cited Bagehot, Literary Studies i 4.

[5] The Westminster Reviewer's defence of Mill.

natural progress of society wages were to tend constantly towards the bare minimum of subsistence, the cost of labour to increase by the increase in the cost of food, and profits were thereby to fall, while the resort to inferior soils only benefited the landlord, the case for a revolution in a society so constituted seemed not only plausible but reasonable." [1]

One section of these more radical and revolutionary reformers questioned the righteousness of all the established theories as to the rights of property. In 1775 Spence, a Newcastle schoolmaster, wrote a famous pamphlet on *The Real Rights of Man*, in which he outlined the consequences of the elimination of landlords. [2] The people would live together in families which owned the land, and each householder would rent his fair share. The state would consist of communities of small cultivators, which communities, out of the rents of the land, would provide for all the needs of government. In the early nineteenth century these theories of Spence inspired Spencean societies which advocated an agrarian communism. The rents received by the state from this communal property, after providing for the expenses of government, were to be divided among the whole people. [3] The doctrines preached by these societies so frightened the Legislature that a statute of 1817 specially singled out the Spenceans for condemnation. [4]

Other writers questioned the righteousness and the expediency of the existence of great estates. Adam Smith regarded them as an anachronism; [5] and, as might be expected, those who followed him made some very radical suggestions for reform. Ogilvie, [6] a professor of Humanity at King's College, Aberdeen, considered that every man has a right to an equal share of the land of his country in its original condition. All the landlord can claim is compensation for the improvements which he has made. The

---

[1] J. S. Nicholson, Camb. Mod. Hist. x 774.

[2] H. W. C. Davis, Age of Grey and Peel 313-314.

[3] Ibid 315.

[4] " Whereas certain societies or clubs calling themselves *Spenceans* or *Spencean Philanthropists*, hold and profess for their object the confiscation and division of the land, and the extinction of the funded property of the kingdom : . . . Be it enacted, that from and after the passing of this Act, all societies or clubs calling themselves *Spenceans* or *Spencean Philanthropists*, and all other societies or clubs . . . who hold and profess . . . the same objects and doctrines shall be and the same are utterly suppressed and prohibited," 57 George III c. 19 § 24.

[5] " When great landed estates were a sort of principalities, entails might not be unreasonable. . . . But in the present state of Europe, when small as well as great estates derive their security from the laws of their country, nothing can be more completely absurd. They are founded upon the most absurd of all suppositions, the supposition that each successive generation of men have not an equal right to the earth, and to all that it possesses ; but that the property of the present generation should be restrained and regulated according to the fancy of those who died perhaps five hundred years ago," Wealth of Nations (Cannan's ed.) i 362.

[6] H. W. C. Davis, Age of Grey and Peel 316-318.

state should take the land and divide it amongst its citizens, so that eventually the land would be divided amongst these small holders. As Davis has said, he inspired some of the land schemes of the Chartists ; and he " anticipated some feature of the Irish Land Purchase Act of 1891, of the English Small Holdings Act of 1892, and of the Finance Act of 1909." [1] Ogilvie's views as to rights to landed property were followed by Paine. We have seen that in the Second Part of his *Rights of Man* he had advocated the taxation of the rich to provide for the needs of the poor.[2] In his *Agrarian Justice*, published in 1797, he subscribed to the thesis that land in its original condition belonged to the state ; that the acquisition of movable property was in part due to the labour of society, so that its owner had no right to an exclusive property ; and that therefore a succession duty on property might rightly be levied which should be applied to relieve the poor.[3]

The projects of Spence, Ogilvie, and Paine were all communistic in character and were all directed to socialistic objects. They were based on the theory that every man has, during his life, a right to a certain portion of the land of the state ; that the state should dispose of the land of the state in such a way as to give effect to his right ; and that it should use the rent which it can derive from land and the taxation it levies on other property to equalize advantages. Other economic theories, almost as divergent from the theories of the classical economists, pursued policies which were not communistic, and tended in some cases to a more socialistic, and in others to a more individualistic, solution of economic problems.

The most famous of these theorists was Robert Owen[4] (1771-1858) who in some respects anticipates the policy pursued by modern legislation.

Owen was a self-made man who became the owner of successful cotton mills. His experience of the evils of the unregulated factory system, which was arising as the result of the industrial revolution, led him to reflect on the evils of a system in which " a great attention was paid to the dead machinery, and the neglect and disregard of the living machinery." [5] Since he had come to the conclusion that all religions were wrong in thinking that men were responsible for their own characters, and that the true view was that character was formed by a man's circumstance and environment, he thought it his duty to conduct his cotton mill

[1] H. W. C. Davis, Age of Grey and Peel 318.   [2] Above 21.
[3] H. W. C. Davis, Age of Grey and Peel 319-320.
[4] F. M. Page, Robert Owen and the Early Socialists, Social and Political Ideas of the Age of Reaction and Reconstruction (ed. Hearnshaw) 82-111 ; H. W. C. Davis, Age of Grey and Peel 321-326; Clapham, An Economic History of Modern Britain i 314-315.
[5] Owen's Autobiography 34, cited F. M. Page, op. cit. 86.

at New Lanark in such a way that the character of his employés should be developed in the right direction. He established stores where goods were sold at 25 per cent below retail prices—an anticipation of the co-operative system. He shortened the hours of labour without reducing wages, and instituted a committee of workmen to suggest improvements and to deal with complaints. He ceased to employ pauper children, and employed no child under ten. He imposed fines for drunkenness and immorality, and devoted the proceeds to a fund, contributed to by the workmen, for the benefit of the old and sick and those injured by accidents. He instituted a remarkable system of education for the children of the workers and his child employés, by means of which he tried to carry out his theory that character depended on environment. This experiment was very successful, and it aroused much public interest at home and abroad ; for it " showed the possibility of producing great wealth without injury to the human element ; the happiness and intelligence of the children showed the forma-tive effects of a careful training from infancy ; the village showed the effect of a bettered environment even upon the hardened adult character." [1] In all these ways Owen was a pioneer. His suggestions were the basis of the first Factory Act [2] which began the long process of humanizing industry ; and he has claims to be considered one of the founders of the co-operative movement and of those saner aspects of the socialistic movement which have been endorsed by the Legislature. Some of his other views, particularly his views on religion and marriage, aroused much opposition ; and his attempts to found communistic labour colonies were, from the first, doomed to failure.

Very different from Owen's mildly socialistic and later com-munistic programmes were the theories and proposals of Thomas Hodgskin (1787-1869). [3] Hodgskin was as much a believer in a natural law, which is superior to positive law, as the classical economists. But he interpreted it in a different way, and he differed from them as to the position of positive law in the state and its relation to this natural law. He maintained that, according to this natural law, the worker has a right to the whole produce of his labour ; for labour alone produces wealth—as Ricardo had admitted. As compared with labour, capital is comparatively unimportant. Circulating capital is not a fixed fund : it is a stream which flows from co-existing labour. Fixed capital, likewise, is produced by labour, and is effective only when

[1] F. M. Page, op. cit. 95.

[2] 42 George III c. 73 ; it applied to wool and cotton factories, and, *inter alia*, regulated the hours of work of apprentices and made some provision for their education ; below 213, 313, 335.

[3] C. H. Driver, Thomas Hodgskin and the Individualists, Social and Political Ideas of the Age of Reaction and Reconstruction (ed. Hearnshaw) 191-219.

used by present labour. He had no use for positive law—the
world and the state is and should be governed by permanent
natural law. Like Godwin,[1] he would abolish positive law and
government. *Laissez faire* and unrestricted competition should
prevail ; for, as might be expected from his views about positive.
law and government, he is an uncompromising individualist.

Hodgskin's views as to the rights of labour made him popular
amongst the working classes. But they naturally aroused the
opposition of the classical economists—James Mill thought that,
if they spread, they "would be the subversion of civilized
society " ; and Place lamented the evil influence of the teaching
both of Owen and Hodgskin.[2] These views did not become really
influential till they were detached from his individualistic creed,
and incorporated by William Thompson into the socialistic creed
in his *Inquiry into the Principles of the Distribution of Wealth
most conducive to Human Happiness.*[3] In that form they influenced the Chartist movement which was, in effect, an attempt,
by means of a revolution, to reorganize society on a socialistic
and labour basis.[4] The Chartist movement influenced the thought
of Karl Marx who advocated class warfare as the only means of
realizing the " labour value theory."[5] He held that it was not
till the proletariat had seized political power and expropriated the
bourgeoisie that the right of the labourer to the whole produce of
his labour could be realized.[6] According to Marx the labourer who
makes these claims is more especially the manual labourer ; and,
since the numbers of these are greater, the menace of this revolutionary and predatory socialism has increased in proportion as the
government of the state has become more completely democratic.

This slight sketch of some of the many ideas on economic
questions, which were making their appearance in this age of
industrial revolution, illustrates the importance which all these
questions had assumed. Some of these ideas were fantastic ; but
others contained more practical suggestions which were destined
to be developed in the latter part of the nineteenth and in the
twentieth centuries. But during this period and during the
greater part of the nineteenth century the ideas of the classical
economists were the dominant ideas. It is true that in the
course of the nineteenth century many of them were being modified as the result of a growing appreciation of their bad effects
upon the health of the workers ; for though these ideas made for
the increase in the wealth of the state by reason of the lead in
manufacturing industries which Great Britain had attained, they
did not make for its health ; and they ceased to make even for its

---

[1] Above, 26, 27.   [2] C. H. Driver, op. cit. 200, 202.
[3] See M. Beer, History of British Socialism i 218-228.
[4] M. Beer, op. cit. i 280 ; below 257.   [5] M. Beer, op. cit. ii 281.   [6] Ibid ii 212.

wealth when that lead in the manufacturing industries began to disappear. In spite of some modifications of these ideas, they retained their predominance too long, and the false assumption of the natural identification of interests, upon which they rested, delayed too long the legislation which was necessary to produce artificially some identification of the opposing interests which arose out of the industrial revolution. Fortunately no such false assumption was made by those who were advocating new ideas of law reform. We shall now see that Bentham, the leader of the law reformers, pursued a policy on questions of law reform which was the reverse of his policy on economic questions, with the result that his ideas on the former set of questions have had a much greater permanence and a much more beneficial effect upon the state than his ideas on the latter set.

Bentham and the New Ideas as to Law Reform

It is the new ideas as to law reform with which this History is directly concerned. But it was necessary to say something of the new ideas on political, religious, and economic questions because, without some knowledge of them, it is hardly possible to understand fully the new ideas as to law reform. The reason is that the new ideas as to law reform are only a part of the series of new ideas which originated in the need to adjust the institutions and the law of the state to the new conditions introduced by the industrial and the French revolutions. Because this series of new ideas had a common origin the proposals made by the advocates of reform in all these spheres of the national life had many points in common. In fact they had so many points in common that, as we shall see in the next section,[1] they were combined in the coherent body of doctrine which is generally known as philosophic radicalism.

At the end of the eighteenth century many thinkers both abroad and in England had seen the need for extensive reforms in the law. We have seen that in 1764 Beccaria had tried to reform and to rationalize criminal law and procedure by the application of the principle which Bentham applied to rationalize all branches of the law—the greatest happiness of the greatest number, and by insisting that the severity of a punishment should be determined only by the consideration that the evil occasioned by the punishment must exceed the good expected from the crime.[2] Helvetius in his book *De l'Esprit* had maintained that, just as the physical universe is subject to the laws of motion, so the moral universe is subject to the laws of self-interest.[3] He taught that the

---

[1] Below 134 seqq.   [2] Vol. xi 575-577.
[3] Halévy, Philosophic Radicalism 19, citing De l'Esprit, discours ii chap. ii.

art of the legislator " consists in forcing men, through their
feeling of self-love, to be always just to one another ";[1] that
" the excellence of laws depends on the uniformity of the views of
the legislator and on the interdependence of the laws themselves ";[2] and that " to establish this interdependence, it must
be possible to reduce all the laws to some simple principle, such as
the principle of the utility of the public, that is to say, of the
greatest number of men subject to the same form of government."[3]
We have seen that in England Burke, Blackstone, Mansfield, and
Gibbon were all conscious of the need to make reforms in the law,
and that they were all ready to welcome reforms to remedy
abuses, and to bring the law into harmony with the needs of the
day.[4] But with the exception of Eden,[5] whose work was confined
to the criminal law, no law reformer had as yet appeared in
England who, having thought out a comprehensive set of
philosophical principles upon which reforms should be made, was
prepared to apply them in detail to the reform of all branches of
English law. Bentham was the first English lawyer to think out a
comprehensive set of philosophical principles upon which reforms
in the law ought to be made. In the light of these principles he
devoted his long life to the production of detailed programmes of
reform in the subject matter of the law, in the form of its statement, in the machinery of its enforcement, in the institutions of
the state ; and he insisted on the duty of the Legislature to make
all these reforms by direct legislation. It is for these reasons that
Brougham could truly say that " the age of law reform and the
age of Jeremy Bentham are one and the same." [6]

At this point I shall deal, in the first place, with Bentham's life
and character ; in the second place, with the principal works in
which he stated his principles and applied them to the reform of
the law ; and, in the third place, with the strong and weak points
of those principles.

---

[1] Halévy, Philosophic Radicalism 20, citing De l'Esprit, discours ii chap. xxiv.
[2] Ibid 21, citing discours ii chap. xvii.
[3] Ibid 21, citing De l'Esprit, discours ii chap. xvii.
[4] Vol. xii 549-551, 730, 732-733, 735.
[5] Ibid 364-365.
[6] " The age of law reform and the age of Jeremy Bentham are one and the same.
He is the father of the most important of all the branches of reform, the leading
and ruling department of human improvement. No one before him had ever
seriously thought of exposing the defects in our English system of jurisprudence.
All former students had confined themselves to learn its principles ; . . . and all
former writers had but expounded the doctrines handed down from age to age. . . .
He it was who first made the mighty step of trying the whole provisions of our
jurisprudence by the test of expediency, fearlessly examining how far each part was
connected with the rest ; and with a yet more undaunted courage, inquiring how
far even its most consistent and symmetrical arrangements were framed according
to the principle which should pervade a code of laws—their adaptation to the circumstances of society, to the wants of men, and to the promotion of human happiness," Brougham, Speeches ii 287-288.

(1) *Bentham's life and character* [1]

Jeremy Bentham was born February 15, 1748. His father was an attorney, whose remarks (recorded by Cooksey) on the Court of Chancery and the Chancellors who presided there, show that he was an observant critic of some of the aspects of the legal panorama of the day.[2] His practice was not large ; but he was so successful a speculator in house property that he left his son a comfortable competence, and thus enabled him to devote all his time to the juristic studies which have made him famous. Bentham as a boy was undersized and physically weak, but intellectually precocious. At the age of three he was found studying Rapin's History of England ; and at four he began to study Latin. The elder Bentham was proud of his precocious son, and imagined that he saw in him a future Lord Chancellor.[3] Though he was disappointed that his son refused to tread the path which might lead to the woolsack, though he never really understood him or gained his confidence,[4] he was always ready to advertise his achievements in branches of learning, legal and otherwise,[5] which were very remote from the sort of learning to which a practising attorney was accustomed.

Bentham went to Westminster school at the age of seven. At school he gained a considerable reputation for his Greek and Latin verses, and at the age of ten he was able to write a letter in Greek and Latin to Dr. Bentham the subdean of Christ Church. Though in later life he thought badly of the education given at Westminster, he made such progress in his studies that at the age of twelve he was sent to Queen's College, Oxford. Before he was matriculated he was obliged to sign the thirty-nine articles. But, on examining them, he came to the conclusion that some were unintelligible, and others contrary to reason or scripture. He applied to the fellow of the college whose duty it was to remove these scruples. But he was merely told that it was presumptuous in an uninformed youth to entertain them.[6] This episode

---

[1] Life by Bowring in vols. x and xi of Bentham's Works ; Leslie Stephen, The English Utilitarians i chaps. v and vi ; Edinburgh Rev. lxxviii 460-516 ; C. M. Atkinson, Jeremy Bentham ; F. C. Montague, Introd. to Bentham's Fragment on Government ; C. W. Everett, A Comment on the Commentaries ; D.N.B. ; Graham Wallas, Pol. Sci. Quart. xxxviii 45-56 ; A. A. Mitchell, Jurid. Rev. xxxv 248-284 ; Dicey, Law and Opinion, Lecture VI.

[2] Vol. xii 214, 215, 239 and n. 12, 244.

[3] That Bentham's father was not wholly mistaken in this opinion is clear from what Romilly said in 1817—" The first eminence at the bar, and the opulence which attends it were at his command ; and, if he could have persuaded himself to accommodate his political principles to the wishes of those in power, the most splendid station and the highest honours would have been infallibly within his reach," Ed. Rev. xxix 218. [4] Bowring, op. cit. x 44-45.

[5] He let out the secret of the authorship of the Fragment on Government ; below 40 ; and published the Defence of Usury, below 49.

[6] Bowring, op. cit. x 37.

illustrates one of Bentham's most marked characteristics—an independence of mind which would take nothing for granted ; and it left a lasting memory of oppression—" I signed : but by the view I found myself forced to take of the whole business, such an impression was made as will never depart from me but with life." [1] Like Gibbon [2] and Adam Smith, [3] Bentham had a very poor opinion of Oxford—its studies, its sports, and his contemporaries, graduate and undergraduate. [4] " I learnt nothing. I played at tennis once or twice. I took to reading Greek of my own fancy ; but there was no encouragement : we just went to the foolish lectures of our tutors, to be taught something of logical jargon." [5] However, he gained some notoriety for a copy of verses on the accession of George III which won a modified approval from Dr. Johnson. [6]

In 1763 Bentham, having begun to keep his terms at Lincoln's Inn, [7] took his place as a student in the court of King's Bench ; [8] and in the December of that year he attended Blackstone's lectures at Oxford. We have seen that Bentham admitted that the lectures were popular, but said that even then he had " detected his fallacy respecting natural rights." [9] But we have seen that at this early period in his career his contempt for the technicalities of the law was not full grown. He was so fascinated by the learning and eloquence of Mansfield that two of his earliest printed compositions were two letters written to *The Gazetteer* in answer to an attack upon him ; [10] and he lamented the destruction of Mansfield's library—a loss, he adds, which I should now think a gain. [11]

Bentham was called to the bar in 1769. [12] He lived in chambers in Lincoln's Inn on a small allowance made him by his father. [13] But, since he had gone to the bar " as a bear to the stake," [14] he made no serious attempt to practise. In the first case in which he had a brief he recommended the parties to come to a settlement ; [15]

---

[1] Bowring, op. cit. x. 37. [2] Vol. xii 750. [3] Vol. xi 507.
[4] Bowring, op. cit. x 39-41. [5] Ibid 41.
[6] After making some criticisms he said, " When these objections are removed, the copy will, I believe, be received ; for it is a very pretty performance of a young man," ibid 41. [7] Ibid op. cit. x 45.
[8] " His father gave Mr. Perkins, the crier of the court, seven shillings and six-pence to secure a particular seat during the term. This seat was immediately below the officers, under the judges," ibid.
[9] Works i 249 ; vol. xii 730.
[10] Bowring, op. cit. x 67 ; his earliest printed composition was a letter to The Gazetteer on December 3, 1770, on the enlistment of seamen, in answer to a letter of Wedderburn, Glynne, and Dunning ; the two letters defending Mansfield appeared March 1 and 18, 1771, C. K. Ogden, Bentham Centenary Lecture 53 ; note that in one of these letters he denies the authority of the Mirror of Justices and calls the author " a *bel esprit* of the thirteenth century "—which is very true, vol. ii 330-333. [11] Works x 51.
[12] Black Books of Lincoln's Inn iii 400. [13] Pol. Sci. Quart. xxxviii 48.
[14] Bowring, op. cit. x 78. [15] Ibid 51, 78.

and he tells us that he never pleaded in public. All he ever did in court was to open a bill two or three times " saying a few words for form " ;[1] and, though he had learnt how to draft a bill in equity,[2] he admits that he was " grossly ignorant " of law. " Instead of pursuing any sound studies, or reading any modern books of law, I was set to read old trash of the seventeenth century ; and I looked up to the huge mountain of the law in despair. I can now look *down* upon it from the heights of utility."[3] In fact, the few years after his call to the bar were the most unhappy of his life.[4]

In the first place, he was disgusted with the expensive, and to his mind the fraudulent, technicalities of the law. As early as 1759 a perusal of the memoirs of a celebrated courtesan, Constantia Philips, had implanted in his mind a hatred of the " Daemon of Chicane " ;[5] and his further studies in the law had deepened that hatred. He tells us that, not long after his call to the bar, he had to appear before a Master in Chancery to defend a bill in equity, which he had drawn, against certain exceptions.

" We shall have to attend on such a day," said the solicitor to me, naming a day a week or more distant, " warrants for our attendance will be taken out for two intervening days, but it is not customary to attend before the third." What I learnt afterwards was—that though no attendance more than *one* was ever bestowed, *three* were on every occasion regularly charged for ; for each of the two falsely pretended attendances, the client being, by the solicitor, charged with a fee for himself, as also with a fee of 6/8 paid by him to the Master : the consequence was—that for every actual attendance, the Master, instead of 6/8, received £1, and that, even if inclined, no solicitor durst omit taking out the three warrants instead of one, for fear of the not-to-be hazarded displeasure of that subordinate judge and his superiors.[6]

On another occasion he was brought up against the inaccessibility of the sources of the law. An opinion which he had given was proved to be wrong " according to a manuscript unseen by me, and inaccessible to me ; a MS. containing the report of I know not what opinion, said to have been delivered before I was born, and locked up, as usual, for the purpose of being kept back or produced according as occasion served." [7]

In the second place he was as yet only feeling his way to his

---

[1] Bowring, op. cit. x 83.   [2] Ibid 84.   [3] Ibid.
[4] " Mine was truly a miserable life. I had been taken notice of by the great when a little boy at Westminster School ; for I was an object of praise from the earliest time of which I have any recollection. *That* filled me with ambition. But I met with all sorts of rebukes and disappointments till I was asked to Bowood," ibid.
[5] Bowring, op. cit. x 35 ; see also Works vii 219 note.   [6] Works v 349.
[7] Bowring, op. cit. x 78—" This incident," he says, " the forerunner of so many others, added its fuel to the flame which Constantia had lighted up."

vocation as a law reformer and to the principles upon which reforms ought to be made.[1] His study of such books as Locke, Hume, Helvetius, and Beccaria was leading him to the conclusion that the time was ripe for extensive reforms in the law, and the principle of utility, plainly taught in these and many other philosophical books of the time, was pointing out to him the principle which such reforms should follow. These books and his own reflection were teaching him his true vocation. As early as the year 1768 Helvetius had convinced him that of all earthly pursuits legislation was the most important ; and that he had become conscious that, if he had a genius for anything, it was for legislation.[2] In 1769-70 a pamphlet written by Priestley, in which occurred the phrase " the greatest happiness of the greatest number," had given him the formula which prescribed, to his mind, the only true standard of right and wrong both for morals and for legislation, and he resolved to make it his guide for his future thought and action.[3] That his mind on both these matters was fully made up in 1771-72 is clear from a letter which he wrote to his father in October 1772, telling him that he was at work on *The Elements of Critical Jurisprudence,* and that " till this great business is disposed of I feel myself unable to think of any other." [4] That he saw clearly how he stood as a philosophical jurist in relation to his predecessors is clear from a memorandum which comes from the year 1773 or 1774, in which he wrote :

A digest of the Laws is a work that could not have been executed with advantage before Locke and Helvetius had written : the first establishing a test of perspicuity for ideas ; the latter establishing a standard of rectitude for actions. The idea annexed to a word is a perspicuous one, when the simple ideas included under it are assignable. This is what we owe to Locke. A sort of action is a right one, when the tendency of it is to augment the mass of happiness in the community. This is what we are indebted for to Helvetius.[5]

---

[1] " Poor *fils* Jeremy ! how I was tormented ! I went on very slowly in my father's conception ; but it was the result of dejection of spirits. I was feeling and picking my way—getting the better of prejudice and nonsense—making a little bit of discovery here—another there—and endeavouring to put the little bits together," Bowring, op. cit. x 86.

[2] " Have I genius for anything ? What can I produce ? That was the first enquiry he made of himself. Then came another : What of all earthly pursuits is the most important ? Legislation was the answer Helvetius gave. Have I a genius for legislation ? Again and again was the question put to himself. He turned it over in his thoughts : he sought every symptom he could discover in his natural disposition or acquired habits. And have I indeed a genius for legislation ? I gave myself the answer, fearfully and tremblingly—Yes," Bowring, op. cit. x 27.

[3] Ibid 79-80, 142 ; but he added that though Priestley had invented the formula, " he did not turn it into a system and knew nothing of its value. He had not connected with happiness the ideas of pleasure and pain," ibid 567.

[4] C. W. Everett, A Comment on the Commentaries i, citing Add. MSS. British Museum 33537 pp. 242-243.

[5] Bowring, op. cit. x 70.

But though Bentham had begun his work on *The Elements of Critical Jurisprudence* in 1772, it was not till 1789 that this book, rechristened *The Principles of Morals and Legislation*, saw the light. The main reason for this delay was a fault which Bentham showed all through his life—an incapacity to finish one piece of work before he began another.[1] Though, as his editor Dumont says, Bentham had formed a vast project for a great work on all parts of the law, though " he had before his eyes the general chart of the science," he never worked steadily at any one part of it. " I have seen him," says Dumont, " suspend a work almost finished, and compose a new one, only to assure himself of the truth of a single proposition which seemed to be doubtful. A problem in finance has carried him through the whole of political economy. Certain questions of procedure obliged him to interrupt his principal work till he had treated of judicial organization." [2] We shall see that this characteristic of Bentham's literary methods accounts for the curious form in which many of his principal works were given to the world.[3] The fact that it manifested itself at the very beginning of Bentham's literary career had important effects upon his future.

While Bentham was engaged on his *Elements of Critical Jurisprudence*, his friend Lind had written a book attacking Blackstone's *Commentaries*, and had sent it to Bentham for his criticism. Bentham had found it so unsatisfactory that he had started to rewrite many passages in it. This rewriting resulted in the production of a substantive book—the *Comment on the Commentaries*. Bentham wrote Lind a long letter explaining what he had done, and offering either to let Lind publish the work as his, or to publish it under their joint names. Lind very generously withdrew his book and left the field to Bentham.[4] Bentham's book was nearly finished in September 1775. But in the meantime Bentham had fallen in love with a Miss Dunkly, a pretty penniless girl, whom he had met at his friend Lind's house ; and he proposed to marry her on the income which he could make by his pen. The *Comment on the Commentaries* would, he thought, bring him in £120, and with that sum he proposed to start married life. He thought that he had sufficient " alacrity " to produce a similar volume each year.[5] But the match was forbidden by his father, and the lady seems to have cooled off—perhaps not liking the prospects of marrying upon the precarious earnings of an unknown author.[6] However that may be, the termination of

---

[1] A good account of this characteristic and of Bentham's method of working is given by Leslie Stephen, The English Utilitarians i 192.

[2] Preface to Dumont's Traités cited C. K. Ogden, in his Introduction to Bentham's Theory of Legislation xlix.

[3] Below 63. [4] C. W. Everett, A Comment on the Commentaries 2-5.

[5] Ibid 5-7. [6] Ibid 9.

Bentham's love affair stopped his work on the *Comment on the Commentaries* ; for, when it was nearly finished, he succumbed to his besetting sin. He turned aside to consider the definition of municipal law given by Blackstone in the second section of his Introduction, and the dissertation, accompanying that definition, on government in general and of the government of Great Britain in particular.[1] Since this was a very separate part of the main work, Bentham detached it, and published it as a separate work under the title of *A Fragment on Government*. The *Comment on the Commentaries* remained unpublished till 1928.[2]

Of the *Comment on the Commentaries* and the *Fragment* I have already spoken,[3] and I shall have something more to say of them later.[4] Though the sales of the *Fragment* diminished when Bentham's father let out the secret of its authorship,[5] though it exposed Bentham to considerable criticism,[6] and though for a few years Bentham continued to be a disappointed man,[7] the tide turned when, in 1781, Lord Shelburne, attracted by the *Fragment*, called on him at Lincoln's Inn and invited him to Bowood. This invitation to Bowood was a turning point in Bentham's career. Shelburne, said Bentham, " raised me from the bottomless pit of humiliation—he made me feel I was something." [8] On the other hand, Shelburne said of Bentham that " his disinterestedness and originality of character refresh me as much as the country air does a London physician." [9] Bentham met at Bowood the leading statesmen of the day, who regarded him as an interesting curiosity.[10] But his social gifts and love of music made him popular with the ladies. Lady Shelburne, like her husband, felt for him a lasting affection. " During her last illness (in 1789) Benjamin Vaughan and Bentham were the only persons of the male sex whose presence she could endure ; and, on her death, he was the only male person who was constantly near Lord Shelburne, of that little party to which he looked for consolation." [11] Bentham never forgot the happy days which he had spent at Bowood—" the happiest of his life " he said in a letter to Shelburne ; [12] and the remembrance of them was the more keen because there he again fell in love with one of the ladies he had met there—Miss Caroline

---

[1] A Fragment on Government, Preface (Montague's ed.) 97-98.
[2] Published by C. W. Everett, with a valuable Introduction, from a MS. found amongst Bentham's papers and letters in the library of University College, London ; for a description of the MS. see Mr. Everett's Preface.
[3] Vol. xii 731-732.   [4] Below 50, 59, 66, 68, 79.
[5] Bowring, op. cit. x 77, 79.   [6] Ibid 82.
[7] Above 45 n. 4.
[8] Bowring, op. cit. x 115 ; see the Preface to the 2nd ed. Works i 248.
[9] Pol. Sci. Quart. xxxviii 50.
[10] See Bentham's description in the Preface to the 2nd ed. of the Fragment on Government, Works i 248-251 ; Bowring, op. cit. x 89-115, 116-119.
[11] Ibid 88.   [12] Ibid 89.

Fox.[1] This was a much more serious affair than the first. He wrote to her and proposed marriage in 1805. She wisely but very kindly refused him;[2] but Bentham never ceased to think of her. In 1827 he wrote to her: " I am alive : more than two months advanced in my 80th year—more lively than when you presented me, in ceremony, with the flower in the green lane. Since that day not a single one has passed (not to speak of nights) in which you have not engrossed more of my thoughts than I could have wished." [3] But her reply was cold and distant, and, says Bowring, who was with him when the reply came, the old man was " indescribably hurt." [4]

In 1785 Bentham visited Russia, where his younger brother Samuel, the distinguished naval engineer, was employed by Prince Potemkin. While in Russia he worked at his books ; and it was there that his *Defence of Usury* was written. It was sent to his friend George Wilson who wished to suppress it. But his father got hold of the MS. and published it.[5] Bentham returned from Russia in 1788. In the meantime his friends had been pressing him to publish his book on Jurisprudence. George Wilson pointed out to him that Paley's *Moral and Political Philosophy* had anticipated many of his conclusions ;[6] and, in a later letter, justly criticized his failure to bring his book to completion.[7] He urged him to publish his *Introduction* separately.[8] Bentham at last complied, and in 1789 his *Introduction to the Principles of Morals and Legislation* was published. It is the best written of all Bentham's works and contains, as we shall see,[9] the gist of the legal philosophy which he applied in detail in many other books and papers to different parts of the law civil and criminal, public and private, substantive and adjective. Ten of these different parts of the law were mentioned in the Preface, which were to be treated of in the light of these principles.[10] The book therefore was an introduction not only to the principles of morals and legislation, but to Bentham's life work.

On Bentham's return from Russia his intercourse with Shelburne, now Lord Lansdowne, was renewed. He had visions of becoming a member of Parliament, for he thought that Lord

---

[1] Bowring, op. cit. x 557-558.　　[2] Ibid 419-420.
[3] Ibid 558.　　[4] Ibid 118.
[5] Leslie Stephen, The English Utilitarians i 190.
[6] Bowring, op. cit. x 163-164.
[7] " With one-tenth part of your genius, and a common degree of steadiness, both Sam and you would long since have risen to great eminence. But your history since I have known you, has been to be always running from a good scheme to a better. In the meantime, life passes away and nothing is completed," Bowring, op. cit. x 171.
[8] Ibid 194.　　[9] Below 68.
[10] Works i iii ; the ten parts were : (1) civil law, (2) penal law, (3) procedure, (4) legislation as to matters of reward, (5) constitutional law, (6) political tactics, (7) international law, (8) finance, (9) political economy, (10) universal jurisprudence.

Lansdowne had offered him one of his seats ; and he went so far
as to sketch out an address to the electors.[1] But this was a
misapprehension, as Lord Lansdowne explained to him in a kind
and tactful answer to Bentham's remonstrance—a remonstrance
which was contained in a letter of sixty-one pages.[2] Lord
Lansdowne knew very well that Bentham was not capable of
shining in the House of Commons. As he said, he never supposed
that Bentham wished for a seat " for this plain reason, that the
same reasons which made you decline the practice of your
profession applied in a great measure to Parliament." [3] Bentham
replied in a friendly apologetic letter, and peace was restored. On
the occasion of Hastings' impeachment he helped Lord Lansdowne
by advice on the law of evidence,[4] and he once wrote an opinion
on a point in that branch of the law which won the approval of
Sir Eardley Wilmot.[5] But for Bentham the most important
result of this renewal of his intercourse with Lord Lansdowne was
his intimacy with Romilly and his introduction to Dumont.

Romilly,[6] like Lord Lansdowne, was a great admirer of the
Fragment and of Bentham's other writings.[7] He was, said
Bentham, " among the earliest, and, for a time, the only efficient
one of my disciples." To him " my works, such as they are, were
from first to last a text book." [8] Romilly tried, with small success,
to effect some of the reforms in the criminal law which Bentham
had advocated ;[9] and on several occasions he probably saved
Bentham from prosecution by his advice to him not to publish
some of his tracts.[10] Two of these tracts were *The Truth v.
Ashhurst*, and *The Elements of Packing*. He also advised him not
to publish *Church of Englandism and its Catechism examined* [11]—
but it would seem that in this case his advice was not taken and
no prosecutions followed. Bentham's association with Dumont,[12]
which was due to Romilly, had very different and very much more
important results. He gave Bentham his world wide reputation,
and that reputation helped to spread his fame in this country.

Bentham had already corresponded with French writers[13]—
we have seen that Helvetius helped him to form his philosophy of
law ; [14] and at the time of the French Revolution he wrote for

---

[1] Bowring, op. cit. x 245.   [2] Ibid 229-243.
[3] Ibid 242.   [4] Ibid 117, 181.
[5] Ibid 185-186 ; for Eardley Wilmot see vol. xii 479-482.   [6] Below 274.
[7] Bowring, op. cit. x 186 ; Romilly, Memoirs (ed. 1842) i 308 ; ii 94, 198, 480.
[8] Works v 370.   [9] Below 185, 186, 235, 236.
[10] Ed. Rev. lxxviii 511.   [11] Romilly, Memoirs (ed. 1842) ii 488-489.
[12] Dumont was a Protestant minister who was born at Geneva in 1759 ; political
troubles had driven him into exile ; he was tutor to Shelburne's son, and in 1788
visited Paris with Romilly ; it was then that Romilly showed him some of Bentham's
papers and that Dumont undertook to edit and publish them. Romilly introduced
him to Scarlett who says of him that " it was impossible to know him without
admiring his wit and his genius," P. C. Scarlett, Memoirs of Lord Abinger 54.
[13] Bowring, op. cit. x 87, 190-194.   [14] Above 4, 46.

the benefit of the Constituent Assembly his *Political Tactics*, and *Draft of a Code for the Organization of the Judicial Establishment in France*; and the French in return had made him a French citizen along with Paine, Priestley, Wilberforce, Mackintosh, and others.[1] Just before the Revolution Dumont had taken some of Bentham's manuscripts and was reducing them to order and form. When it broke out he used some of Bentham's matter to supply Mirabeau (with whom he was on intimate terms) with some of the material for his speeches and addresses.[2] In the course of the next ten years he succeeded in reducing, with great skill, Bentham's scattered matter to literary form. During the composition of the work he got very little assistance from Bentham, who would never willingly reconsider or discuss a manuscript which he had put aside.[3] On the other hand, Bentham, rather inconsiderately, made some rather captious criticisms when the MS. was in proof.[4] The work was published in 1802 under the title of *Traités de Législation civile et pénale, Précédés de Principes généraux de Législation, et d'une Vue d'un Corps complet de Droit*; and in later years Dumont published other *Traités* from Bentham's MSS.[5] The service which Dumont thus performed for Bentham was invaluable. He interpreted Bentham's message so clearly that he gave Bentham an international reputation as a great jurist long before his merits were recognized by his own countrymen; and, though his countrymen were slow to recognize his merits, his international reputation and the merits of Dumont's interpretation at length led them to realize that his genius as a jurist was unique, and to accept his guidance in matters of law reform.[6] Macaulay's summary of Dumont's service to Bentham is, I think, the best description of the results of this extraordinary literary partnership. He says:

Never was there a literary partnership so fortunate as that of Mr. Bentham and M. Dumont. The raw material which Mr. Bentham furnished was most precious; but it was unmarketable. He was, assuredly, at once a great logician and a great rhetorician. But the effect of his logic was injured by a vicious arrangement, and the effect of his rhetoric by a vicious style. His mind was vigorous, comprehensive, subtile, fertile of arguments, fertile of illustrations. But he spoke in an unknown tongue. . . . His oracles were of high import; but they were

---

[1] Bowring, op. cit. x 280-281.
[2] Leslie Stephen, The English Utilitarians i 187; Bowring, op. cit. x 185.
[3] " While pushed on by a creative force he [Bentham] feels only the pleasure of composition; when it becomes necessary to shape, to put in order, to finish, he experiences nothing but fatigue. . . . This same turn of mind has prevented him from taking any part in the compilations which I now present to the public. It was rarely that I was able to obtain any explanations, or even the aid of which I was absolutely in need," Dumont, Preface to the *Traités*.
[4] C. K. Ogden, Bentham's Theory of Legislation xliv-xlvi.
[5] Below 64.   [6] C. M. Atkinson, Jeremy Bentham 147-151.
[7] Essay on Mirabeau.

traced on leaves and flung loose to the wind. So negligent was he of the arts of selection, distribution, and compression, that to persons who formed their judgment of him from his works in their undigested state he seemed to be the least systematic of all philosophers. The truth is, that his opinions formed a system, which, whether sound or unsound, is more exact, more entire, and more consistent with itself than any other. . . . Many persons have attempted to interpret between this powerful mind and the public. But, in our opinion M. Dumont alone has succeeded. It is remarkable that, in foreign countries, where Mr. Bentham's works are known solely through the medium of the French version, his merit is almost universally acknowledged. Even those who are most decidedly opposed to his political opinions—the very chiefs of the Holy Alliance— have publicly testified their respect for him. In England, on the contrary, many persons who certainly entertained no prejudice against him on political grounds were long in the habit of mentioning him contemptuously. Indeed, what was said of Bacon's philosophy may be said of Bentham's. It was in little repute amongst us, till judgments in its favour came from beyond the sea, and convinced us to our shame, that we had been abusing and laughing at one of the greatest men of the age.

In fact it is true, even now, that the best known of Bentham's works—*The Theory of Legislation*—is an American translation of Dumont's *Traités* made by Robert Hildreth in 1864.[1]

It was owing to Dumont that Bentham's continental reputation was acquired. Many countries in Europe and in North and South America expressed their wish to enlist his services for the work of law reform ; and he was very ready to respond ; for he had no doubt of his capacity to legislate for any country in the world.[2] It is true that in his tract upon *The Influence of Time and Place in Matters of Legislation*[3] he admitted that allowances must be made for local conditions and prejudices. But, like Helvetius,[4] he regarded these local conditions and prejudices as comparatively unimportant, and held that legislation, based on the broad principles of utility, must be suitable to all nations in all ages.[5] He said :[6]

In comparison of the *universally-applying*, the extent of the *exclusively-applying circumstances* will be found very inconsiderable. Moreover, throughout the whole of the field, the exclusively-applying circumstances will be found to be circumscribed as it were by, and included in, the universally applying circumstances. The great *outlines*, which require to be drawn, will be found to be the same for every *territory*, for every *race*, and for every *time*. . . . In every country, and for every race, at every time—of the all-comprehensive and only defensible end—the *greatest happiness* of the greatest number—of the four most comprehensive particular and subordinate *ends*, viz. *subsistence, abundance*,

---

[1] For Hildreth see C. K. Ogden's edition of Bentham's Theory of Legislation l-li.

[2] See Codification Proposal addressed by Jeremy Bentham to all Nations professing Liberal Opinions, Works iv 535 ; below 107.

[3] Below 76.   [4] Halévy, Philosophic Radicalism 20, 67.

[5] Leslie Stephen, The English Utilitarians i 300.

[6] Works iv 561 ; below 73, 74.

security, and *equality*— . . . will the description be found the same : only of the *means* best adapted to the accomplishment of those great *ends*, in this or that country, or for this or that race, at this or that time, will the description, in this or that particular be found, in a greater or less degree different.

In fact, unless Bentham had held this view, he could not have undertaken to create a science of morals and legislation, the principles of which were as exact as those of the physical sciences.[1] Therefore he was ready to legislate for India,[2] Tripoli,[3] the United States,[4] the South American states,[5] Russia,[6] Portugal,[7] and Spain.[8] This readiness to legislate and to advise on legislative problems brought him into contact with many leaders of thought and many statesmen. He corresponded with English,[9] American,[10] and European[11] statesmen, with European princes,[12] and Greek patriots ;[13] and his close relations with some of the South American states and their leaders led him to think of emigrating at one time to Mexico,[14] and at another time to Venezuela.[15] As he grew older his European reputation grew. He had been made a French citizen in 1792 ; and when in 1825 he visited the law courts at Paris the whole court rose to do him honour, and he was invited to take a seat on the bench.[16] Talleyrand said of him that he was more pre-eminently a genius than any man he had ever known, and that, copied by others without acknowledgment, " *pillé de tout le monde il est toujours riche.*" [17]

These were the eventual results of Bentham's partnership with Dumont. We must return to England, and to the events of his career which shaped the development of his ideas.

Bentham, throughout his life, continued to follow the pro-gramme sketched out in the Preface to *The Principles of Morals and Legislation*,[18] and to work at different departments of the law. We shall see that his most extensive works were done in the

---

[1] In the draft of a preface to an unwritten book in the library of University College, London, he says, " the present work, as well as any other work of mine that has been or will be published on the subject of legislation or any other branch of moral science, is an attempt to extend the experimental method of reasoning from the physical branch to the moral," cited by Graham Wallas, Pol. Sci. Quart. xxxviii 47 ; cp. Works i 193 cited below 77.

[2] Bowring, op. cit. x 292, 590-591.   [3] Works viii 555-600 ; below 107, 108.

[4] Works iv 451-507 ; below 107 ; Works x 462-463.   [5] Ibid x 458.

[6] Ibid 408, 413, 478 ; ibid iv 514-516.

[7] In 1821 the Cortes of Portugal accepted Bentham's proposal to prepare a code ; below 109.

[8] Works x 465-467 ; for Bentham's influence in Spain see two articles by Kenny L.Q.R. xi 48, 175 ; below 108, 109, 110.

[9] E.g. Sidmouth, Brougham, and the Duke of Wellington.

[10] E.g. Madison, Livingston, Miranda, Bolman.

[11] E.g. Talleyrand, Brissot, and the Duc de Broglie.

[12] E.g. the Emperor of Russia and the King of Bavaria.

[13] Bowring, op. cit. x 538-539.   [14] Ibid 439.   [15] Ibid 457.

[16] Ibid 551.   [17] Ibid xi 75.   [18] Above 46, 47.

spheres of evidence, procedure, criminal law, and constitutional law.[1] But, throughout his life, his interest was always liable to be deflected by current legislative proposals, by passing legal events, and, in later life, when he had thrown in his lot with the radicals,[2] by political controversies. And so, concurrently with his larger works, he wrote many pamphlets and criticisms on all these topics. The topics which were the first to interest him after his return from Russia were the questions of prisons and the poor law. His proposals for dealing with these problems by means of an institution called a Panopticon, absorbed a large part of his time for many years, and a large part of the fortune which in 1792 he had inherited from his father.[3]

This Panopticon proposal arose directly out of Bentham's visit to Russia. His brother had designed a large round workshop divided into partitions which converged in the centre, where there was to be a compartment for an inspector, who from his central position could survey the establishment—hence the name Panopticon. As early as 1778 Bentham had criticized some of the proposals made by Blackstone and others for prison reform.[4] He had kept the subject in his mind, and had come to the conclusion that a large round building, like that which his brother had designed, would answer the purposes both of a prison and a workhouse. The failure of Blackstone's proposals led Bentham to press his own proposals on the attention of the government ;[5] the return of his brother in 1790 enabled him to get his help in designing the building ; and the death of his father gave him the pecuniary means to pursue the project. In 1792 he laid it before the government. He proposed that a building on this plan, capable of holding a thousand prisoners, should be built, and he offered to maintain, employ, and educate the prisoners, and to pay a rent for the building. The expenses and his own remuneration were to be made out of the prisoners' labour. The government at first favoured the scheme, and in 1794 an Act was passed to enable a site to be purchased.[6] But, in spite of favourable reports, the project hung fire. Bentham spent time and money on it in vain ; and in vain he suggested, when Pitt brought in his bill for the reform of the Poor Law, that the Panopticon principle should be applied to houses for the poor. The Panopticon was, as he expressed it, to be " a mill for grinding rogues honest, and idle

---

[1] Below 82, 83-87, 88-95.   [2] Below 104, 105.

[3] Works x 301 ; Panopticon Correspondence, Bowring, op. cit. xi 96-170 ; Leslie Stephen, The English Utilitarians i 193-206 ; Works iv 171-172. Mr. Ogden, Bentham Centenary Lecture 114, tells us that in 1932 a panopticon penitentiary was built in Cuba on Bentham's model.

[4] A view of the Hard Labour Bill, Works iv 6-33.

[5] C. M. Atkinson, Jeremy Bentham 38-39.

[6] 34 George III c. 84.

men industrious."[1] Though the scheme was favourably reported on in 1797, and though an estate at Millbank was acquired, the project still hung fire. It was in vain that Bentham appealed to Wilberforce and other members of Parliament. "Never," says Wilberforce,[2] "was any one worse used. I have seen the tears run down the cheeks of that strong-minded man through vexation at the pressing importunity of his creditors, and the indolence of official underlings when day after day he was begging at the Treasury for what was indeed a mere matter of right."

It was not till 1811 that the end came. A committee of the House of Commons committee reported against it, on the obvious ground that it would be quite impossible to run such an institution on the profits to be made from the prisoners' work.[3] Parliament voted a compensation to Bentham for his expenditure of time and money, and he was ultimately paid £23,000.[4] In fact, as Leslie Stephen has pointed out, Bentham was well out of the scheme. "There were probably few men in England less capable of managing a thousand convicts, in spite of his theories about springs of action. If anything else had been required to ensure failure, it would have been association with a sanguine inventor of brilliant abilities."[5] The scheme, too, illustrates the interest which Bentham always showed in mechanical inventions ;[6] and that interest, when coupled with his habit of testing his principles by applying them in detail to concrete facts,[7] led him to fail to distinguish between the feasibility of the rules logically deduced from the principle and the mechanical means for making the rule work. He thus became the easy victim of a common delusion : "if a system will work, its minutest details can be exhibited. Therefore, it is inferred, an exhibition of minute detail proves that it will work."[8] Bentham, of course, could never see these obvious objections to his scheme. Deceived by a story told him by Lord Lansdowne, which was meant as a joke,[9] he ascribed the delay and final failure of his scheme to the hostility of George III.[10] But, naturally, he felt his failure deeply,[11] and the vexation which it

[1] Bowring, op. cit. x 226.
[2] Ibid 390 n., citing Wilberforce's Life ii 71.
[3] Leslie Stephen, The English Utilitarians i 205.
[4] 52 George III c. 44 § 4.
[5] Leslie Stephen, The English Utilitarians i 305.
[6] See Bowring, op. cit. x 260, 344, 346-347, 381 ; as Dicey says, Law and Opinion 129, " a jurist's capacity for the grasp of general principles and the acumen of a natural born logician were blended with the resourcefulness of a mechanical inventor."
[7] Below 89, 90, 115, 123-125.
[8] Leslie Stephen, The English Utilitarians i 283.
[9] Ibid 193.
[10] Bowring, op. cit. x 211-212, xi 96-97.
[11] " I do not like," he would say, " to look among Panopticon papers. It is like opening a drawer where devils are locked up—it is breaking into a haunted house," ibid. x 250.

caused him had an important effect on the development of his political opinions and some effect on his views on law reform.[1]

Bentham had begun life as a Tory. In 1782 he praised " the constitutional branch of the law of England " ;[2] and it is said that in 1795 he contemplated writing a defence of the rotten boroughs.[3] In fact, the theories of natural right which figured so largely in the American and the French Revolutions tended to prevent any change in his political creed. He tells us that he was opposed to the Americans because of the badness of the arguments which they used ; and that he had always considered that their Declaration of Rights was a "hodge-podge of confusion and absurdity."[4] His treatment of the French Declaration of Rights in his *Anarchical Fallacies*[5] is even more severe. We have seen that it is the most complete exposure of the logical absurdity of the doctrine of natural rights which has ever been written.[6] If it had been published when it was written the French would certainly not have made him a French citizen.[7] In fact, Bentham was one of the few persons whose opinions were not changed by the French Revolution. He was not then a politician : he was a jurist interested in teaching and spreading the true principles upon which a system of laws should be based. The French Revolution was, to him, simply an event which seemed to give an excellent chance for the furtherance of these principles.[8] The destruction of the old *régime* gave a magnificent opportunity for the establishment of a system of law based on the right principles.[9] It was for this reason that he sent to the French his *Political Tactics*,[10] his proposals for the organization of the French judicial system,[11] and his Panopticon proposals.[12] He seems to have thought that his arguments for the reform of the law were so obviously reasonable, that as soon as they had been submitted to the politicians—

[1] Wilberforce says, Life 71, cited Bowring op cit. 390 n., " He was quite soured by it ; and I have no doubt that many of his harsh opinions afterwards were the fruit of this illtreatment."

[2] " The constitution branch of the law of England, taking it in its leading principles, would probably be found the best beyond comparison that has hitherto made its appearance in the world ; resting at no great distance, perhaps, from the summit of perfection," Works i 185 ; later Bentham inserted on the MS. a warning that this was written in 1782, Halévy, Philosophic Radicalism 519-520.

[3] C. M. Atkinson, Jeremy Bentham 109.

[4] " The Declaration of Rights presented itself to my conception from the first, as what it has always continued to be, a hodge-podge of confusion and absurdity, in which the thing to be proved is all along taken for granted," Bowring, op. cit. x 63.

[5] Works ii 489-534.   [6] Above 6, 22.

[7] Bowring, op. cit. x 317.

[8] " Il ne dit point aux peuples : ' Emparez-vous de l'authorité, changez la forme de l Etat.' Il dit aux gouvernements : ' connaissez les maladies qui vous affaiblissent, etudiez le régime qui peut les guerir,' " Dumont, Pref. to the *Traités*.

[9] Leslie Stephen, The English Utilitarians i 196-197.

[10] Works ii 299-373.   [11] Ibid iv 285-406.

[12] Bowring, op. cit. x 270.

English or French—they would be received with gratitude and acted upon. It was a belief which came naturally to an academic speculator who knew little of the world of practical affairs—legal or political. The insight which he got into that world in his endeavour to realize his Panopticon proposals, and the course of events in France,[1] disillusioned him. Statesmen and lawyers were not so ready as he thought to see the reasonable course which seemed to him so obvious. Why was this ? The conclusion to which Bentham came was that they refused to see the reasonable course because they did not desire the greatest happiness of the greatest number. They desired only their own interests.[2] It was this sinister influence which had defeated all his efforts. But how was this sinister influence to be combated ? The only way to combat it was to give to all citizens a share in the government. Thus Bentham was converted to the radical creed, and thus he came to support at the end of his life a form of government which was identical with that advocated by the upholders of that theory of natural rights which he had so effectively denounced.[3] The man who in 1782 had regarded English constitutional law as not far short of perfection,[4] could in 1830 describe the English constitution as anarchy, because it gave no security to person, property, reputation, or condition in life.[5]

It was at this period, when the Panopticon schemes were failing and Bentham was coming to these conclusions as to the reasons for their failure, that he made the acquaintance of James Mill.[6] Bentham helped Mill when he was eking out a precarious livelihood by writing articles for reviews,[7] and Mill more than repaid this debt. This capable dour Scot, possessed of the typical Scottish capacity for systematic philosophizing, was exactly the sort of helper that Bentham needed to correct his intellectual deficiencies. M. Halévy has truly said :[8]

The truth is that Bentham could not do without this man at his side, who, with as much zeal and more perseverance, took up the role of editor and expositor which had hitherto been filled by Dumont alone. With his " need of someone to admire," which made him the ideal disciple for Bentham, with his energetic temperament and despotic character which

---

[1] Bowring, op. cit. x 296.
[2] He tells us, Works ii 463 n., that when in 1789 Lord Loughborough denounced the principle of utility as " dangerous," he thought that the criticism was merely absurd ; but that he had come to see that he was mistaken, and that the criticism was really sagacious, because he had not then realized that the greatest happiness of the greatest number was not the object aimed at by statesmen of the type of Lord Loughborough, but that what was aimed at was the " greatest happiness of the ruling few "—an object which is generally in direct opposition to that of the greatest of the greatest number.
[3] Above 6, 22, 56 ; below 104, 105.   [4] Above 56.
[5] Works iv 449.   [6] Below 135 seqq.
[7] Halévy, Philosophiç Radicalism 250.   [8] Ibid 251.

made him, to all except to Bentham, a dreaded master, with his genius for logical deduction and exposition, which gives a kind of originality to his works even when they are expressing someone else's ideas, Mill rendered Bentham as much service as Bentham rendered Mill. Bentham gave Mill a doctrine, and Mill gave Bentham a school.

Mill made Bentham the oracle of that school of philosophic radicals[1] which helped to shape the course of legislation to some extent before, and to a much greater extent after 1832.[2] Under this influence Bentham wrote his *Catechism of Parliamentary Reform*, his *Radical Reform Bill*,[3] and some of his most scathing tracts on the abuses of the English law, such as the *Elements of the Art of Packing as applied to special Juries in cases of Libel*,[4] *Swear not at all*,[5] *Equity Dispatch Court Proposal*.[6] His great work on *The Rationale of Judicial Evidence*[7] is coloured by his new political views ; and it was these views which led him at the close of his life to concentrate all his energies on his *Constitutional Code*[8] and on numerous separate papers connected therewith. Moreover his connection with the philosophic radicals led him to reflect upon other topics connected with his utilitarian philosophy. This reflection led him to write books on philosophy—such as his *Table of the Springs of Action*,[9] and *Logic* ;[10] and, just as the failure of the government to carry out his Panopticon proposals had made him a radical,[11] so the opposition of the church to his chresto-mathic proposals[12] led him to write some very heretical books on religion,[13] in which not only the Church of England, but also Christianity itself was attacked.[14] He came to regard religion, and more especially religion as taught by the Church of England, as one of those sinister influences which impeded the spread of the true gospel of utilitarianism.[15] Under these influences it soon became clear to Bentham that, if the radical proposals for the reform of the state were to be realized, the people must be sufficiently educated to understand the basis upon which they rested. Hence his collection of papers entitled *Chrestomathia*[16]—a collection of papers explaining a proposed Chrestomathic day school " for the extension of the new system of instruction to the higher branches of learning for the use of the middling and higher ranks of life." It was to some extent his interest in education which led him to

---

[1] Below 135, 136.　　　　　　　　[2] Below 154, 155.
[3] Works iii 558-597 ; below 104.　　[4] Works v 61-186 ; below 99.
[5] Works v 187-229 ; below 83.
[6] Works iii 297-317, 319-431 ; below 99.
[7] Works vols. vi and vii ; below 83-88.　　[8] Works vol. ix ; below 88-95, 101, 106.
[9] Works i 195-219.　　　　　　[10] Works viii 213-293 ; below 114, 115.
[11] Above 57.　　　　　　　　　[12] For these proposals see below 113.
[13] C. K. Ogden, Bentham Centenary Lecture 24-25 ; these books were not included by Bowring in his collected works.
[14] Below 116, 117.　　　　　　　[15] Below 116.
[16] Works viii 1-191 ; Bowring, op. cit. x 485 ; below 66.

become a partner in Owen's model factory at New Lanark ;[1] and it was for the same reason that he was induced in 1823 to find the friends needed to found the *Westminster Review*. " What think you," he wrote,[2] " of your old antediluvian having, in as great a degree he could wish, at his disposal, a rival—a professed rival—to the *Edinburgh* and *Quarterly*—an organ of the radicals, as the *Edinburgh* is of the Whigs, and the *Quarterly* of the Tories ? . . . The capital thing is, the circumstantial evidence this affords of the growth of Radicalism."

But Bentham's new interests did not deflect him from the pursuit of the main interest of his life—the application of the principles of utility to the reform of the law. From 1814 to 1818 he lived at Ford Abbey—" a superb residence with chapel, cloisters, and corridor, a hall eighty feet long by thirty high, and a great dining parlour."[3] There he devoted six to ten hours a day[4] to writing many papers advocating projects of law reform, such as his *Commentary on Mr. Humphrey's Real Property Code*,[5] and to his work of codification. In the intervals he gardened, played on a large organ which he had erected, and played battledore and shuttlecock.[6] In 1818 he returned to his home in Queen's Square Place which he seldom thereafter quitted. He was reluctant to make new acquaintances, or to receive miscellaneous visitors.[7] His intimates were Romilly, James Mill, the Austins, and later Bowring whom he made his literary executor. But though his main interest was still the scientific reform of the law, and its statement in the form of a code, it was inevitable that his outlook upon English law should be affected by his new political creed. In his *Fragment on Government*,[8] in the *Comment on the Commentaries*,[9] and in his *General View of a Complete Code of Laws*[10] he had recognized some of the merits of Black stone's Commentaries. But we have seen that in later years his hostility to Blackstone led him to condemn him wholesale in very abusive

[1] Bowring, op. cit. x 476-477 ; above 38, 39.   [2] Bowring, op. cit. x 540.
[3] Leslie Stephen, The English Utilitarians i 214.
[4] Dr. Southwood Smith, Bowring, op. cit. xi 94 said eight, ten, and occasionally twelve hours a day ; Romilly, ibid x 478 n. says six or eight hours.
[5] Works v 387-416.
[6] Bowring, op. cit. x 480, 540.   [7] Ibid x 467.
[8] Vol. xii 724, 728 ; " embarrassed, as a man must needs be, by this blind and intractable nomenclature, he will be found to have done . . . more and better than was ever done before by anyone," Preface (Montague's ed.) 122 ; " not even in a *censorial* view would I be understood to deem them altogether without merit," ibid 123.
[9] Vol. xii 716 n. 7, citing A Comment on the Commentaries 147.
[10] " Blackstone, who confined himself to making a picture of the laws of England, has only sought commodiously to arrange the technical terms most frequently used in English jurisprudence. His plan is arbitrary, but it is preferable to all those which have preceded him. It is a work of light in comparison with the darkness which previously covered the whole face of law," Works iii 163 ; this was written at the end of the eighteenth century.

language.[1] Similarly his condemnation of the common law,[2] of English lawyers,[3] and of the British constitution, which he had once highly praised, grew more sweeping as he got older.[4]

In spite of the increased bitterness of Bentham's criticisms of English institutions and English law, which was caused by his new political views, his devotion to the cause of scientific legal reform, and the growing perception of all parties that some reforms were needed, gave him in the latter part of his life as great a reputation in England as he had acquired abroad. Lincoln's Inn showed that liberality in the recognition of legal merit of the academic kind which has always distinguished it, when, in 1817, it called him to the Bench.[5] In 1831, in the year before his death, Brougham, referring to a pamphlet which he had written on the Bankruptcy Act, said that he was " the father of law reform."[6] He worked on at his constitutional code, he kept in close touch with Mackintosh, Brougham, and others who were advocating law reforms, and he was always ready to help correspondents in all parts of the world who asked his advice on matters connected with law reform and the codification of the law. In 1830 he was beginning to feel his age ;[7] but in the same year he wrote to Admiral Mordvinoff, " I am still alive ; though turned of eighty-two, still in good health and spirits, codifying like any dragon." [8] To the end his actions were dictated by the philosophy which he had spent his

[1] Bowring op. cit. x 141, cited vol. xii 730 n. 3.

[2] " By force of his imagination he [the lawyer] creates a sort of god or goddess upon earth, a sort of divinity which he calls common law. Of this goddess the principal occupation is the finding pretences for giving fulfilment to the monarch's sinister will," Works ix 135.

[3] " Such is the arithmetic of lawyer craft—confederate partner and instrument of tyranny—of lawyer craft in its most rapacious character and elaborate garb— the character and garb of the English lawyer," ibid. 23.

[4] In 1782 he said " The constitutional branch of the law of England, taking it in its leading principles, would probably be found the best beyond comparison that has hitherto made its appearance in the world ; resting at no very great distance, perhaps, from the summit of perfection," Works i 185 ; but in 1827 he said, " Of the several arrangements in the English system, in no one instance has the greatest happiness of the greatest number been the end in view. At all times— on every occasion—in every instance, the end actually pursued by the several sets of rulers, has been the promotion of the particular, and thence sinister, interest of these same rulers," Works ix 2, and see ibid 59-60 ; in 1831 he said, " under matchless constitution, the *end* aimed at is maximization of degradation and oppression," Bowring, op. cit. xi 73—though shortly before he admitted that it was better than any other except that of the U.S.A., ibid. 62 ; above 56, 57.

[5] Black Books of Lincoln's Inn iv 147 ; he said, Bowring, op. cit. x 584, " when I was made a bencher I accepted the rank, as I thought it would be the means of saving me from persecution. They were some time in choosing me, and I was some time—I believe six months—in accepting."

[6] Hansard (3rd Series) viii 821.

[7] He wrote to O'Connell, " my eyes are waxing every day dimmer and dimmer, and my mind more and more oscillatory. . . . I neither see what I am writing, nor remember one moment what I had just been writing the moment before. But this does not in any material degree diminish my cheerfulness," Bowring, op. cit. xi 32-33.   [8] Bowring, op. cit. xi 33.

life in preaching. " Some time before his death, when he firmly believed he was near that last hour, he said to one of his disciples who was watching over him :—' I now feel that I am dying : our care must be to minimize pain. Do not let any of the servants come into the room, and keep away the youths : it will be distressing to them, and they can be of no service.' " [1] He did his last bit of work on his constitutional code on May 18, 1832.[2] On June 6, 1832—the day before the royal assent was given to the Reform bill—he died peacefully, in Bowring's arms.[3] His skeleton, clothed in his garments and his face covered by a wax mask, is kept in University College, London. It presided over a centenary dinner held in his honour in 1932.

Though Bentham, after the failure of his Panopticon scheme, lived a secluded life, he kept in touch with the politics of the day, and was always ready to deal drastically with abuses, to suggest reforms, and to criticize schemes of legislative reform advanced by others. His absorption in his work, his small knowledge of the practical world, and his certainty that his conclusions were correct, sometimes led him to criticize harshly the proposals of disciples who were trying to carry out some of his suggested reforms.[4] For the same reasons he was too apt to take offence, and to say unjust and cutting things of friends who had helped to spread his fame. He was unjust to James Mill[5] and to Dumont.[6] But I do not think that we must therefore conclude that he was an essentially vain man, or that he had a cold heart which made him indifferent to the ties of friendship.[7] He put his work first ; and his absorption in it, and the deference with which he was treated by his numerous disciples, made him, as he grew older, increasingly impatient of trifles which annoyed him. At the same time he had, as J. S. Mill has pointed out,[8] some of the qualities of a child for good and for evil ; and these qualities led him to say things which he would not have said if he had stopped to reflect. But though he was first and foremost a philosopher who lived apart in a world of

[1] Bowring, op. cit. xi. 95.

[2] Leslie Stephen, The English Utilitarians i 229 ; he wrote several pages of his constitutional code on May 9, 10, and 11, 1832, Works ix Preface *note* ; one of the last tracts he wrote was called " Auto-Icon, or further uses of the Dead to the Living," see C. K. Ogden, Bentham Centenary Lecture 118.

[3] Bowring, op. cit. xi 76. [4] Below 103.

[5] Bentham once said of him, " his creed of politics results less from love for the many than from hatred of the few," Bowring, op. cit. x 450 ; this dictum was naturally resented by J. S. Mill, Ed. Rev. lxxix 267-269—but there was just enough truth in it to make it an effective caricature.

[6] " Dumont could never form any the least conception of our law. He was utterly incapable of doing so," Bowring, op. cit. x 563 ; and in 1827 Bentham refused to see him, saying that he did not understand a word of his meaning, Ed. Rev. lxxviii 466 n.—though Dumont never ceased to admire Bentham, see his letter written a few days before his death, Bowring, op. cit. xi 24.

[7] This is the view taken in Ed. Rev. lxxviii 465-468.

[8] Dissertations and Discussions i.

his own, he had many social qualities and many human interests. We have seen that he always cherished the memory of his most serious love affair.[1] He loved flowers and music and animals, and could be an entertaining host to his intimates.[2] His cat Sir John Langborn, his stick Dapple, and his teapot Dicky were familiar objects of his hermitage in Queen's Square Place.[3] The fact that he gathered round him the band of devoted admirers who regarded him as their oracle, and who, as we shall see, were ready to devote themselves to the laborious task of editing his scattered papers, shows that his attraction was due not only to intellectual qualities which inspired admiration, but also, in part at least, to human qualities which inspired affection. In October 1831 he wrote :[4] " The way to be comfortable is to make others comfortable. The way to make others comfortable is to appear to love them. The way to appear to love them is to love them in reality. *Probatur ab experientia* Jeremy Bentham." No small part of his influence is due to the fact that these words summed up the principle which had guided him throughout his life.

No doubt Bentham owed some part of his influence to two pieces of good fortune—to the length of his life and to the fact that he had inherited an income which enabled him to devote his whole time to his work. But he owed more to the industry and ability with which these two pieces of good fortune were exploited. Similarly, it was his intellectual and human qualities which account for three other pieces of good fortune, which added enormously to the effectiveness of his work by curing some of the consequences of two of his chief intellectual defects—his incapacity to finish one piece of work before he began another[5] and the unpractical character of some of his concrete proposals for reform.[6] The first of these three other pieces of good fortune was the fact that friends and admirers like Dumont, J. S. Mill, Doane and others were willing to spend time and trouble in preparing his scattered MSS. for publication. The second was the fact that friends like Romilly and Mackintosh and Brougham were willing to present to Parliament his ideas as to law reform in such a shape that it was possible to induce Parliament to give effect to some of them. The third was the fact that friends like James Mill and others used Bentham's scattered writings on legal and ethical and political philosophy to create a coherent

---

[1] Above 49.

[2] T. E. Holland, in his article on Bentham in the Encyclopædia Britannica, cites an account given by Rush, the United States minister, of a dinner at Bentham's house in 1818, at which Brougham, Romilly, James Mill, and Dumont were present ; he says, " Mr. Bentham did not talk much. He had a benevolence of manner suited to the philanthropy of his mind. He seemed to be thinking only of the pleasure and convenience of his guests."

[3] Bowring, op. cit. xi 80, 81, 82.   [4] Ibid 71.

[5] Above 51.   [6] Above 55 ; below 83.

body of doctrine. With these matters I shall deal in the sections in which I shall give some account of the writings in which Bentham stated his principles and applied them to the reform of the law, estimate the strong and weak points in these principles, and describe the rise of the school of philosophic radicalism.

(2) *The principal works in which Bentham stated his principles and applied them to the reform of the law*

I have already said something of Bentham's unsystematic methods of literary composition—of his incapacity to finish a piece of work on which he was engaged, of his habit of rewriting an almost finished manuscript to embody some new idea, of his tendency to abandon an almost finished piece of work and embark on a new work suggested by some line of thought suggested by the abandoned work, of his reluctance to revise his manuscripts finally for the press.[1] It was these unsystematic methods of literary composition which explain, first, the curious manner in which some of Bentham's most important works were originally published; secondly, the chaotic condition in which Bentham left his manuscripts; and, thirdly, to some extent, the form in which Bowring, Bentham's literary executor, produced his collected edition of Bentham's works.

(i) A large number of Bentham's most important works were not published by their author. They were published by disciples who edited his manuscripts, gave them a logical and a systematic form, and sometimes did a little to correct the intricate and involved style of his later works. Bentham wrote his earlier works in a clear bright style enlivened by apposite illustrations and an occasional epigram.[2] In his later works, in order to obtain an impossible precision, he used an intricate and involved style,[3] which is still further obscured by a jargon of invented words.[4] We have seen that of all Bentham's editors Dumont was, in Macaulay's opinion, the most successful and the most important;[5] and with this opinion John Stuart Mill, who edited Bentham's manuscripts on the law of evidence,[6] agreed.[7] That these opinions are correct is proved by the fact that it was Dumont's recension

---

[1] Above 51, 62.
[2] " A Benthamania might be made of passages worthy of Addison or Goldsmith," J. S. Mill, Dissertations and Discussions i 390.   [3] Ibid.
[4] " Preoccupation with terminology never ceased to engage Bentham's attention ; he attempted to solve its problems by inventing a vocabulary of his own. Thereby he incurred the reproach which he levelled at lawyers, of fashioning their notions ' as unlike as possible to those of other men's ' ; and though in some instances, like the terms ' codify ' and ' international law,' he definitely added to the language, too often he merely substituted one difficulty for another," C. K. Allen, The Young Bentham L.Q.R. xliv 506.
[5] Above 51.   [6] Below 65.
[7] " That first of translators and *rédacteurs* as he has justly been termed," Mill's Preface to the Rationale of Judicial Evidence, Works vi 195.

of Bentham's manuscripts which gave him his continental reputation, and so helped to make his countrymen realize that he was a great juridical thinker.[1] Of Dumont's work, therefore, I must, in the first place, say something.

Dumont's *Traités* were published in 1802 in three books. The first book contains the Principles of Legislation, which set forth Bentham's general theory and the mode of its application to the problems of legislation and the reform of the law, and the Principles of the Civil Code ; the second contains the Principles of the Penal Code ; and the third consists of four essays—on the Panopticon, on the promulgation of law, on the influence of time and place in matters of legislation, on a general view of a complete code of law. For these *Traités* Dumont used manuscripts, most of which had been written by Bentham between 1783 and 1789.[2] The principal manuscripts were a theory of civil law in three books, Bentham's *Introduction to the Principles of Morals and Legislation*, parts of a manuscript dealing with the principles of the penal code, a manuscript entitled *Indirect Legislation*, a manuscript entitled *A General View of a Complete Code of Law*, and three other manuscripts—the Panopticon, which was a memorandum sent to a member of the French Legislative Assembly, an essay on the promulgation of laws written in French, and a French translation of the essay entitled *Of the Influence of Time and Place in Matters of Legislation*. Dumont converted these MSS. into logical treatises. " I have not," he said, " translated words, I have translated ideas ; I have made sometimes an abridgement and sometimes a commentary." [3] He toned down the irreligious passages, he corrected Bentham's French style, he developed and explained by examples his arid metaphysical disquisitions, and he omitted "forms which were too scientific, subdivisions which were too numerous, and analyses which were too abstract."[4] These, in M. Halévy's opinion, were " the most important and the most happy of the modifications which Dumont made to Bentham's text." He did a similar work in four other books entitled *Théories des Peines et des Recompenses* published in 1811, *Tactique des Assemblées législatives suivie d'un traité des sophismes politiques* published in 1816, *Traité des Preuves Judiciaires* published in 1823, and *De l'Organization judiciaire et de la Codification* published in 1828. All these books of Dumont and Bentham's MSS. were used by the editors of the collected English edition of Bentham's works. Some of these MSS. date from an early period in Bentham's career. Thus Dumont

¹ Above 52.
² On this question of the manuscripts used by Dumont see Halévy, Growth of Philosophic Radicalism App. 515-521.
³ Preface to the *Traités*.   ⁴ Halévy, op. cit. 520-521.

tells us that the MSS. on which the *Théorie des Peines* is based come from the year 1775, and those on which the *Théorie des Recompenses* is based are a little later in date.[1]

The *Traité des Preuves Judiciaires* contained Bentham's main proposals for the reform of the law of evidence. But, because it was addressed to continental readers, it omitted Bentham's criticisms of English law.[2] It was obviously desirable that in an English version these criticisms should be included ; and the task of preparing an English edition which included them was entrusted to John Stuart Mill.

John Stuart Mill did for Bentham's work on the law of evidence a service similar to that done by Dumont on Bentham's theory of legislation and on many branches of the law substantive and adjective. Mill's account of his labours on Bentham's manuscripts is a good illustration of the heavy burden which his editors assumed, and the extent to which Bentham's reputation is indebted to their labours. He says :[3]

About the end of 1824 or beginning of 1825, Mr. Bentham, having lately got back his papers on Evidence from M. Dumont (whose Traité des Preuves Judiciaires, grounded on them, was then first completed and published) resolved to have them printed in the original, and bethought himself of me as capable of preparing them for the press ; in the same manner as his Book of Fallacies had been recently edited by Bingham. I gladly undertook this task, and it occupied nearly all my leisure for about a year, exclusive of the time afterwards spent in seeing the five large volumes through the press. Mr. Bentham had begun this treatise three times, at considerable intervals, each time in a different manner, and each time without reference to the preceding : two of the three times he had gone over nearly the whole subject. These three masses of manuscript it was my business to condense into a single treatise ; adopting the one last written as the ground work, and incorporating into it as much of the two others as it had not completely superseded. I had also to unroll such of Bentham's involved and parenthetical sentences, as seemed to over pass by their complexity the measure of what readers were likely to take pains to understand. It was further Mr. Bentham's particular desire that I should myself, endeavour to supply any *lacunae* which he had left ; and at his instance I read, for this purpose, the most authoritative treatises on the English Law of Evidence, and commented on a few of the objectionable points of the English rules, which had escaped Bentham's notice. I also replied to the objections which had been made to some of his doctrines by reviewers of Dumont's book, and added a few supplementary remarks on some of the more abstract parts of the subject, such as the theory of improbability and impossibility.

Bingham, as Mill notes, did for Bentham's *Book of Fallacies*[4] what Mill had done for his work on Evidence. Like Mill, he

[1] Preface to the Théorie des Peines et des Recompenses.
[2] " The strictures on English law, which compose more than one-half of the present work, were judiciously omitted by M. Dumont," Mill's Preface to the Rationale of Judicial Evidence, Works vi 195.
[3] Autobiography 114-115 ; see also his Preface, Works vi 195 n.
[4] Works ii 375-387.

restored the references to English institutions which Dumont had omitted.[1] After Bentham's death Richard Doane produced from " an immense mass of MSS. extending to several thousand pages " the work on *Principles of Judicial Procedure, with the Outlines of a Procedure Code*,[2] and from the voluminous MSS. dealing with constitutional law, which Bentham had been writing from 1818 till his death in 1832, he produced the *Constitutional Code*.[3] Francis Place put together *Not Paul but Jesus* in 1817, and helped to prepare the *Reform Catechism*.[4] Southwood Smith edited Bentham's *Chrestomathia*;[5] and we shall see that Bowring undertook the general editorship of a collected edition of Bentham's works.[6] James Mill edited his *Introductory View of the Rationale of Evidence*;[7] and we shall see that by his foundation of the school of philosophic radicals, he did more than any one single person to gain recognition for Bentham's ideas, and to give practical effect to some of them.[8]

(ii) From this account of the manner in which some of Bentham's most important works were originally published, it follows that Bentham left his manuscripts in a chaotic condition. These MSS. are in the custody of University College, London ; and in 1892 they were reported on, catalogued, and indexed by Thomas Whittaker. Whittaker says :[9]

Having worked through the Bentham MSS. I find that, with few exceptions, they are not treatises actually printed from or intended to be printed from, but are material in the form of chapters and fragments, written at different periods, and marked, according to Bentham's custom, with the subject and date. In nearly all cases, though some material may have been left aside, the substantial equivalent is to be found in the published works.

He arranged this mass of MSS. in 148 boxes and portfolios, of which half consisted of legislative matter. Other MSS. have since emerged ; and at the present day they are contained in 172 boxes and portfolios each containing about 300 sheets.[10] They have been recatalogued by Mr. Everett who was preparing a life of Bentham ; and in the course of his researches he discovered and published the *Comment on the Commentaries* from which the *Fragment on Government* had been detached by Bentham. It is possible that other discoveries may be made in this mass of papers ; but it is more probable that Whittaker is right when he

[1] Preface, Works ii 376.   [2] Works ii 1-188 ; see the editor's note.
[3] Works ix, and see the editor's note.
[4] Graham Wallas, Francis Place 83-84.
[5] Works viii 1-191, and see the editor's introduction.   [6] Below 67.
[7] Halévy, op. cit. Everett's Bibliography 533 ; Works vi 1-187 ; other helpers were Grote, and Hobhouse, Graham Wallas, Life of Francis Place 83-84.
[8] Below 135.
[9] Report on the Bentham MSS. at University College, London.
[10] Everett, A Comment on the Commentaries, Preface.

said that most of Bentham's material has already been published either separately or in the Collected Works. It is certain that enough has been published to enable us to predict pretty clearly what Bentham's opinion was on any given topic, and the point of view from which he would attempt the solution of any given problem.

(iii) The collected edition of Bentham's works was published under the superintendence of John Bowring, Bentham's literary executor. Bowring[1] (1792-1872) was a man of many talents who had a distinguished and a variegated career. He was a linguist and a man of letters, a merchant and an authority on finance, an enthusiast for free trade and an efficient plenipotentiary in China and other countries in the far East, a Fellow of the Royal Society and of many other learned societies in Europe ; but not, according to Selborne, a success in the House of Commons.[2] But both his life of Bentham, which is contained in volumes x and xi of the Collected Works, and the Collected Works themselves, have considerable defects. Leslie Stephen says of his biography that it is " one of the worst in the language," though he had materials " which might have served for a masterpiece." [3] The Collected Works contain most of Bentham's important works as they were given to the world by Bentham himself or as they existed in Bentham's MSS. or in the recensions of his editors ; and there is prefixed to them a general preface, and a very valuable introduction to the study of Bentham's works by John Hill Burton. But the small type and double columns of the volumes make them difficult to read ; and, what is more important, they are not complete. Bowring was an orthodox Christian and a writer of hymns ; and for that reason omitted all Bentham's writings on religious topics.[4] Moreover he is suspected of having garbled Bentham's notes on ethics[5] in his edition of Bentham's *Deontology*.[6] There are also other omissions—notably Bentham's revolutionary views on sexual offences,[7] his curious tract entitled *Auto-Icon, or further uses of the dead to the living*; and, as we have seen,[8] his *Comment on the Commentaries*.

Nevertheless, when all deductions have been made, a very substantial proportion of Bentham's writings are contained in the Collected Works, and a certain amount of Bentham's extensive correspondence is preserved in Bowring's biography. I shall first

---

[1] D.N.B.

[2] " A *doctrinaire* radical who had been for some years one of the established bores of the House of Commons," Memorials, Family and Personal ii 319.

[3] The English Utilitarians i 225.   [4] Ibid.

[5] Ibid ; Mill, Dissertations and Discussions i 365.

[6] This is not contained in the Collected Works, because Bowring's edition of the work was not exhausted. Works, Burton's Introd. 19 n.

[7] Printed by Ogden, in his edition of Bentham's Theory of Legislation 476-497.

[8] Above 47, 48.

say something of those writings which illustrate the main
principles underlying his proposals for the reform of the law;
and, secondly, I shall give a brief account of his other writings.

(a) Writings which illustrate Bentham's main principles underlying his proposals for the reform of the law

The works which illustrate the principles upon which Bentham
proposed to reform the law are his *Introduction to the Principles
of Morals and Legislation*;[1] his *Rationale of Reward*;[2] his
General View of a Complete Code of Laws;[3] and Dumont's
Theory of Legislation,[4] which contains parts of Bentham's *Introduction*, parts of his *Principles of the Civil Code*, parts of his
Principles of Penal Law, and the gist of various passages in his
Book of Fallacies.[5] These works are supplemented by his *Essay
on the Influence of Time and Place in Matters of Legislation*.[6]
Principles which are in opposition to Bentham's principles and
theory of legislation are dealt with in his *Fragment on Government*,[7]
his *Comment on the Commentaries*,[8] his tract entitled *Truth v.
Ashhurst*,[9] his *Book of Fallacies*,[10] and his essay on *Anarchical
Fallacies*.[11]

The first words of Bentham's *Introduction* set out the theory
which he spent his life applying in detail, both in his work of
criticizing the rules of English law and in his work of constructing
a reformed body of laws in accordance with it. He says:[12]

Nature has placed mankind under the governance of two sovereign
masters, *pain* and *pleasure*. It is for them alone to point out what we
ought to do, as well as to determine what we shall do. On the one hand
the standard of right and wrong, on the other the chain of causes and
effects are fastened to their throne. They govern us in all we do, in all we
say, in all we think : every effort we make to throw off our subjection,
will serve but to demonstrate and confirm it. In works a man may pretend to abjure their empire ; but in reality he will remain subject to it all
the while. The *principle of utility* recognizes this subjection, and assumes
it for the foundation of that system, the object of which is to rear the
fabric of felicity by the hands of reason and law. Systems which attempt
to question it, deal in sounds instead of sense, in caprice instead of reason,
in darkness instead of light.

After analysis of the principle of utility, Bentham then disposes
of rival principles which legislators have taken as their guide—the
principle of asceticism, the principle of sympathy and antipathy

---

[1] Works i 1-154. The Limits of Jurisprudence Defined, unearthed by Mr. C. W.
Everett and published in 1948, was clearly intended to form Part II of this work :
see Pound, Texas Law Review (1948) ; see also Friedmann, in Jeremy Bentham
and the Law, 23a. [Eds.]   [2] Works ii 189-266.   [3] Works iii 155-021.
[4] My references are to the edition by C. K. Ogden.
[5] C. K. Ogden's Introd. xxxviii.   [6] Works i 171-194.
[7] Works i 221-295 ; my references are to Montague's edition.
[8] Edited by C. W. Everett.   [9] Works v 231-237.
[10] Works ii 375-487.   [11] Works ii 488-529.   [12] Works i 1.

and the religious principle. To base morals and legislation upon the principle of utility is not, Bentham contends, mere epicurism : " The most exalted acts of virtue may be easily reduced to a calculation of good and evil. This is neither to degrade nor to weaken them, but to represent them as the effects of reason." [1]

The practical consequences in the sphere of politics and legislation of admitting any other principle than that of utility were later developed by Bentham in his *Book of Fallacies*, and his essay on *Anarchical Fallacies* of which I have given some account. [2] In his *Book of Fallacies* the following fallacies are exposed at length and with a wealth of illustration : [3]

First, fallacies of *authority* (including laudatory personalities) ; the subject matter of which is the suggestion of danger in various shapes— and the object to repress altogether on the ground of such danger, the *discussion* proposed to be entered on. Secondly, fallacies of *danger* (including vituperative personalities) ; the subject matter of which is the suggestion of danger in various shapes—and the object to *repress altogether* on the ground of such dangers, the *discussion* proposed to be entered on. Thirdly, fallacies of *delay* ; the subject matter of which is an assigning of reasons for delay in various shapes—and the object is to *postpone* such *discussion*, with a view of eluding it altogether. Fourthly, fallacies of *confusion* ; the subject matter of which consists chiefly of vague and indefinite generalities—which the object is *to produce*, when discussion can no longer be avoided, such *confusion* in the minds of the hearers as to incapacitate them for forming a correct judgment on the question proposed for deliberation.

Sydney Smith's essay, in which he reviewed this book, wittily summed up the manner in which these fallacies were used in his celebrated Noodle's Oration. [4]

Since to increase pleasures and to diminish pains ought to be the sole object of the legislator, the question arises how he is to effect this result. The answer is by means of the four sanctions which nature, the state, the community, or religion provide— i.e. the physical, the political, the moral, or the religious sanction. Because these four sanctions are the sources of pleasures and pains, they are the instruments with which the legislator must work. Therefore to do his work efficiently the legislator must consider the value of each pleasure and pain to the individual and the community, and the various kinds of pleasures and pains. Bentham analyses the value of pleasures and pains by reference to their intensity, duration, certainty, propinquity, fecundity, purity, and extent ; and he enumerates twelve simple pleasures and fourteen simple pains. But it is obvious that different persons are affected by these pleasures and pains in different ways. Therefore the legislator must always take into consideration circumstances which may affect sensibility. Bentham enumerates

[1] Works i 13. [2] Above 22, 56. [3] Works ii 382. [4] Ibid (ed. 1869) 498-499.

thirty-two such circumstances, of which a legislator, like a physician, must always take account.[1]

Having thus analysed the conception of pleasure and pain, it is necessary to analyse the conception of a human act and its material consequences, because it is with these acts that a legislator is concerned. In considering whether any given act is punishable we must have regard to the act itself, to the circumstances in which it is done, to the intention and consciousness of the actor, to his motives, and to the disposition which it indicates. Bentham, having analysed minutely all these matters, passes to the consideration of the mischievous consequences of acts, for it is with these mischievous consequences that the legislator is concerned.[2] Those consequences may be either primary, i.e. the consequences to a definite individual or individuals, or secondary, i.e. the consequences to the whole community or some indefinite part of it. Thus, if a man is robbed, the primary mischief is the loss suffered by the owner of the property, the secondary mischiefs are, first, the alarm created in the neighbourhood, and, secondly, the danger that further robberies will be committed. These various mischiefs, primary and secondary, Bentham calls evils of the first, second, and third orders.[3] At the same time it must always be remembered that in all cases the circumstances in which the act is done and the motives and intention of the actor have an important bearing on the extent of the mischief, whether primary or secondary.[4]

Having thus analysed acts and their mischievous consequences, it becomes possible to consider what acts should be regarded as crimes. All agree that certain acts should be accounted crimes, but, says Bentham, " the agreement which exists is only founded upon prejudices ; and those prejudices vary according to times and places, according to opinions and customs." [5] These prejudices should be tested by the principle of utility. Therefore he says :[6]

I suppose myself a stranger to all our present denominations of vice or virtue : I am called to consider human actions only with relation to their good or evil effects. I open two accounts ; I place on the side of pure profit all pleasures ; I place on the side of loss all pains : I faithfully weigh the interests of all parties ; the man whom prejudice brands as

---

[1] " In this respect there is a striking analogy between the art of the legislator and that of the physician. The catalogue of circumstances influencing sensibility is necessary in both their sciences. What distinguishes the physician from the empiric is the attention which the first pays to everything which constitutes the particular state of the individual. But it is especially in diseases which affect the mind ; in those which concern morality . . . that it is necessary to study everything which affects the dispositions of the invalid," Works i 35.

[2] " Such part of this tendency as is of a mischievous nature, is all that we have any direct concern with," Ibid i 69.

[3] Ibid i 69-70, 81. [4] Ibid 73-80. [5] Ibid 81. [6] Ibid.

vicious ; he who is accounted virtuous, are, for the moment, equal before me. I wish to judge the prejudice itself, and to weigh in this new balance all actions, with the intention of forming a catalogue of those which ought to be permitted, and of those which ought to be prohibited. The operation which at first appears so complicated, becomes easy, by means of the distinction which we have made between the evil of the first, the second, and third orders. Have I to examine an act attacking the security of an individual ? I compare all the pleasure, or, in other terms, all the profit which arises from this act to its author, with all the evil, or all the loss, which results from it to the party injured. I see at once that the evil of the first order surpasses the good of the first order. But I do not stop there. This action is followed by danger and alarm to society ; the evil which was confined at first to a single person, spreads itself over all in the shape of fear. The pleasure resulting from the action is only for one : the pain is for a thousand, for ten thousand, for all. This disproportion, already prodigious, appears almost infinite, if I pass on to the evil of the third order, by considering, that if the act in question were not repressed, there would result from it an universal and durable discouragement, a cessation of labour, and at last the dissolution of society.

It is on these grounds that we must decide first whether any given act should be punished as a crime, and, secondly, what the punishment should be.

First, an act should not be punished at all if it produces no mischief, if it is inefficacious to prevent the mischief, if the mischief produced by the punishment would be greater than that produced by the act, or if the act can be prevented by means other than punishment. It is at this point that ethics and law diverge.[1] Ethics and law have the same end—utility ; they are concerned with the same persons ; and, to a large extent, the acts with which they are concerned are the same. But they are not wholly the same ; for ethics may intervene where it would be impossible or inexpedient to punish. So that while ethics teach a man how to conduct himself in such a way as to secure his happiness " by means of such motives as offer of themselves," [2] legislation teaches a community how to conduct itself in such a way as to secure its happiness " by means of motives to be applied by the legislator."[3] Secondly, in considering the nature of the punishment Bentham lays down thirteen rules. The first and the most important is the rule that, as the main object of punishment is to prevent, " the value of the punishment must not be less in any case than what is sufficient to outweigh that of the profit of the offence." [4] In all cases the legislator must bear in mind the character of the offence, the nature of the punishment, the character of the offender, and the state of public opinion. It follows that a punishment should be variable, it should be proportionate to the offence, characteristic, and no more severe than is necessary ; further and minor objects which the legislator should bear in mind are the reform of the criminal, the disabling him to commit similar offences, and its effect in compensating the victim of the offence.

Bentham then proceeds to classify the offences which are the proper objects of punishment.[1] He divides them into five classes,[2] which, in his *General View of a Complete Code of Laws*, he reduced to the following four classes :[3] private offences, i.e. offences detrimental to private persons ; self-regarding offences, i.e. offences detrimental primarily to the offender himself ; semi-public offences, i.e. offences against some definite portion of the community ; and public offences, i.e. offences against the state. The offences falling under each head are elaborately classified.

It is clear that the most potent of the sanctions which the legislator has at his command is the sanction of pain. But we have seen that, in Bentham's view, pleasure can also be regarded as a sanction.[4] The degree in which the giving of pleasure should operate as a sanction in a legal system is considered by Bentham in his tract on the *Rationale of Reward*.[5] He defines reward as " a portion of the matter of good which, in consideration of some service supposed or expected to be done, is bestowed on someone, in the intent that he may be benefited thereby " ;[6] and adds that " when employed under the direction of the principle of utility, it operates as a motive for the performance of actions useful to society, in the same manner as, under the same guidance, punishment operates in prevention of actions to which we ascribe an injurious tendency."[7] It is clear, however, that reward can never be so universal a sanction as punishment, for the state could not afford to reward all who obeyed the law ; and, if it tried to do so, the result would be universal suffering :

When a punishment is denounced against a breach of the law, if the law be not broken, no one need be punished. When a reward is promised to obedience, if every body obey the law, every body ought to be rewarded. A demand for rewards is thus created, and these rewards can only be derived from the labour of the people, and contributions levied upon their property.[8]

Generally, punishment ought to be the sanction for the breach of negative duties—not to murder, rob, or steal : reward for positive services which cannot be enacted by law—services to the state or

---

[1] Works i 96-142 ; there is a more detailed classification in his General View of a Complete Code of Laws, Works iii 163-176.

[2] Works i 97-98.   [3] Ibid iii 164.   [4] Above 69.
[5] Works ii 189-266.   [6] Ibid 192.   [7] Ibid 192-193.

[8] Ibid 204 ; hence " reward ought never to be employed, when the same effect can be produced by punishment. And, in support of this paradox, I employ another : Let the means be penal, and the desired effect may be attained without giving birth to suffering : let the means be remuneratory, and suffering is inevitable," ibid ; cp. A Comment on the Commentaries 90-92.

to the cause of learning.[1] On this principle rewards to informers and accomplices may be justified ; and also endowments for the diffusion of the arts and sciences. A separate part of this tract discusses the principles upon which state officials should be remunerated. This discussion is marked by a curious mixture of modern and eighteenth century ideas. All fees and perquisites are denounced, fair salaries in proportion to the duties imposed should be paid, and retiring pensions should be provided. On the other hand he does not wholly condemn the sale of offices,[2] and he prefers the system of administration by contractors to direct administration by the state.[3]

Bentham's *Introduction* originally dealt mainly with criminal law. He added some notes on the civil law and the differences between civil and penal law before it was published in 1789. But for a more complete treatment of the civil law we must turn to his *View of a Complete Code of Laws*, and to Dumont's *Theory of Legislation*.

There is, Bentham points out, an intimate connection between the penal and the civil code. In general it may be said that " a civil law is that which establishes a right : a penal law is that which, in consequence of the establishment of a right by the civil law, directs the punishment in a certain manner of him who violates it." [4] Dumont neatly paraphrased Bentham's thought when he said in his Introduction to the principles of the civil code :[5]

The civil law is only another aspect of the penal law ; one cannot be understood without the other. To establish *rights*, is to grant permissions ; it is to make prohibitions ; it is, in one word, to create offences. To commit a private offence is to violate an obligation which we owe to an individual—a right which he has in regard to us. To commit a public offence is to violate an obligation which we owe to the public—a right which the public has in regard to us. Civil law, then, is only penal law viewed under another aspect. If I consider a law at the moment when it confers a right, or imposes an obligation, this is the civil point of view. If I consider a law in its sanction, in its effects as regards the violation of that right, the breaking through that obligation, that is the penal point of view.

Therefore the subject matter of civil law is rights and obligations, which the Legislature creates in order to promote the happiness of the community. That happiness consists chiefly in four things— subsistence, abundance, equality, and security.[6]

Amongst these objects the two most important are sub-sistence and security. " Abundance and equality are manifestly

---

[1] Works ii 205.   [2] Ibid 246-248.
[3] Ibid 249-251 ; for the extent to which this system of contracting was used in eighteenth century local government see vol. x 177 ; Bentham proposed to use it on a large scale in his Panopticon scheme, above 54, 55 ; below 93, 118.
[4] Works iii 160.   [5] Theory of Legislation 89.   [6] Ibid 96.

of inferior importance. Without security, equality could not last a day ; without subsistence, abundance could not exist at all." [1] As between subsistence and security the latter is the more important, for without it subsistence cannot exist. [2] Equality should only be favoured in so far as it does not interfere with security. [3] In fact, it is impossible to establish absolute equality. If all property were equally divided at fixed periods there would soon be no property to divide. If all men were given equal rights there would be no subordination—no political society. [4] The law cannot directly promote the ends of subsistence and abundance. Nor can it do much positively to secure equality—though it can do something positively by promoting a practice of insurance or by indemnifying those who have suffered by public calamities or war, [5] and negatively by death duties and the removal of restraints upon trade. [6] Hence the principal object of the law is security. [7] Its main object should be to protect property, and to promote the realization of those expectations which the law has created by its protection of property. [8] By pursuing this object it will indirectly and gradually promote a measure of equality ; for it will thereby promote the growth of a middle class, [9] upon whose progressive increase and enlightenment Bentham mainly relied to secure the gradual conversion of the state to his principle of utility and the reforms in the law founded upon it. [10]

But to attain the security of property some sacrifice of property must be made in order to enable the state to maintain the machinery for warding off attacks upon it ; and it may be maintained that the state should demand a similar sacrifice to relieve the poor, to support religion, and to encourage the arts and sciences. But in all cases there must be an equality of sacrifice—taxes must be equally levied, [11] and if, to secure economy, places or pensions are suppressed, full indemnity must be paid. [12]

These then should be the objects of the law. But to attain these objects the legislator must bear in mind the following principles : the laws must not run counter to expectation founded on old

---

[1] Theory of Legislation 98 ; above 52, 53.

[2] Theory of Legislation 98.   [3] Ibid 99.

[4] Ibid ; these conclusions were enforced by an appendix on The Levelling System printed at the end of the civil code, ibid 358-364.

[5] Ibid 107.   [6] Ibid 122-123.   [7] Ibid 110.   [8] Ibid 111.

[9] " It is worthy of remark that, in a nation prosperous in its agriculture, its manufacture, and its commerce, there is a continual progress towards equality. If the laws do nothing to combat it, if they do not maintain certain monopolies, if they put no shackles upon industry and trade, if they do not permit entails, we see great properties divided little by little, without effort, without revolution, without shock, and a much greater number of men coming to participate in the moderate favours of fortune. . . . Thus we may conclude that *Security*, while preserving its place as the supreme principle, leads indirectly to *Equality* ; while equality, if taken as the basis of the social arrangement, will destroy both itself and security at the same time," ibid 123.

[10] Below 113.   [11] Theory of Legislation 139-142.   [12] Ibid 143-145.

customs, they must be known, they must be consistent with one another, they must be consistent with the principle of utility, they must be methodically arranged, they must be certain in their execution, they must be literally, not arbitrarily, interpreted.[1]

Bentham then proceeds, in the light of these principles, to sketch the principles of the law of property. He considers, first, original titles to property; title by consent, which involves a consideration of some of the principles of the law of contract, and of restraints on alienation; title by succession, which involves a discussion of the rules of intestate succession and of the power of making a will—it may be noted that Bentham approves of the French *légitime* because it is "a convenient medium between domestic anarchy and paternal tyranny."[2] Bentham then proceeds to discuss rights to services, in other words, the law of obligations. These rights to services, he thinks, depend either on superior need, on anterior service, or on agreement.[3] Agreement, he maintains, is not, as is usually supposed, a reason in itself for the creation of an obligation.[4] It merely proves the existence of a mutual advantage to the contracting parties. "It is this reason of utility which gives the contract all its force."[5] The same principle will tell us when and why the law should make a contract void. Finally Bentham condemns tenancy in common, approves enclosures,[6] and condemns copyhold tenure as a remnant of the feudal system which "has produced in modern laws a confusion and complexity from which it is very difficult to deliver them."[7]

Lastly, Bentham considers the law of status under the four heads of master and servant, guardian and ward, father and child, husband and wife. Under the first head he discusses the institution of slavery, and the best methods of getting rid of it. He favours a gradual abolition.[8] He condemns the Elizabethan system of apprenticeship; and, in accordance with the dominant economic theories, he thinks that the best way to secure skill in the workman is "to leave everybody a perfect liberty of choosing the good and rejecting the bad, of being governed in their preferences by merit; and to excite the emulation of artisans by the freedom of competition."[9] Under the last head he discusses and justifies the institution of marriage. On grounds of utility he favours a considerable facility of divorce.[10]

---

[1] Theory of Legislation 148-157.   [2] Ibid 185.
[3] Ibid 189.   [4] Ibid 194.   [5] Ibid.
[6] " In passing through the lands which have undergone that happy change, we are enchanted as by the sight of a new colony. Harvests, flocks, smiling habitations, have succeeded to the dull sterility of a desert. Happy conquests of peaceful industry ! " ibid 195-196 ; Bentham takes the view of the advantages of enclosures taken by the orthodox economists, and ignores the hardships to the small cultivators which they caused, see vol. xi 455-457.
[7] Theory of Legislation 197.   [8] Ibid 207.
[9] Ibid 200.   [10] Ibid 221-230.

The detailed contents of the penal and civil codes are set out by Bentham in his *General View of a Complete Code of Laws*.[1] But these two codes did not exhaust the whole field of law. He provides for and sketches the contents of a constitutional code,[2] and less elaborately the contents of international, maritime, military, ecclesiastical, and procedure codes.[3] These codes should contain the whole of the law ; and nothing not in the code should be law. Unwritten law is merely conjectural law and should not be admitted as law.[4] The style of the code should be clear, precise, and as concise as possible. Words should always be used in the same sense, and when necessary, terms should be defined.[5]

" A code formed upon these principles would not require schools for its explanation, would not require casuists to unravel its subtilties. It would speak a language familiar to everybody : each one might consult it at his need. It would be distinguished from all other books by its greater simplicity and clearness. The father of a family, without assistance, might take it in his hand and teach it to his children, and give to the precepts of morality the force and dignity of public morals." [6]

To preserve its purity all commentary upon it, whether in the shape of decided cases or text books, should be regarded as unauthoritative. If defects should be found such defects should be brought to the notice of the Legislature which should provide the necessary amendment.[7] Finally, once in each century, the codes should be revised, in order to eliminate obsolete terms or formularies—" remembering that this will be more needful in regard to the language of the legal formularies in use than that of the text of the laws themselves." [8]

This last sentence shows that Bentham thought that the contents of codes of laws based upon the principle of utility would lay down rules as eternally and universally true as the principle of utility itself, so that those contents would be as little subject to variation as the laws of the mathematical or physical sciences.[9] But it was obvious that the laws of different nations were diverse, and that the laws of the nation had been changed and modified in process of time. How then could this diversity be reconciled with the idea of uniform laws founded on the one universally true principle of utility ? It is to this problem that Bentham addresses himself in his essay on *The Influence of Time and Place in Matters of Legislation*.[10]

Bentham admits that time and place must be considered ; for they are circumstances which influence sensibility, and so they must be taken into account in " estimating the force of a lot of

[1] Works iii 155-210. [2] Ibid 195-200. [3] Ibid 200-205.
[4] Ibid 206. [5] Ibid 207-209. [6] Ibid 209.
[7] Ibid 209-210. [8] Ibid 210.
[9] Above 52, 53; below 131. [10] Works i 171-194.

punishment." [1] He admits, too, that there is some force in Montesquieu's view that the laws must be adapted to the people for whom they are made. He says : [2]

Before Montesquieu, a man who had a distant country given him to make laws for, would have made short work of it. " Name to me the people " he would have said ; " reach me down my Bible, and the business is done at once. The laws they have been used to, no matter what they are, mine shall supersede them : manners, they shall have mine which are the best in nature ; religion, they shall have mine too which is all of it true and the only one that is so."

Since Montesquieu the number of documents which a legislator would require is considerably enlarged. " Send the people," he will say, " to me, or me to the people ; lay open to me the whole tenor of their life and conversation ; paint to me the face and geography of the country ; give me as close and minute a view as possible of their present laws, their manners, and their religion." But we have seen that the essay shows that circumstances of which Bentham would take account are really superficial. [3] He would take account of climate, physical geography, religious beliefs, social customs, national prejudices ; but he maintains that, though early laws were imperfect, it is a fallacy to think that they were more suited to the age than perfect laws would have been. [4] His real belief is that laws grounded on the true principle of utility are suited to all times and places. He " reaches down " the principle of utility, and uses it in much the same way as a man, before Montesquieu, used his Bible. He says : [5]

Were I to choose to what I would . . . attribute these magnificent prerogatives of universality and immutability, it should rather be to certain grounds of law, than to the laws themselves : to the principles upon which they should be founded : to the subordinate reasons deducible from those principles, and to the best plan upon which they can be put together : to the considerations by which it is expedient the legislator should suffer himself to be governed, rather than to any laws which it is expedient he should make for the government of those who stand committed to his care.

Thus, to take an example from the criminal law,

The rules concerning the cases that are respectively meet and unmeet for punishment and for reward ; the rules concerning the proportion proper to be observed between offences and punishments, between acts of merit

---

[1] Works i 173 n.   [2] Ibid.   [3] Above 52, 53.   [4] Works i 189.
[5] Ibid 193 ; above 5 n. 9 ; Halévy, Philosophic Radicalism 678 ; see Maine's criticism, Ancient Law 118, " That which seems expedient to a society, or rather to the governing part of it, when it alters a rule of law, is surely the same thing as the object, whatever it may be, which it has in view when it makes the change. Expediency and the greatest good are nothing more than different names for the impulse which prompts the modification "—in other words since the impulses to modification vary in different times and places, there is no fixed rule, as Bentham thought, as to what is and what is not expedient.

and reward ; the rules concerning the properties to be wished for in a lot
of punishment and reward ; the principles on which the division of
offences has its foundation : . . . all these, if they are just and proper
now, would at any time have been so, and will be so everywhere, and to
the end of time. They will hold good so long as pleasure is pleasure and
pain is pain ; so long as steel wounds, fire burns, water seeks a level,
bread nourishes, inanition destroys.[1]

Bentham's real belief was that, just as science enables man " to
transform physical nature at will and without limits," so
" education has the faculty of transforming the human character
to an unlimited extent." [2]   Therefore a thorough grounding in the
principle of utility and all that it implies will eliminate all
diversities, and make it unnecessary to consider such factors as
time and place.

But it should be noted that Bentham, unlike visionaries like
Rousseau[3] or Godwin,[4] is too sensible to think that even the
complete carrying out of his proposals for reform, would inaugurate a golden age. They would obviate a certain quantity of evil
by diminishing pain ; but

everything beyond this is chimerical. Perfect happiness belongs to the
imaginary regions of philosophy, and must be classed with the universal
elixir and the philosopher's stone. In the age of greatest perfection, fire
will burn, tempests will rage, man will be subject to infirmity, to
accidents, and to death. It may be possible to diminish the influence of,
but not to destroy, the sad and mischievous passions. The unequal gifts
of nature and of fortune will always create jealousies : there will always
be opposition of interests ; and, consequently, rivalries and hatred.
Pleasures will be purchased by pains ; enjoyments by privations.
Painful labour, daily subjection, a condition nearly allied to indigence,
will always be the lot of numbers. Among the higher as well as the lower
classes, there will be desires which cannot be satisfied ; inclinations which
must be subdued : reciprocal security can only be established by the
forcible renunciation by each one, of everything which might wound the
legitimate rights of others. If we suppose, therefore, the most reasonable
laws, constraint will be their basis : but the most salutary constraint in
its distant effect is always an evil, is always painful in its immediate
operation.[5]

But though legislative reforms based on the principle of utility
will not inaugurate a golden age, that principle has at least done
this :— it has enabled us to attain a vision of what a perfect
system of legislation should be and what benefits it would confer
upon mankind ; and so

[1] Works i 193.
[2] Halévy, Philosophic Radicalism 52-53 ; it may be noted that Bentham had
translated a work of the Swedish chemist Bergmann, and that James Mill was a
friend of Thomson, a defender of Daltonian Atomism, Halévy, History of the English
People in 1815 (Pelican ed.) iii 209.
[3] Vol. x 13, 16 n. 4.   [4] Above 26, 27, 40.   [5] Works i 194.

though no one now living may be permitted to enter into this land of promise, yet he who shall contemplate it in its vastness and beauty may rejoice, as did Moses, when on the verge of the desert, from the mountain top, he saw the length and breadth of that good land into which he was not permitted to enter and take possession.[1]

It is obvious that the principle of utility, applied as Bentham proposed to apply it to the form and substance of the law, would effect a revolution in the traditional methods of legal thought, and in the traditional methods of stating the law. Therefore it was necessary for Bentham not only to state his principles and show how they ought to be applied to the reform of existing systems of law, but also to explain in what respects they were superior to the traditional methods. This involved a criticism of those methods in some detail. This criticism he applied in his two books on Blackstone's *Commentaries*—the *Fragment on Government* and the *Comment on the Commentaries*. Of these two books I have already said something.[2] The *Fragment* is, as we have seen, a detailed criticism of a passage in the second section of Blackstone's Introduction, which deals with government in general and the British constitution in particular.[3] In the Preface he states his principle of utility, his contempt for the race of lawyers and politicians,[4] his indictment of their representative Blackstone as a base apologist for all things established,[5] and an enemy to " beneficent legislators whose care it has been to pluck the mask of mystery from the face of jurisprudence."[6] In the work itself he criticizes Blackstone's account of the origin of government, and, with the help of the doctrine of sovereignty, he turns to ridicule Blackstone's laudatory description of the British constitution. The *Comment on the Commentaries* is a detailed criticism of the rest of Blackstone's Introduction. In it Bentham emphasizes his central theory that the only true law—the only law properly so called—is the enacted law. " What is the *Common Law* ? What but an assemblage of fictitious regulations feigned after the image of these real ones that compose the Statute Law."[7] It is wholly uncertain, and ought to be set out in plain terms by the Legislature[8]—not in the verbose and inaccurate style in which

[1] Works i 194. [2] Vol. xii 731-734 ; above 43, 46, 47, 48, 50, 59, 66. [3] Above 48.

[4] " A passive and enervate race, ready to swallow anything, and to acquiesce in anything : with intellects incapable of distinguishing right from wrong, and with affections alike indifferent to either : insensible, shortsighted, obstinate : lethargic, yet liable to be driven into convulsions by false terrors : deaf to the voice of reason and public utility : obsequious only to the whisper of interest, and to the beck of power," Preface to the Fragment (Montague's ed.) 104.

[5] Ibid 108-114. [6] Ibid 113.

[7] A Comment on the Commentaries 126.

[8] " Judged by a standard the parts of which are everywhere and no-where, commanded to do they know not what, and punished they know not why, such, O Legislators, is the state of uncertainty and distraction in which the people lie abandoned, while ye are sleeping," ibid 248.

statutes are generally drawn ;[1] and really notified to those who are required to obey it.[2] In fact it is one of the worst features of judge-made law that it is never effectively notified, and is therefore unknowable.[3] As for divine law, with which Blackstone had made some play, it is even more unknowable than the common law.[4] It is quite obvious that the Mosaic law cannot be taken over in bulk.[5] If we ask what parts of the divine law as stated in the Bible is to be taken over, we must, in effect, have recourse to the principle of utility, which " once adopted as the governing principle, admits of no rival, admits not even of an associate." [6] Our principal concern should be to study, by the light of this principle, what ought to be law. History is mainly valuable as an object lesson as to the mistakes which we ought to avoid.[7] The detailed criticism of the Introduction to the *Commentaries* contained in the book is thus directed to prove the confused state of English law, the evil results of the traditional methods of stating it, and the improvement which would result from the adoption of Bentham's principles.

The short tract entitled *The Truth v. Ashhurst* [8] supplements the *Fragment* and the *Comment on the Commentaries*. It was inspired by a charge to a Middlesex grand jury delivered by Ashhurst J. in 1792, in which he had stated a number of commonplaces as to the excellencies of the British constitution and of English law. " No man is so low," he said, " as not to be within the law's protection." That is not true, said Bentham, because ninety-nine men out of a hundred cannot afford the cost of bringing an action.[9] The law only lays upon individuals such restraints as are necessary for the good of the community. The game laws and the law of settlement show that that is not true.[10] The subject is not bound by any laws other than those to which he has virtually consented. If we look at the enacted law, it is obvious that few subjects have any vote for members of Parliament ; and the common law is made by the judges on the same principle as a man makes laws for his dog—he waits till the dog has done something he does not like and then punishes him for it.[11] Consequently

---

[1] A Comment on the Commentaries 143.   [2] Ibid 66-68.

[3] " The Judge in a narrow ill-contrived room, where a hundred perhaps can see, where fifty perhaps hear, where twenty perhaps can bestow themselves at such ease as to profit from their hearing, announces these judicial acts viva voce : of these twenty, if any one publish what is announced, he is to be punished : so saith the Law. Thus it is that the acts of Judges are made known to 8 millions of people," ibid 187 ; but Bentham was mistaken in supposing that a reporter who published his reports, was liable to punishment, vol. xii 112-113.

[4] A Comment on the Commentaries 192.   [5] Ibid 49-50, 192-193.

[6] Ibid 51.   [7] Ibid 136 ; below 107, 118.   [8] Works v 231-237.

[9] Ibid 233-234.   [10] Ibid 235.

[11] Ibid 235-236 ; see vol. xii 158 for Bentham's comparison of case law to dog law.

it is wholly false to say that all men have the means of knowing the law.

These, then, were the principles which he spent his life in expounding, and this was his attitude to the rules and institutions of English law. But, in the course of his long life spent in expounding and applying these principles, he wrote many works and tracts, not only on the theory of legislation and on the form and substance of the law public and private as he thought it ought to be, but also on cognate subjects such as political economy, education, logic, philosophy, and religion ; and, since he kept a close watch on legal and political events at home and abroad, he also wrote letters and tracts on many topics suggested by them. We must now glance briefly at the way in which his principles were developed and applied in this large and miscellaneous mass of writings.

(b) Bentham's other writings

Bentham's other works fall into the following groups : (i) Writings on different branches of the law ; (ii) writings connected with English politics ; (iii) writings connected with foreign politics ; (iv) economic writings ; (v) writings connected with education ; (vi) philosophical and religious writings.

(i) Writings on different branches of the law

Bentham's main work and main interest were the reform and the restatement of the law. Therefore his writings on different branches of the law are the most numerous and most important. They can be grouped under the following heads : (a) works on civil and criminal law ; (b) works on evidence and procedure ; (c) works on constitutional law ; (d) works on international law ; (e) works on codification and the drafting of statutes.

(a) Works on civil and criminal law

Bentham's *Principles of the Civil Code*[1] are in effect the same as the part of Dumont's Theory of Legislation which deals with the civil law of which I have given some account. To it is added in the Collected Works an appendix on *The Levelling System*[2] in which he reiterates his arguments against legislative attempts to equalize property. It would, he contends, " be destructive both of security and wealth." [3] The only other part of the civil law of which he has anything to say is the law of real property. In 1826 he wrote an article in the *Westminster Review* entitled a *Commentary on Humphreys' Real Property Code*.[4] In it he advocated reforms in the forms of conveyances, registration of

---

[1] Works i 299-358.   [2] Ibid 358-364.
[3] Ibid 358.   [4] Works v 387-416.

conveyances, the abolition of gavelkind and borough-English, the conversion of copyholds into freeholds, the partition of all common lands, and a codification of the law of real property,[1] an increase in the number of the judges if needed to give effect to the code, and improvements in the law of procedure directed to the same object. The term heirs should " be, in all its applications, eliminated out of the code, and abandoned to the society of antiquaries."[2] Another paper on the same subject is an *Outline of a Plan of a General Register of Real Property*[3] addressed to the real property commissioners. A good deal is said as to the general utility of such a register, and of the mechanical details of its compilation ; but the substantial difficulties arising from the substantive rules of the law of real property are not discussed.

Bentham's work on the *Principles of Penal Law*[4] is, to a large extent, reproduced in Dumont's *Traités* ; but in the *Principles* there is a good deal of additional matter. Bentham exposes many of the absurd and archaic rules of the English criminal law and the law of tort—the theory upon which the action for seduction was based.[5] The effect of death upon a cause of action,[6] the consequences of suicide,[7] the conception of felony,[8] the doctrine of corruption of blood,[9] deodands,[10] benefit of clergy,[11] outlawry,[12] excommunication.[13] He exposes also abuses which were the result of archaic ideas such as gaolers' fees,[14] or of existing institutions such as the state of the prisons,[15] the system of transportation,[16] the indiscriminate infliction of capital punishment—the punishment of death should be inflicted only for treason, and then only occasionally.[17] But he has none of that morbid sentimentality which looks too exclusively at the feelings of the criminal and pays little attention to the sufferings of his victims. He advocated the use of a whipping machine,[18] he dwelt upon the efficacy of solitude, and upon darkness and hard diet as aids to the reformation of the criminal.[19] He advocates the spread of education,[20] the liberty of the press,[21] laws against cruelty to animals,[22] laws against attempts to commit crimes.[23] In *The Principles*, as in his other works, he minimizes the influence of

---

[1] Works v 412.

[2] Ibid 405 ; as Maitland said, " This is his doom, ' abandoned to the Society of Antiquaries,' yes, with all his rights, privileges, and appurtenances. Or if our antiquaries will not have him as a gift . . . we will hand him over to the tender mercies of the *Gradualisten* and *Parentelisten*, who shall write monographs upon him to the end of time," Collected Papers i 200-201.

[3] Works i 417-435.	[4] Ibid 365-580.	[5] Ibid 373.
[6] Ibid 523-525.	[7] Ibid 479-480.	[8] Ibid 503-511.
[9] Ibid 480.	[10] Ibid 485.	[11] Ibid 505-509.
[12] Ibid 512-514.	[13] Ibid 514-516.	[14] Ibid 423-424.
[15] Ibid 427-429.	[16] Ibid 490-497.	[17] Ibid 441-450, 449-450.
[18] Ibid 415.	[19] Ibid 425-427.	[20] Ibid 536.
[21] Ibid 568, 574-575.	[22] Ibid 562.	[23] Ibid 561.

religion, he is opposed to all disabilities on religious grounds,[1] and he exposes the futility of the practice of exacting an oath as a test of opinion or on trifling occasions.[2] On the other hand, some of his ideas are quite unpractical, e.g. his suggested mitigation of the rule of employer's liability when the employer of the tort-feasor is poor and the injured party is rich;[3] and some are mischievous. Thus he condemns many of the principles of English law which are designed to protect an accused person. They are, he thinks, the cause of the frequency of crime in England. The model upon which criminal procedure should be based is that adopted by the father of a family who is searching after the truth.[4] He approves of secret and anonymous informations as to the commission of crime. They can be justified upon the same principle as the ballot is justified.[5] He is opposed to all restrictions on the right of association.[6] In fact in Bentham's *Principles of Penal Law*, as in other parts of his works, there is a mixture of wise and foolish suggestions for the reform of the law. We shall see that he owes no small part of his reputation to the fact that his suggestions were translated into concrete reforms by practical lawyers whose training enabled them to separate the wheat from the chaff.[7]

The Principles are supplemented by a series of papers on prison reform, on the abuses of the system of transportation, and on the merits of the Panopticon scheme of prison management.[8]

(b) Works on evidence and procedure

Bentham's two principal works on evidence and procedure are *An Introductory View of the Rationale of Evidence*[9] and the *Rationale of Judicial Evidence*.[10] Two supplementary works are the tract entitled *Swear not at all* " containing an exposure of the needlessness and mischievousness as well as anti-Christianity of the ceremony of an oath ";[11] and the work entitled *Justice and Codification Petitions* which is supplementary partly to his works on evidence and procedure and partly to his works on constitutional law.[12] The *Introductory View of the Rationale of Evidence* is an introductory sketch : the *Rationale of Judicial Evidence* is a finished treatise compiled, as we have seen, with great skill by J. S. Mill from Bentham's MSS.[13] These works on evidence and

---

[1] Works i 564-565. [2] Ibid 567 ; cp. below 86. [3] Works i 384.
[4] Ibid 568. [5] Ibid 573. [6] Ibid 576-578.
[7] Below 127, 128. [8] Works iv 1-284. [9] Ibid vi 1-187.
[10] Ibid 190-585 and vol. vii. [11] Works v 187-229.
[12] Ibid 436-548 ; as Halévy points out, Philosophical Radicalism, 374, the two topics of constitutional law and adjective law are, according to Bentham, closely connected ; the former gives powers and imposes duties on officials ; the latter describes the powers and duties needed to enforce the law.
[13] Above 63, 65.

procedure are the most finished of Bentham's works, and the most fruitful in their suggestions of practical reforms. His work on constitutional law [1] is as elaborate ; but we shall see that it is not so well balanced, and, that though it contains some fruitful ideas, many of the suggestions it makes are unpractical and even foolish. [2] J. S. Mill, in his summary of Bentham's services to the law, singled out his work on evidence and procedure for special praise. He said : [3]

He found the philosophy of judicial procedure, including that of judicial establishments and of evidence, in a more wretched state than even any other part of the philosophy of law ; he carried it at once almost to perfection. He left it with every one of its principles established, and little remaining to be done even in the suggestion of practical arrangements.

This praise is perhaps a little exaggerated ; for we shall see that though Bentham made many useful suggestion for reform which have been carried out, some of his suggestions have fortunately not been endorsed by the Legislature. [4]

The most important of these two books is the *Rationale of Judicial Evidence*. In it the ideas contained in the *Introductory View* are elaborated and many additional topics are introduced. It is divided into ten Books. The first Book deals with the theoretic grounds of the law of evidence ; the second with the securities for the trustworthiness of testimony ; the third with the extraction of testimonial evidence ; the fourth with pre-appointed evidence ; the fifth with circumstantial evidence ; the sixth with makeshift evidence ; the seventh with the authentication of evidence ; the eighth with the cause of the exclusion of evidence—the technical system of procedure ; the ninth (which is in six parts) with the exclusion of evidence ; the tenth with the the instructions to be delivered from the legislator to the judge for the estimation of the probative force of evidence. The work contains, first, a searching exposure of the many defects in the English system of procedure, and of the illogical character of most of the rules of the law of evidence ; and, secondly, an account of the shape which a system of procedure and the rules of the law of evidence ought to take in the light of the principle of utility. The gist of the work, Bentham tells us, can be summarized in three propositions—the first a theorem to be proved, the other two problems to be solved : [5]

The theorem is this : that, merely with a view to rectitude of decision, to the avoidance of the mischiefs attached to undue decision, no species of evidence whatsoever, willing or unwilling, ought to be excluded : for that although in certain cases it may be right that this or that lot of

---

[1] Below 88 seqq.   [2] Below 92-94.   [3] Dissertations and Discussions i 374.
[4] Below 87.   [5] Works vi 203-204.

evidence, though tendered, should not be admitted, yet in these cases the reason for the exclusion rests on other grounds ; viz. avoidance of vexation, expense, and delay. . . . To give instructions pointing out the means by which what can be done may be done towards securing the truth of evidence : this is one of the two main problems, the solution of which is here attempted. . . . To give instructions serving to assist the mind of the judge in forming its estimate of the probability of truth, in the instance of the evidence presented to it ; in a word, in judging of the weight of evidence : this is the other of the two main problems which are here attempted to be solved.

Bentham's main thesis is that all evidence, even hearsay evidence,[1] ought to be admitted ; that it was for the judge to determine its probative force ;[2] and that the only grounds for the exclusion of evidence were expense, vexation, or delay.[3] The procedural model, to which he thought judicial procedure and the rules of evidence should conform, was the method adopted by the father of a family to settle family disputes. If, he said, the artificial rules of the English law of evidence and procedure were applied to the family it would soon cease to exist ;[4] and it was only the fact that these rules were not known that preserved society—" if rogues did but know all the pains that the law has taken for their benefit, honest men would have nothing left they could call their own." [5]

Some instances of the chief changes in the rules of the law of evidence which, in Bentham's opinion, were needed to give effect to the principles upon which a rational law of evidence should be based can be summarized as follows : the admissibility of the evidence of accused persons,[6] of the parties to an action, and of persons interested ;[7] the recognition of the superiority of oral evidence over written evidence,[8] and, more especially, the efficacy of cross-examination as a means of eliciting the truth ;[9] an analysis of the collection of different rules included under the principle that only the " best evidence " is admissible, and an examination of the reasonableness or otherwise of these rules ;[10] a revision of the rules as to the conditions in which oral evidence can be admitted to explain or vary a written document,[11] and of

---

[1] Works vi 165, vii 132-137 ; Halévy, Philosophic Radicalism 388, 390-391.

[2] " What, then, is the practical conclusion here contended for ? It is this : viz. that every article of evidence, the nature of which is to operate in the character of circumstantial evidence—whether it be presented in the form of oral or written evidence, and (if in the form of written evidence) whether in the form of a judicial document or any other—ought equally to be admitted : the judge of fact being left equally free, in all these cases, to form his judgment of its probative force," Works vii 72.

[3] Ibid 335-336.   [4] Works vi 205, vii 198.   [5] Works vi 205.

[6] Works vii 455 seqq. ; cp. Halévy, Philosophic Radicalism 391-393.

[7] Works vi 138, vii 487-489, 506-517.   [8] Works vi 331-332, 505.

[9] Ibid 499 ; Bentham thought that the superiority of English to continental modes of trial was due, not to trial by jury, but to trial " by oral and cross-examined evidence," ibid 507.

[10] Ibid vi 115, 126, vii 554-558.   [11] Ibid vii 556-557.

the rules as to the proof of documents by attesting witnesses ;[1] the recognition of the illogicality of requiring in certain cases two witnesses ;[2] the recognition of the absurdity of supposing that an oath is any safeguard against perjury,[3] accompanied by suggestions, if oaths were to be retained, for making the ceremony more efficacious.[4] Because Bentham was opposed to the exclusion of evidence he disapproved of the rules which disqualified husband and wife from giving evidence on one another's behalf,[5] and the privilege of refusing to give evidence allowed to legal advisers with respect to communications passing between them and their clients.[6]

In dealing with the defects of the English system of procedure Bentham enumerated twelve different defects,[7] amongst which were the absence of local courts,[8] the fact that the courts did not sit continuously,[9] the system of pleading and especially special pleading,[10] the use of fictions,[11] the use of technical jargon,[12] case law,[13] useless offices,[14] the separation of courts of law and equity.[15] We have seen that Bentham was well warranted in dwelling upon the evil effects of some of these features of the English system of procedure. His denunciation of the form of the pleadings in a Chancery suit,[16] of sham bail and pledges for the prosecution,[17] of the abuse of common injunctions,[18] are completely justified. His criticism of the common saying that the judge ought to be of counsel with the prisoner is acute,[19] and his condemnation of the uselessness of the secret enquiry by the grand jury[20] has recently been endorsed by the Legislature.[21] There is much to be said for his view that the use of a seal is an old and useless formality,[22] and for his very just criticisms upon the technical definition of a court of record.[23] Occasionally, it is true, Bentham admits that the English system of procedure has a few merits, such as the

[1] Works vii 190-192.   [2] Ibid 520-531.
[3] Ibid vi 308-315 ; Halévy, Philosophic Radicalism 388.
[4] Works vi 318-321.   [5] Ibid vii 480-486.
[6] Ibid 474-476 ; but Bentham was in favour of allowing a Roman Catholic priest to refuse to give evidence as to what he had heard under seal of confession, ibid 366-368—he thought that it would not diminish the amount of evidence available, since, if confessions were not privileged, less would be confessed, and that the contrary rule would give rise to vexation out of all proportion to any possible gain.

[7] Ibid 225 ; cp. ibid v 446 when fourteen defects are enumerated.
[8] Vol. i 187-191.   [9] Vol. iii 674-675.
[10] Ibid 627-639 ; vol. ix 262-315.   [11] Ibid 247-262.   [12] Ibid 260.
[13] Below 89, 90.   [14] Vol. i 246-252, 256-262.
[15] Ibid 635 ; cp. vol. xii 583-605.   [16] Works vi 307-308 ; vol. ix 379-406.
[17] Works vii 284-285.   [18] Ibid 298-300 ; cp. vol. i 465.
[19] Works vi 349-351.   [20] Ibid 375.
[21] 23, 24 George V c. 36 § 1.   [22] Works vi 515-516.
[23] Ibid 565 ; cp. vol. v 157-160 ; Bentham said, loc. cit., " Among those inferior courts [not of record] which stands first on the list ? The Court of Chancery, of which the daily functions are to impede and overrule the decisions of them both [the King's Bench and Common Pleas]."

publicity of its proceedings, the use of cross-examination, and the use of juries—these merits, he says, make it " the least bad extant instead of being amongst the worst." [1] But on the whole Bentham maintains that, though as a rule, it is absurd to suppose that ancient and savage states of society are superior to our own, in the case of the law of evidence and procedure it would be possible to maintain this thesis.

By doing away the work of five or six hundred years, and throwing back the system of procedure, as to the most fundamental parts, into the state in which it was at the time of Edward I and much earlier, a mountain of abuse might be removed, and even a near approach to perfection made. [2]

Then no evidence was excluded, the parties were always present in court, and there was an efficient system of local courts. [3] The reforms most urgently needed were the abolition of payment of the officers of justice by fees, the substitution of the " natural " for the technical system of procedure, codification, and the constitution of a standing committee to watch the working of the law and to suggest reforms to the Legislature. [4]

For the most part, Bentham's analyses of the defects of the law and his suggested remedies are both acute and sensible. But occasionally they are impracticable or unwise. Perhaps the most absurd, and indeed unjust, of his suggestions is that the plaintiff's statement of claim should be taken as prima facie evidence, and that the burden of disproving it should lie on the defendant. [5] It was not a very practical suggestion that each particular contract should be written on a particular form which contained on the margin an abstract of the law relating to that contract ; [6] and his objections to prescribing a particular form for wills on pain of nullity have proved to be groundless. [7] His objections to some of the cases of estoppel in pais, e.g. the rule that a tenant is estopped from disputing his landlord's title, [8] overlook the fact that these rules are based on a sensible principle which tends to expedite legal proceedings, and so to diminish their vexation and delay. There was more to be said than he realized for allowing a privilege from compulsory disclosure to communications as between husband and wife and as between legal adviser and client. [9] But these aberrations are rare. For the most part Bentham's criticisms of the rules of English law are completely justified, and a very large number of his suggestions for reform have, in the century which has elapsed since his death been adopted by the Legislature. [10]

---

[1] Works vi 373.
[2] Ibid vii 599.
[3] Ibid ; and see ibid 594-595.
[4] Ibid 320.
[5] Ibid vi 136-137.
[6] Ibid 522.
[7] Ibid 532-535.
[8] Ibid vii 554.
[9] Above 86.
[10] Below 132-134.

(c) Works on constitutional law

Bentham's *Constitutional Code* [1] was the latest of his important works. He projected a work in three volumes dealing with both the central and the local government. He began the work in 1820. The first volume was printed in 1827, and the first chapter of the second volume was printed in 1830, and published with the first volume in that year. When Bentham died in 1832 the two succeeding chapters were nearly ready to be printed ; but the rest of the volume was in an imperfect state, and much unarranged matter, intended to form an introductory dissertation, was in existence. As usual, the MSS. were both voluminous and confused, and none had been revised. Richard Doane, Bentham's editor, arranged the work in two Books. The first Book forms the introductory dissertation. It deals with Bentham's general theory of legislation, with the relation of constitutional law to other branches of law, and with the leading principles of the *Constitutional Code*. The second Book contains the code arranged according to Bentham's plan. To produce a coherent text arranged in this way it was necessary to arrange and classify the MSS. Doane's plan was, he tells us,

to incorporate into one chapter all that related to the same subject matter ; to place those chapters first, which were of most general application, and to make those follow, which discussed more particularly the leading provisions of the Code itself, and constituted as it were, a general Rationale to the whole work. [2]

Doane thus did for the MSS. of the *Constitutional Code* a work similar to that done by J. S. Mill for the MSS. of the *Rationale of Judicial Evidence*. [3]

The Code embodies the latest version of Bentham's democratic and republican [4] ideas. He hoped that a Code embodying these ideas would be useful to Spain and Portugal, and to the American states which were growing up out of the wreck of the Spanish monarchy. [5] He hoped also that at some time in the future it might be useful to the British empire. [6] At the outset, therefore, he states the theory upon which he justifies these ideas. An absolute monarchy has for its end the greatest happiness of one individual only. A limited monarchy has for its end the greatest happiness of the monarch and the ruling few. It is only a

---

[1] Works ix. [2] Ibid, Note by the Editor.
[3] Above 63, 65, 83. [4] See Halévy, Philosophic Radicalism 415.
[5] Works ix ; Note by the Editor.
[6] " For England (independent of any such sudden revolution as, under the provocations given, will be always upon the cards), it may, in proportion as it is well adapted to its purpose, be of use in giving direction to the views of all such persons as may feel disposed to occupy themselves in the effecting of melioration by gradual changes, which, in so far as they are conducive to the professed end, will be so many approaches towards republicanism," Works ix 2.

representative democracy that has for its end the greatest happiness of the greatest number.[1] The ruling few are always the enemies of the subject many ; and the only remedy against their oppression is a constitution based on universal suffrage, annual elections, and vote by ballot.[2] But Bentham illogically maintained that the converse is not true—that the many poor would not oppress the rich few—on the ground that the poor could not oppress the rich except by plundering them, which would mean that all property—that of the poor as well as that of the rich—would be destroyed.[3] In fact Bentham convinced himself that, given education and a moderate subsistence, the less a man has of wealth, power, and dignity, the better is his aptitude for politics—in other words, his favourite middle classes are politically the most able.[4] Obviously in such a constitution there is no place for a second chamber.[5] The House of Lords is more dangerous than a pack of wolves ;[6] and, even if a second chamber were an elected body, it would be objectionable on account of delay, expense, and factitious differences between the two Houses.[7] The same democratic principles as are applied to the central government are applied to the local government. Each district has a sub-legislature which is elected on the same plan as the central legislature.[8]

The legislature thus elected is " omnicompetent." That is, it is sovereign.[9] Any restriction upon its legislative power would fetter its capacity to act for the interest of the whole community, so that any restriction would be contrary to the greatest happiness principle.[10] It is only in the case of governments which are based on the wrong principles that such restrictions are of any use. Indeed the fact that it has been found to be of use is " a conclusive proof of the badness of the government." [11] It follows that the legislature is the only source of law. Law enacted by the legislature is real law, as contrasted with the " unreal . . . imaginary, fictitious, spurious, judge-made law." [12] The legislature appoints the premier—the head of the state—for four years, and may dismiss him ;[13] and he appoints the other ministers.[14] The functions and departments of the other ministers are described at great length, and with an emphasis on mechanical minutiae which is sometimes ridiculous.[15] Some of them—the Preventive

---

[1] Works ix 10, 143.   [2] Ibid 107.
[3] Ibid 143-144 ; Halévy, Philosophic Radicalism 428-429 ; below 138, 139.
[4] Works ix 110-113 ; Halévy, Philosophic Radicalism 427-428.
[5] Cp. Works ii 307-310 ; ix 114-117, 144-145.
[6] Ibid 114.   [7] Ibid 114-115.   [8] Ibid 640-643.
[9] Ibid 119.   [10] Ibid.   [11] Ibid 122.
[12] Ibid 8 ; cp. ibid 480.   [13] Ibid 207-209.
[14] Ibid 205—except the minister of justice, below 93.
[15] See Works ix 42—arrangement of the public offices, and rules for the conduct of officials ; 234—the books to be kept by the ministers and how they should be

Service Minister,[1] the Indigence Relief Minister,[2] the Educations Minister,[3] the Health Minister[4] a Public Prosecutor and Eleemosynary Advocates for the poor[5]—foreshadow a policy of the supply by the state of social services which was long in developing. But, as M. Halévy has said, Bentham had realized that " when popular sovereignty is recognized, all increase of the administrative power is favourable to the rights and to the interests of the people, precisely because it strengthens the power of the sovereign." [6] These ministers are dismissible either by the premier or by the legislature.[7] They may take part in the debates of the legislature, they may propose motions, and they may answer questions ; but they cannot vote.[8] This denial to ministers of the power to vote is curious, since Bentham strenuously denies the need for any division of powers in a government. The theory that liberty is protected by a division of powers is condemned partly because it is " destitute of all reference to the greatest happiness of the greatest number," and partly because a complete separation would spell anarchy.[9]

The judicial department of the state is entrusted to a series of local courts. Each subdistrict has a court and there is a single appeal to the district court.[10] To allow any further appeal would entail increase of expense without any corresponding advantage.[11] The judiciary should be completely separated from the bar, because " in quality of his profession a law practitioner, in the pay of a litigant party, acts under the impulse of an interest incurably adverse to the several ends of justice." [12] His is a " sinister " interest.[13] Since judge-made law is prohibited some provision must be made for dealing with the defects in the law which litigation discloses. The judges must report all cases in which difficulty has occurred to the minister of justice and the minister for legislation, and the law must be amended by the legislature.[14] The advantage of the jury was, in Bentham's opinion, very questionable, and the system itself was very defective.[15] He objected to the mode in which juries were chosen, to the need for

---

used ; 239-240—how to register the stock kept by a naval yard and by government warehouses ; 274-275—the exact mode of voting for a candidate for government employment ; 280-281—how the examination of these candidates is to be conducted ; 327-329—how the different ministers should communicate with each other and with the public ; Bentham had some of the mechanical gifts of his brother Samuel whose inventive genius was remarkable. Clapham, An Economic History of Modern Britain, i 153.

[1] Works ix 213, 439.   [2] Ibid 213, 441.
[3] Ibid 213, 441-442.   [4] Ibid 214, 443-445.
[5] Ibid 570, 577.   [6] Philosophic Radicalism 431.
[7] Works ix 294.   [8] Ibid 316.
[9] Ibid 122-124 ; cp. Halévy, Philosophic Radicalism 408-409.
[10] Works ix 468-469.   [11] Ibid 469.
[12] Ibid 592.   [13] Ibid 594.   [14] Ibid 504-508.
[15] Ibid 555-556 ; Halévy, Philosophic Radicalism 400-401.

unanimity, to the juryman's oath, to lack of ability, to the additional expense and complication which a jury trial entailed. In its place he advocated what he called a quasi-jury, which he thought would retain the beneficial effects of the jury system. They were to hear the case, read the relevant documents, put questions to the judge and witnesses, comment on the case as it proceeded, suggest amendments to the judgment, give leave to appeal.[1] Each quasi-jury was to be divided into two sections— the erudite, and " the more popular and more numerous." In case of disagreement the will of the latter was to prevail, but, it was thought, the former would be able to guide them to a right decision.[2] The courts, like the legislature, were to be in continual session, and each judge, like each member of the legislature,[3] was given a deputy to act for him if he was unavoidably absent.[4] The judges were to be appointed by the minister of justice and dismissible by him for certain defined causes.[5]

Though Bentham suggested many detailed provisions for securing the competence of the various bodies and officials entrusted with the government of the state, and for securing economy in its administration,[6] he was always suspicious that some sinister influence would introduce abuses. The only corrective to this risk was the mobilization of public opinion, which, he thought, already coincided in most cases, and soon would coincide in all, with the teachings of the principle of utility.[7] In order to mobilize public opinion Bentham devised what he called a Public-Opinion Tribunal, in order that " every individual, taken individually, might not escape from the control of all the individuals taken collectively."[8]

The members of the public-opinion tribunal in a community are the members of that same community, the whole number of them, considered in respect of their capacity of taking cognizance of each other's conduct, sitting in judgment on it, and causing their judgments in the several cases to be made known. In the English House of Commons, in the

---

[1] Works ix 561-563.   [2] Ibid 556.   [3] Ibid 167.
[4] Ibid 483-484.   [5] Ibid 529, 532.
[6] He says, ibid 191, " The assemblage of securities, here proposed with reference to the highest department, the legislature, forms the commencement of an all pervading system of the like securities, covering the whole field of the official establishment, and applying to all public functionaries in every department and subdepartment."
[7] Public opinion may be considered as a system of law, emanating from the body of the people. . . . To the pernicious exercise of the power of government, it is the only check ; to the beneficial and indispensable supplement. Able rulers lead it ; prudent rulers lead or follow it ; foolish rulers disregard it. Even at the present state in the career of civilization, its dictates coincide, on most points, with those of the *greatest happiness principle* ; on some, however, it still deviates from them ; but, as its deviations have all along been less and less numerous, and less wide, sooner or later they will cease to be discernible ; aberration will vanish, coincidence will be complete," Works ix 158.
[8] Halévy, Philosophic Radicalism 432.

formation of a committee of members for this or that particular purpose, an order that now and then is seen to have place is, that all who come to the committee, shall have voices. The members of the public-opinion tribunal are to the members of the community at large what the members of the House of Commons' committee thus formed, are to the members of the house. The public-opinion tribunal may be conceived as sitting and acting in full assembly, or through the medium of a committee, a specially and actually appointed committee. . . . As this tribunal, by the counterforce, which, by its punitive power, it applies to the power of government, contributes to keep it in check, and to keep its course within the paths indicated by the greatest happiness principle . . . so, may it, in no inconsiderable degree, by its remunerating power.[1]

Thus those present at meetings of the Legislatures or Sub-legislatures, at sittings of the courts, those doing business with officials, those present at public meetings, can be regarded as so many committees of this Public-Opinion Tribunal.[2] They can express their approbation or disapprobation of the conduct of officials or elected representatives, and give effect to their views by their votes at elections.[3]

It was his desire to safeguard the subject against oppression which led Bentham to give both to private citizens and to civil servants a right to have recourse either to the ordinary courts of law, or to the minister who presided over the department to which the official complained against belonged.[4] Bentham proposed to give them the right to appeal to the minister because, as in the case of the army and the navy, a specialized referee of this kind could do better justice than the ordinary courts[5] as then constituted. But Bentham was not in favour of abridging the supremacy of the law. In all cases he would allow an appeal to the courts,[6] but he seems to admit that if the procedure of the ordinary courts[7] was reformed and if the terms on which officials held their office was more clearly defined,[8] there would be no objection to bringing such cases before their original jurisdiction.

The *Constitutional Code* is a logical code, which contains very few inconsistencies. There is perhaps an inconsistency between Bentham's suspicion of all governmental action,[9] and his suggestion that the state should take control of many various social services;[10] and between the denial of any division of powers

---

[1] Works ix 41.   [2] Ibid 157-158.   [3] Ibid 41-42, 158-159.
[4] On this topic see Arndt, Bentham on Administrative Jurisdiction, Journal of Comparative Legislation xxi 198-204; but I am not sure that Arndt, any more than other critics of Dicey, understands exactly what Dicey meant by the "rule of law," see L.Q.R. lv 586-588; for a passage in which Bentham expounds this option, see Works ix 303-307.
[5] Ibid 294, 323. "Referring a complaint to the one great penal justice shop, the King's Bench, a man by whom a wrong is sustained places his complaint in the hands of a Judicatory in which every one of the requisites necessary for the administration of relief is completely wanting," ibid 324.
[6] Ibid 306.   [7] Ibid 307-308.   [8] Ibid 323-324.
[9] Below 93.   [10] Above 89, 90.

in the constitution, and the rule that acceptance of office vacates a seat in the legislature,[1] and his denial to the Prime Minister of the power to appoint the Minister of Justice.[2] There is also an inconsistency between the condemnation of judge-made law[3] and the admission that in the past the judges have made much good law, and, by so doing, have furnished " a rich and apposite stock of materials for legislation."[4] Bentham, having convinced himself of the absolute and final perfection of a code based on the principle of utility, failed to see that a mode of developing law, which had led to good results in the past, was equally necessary for its future development.

It is a code which contains a curious mixture of eighteenth century and modern ideas. Bentham's suspicion of all governmental action and his desire to minimize its power ;[5] his desire to minimize its expense,[6] which led him to prefer a man who offered to accept the lowest salary[7] and to condemn all retiring pensions ;[8] his preference for the system of doing government work by contract[9]—are all ideas which are characteristic of the eighteenth century. On the other hand, his condemnation of the system of allowing ministers to profit by money in their hands,[10] and of the system of payment by fees, and his advocacy of a system of fixed salaries ;[11] his advocacy of a Preventive Service Minister, of an Indigence Relief Minister, of an Education Minister, of a Health Minister,[12] and of a Public Prosecutor ; his advocacy of something like a competitive examination as a test of fitness for employés ;[13] his advocacy of an extended franchise, votes for women, and the ballot ;[14] his advocacy of an efficient

---

[1] Works ix 191 ; above 90.

[2] Works ix 609 ; cp. Halévy, Philosophic Radicalism 413. [3] Above 80, 89, 90.

[4] " On any part of the field of human action, a body of law, conceived in general terms, cannot have been framed on adequate grounds, except in so far as a certain stock of individual cases spread over that same ground, and constituting a demand for legislation have rendered themselves present to the mind of the legislator. The greater the length of time during which the government in question has continued in existence . . . the greater will have been the number of those individual cases, that will have presented themselves to the cognizance of the judge. . . . Memorials affording indication, more or less particular, of individual cases of this sort . . . are in the language of English jurisprudence called by the common appellation of *Reports*. In no other country upon earth have those indispensable grounds for apt legislation presented themselves . . . in any variety or extent, comparable to that which stands exemplified in English jurisprudence. Thus it is, that, from a combination of causes . . . no country upon earth affords so rich and apposite a stock of materials and grounds for legislation," ibid 26 ; Bentham characteristically added that no country was less likely to make a good use of this material.

[5] Works ix 49.

[6] Ibid 228, 231—a mere clerk is normally to have greater pay than a minister, since the minister is compensated sufficiently by the greater power which he has.

[7] Ibid 113, 283—the principle of the " patriotic auction," see Halévy, Philosophic Radicalism 414.

[8] Works ix 31, 269.   [9] Above 73.   [10] Works ix 28.

[11] Ibid 524-525.   [12] Above 89, 90.

[13] Works ix 128, 271-279.   [14] Above 89.

system of local courts, and local sub-legislatures[1]—are all ideas which have in various forms been adopted in modern times.

It is a code which contains many ideas which are wholly unpractical[2] and even nonsensical ;[3] and it is not well balanced. Too much attention is paid to mechanical minutiae.[4] But what I have said of the *Principles of the Penal Code* [5] applies with even greater force to the *Constitutional Code*—the wise suggestions were taken and the foolish left by the practical statesmen who, consciously or unconsciously, used Bentham's ideas to make the reforms in the British constitution which were demanded by the new conditions of the nineteenth century.[6]

Bentham, at different periods of his life, wrote several minor works on constitutional law. The earliest is *An Essay on Political Tactics* [7] which, as we have seen,[8] he wrote for the benefit of the French Constituent Assembly. It was the first and only purely theoretical and scientific treatise on Parliamentary procedure that has ever been written ; for, as Redlich says, the standard works of Hatsell and Erskine May are purely empirical.[9] Bentham, using his knowledge of the existing rules of the procedure of the House of Commons, deduces from them the following principles for the guidance of a representative assembly :[10] publicity of its proceedings, the need for an impartial president, the need for maintaining a definite order in the different stages in the formation of the will of the assembly, freedom of speech, the principle that the will of the majority must prevail. These principles

are enunciated as if they were deduced from the " Idea of a political assembly " ; but, to tell the truth, they are nothing but the results of a discriminating study of the characteristics of the British Parliament at the end of the eighteenth century : the utilitarian standpoint is maintained with sufficient clearness to enable Bentham to take a critical measure of the positive law, and to detect the divergence of certain elements in English parliamentary procedure from the universal and rational standard.   It was in the theoretical shape given it by Bentham, admirable in clearness and consistency, that English parliamentary procedure was introduced to Continental notice, was received into constitutional theory, and became effective as an important component in the formation of Continental constitutional practice.[11]

---

[1] Above 92.

[2] E.g. the Public-Opinion Tribunal, above 91, 92 ; his method of supplying the place of case law, above 90.

[3] E.g. his ideas as to the remuneration of ministers above 89, 93 ; and his notion that in a pure democracy no such offences as treason or libel could ever be known, Works ix 38-39.

[4] Above 89.   [5] Above 83.   [6] Below 132-134.

[7] Works ii 299-373.   [8] Above 51, 56.

[9] Redlich, Procedure of the House of Commons iii 177-178.

[10] Ibid 184-188.   [11] Ibid 188.

Its logical arrangement, its acute criticism, and its clear style have won for this essay high praise from continental jurists.[1]

Bentham's other works on constitutional law for the most part advocate ideas which he later embodied in his *Constitutional Code*. They are a short tract entitled *Leading Principles of a Constitutional Code for any State*[2] which was written in 1823 ; a treatise entitled *Principles of Judicial Procedure with the Outlines of a Procedure Code*,[3] written for the most part between 1820 and 1827, and in effect an appendix to the part of the *Constitutional Code* which deals with judicature and to his *Rationale of Judicial Evidence* ; and a collection of tracts entitled *Official Aptitude Maximized ; Expense Minimized*,[4] written between 1816 and 1825, which are partly political and partly an appendix to the *Constitutional Code*.

(d) Works on international law

Between the years 1787 and 1789 Bentham wrote four short essays on *The Principles of International Law*.[5] The first deals with the objects of international law, the second with its subjects i.e. states and the persons who owe allegiance to the state, the third with war, and the fourth with a plan for a universal and perpetual peace. Bentham considered that the object of international law should be, like the object of all law, the greatest happiness of mankind—of " all nations taken together." [6] The laws of peace were, in his opinion, the substantive branch of the law, and the laws of war the adjective branch.[7] States and their subjects were the persons of whom the rules of international law must take cognizance, and therefore the question of who is a subject for this purpose is discussed.[8] The incentives to war are discussed and the means of preventing it ;[9] and then, at considerably greater length, the plan for a universal and perpetual peace.[10] Armaments should be reduced, colonies should be emancipated, and trade should be free. If this was done, no greater navy would be needed beyond what would be sufficient to defend commerce against pirates. There should be a court to decide differences between nations,[11] the rules of international law should be restated,[12] and a congress, composed of two deputies from each state, to determine and to circulate the common opinion of Europe.[13] If a court were established its obvious utility

[1] Redlich, Procedure of the House of Commons iii 183.
[2] Works ii 267-274.
[3] Ibid 1-188 ; see above 88 n. 6 for the close connection between Bentham's idea of constitutional law and adjective law.   [4] Works v 263-386.
[5] Ibid ii 535-560 ; cp. Nys, Notes Inédites de Bentham sur le Droit International, L.Q.R. i 225-226 ; Nys, Droit Internationale i 179-180.
[6] Works ii 538.   [7] Ibid 539.   [8] Ibid 540-544.
[9] Ibid 544-546.   [10] Ibid 546-560.   [11] Ibid 552.
[12] Ibid 540.   [13] Ibid 554.

would soon convince nations that it was no visionary proposal.[1] If secret diplomacy were abolished,[2] if the harm which war does to both sides—to conqueror or conquered—were realized,[3] war would be banned, and resort to the arbitration of the court would become usual. For the purpose of coercing a refractory state, the several states of Europe might provide an armed force.[4]

At the end of his life Bentham returned to the subject of international law. In 1829, in a letter which he wrote to Jabez Henry,[5] he sent a sketch of a preliminary title to a code of international law which he had written in 1827 ;[6] and, in some notes appended thereto, he suggested a congress to draw up a body of international law, in order to minimize the occasion of conflicts between states, and a court appointed by the congress to settle international disputes.[7] This court he said " would in effect be the Public Opinion Tribunal, composed of all the several individuals belonging to all the several states." [8]

Appended to his *Principles of International Law* is a curious proposal for establishing a Junctiana Company for cutting a canal through the isthmus of Panama.[9]

(e) *Works on codification and the drafting of statutes*

We have seen that the word " codify," like the word " international," was one of Bentham's few successful attempts to coin words ;[10] and throughout his works he preaches the gospel of codification. Three works are more especially devoted to this topic—*A General View of a Complete Code of Laws*,[11] *Pannomial Fragments*,[12] and a short tract on *The Promulgation of Laws and the Reasons thereof with Specimen of a Penal Code*.[13] Of the first of these works I have already said something.[14] In addition to the sketch of the various codes of which a complete system of law should consist, it contains some general reflections upon the qualities which a code should possess. It should be complete—" whatever is not in the code of laws ought not to be law."[15] It should state the commands of the Legislature without argument, for as Bacon said " leges non decet esse disputantes sed jubentes." [16] It should be drawn up in a clear precise style ; and the courts in interpreting it should attend only to the text and disregard commentaries.[17]

---

[1] Works ii 553.   [2] Ibid 554-556.   [3] Ibid 557-558.   [4] Ibid 554.
[5] For an account of Jabez Henry, who had occupied judicial positions abroad and in the colonies, and written some able law books, see Nys, L.Q.R. i 226.
[6] Ibid 227-229.   [7] Ibid 229-231.   [8] Ibid 230.
[9] Works ii 561-571.   [10] Above 63.   [11] Works iii 155-210.
[12] Ibid 211-230.   [13] Ibid i 155-168.
[14] Above 59, 68, 72, 73.   [15] Works iii 205.
[16] Ibid 206 ; Bacon said in Chudleigh's Case, Works (ed. Spedding) vii 625, nil ineptius lege cum prologo, jubeat non disputet . . . for the law carries authority in itself," cited vol. iv 186.   [17] Works iii 210.

The *Pannomial Fragments* explain, in the first place, the under-lying object—utility—at which the legislator should aim, and how it should be applied to the problems arising in various branches of the law.[1] Something is said, in the second place, of the psycho-logical problems involved in the application of the principle of utility ; of the meaning of such terms as " principle," " rule," " axiom," " law," " title," " right," " obligation," " possession," " power," " command " ; of the relations of law and government ; of the fallacy of natural rights.[2] In the third place, various classes of axioms, which the Legislature must bear in mind, are analysed [3] —axioms of mental pathology, axioms relating to the security of the person, axioms relating to subsistence, axioms relating to abundance, axioms relating to equality in respect of wealth, and axioms relating to power, rank, and reputation. The explanation of these axioms gives in a concise form the gist of the principles which underlie all Bentham's works. The *Essay on the Pro-mulgation of Laws* contains various suggestions for bringing laws to the notice of the people, and some arguments for accompanying them with a statement of the reasons for their enactment.[4]

The work which is specially concerned with the drafting of statutes is entitled *Nomography or the Art of Inditing Laws*.[5] In this tract Bentham elaborates some of the principles which he had laid down in his *General View of a Complete Code of Laws*. It is a very complete analysis of the rules which a draftsman of statutes should observe in order to attain clarity in style and arrangement, and of the various imperfections which he should avoid. These imperfections are illustrated from the statute book ; and we have seen that they are a very thorough exposure of the chief defects in draftsmanship which disfigured it.[6] But we have seen that Bentham's neglect of the historical causes for these de-fects caused his diagnosis to be somewhat superficial.[7] He makes a number of acute suggestions as to the literary style which a draftsman should adopt ; but, since he is ignorant of the substantial causes for the defects of the statute book he fails to appreciate the need for the more fundamental reforms which, in the nineteenth and twentieth centuries, have been applied to remedy the evils which he exposes.[8]

(ii) *Writings connected with English politics*

These works fall under three heads : (*a*) works dealing with the exposure of abuses and the advocacy of reforms in the law

---

[1] Works iii 211-213.   [2] Ibid 213-221.   [3] Ibid 224-230.
[4] For early methods of publishing the statutes see vol. xi 291 ; for later measures see ibid 309-320.
[5] Works iii 231-283.   [6] Vol. xi 375-376.
[7] Ibid 376-377.   [8] Ibid 377-387.

or its administration ; (b) criticism of particular persons and
cases ; and (c) works explaining and justifying the position of
radical reformer which Bentham took up at the latter part of his
life.

(a) *Works dealing with the exposure of abuses and the advocacy of
reforms in the law or its administration*

One of the earliest of these works is a tract entitled *A Protest
against Law-Taxes* which was printed in 1793 and published in
1795.[1] These taxes, Bentham contended, were a tax on the first
of all necessaries—justice, and in many cases amounted to the
denial of it, which is " the very quintessence of injury, the sum and
substance of all sorts of injuries." [2] They did not, as was sometimes said, make those pay who benefited by the law—those
benefit who are not obliged to go to law, and they pay nothing.[3]
On the contrary, they were a tax upon distress.[4] Nor could they
be said to check groundless suits. They favoured the rich and the
litigious at the expense of the poor, and so prevented the
dispensation of equal justice.[5] The tract made some impression
at the time ; but the need for money prevented effect from being
given to Bentham's suggestions.[6] Supplementary to this tract is a
tract entitled *Supply without Burden or Escheat vice Taxation*[7]
which was published in the same year. Bentham proposed to
substitute for law taxes a new kind of death duty. If a man died
intestate laving no " near " relatives, which was to mean no
relatives within the prohibited degrees,[8] the state was to get the
whole of the property : if he left a will the state was to take half
i.e. he could only dispose by will of half his property.[9] Such a tax,
Bentham pointed out, would tend to diminish speculative
litigation, and would favour large families.[10] Indeed in the latter
respect Bentham's suggestion is a great deal more statesmanlike
than our modern death duties. They penalize and indeed make it
impossible for the most prudent and industrious citizens to have
large families, and so the best stocks are not bred from. At the
same time our socialistic legislation hands over some part of the
the produce of these duties to the most needy, who are often the
most shiftless and stupid. They see no objection to large families
for which the state, i.e. the industrious members of the state, will
provide, and so the worst stocks are bred from. Much of this
socialist legislation will in time have the same effect as religious
persecution had in some continental countries in the sixteenth and

---

[1] Works ii 573-583.   [2] Ibid 574.   [3] Ibid 576.
[4] Ibid 573.   [5] Ibid 578-579.   [6] Ibid 582.
[7] Ibid 585-598 ; appended to this tract, ibid 599-600, there is a short paper
entitled Tax with Monopoly in which a tax on the profits of stockbrokers and
bankers is recommended.
[8] Ibid 586.   [9] Ibid.   [10] Ibid 591.

seventeenth centuries. In the future as in the past the elimination of the most independent and progressive minds in a nation will permanently lower its moral and intellectual standards.[1]

We have seen that some of Bentham's attacks upon the legal and political abuses of his time were so outspoken that Romilly advised him not to publish them.[2] He feared, not without reason, that, if he were prosecuted for libel, a special jury of the late eighteenth or early nineteenth century would be very likely to convict. This state of the law inspired a tract entitled *The Elements of the Art of Packing as applied to Special Juries particularly in Cases of Libel Law* ;[3] which was published in 1821. It had been originally inspired by an article in *The Times* of February 20, 1809, and had been printed many years before 1821.[4] Bentham accuses the Crown of choosing its special juries from a special list of persons selected by officials of the common law courts who were corruptible and were in fact corrupted.[5] This, he said, was in pursuance of a design to crush the liberty of the press.[6] The uncertainty as to what publication might be ruled by the judge to be a libel, coupled with the obsequiousness of those special juries,[7] made the Star Chamber a fairer tribunal than a judge and a special jury.[8] He suggested a radical reform of the system of selecting jurors—keep the special and common jury lists, but let all juries be chosen from both lists,[9] abolish the rule of unanimity and allow a majority verdict,[10] codify the existing statute law and the existing judicial practice relating to juries.[11] In conclusion Bentham assembles a number of cases in which both in relation to jury trials, and in relation to other matters, the courts have violated the spirit and sometimes the letter of statutes by the manner in which they have interpreted them.[12]

The court of Chancery was the first and only court in which Bentham attempted to practice.[13] It was its abuses which played a large part in turning his attention to the topic of law reform ; [14] and to the end he was ready to propose projects for its reform. Two tracts entitled *Equity Dispatch Court Proposal*,[15] and *Equity Dispatch Court Bill* [16] were two of the works upon which Bentham

---

[1] Lecky, History of England i 235, speaking of the effects of the revocation of the Edict of Nantes, says, " The destruction of the most solid, the most modest, the most virtuous, the most generally enlightened element in the French nation, prepared the way for the inevitable degradation of the national character, and the last serious bulwark was removed that might have broken the force of that torrent of scepticism and vice which, a century later, laid prostrate, in merited ruin, both the altar and the throne."

[2] Above 50.	[3] Works v 61-184.	[4] Ibid 65.
[5] Ibid 71-72, 76-77, 79-81.	[6] Ibid 97.	[7] Ibid 75-6, 102-4.
[8] Ibid 115-116.	[9] Ibid 165-167.	[10] Ibid 174.
[11] Ibid 175.	[12] Ibid 178-180.	[13] Above 44, 45.
[14] Above 45.	[15] Works iii 297-317.	[16] Ibid 319-431.

was engaged at the very end of his career, between the years 1829 and 1831.[1] In the first Bentham explains to the suitors of the court of Chancery and others interested the purport of a proposed petition to Parliament for legislation, the steps which they must take if such legislation were passed, and an abstract of the suggested bill. Though the suitors and others did not come forward in sufficient numbers to sign the petition, Bentham, in the second of these tracts, drew up a bill to give effect to his proposals.[2] His suggestions for the constitution of a Dispatch Court are, as his editor says,[3] closely related to his proposals relating to the machinery of judicial procedure contained in his Constitutional Codes.[4] The Judge of the Court was to be elected by the suitors and commissioned by the King.[5] He was to have the power to appoint a deputy, auxiliary judges, and accountants, who were to perform the functions of the Masters in the court of Chancery, and other officers.[6] All these officials were to be paid by salary and not by fees.[7] Evidence of all kinds was to be admissible, and it was to be given orally in court.[8] The judge could make rules to give effect to the Act, which rules were to be laid before Parliament, and could be disallowed by it.[9] All suits pending before the existing courts of Equity could be removed to this court.[10] The judge was not to be bound by any of the existing rules of equity. He was to judge all cases according to the " non-disappointment principle," that is, he must consider which of two suggested solutions would cause the least pain to the parties.[11] " By the exclusion put upon all mention of the rules and decisions of the existing Equity courts, saved will be the prodigious quantity of time and expense employed in the reference to them in the existing practice."[12] Bankruptcy business was excluded from the court's jurisdiction;[13] and, if counsel were employed, no more than one was to be allowed.[14] The last two suggestions were sensible; for we have seen that the assumption by the court of Chancery of a jurisdiction in bankruptcy added materially to the congestion of its business,[15] and that the fact that an unlimited number of counsel could be employed lengthened the time taken to hear cases.[16] The suggestion that all evidence should be given orally in court was also sensible and has, with limitations, been adopted.[17] But many of the suggestions were quite impossible—in particular the suggestion that all the rules of equity should be scrapped. Though this suggestion was made in order to further the " non-disappointment principle," it was

---

[1] Editor's Note, Works iii 320.   [2] Works iii 322.   [3] Ibid 320.
[4] Above 91, 92.   [5] Works iii 332, 334.   [6] Ibid 341-345, 395-406
[7] Ibid 335-336.   [8] Ibid 364.   [9] Ibid 367.   [10] Ibid 348.
[11] Ibid 388-389.   [12] Ibid 389.   [13] Ibid 392, 428.
[14] Ibid 416.   [15] Vol. i 470-471.   [16] Vol. ix 365-366.
[17] Ibid 375; 15, 16 Victoria c. 86 § 28 R.S.C. O. 37 r. 1.

in reality completely hostile to it ; for it tended to frustrate the expectations based upon ascertained rules of equity which had guided the transactions entered into by suitors.

Bentham had always been interested in the poor law. In fact his schemes of prison reform and poor law reform were closely connected—both problems were to be solved by his Panopticon schemes.[1] Since the problem of the poor was a very pressing problem all through this period, Bentham was drawn into its discussion. His contribution to its solution is contained in a number of tracts on *Poor Law and Pauper Management*.[2] His suggestion that the management of paupers should be entrusted to a joint stock company to be called the National Charity Company, which should be self supporting,[3] is typical of his eighteenth century mentality ; for it depends on the then prevalent belief in the efficacy of contract to supply those defects in the administrative powers of the state which were caused by the inadequacy of its machinery and the jealousy of entrusting increased powers to it,[4] and the then prevalent fallacy that profit could be made from the employment of paupers.[5] Bentham did not make these mistakes in his *Constitutional Code*, for he suggested an Indigence Relief Minister and a centralized system of poor relief[6] which was in fact carried out after 1832.[7] These suggestions were perhaps partly due to Owen's influence,[8] for he was interested in and subscribed money for Owen's model factory at New Lanark,[9] partly to the fact that he had come to see that the principle of utility demanded that the sphere of state interference must be enlarged and its machinery strengthened,[10] partly to his realization that his doctrine of popular sovereignty destroyed many of his objections to government action.[11] Many of his other suggestions may be due to the same causes. His suggestions that work-houses on a larger scale should be erected,[12] that there should be measures of segregation and classification of their inmates,[13] that proper measures should be taken to educate pauper children,[14] that a system of employment registries should be set up,[15] that the poor should be encouraged to save by setting up a system of frugality banks and the encouragement of insurance against various causalities[16]—have all borne fruit. His tract entitled *Observations on the Poor Bill*[17] which Pitt introduced in 1796 was not published till long after the bill had been

---

[1] Above 54, 55 ; Works viii 375.   [2] Ibid 358-439.
[3] Ibid 369 ; cp. Halévy, Philosophic Radicalism 84-85.
[4] Vol. x 177, 194, 208, 217, 233.   [5] Ibid 275 and n. 7.
[6] Works ix 441 ; cp. Webb, English Poor Law History Pt. II. i 29-30.
[7] Ibid 31, 79, 191.   [8] Above 38, 39.   [9] Above 58, 59.
[10] Dicey, Law and Opinion 305.   [11] Above 90.
[12] Works viii 374.   [13] Ibid 372-373.   [14] Ibid 395.
[15] Ibid 398.   [16] Ibid 407-417.   [17] Ibid 440-461.

withdrawn.[1] But it was printed for private circulation, and
" may probably have impressed the Prime Minister with whom
Bentham was personally acquainted." [2] It is almost entirely
critical, and the main burden of Bentham's criticism is that the
bill draws no clear line between the idle and the industrious,
between the deserving and the undeserving poor.[3]

Various proposals for reform in the administration of justice in
Scotland induced Bentham to write in 1807 a series of five letters
to Lord Grenville, in the first four of which he set out his ideas as
to the reforms needed in the machinery and the procedure of the
courts, and in the last of which he criticized Lord Eldon's bill for
the reform of the Scottish judicial system.[4] In the first four letters
he sums up the ideas which he had already set forth in his
Introductory View of the Rationale of Evidence,[5] and applies them
to the Scottish system. He advocates his idea of a " single-seated
judicature " as compared with a court staffed by a board of two
or more judges. " A board," he said,[6] " is a screen " ; and, as we
might expect, he was wholly opposed to Lord Eldon's Act for the
extension of the jury system to Scotland in civil cases[7]—a view
in which he agreed with Lord Mansfield.[8] Similarly proposals for
the reform of the House of Lords as the final appellate tribunal
produced a tract entitled *The Plan of Judicatory under the name of
the Court of Lords Delegates*.[9] In each session the Lords were to
elect by ballot a salaried president and three salaried puisne judges
—one from each of the three kingdoms.[10] They were to exercise
all the powers of the House as the final court of appeal,[11] and,
though the other Lords were to have the right to be present, they
were to have no right to vote.[12] The judges chosen need not
necessarily be members of the House, and thus an opportunity
would be given to choose the best lawyers.[13] If they were members
of the House they were to have no right to vote while they held
office, " lest of the time purchased for judicature any part be
diverted to politics, lest the politician corrupt or be suspected of
corrupting the judge." [14]

(b) Criticism of particular persons and cases

Bentham was so convinced of the absolute truth of his theories
that he was very intolerant not only of persons who represented

---

[1] Note by the Editor, Works viii 440.
[2] Webb, English Poor Law History, Pt. II. i 35 n.
[3] Works viii 442-443 ; Webb, op. cit. 35 n.
[4] Works v 1-53.   [5] Above 83, 84.
[6] " A *board*, my Lord, is a *screen*. The lustre of good desert is obscured by it ;
ill desert, slinking behind, eludes the eye of censure," Works v 17.
[7] Ibid 29-38 ;   55 George III c. 42 ; Twiss, Life of Eldon ii 259-260.
[8] Vol. xii 551.   [9] Works v 55-60.   [10] Ibid 55-56.   [11] Ibid.
[12] Ibid 56.   [13] Ibid 57, 59.   [14] Ibid 58.

modes of thought which were wholly opposed to his own, but even of persons who, though in general agreement with his theories, refused to go the whole way with him. It is not surprising that he should have used violent language about men whose mental outlook was so opposed to his own as Blackstone[1] and Eldon[2]—though it cannot be said that he improved his case by his unnecessary violence and imputation of motives. But it is surprising that he should sometimes attack a supporter in very violent language. Brougham had done more than any other person to forward the cause of law reform. We shall see that his great speech in 1828, in which the long list of abuses urgently needing reform were set forth, made it impossible to shelve the subject of law reform, and so inaugurated the period which gave practical effect to many of Bentham's proposals.[3] And yet in *Lord Brougham Displayed*[4] which was published in 1832, Bentham fiercely attacked Brougham because Brougham did not see eye to eye with him on the form which the reforms of the court of Chancery and the Bankruptcy court should take—because he preferred bit by bit reform to the adoption of Bentham's impracticable measures.[5] Brougham, he said, had not tried to further the two reforms on which all effective law reform depends—codification and " appropriate judicial establishment with its system of procedure " ; and so Bentham represented him as given up to " sinister influence, interest-begotten prejudice, and interest-begotten sympathy." [6] It was not till the very end of his paper that Bentham had the grace to acknowledge Brougham's professional and private virtues, and his kindness to himself, and thus to get as near to an apology as he ever got.[7]

Bentham always kept his eye on current events and on the cases heard in the courts. We have seen that Ashhurst J.'s charge to a Middlesex Grand Jury in 1792 furnished him with a text which he used to show up the baselessness of the praise generally bestowed on the " matchless constitution." [8] In 1820 he published comments on the two cases of *R. v. Edmonds and Others*,[9] and *R. v. Wolseley and Harrison*.[10] He used the two cases to make an attack on the law of libel, conspiracy, and sedition. His attack on the law of conspiracy shows that he was very ignorant of the history of the development of this offence.[11]

---

[1] Above 44, 47, 48, 59, 60.
[2] See Indications respecting Lord Eldon, Works v 348-382.
[3] Below 273, 296-307.   [4] Works v 549-610.   [5] Ibid 564.
[6] Ibid 609.   [7] Ibid 610.   [8] Above 56, 57, 60.
[9] Works v 239-251.   [10] Ibid 253-361.
[11] Ibid 248-249 ; for the history of conspiracy see vol. iii 401-407 ; vol. v 203-205 ; vol. iii 378-397.

(c) Works explaining and justifying his new position of radical reform

Bentham signalized his conversion to the creed of the radical reformers[1] by writing in 1809 a book called *Plan of Parliamentary Reforms in the Form of a Catechism.*[2] It was published in 1817 ; and it was followed in 1819 by *A Radical Reform Bill,*[3] and in 1819-20 by a tract entitled *Radicalism not Dangerous.*[4] In the first of these works Bentham maintained the thesis that the only remedy for the evils which were afflicting the country was a reform of Parliament which would ensure " democratical ascendancy." [5]   He maintained that the experience of the United States, the constitution of which he considered to be almost perfect, showed that an entirely democratic constitution was by far the best.   He poured scorn on mixed or balanced constitutions.   " Talk of balance," he said, " never will it do : leave that to Mother Goose and Mother Blackstone " [6]— ignoring the fact that the American constitution, with its separation of powers, reproduced many of the features of the mixed and balanced English constitution of the eighteenth century.[7]   He advocated virtually universal suffrage—the only persons excluded were to be infants, idiots, and persons unable to read.[8]   Voting was to be by ballot,[9] no placemen were to have a vote in the legislature,[10] and Parliaments were to last one year only.[11]   But he realized that it was useless to look either to Tories or to Whigs to support such a measure of reform—" The Tories are the people's avowed enemies.   Man must change his nature, ere, to any radical remedial purpose, the Whigs can be their friends." [12]   The *Radical Reform Bill* is an elaborate bill designed to give effect to those ideas.   It deals in great detail with electoral districts, the franchise, the machinery of elections, qualifications of members, causes for the vacation of a seat.   The third tract—*Radicalism not Dangerous* —attempts to prove that the enactment of *The Radical Reform Bill* would not be dangerous to the constitution or to the rights of property.   Bentham argued from the experience of the United States, and from that of Ireland during the volunteer movement (1778-1783), that democratical ascendancy is compatible with good government.[13]   As in his appendix to the civil code on the " Levelling System," [14] he used the laws of political economy to prove that if, as a result of democratical ascendancy, any general scheme of confiscation of property were attempted, the poor would suffer the most ;   and from this premise he concluded that they

[1] Above 57.   [2] Works iii 433-557.   [3] Ibid 558-597.
[4] Ibid 599-622.   [5] Ibid 445-446.   [6] Ibid 450.
[7] Vol. xi 133-139.   [8] Works iii 452, 464.   [9] Ibid 453.
[10] Ibid 456-457.   [11] Ibid 521.   [12] Ibid 534.
[13] Ibid 612-615.   [14] Above 74, 81 ; Works i 358-364.

would not attempt any such scheme.[1] It is no doubt true that a general confiscation of property would in the long run make a nation poorer ; but the poor are the last people to take long views ; and the immediate result would certainly be the enrichment of considerable numbers of them. A similar argument was used by Bentham's disciple James Mill ;[2] and its fallacy was exposed by Macaulay : [2a]

It may perhaps be said that, in the long run, it is for the interest of the people that property should be secure, and that therefore they will respect it. We answer thus :—It cannot be pretended that it is not for the immediate interest of the people to plunder the rich. Therefore, even if it were quite certain that, in the long run, the people would, as a body, lose by doing so, it would not necessarily follow that the fear of remote ill consequences would overcome the desire of immediate acquisitions. Every individual might flatter himself that the punishment would not fall on him. . . . Scarcely any despotic sovereign has plundered his subjects to a large extent without having reasons before the end of his reign to regret it. . . . But despots do plunder their subjects, though history and experience tell them that, by prematurely enacting the means of profusion, they are in fact devouring the seed corn from which the future harvest of revenue is to spring. Why then should we suppose that the people will be deterred from procuring immediate relief and enjoyment by the fear of distant calamities, of calamities which perhaps may not be fully felt till the times of their grandchildren ?

We have a much larger experience of the doings of democracies than Bentham possessed, and that experience has abundantly justified Macaulay's criticism.

(iii) *Writings connected with foreign politics*

We have seen that for many years Bentham's works were better known and appreciated in foreign countries than they were in England.[3] It is not surprising, therefore, that, throughout his life, he was interested in foreign politics, and either corresponded with foreign rulers or wrote books or tracts to assist the cause of law reform, or, in the later years of his life, to assist the cause of democratic government.

It was in France that his writings were first published in Dumont's skilful version ;[4] and his earliest incursions into foreign politics were into French politics after the Revolution, because revolutionary France seemed to afford a magnificent field on which his projects of law reform could be tried out.[5] Besides his work on *Political Tactics*,[6] Bentham wrote several other works for the benefit of the French people. The most considerable was the *Draft of a Code for the Organization of the Judicial Establishment*

[1] Above 89.
[2] Mill's Essay on Government (Barker's ed.) 68-73 ; cp. Halévy, Philosophic Radicalism 410-411. [2a] Miscellaneous Writings, vol. i 310, 312.
[3] Above 52, 53. [4] Above 50-53. [5] Above 50, 51, 56, 57. [6] Above 51, 56.

in France.[1] The work was published in 1790, and it was
accompanied by comments on the draft code proposed by a
committee of the National Assembly. Bentham suggested the
creation of a hierarchy of courts, from parish courts to a metropolitan supreme court.[2] The judges were to be elected by those
subject to their jurisdiction, but the judges of the metropolitan
court were to be elected by the National Assembly.[3] These
electors were to have power to remove their appointees;[4] but
such removal was not to entail loss of salary or incapacity to be
again elected.[5] When dealing with the judges' tenure of office,
Bentham gave some very good reasons why the system of electing
judges for short periods was undesirable.[6] As in his *Constitutional
Code*[7] he proposed that the courts should sit continuously, and
that therefore each judge should be able to appoint a deputy;[8]
that each court should have a single judge;[9] that each court
should be omnicompetent;[10] that all judges should be paid by
salary and not by fees;[11] and that of the competent candidates
that one should be elected who at a " patriotic auction " offered
to give most to the common fund of the locality.[12] No judge was
to have any legislative power—he was not even to be able to make
rules of procedure.[13] He must report to the Assembly any matter
in respect of which an amendment of the law was desirable.[14]
There was to be both a pursuer and a defender-general, both of
whom were to be ready to undertake the causes of poor litigants.[15]
Though Bentham approved the jurisdiction exercised by the
court of King's Bench by means of the prerogative writs, and did
not approve a separate system of administrative courts,[16] he was,
in other respects, a severe critic of many aspects of the English
judicial system—the system of new trials as compared with an
appeal by way of rehearing,[17] the capacity of the House of Lords
to act as the final court of appeal,[18] the powers of the Attorney-
General;[19] and it was in this work that he inserted his caustic
and substantially true account of the heterogeneous powers of the
Lord Chancellor.[20]

In 1793 he addressed to the National Convention a tract
entitled *Emancipate your Colonies*.[21] Colonies, he argued, were
expensive to protect, and were, from an economic point of view,
worse than useless—a fallacious argument which gained some
support from the " little Englanders " of the middle of the
nineteenth century, who were obsessed by the economic argu-

---

[1] Works iv 285-406.   [2] Ibid 289.   [3] Ibid 286, 300.
[4] Ibid 290.   [5] Ibid 290, 358-362, 367-368.   [6] Ibid 363-367.
[7] Above 91.   [8] Works iv 291, 293-294.   [9] Ibid 325.
[10] Ibid 331-332.   [11] Ibid 287.   [12] Ibid 290-291.
[13] Ibid 287.   [14] Ibid 312-313.   [15] Ibid 406.
[16] Ibid 316.   [17] Ibid 343 n.   [18] Ibid 353.
[19] Ibid 405-406.   [20] Ibid 381, cited vol. i 397.   [21] Works iv 407-418.

ments of the classical economists.[1] But, before the tract was published in 1830, Bentham had revised his views. He did not wish to see the British Empire dissolved;[2] but he made the acute prophecy that before a century was over Australia would have become a representative democracy and free from the control of Great Britain.[3] In 1830, at the very end of his life, he wrote an address to his fellow citizens of France[4] in which he attacked all second Chambers, and denounced the sinister influence of Kings and aristocracies.[5] He ridiculed the appeal made to history to support such institutions, and made some sarcastic remarks upon Savigny's historical school and legal history in general.[6]

Russia and the United States of America were two other states whom he advised on questions of law reform and constitutional matters. His *Papers relative to Codification and Public Instruction*[7] contain correspondence with James Madison and other prominent United States citizens, in which he offered to draw up a code of law for the United States. He also addressed a series of eight letters to all citizens of the United States, in which he advised them as to the ideals to be aimed at in the compilation of a body of law.[8] He wrote to the Emperor of Russia and offered to draw up a code of law for his empire.[9] Other letters written to the governors of the states of the United States give advice as to the establishment of a system of public instruction.[10] In 1822 Bentham drew up what he called a *Codification Proposal*,[11] which was addressed to "all nations professing liberal opinions," in which he gave reasons why all states ought to provide themselves with "an all-comprehensive body of law." The first part of the paper consists of arguments, based on the principle of utility, for the proposals, and suggestions as to how the code should be drawn up. It should, Bentham thinks, be the work of a single hand.[12] Very characteristically (but very foolishly) he thinks that a foreigner could draw up a better code than a native.[13] He is less exposed to sinister influences; and the parts of a code which are of universal application to all nations are greater and of more importance than those parts which apply only to a particular nation.[14] The second part contains testimonials from eleven countries as to Bentham's fitness to draw up such a code. In 1822-3 Bentham wrote a series of papers entitled *Securities against Misrule adapted to a Mahommedan State*.[15] They were written with special reference to Tripoli, since

[1] Dicey, Law and Opinion 448-450.
[2] Works iv 418.   [3] Ibid.
[4] Jeremy Bentham to his Fellow Citizens of France on Houses of Peers and Senates, Works iv 419-450.
[5] Ibid 430.   [6] Ibid 425 ; below 118.   [7] Works iv 451-533.
[8] Ibid 478-507.   [9] Ibid 514-515, 516-528.   [10] Ibid 531-532.
[11] Ibid 535-594.   [12] Ibid 554-559.   [13] Ibid 560-563.
[14] Ibid 561 ; below 124, 125.   [15] Works vii 555-600.

his attention had been directed to the subject by the ambassador from Tripoli.[1] Bentham discourses on misrule and the various shapes it might take, recommends his favourite panacea—a Public-Opinion Tribunal,[2] explains the important role which the newspapers should take in forming public opinion,[3] explains what securities should be provided for liberty and for the protection of person or property,[4] and gives arguments why the sovereign should consent to the necessary restrictions on his own power.[5] That Bentham should have thought that such a discourse addressed to the absolute ruler of an Eastern state could have the smallest effect is a curious instance of his faith in the absolute truth of his principles, and in their power to induce a similar faith in others, and action based on that faith.

The disturbances in Spain and Portugal in the second decade of the nineteenth century produced several pronouncements from Bentham.[6] Between 1808 and 1812 the four years struggle against Joseph Bonaparte produced the constitution " drafted in 1811 at Cadiz whilst French shells were exploding under the draftsmen's windows," [7] and adopted in 1812. In 1814 this constitution was overthrown, but in 1820 there was another rising, as the result of which the constitution was restored.[8] Spain's example was copied by Naples, Sardinia, and Portugal. But in Spain the Holy Alliance intervened, and constitutional government came to an end in 1823.[9] As Kenny has said :

These years 1820-23 are in the life of Jeremy Bentham what 1808-13 are in English military annals—the great Peninsular period. His writings obtained for some time a greater celebrity in Spain and Portugal than anywhere else in Europe, rivalling indeed the celebrity which at a much later date they won in England itself.[10]

One of the first of his communications to Spain was a series of four letters to the Spanish people on the liberty of the press [11] in which not only the liberty of the press, but liberty of public meetings is advocated. The letters were published in English in 1821, but they were never published in Spanish, because Mora, the translator, was imprisoned for a political offence before the translation was finished.[12] In the same year Bentham published *Three Tracts relative to Spanish and Portuguese Affairs with a continual Eye to English Ones.*[13] The first is a letter to the Spanish nation on a proposal to establish a House of Lords.[14] The letter does not

---

[1] Note by the editor, Works vii 555.   [2] Works vii 566-568; above 91, 92, 94, 96.
[3] Works viii 579-583.   [4] Ibid 583-592.   [5] Ibid 596-600.
[6] On this subject see Kenny, A Spanish View of Bentham's Influence, L.Q.R. xi 48-63.
[7] Ibid L.Q.R. xi 48.   [8] Ibid.   [9] Ibid 49.   [10] Ibid.
[11] Works ii 275-297.   [12] L.Q.R. xi 50.   [13] Works viii 463-485.
[14] L.Q.R. xi 54-58; Kenny proves that it was addressed to the Spanish people and not, as it had been conjectured, to the people of Portugal.

discuss second chambers in general, but concentrates on a consideration of the advisability of a second chamber constituted like the House of Lords—an impossible assembly to set up in Spain. The arguments contained in the letter against such a second chamber are directed to England rather than to Spain or Portugal.[1] The second tract was occasioned by a massacre which took place at Cadiz in 1820. On March 10, 1820, the constitution of 1812 was to be proclaimed. As the proceedings were beginning, the soldiers attacked the crowd killing some three hundred and wounding some thousand persons. But, at the time when the massacre took place, the King, without having informed the military authorities at Cadiz, had surrendered to the demand for the constitution. When this was known there was an outcry against the military authorities and a demand for a prosecution.[2] A prosecution was ordered, but it dragged on for years and nothing was done. The official prosecutor tried to excuse this delay by saying that in such proceedings it was necessary to be deliberate if justice was to be done. This provoked Bentham to protest against this sort of excuse—a protest which was justified by the result of the trials.[3] It is interesting to note that, when attacking technical " Rome-bred " systems of procedure, he inserts an attack on Montesquieu in somewhat the same terms as he used in his attacks on Blackstone, and for much the same reasons.[4] The third tract deals with certain defects in the Spanish constitution of 1812, which had been adopted in principle by Portugal in 1820.[5] Since the Cortes of Portugal was about to draft a constitution, Bentham sent them this letter. He objected to the Spanish constitution because it could not be amended for eight years, because a deputy who had sat in one Cortes was not re-eligible for the next—a criticism which he later recanted,[6] because the Cortes only met for four months in each year, and because the Cortes was to last so long as two years. But, though Bentham could discover only these defects in the constitution, it lasted a very short time.[7]

Bentham's last publication is a series of seven letters addressed to Count Toreno on a proposed penal code for Spain.[8] In April

---

[1] " The cosmopolitan philosopher, . . . did not really utter this oracle of his for the world at large, nor even for the Spaniards to whom he seems to address it, nor even for the Portuguese who may have needed it, but simply for his fellow-citizens of the United Kingdom of Great Britain and Ireland. Bentham's letter to Madrid belongs (as Senor Silvola says) to the homeward mail," L.Q.R. xi 58.

[2] Ibid 51.

[3] " After fifty-four offenders had been indicted, and some seven thousand pages of evidence had been taken [this state trial] dragged itself on for more than three years, and finally terminated in handing over to punishment one solitary sentinel, who was in no way more guilty than his fifty-three fellow prisoners," ibid 52.

[4] Works viii 481.   [5] L.Q.R. xi 52.   [6] Ibid 53.

[7] Ibid 54.   [8] Works viii 487-554.

1821 a committee of the Spanish Cortes had prepared a draft penal code. The draft was sent to learned societies in Spain, to the judges, and to experts in the study of law and legal theory, inviting their criticisms.[1] No special appeal had been made to Bentham ; but Count Toreno, the president of the Cortes, wrote to Bentham, sent him a copy of the Code, and asked for his criticisms.[2] These seven letters are Bentham's reply. They do not contain any helpful criticisms ; for Bentham was annoyed that he had not been formally consulted. They consist of a series of severe animadversions on the action of the legislative committee of the Cortes in preventing any adequate discussion of their proposed code.[3] Naturally Toreno ignored these letters and did not even preserve them.[4] In fact Bentham's ignorance of the facts of the political situation in Spain made many of his criticisms absurd.[5] At the same time the style in which they were expressed offended the Cortes which, like Toreno, treated them with contempt.[6] These seven letters were the least successful of all Bentham's interventions in foreign politics, and are perhaps the best illustration of his mistaken belief that his views of utility, and his deductions from them, afforded an absolutely true criterion of the qualities which a code of laws should possess, regardless of considerations of time and place, and of national characteristics which are the product of time and place.[7]

(iv) *Economic writings*

The first of Bentham's economic writings, and one of the earliest of all his writings, was his *Defence of Usury*.[8] It is a series of thirteen letters written in 1787 from Crichoff in Russia. It was published by Bentham's father in that year.[9] We have seen that it is a more logical application of Adam Smith's *laissez faire* principles to the usury laws than Adam Smith himself made ; for Adam Smith never lost sight of the concrete facts of life, and was ready to modify his theories if he saw that they produced bad results in practice.[10] On the same principle Bentham condemned the laws against maintenance and champerty ;[11] and, with more reason, he criticized Adam Smith's indiscriminate condemnation of prodigals and " projectors." To condemn the

---

[1] L.Q.R. xi 58.   [2] Ibid. 59.   [3] Ibid 60-61.
[4] Ibid 59-60.   [5] Ibid 61-62.
[6] " This evident gulf between Bentham's abstract theories and the actual facts of Spanish life, the contempt which he showed for the committee and their draft code, the attitude of superiority which he assumed towards the Cortes, the lack of exactness in many of his criticisms, and the frivolity with which he expressed them—a frivolity unbecoming in a man of his nationality and of his eminence—caused these letters and their counsels to be completely ignored in Spain," ibid 62.
[7] Above 76, 77 ; below 124, 125.   [8] Works iii 1-29 ; above 29, 43, 49.
[9] Above 43.   [10] Vol. xi 515-516 ; above 29.   [11] Works iii 19-20.

latter, he said, is to condemn all persons who " in the pursuit of wealth, or even of any other object, endeavour by the assistance of wealth to strike into any channel of invention." [1] We have seen that Bentham's criticisms foreshadow the growth of those more rigid economic theories which were produced by the classical economists. They, like Bentham in these letters, accepted Adam Smith's principles, and pushed them to their logical consequences. [2]

This development was, in fact, inevitable ; for there was a fundamental agreement between Bentham's theory of utility and Adam Smith's economic theories. Let men be free to pursue their own interests and they will naturally pursue the course which will make for their greatest happiness. We have seen that this fundamental agreement clearly emerges in his *Manual of Political Economy*. [3]

On the other hand, Bentham was not quite so rigidly governed by the policy of *laissez faire* as many of the economists. He was not primarily an economist. His main object was the reform of the law by the application of the principle of utility. To leave every man free to follow his own interests might conduce to this result in a large number of cases. It could not conduce to this result in all cases. In fact, it was because an unfettered permission to every man to follow what he considered to be his own interest did not lead to the greatest happiness of the greatest number, that legislation was needed. Hence Bentham was prepared to admit that upon some economic matters, the government might and ought to interfere. He therefore admitted a longer list of " agenda " than many of the economists. Thus he thought that the government could and should encourage the increase of knowledge and useful inventions in various ways [4]—by a reform of the laws as to the granting of patents, [5] by the establishment of a register of trade marks, [6] by introducing the principle of limited liability, [7] by providing statistics of various kinds. [8] He thought, too, that the government ought to provide not only for the defence of the nation against attacks, but also against such casualties as famine ; [9] that it ought to provide hospitals for the sick, to maintain the poor, and " establishments for the prevention or mitigation of contagious diseases." [10] As the Webbs have pointed out, Bentham's attitude to economic questions was that of an eclectic. They say : [11]

[1] Works iii 21 ; and see Manual of Political Economy, ibid 48-49.
[2] Above 30, 33, 36.   [3] Above 29.   [4] Works iii 36, 71.
[5] Ibid 71-72.   [6] Ibid 72.   [7] Ibid 48.
[8] Ibid 82-83.   [9] Ibid 42.   [10] Ibid 72-73.
[11] English Poor Law History Pt. II. i 28 ; the treatment of these topics in his constitutional code shows that he was prepared to allow the state to undertake a considerable number of social services, above 89, 90, 93.

In industry and commerce—spheres in which pecuniary self-interest was the dominant motive—the adjustment of private interests to public ends might, for the most part, be left to the automatic working of free contract and free competition. On the other hand, criminals, lunatics, the sick and the destitute, were manifestly incapable of managing their own affairs ; whilst other national interests, such as public health and public education might not be adequately attended to if left to the pecuniary self-interest of the individuals of a single generation. Jeremy Bentham was, in fact, in respect to the modern controversy between Individualism and Socialism, a practical eclectic.

We shall see that it is for this reason that his influence over the course of legislation has been so long-lived.[1]

Two other short papers on economic subjects are of less importance. The first is a plan for the conversion of government stock into note annuities.[2] The second is a paper entitled *Observations on the Restrictive and Prohibiting Commercial System*,[3] which was occasioned by a decree of the Spanish Cortes of July 1820. " Leave us alone " is the motto printed on the tract, and this indicates the character of its argument in favour of free trade.[4]

(v) *Writings connected with education*

During the first decade of the nineteenth century there was a growing movement for the education of all classes of the community, which had almost immediately become the centre of a religious controversy.[5] Bell, an Anglican clergyman, had devised a new scheme of education, which centred round the use of pupil teachers. About the same time Lancaster, a quaker, had devised a similar scheme. For a short time Bell and Lancaster were on friendly terms. The split came when theological considerations intervened. The Royal Lancastrian Society was formed in 1810 to support Lancaster, and was supported by the Edinburgh Review and by Place and Mill.[6] The National Society, founded in 1811 to educate the poor in the principles of the Established Church, supported and was supported by the Quarterly Review and by Coleridge.[7] But though the supporters of popular education were thus divided, all, and especially the utilitarians, were agreed

[1] Below 122.
[2] Works iii 105-153 ; the full title is " A Plan for saving all trouble and expense in the transfer of stock and for enabling the proprietors to receive their dividends without powers of attorney, or attendance at the Bank of England by the conversion of stock into note annuities."
[3] Ibid 85-103.
[4] For two other papers which have economic as well as political bearings see above 104, 105.
[5] For this movement see Graham Wallas, Life of Francis Place chap. iv ; Leslie Stephen, The English Utilitarians i 218-219, ii 17-22.
[6] Graham Wallas, op. cit. 93 ; it became in 1813 the British and Foreign School Society, ibid 95 ; Leslie Stephen, op. cit. ii 18-19.
[7] Graham Wallas, op. cit. 94 ; Leslie Stephen, op. cit. ii 19-20.

that the pupil teacher method of instruction devised by Bell and Lancaster was a wonderful discovery, which would cheapen, and so render more possible, a scheme of popular education. "Believers in the ' Panopticon ' saw in it another patent method of raising the general level of intelligence," [1] and therefore of spreading the true faith in the principle of utility.[2] Mill and Place having failed to found a " West London Lancastrian Institution," embarked, at Francis Place's suggestion, upon a scheme for the higher education of the middle classes[3]—a Chrestomathic school, i.e. a school of useful learning, from which all theology was to be excluded.[4] Bentham was a whole-hearted supporter, and offered his garden at Queen Square Place as the site of the school.[5] To his mind, it was obvious that the better educated the community, and especially the middle classes,[6] the more ready it would be to accept his utilitarian measures of reform ; and so, to explain the merits of the scheme and the principles upon which it was to be based he wrote his *Chrestomathia*. But the scheme failed ; and Bentham, who, not without reason, attributed the failure to the hostility of the Church of England, became convinced that the Church of England and the Christian religion itself were sinister influences which impeded the spread of the utilitarian faith.[7]

The *Chrestomathia*[8] begins with two Tables accompanied by explanatory notes. The first Table explains the courses of instruction which were to be given, and the stages at which they were to be given. They were to be scientific, literary, and philosophical ; but the main emphasis was upon the natural sciences. Greek and Latin were not to be taught. Nothing, Bentham thought, could be learnt from the classical authors ; and it was waste of time to learn the languages, since, if necessary, the books could be read in translation.[9] Bentham thus anticipated much that has been advocated and much that has been accepted in the sphere of education during the century which succeeded his death. The second Table showed how the principles of instruction by pupil teachers were to be applied to the teaching of these different

[1] Leslie Stephen, op. cit. ii 19 ; but as Graham Wallas says, op. cit. 100, " The monitorial system is now amply discredited, but one can imagine that it was, at any rate, better than the dreadful old method, whereby, for hours together, one boy at a time translated, while two hundred played. It was indeed, the first serious attempt in England to think out any system of class teaching whatsoever ; " the plan of the school was reminiscent of the Panopticon, ibid 104-105.

[2] Above 54.

[3] Graham Wallas, op. cit. 98.

[4] Bentham, Works viii ii.

[5] Graham Wallas, op. cit. 99 ; but on reflection Bentham repented—" he imposed harder and harder conditions, and in 1820, after an enormous correspondence, his offer of a site was finally declined and the project was given up," ibid 111-112.

[6] Above 58, 59 ; below 113, 136.   [7] Above 58 ; below 116, 117.

[8] Works viii i-191.   [9] Ibid 18.

subjects. In the notes to this Table the advantages of this system are set out at great length. These two Tables and the notes thereto are followed by nine Appendices. The first contains the proposal for the institution of the Chrestomathic school; the second and third consist of testimonials as to the efficacy of the pupil teacher system of teaching; the fourth and longest is an essay on nomenclature and classification, which is accompanied by a diagram illustrating a plan of a possible arrangement of the various sciences and arts; the fifth is an analytical sketch of the several sources of motion;[1] the sixth is a sketch of the field of technology,[2] and the seventh contains hints towards a system and course of technology; the eighth consists of an account of certain new principles of instruction applicable to geometry and algebra; and the ninth contains hints toward the composition of an elementary treatise on universal grammar. Most of these appendices were meant to be guides to writers of the elementary text books which were urgently needed for the courses of study which were to be pursued at the Chrestomathic school. The editor of these papers—Southwood Smith—shows that there is reason to think that they then gave many useful suggestions to specialists who contemplated writing such books.[3]

(vi) *Philosophical and religious writings*[4]

Bentham was interested primarily in applying his principle of utility to the reform of the law substantive and adjective, and to the reform of legal and political institutions. But his minute analysis of all that was involved in the application of the principle of utility to concrete legal rules and political institutions, necessarily brought him into contact with philosophical problems, and more especially with psychological, logical, and linguistic problems. In fact, it is possible that he thought of writing a comprehensive work on psychology, in which his studies on logic and language and grammar were to be united.[5] But he never wrote more than detached works dealing with parts of the subject; and he never, like his disciple James Mill,[6] wrote a clear statement of the philosophy assumed by him as the basis of his theory of

[1] At p. 136 there is an account of what was apparently an attempt to make an internal combustion engine.

[2] This is defined as " the aggregate body of the several sorts of manual operations directed to the purposes of art, and having, for their common and ultimate end, the production and preparation of the several necessaries and conveniences of life," Works viii 148.

[3] He says in his Introduction, Works viii iii, that he had submitted the papers on geometry and algebra to an expert, who said that, though knowledge on these subjects had advanced since Bentham wrote, yet the papers contained many useful suggestions and ought to be published.

[4] For a more detailed account of these works see John Hill Burton's Introduction to Bentham's Works, Works i 80-83.

[5] Essay on Logic, Editor's Note, Works viii 214.   [6] Below 138.

utility.   These detached works are :   *A Fragment of Ontology*[1]
pieced together by Bowring from Bentham's MSS. in a manner
which the Mills considered to be very unsatisfactory ;[2]   an
Essay on Logic ;[3]   an *Essay on Language* ;[4] and *Fragments on
Universal Grammar*.[5]   But all these works, and indeed all that he
wrote, presuppose a philosophy.   That philosophy, upon which
his theory of utility was based, rests upon a belief that " all
knowledge consists of generalizations from experience " ;   that
" there is no knowledge *a priori*—no truths cognizable by the
mind's inward light, and grounded on intuitive evidence " ;
that " sensation, and the mind's consciousness of its own acts,
are not only the exclusive sources, but the sole materials of our
knowledge." [6]   These were the commonplaces of the school of
philosophy to which Bentham subscribed.   " It was a school,"
says Lord Morley, " whose method subordinates imagination to
observation, and whose doctrine lays the foundation of knowledge
in experience, and tests of conduct in utility." [7]   What constitutes Bentham's originality is, as Mill has said, not his
philosophy, but the use which he made of it.   Mill says :[8]

He brought into philosophy something which it greatly needed and for
want of which it was at a stand.   It was not his doctrines which did this,
it was his mode of arriving at them.   He introduced into morals and
politics those habits of thought and modes of investigation which are
essential to the idea of a science ;   and the absence of which made those
departments of enquiry, as physics had been before Bacon, a field of
interminable discussion, leading to no result.   It was not his opinions, in
short, but his method, that constituted the novelty and value of what he
did. . . .   Bentham's method may be shortly described as the method of
detail ;   of treating wholes by separating them into their parts,
abstractions by resolving them into Things—classes and generalities by
distinguishing them into the individuals of which they are made up ;
and breaking every question into pieces before attempting to solve
it. . . .   Hence his interminable classifications.   Hence his elaborate
demonstrations of the most acknowledged truths.

With this opinion Maine in substance agrees.   He says that it is
" to Bentham, and even in a higher degree to Austin, that the
world is indebted for the only existing attempt to construct
a system of jurisprudence by strict scientific process and to found
it, not on *a priori* assumption, but on observation, comparison,
and analysis of various legal conceptions." [9]

It was the character of Bentham's philosophy, and the mode of
its application to the concrete problems of law and politics, that

[1] Works viii 192-211.   [2] Mill, Dissertations and Discussions i 365.
[3] Works viii 213-293.   [4] Ibid 294-338.   [5] Ibid 339-357.
[6] Mill, Dissertations and Discussions i 404.
[7] The Death of Mr. Mill, Critical Miscellanies iii 40.
[8] Mill, Dissertations and Discussions i 439-440 ;   cp. Halévy, Philosophic
Radicalism 58-59, 76.
[9] Early History of Institutions 343.

determined his attitude to religion. As Leslie Stephen has said, utilitarianism and the philosophy on which it rested, was fundamentally opposed to religion :[1]

Religion—on their understanding of the word—must, like everything else, be tested by its utility, and it was shown to be either useless or absolutely pernicious. The aim of the Utilitarians was to be thoroughly scientific. The man of science must be opposed to the belief in an inscrutable agent of boundless power, interfering at every point with the laws of nature, and a product of the fancy instead of the reason. Such a conception, so far as accepted, makes all theory of human conduct impossible, suggests rules conflicting with the supreme rule of utility, and gives authority to every kind of delusion, imposture, and "sinister interest."

The utilitarians were as much opposed to Christianity as Paine. But just as they advocated a democratic theory of government, essentially similar to Paine's, but on grounds very different to his ; so they approved an anti-Christain set of ideas, essentially similar to his, but on very different philosophical grounds. Bentham's utilitarian philosophy made him a sceptic in matters of religion ; and his personal experiences, which always had some share in determining his opinions, inspired him with an especial dislike of the teachings of the Church of England.[2] " In Bentham's MSS. the Christian religion is nicknamed ' Jug ' as short for ' Juggernaut.' He and his friends were as anxious as Voltaire to crush the infamous."[3]   In an anonymous book Bentham attacked the church catechism and the church of England.[4] The Church to his mind was an organization like " Judge and Co." which bolstered up all sorts of abuses and sinister interests.[5] He attacked St. Paul, under the pseudonym of Gamaliel Smith, because he thought that he was responsible for dogmatic theology, and therefore for the catechism.[6] He dwelt upon the discrepancies in the accounts of his conversion, and " in one of the MSS. at University College the same method is applied to the gospels."[7] These books were published either anonymously or under a pseudonym because it was a criminal offence to attack the Christian religion[8]—as Richard Carlile and other atheists had found to their cost.[9]

---

[1] The English Utilitarians ii 348.

[2] Leslie Stephen, op. cit. i 315 : he never forgot the fact that he had been forced to subscribe to the thirty-nine articles before he was allowed to matriculate at Oxford, above 43, 44, or the hostility of the Church to his Chrestomathic proposals, above 58, 113.

[3] Leslie Stephen, op. cit. ii 339.

[4] Church of Englandism and its Catechism examined (1818).

[5] Leslie Stephen, op. cit. i 315.

[6] Not Paul but Jesus (1823)—put together by Francis Place from Bentham's MSS., Halévy, Philosophic Radicalism 544.

[7] Leslie Stephen, op. cit. i 316.

[8] Vol. viii 407-409.   [9] Ibid. 413 nn. 8 and 9.

It was for the same reason that another book, embodying Bentham's ideas, which was edited by George Grote, was published in 1822 under the pseudonym of Philip Beauchamp.[1] It is entitled *The Analysis of the Influence of Natural Religion on the Temporal Happiness of Mankind*. Under the disguise of natural religion it attacked all revealed religion,[2] and in effect it condemned Christianity as fundamentally immoral.[3] But it did not attack Christianity *eo nomine* and so it escaped prosecution.[4] But though the utilitarians thus took care not to parade their anti-religious views, the anti-religious consequences of the utilitarian philosophy were sufficiently obvious ;[5] and there is no doubt that their anti-religious attitude diminished their influence, and helped to rally the forces opposed to the new ideas on political, economic and legal matters.[6]

Bentham's incursion into these philosophical and religious questions were in the nature of by-products and add little or nothing to his reputation. He was in no sense a great philosopher and quite incapable of understanding the appeal made by religion.[7] It is true that some think that he was a great psychologist ; and that his contributions to the theory of language and linguistic fictions, and to the problem of an international language, are of permanent value ;[8] but, whether or not this is so, it is not of the first importance to the legal historian. To the legal historian the important matter is the influence of his new legal ideas upon the development of English law public and private and upon English institutions. The account which I have just given of the works in which these ideas were expounded will help us to understand their strong and weak points, and their influence upon the development of English law. With these matters I shall deal in the following section.

(c) The strong and weak points of Bentham's principles

John Stuart Mill said of his father, James Mill, that he was " the last of the eighteenth century." [9] Bentham, who died in 1832, four years before James Mill, can with quite as much truth, be regarded as the last but one of the eighteenth century ; for,

---

[1] For an analysis of this book see Leslie Stephen, op. cit. ii 339-361.

[2] Leslie Stephen, op. cit. ii 340.

[3] " Taken as a serious statement of fact, the anthropomorphism of the vulgar belief was open to the objection which Socrates brought against the Pagan mythology. The supreme ruler was virtually represented as arbitrary, cruel and despotic," ibid 358-359.

[4] " James Mill could safely argue in perfect safety against the foundations of theology, while Richard Carlile was being sent to gaol again and again for attacking the superstructure," ibid 338.

[5] Ibid 347-348.   [6] Below 143 seqq.   [7] Below 123.

[8] See C. K. Ogden, Bentham's Theory of Legislation xi-xviii, xxix-xxx.

[9] Autobiography 204.

as Dicey has said,[1] " he was in spirit entirely a child of the eighteenth century, and in England was the best representative of the humanitarianism and enlightenment of that age." Like other representative men of that century, he believed in its intellectual superiority to all other centuries.[2] Like them, he was prepared to apply a reasoned criticism of an analytical kind to laws and institutions and to projects for reforming them ; [3] and he was not prepared to attach weight to arguments for delaying such projects for reforms which were founded upon historical explanations of the genesis of these rules and institutions. As we might expect, he scorned Savigny's German historical school. In 1830 he wrote :[4]

It is not every man that knows, that by this same school a *history of law* is spoken of—and with no small assurance—as a most advantageous substitute to *law* itself ; . . . and that, by these same philosophers, it is mentioned with perfect sincerity, and no small earnestness, that by an historical work of this sort, direction sufficient may be given to the political conduct of men in that same country.

His dislike of governmental interference with individual liberty was shared by many representative men in the eighteenth century.[5] If the result was a weak government, which was unable to perform the duties which changing social conditions placed upon it, Bentham was prepared, in his earlier years, to eke out its deficiencies by a recourse to the expedient of contracting with an individual or a corporation for their performance.[6] We shall see that his principle of utility was then generally accepted as the test by which new legislative proposals ought to be tried.[7]

These intellectual characteristics Bentham shared with many of his eighteenth century contemporaries. But he had other and more important intellectual characteristics which caused him to differ profoundly from them. We have seen that the majority of Englishmen were contented with the balanced eighteenth century constitution, and with the main principles of the law on which it rested.[8] Its inconveniences and anomalies were, they thought, a small price to pay for the advantages which it secured to them. In the opinion of many they were hallowed by their antiquity, and, therefore, they thought that it was the duty of good citizens " to understand their constitution and their law according to their measure," and " to venerate when they were not able presently to comprehend." [9] Paley was as convinced a believer in the utilitarian philosophy as Bentham ; but, like Burke, he venerated the British constitution, and he used his philosophy to

---

[1] Law and Opinion 127.
[2] Vol. x 5-6 ; vol. xi 278 ; vol. xii 729-730.
[3] Vol. x 113 ; Vol. xii 729-730.   [4] Works iv 425.
[5] E.g. Johnson, vol. x 419, 454 n. 8, vol. xi 284 ; Blackstone vol. x 419, 420.
[6] Above 73, 93.   [7] Below 129.   [8] Vol. x 11 ; vol. xi 278.
[9] Burke, Works (Bohn's ed.) iii 114, cited vol. xi 278.

defend its anomalies.[1] Similarly Blackstone, though he made many suggestions for the reform of the law, is its convinced admirer ; and he used his knowledge of its underlying principles and the reasons on which they were based, to defend effectively principles and rules and institutions which could not be defended by a believer in the sole authority of the utilitarian principle and all its logical consequences.[2] It is at this point thatBentham parted company with these eighteenth century lawyers and philosophers. Bentham was not contented with English law and English institutions, and he was a believer in the sole authority of the utilitarian principle and all its logical consequences. Therefore, unlike them, he did not recognize Horace Walpole's distinction between the correction of abuses and the removal of landmarks[3] —a distinction which was emphasized by Burke.[4]

There was no limit to Bentham's critical analysis of existing laws and institutions, and of his application to them of his principle of utility ; and, as we have seen, it was his method of analyzing and applying in detail the results of his analysis to English laws and institutions which justifies his title to be considered an original thinker.[5] Take, for instance, the example given by Dicey :[6]

At the time when Bentham became the preacher of legislative utilitarianism the English people were proud of their freedom, and it was the fashion to assert, that under the English constitution no restraint was placed on individual liberty which was not requisite for the maintenance of public order. Bentham saw through this cant, and perceived the undeniable truth, that, under a system of ancient customs modified by haphazard legislation, unnumbered restraints were placed on the actions of individuals and restraints which were in no sense necessary for the safety and good order of the community at large, and he inferred at once that these restraints were evils.

He applied this criticism in detail to all the principles and rules of English law, and so he was, as Mill has said, " the great questioner of things established." [7]

If the superstition about ancestorial wisdom has fallen into decay ; if the public are grown familiar with the idea that their laws and institutions are in great part not the product of intellect and virtue, but of modern corruption grafted upon ancient barbarism ; if the hardiest innovation is no longer scouted *because* it is an innovation—establishments no longer considered sacred because they are establishments—it will be found that

---

[1] Dicey, Law and Opinion 142 ; Halévy, Philosophic Radicalism 80-81 ; cp. vol. x 633 for his view of the advantages of the influence which the state of the representation enabled the King and the House of Lords to exercise over the House of Commons.
[2] Vol. xii 728-730, 734-735.   [3] Letters (ed. Toynbee) xiii 86.
[4] Works (Bonn's ed.) vi 152, cited vol. x 113 n 1.
[5] Above 68, 69.   [6] Law and Opinion 146 ; above 57, 60.
[7] Dissertations and Discussions i 332.

those who have accustomed the public mind to these ideas have learnt them in Bentham's school, and that the assault on ancient institutions has been, and is, carried on for the most part with his weapons.[1]

It is not only the thoroughness with which Bentham exposed the abuses and anomalies which existed in the English legal system, it is not only the thoroughness with which he applied the principle of utility to test the soundness of all laws and institutions, which gives him so great a place in English legal history ; it is also the means which he advocated for the reform and restatement of the law.   Abuses and anomalies must be removed and the law must be reformed and restated by the direct action of the Legislature.[2]   These three things—his method of exposing abuses, his application of the principle of utility, and his advocacy of the direct action of the Legislature—are his titles to fame as a legal theorist and a reformer of the law.   Many others saw the need for reform ; but he alone had both the industry and the capacity to elucidate the principles upon which the many reforms needed in all branches of the law should be made, to make concrete suggestions as to the shape which these reforms should take, and to prove that it was the duty of the Legislature to enact the laws needed to give effect to them.   It is these qualities and these achievements which entitle him to his fame as a legal philosopher.   They have made him, in spite of his intellectual affinities with eighteenth century thinkers, the pioneer of the age of law reform.

But we must not underrate the effects of Bentham's intellectual affinities with eighteenth century thinkers.   It is because Bentham combined these intellectual affinities with the intellectual characteristics which made him the pioneer of the age of law reform that he has exerted so great an influence upon the development of English law in the nineteenth century and down to the present day.   It is the extent of this influence which gives to him and his ideas so large a place in this latest phase of our legal history.   The causes of this influence have been acutely analysed by Dicey in his *Law and Opinion*.   They can be summarized as follows :

First, when, in the second and third decades of the nineteenth century, the majority of thinking men were beginning to realize that the law and institutions of England required a thorough reform, Bentham supplied them with an ideal and a programme.   Neither were revolutionary and both were intelligible.

Even the prosaic side of Bentham's doctrines, which checks the sympathy of modern readers, reassured sensible Englishmen who in 1830 had come to long for reform but dreaded revolution.   Bentham and his friends

---

[1] Dissertations and Discussions i 333.   [2] Below 131.

might be laughed at as pedants, but were clearly not revolutionists ; and, after all, whatever were the defects of Bentham as a jurist, critics who really understood his life and work knew that the first of legal philosophers was no agitator, but a systematic thinker of extraordinary power, and a thinker who kept his eyes fixed, not upon vague and indefinite ideals, but upon definite plans for the practical amendment of the law of England. Where could a teacher be found so acceptable to men of common-sense as a lawyer who had studied the law of England more profoundly than had many Lord Chancellors, and had studied it only with a view to removing its defects ? [1]

Therefore Bentham appealed to the conservative instincts of Englishmen. The reforms which he proposed aimed, not at revolution, but at giving a better security to liberty and property.

Secondly, Bentham's creed of utility had long been the accepted creed of many thinkers of many different political parties.

Dr. Johnson, the moralist of the preceding generation, had admitted, and Paley, still the accepted English theologian of the day, had advocated, the fundamental dogma of Benthamism, that the aim of existence was the attainment of happiness. The religious teachers who touched the conscience of Englishmen tacitly accepted this doctrine. The true strength of Evangelicalism did not, indeed, lie in the fervour with which its preachers appealed, as they constantly did, to the terrors of hell as a sanction for the practice of virtue on earth, but the appeal was in fact a recognition of the principle of utility. [2] When Bentham applied this principle to the amendment of the law he was in thorough harmony with the sentiment of the time ; he gave no alarm to moderate reformers by applying to the appropriate sphere of legislation that greatest happiness principle which the public had long accepted as something like a dictate of common-sense. [3]

Therefore Bentham's creed appealed to a belief widely held by Englishmen of many different schools of thought.

Thirdly, Bentham's creed appealed to that distrust of state interference and that suspicion of socialistic measures which were old established instincts amongst the majority of Englishmen. [4]

During the long conflicts which have made up the constitutional history of England, individualism has meant hatred of the arbitrary prerogative of the Crown, or, in other words, of the collective and autocratic authority of the State, and has fostered the instinctive and strenuous effort to secure for the humblest Englishman the rule of law. Benthamism was, and was ultimately felt to be, little else, than the logical and systematic development of those individual rights, and especially of that individual freedom which has always been dear to the common law of England. [5]

[1] Law and Opinion 171-172.
[2] For an instructive parallel between the Evangelical and the Utilitarian movements see G. M. Young, Victorian England 12 ; below 138.
[3] Dicey, Law and Opinion 172-173.
[4] Above 32, 92, 93, 111, 118.   [5] Dicey, Law and Opinion 174-175.

Fourthly, and as the result of these three causes, Bentham's creed attracted men of all parties. Whigs and the followers of Peel, Place and the trade unionists, joined with Mill and the philosophic radicals in subscribing to some at least of the legal and economic ideas of Benthamism.[1] This had an important effect on the extent of Bentham's influence. It would, as we have seen,[2] have been impossible to have accepted many of Bentham's detailed suggestions. But, because his ideas appealed to statesmen and lawyers of all parties, they were put into workable form and fitted into the fabric of English law by these statesmen and lawyers.[3] And so, such of his basic ideas as were practicable, were accepted and adjusted to the technical needs of the English legal system.

Bentham's main object was the reform and the restatement of English law and the institutions of the English state, in order that they might be made to conform to the dictates of the principles of utility. In the pursuit of this objective he necessarily made incursions into topics on the borderline of law and legal theory. It is for this reason that he has something to say on such subjects as philosophy, economics, and religion.[4] But his writings on these topics were, as we have seen, in the nature of by-products.[5] It is generally agreed that Bentham was no philosopher. Mill said that he was no metaphysician,[6] and Leslie Stephen said that he was weak in psychology and sociology, and unsatisfactory in ethics.[7] He never distinguished satisfactorily between law and morals.[8] As Leslie Stephen points out, the elimination of motive, which is justifiable from the point of view of the legislator, takes all meaning out of morality.[9] Bentham's philosophy will thus " do nothing for the conduct of the individual beyond prescribing some of the more obvious dictates of worldly prudence, and outward probity and beneficence."[10] As Maine points out, he reasons about morals in the same way as he reasons about legislation, without any perception of the fact that the considerations applicable in these two spheres are fundamentally different.[11] In economics he was for the most part a follower of Adam Smith. We have seen that he anticipated the logical conclusions which the classical economists drew from Adam Smith's doctrines[12]—though in some respects he departed from the strict *laissez faire* conclusions which some of those economists deduced from those

---

[1] Dicey, Law and Opinion 168-169.   [2] Above 87, 92, 93, 100, 101.
[3] Dicey, Law and Opinion 169 ; below 155.
[4] Above 110-112, 114, 116, 117.   [5] Above 117.
[6] Dissertations and Discussions i 335.
[7] The English Utilitarians i 269-270.
[8] Halévy, Philosophic Radicalism 26-27.
[9] The English Utilitarians i 258 ; cp. Halévy, Philosophic Radicalism 32-33.
[10] Mill, Dissertations and Discussions i 363.
[11] Early History of Institutions 400 ; below 124, 125.   [12] Above 29, 110, 112.

doctrines.[1] His speculations on religious matters were the logical consequences of his utilitarian philosophy, and show that he was as incapable of any real understanding of religion as he was of appreciating poetry.[2] As Mill said, " man is never recognized by him as a being capable of pursuing spiritual perfection as an end."[3] Logically enough, he does not recognize such a thing as conscience, " as a thing distinct from philanthropy, from affection for God or man, and from self interest in this world or in the next." [4] These defects in Bentham's intellect are the natural consequences of his devotion to the study of legal theory and to the problems of law reform. As we shall now see, they help to explain both his defects and his merits in both these capacities.

Defects. First, Bentham tries all institutions and all laws by one criterion and one standard—his own opinion as to what will make for the greatest happiness of the greatest number. His criterion and standard are those of the average man of his own day—" the respectable citizen with a policeman round the corner," [5] " the qualities obvious to an inhabitant of Queen's Square Place about the year 1800." [6] All speculations which failed to apply this criterion and this standard he ignored or ridiculed. As Mill says :[7]

He had a phrase, expressive of the view he took of all moral speculations to which his method had not been applied, or (which he considered the same thing) not founded on a recognition of utility as the moral standard ; this phrase was " vague generalities." Whatever presented itself to him in such a shape, he dismissed as unworthy of notice, or dwelt upon only to denounce as absurd. He did not heed, or rather the nature of his mind prevented it from occurring to him, that these generalities contained the whole unanalysed experience of the human race.

If we compare this attitude of mind with that of his great opposite Blackstone, we can see that Blackstone often shows a greater knowledge of, and a greater appreciation for, those various prejudices and characteristics of the men of his own day, of which those who would legislate effectively for them must take account. As I have pointed out, he realized that the principle of utility was only one amongst many principles upon which the rules of a legal system is based ; and that for the understanding of that

[1] Above 110, 111.
[2] Above 117 ; " Prejudice apart, the game of pushpin is of equal value with the arts and sciences, of music and poetry If the game of pushpin furnish more pleasure it is more valuable than either," Works ii 253 ; cp. ibid. x 583.
[3] Dissertations and Discussions i 359.   [4] Ibid.
[5] Leslie Stephen, The English Utilitarians i 314.
[6] Ibid 300 ; as Coleridge said (Table Talk, April 20, 1831), " What happiness? That is the question. The American savage in scalping his fallen enemy, pursues *his* happiness actually and adequately. A Chicksdaw or Pawnee Bentham . . . would necessarily hope for the most frequent opportunity of scalping the greatest possible number of savages for the longest possible time."
[7] Dissertations and Discussions i 356.

system, and therefore for reforms which are practicable because they are based on understanding, account must be taken of these competing principles.[1] Moreover it may well be that these competing principles have more truth in them than those who are blinded by a belief in a single principle will admit.[2] We have seen that Sydney Smith condensed the substance of Bentham's *Book of Fallacies* in his " Noodle's Oration." [3]

The noodle utters all the commonplaces by which the stupid conservatives, with Eldon at their head, met the demands of the reformers. Nothing could be wittier than Smith's brilliant summary. Whigs and radicals for the time agreed in ridiculing blind prejudice. The day was to come when the Whigs at least would see that some principles might be worse than prejudice. All the fools, said Lord Melbourne, were against Catholic Emancipation, and the worst of it is, the fools were in the right. Sydney Smith was glad to be Bentham's mouthpiece for the moment : though when Benthamism was applied to church reforms Smith began to perceive that Noodle was not so silly as he seemed.[4]

Secondly, because Bentham had convinced himself that all institutions and all laws could be tried by one criterion and one standard, he emphasized the equality of all men. Such differences as existed he thought were due to difference in circumstances which could be easily removed, and could for many purposes be ignored.[5] " Bentham's tacit assumption, in fact, is that there is an average ' man.' Different specimens of the race, indeed may vary widely according to age, sex, and so forth ; but for purposes of legislation, he may serve as a unit." [6] Whatever truth there may be in this assumption if confined to the men of a particular country at a particular time, it is obviously not universally true of men of all times and places.[7] Yet this was the assumption made by Bentham and by all his followers.

Thirdly, because he made this assumption, he convinced himself that a science of law and legislation could be created which was governed by laws as invariable as those which governed the physical world.[8] It is for this reason that, as Maine said,[9] Bentham and his disciple Austin " sometimes write as if they thought that, although obscured by false theory, false logic, and false statement, there is somewhere behind all the delusions which they expose a framework of permanent legal conceptions which is discoverable

---

[1] Vol. xii 734.   [2] See Vol. v 480.   [3] Above 69.
[4] Leslie Stephen, The English Utilitarians i 227-228.   [5] Above 76, 77.
[6] Leslie Stephen, The English Utilitarians i 299 ; " What Bentham is teaching, under new formulæ, is still a law founded on knowledge of the universal nature of man (Bentham uses the word in this sense), a law that can be used for the jurisprudence of all nations, a law whose ' language will serve as a glossary by which all systems of positive law might be explained, while the matter serves as a standard by which they might be tried,' " Halévy, Philosophic Radicalism 63.
[7] Above 123.   [8] Halévy, Philosophic Radicalism 29-30, 34.
[9] Early Law and Custom 360.

by a trained eye, looking through a dry light, and to which a rational Code may always be fitted." It was a common fallacy of the utilitarians, and the logical consequence of their philosophy, that sciences of law and economics[1] and even of history[2] itself could be constructed on the model of the exact sciences.

Fourthly, it followed, as we have seen,[3] that Bentham had very little use for history and its lessons. In fact he despised and distrusted it. He saw, as Dicey points out,[4] that interest in history tends to shift the aim of legal study from reform to research ; that a study which enables explanation to be given of the reasons for abuses will provide arguments against their removal ; and that historians tend to emphasize the dissimilarities between classes and nations, and to cast doubts on the paramount importance of those uniformities in the physical and mental characteristics of mankind which was the postulate of the utilitarian philosophy. This contempt and distrust for history meant that he ignored the accumulated experience of the race, and ignored all those national characteristics which are the result of that history and that experience. But, as Mill points out,[5] to reform effectively the laws and institutions of a nation, an understanding of its national character is essential :

The true teacher of the fitting social arrangements for England, France or America, is the one who can point out how the English, French, or American character can be improved, and how it has been made what it is. A philosophy of laws and institutions, not founded on a philosophy of national character, is an absurdity. But what would Bentham's opinion be worth on national character ? How could he, whose mind contained so few and so poor types of individual character, rise to that higher generalization ? All he can do is but to indicate means by which, in any given state of the national mind, the material interests of society can be protected ; saving the question, of which others must judge, whether the use of those means would have, on the national character, any injurious influence.

It is to these four defects of Bentham's intellect that his greatest mistakes in the spheres of politics and law are due.

In his criticisms of the " matchless constitution "[6] and of the established church[7] he entirely ignores deep-seated national feelings and prejudices. His denunciation of Kings and the House of Lords did not represent the feelings of the intelligent majority ; and, in fact, the nineteenth century has illustrated the usefulness of a King, and the need for a second chamber. He failed to see that

[1] Above 4, 76.
[2] The aim of Buckle's History of Civilization in England was " to fill the gap in the Utilitarian scheme by placing historical science upon a basis as firm as that of the physical sciences," Leslie Stephen, The English Utilitarians iii 347.
[3] Above 80, 118.   [4] Law and Opinion 457-459.
[5] Dissertations and Discussions i 366.
[6] Above 60.   [7] Above 58, 113, 116.

annual Parliaments would make effective Parliamentary government impossible. His simple belief that a pure democracy would
eliminate all sinister influences and would ensure enlightened
government is logically absurd and has been proved to be absurd.
It is logically absurd for the reasons given by Mill :[1]

The numerical majority of any society whatever must consist of persons
all standing in the same social position and having, in the main, the
same pursuits, namely, unskilled manual labourers ; and we mean no
disparagement to them : whatever we say to their disadvantage, we say
equally of a numerical majority of shopkeepers, or of squires. Where
there is identity of position and pursuits, there also will be identity of
partialities, passions, and prejudices, and to give to any one set of
partialities, passions and prejudices absolute power, without counterbalance from partialities, passions, and prejudices of a different sort, is
the way to render the correction of any of those imperfections hopeless ;
to make one narrow, mean type of human nature universal and perpetual, and to crush every influence which tends to the further improvement of man's intellectual and moral nature.

It was the great merit of that unreformed Parliament, which
Bentham attacked,[2] that the varieties in the franchise did provide
a counterbalance to the prejudices of any single class.[3] In fact,
in 1818, Mackintosh, the representative of the Whigs, who had not
yet been converted to the principle of the uniformity of the
franchise, attacked Bentham's proposals on the ground that he
had advocated a uniform and not a varied franchise.[4]

In his criticisms of the English legal system and of English
law he entirely ignored the fact that it is work of the lawyers
which has made both English law and Roman law great legal
systems. He regards the activities of " Judge and Co." as merely
harmful—though, as we have seen,[5] he admits that in the past
they had supplied good legal material. He entirely failed to see
that, however much the law may be codified, whatever benefits
may be derived from the codification of judge-made law, the work
of interpreting the law, of systematizing its principles and rules,
of applying the law to the facts, of elucidating the facts from
conflicting evidence, needs the collaboration of learned lawyers.[6]
He failed to see that the complexity of life, and therefore of the
rules of law needed to regulate it, must increase with the complexity of civilization, so that his ideal of a code of substantive and
adjective law, so simple that it could be understood by all,[7] was
quite illusory. His scheme of administering justice through small
local courts, in which the judge was not allowed to look at

[1] Dissertations and Discussions i 379-380.
[2] Above 88, 89.
[3] Above 23 ; Vol. x 565-568.
[4] Halévy, Philosophic Radicalism 418-419.
[5] Above 93.
[6] See Maine, Early History of Institutions 49-50.
[7] Works iii 209 ; Halévy, Philosophic Radicalism 378-379, 381-382.

anything but the text of the enacted law,[1] and his idea that the
shortcomings of the court of Chancery could be got rid of by
scrapping the rules of equity,[2] would have made short work of
the English legal system. In fact, when he represented that
system as a mere chaos studded with abuses he was guilty of gross
exaggeration. Mill's statement that Bentham "found the
philosophy of law a chaos and left it a science "[3] is a similar
exaggeration. If English lawyers were destitute of any philosophy
of law, how was it that they were able to make their legal system
one of the great legal systems of the world ? How did they manage
in the eighteenth century to construct and work a Constitution
which was universally admired ? How did they manage to think
out for themselves wholly original ideas on the law of property,
contract, and tort ?

The truth is that English lawyers have never ignored legal
theories, but they have declined, as Blackstone's *Commentaries*
show,[4] to be mastered by any one of them. They have preferred to
build upon the stable foundation of the concrete facts of life and
the needs of human beings, rather than upon the shifting sands of
the conflicting theories of ingenious philosophers. Mill was nearer
the truth when he said that "bad as the English system of
jurisprudence is, its parts harmonize tolerably well together,"
so that it was difficult to reform particular abuses without creating
difficulties in those parts of it which remained unreformed.[5] The
solution was not, as he and Bentham thought, to reform it root
and branch by the wholesale adoption of Bentham's suggestions,
but to adopt the expedient which English lawyers in fact adopted,
of using the talents of lawyers who were masters of the system, to
make gradually the reforms which were needed in such a way that
the changed rules were harmonized with the existing system.[6]
Bentham, as we have seen, disapproved of this method of
conservative reform ;[7] and if it be said that the fact that English

---

[1] Above 90.   [2] Above 90, 100.
[3] Dissertations and Discussions i 368.   [4] Vol. xii 734.
[5] " The truth is that, bad as the English system of jurisprudence is, its parts
harmonize tolerably well together ; and if one part, however bad, be taken away,
while another part is left standing, the arrangement which is substituted for it may,
for the time, do more harm by its imperfect adaptation to the remainder of the old
system, than the removal of the abuse can do good. The objection so often urged
by lawyers, as an argument against reforms, ' that in so complicated and intricate a
system of jurisprudence as ours, no one can fore-tell what the consequences of the
slightest innovation may be ' is perfectly correct ; although the inference to be
drawn from it is not, as they would have it to be understood, that the system
ought not to be reformed, but that it ought to be reformed thoroughly, and on a
comprehensive plan ; not piecemeal, but at once. There are numerous cases in
which a gradual change is preferable to a sudden one ; because its immediate
consequences can be more distinctly foreseen. But in this case, the consequences
even of a sudden change can be much more easily foreseen than those of a gradual
one," J. S. Mill's Preface to Bentham's Rationale of Judicial Evidence, Works
vi 202-203.   [6] Below 155.   [7] Above 102, 103.

lawyers pursued it shows their indifference to legal theory and the
philosophy of the law, the answer is that it shows, not indifference,
but an appreciation of the part which theory and philosophy on
the one hand, and the conditions imposed by an existing system
of law on the other hand, impose on law reform.   Workable
reforms can only be made by men who pay due attention both to
theory and to the practical limitations imposed by the system of
law which is to be reformed, by men who can not only appreciate
the theory but who have sufficient knowledge of the existing
system to work deductions from the theory into the technical
fabric of that system.[1]   It is well to remember that it was not only
English lawyers who refused to accept Bentham's proposals in
bulk. As M. Halévy has pointed out,[2] his influence was greatest in
those countries like Russia which had no legal tradition of their
own. Lord Campbell, though he praised the Code Napoleon, said
truly that it was " wholly insufficient to solve the vast majority
of questions coming before the tribunals " :

Joseph Hume and other such ignorant coxcombs think that the whole
law of England might be comprised in an octavo volume, and that all
other books connected with the law might be burned.   Were he to attend
in the Palais de Justice, he would find the advocates and judges . . .
referring to the Civil Law, to the *droit coutumier* before the Revolution,
to the works of Daguesseau and Pothier, or to a body of recent decided
cases little less bulky than the Reports which load the shelves of an
English lawyer.[3]

These, then, are Bentham's defects as a legal philosopher and
a law reformer : let us now examine his merits which more than
compensate for his defects.

Merits. At the end of the eighteenth and the beginning of the
nineteenth centuries the need for a thorough reform of English
law, to bring it into conformity with the needs of a new age, was
obvious.   Its continuous and haphazard growth, and its " bit by
bit " development[4] had resulted in a system marked by many
archaic rules, by many legal fictions, and by many needless forms
which were bidding fair to choke the sound principles and rules
which it contained, and to make its administration so expensive

---

[1] " The bold vehement man who exposes an abuse has rarely the skilful, painful,
dissecting power to expunge it. . . . A law reformer, in order that his work may be
perfect, requires conveyancing abilities.   He must be able to bear in mind the
whole topic—to draw out what is necessary of it on paper—to see what is necessary—
to discriminate the rights of individuals—to distinguish, with even metaphysical
nicety, the advantages he would keep from the abuse he would destroy.   He must
elaborate enacting clauses which will work in the complicated future, repealing
clauses which will not interfere with the complicated machinery of the past,"
Bagehot, Literary Studies ii 73-74 ; cp. Brougham's criticism of this failing of
Bentham in the introduction to his speech of 1828 on Law Reform, Speeches ii
293-294.
[2] Philosophic Radicalism 296.   [3] Life of Campbell i 363.
[4] See Bagehot, Biographical Studies 284, cited vol. i 633.

that justice was in effect denied to the poor man. Mill's picturesque summary gives a substantially true picture of the result : [1]

The law had come to be like the costume of a full grown man who had never put off the clothes made for him when he first went to school. Band after band had burst, and, as the rent widened, then, without removing anything except what might drop off of itself, the hole was darned, or patches of fresh law were brought from the nearest shop and stuck on. Hence all ages of English history have given one another rendezvous in English law ; their several products may be seen all together, not interfused, but heaped one upon another, as many different ages of the earth may be read in some perpendicular section of its surface —the deposits of each successive period not substituted but superimposed on those preceding. . . . The whole history of the contest about trusts may still be read in the words of a conveyance, as could the contest about entails, till the abolition of fine and recovery by a bill of the present Attorney-General.

Bentham's principle of utility, and the method in which he applied it, was exactly what was required by those who set out to reform a system of law which had got into this condition. It gave reformers, as Maine said, [2] " a distinct object to aim at in the pursuit of improvement " ; so that, in that respect, it did for English law somewhat the same service as the theory of a law of nature did for Roman law.[3] Though Bentham's philosophy was defective, both his method and his test of utility applied a workable and, Maine thinks, [4] the only possible, criterion for the guidance of a legislature ; and with this verdict Leslie Stephen agrees :[5]

Bentham's method involved a thoroughgoing examination of the whole body of laws, and a resolution to apply a searching test to every law. If that test was not so unequivocal or ultimate as he fancied, it yet implied the constant application of such considerations as must always carry weight, and, perhaps, be always the dominant considerations, with the actual legislator or jurist. What is the use of you ? is a question which may fairly be put to every institution and to every law ; and it concerns legislators to find some answer, even though the meaning of the word " use " is not so clear as we could wish.

In fact, it may be said that some of the defects of Bentham's philosophy helped to make him the more effective as a legal

[1] Dissertations and Discussions i 369-370 ; good illustrations in the sphere of procedure will be found in the system of common law procedure, vol. ix 247-262, and equity procedure, ibid 336-371. [2] Ancient Law 78.

[3] " It is not an altogether fanciful comparison if we call the assumptions we have been describing [the assumptions made by the jurists who believed in a simple and symmetrical Law of Nature] the ancient counterpart of Benthamism. The Roman theory guided men's efforts in the same direction as the theory put into shape by the Englishman ; its practical results were not widely different from those which would have been attained by a sect of law reformers who maintained a steady pursuit of the general good of the community," ibid 79.

[4] Early History of Institutions 399-400.

[5] The English Utilitarians i 271.

philosopher and a law reformer. He was, as Mill said, a " one-eyed man " ;[1] and, because he was a one-eyed man, he was able to state and explain his ideas and proposals with a clarity and force which a clearer view of the complexities and innate conservatism of human nature would probably have obscured.[2] However that may be, the fact that the verdicts of Maine and Leslie Stephen are right is proved, first by the services which Bentham has rendered to the philosophy of law and to men's ideas as to the machinery for its improvement ; and secondly by the large number of reforms in the law which can be traced back to his ideas.

(i) Services to the philosophy of law and the machinery for its improvement

Philosophy. Because Bentham was determined to criticize abuses in all departments of the law, and to submit all laws to the test of utility, " he expelled mysticism from the philosophy of law, and set the example of viewing laws in a practical light, as means to certain definite and precise ends." [3] As Maine has said :[4]

If the analytical jurists failed to see a great deal which can only be explained by the help of history, they saw a great deal which even in our day is imperfectly seen by those who, so to speak, let themselves drift with history. Sovereignty and Law, regarded as facts, had only gradually assumed a shape in which they answered to the conception of them formed by Hobbes, Bentham, and Austin, but the correspondence really did exist by their time, and was tending constantly to become more perfect. They were thus able to frame a juridical terminology which had for one virtue that it was rigidly consistent with itself, and for another that, if it did not completely express facts, the qualifications of its accuracy were never serious enough to deprive it of value and tended moreover to become less and less important as time went on. No conception of law and society has ever removed such a mass of undoubted delusions.

Because Bentham was not only a critical thinker but a positive reformer who suggested remedies for the abuses which he criticized he accomplished results far greater than any merely critical thinker has ever accomplished. The merely critical thinkers,

took for their starting point the received opinion on any subject, dug round it with their logical implements, pronounced its foundations defective, and condemned it : he began *de novo*, laid his own foundations deeply and firmly, built up his own structure, and bade mankind compare the two ; it was when he had solved the problem himself, or thought he had done so, that he declared all other solutions to be erroneous.[5]

---

[1] Dissertations and Discussions i 357.
[2] Halévy, Philosophic Radicalism 33-34.
[3] Mill, Dissertations and Discussions i 373.
[4] Early History of Institutions 396-397.
[5] Mill, Dissertations and Discussions i 338.

It is for this reason that, as we shall see, so many of Bentham's suggested reforms have been adopted by the Legislature.[1]

Machinery. Bentham emphasized the fact that, to make the reforms which he advocated, direct legislation by a sovereign legislature was the only possible means. He not only " took up the theory of sovereignty where Hobbes left it," [2] he made one considerable addition to it. Not only did he use it to define the State and the law, not only did he use it to prove that law enacted by a sovereign is the only law of which a legal system should consist, and that it attained its most perfect shape in a code, he also maintained that it was the duty of the sovereign to be an active legislator in order to make the principle of utility prevail throughout the legal system. " The formula of the greatest happiness is made a hook to put in the nostrils of Leviathan, that he may be tamed and harnessed to the chariot of utility." [3] Naturally, he emphasized the deficiencies of judge-made law and, both he and Austin poured scorn on Lord Mansfield's idea[4] that the judges were better fitted for the work of law reform than the Legislature.[5]   Bentham, as Dicey says,[6] " forced the faith in scientific legislation upon the attention of a generation of Englishmen by whom its truth or importance was denied or forgotten." We have seen that he made many valuable suggestions as to the manner in which this legislation should be drafted ;[7] and that he not only invented the word ' codification,'[8] but advocated the reduction of all law to the form of a scientifically constructed code.[9]

These services rendered by Bentham to the philosophy of law and to the machinery of law reform largely outweigh his defects. We may not agree with all his criticisms of the English legal system and the English constitution, we may think that some of the rules of English law and some of the institutions of the English state which he called abuses were not abuses, we may not agree with some of his suggested reforms, we may doubt whether it is possible or desirable to restate all the law in the form of a code. At the same time we cannot deny that a very large part of his criticisms were justified, that many of his suggested reforms are sensible, and that it is desirable to restate in the form of a code those parts of the law which are ripe for codification. As we shall now see, it is the merits of Bentham's principles, and the needs of the English legal system for a reformer convinced of the truth of those principles, and prepared to apply them in detail to all parts

---

[1] Below 132-134.   [2] Pollock, History of the Science of Politics 96.
[3] Ibid 101.   [4] Cited vol. xii 551.
[5] Works vii 311 ; Austin's views on this matter are cited by Mill, Dissertations and Discussions iii 252.
[6] Law and Opinion 135.   [7] Above 97 ; vol. xi 375-377.
[8] Above 96.   [9] Above 96, 97.

of the English legal system, that account for the large number
of reforms in the law, which can be traced back to his ideas.

(ii) *The reform in the law which can be traced to Bentham's ideas*

Bentham's principles had won some victories before 1832,
but the major victories of his principles were won in the period
which stretches from the Reform Act of 1832 to the Judicature
Acts of 1873 and 1875. That was the period when his philosophical,
legal, and economic ideas were dominant. But his influence has
lasted beyond this period, when the individualistic ideas of his
followers were dominant, into the new age of collectivism and
socialism. This is due partly to the fact that his ideas as to law
reform were not dependent upon his fallacious political ideas or
his fallacious economic ideas, partly to the intrinsic sense of many
of his ideas as to law reform which have overcome the outworn
prejudices which prevented their immediate realization, and
partly to the fact that Bentham's individualism and distrust
of the state were necessarily weakened by the fact that the
application of his principle of utility to the government of the
state had shown him that various social services such as health
services, care of the poor, and national education, must be undertaken by the state.[1] Let us look first at some of the reforms which
can be traced back to Bentham's ideas, (*a*) in the period before,
and (*b*) in the period after 1875.

(*a*) John Hill Burton, who wrote the Introduction to Bowring's
1843 edition of Bentham's works, said that the following
suggestions for reform made by Bentham had then been wholly
or partially carried out : [2]

Reform in the representative system.[3] Municipal Reform in the abolition
of exclusive privileges.[4] Mitigation of the Criminal Code.[5] The abolition
of Transportation, and the adoption of a system of Prison discipline
adapted to reformation, example, and economy.[6] Removal of defects in
the Jury system.[7] Abolition of arrest in Mesne Process.[8] Substitution
of an effectual means of appropriating and realizing a Debtor's property,
for the practice of Imprisonment.[9] Abolition of the Usury Laws.[10]
Abolition of Oaths.[11] Abolition of Law Taxes, and Fees in Courts of
Justice. Removal of the exclusionary rules in [the law of] Evidence.
Repeal of the Test and Corporation Acts, the Catholic Disabilities Acts,
and other laws creating religious inequalities.[12] Abolition or reduction of
taxes on knowledge. A uniform system of Poor Laws under central
administration, with machinery for the eradication of mendicancy and

---

[1] Above 89, 90, 93, 111.   [2] Works i, Advertisement to the Introduction p. 3 n.
[3] Below 239-247.   [4] Below 447, 448.   [5] Below 226.
[6] Vol. xi 575 ; below 317-320.   [7] Below 262, 406.   [8] Below 405.
[9] Vol. viii 231-233 ; vol. xi 524-525, 595-597 ; below 226, 264-266, 377, 412.
[10] Vol. viii 112.   [11] Below 168, 203.   [12] Below 230, 231.

idleness.[1] A system of training Pauper children, calculated to raise them from dependent to productive members of society.[2] Savings banks and Friendly Societies on a uniform and secure system.[3] Postage cheap, and without a view to revenue.[4] Post-office money orders. A complete and uniform Register of Births, Marriages, and Deaths. A Register of Merchant seamen, and a Code of Laws for their protection. Population Returns, periodical, and on a uniform system, with names, professions, etc. of individuals. The circulation of Parliamentary Papers as a means of diffusing the information contained in them. Protection to Inventions without the cumbrous machinery of the Patent Laws.

In the period between 1843 and 1875 many of these reforms were more fully developed. In public law the franchise was extended and voting by ballot was introduced. Trade was entirely freed, a system of national education was introduced, and an efficient system of local courts was provided.[5] The judicial system was recast by the Judicature and Appellate Jurisdiction Acts ;[6] and, though law and equity were not fused,[7] the courts of law and equity and of probate divorce and admiralty were amalgamated,[8] and his idea of a "single seated" judge was adopted.[9] The law of procedure and pleading was simplified,[10] and facilities were provided for divorce.[11] Companies with limited liability were introduced. Patronage was eliminated in the civil service, and its place was supplied by a system of competitive examination.[12] Laws providing for the care of public health were enacted, and a machinery for their enforcement was provided. Great improvements were made in the classification and drafting of Acts of Parliament.[13]

(b) In the period since 1875 more of Bentham's ideas have been realized. Complete democracy has been introduced, and the House of Lords has been shorn of its powers. Many of his suggestions for the reform of the law of real property had been adopted by the legislation of the nineteenth-century ; and those reforms have culminated in the Property Acts which have, amongst many other things, almost adopted his suggestion of "abandoning the heir at law to the Society of Antiquaries." Women have gradually been placed on an equality with men in public law ; and married women have, contrary to Bentham's views,[14] been given the same capacity in private law as unmarried women. Though his plan of a quasi-jury has not been adopted, his

---

[1] Below 311-315.
[2] Below 313, 314.
[3] Below 333, 334, 335.
[4] Below 234.
[5] Vol. i 191-193.
[6] Ibid 638-645.
[7] Vol. xii 601-605.
[8] Vol. i 638.
[9] Vol. i 641.
[10] Vol. ix 262, 328-330, 375-376, 406-407.
[11] Vol. i 624.
[12] Vol. x 511.
[13] Vol. xi 377-387.
[14] Works i 536.

criticism of the jury as a tribunal to decide the facts in civil cases has been given some effect by its disuse in many classes of civil cases ; and grand juries have for the most part [1] been abolished. Though English law has not been completely codified, many important parts of it have been codified. His criticism of the law which attaches a sacramental efficacy to a seal is now generally accepted. Reforms in the theory of punishment have gone far beyond his suggestions ; and in 1938 the power of a man entirely to disinherit his wife and children was abridged by the legislature. [2]

The continued influence of Bentham's ideas upon legislation is due in large part to their merits. They were the logical results of his detailed application of that principle of utility which (whatever its deficiencies may be as a guide to morality) must always be the paramount consideration of a legislature. [3] That so many of them were so quickly adopted is due to the fact that a small party of lawyers and political thinkers, who regarded Bentham as their oracle, summed up all the new ideas of this age— legal, political, economic, and religious—in the form in which he approved them, and made of them a coherent body of philosophical, political, economic, and religious doctrine. This group of philosophic radicals was a small and unpopular party ; but, as we shall now see, they gave a coherence and definiteness to the new ideas upon all these topics which had been coming to the front in this age of transition.

Philosophic Radicalism

This school of thought is important in the history of English law because its teaching summed up and justified the main points of Bentham's theories as to politics, religion, economics, and law reform ; because it supplied those theories with a more definite philosophic backing than that supplied by Bentham ; and because, in consequence, it made for the more rapid adoption of some of Bentham's suggestions for reform. The fact that Bentham's influence on law reform was so marked during the third and fourth decades of the nineteenth century[4] is largely due to this school of thought. Its adherents were never numerous, and, as we shall see, they were never popular. [5] But they comprised important men who made their mark both in literature and politics ; they held a set of clear-cut and logically connected beliefs ; and they advocated a set of reforms in the law and constitution of England based on those beliefs. For those reasons they were able to exert an influence upon legislation out of all proportion to their numbers.

---

[1] Above 71.   [2] 1 and 2 Geo. 6, ch. 45.
[3] Above 59, 68, 69, 114.   [4] Above 132.   [5] Below 142-144.

The founder of this school was James Mill. He, as we have seen, derived his beliefs and doctrines from Bentham,[1] and in return he reverenced Bentham as the master whose theories had inspired his school of thought. Therefore I shall, in the first place, say something of James Mill; secondly, I shall sum up briefly the main articles of the creed of this school of thought; and, thirdly, I shall say something of the reasons why, though it was an influential, it was never a popular creed.

(1) James Mill[2] (1773-1836) was born at Northwater Bridge, Forfarshire. He was the son of a shoe-maker. At the parish school his abilities attracted the notice of Peters the minister, who recommended him to Sir John and Lady Jane Stuart of Fettercairn. Lady Jane was interested in promising young men, and had started a fund to educate young men for the ministry. Mill interested her, she employed him as tutor to her daughter, and it was through the help of her and her husband that he was able to go to Edinburgh University in 1790. At Edinburgh he studied the classics and philosophy. In 1794 he began the study of divinity, and was licensed to preach in 1798. But he failed to secure a ministry, and in 1802 he went to London. In two years' time, by literary and editorial work, he was earning £500 a year, and in 1805 he married. But he lost his editorships, and at first had a hard struggle to keep himself and his growing family. In 1806 he began his *History of India* in order that he might make for himself a permanent place in literature ; and he did not cease to work at it in spite of his numerous literary activities by means of which he supported his family, and in spite of the hours he devoted to the education of his children. In 1808 he made the acquaintance of Bentham. From that time onwards he was his devoted disciple, the chief propagator of his doctrines, and the founder of the school of philosophic radicals which reduced the utilitarian doctrines to systematic dogmas. In the succeeding years Mill lived next door to Bentham in London, and spent many months at Bentham's homes at Barrow Green House and Ford Abbey. Throughout his life he never wavered in his faith in Bentham's creed. The inevitable result of his new faith was the abandonment of all belief in Christianity, and the adoption of the agnostic creed.

Mill helped to propagate the Benthamite creed by occasional articles in the *Edinburgh Review*, and in a paper called the *Philanthropist*, which was financed by the quaker William Allen, who supported the anti-slavery agitation and many other philanthropic schemes. He soon gathered round him a party of men who believed in Bentham's creed. He had met Hume, the radical

[1] Above 57, 58.
[2] Leslie Stephen, The English Utilitarians ii 1-40 ; J. S. Mill, Autobiography ; D.N.B.

reformer, and Brougham at Edinburgh University ; and in 1811 or 1812 he became an ally of Francis Place—the organizer of the radical party in the Westminster constituency. Place helped Bentham to put some of his writings into shape ;[1] and Mill, Place, and Bentham supported Lancaster's educational schemes and tried to found the Chrestomathic school.[2] About the same time Mill had acquired in Ricardo a still more important ally. He encouraged Ricardo to publish his book and to stand for Parliament ; and meetings in Ricardo's house led to the formation of the Political Economy Club in 1821, which brought him into connection with Malthus.[3] Grote, the historian, introduced to Mill by Ricardo, was another defender of the utilitarian theory of government, and of Bentham's anti-religious views.[4]

Mill's series of articles in the *Encyclopaedia Britannica* (1817-1823)[5] put him at the head of the utilitarian school of philosophic radicals, which was now attracting a number of brilliant young recruits such as McCulloch, Bickersteth (afterwards Lord Langdale), John Stuart Mill, Black the editor of the *Morning Chronicle* and his assistant Fonblanque, and John and Charles Austin. J. S. Mill founded the Utilitarian Society—coining the word " utilitarian," which became the name generally used to denote the adherents to Bentham's creed ;[6] and he and others founded a debating society in which the Tories and the philosophic radicals argued their cases.[7] Mill himself was now prosperous. He had completed his *History of India* in 1818 ; and it was due to it that in 1819 he was appointed to the post of assistant to the examiner of Indian correspondence at a salary of £800 a year. By 1830 he had become head of the office, and exercised considerable influence upon the new settlement which Parliament made with the East India Company in 1833.[8] Mill's new position did not prevent him from continuing, as the leader of the utilitarians and radicals, to preach Bentham's creed. After the failure of the Chrestomathic scheme of education,[9] he helped to found London University, which was meant to develop Chrestomathic principles and the utilitarian cause ; and in 1824, when the *Westminster Review* was founded to provide an organ for

---

[1] Above 66.   [2] Above 113.
[3] The club discussed not only economic questions but also logic and psychology, J. S. Mill, Autobiography 119-123.   [4] Above 113, 116, 117.
[5] Besides the article on Government, he wrote articles on Jurisprudence, Liberty of the Press, Prisons and Prison Discipline, Colonies, the Law of Nations, Education, Economists, see Barker's ed. of the Essays on Government ix.
[6] " The name I gave to the society I had planned was the Utilitarian Society. It was the first time than anyone had taken the title of Utilitarian ; and the term made its way into the language from this humble source. I did not invent the word, but found it in one of Galt's novels, the ' Annals of the Parish ', in which the Scotch clergyman . . . is represented as warning his parishioners not to leave the Gospel and become utilitarians," J. S. Mill, Autobiography 79-80.
[7] Ibid 125-129.   [8] Below 142, 143.   [9] Above 113.

the utilitarians and radicals side by side with the Whig *Edinburgh*
and the Tory *Quarterly*, he gave it his support, though he distrusted Bowring, its editor. He continued his advocacy of the
various articles of the utilitarian creed down to his death, June 23,
1836. His last writings were an article upon the aristocracy, and a
dialogue on the utility of political economy, which appeared in
the *London Review* for January 1836.

Mill was a dour Scot "whose austere, energetic, imperious,
and relentless character showed the temperament of the Scots
Covenanter of the seventeenth century, inspired by the principles
and philosophy of France in the eighteenth." [1] He had the typical
Scots intellect—logical, deductive, systematizing. These intellectual characteristics, which are analogous to those of other
typical Scots—to those displayed by James I in his *Trew Law of
Free Monarchies*, [2] and by Lord Mansfield, [3] were admirably suited
to create from the new ideas upon politics, religion, economics, law,
and philosophy a fixed and logical system. In fact he was a
typical, almost an exaggerated, example of that one of those
"two ways of thinking" which Lord Macmillan shows as
characteristics of the Scottish mind ; [4] for, as his son said, " he
trusted too much to the intelligibleness of the abstract, when not
embodied in the concrete." [5] And Mill's personal characteristics
were similar to his intellectual characteristics. He was as inflexible
in the observation of his high standards of duty as he was logical in
the exposition of his intellectual conclusions. He rarely showed his
feelings—men were surprised at the grief he showed when Ricardo
died ; and his stoical, epicurean, and cynical qualities [6] inspired
the gibe that he was a democrat less from love of the many than
from hatred of the few [7]—a caricature no doubt, but, like all
caricatures, based on at least an appearance of the truth. He
took an infinity of pains to educate his children in his creed—more
especially his brilliant son John Stuart, whose precocious intellect
he so forced that in his early twenties it nearly broke down. [8]
He had great intellectual gifts, and some social gifts ; [9] but he was

[1] Morley, Critical Miscellanies iii 66.
[2] Vol. vi 11-12.   [3] Vol. xi 16 ; Vol. xii 556.
[4] Law and Other Things 76-101 ; ibid 110-111 ; vol. xi 14-16.
[5] J. S. Mill, Autobiography 23-24.
[6] His son said of him, " In his views of life he partook of the character of the
Stoic, the Epicurean, and the Cynic, not in the modern but the ancient sense of the
word. In his personal qualities the Stoic predominated. His standard of morals
was Epicurean, inasmuch as it was utilitarian, taking as the exclusive test of right
and wrong, the tendency of actions to produce pleasure or pain. But he had (and
this was the Cynic element) scarcely any belief in pleasure. . . . He was not insensible to pleasures ; but he deemed very few of them worth the price which, at
least in the present state of society, must be paid for them. . . . He thought human
life a poor thing at best, after the freshness of youth and of unsatisfied curiosity had
gone by," J. S. Mill, Autobiography 47-48.   [7] Above 61.
[8] J. S. Mill, Autobiography 132-141.   [9] Ibid 101-102.

so absorbed in his high intellectual quests that he inspired, even in his own family, respect rather than affection.[1]

Such a man was well fitted to make a creed out of the new ideas of the age. Building on the basis of Bentham's doctrines, and on his own speculations, he formulated a set of opinions which were, his son tells us, " the principal element which gave its colour and character to the little group of young men who were the first propagators of what was afterwards called ' Philosophic Radicalism '." [2] It was, says Bagehot,[3] " a curious, hard, compact, consistent creed " ; and its adherents have been described with substantial accuracy as " a party, almost a sect, with formularies as compact as the Evangelical theology, and conclusions not less inexorable." [4] This logical system of connected ideas upon politics, religion, economics, law, and philosophy would, its adherents vainly hoped, guide the thought of the nation upon all these matters.

(2) The main articles of this creed can be summed up as follows:

In *politics* Mill's *Encyclopaedia* article on *Government* (reprinted under the title of *An Essay on Government*) was the bible of the sect. It embodied most of Bentham's democratic ideas, and, in particular, it based the argument for democracy on Bentham's theory that it is only a representative assembly elected at frequent intervals and with the widest possible franchise that can secure the community from " sinister " influences, and so promote the greatest happiness of the greatest number.[5] Like Bentham, Mill was confident that the majority would not mis-use their power. Given education, he was sure that the mass of the people would follow the wisest and the most virtuous—whom Mill, like Bentham, identified with the middle classes.[6] He says :[7]

Another proposition may be stated, with a perfect confidence of the concurrence of all those men who have attentively considered the formation of opinions in the great body of society, or, indeed, the principles of human nature in general. It is, that the opinions of that class of the people, who are below the middle rank, are formed, and their minds are directed by that intelligent and virtuous rank, who come the most immediately in contact with them, who are in the constant habit of intimate communication with them, to whom they fly for advice and assistance in all their numerous difficulties, upon whom they feel an immediate and daily dependence, in health and in sickness, in infancy and in old age ; to whom their children look up as models for their imitation, whose opinions they daily hear repeated, and account it an honour to adopt. There can be no doubt that the middle rank, which gives to science, to art, and to legislation itself, their most distinguished ornaments, the chief source of all that has exalted and refined human nature, is that portion of the community of which, if the basis of

---

[1] J. S. Mill, Autobiography 51-52.   [2] Ibid 105.
[3] Literary Studies (Silver Library ed.) iii 391.
[4] G. M. Young, Victorian England 8.   [5] Above 88, 89.
[6] Above 58, 89, 113.   [7] Essay on Government (Barker's ed.) 72.

Representation were ever so far extended, the opinion would ultimately decide. Of the people beneath them, a vast majority would be sure to be guided by their advice and example.

It was no answer to say that the behaviour of the lower classes in towns and manufacturing districts disproved this thesis—the fact that the mob in a manufacturing district sometimes created riots and disorders was merely an occasional incident, produced by some transitory cause. " The great majority of the people never cease to be guided by that rank [the middle classes] ; and we may, with some confidence, challenge the adversaries of the people to produce a single instance to the contrary in the history of the world."[1] It is, I think, clear that Mill was making the enormous mistake of supposing that the behaviour of the lower classes in a manufacturing town and under a democratic constitution would be the same as the behaviour of the lower classes in the country or a country town under the aristocratic constitution of the eighteenth century.

In the matter of *religion* Mill and his school followed Bentham.[2] They were careful not to parade their agnostic views, but the trend of their thought was quite unmistakable. To their minds the Church of England was " a mere state machine worked in subservience to the sinister interest of the governing classes."[3] It should therefore be disestablished and disendowed. The money should be used to establish a system of ethical and scientific education under the Minister of Public Instruction. James Mill's suggestions are thus summarized by Leslie Stephen :[4]

Let the clergy be appointed by a " Minister of Public Instruction " or the county authorities ; abolish the articles and constitute a church " without dogmas or ceremonies " ; and employ the clergy to give lectures on ethics, botany, political economy, and so forth, besides holding Sunday meetings, dances (decent dances are to be specially invented for the purpose), and social meals, which would be a revival of the " agapai " of the early Christians. For this purpose, however, it might be necessary to substitute tea and coffee for wine. In other words the church is to be made into a popular London University.

The scheme, as Leslie Stephen says, " illustrates the incapacity of an isolated clique to understand the real tone of public opinion."[5]

In *economics* Mill and the philosophic radicals were the exponents of all the doctrines of the classical economists ;[6] for they numbered among their members Ricardo and M'Culloch, and they accepted the conclusions of Malthus.[7] In fact, it was Mill who

---

[1] Essay on Government (Barker's ed.) 73.
[3] Leslie Stephen, The English Utilitarians ii 61.
[5] Ibid 62.
[7] Halévy, Philosophic Radicalism 274.

[2] Above 58, 113, 116, 117.
[4] Ibid 61-62.
[6] Above 30, 33, 34. 40.

induced Ricardo to publish his *Principles* and other economic writings ;[1] and M. Halévy thinks that it was to Mill's influence that " political economy owes the systematic and deductive character which it assumed in Ricardo." [2]   In his *Elements of Political Economy* he summed up the conclusions of Ricardo ; and both he and M'Culloch gave to Ricardo's doctrines a logical hardness and fixity which was typically Scottish.[3] Their doctrines, it is true, helped to explode many popular fallacies. They showed that " it was absurd to suppose that by simply expanding the currency, or by making industry less efficient, or by forcing it to the least profitable employments, you were increasing the national wealth ; or to overlook the demoralising effects of a right to support because you resolved only to see the immediate benefits of charity to individuals." [4] But their postulates, and the axioms founded on them, were too simple and too rigid. Too many essential factors were omitted when they forgot or treated as negligible the variations of human beings, and the complexities of an old and an organized society.[5] Moreover their conclusions were not always logical. We have seen that their adoption of Adam Smith's assumption that there is a natural identification of interests, so that the beneficent effect of natural laws should not be interfered with by the state,[6] was hardly compatible with the theories of Malthus as to population and as to rent.[7] But, notwithstanding this difficulty, the economists still maintained that the state should not interfere to establish artificially any identification of these naturally divergent interests. They justified this illogical conclusion by the proposition that, if men were sufficiently educated, they would learn lessons of prudence, which would counteract the causes of poverty arising from too rapid an increase of population.[8] The idea of the advisability of checking births by artificial means —neo-malthusianism—was taken up by the philosophic radicals, and helped to add to their unpopularity amongst the religious.[9] In these circumstances it is not surprising that the economic doctrines of the philosophic radicals should not only have made them unpopular but also have aroused hostility to the political economy which they expounded.

In the sphere of *law reform* the philosophic radicals did little more than expound and defend Bentham's proposals. Mill did much to further these proposals by his writings ;[10] and we have

---

[1] Halévy, Philosophic Radicalism 266.
[2] Ibid 281.   [3] Ibid 343.
[4] Leslie Stephen, The English Utilitarians ii 218-219.
[5] Ibid 219-222.   [6] Vol. xi 505-506.   [7] Above 31-33.
[8] Halévy, Philosophic Radicalism 363-364 ; above 36.
[9] Halévy, Philosophic Radicalism 364-365 ; J. S. Mill, Autobiography 105 ; above 116, 117.
[10] Leslie Stephen, The English Utilitarians ii 10-12.

seen that both he and his son edited Bentham's works on evidence.[1]

It was in the sphere of *philosophy* that Mill and the philosophic radicals added most to Bentham's teaching. Bentham was not, as we have seen, a philosopher :[2] Mill was ; and, because he was a philosopher, he supplied the intellectual cement to the disparate parts of the creed of philosophic radicalism.[3] As M. Halévy has said,[4] the utilitarians " had long neglected theoretic researches concerning psychology, logic, and morals." They were more interested in practical reforms. But " at the end of his career Bentham at last became aware that it was necessary to define the moral theory on which his social system rested. Towards the same time James Mill likewise came to understand that the psychology on which Bentham's moral theory rested had to be scientifically constituted." It was with that object that he wrote his *Analysis of the Phenomena of the Human Mind*, which he hoped would make " the human mind as plain as the road from Charing Cross to St. Paul's." [5]

I have described in general terms the conclusions of the philosophical school of Mill and Bentham.[6] In fact, just as Bentham wished to found a science of law and legislation which should be governed by laws as universal as those of the physical sciences,[7] so Mill wished to found a science of mental phenomena which was governed by laws as ascertainable as those which govern the physical world. Leslie Stephen says :[8]

Mill applies " Baconian "' principles. The inductive method, which had already been so fruitful in the physical sciences, will be equally effective in philosophy, and, ever since Locke, philosophy had meant psychology. The " philosophy of the mind " and the philosophy of the body may be treated as co-ordinate and investigated by similar methods. In the physical sciences we come ultimately to the laws of movement and their constituent atoms. In the moral sciences we come in the same way to the study of ideas. The questions, How do ideas originate ? and How are they combined so as to form the actual state of consciousness ? are therefore the general problems to be solved. Hume had definitely proposed the problem. Hartley had worked out the theory of the association of ideas which Hume had already compared to the universal principle of gravitation in the physical world ; and had endeavoured to show how this might be connected with physiological principles . . . Mill, as his son testifies, had been profoundly influenced by Hartley's treatise—the " really master-production," as he esteemed it, " in the philosophy of the mind."

With the help of this associationist principle Mill proceeded to construct a system of morals which depended simply upon a series

---

[1] Above 65, 66, 83-86.
[2] Above 117.
[3] Halévy, Philosophic Radicalism 457.
[4] Ibid 487.
[5] Cited Halévy, Philosophic Radicalism 451.
[6] Above 134 seqq.
[7] Above 124.
[8] The English Utilitarians ii 288-289.

of applications of the principle of utility—" the whole effort of the utilitarian moralist was to subordinate the sentimental impulses, whether egotistical or disinterested, to a reflective egoism." [1] It was a morality well suited to those middle classes whose political virtues Bentham and Mill regarded as the mainstay of their democratic state ; for as M. Halévy has said : [2]

It is no longer the religious or aristocratic, ascetic or chivalrous morality which makes current antipathies or sympathies the sentimental rule of its practical judgments, which exalts the rare and showy virtues, and recommends to the masses, in the interest of a governing class, humility or sacrifice. It is a plebeian or rather a bourgeois morality, devised for working artisans and shrewd tradesmen, teaching subjects to take up the defence of their interests ; it is a reasoning, calculating, and prosaic morality. The morality of the Utilitarians is their economic psychology put into the imperative. Disraeli was right when he said that the great fault of the utilitarians was that they wanted that imagination which plays a decisive part in the government of mankind. [3]

(3) It is not difficult to see why such a creed aroused opposition. Its various articles were calculated to offend many different schools of thought as well as many vested interests.   Mill's democratic theories, stated as he stated them in logical and dogmatic form, aroused the opposition of Englishmen of many shades of opinion, who like to think about politics in the traditional empirical fashion.   Their views were voiced in Macaulay's criticism of Mill. [4]   The tone of his criticism was resented by the philosophic radicals [5]—but after all the two antagonists were reconciled.   Macaulay was an admirer of Bentham's qualities as a jurist ; at the crisis of the Reform Act, when the Whigs and radicals came together, he used in one of his speeches one of Mill's arguments from his *Essay on Government* ; [6] and it was due to Mill that he was appointed the first legal member of the Governor-General's Council, and thus given the opportunity to vindicate with remarkable success the feasibility of Bentham's panacea of codification. [7]   On the other hand, Mill showed by the evidence which he gave to Parliament in 1831 and 1832 that on Indian questions he was not so blinded by his democratic dogmas or his economic theories that he had lost all sight of realities.   He

[1] Halévy, Philosophic Radicalism 477.   [2] Ibid 477-478.
[3] " The Utilitarian politics are like the Unitarians' religion ; both omit imagination in their systems, and imagination governs mankind," Monypenny and Buckle, Life of Disraeli (Res. ed.) i 241.
[4] Mill on Government ; The Westminster Reviewer's Defence of Mill ; the Utilitarian Theory of Government.
[5] J. S. Mill, Autobiography 157.
[6] Halévy, Philosophic Radicalism 421-422.
[7] Leslie Stephen, The English Utilitarians ii 36 ; vol. xi 225 ; Macaulay admitted that Mill had behaved handsomely, and showed his gratitude by not including these papers on Mill in his Essays ; they were included in his miscellaneous works published after his death, Leslie Stephen, op. cit. ii 85.

told Parliament that it was quite impossible to introduce self-government into India, and he defended the commercial monopoly of the East India Company.[1] But there is no doubt that their democratic theories did not make them popular—"they liked the people but the people did not like them or their ideas."[2]

Both the agnostic theories and the neo-malthusianism of the philosophic radicals aroused the hostility of all religious sects. At the same time the gross abuses of the factory system, and the misery of the workmen, made their economic theories increasingly unpopular, because those theories assumed that the abuses were inevitable, and denied the right and even the power of the state to give effective redress.[3] On the other hand, Bentham's proposals for law reform received an increasing measure of support from men of all parties. They never aroused the hostility which was excited by the other articles of the creed of the philosophic radicals, largely because, as I have said,[4] they were translated into practice by practical lawyers who adapted them to the existing legal system. Naturally Mill's philosophical theories[5] aroused the hostility of the opposite school of philosophic thought which denies that all truths are simply generalized experience, and asserts that our reason enables us to grasp intuitively truths, such as the truths of religion and moral laws, which are not cognizable by the senses.[6] For as J. S. Mill points out :

The difference between these two schools of philosophy, that of Intuition and that of Experience and Association, is not a mere matter of abstract speculation ; it is full of practical consequences, and lies at the foundation of all the greatest differences of practical opinion in an age of progress. The practical reformer has continually to demand that changes be made in things that are supported by powerful and widely spread feelings, or to question the apparent necessity and indefeasibleness of established facts ; and it is often an indispensable part of his argument to show how those powerful feelings had their origin ; and how these facts came to seem necessary and indefeasible. There is therefore a natural hostility between him and a philosophy which discourages the explanation of feelings and moral facts by circumstances and association, and prefers to treat them as ultimate elements of human nature ; a philosophy which is addicted to holding up favourite doctrines as intuitive truths, and deems intuition to be the voice of Nature and of God, speaking with an authority higher than that of our reason.[7]

[1] Leslie Stephen, op. cit. ii 35-36 ; D.N.B.
[2] Bagehot, Literary Studies (Silver Library ed.) iii 391.
[3] Above 140.   [4] Above 127.   [5] Above 141, 142.
[6] Mill, Dissertations and Discussions i 405 ; as Mill says, ibid, " it is not necessary to remind anyone who concerns himself with such subjects, that between the partisans of these two opposite doctrines there reigns a *bellum internecinum*. Neither side is sparing in the imputation of intellectual and moral obliquity to the perceptions, and of pernicious consequences to the creed, of its antagonists. Sensualism is the common term of abuse for the one philosophy, mysticism for the other."
[7] Autobiography 273-274.

This school of philosophy, Mill thought, was "the great intellectual support of false doctrines and bad institutions"; for it enabled men to dispense with the necessity of justifying their conclusions by reason.[1]

As we shall now see, these various elements of opposition to the new ideas which made up the articles of the creed of the philosophic radicals, were producing an opposition which, in order to make itself effective, was developing and transforming its own ideas upon many of the topics comprised in these articles. Just as these new ideas were creating a liberal and a radical party from the different sections of the old Whig party, so this opposition was creating a conservative party from the old Tory party.

The Opposition to the New Ideas

Some of the new ideas of Bentham and the philosophic radicals became the most influential of the ideas which guided reforming movements of different kinds in the second and third decades of the nineteenth century. But these ideas necessarily aroused considerable opposition both from those who denied the necessity for some or all of these reforms, and from those who thought that some or all of these reforms should go further or should take a different shape. In other words, they were criticized by opponents both of the right and the left wing. Of some of the socialistic and communistic critics of the left wing I have already spoken.[2] At this point I shall deal very shortly with some of the critics of the right wing. I shall describe the extent to which the discussion of the new ideas had compelled them to think out a reasoned opposition; and how, on the basis of the old ideas and traditions and institutions, they had begun to construct a new conservative creed, which, while admitting the need for some reforms, differed fundamentally from the opposing creed in the sort of reforms which were desirable, and rejected most of the principles upon which, and the methods by which, the believers in the opposing creed proposed to proceed in making those reforms which all thinking men saw were needed.

It is no doubt true that the utilitarian system had no "clear and assignable rival,"[3] and that the Tory or conservative party had no definite philosophy.[4] But both abroad and in England there was a definite reaction against the rationalistic philosophy of the eighteenth century, because it had led men to destroy or to advocate the destruction of, not only obvious abuses, but also many things which many rightly prized.

Abroad "the disillusionment brought about by the excesses

---

[1] Autobiography 225-226.
[3] Leslie Stephen, The English Utilitarians ii 362.
[2] Above 40.
[4] Ibid ii 366.

of the French Revolution brought discredit on the cult of reason as preached by the Terrorists." [1] The revival of national feeling, and, with it, the revival of patriotic pride in the nation's history, and the revival of religious beliefs, set in motion " a tide of romantic reaction," which made for " a restoration of organic ties broken by the sacrilegious violence of rationalistic reformers." [2] This romantic revival had many repercussions and influenced many different branches of learning. [3] In all it tended to emphasize the historical point of view. In law its most remarkable effect was the rise of Savigny's historical school. [4] We have seen that Bentham poured scorn on that school ; [5] and it was inevitable that he should do so ; for it stood for a wholly different manner of regarding law from his. As Vinogradoff has said, [6] that school regarded law,

not in its formal aspect as the command of a sovereign, but in its material content as the opinion of the country on matters of right and justice. Instead of being traced to the deliberate will of the legislator, its formation was assigned to the gradual working of customs, the proper function of legislation being limited to the declaration of an existing state of legal consciousness, and not as the creation of new rules by individual minds. As regards the State, law was assumed to be an antecedent condition, not a consequence of its activity. In this way direct legislation was thrust into the background, while customary law was studied with particular interest and regarded as the genuine manifestation of popular consciousness.

England felt the same influences as the continent. Sir Walter Scott typically demonstrated the sway wielded by the romantic and historical influences.

He loves with his whole heart the institutions rooted in the past and rich in historical associations. He transferred to poetry and pictures the political doctrine of Burke. To him the revolutionary movement was simply a solvent, corroding all old ties because it snapped the old traditions, and tended to substitute a mob for a nation. [7]

Southey, in his *Colloquies on Society*, [8] takes a substantially similar view. The spectacle of the new industrial society, thinking only of accumulating wealth, with no care for the thousands of workers growing up in the slums of the industrial towns, without religion and without a definite place in the social order, and indifferent to the cruelties inflicted on children in the factories, led him to doubt whether, in spite of all the discoveries of science, there had been any material progress. The state, he thought, should

---

[1] Vinogradoff, Outlines of Historical Jurisprudence i 124.
[2] Ibid 125.   [3] Ibid 126-127.   [4] Ibid 128-129.
[5] Above 107, 118.   [6] Outlines of Historical Jurisprudence i 129.
[7] Leslie Stephen, The English Utilitarians ii 367.
[8] For an account of this book see ibid ii 109-114 ; Dicey, Law and Opinion 215-2215, 2232-2234.

educate, should teach sound religious principles, should aid schemes of colonization and any other schemes likely to improve the condition of the people. And at this point Southey was in agreement with some of the critics of the left wing. He approved of many of the schemes of Owen—though he differed entirely from him as to the place which religion should take in the state.[1] Macaulay, taking the popular *laissez faire* attitude of the philosophic radicals, mocked at these ideas;[2] and, in truth, much of Southey's history and many of his suggested remedies laid him open to legitimate criticism. But both his religious beliefs and his knowledge of history led him to see many things to which Macaulay was blind; and so, in spite of Macaulay's criticisms, he is to us "the prophetic precursor of modern collectivism."[3] Men like Oastler, Sadler (Macaulay's literary and political opponent), and Ashley (afterwards Lord Shaftesbury), agreed with Southey in their detestation of the principle of *laissez faire* and their denunciation of the iniquity of child labour in the factories.[4]

Southey had been a Jacobin in his youth because he sympathised with the poor and oppressed, so that, when the excesses of the French Revolution disgusted him with the revolution movement, he naturally became a Tory who opposed revolutionary principles on humanitarian lines. Wordsworth also was in his youth an enthusiastic admirer of the French Revolution. But, as Napoleon's star rose, he began to see that France was the enemy of the liberties of the nations of Europe. And so he too became a Tory, and adopted the creed of Burke. As Dicey has said,[5]

You can hardly give higher praise to Burke than the statement that his teaching freed Wordsworth, and thousands of other Englishmen with him, from revolutionary sophisms and delusions; you cannot better sum up the peculiarity of Wordsworth's political creed than by the statement that he imbibed the best truth which Burke could teach, and yet at the same time retained unshaken that complete faith in freedom, and that hope of human progress, which formed the truest part of the revolutionary dogmas.

[1] Leslie Stephen, The English Utilitarians ii 112-113.
[2] Essay on Southey's Colloquies.
[3] Dicey, Law and Opinion 224, and see ibid 214 n.
[4] Ibid 224-231.
[5] The Statesmanship of Wordsworth 67; as Dicey points out, ibid 108, "The ideals of the Whigs were, many of them, such as Wordsworth could not possibly have accepted; they were hostile to the local liberties and the local traditions which he valued above all things. The Whigs cared for nothing in the life of the country but the development of its industries. The Benthamites, and in later days the Manchester School, were opposed to Wordsworth's ideals, and even in the matter of foreign policy, by the interpretation they put on the duty of non-intervention, went very near to denying the duty of England, which he had preached with so much fervour, to interpose for the protection of any small state whose independence was menaced by the gigantic power of some great and well armed neighbour."

The Oxford Movement was primarily a protest against the anti-church and anti-religious views of the radical party; and it enforced its views as to the position and duties of the church by an appeal to history. Because it was a religious movement within the Church of England, it added strength to the forces of conservatism and helped to forward the views of Southey, Wordsworth, and Coleridge.[1]

Thomas Carlyle, another opponent of the creed of philosophic radicalism, who was outside all the churches, was beginning his literary career at the end of this period. As the authors of the standard life of Disraeli have truly said:[2]

Newman, Carlyle, and Disraeli were far different figures; but, little as they may have known it, they were in a sense spiritual brethren, engaged in a desperate fight against a common enemy, working in their several ways with a common purpose. Beneath a thousand superficial differences they all three had the same romantic temperament; all three had in them something of the artist; and all three were deeply imbued with that historical sentiment which is the fatal enemy of Benthamism, as of every kind of system-mongering.

In fact we shall see that Disraeli had also much in common with Coleridge.[3]

Disraeli belongs to the following period; and it was then also that Carlyle's influence was at its height. But Carlyle's protests against the dominant philosophical, political, and economic ideas began in this period, so that he can be reckoned as one of the forces which helped to create an effective opposition to them. Though it is difficult to construct any very positive creed from Carlyle's eloquent and sometimes hysterical denunciations of ideas and tendencies which he disliked, it is not difficult to construct a negative creed. He used his great literary and historical gifts to oppose the utilitarian, economic, democratic, and scientific ideas of his day. He enforced the lesson that

we are not entitled to regard ourselves as the centres of the universe; that we are but atoms of space and time, with relations infinite beyond our personalities; that the first step to a real recognition of our duties is the sense of our inferiority to those above us, our realization of the continuity of history and life, our faith and acquiescence in some universal law.[4]

A mystic and a believer in the inequality of man, he stressed the absurdities and dangers of the democratic creed, and the duty of loyalty to the strong man who could rule. And his protests against the social conditions which resulted from the acceptance

---

[1] See R. W. Church, The Oxford Movement 107, 147-149; for Coleridge see below.

[2] Monypenny and Buckle, Life of Disraeli (Rev. ed.) i 301.   [3] Below 154.

[4] John Nichol, Thomas Carlyle (English Men of Letters) 190.

of the *laissez faire* doctrines of the economists helped to rouse the country to insist that the state should take a larger view of the scope of its duties, and so seconded the humanitarian protests against some of the iniquitous consequences of the new industrial system.[1] Though he did not succeed in stemming the tide of democracy, though scientific discovery continued its task of transforming the physical world, he seconded powerfully the efforts of those who, in opposition to the dominant political and economic ideas of the day, were stressing the claims of the individual, and of those who, in the light of history, saw in the state and society something more than a body of persons who had united merely to promote the greatest happiness of the greatest number of its existing members.

The most important of the opponents of the new ideas embodied in the creed of the philosophic radicals was Coleridge ; for his opposition was founded, as the creed of the philosophic radicals was founded, on a philosophy. He was the great exponent of the intuitionist school of philosophy, as the two Mills were of the school of experience and association.[2] It is for this reason that he played so great a part in transforming the old Tory into the new Conservative party. As J. S. Mill has said :[3]

He has been the great awakener in this country of the spirit of philosophy within the bounds of traditional opinions. He has been, almost as truly as Bentham, the great questioner of things established ; for a questioner needs not necessarily be an enemy. By Bentham beyond all others, men have been led to ask themselves, in regard to any ancient and received opinion, Is it true ? and by Coleridge, What is the meaning of it ? The one took his stand *outside* the received opinion, and surveyed it as an entire stranger to it : the other looked at it from within, and endeavoured to see it with the eyes of a believer in it ; to discover by what apparent facts it was at first suggested, and by what appearances it has ever since been rendered continually credible—has seemed, to a succession of persons, to be a faithful interpretation of their experience. Bentham judged a proposition true or false as it accorded or not with the result of his own enquiries ; and did not search very curiously into what might be meant by the proposition, when it obviously did not mean what he thought true. With Coleridge, on the contrary, the very fact that any doctrine had been believed by thoughtful men, and received by whole nations or generations of mankind, was part of the problem to be solved, was one of the phenomena to be accounted for.

Coleridge, like Southey and Wordsworth, welcomed the outbreak of the French Revolution ; and, like them, came to be the bitter opponent of the principles upon which it was supported. But his opposition was based upon different and more far-reaching principles, because he was essentially a philosopher, and a

[1] See Dicey, Law and Opinion 215-216.
[2] See above 143 for these two schools of philosophy.
[3] Dissertations and Discussions i 393-394.

philosopher of the intuitionist school, who also believed that the essential doctrines of the Christian religion were the ultimate truths upon which all philosophy should rest. We are not concerned with the reasoning by which Coleridge arrived at his philosophical creed. But we are concerned with the practical conclusions upon the political questions of the day which he drew from it, and with the reasoning by which he established them, because these conclusions and this reasoning united and based upon intelligible principles the various elements of opposition to the dominant utilitarian creed of the philosophic radicals. It is because they did for the opponents to Bentham's creed what James Mill and the philosophic radicals had done for its exponents,[1] that J. S. Mill rightly regarded Bentham and Coleridge as the two protagonists in the conflict of ideas.

A short account of Coleridge's ideas upon history, religion, politics, and economics will illustrate the intellectual basis of his opposition to the utilitarian creed, and indicate the nature of the debt which the new Conservative party owes to him.[2]

History is not to Coleridge, as it was to Bentham, merely a collection of instances which proved the folly of men who ignored the teachings of his philosophy.[3] Coleridge regarded history as the only means by which the spirit, or the " idea," as he called it, of any given institution or rule of law could be grasped. Expediency might be all very well as a guide to the routine of conduct in the daily life of an organized society :[4]

But whence did this happy organization first come ? Was it a tree transplanted from Paradise with all its branches in full fruitage ? Or was it sowed in sunshine ? Let history answer these questions. With blood was it planted ; it was rocked in tempests ; the goat, the ass, and the stag gnawed it ; the wild boar has whetted his tusks on its bark. The deep scars are still extant on its trunk, and the path of the lightning may be traced among its higher branches. Mightier powers were at work than expediency ever yet called up, yea, mightier than the mere understanding can comprehend.[5]

We cannot, for instance, understand the British constitution without history because " a constitution is an idea arising out of the idea of a state ; and because our whole history from Alfred onwards demonstrates the continued influence of such an idea." [6] Nor can we understand its various parts or suggest wise measures of reform without a knowledge of the ideas at their back, which only a knowledge of history can give.

---

[1] Above 135, 136, 138.
[2] In my illustration of Coleridge's views on these matters I have used R. J. White's Political Thought of Coleridge ; my quotations from Coleridge's works are taken from Mr. White's selection from Coleridge's works.
[3] Above 80.   [4] White, op. cit. 94.
[5] Ibid 95.   [6] Ibid 37.

How fine, for example, is the idea of the unhired magistracy of England, taking in and linking together the duke to the country gentleman in the primary distribution of justice, or in the preservation of order and execution of law at least throughout the country ! [1] Yet some men never seem to have thought of it for one moment, but as connected with brewers and barristers and tyrannical Squire Westerns. The corruptions of a system can be duly appreciated by those only who have contemplated the system in that ideal state of perfection exhibited by the reason. . . . Those, on the other hand, who commence the examination of a system by identifying it with its abuses or imperfections, degrade their understanding into the pander of their passions, and are sure to prescribe remedies more dangerous than the disease. [2]

It follows that a knowledge of history is needed for true statesmanship. Without it measures of policy will be " either a series of anachronisms or a truckling to events, substituted for the science that should commend them ; for all true insight is foresight." [3]

Religion, Coleridge holds, is absolutely necessary both for the stability of the state and as a guide to individual action. It is necessary for the stability of the state because its teachings will help to alleviate the lot of the poor, to improve their minds, and to fit them to rise in the social scale. [4] It is necessary as a guide to individual action because to base actions on a calculation of consequences is a very perilous course. No one has perfect foresight even if he is undisturbed by passion. " The intervention of accidents ' between the cup and lip ' is the subject of a hundred proverbs in all languages, and our incapacity for praying wisely for any particular object of our desire among the primary articles of all rational religions." [5] This religion ought to be taught by a national church. By a national church Coleridge meant " a permanent, nationalized, learned order," " a national clerisy." [6] Such an order was, in the days of Elizabeth, regarded as the third estate of the realm. Of its members,

A certain smaller number were to remain at the fountainheads of the humanities, in cultivating and enlarging the knowledge already possessed, and in watching over the interests of physical and moral science ; being likewise the instructors of such as constituted, or were to constitute, the remaining more numerous class of the order. This latter and far more numerous body were to be distributed throughout the country, so as not to leave the smallest integral part or division without a resident guide, guardian, and instructor ; the objects and final intention of the whole order being these—to preserve the stores, to guard the treasures, of past civilization, and thus to bind the present with the past ; to perfect and add to the same, and thus to connect the present with the future ; but especially to diffuse through the whole community, and to every native entitled to its laws and rights, that quantity and quality of knowledge which was indispensable both for the understanding of those rights and for the performance of the duties correspondent. [7]

---

[1] This was the view taken by Bacon, Spedding, Letters and Life of Bacon vi 303 ; cited vol i 291-292.

[2] White, op. cit. 139.   [3] Ibid 101.   [4] Ibid 42-43.
[5] Ibid 125.   [6] Ibid 96.   [7] Ibid 165.

If the property of this national clerisy had not been wrongfully alienated by Henry VIII, it would have been able to maintain universities, to maintain a parson in every parish who would be a centre of civilization and a link between all classes in the parish, to maintain a school master in every parish, and to maintain an organization for the relief of the infirm poor.[1] Those who would refuse the benefits of education to the poor are acting on the principle " that the *status belli* is the natural relation between the people and the government." [2] Such an idea is as foolish as it is dishonest. " The Philistines had put out the eyes of Samson, and thus as they thought fitted him to drudge and grind. But his darkness added to his fury without diminishing his strength, and the very pillars of the temple of oppression he tugged, he shook, till down they came." [3] Coleridge admits that these functions of the national church were most inadequately fulfilled. The Church of England had clung to the court instead of cultivating the people. It did not act as a mediator between the people and the government, between rich and poor, and so " the hearts of the common people are stolen from it." [4]

The basis of Coleridge's political thinking was his view that " the subjects of Christian Government should be taught that neither historically or morally, in fact or by right, have men made the State ; but that the State, and that alone, makes them men." [5] The aim of the state should be to make them civilized men. To do this it must not only protect person and property, it must also make the means of subsistence more easy for its citizens, secure to them a chance to better their condition, and develop their moral and rational faculties.[6] But how should a state be organized in order to attain these objects ? It could not be organized as a pure democracy—only a church which looks at men entirely as individuals could be so organized.[7] The state must be organized so as to give due weight to the interests of various sorts of property and to the claims of ability.[8] Due weight must be given to maintaining the balance between the landed interest and other forms of property ;[9] but, as a general rule, the claims of mere intellect, unaccompanied by property, should not be regarded. Otherwise " political power might be conferred as an honorarium or privilege on having passed through all the forms in the National Schools."[10] The wiser course was to allow intellect the opportunity to acquire property, for then " intellectual power will be armed with political power only when it has previously been combined with and guarded by the moral qualities of prudence, industry, and self-control."[11] Coleridge has no use for a class of mere intellectuals.

[1] White, op. cit. 171-173. [2] Ibid 223. [3] Ibid 223-224.
[4] Ibid 239. [5] Ibid 215. [6] Ibid 152. [7] Ibid 154.
[8] Ibid 160. [9] Ibid 178. [10] Ibid 177. [11] Ibid.

He did not object to Parliamentary reform. He admitted that it was necessary if the balance between the various interests in the nation had altered.[1] He did not object to the Reform Act of 1832 because it extended the franchise,[2] but because it reconstructed the House of Commons, not on the principle of a representation of interests, but on the principle of a delegation of men.[3] That principle, he held, led straight to universal suffrage, and the logical consequence of the principle of universal suffrage was Communism.[4] Property, and a proper representation of various kinds of property, were the principles upon which the state should be organized. But it should be noted that Coleridge held strongly that property was a trust.

When shall we return to a sound conception of the right to property— namely as being official, implying and demanding the performance of commensurate duties? Nothing but the most horrible perversion of humanity and moral justice, under the spacious name of political economy, could have blinded men to this truth as to the possession of land—the law of God having connected indissolubly the cultivation of every rood of earth with the maintenance and watchful labour of men. But money, stock, riches by credit, transferable and convertible at will, are under no such obligations; and, unhappily, it is from the selfish, autocratic possession of *such* property, that our landowners have learnt their present theory of trading with that which was never meant to be an object of commerce.[5]

The current must be reversed. " Our manufacturers must consent to regulations."[6] All classes of property owners must recognize the duties which the ownership of property imposes.[7]

In the sphere of economics Coleridge saw many things to which the classical economists were blind:

You talk about making this article cheaper by reducing its price in the market from 8d. to 6d. But suppose, in so doing, you have rendered your country weaker against a foreign foe; suppose you have demoralized thousands of your fellow-countrymen, and have sown discontent between one class of society and another, your article is tolerably dear, I take it, after all.[8]

With some justice he ascribed the economic evils of the time, and the industrial distress and consequent unrest, to an " overbalance of the commercial spirit in consequence of the absence or weakness of the counterweights "[9]—such counterweights as

---

[1] White, op. cit. 178-179.
[2] Ibid 230—In fact he advocated votes for women, ibid 242.
[3] Ibid 229. [4] Ibid 121. [5] Ibid 163-164. [6] Ibid 209.
[7] " Our gentry must concern themselves in the education as well as in the instruction of their natural clients and dependents, must regard their estates as secured indeed from all human interference by every principal of law and policy; but yet as officers of trust, with duties to be performed in the sight of God and their country," ibid.
[8] Ibid 223.   [9] Ibid 194.

obligations of rank and ancestry, the decline of the study of philosophy, the waning influence of religion.[1] Coleridge here joined hands with Southey and other humanitarians[2] in denouncing the evils which flowed from so exclusive a regard to the purely economic point of view that the interests of the hands who tilled the land or who worked in the factories were wholly disregarded. No doubt the power and prosperity of the country had increased ; and it was said that though suffering might be caused by bad times, yet in the long run things found their level.[3]   But

persons are not things—but man does not find his level. After a hard and calamitous season, during which the thousand wheels of some vast manufactory had remained silent as a frozen waterfall, be it that plenty has returned and that trade has once more become brisk and stirring ; go, ask the overseer, and question the parish doctor, whether the workman's health and temperance with staid and respectful manners best taught by the inward dignity of conscious self-support, have found their level again ? Alas ! I have more than once seen a group of children in Dorsetshire, during the heat of the dog-days, each with its little shoulders up to its ears, and its chest pinched inward, the very habit and pictures, as it were, that had been impressed on their frames by the former ill-fed, ill-clothed, and unfuelled winters.[4]

And such suffering had even worse effects on the minds of all classes—both on the poor and the rich.[5] Malthusianism, which taught that this suffering was inevitable, he regarded as the most abominable tenet that had ever been preached.[6] Another evil result of this new political economy was its tendency to " denationalize," " to make love of our country a foolish superstition."[7]

The essence of Coleridge's teaching was to be found in Burke,[8] whom he recognized as " a scientific statesman and therefore a seer."[9] His political teaching was in fact an application of Burke's principles to the needs and intellectual conditions of his day ; for just as Burke had protested against the deductions drawn from the *a priori* philosophy of Rousseau, so Coleridge protested against the deductions drawn from the *a priori* philosophy of Bentham and the philosophic radicals.[10]

[1] White, op. cit. 195-197.   [2] Above 147, 148.
[3] White, op. cit. 188.   [4] Ibid 189.
[5] " But, as with the body, so or still worse with the mind. Nor is the effect confined to the labouring classes. . . . I cannot persuade myself that the frequency of failures, with all the disgraceful secrets of fraud and folly, of unprincipled variety in expending and desperate speculation in retrieving, can be familiarized to the thoughts and experience of men as matters of daily occurrence without serious injury to the moral sense," White, op. cit. 189.
[6] Table Talk, Aug. 12, 1832.
[7] Ibid 222 ; cp. Table Talk, Jan 20, 1834.
[8] For Burke's principles see vol. x 93-97.   [9] White, op. cit. 237.
[10] Feiling in his paper on Coleridge and the English Conservatives at p. 73 (in the volume edited by Hearnshaw entitled Social and Political Ideas of the Age of Reaction and Reconstruction) contrasts Burke with Coleridge in the use which

J. S. Mill was quite right when he said that Coleridge's philo-sophy " expressed the revolt of the human mind against the philosophy of the eighteenth century " ;[1] and that the great defect of the opposite school of philosophy was its failure to appreciate what it owed to the past.[2] Because the philosophers of Bentham's school looked only at individuals living in the organized states familiar to them, they failed to recognize the need for, and the effect of, the discipline exercised by the state upon its citizens ; the need for a feeling of loyalty to the state and its fundamental institutions ; and the need for the feeling of a common nationality in order to create a community of interest amongst its members.[3] The philosophers of Coleridge's school, by restoring history to its proper place in social studies, secured the recognition of the fact that history, " by unfolding the agencies which have produced and still maintain the present," affords " the only means of predicting and guiding the future." [4] Mill pointed out that it was a mistake to think that Coleridge was an enemy to reform. On the contrary he elucidated the true meaning and purpose of established institutions, and advocated the reforms needed to enable them to fulfil that purpose.[5] Mill was a wise statesman and a true prophet when he pointed out that the best chance of effective reform was to educate con-servatives " to adopt one liberal opinion after another as a part of Conservatism itself." [6] It is this process of education, in, which Coleridge took a leading part, that converted the old Tory into the new Conservative party, which, to use Mill's words " rescued from oblivion truths which Tories had forgotten, and which the prevailing school of Liberalism never knew." [7]

they made of history; he says, " with the historical experience of this, or any other question, if designed as the basis of a philosophy, Coleridge had nothing to do " ; this may be true of the basis of Coleridge's philosophy; it is not true of the practical conclusions drawn from that philosophy.

[1] Dissertations and Discussions i 403—" It is ontological, because that was experimental ; conservative, because that was innovative ; religious, because so much of that was infidel ; concrete and historical, because that was abstract and metaphysical ; poetical, because that was matter-of-fact and prosaic."

[2] Ibid 424.   [3] Ibid 414-421.   [4] Ibid 427.

[5] Ibid 437-449, 452-458.

[6] Dissertations and Discussions i 466 ; " ' Hush ', said Mr. Tadpole, ' the time has gone by for Tory governments ; what the country requires is a sound Conservative government.' ' A sound Conservative government,' said Taper musingly. ' I understand : Tory Men and Whig measures,' "Disraeli's Coningsby Bk. II chap. vi.

[7] Dissertations and Discussions 465 ; that Coleridge's thought was made the basis of the ideas preached by the new Conservative party can be illustrated by two passages from Disraeli's Coningsby, in Bk. IV chap. xiii Sidonia is made to say, " There has been an attempt to reconstruct society on a basis of material motives and calculations. It has failed. It must ultimately have failed under any circumstances ; its failure in an ancient and densely peopled kingdom was inevitable. How limited is human reason the profoundest enquirers are most conscious " ; in Bk. VII chap. ii Millbank is made to say that it is " by the Church alone that I see any chance of regenerating the national character."

The new ideas as to law reform encountered less opposition than any of the other ideas. We have seen that many of Bentham's ideas were accepted by men of all parties on the continent;[1] and we shall see that this was also true in England in the second and third decades of the nineteenth century. Reforms in the law were so obviously necessary, and Bentham's principle of utility and many of his suggestions based on it, were so obviously reasonable, that they were very generally accepted. But we have seen that Bentham's suggestions were not accepted literally, but were worked into the fabric of English law by learned lawyers.[2] Those lawyers were saturated with that historical tradition which, as I have shown, has been one of the great forces which have made for the continuity of English law.[3] And so the reforms in the law were made by men who unconsciously combined the strong points of the teaching of Bentham and Coleridge. This method of reforming the law has, it is true, made the process of reform slow, but it has had advantages which more than compensate for this defect. By preserving the continuity of English law it has helped to preserve that respect for and trust in the law which, from early periods in our history, has been a marked characteristic of the national character.[4] By ensuring a large measure of agreement as to the substance of the reforms which were desirable, it has put the law to a large extent above party, and so has provided a basis of agreed principles, without which a system of party government is a constant menace to the peace of the state.

We must now turn from the consideration of these new ideas to their effects upon the development of English law, public and private, during this period of transition.

II

The Political and Constitutional Background

In this section I shall give some account of the political and constitutional events of this period, and show how, in the light of the new ideas which I have just described, they have influenced the development of English constitutional law. The period, both naturally and chronologically, can be divided into the following three parts : from 1793 to the death of Pitt in 1806 ; from 1806 to the close of the war with France in 1815 ; from 1815 to the passing of the Reform Act in 1832. Having dealt with the political and constitutional events of the period under these three heads, I

---

[1] Above 107, 108, 127.   [2] Above 127.   [3] Vol. xii 415-417.
[4] Vol. ii 417, 435-436, 477 ; vol. v 435-436, 444.

shall, in conclusion, say something of the Reform Act of 1832 and its constitutional effects.

From 1793 to the death of Pitt in 1806

Until late in 1792 Pitt believed that England could be kept out of the European war against the French Revolution.[1] But all over England passions were being roused and sides taken in the war of ideas which the outbreak of the Revolution had let loose. Burke's *Reflections*[2] and Paine's *Rights of Man*[3] were circulating in thousands ; and Tory and Radical societies and pamphlets and newspapers fanned the flame. Some of the radical societies began, as we shall see, to correspond with the French Clubs,[4] and after the arrival of the *emigrés* and expelled priests, radical demonstrations of sympathy with the Revolution produced Tory riots, in one of which Priestley's house at Birmingham was wrecked.[5] The September massacres in 1792, and the assembly or projected assembly of conventions in England, Scotland, and Ireland, to fraternize with the French, increased the tension.[6] In the following November the French, in defiance of treaties, declared that by the law of nature the navigation of the Scheldt was freely open to all, and offered to help all peoples who wished to recover their liberty.[7] In these circumstances the government issued a proclamation against seditious writings,[8] which the opposition stigmatized as unnecessary, malicious, and calumnious,[9] prosecuted Paine, who, as we have seen, was condemned in absence ;[10] and embodied part of the militia.[11] Though for a short time the government made little use of the proclamation against seditious writings,[12] prosecutions for sedition and seditious libel soon followed ;[13] for Pitt had come to believe

---

[1] In his budget speech of February 1792, Pitt had said, " There never was a time in the history of this country when from the situation of Europe we might not more reasonably expect fifteen years of peace than at the present moment," and he reduced taxation and the vote for seamen, Rosebery, Pitt 121 ; as late as November 1792 he hoped to keep out of the war, and to mediate between France and her enemies, ibid 122 ; cp. Feiling, The Second Tory Party 186.

[2] Above 13.   [3] Above 17.   [4] Below 159, 160.

[5] For a debate on these riots in which the supineness of the magistrates was attacked unsuccessfully see Parlt. Hist. xxix 1431-1436 ; for an account of the trials arising out of the riots see Romilly, Memoirs (ed. 1842) i 339-343.

[6] Feiling, The Second Tory Party 189.   [7] Ibid 190.

[8] Parlt. Hist. xxix 1477-1478.

[9] See Grey's speech ibid 1480-1489.   [10] Above 18.

[11] Feiling, The Second Tory Party 191.

[12] Davis, Age of Grey and Peel 76-77 ; Davis points out the government did not oppose Fox's Libel Act ; but this may well be because it thought that it would be easier to get convictions under the new law—as indeed it was, vol. x 693.

[13] R. v. Frost (1793) 22 S.T. 471 ; R. v. Eaton (1793) 22 S.T. 753, 785 ; R. v. Winterbotham (1793) 22 S.T. 823 ; R. v. Briellat (1793) 22 S.T. 909 ; R. v. Lambert (1793) 22 S.T. 953 ; R. v. Hudson (1793), 22 S.T. 1019 ; R. v. Holt (1793), 22 S.T. 1189 ; R. v. Eaton (1794) 23 S.T. 1013—the accused was in this case acquitted ; Trevelyan, Lord Grey of the Reform Bill 77.

in the existence of a widespread conspiracy to overturn the government.[1] It was probably for this reason that he declined to interfere with the iniquitous sentences passed upon Muir and Palmer in 1793.[2] In January 1793 Louis XVI was executed, and on February 1 France declared war.

The French Revolution had already, as we have seen, divided the Whig party.[3] In 1792 negotiations were begun by the government to take in the section of the Whig party who were opposed to the Revolution—the ' Old Whigs.' But it was not till 1794 that a coalition was effected,[4] and four of their number entered the government.[5] The section of the Whigs who still welcomed the Revolution—the " New Whigs "—were a very small party. It was led by Fox, and it included Grey and Sheridan. The result was that the opposition to Pitt was reduced to very small dimensions.[6] Pitt himself abandoned most of his liberal principles. When Grey in 1792 gave notice of motion for Parliamentary reform, and advocated it on the ground that reform would increase the confidence of the people in the House,[7] Pitt opposed him on the ground that, though he favoured a moderate reform on which all parties could agree, reform was then unnecessary, and it was " not a time to make hazardous experiments." [8] He feared that " the motion for a reform was nothing more than the preliminary to the overthrow of the whole system of our present government ; and if they succeeded they would overthrow what he thought the best constitution that was ever formed on the habitable globe." [9] He opposed a similar motion by Grey in 1793,[10] and still more decidedly another motion by Grey in 1797, which proposed to introduce household franchise and electoral districts for all but county members.[11] Pitt did not, it is true, abandon all his liberal sympathies. He consistently supported Wilberforce's motions for the abolition of the slave trade ; and in 1796, moved by the misery of the poorer classes[12] he tried to pass a poor law bill which provided for parish schools, relief for the aged and sick, allowances for children, supplements to wages, money to purchase for poor persons who had rights of common " a cow or other animal yielding profit," the apprenticing

---

[1] Rosebery, Pitt 166-167.
[2] In the debate on their trials in 1794, Parlt. Hist. xxx 1486 seqq. Pitt at pp. 1572-1576 defended the legality of the trials and the sentences ; of Muir's trial Romilly wrote to Dumont that he was not surprised that he was shocked, and he said, " You would have been more shocked if you had been present at it as I was ", Memoirs ii 23 cited Davis, Age of Grey and Peel 83 n. 1.
[3] Vol. x 124 ; above 13, 16.
[4] Davis, Age of Grey and Peel 38-39.
[5] Portland, Fitzwilliam, Spencer and Windham.
[6] Davis, Age of Grey and Peel 39-40.
[7] Parlt. Hist. xxix 1301.
[8] Ibid 1311.   [9] Ibid 1312.
[10] Ibid xxx 890-902.
[11] Ibid xxxiii 644-681.
[12] Rosebery, Pitt 169.

of poor children. Large powers were given to justices, wardens,
and guardians to carry out the provisions of the Act. They were
given powers to employ, and powers to buy raw material and sell
the manufactured article.[1] But the bill aroused the opposition of
Bentham who criticized both its policy and its draftsmanship,[2]
and the hostility of the economists who believed in *laissez faire* :
and so it was ultimately dropped. But Pitt opposed all large
measures of reform. And there is no doubt that this policy
commanded the approval of the majority of Englishmen.
Romilly had published some essays which advocated a democratic system of Parliament, but the excesses of the French
revolutionists caused him to burn all copies which had not been
sold.[3] It is true that among the educated the Nonconformists and
Unitarians furnished some supporters of the Revolution—men
like Priestley and Price and Robert Hall ; and there were groups
of advanced thinkers such as Horne Tooke, Mary Wollstonecraft,
the advocate of women's rights,[4] and, in the early stages of the
Revolution, Wordsworth, Southey, and Coleridge.[5] It is true
that among the lower classes many, taught by Paine, were firm
believers in the rights of man. But they were not the majority.
As we have seen, loyalist mobs destroyed Priestley's house ;[6]
and Place testifies that the Acts of 1795 and 1799 which destroyed
societies like the Corresponding Society, were popular even
amongst the mass of shopkeepers and working men.[7] In the
opinion of many Englishmen " Great Britain was the best
government in Europe, and most responsive to popular demand "[8]
and this opinion was endorsed by foreign observers.[9]

The small but active minority amongst the higher classes who
wished for a moderate reform of Parliament, and the larger
minority amongst the lower classes who wished for revolutionary
changes, frightened the majority. The effect of this fear was, as it
always is, cruelty.

" If," said Romilly in 1808, " any person be desirous of having an adequate
idea of the mischievous effects which have been produced in this country
by the French Revolution and all its attendant horrors, he should attempt
some legislative reform on humane and liberal principles. He will then
find not only what a stupid dread of innovation, but what a savage
spirit, it has infused into the minds of many of his countrymen."[10]

But the natural result of this dread of innovation, and the refusal
to consider any kind of reform, was the growth of a party of

---

[1] Rosebery, Pitt 168-170, parts of the bill are printed by Bentham, Works
viii 440-446.   [2] Ibid ; above 101, 102.
[3] P. C. Scarlett, Memoirs of Lord Abinger 551.
[4] Camb. Mod. Hist. 764-765.
[5] Ibid 765-767 ; above 148.   [6] Above 156.
[7] Graham Wallas, Francis Place 25 n. 1.
[8] Woodward, The Age of Reform 28.   [9] Ibid.
[10] Romilly, Memoirs ii 90.

radical reformers, who, as Romilly said, desired " to try the boldest political experiments, and a distrust and contempt for all moderate reforms." [1] And this war of ideas was made the more acute, and the more dangerous to the peace of the country, by the fact that all these parties had formed associations or societies to forward their views. Of these associations or societies I must say something, because the activities of some of them resulted both in important state trials, and in legislation.

We have seen that in the sixth decade of the eighteenth century the dangers to the constitution arising from the way in which George III and his ministers had used their influence over the House of Commons—dangers which had been made abundantly clear by the attitude of the government on the question of general warrants (1763-1769) and of the House on the question of the Middlesex election (1769)[2]—had given rise to associations and county committees formed to advocate measures of economic and Parliamentary reform.[3] One of these associations was the Society of the Supporters of the Bill of Rights founded in 1769,[4] and another, founded in 1780 by Horne Tooke and Major Cartwright, was the Society for Constitutional Information.[5] The latter society survived till the period of the French Revolution, and, as a result of that event, it began a new period of activity.

In 1792 it held a great dinner at the Crown and Anchor in the Strand to celebrate the fall of the Bastille, it sent addresses to the National Convention and the Jacobin Club, and it reprinted Paine's *Rights of Man*.[6] Its members, says Davis,[7] " Were men of mediocre abilities and politically insignificant ; but they were educated men, possessing some knowledge of constitutional law and some experience of the art of agitation." They were thus very useful to other middle class and popular associations which were springing up in London and the provinces. One of these provincial societies was the Manchester Constitutional Society formed in 1790 to resist the Tory, Church and King Society.[8] The fact that both this society and the Society for Constitutional Information, sent addresses to the Jacobin Club, helped to convince public opinion that their members wanted not reform but revolution. In 1791-1792 a number of provincial societies were formed both in England and Scotland to advocate Paine's principles.[9] It was to link together these societies that the London Corresponding Society was founded by Hardy, a Scotch shoemaker, in January 1792. It was organized in local branches, each of which sent a delegate to an executive committee, which met once a week. In

---

[1] Memoirs ii 537 cited vol. x 19 n. 2.   [2] Vol. x 99-100.
[3] Ibid 102.   [4] Ibid.
[5] Veitch, The Genesis of Parliamentary Reform 71 ; Davis, Age of Grey and Peel 71-72.
[6] Ibid 72.   [7] Ibid 72-73.   [8] Ibid 74.   [9] Ibid 77-79.

November 1792 it sent addresses to the French National Convention, one of which assured the French that the King would not be allowed to use British troops against the French as he was using those of Hanover.[1] In 1792 it issued a manifesto declaring its principles—reform not anarchy, universal suffrage, and a fair and equal representation of the people in Parliament.[2]

In March 1792 another very different society was founded—the Society of the Friends of the People.[3] It had aristocratic leaders—among them were Lords Lauderdale and Grey. Grey in later years lamented his association with this Society;[4] for though it kept strictly to its programme of Parliamentary reform, though it would have nothing to do with Paine's principles, and thought it declined an alliance with the Society for Constitutional Information,[5] it was approved by the Corresponding Society.[6] It was at the request of the Society of the Friends of the People that Grey gave notice of a motion for Parliamentary reform in 1792.[7] His motion was to have been based on a report of a committee of the Society on the state of the representation "which remained until 1832 the great magazine of facts and arguments for reformers of every shade."[8] Other societies of Friends of the People sprang up which were of a much more radical complexion[9]—perhaps Grey was thinking of these societies, and the discredit which they brought upon his Society and upon Whig projects of moderate reform, when he regretted his association with his Society. However that may be, the Society expired in 1795,[10] after adopting the principle of household suffrage, which Grey proposed in his motion for Parliamentary reform in 1797.[11]

In the meantime the Tory opposition had followed the example of these different classes of reformers. Reeves, the historian of English law, founded, as we have seen, an association "for preserving liberty and property against levellers and republicans,"[12] which soon had branches all over England.[13] The association, it was said in the House of Commons, had used

---

[1] Davis, Age of Grey and Peel 79-80; Veitch, The Genesis of Parliamentary Reform 191-193, 195.   [2] Ibid 206.

[3] Davis, Age of Grey and Peel 100-102; Veitch, op. cit. 196-198.

[4] Trevelyan, Lord Grey of the Reform Bill 44-45.

[5] Davis, Age of Grey and Peel 101; but it should be noted that Scott in opening the case against Hardy, R. v. Hardy (1794) 24 S.T. at p. 299, said that though the Friends of the People declined to correspond with the Society for Constitutional Information, they had many common members so that "the work of both societies went on by the same instruments."

[6] Trevelyan, op. cit. 45.

[7] Above 157; Veitch, op. cit. 198; Trevelyan, op. cit. 47.

[8] Ibid 60.   [9] Ibid 46.

[10] Davis, Age of Grey and Peel 102.

[11] Above 157.   [12] Vol. xii 412.

[13] Veitch, Genesis of Parliamentary Reform 231.

methods of intimidation which were discreditable,[1] had got anonymous informations and used them to stir up the government to initiate prosecutions,[2] and, at the trial of Thomas Walker, its agents were shown to have been guilty of something like subornation of perjury.[3] The spread of this association illustrates the widespread fear of the principles advocated by the revolutionary associations, and the hatred which they aroused by reason of their obvious sympathy with the French. In these circumstances the proclamation of the government against seditious writings [4] was a wise attempt to allay that fear. It was attacked, as we have seen, by Grey as a malicious attempt to throw odium upon the Friends of the People.[5] But it is obvious that, though that Society was being confused with other more revolutionary societies, its principles were very different, and it had little to fear from the proclamation.[6]

The outbreak of the war hardened public opinion against the activities of the revolutionary societies. The trials of Muir and Palmer, the animus of the judges, and the severe sentences passed,[7] roused the fears of the Corresponding and other similar Societies. The Corresponding Society sent two delegates—Margarot and Gerrald—to a convention at Edinburgh, and instructed them that it was " the duty of the People to resist any Act of Parliament repugnant to the constitution, as would be every attempt to prohibit associations for the purpose of reform." [8] The convention proceeded to discuss reform, and then defined the various emergencies upon the happening of which a British convention was to be summoned.[9] A secret committee was to determine the place of meeting, which was to remain a secret till the meeting was summoned.[10] Any illegal dispersion of the present convention was to be a signal for a meeting of the British convention.[11] As a result of these resolutions the leaders—Margarot, Gerrald, and Skirving—were tried for sedition, convicted, and transported.[12] These proceedings led the London Corresponding Society to adopt some very dangerous measures. It issued an address in which the Scotch trials and the war were denounced, and resolved that, in case of emergency, a general convention of the people should be summoned.[13] The presenting to Parliament of any bill or measure hostile to the liberties of the people was to

---

[1] Parlt. Hist. xxx 620-621. [2] Ibid 547.

[3] (1794) 23 S.T. 1055, 1105 ; Dunn, the principal witness for the prosecution was committed for perjury, ibid. at p. 1164 ; Davis, Age of Grey and Peel 147.

[4] Above 156. [5] Above 156. [6] Below 165.

[7] Davis, Age of Grey and Peel 81-84 ; Veitch, Genesis of Parliamentary Reform 255-263. [8] Ibid 84.

[9] Ibid 85 ; those emergencies were a foreign invasion, the landing of foreign troops, the passing of a Convention Act, or the suspension of the Habeas Corpus Act. Ibid. [10] Ibid 86.

[11] Ibid. [12] Ibid. [13] Ibid 88.

constitute such an emergency.[1] These resolutions were approved at an open-air meeting at Halifax, a convention at Bristol was proposed,[2] and a London meeting was held at Chalk Farm.[3]

There is little doubt that the resolutions of the Corresponding Society were seditious. But they were clearly not treasonable. Dundas thought that he had evidence of a plot to levy war in Scotland, and of the manufacture of arms for that purpose.[4] Seven persons were tried and convicted in Scotland, and one was executed for treason.[5] But the trials made it clear that there was no widespread plot, and no extensive manufacture of arms. In spite of these facts, the English government resolved to take action against leading members of the Corresponding Society. After hearing two reports from secret committees of the House of Lords and the House of Commons,[6] a bill suspending the right to a writ of Habeas Corpus was passed,[7] and Hardy, Horne Tooke, Thelwall, and ten others were arrested and put on their trial for high treason.

Sir John Scott, the attorney-general, took nine hours to open the prosecution. His speech was rather dull and heavy but it stated the Crown case clearly,[8] and developed with precision the doctrine of constructive treason on which it rested.[9] Erskine's speech for the defence is a far finer forensic effort.[10] In it he disputed the Crown's application of the doctrine of constructive treason,[11] defended the rights of the subject to criticize and suggest reforms in the constitution,[12] and made some devastating criticisms on the evidence of the witnesses called by the Crown[13] and on other evidence offered for the Crown.[14] The effect of his speech on the spectators and the public was so great that " an irresistible acclamation pervaded the court, and to an immense distance round " ; and it was not till he had gone out and addressed the crowd, and asked them to disperse, that it was possible for the judges to get to their carriages.[15] After a long, able, and impartial summing up by Eyre, C. J., which lasted for a day and a half,[16] the jury on the eighth day of the trial, having deliberated for three hours and five minutes, acquitted the accused. The case against Horne Tooke was not so strong as the case against Hardy.[17] He called Pitt and the Duke of Richmond in order to prove that his proposals for Parliamentary reform were not materially different

---

[1] Veitch, Genesis of Parliamentary Reform 88.   [2] Ibid.
[3] See R. v. Hardy (1794) 24 S.T. at pp. 363, 365.
[4] Davis, Age of Grey and Peel 89.
[5] Ibid ; R. v. Watt (1794) 23 S.T. 1167 ; cf. R. v. Downie (1794) 24 S.T. 1.
[6] Parlt. Hist. xxxi 475-497, 688-879 (House of Commons) ; 573-574, 886-903 (House of Lords).   [7] 34 George III c. 54.
[8] (1794) 24 S.T. at pp. 241-370.   [9] Ibid at pp. 252-268.
[10] Ibid at pp. 877-970.   [11] Ibid at pp. 881-911.
[12] Ibid at pp. 913-927.   [13] Ibid at pp. 953-963.
[14] Ibid at pp. 963-965.   [15] Ibid at p. 970 n.
[16] Ibid at pp. 1293-1384.   [17] (1794) 25 S.T. 1.

from theirs ;[1] and there was very little evidence that he had done more than press proposals of this kind. The jury acquitted him after deliberating for only eight minutes.[2] After this acquittal the Crown, except in the case of Thelwall, accepted its defeat, and did not offer any evidence against the other accused, who were therefore acquitted.[3] Thelwall was indicted ; but after a four days' trial he too was acquitted.[4]

There is no doubt that the actions and correspondence of the Corresponding Society and the Society for Constitutional Information laid them open to suspicion. They had corresponded with the Scotch societies, they had designed a British Convention, and they had been in full sympathy with doings of the Scotch societies which had ended in convictions for sedition or for treason. It was by no means clear from their correspondence that they had intended to limit their activities merely to a constitutional agitation for Parliamentary reform. It was by no means clear that they were not in favour of a radical reform, on the model advocated by Paine, which involved the elimination of the King and the House of Lords—a purely democratic representative government which, as the attorney-general said, was wholly opposed to the mixed British constitution.[5] It was by no means clear that their convention was not intended to force these changes upon Parliament. On the other hand, there is little real evidence that they intended to effect their purposes by force of arms. The evidence offered by the Crown to prove this broke down. It was therefore possible for Erskine to contend that there had been nothing more than a constitutional agitation for the reform of Parliament, on radical lines no doubt, but on lines which were no more radical than the scheme proposed by the Duke of Richmond in 1780.[6] I think the evidence shows that rather more than this was intended. The expressions of hostility to the King and the House of Lords, taken in connection with the approbation of Paine's books, are evidence of designs of a seditious character ; and if Hardy had been indicted for a seditious, and not a treasonable, conspiracy he would probably have been convicted.[7] To have convicted him of constructive treason on the evidence offered by the Crown could perhaps be logically defended ; but it would have meant pressing that unpopular doctrine further than it had ever been pressed before.[8] It is well to remember that Thurlow, in the debate on the report of the House of Lords committee, thought that the evidence would only support a charge of sedition.[9]

[1] (1794) 25 S.T. 1.   [2] Ibid.   [3] 25 S.T. 745-748.
[4] Cp. Veitch, Genesis of Parliamentary Reform 316-317.
[5] 24 S.T. at p. 326.   [6] Veitch, Genesis of Parliamentary Reform 70.
[7] Davis, Age of Grey and Peel 89.   [8] Vol. viii 317-318.
[9] " From what he had seen of the report, there were many things that, in his opinion, were seditious, but he did not think that they amounted to any higher crime," Parlt. Hist. xxxi 587.

Why then did the government prosecute for treason and not for sedition ? The main reasons were, I think, these : Public opinion was very hostile to these societies. They were both hated and feared, partly on account of their opinions, and partly on account of their connection with France ; and this hatred and fear was naturally aggravated after the outbreak of war with France. The secret committees of the House of Commons and the House of Lords had endorsed the view that something must be done to stop their activities ; and the result of the Scotch trials gave countenance to the idea that seditious if not treasonable conspiracies were being set on foot by these societies. Coleridge in 1830 said that, in his opinion, the danger of revolution was then a real danger.[1] It may be said, and it has been said, that these fears were foolish because it was absurd to think that a set of working men with no pecuniary backing, and no armed force behind them, could hope to overturn a settled government. That is a retrospective criticism which it is easy to make. The answer given was that France had shown what an active club of deter-mined men could do ;[2] that in England there was no adequate police force to nip in the bud attemps at armed violence ;[3] and that the Gordon riots had shown the power for mischief which even an unarmed mob possessed.[4] The weight of these con-siderations were aggravated by the war mentality of the period ; and the Scotch trials, it might seem to the ministers, had shown that a conviction might be got which would end the activities of these societies, and so, by strengthening the hands of the govern-ment, help them in the prosecution of the war. No doubt it was true that the conditions of revolutionary France were very different from those of England ; no doubt the widespread hatred of revolutionary ideas was quite sufficient to prevent any rising in support of them ; and no doubt the manner in which the Scotch trials were conducted should have prevented any general deductions from their results. But, naturally, it would, in any circumstances, have been difficult for a ministry in the midst of a war and in the face of the opinion of the country and of Parliament to give due weight to these considerations ; and, seeing that the ministers had come to believe in the existence of widespread plots,[5] it was impossible even that any attempt should be made to give weight to these considerations.

There is no doubt, however, that the effect of the acquittals was most salutary. In the first place, the thorough investigation

---

[1] " The Jacobins played the whole game of religion, and morals, and domestic happiness into the hands of the aristocracy. Thank God ! that they did so. England was saved from civil war by their enormous, their providential blundering ", Table Talk, May 8, 1830.

[2] 24 S.T. at pp. 270-272.   [3] Vol. x 143-144.

[4] 24 S.T. at p. 272.   [5] Above 162, 163.

of the activities of the societies did much to show that the fear of them was exaggerated. In the second place, they stopped the attempt to develop and use the doctrine of constructive treason to fetter the discussion of projects of reform. Grey was present during the trials, and wrote to his fiancée :

Of this trial I will say nothing. I have no power to express my abhorrence of the whole proceeding. If this man is hanged there is no safety for any man. Innocence no longer affords protection to a person obnoxious to those in power, and I do not know how soon it may come to my turn.[1]

Grey had no occasion to fear for himself ; for Sir John Scott had drawn a distinction between the activities of Grey's Society of the Friends of the People and those of the Corresponding Society,[2] though he commented on the fact that some of its members were also members of the Society for Constitutional Information.[3] But there is no doubt that Grey was right in thinking that a conviction would have struck a heavy blow against the right of freedom of discussion.

The Corresponding Society held a meeting in St. George's Fields in June 1795, and a petition was drawn up which asked for annual Parliaments, universal suffrage, and peace with France.[4] A second meeting later in the year to protest against the neglect of this petition, was the occasion of the first of the statutes passed to fetter the activities of these societies ;[5] and the fact that the King had been hooted and shot at by an air gun when he went to open Parliament,[6] was the occasion of another statute to strengthen the law of treason.

The first of these statutes was entitled "An Act for the more effectually preventing Seditious Meetings and Assemblies."[7] With certain exceptions, it was made unlawful to hold a meeting of more than fifty persons to petition for the alteration of matters established in church or state, or to discuss grievances in church or state, unless either a notice of the meeting signed by seven householders resident in the place where the meeting was to be held was advertised five days before the meeting, or a notice five days before the meeting was sent to the clerk of the peace.[8] Persons who assembled contrary to the Act, and who did not disperse within an hour of the reading of a proclamation ordering them to disperse, were to be guilty of felony without benefit of clergy.[9] If at any such meeting it was said that the law could be altered otherwise than by the authority of Parliament, or if the

---

[1] Trevelyan, Lord Grey of the Reform Bill 85.
[2] 24 S.T. at p. 298 and cp. p. 365.
[3] Ibid at p. 299 ; above 162.
[4] Davis, Age of Grey and Peel 90.
[5] Ibid 90-91.   [6] Feiling, The Second Tory Party 203.
[7] 36 George III c. 8.   [8] §§ 1 and 2.   [9] §§ 4 and 5.

people were incited to the hatred or contempt of the King or government, the meeting could be ordered to disperse, and if it did not disperse within an hour, those remaining were guilty of felony without benefit of clergy ;[1] and any justices present at a meeting where these things were said, could order the arrest of the guilty members of the meeting.[2] Justices were empowered to attend at these meetings to see that the law was observed, and severe penalties were imposed on those obstructing them in the execution of their duties.[3] Places used for giving lectures upon public grievances or matters relating to the government must be licensed by the justices, and the justices must be allowed admittance to these lectures.[4]

The second of these statutes[5] gave, as we have seen,[6] statutory force to many of the acts which had been held to be treason on the construction of Edward III's statute. It further provided that anyone who, by writing or speeches, stirred up the people to hatred or contempt of the King or his government, was to be guilty of a misdemeanour.[7]

Naturally the opposing parties attacked one another in the press. On the conservative side the wittiest of these productions was the *Anti-Jacobin*. Canning, Frere, the first Lord Granville, George Ellis, and Gifford the first editor of the *Quarterly* " made it their business to show the ridiculous side of the radicals—the swollen head of Paine, or the sponging Godwin." [8] They satirized the friends of France, the ill digested projects for the reform of Parliament,

> Whatever is in France is right ;
> Terror and blood are my delight ;
> Parties with us do not excite
>   Enough rage.
> Our boasted laws I hate and curse,
> Bad from the first, by age grown worse,
> I pant and sigh for universal suffrage.
>
> *The Jacobin.*

> That British Liberty's an empty name,
> Till each fair burgh, numerically free
> Shall choose its Members by the Rule of Three.
>
> *The New Morality.*

---

[1] § 6.   [2] § 7.   [3] §§ 8, 9, 10.   [4] §§ 12, 13, 14, 15, 16.
[5] 36 George III c. 7   [6] Vol. viii 318, 321.
[7] 36 George III c. 7 § 2 ; an Act of 1800, 39, 40, George III c. 93 provided that when the overt Act alleged was the killing of the King or any attempt against his life or person endangering his life, the accused should not have the benefits of the statutes 7, 8, William III c. 3 and 7 Anne c. 21 ; for the first of these statutes see vol. vi 232-234 ; the second was the Act of Union with Scotland which (§ 7) extended the English law of treason to Scotland.
[8] Feiling, The Second Tory Party 201-202.

and the propaganda designed " by the friends of every country but their own " to encourage the Nore mutinies and disaffection in the army.[1] It was this propaganda which induced Pitt to pass in 1798 a law for the better control of the press. In order, as he said, to stop " treasonable slanders and seditious abuse," [2] an Act was passed which required the names of printers, publishers, and proprietors to be registered,[3] and the names and addresses of the printers and publishers to be printed in the paper;[4] and penalized the publication of seditious matter under colour of its being the copy of matter taken from foreign newspapers.[5]

The war went on. It was marked by failures on the continent, for, as Macaulay has said,[6] Pitt did not understand the peculiar character of the war; and by successes at sea. French colonies were acquired, Napoleon's fleet was destroyed at the battle of the Nile (1798), and Sydney Smith compelled the French to retire from Acre (1799). But bad harvests, the pressure of taxation, and the measures taken to man the navy and the army were rendering the war more and more unpopular. Pitt was insulted in the streets, and was convinced that his life was in danger.[7] But he never lost heart, nor did he relax his efforts for peace if an opportunity opened. But his peace overtures were rejected,[8] and an overture from Napoleon in 1799 was also rejected.[9]

After Grey's reform motion had been defeated in 1797 some of the Whig leaders seceded from Parliament. This secession was never complete, and it only lasted for about three years.[10] It was not only a tactical mistake but also a betrayal of Whig principles; for it deprived the nation of all chance of criticizing the government measures, and so of educating the nation.[11] It enabled Pitt to pass without effectual protest measures to suppress the political associations,[12] to restrain the press,[13] and to pass the Combination Acts.[14]

The worst crisis of the war came in 1797-8 at the beginning of this period of Whig secession. There were mutinies of the fleet at Portsmouth and the Nore in 1797, and in 1798 the Irish rebellion broke out.

The naval mutinies gave rise to an Act which made it felony

---

[1] Feiling, The Second Tory Party 202.   [2] Parlt. Hist. xxxiii 1420.
[3] 28 George III c. 78 §§ 1-7.   [4] § 10.   [5] § 24.
[6] Essay on Pitt.   [7] Rosebery, Pitt 167.
[8] Feiling, The Second Tory Party 215.   [9] Rosebery, Pitt 142-146.
[10] Trevelyan, Lord Grey of the Reform Bill, 98-100; Camb. Mod. Hist. ix 676.
[11] " They said it was a protest against Government tyranny, but the floor of the House was the one place in England where that tyranny was not exercised to silence debate. Attacks made on the government in the House could be reported in the newspapers without fear of prosecution," Trevelyan, op. cit. 98-99.
[12] Below 173.   [13] Above n. 3 (this page).
[14] Vol. xi 496-498; below 339, 341.

to attempt to seduce any soldier or sailor from his allegiance,[1] and another Act which made it felony to administer unlawful oaths to persons so seduced.[2] A third Act was passed to restrain intercourse with ships, the crews of which had mutinied, and to give the Admiralty power to accept their submission.[3]

The Irish rebellion was the immediate cause of the Act of Union between Great Britain and Ireland.

We have seen that the Irish rebellion of 1798 was due ultimately to the policy pursued by the government after Ireland had attained legislative independence in 1782.[4]   Influence and corruption were the means used to induce the Irish Parliament to assent to the policy of the English executive ;[5] and because sole reliance was placed on this expedient all projects of Parliamentary reform were opposed.[6] The only concession made—a concession opposed by the Irish Chancellor Fitz-Gibbon (afterwards Lord Clare)—was the Act of 1793 which gave Catholics the vote.[7] After the fusion of the Whig and Tory parties, the Whig Fitz-William was made viceroy. His tenure of office was marked by a series of flagrant indiscretions which amounted to insubordination. Before he left England he was told that no change in the system of governing Ireland must be undertaken, and, in particular, that Fitz-Gibbon the Chancellor must not be removed, and the question of Catholic emancipation must not be raised. But when he got to Ireland he proceeded to remove many of the officials whom Pitt had appointed, and to press for Catholic emancipation. The result was his dismissal—a dismissal in which his Whig friends in the government concurred.[8] The results were disastrous. Fitz-William's actions and declarations had given the Irish the expectation that the system of government was to be completely changed. They naturally thought that he had been removed because he was in favour of reform. " Dublin shut its shutters and went into mourning ; while ardent patriots made up their minds that any amendment must come from France or from an appeal to arms."[9] A period of anarchy ensued. Orange and Catholic associations fought one another, and the society of the United Irishmen, which had quite changed its original character, organized itself on a military basis, and prepared for rebellion in alliance with the French.[10] France sent an expedition under Hoche in 1796 and, if the weather had not prevented a landing, Ireland might well have been lost.[11] The measures taken by the

---

[1] 37 George III c. 70.
[2] 37 George III c. 123 ; amended and extended 52 George III c. 104.
[3] 37 George III c. 71.   [4] Vol. xi 33.
[5] Ibid 32-33.   [6] Ibid 33.   [7] Ibid.
[8] Lecky, History of Ireland iii 238-324 ; Rosebery, Pitt 174-184.
[9] Ibid 185.   [10] Lecky, History of Ireland iii 13-16, iv 250-257.
[11] Ibid iii 522-537.

soldiers and militia added to the confusion by producing reprisals. The rebellion broke out in 1798. "That it was not more formidable may be attributed to two causes. Ulster held aloof, and the French came too late. As it was, the rebellion lasted barely a month, and was both local and partial." [1]

It was the rebellion which made Pitt determined to force a legislative union between England and Ireland, and Cornwallis was sent over as viceroy to effect it. The Irish House of Lords under the leadership of Fitz-Gibbon was ready to accept it ; but when the project was first introduced into the Irish House of Commons it was rejected. [2] Foster the Speaker led the opposition ; and there is no doubt that the opposition represented independent public opinion in Ireland—the opinion of the bar, the bankers, and the merchants. [3] But that was of little avail. The machinery of influence and corruption was set to work.

Between the close of the session of 1799 and the beginning of that of 1800, between June and January, sixty-three seats out of a total of three hundred were vacated. Some of those who held them were cajoled ; some were bribed into office and out of Parliament ; the mass departed because the patrons of their boroughs had been bought over to the Union. [4]

The debating in the House of Commons was on a very high level of oratory and political thinking—particularly the speech of Foster who set himself to answer Pitt's arguments for the Union. [5] In the face of the bought majority, all argument was vain. But, from the purely legal point of view it is interesting to note that it is in the debates on the union that we get the last echoes of the idea that there are some limitations upon the sovereignty of Parliament. [6] Just as in 1793 Fitz-Gibbon had maintained that the extension of the franchise to the Catholics was beyond the competence of Parliament, because it was beyond the power of Parliament to repeal the Act of Supremacy ; [7] so Grattan now contended, [8] as he had contended in 1785, that the Irish Parliament was incompetent to pass an Act of Union.

[1] Rosebery, Pitt 187.
[2] Lecky, History of Ireland v 223-227.   [3] Ibid 181-197.
[4] Rosebery, Pitt 189-190.
[5] Lecky, History of Ireland v 388-394.
[6] For the earlier history of this idea in England see vol. x 527-531 and the references to earlier volumes there cited.
[7] He said, " I consider a repeal of the Act of Supremacy in any of the hereditary dominions of the Crown of Great Britain, to be as much beyond the power of Parliament as a repeal of the Great Charter, or a repeal of the Bill of Rights," Lecky, History of Ireland iii 174.
[8] Ibid v 135-136 ; it may be noted that in the debates on the Act in England some allusion was made to this controversy in the speech of Hobhouse, Parl. Hist. xxxiv 474-476, in which there was some loose talk of the right of resistance; but he in substance admits the competence of Parliament.

The main provisions of the Act of Union[1] are as follows :
From January 1, 1801, the two kingdoms of Great Britain and
Ireland were united under the name of the United Kingdom of
Great Britain and Ireland.[2] The succession to the Crown of the
United Kingdom was to remain as already settled by law.[3] The
United Kingdom was to be represented by one Parliament.[4]
Ireland was to be represented in that Parliament by twenty-
eight lords temporal elected for life from the Irish peerage and
four lords spiritual " by rotation of sessions," who were to sit in the
House of Lords ; and by one hundred commoners, who were to
sit in the House of Commons. Irish peers, other than the representative peers, were to be eligible for election to the House of
Commons by any constituency in Great Britain. So often as any
three Irish peerages became extinct the Crown could create
another Irish peer, until the number of Irish peerages was reduced to one hundred. When that reduction had been effected
the number could be kept up to one hundred.[5] The churches of
England and Ireland were to be " united into one protestant
episcopal church to be called The United Church of England and
Ireland." Its continuance and preservation were to be " deemed
and taken to be an essential and fundamental part of the Union." [6]
With certain exceptions, free trade was established between
Great Britain and Ireland. Elaborate provisions were made with
regard to certain duties which were to be retained for the protection of Irish industry.[7] Provision was made for the contributions
of Great Britain and Ireland to the expenses of the government
of the United Kingdoms.[8] The proportion of the Irish contribution was fixed at two-fifteenths of the whole—an arrangement
which the great expenditure on the French war soon wrecked.[9]
The laws and the courts of the two kingdoms were to remain as
they were before the union ; but the final court of appeal for
common law and equity cases was to be the House of Lords of the
United Kingdom. In Admiralty cases the final court of appeal was
to be " his Majesty's Delegates and his court of Chancery in
Ireland." [10] These articles were given the form of law as from
January 1, 1801, provided that before that date a similar Act
had been passed by the Irish Parliament.[11] An Act of the Irish
Parliament regulating future elections to the Houses of Lords
and Commons of the United Kingdom was recited, and made
part of the Act of Union.[12] Lastly, provision was made for the use

[1] 39, 40 George III c. 67.　　　[2] Art. 1.　　　[3] Art. 2.　　　[4] Art. 3.
[5] Art. 4.　　[6] Art. 5.　　[7] Art. 6 ; see Lecky, History of Ireland v 364-366.
[8] Art. 7.　　　[9] Lecky, op. cit. v 362-364, 475-477.　　　[10] Art. 8.
[11] 39, 40 George III c. 67 § 1.
[12] § 2 ; no elections took place to the House of Commons; in those constituencies in which representation was unchanged the sitting member took his
seat at Westminster ; when it was curtailed one of the two sitting members was
selected by lot, Lecky, History of Ireland v 410.

of the Irish great seal in Ireland, and for the continuance of the Irish Privy Council.[1]

The Act of Union with Ireland, unlike the Act of Union with Scotland,[2] was passed by a Parliament which was not elected for the purpose of considering a project of Union ; it was passed in defiance of the wishes of the majority of independent Irishmen ; and it was passed by means of wholesale and gross corruption. To modern critics these facts are sufficient to condemn it. But, in the eighteenth century, they were not regarded as being quite so decisive. It was by corruption of the kind used to carry the Union that a liaison was maintained between the English and Irish government,[3] just as corruption of a similar but less flagrant kind was the chief link between the executive and the legislature in England.[4]

As against the corrupt means by which the Union was carried we must set off the supreme importance of a united Legislature in time of war,[5] and remember that, at the general election in 1802, the fact that a candidate had voted for the Union was not regarded as a reason for displacing him.[6] The failure of the Act of Union to produce better relations between England and Ireland was due, not to the Union itself and the means by which it was carried, but to the fact that it was not accompanied by any of those measures which were needed to ensure its success. Catholic emancipation had been promised to induce the Catholics to consent.[7] The insane prejudice of the King, which was shared by many Englishmen, made that impossible.[8] But an attempt should have been made to carry two other measures which Pitt had originally designed to follow the Union—endowment of the Roman Catholic priesthood and tithe commutation. If the first of these measures had been carried the priesthood would have been recruited from a higher class, inclined to side with the law rather than with a disloyal peasantry, who were accustomed to conduct agitations by means of leagues of persons whose method of action was the commission of crimes against person and property.[9] If the second of these measures had been carried one of " the most fertile of all the sources of Irish anarchy and crime " would have been removed.[10] It was not till 1838 that such a measure was passed, and then it was too late.[11] The result was that the Union produced not peace but a sword ; and the Irish membership of the House of Commons came to exert upon the

---

[1] § 3. [2] For this Act see vol. x 41-42, vol. xi 4-10.
[3] Vol. xi 32-34 ; cp. Rosebery, Pitt 193-195.
[4] Vol. x 632-634. [5] See Rosebery, Pitt 196-197.
[6] Lecky, History of Ireland v 465.
[7] Ibid 429, 433-437. [8] Below 173, 182.
[9] Lecky, History of Ireland v 468-471.
[10] Ibid 472. [11] Ibid 472-473.

Parliament of the United Kingdom and upon English parties a most disastrous influence.[1]

It was clear that some of the members of the Corresponding Society and of the United Irishmen had been implicated in the naval mutinies ; and "it is probable that the leaders of the mutineers had learned the art of organization from the reform associations."[2]   In 1796 Binns and Jones,[3] delegates of the Corresponding Society, were tried for using seditious words at a meeting at Birmingham.   Binns, defended by Romilly, was acquitted[4] but Jones was convicted.[5]   In July the Corresponding Society held a meeting in London, in spite of the prohibition of the magistrates, which was dispersed.[6]   In 1798 Binns tried to help O'Connor, a leading member of the United Irishmen, to get to France.   At Margate Binns, O'Connor, and O'Coigley, an Irish priest who had a letter from "the Secret Committee of England" to the French Directory, were arrested.   They were all tried for treason ;[7]   O'Coigley was convicted and executed, but Binns and O'Connor were acquitted.   Binns was detained in prison under the Habeas Corpus Suspension Act till that Act expired in 1801 ;[8] and in 1798 several members of the committee of the Corresponding Society were arrested and kept in prison.   Among the papers of the Society was found an address to the United Irishmen.[9]   This and other facts were reported by a secret committee of the House of Commons in 1799.[10]   Its general conclusion was that there was a systematic design, in conjunction with France, to overturn the government ;   that the chief hope of these conspirators lay in the propagation of the principles of the French revolution ;   and that the chief means which they employed was "the institution of political societies, of a nature and description before unknown in any country, and inconsistent with public tranquility, and with the existence of regular government."[11] It reported also that, in spite of legislation,

The utmost diligence is still employed in endeavouring, not only to sustain and revive these societies whose seditious and treasonable purposes long since attracted the notice of Parliament, but to extend

[1] Coleridge said of the Union with Ireland (Table Talk, Dec. 17, 1831), "I believe it will sooner or later be discovered that the manner in which or the terms upon which Pitt effected it, made it the most fatal blow that was ever levelled against the peace and prosperity of England.   From it came the Catholic Bill.   From the Catholic Bill came this Reform Bill !   And what next ?"   Ibid cited vol. x 22 n. 2.

[2] Davis, Age of Grey and Peel 91.

[3] For these men see Veitch, Genesis of Parliamentary Reform 328-329.

[4] (1797) 26 S.T. 595.

[5] Davis, Age of Grey and Peel 91 ; the statement of Veitch, op. cit. 330, that no sentence was passed seems to be incorrect.

[6] Davis, Age of Grey and Peel 91-92.

[7] Ibid 92 ; (1798) 26 S.T. 1191   [8] Davis, Age of Grey and Peel 92.

[9] Ibid 92-93.   [10] Parlt. Hist. xxxiv 579-656.   [11] Ibid 579-580.

their correspondence to every part of the kingdom, to Ireland, to France, and to those places on the continent where French emissaries are established ; and to initiate new societies, formed precisely on the same plan, and directed by the same object, as those whose influence in Ireland has produced such pernicious and formidable effects.[1]

It was the report of this committee which produced the Act which suppressed for the time being these reforming societies.[2]

The main provisions of the Act were as follows : the societies of United Englishmen, United Scotsmen, United Irishmen, and United Britons, the London Corresponding Society and its branches, were suppressed as being unlawful combinations.[3] For the future societies which obliged their members to take an oath within the meaning of the Act of 1797,[4] or other oath not authorized by law, or which kept secret their list of members or which had a secret committee or secret offices, or which had separate branches, were to be unlawful combinations.[5] Persons permitting the meetings of such societies on their premises were to be guilty of a breach of the Act, and, if the premises were licensed, the licence was to be forfeited.[6] Every house or other place at which a lecture was given or a debate held, or which was used as a place for the reading of books or newspapers, on payment of money for admission, was to be deemed a disorderly house within the meaning of the Act of 1736, unless such house or place had been licensed by two justices for these purposes.[7] Printing presses, type founders, and makers of printing presses must be registered with the clerk of the peace ;[8] the name of the printer must be printed on every paper or book ;[9] and the name of the person for whom it is printed must be kept by the printer.[10] There were saving clauses for the societies of freemasons, and for lectures delivered at the Universities, the Inns of Court, and Gresham College.[11]

The first effect of the Act of Union was the resignation of Pitt. Pitt told his cabinet that he intended to follow up the Act by Catholic emancipation, by a commutation of tithes, and by the endowment of Catholic priests and dissenting ministers.[12] But, as early as 1795, the King had been persuaded by Fitz-Gibbon that if he assented to any measure of Catholic emancipation he would break his coronation oath.[13] Loughborough showed his characteristic lack of statesmanship and his self-seeking[14] by

---

[1] Parlt. Hist. xxxiv. 580.   [2] 39 George III c. 79.   [3] § 1.
[4] Above 168.   [5] § 2.   [6] §§ 13 and 14.
[7] §§ 15, 17, 18.   [8] § 23.   [9] § 27.
[10] § 29.   [11] §§ 5, 6, 22.   [12] Rosebery, Pitt 222.
[13] Lecky, History of Ireland iii 305-307, 310-312.
[14] For an account of Loughborough's career and character see vol. xii 569-576 ; it should be noted that in 1795 Lord Kenyon and Sir John Scott had told the King that the alteration of the Test Act was compatible with his coronation oath, Lecky, op. cit. v 438.

betraying the secrets of the Cabinet to the King, and engineering
opposition to Pitt's policy.[1] Pitt resigned, and was succeeded by
his friend Addington, then Speaker of the House of Commons,
whose father had been the family doctor of the Pitt family. Pitt
gave Addington's ministry his support, and it was that ministry
which, with Pitt's help, negotiated the transient peace of Amiens.
But the renewal of the war necessarily recalled Pitt to office. In
1804 he again became Prime Minister ; and it was only the
opposition of the King which prevented him from including Fox
and his party, and so forming a really national government.[2] The
result was a weak government—" so null was it that it was wittily
called ' the new administration composed of William and Pitt '."[3]
It was further weakened by the attack upon Lord Melville, and
his subsequent impeachment for malversation.[4] Pitt urged the
King to include Fox and Grenville in the government. It was a
measure which would have lightened the load of responsibility
which rested upon him, and might have prolonged his life. But
the King was adamant.[5] Pitt was obliged to go on alone. Though
his health was giving way his energy was untiring. He engineered
a great coalition of Austria, Prussia, and Russia against Napoleon.
Austria was put out of action by Napoleon's victory at Ulm ; and
though the victory of Trafalgar a few days later removed all
danger of invasion, Napoleon's victory of Austerlitz shattered the
coalition. At the Lord Mayor's banquet, held a few days after
Trafalgar, Pitt had said in his last speech, " England has saved
herself by her exertions, and will, as I trust, save Europe by her
example " ; and after Austerlitz he had shown his foresight when
he said that " nothing but a war of patriotism, a national war,
could save Europe, and that war should begin in Spain."[6] But
Austerlitz broke his heart. He was at Bath when he heard the
news, and he returned to his house at Putney only to die on
January 23, 1806.

I have given some account of the principal statutes of constitutional importance passed during this period—the Act of Union,[7]
the Acts amending the law of treason,[8] the Acts controlling and
finally suppressing the reforming societies of different kinds,[9] the
Act regulating the press,[10] and Acts of 1799 and 1800 prohibiting
industrial combinations.[11] The earlier of the two Acts directed
against industrial combinations dealt only with combinations of
men.[12] The generality of its provisions made it a new departure

---

[1] Rosebery, Pitt 222-223.
[2] Davis, Age of Grey and Peel 111-113 ; Rosebery, Pitt 241-243.
[3] Ibid 245.   [4] Ibid 249-252.   [5] Ibid 252-253.
[6] Rosebery, Pitt 256.   [7] Above 169, 170, 171.   [8] Above 165-167.
[9] Above 173.   [10] Above 167.
[11] Vol. xi 496-498 ; 39 George III c. 81 ; 39, 40 George III c. 106.
[12] Vol. xi 496-497.

in the industrial world ;[1] and it is probable that the policy underlying this new departure was the same as the policy of the Act for
suppressing the reforming societies.   The only other statutes
dealing with constitutional law are the numerous statutes, most
of which are of temporary importance, which were demanded by
the exigencies of the war.   There are statutes dealing with the
army, e.g. an Act to permit French royalists to enlist or to serve as
officers in the army,[2] and later Acts [3] to allow foreigners to enlist
or to serve as officers ; and Acts relating to the *militia*, e.g. an
Act for getting the numbers required for the militia by ballot and
for punishing deserters,[4] an Act to allow militia men to enlist in
the regular army or the marines,[5] a consolidating Act to provide
relief for the families of militia men called up for active service.[6]
There are statutes dealing with the *navy*, e.g. an Act to enable
magistrates to compel able bodied and idle persons to serve in the
navy,[7] Acts to enable seamen to allot part of their pay for the
maintenance of their wives and families,[8] an Act as to convoy,[9]
Acts modifying the provisions of the Navigation Acts with respect
to the manning of ships,[10] and with respect to imports in other
than British ships, [11] an Act for the encouragement of sea-men by
provisions for the disposal of prizes and the payment of bounties
and prize money, and for the issue of letters of marque.[12] There are
a number of statutes relating to the *defence of the realm*, e.g. Acts
relating to the export of munitions,[13] as to correspondence with
the enemy,[14] as to the detention of suspected persons,[15] as to the
purchase of land for national defence,[16] as to the compensation
payable to persons whose property was injured by defence
measures,[17] as to the prevention of subjects from going to France
or to countries occupied by the enemy.[18]   There are a number of
statutes relating to *trade* e.g. an Act to prohibit the circulation of
French paper money,[19] an Act to prevent money payable to persons
resident in France coming under the control of the French government,[20] an Act allowing the issue of promissory notes and inland
bills of exchange for less denominations than £5,[21] and Acts
suspending cash payments by the Bank of England.[22]   Various

[1] Vol. xi 491, 498.   [2] 34 George III c. 43.
[3] 44 George III c. 75 ; 46 George III c. 23.
[4] 43 George III c. 50.   [5] 45 George III c. 31.
[6] 43 George III c. 47.   [7] 35 George III c. 34.
[8] 35 George III c.c. 28, 95.   [9] 41 George III c. 57.
[10] 33 George III c. 26 ; 43 George III c. 64.
[11] 44 George III c.c. 29, 30, 101 ; 45 George III c. 34.
[12] 45 George III c. 72.   [13] 33 George III c. 2.
[14] 33 George III c. 27.   [15] 34 George III c. 54.
[16] 34 George III c. 76.
[17] 38 George III c. 27 ; cp. Parlt. Hist. xxxiii 1357-1358.
[18] 38 George III c. 79.   [19] 33 George III c. 1.
[20] 34 George III c. 9.   [21] 37 George III c. 32.
[22] 37 George III c.c. 45, 91 ; cp. Parlt. Hist. xxxii 1517-1520, 1524-1567.

incidents of the war gave rise to other statutes, e.g. there is legislation consequent on the surrender of certain French colonies,[1] legislation giving indemnity for illegal acts done by the executive, whether by means of orders in council,[2] or by officers of the government.[3] Lastly there are Acts as to the *exclusion of aliens* of which I have given some account in an earlier chapter.[4]

FROM 1806 TO 1815

I shall deal in the first place with the main events of this period ; in the second place with the beliefs and programmes of the component parts of the Tory and Whig parties and the beginnings of a new radical party ; and in the third place with the character of the legislation on constitutional law and matters related thereto which resulted from this grouping of parties and their component parts.

(1) *The events of this period*

Pitt's ministry dissolved at his death, and the King was obliged to send for Fox and Grenville.[5] They formed the " ministry of all the talents "—Fox, Petty (the future Lord Lansdowne), Grey, Spencer, Windham, Fitzwilliam, Sidmouth, and Erskine[6] as Chancellor. It included also Lord Ellenborough, the Chief Justice of the King's Bench ;[7] and, though his inclusion in the cabinet was defended by Romilly, the new Solicitor-General,[8] it was obviously objectionable. As was pointed out in debates in the House of Lords and Commons, a man who, as cabinet minister had adopted a particular policy based on a particular view of the law, could hardly be an impartial judge if the question of law came to be argued before him.[9] It tended, as the Earl of Bristol said,[10] " to blend and to amalgamate those great elementary principles of political power, which it is the very object of a free constitution to keep separate and distinct." The ministry's conduct of the war was futile. Eight months were wasted in negotiations because Fox foolishly thought that Napoleon could be induced to negotiate.[11] Their chief war activity was the promulgation of the first of the Orders in Council in answer to Napoleon's Berlin decrees.[12] We shall see that the Orders in Council

---

[1] 34 George III c. 42 ; 37 George III c. 63.   [2] 41 George III c. 46·
[3] 41 George III c. 66—arrests of persons suspected of treason, see Parlt· Hist. xxxv 1507-1541.
[4] Vol. x 397.   [5] Feiling, The Second Tory Party 247.
[6] For Erskine see below 580-595.
[7] For Ellenborough see below 499-516.   [8] Memoirs (ed. 1842) ii 4.
[9] Cobbett, Parlt. Debates vi 254-284, 286-341 ; see 502.503 for the arguments by which Ellenborough tried to justify his acceptance of a place in the cabinet.
[10] Cobbett, Parlt. Debates vi 255.
[11] Davis, Age of Grey and Peel.   [12] Ibid.

were passed to counter Napoleon's Berlin and other decrees, which established a blockade of Great Britain, by establishing a blockade of France and all countries in Europe allied with or subject to her.[1] The main achievement of the ministry was the abolition of the slave trade[2]—a measure which Pitt and Fox had always supported. The dying Fox had urged his colleagues to pass the measure ; and Wilberforce had given the government the support of his party, " the Saints," in return for its help in carrying abolition.[3] The bill passed both Houses, but it was only just before the ministry fell that it received the Royal assent.[4] We shall see that the Act of 1807 was followed by other Acts against slave trading,[5] and in 1814, in order that British commercial interests might not be damaged, by treaties with France and other nations for its abolition in their dominions.[6]

The ministry was dismissed in 1807 owing to a mis-understanding with the King as to a measure of relief for Catholic officers in the Irish army. The King had consented that commissions tenable by Irish Catholic officers in Ireland should also be tenable by those officers in England. But the bill to effect this did a great deal more. It enabled Catholics in Great Britain to hold even the highest commissions in the army and navy. Sidmouth called the King's attention to this enlargement of the bill. The cabinet withdrew the bill, stating, however, that it reserved its right to give free and full advice on Irish questions. The King demanded a pledge that it would never advise further concessions to the Catholics. The pledge was refused and the ministry was dismissed.[7]

The ministry of all the talents was succeeded by a ministry under the nominal headship of Portland. Its leading members were Lord Hawkesbury (the future Earl of Liverpool), Eldon,[8] and Perceval—a successful lawyer who had been solicitor and attorney-general and an orthodox and pious churchman of considerable debating power[9]—who took the lead in the House of Commons, and Canning. Its conduct of the war was more ener-getic than that of its predecessor.

In the first sixteen months of its existence the Danish fleet was seized (Sept. 1807) ; the Crown Prince of Portugal was induced to sail from Brazil with a Portuguese fleet, which was thus placed beyond Napoleon's reach (Nov.) ; three Orders in Council were issued to strangle the

---

[1] Below 178, 179.　　　　　　　　[2] 47 George III Sess. 1, c. 36 ; below 192.
[3] Davis, op. cit. 117-118.
[4] Trevelyan, Lord Grey of the Reform Bill 158-159.　　　[5] Below 184, 192.
[6] Halévy, History of the British People in 1815 (Pelican Books) iii 80-81, 82.
[7] Davis, op. cit. 119-120; Feiling, The Second Tory Party 252-253; there was much truth in Wilberforce's criticism that Grenville had run his ship aground " on a rock above water," and of Sheridan's criticism that " he had built a brick wall in order to run his head against it."
[8] For Eldon see below 595 seqq.　　　　　　　[9] See Feiling, op. cit. 254-255.

foreign trade of France and her allies (Nov.) ; an expeditionary force was
sent to Portugal (July 1808) ; the Russian fleet was seized in the Tagus ;
Heligoland was occupied as a base for the smuggling trade with the
Continent : and a British expeditionary force appeared in the Baltic.[1]

Canning, to whose initiative the seizure of the Danish fleet was
due,[2] was critical of the way in which his colleagues, and
especially Castlereagh, were conducting the war. The failure of
the Walcheren expedition, and the quarrel resulting therefrom
between Canning and Castlereagh, which ended in a duel and
their retirement from the ministry, broke up the government.[3]
The Whigs unpatriotically refused to join in a national government. Perceval and Lord Liverpool managed to reconstruct the
government without them, and by their steady support of the
Peninsular campaign, which the Whigs (except Lord Holland)
opposed, they took a long step towards winning the war.[4]

Helped by Wellington's victories in the Peninsular Perceval's
government held on ; and it was attracting some brilliant younger
men. Peel made his first speech in 1810 ; and Croker at the
Admiralty and Arbuthnot at the Treasury were beginning to
make names for themselves.[5] But the policy of replying to
Napoleon's Berlin and later decrees by the Orders in Council was
raising new difficulties.[6] Napoleon by his decrees[7] tried to
establish an economic blockade of Great Britain. No foodstuffs
or raw material were to be imported, and no British goods were
to be sold in continental markets. The effect of the various
Orders in Council, issued in reply to Napoleon's various decrees,
was to blockade the coast of France and of those countries which
were subject to or in alliance with France. The Navigation Acts
were relaxed[8] so as to allow neutrals to import goods more freely,
and to export them, provided they landed them first in England
and paid a duty.[9] The result of these measures has been summed
up as follows :

Napoleon issued a prohibition of all commerce between England and
countries subject to his authority or influence. The English Government
replied by a prohibition of all commerce between neutrals and France,
unless the neutral ships put in at an English port on their way and paid
a duty to the English Exchequer. Napoleon defied England to do

[1] Davis, Age of Grey and Peel 121.
[2] Temperley, Life of Canning 74-79.
[3] Davis, op. cit. 121-122 ; Feiling, op. cit. 259-261.
[4] Davis, op. cit. 122-123.   [5] Feiling, op. cit. 264.
[6] A very clear account of the Orders in Council and the controversies roused
by them is given by Halévy, History of the English People in 1815 (Pelican
books) ii 149-158.
[7] Decree of Berlin 1806, Decree of Milan 1807, Decrees of Fontainebleau 1810 ;
for the list of the Orders in Council see Halévy, op. cit. ii 152 ; for attacks on them
in the House of Lords in 1808 see Cobbett, Parlt. Debates x 150-154, 465-486,
780-786, 1235-1242.
[8] Below 188.   [9] Halévy, op. cit. ii 152.

without the Continental market and the British Government in return defied the French Empire to dispense with all goods which were either of English manufacture or had passed through the English customs. The two nations, to employ the illustration of a minister, George Rose, were in the position of two men who had both put their heads in a bucket, and were trying to see who could keep his head under longer.[1]

This policy aroused hostility both at home and abroad. The merchants resented the restrictions on their export trade ; and the system of licences issued to individuals to import and export, notwithstanding the Orders in Council, roused the enmity of ship-builders and ship-owners, since these licences were generally issued to the owners of neutral ships.[2] The United States resented the restrictions on their trade,[3] and their resentment was aggravated by the claim to take sailors from American ships on the ground that they were British subjects.[4] The result was that they had, by their Non-Intercourse Act, stopped all trade with Great Britain. The merchants agitated against this further dislocation of trade, which prevented them from earning money and caused much industrial unrest. Brougham[5] made his name by voicing the complaints of the merchants ; and in 1812 the Orders in Council were revoked so far as they applied to American ships. But the revocation came just too late to avert the outbreak of war between Great Britain and the United States.[6]

The merchants had won a victory for free trade by securing the modification of the Orders in Council ;[7] and we shall see that, under the influence of the new economic doctrine of *laissez-faire*, old restrictions on trade were being released in many directions.[8] Both the agricultural and the manufacturing industries were coming to be organized more and more on a capitalistic basis ; and the modern system of finance and banking was arising. But as yet this new system of industry and finance was both unregulated and unorganized. The results were periodic periods of good and bad trade. In the latter periods banks broke, bankruptcies multiplied, and men were thrown out of work. Since labour in the agricultural and manufacturing districts was also to a large extent unorganized, and since low wages eked out by poor

---

[1] Halévy, op. cit. 153.   [2] Ibid 154-155.
[3] Ibid. 155-156.   [4] Vol. ix 90-91.
[5] For Brougham, see below 195 seqq., 639 seqq. ; for his speeches in 1812 on the motion for an enquiry on the effect of the Orders in Council on trade see Cobbett's Parlt. Debates xxi 1092, 1116, xxiii 486-522.
[6] Halévy, op. cit. ii 158-159.
[7] James Mill's Commerce Defended (1807) was, says Halévy op. cit. ii 153-154, " the first work, explicitly and dogmatically preaching Free Trade, which had appeared in England since the beginning of the war. It reflected the opinion of the manufacturers and merchants. From 1807 onwards Liverpool was in open protest against the Orders in Council. As the years went by all the seaports and manufacturing towns joined the movement of protest."
[8] Below 212.

relief prevailed in many industries, riots resulted.[1] Among the most serious of these outbreaks were the Luddite riots of 1811-12 which began in Nottinghamshire and spread to Yorkshire, Lancashire, Cheshire, and the lowlands of Scotland.[2] Organized gangs destroyed the knitting frames which it was thought threw men out of work. Almost the only remedy which the government applied was repression. Repressive legislation was passed to deal with the Luddites ;[3] and, since the publication of Cobbett's *Political Register*, which began in 1806, was reviving the democratic movement,[4] the critics of government measures, industrial or otherwise, were dealt with by informations for libel, the number of which aroused criticism in both Houses of Parliament.[5] By 1813 a return of prosperity caused the Luddite riots to subside ; but we shall see that the Legislature did little to remedy the grievances of the workmen. It repealed the old restrictions, but put little that was effective in their place.[6]

In 1811 the King had gone permanently mad ; and a Regency Act was passed which followed the model of that of 1788.[7] But the Regent did not change his ministers. He disliked both Grey and Grenville, and the Whigs themselves were divided.[8] In May 1812 Perceval was shot in the lobby of the House of Commons by a madman named Bellingham. It was necessary to reconstruct the ministry ; and overtures were made to the two leading Tories out of office—Wellesley and Canning—which were refused.[9] Wellesley and Canning failed to form a ministry of their own,[10] and Liverpool came back to power as prime minister. Again overtures were made to Canning,[11] for he was by far the ablest, most far-seeing, most liberal and most eloquent of the Tories. He was the disciple and the political heir of Pitt on whom he modelled himself—the liberal Pitt of pre-revolution days as well as the Pitt whom he had apostrophized in verse as " the pilot who weathered the storm." He made a great mistake when he refused the very liberal offers which were made to him, because he insisted on the leadership of the House of Commons.[12] If he had then taken office, and if in the difficult years which followed 1815 he had become the leader of his party, he might have been able to carry a programme of law reform, and of social and industrial

---

[1] " Neither the new class of employers nor the new class of workmen had yet learnt to organize. Not only was there open war between Capital and Labour but also in the ranks of Capital and Labour alike, confusion and anarchy prevailed." Halévy, op. cit. ii 145-146.

[2] Ibid 172-176 ; for the trials of the rioters in 1813 see 31 S.T. 959.

[3] 52 George III c.c. 16, 17 ; below 192, 193.

[4] Graham Wallas, Francis Place 41.

[5] Cobbett's Parlt. Debates xix 129-174, 548-612.   [6] Below 342-351.

[7] Feiling, op. cit. 266-277 ; 51 George III c. 1, amended by 58 George III c. 90 ; below 588 ; for the Act of 1788 see vol. x 439-444.

[8] Feiling, op. cit. 267.   [9] Ibid 271.

[10] Ibid 272.   [11] Ibid 273-274.   [12] Ibid 274.

legislation, which would have enabled the Tory party to take the chief part in adapting the law and institutions of England to the new political and economic conditions.[1] Liverpool improved his position after a general election in 1812; and it was he and Castlereagh who made peace with America in 1814 and with France in 1815.

We shall see that the England which emerged from the war in 1815 was a very different England from that which had entered it in 1793. Economic conditions and problems, political and to some extent religious ideas, had been changing. The anomalies and anachronisms in the law which existed in 1793 were more obvious and more mischievous in the changed conditions of 1815, and therefore new ideas as to law and law reform were emerging.[2] For these reasons the creeds of the two great political parties were changing their shape. Both in the Whig and in the Tory parties groups were emerging whose ideals and programmes were divergent; and in the masses of workers which the new industrial conditions were calling into existence, and in open constituencies such as Westminster, where the franchise was wide, we can see the beginnings of a new radical party, whose ideals were voiced and justified by men like Bentham and James Mill. It was a significant sign of the times that in 1807 Francis Place was able to secure the return of Burdett, and defeat both the official Whig and the official Tory candidate.[3] If we look at the manner in which different groups were emerging in the Whig and Tory parties under the pressure of the new conditions, and at the beginnings of this new radical party, we shall be better able to understand the legislation of these years on constitutional and cognate topics, and the beginnings of the process which will convert the old Whig and Tory parties into the modern Liberal and Conservative parties.

(2) *New groupings in the Whig and Tory parties and the beginnings of a new radical party*

After 1807 and until 1830 the government was a Tory government. But it is a mistake to suppose that the Tories were impervious to all ideas of reform. Although Pitt's reforming zeal had been damped down by the French Revolution and the war, although Tories like Eldon[4] and Ellenborough[5] opposed any but the smallest change in the *status quo*, some small reforms were made. The Board of Agriculture, which had been founded in 1793 and lasted till 1818, was subsidized by the State, and did good

---

[1] Below 222.   [2] Below 259 seqq.
[3] Graham Wallas, Francis Place 47; for Burdett see below 186, 187.
[4] For Eldon see below 595 seqq.   [5] For Ellenborough see below 499-516.

work for the improvement of agriculture.[1] We shall see that
changes were made in the machinery of the executive government,[2]
that attempts were made to tighten up the law against corrupt
practices at elections and to prevent the sale of seats,[3] that the
House of Commons passed bills to abolish sinecures,[4] and that the
practice of granting offices in reversion had been suspended.[5]
But the rank and file of the Tories were opposed to all large
changes. " Either they would defend anomalies as the fruit of the
unconscious wisdom of the past, or they would take it for granted
that the wit of man was incapable of patching and repairing
the old constitution without destroying it altogether."[6] Fear of
the French Revolution made them hostile to all large changes,
and produced a scepticism as to the good to be derived from any
change. Naturally they opposed Parliamentary reform, for a
large measure of reform would upset the balance of the constitution.[7] Partly for the same reason they opposed Catholic
emancipation. But on this question Protestant prejudice, and
fear and dislike of the Irish Catholics, co-operated.[8] It is true that
some of the Catholic disabilities had been removed and some of the
penal laws against them had been repealed.[9] But the Catholics
still suffered under disabilities in public law. They were disfranchised, and they could not hold office. There is no doubt that
the unwillingness of George III to emancipate the Catholics
reflected the prejudices of a large number of his subjects, and
added to his popularity which had, as Romilly says, been increasing
ever since 1784.[10]

In fact it was the attitude taken by the rank and file of the
Tories to the King and to the Church of England which was the
clearest line of demarcation between them and the Whigs.[11] The
King, the Tories thought, should not only reign, but should take
some part in the government. After all, the government was
his government, and all honest men should help the King to carry
out his policy. In fact, as Davis has said,[12]

the plea of personal devotion to the sovereign was used, and used with
complete success, to justify deviations from the current code of political
morality. It was so used by Pitt (in 1801) to justify the repudiation of

---

[1] Halévy, History of the English People in 1815 39.
[2] Below 189, 190 ; Halévy, op. cit. i 40.
[3] Below 191, 192 ; Halévy, op. cit. i 236-237.
[4] Below 189 ; Halévy, op. cit. i 40.   [5] Ibid.
[6] Davis, Age of Grey and Peel 142.   [7] Vol. x 631-632.
[8] Halévy, op. cit. 99-100, 108-109.   [9] Vol. x 114.
[10] Memoirs (ed. 1842) ii 129-131 ; Romilly, op. cit. 31 n., tells us that Wilkes,
who had just " manifested his attachment to the King in a very extravagant way,"
was asked by the Prince of Wales, how long it was that he had been so loyal, and
that he replied, " ever since I have had the honour of being acquainted with your
Royal Highness " ; that, as Romilly says, " conveys a very exact explanation of
many a man's loyalty."
[11] Davis, Age of Grey and Peel 146.   [12] Ibid 147-148.

the understanding with the Irish Catholics. Lord Eldon was accustomed to boast that he held the great seal as the King's servant, and not as a minister in the ordinary sense . . . . A greater man than Eldon, but bred in the same school of thought, the Duke of Wellington, maintained (in 1832) that he could not, in honour or loyalty, refuse office when he was pressed by the King to undertake it, even though the policy to be pursued was repugnant to his own convictions. It is permissible to doubt whether these statesmen were actually convinced by their own arguments. But they were much too shrewd to use arguments which would fail to convince their followers.

The Church was always in the thoughts of the Tories. " Lord Sidmouth was the leader of a movement for building new churches in great industrial centres, and in 1818 Lord Liverpool agreed to allot a million of public money for this purpose.' [1] Wilberforce's party of " the Saints " was a force to be reckoned with.[2] The evangelical Christianity which they represented had many beliefs, and made many practical suggestions based on those beliefs, which sometimes coincided with, and sometimes differed from, the new school of economic thought. Both these schools—the economists and the Saints—were introducing new ideas into the Tory party.

Pitt was a student of Adam Smith, and in the pre-revolutionary period his commercial treaty with France showed that he had been influenced by his ideas.[3] Some of the new leaders of industry like the Peels, and the new leaders of finance like the Thorntons, were attracted to the Tory party. Others, like Horner and Huskisson, gravitated to the Whigs. But all these men were supporters of free trade. They supported the repeal of the old laws which enabled magistrates to fix wages, and the old apprentrceship laws ;[4] the agitation against the Orders in Council ;[5] the repeal of the trading monopoly of the East India Company ;[6] and the resumption of cash payments by the Bank of England.[7] These new economic ideas, which were supported by Tories as well as Whigs, helped to introduce new ideas into the Tory party, and induced that party to consent to a number of legislative changes.[8] It was not till the latter part of this period that the proposed corn law of 1815 showed a rift between the commercial men and the agriculturists,[9] which, in the future, was destined to exercise a large effect upon the groupings of political parties by putting the commercial men into the Whig or Liberal, and the agriculturists into the Tory or Conservative camp.[10]

[1] Davis, Age of Grey and Peel 149 ; below 215.
[2] See James Stephen's Essay on the Clapham Sect, Essays in Ecclesiastical Biography ii 287-338.
[3] Vol. x 121.
[4] Vol. xi 421, 471-472 ; below 327, 328.
[5] Above 179.
[6] Vol. xi 214 ; below 365.
[7] Below 375.
[8] Below 187, 194.
[9] Halévy, op. cit. 162-3 ; Romilly, Memoirs ii 352-353 ; below 357-358.
[10] Below 185, 187.

" The Saints," led by Wilberforce, were another very detached
section of the Tory party. They were men who belonged to the
evangelical party in the Church of England. Their great triumph
was the Act of 1807 which abolished the slave trade.[1] But for a
long time they had been the great supporters of a strict scriptural
morality, which included a rigid sabbatarianism.[2] They protested
against duelling, cock-fighting, and bull and bear baiting.[3] They
attempted to alleviate the evils of child labour,[4] to reform the
prison system,[5] to mitigate the savagery of the penal code.[6] And
in many of these parts of their programme, as in their movement
for the abolition of the slave trade, they joined hands with the
utilitarians, and the left-wing Whigs, such as Brougham, who
worked with Wilberforce,[7] and was the author of an Act to make
more effective the Act prohibiting the slave trade.[8] Nor were
their ideals wholly opposed to those of the commercial men.
Some of the most enlightened of the large employers of labour,
such as Dale and Owen and others, tried to improve the social
conditions of their workmen ;[9] and " manufacturers who had
improved the conditions of labour in their own establishments
were indisposed to tolerate in the factories of their neighbours
the abuses suppressed by themselves." [10] Peel's father, a great
cotton manufacturer, carried the first Act to regulate pauper
child labour in cotton factories.[11] The Act was approved by
Wilberforce and his party who wished to see it extended to all
factories and all children. An attempt so to extend it was made
in 1815 and failed.[12]

At first sight there is not much in common between the creed
of the economists and the creed of " the Saints." But as Mr.
Young has pointed out,[13] " the virtues of a Christian after the
evangelical model were easily exchangeable with the virtues of
a successful merchant or a rising manufacturer." And just as there
is a similarity between the evangelical and the economic creed, so
there is a similarity between the new utilitarian creed, which had
adopted the new economic creed,[14] and the evangelical creed.

Both rested upon a body of doctrine which to question was impious or
irrational ; in both cases the doctrine was the reflection of an exceptional
experience, the religious experience of a nation undergoing a moral
revival, its social experience during a revolution in the methods of production. . . . With their almost Genevan rigour, and almost Latin

---

[1] Above 177 ; below 192.   [2] Halévy, op. cit. iii 75-76.
[3] Ibid 76-77.   [4] Ibid ii 115-116.
[5] Ibid iii 78.   [6] Ibid 78-79 ; below 279, 280.
[7] A. Aspinall, Brougham and the Whig Party 10-11.
[8] Ibid 23-24 ; below 215.
[9] A. Aspinall, Brougham and the Whig Party ii 114-115.
[10] Ibid 115.   [11] Ibid 115-118 ; below 213.
[12] Aspinall, op cit. 118.   [13] Victorian England 2.
[14] Above 138-140.

clarity, they imposed themselves like foreign taskmasters on the large ironic English mind.[1]

These two detached wings of the Tory party were profoundly modifying its ideals. They were making some of its leaders, and some of its younger members, more receptive to new ideas. They were giving them some perception of the sort of reforms in the law and institutions of England which were needed to adapt them to the needs of a new age.

Similar developments were at the same time going on in the Whig party. There was much in common between the old Whig party led by Whig territorial magnates and the Tory party. As Davis says :[2]

The early numbers of the *Edinburgh Review* contain some articles which, twenty years later, would have been cheerfully printed by Mr. Croker in the *Quarterly*. In 1807 an Edinburgh reviewer gravely states that the balance of the constitution can only be maintained by the exercise both of royal and of aristocratical influence in the House of Commons. It is essential, he maintains, that there should be some members in that House who owe their seats to the help of the Treasury, or to the patronage of noble lords. The sale of seats for money had not yet been made illegal ;[3] and the reviewer thinks the practice not wholly indefensible . . . the reviewer protests that he has no great affection for rotten boroughs, since the sale of seats cannot fail to demoralize the electorate. But he does not believe that the efficiency of the lower House would be destroyed by the extension of the system or much improved by its suppression.

An *Edinburgh Review* article of 1809 defends the hereditary landed aristocracy—though it thinks that some increase of Parliamentary reform should be conceded in order to preserve and increase the popularity of the House of Commons.[4] But the Whigs were more ready to admit the need for reform than the Tories. They did not fear change, nor were they sceptical as to its good results. They did not profess such exaggerated loyalty to the King or the Church as the Tories. They favoured the removal of religious disabilities and therefore the emancipation of the Catholics. Both Landowne House and Holland House were nurseries of brilliant young men, some of whom went further in their proposals for reforms than the older and more orthodox Whigs approved.[5]

Of these younger men Romilly,[6] the friend and disciple of Bentham,[7] worked for the reform of the penal law. In fact "he contributed materially to the education of the Whigs when he compelled them to take account of Bentham's work on

---

[1] Young, Victorian England 12.
[2] Davis, Age of Grey and Peel 144.
[4] Davis, Age of Grey and Peel 145.
[5] Halévy, op. cit. i 231-232.
[6] Below 235, 236, 260, 274, 279, 296.

[3] Below 191.

[7] Above 43, 50, 59, 62, 99.

jurisprudence ";[1] and in this work he was helped by such enlightened Tories as Canning and Wilberforce. Whitbread, Grey's brother-in-law, advocated a minimum wage for labourers to be fixed by the justices, reform of the poor law, and free and compulsory education for poor children.[2] Horner was the economist of the Whig party, who advocated the resumption of cash payments and the cause of free trade.[3] Brougham, never, as we shall see,[4] an orthodox Whig, was always an advocate of educational and social reform, and sometimes made approaches to the radical party,[5] though he never adopted their scheme of Parliamentary reform.[6] A group of advanced Whigs, known as "the Mountain," because their principles were supposed to resemble those of the Jacobins, supported Whitbread, and were ever on the look-out to expose corruption and incompetence.[7] In 1812 a motion to enquire into the enormous fees paid to the tellers of the Exchequer was opposed by both the orthodox Whigs and the Tories, and was supported by "the Mountain."[8]

The Whigs were rich in talent; but their influence as a party was small. This was partly due to their mistaken attitude to the war—they were constantly prophesying disaster in the Peninsular,[9] and partly to differences amongst themselves.[10] They differed as to the attitude to be taken to the scandals connected with the Duke of York and Mrs. Clark,[11] on the subject of Parliamentary reform,[12] on Whitbread's reforming policy,[13] and later on the subject of the Queen's trial.[14] But though some Whigs were more advanced than others on particular topics, hardly any of them at this period had any sympathy with the new radical party which was beginning to revive at the end of the first decade of the nineteenth century.

We have seen that in 1807 Place secured the election of Burdett, who favoured a liberal measure of Parliamentary

[1] Davis, Age of Grey and Peel 131.   [2] Ibid 127.   [3] Ibid 135.
[4] Below 199.   [5] Davis, op. cit. 136-137.
[6] Ibid 137; below 252.   [7] Ibid 127.
[8] "On this occasion Ponsonby, Tierney and the greatest part of the Opposition joined the Ministers. Lord Grenville, indeed, had said that he considered the motion as aimed personally at himself, his family, and his friends; and most of the firm adherents to the Opposition party voted accordingly, or stayed away. In the minority, however, were Whitbread, General Ferguson, Lord Tavistock, Lord Archibald Hamilton, and Brougham," Life of Romilly (ed. 1842) ii 255.
[9] Above 178; Davis, op. cit. 123.
[10] In 1811 Lord Holland wrote, "There is a want of popular feeling in many individuals of the party. Others are exasperated with the unjust and uncandid treatment they have received, and are every day receiving, from the modern Reformers. Another set are violent anti-Reformers and alarmed at every speech or measure that has the least tendency towards reform," the Creevy Papers i 144.
[11] Trevelyan, Lord Grey of the Reform 166-168.
[12] Ibid 169-170; Davis, op. cit. 139.
[13] Trevelyan, op. cit. 165; the Creevy Papers i 156.
[14] Trevelyan, op. cit. 192-193; below 219, 220; the Creevy Papers i 341 n.

and other reforms.[1] In 1811 a new society of friends of Parliamentary reform was founded by the veteran reformer Major
Cartwright, and in 1812 a Hampden Club consisting of persons of
higher social status was also founded.[2] These examples were
followed ; political clubs of reformers were established in many
places ;[3] and in 1813 Major Cartwright set out on a political tour
to preach reform.[4] In 1809 Bentham had gone over to the cause.[5]
But as yet all sections of the Whigs held aloof from projects of
radical reform ; and the cause of radical reform was not helped
by Burdett's dispute with the House of Commons on a question
of privilege,[6] or by the riotous conduct of his supporters when he
was committed to prison.[7] Though no doubt some of the radicals
approved measures of social reform, such as those suggested by
Whitbread,[8] they were as hostile to the Whigs as to the Tories ;
and many of the Whigs reciprocated their dislike, because, they
thought, they made all reform odious.[9] It was not till the rise of
the philosophical radicals [10] in the following period that this party
was able to exercise some influence on politics.[11]

This analysis shows that the creeds and ideals of the two great
parties in the state were very fluid. Some measures proposed by
sections of the Tory party who believed in free trade, and some
measures proposed by " the Saints," were approved by the Whigs ;
and though no section of the Tory party supported a measure of
Parliamentary reform, the Whigs and the Tories were basically
more agreed upon the principles of Parliamentary representation
than the Whigs and the Radicals. Moreover, on the question of
Catholic emancipation, some Tories agreed with the Whigs ;
and some sections of the Tories approved reforms in the machinery
of government, and reforms of obvious abuses. We shall now see
that it is this fluid state of the creeds and ideals of the Whig
and Tory parties which accounts for the character of the legislation
on matters of public and semi-public laws during this period.

[1] Above 181 ; Veitch, The Genesis of Parliamentary Reform 343 ;   Graham
Wallas, Francis Place 43 ; see Cobbett, Parlt. Debates xiv 1041-1056 for Burdett's
motion on Parliamentary reform in 1809 ;   he proposed a uniform household
suffrage, equal electoral districts, all elections to be held and finished on one day,
and shorter Parliaments.
[2] Veitch, Genesis of Parliamentary Reform 343-344 ;   to belong to the
Hampden Club it was necessary to have £300 a year in land.
[3] Ibid 345.   [4] Ibid 346-347.   [5] Above 57, 104.
[6] (1811) 14 East 1.
[7] See Graham Wallas, Francis Place 49-53, for a good account of these
proceedings.
[8] Above 186.
[9] In 1810 Grey wrote to Holland, " the persons whom you designate Burdettites
and Jacobins are in truth the best friends of the Court.   By diverting the public
attention from all useful and practical objects, they provide the best means of
escape for the Ministers from those difficulties in which their folly and wickedness
have involved them," cited Trevelyan, Lord Grey of the Reform Bill 169.
[10] Above 134 seqq.   [11] Below 239 seqq.

(3) *The legislation on constitutional and other matters related thereto*

As we might expect, during a period of war there is no legislation on those topics of first rate importance. But, as in the preceding period,[1] there is much legislation mainly of a temporary kind occasioned by war conditions. Thus, as in the preceding period, the Navigation Acts were several times modified in order to provide for the exigencies of foreign trade under war conditions.[2] There was much legislation as to the militia,[3] as to the regular army,[4] as to volunteers for the army,[5] as to the navy,[6] as to Prize,[7] as to convoy.[8] War conditions made it necessary to give enlarged powers to the executive—powers to purchase land for the defence of the realm,[9] power to the Postmaster-General to open returned letters directed to places abroad,[10] powers in relation to foreign trade.[11] We shall see that the fact that the Legislature had, as the result of war conditions, become familiarized with the practice of giving increased powers to the executive, helped to induce it, in the following period, to be more liberal in the grant of these powers than it had been in the eighteenth century.[12] Further provisions were made for the maintenance of the military canal at Shorncliff,[13] and provision was made for the more effective punishment of persons who aided the escape of prisoners of war.[14]

Though there is no legislation of first rate importance on constitutional and other matters related thereto, there is a certain amount of reforming legislation, both in relation to the executive government and the courts, and in relation to Parliament, which indicates the growth of a feeling that it is desirable to get rid of abuses and anomalies, and to give effect to modern ideas of efficiency ; and that feeling is still more clearly indicated by the Parliamentary debates and by proposals for even more drastic reforms.

[1] Above 175, 176.

[2] 47 George III Sess. 1 c. 26 ; 48 George III c.c. 11, 69 ; 49 George III c.c. 47, 59, 60.

[3] E.g. 47 George III Sess. 2 c. 57 ; 49 George III c. 4 (allowing a certain proportion of the militia to enlist in the regular army) ; 48 George III c 111 ; 49 George III c. 40 (provision for a permanent militia) ; 49 George III c. 53 ; 50 George III c. 24 (enlistment and the ballot) ; 50 George III c. 25 ; 52 George III c. 38 ; 55 George III c. 65 (organization) ; 55 George III c. 77 (embodiment).

[4] 47 George III Sess 2 c. 57 ; large additions were made to some of the annual Mutiny Acts, e.g. 53 George III cc. 17 and 99 ; 54 George III c. 86 (army prize money).

[5] 49 George III c. 113 ; 52 George III c. 152 ; 54 George III c. 151 ; 55 George III c. 170 (agent-general for volunteers and militia).

[6] E.g. 49 George III c. 108 ; 53 George III c. 85 ; 54 George III c. 93 (wages and prize money).

[7] 48 George III c. 70 ; 55 George III c. 160 (prize and bounty money, letters of Marque).   [8] 55 George III c. 173.

[9] 49 George III c. 112, amending 43 George III c. 55, and 44 George III c. 92.   [10] 47 George III Sess. 2 c. 53.

[11] 48 George III c. 37 ; 52 George III c. 119 § 2.

[12] Vol. x 516 ; vol xi 283-286.

[13] 47 George III c. 70.   [14] 52 George III c. 156.

In relation to the executive government there are a series of Acts which are directed to the abolition of practices which were generally recognized to be abusive or anomalous. Thus the process of abolishing useless patent offices in the customs, begun by an Act of 1798, was continued.[1] The practice of granting offices in reversion—a practice which rested upon the mediæval idea that an office was a species of property[2]—was, except in respect to offices in the courts, suspended for several years.[3] Attempts were made to abolish all sinecures. In 1807 a motion to enquire into " offices, posts, places, sinecures, pensions, fees, perquisites, and emoluments " arising from the public revenues or from the fees of the courts, held by or for any member of the House of Commons or his relatives, was lost;[4] but a modified resolution to the same effect was passed on the motion of the Chancellor of the Exchequer.[5] In 1809 the finance committee of the House of Commons submitted a statement as to sinecure offices, offices held in reversion, and offices executed by deputy.[6] In 1810 a motion to abolish sinecures and to substitute a fund for pensioning deserving officials was lost.[7] In 1812 a sinecure offices bill passed the House of Commons,[8] but was rejected by the House of Lords.[9] The Act of Edward VI against the sale of offices[10] was extended, and made more effective—though exceptions with respect to offices in the courts and with respect to the sale of commissions in the army were still allowed.[11] The emergence of modern ideas as to the position of officers of the central government can be seen in the requirement that officers appointed to positions of trust must give security,[12] in the

[1] 38 George III c. 86 ; 48 George III c. 9 ; 51 George III c. 71.

[2] Vol. i 246-252 ; a private Act of 1810, 50 George III c. clxiv, passed to reform the examiner's office of the court of Chancery, illustrates the difference between mediæval and modern ideas ; it is there recited that the office of examiner was held for life, so that an examiner was practically irremovable, and that one Henry Fitzcroft, who held the office " is now and hath for a considerable time been a lunatic ward of the said court " ; the Act then goes on to provide for the office of examiner and of the clerks of the office, gives power to appoint and remove examiners, who are to perform their duties in person, settles the amount of the fees payable, and provides for the salaries of clerks and for superannuation allowances.

[3] 48 George III c. 50 ; 50 George III c. 88 ; 52 George III c. 40 ; for the opposition to a bill to prevent the grant of such offices in 1807 see Life of Romilly (ed. 1842) ii, 69-70—the bill, Romilly says, was bitterly opposed by Mansfield, the Chief Justice of the Common Pleas ; Cobbett, Parlt. Debates ix 178, 187, 1158-1167 (1807) ; x 870-872, 1086-1088 (1808) ; xi 18-23, 32, 139-141, 159-160; in 1814 Eldon successfully opposed the suspending bill on the ground that these Acts were intended to force the Lords to do what they had refused to do, i.e. pass a permanent act, ibid xxviii 635.

[4] Ibid ix 746, 739.*

[5] Ibid 740.*

[6] Ibid xiii, cclxx-cclxxxvii.

[7] Ibid xvi 1083-1103.

[8] Ibid xxii, 1178, xxiii 552.

[9] Ibid xxiii 895.

[10] 5, 6 Edward VI c. 16 ; vol. i 250.

[11] 49 George III c. 126.

[12] 50 George III c. 85 ; 52 George III c. 66.

substitution of fixed salaries for payment by fees,[1] and in the provision of pensions for superannuated officers.[2] Several of the government departments were reformed and reorganized;[3] and reforms were made in the machinery for managing the land revenues of the Crown.[4] We shall see that the Act of 1782,[5] which compelled the holders of offices in the colonies granted by letters patent to reside in their colony, was amended and extended to offices granted by commission ; and that provisions were made as to the granting of leave of absence.[6]

Similar reforms were made in the judicial machinery of the state. We have seen that an attempt was made, which was not very successful, to cope with the growing arrears of business in the Court of Chancery by the appointment of a Vice-Chancellor.[7] Romilly opposed the bill on the ground that it would make a radical alteration in the position of the Lord Chancellor. If as a result of the bill he confined himself to his appellate work in the House of Lords, he would no longer be mainly responsible for the development of equity, and he would become more of a political and less of a judicial officer.[8] This criticism was perhaps open to the reply that it took too small an account of the fact that, now that equity had become a regular and settled system, its develop-ment no longer depended so exclusively on the Lord Chancellor as in earlier periods. There was no reason why the administration of the system of equity should not, like the administration of the common law, be entrusted to a number of judges. Others opposed it on the ground, which in fact was found to be true, that appeals would be multiplied, so that not much relief to the suitor would result ;[9] and it was said with considerable justice that a better method of coping with the Chancery arrears would be to take away from the Chancellor his jurisdiction in bankruptcy.[10] We have seen, too, that reforms were made in the process and procedure of the ecclesiastical courts, and that for the writ *de excommunicato capiendo* a writ *de contumace capiendo* was substituted.[11] An Act was passed to regulate the office of registrar of the Court of

---

[1] 50 George III c. 117 ; 51 George III c. 71 ; above 189 n. 1.
[2] 50 George III c. 117 ; 51 George III c. 55.
[3] 53 George III c. 150 (the audit office) ; 54 George III c. 157 (the office of works) ; 54 George III c. 159 (harbours, dockyards and arsenals).
[4] 48 George III c. 73 ; for these revenues see Vol. x 348-349.
[5] 22 George III c. 75 ; vol. x 523, vol. xi 42, 53, 74.
[6] 54 George III c. 6 ; see Cobbett, Parlt. Debates xxvii 369-370, 365-370, 434-448.
[7] 53 George III c. 24 ; vol. i 442 ; he at first sat in the council chamber at Lincoln's Inn, but in 1816 an Act was passed to build him a court in Lincoln's Inn, 56 George III c. lxxxiv.
[8] Life of Romilly (ed. 1842) ii 208-209, 299 ; Hansard (1st series) xxiv 491-494, xxv 22.
[9] Ibid xxiv 470-471, 485-486.   [10] Ibid xxv 16-18, 21-22.
[11] 53 George III c. 127; vol. i 632; below 269.

Admiralty and the Prize Court.[1] It prevented the registrar from making a profit by the use of the money in court and required him to pay it into the Bank of England[2] just as Acts of 1725 had deprived the masters in Chancery of the control of the suitors' money.[3] We shall see that the reforms were made in the organization of the London stipendiary magistrates ;[4] and all gaol fees and similar fees payable to clerks of the court were abolished.[5]

In relation to Parliament there are several Acts which make small reforms of a similar kind. The Grenville Act, which regulated the trial of contested elections to the House of Commons, was amended and made perpetual ;[6] and provision was made for the improvement of the procedure on such trials.[7] The Act of William III's reign, which prohibited the splitting of interest in land in order to multiply votes,[8] was made more effectual.[9] The process of reforming the offices of the House of Commons, which had begun in 1800,[10] was continued. After the death of the present holders of the offices of Clerk of the House of Commons and Serjeant at Arms, these officers and their assistants were no longer to be paid by fees, but by a fixed salary.[11] A member of the House of Commons who became bankrupt was to be suspended, and, if he did not get his discharge within twelve months, he was to lose his seat.[12] The Act which most clearly shows the growth of modern ideas as to election to, and representation in, Parliament is the Act, generally known as Curwen's Act, which declared to be illegal the purchase and sale of seats in the House of Commons, and all express contracts to procure any seat in the House in consideration of office, place, or employment.[13] Romilly[14] and others[15] considered that the fact that the contract must be " express " made the Act useless, and in effect gave the government a

---

[1] 53 George III c. 151 ; for similar bill of 1810 see Life of Romilly ii 157-158 ; Cobbett, Parlt. Debates xvii 650-654.

[2] Romilly, ibid ii 263, says that " it appeared that Lord Arden, the registrar, whose fees amount to about £12,000 a year, has made £7,000 a year more by interest and profits of suitors' money, and that he has sometimes employed above £200,000 of such money at interest for similar practices in the office of the Deputy-Remembrancer of the court of Exchequer " ; see ibid 158-159.

[3] 12 George III c.c. 32, 33 ; vol. i 440.

[4] 51 George III c. 119 ; vol. i 147-148 ; below 235.

[5] 55 George III c. 13 ; 56 George III c. 116 ; it was said in 1814, Cobbett, Parlt. Debates xxviii 91, that," in a large number of gaols, and even of county gaols, no table of fees was kept. In others the greatest irregularity prevailed. In some, these fees were very exorbitant, and it often happened that the prisoners were compelled to sell their clothes and bedding in order to pay the fees."

[6] 47 George III Sess. 1 c. 1 ; vol. x 548-550.

[7] 53 George III c. 71.   [8] 7, 8 William III c. 25 ; vol. vi 246.

[9] 53 George III c. 49.   [10] 39, 40 George III c. 92.

[11] 52 George III c. 11.   [12] 52 George III c. 144.

[13] 49 George III c. 118.   [14] Life of Romilly (ed. 1842) ii 120-121.

[15] Earl Grosvenor said in the House of Lords, Cobbett, Parlt. Debates xiv 1037, that the bill, " by the introduction of the word ' express ' has transferred the power of corruption to his majesty's ministers, to be exercised by them without control."

monopoly in the purchase of seats.[1] But this was perhaps too extreme a view. The Act did recognize the principle that seats ought not to be sold or procured for money or money's worth ; and it may be noted that Liverpool, writing to Peel, the Irish Secretary, on the subject of the Irish elections, said that Curwen's bill had put the government "under considerable difficulties," [2] and that Croker wrote to Peel that "Curwen's Bill is not quite the *caput mortuum* that people supposed."[3]

The growth of toleration is illustrated by the Act of 1812[4] which repealed the Act of Charles II's reign against Quakers,[5] and the Acts of his reign which prohibited non-conformist preachers or teachers from residing in corporate towns,[6] and suppressed conventicles.[7] For the future Protestant non-conformists could conduct their services in certified and registered places of worship. In 1813 it was provided that Unitarians should no longer be exempted from the Toleration Act of 1688.[8]

The Act of 1807 which abolished the Slave Trade[9] was a great victory for "the Saints" ; and, as we shall see, it was followed up by later Acts directed to make the prohibition more effectual.[10] We shall see that the growth of humanitarianism is further illustrated by Acts for making better provision for the care of pauper and criminal lunatics.[11] The immediate cause for the passing of the first of these Acts was the Act of 1800,[12] passed in consequence of *Hadfield's Case*,[13] which gave the Crown power to detain a criminal lunatic during pleasure. Before that Act, it was said, "several unfortunate persons were now lying in public gaols—of all places the most improper for their abode" ; and an instance was given of a homicidal maniac so detained who had murdered a fellow prisoner.[14]

Lastly there are the Acts which gave the justices extended powers to deal with the Luddite disturbances.[15] One Act of 1812 increased the punishment of persons who destroyed stocking or lace frames or other machinery,[16] and two other Acts provided for

---

[1] Romilly, op. cit. 120-121, said that the government " have struck out the clause which required an oath of the member, and which annexed the penalties of perjury to the taking of such an oath falsely, and every other clause that could make the bill effectual. With their alteration the Bill is, in truth, what Lord Folkestone proposed to entitle it, " A Bill to secure the Purchase of Seats exclusively to Government." I could have no hesitation in voting against it."

[2] C. S. Parker, Sir Robert Peel i 38. [3] Ibid 47.

[4] 52 George III c. 155. [5] 14 Charles II c. 1 ; vol. vi 198.

[6] 17 Charles II c. 2 ; vol. vi 198. [7] 16 Charles II c. 4 ; vol. vi 198.

[8] 1, 2 William and Mary, Sess. i c. 18, § 17 ; 53 George III c. 160.

[9] 47 George III, Sess. 1 c. 36. [10] Below 215.

[11] 48 George III c. 96 ; 51 George III c. 79 ; 55 George III c. 46 ; below 320, 321. [12] 39, 40 George III c. 94. [13] (1800) 27 S.T. 1281.

[14] Cobbett, Parlt. Debates viii 514.

[15] Above 180. [16] 52 George III c. 16.

the more effectual policing of the disturbed districts,[1] and for the seizure of arms. Assemblies of persons for the purpose of being drilled or trained in the use of arms or for the purpose of aiding and abetting such assemblies, were declared to be unlawful assemblies. They could be dispersed, and those taking part in them could be arrested. Secretaries of and delegates to such assemblies could be arrested and their books seized.

This legislation shows, as I have said, that even in the war years, the need to adapt the law and institutions of the state to modern needs was not wholly lost sight of. Naturally the return of peace seemed to those who were conscious of the need for larger reforms to open a bright prospect. In 1814 Brougham wrote[2] that the elimination of war expenditure at once deprived the Crown of a fertile source of patronage. " Besides," he added, " the *gag* is gone, which used to stop our mouths as often as any reform was mentioned—' Revolution ' first, and then ' Invasion.' These cries are gone. It really appears to me that the game is in the hands of the Opposition. Every charge will now breed more and more of discontent. The dismissal of officers and other war functionaries will throw thousands out of employ, who will sooner or later ferment and turn to vinegar. All this will tell against Government and the benefits of the peace." In 1816 he sketched the plan of campaign which the Opposition should pursue.[3] " Retrenchment in all ways, with ramifications into the Royal family, property tax, jobs of all sorts, distresses of the landed interest, etc. . . . Last of all, but not least, the proposal of measures and exigencies unconnected with the ordinary party topics, whereby much immediate real good is done to the country, and great credit gained by the party, as well as, ultimately, a check secured to the Crown, and to abuses generally. For example —prison reform—education of the poor—tithes—above all the Press, with which last I think of leading off immediately, having long matured my plan. . . . It embraces the whole subject—of allowing the truth to be given in evidence—limiting the *ex officio* powers, both by filing informations and other privileges possessed by the Crown, and abolishing special juries in cases of libels,[4] or rather of misdemeanour generally."

Brougham was right in thinking that many reforms were urgently needed. But he did not foresee all the difficulties which lay in the path of the reformer. He did not foresee that the economic difficulties, which arose from the change over from war to peace conditions, would give rise to disturbances which would help the Tory party to retain power for several years to come, and

---

[1] 52 George III c.c. 17 and 162 ; below 311.
[2] The Creevy Papers i 192.   [3] Ibid 248.
[4] For Bentham's views on this question see above 58, 99.

delay the advent of the larger measures of reform which were urgently needed. He did not foresee that when, in the third decade of the century, the more farseeing Tories began to undertake the work of reform, the very fluid condition of parties, and the divergent creeds and ideals of different sections of those parties, would open the possibility of a coalition between Whig and Tory reformers. In fact in that third decade, when it had become clear that large measures of reform were inevitable, it was by no means certain whether they would be undertaken by a coalition of Whigs and left-wing Tories, or by a coalition of Whigs and Radicals. The question which of these two coalitions would control the movement for reform was a momentous question, for upon it would depend very largely the character of the constitutional development of the English state in the nineteenth century. We shall now see that the fact that the movement for reform was controlled by a coalition of Whigs and Radicals was due partly to the accidents of history—if Canning had lived a coalition between Whigs and left-wing Tories might have been effected ;[1] and partly to the disturbing influence of the Irish politics.[2]

From 1815 to the passing of the Reform Act of 1832

The end of the war enabled statesmen to turn their undivided attention to the internal condition of the country. The dominating feature of that condition was the rapid progress of the industrial revolution and its effects upon many aspects of the national life. That revolution had created, on the one hand, a class of wealthy merchants and a numerous and prosperous middle class of traders and, on the other hand, a class of workmen many of whom were badly paid, hard-worked, and liable to intervals of unemployment when trade was bad.[3] It was obvious that many reforms were needed to adjust the political institutions and the law to these new economic conditions, to determine the position in the state of these new classes of persons, to give effect to their ideas, and to adjust their relations to the aristocracy of landowners which, all through the eighteenth century, had exercised predominant power. During the war years this process of adjustment had begun ;[4] but it had made very little progress. During this period the progress is much more rapid ; and, at the end of the period, the passing of the Reform Act ensured its greatly increased acceleration. In the latter years of this period both Whigs and Tories assisted in this process of adjustment.[5] Of the Tories the two greatest names are Canning and Peel, and of them and their work I shall speak later.[6] Of the Whigs the man who did most to

---

[1] Below 228.   [2] Below 228, 241.
[3] Temperley, Camb. Mod. Hist. x 573, 575-576.
[4] Above 188 seqq.   [5] Below 230, 231.   [6] Below 221-227.

forward its progress all through this period was Henry Brougham, who, as we have seen, had been quick to see the opportunites for the reformer which the peace gave.[1] He has left a considerable mark upon English political and constitutional history as a politician, and upon legal history as a law reformer. Of his achievements as a law reformer,[2] and of his qualities as Lord Chancellor[3] I shall speak later in this chapter. At this point I shall say something of his position as a politician and of his character.

Henry Brougham[4] (1778-1868), the son of a small Westmorland landowner, was born at Edinburgh and educated at Edinburgh University. He was a precocious child and youth. He entered the University at fourteen, where he studied the classics—more especially the Latin classics, philosophy, mathematics, and science. In 1800 he was admitted as an advocate to the Scotch bar ; but he found little opening there ; and so, like Wedderburn[5] and Erskine,[6] he determined to try the English bar. He became a student of Lincoln's Inn, Nov. 14, 1803, and was called to the bar Nov. 22, 1808. Before his call his name was beginning to be known. Besides writing a book on the *Colonial Policy of the European Powers*, which was remarkable for its promise rather than its performance,[7] he had become one of the principal writers in the *Edinburgh Review*,[8] over which in later years he came, to Macaulay's disgust,[9] to wield a despotic sway. After a year spent in foreign travel with an American passport, he settled in London in 1805. He allied himself with the Whigs, was elected to Brooks's, and had the entrée at Holland House. In 1807 he helped the Whigs to run the general election of that year. In that capacity he showed his powers of organization. Lord Holland says :[10]

With partial and scanty assistance from Mr. Allen, myself, and two or three more, he, in the course of ten days, filled every bookseller's shop with pamphlets, most London newspapers and all the county ones without exception with paragraphs, and supplied a large portion of the boroughs throughout the kingdom with handbills adapted to the local interests of the candidates.

[1] Above 193, 194.   [2] Below 296-307.   [3] Below 639-651.
[4] Atlay, The Victorian Chancellors i 168-378 ; Campbell, Lives of the Chancellors viii 213-596 ; A. Aspinall, Lord Brougham and the Whig Party ; Bagehot, Biographical Studies 40-83.
[5] Vol. xii 570.   [6] Below 581.   [7] Atlay, op. cit. i 176.
[8] Creevy's first mention of Brougham, the Creevy Papers i 30, was occasioned by a review written by Brougham in the *Edinburgh*, which his friend Currie considered to be " unfair and foul " ; Currie says of Brougham and his book, " he has got a sort of philosophical cant about him, and a way of putting obscure sentences together, which seem to fools to contain deep meaning, especially as an air of consummate petulance and confidence runs through the whole."
[9] Trevelyan, Life of Macaulay i 198.
[10] Memoirs of the Whig Party ii 225, cited Atlay ; The Victorian Chancellors i 183.

In spite of all his efforts the Whigs were defeated, and so he turned to the bar, and entered the chambers of Tindal,[1] then a special pleader. As a Scottish advocate he could appear in Scottish appeals and before the Privy Council. There he got some work ; but his real chance came when in 1807 he was briefed by the Liverpool and Manchester merchants to appear before the Parliamentary committees of the two Houses in support of their petition against the Orders in Council.[2] His efforts before these committees made his name ; and in 1810 the Duke of Bedford, at the instance of Lord Holland, found a seat for him in Parliament. By the end of the session he had become one of the leaders of the Opposition. As Mr. Atlay has said :[3]

No subject was too small, too complicated, or too abstruse for his notice, and on all alike he was ready to pour out a fluent, if sometimes a discursive, stream of eloquence, lightened by flashes of bitter sarcasm and invective, and relieved occasionally by extravagant banter. He had a watchful eye on the whole working of the State Machine. Nothing that savoured of an increase in the Royal prerogative could escape his notice ; he was adamant as to parliamentary control over the public money, and equally jealous of parliamentary privilege when exercised at the expense of the people. He was as one crying in the wilderness in his advocacy of the Catholic claims ; he was loud for purity in election and the abolition of sinecures. Acts of cruelty perpetrated under cover of naval or military discipline, the illegal oppression of prisoners in gaol or mad house, were dragged by him into the glare of day. It is perhaps the highest tribute to his abilities that, instead of being looked on as a bore or a busy body, " Counsellor Brougham in a terrible fume " was accepted as an invaluable auxiliary.

In 1812 it was largely due to his efforts that the Orders in Council were revoked. Even before Brougham had entered Parliament Lord Grey had been impressed by his talents. He said of him that he was " the first man this country has seen since Burke's time " ;[4] and in 1811, when the approach of the regency seemed to indicate a possibility of the return of the Whigs to power, he was prepared to offer Brougham the post of President of the Board of Trade.[5] But this prospect never materialized, since the Prince decided to go on with the existing Tory ministry. Brougham's success in Parliament reacted on his position at the bar ; and he made a considerable name by his defence of the two Hunts in two prosecutions for seditious libel.[6]

Brougham failed to secure a seat in the new Parliament which met in 1813. In spite of all his efforts he failed to win a seat at

---

[1] Afterwards Chief Justice of the Common Pleas, below 549-555.
[2] For the Orders in Council see above 178, 179.
[3] The Victorian Chancellors i 189.
[4] The Creevy Papers i 108 ; Trevelyan, Lord Grey of the Reform Bill 190—though he afterwards came to mistrust him, ibid 223, 256-257.
[5] Atlay, op. cit. i 190.   [6] Ibid 192-195 ; (1811) 31, S.T. 367, 495.

Liverpool. It was during these years of exclusion that he made the acquaintance of the Princess of Wales, who had been much impressed by his manners and his talents. From the first he realized that her wrongs could be made a valuable weapon wherewith to attack the government.[1] Meanwhile he kept in close touch with Lord Grey and the Whig party, and for the Parliament of 1816 Lord Darlington, at the request of Lord Grey, found him a seat. Brougham therefore got an opportunity of carrying into effect the plan of campaign which he had outlined.[2]

Brougham's combination of abilities was remarkable and unique. " The distinctive quality of Brougham, the source . . . of his greatness, was his impulsive power, his propelling force, resulting from his grasp of mind, his prodigious capacity for labour, his indomitable energy, and his excitability," [3] He was a great orator in Parliament and on the hustings,[4] a great debater and a great organizer. His industry was as great as his abilities ;[5] and this combination of industry and ability enabled him to master the details of any subject, scientific or literary, and to speak or write about it in such a way that his hearers or readers, unless they were specialists, were persuaded that he was a master of the subject.[6] It has been truly said that

What Brougham did for literature and science must be taken in the block, and not judged individually or by the pieces. His multifarious writings were the wheels and cogs of the machinery by which he upheaved prejudice and bigotry, the slings and arrows with which he assailed ignorance, the aqueducts and sluices by which he diffused knowledge. The real aim of the essay or article was attained by the enquiry it stimulated or the example it set. Brougham may not have contributed the best papers published by the Society for the Diffusion of Useful Knowledge. But he set the Society afloat.[7]

He waged a life-long war against abuses of all sorts, and was a whole-hearted supporter all his life of the causes of education, law reform, a freer trade, Catholic emancipation, and Parliamentary reform. While he was out of Parliament he had

---

[1] In 1813 Brougham wrote to Creevy, " my principle is—take her [the Princess] along with you as far as you both go the same road. It is one of the constitutional means of making head against a revenue of 105 millions . . . an army of ½ million, and 800 millions of debt," the Creevy Papers i 179.

[2] Above 193.   [3] Quart. Rev. cxxvi 36.

[4] Of his oratory Bagehot, Biographical Studies 62, said, " it is rough and ready. It abounds in sarcasm, in vituperation, in aggression. It does not shrink from detail. It would batter anything at any moment "; but with important speeches he took great pains, e.g. he wrote out the peroration of his speech for Queen Caroline seven times, Quart. Rev. cxxvi 44 ; Greville, Memoirs iii 343, says that " he wrote and rewrote over and over again whole speeches."

[5] Greville, Memoirs, iii 343, says " he has been known to work fifteen hours a day for six weeks together."

[6] Atlay, op. cit. i 277-278 ; Campbell, Lives of the Chancellors viii 493-494

[7] Quart. Rev. cxxvi 60-61.

coquetted with the projects of the more radical reformers ;[1] but after 1816 he threw in his lot with the Whigs,[2] with the result that his advocacy of more moderate reforms played no small part in educating the aristocratic Whig party, and in bringing the left wing of that party into line with the ideas and wishes of the rising middle class of commercial men.[3]

At the same time he had some very remarkable defects which prevented him from gaining the leading position in his party to which his abilities entitled him. His vehemence as an orator sometimes made him guilty of gross want of tact and judgment, which disgusted his own party and ruled him out as its official leader.[4] His attack on the Regent in 1816 turned votes against him and earned the reproaches of Romilly and many others.[5] Though this speech had made him very unpopular, he soon recovered his ground—a few days after he led the successful assault on the income tax.[6] But though his manners and social qualities united with his abilities to help him to extricate himself from difficulties into which he had got himself,[7] his vanity and selfishness were a constant handicap both at the bar and in politics. At the bar the multifariousness of his interests and his studies made him inferior as a lawyer to lesser men ;[8] and he sometimes showed himself

more solicitous to gain distinction for himself than to succeed for his client ; he could not resist the temptation to make a joke at his client's expense ; he showed no tact in conducting a difficult case, and, if he was a vigorous, he was never a verdict-getting, counsel.[9]

[1] A. Aspinall, Lord Brougham and the Whig Party 31, 53-54; Graham Wallas, Francis Place 117-119, 124-125.
[2] Aspinall, op. cit. 68, 71-72, 85-86; Graham Wallas, op. cit. 122-123.
[3] Aspinall, op. cit. 50.   [4] The Creevy Papers i 250-265.
[5] Life of Romilly (ed. 1842) ii 412-413; Gore, Creevy's Life and Times 107; The Creevy Papers i 249-250.   [6] Atlay, op. cit. i 205.
[7] Mackintosh said in his Journal for Jan. 30, 1818 : "The address and in-sinuation of Brougham are so great that nothing but the bad temper which he cannot always hide could hinder him from mastering everybody as he does Romilly. He *leads* others to his opinion ; he generally appears at first to concur with theirs, and never more than half opposes it at once. This management is helped by an air of easy frankness that would lay suspicion itself asleep. He will place himself at the head of an opposition with whom he is unpopular ; he will conquer the House of Commons, who hate, but now begin to fear him," cited Bagehot, Biographical Studies 59 ; a good illustration is the way he conciliated Grey in Scotland in 1834 after their quarrel, Campbell, Chancellors viii 454-455.
[8] Horner, speaking of his arguments in Banc, says that they were defective in lawyer-like qualities—" Precision and clearness in the details, symmetry in the putting of them together, an air of finish and unity in the whole are the merits of that style ; and there is not one of them in which he is not very defective," Memoirs ii 123, cited Atlay, The Victorian Chancellors i 192.
[9] Campbell, Chancellors viii 256 ; Pollock was the more effective advocate in the Northern Circuit, Life of Campbell i 448 ; as Hanworth says, Life of Chief Baron Pollock 42, "Brougham starved the case to his own glory, while Pollock set out to win for his client."

Tindal once said that Scarlett had invented a machine by means of which, when he argued, he could make the judges' heads nod at his pleasure ; but that Brougham had got hold of it, but, not knowing how to manage it, when he argued the judges, instead of nodding, shook their heads.

In his advocacy of the cause of the Princess of Wales and her daughter he always had at the back of his mind the political capital which could be made out of their misfortunes ;[1] and it was said, I think not without justification, that he was prepared to subordinate the interests of his client, Queen Caroline, to his own advancement.[2] As a politician the same causes inspired distrust throughout his career. Creevy, in company with whom he contested Liverpool in 1812, after expressing admiration for his oratorical feats adds :

still I cannot like him. He has always some game or underplot out of sight—some mysterious correspondence—some extraordinary connection with persons quite opposite to himself.[3]

" Wicked Shifts " was one of the nicknames which he coined for him. We shall see that his later career, and more especially his career as Chancellor, affords considerable justification for this distrust.[4] The qualities which make a successful agitator are not the qualities which made a successful leader of a party or a successful minister. Brougham had, as Bagehot has said,[5] that most essential quality of a successful agitator—a vast amount of " devil " :

What it is one can hardly explain in a single sentence. It is most easily explained by physiognomy. There is a glare in some men's eyes which seems to say, " Beware I am dangerous ; noli me tangere." Lord Brougham's face has this. A mischievous excitability is the most obvious expression of it. If he were an horse, nobody would buy him ; with that eye no one could answer for his temper.

It is the possession of this quality which goes far to explain Brougham's success in exposing abuses and supporting reforms, and his failure as an administrator ; his capacity in a crisis such

---

[1] Above 197 n. 1.

[2] On April 12, 1820 Croker noted that, " Brougham, it is said *grossly*, has sold the Queen" ; and on April 22 that, " Brougham wished to secure the profits without the inconveniences of this appointment [attorney-general to the Queen], and offered not to assume it if the Government would give him a patent of precedence, but the Chancellor refused," The Croker Papers i 172-173 ; Creevy had similar suspicions, The Creevy Papers ii 23-24.

[3] Ibid i 171 ; on the premature report of his death in 1839, Barnes, the editor of The Times, wrote an article in which, " admitting his wondrous versatility," admitting that he was " one of the most agreeable, amusing, kindly and convivial of associates," he declared him to be a man in whom no one could confide, " whom no party could venture to employ otherwise than as a transient ally ; as a partner or a colleague, never," Quart. Rev. cxxvi 53.

[4] Below 639-644.   [5] Bagehot, Biographical Studies 64.

as the crisis of the Reform Bill, and his incapacity to settle down
to the routine work of his office ; the admiration which his great
qualities excited both in the country and the House of Commons,
and the distrust which he inspired in the men with whom he
worked. As Greville said, all his splendid talents were neutralized
by his want of ballast[1]—the want, that is, of settled calculable
principles.

We must now turn from the consideration of Brougham himself to the position of the two parties in the House of Commons,
and the condition of the country, when he re-entered the House
in 1816.

The victorious close of the war gave the Tory party a position
of great strength. The Whigs were divided, and the war record
of many of their leaders was bad. They had been constant critics
of Wellington's Peninsula campaign, and some of them had wished
to make terms with Napoleon when he broke out of Elba.[2] But
the Tories, under the leadership of Liverpool, Eldon, and Castlereagh made the mistake of thinking that, with the restoration of
peace, the nation could and ought to settle down without substantial change in the laws and institutions which had governed
it when the war broke out.

Their general aim was professedly to carry out the policy of Pitt, but the
policy of Pitt after, and not before, 1793. . . . To secure the stability of
the State, not to provide for its growth, was . . . the true end and object
of all statesmanship.[3]

Events were soon to show the impossibility of this policy, and
prove the truth of Brougham's diagnosis[4] of the opportunities
offered to an intelligent opposition ; for at the end of the war
the country, it has been truly said, was " in the position of a
county family which has spent half as much as it is worth in a
contested election." [5]

The change over from war to peace conditions necessarily
occasioned much distress both in the manufacturing industries
and in the agricultural industry. The cessation of the demand for
munitions at home and abroad, the falling off of foreign trade
occasioned partly by the poverty of countries ruined by war and
partly by hostile tariffs, the discharge of soldiers and sailors,
created an industrial crisis, widespread unemployment, and a
lowering of wages to starvation levels. The price of corn fell,

---

[1] " Brougham is only a living and very remarkable instance of the inefficacy of
the most splendid talents, unless they are accompanied with other qualities which
scarcely admit of definition, but which serve the same purpose that ballast does
for a ship," Memoirs i 121.

[2] Feiling, The Second Tory Party 276-277.

[3] Temperley, Camb. Mod. Hist. x 574.

[4] Above 193. [5] Quart. Rev. cxxvi 189.

farm labourers were discharged, and land went out of cultivation. Naturally the attempt to keep up the price of corn was unpopular with the starving population of the great towns, and with the agricultural labourers who got little benefit from this protection. All these causes of distress were aggravated by the bad harvest of 1816. It is not therefore surprising that all over the country there were epidemics of rioting. In 1815 there were riots at Nottingham and Newcastle-on-Tyne.[1] In 1815-16 there were agricultural riots in the eastern counties—five rioters were hanged after a special assize at Ely in 1816.[2] There was industrial unrest at Birmingham in 1816;[3] and " in Worcestershire and Staffordshire a large number of colliers, forgemen, mailers, and labourers were roaming over the countryside in small parties, some begging and others demanding money and provisions."[4] There was much distress amongst the cotton operatives and hand-loom weavers in Lancashire.[5]   In South Wales reductions of wages resulted in strikes, and it was necessary to call out troops.[6] In 1816 machine breaking societies were at work in the counties of Leicester and Nottingham.[7]

In this atmosphere it is not surprising that the radical agitation, which had been suppressed in the last years of the eighteenth century,[8] revived. Working through Hampden Clubs and political unions which were spread over the country,[9] they voiced the demand for Parliamentary reform and all sorts of other reforms—possible and impossible. Cobbett's *Political Register*, Wooler's *Black Dwarf* and other papers familiarized the people with Paine's democratic and irreligious views.[10] In London the radicals organized two great demonstrations in Spa fields on November 15 and December 2, 1816;[11] and, after the second of these meetings, there was rioting and the looting of gunshops.[12] In January 1817 the Regent was stoned and fired at by an airgun;[13] in March an attack on the prisons and barracks at Manchester was planned;[14] and in June there was an armed insurrection in Derbyshire led by Brandreth, who in the course of the proceedings committed murder.[15]

The riot which followed the Spa fields meeting of December 2, 1816, and the Derbyshire insurrection led by Brandreth in June 1817 had their sequels in the courts.

The riot which followed the Spa fields meeting resulted in the

[1] Davis, Age of Grey and Peel 169.
[2] Ibid 169-170.
[3] Ibid 170.   [4] Ibid.   [5] Ibid 171.
[6] Ibid 171-172.   [7] Ibid.   [8] Above 173, 174.
[9] Davis, Age of Grey and Peel 177-180.
[10] For Paine's views see above 18-26.
[11] Davis, op. cit. 176.
[12] Feiling, The Second Tory Party 290.   [13] Ibid.
[14] Ibid Davis, op. cit. 188-189.
[15] Martineau, History of the Peace i 152-155.

prosecution of Watson, Thistlewood, Hooper, and Preston for high treason.[1] Watson was tried first. He was ably defended by Wetherall and Copley—the future Lord Lyndhurst. Copley's speech[2] was a very effective defence, and he succeeded in very thoroughly discrediting Castle, the chief witness for the prosecution. Watson was acquitted, and the government abandoned the prosecution of the other three accused.[3] In putting these men on their trial for high treason, the government made the same mistake as they had made in the case of Hardy.[4] The facts proved showed that the accused had been engaged in a serious riot, and that acts of violence and robbery had been committed : they did not show that there had been a levying of war.[5] As Romilly said,[6]

If they had been committed to Newgate, tried at the Old Bailey, and indicted merely for a very aggravated riot, they would without doubt have been convicted. Instead of this they are declared innocent, and they escape all punishment, except, indeed, a long and close imprisonment previous to trial, which, as they have been finally acquitted, has the appearance of a great injustice done to them.

Brandreth and thirty-four others were indicted for high treason.[7] Brandreth and three others were tried and convicted. Nineteen others then pleaded guilty,[8] and against twelve the Crown offered no evidence—mainly on the ground of their youth—so that they were acquitted.[9] Three were executed, eleven were transported for life, three were transported for fourteen years, one was imprisoned for two years, two for one year, and three for six months.[10]

Having regard to all these events and signs of discontent, having regard to reports from the country by magistrates and government spies,[11] and having regard to the doings and boastings of the London radicals,[12] it is not surprising that the government should have believed in an organized and widespread conspiracy against government and property, and that secret committees of both Houses of Parliament should have endorsed that belief,[13] and framed legislation to suppress it. Peel, writing to Lord Whitworth in January 1817, said : " Lord Liverpool told me

---

[1] R. v. Watson (1817) 32 S.T. 1. [2] At pp. 499-538.
[3] At p. 674. [4] Above 162, 163.
[5] See Copley's defence 32 S.T. at pp. 510-511.
[6] Life of Romilly (ed. 1842) ii 460.
[7] (1817) 32 S.T. 755. [8] At p. 1387.
[9] At pp. 1387-1389. [10] At p. 1394.
[11] The most notorious of these spies was Oliver who acted as an agent provocateur, but as everyone now admits, without any authority from the government, Davis, op. cit. 189 ; see Hammond, The Skilled Labourer, chap. xii.
[12] Their game in 1816, says Davis, op. cit. 173, " was to create the illusion that all the distressed and discontented classes in the country were linked together in the closest correspondence for a common purpose."
[13] Hansard xxxv 411-420 (House of Lords); ibid 438-447 (House of Commons).

yesterday that he had been a member of the secret committees of
1794, and that nothing came to light then which showed nearly
so disaffected and seditious a feeling among the people as exists
at present." [1]

In 1817 an Act was passed which recited that a traitorous
conspiracy had been formed " for the purpose of overthrowing by
means of a general insurrection the established government, laws,
and constitution of this kingdom," and suspended the Habeas
Corpus Act with respect to persons charged with high treason or
treasonable practices. [2] Another Act of the same year re-enacted
with important additions the Act of 1795[3] for the prevention of
seditious meetings and assemblies. [4] The most important of these
additions were a clause forbidding the meeting of more than
fifty persons for the purpose of considering any petition to Parliament or address to the Regent for the alteration of matters in
church or state within a mile of Westminster Hall on the days when
Parliament or the courts were sitting ;[5] a clause suppressing the
Spencean and other like societies ;[6] and a clause suppressing
societies which enacted oaths made unlawful by Acts of 1796
and 1812,[7] or which elected delegates or representatives to confer
with other societies. [8]

This legislation did not pass unopposed. For the suspension of
the Habeas Corpus Act, it was said, there was no real need. Lord
Grey maintained that there was no evidence of any formidable
conspiracy. Who, he asked, were the conspirators ?[9]

They were miserable wretches reduced to the lowest poverty and distress,
who would probably have been driven to seek relief upon the highway,
if there had not been a prospect that the discontents of the country were
such as might prompt many to follow their wild schemes. What was
their object ? to produce insurrection, by calling persons together under
the pretence of parliamentary reform, without any previous concert or
design, and trusting wholly to chance for the means of stimulating their
instruments in the work of sedition. That was the whole extent of the
plot ; and the attempt was made in the way that was projected. The
mob assembled at Spa-fields ; they were addressed in inflammatory
language ; to be sure they were provided with ammunition, having
about twenty or thirty balls and a pound of gun powder concealed in the
foot of an old stocking. They were not followed by more than two or
three hundred persons, who plundered a few gunsmiths' shops, and a
gentleman received a wound, from which he sincerely hoped he would
recover. Such excesses ought, undoubtedly, to be repressed and punished,
but in order to do so, was it necessary to suspend the Habeas Corpus ?

Romilly opposed the bill on the same grounds ; and both he
and Lord John Russell pointed out that what might have been

---

[1] C. S. Parker, Sir Robert Peel i 237.
[2] 57 George III c.c. 3 and 55.
[3] Above 165, 166.
[4] 57 George III c. 19.
[5] § 23.
[6] § 24.
[7] Above 168, 173.
[8] § 25.
[9] Hansard xxxv 578-579.

justifiable in 1794 or 1799, when the country was at war and when plots had been made to supersede Parliament, was not justifiable in 1817.[1] Brougham contended that the government had been deluded by worthless spies like Castle and Oliver.[2] On the same grounds the opposition objected to the Act[3] to indemnify persons who had arrested and detained persons while the Habeas Corpus Act was suspended. Lambton opposed it because it stopped all enquiry into the conduct of the ministers.[4] Romilly and Brougham opposed it because it was too sweeping in its character and protected not only ministers and magistrates but spies and informers.[5]

The Act to prevent seditious meetings was opposed on the same grounds. The existing law, Romilly said, was quite sufficient.[6] Moreover it was dangerous to curtail the very valuable right of public meeting because it would tend to diminish the people's attachment to the constitution.[7] Brougham ridiculed the fear of the followers of Spence[8]—" the visionary author of the new system, who lived twenty years ago, and published his opinions in the most miserable prose that ever issued from the press." [9] On the other hand, Canning, with some reason, defended the bill on the ground that, so far from abridging the right to petition or the right of public meeting, it protected it from abuse. He said :[10]

Why is it that popular meetings require extraordinary control at the present moment ? Because the great multitude of the individuals who attend them go there with the intention to subvert the constitution ?— because they go with a disposition to be led on to acts of outrage ? No. But because, in the peculiar circumstances of the country, there is an unusual degree of inflammability in the public mind ; because there are incendiaries abroad who would avail themselves of this extraordinary inflammability to kindle the fires of rebellion in every corner of the kingdom. This is the true reason why restraints ought to be put upon popular assemblies. . . . It is true that great distress prepares the minds of sufferers for listening to every fantastic and delusive project. This state of mind . . . exposes the unemployed manufacturers [11] and artisans to be misled by the artifices of enemies, who, neither sharing, nor commiserating, nor wishing to relieve their distresses, consider them as only prepared by those distresses to be the instruments of most nefarious designs. Even the benevolent exertions of the wealthier orders of the community, and the last and best exertion of benevolence, the diffusion of knowledge among the poor classes, are turned by these corruptors into evil. Education itself, the greatest of all blessings in a state . . . has been thus converted into one of the blackest curses that could afflict mankind.

---

[1] Hansard xxxv 736-737, 743-744.   [2] Ibid xxxvi 1134-1135.
[3] 58 George III c. 6.   [4] Hansard xxxvii 891-899.
[5] Ibid xxxvii 965-980, 1011-1012, 1019-1020.   [6] Ibid xxxv 618-619.
[7] Ibid 1097.   [8] For Spence see above 37, 38.
[9] Hansard xxxv 626.   [10] Ibid 1118-1119.
[11] The word " manufacturer " is here used in its older sense of " workman " vol. xi 412 n. 1, 462-463.

That the distinction drawn by the opposition speakers between the condition of the country in 1794 and 1817 was a valid distinction is shown by the fact that the legislation of 1817 did not, like that of 1795 and 1799, suppress all radical agitation. In Place's opinion the government had less power than in Pitt's time, for "the people had become too well informed to be deceived." [1]

Trade improved in 1818-19; but there was much distress in Lancashire.[2] Trade unions and strikes multiplied.

Manchester and London were co-operating to make one great Trades Union and issuing literature which declared labour the corner stone of society. Taking their models from the London Hampden clubs, political unions spread over Lancashire and the Midlands, distributing propaganda, signing reform petitions, organizing mass meetings, singing "Millions be free." . . . A Tyne colliery manager noted *The Black Dwarf* or 'The Black Book' of sinecures and rotten boroughs was to be found in the hat crown of almost every pitman you meet.[3]

At Birmingham a meeting reflected upon the constitution of the House of Commons, and resolved to appoint a legislatorial attorney who was to demand admittance to the House of Commons as the representative of Birmingham, and propose a radical measure of reform. The result was that five of those attending the meeting were convicted of a seditious conspiracy.[4] At Manchester there were reports of terrorism and secret drilling. It was in this atmosphere that a meeting of sixty to eighty thousand persons met at St. Peter's Field, Manchester, to hear the great radical speaker Hunt.[5] The magistrates had issued a warrant for the arrest of Hunt and others. Since the constables could not execute this warrant, the yeomanry were summoned to assist. They got mixed up with the crowd and were quite unable to act or escape. Orders were then given to the hussars to disperse the mob, which they did at the expense of eleven killed and many injured, and Hunt and some of his friends were arrested.[6] This "Manchester Massacre" or "Peterloo" gave rise to two important criminal cases—*R. v. Hunt*[7] and *R. v. Burdett*;[8] and there were other cases which arose out of it.

Hunt and nine others were indicted[9] for conspiracy to disturb the peace and to excite discontent and disaffection, and to excite hatred and contempt of the government and constitution, and for unlawful assembly. Hunt and four others were convicted of

---

[1] Graham Wallas, Francis Place 126.
[2] Feiling, The Second Tory Party 297.   [3] Ibid 297-298.
[4] R. v. Edmonds and Others (1821) 1 S.T.N.S. 785.
[5] For Hunt see below 211, 505, 537.
[6] Martineau, History of the Peace i 296-305.
[7] (1820) 3 B. and Ald. 566.
[8] (1820) 1 S.T.N.S. 1.   [9] (1820) 1 S.T.N.S. 171.

holding an unlawful and seditious assembly for the purpose of exciting discontent and exciting hatred and contempt of the government and the constitution.[1] The others were acquitted.[2] Bayley, J. laid it down that to cause persons to meet for the purpose of disturbing the peace, of creating disaffection in the King's subjects, or of exciting hatred of the government, was a criminal conspiracy;[3] that an assembly to effect any of these purposes was an unlawful assembly;[4] and that if an assembly was so numerous, and held in such circumstances that it caused " fears and jealousies amongst the King's subjects " it was an unlawful assembly[5]—" in all cases of unlawful assembly " he said, " you must look to the purpose for which they meet ; you must look to the manner in which they come ; you must look to the means which they are using."[6] He said that those present at such an assembly who knew nothing of its purpose, and did nothing to carry out the purpose, were not guilty of unlawfully assembling.[7] With respect to unlawful drilling of those assembled he held that drilling merely for the purpose of the better management of the crowd was lawful ; but that drilling, if for an illegal purpose, was a misdemeanour.[8] Burdett was indicted for a seditious libel contained in a letter which he wrote on the Manchester massacre.[9] Best, J. told the jury that the truth or falsehood of the statements in the letter was immaterial. " It is," he said,[10] " not the truth or falsehood that makes a libel, but the temper with which it is published. Criticism of the government," he said, was no offence— " the question always is as to the manner." Has the writer tried " to instruct by appealing to the judgment, or to irritate and excite to sedition ? " Has he appealed " to the sense or the passions ? "[11] Burdett was convicted. He was fined £2,000 and imprisoned for three months.[12]

Two other criminal cases are connected with the Manchester massacre. In *R. v. Dewhurst and Others*,[13] Dewhurst and seven others were indicted for unlawful assembly. It was proved that a large meeting, some of whom were armed, assembled to protest against the Manchester massacre, and to advocate the reform of Parliament. Dewhurst and five of the accused were convicted and two were acquitted.[14] Bayley, J., after defining the offence of unlawful assembly, laid it down that the issue by the magistrates of a warning not to attend the meeting would not by itself make an assembly unlawful.[15] In *R. v. Knowles*[16] it appeared that a meeting was to be held at Bolton. The day before the meeting

[1] (1820) 1 S.T.N.S. 487.   [2] Ibid.   [3] Ibid 432-433.
[4] Ibid 433.   [5] Ibid 434.   [6] Ibid 435.
[7] Ibid 434-436.   [8] Ibid 446.   [9] Ibid 1.
[10] At p. 49.   [11] (1820) 1 S.T.N.S. 50-51.   [12] Ibid 170.
[13] Ibid 530.   [14] Ibid 605.   [15] Ibid 600.
[16] Ibid 498.

Knowles sold two pike heads and said, while selling them, that he hoped that the people would meet to-morrow to avenge Peterloo. He was convicted of making and selling pike heads for an unlawful purpose. The proceedings at Manchester also gave rise to the civil action of *Redford v. Birley and Others*,[1] all members of the yeomanry, for assault. The defendants justified their actions on the ground that the assault was committed while dispersing an unlawful assembly in which the plaintiff was taking part. The jury found for the defendants, and a motion for a new trial on the ground of misdirection and misreception and rejection of evidence was refused.

The action of the magistrates at Manchester was at once approved by the government.[2] But, in addition to the protests which involved their makers in criminal proceedings,[3] other protests soon began to be heard. One came from the Common Council of the City of London; and Fitz-William, the Lord Lieutenant of Yorkshire, summoned a county meeting at York for the purpose of demanding an enquiry. The government replied by dismissing Fitz-William and by proposing the Six Acts;[4] and in this action they had the support of the upper and middle classes. Such men as Zachary Macaulay and Wilberforce supported the action of the magistrates, and even Brougham recognized the danger of these mass meetings.[5]

The first of these Acts was an Act to prevent meetings for the training of persons to the use of arms.[6] The second Act gave power to the justices of the peace in certain counties to issue warrants to search for and seize arms, and to arrest persons found carrying arms in such manner and at such times as, in the judgment of the Justice, afforded ground for suspicion that they were carried for purposes dangerous to the peace.[7] The third Act was passed to prevent procedural delays in prosecutions for misdemeanour.[8] Accused persons must plead or demur within four days of appearance, and could not delay the final by imparling and so putting off the trial to a later term.[9] In default of a plea, a judgment could be entered against the accused.[10] Persons in custody or released on bail must, within twenty days of the sessions of the court, plead at once unless the case was removed by writ of certiorari.[11] On the other hand, prisoners, if prosecuted by the attorney or solicitor-general, were given the right to a copy of the information or indictment,[12] and, if they were not brought

---

[1] (1822) 1 S.T.N.S. 1071.
[2] Feiling, The Second Tory Party 299.
[3] Above 205, 206.   [4] Feiling, op. cit. 229-300.
[5] Ibid 300; for Brougham's views see Hansard xli 665.
[6] 60 George III and 1 George IV c. 1.   [7] Ibid c. 2.
[8] Ibid c. 4.   [9] § 1.   [10] Ibid.
[11] § 3.   [12] § 8.

to trial within twelve months after a plea of not guilty, they could apply to the court to bring on the trial.[1]

The fourth and most elaborate of these Acts was passed to strengthen the law against seditious assemblies.[2] No meeting of more than fifty persons, except county meetings called by the Lord Lieutenant or sheriff, was to be held to discuss public grievances, or anything relating to any trade, manufacture, business or profession, or any matter in church or state, except in the parish which the persons calling the meeting usually inhabited ; and a notice of the meeting, subscribed by seven householders of the parish, must be given to a justice of the peace residing near the parish six days before the meeting.[3] If a meeting was held in pursuance of such notice, and the notice

shall express or purport that any matter or thing by law established may be altered otherwise than by the authority of King, Lords and Commons in Parliament assembled ; or shall tend to incite and stir up the people to hatred and contempt of the person of his majesty, his heirs or successors, or of the government and constitution of this realm as by law established ; every such meeting shall be deemed and taken to be un-lawful assembly.[4]

It was made unlawful to adjourn such meetings to another date or place.[5] With the exception of justices of the peace and other peace officers, only freeholders or inhabitants of the county or corporate town where the meeting was held could attend such meetings.[6] Justices of the peace and other peace officers could attend such meetings with such a force of constables as they considered necessary, and take such steps as the case might require and other steps which this Act or the law entitled them to take ; and penalties were provided for those who obstructed them.[7] Persons attending meetings or persons assembled contrary to the Act could be ordered to disperse within a quarter of an hour—disobedience was made a felony punishable with transportation for a maximum time of seven years.[8] To attend a meeting with arms, flags, drums or other music, or in military array, was made an offence.[9] Lectures or debates for the purpose of raising money, or to which persons were admitted on payment

---

[1] § 9 ; this was an amendment proposed by Lord Holland, Hansard xli 957, which was accepted by Lord Eldon who reduced the period of eighteen months, proposed by Lord Holland to twelve months, ibid 1008-1009 ; as so amended Lord Holland assented to the bill ibid 1009.

[2] 60 George III and I George IV c. 6.

[3] § 1 ; Justices were given power to subdivide large parishes for the purpose of the Act, § 21.   [4] § 7.   [5] § 3.

[6] § 4 ; there were exceptions in the case of members of Parliament, and voters for Parliament in corporate towns.   [7] §§ 6, 13, 14.

[8] §§ 8-12 ; § 15 indemnified the justices and their officers in case any person was killed or maimed in carrying out their orders.

[9] §§ 18 and 19.

of money, must be held in places previously licensed ;[1] and magistrates could demand admission to any lecture whether held in a
licensed or an unlicensed place.[2] If lectures were given of a
seditious, irreligious or immoral tendency the licence was to be
forfeited.[3]

The fifth and sixth of these Acts dealt with the press. The
former Act gave power to the court, on a conviction for blasphemous or seditious libel, to order copies of the libel in the
possession of those convicted to be seized ;[4] and it gave power to
the court on a second conviction to order the offender to be
banished.[5] The latter Act subjected certain pamphlets containing
news or comments thereon to the newspaper stamp duties.[6]
Publishers of such pamphlets must enter into a recognizance
with sureties for payment of any fines or penalties incurred for
the publication of blasphemous or seditious libels.[7] Copies of
such pamphlets must be delivered to the commissioners of
stamps.[8]

The Acts were justified by the government on the ground that
the evidence showed that there was a widespread conspiracy to
subvert the law and the existing institutions of the country.[9]
As in 1817,[10] the existence of such a conspiracy was denied by the
opposition ;[11] and, though it was admitted there was justification
for strengthening the law in some directions,[12] some of the Acts,
e.g. the Acts giving the right to seize arms and the seditious
meetings bill, were criticized as too severe.[13] On the whole the
tone of the opposition speakers was moderate ; for though they
denied the existence of any widespread conspiracy, they could
not deny that the state of feeling in many parts of the country
was a menace to the maintenance of the peace.[14] I think that the
opposition speakers were right when they denied the existence of
a widespread conspiracy ; and that there was abundant justification for a protest made by the Earl of Lauderdale to the
Seditious Meetings Bill, in which he pointed out that economic
ills were at the root of the trouble, and maintained that public
money should be more generously spent in relieving distress.[15]
Lauderdale was not very ready to support bills designed to

[1] § 26.   [2] §§ 28 and 30.   [3] § 32.
[4] 60 George III and 1 George IV c. 8 § 1.
[5] § 4 ; this clause was repealed by 11 George IV and 1 William IV c. 73 § 1 ;
the punishment had never been inflicted, see Hansard (N.S.) xxv 1275-1276.
[6] 60 George III and 1 George IV. c. 9.   [7] § 8.   [8] § 12.
[9] Hansard xli 344 (Sidmouth), 624-625 (Peel).
[10] Above 203.   [11] Hansard xli 352, 753 (Grey).
[12] Both Lord Holland, above 208 n. 1, and Denman, Hansard xli 1302,
approved the bill for improving the procedure on trials for misdemeanour.
[13] Hansard xli 665-666, 672-673 (Brougham).
[14] " In the debates on the Six Acts the Whigs occasionally made good speeches
but offered no really serious resistance," Graham Wallas, Francis Place 148.
[15] Hansard xli 1385-1390.

mitigate some of the evil results of the industrial revolution,[1] so that his protest is the more significant.

" I cannot think," he said,[2] " it is fitting in the parliament of this country, who have expended millions in protecting foreign emigrants and African negroes, as well as in the relief of the peasantry of the various states of Europe, to abstain from all attempts to relieve the wants of our manufacturers, on the ground stated in these debates—that nothing can be done to mitigate their sufferings without violating the true principles of political economy."

Why then was the government, both in 1817 and in 1819, able to obtain a very general approval of these severe measures ? Why did the government refuse to give adequate effect to the policy suggested by the Earl of Lauderdale ?

To the first of these questions the answer is, I think, as follows : The evidence which the government got from the justices of the peace, from other officials of the local government, and from spies, seemed at first sight to indicate a widespread conspiracy. Clubs up and down the country were passing resolutions for various reforms and sometimes circulating seditious literature.[3] Sometimes the local clubs or unions sent delegates to London,[4] and some were in communication with the Spencean clubs.[5] Rumours were in circulation as to the revolution which, it was said, had followed the December Spa Fields meeting.[6] The fact that the proceedings of the clubs were secret, and the fact that there was some evidence of the purchase of arms, helped to increase the alarm.[7] All these facts, the government thought, pointed to the existence in London of " a central committee of revolutionaries ";[8] and the committees of both Houses before whom the evidence was laid agreed with it. It is not surprising that they did so. The discontent in the industrial districts was obvious and might easily lead to serious and widespread riots ; and the government's power to suppress such riots was small.[9] The lesson to be learnt from the Gordon riots was always present to its mind ; and it did not forget that the French Revolution had shown that an organized and fanatical minority could overturn a constitution. Therefore the government is hardly to be blamed for employing spies to get information, for passing repression measures, and for carrying them into effect with severity.[10]

---

[1] He held up the progress of the Factory Bill, below 213, by supporting a demand that counsel should be heard against it, Hansard xxxviii 578-582 ; and he opposed the Chimney Sweepers Bill, below 266, Hansard xxxix 905-982.

[2] Hansard xli 1389.

[3] Davis, Age of Grey and Peel 177-182.

[4] Ibid 182.   [5] Ibid 184.

[6] Ibid 177, 184-185 ; Hansard xxxv 414-415.

[7] Davis, op. cit. 187.   [8] Ibid ; Hansard xxxv 412-415.

[9] Davis, op. cit. 190.   [10] Ibid.

It was alleged by the opposition that the government had over-estimated the danger, and, in particular, that it had been increased and largely created by spies like Oliver and Castle.[1] Probably the latter allegation is not true.[2] There was more to be said for the former allegation ; but it must be remembered that it is an allegation which is easily made when a revolution has not materialized, that the evidence for the danger in the hands of the government was of a nature to convince officials responsible for the maintenance of order, and that the opposition had less knowledge of the state of the country. Looking at the situation from the point of view of a contemporary, and having regard to the information available to the government, it is not surprising that the government should have believed in the existence of a widespread conspiracy, and that Parliament should have endorsed that belief. It might with some justice be said that the opposition's view that the danger was negligible, and that no such conspiracy existed, rested rather on conjecture than on evidence. Nevertheless it is probable that on this matter the opposition was right. As Davis has pointed out, the leaders of the Radical party were persons of such varying aims and ideas that it is impossible to suppose that they could ever enter into such a conspiracy.[3] A man like Cobbett who distrusted radical clubs, hated commerce and commercial men, and desired above all things to rescue the agricultural labourer from the position of semi-pauperism to which he had sunk,[4] had little in common with radicals of the type of Bentham, Place, Mill, and Ricardo.[5] The sole bond of union was a belief in Parliamentary reform and the abolition of sinecures and other abuses in the executive government. None of these radicals had much in common with the physical force party represented by Thistlewood, who engineered the Cato Street conspiracy in 1820.[6] It was difficult for contemporaries to see through the pretensions of Hunt—the mob-orator with the white hat and a voice which could hold the attention of the largest crowds.[7] These things which are plain to us were not plain to

[1] Above 202, 204.

[2] " Sidmouth was not wrong in believing that the position in the industrial districts might easily become critical.   On later occasions it did become critical, in Lancashire and the West Riding, in Nottingham and Birmingham, and many other places ; it was critical in 1819 and 1820 ; it was critical in 1830. At those dates no Oliver was in the field," Davis, op. cit. 190.

[3] Age of Grey and Peel 173.   [4] Ibid 193-195.

[5] For Place's views on Cobbett see Graham Wallas, Francis Place 177 ; for his views on Hunt see ibid 119-120 ; for Bentham's political views see above 56, 57, 104, 105 ; for Mill's view see above 138, 139 ; for Ricardo see above 34, 136.

[6] 33 S.T. 681 ; a conspiracy to murder the whole cabinet, Thistlewood was convicted and executed for high treason ; for his earlier appearance in the courts on the same charge see above 202.

[7] He was as Davis says op. cit. 176, " *Vox et praeterea nihil.*   But to the country clubs, regarding him from a distance, he seemed to be a lion-hearted philanthropist, and the one militant leader that the popular cause had yet produced."

contemporaries ; and it is upon the facts known to contemporaries that the contentions of the government and the opposition must be judged. Judged by this test, we must conclude that, though the opposition did good work in exposing the actions of some of the government spies, and in criticizing the government case in general and its treatment of individuals, there was very considerable justification for the policy pursued by the government.

To the second of these questions, why did the government refuse to give adequate effect to the policy suggested by the Earl of Lauderdale there are several answers. In the first place the influence of the orthodox *laissez faire* school of political economists was increasing. All parties, Whig, Tory, and Radical, were coming to believe that more harm than good would be done by interfering with individual liberty, and so impeding the free working of economic laws.[1] For instance, the radical Francis Place[2] was in favour of free trade in liquor, and maintained that no restrictive laws on industry should exist, even though he lamented that this freedom was more favourable to the employer than to the workman.[3] Throughout this period there was an unsuccessful attempt to carry out that abolition of the usury laws which Bentham had advocated as the logical consequence of Adam Smith's principles.[4] In the second place, the financial position of the government was bad. It had been forced to abandon the income tax in 1816, and, consequently, had had to meet recurring deficits by fresh borrowing.[5] No money was available for large schemes of relief. In the third place, the government had no adequate machinery to set in motion or work such schemes. A proposal to set up any kind of central department of the government to administer such schemes, would have been opposed by the Whigs and Radicals, because the establishment of such a department would have given the government more patronage and more opportunity for jobbing ; and it was hopeless to expect that the overworked machinery of local government could have been effectively used.

These were the reasons why nothing adequate was done to deal with the causes of the existing discontents. But it is not quite true to say that the government did nothing to deal with its causes. Both the statute book and the debates in Parliament show that some attempts were made to deal with them. There were a few attempts, first, to mitigate some of the worst effects of the industrial revolution ; secondly, to make some reforms in

---

[1] Above 187.   [2] Graham Wallas, Francis Place 173   [3] Ibid 175.
[4] Hansard xxiv 723-739 ; xxxiv 100-106, 1266-1268 ; xxxviii 236-239, 995-996 ; xxxix 420-422 ; below 330 ; for Bentham's tract on this subject see above 110.
[5] Feiling, The Second Tory Party 287, 296 ; Davis, Age of Grey and Peel 190-191.

the machinery of the central government ; and, thirdly, to make some reforms in the law.

(1) We have seen that some regulation of the hours of work of apprentices had been made in 1802 by the first Factory Act.[1] But the Act was almost a dead letter for want of adequate machinery for its enforcement.[2] In 1817-18 the abuses of child labour in factories were brought to the attention of the House of Commons by the elder Sir Robert Peel. He succeeded in passing his bill through the House in 1818, but it was held up in the Lords,[3] and it was not till 1819 that a similar bill was passed. No child under nine was to be employed in a cotton mill, and no person under sixteen was to be employed for more than twelve hours a day.[4] This Act was repealed in 1831 by a new Act which provided that persons under twenty-one were not to work between the hours of 8.30 p.m. and 5.30 a.m.,[5] that persons under eighteen were not to work more than twelve hours a day,[6] and that no child under nine could be employed in a cotton mill.[7] But these Acts, like the 1802 Act, were almost a dead letter for want of machinery for their enforcement.[8] In 1817 the Truck Acts were extended to labourers in the steel and iron industries,[9] and to workmen employed in the collieries.[10] In 1816 it was provided that discharged soldiers could set up trades in any part of the kingdom, and that they could not be removed to their place of legal settlement till they became chargeable to the parish.[11] In 1817 an Act was passed for the encouragement of saving banks,[12] and in 1819 an Act "for the further protection and encouragement of friendly societies, and for preventing frauds and abuses therein." [13] In 1817 an attempt was made to deal with the problem of unemployment by empowering the Crown to advance money on loan for the carrying on of public works and fisheries in the United Kingdom, and the employment of the poor in Great Britain.[14]

[1] Above 39; for these Acts see Hammond, the Town Labourer 167 seqq. ; below 335.   [2] Below 338.   [3] Below 215.
[4] 59 George III c. 66 ; amendments and further provisions were made by 60 George III c. 5 ; 6 George IV c. 63, and 10 George IV c.c. 51 and 63.
[5] 1 and 2 William IV c. 39 § 2.
[6] § 3 ; nine hours on a Saturday.
[7] § 8.   [8] Below 338.
[9] 57 George III c. 115 ; for the earlier Acts see vol. xi 473 and n. 4.
[10] 57 George III c. 122 ; this and other Truck Acts were slightly amended in 1818, 58 George III c. 51 ; all the existing Acts were repealed in 1831 and the law was consolidated and restated, 1, 2 William IV c.c. 36 and 37 ; below 336.
[11] 56 George III c. 67 ; below 315.
[12] 57 George III c. 130 ; amended by 58 George III c. 48 ; below 334.
[13] 59 George III c. 128 ; it considerably amended the earlier Acts, 33 George III c. 54, 35 George III c. 111, 43 George III c. 111, 49 George III c. 125 ; below 333.
[14] 57 George III c. 34 ; amended 3 George IV c. 86, 7 George IV c. 30, and 7, 8 George IV c. 47.

Though the state did nothing as yet for the secular education of the people, Brougham did not allow the government to lose sight of its importance.[1] In 1816 he had persuaded the House to consent to the appointment of a committee to enquire into the state of the education of the lower classes in London.[2] The first report of this committee showed that enormous abuses existed in the administration of educational charities, and urged an enquiry into the application of educational charities throughout the country.[3] In 1818 the committee was given power to enquire into the state of the education of the lower classes throughout the country.[4] Like its predecessor, which had enquired into the administration of Westminster, the Charter House, and Christ's Hospital,[5] it proceeded to enquire into all sorts of educational endowments, including those administered by Eton and Winchester and St. John's College, Cambridge.[6] Brougham, after pointing out that England was behind Scotland, Switzerland, and some of the German states in making provision for education,[7] suggested the appointment of a permanent body of commissioners to supervise the administration of these endowments. In spite of Eldon's opposition,[8] the government adopted this suggestion, and passed Brougham's bill in a much modified form.[9] Brougham objected strongly to the emasculation of his bill,[10] and though he praised Eldon's legal abilities,[11] he made a scathing attack upon the inadequacy of the procedure of the court of Chancery,[12] which was based upon cases which had come before his committee.[13] The Act appointed commissioners, eight of whom were to be paid,[14] to enquire into the nature, amount, and management of charities

---

[1] A very good account of Brougham's efforts on behalf of education will be found in Atlay, Victorian Chancellors i 207-212.

[2] Hansard xxx iv 633.   [3] Ibid 1230-1234 ; xxxvi 1303.

[4] Ibid xxxvii 815.   [5] Ibid xxxiv 1231.

[6] Atlay, op. cit. i 209 ; for Peel's attack on the proceedings of the committee see Hansard (1st Series) xl 1300-1308.

[7] Hansard xxxviii 592-594.

[8] He objected to exposing trustees to vexatious enquiries and to trenching upon the jurisdiction of visitors, Hansard xxxviii 977.

[9] 58 George III c. 91 ; amended by 59 George III c. 81.

[10] 6 Hansard xxxviii 1212 seqq.   [11] Ibid 1224.

[12] " The conclusion from all this was that the court of Chancery might be excellent for many purposes, but that to the suitors in it it was ruinous. . . . Notwithstanding all these good qualities on the part of the noble and learned lord [Eldon] it was his duty to say that there was a something in the court of Chancery that set at defiance all calculations of cost and time, and rendered the celebrated irony of Swift, when he made Gulliver tell the worthy Hynynham his master . . . that his father had been wholly ruined by the misfortune of having gained a Chancery suit with full costs," ibid ; for these abuses of Chancery procedure see vol. ix 339-342, 370-371, 375 ; cf. Life of Romilly (ed. 1842) ii 500.

[13] Hansard xxxviii 1221-1223 ; for a gross abuse discovered in a town in the county of Huntingdon in which the corporation had used Charity land to consolidate its Parliamentary influence, see ibid 1294-1296 ; for other abuses see ibid 761-763.

[14] 58 George III c. 91 § 4.

for the education of the poor.[1] From the jurisdiction of the commissioners were excluded the two universities and their colleges and schools of which they were trustees, six public schools, and certain other schools.[2] For the religious education of the people more direct provision was made. One million pounds was granted in 1818 for the building of additional churches in populous places.[3]

Some of these measures were supported by " the Saints." Wilberforce, for instance, strongly supported Brougham's educational crusade,[4] and the bill, which was lost in the Lords, to prevent the employment of small children as chimney sweepers.[5] In return Brougham had constantly supported Wilberforce's efforts to make the suppression of the slave trade effectual[6]— notably the Act of 1811 which made it felony to be engaged in the trade.[7]

(2) There are a number of statutes which make small reforms in the machinery of the central government. Several Acts made small changes in the machinery for the collection of the revenue.[8] The old abuses of sinecures, the execution of offices by deputy, and the existence of useless offices, were stressed by the opposition. In 1816 Lord Althorp moved for a committee on the number and cost of the public offices, which was lost.[9] In the same year and in 1817 Lord Grosvenor moved for an enquiry into the state of the public offices with a view to the abolition of sinecures, which was also lost ; [10] and in 1818 he submitted resolutions as to the grants of offices and reversion, as to sinecures, and as to the emoluments of offices, which were negatived without a division.[11] But the government did something to meet this agitation. In 1816 the consolidated funds of Great Britain and Ireland were united.[12] In 1817 certain offices in the court of Exchequer were no longer to be executed by deputy, and their duties and emoluments were to be regulated by the Treasury ; [13] the sinecure officers, wardens and chief justices in Eyre of the forests north and south of the Trent were abolished ; [14] and new regulations were made for the

---

[1] § 1.
[2] § 12 : Westminster, Eton, Winchester, Charterhouse, Harrow, Rugby.
[3] 58 George III c. 45.
[4] Atlay, The Victorian Chancellors i 211.
[5] Hansard xxxvii 1157 ; xxxvii 216-217, 506-508 ; xxxix 899-903, 981-984.
[6] Campbell, Chancellors vii 264-267.
[7] 51 George III c. 23; two Acts were passed in 1818 to carry out treaties with Spain and Portugal to abolish the slave trade, 58 George III c.c. 36 and 85.
[8] E.g. 56 George III c. 16 (receivers of Crown rents) ; c. 20 (the customs) ; c. 46 (the civil list) ; 57 George III c. 59 (post horse duties).
[9] Hansard xxxiv 310-362.
[10] Ibid 807-819 ; xxxv 945-968.
[11] Ibid xxxviii 1253-1256.
[12] 56 George III c. 98.   [13] 57 George III c. 60.
[14] Ibid c. 61 ; Hansard xxxv 689-691.

offices of clerks of the signet and privy seal, for the board of trade, and for the mints of England and Scotland.[1] An Act which originated from a report of the finance committee,[2] gave the Crown power to give pensions to those holding high office in the civil service, and so removed the chief argument for the retention of sinecure offices.[3] Camden's relinquishment of a large part of his emoluments as teller of the Exchequer, which resulted in a gain to the Exchequer of £244,000, is an illustration of the growing feeling that large sinecures paid by fees were indefensible.[4] In 1817 it was provided that the tenure of civil or military offices in Great Britain, Ireland, and the colonies should not be affected by the death of George III.[5] The only Act relating to Parliament was an Act of 1819 which provided that the land required to be owned by members of the House of Commons could be in England, Scotland, or Ireland.[6]

Turning from the machinery of government to substantive law, there are one or two statutes which attempted to correct abuses or to settle new problems. We shall see that in 1819 better provision was made for pauper lunatics, and for the regulation of Millbank prison.[7] In the same year a motion for the select committee to enquire into the state of the prisons was carried.[8] Foreign affairs were the cause of legislation to carry into effect a commercial treaty with the United States;[9] to regulate Napoleon's detention at St. Helena, and intercourse with the island while he was detained there;[10] to regulate the trade of Dutch subjects in certain of the West India Islands in accordance with a treaty made between Great Britain and the Netherlands,[11] and to appoint commissioners to carry into effect the treaty of 1815 as to claims of British subjects against the French government.[12] The most important of this class of Acts is the Foreign Enlistment Act of 1819, which repealed the earlier Acts.[13] The Act recited that

the enlistment or engagement of His Majesty's subjects to serve in war in foreign service, without His Majesty's licence, and the fitting out and equipping and arming of vessels by His Majesty's subjects, without His

---

[1] 57 George III c.c. 63, 66, 67.   [2] Hansard xxxvi 128-158.

[3] 57 George III c. 65 ; vol. x 504 ; the Act was opposed very unreasonably by Brougham and some of the Whigs, though it was supported by Bankes, Hansard xxxvi 691-701, 915-916, 933-938.

[4] 59 George III c. 43 ; Anson, the Crown (4th ed.) ii Pt. ii 175.

[5] 57 George III c. 45 ; for the history of this topic see vol. x 433-435 ; the Act of 1817 was passed because it would have been absurd that the tenure of the office of those holding office in effect under the Regent, should have been affected by the fact that he had become King.

[6] 59 George III c. 37.   [7] Ibid c.c. 127, 136 ; below 318, 321.

[8] Hansard xxxix 740-760.   [9] 56 George III c. 15.

[10] Ibid c.c. 22, 23.   [11] Ibid c. 91.

[12] 59 George III c. 31.

[13] Ibid c. 69 ; for the earlier Acts see vol. x 376, 400.

Majesty's licence, for warlike operations in or against the dominions and territories of any foreign prince, state, potentate, or persons exercising or assuming to exercise the powers of government in or over any foreign country, colony, province or part of any province, or against the ships, goods, or merchandize of any foreign prince, state, potentate, or persons as aforesaid, or their subjects, may be prejudicial to and tend to endanger the peace and welfare of this kingdom.

It then made it a misdemeanour for any British subject without the licence of the Crown to enlist or accept a commission in the military or naval service of a foreign power, or to procure others to enlist or accept commissions in such services.[1] Ships having such persons on board could be detained;[2] and masters of ships knowingly taking such persons on board were subjected to penalties.[3] It was also made an offence to fit out, without the licence of the Crown, armed ships to help the operations of foreign powers with which this country was at peace;[4] and also to increase the armament of such ships.[5] The Act was opposed because the opposition considered that it was directed principally against the South American states which had rebelled against Spain;[6] and it was even said that a neutral state was not obliged by international law to prevent its subjects from enlisting in the service of a foreign power at peace with this country, or from fitting out armed ships.[7] The fallacy of this view was thoroughly exposed by Sir William Scott[8] and Sir Robert Grant;[9] and there is no doubt that the Act gave a much needed but, as events later in the century showed, an insufficient power to the state to compel its subjects to observe the obligations of neutrality.

(3) With the statutes which made reforms in the law I shall deal later.[10] At this point I shall only call attention to one or two of these statutes in order to show that during the years 1815-1820 the government did not wholly lose sight of the need for some reforms. We have seen that in 1816 the Habeas Corpus Act of 1679 was applied to persons deprived of their liberty otherwise than on a charge of crime, except when they were imprisoned for debt or on civil process;[11] and that in 1819 trial by battle was abolished[12]—Eldon for once supporting a change in the law.[13] In 1816 the punishment of the pillory was abolished except for those found guilty of perjury;[14] and in 1817 whipping as a punishment

---

[1] § 2. [2] § 5. [3] § 6. [4] § 7. [5] § 8.
[6] Hansard xl 366 (Mackintosh).
[7] Ibid 871 (Sir Robert Wilson), 1235 (Scarlett).
[8] Ibid 1232-1235. [9] Ibid 1239-1260.
[10] Below 308 seqq.
[11] 56 George III c. 100; vol ix 121-122.
[12] 59 George III c. 46; vol. i 310.
[13] Hansard xl 1203-1207; he moved that the bill be committed.
[14] 56 George III c. 138; for the abuses of this form of punishment see vol. xi 557.

for females was abolished.[1] In 1819 the procedure of the court of Chancery in relation to charitable trusts was improved,[2] and in the same year Mackintosh carried a motion for the appointment of a select committee to consider the question of capital punishment for felonies.[3]

There is no doubt that all through this period the efforts of the government to maintain order, and at the same time to introduce some few reforms, were handicapped by the unpopularity of the Regent and his brothers. The Regent himself, though he was handsome in his youth and not without social gifts, and though he was often generous to friends and dependents,[4] was a false and selfish debauchee who thought only of his own enjoyments.[5] He had separated from his wife immediately after the birth of their daughter,[6] and his behaviour to them both was scandalous.[7] In 1806 he had made charges against the Princess which were disproved—though the committee reflected on her conduct.[8] Brougham took up the case of the Princess and her daughter—mainly from party considerations[9]—and became her chief adviser. In 1814 she was excluded from the royal drawing room ; and in that year, worn out by persecution, she had left the country.[10] Her daughter Charlotte refused to marry the Prince of Orange, and in 1816 she married the Prince of Saxe-Coburg. In 1817 she died in childbirth.[11]

The royal brothers, the dukes of York, Clarence, Kent, Cumberland, and Cambridge, were now in the direct line of succession to the throne. They were, Wellington said " the damnedest millstone about the necks of any government " ; and he added that they had " personally insulted two-thirds of the gentlemen of England." [12] What Parliament thought of them can be seen from what happened when they proceeded to marry in order to get an heir to the throne, and applied for increased allowances. Though Parliament reluctantly gave the Duke of York an extra £10,000 a year when, on the death of the Queen, the custody of the King was entrusted to him,[13] it refused to give

---

[1] 57 George III c. 75. [2] 59 George III c. 91.
[3] Hansard xxxix 777-846.
[4] Aspinall, Letters of George IV, Webster's Introd. i lxv.
[5] Feiling, The Second Tory Party 284.
[6] Atlay, The Victorian Chancellors i 218.
[7] Ibid 221-224. [8] Ibid 219-220.
[9] Above 197. [10] Atlay, op. cit. i 227.
[11] Feiling, The Second Tory Party 284; 56 George III c.c. 12 and 13 (naturalization of the Prince of Saxe-Coburg), c. 115 (the settlement of the Claremont estate on the Princess).
[12] Cited Feiling, op. cit 284 ; but Professor Webster points out that the Dukes of York and Cambridge showed some administrative ability, and that the Duke of Cumberland was a successful ruler when he became Elector of Hanover, Aspinall, Letters of George IV i lxvii-lxix.
[13] 59 George III c. 22 § 4.

the Duke of Cumberland an increased allowance, and it gave the Duke of Clarence only £6,000 a year instead of the £20,000 a year for which the government asked.[1]

Meanwhile the Princess of Wales was leading a wandering life in Europe and the near East. She had surrounded herself with Italian attendants, notorious amongst whom was her courier Bergami whom she made her chamberlain.[2] These doings encouraged the Regent to hope that he might at last get rid of his wife. A commission of three[3] was sent to Milan to collect evidence. It reported to the cabinet in 1819, which resolved that the facts stated in the depositions would, if supported by witnesses, prove adultery.[4] In January 1820 George III died, and the King at once pressed his ministers to get him a divorce. They at first resisted, but at last acquiesced in the omission of the Queen's name from the liturgy.[5] The Queen was furious, and in spite of Brougham's advice who would have liked to have arranged a separation,[6] resolved to act on the advice of Alderman Wood, and to come to England to assert her claims. A last minute attempt at a compromise at a conference held at St. Omer broke down, and the Queen started for England.[7] On the day of her arrival the King laid the evidence taken in Italy before Parliament.[8] A bill of pains and penalties, depriving the Queen of her title and privileges and dissolving her marriage with the King, was introduced into the House of Lords. The Queen was represented by Brougham and Denman, whom she had appointed her attorney and solicitor-general, by Williams, Tindal, Wilde, and Dr. Lushington. The King's case was presented by Gifford, the attorney-general, Copley, the solicitor-general, James Parke, Christopher Robinson, and Dr. Adams.[9]

Popular opinion was overwhelmingly in favour of the Queen— not so much on account of any belief in her innocence as on account of the conduct of the King. In fact, Brougham had grave doubts of the possibility of disproving the charges against her;[10] and

---

[1] Feiling, The Second Tory Party 284-285 ; it settled £6,000 a year on the Duchesses of Cambridge and Cumberland after the deaths of their husbands, 58 George III c.c. 24 and 25.

[2] Atlay, The Victorian Chancellors i 227-229.

[3] Cooke, K.C., Browne of the Cavalry, and Powell a solicitor, ibid 229.

[4] Ibid 230.   [5] Ibid 231.

[6] He had actually proposed this to the government, ibid 230-231.

[7] Ibid 231-235 ; Brougham has been blamed for not letting the Queen know at St. Omer the terms of the King's offer, which was substantially simiiar to the offer which he himself had made ; but the Queen knew of the offer, and was obviously resolved not to accept any offer ; Brougham's defence of his conduct in the House of Commons was lame, but, as Atlay says, he " could not tell the whole truth without damaging his client," ibid 234.

[8] Ibid 235.   [9] Ibid 237, 240.

[10] Mrs. Brougham did not call on the Queen, and Brougham knew of the indiscretions not known to the commissioners ; it was for these reasons that he tried to arrange a separation, ibid 230-231, 238-239 ; Atlay thinks that we may

Grey at first was doubtful.[1] But the Italian witnesses against her broke down ; and whether or not she was guilty, it became increasingly clear that in spite of all the efforts of the Crown's advocates and especially of Copley,[2] the promoters of the bill had not proved and could not prove her guilt. Brougham and Grey came to believe in her innocence ;[3] and Brougham's great speech in her defence was, in spite of all the efforts of the Crown's advocates, decisive. The critical Creevy wrote :[4]

Brougham has just finished his opening. I never heard him anything like the perfection he has displayed in all ways. In short, if he can prove what he has stated in his speech, I for one believe she is innocent, and the whole case a conspiracy. He concluded with a most magnificent address to the Lords—an exhortation to them to save themselves—the Church—the Crown—the Country, by their decision in favour of the Queen. This last appeal was made with great passion, but without a particle of rant. I consider myself infinitely overpaid by these two hours and a half of Brougham, for all the time and money it has cost me to be here.

The bill was abandoned ; but the Queen, though she remained Queen, took little other benefit. She was excluded from the Abbey when the King was crowned, and she died a fortnight afterwards.

The abandonment of the bill was due mainly to Brougham's advocacy and his conduct of her case.[5] His practice at the bar increased enormously, and in the House of Commons he was recognized as the most formidable member of the opposition. When, on the suicide of Castlereagh in 1822, there seemed a slight chance that the Whigs might at length come into power, Grey recognized that Brougham must lead the House of Commons.[6]

accept as genuine the statement he made during the course of the trial—" at first he did not think it possible she *could* be innocent. But the more the case opened, the more had her innocence appeared, and now in his conscience he believed her guiltless," citing Life of Plumer Ward ii 60 ; in view of James Brougham's letter to his brother written after March 11, 1819, Aspinall, Letters of George IV ii no. 767 it is not surprising that Brougham should have despaired of disproving the charges against her. In view of her " attempt to corrupt or compromise her daughter," ibid i nos. 508, 509, ii no. 547 A, and of the evidence of these documents as to her conduct, there is little doubt that Professor Webster is right when he says that "she was not so much immoral as incapable of understanding in what morality consists," ibid i lxxi.

[1] Trevelyan, Lord Grey of the Reform Bill 193.

[2] " Copley more than held his own against Brougham and Denman. His handling of one of the Queen's witnesses, a certain Lieutenant Flynn, dealt a blow to her case from which it never fully recovered ; and the speech in which he summed up the evidence for the Bill went a long way to destroy the effect produced by the furious cross-examination of Brougham and his colleagues," Atlay, The Victorian Chancellors i 35.

[3] Above 219 n. 9.

[4] The Creevy Papers i 321 ; for a good description see Atlay, op. cit. i 246-248.

[5] " Though Brougham was assisted by some of the most learned, the most eloquent, and the most courageous members of the English bar, the main credit for Caroline's defence must always rest with him," Atlay, op. cit. i 260.

[6] Ibid i 272, citing a letter from Grey to Brougham.

The death of Castlereagh is the beginning of a new epoch in legal history. He had been an able war minister and an able foreign minister. He had brought to a victorious conclusion the war against Napoleon, he had made a just peace, and he had refused to commit England to the policy of the Holy Alliance.[1] And yet his death was hailed by the populace as a great deliverance, and "his memory was pursued with a bitterness unique in the history of public men." [2] The answer, Mr. Hammond says, is symbolized in two words—Oliver and Peterloo.[3] He was identified with all the stern measures taken to repress revolution. It was forgotten that law and order had been preserved by these measures—only their sternness was remembered. The reason why Castlereagh's death opens a new epoch in legal history is this: Castlereagh had introduced few measures of domestic reform, and he allowed no one else to do so.[4] His duties as foreign minister left him little time to consider such measures. But the government which was reformed after his death passed under the control of men like Canning, Peel, and Huskisson—representatives of the new commercial and middle classes, and well aware of the need for large reforms in the law and institutions of the country. Dr. Temperley has concisely and accurately described this change and its effects on legislation. He says:[5]

Between 1815 and 1822, such reforms as were accomplished resulted almost wholly from private member legislation; and the Opposition exhausted their vocabularies in denunciation and abuse of the Government. Between 1822 and 1827, ministers were found adopting the suggestions and encouraging the motions of individual members; and the Opposition not infrequently praised and supported Government proposals. The result was an outburst of reforming activity, proceeding on the model of Pitt's legislation between 1784 and 1793, but far surpassing it in effect and importance.

Just as the latter part of the eighteenth century, in which many princes had become converts to new ideas which taught the necessity for reforms, has been called the age of "repentance of monarchy," [6] so these years may be called the age of the repentance of the Tory party.

The two men who did most to introduce this new spirit into the government were Canning and, more especially, Peel. Because they both influenced the development of English law I must say a few words about them.

Of Canning's earlier career I have already said something.[7] He was foreign secretary in 1807; but, in consequence of his

---

[1] See Temperley, Foreign Policy of Canning 448-449.
[2] Hammond, The Skilled Labourer 375.   [3] Ibid.
[4] Temperley, Camb. Mod. Hist. x 584.   [5] Ibid.
[6] Vol. x 10.   [7] Above 177, 178, 180.

intrigues against Castlereagh which ended in a duel, he was out of
office from 1809 ; and we have seen that he made a great mistake
when he refused to take the foreign office in 1812 because Castlereagh was to lead the House.[1] In 1814 he went on an embassy to
Lisbon. In 1816 he had again become a member of the government as President of the Board of Control ; but in 1820 he resigned because he did not wish to take part in the proceedings
against the Queen. In 1822 he accepted the post of Governor-
General of India. But before he sailed Castlereagh had died ;
and Canning succeeded him as foreign minister with the lead of
the House of Commons. With Canning's foreign policy we are not
here concerned. It is sufficient to note that he conciliated
liberal opinion by recognizing the independence of the Spanish
colonies after France had invaded Spain to put down the Spanish
rebels ; and he played a large, some think the largest part, in
rescuing Greece from the Turks.[2] In his domestic policy he
encouraged reforms of the tariff in the direction of a freer trade,
relaxations of the Navigation Acts, and the reforms in the law
which Peel suggested. In his economic policy he was very ably
assisted by his faithful disciple Huskisson—the foremost financier
of his day—who in 1823 became President of the Board of Trade,
and a member of the cabinet. He was in favour of Catholic
emancipation, but he was wholly opposed to Parliamentary
reform, since he saw that any considerable measure of reform
would be the end of the balanced eighteenth century constitution,
and would lead ultimately to democratic government. In all
other respects he was a liberal, and his gifts of oratory and his
powers of close and clear reasoning were used to persuade
Parliament to accept the reforms in the law which new social and
economic conditions demanded. His greatest service to the
development of the law, public and private, is that he began the
process of educating the Tory party out of the blind obstructive-
ness of men like Eldon and Ellenborough, and so made it fit to
survive as a Conservative party, which applied a steadying, an
informed, and a business-like corrective to the wild proposals for
reform which are produced in an age of change. By thus helping
to preserve continuity in the development of the state and the law,
he showed himself to be a true disciple of Burke and the true
successor of Pitt. If he had not died a few months after he became
prime minister he might have given the Tories a new lease of
power, for, though he was at first disliked by the King, he had,
while he held office, won his confidence, and " with his aid had
triumphed over the aristocratic clique which disliked and distrusted him." [3] The fact that he was a leader of the Tory party,

---

[1] Above 180.   [2] Temperley, Foreign Policy of Canning 409.
[3] Aspinall, Letters of George IV i lxxx.

and yet pursued a liberal programme, caused some of the Whigs and many of the Tories to doubt unjustly his sincerity ; and we shall see that when in 1827 he became prime minister and co-alesced with a section of the Whigs, these doubts were, equally unjustly, intensified.[1]

Though the impulse towards the adoption of an enlightened conservatism came largely from Canning, it was given effect to in detail by the less brilliant but more business-like and pedestrian mind of Peel.[2]

Sir Robert Peel was the son of the first baronet Sir Robert Peel, who made a fortune out of his cotton mills. The first Sir Robert was a Tory, a follower of Pitt, and, as we have seen, the author of the first and second Factory Acts.[3] Like the elder Pitt, he determined to make his son a statesman, and, like him, he succeeded.[4] After a brilliant career at Oxford, Peel entered Parliament in 1809 at the age of twenty-one. He became Chief Secretary for Ireland in 1812, and in that difficult position he served his apprenticeship as a minister. When he resigned that office in 1818 his abilities, his industry, and his character had so firmly established his reputation in Parliament that many prophesied that he would become prime minister.[5] He was out of office till 1821, when he became Home Secretary.

Peel had two sets of qualities seldom found together. He had the qualities of a first rate head of a department in the permanent civil service,[6] and at the same time he had the qualities of a great Parliament man—"a nearly unequalled master," it was said, "of the art of political advocacy,"[7] and "the greatest member of Parliament who ever lived,"[8] who could "play upon the House of Commons as on an old fiddle." But, necessarily, he had the defects of both those sets of qualities. The business of the head of a government department in the permanent civil service is to administer it, and not, except within narrow limits, to originate its policy. Peel, because he was an admirable administrator, could see what laws worked badly, why they worked badly, and how they could be amended ; but "when it was a question, as in the case of the Reform Bill, not of simple abolition, but of extensive and difficult reconstruction, he could not see his way."[9] As Davis has said,[10]

---

[1] Below 227, 228.
[2] J. R. Thursfield, Peel ; Bagehot, Biographical Studies i 39.
[3] Above 213. [4] J. R. Thursfield, Peel 10-12.
[5] Ibid 31. [6] See Bagehot, op. cit. 16-19.
[7] Ibid 26. [8] Disraeli, Life of Bentinck 320.
[9] Bagehot, op. cit. 37.
[10] Age of Grey and Peel, 297-298 ; Woodward, The Age of Reform 105-106 agrees ; he says, "he carried out reform after reform of a practical and limited kind ; but his measures were never part of a widely envisaged plan of social change. They were always set against the larger mass of English institutions and habits which Peel did not want to alter."

the reforms which he liked to undertake were safe reforms, reforms which would not give his enemies a handle, or leave any large section of his followers with a grievance. . . . His correspondence shows that he was always on the alert to discover some possibility of uncontentious reforms, and always both ingenious and indefatigable in working out the details of any reform which he took in hand.

The business of a minister is to defend the policy of his department and of the government. Peel's debating powers enabled him to make a good case for any project he was advocating or defending.[1] But a man who has spent his life in administration and in political advocacy will not have had the time, or probably the inclination, to think out the ultimate consequences of the policy of all the articles of his political creed, unless and until they come to be an immediate and pressing problem. Obviously this mental attitude created a difficult problem for an able and practised minister who had been educated as a Tory in the early years of the nineteenth century, for, when he reached his political maturity, the changing circumstances of the nation necessitated the modification, if not the jettison, of some of the articles of his political creed. Such a man would be likely to be blind to the need to modify or jettison till the last moment ; and then suddenly, struck by arguments to which new circumstances had given a new meaning, he would be likely to turn round and advocate that which he formerly condemned.[2] This was the cause of Peel's three sudden changes in his political views—his changes on the policy of the resumption of cash payments, Catholic emancipation, and the Corn Laws. The last two changes shattered his party. He did not see that they must have this effect because his hard and unsympathetic temperament (except with a few intimates), which was shown in his repellent manners,[3] his egotism,[4] his want of "knowledge of human nature," and his sometimes overweening confidence in his own abilities,[5] deprived him of the power to judge correctly the effect of such a course of conduct. It is for this reason that it is true to say that " he had insight but not foresight " ;[6] and that " wanting imagination, he wanted prescience."[7] It is arguable, indeed, that this defect increased his capacity as a leader of the Tory party in this age of rapid change. Having, as Bagehot has

---

[1] Once when they were opposed on a railway bill, the keen irascibility of Lord Derby stimulated him to observe, that " no one knew like the right honourable baronet how to *dress up* a case for the House," Bagehot, Biographical Studies 26.

[2] As Disraeli said, Life of Bentinck 305-306, he had not got a creative faculty, his mind could not "create a substitute for the creation which was crumbling away," so that he was on the lookout for new ideas which he embraced with precipitancy.

[3] Thursfield, op. cit. 41-42.

[4] Ibid 40.

[5] Davis, Age of Grey and Peel 300.

[6] Thursfield, op. cit. 69.

[7] Disraeli, Life of Bentinck 305.

said, "the powers of a first rate man and the creed of a second rate man," [1] he was admirably fitted to take up the work of educating and purifying the Tory party, and so enabling it to take its share in the government of the state in the new conditions which the Reform Act had introduced. But if, instead of being a first rate statesman of the second class, he had been a statesman of the first class, the Tories and not the Whigs might have guided the transition of the state from the eighteenth to nineteenth century conditions.

That Peel, when he took office in 1821, was well aware that public opinion was demanding the extensive reforms in public and private law which were needed to adapt the law to the new social and economic conditions which the industrial revolution was producing, to the new political ideas of the commercial men of middle classes, and to the new ideas as to law reform preached by the followers of Bentham, is shown by a letter which, in March 1820, he wrote to Croker. It runs as follows: [2]

Do you not think that the tone of England—of that great compound of folly, weakness, prejudice, wrong feeling, right feeling, obstinacy, and newspaper paragraphs, which is called public opinion—is more liberal, to use an odious but intelligible phrase, than the policy of the Government? Do not you think that there is a feeling, becoming daily more general and more confirmed, that is, independent of the pressure of taxation or any immediate cause, in favour of some undefined change in the mode of governing the country? It seems to me a curious crisis, when public opinion never had so much influence on public measures, and yet never was so dissatisfied with the share which it possessed. It is growing too large for the channels which it has been accustomed to run through. God knows it is very difficult to widen them exactly in proportion to the size and force of the current which they have to convey, but the engineers that made them never dreamt of various streams that are now struggling for a vent. Will the Government act on the principles on which, without being very certain, I suppose they have hitherto professed to act? Or will they carry into action moderate Whig measures of reform? Or will they give up the Government to the Whigs, and let them carry those measures into effect? Or will they coalesce with the Whigs, and oppose the united phalanx to the Hobhouses and Burdetts of radicalism? I should not be surprised to see such a union.

Peel and Canning and Huskisson, with the co-operation of the prime minister Lord Liverpool, adopted the second of these alternatives, and proceeded to carry out moderate Whig measures of reform both in the sphere of law and in the spheres of commerce and industry

In the sphere of law reform, in addition to improvements in the mechanism of government,[3] we shall see that Peel amended, re-stated, and consolidated important branches of the law.[4]

---

[1] Biographical Studies 6.   [2] Cited, J. R. Thursfield, Peel 19-20.
[3] Below 234, 237.   [4] Below 226.

There are Acts of this class dealing with the registration of British ships,[1] the punishment of rogues and vagabonds,[2] bankruptcy,[3] the slave trade,[4] jurors,[5] quarantine,[6] the law as to the customs,[7] the law as to weights and measures,[8] the law as to insolvent debtors,[9] the law as to larceny and kindred offences,[10] the law as to malicious injuries to property and as to remedies against the hundred for damage caused by rioters,[11] the law as to offences against the person,[12] the law as to forgery,[13] the law as to savings banks[14] and the law as to friendly societies,[15] and the law as to the property of infants, married women, and persons of unsound mind.[16] He abolished benefit of clergy ;[17] and, as Lord Lyndhurst pointed out, he humanized the criminal law by abolishing the death penalty in nearly three hundred cases. And the way was being prepared for more drastic amendments in the law. The long continued attacks on the court of Chancery, in which Michael Angelo Taylor, Romilly, and John Williams,[18] assisted by Brougham, had been the protagonists,[19] had resulted in the appointment of a commission in 1824 which had reported in 1826.[20] Copley introduced two bills to give effect to its proposals which never became law ; and, later, as Lord Lyndhurst, he introduced two other abortive bills for the reform of the court and its procedure.[21] We shall see that in 1828 Brougham, in a speech which lasted for six hours and three minutes,[22] exposed the abuses and defects of the procedure of the courts of common law, the local courts, and of all branches of the common law and the ecclesiastical law ; and that this great speech was followed by the appointment of two commissions—one to enquire into the law of real property, and the other to enquire into the practice and procedure of the common law courts.[23]

In the sphere of commerce and industry Huskisson revised

---

[1] 4 George IV c. 41 ; 6 George IV c. 110.
[2] 3 George IV c. 40 ; 5 George IV c. 83.
[3] Ibid c. 98.   [4] 6 George IV c. 50.
[5] 5 George IV c. 74.   [6] 6 George IV c. 113.
[7] 3 George IV c.c. 41, 42 ; 6 George IV c.c. 104-108, 111-115.
[8] 5 George IV c. 74.   [9] 7 George IV c. 57.
[10] 7, 8 George IV c. 29.   [11] Ibid c.c. 30, 31.
[12] 9 George IV c. 31.
[13] 11 George IV and 1 William IV c. 66.
[14] 9 George IV c. 92.   [15] 10 George IV c. 56.
[16] 11 George IV and 1 William IV c. 65.
[17] 7, 8 George IV c. 28 ; for benefit of clergy see vol. iii 294-302.
[18] He became a judge, below 292.
[19] Atlay, The Victorian Chancellors i 42-43 ; below 274 seqq., 288 seqq., 290 seqq.   [20] Vol. i 442-443 ; vol. ix 371, 375.   [21] Atlay, op. cit. i 43-45, 68-71.
[22] " Brougham spoke, according to Hayward, who timed him, exactly six hours and three minutes by the clock, and he exhausted a hatful of oranges, which were all the refreshment then tolerated by the custom of the House," Atlay, op. cit. i 284.
[23] Below 306 ; Atlay, op. cit. i 285.

and modified the Navigation Acts ;[1] and in the interest of the colonies he gave a preference to colonial corn and encouraged and subsidized emigration.[2] He modified the customs tariff in the direction of a freer trade,[3] and he reformed the sinking fund.[4] The laws forbidding the emigration of workmen,[5] and the export of machinery[6] were repealed. But when, in obedience to the *laissez faire* school of economists, the combination laws were repealed,[7] the results were so disastrous that it was found necessary to impose some restrictions and limitations upon the activities of industrial combinations.[8] The laws relating to the arbitration of industrial disputes were amended and consolidated.[9] Huskisson and Canning were preparing to modify the Corn Laws when, in 1827, the ministry was dissolved by the paralytic stroke which incapacitated Lord Liverpool.[10]

Lord Liverpool, described by Disraeli in *Coningsby* as the " arch-mediocrity," had nevertheless been prime minister for fifteen years, during which the Napoleonic War had been brought to a victorious conclusion.[11] He had kept the peace in the difficult post-war years, and had co-operated with Canning, Peel, and Huskisson in their work of reconstruction.[12] As Coleridge said, he was the " single stay of the cabinet " because, though not a man of " directing mind," he served " as an isthmus to connect one half of the cabinet with the other." [13] The years from 1822 to 1827 had been years of steady progress in this work of reconstruction. But it was largely because two burning questions had been kept in the background—the questions of Catholic emancipation and Parliamentary reform. It was the emergence of these questions after Liverpool's disappearance which split the Tory party, and enabled the Whigs at length to gain power. Peel was opposed to any concession to the Catholics : Canning was opposed to any measure of Parliamentary reform. If in 1827 they had been able to make concessions on these points the future history of England might have been different.

Canning became prime minister in April 1827, and Wellington, Eldon, Peel, and three others resigned.[14] Eldon was succeeded as

[1] See 3 George IV c.c. 43 and 44 ; 6 George IV c. 73 ; Camb. Mod. Hist. x 585-587 ; for the Navigation Acts see vol. vi 316-319, 321-323 ; vol. xi 84-88, 407-411 ; below 262, 325, 360-362.
[2] Camb. Mod. Hist. x 587 ; below 327, 346.
[3] Camb. Mod. Hist. x 588 ; below 363.
[4] Camb. Mod. Hist x 588 ; for the sinking fund see vol. x 121-122.
[5] 5 George IV c. 97 ; 6 George IV c. 105, 163 ; vol. xi 432-433.
[6] 6 George IV c. 105 §§ 163, 174 ; vol. xi 433.
[7] 5 George IV c. 95 vol. xi 486-498.
[8] 6 George IV c. 129 ; below 348, 351.   [9] 5 George IV c. 96.
[10] Camb. Mod. Hist. x 591.   [11] J. R. Thursfield, Peel 23-24.
[12] Feiling, The Second Tory Party 349.
[13] Table Talk, April 27, 1823.
[14] Feiling, The Second Tory Party 352.

Chancellor by Copley who became Lord Lyndhurst.[1] Many of the Tories had persisted in regarding Canning as a mere adventurer, Wellington disliked his foreign policy and his liberal home policy,[2] and Peel refused to serve under him because he was in favour of Catholic emancipation.[3] The result was that Canning made a coalition with the Whigs. Some few of the Whigs stood out—including Lord Grey who personally disliked Canning and attacked him savagely in the House of Lords. But he was supported by Brougham, Tierney, Lambton, Holland, and Lansdowne.[4] What this coalition would have effected is a matter of speculation; for Canning died in August 1827.

Lord Goderich, Disraeli's "transcient and embarrassed phantom," formed a government which fell to pieces before it met Parliament.[5] Wellington formed a ministry in 1828 composed of Tories and the Tory following of Canning—Peel, taking the lead in the House of Commons, and Lyndhurst continuing as Chancellor.[6] The House of Commons was more liberal than the government. It repealed the Corporation and Test Acts so far as they applied to Protestant dissenters in spite of the opposition of the government;[7] there were differences of opinion on the new Corn Law; and a resolution in favour of Catholic emancipation was carried.[8] The question of the transfer of the representation of the corrupt boroughs of Penrhyn and East Retford to Manchester and Birmingham produced further differences of opinion. Huskisson, who had voted with the Whigs and against the government for the transfer of representation of East Retford to Birmingham, made a tentative offer to resign, which the duke at once accepted—though Huskisson explained that he had not meant to tender a definite resignation.[9] With him the other leading followers of Canning resigned—Palmerston, Grant, Dudley, and Lamb.[10] Peel appointed Vesey-FitzGerald to succeed Grant at the Board of Trade. But, though he was in favour of Catholic emancipation, when he stood for re-election in County Clare he was defeated by O'Connell. The Clare election was the end of the government of Ireland through the Irish landlords; and the sudden change in the policy of the government which followed it broke the Tory party.[11]

After the Act of Union Ireland had been governed, as before,

[1] Below 578, 638, 639.   [2] Feiling, op. cit. 351.   [3] Parker, Peel i 459-464.
[4] Feiling, The Second Tory Party, 353-354; Davis, Age of Grey and Peel 220; Trevelyan, Lord Grey of the Reform Bill 201-205.
[5] Feiling, op. cit. 359-360.   [6] Ibid 361-363.
[7] Ibid 365; 9 George IV c. 17; for the sacramental test there was substituted a declaration " on the true faith of a Christian " that the office-bearer would do nothing by virtue of his office to weaken the Protestant Church as by law established in England, §§ 2-5.
[8] Feiling, op. cit. 365-366.   [9] Ibid 366-367.
[10] Ibid 367.   [11] J. R. Thursfield, Peel 80.

by the expedient of using government influence to induce the landlords and borough proprietors to return members favourable to it.[1] Only in that way could the Protestant ascendancy continue unimpaired. But, as might have been expected, the country could only be kept relatively quiet by a large force of soldiers and coercion Acts.[2] For a few years the question of the veto divided the Catholics ;[3] but in 1823 this dispute was healed, and O'Connell and his Catholic Association took up the question of emancipation.[4] The Catholic Association was suppressed in 1825 ;[5] but in the same year the House of Commons voted in favour of emancipation, and it was supported by Canning.[6] We have seen that it was Canning's view on this question which caused Peel not to serve under him.[7] But O'Connell had organized a new Catholic Association ; and, with its help, he and the priests persuaded the 40/- freeholders to break loose from the domination of their landlords, and at the election for Waterford in 1826 to vote for the Protestant candidates who favoured emancipation.[8] The election of the Catholic O'Connell for County Clare in 1828 showed that the Catholic party was now prepared to go a great deal further, in that it was prepared to take the offensive against the Protestant landlords, whether or not they supported the cause of Catholic emancipation.

In a moment the fabric of resistance to the Catholic claims had crumbled to pieces. What had happened in Clare might happen at a general election in every county constituency in Ireland. O'Connell, it is true, could not take his seat in the House of Commons, nor could any other Catholic who might be elected. But that merely aggravated the difficulty of the situation. It made civil war the only alternative to concession ; and even civil war, a conflict between classes and creeds in Ireland, was not the worst evil to be feared. The Duke of Wellington, the first soldier of the age, was Prime Minister of England. The Marquis of Anglesey, another soldier of renown, was Lord Lieutenant of Ireland. Neither could be confident that the contagion of Catholic sympathies would not spread to the Catholic soldiery of the Crown, and add to the horrors of civil war the confusion of military discord.[9]

Wellington and Peel saw that Catholic emancipation could no longer be resisted. It would perhaps have been better for Peel's reputation if he had persisted in his first resolution to resign. In a letter to the Duke of Wellington offering to resign and promising his support to a measure of Catholic emancipation, he said that he thought that, having regard to his past opposition to such a measure, "it would not conduce to the satisfactory adjustment of

[1] Vol. xi. 32-34 ; J. R. Thursfield, Peel 34-35.
[2] Ibid 35-36.   [3] Ibid.
[4] Davis, Age of Grey and Peel 290-291.
[5] Thursfield, Peel 70.
[6] Ibid 71.   [7] Above 228.
[8] J. R. Thursfield, Peel 74-75.   [9] Ibid 80-81.

the question that the charge of it in the House of Commons should be committed to my hands." [1] But he all along assumed that it was the Tory party who must carry this reform, and was somewhat easily persuaded that, since the duke could not overcome the opposition of the King and the bishops without him, he, as the leader of the Tory party in the House of Commons, must take charge of the measure. [2]

It was necessary to act quickly if an outbreak of civil war was to be avoided. The King's consent to the introduction of the measure was extorted ; and in March 1829 Peel introduced the bill in the House of Commons. It was easily carried in the House of Commons ; but the minority of 173 Tories, and Peel's rejection by Oxford University when he stood for re-election after the resignation of his seat, [3] showed what effect it was likely to have on the party. In the House of Lords it was carried by a majority of 105, in spite of the opposition of Eldon and the bishops. The bill was justified both in the House of Commons and the House of Lords not only on the ground that it was necessary to avert civil war, but also by the argument that it would end Irish discontent, and would operate to the advantage of the Protestants. [4] Both these propositions were denied by the opposition [5]— and they were more correct in their forecast than the government, for the concession had come a quarter of a century too late. [6] " All the wise men," said Melbourne at a later day, "were on one side and all the fools on the other, and the worst of it was that the fools were right." An alien element was introduced into the Parliament of the United Kingdom, which, in the name of a nationalism founded on dubious history and past grievances, intrigued with any party that seemed likely to embarrass the government, and, to the detriment of both countries, refused to co-operate in the work of government. [7]

The Act [8] repealed all the Acts requiring a declaration against transubstantiation as a condition for taking a seat in Parliament or holding office under the Crown. [9] Catholics were allowed to be elected and to sit in Parliament on taking the oath set out in the Act ; [10] but no Catholic priest was to be capable of sitting in the House of Commons. [11] Catholics were made capable of holding military and civil offices, subject only to six exceptions. [12] They

---

[1] Parker, Peel ii 56.   [2] Davis, Age of Grey and Peel 300-301.
[3] Feiling, The Second Tory Party 371.
[4] Hansard (N.S.) xx 778 (Peel) ; ibid xxi 58 (Wellington) ; 215 (Lyndhurst).
[5] Hansard (N.S.) xx 792-793 (Inglis) ; 1183 (Bankes) ; xxi 627-638 (Eldon) ; 678-680 (Redesdale).   [6] Above 124.   [7] Above 168, 173.
[8] 10 George IV c. 7.   [9] § 1.   [10] §§ 2 and 5.   [11] § 9.
[12] §§ 10-12 ;   the offices were Guardians or Justices of the United Kingdom, Regent, Lord Chancellor, Lord Keeper or Commissioner of the Great Seal, Lord Lieutenant of Ireland, High Commissioner to the General Assembly of the Church of Scotland.

could be members of lay corporations,[1] but could not take part
in any appointments made by such corporations to ecclesiastical
benefices,[2] nor could they be appointed to offices in the established churches of England, Scotland, or Ireland, or in the
ecclesiastical courts, or in the universities or colleges or in the
colleges of Eton, Westminster, or Winchester.[3] If a Catholic
held an office which entitled him to appoint to an ecclesiastical
benefice the right of presentation was to devolve on the Archbishop of Canterbury;[4] and no Catholic was to be capable of ad-
vising the Crown as to the appointment to offices in the established
Church.[5] Catholics were not to assume the titles of English sees
or deaneries,[6] nor were municipal officers to attend Catholic
churches with the insignia of their office,[7] nor were Catholic
priests to officiate anywhere except in private houses or in their
usual places of worship.[8] The Act concluded with a group of
sections for the suppression of the Jesuits and other such
Catholic orders.[9] Two other Acts were passed supplementary to
the principal Act. In the first place, the qualification for voting
was raised from a freehold of the annual value of 40/- to a freehold
of the annual value of £10.[10] In the second place, the Catholic
Association was suppressed, and the Lord Lieutenant was given
power to suppress any association or assembly or meeting which
he considered to be dangerous to the public peace or safety.[11]

The bill received the royal assent on April 14, 1829. In the
ensuing session the government's position was made difficult by
the hostility of the ultra-Tories who had opposed it. There was
distress in the industrial north and in the agricultural counties of
the south; and economists, and writers like Southey and
Coleridge who denounced the economists, and Malthusians and
anti-Malthusians, were all advocating different cures for the evils
which afflicted the state.[12] It is not surprising that in these
circumstances Parliamentary reform again came to the front.
Russell's proposals to enfranchise Birmingham, Manchester, and
Leeds was lost by only forty-eight votes;[13] and moderate Tories
like Croker began to see the necessity of a limited measure of
reform.[14] On June 26, 1830, George IV died. In the election for

[1] § 14.   [2] § 15.   [3] § 16.   [4] § 17.   [5] § 18.
[6] § 24.   [7] § 25.   [8] § 26.   [9] §§ 28-37.
[10] 10 George IV c. 8.   [11] Ibid c. 1.
[12] Feiling, The Second Tory Party 374-375.   [13] Ibid 376.
[14] Ibid 377; in 1819 Croker was in favour of handing over the representation
of boroughs proved guilty of corruption to the large towns, The Croker Papers
i 137, and he was of the same opinion in 1828-1830, ibid 410 ii 15, 52-54, 97;
his idea and that of the more enlightened Tories was to reform abuses when
proved, as in the cases of Grampound, Penrhyn, and East Retford, to give the franchise to large towns as seats came to be available by the disfranchizement of
corrupt boroughs, but to oppose any general measure of reform, because such
a measure would imperil the monarchy and the House of Lords since it would
lead to universal suffrage and an unchecked democracy, below 257.

the new Parliament the feud in the Tory party secured some Whig victories ; and Brougham was returned without expense to himself by Yorkshire, pledged to a revision of the Corn Laws and Parliamentary reform.[1] If the Tories had listened to the last minute overtures of some of the followers of Canning, and had consented to introduce a measure of Parliamentary reform, they might have retained power.[2] But *quos Deus vult perdere prius dementat.* The reply to these overtures was a point blank refusal. It was given by the Duke of Wellington in the debate on the address. Grey, alluding to our doubtful relations with foreign powers, had argued that the best way to guard against this danger was to gain the affections of the people   and that the best way to gain their affections was to redress their grievances, and, above all, to reform Parliament. He said :[3]

Through my whole life I have advocated Reform, and I have thought that if it were not attended to in time, the people would lose all confidence in Parliament . . . . I trust that it will not be put off as the Catholic Question was put off, but considered in time, so that measures may be introduced by which gradual Reform can be effected without danger to the institutions of this country. Whether it can be expected that Ministers will bring forward such measures, I cannot say ; but of this I am sure, that if they do not bring them forward, and carry them into effect, they will in time be pressed by this question as they have been pressed by the question of Catholic Emancipation, and compelled to yield to expediency what they refuse to concede upon principle.

Wellington in his reply said :[4]

The noble Earl had alluded to the propriety of effecting Parliamentary Reform.   The noble Earl had, however, been candid enough to acknowledge that he was not prepared with any measure of reform, and he could have no scruple in saying that his Majesty's Government was as totally unprepared with any plan as the noble Lord. Nay, he, on his part would go further, and say, that he had never read or heard of any measure up to the present moment which could in any degree satisfy his mind that the state of the representation could be improved, or be rendered more satisfactory to the country at large than at the present moment . . . . He was fully convinced that the country possessed at the present moment a Legislature which answered all the good purposes of legislation, and this to a greater degree than any Legislature ever had answered in any country whatever. He would go further and say, that the Legislature and the system of representation possessed the full and entire confidence of the country—deservedly possessed that confidence . . . . He would go still further and say, that if at the present moment he had imposed upon him the duty of forming a Legislature for any country, and particularly for a country like this, in possession of great property of various description, he did not mean to assert that he could form such a Legislature as they possessed now, for the nature of man was incapable of

[1] Atlay, The Victorian Chancellors i 286-288.
[2] For these overtures see Parker, Peel ii 163-167.
[3] Hansard (3rd Series) i 37.   [4] Ibid 52-53.

reaching such excellence at once ; but his great endeavour would be, to form some description of legislature which would produce the same results . . . . Under these circumstances he was not prepared to bring forward any measure of the description alluded to by the noble Lord. He was not only not prepared to bring forward any measure of this nature, but would at once declare that so far as he was concerned, as long as he held any station in the Government of the country, he would always feel it his duty to resist such measures when proposed by others.

Wellington was stating the view held by those who knew and understood the manner in which the eighteenth century con-stitution worked in practice. He knew that it was the link of influence which enabled the executive and the Legislature to work together. He saw that any extensive measure of Parlia-mentary reform would destroy that link From this point of view there was much to be said for his panegyric on the *status quo*.[1] Where he was disastrously wrong was in supposing that the nation was content with this *status quo*. He and many others believed with some reason that, by a series of historical accidents and by the working of a curious set of conventional practices, a system of representation had come into existence which, though full of anomalies, did represent most of the important interests in the nation, and did respond to great waves of public feeling ; and he was quite right when he said that such a system could never have been thought out by any single man. But again he was disastrously wrong in supposing that the nation forgave the anomalies of this system because it believed in its fundamental excellence. On the contrary it was blind to its excellence and was conscious only of the absurdity of its anomalies.

In fact the Duke of Wellington's speech sealed the fate of the Tory party. The followers of Canning joined forces with the Whigs, and the Ultra-Tories were not conciliated. They helped to defeat the government on an opposition motion to appoint a committee on the civil list ; and there was every reason to think that they would vote for Brougham's motion for a reform of Parliament, of which he had given notice on the first day of the session.[2] The government resigned, and the King, on the advice of Wellington, sent for Lord Grey.[3] The Whigs, who had been in opposition since 1784, with the brief interval of the ministry of all the talents in 1806-7, at last regained office. Grey proceeded to form a ministry pledged to introduce a measure of Parlia-mentary reform.

Before dealing with Grey's ministry and the history of the passing of the Reform Bill, I must say a few words as to the

[1] Vol. x 631-632.
[2] Feiling, The Second Tory Party 382.
[3] Trevelyan, Lord Grey of the Reform Bill 240.

legislation of George IV's reign on constitutional law and on questions of public or semi-public law.

The statutes on these topics are on lines similar to those of the years after 1815. First, small changes are made in the machinery of executive government ; secondly, there is legislation as to the officials of Parliament and as to elections to the House of Commons; thirdly, anomalies in the law are removed and some amendments are made ; and, lastly, changes in the royal family give rise to some legislation.

(1) There are a number of small changes in the machinery of the executive government. Reforms were made in the Exchequer and audit office, and better provision was made for taking the public accounts and for examining the accounts of certain colonial revenues ;[1] the boards of customs and excise of England and Ireland were consolidated,[2] trade between England and Ireland was regulated,[3] and the currencies of England and Ireland were assimilated ;[4] there was regulation of the post office,[5] of the department of woods and forests,[6] of the commissioners of excise,[7] of the treasurer of the navy,[8] of the offices of clerks of the signet and privy seal,[9] and the president of the board of trade was given a salary.[10] Other statutes carried on the work of modernizing the machinery of government. Further provision was made for the regulation of the salaries and pensions of public servants,[11] and their remuneration by fees paid by the public was further restricted.[12] Some of the inconvenient consequences of a demise of the Crown were remedied by an Act which excused persons, who had lost their offices by that event and had been re-appointed, from paying the fees and duties chargeable on a new appointment ;[13] and the salaries of the judges and of persons in the diplomatic service were for the future to be charged, not on the civil list, but on the consolidated fund.[14] We have seen that this process of modernization had been begun in connection not only with the executive but also with the judicial machinery of the state.[15] Useless offices and saleable offices were being got rid of, and the system of payment by fees was being eliminated.[16]

---

[1] 1, 2 George IV c. 121 ; 2, 3 William IV c. 26.
[2] 4 George IV c. 23.   [3] Ibid c.c. 26, 30.
[4] 6 George IV c. 79.   [5] 5 George IV c. 20.
[6] 10 George IV c. 50 ; 2, 3 William IV c. 1.
[7] 2, 3 William IV c. 16.   [8] 11 George IV, 1 William IV c. 42.
[9] 2, 3 William IV c. 49.   [10] 7 George IV c. 32.
[11] 3 George IV c. 113.   [12] 1, 2 William IV c. 40.
[13] 11 George IV, 1 William IV c. 43.
[14] 2, 3 William IV c. 106 ; for the civil list and its history see vol. x 482-485.
[15] Vol. i 262, 442-443.
[16] 6 George IV c.c. 82, 83 (abolition of saleable offices in the King's Bench and Common Pleas) ; ibid c. 84 (augmentation and fixing of the salaries of the judges) ; 11 George IV, 1 William IV c. 58 (fees of the officials of the common

Another series of statutes show that the government was being obliged to undertake new duties either directly or through the agency of the officials of the local government, and to assume new powers. We shall see that provision was made for the advance of money by the government to the justices for the building and repair of prisons,[1] and that a comprehensive set of rules was enacted for the regulation of prisons and the treatment of the prisoners.[2] We shall see also that further provision was made for the treatment of pauper and criminal lunatics ;[3] and that, by a later statute, the law on this subject was consolidated and amended.[4] The destruction wrought by the cholera in 1831-2 was the occasion of an Act which gave large powers to the Privy Council to make orders to prevent the spread of the disease.[5] But the most striking instance in which the government found itself obliged to assume new powers was in reference to the London police.

We have seen that the growth of London in the eighteenth century had rendered the old system of unpaid constables quite inadequate to maintain the peace and to protect life and property.[6] The beginnings of a new system was connected with the institution of magistrates paid by the government. We have seen that the earliest of these paid magistrates was the chief magistrate at Bow Street ;[7] and that the great novelist Henry Fielding, when he held this office, established a body of paid police which had a very considerable success.[8] A proposal in 1785 to establish nine " public offices," that is police-courts, staffed by paid magistrates, and a paid body of police commissioners, who were to employ a paid body of police, aroused such violent opposition that it was abandoned.[9] But seven " public offices " in addition to the Bow Street office were established in 1792 staffed by paid magistrates who were empowered to employ a few paid police ;[10] and a ninth public office was established in 1800 at Wapping to provide for the policing of the Thames and the trial of offences committed thereon. But, though these statutes were frequently revised,[11] they were quite inadequate. In 1812 Romilly noted the increase

law courts) ; ibid c. 70 (abolition of Welsh Judges) ; 2, 3 William IV c. 111 (abolition of sinecure offices in the court of Chancery and a consequential annuity to the Lord Chancellor on resignation) ; ibid c. 122 (Lord Chancellor to be paid by a fixed salary).
    [1] 4 George IV c. 63 ; below 318.   [2] 4 George IV c. 64 ; below 318, 319.
    [3] 5 George IV c. 71 ; below 321.   [4] 9 George IV c. 43 ; below 309.
    [5] 2, 3 William IV c. 10 ; Macaulay writing in June 1831 said, " the great topic now in London is not, as you perhaps fancy, Reform, but Cholera," G. O. Trevelyan, Life and Letters of Macaulay i 223.
    [6] Vol. x 143-144.   [7] Vol. i 146-147 ; vol. x 144.
    [8] Ibid 144 ; 32 George III c. 53.   [9] Vol. i 147.
    [10] Vol. i 147 ; 32 George III c. 53.
    [11] 42 George III c. 76; 47 George III c. 37; 51 George III c. 119; 54 George III c. 37; 1, 2 George IV c. 118; 3 George IV c. 55; 6 George IV c. 21.

of crime. " Two whole families," he said, " one consisting of four and the other of three persons had, at a very short distance of time, been murdered in their houses." This increase of crime was due, he said, partly to the absence of efficient police, partly to the punishment of " promiscuous imprisonment in gaols " which turned out hardened offenders, and partly to the system of rewards paid for convictions which gave " a direct interest to the police and thief taking that crimes of great atrocity, but extremely profitable to them, should greatly multiply." [1] The powers of these paid magistrates to appoint and dismiss a sufficient number of police subject to the approbation of the Home Secretary was confirmed in 1821 ; [2] and the justices attached to the Thames police court were empowered to employ men (not exceeding thirty in number) to police the Thames. [3] In order to increase the efficiency of the magistrates, and to induce persons with some legal knowledge to take office, [4] their pay was increased from £400 to £600 a year, and in 1825 to £800 ; [5] additional powers of arrest were given to the paid police ; [6] they were given power to take bail from persons arrested at night ; [7] and special powers were given to the magistrates and the Thames police with respect to offences committed on the Thames. [8] The magistrates of the Thames police court were also given power to settle disputes as to the wages due to persons employed on the river or the docks ; [9] and other powers were given to all those magistrates. But it was little use to give powers to magistrates without giving them a competent and sufficient police force to enforce their orders. [10] In 1821 the police force was said by one of the magistrates to be " essentially corrupt " ; and the reason was " that there was great service, great temptation, and little pay." There were no pensions, and no allowance for wounds or injuries received while doing their duty. Moreover their numbers were insufficient—" in the Marlborough Street district there was a population of 270,000, yet attached to this office there were no more than eight

[1] Memoirs of Romilly ii 232.
[2] 1, 2 George IV c. 118 § 5 ; see also 3 George IV c. 55 ; 6 George IV c. 21.
[3] § 6.
[4] In 1825 Peel said, that when police magistrates were first instituted, in-competent persons were appointed—out of twelve persons appointed there were only three barristers, " the rest were composed of a major in the army, a starch-maker, three clergymen, a Glasgow trader, and other persons who, from their previous occupations, could not but be utterly unqualified " ; he said that he and his predecessor (Lord Sidmouth) had only appointed barristers ; but that to adhere to this rule the salaries must be augmented.
[5] 1, 2 George IV c. 118 § 1 ; Hansard (N.S.) xii 1128-1129.
[6] 1, 2 George IV c. 118 § 21.
[7] Ibid c. 118 § 28.   [8] §§ 6, 29-39.
[9] § 44 ; this power had been first given in 1807, 47 George III c.c. 37, 64.
[10] E.g., power to regulate coffee shops, 1, 2 George IV c.c. 108-118 ; to regulate fairs, to stop hawkers from using noisy instruments, to stop the beating of bullocks on the streets, 3 George IV c. 55 §§ 17, 19 seqq.

constables." [1] The necessity for a drastic reform had long been apparent. But, since the institution of a paid police force had grown up round the public offices controlled by paid magistrates, it was inevitable that, when it became necessary to extend the system of paid police, this extension should take the form of the creation of a new public office entrusted with the appointment and management of this new force.

By Peel's Act of 1829[2] a police officer under the control of two paid justices was established in Westminster.[3] They were to appoint, and, subject to the control of the Home Secretary, were to manage a force of paid police,[4] for parts of Middlesex, Surrey, and Kent, which were to be known as the Metropolitan Police District.[5] This police force was to supersede the old watchmen or night police employed by the parishes.[6] The expenses of the new police were to be defrayed by a police rate levied in all the parishes of the Metropolitan Police District.[7] This assumption of control by the government over the most important of all government services is perhaps the best illustration of the fact that the needs of the new age were demanding an increase in governmental control. We shall see that in the following period this need was emphasized, and that other services were either undertaken or more strictly controlled by the government.

(2) There are a few Acts which relate to officials of Parliament and to elections to the House of Commons. The office of Clerk of the Parliaments was a patent office held for life and executed by deputy. On the resignation of the present holder, Sir George Rose, the Clerk's Assistant was to become Clerk of the Parliament. He was to execute the office in person, and to hold it during pleasure ; and the other clerks were to be appointed by the Lord Chancellor.[8] Another Act provided that the Speaker of the House of Commons was to receive a fixed annual salary of £600 in lieu of fees.[9] These Acts show that the process of modernizing the appointment and tenure of public offices was being applied to offices of Parliament as well as to offices of the Crown. The Grenville Act[10] and a number of Acts which had amended it were consolidated and amended in an Act which settled the procedure to be followed in the case of contested elections.[11] Persons employed by the candidates at elections were disqualified from voting,[12] and candidates were prohibited from giving ribbons or cockades to their supporters.[13] Voters were to be exempt from being compelled to serve as special constables at the place of

[1] Hansard (N.S.) v 492-494.   [2] 10 George IV c. 44 ; vol. i 147.
[3] 10 George IV c. 44 §§ 1-3.   [4] § 5.   [5] § 4.   [6] § 19.
[7] § 23.   [8] 5 George IV c. 82.
[9] 2, 3 William IV c. 105.   [10] Vol. x 548-549.
[11] 9 George IV c. 22.   [12] 7, 8 George IV c. 37 § 1.   [13] § 2.

the election.[1] Municipal corporations were forbidden to spend the corporation property on elections.[2] Better provision was made for the provision of polling stations at different places in Yorkshire.[3] The corruption of the borough of Grampound was the cause of the Act which disfranchized it and transferred its two members to Yorkshire ;[4] and the corruption of the borough of East Retford was the cause of the Act which enabled freeholders of the adjoining hundred of Bassetlaw to vote at elections for East Retford.[5]

(3) Some of the Acts of this period recall surviving anomalies in the law. Till 1837[6] the Master of the Rolls was paid from the rents of the Rolls estate ; and in 1820 an Act was passed repealing earlier legislation and appropriating those rents to his use.[7] In 1822 the antiquated procedure for recovering damages against the hundred for damage done by rioters was reformed. For the expensive method of bringing actions against individual inhabitants of the hundred there was substituted, in cases where the damage did not exceed £30, proceedings before the petty sessions.[8] It was a rule which went back to the early mediæval period that in any place in which the King's Bench was sitting all other commissions were superseded.[9] It was necessary to pass an Act in 1828 to enable the justices of the peace for Westminster to hold their sessions during term time when the Court of King's Bench was sitting at Westminster.[10]

(4) The beginnings of the reigns of George IV[11] and William IV[12] were the occasion of Acts for the settlement of their civil lists. In 1821 power was given to George IV to grant an annuity of £50,000 to his Queen ;[13] and in 1825 power was given to him to grant an annuity of £6,000 to the Duke of Cumberland to provide for the support and education of his son,[14] and to grant a similar annuity to the Duchess of Kent for the support and education of her daughter Victoria.[15] In 1830 the King's last and fatal illness

---

[1] § 5.   [2] 2, 3 William IV c. 69.   [3] 7 George IV c. 55.

[4] 1, 2 George IV c. 47 ; ibid c. 21 indemnified witnesses implicated in this corruption who give evidence of it.

[5] 11 George IV, 1 William IV c. 74.

[6] 7 William IV and 1 Victoria c. 46, vested the Rolls estate in the Crown and gave the Master of the Rolls in lieu thereof a salary of £7,000 a year.

[7] 1 George IV c. 107.

[8] 3 George IV c. 33 ; it was said that in one case eleven actions had been brought to recover £69 7s. 6d., the costs of which amounted to £1,106 9s. 10d.; that four actions had been brought to recover £7 6s. 5d., the costs of which amounted to £501 6s. 10d. ; and that the costs of an action to recover 18s. amounted to £112 8s. 6d., Hansard (N.S.) vi 916.

[9] Vol. i 212 and n. 3 ; Putnam, Proceedings before the Justices of the Peace (Ames Foundation) lxi-lxii ; the rule was the same for any place in which the general Eyre was sitting, vol. i 266-267.   [10] 9 George IV c. 9.

[11] 1 George IV c. 1.   [12] 1, 2 William IV c. 21

[13] 1, 2 George IV c. 1.   [14] 6 George IV c. 71.

[15] Ibid c. 72 ; an additional annuity of £10,000 was granted in 1831, 1, 2 William IV c. 20.

was the occasion of an Act to enable him to appoint one or more persons to affix the sign manual by means of a stamp, in pursuance of a memorandum in writing signed by certain officers of state.[1] In 1830 provision was made for a regency in case the Crown descended upon Victoria before she was eighteen.[2]

Many of those statutes which made small reforms in public and semi-public law, most of the statutes which reformed the criminal law,[3] and the reports of commissions which prepared the way for large reforms in the law of procedure and in the judicial machinery of the state,[4] and most of the statutes which made large reforms in the law as to commerce and industry,[5] reflected the legal ideas of Bentham and the classical economists. But we have seen that, though the reforms made in the laws as to commerce and industry were dominated too exclusively by the new economic theories,[6] the reforms made in the criminal law and other branches of law, public and private, were by no means exclusively dominated by Bentham's ideas. Those ideas were used by English lawyers ; but they did not adopt Bentham's detailed suggestions as to the manner in which his ideas should be carried out. On the contrary, they carried them out in such a way that they were fitted into the existing system of English law.[7] The fact that this method of reforming English law had been adopted in this period before the reign of the Whigs had begun, and before the influence of the philosophic radicals[8] had become marked, was of considerable benefit both to English law and to the English constitution. After 1832 the speed and thoroughness with which reforms in the law were made was increased. But the methods of law reform pursued in the last years of the Tory régime persisted. The inauguration of these methods of reform by Peel and Canning is not the least of the services of the Tory party, during the last ten years of its existence, to the law and to the constitution.

Since 1815 popular interest in the question of Parliamentary reform had fluctuated. It increased in years of economic de-pression and diminished in years of prosperity. In the decade which followed 1815 there was so little sustained interest in it that, in 1820, Grey had said to his son-in-law Lambton[9] that there was no hope of carrying a reform bill " in my life-time, or even during yours."[10]   But when Grey took office the question of

---

[1] 11 George IV and William IV c. 23.
[2] 1, 2 William IV c. 2.   [3] Above 217, 218, 226 ; below 386-392, 394.
[4] Above 190, 191 ; below 403-407.   [5] Above 226, 227 ; below 328 seqq.
[6] Above 226, 227 ; below 323, 324.   [7] Above 127, 155.
[8] For this school of thought see above 134 seqq.
[9] He became Lord Durham in 1828 ; for his famous report on the Government of Canada, see below 651, 652.
[10] Davis, Age of Grey and Peel 214.

Parliamentary reform had become the question of the day. All sections of the Whig party, the followers of Canning who had joined the Whigs, and even some of the Tories[1] had become convinced that some reform of Parliament was inevitable. The reasons for this change in public opinion are as follows :

In the first place, Cobbett and the radicals were preaching the need for Parliamentary reform and putting it forward as the measure needed to cure the economic and other evils from which the country was suffering.[2] The London Radical Reform Association and the *Westminster Review* kept the subject alive ;[3] and Cobbett undertook a tour of the Northern cities and addressed many meetings at which he urged the necessity for reform.[4] At Birmingham Attwood " a typical merchant prince of the early nineteenth century " [5] had formed his Political Union, the object of which was to obtain Parliamentary reform.[6] At Westminster Place, Bentham's disciple, had organized the Westminster Radicals.[7] The result was that the question of Parliamentary reform was the most prominent issue. The return of Brougham for Yorkshire, without expense to himself, and pledged to a large measure of reform, shows that this question had taken the first place in the minds of the electors.[8] In the second place, the French Revolution of July 1830, which dethroned Charles X, exercised a considerable influence. " This is a revolution," said Cobbett,[9] " made by the industrious classes, and by the working part of those classes ; and will any man now be so impudent as to assert that these people are unworthy of being permitted to vote for representatives." It was a revolution which "fulfilled every condition of justification which Locke and Burke had required and found in the events of 1688." [10] What the French had effected by their revolution could easily, it was argued, be effected in England by an extensive measure of Parliamentary reform.[11]

For these reasons the question of Parliamentary reform had become insistent. At the same time the character and opinions of William IV made the task of carrying of a measure of reform much more possible than it would have been under George IV. William IV, though he distrusted the people, was determined to hold the balance impartially between the two parties.[12] This attitude of mind was of immense value to the Whigs during the struggle for reform ; for it meant that he could be persuaded by

[1] Above 187, 231 ; J. R. M. Butler, The Passing of the Great Reform Bill 62-63.
[2] Ibid 56-57.   [3] Ibid 57-58.   [4] Ibid 58.   [5] Ibid 61.
[6] Ibid 61-64 ; to it " even Whig statesmen largely attributed the passing of the Great Reform Bill," ibid 59.
[7] Above 136.   [8] Above 232.
[9] Political Register, August 7, 14 cited Butler, op. cit. 86.
[10] Butler, op. cit. 88.
[11] Ibid 85-86 and 87, citing the Manchester Guardian of Aug. 28.
[12] Ibid 78-79.

his ministers to use his prerogative to help them to carry out their policy.

Grey's ministry was a coalition of Whigs and Canningites.[1] The greatest difficulty he had was in assigning a place to Brougham. If Brougham was left out his independent criticism, backed by his great popularity, would be dangerous to the government. Already he had been with difficulty persuaded to postpone for a few days his motion or Parliamentary reform ;[2] and he had indignantly refused the office of attorney-general.[3] If he had been given the post of Master of the Rolls, which he wanted, he would have been in as independent position as if he had no office, and, as Althorp pointed out, could have made his position as leader of the House of Commons impossible.[4] At length he was persuaded to give up his great position in the House of Commons and take the office of Lord Chancellor. He was persuaded to take this office by the argument that, if he refused it, the formation of a Whig government would be impossible, and the Tories would come in again.[5] Brougham's acceptance of the office of Lord Chancellor completed the ministry ; and its construction was no small testimony to Grey's statesmanship. Professor Trevelyan says :[6]

In four days Grey had accomplished what no other man in the country could have done. He had made out of scattered and divergent elements a Cabinet and thereby a new Parliamentary party, at once sufficiently advanced in opinion to accept a sweeping Reform Bill, and yet sufficiently broad-bottomed to muster the votes to carry it. In that age, with that King, with those nobles, a less imposing an aristocratic personality than Grey . . . would have failed to create and hold together a Government capable under the existing Constitution of peacefully handing over the power of the aristocracy to the middle class. People complained then and still complain that Grey's Government was very aristocratic in its personnel. It certainly was, but it passed the Reform Bill ; and the question is whether it would have been permitted to do so if it had not been so largely made up of aristocrats ; for the measure was, in effect, one by which the aristocracy, under the combined influence of persuasion, cajolery, and intimidation laid down its monopoly of political power.

The new ministry took office at a time of great economic depression. The wages of the manufacturing population were low,

---

[1] For a list of the ministers see Trevelyan, Lord Grey of the Reform Bill 247-249.

[2] Above 232 ; Trevelyan, op. cit. 242.

[3] The Croker Papers ii 80 ; Atlay, The Victorian Chancellors i 290.

[4] Trevelyan, op. cit. 243.

[5] Ibid 244 ; Butler, op. cit. 149 says, " It seems fair to give him credit for a genuine sacrifice of self-interest in the cause of reform . . . and Brougham fully realised that on the day he took his seat on the Woolsack he had said a long farewell to all his real greatness " ; his mother advised him not to leave the House of Commons—she said, truly enough, that " as member for Yorkshire . . . you are more powerful than any official that ever existed, however high in station or in rank," cited Atlay, Victorian Chancellors i 291-292.

[6] Lord Grey of the Reform Bill 245-246.

and many industries were depressed.[1] At the same time the rise
of the Trade Union movement,[2] which had been rendered possible
by the repeal of the Combination Acts,[3] had made the operatives
more conscious of their distress and more determined to take
measures, political or otherwise, to remedy it. Strikes, lock-outs,
and accompanying disturbances inspired fears of revolution.
Trade Unionism, it was said, "was becoming a public menace." [4]
At the same time revolution had broken out in the agricultural
districts of the south and south east of England.[5] The revolt was
suppressed, and the rioters were punished with the ruthless
severity[6] which was born of fear that a widespread revolution
was being engineered by radical agitators or French Jacobins.[7]
Carlile and Cobbett, who had taken up the cause of the labourers,
were prosecuted. Carlile was convicted and condemned to two
years imprisonment.[8] Cobbett defended himself, and secured his
acquittal.[9] Hetherington and others who had defied the newspaper stamp Acts and issued cheap pamphlets to educate the
working classes were prosecuted and convicted.[10] The ministry
have been generally condemned for the savage sentences on the
rioters. But again we must remember that then, as in the earlier
years of the century, the power of the government to suppress
disorder was small, and that a revolution not suppressed might
easily have spread.[11] If the government had failed promptly to
suppress the revolt the impression, held by many, and confirmed
by the failure of their budget,[12] that the Whigs, long excluded from
power, were unable to govern, might easily have been fatal to
them. As Professor Trevelyan says :[13]

If Grey had shown in this matter the real statesmanship which our age
would approve, he would have lost the confidence not only of the King
and of all the aristocracy, but the greater part of the middle class
opinion to whom he was about to make his great appeal. If the Whigs had
seemed to palter with " anarchy " and " Jacobinism," the ship of Reform
could never have been launched.

At the beginning of 1831 it was obvious that the fate of the
ministry would depend on their Reform Bill. Grey asked his
son-in-law Lord Durham and Lord John Russell to make the
first draft of the bill, and they with Sir James Graham and Lord

---

[1] Butler, op. cit. 117, 119, 120.   [2] Ibid 126-130 ; below 324.
[3] Above 227 ; below 346-348.   [4] Butler, op. cit. 129.
[5] Ibid 130-134.
[6] Nine were hanged, four hundred were imprisoned and four hundred and
fifty seven were transported, Hammond, The Village Labourer 308.
[7] Butler, op. cit. 133 ; Davis, Age of Grey and Peel 225.
[8] R. v. Carlile (1831) 2 S.T. (M.S.) 459.
[9] R. v. Cobbett (1831) ibid 789 ; Hammond, The Village Labourer 317-319.
[10] Butler, op. cit. 135, 167.   [11] Above 164, 165.
[12] Trevelyan, Lord Grey of the Reform Bill 256.   [13] Ibid 253.

Duncannon undertook the task.[1]   Brougham was not included. His work as Chancellor left him little leisure ; and his more limited views as to the scope which such a measure should take, and his disputatious and difficult temperament, would have ensured serious disagreement.[2] The committee were instructed by Grey to prepare a measure " large enough to satisfy public opinion and to afford sure ground of resistance to future innovation." [3] It was to be based on " property and existing franchizes "—there was to be no manhood suffrage. It was to be based on " existing territorial divisions " not, as the radicals wished, " on equal constituencies." [4]

The proposals of the committee were as follows : fifty boroughs were to be disfranchized, and one member was to be taken from fifty others ; about thirty large towns were to elect two members ; four or five additional members were to be given to London ; twenty counties were to have two more members ; votes were to be given to copyholders and leaseholders for twenty-one years in the counties ; in the boroughs the franchize was to be given to £20 householders ; the duration of Parliament was to be reduced to five years ; and voting was to be by ballot.[5] The cabinet refused to accede to Brougham's pleas for a few nomination boroughs to provide a "safe means for getting seats for persons in the Government." ; [6] but it dropped the last two proposals of the committee, and it lowered the £20 household franchize to £10. With these modifications the report of the committee was the basis of the bill, to the principles of which Grey, by his tactful management, induced the King to consent.[7] The bill as first introduced proposed to give two members to seven towns,[8] to give one member to twenty towns,[9] to give eight members to the unrepresented parts of London,[10] to give two additional members to twenty-seven counties,[11] and one member to the Isle of Wight.[12] Sixty boroughs with a population of less than 2,000 named in Schedule A of the bill were to be disfranchized,[13] and forty-seven boroughs with a population of less than 4,000 named in Schedule B of the bill were to lose one member.[14] There was to be a £10 household franchize for the boroughs,[15] and in the

---

[1] Butler, The Passing of the Great Reform Bill 159-160.
[2] Ibid 172 ; Brougham wanted to keep some nomination boroughs, below 252, 652.   [3] Butler, op. cit. 173-174.
[4] Davis, Age of Grey and Peel 229.
[5] For the text of the report see C. W. New, Lord Durham 126-129 ; Butler, op. cit. 179-181.
[6] Davis, Age of Grey and Peel 230 ; for Brougham's views on this matter see Butler, op. cit. 184, 243 ; C. W. New, op. cit. 129.
[7] Butler, op. cit. 187-188.   [8] Hansard (3rd Series) ii 1071-1072.
[9] Ibid 1072.   [10] Ibid.   [11] Ibid 1072-1073.
[12] Ibid.   [13] Ibid 1076-1077.
[14] Ibid 1077-1078.   [15] Ibid 1070.

counties, in addition to the 40/- freeholders, copyholders holding
property of the annual value of £10, and leaseholders of not less
than twenty-one years of the annual value of £50, were to have a
vote.[1]

It was all important that the contents of the bill should not be
known till it was introduced. A premature disclosure would have
provoked the rage of the Tories, and frightened the King and a
section of the Whigs. To ensure that the secret should be kept
" several of the Grey ladies were made partners in it as ammanu-
enses to prevent the employment of clerks." [2]

On March 1 Lord John Russell explained the outlines of the
bill and moved for leave to bring it in. Shouts of ironical laughter
greeted the reading of the lists of boroughs in Schedules A and B ;
and the day after it had been introduced Sir Robert Inglis, who
had made the first speech in opposition, told a friend that " up
to the previous night he had been very anxious, but that his fears
were now at an end, inasmuch as the shock caused by the
extravagance of the ministerial proposals would infallibly bring
the country to its senses."[3]   Inglis was not alone in that opinion ;[4]
and it gives countenance to the view that, if Peel had moved
that the House divide at once, the bill might have been killed
before the country was aroused.[5] But Peel had no talent for
Napoleonic strategy of this order. The debate went on for seven
nights ; and at the end of the second night, after Macaulay had
made his name by the first of his speeches on the bill, " the
Speaker sent for him and told him that in all his prolonged
experience he had never seen the House in such a state of excitement." [6] After the seven days debate that excitement spread over
the whole country.

The bill was introduced and read a first time. The real
struggle came with the debate on the second reading. It was
carried by a majority of one (302-301) amid a scene of excitement
which Macaulay has described in an often cited passage in a letter
to his friend Ellis.[7] It was in effect carried by the votes of the
Irish members.[8] But with opinions so equally divided it was clear
that the bill as it stood could not pass through the Committee
stage. The Government were, in fact, defeated on Gascoigne's

---

[1] Hansard (3rd Series) ii 1070-1071.
[2] Trevelyan, Lord Grey of the Reform Bill 275.
[3] G. O. Trevelyan, Life and Letters of Macaulay i 171-172.
[4] Butler, op. cit. 197 citing some letters of the future Lord Campbell.
[5] Ibid. 195-196 ; The Croker Papers ii 110 ; see Greville Memoirs iv 129.
[6] G. O. Trevelyan, op. cit. i 172.   [7] Ibid 201-204.
[8] " It is an interesting fact, particularly in view of later history, that the bill was
carried on this its first and supreme trial in the Commons by the votes of the
Irish members. England and Scotland were against it, though in England
the closed boroughs only just outweighed the open boroughs and the counties,"
Butler, op. cit. 207-208.

motion that the number of members for England and Wales should not be diminished.[1] The King had told Grey that he would not grant a dissolution.[2] But it was clear that if the King persisted in his refusal the Government must resign. At the last moment Grey's arguments prevailed, and the King consented to grant a dissolution.[3] Knowledge of this fact precipitated the dissolution. A motion was proposed in the Lords praying the Crown not to dissolve. The only way to stop the motion was to get the King to come in person and dissolve Parliament. The King, indignant at the motion, which he regarded as an interference with his prerogative, consented.[4] Before the King's arrival at the House of Lords there were scenes of confusion and uproar in both Houses.[5] But the King arrived before the motion in the House of Lords was carried, and prorogued Parliament with a view to its immediate dissolution.[6]

That was the end of the Tory party and of the old balanced eighteenth century constitution. An overwhelming majority of the nation demanded the passage of the bill. In the new Parliament the second Reform Bill passed its second reading by a majority of 136 on July 6, 1831.[7] After long debates in committee the bill was taken to the Lords who, after a five nights debate, and in spite of great orations by Grey and Brougham, rejected it by a majority of forty-one on October 7, 1831.[8] The Government decided not to resign on condition that the King would give his support to a similar bill to be introduced in the next session.[9] But riots in some of the larger towns, the worst of which was at Bristol, and the activities of the political unions and reform associations, were making it clear that, unless the bill was soon carried, civil war was certain. In those circumstances there was a growing demand that the King should create a sufficient number of peers to pass the bill.[10]

A short prorogation and peers at once was the demand of the forward section ; the more timid were for some modification of the bill, and no creation unless absolutely necessary.[11]

---

[1] Butler, op. cit. 212.　　　　[2] Ibid 203-204.　　　　[3] Ibid 213.

[4] Ibid 215-217 ; Trevelyan, Lord Grey of the Reform Bill 294-296 ; there is no evidence for the imaginative account of the way in which Grey and Brougham induced the King to consent to a dissolution, contained in Brougham's memoirs, and in Roebuck's History of the Whig Administration, which is based on Brougham's statement to Roebuck, see Roebuck's story printed by Atlay, Victorian Chancellors i 303-304.

[5] Butler, op. cit. 217-218.

[6] Greville says, Memoirs ii 140-141, " George Villiers said that in his life he never saw such a scene, and as he looked at the King upon the Throne with the Crown loose upon his head, and the tall, grim figure of Lord Grey close beside him, with the sword of state in his hand, it was as if the King had got his executioner by his side, and the whole picture looked strikingly typical of his and our future destinies."

[7] Butler, op. cit. 278.　　　　[8] Ibid 284-286.　　　　[9] Ibid 287.
[10] Ibid 291.　　　　[11] Ibid.

This difference of opinion was reflected in the cabinet, and it made the preparation of the new bill difficult. The King objected to create peers, and some members of the Government wanted to win over the Lords by concessions[1]—a fatal course to pursue because, as Durham pointed out,[2] by such a policy the Government would lose the support of the nation which alone kept them in office. His reason was decisive ; and a third bill only slightly modified was introduced on December 11, 1831, and was carried by a majority of 162 (324-162).[3] In January 1832 Grey had extracted a promise from the King to create peers if, in the last resort, it should be necessary.[4] The second reading of the bill in the Lords was carried by a majority of nine (184-175).[5] But in committee the opposition attempted to take the conduct of the bill out of the hands of the Government, by carrying an amendment to postpone the consideration of the disfranchizing clause till the enfranchizing clause had been considered.[6] Grey decided to resign unless the King would consent at once to create fifty peers. The King refused and the Government resigned on May 9.[7] The King asked Wellington to form a ministry and pass the bill— thinking that in this way he might avoid a large creation of peers.[8] But Peel wisely refused to have anything to do with so mad a scheme ;[9] and it was clear that the House of Commons would give no support to such a ministry.[10] The attitude of the House of Commons was decisive. On May 15 Wellington gave up his attempt to form a ministry, and Grey was again sent for. There is no doubt that if Wellington had persisted and had taken office a revolution would have broken out. As Professor Trevelyan has said :[11]

The Commons, by preventing the formation of a Tory ministry, had averted an organized insurrection in the great cities of England and Scotland, though if we are to judge of the debates very few members were aware of it. Still less did the Whig and Tory magnates, with whom lay the decision of the Cabinet crisis, discuss their conduct in relation to the impending insurrection. Yet few contingent historical propositions are more certain than this, that if the Duke had taken office there would have been a rebellion.

---

[1] Butler, op. cit. 317-318.

[2] He wrote, " Public support once withdrawn from you, you will not have that of the King for four-and-twenty hours. Do you think he keeps you in now because he likes you on Whig principles ? Far from it. He does so because the people would not sanction a Tory government for an hour," cited, ibid 318.

[3] Ibid 325-326. [4] Ibid 333, 337-338. [5] Ibid 360.

[6] Trevelyan, Lord Grey of the Reform Bill 337-338 ; Grey said of the amendment that " if it did not entirely subvert the principle of the Bill, it materially affected it, and therefore, it was quite impossible that he could accede to it," Hansard (3rd Series) xii 716.

[7] Butler, op. cit. 371-372. [8] Trevelyan, op. cit. 340.

[9] Ibid 341 ; see his letter to Croker, The Croker Papers ii 180-181.

[10] Trevelyan, op. cit. 343. [11] Ibid.

But it was not till May 18 that the consent of the King to create the number of peers needed to pass the bill removed the danger of civil war.[1] The King's action induced the Lords to abandon their opposition—reluctantly and with many misgivings.[2] The bill passed the House of Lords on June 4, and the royal assent was given to it on June 7.[3]

The Act made as great a constitutional revolution as the Revolution of 1688. We shall now see that just as the Revolution of 1688 was the condition precedent for the growth during the eighteenth century, of a mixed, though predominantly aristocratic constitution, with its checks and balances and separated powers ; so the Reform Act was the condition precedent for the growth, during the nineteenth and twentieth centuries, of our modern democratic constitution, in which there are very few checks upon the sovereignty of the majority of the House of Commons and its agent and master, the cabinet.

The Reform Act of 1832 and its Constitutional Effects.

The main provisions of the Act [4] can be summarized as follows : Fifty-six boroughs were wholly disfranchized,[5] and thirty boroughs lost one member.[6] Twenty-two towns and London suburban districts were given the right to elect two members,[7] and twenty towns were given the right to elect one member.[8] Provision was made for ascertaining the boundaries of the enfranchized boroughs.[9] The boroughs of Shoreham, Cricklade, Aylesbury, and East Retford were to include certain adjoining districts ;[10] and the boroughs of Weymouth and Melcombe Regis, Penryn and Falmouth, and Sandwich, Deal and Walmer were to be united and were each to return two members.[11] Provision was made for extending the franchize in certain specified Welsh boroughs to certain specified neighbouring towns,[12] and for

---

[1] Trevelyan, op. cit. 348 ; Grey and Brougham at length induced the King to write, " His Majesty authorizes Earl Grey, if any obstacle shall arise during the further progress of the Bill, to submit to him a creation of Peers to such extent as shall be necessary to enable him to carry the Bill."

[2] " The reformers are triumphant," said Lord Lyndhurst, " the barriers are broken down, the waters are out—who can predict their course or tell the devastation they will occasion ? " Hansard (3rd Series) xii 1002.

[3] Ibid 349.

[4] 2 William IV c. 45 ; the Scotch Reform Act is 2 William IV c. 65, and the Irish Act is 2 William IV c. 88.

[5] § 1 and Schedule A.   [6] § 2 and Schedule B.

[7] § 3 and Schedule C.   [8] § 4 and Schedule D.

[9] § 7 and 2 William IV c. 64 ; a similar Act was passed for Ireland 2 William IV c. 89.

[10] § 5.   [11] § 6.   [12] § 8 and Schedule E.

ascertaining their boundaries;[1] and the towns of Swansea, Loughor, Neath, Aberavon and Kenfig, were to form one borough returning one member, and were to be separated from Cardiff.[2] Provision was made for the appointment of returning officers in the new boroughs.[3]

Additional members were given to certain counties. Yorkshire was to have six members—two for each Riding;[4] Lincolnshire was to have four members;[5] twenty-five counties were to be divided into two divisions, and were to return two members for each division;[6] seven counties were to return three members;[7] the Isle of Wight was to return one member;[8] and thirteen towns which were counties in themselves were, for election purposes, to be included in their counties.[9]

Existing franchizes in the counties and the boroughs were to be retained during the lives of those entitled to exercise them,[10] except in the case of persons created freemen in boroughs since March 1, 1831.[11] For the future the right to the franchize was to be regulated as follows: in the counties the 40/- freeholders; but those holding freeholds for life were not to have the vote unless they were in occupation, or were entitled by marriage, devise, or by virtue of a benefice or office, or unless the freehold was of the annual value of £10.[12] In addition, copyholders holding property of the annual value of £10,[13] and leaseholders of terms created, for not less than sixty years, of the annual value of £10, or terms created for not less than twenty years, of the annual value of £50, or tenants holding at a rate of not less than £50.[14] A freehold, copyhold, or leasehold house, which gave a vote for a borough, was not to give the right to vote in a county election.[15] In the boroughs the vote was given to occupiers of houses of the annual value of £10,[16] and to freemen by birth or servitude registered and residing within seven miles of the borough.[17] Receipt of parish relief was a disqualification. In all cases the voter must have been resident for six months previous to the last day of July in each year, and in all cases he must have been registered as a voter.[18] Provision was made for the preparation of registers by the overseers of the poor,[19] and for objections to insertions or omissions in the register.[20]

---

[1] § 9 and 2 William IV c 64.

[2] § 10.   [3] § 11.   [4] § 12.

[5] § 13—two for parts of Lindsey, and two for parts of Kesteven and Holland.

[6] § 14 and Schedule F; boundaries were settled by 2 William IV c. 64.

[7] § 15 and Schedule F 2.   [8] § 16.

[9] § 17 and Schedule G.   [10] §§ 18, 31-35.

[11] § 32; the reason was that very many persons had been made freemen in order to vote against the reform candidates at the general election of 1831, Erskine May, Constitutional History i 428; there was a similar provision with respect to burgess tenements acquired after March 1, 1831, § 35.

[12] § 18.   [13] § 19.   [14] § 20.   [15] §§ 24, 25.

[16] § 27.   [17] § 32.   [18] §§ 26, 27, 32, 33.

[19] §§ 37, 38.   [20] §§ 38, 39, 44-48.

The registers of county voters with the objections were to be forwarded to the clerks of the peace,[1] and the borough lists to the returning officer.[2] Objections were to be adjudicated on by revising barristers, who were to be appointed by the Chief Justice of the King's Bench.[3] The register of voters when settled was to be in force for one year.[4] The fact that a name was on the register was to be conclusive as to the right of the voter to vote ;[5] but on an election petition the committee of the House of Commons was to have power to enquire into the correctness of the register.[6]

No election was to last for longer than two days ;[7] and provision was made for the creation of polling districts,[8] and the erection (at the expense of the candidates) of polling booths.[9] The polling could be adjourned in case of riot.[10]

Many of the provisions of the Act cannot be understood without some knowledge of the history of the agitation for reform during the earlier years of the century, and of the views held by Grey and his principal ministers—notably Lord Durham. Of these matters I shall, in the first place, say something ; and then I shall try to sum up shortly the principal effects of the Act—both immediate and remote.

(1) I have already said something of the movements in favour of Parliamentary reform before the outbreak of the French Revolution. They began after the agitation aroused by Wilkes and the Middlesex election, and were fomented by the mismanagement of the war with America.[11] The reformers aimed at the curtailment of the influence of the Crown. " As a rule they accept the existing constitution as the basis of moderate change ; divisions run on non-party lines ; the subject is rather academic and makes no appeal to the mass of the people." [12] The reform movement died down after Pitt's failure to carry a very moderate measure of reform in 1785,[13] because some of the abuses which called it into existence were remedied by Pitt.[14] After the French Revolution the agitation revived. By some, who drew their inspiration from Paine, reform was advocated on democratic and republican lines.[15] By the more advanced Whigs proposals for an extensive reform on more orthodox lines were put forward.[16] But the French Revolution had made all such proposals unpopular. Grey's motion in 1793 for a committee to enquire into the state

---

[1] § 40.   [2] § 54.
[3] § 41 ; the judges of assize were to appoint the revising barristers for the boroughs § 49.
[4] § 54.   [5] § 58.   [6] § 60.   [7] §§ 62, 67.
[8] §§ 63, 69.   [9] §§ 64, 68, 71.   [10] § 70.   [11] Vol. x 102.
[12] Butler, The Passing of the Great Reform Bill 3 ; Leslie Stephen, The English Utilitarians i 17-18.
[13] Butler, op. cit. 11.   [14] Ibid 12-13.
[15] Above 163, 201.   [16] Above 239 seqq.

of the representation, based on a report prepared by the Friends of the People, was defeated by a majority of 241 (282-41) ;[1] and his proposal in 1797 was defeated by a majority of 165 (256-91).[2] The latter proposals were far reaching. They included an addition of twenty-one members to the counties, the extension of the franchize to copyholders, leaseholders, and householders, triennial Parliaments, a scheme for the redistribution of borough seats which would have abolished rotten boroughs and given representation to the large towns, and the abolition of plural voting.[3]

In the earlier years of the nineteenth century the Whigs advocated Parliamentary reform ; but there was no popular demand for reform ; and the Whigs were divided as to the kind of reform which was needed. In 1809 Burdett proposed a radical scheme of reform[4] which was lost by a majority of 59 (15-74).[5] It was criticized by the *Edinburgh Review* which defended inequality of representation, provided that this inequality was diminished by disfranchizing a few rotten boroughs and enfranchizing a few large towns.[6] The reviewer advocated some reforms in the franchize—raising the pecuniary qualification in some of the open boroughs, and adding new qualifications for the county vote ;[7] and he advocated measures to prevent riots and disorders at elections.[8] He defended the influence over elections exercised by the Crown and by members of the House of Lords :

If we apprehended that the House of Commons would be freed from all but popular influence, by making the scheme of representation more comprehensive and more consistent, we should certainly be vehement against any such change in its present constitution. We have no fears, however, on this head ; and are perfectly satisfied, that so long as the administration retains any considerable share of its present patronage, and so long as the great families retain their popularity and riches, there will always be a due proportion of their influence to prevent that omnipotent assembly from being guided by the feelings of only one class of the community.[9]

It is therefore not surprising that the reviewer considered that the adoption of the schemes of radicals like Burdett or Cobbett would be " by far the greatest calamity which could be inflicted upon us by our own hands."[10] Thus in 1809 the differences between the Whigs and radicals on the subject of Parliamentary reform are foreshadowed.

---

[1] Trevelyan, Lord Grey of the Reform Bill 76.   [2] Ibid 96.
[3] Ibid 95-96 ; Butler, op. cit. 16 ; above 243, 244.
[4] Hansard (New Series) xiv 1041 ; all householders were to have the vote, and the counties were to be divided into electoral districts according to the taxed male population, elections were only to last one day, and the duration of Parliament was to be shortened, ibid 1053.
[5] Ibid 1070.   [6] Vol. xiv 299.   [7] Ibid.
[8] Ibid 299-300.   [9] Ibid 303-304.   [10] Ibid 302.

These differences became acute when the radical party, strengthened by the adhesion of Bentham and James Mill,[1] and by the growth of the party of philosophic radicals,[2] put forward their schemes of radical reform, and justified them on logical grounds.[3] The proposals of the radicals were anathema to the Whigs. In 1818 the *Edinburgh Review* attacked Bentham's *Plan of Parliamentary Reform*,[4] and, while admitting the increased public interest in Parliamentary reform,[5] denounced projects of universal suffrage because they were sure to lead to attacks on property.[6] All classes, it was said, should be fairly represented ; and to secure the fair representation of all classes diverse and various rights of suffrage must be permitted.[7] We have seen that in 1829 Macaulay made an incisive attack upon James Mill's purely logical arguments in favour of a completely democratic constitution.[8] But though the Whigs were united in their attack on the radicals, they were still divided amongst themselves as to the form which Parliamentary reform should take.

One section of the Whigs advocated very moderate schemes of Parliamentary reform. Lord John Russell's motion in 1819 that corrupt boroughs should be disfranchized and their members given to large towns or counties ;[9] a substantially similar motion in 1821 ;[10] proposals in 1822[11] and 1823[12] to take one member from the hundred smallest boroughs and add sixty to the counties and forty to the large towns ; and his proposal in 1830 to transfer the representation of boroughs convicted of corruption to Leeds, Manchester, and Birmingham[13]—were all measures of very moderate reform. In fact in 1830, he expressly dissociated himself from O'Connell's proposals for universal suffrage, triennial Parliament, and vote by ballot.[14] The other section of the Whigs, without going so far as the radicals, went some way to meet them. They were convinced, and rightly convinced, that unless they proposed a thoroughgoing reform they would never get a sufficient popular backing to carry any reform. The leader of this section of the Whigs was Lambton (the future Lord Durham). In 1821

---

[1] Above 58, 105, 138.   [2] Above 134 seqq.

[3] In the debate on Burdett's motion in 1817 for a committee on the state of the representation it was said, Hansard (N.S.) xxxvi 76, that reformers were divided into two main classes, radical reformers who wanted annual Parliaments and universal suffrage, and moderate reformers who wanted partial alterations for particular grievances.

[4] Vol. xxi 165-203.   [5] Ibid 171-172.

[6] Ibid 172-173.   [7] Vol. xxxi 180-182, 191-192.

[8] Essay on Mill's Essay on Government ; above 142.

[9] Hansard xli 1091-1122 ; his concrete proposals are given at pp. 1106-1107.

[10] Hansard (N.S.) v 604, 626.   [11] Ibid vii 51-141.

[12] Ibid viii 1260-1289.   [13] Ibid xxii 858-918.

[14] " The hon. and learned member for Clare has now moved a resolution containing three main features. The first is that of triennial parliaments ; the second, universal suffrage ; and the third, vote by ballot—from all of which, I beg leave to say, that I most decidedly dissent," ibid xxiv 1222.

he proposed that the country should be divided into equal electoral districts in which each householder should have a vote, that copyholders and leaseholders should have a vote, that the duration of Parliament should be limited to three years, and that measures should be taken to secure the proper conduct of elections.[1] Canning on the second day of the debate pursued the course which some thought Peel should have taken on the introduction of the Reform Bill.[2] Instead of speaking on the motion, he divided the House on it and threw it out.[3] Lambton's scheme was attacked in the *Edinburgh Review* mainly because he proposed to disfranchise the rotten boroughs without compensation.[4] In fact Lambton's scheme and Russell's scheme, which were both submitted to Parliament in 1821, are a striking illustration of the divergence of the ideas of the two sections of the Whig party.

When Grey took office in 1830 pledged to a measure of Parliamentary reform, all depended upon the question whether he would adopt the views of the right or the left wing of the Whig party. His own views had fluctuated. In 1797 he had, as we have seen, proposed a large scheme of reform.[5] But in the succeeding years he had gravitated to the views of the right wing, and had sometimes despaired of seeing reform carried in his lifetime.[6] When taunted in 1831 with having changed his opinions, he admitted that in 1810 he had advocated a less extensive reform ; but, as he said, "if a smaller reform had at that time been adopted, it might have obviated the necessity of the larger reform which I now propose."[7] In fact, as early as 1820, he had made up his mind that, if and when reform came, it ought to be no half measure.[8] Probably he was influenced by his son-in-law Lambton[9] —Croker once said of him that he was " much under the influence of people about him."[10] Certainly when Wellington advised the King to send for Grey he believed that he was an advocate of a moderate measure of reform.[11] However that may be, in spite of the fact that many of his colleagues—the Canningites and Brougham[12] amongst others—were friends of moderate reform, his decision to adopt a more drastic measure is shown by his request to Durham to take the chairmanship of the committee which prepared the bill.[13] He may have been influenced by the consideration that, since the disturbed state of the country was

---

[1] Hansard (N.S.) v 375-380 ; C. W. New, Lord Durham 69, says of this bill that it " so closely resembled the Great Reform Bill of 1832 that it may be regarded as the model from which his committee constructed this measure."

[2] Above 249, 250.   [3] C. W. New, Lord Durham 70-71.
[4] Vol. xxxiv 488-489.   [5] Above 160, 167.
[6] Above 239, 240.   [7] Hansard (3rd Series) viii 314.
[8] Trevelyan, Lord Grey of the Reform Bill 183.
[9] C. W. New, Lord Durham 125.
[10] The Croker Papers ii 104.   [11] C. W. New, op. cit. 125.
[12] Above 240 seqq. ; C. W. New, op. cit. 129.   [13] Above 242, 243.

making the position of his ministry somewhat precarious,[1] a large measure of reform would set it on its feet. But he was chiefly influenced by the consideration that the only chance to remove the danger of radical reform and revolution was to introduce a measure which would give more power to the middle classes ;[2] and it was partly this consideration, and partly the arguments of Durham and the opinions of the committee, which induced Lord John Russell to assent to a measure far more drastic than any which he had previously proposed.[3] Grey wished the question of reform to be settled finally. He saw that it was only a large measure which " would satisfy public opinion and afford a sure ground for resisting further innovations." [4]

It was this need to propose a drastic measure, and at the same time to conciliate those members of his ministry who would have preferred a more moderate measure of reform, which explains the form which the Reform Act took. It was a radical measure in that it suppressed the rotten boroughs, diminished the representation of the smaller boroughs, gave additional members to the counties, enfranchised the large towns, and introduced a uniform and enlarged franchise. It was a moderate measure in that existing rights of voting were preserved, existing constituencies (except in the case of boroughs in Schedule A) were preserved, the duration of Parliament was unchanged, and the ballot was not adopted. But there is no doubt that its radical characteristics, which were due mainly to Lord Durham, predominated, and that it was this fact that united by far the greater part of the nation in its demand for the whole bill. This fact is clear from the arguments both of the supporters and the opponents of the bill.

Lord John Russell, in his speech introducing the bill, said that the real question was whether, without such a measure of reform, it was possible to enlist on behalf of the government that confidence and support of the people without which the constitution must perish.[5] It was only, he said, by a reform of this extent and kind that

we shall be enabled to give permanency to that Constitution which has been so long the admiration of nations, on account of its popular spirit, but which cannot exist much longer unless strengthened by an additional infusion of popular spirit, commensurate with the progress of knowledge and the increased intelligence of the age.[6]

---

[1] Above 241.
[2] Trevelyan, Lord Grey of the Reform Bill 237 and n. 1, citing a letter from Grey to the Knight of Kerry ; Davis, Age of Grey and Peel 227.
[3] Ibid 264 ; C. W. New, op. cit. 115-124.
[4] Davis, Age of Grey and Peel 229.
[5] Hansard (3rd Series) ii 1087.
[6] Ibid 1088-89.

As Mackintosh said, the bill was extensive in its scope because it was a payment of large arrears of reform.[1] Brougham pronounced a somewhat exaggerated panegyric on the virtues of those middle classes to whom the bill proposed to give the franchize ;[2] and Grey truly pointed out that to enfranchize these classes did not, as it had been alleged, give power to a " fierce democracy." [3] It was only by a measure of this kind, he said, that a permanent settlement of the question could be made—permanent in this sense, that the question would not be constantly revived, as formerly it had been revived, in times of distress which " called into action all the elements of political division and discontent." [4] Macaulay in the peroration of his first speech on reform stressed the need for a measure of this kind in order to save the country from the revolution which must break out if all reform were denied.[5] It was denied that its passage would diminish the real and only legitimate influence of the King and the House of Lords—rather it would increase their influence by proving that they were prepared to give effect to the national demand for reform.[6] To disfranchize the rotten boroughs was not an attack on property, for the power of returning members of Parliament was "not property but a trust." [7] Mackintosh truly said that to argue that the disfranchizement of Gatton and Old Sarum was an attack on property, was dangerous to the principle of property, because it tended to identify property with political abuses.[8] To the argument, which was generally believed and was to a large extent true, that the rotten boroughs helped to preserve the balance of power as between King, Lords, and Commons,[9] the short answer was given that no such theory was recognized by the constitution.[10] It was an insufficient answer because, both in the eighteenth century[11] and in the Whig projects for moderate reform in the earlier years of the century,[12] the fact that the rotten boroughs had this beneficial result was well recognized. In fact, though this beneficial result was wholly unrecognized by the law of the constitution, it was, as we have seen,[13] a well

---

[1] Hansard (3rd Series) iv 678.　　[2] Ibid viii 251-252.

[3] Ibid 328.　　[4] Ibid 334.

[5] " The danger is terrible.   The time is short.   If this bill should be rejected, I pray to God that none of those who concur in rejecting it may ever remember their votes with unavailing remorse, amidst the wreck of laws, the confusion of ranks, the spoliation of property, and the dissolution of social order," speech of March 2, 1831 ;   cp. Hansard (3rd Series) iv. 696 (Mackintosh).

[6] Hansard (3rd Series) vii 954, 955-956 ;   viii 335.

[7] Ibid vii 946-947 ; the view that the power to return members was property was held by those who proposed in earlier bills to compensate the owners of disfranchized boroughs ;   it was taken by the writer in the *Edinburgh Review* in 1820, above 252 n. 4 ;   and it was strenuously contended for by Eldon in 1831, Hansard (3rd Series) viii 210-212.

[8] Ibid iv 685.　　[9] Above 23, 126 ; vol. x 565.

[10] Hansard (5th Series) vii 942-943.　　[11] Vol. x 633-634.

[12] Above 251 ; vol. x 565.　　[13] Vol. x 579-580, 632-635.

recognized convention of the constitution which, in the eighteenth century, was regarded as possessing an importance comparable to that of the nineteenth century conventions upon which the modern system of cabinet government depends.

The opponents of the bill denounced it as a revolutionary measure because it would set up a House of Commons which, being dependent solely on the will of the people, would soon reduce the two other branches of the Legislature to impotence.[1] It was a stepping stone to the realization of the ideal of the radical reformers who wanted a single House based on universal suffrage.[2] The bill would destroy the old balanced constitution in which, by means of the influence exercised by the Crown and the Lords over the House of Commons, each of the three partners in legislation could make their influence felt; for, however logically indefensible the rotten boroughs might be, they performed the vital service of preserving the balance of the constitution.[3] For that old balanced constitution there would in no long time be substituted a pure democracy; and if the duration and the achievements of the democratic constitutions recently set up in Europe were compared with the duration and achievements of the British constitution, there could be no doubt as to which produced the best results.[4] It was a fallacy to suppose that, because an admixture of democracy in a constitution was beneficial, the constitution would be improved in proportion as that democratic admixture was increased.[5] The existing system of representation might not be logical, for it was not the product of a single mind working out the results of an abstract theory.[6] But, as Wellington, in his very ill-advised speech in which he opposed all reform,[7]

---

[1] Hansard (3rd Series) ii 1104, 1122-1123 (Robert Inglis); ibid iii 103-105 (Croker). Sir John Rolt, Memoirs 126, tells us that he was opposed to the bill, first because that he thought that a House of Commons elected on the basis of the bill could not " permanently work with, or form part of, a limited monarchy, and secondly, because it would lead to further reforms which would lead to a pure democracy."

[2] Ibid vii 1384-1385 (Earl of Haddington citing Huskisson); vii 201, 204 (Lord Wynford).

[3] Ibid ii 1132-1133 (Twiss); vii 971 (Lord Wharncliffe) 1199-1200 (Duke of Wellington); viii 287-288 (Lord Lyndhurst).

[4] Hansard (3rd Series) ii 1351 (Peel). With this view Gladstone is said to have agreed. C. R. L. F., Mr. Gladstone at Oxford, 1890, 42-43, reports the following dicta : " I remember his rather staggering me by observing that the Duke of Wellington was quite right when he said in 1830 that the Constitution was incapable of improvement and by his defending the saying on the ground that the control which the House of Lords exercized by means of the pocket boroughs over the House of Commons, established an ideal as well as a real equilibrium between component parts of Parliament. He went on to say that the Reform Bill of 1832 destroyed this equilibrium and that henceforward the Constitution logically had to develop on purely democratic lines, a result which he seemed to regard as a doubtful blessing." He also told C. G. L. that in point of ability and efficiency he thought the country had never been better governed than in the period preceding the first Reform Bill.

[5] Ibid xi 742-743 (Peel).   [6] Ibid ii 1339-1345 (Peel).   [7] Above 232, 233.

and as Peel[1] and many others in the debates on the Reform Bill,
said, it was because the existing system of representation was the
product of the practical experience of many minds and of many
periods of history, that it produced results which mere logic and
abstract theory were incapable of producing. Thus the variety
of franchises to be found in the boroughs in effect gave a representation to every class in the community—but in such a way
that the enlightened few were not overwhelmed by the ignorant
many.[2] For this variety of franchise which ensured that al
classes could make their views heard in the House of Commons,
there was to be substituted the dominance of a single class, the
majority of whom were very ignorant.[3] Those below the line
fixed by the bill were disfranchised : the more wealthy and enlightened were swamped by the mass of the poorer and more
ignorant who were above the line. It was argued, therefore, that
both the rotten boroughs, and the variety in the franchise which
the logical maker of constitutions condemned, were in effect
essential parts of the constitution, so that their removal amounted
to a change which could only be described as revolutionary.
Moreover, as Peel showed, the rotten boroughs had very often
given seats to brilliant men for whom it would have been
difficult otherwise to find seats.[4] It was no doubt true that
some of the members for these boroughs were mere delegates for
their patrons ; but some were not ;[5] and there was something
to be said for the view, urged by Peel and supported by evidence,
that, in proportion as the democratic principle prevailed,
members of Parliament would cease to be representatives of
the people of England, and become mere delegates for their
constituents.[6]

We must now consider the question of the extent to which
the hopes of the supporters of the Act and the fears of its
opponents have been realized. This question I must consider
under my second head—the principal effects of the Act both
immediate and remote.

[1] Hansard (3rd Series) xi 742-743.
[2] Ibid ii 1346-1347 (Peel) ; iii 89-90 (Croker) ; vii 116 (Earl of Harrowby).
[3] Ibid vii 1162-1163 (Earl of Harrowby) ; this was also the view of Scarlett,
in his letter to Lord Milton, P. C. Scarlett, Life of Lord Abinger 141-143; cp.
Coleridge, Table Talk, June 25, 1831, Nov. 20, 1831.
[4] Hansard (3rd Series) ii 1349-1350 ; both Macaulay, speech of March 2,
1831, and Mackintosh, Hansard (3rd Series) iv 686-687, treated this as a merely
accidental result of a bad system ; but Peel's imposing list of distinguished men
returned by these boroughs cannot be disposed of in so easy a fashion ; in 1855
Campbell and Brougham agreed that although the Act has had other results
" it had not improved the *matériel* of the House of Commons," Life of Lord
Campbell ii 332-333.
[5] Vol. x 567 ; Bagehot, Essays on Parliamentary Reform 103, 124, 172-180 ;
Porritt, The Unreformed House of Commons i 362-363.
[6] Hansard (3rd Series) xii 168-169 ; ibid 682 (Lord Lyndhurst).

(2) The Reform Act settled the question of Parliamentary reform for thirty-five years—till 1867. It was by no means a final settlement in the sense that Grey hoped it would be. As early as 1834 Lord Durham wished to go further in the path of reform. He wanted shorter Parliaments and the ballot ;[1] for, as Mr. New has said, while Grey supported the bill " in order to secure a basis on which all further reforms—perilous in his eyes—could be permanently refused," Durham supported it " in order that it might inevitably lead to successive measures of advance."[2] In the succeeding years the agitation for further reform became vocal during the Chartist agitation in 1842, and never wholly died down.[3] But it was final in the sense in which Macaulay used that term—it staved off the demand for further reform for a generation. On the other hand, the Tories were right when they said that it was the first step towards the establishment of a purely democratic constitution. It was because the radicals realized this fact that they gave a whole-hearted support to it.[4] As I have said, though it introduced a very moderate measure of democracy, it created a set of conditions in which this moderate measure could be easily increased.[5] That it was increased in so short a time was due, as we shall see, to the tacit acceptance of ill-digested democratic theories as to the presumptive right of every man to a vote, to fanciful and mistaken views, as to the effects of lowering the property qualification for a vote, to the exigencies of party politics, and to the defects of the rule of a middle class dominated by the principles of free trade and *laissez faire*.

The Act, by abolishing the rotten boroughs, put an end to that link of influence which had been the principal method in the eighteenth century of securing harmony between the Executive and the Legislature, and between the House of Lords and the House of Commons.[6] The result was that the cabinet became the only link which secured harmony between the Executive and the Legislature.[7] The modern history of the cabinet begins with the Reform Act.[8] No means were provided for securing harmony between the House of Lords and the House of Commons, with

---

[1] Davis, Age of Grey and Peel 236.

[2] C. W. New, Lord Durham 127.

[3] " For my part I do believe that the settlement proposed by His Majesty's Ministers will be final, in the only sense in which a wise man ever uses that word. I believe that it will last during that time for which alone we ought at present to think of legislating. Another generation may find in the new representative system defects such as we find in the old representative system . . . for our children we do not pretend to legislate," speech of July 5, 1831 ; cp. Hansard (3rd Series) iv 697 (Mackintosh).

[4] See Place's view cited above 205.

[5] Vol. x 22.

[6] Ibid 630-635.

[7] Ibid 632.

[8] For the early history of the cabinet see vol. x 636-643.

the result that the House of Lords ceased to be, as it had been in the eighteenth century, the " poise " or centre of the constitution, and became, far more definitely than it had become in the eighteenth century,[1] a second chamber,[2] which might delay, but could not prevent a constitutional change which the House of Commons and the nation were determined to effect. As Coleridge said,[3] " its supremacy as a co-ordinate estate of the nation " was destroyed.

As the Tories had prophesied, the abolition of the rotten boroughs, and of the varieties in the franchize which had characterized the old system of representation, tended to give undue weight to the most numerous and the least educated class in the community. For some years the anomalies in the representation still retained by the Reform Act obscured this result. We have seen that Bagehot, writing in 1866, said that the influence of the landed gentry in the House of Commons was still very great.[4] But in the middle years of the nineteenth century, when the question of further reforms on logical lines was becoming a burning question, the problem of how to guard against this evil was considered by many—notably by Bagehot[5] and J. S. Mill.[6] But no one of the artificial expedients suggested to attain this result was found to be practicable. The anomalies of the old representative system, which did guard against this evil, had been scrapped ; and it was found to be impossible to construct artificially any expedient to take their place. The lesson to be learned from the course pursued by the framers of the Reform Act is, I think, this : It is dangerous to scrap, merely on theoretical grounds, what appear to be anomalies without a most careful consideration of the question whether in fact they serve a useful purpose. This was the principle laid down by Burke[7] when he said,

Let us improve it (the constitution) with zeal, but with fear. Let us follow our ancestors, men not without a rational, though without an exclusive confidence in themselves ; who, by respecting the reason of others, who, by looking backward as well as forward, by the modesty as well as by the energy of their minds, went on, insensibly drawing this constitution nearer to its perfection, by never departing from its fundamental principles, nor introducing any amendment which had not a subsisting root in the laws, constitution and usages of the kingdom.

[1] For its position in the eighteenth century see vol. x 604-605, 614-618.
[2] Ibid 619, 626-627.   [3] Table Talk, Feb. 24, 1832.
[4] English Constitution 163-164, cited vol. x, 566 n. 5.
[5] Essays on Parliamentary Reform 31, 61-73.
[6] Representative Government, Chap. vii ; ibid 71-72 where the expedient of plural votes for better educated people is suggested; cp. J. S. Mill's Autobiography 256-260, 309-310.
[7] Appeal from the New to the Old Whigs, Works (Bohn's ed.) iii 114 ; cp. Peel's argument on the second reading of the first Reform Bill, Hansard (3rd Series) ii 1339-1344.

In fact many of the most valuable principles of the constitution owe their existence to the fact that what appeared to be anomalies to constitutional theorists were not scrapped in obedience to a logical theory. In the seventeenth century Coke's insistence on the mediæval concept of the supremacy of the common law, preserved the concept of the rule of law at a time when the dominant political theory favoured the sovereignty of a single person.[1] At the time of the Reform Act the House of Lords and the Crown were preserved as essential parts of the constitution at a time when, according to the logical theories of the philosophic radicals, both ought to have been eliminated.[2] The succeeding years were to show that both the House of Lords and the Crown fulfil some very essential functions. The House of Lords provides a second chamber, the average ability of whose active members is equal if not superior to the average ability of the members of a democratically elected House of Commons. No such claim can be made for the democratically elected second chambers of modern constitutions ; and, notwithstanding the preamble to the Parliament Act,[3] it is fortunate that as yet no one of the many schemes for the reform of the House on democratic lines has materialized. Without the connecting link of the Crown the leading members of the British Commonwealth of Nations would have become entirely separate states. The House of Lords and the Crown were fortunately not eliminated, as the Tories prophesied, by the growth of the democratic elements in the constitution. On the contrary they entered upon different but no less real careers of usefulness.

In so far as these results of the Reform Act were attained before 1875, I shall deal with them in the next chapter of this History. I must now turn back to this period, and, in the two following sections of this chapter, give some account of the growth of the movement for the reform of the law, and of the changes in the enacted law effected as the result of this movement.

III

THE MOVEMENT FOR REFORMS IN THE LAW (1793-1832)

We have seen that the effect of the French Revolution and of the war with France was almost to put an end to all hope of persuading the Legislature to consider projects for reform.[4] No project for major reforms in any of the institutions of the state or

---

[1] Vol. v 428, 430, 454 ; Vol. vi 67-69, 83-84.   [2] Above 163.
[3] " Whereas it is intended to substitute for the House of Lords as it at present exists a Second Chamber constituted on a popular instead of hereditary basis," 1, 2 George V c. 13.   [4] Above 249, 250.

in the laws which governed its policy in economic or social matters could get a hearing ; and, still less, any projects for the reform of the rules of law, criminal or civil. At the same time it would not be true to say that the advocates for reforms in the law were quite powerless. They were, it is true, an inconsiderable minority in Parliament. But in the unreformed Parliament even an inconsiderable minority had many more chances of making its voice heard than in an age in which the procedure of Parliament is no longer a procedure designed to give facilities to the opposition,[1] but a procedure designed to give facilities for the rapid transaction of the business of the government. And so, although the last ten years of the eighteenth century and the first ten years of the nineteenth century were the most difficult years for those who advocated reforms in the law, even in those years reforms were suggested and discussed. The cause of reform was never wholly abandoned ; and projects which were voted down in those years were realized in the two following decades of the nineteenth century because, the need for reform having become more urgent, the reasons advanced by the reformers, inspired partly by the obvious unreasonableness of the existing rules and partly by Bentham's principles, gained an ever increasing measure of acceptance.[2] I shall, in the first place, give some illustrations of the various reforms in the law suggested during this period, and of the reasons advanced by their advocates. In the second place, I shall say something of the work of the principal pioneers of law reform—of the work done by Romilly, Mackintosh and Peel for the reform of the criminal law ; of the work done by Michael Angelo Taylor, C. P. Cooper, John Williams and Joseph Parker for the reform of the court of Chancery ; of Humphreys's proposals for the reform of the law of real property ; and of Brougham's great speech in 1828 in which he surveyed a large part of the field of common law jurisdiction, proved the urgent need for reform in many parts of the law substantive and adjective, and gave a great impetus to the existing movement for law reform.

(1) In the first place, reforms in many different branches of the law were suggested and discussed in both Houses of Parliament all through this period. In the second place, several royal commissions were appointed which collected and published information as to the courts and some of the other institutions of government, and so enabled the reformers to get a clear view of

---

[1] Vol. x 536-538.

[2] In 1830, Mackintosh, contrasting that period with the preceding two decades when Romilly was trying to effect reforms in the criminal law, said that " he almost thought that he lived in two different countries, and conversed with people who spoke different languages," Hansard (3rd Series) xxiv 1033.

the abuses and anomalies which needed abolition or reform, and made it possible for them to make informed and intelligent suggestions for legislative changes. Of these two methods of promoting reforms in the law I shall say something.

(i) The principal branches of the law in which reforms were suggested or discussed were the following : the state of the statute book ; the courts ; the law of debtor and creditor ; the criminal law ; ecclesiastical law ; equity and allied topics.

The state of the statute book. In 1796[1] and 1799[2] the confused state of the statute book induced the House of Commons on the motion of Charles Abbott (afterwards Speaker and later Lord Colchester) to appoint a committee to enquire into the subject of expiring laws, and to make recommendations as to their continuance or revival ;[3] and in 1796 Abbott persuaded the House to appoint a committee to enquire into the defective methods of promulgating the statutes.[4] In 1800 he persuaded the House to appoint a committee on the public records,[5] which led to the appointment of the Record Commission, and the publication by it of a more complete and authoritative edition of the statutes than had ever been published before.[6] In 1816 Earl Stanhope persuaded the House of Lords to accept a motion, which Eldon did not oppose, for undertaking a revision and rearrangement of the statute book ;[7] and the House of Commons concurred in it.[8]

In the second decade of the nineteenth century a reform of certain parts of the statute law was effected by Acts which repealed large numbers of statutes from all periods in legal history, and replaced and amended them by consolidating Acts. The three branches of law which were reformed in this way were the law as to the customs revenue and matters cognate thereto, the law as to juries, and the criminal law.

The revision of the law as to the customs revenue was effected by a series of twelve statutes passed in 1825.[9] The first of these statutes [10] repealed 387 English statutes, beginning with 17 Richard II c. 5 and ending with 5 George IV c. 94, and 55 Irish statutes, beginning with 25 Henry VI c. 3 and ending with 4 George IV c. 72. The second [11] and third [12] of these statutes created

---

[1] Parlt. Hist. xxxii 992-994 ; for the history of the revision of the statute book see vol. xi 309-316.   [2] Parlt. Hist. xxxiv 516-518.

[3] Abbott said, ibid 517, " The trading interests which are deeply concerned in the laws of bankruptcy and insolvency, have repeatedly suffered by the expiration of Acts of this nature."

[4] Parlt. Hist. xxxii 1239-1241 ; for the history of this subject see vol. xi 290-291, 303-304, 319-320.

[5] Parlt. Hist. xxxiv 1458-1465.   [6] Vol. xi 310-313 ; below 272.

[7] Hansard (1st Series) xxxiv 173-183, 425.   [8] Ibid 1041-1043.

[9] 6 George IV c.c. 105-116.   [10] C. 105.

[11] C. 106, containing 54 sections.   [12] C. 107, containing 44 sections.

a new code of rules for management of the customs, and for their general regulation. The fourth statute[1] codified the law as to the prevention of smuggling. The fifth[2] and sixth[3] statutes codified the Navigation Acts and the Acts for the registration of British shipping. The seventh[4] statute imposed new customs in place of those imposed by the repealed statutes. The eighth[5] statute dealt with the subject of bonded warehouses. The ninth statute [6] dealt with bounties and allowances. The tenth statute [7] regulated the trade of British possessions abroad. The eleventh[8] statute regulated trade with the Isle of Man. The twelfth statute[9] laid down the rules with which passenger ships must comply. This series of twelve statutes was by far the greatest feat in the consolidation of the statute law that had ever been made. It was followed in 1827 by an Act which consolidated and amended the laws relating to the collection and management of the revenue of excise; [10] and in 1829 by " an Act to consolidate and amend the laws relating to the management and improvement of his Majesty's woods, forests, parks, and chases; of the land revenue of the Crown within the survey of the Exchequer in England; and of the land revenue of the Crown in Ireland; and for extending certain provisions relating to the same to the Isles of Man and Alderney," [11] which repealed 17 Acts except so far as they related to the Duchy of Lancaster.

The law as to juries was consolidated and amended by an Act of 1825 which repealed wholly or in part 63 statutes, beginning with 43 Henry III and ending with 22 George II c. 3.[12] The criminal law was consolidated by a series of statutes passed between the years 1826 and 1832. The Act of 1826 dealt with criminal procedure.[13] In 1827 five consolidating Acts were passed.[14] The first of these statutes [15] repealed 137 statutes or parts of statutes, beginning with 9 Henry III St. 2 c. 10 and ending with 7 George IV c. 69. The second statute effected reforms in criminal procedure, the punishment of felony, and the interpretation of criminal statutes.[16] The third statute [17] consolidated and amended the law as to larceny and offences connected therewith. The fourth

---

[1] C. 108, containing 107 sections.   [2] C. 109, containing 23 sections.
[3] C. 110, containing 51 sections.
[4] C. 111, containing 29 sections and tables of customs duties inwards, outwards and coastwise.
[5] C. 112, containing 46 sections.   [6] C. 113, containing 15 sections.
[7] C. 114, containing 86 sections and tables of duties.
[8] C. 115, containing 18 sections.   [9] C. 116, containing 21 sections.
[10] 7, 8 George IV c. 53, containing 130 sections.
[11] 10 George IV c. 5, containing 135 sections; for some account of the land revenue of the Crown see vol. x. 348-349.
[12] 6 George IV c. 50, containing 64 sections.
[13] 7 George IV c. 114.   [14] 7, 8 George IV c.c. 27-31; below 397, 398, 400.
[15] C. 27.   [16] C. 28.
[17] C. 29, containing 77 sections.

statute[1] consolidated and amended the law as to malicious injuries to property. The fifth statute[2] consolidated and amended the law as to the remedies against the hundred. In 1828 the law as to offences against the person was consolidated and amended by a statute which repealed 57 statutes or parts of statutes, beginning with 9 Henry III c. 26 and ending with 3 George IV c. 114.[3] In 1830 the law as to those forgeries which were to be punishable with death was consolidated and amended by a statute which repealed 27 statutes or parts of statutes.[4] In 1832 the law as to coinage offences was consolidated and amended by a statute which repealed 35 statutes or parts of statutes.[5] With the reforms effected in the criminal law by some of these statutes I shall deal later.[6]

The courts. We shall see that between 1810 and 1826 royal commissions were enquiring into the saleable offices in the courts,[7] into the officers of the courts of law and equity, the ecclesiastical courts, and the court of Admiralty,[8] and into the procedure of the court of Chancery.[9] In 1817 a motion to refer some of their reports to a committee was lost,[10] but in 1818 a motion in the House of Lords for copies of some of these reports was acceded to.[11] In 1811 Eldon moved for a committee to consider the arrears of business in the House of Lords [12]—there were then 42 writs of error and 296 appeals waiting to be heard.[13] It was suggested that the House should sit three days a week to hear appeals, and that, to relieve the Lord Chancellor, an additional judge of the court of Chancery should be appointed [14]—a proposal which, as we have seen was carried out when a vice-chancellor was appointed in 1813.[15] With the other proposals for dealing with the arrears of business in the court of Chancery, and its dilatory procedure, I shall deal later.[16] In 1820[17] and 1824[18] Lord Redesdale proposed to establish efficient county courts for the recovery of small debts ; and in 1824 Eldon agreed that some such measure was necessary. In 1823 Lord Althorp, on the report of a committee of the House of Commons, proposed the establishment of local courts. The judge was to be a barrister, acting as assessor to the sheriff, who was to be appointed by the Lord Lieutenant and paid out of the county rate.[19] In 1824 a bill to establish these courts was proposed ; [20]

---

[1] C. 30, containing 43 sections.   [2] C. 31, containing 16 sections.
[3] 9 George IV c. 31, containing 38 sections.
[4] 11 George IV and 1 William IV c. 66, containing 32 sections.
[5] 2 and 3 William IV c. 34.   [6] Below 400, 401, 402.
[7] Below 272 ; see vol. 1 686-688 for some extracts from this report.
[8] Below 273.   [9] Below 273.
[10] Hansard (1st Series) xxxv 971-979.   [11] Ibid xxxvii 1255-1259.
[12] Ibid xix 232.   [13] Ibid xx 338.   [14] Ibid.
[15] Above 190.   [16] Below 288, 289, 290.
[17] Hansard (2nd Series) i 742.   [18] Ibid xi 1315-1316.
[19] Ibid ix 543-546 ; Lord Althorp, at p. 543 said, " no man to whom a sum of under £15 was due, would now think of attempting to recover it unless he was actuated by motives of a vindictive nature."   [20] Ibid x 210-212.

in 1828 the subject was taken up by Peel;[1] and in 1830 by
Brougham.[2] In fact such a measure was needed not only to give
creditors a less expensive remedy than that afforded by the
common law courts, but also to protect them against the manner
in which debtors could make use of the technicalities of the
procedure of those courts to delay their actions and put them
to expense. In 1817 Romilly brought to the notice of the House
of Commons a circular sent out from the Temple giving debtors
advice as to how best to annoy and harass their creditors, and
cause them expense by means of sham pleas, writs of error,
and by filing bills for injunctions. It was stated in the circular
that " a debtor might, at the expense of five guineas to himself,
put his creditor to the expense of £100 ; and for £24 and a fraction,
oblige him to pay, in fees and expenses, above £300." [3] The main
hindrance to the acceptance of these bills came from officials
of the courts local and central, who held offices for life, and
who claimed compensation for the loss of fees which the establishment of these courts would cause.[4] Peel admitted that these
claims raised difficult questions ; [5] and in fact it was a very
old standing difficulty.[6] It was not till the emoluments of these
freehold offices were commuted by an Act of 1830 that this
impediment to reform was removed.[7]

The law of debtor and creditor. I have already said something
of the abuses of and the hardships caused by the law which allowed
a creditor to arrest his debtor on mesne process.[8] In 1800 a
bill to reform the law on this subject was proposed in the House
of Lords by Earl Moira,[9] but it was opposed by Lord Ellenborough and rejected.[10] In 1814 Earl Stanhope said that arrests

---

[1] Hansard (2nd Series) xix 876.   [2] Ibid xxiv 243-274.
[3] Romilly, Memoirs ii 453.
[4] When the bill of 1824 to establish small debt courts was before the House, the
following officials claimed compensation : the chief clerk on the plea side of the
court of King's Bench, the clerk of the rules and the clerk of the papers of the
court of King's Bench ; the prothonotaries, secondaries, and filacers of the court
of Common Pleas ; the Master, senior attorney, and secondary of the plea side
of the court of Exchequer ; the prothonotaries of the courts of Great Sessions
in Wales.   Althorp contested these claims—if, he said at p. 1431, a man's property
was taken he was entitled to compensation, but he was not so entitled if as the
result of legislation his property was made less valuable ; to which the reply was
given (p. 1432) that if a bridge was built the owner of an existing ferry was always
compensated.
[5] In 1830 Peel said that the reason why he had not again brought forward
his bill was " the great difficulty of making compensation to the different persons
who held freehold offices.   There was at present a bill in progress for compensating the holders of all such offices, and when that had passed into law, he
would be ready to bring forward his bill again, or to support the more extensive
bill of the hon. and learned member for Knaresborough (Brougham)," Hansard
(2nd Series) xxiv 1202.   [6] Vol. i 251 n. 5.
[7] 11 George IV, 1 William IV c. 58 ; see Spencer Walpole, History of England
iii 49-50.   [8] Vol. xi 595-597.
[9] Hansard (1st Series) x 1068-1069.   [10] Ibid 1069-1070.

on mesne process had resulted in a state of affairs which might be called the " English slave trade," [1] and he exposed some of the abuses to which it gave rise ; [2] but again Ellenborough's opposition to its abolition was successful. [3] In 1829 and 1830 protests against imprisonment for debt on mesne or final process were made in the House of Commons. [4] We have seen also that the power of creditors to arrest their judgment debtors for non-payment of their debts had caused the enactment of frequent temporary insolvent Acts by means of which these debtors could get released. [5] These Acts, though sometimes opposed on the ground that they were *ex post facto* [6] laws, injurious to trade and tending to promote fraud, [7] were in fact so necessary that Eldon did not oppose Lord Redesdale's permanent Act in 1813, [8] and made the wise suggestion that it might be expedient to extend the bankruptcy law to non-traders. [9] In 1823 he proposed a bill to reform and consolidate the law of bankruptcy. [10] In 1806 [11] and 1809 [12] Romilly had managed to get two Acts passed which effected small reforms in the law of bankruptcy ; and in 1807 he had succeeded in carrying an Act to make the land of deceased traders equitable assets for the payment of their simple contract debts. [13] " Country gentlemen " he said, " have no objection to tradesmen being made to pay their debts ; and to the honour of men in trade, of whom there are a good many in the House, they, too, had no objection to it." [14] But he tried in vain to extend this liability to the land of non-traders. It was in vain that he pointed out that the law of no other country thus freed land from liability, and that cases of great

[1] Hansard (1st Series) xxvii 618.

[2] One instance was an arrest to prevent the person arrested from giving evidence in the case of fraud in which he was the prosecutor.

[3] Ibid xxvii 739-740, 959-962.

[4] Hansard (2nd Series) xx 431 ; xxii 267. In 1830 Hume said that there was an instance of a person being imprisoned for forty days by the judgment of the court of Requests for a debt of 1s. 6d. and being put to great expense to get his release.   [5] Vol. xi 597-598 ; Hansard (1st Series) ii 648.

[6] Romilly said, Memoirs ii 212, that nothing could justify these *ex post facto* laws " but the intolerable mischief of the law as it at present stood."

[7] Hansard (1st Series) ii 648, 879, 1111 ; ibid vii 146.

[8] 53 George III c. 102 ; vol. xi 598 and n. 5 ; see Romilly, Memoirs ii 314-318, for an account of the passing of this Act ; it appears that Lord Ellenborough was opposed to it, see ibid 323-324, and only let it pass " because he was weary of opposing such bills."

[9] Hansard (1st Series) xxiii 320, 324.

[10] Hansard (2nd Series) viii 705-706.

[11] Memoirs of Romilly ii 18-19, 22-23 ; 46 George III c. 135.

[12] Memoirs of Romilly ii 96-97, 102, 114-115 ; it was so altered by the Lords that Romilly thought of abandoning it, ibid 123-124 ; 49 George III c. 121 ; below 275, 276, 376.   [13] 47 George III Sess. 2 c. 74 ; below 414.

[14] Memoirs of Romilly ii 54 ; Eldon made considerable difficulties, but he at last decided to let it pass ; Redesdale opposed it, and proposed to make it apply not only to traders but to all persons, so that when it came back to the Commons in that form they might throw it out, ibid 72-73.

hardship resulted from it.[1] Flimsy arguments, that it was hard
on the heir if he were penalized by the extravagance of his
ancestor,[2] that such a law was contrary to the " genius and manners of the people," [3] that it would make land unsaleable,[4] that
the creditor should have bargained for a better security,[5] that
the effect of the bill would be to bring all freehold estates into
the court of Chancery, and would destroy the law of primo-
geniture,[6]—for the time being carried the day. It was not till
1834 that this reform was effected.[7] Before it was effected
Sugden had succeeded in effecting a much needed extension of
William III's statute of fraudulent devises.[8]

The criminal law. The many different proposals made to
reform the criminal law show a very distinct humanitarian
tendency. In 1819 Lord Auckland tried to pass a bill to protect
the boy chimney sweepers—the work, he pointed out, could
just as well be done by machines; [9] and we have seen that the
first factory Acts were passed for the protection of children
in spite of the objection of the more rigid economists.[10] Many
attempts were made to legislate against cruelty to animals and
against cruel sports such as bull baiting and dog-fighting. In
1809 Lord Erskine introduced a bill to prevent cruelty to animals.[11]
Lords Eldon and Ellenborough approved the principle of the bill,
but thought that it should be limited to beasts of draught and
burden.[12] In the House of Commons Romilly supported the
bill " not merely as a measure of humanity but of sound policy,"
because " habits of cruelty towards animals led to the exercise
of cruelty towards human beings," and so made them bad citizens.[13] But it was successfully opposed because it introduced
a new principle into the criminal law.[14] Moreover, it was said
definition would be difficult, and it would throw difficulties
in the way of the use of animals for food and sport.[15] In 1822
a bill to prevent the ill-treatment of horses was opposed on
similar grounds; [16] but in the same year a bill to prevent the
ill-treatment of cattle was passed.[17] In 1825, however, Peel

[1] Hansard (1st Series) viii 561-563 ; it was said that there was a case where
an estate worth £4,000 a year descended to the heir, and the undertaker's and
doctor's bills were unpaid, ibid ix 83 ; in 1814 Romilly pointed out that the length
to which judges went to find a direction in the will to pay debts showed the hardship of the law, ibid xxvii 594, and that Blackstone had advocated this reform,
ibid 605.

[2] Ibid ix 161. [3] Ibid 162. [4] Ibid 163. [5] Ibid 748-749.
[6] Romilly, Memoirs ii 376. [7] 3, 4 William IV c. 104.
[8] 11 George IV and 1 William IV c. 47 ; Hansard (2nd Series) xix 368-371 ;
for William III's statute of fraudulent devises, 3 William and Mary c. 14 see vol.
vi 397-398 ; below 408, 414.
[9] Hansard (1st Series) xxxix 899. [10] Above 36, 39.
[11] Hansard (1st Series) xiv 553. [12] Ibid 571, 807.
[13] Memoirs of Romilly ii 121. [14] Hansard (1st Series) xiv 1029.
[15] Ibid 1032-1033. [16] Hansard (2nd Series) v 1099.
[17] 3 George IV c. 71 ; Hansard (2nd Series), vii 758-759, 874 ; below 392.

successfully opposed any extension of this Act.[1] Just as the arguments of the more rigid economists were an obstacle in the way of the factory Acts, so the needs of sport were an obstacle in the way of preventing legislation against cruel sports. In 1800 Pulteney failed to persuade the House of Commons to stop the practice of bull baiting.[2] Canning went so far as to say that " it inspired courage, and produced a nobleness of sentiment and elevation of mind." [3] In 1823 Brougham opposed a bill to prevent bull baiting and dog-fighting on the ground that it was unfair to draw a distinction between the blood sports of the higher and lower classes.[4] Similar bills in 1824[5] and 1825[6] were rejected on the ground that they interfered with sport.

In these circumstances it was impossible to effect any reforms in the irrational code of the game laws.[7] Nevertheless several attempts to reform them were made. In 1796 Curwen moved for their repeal, and induced the House of Commons to consider them.[8] But he failed to carry a bill enabling every landowner to kill game on his own land.[9] Pitt defended the game laws on the ground that they tended " to induce gentlemen to live in the country " ; [10] and even on such a subject the influence of the French Revolution was felt. " Many of the evils that existed in a neighbouring nation," said Jenkinson, " were in a great degree occasioned by gentlemen not residing on their estates."[11] In 1827 an attempt was made to prohibit trespassing on another's land in pursuit of game, and to permit the sale of game.[12] As Romilly pointed out in 1818,[13] the game laws consisted of a body of criminal law " which has so little the sanction of public opinion that no man is thought the worse of, by persons in his own rank of life, for incurring its penalties." Moreover, the severe punishments inflicted on poachers made them desperate, and so formed a body of men ready for the commission of the most enormous crimes. The one piece of legislation directed against the methods of game preservers which met with the approval of Lord Eldon, though it was opposed by the Duke of Wellington, was the legislation against the setting of spring guns.[14] Eldon agreed that the law on this matter was uncertain,[15] and he was perhaps influenced by the

---

[1] Hansard (2nd Series), xiii 418-419. [2] Parlt. Hist. xxxv 202-214.
[3] Ibid 211. [4] Hansard (2nd Series) ix 433.
[5] Ibid x 131-132, 492. [6] Ibid xii 657, 661, 1002-1003, 1013.
[7] For the same laws see vol. i 107-108 ; vol. iv 505-506 ; vol. vi 403 ; vol. xi 543-545.
[8] Parlt. Hist. xxxii 831-846. [9] Ibid 847-854.
[10] Ibid 851. [11] Parlt. Hist. xxxii 853.
[12] Hansard (2nd Series) xvi 1286. [13] Memoirs ii 496.
[14] Hansard (2nd Series) xii 641-642, 922-925, 937-938, 939-940 ; ibid xvii 235-239, 296 ; 7, 8 George IV c. 18 ; below 390, 605.
[15] Ibid xii 939-940.

statement that on one occasion one of these guns had nearly caused royal blood to be shed.[1]

We shall see that the mitigation of the severity of the punishments inflicted by the criminal law was the main work first of Romilly [2] and then of Mackintosh,[3] with some help from Peel.[4] But they were not the only persons who advocated this cause. In 1799 there was a debate on the question of the justification of forfeiture[5] as an additional penalty for high treason. It was attacked by Hobhouse and defended by Charles Abbot.[6] In 1825 both forfeiture and the doctrine of corruption of blood were attacked by Lord Holland, and both were defended by Eldon on the ground that they were "a vast security to the public peace."[7] In 1815[8] and 1816[9] bills to abolish the punishment of the pillory, on the very good ground that it was a very unequal punishment,[10] were introduced, and the bill of 1816 met with partial success.[11] In 1817 the public whipping of females was abolished.[12]

Ecclesiastical Law. The growing frequency of applications for divorce Acts and the anomalous state of the law[13] aroused discussion in 1800 and 1830.

In 1800 there were long but inconclusive debates in both Houses on a bill proposed by Lord Auckland to make it illegal for an adulterer, after the dissolution of the marriage, to marry the guilty lady, and to make adultery a common law misdemeanour.[14] Lord Eldon was in favour of passing the bill because he was certain that in nine out of ten cases there was "the most infamous collusion." [15] In 1830 the House of Commons on the motion of Dr. Phillimore discussed the question. Phillimore pointed out that the House of Lords, and still more the House of Commons, were most unfit tribunals to discuss these cases ; and that the expense of getting these Acts amounted to at least £600 or £700, whereas in Scotland a divorce could be got for £10 or £15.[16] He advocated the handing over of the whole matter to the ecclesiastical courts, and giving to those courts power to grant a decree *a vinculo*—an expedient which Lord Thurlow

---

[1] Hansard (2nd Series) xii 641-642. [2] Below 279-281.
[3] Below 283, 284, 287. [4] Below 286, 287.
[5] For forfeiture for high treason see vol. iii 70-71 ; vol. iv 500 ; vol. xi 558-559; vol. xii 362-363.
[6] Parlt. Hist. xxxiv 1067-1085. [7] Hansard (2nd Series) xiii 835-836.
[8] Hansard (1st Series) xxx 354-356 ; ibid xxxi 1121, 1126 ; to the surprise of Romilly it passed the House of Commons unanimously, Memoirs ii 359-360, but was rejected by the House of Lords, ibid 376-377, which ordered the matter to be referred to the judges.
[9] Hansard (1st Series) xxxii 803. [10] Vol. xi 557.
[11] 56 George III c. 138 ; below 392. [12] 57 George III c. 75.
[13] For the anomalous state of the law see vol. i 622-624 ; xi 622-623.
[14] Parlt. Hist. xxxv 225-326. [15] Ibid 237.
[16] Hansard (2nd Series) xxiv 1265-1266.

had approved in 1800.[1] Dr. Lushington did not agree that cases of collusion were so common, but admitted that the law needed reform.[2] Peel took the same view, and said that " it would be much better to retain all the existing inconveniencies than to make divorces so easily attainable."[3] It is obvious from this discussion that public opinion was being aroused by the anomalous state of the law; but it is also obvious that the feelings aroused by an attempt to alter the law on this matter would make the path of the reformer very difficult.[4]

In 1812 *Dix's Case*[5] caused a debate on a motion for an enquiry into the inferior ecclesiastical courts.[6] We have seen that it led to an Act which abolished excommunication as part of the process of the ecclesiastical courts and as a punishment for contempt.[7] The Act also contained provisions for the better recovery of tithes of small amount and of church rates.[8] The bill as originally introduced by Sir William Scott introduced other reforms, including the abolition of certain minor ecclesiastical courts, and the requirement of a legal qualification for the judges of these courts. To the indignation of Romilly, the hostility of the bishops led Scott to abandon these two clauses;[9] but Romilly succeeded in adding a clause imposing a period of limitation to suits for the recovery of tithes.[10] In 1813 Romilly exposed the abuses of actions for defamation in the ecclesiastical courts. He thought that this jurisdiction should be abolished because all such actions ought to be tried by a jury.[11]

Equity and allied topics. In 1825 Eldon told the House of Lords that it was necessary to legislate against the abuse of dealings in the shares of joint stock companies not yet incorporated.[12] In the House of Commons it was pointed out that what was wanted was a law to settle the position of joint stock companies, and in particular a law to repeal the Bubble Act which made the legal position of those companies wholly uncertain.[13] " As things were," it was said,[14] "the various

---

[1] Hansard (2nd Series) xxiv 1267. [2] Ibid 1276-1281.
[3] Ibid 1287. [4] Below 674. [5] Vol. i 632.
[6] Hansard (1st Series) xxi 99, 295.
[7] 53 George III c. 127 § 1; vol. i 632; above 190.
[8] §§ 4 and 7; for another bill on the subject of tithes introduced by Curwen see Romilly, Memoirs ii 461-462, 484-485, 487-488.
[9] Memoirs ii 318-319. [10] Ibid 319; § 5.
[11] Hansard (1st Series) xxvi 706; vol. i 619, 620; below 674.
[12] " Whatever might be the existing law, it could never be intended that the public should stand in this situation. That before the authority of the Crown or of Parliament shall be given to constitute a joint stock company, persons should be permitted to sell at an enormous profit the shares of that company; which was nothing more or less than laying a bait for their own benefit, by which innocent individuals were great sufferers," Hansard (2nd Series) xii 127-128.
[13] Ibid 1279-85; for the Bubble Act (6 George I c. 18 §§ 18-22) see vol. viii 220-221. [14] Hansard (2nd Series) xii 1284.

companies possessing a capital of 250 millions, were left at sea, without rudder or compass, not knowing whether they were acting right or wrong." It was agreed that the repeal of the Bubble Act, which was a dead letter,[1] was necessary, and also reforms of the law as to chartered companies.[2] In these discussions we can see that changes in the mechanism of commerce were beginning to show a need for the reform of the law as to commercial companies which will, in the following period, revolutionize the law on this topic. At the end of this period Sugden introduced bills to reform the law as to illusory appointments; as to the property of infants, married women and lunatics ; and as to lunatic and infant mortgagees and trustees.[3] He also proposed to amend the law as to commitments for contempt of the court of Chancery :[4]

Now a man might be left in gaol year after year to the end of his life without the slightest notice of his being still in existence ; by the change he proposed, the imprisonment of no man could be prolonged without special application to the court, and that with due notice to the party.[5]

Further, he proposed that if an order, e.g. to execute a deed, were disobeyed, the court, instead of imprisoning the man who disobeyed, should itself execute the deed.[6]

(ii) These suggestions and discussions of reforms in the law were assisted by the reports of royal commissions and committees of the two Houses of Parliament.[7]

Royal commissions to conduct enquiries into topics connected with law and government, or into some subject upon which the government requires information, have been known from a very early period in English history. " The Domesday survey may be regarded as the result of the first royal commission of enquiry ;"[8] and out of some of Henry II's commissions of enquiry the system of itinerant justices developed.[9] In Edward I's reign the *quo warranto* enquiries, which are embodied in the Hundred Rolls, is another famous instance of a commission of enquiry.[10] Though the rise of Parliament—the Grand Inquest

---

[1] Hansard (2nd Series) xii 1285 ; ibid xiii 1019.   [2] Ibid 1020.
[3] Hansard (2nd Series) xxii 363-365, 388-389 ; for his Act to amend the statute of Fraudulent Devises see above 266.
[4] Ibid 369-374.
[5] Ibid 371 ; vol. ix 352-353 ; cp. Holdsworth, Charles Dickens as a Legal Historian, 109-113.
[6] Hansard (2nd Series) xxii 373-374.
[7] A good account of this topic will be found in H. M. Clokie and J. W. Robinson's book on Royal Commissions of Inquiry.
[8] Clokie, op. cit. 28; for the Domesday Survey see vol. ii 155-165.
[9] Vol. i 49-51, 265-272.
[10] Vol. i 88-90 ; for other enquiries see vol. ii 184.

of the Nation—obviated the necessity for some of these commissions,[1] their use continued, in spite of the objections of Parliament.[2] Indeed Parliament sometimes asked for the appointment of a commission to enquire into particular abuses.[3] We
have seen that the Tudors made an extensive use of these commissions [4]—one famous instance is the "Domesday of Enclosures"
of 1517.[5] Other instances are the numerous commissions set
up to deal with religious matters,[6] from one of which the court
of High Commission sprang.[7] Use continued to be made of
these commissions by the Stuarts, e.g. James I issued a commission
to enquire into the statutes, and to reduce the statute book
to some sort of order.[8] But we have seen that in the latter
part of the Tudor period the legality of some of these commissions
had been called into question ; [9] that in the Stuart period Coke
laid it down that though the Crown could issue a commission
to enquire into matters of state, it could not issue a commission
to enquire into offences which were determinable at common
law ; [10] and that after the Restoration it was said that it could
not issue a commission to determine complaints, and that therefore it could not give to such commissioners power to administer
an oath to the witnesses who appeared before them.[11] But since
commissions to enquire into matters of state were still lawful
they continued to be issued. "Even the Long Parliament,
which swept aside scores of prerogative royal commissions,
provided for enquiry into the metes and bounds of the forest
by ' commissions under the Great Seal of England '."[12] Comparatively little use was made of royal commissions of enquiry
in the eighteenth century ; and those which were issued were

---

[1] Vol. i 272 ; Clokie, op. cit. 33.

[2] Ibid 34, citing R. P. ii 148-149—a demand that " novelle enquerez " should
cease, and the statute 34 Edward III c. I that all general enquiries should cease ;
this statute may have referred to the general eyre, see R. P. ii 200 no. 4 cited
vol. i 272.

[3] In 1325 there was a petition for an enquiry into the violation of the charter
of the forest, R.P. i 430, cited Clokie, op. cit. 34, and there are other instances,
ibid.

[4] Vol. iv 68-70.   [5] Vol. iv 366.
[6] Clokie, op. cit. 40-41.   [7] Vol. i 605-611.

[8] Clokie, op. cit. 39 ; as he says, " that the labours of the commissioners
resulted in nothing more than a manuscript, now preserved in the British Museum,
reveals that nineteenth century commissions are not the only ones which have
proved abortive " ; schemes for the revision of the statute book were then being
considered, see vol. ii 428 and n. 2 vol. v 487.

[9] Vol. iv 70.   [10] Vol. v 432-433.

[11] Vol. v 433 n. 5 ; it was assumed that the Crown could give this power to a
commission which it had power to appoint, though a committee of the House of
Commons had not got this power unless it was given to it by statute, see Clokie,
op. cit. 87 n. 12 ; but whereas a committee of the House of Commons could
compel witnesses to appear and testify, a commission unless authorized by statute
had not got this power, ibid 85-87.

[12] Ibid 44.

generally approved of or asked for by Parliament.[1] Their place was to a large extent taken by enquiries made by select committees of one or other House of Parliament.[2]

The great social and economic changes which accompanied the industrial revolution, the changes in men's political ideas which resulted directly or indirectly from the French Revolution, the changes in men's ideas as to the expediency of reforms in the law, caused partly by the obvious need for making the reforms required by new social and economic conditions and partly by Bentham's teaching—all contributed to revive enquiries by means of royal commissions, and to stimulate enquiries by means of committees of the two Houses of Parliament, into many legal, social, and economic problems.

From 1800 to 1831, "some sixty or more commissions of enquiry were appointed, some with statutory authority, most without ".[3] Those which are of most importance in legal history are the following. In 1800 a commission on public records was issued in consequence of a report of a committee of the House of Commons [4] which did good work in producing a new edition of the statutes [5] and in printing a considerable quantity of records.[6] In 1810 a commission was issued to enquire into saleable offices in the law courts.[7] In 1815 a commission was issued to examine into the duties, salaries and emoluments of officers, clerks and ministers of the courts of justice in England and Wales. Its first report, issued in 1816 [8] and 1818,[9] dealt with the officials of the court of Chancery. Its second report, issued in 1818, dealt with the officials of the court of King's Bench.[10] Its third report, issued in 1819, dealt with the officials of the court of Common Pleas,[11] and its fourth report, issued in 1822, with the officials of the courts of Exchequer and Exchequer Chamber.[12] Its two next reports, issued in 1823 [13] and 1824,[14] dealt with the officials

---

[1] Clokie, op. cit. 48 ; several were appointed in the later years of the eighteenth century, one of the most important of which was the statutory committee to audit the public accounts which was first set up in 1780, ibid 56 ; vol. x 522.

[2] Ibid 50-51.

[3] Ibid 57, 58-59 ; for a complete list see Parlt. Papers 1825 v 45-62.

[4] Above 261.   [5] Vol. xi. 310-313.

[6] See vol. ii 601, and Maitland's Introduction to the Memoranda de Parliamento of 1305 (R.S.) xxviii for the disputes which caused a cessation of the publication of records.

[7] Parlt. Papers (1810) vol. ix ; some extracts are printed in vol. i, 686-688.

[8] Parlt. Papers (1816) vol. viii.   [9] Parlt. Papers (1818) vol. vii.

[10] Ibid.   [11] Parlt. Papers (1819) vol. ii.

[12] Parlt. Papers (1822) vol. xi.

[13] Parlt. Papers (1823) vol. vii. This report dealt with the court of the Arches, the Prerogative court, and the court of peculiars of the Archbishop of Canterbury ; for these courts see vol. i 601, 602.

[14] Parlt. Papers (1824) vol. ix. This report dealt with the consistory court of the Bishop of London, and the court of the commissary of the Bishop of London for London and the suburbs and for the deaneries of Middlesex and Barking.

of the principal ecclesiastical courts; and a further report, issued in 1824, with the officials of the court of Admiralty, the court of Delegates, and the court of appeals for Prize cases.[1] We have seen that in 1825 a commission was appointed to enquire into the practice and offices of the court of Chancery, which reported in 1826.[2] Many other commissions were appointed to enquire into specific topics connected with the law. There were enquiries into particular prisons, into educational charities, into weights and measures, into colonial problems. In 1830 a new commission to enquire into the ecclesiastical courts was issued.[3] We shall see that the two most important of these commissions from the point of view of the reform of the law were issued as the results of Brougham's great speech on the state of the common law and common law courts in 1828.[4] We shall see also that a greatly extended use was made of these commissions in the following period.

The enquiries set on foot by these commissions were supplemented by the enquiries of select committees of the two Houses. After 1800 the same reasons which led to the great increase in the enquiries conducted by royal commissions led also to a great increase in the number of enquiries conducted by select committees:

Whereas the reports of the eighteenth century (1715-1801) which were selected for republication occupied only fifteen volumes, this number was soon equalled each year in the next century. In the first third of the nineteenth century over five hundred committees presented printed reports to the Houses of Parliament, the average number being sixteen per annum.[5]

In 1825 a select committee of the House of Commons emphasized their value to many different classes of seekers after knowledge. It said :

In these reports there is scarcely a subject connected with the laws, institutions, commerce, and morals of the country, but what will be found treated on: the administration of justice, the privileges of Parliament, the national church, arts and manufacturing, agriculture and trade, criminal law, police and education—all have their place ; and it may be observed that on all subjects relating to arts and commerce more information will be found than in the reports of former periods, arising from the superior intelligence of those who are called upon to impart knowledge, the willingness with which it is communicated, and the greater accuracy with which the evidence and documents are prepared.[6]

---

[1] Parlt. Papers (1824) vol. ix.
[2] Vol. i 442-443 ; vol. ix 375, 401-402 ; Parlt. Papers (1826) vol. xv.
[3] Clokie, op. cit. 59. [4] Below 306.
[5] Clokie, op. cit. 62.
[6] Parlt. Papers (1825) vol. v 9 ; for a list of the reports of these committees see ibid 13-44.

It was due largely to those who were advocating reforms in many different branches of the law that many of these royal commissions and committees of the two Houses of Parliament were appointed, and, conversely, it was the information which they supplied which enabled these advocates of reform to propose measures which were intelligent because they were founded upon information as to the defects in the law which needed to be remedied. This we shall see more clearly when we have examined the work of some of the leading advocates of law reform.

(2) I shall deal first with the two advocates for the reform of the criminal law—Romilly and Mackintosh, and with the work done by Peel as the result of their advocacy.

Romilly [1] was born March 1, 1757. He came of a Huguenot stock which had come to England on the revocation of the edict of Nantes. At one time he had thought of entering his father's business as a jeweller, and for some years he kept his father's accounts. But he had begun to study Latin, and developed a taste for literature which made him dislike this career. A fortunate legacy enabled him to strike out a new line. He was articled at the age of sixteen to Lally, one of the sixty sworn clerks in the Six Clerks office in Chancery. [2] But at the end of his articles he decided not to purchase a seat in the Six Clerks office. He entered Gray's Inn on May 5, 1778, and was called to the bar June 2, 1783. We have seen that he pursued the then usual course of legal education. He read in the office of an equity draftsman—a Mr. Spranger, who let him have the use of his library and directed his reading; he made a commonplace book; and he formed a small moot club with some of his friends. [3] In 1781 while on a continental tour he made the acquaintance of Dumont and Mirabeau; and after his return to England it was through Mirabeau that he was introduced to Lord Lansdowne. He introduced Dumont to Lord Lansdowne; it was at the latter's house that Dumont and Bentham met and entered upon their famous literary partnership; [4] and it was then that Romilly first met Bentham. [5] We have seen that Romilly never ceased to be a friend, an admirer, and a sound adviser of Bentham; [6] and even when Bentham in his radical days opposed Romilly's candidature for Westminster there was no break in their friendship. [7]

---

[1] The Life of Samuel Romilly, written by himself. With a selection from his correspondence. Edited by his sons (ed. 1842), hereinafter referred to as Memoirs; Brougham, Statesmen of the Time of George III i 290-298; D.N.B.

[2] For the six and the sixty clerks see vol. i 421-423; vol. ix 369-370.

[3] Vol. xii 86-87.   [4] Above 50.   [5] Above 50.   [6] Above 50.

[7] Romilly says, Memoirs ii 512-513, " Some of my friends were very angry with Bentham for this hostile interference against me. For myself I feel not the least resentment at it. Though a late, I know him to be a very sincere, convert to the expediency of universal suffrage; and he is too honest in his politics to suffer them to be influenced by any considerations of private friendship."

Romilly's liberal opinions were shown in his first published work—a tract on the constitutional power and duty of juries on trials for libel, which was suggested by the *Dean of St. Asaph's Case* ;[1] his attack on Madan's *Executive Justice*[2] shows that he had already begun to think of the problems connected with the criminal law ; and his sympathy with the French Revolution is shown by his summary of the procedure of the House of Commons which he drafted for the use of the States General. In a work entitled *The Letters of Harry Greenville* he advocated a reform of Parliament on very democratic lines. But, says Scarlett, "shortly after it issued from the press, commenced the violent passages of the French Revolution which disgusted and terrified most of those who had been friendly to it, so Romilly, without hesitation, committed to the flames every copy that had not been sold."[3] In the last years of his life he contributed to the *Edinburgh Review*[4] an appreciation of Bentham's work, with special reference to his work on codification, in which he dwelt on the disadvantages of the system of case law.[5] He justly criticized the defects of Bentham's later literary style, and his habit of pouring exaggerated abuse on his opponents.[6] But he acclaimed Bentham as a great citizen of the world, who had worked for all nations, and who in future ages would be regarded by many nations as their teacher and legislator.[7]

Romilly, when he was first called to the bar, joined the Midland circuit, attended the Warwick Sessions, and practised in the court of Chancery. In 1797 he successfully defended at Warwick, John Binns—a member of the London Corresponding Society.[8] But by that time the increase of his Chancery business was beginning to make circuit business a minor consideration.[9] In 1800 he took silk, and by 1802 he was one of the leaders of the Chancery Bar. In 1805 he became Chancellor of the county palatine of Durham, and in 1806 he became solicitor-general in the ministry of " all the talents ". That ministry was dismissed in 1807 ; and this one year was the only year of office that Romilly ever had. He signalized it by carrying a reform

---

[1] For this case see vol. x 677-679.
[2] For this book and Romilly's attack see vol. xi 564.
[3] P. C. Scarlett, Memoirs of Lord Abinger 55.
[4] Vol. xxix (1817).
[5] pp. 222-223.
[6] pp. 236-237 ; see above 261.
[7] pp. 218-219.   [8] 26 S.T. 595.
[9] He says, Memoirs i 69, that " it was more for the sake of cultivating the habit of addressing juries, of examining and cross-examining witnesses, and of exercising that presence of mind which is so essential to a *nisi prius* advocate, and which I thought might be of great use to me in the higher states of the profession to which I began to aspire, than on account of the emoluments I might derive from it, that I remained on the circuit."

of the bankruptcy law [1] and an Act making traders' real estate equitable assets for the payment of their debts. [2]

Romilly's reading in English and continental literature was wide. His study of Rousseau and Beccaria and Bentham, his liberal opinions, and his knowledge of English law, made him the earliest of the men of first rate ability and standing at the bar and in Parliament to devote himself to the cause of law reform. If the Whigs had regained office in the second decade of the nineteenth century Romilly might have become Lord Chancellor ; and in 1801 and 1807 he wrote some letters addressed to an imaginary friend which relate to that office. In the first two letters written in 1801 he argues for the proposition that the Lord Chancellor should devote himself to the cause of law reform. [3] But in the third letter written in 1807 he was obliged to admit that the times were most unpropitious for any such schemes. [4] Connected with these letters he drew up papers on the duties of a Lord Chancellor in his capacity as a legislator, a minister, and a judge. Among the papers relating to the Chancellor's legislative duties are resolutions as to the reform of the civil code and of the penal law, which refer to manuscripts in which the particular reforms needed are set out, with reasons and with references to the authorities. [5] These manuscripts are a set of proposals, sometimes mere sketches, but in many cases finished essays on the reforms which were needed in the law. [6] Their number and varied subject matter illustrate the very thorough manner in which he had studied the question of law reform. [7]

---

[1] Above 265.   [2] Above 265.   [3] Memoirs ii 522-531.
[4] Ibid 534-543.   [5] Ibid 516-517.   [6] Ibid 518-519.
[7] The following list of forty-three of the most complete of these essays is given in the Memoirs ii 518 n.1 : 1. On the Promulgation of Laws ; 2. On a written Code of Laws ; 3. Project of a New Code ; 4. On unauthorized Reports of Judicial Proceedings ; 5. On certain Rules of Evidence ; 6. On the imposition of Taxes on Law Proceedings ; 7. On Irrevocable Laws ; 8. On the Law of Libel ; 9. On Apprenticeships ; 10. On Bankrupts ; 11. On the Poor Laws ; 12. On Divorces among the Poor ; 13. On Superstition ; 14. On Judicial Superstition ; 15. Attempts to Reform Defects and Abuses in Criminal Law ; 16. On a Public Prosecutor ; 17. On Ignominious Punishments ; 18. On Cruel Punishments ; 19. On Military Punishments ; 20. On the Regard to be had to Sex, Age, and condition of Life in inflicting Punishment ; 21. On Punishments to Children ; 22. On Transportation ; 23. On Conspiracies to convict innocent men ; 24. On Confession and Denial after Conviction ; 25. On Perjury ; 26. On the Punishment of Perjury ; 27. On Shop-lifting ; 28. On Petty Treason and Murder ; 29. On Appeals of Death ; 30. Account of a Criminal Trial in Scotland ; 31. On Suicide ; 32. On Blasphemy ; 33. On Bigamy ; 34. On Felony ; 35. On the Clergy as amenable to Criminal Law ; 36. On Forestalling and Regrating ; 37. On laws against unusual Crimes ; 38. On allowing Counsel to Persons accused ; 39. On Compensation to Persons wrongfully accused ; 40. On the Policy of giving Rewards on Conviction ; 41. On frequent Public Executions ; 42. Observations on Eliza Fenning's Case ; 43. Observations of Bentham on Punishment. It will be noted, first, the number of essays on the criminal law is large, and, secondly, that his study of Bentham's works has obviously inspired a good many of them.

Romilly had entered the House of Commons as member for Queensborough when he became solicitor-general. In the general election for 1807 he was returned for Horsham, but, being unseated on petition, he bought the seat for Wareham.[1] He had refused offers of seats from Lord Lansdowne and the Prince of Wales because he wished to preserve complete independence of action in the House of Commons.[2] In 1818, in the last year of his life, his consistent support of measures of law reform and all other liberal measures secured his return for Westminster at the head of the poll.[3] In his advocacy of these measures Romilly had a very uphill fight, and did not succeed in effecting many reforms. But he led the attack, and his successors, Mackintosh[4] and Brougham,[5] recognized him as their leader. His high, if somewhat austere[6] principles, and his consistent devotion to the cause of reform, caused him to be universally respected by men of all parties. He was consoled for his failures by a very happy home life—so happy that his wife's death in October 29, 1818, unhinged his mind and led him to commit suicide four days later.

Romilly was one of the best lawyers of his day, and he had a leading practice in the court of Chancery. His mastery of equity is shown by his famous argument in *Huguenin v. Baseley*,[7] which is a classical summary of the law as to undue influence. Of this argument Lord Cottenham said in 1839 that he had " received so much pleasure from hearing it that the recollection of it has not been diminished for the lapse of more than thirty years."[8] His speeches advocating reforms in many different branches of the law show that he was also a good common lawyer. He was an effective speaker both in the court of Chancery and in the House of Commons. Of his merits as an advocate in the court of Chancery Lord Kingsdown says :

[1] He insisted on paying the whole price (£3,000) himself and refused to allow £1,000 of it to be paid from a fund raised by members of the opposition " for extraordinary occasions," Memoirs ii 83-84.

[2] For the obligations of a member to the patron who had given him the seat see vol. x 567.

[3] Memoirs ii 510 ; he had been defeated at Bristol in 1812, and had got a seat in the Duke of Norfolk's borough at Arundel.

[4] In 1819, after praising his attempts to " rescue his country from the disgrace " of its criminal code, and his success in stopping " that career of improvident and cruel legislation which, from session to session was multiplying capital felonies," he said that " while private virtue and public worth are distinguished among men, the memory of Sir Samuel Romilly will remain consecrated in the history of humanity," Hansard (2nd Series) xxxix 793.

[5] Preface to his speech on Law Reform in 1828, Speeches ii 307 ; in his speech at p. 321 he referred to Romilly as " a name never to be pronounced by any without veneration, nor ever by me without sorrow."

[6] Ibid 308.

[7] (1807) 14 Ves. at pp. 284-288.

[8] Dent v. Bennett (1839) 4 My at §2 at p. 277 ; Brougham, op. cit. i, 292.

As an advocate I think Sir Samuel Romilly approached in his own line as near perfection as it is possible for man to attain . . . . When any great occasion arose, especially when he came to reply at the close of a long and important case, in which the feelings were at all engaged, nothing could be finer. Usually restating his case . . . . not always exactly as he had opened it, but as, after the discussion which it had undergone, it could be presented with the best prospect of success ; not using all the arguments which had been used against him, and which admitted of an answer ; . . . . clear, powerful, and logical when he was right ; discreet and adroit when he was wrong ; never introducing an unnecessary sentence, seldom using a word that could be altered for the better ; always energetic, often earnest and impassioned, never degenerating into violence, either of language or tone ; with a noble countenance, a stately figure . . . . and a voice distinct, deep, and mellow, always, as it seemed to be modulated with singular skill, the exhibition was one which it was impossible to witness without admiration and delight. Probably those who have heard Sir William Grant and Sir Samuel Romilly have heard the most exquisite specimens of eloquence ever addressed from the Bar to the Bench or from the Bench to the Bar.[1]

In the House of Commons he was a clear and logical reasoner, eloquent on occasion, quick to detect a fallacy, and possessed of powers of sarcasm and invective which enabled him to reply effectively to his opponents. Brougham says :[2]

No man argued more closely when the understanding was to be addressed; no man declaimed more powerfully when indignation was to be aroused or the feelings moved. His language was choice and pure ; his powers of invective resembled rather the grave anthority with which the judge puts down a contempt, or punishes an offender, than the attack of an advocate against his adversary and equal. . . . His sarcasm was tremendous, not always very sparingly employed. His manner was perfect, in voice, in figure, in a countenance of singular beauty and dignity ; nor was anything in his oratory more striking or more effective than the heartfelt sincerity which it throughout displayed, in topic, in diction, in tone, in look, in gesture.

Except among his intimate friends he was apt to be somewhat taciturn and reserved.[3] But like many other reserved men, he was very sensitive. Mackintosh said : " I have never observed any man so deeply and violently affected by the recital of cruelty as Romilly."[4] It was this trait in his character which led him to embark upon his crusade for the reform of the criminal law, which is generally regarded as his chief title to enduring fame.

---

[1] Recollections cited Ed. Rev. cxxix, 48-49.

[2] Historial Sketchings of Statesmen in the Time of George III i 293–294 ; Scarlett's estimate is very similar to that of Brougham, P. C. Scarlett, Memoir of Lord Abinger 51–52.

[3] Bentham, in a somewhat uncharitable notice of Romilly, says that " he was a man of great modesty—of few words—of no conversation. Dumont used often to dine there, and after dinner they would sit together for half an hour without either uttering a word," Works x 186; but Brougham, op. cit. i 295, tells us that in his family and in society he was " amicably simple, natural, and cheerful."

[4] Memoirs of the Life of Mackintosh ii 349.

In 1808 Romilly made a great speech on what had long been recognized as one of the greatest blots of the English criminal law—the frequency of capital punishment.[1] It was true, he said, that only one in twenty of the persons condemned to death were executed ; but the fact that the enforcement of the law was the exception was a sufficient condemnation of it. It was obvious that though the criminal law of all other civilized countries had been influenced by the speculations of Beccaria, the English criminal law was the unfortunate exception. He therefore moved the repeal of a statute of 1565 [2] which made privately stealing from the person a felony without benefit of clergy. He succeeded in getting this statute repealed.[3] In 1810, in moving to take away the death penalty for privately stealing in a dwelling house, he pointed out that in 1808-9 on an average of 7,196 of persons committed for trial only one was executed.[4] This bill was lost in the House of Commons. In 1811 a bill to take away the death penalty for robbery on navigable rivers was withdrawn.[5] But in that year a bill which took away the capital penalty for stealing from bleaching grounds in Ireland was passed,[6] and a bill to repeal the death penalty for privately stealing in a shop to the value of 5s. passed the Commons without a division,[7] but was rejected by the Lords.[8] In 1818 it was said that this bill had passed the Commons four times and had been four times rejected by the Lords ;[9] and it was pointed out that over a period of eight years 1,228 persons had been tried for this offence, 343 had been convicted, and only one executed.[10] Some peers, it is true, sympathized with these attempts to humanize the criminal law. In 1811 Grenville induced the House of Lords to condemn the practice of creating capital offences in the revenue law by reference to old laws, the provisions of which were not generally known, and to resolve that all revenue offences capitally punishable should be consolidated into one Act.[11] But there is no doubt that the growing feeling that the severity of the criminal code ought to be mitigated, which is illustrated by petitions for mitigation from the City of London and from the Quakers in 1818,[12] influenced the House of Commons sooner than it influenced the House of Lords.

Various arguments were used by the opponents of any mitigation in the severity of the criminal code. It was not right, it was said, that the public should be led by the advocacy

[1] Hansard (1st Series) xi 395 ; vol. xi 562-563.
[2] 8 Elizabeth c. 4 ; vol. iv 514. [3] 48 George III c. 129.
[4] Hansard (1st Series) xv 368. [5] Ibid xvii 531-533.
[6] 51 George III c. 39. [7] Hansard (1st Series) xix App. lxxxvii.
[8] Ibid cxxii. [9] Ibid xxxvii 610. [10] Ibid 611.
[11] Ibid xviii 1238-1239 ; this was effected by 52 George III c. 143.
[12] Ibid xxxix 81, 396.

of these proposals to think that the criminal law was defective.[1] Windham pointed out that, at the beginning of the French Revolution, capital punishment had been abolished.[2] Another member said that by altering the criminal system " we should destroy those high and lofty sentiments which were the best safeguards of our constitution " ; and that " it prevented crimes without recurring to punishment " ![3] It was said by Ellenborough that the removal of the death penalty for privately stealing from the person had increased the number of these offences " to a serious and alarming degree " ;[4] and it was in vain pointed out that the mitigation of the penalty had led to a greater willingness to prosecute and therefore to a larger number of convictions.[5] Eldon once went so far as to say that " as long as human nature remained what it was, the apprehension of death would have the most powerful co-operation in deterring from the commission of crimes ; and he thought it unwise to withdraw the salutary influence of that terror."[6] In 1811 the recorder and the common serjeant of London, reasoning from the increase in the number of convictions for privately stealing from the person, said that they were sure that any mitigation of punishment would have very evil effects.[7]

As an essential part of his crusade for the abolition of indiscriminate capital punishment, Romilly tried to induce the House of Commons to take some interest in the question of the objects at which the legislator should aim in awarding punishment. He agreed that the primary objects should be to deter and to prevent ; but he pointed out that abroad it was recognized that a secondary object was to reform. This object, he said, had been completely lost sight of in England, in spite of the efforts of Blackstone and Howard.[8] The Act for prison reform which they had induced the Legislature to pass had been a dead letter for thirty-six years.[9] Instead of building suitable prisons, the Legislature had ordered the transportation of criminals—with very evil effects.[10] The state of the gaols was disgraceful. Newgate combined every possible defect of which a prison was capable.[11] " At the same time," he said,[12] " as we have erected a national monument to Mr. Howard, as a reward for his exertions to reform our prisons the City of London leaves, close to the statue we have raised, this gaol as a monument of our disgrace and our inhumanity, in which not one of the regulations which Howard recommended has been observed." As Romilly said, the

---

[1] Hansard (1st Series) xvi 763.   [2] Ibid 768.   [3] Ibid 772.
[4] Ibid xx 299.   [5] Ibid xvii 531-532.   [6] Ibid xx 301.
[7] Ibid xix 643-645.   [8] Ibid xvi 944-945.
[9] Ibid 945 ; vol. x 182-183 ; vol. xi 568.
[10] Hansard (1st Series) xvi 945-946 ; ibid xvii 325-328.
[11] Ibid 324.   [12] Ibid.

Legislature would do well to pay some attention to " the masterly and valuable " work of Bentham on these subjects.[1] In 1808 he argued that persons who were imprisoned, sometimes for as long as eight months, and in the four northern counties for over a year, before trial, ought to be compensated if they were acquitted.[2]

In 1813 Romilly, with the support of Preston, the conveyancer, tried to induce the House of Commons to abolish the doctrine of corruption of blood—a reform, he pointed out, which Blackstone had supported.[3] In 1814 he again introduced a bill to abolish this doctrine, and induced the House to assent to its abolition in cases of felony ;[4] but we have seen that Eldon and the House of Lords successfully resisted any change.[5]

In the debate on this bill in the House of Commons Romilly was supported by Mackintosh, who pointed out that, though the law of other countries recognized the doctrine of forfeiture for treason, the law of no other country recognized the doctrine of corruption of blood.[6] Of Mackintosh and his work for the reform of the criminal law I must now say something.

James Mackintosh[7] was born October 24, 1765, at Aldowrie, near Inverness. From 1780 to 1784 he studied at King's College, Aberdeen. In 1784 he went to Edinburgh to study medicine and took his degree in 1787. He went to London in the following year. Because he had always been more interested in philosophy, politics, and literature than in medicine, he resolved to give up medicine and go to the bar. It was while he was studying for the bar that he wrote the *Vindiciae Gallicae*[8] and thereby made his name as a liberal political thinker. He was called to the bar by Lincoln's Inn in 1795, and succeeded in getting a fair practice both on the northern circuit and before Parliamentary committees in cases involving a knowledge of constitutional and international law. His greatest success at the bar was his speech in defence of Peltier who was indicted for a libel on Napoleon. Though his client was convicted, his speech won praise from Perceval the attorney-general, and from Lord Ellenborough and Erskine.[9]

---

[1] Hansard (1st Series) xix 659.

[2] Ibid xi 399-400 ; on this subject see Lord Justice Mackinnon's book, Grand Larceny, which gives an account of how Mrs. Leigh-Perrot, Jane Austen's aunt, was imprisoned from Oct. 1799 to the end of March 1800 before she was tried and acquitted.

[3] Ibid xxv 576-578, 580.

[4] Ibid xxvii 342-344, 538.

[5] Above 181, 189.   [6] Hansard (1st Series) xxvii 528-529.

[7] Memoirs of the Life of Mackintosh by his sons ; D.N.B.

[8] Above 13, 14, 15, 16.

[9] (1803) 28 S.T. at pp. 563-608 ; since the war with France was shortly after renewed Peltier was never called up for judgment, ibid 620.

His studies in philosophy and history naturally led him to study the philosophy of law. In 1799 he gave a course of thirty-nine lectures in Lincoln's Inn Hall on the Law of Nature and Nations which were attended by many distinguished men, including six peers and twelve members of the House of Commons.[1] They were an interesting set of lectures on jurisprudence, which dealt with the relations between law and morals and with some of the underlying principles of public law, private law, and international law. His inaugural lecture, which he published under the title of *A Discourse of the Law of Nature and Nations*, is an able introduction possessed of literary qualities which were then not usually found in law books. In that lecture he recanted some of the opinions expressed in the *Vindiciae Gallicae*; for he had been introduced to Burke, and the course taken by the French Revolution had caused him to be converted to many of Burke's views.

In 1803 he accepted the post of recorder[2] of Bombay, and went to India. But he was never happy there, and, though he read widely, his natural indolence and unbusinesslike habits prevented him from producing any considerable literary work. His health compelled him to return to England in 1811—to the regret of the English residents.

On his return he was offered a seat in Parliament by Perceval. He refused it because its acceptance would have obliged him to vote against a proposal to take immediate steps to grant Catholic emancipation. Lord Cawdor gave him a seat for Nairn, and later, the Duke of Devonshire gave him a seat for Knaresborough. He had intended after his return to write a history of England from 1688 to the French Revolution; but his health disabled him from accomplishing the double task of writing the history and attending to his Parliamentary duties. He wrote only a small fragment of the history, and further dissipated his energies by writing books and articles of a more ephemeral character—articles for the *Edinburgh Review*, an article on ethical philosophy for the *Encyclopaedia Britannica*, a short history of England for *Lardner's Cabinet Encyclopaedia*, and a life of Sir Thomas More. In Parliament he was a steady supporter of all liberal measures, and more especially of Romilly's proposals for the reform of the law. He took rank, therefore, as a distinguished member of the Whig party; and both for this reason and by reason of his literary abilities he was one of that band of literary celebrities which foregathered at Holland House. When the Whigs gained power in 1830 he was made

[1] Vol. xii 81-82.
[2] The Act of 1797, which empowered the Crown to establish courts at Madras and Bombay, provided that the president of those courts should be styled " recorder," 37 George III c. 142 § 9.

a commissioner of the board of control. There was some surprise that he was not given a more important office.[1] But his health, and his comparative failure as a debater and speaker in the House of Commons, were obstacles. He died May 30, 1832.

Mackintosh had a great reputation in his own day as an historian, a philosopher, and a man of letters. Macaulay regrets that he did not devote the whole of his later years to philosophy and literature ;[2] for, though he distinguished himself in Parliament, he was not an effective speaker. His speeches were too academic in tone. His speech in July, 1831 on the Reform Bill, which, Macaulay tells us, was "luminous and philosophical," was "spoken to empty benches " ; and " the effect of his most successful speeches was small when compared with the quantity of ability and learning expended on them."[3] But, if Mackintosh had devoted all his later years to philosophy and literature, he would not have gained his place in legal history as one of the leaders in the reform of the law and especially of the criminal law. As we shall now see, he carried on the fight for reform after Romilly's death. In this campaign it may well be that his defects as a speaker and debater in Parliament helped his effectiveness. The philosophical character of his speeches, and the historical knowledge and the knowledge of other systems of law which they displayed, helped to convince those capable of being convinced that reforms were necessary.[4] It was the speeches of men like Romilly and Mackintosh which went some way towards persuading Peel that it was necessary to take up in earnest the cause of law reform.

In 1819 Mackintosh moved for a committee to consider so much of the criminal law as related to capital punishment for felony.[5] He pointed out that in London and Middlesex between 1749 and 1819, out of two hundred capital felonies, only twenty-five were regularly punished with death ;[6] that the letter of the law ought to be brought nearer to its spirit ; and that the execution of the law, and not the remission of its penalties, ought to be the rule and not the exception.[7] As matters stood the law and the practice could not both be right.[8] He was ably seconded by Foxwell, Buxton, and Scarlett, and the motion was carried. The committee reported later in the

---

[1] See Brougham's remarks in his introduction to his speech of 1828, Speeches ii 311-312.

[2] Essay on Mackintosh.

[3] Brougham's verdict was much the same as Macaulay's—he says, Speeches ii 309-310, " even his most celebrated performances were less remarkable for reasoning than for dissertation."

[4] See Brougham, Speeches ii 307-308.

[5] Hansard (1st Series) xxxix 777.

[6] Ibid 787.   [7] Ibid 783.   [8] Ibid 788.

same year.[1] In his speech on the motion that the report be printed
Mackintosh said that the report proposed first to repeal a number
of obsolete Acts which created misdemeanours, and, secondly
to substitute imprisonment or transportation as the penalty
for a number of other crimes.[2] The evidence of judges, magistrates, traders, and bankers in favour of the latter recommendation was conclusive. Sir Archibald Macdonald—Chief Baron
of the Exchequer 1793-1813[3]—said that

The infliction of capital punishment on crimes not of the most atrocious
nature, renders prosecutors reluctant to proceed, witnesses reluctant to
give evidence, and juries reluctant to convict ; and therefore the chance
that a criminal has of escaping with impunity is greatly increased by the
existence of that punishment for such crimes.[4]

Harmer, the solicitor for crown prosecutions at the Old Bailey,
said that he knew many cases in which persons who had suffered
from acts of larceny or forgery had declined to prosecute because
the punishment was capital ;[5] and several bankers gave evidence
to the same effect.[6] The committee proposed two bills—one
to abolish thirty-five or more capital felonies, and the other to
consolidate the law as to forgery.[7]

In 1820 Mackintosh, pursuant to the report of the committee,
moved for a select committee on the criminal law, and for leave
to bring in certain bills abolishing the death penalty.[8] Some of
these bills were opposed with the usual arguments in the House of
Lords and rejected.[9] In 1821 Mackintosh introduced a bill to
mitigate the punishment for forgery, which secured a large amount
of support. But it was lost by a trick. It had passed its third
reading, and many of its supporters had left the House. A division
was challenged on the question that the bill do pass, and it was
rejected.[10] In 1822 Mackintosh made another motion on the
criminal law, in which he pointed out that while in England the
number of capital crimes was two hundred and twenty-three,
in France the number was only six.[11] He urged the House to assent
to the proposition that the efficiency of the criminal law would be

[1] For an account and criticism of this report see Miller, An Enquiry into
the present State of the Statute and Criminal Law 95 seqq. ; for Miller see
below 292.
[2] Hansard (1st Series) xl 1525.
[3] Below 499, 556-557.   [4] Hansard (1st Series) xl 1527.
[5] Ibid 1530-1531.   [6] Ibid 1532-1533.
[7] Ibid 1533.   [8] Ibid (2nd Series) i 227.
[9] On two bills, for removing the death penalty for privately stealing in a
dwelling house, and for robbery on rivers, Eldon said that he had at one time
thought that the law was too severe, but " after the experience of many years he
took a different view," and that the best way was to leave the question whether or
not the death penalty was to be inflicted to the discretion of the judges, ibid
v 1232-1233.
[10] Ibid v 1114.   [11] Ibid vii 795-796.

increased by abating the rigour of its punishments, by improving
the police, and by reforming the system of imprisonment and
transportation.[1] The motion was carried, and Peel agreed that
prison discipline and transportation were subjects which needed
reform.[2] In 1823, Mackintosh, in pursuance of this motion,
proposed that capital punishment in a number of cases,[3] and
forfeiture of the chattels of a suicide and the indignities practised
on his body should be abolished.[4] He proposed also that sentence
of death should not be pronounced in cases where it was well
known that it would not be carried out.[5] At the present day, he
said,

the sentence of death was reduced to a contemptible, frivolous and even
ridiculous ceremony. Ten-elevenths of the persons condemned to death
never suffered ; yet, in every case, the terrors of religion, and the dictates
of morality were called in aid, while the spectators, and even the prisoner
himself, knew the whole to be a mere mockery.[6]

Peel agreed that the criminal law must be taken into consideration.[7] But he tried to find specious excuses for many of its
obvious defects,[8] so that he laid himself open to Mackintosh's
retort that " he was a great friend to general principles, but had an
exception for every particular case." [9] If, he said, his resolutions
were negatived, he would introduce no more measures to amend
the criminal law, because " he must fore-know their fate." [10]

In 1821[11] and 1824[12] Mackintosh had tried in vain to induce
the House to pass a bill to allow persons accused of felony to
be defended by counsel ; and in 1826 a similar motion made by
George Lamb failed to pass.[13] But Horace Twiss exposed the
usual argument against the change—that the judge was counsel
for the prisoner. It would be more correct, he said, to call him
counsel for the prosecution, for the only instructions he has are
the depositions for the prosecutor. Moreover the duties clashed.
" Did the judge take all advantages to defeat the prosecutor and
acquit the prisoner ? Then, as judge, he betrayed his oath of
office. Did he decline to take those advantages ? Then as counsel
for the prisoner he deserted his client."[14] Scarlett said that he had
changed his former opinion against the bill, which was grounded on
the view that it would be disadvantageous to the prisoner because

---

[1] Hansard (2nd Series) vii 790. [2] Ibid 803.
[3] Ibid ix 419. [4] Ibid 420.
[5] Ibid 419 ; this reform was effected in 1823, 11 George IV c. 48.
[6] Ibid 413. [7] Ibid 420-429.
[8] Thus at p. 427, dealing with the pious perjury of juries who found property
worth large amounts to be of the value of 39s., he said that when property of a
large amount was stolen it might not be possible to prove that all was stolen at
once, so that the finding of the jury was correct.
[9] Ibid 431. [10] Ibid 532. [11] Ibid iv 945.
[12] Ibid xi 182. [13] Ibid xv 589, 633. [14] Ibid 610.

though under the present law the innocent were sometimes convicted and the guilty acquitted, it was erroneous acquittals which were the more frequent.[1] He had come to the conclusion that that view was grounded upon fallacious and superficial reasoning. A large number of these acquittals were due to the fact that prosecutors or the jury thought that the law was unfair. To allow prisoners counsel would tend to produce more convictions, and more just and satisfactory convictions.[2] This reform was made in 1837 ;[3] and there is no doubt that Scarlett's view of its effect was correct.

After 1823 the reform of the criminal law was taken up by Peel.[4] In 1830 he said that he agreed with the views of the committee on the criminal law which had reported in 1819,[5] " and wished to remove where it was practical the punishment of death."[6] Later in the same year he said that, while he was prepared to abolish the death penalty in some cases of forgery, he was not, as Mackintosh wished, prepared to abolish it in all cases ; and he took this occasion to explain his policy with regard to the reform of the criminal law. He said :[7]

From the right honourable gentleman's (Mackintosh) general doctrines respecting the punishment of death he did not dissent ; but he wished to state his opinion, with the reasons and the facts on which it had been formed, on the question whether the punishment of death ought to be preserved or abandoned. There were no reasons that he knew of, nor any circumstances in his situation, why he should not be ready to adopt the views of the right hon. gentleman. By the bill which he had introduced into the House he proposed to meliorate one part of our criminal code, and his course had uniformly been towards mitigation of its severity. . . . He had found, however, that the habits and usages of the country were adapted to and formed on the severity of our code, and he found it necessary to proceed in the mitigation of this severity with great caution. He thought it advantageous to continue the severity of the law in its letter, but gradually to meliorate its practical application. The bills he had introduced into Parliament, consolidating the criminal laws, had, in part, abandoned capital punishment ; but he looked forward to a time when the criminal law, after the consolidation of its various parts had been carried into effect, should be again brought under consideration. When that was the case, the House might, with propriety, take into consideration whether further mitigation of its severity should not be attempted.

The way was prepared for the enactment of Peel's Acts by a digest and code which was prepared by Anthony Hammond (1758-1838)[8] who was the author of several books on pleading and practice,[9] a student of jurisprudence, and an advocate of

[1] Hansard (2nd Series) xv 622.
[2] Ibid 624.
[3] 6 and 7 William IV c. 114 § 1 ; vol. ix 235.
[4] Above 225, 226 ; below 296.
[5] Above 283, 284.
[6] Hansard (2nd Series) xxiii 1179.
[7] Ibid xxiv 1043-1044.
[8] D.N.B.
[9] Below 287, 443.

codification.[1] He had submitted a draft measure to the select committee of the House of Commons, which had been appointed in 1824 to consider the question of consolidating and amending the criminal law. This draft developed into an elaborate digest and code which Peel had presented (1825-1829).[2] It is comparable to the draft code founded on Stephen's *Digest of the Criminal Law* which was prepared by the criminal code commissioners in 1878-9.[3] In his preface the author explains that his objects were to prepare the way for the consolidation and amendment of the criminal law, and the codification of the whole of the criminal law. The last-mentioned project he defends from objections based on the allegation that the Code Napoléon had caused many uncertainties in the law. The object of the Code Napoléon, he said, was to make new law : the object of his digest was to reduce to certainty the existing law. The difference of object and execution was therefore an answer to objectors who relied on a precedent of the Code Napoléon. Hammond's work was exhaustive and complete. It involved much labour and research but it was labour and research well spent since it ensured the success of Peel's great measures of consolidation and amendment.

Both Brougham[4] and Mackintosh[5] thought that more immediate action should be taken to mitigate the severity of the criminal law ; but Mackintosh said that he was happy to have lived to see the day when a minister of the Crown advocated the policy of mitigating the severity of the law ;[6] and we have seen that he testified to completeness of the change in the attitude of Parliament to this question of the reform of the criminal law.[7] In fact, by the end of this period, the number of crimes punished by death had been very greatly diminished.[8]

I now pass to the work done by Michael Angelo Taylor, C. P. Cooper, John Williams, and Joseph Parker for the reform of the court of Chancery.

Michael Angelo Taylor (1757-1834)[9] was called to the bar by Lincoln's Inn in 1774 ; but he was much more of a politician than a lawyer. He was a member of the House of Commons almost continuously from 1784 till his death in 1834. At first a

---

[1] He produced a scheme for a digest of English law with introductory essays on natural jurisprudence.

[2] The different volumes are as follows : 1825—coining ; 1826—forgery ; 1826—burglary, house breaking, and church robbing ; 1828 and 1829—simple larceny, robbery, stolen goods, fraud, mischief, restitution, and compensation (two volumes and vol. ii is in two parts) ; 1828 on Game Laws.

[3] Stephen, H.C.L. chap. vi ; the commissioners were Stephen, Lord Blackburn, Barry, J. and Lush, L.J.

[4] Ibid 1054-1059.　　　　　　　　　　[5] Ibid 1032-1043.
[6] Ibid 1033.　　　　　　　　　　　　　[7] Ibid ; above 285.

[8] Stephen, H.C.L. i 472-474 ; illustrations are 1 George IV c.c. 105-107 ; 4 George IV c. 46 ; ibid c.c. 53 and 54 which extended benefit of clergy to certain crimes ; 2, 3 William IV c.c. 62 and 123.　　　　[9] D.N.B.

Tory, he went over to the Whig party, and, when the French Revolution split the Whig party, he adhered to Fox. He gave his name to an Act of 1817 for paving and lighting the streets of London ;[1] and from 1811 onwards he made it his business to expose the abuses in the procedure of the court of Chancery, and the delays in the hearing of appeals by the House of Lords.

We have seen that in 1811 the arrears of appeals waiting to be heard by the House of Lords had induced Eldon to move for a committee to consider the question : and that the Government decided in 1813 to appoint a Vice-Chancellor to relieve the Chancellor of some of his work.[2] In the same year Michael Angelo Taylor moved for a committee to consider the same subject ; and in moving it he strongly criticized the state of business in the court of Chancery.[3] He pointed out that legatees could not get their legacies paid. There was one case in which a husband had left a legacy to his wife. He died, and the question arose whether the legacy barred dower. The question had been pending for some fourteen years, and was not yet decided ; and, in the meantime, the widow was in great distress.[4] In another case a writ of error, brought in 1801, had not yet been heard ;[5] for there were three hundred appeals waiting to be heard, and they were only heard at the rate of thirteen a year.[6] Later in the same year Taylor said that the appointment of an additional judge would not relieve the congestion in the court of Chancery. What was wanted was a Commission on the court of Chancery, and a separation of the bankruptcy business from the equity business.[7] In 1819 he was able to show that the appointment of a Vice-Chancellor in 1813 had not relieved the congestion of business, and again urged the separation of the equity from the bankruptcy business, and also from the lunacy business.[8] He pointed out, too, that there was no effectual appeal from the court. If the suitor appealed from the Chancellor to the House of Lords he appealed to the Chancellor assisted by two lay lords.[9] Later in the year he told the House that there was not less than £10,000,000 in court which ought to have been distributed.[10] He again enforced these points in 1821[11] and 1822.[12] In 1821 he showed how the delay in hearing cases set down entailed the automatic piling up of costs. He said :[13]

---

[1] 57 George III c. xxix.
[2] Above 263.
[3] Hansard (1st Series) xix 260-265.
[4] Ibid 263.
[5] Ibid 264.
[6] Ibid 262.
[7] Ibid xx 442-445.
[8] Ibid xxxix 1261-1263.
[9] Ibid 1262 ; in 1828 he said, " it was an appeal from a judge in a tie wig in Lincoln's Inn Hall, to the same judge in a full bottom wig in the House of Lords, with a snoring bishop perhaps on one side and a Scotch peer on the other, wishing him and the cause together at the devil," Hansard (2nd Series) xix 61.
[10] Ibid (1st Series) xl 564.
[11] Ibid (2nd Series) v 1025-1037.
[12] Ibid vii 1374-1379.
[13] Ibid v 1030-1031.

A cause which related to the title of some charity estates was set down in Easter Term 1812 ; and it remains still unheard. Being within the last twelve, it has been in the paper for two years, and from that time counsel, solicitor, and clerks in court are entitled to their fees for attendance, which, in addition to the charge for term fees, may be calculated for both parties at no less a sum than £120 a year.

In 1827 he attacked the report of the Chancery commission of 1825—" he was inclined to believe that the commission had never intended to do much, and the little that they had intended to do they had been frightened out of " ;[1] in the same year he again urged the separation of the bankruptcy from the equity jurisdiction ;[2] and in 1828 he again attacked the report of the Chancery commission, and the futility of the attempts made to reform the practice of the court.[3] Sugden, it is true, attempted a defence of what was in truth indefensible by showing that equity causes necessarily took more time to hear than common law causes, and that the judges of the court were industrious men.[4]

In the earlier attacks on the court Eldon had been treated with courtesy and exonerated from blame. In 1811 Romilly said that he would not consent to any motion which in any way reflected upon him ;[5] and in 1819 Taylor said he did not mean to impute blame to him.[6] But, as we shall now see, John Williams, in the very able attacks on the court which he made in the second decade of the century, abandoned this attitude, and attributed to Eldon a considerable share of blame for the state of business in his court, and for the refusal of the government to take any adequate measures of reform ; and his example was followed by others.

C. P. Cooper (1793-1873),[7] after a distinguished career at Oxford, where he was a contemporary at Wadham College of the future Lord Westbury, became a distinguished practitioner in the court of Chancery, a bencher and Treasurer of Lincoln's Inn, and a benefactor to its library. He was one of the leaders in the cause of law reform, and secretary of the second record commission. His study of the legal history both of England and of other countries which spread his fame abroad,[8] and his experience as a practising barrister, helped to give his suggestions for law reforms, and especially his suggestion for the reform of the court of Chancery, considerable value. His most important suggestions for its reform were made in a book which was published in 1828.[9] This

---

[1] Hansard (2nd Series) xvi 708.   [2] Ibid xvii 729-961.
[3] Ibid xix 53.   [4] Ibid 85-89.
[5] Ibid (1st Series) xix 267-268.
[6] Ibid xl 562.   [7] D.N.B.
[8] He was an honorary doctor of Louvain and Kiel, and a corresponding member of the royal academies of Lisbon, Munich, Berlin, and Brussels. In 1828 he wrote in French some letters on the Court of Chancery and on certain other matters relating to English Law and jurisprudence.
[9] " A Brief Account of some of the most important proceedings in Parliament relative to the defects in the administration of justice in the Court of Chancery,

book, which is dedicated to Michael Angelo Taylor, collects and presents in a convenient form the criticisms which had been made on the court of Chancery in Parliament between the years 1810 and 1827, and of the witnesses who had given evidence before the Chancery Commission of 1824 ; and it contains the author's own suggestions for reform. He proposed that there should be three courts of first instance sitting at the same time,[1] and that each case in all its stages should be heard by the same judge.[2] Only one appeal should be allowed which should be, not to the House of Lords, but to a council of last resort which should consist of the Lord Chancellor and retired common law and equity judges.[3] The jurisdiction on bankruptcy should be reformed and separated from the court of Chancery, that jurisdiction should be considered by a court of Bankruptcy staffed by four or five judges chosen from barristers of not less than twelve years standing.[4]

John Williams (1774-1846)[5] was educated at Manchester Grammar School and Trinity College, Cambridge. He was a distinguished classical scholar, and was elected a fellow of Trinity in 1801. Throughout his life he never lost his love for the classics, and contributed several articles on the Greek orators to the *Edinburgh Review*. He was called to the bar by the Inner Temple in 1804. He made his name at the bar by the part which he took, as junior counsel for the defence, in the trial of Queen Caroline. Brougham specially commends his cross-examination of Dumont, one of the Queen's waiting women, and his speech at the opening of the defence. He sat in the House of Commons from 1822 till 1832, where he made it his business to attack both the court of Chancery and Lord Eldon. In 1834 he became a baron of the Exchequer, but in the same year he migrated to the King's Bench, and continued to be a judge of that court till his death.[6] He was an effective speaker in the House of Commons, a sound lawyer, and well liked by the bar and by his brethren. " In banc," says Brougham, " his attention was ever awake . . . At *nisi prius* he distinguished himself as might be expected from one of his long experience and judgment. In the House of Lords his judgments, when there arose a difference of opinion, were firstly admired for the close texture of the arguments, and the uniform rejection of all extraneous matter." Pollock, the Queen's

---

the House of Lords and the court of the commissioners of Bankrupts. Together with the opinions of different statesmen and lawyers and the remedies to be applied."

[1] At p. 344.   [2] At p. 352.

[3] At pp. 3, 8, 36 c. ; he thought that this court should hear colonial appeals, and should in addition watch over the law, suggest reforms and draft bills.

[4] See pp. 382 seqq.

[5] D.N.B. ; Foss, Judges ix 313-315 ; Brougham, Historical Sketches ii 312-314.

[6] 10 Bing 570.

Remembrancer, tells a good story of one of his dinners to the bar of the northern circuit :[1]

Lady Williams and himself had their separate sets of friends and acquaintances—his chiefly legal, hers chiefly fashionable ; and they gave separate entertainments accordingly. It was the coronation year (1838), and a certain French nobleman in the suite of Marshal Soult, who came over to represent Louis Philippe, the King of the French, was in London on the occasion, and he had been asked to dinner by Lady Williams. By some mistake he made his appearance as a guest of the judge's at the Northern circuit dinner. Williams could speak no French, nor, so far as could be seen, were any of the company able to converse with ease in it. But the best had to be made of the affair. The duke occupied the seat on the right of the judge, which otherwise would have been filled by Cresswell, as leader of the circuit ; I, as junior, sat at the bottom of the table. Of course this incident was turned to good account by Adolphus,[2] who was Circuit Attorney-General at the next Grand Court at York. Alexander, whose foible was not that of retiring modesty, was represented as having introduced himself to the duke, and saying, " Je suis Monsieur Alexandre," and the bewildered guest as replying, " Ah ! oui, ventriloque célèbre "—a ventriloquist of that name being then performing in London. At last, and after many other equally unsuccessful attempts to promote conversation, Wightman[3] was supposed to have bethought himself of the store of Norman law French accumulated by him in his study of the old Year Books, and, taking courage, to have addressed the duke with " Nota que ceo est meason de Williams Justice ; il done feed als apprentices del Northern Circuit ; peradventure vous estes nemy invite."

In 1823 Williams pointed out that none of the remedies which had been suggested and tried had succeeded in curing the defects of the court of Chancery.[4] Then, after praising the abilities of Lord Eldon, he went on to say that " unfortunately those great and estimable talents were joined to a degree of indecisiveness and over-caution which neutralized, and he might say annihilated, the high advantages which should have resulted from them. "[5] After giving many instances from the cases of the ruinous effects of Eldon's long-continued doubts, he said that a solicitor's bill on one occasion contained this item : " attending the Lord Chancellor in his private room, when his Lordship begged for further indulgence till tomorrow, 13/4 ".[6] In 1824 he again brought to the notice of the House cases in which there had been scandalous delays ;[7] instances of the way in which, in consequence of these delays, the costs had been piled up ;[8] the abuses of the procedure in the masters' offices ;[9] the futility of appealing from the Lord Chancellor in his court of Chancery to the Lord Chancellor in the

[1] Personal Remembrances of Sir Frederick Pollock i 116-118.
[2] For Adolphus see vol. ix 413-414 ; below 428.
[3] Below 306.
[4] Hansard (2nd Series) ix 707-708.
[5] Ibid 709.
[6] Ibid 719.   [7] Ibid x 379-390.
[8] Ibid 391-393.
[9] Ibid 394-397 ; cp. vol. ix 360-365.

House of Lords.[1] He added that he had had great difficulty in eliciting the facts of the cases which he had brought to the notice of the House. One solicitor told him that he was afraid to give him information because, if he did, he would become a marked man—not in the court, but in the offices of the court, where his business would be " traversed and impeded." [2] In 1825 he pointed out that at the present rate of progress it would take forty years to clear off the existing arrears.[3] He attacked the system which permitted two systems of judicature to co-exist in the same country,[4] the system of the transfer of real property,[5] and the annexation to the court of Chancery of the jurisdiction in bankruptcy;[6] and he cited with approval a bitter attack on Eldon,[7] made by John Miller at the end of his book on the Civil Law of England. In 1827 Brougham went so far as to say (unjustly) that it was " the man, the individual judge, more than the system, that was to blame for the delay existing in the court of Chancery ";[8] and he accused him of deliberately using his learning and his charm of manner to mislead the commission.[9] It was perhaps hardly surprising that Eldon refused to give silk gowns to Williams and Brougham.

Joseph Parkes (1796-1865)[10] was a Birmingham solicitor and one of Bentham's disciples. From the time that the Reform bill was introduced he took an active part in all the measures to secure its passage. When Grey's ministry resigned he became a member of the Birmingham political union, and took part in the preparations for a rebellion against a Tory ministry. In 1833 he became the secretary of the municipal reform commission, moved to London, and got into good business as a Parliamentary solicitor. Cobden, who was introduced to him in 1837, said that he was one

[1] Hansard (2nd Series) x 398-399; above 289.
[2] Hansard (2nd Series) x 379.
[3] Ibid xiii 960. [4] Ibid 962.
[5] Ibid 965-966; " the law affecting the transfer of real property was reserved for the consideration and profit of a select few, removed from the general practice of the profession, ' whose ways were past finding out '," ibid 966.
[6] Ibid 967-968. [7] Ibid 980-981.
[8] Ibid xvi 733.
[9] " He the noble and learned lord, attended the commission, endowed with all the graces of a complete courtier, with the most entire and unbroken good humour, with all the fascination of manner which his experience had taught him to ingraft upon a naturally affable temper, with all the weight which invariably attends upon a man of influence in a learned profession, with a great reputation for profound research in the laws of his country, with a name already associated with its legal history—the noble and learned lord . . . came down to the commission clothed in smiles and courtesies, and laying aside the authority which he had a right to assume, endeavoured to mislead those whom he had no right to attempt to influence. The noble and learned lord eventually succeeded in his endeavours : he prevailed, as the House well knew, over the hopes of some, the fears of others, and the good nature of all, till the inquiry, dwindling away step by step, was paralyzed as to its power, and neutralized in its results," ibid 729.
[10] D.N.B.

of the cleverest men that he had ever met.[1] In 1847 he became a
taxing master in Chancery. His contribution to the agitation for
the reform of the court of Chancery is his *History of the Court of
Chancery*[2] which he published in 1828.

Parkes, before he took up practice in Birmingham, had been
a clerk in an attorney's office in London, so that he had a practical
knowledge of the existing state of the procedure of the court.[3]
His book is an attempt to trace the causes of the lamentable
condition of the procedure and practice of the court. Considering
that it is the first detailed history of the court, it is a work of
considerable merit. The author made an intelligent use of the
available printed sources, and more especially of the literature
which, from the seventeenth century onwards, had criticized the
shortcomings of the court, of the reports of Parliamentary
committees, and of debates and other Parliamentary proceedings.
He succeeded in showing that the delays and expense from which
the suitor was suffering were abuses of very old standing, which
had been gradually aggravated, partly by the growth of the
business of the court, and partly by the failure of the Lord
Chancellors to use their powers to apply a remedy. Though he
admitted that it was the system which was partly to blame,[4] he
adopted the view expressed by Williams and Brougham that the
evil effects of the system had been increased by Eldon's delay
in giving judgment, and by his hostility to all effective reform.[5]
His criticism,[6] and the criticism of *The Times* (which he reprints),[7]
of the ineffectiveness of the remedies suggested by the Chancery
commission, are entirely justified. He made some suggestions
for reform, which were inspired partly by his own experience,
partly by the criticisms of Taylor, Williams, and Brougham, and
partly by his study of Bentham's works. The jurisdiction in
bankruptcy,[8] in lunacy,[9] and various detached pieces of jurisdiction given to the Chancellor by special Acts,[10] should be
separated from his equitable jurisdiction ; and some subjects
of equitable jurisdiction e.g. jurisdiction over infants,[11] might be
entrusted to a separate court. A statutory reform of the law
of real property,[12] and of the law as to public charities and

---

[1] Morley, Life of Cobden i 138.
[2] A History of the Court of Chancery ; with Practical Remarks on the recent
Commission, report and evidence, and on the means of improving the administration of justice in the English courts of equity.
[3] Ibid, Preface xix.   [4] Ibid 352.   [5] Ibid 352-354.
[6] Ibid 359-372.   [7] Ibid 529-582.
[8] Ibid 413-424 ; cp. vol. i 470-473 ; vol. viii 236-244.
[9] Parkes, op. cit. 428-435 ; cp. vol. i 473-476.
[10] Parkes, op. cit. 424-429 ; cp. vol. i 469.
[11] Parkes, op. cit. 402-404 ; he points out that in some of the American
States there were courts called Orphans' courts ; the City of London had such a
court, vol. iii 273 n. 2, 512.
[12] Parkes, op. cit. 390-402.

corporations,[1] would go far to obviate the need of recourse to
the court of Chancery. It should be made possible to try equity
cases in local courts.[2] The jurisdiction of the judges administering
equity should be rearranged ;[3] and the Chancellor " should be
abstracted wholly from his political or his judicial duties."[4]
Merit, not patronage or political influence, should govern in the
appointments of the judges and officers of the court.[5] The
system of payment by fees should be abolished.[6] The practice
of the court should be reformed ;[7] and evidence should be given
publicly and orally, and not secretly and in writing.[8]

No effectual reform of the court and its practice and procedure was effected in this period. We have seen that it was not
till after 1832 that the long task of reform was taken in hand.[9] But
it was in this period that the preliminary work was done. The
abuses of the court had been fully exposed in Parliament, and in
the evidence given to the Chancery commission ; and they had
been ably summarized by Parkes and others. It was the information thus made public, and the suggestions for reform which
were based upon that information, which were the basis of the
reforms made in the following period.

I pass now to the suggestions for the reform of the law of real
property made by James Humphreys. Humphreys was a
conveyancer who had read in Charles Butler's chambers, and a
Benthamite who had given lectures in London University.[10]
The first edition of his book[11] was published in 1826. It was so
successful that a second edition was called for in 1827, in which
the author, in order to attract support for some of his suggested
reforms, modified some of his more radical proposals.[12] His book
consists of two parts. The first part is a critical account of some of
the salient features of the law of real property. The second part
contains a code embodying the reforms suggested by Humphrey
with explanatory notes. They include the abolition of copyhold
tenure ; changes in the law of inheritance which, though they did
not assimilate it to the law of succession to personalty [13] tended
in that direction ; a deed was to be the method of conveying
land ; a will of land was to speak as from the death of the
testator ; executed uses and passive trusts were to be abolished ;
entails were to be barred by deed ; powers were to be given to the

[1] Parkes, op. cit. 405-412.   [2] Ibid 444-445.
[3] Ibid 445.   [4] Ibid 446.   [5] Ibid 446-449.
[6] Ibid 449-451 ; cf. vol. i 424-425, 441-442 ; vol. ix 360-364.
[7] Parkes, op. cit. 451-453.
[8] Parkes, op. cit. 453-459 ; cf. vol. ix 353-358.
[9] Vol. i 442-445 ; vol. ix 375-376, 406-407.   [10] D.N.B.
[11] Observations on the actual state of the English Law of Real Property
with outlines for a systematic Reform.
[12] Preface to the second edition.
[13] The preference of male to female is retained throughout.

tenant for life holding under a strip settlement somewhat similar to those given by the Scottish Land Acts ; real property was to be held for all the debts of a deceased person and the distribution between legal and equitable assets was to be abolished ; there was to be a register of conveyance and wills of land ; possession or enjoyment for thirty years was to give a title both to corporeal and incorporeal hereditaments. Bentham gave an enthusiastic welcome to Humphreys' proposals in an article in the *Westminster Review*.[1]

These proposals were criticized both by real property lawyers and by historical jurists who disliked Bentham's purely analytical standpoint. Sugden, in a letter to which Humphreys replied, though he admitted the need for reforms in the law of inheritance, and the statutes of limitation, in the mode of barring estates tail, and in the decrees for the protection of contingent remainders, was opposed to sweeping reforms such as the creation of a uniform law of intestate succession. He thought that the main principles of the law of real property were sound, and that strict settlement was " free from all objection." He was opposed to codification, and was sure that the effect of Humphrey's reforms would be to weaken the aristocracy and leave the peers with insufficient estates to support their dignities. Another critic, J. J. Park,[2] was also a real property lawyer, but his criticisms[3] were jurisprudential in character. Park was a pupil of Preston, the famous conveyancer, the author of a learned work on Dower[4], and a professor of law and jurisprudence at King's College, London. He was also a jurist of the historical school who had studied law at Göttingen. He argued that though a measure of codification, like that suggested by Humphreys, might benefit a nation whose laws suffered from a lack of uniformity, it would not necessarily benefit English law which was a uniform system. He rightly pointed out that the question whether or not codification was expedient depended on time, place, and circumstance.[5] In fact his book is more than a criticism of Humphreys' proposals. It is a good historical survey of various projects for the restatement of English law. We shall see that the Real Property Commissioners agreed with Humphrey's critics, so that his suggestions for large measures of reform were for the time being shelved.

[1] Works v 387 ; above 81.
[2] D.N.B.
[3] " A Contra-Project to the Humphreysian Code, and to the projects of redaction by Messrs. Hammond, Uniacke, and Twiss " (1828).
[4] Below 474.
[5] At p. 89. Another book which discussed on conservative lines the proposals made by the Chancery Commission on proposals for the reform of the law of real property was published by R. Barnes in 1823 ; it is entitled " An Enquiry into Equity Practice and the Law of Real Property with a view to Legislative Revision."

But they indicate the direction which the reform of the land law will take in the late nineteenth and twentieth centuries.

All these reformers had concentrated their efforts upon particular parts of English law. The greatest single effort to deal with the defects of English law as a whole was made by Brougham in the great speech on the reform of the law which he made in the House of Commons on February 7, 1828;[1] and the royal commissions appointed as the result of it[2] effected more for the reform of the law than any royal commissions or reports of Parliamentary committees had ever done before.

Brougham's Speech of 1828

Brougham's speech [3] covered a large part of the field of English law—but not the whole. At the outset he explained that he should omit equity, since equity had recently been reported on by a royal commission; criminal law, since criminal law had been taken over by Romilly, Mackintosh and Peel; commercial law, since it was more modern and less defective than older branches of English law; and much of the law of real property since that topic was the peculiar province of Humphreys.[4] With these exceptions the speech set out to give a survey of the main defects in English law, and to suggest remedies for those defects. The main subjects dealt with were the courts, procedure, pleading, evidence, and some of the rules of substantive law.

The courts

Brougham dealt first with the common law courts. He explained how, by the fictitious processes of latitat and quominus, they had come to exercise a concurrent jurisdiction;[5] but that the advantages possessed by the King's Bench had given to that court by far the largest share of the common law jurisdiction.[6] The result was a waste of judicial time. The judges

---

[1] Above 273.　　　　　　　　　　[2] Below 306 seqq.
[3] Speeches of Lord Brougham with Historical Introductions (1838) vol. ii 319-486, hereinafter referred to as Speeches.
[4] Speeches 320-323.
[5] Ibid 325-327; vol. i 199-200, 219-222, 240; ix 249-250.
[6] Ibid 327-331; in the Common Pleas the sergeants-at-law had a monopoly of practice, and in the Exchequer only four attornies and sixteen clerks were allowed to practice; see vol. i 200 n. 8 for the comparative number of cases begun in the three courts of common law between 1823 and 1827; Brougham said, Speeches 338-339, that the business of the King's Bench was so heavy that the court " with the exception of a day or two of respite at Easter, and a week at Christmas, sat for above eleven months last year, taking the circuits as part of the year's work."

of the King's Bench had so much to do that arrears piled up ; the judges of the Common Pleas and more especially of the Exchequer were never fully employed.[1] Various attempts made to lighten the work of the King's Bench had failed. One of these expedients had resulted in the full court of King's Bench presided over by the Chief Justice doing mainly the formal business, while the really important cases were heard by three judges sitting in a back room with no one present but the practitioners and the parties.[2] Moreover, the arrangement of the business of the court was so defective that the full court, instead of sitting for six hours a day, could never sit for more than three or four hours.[3] What was really wanted was an increase in the number of the judges. If twelve judges were needed in the time of Coke, it is clear that the number of cases to be tried now, as compared with the time of Coke or even the time of Mansfield, made an increase in the number of judges obviously necessary.[4] If the unsatisfactory separate system of Welsh judges were done away with, and two extra judges were appointed, much could be done to clear off all arrears.[5] Minor improvements would be to abandon " the vexatious folly of regulating Easter term by means of the moon,"[6] and cease the practice of appointing as judges only those lawyers whose political opinions were those of the government of the day.[7]

Brougham then proceeded to criticize the manner in which the judges of the courts staffed by civilians were appointed and paid. He contended that it was a solecism that judges " who determine the most grave and delicate questions of spiritual law, marriage and divorce, and may decide on the disposition by will of all the personalty in the kingdom," should be appointed by the two archbishops and the bishops.[8] The judge of the court of Admiralty, who decided questions of great national importance and questions involving large sums of money, was underpaid in time of peace ; but in time of war the fees from Prize Cases caused him to be overpaid.[9] The composition of the court of Delegates, which heard appeals from the ecclesiastical courts, was absurd. The civilian delegates, who always outnumbered the common law judges, were the youngest and least experienced civilians. The appeal was thus from the most learned of the civilians to the least learned and the least employed :

---

[1] Speeches 330-331.   [2] Ibid 331-334.
[3] Ibid 334-335 ; chamber business and business in the bail court took a judge away from the court for several hours a day.
[4] Ibid 336.
[5] Ibid 338, 347-349 ; for the history of the Welsh judicial system see vol. i 124-125, 128-132.
[6] Ibid 349 ; for the history of the law terms see vol. iii 674-675.
[7] Ibid 341-347.   [8] Ibid 354.   [9] Ibid 352-354.

The absurdity is really much the same as if you were to appeal from a solemn and elaborate judgment, pronounced by my Lord Tenterden, Mr. Justice Bayley, Mr. Justice Holroyd, and Mr. Justice Littledale, to the judgment of three young barristers, called but the day before, and three older ones, who never could obtain any practice.[1]

The Privy Council, which heard appeals from India and from all the colonies with their widely different systems of law, and also appeals from the Admiralty and Prize Courts, only sat for about nine days in the year;[2] and the composition both of the courts from which appeals were brought, and of the Privy Council itself, was most defective:[3]

That the sentences in the colonies should oftentimes be found ill-digested, or hasty, or ignorant, can be no matter of astonishment, when we find a bold Lieutenant-General Lord Chancellor in one Court, and an enterprising Captain President in another, and a worthy Major officiating as Judge-Advocate in a third. In many of these cases, a gallant and unlearned Lord Chancellor has decided, in the Court below, points of the greatest legal nicety and the Judges of Appeal who are to set him right here, are chosen without much more regard to legal aptitude; for you are not to suppose that the business of these nine days upon which they sit is all transacted before lawyers; one lawyer there may be, but the rest are laymen . . . the Master of the Rolls alone is always to be seen there, of the lawyers; for the rest, one meets sometimes in company with him, an elderly and most respectable gentleman, who has formerly been an ambassador, and was a governor with much credit to himself in difficult times; and now and then a junior Lord of the Admiralty, who has been neither ambassador nor lawyer, but would be exceedingly fit for both functions, only that he happened to be educated for neither. . . . This is the Court which determines, without appeal, and in a manner the most summary that can be conceived in this country, all those most important matters which come before it. For instance I once saw property worth thirty thousand pounds sterling per annum disposed of in a few minutes after the arguments at the bar ended, by the learned members of the Privy Council, who reversed a sentence pronounced by all the Judges in the Settlement, upon no less than nineteen days' most anxious discussion. Such a Court . . . is the supreme tribunal which dispenses the law to eighty millions of people, and disposes of all their property.[4]

Some reforms were needed in the system of justices of the peace. It was not reasonable that in practice they should be appointed by the Lords Lieutenant "without the interference of the Crown's responsible ministers."[5] The Lord Chancellor might, it is true, interfere, but he never did;[6] and in particular it was very doubtful whether it was expedient to appoint clergy-

---

[1] Speeches 355-356; for the Court of Delegates see vol. i 603-605.
[2] Ibid 359; for the history of the appellate jurisdiction of the Privy Council see vol. i 516-518, 520-524.
[3] Ibid 360-362.   [4] Ibid.   [5] Ibid 367.
[6] Ibid 367-368; vol. i 291; x 134.

men.[1] There was reason to think that the absolute discretion
of the justices in the granting or withholding liquor licenses
was sometimes abused;[2] and to distrust the impartiality of
some of them in their enforcement of the game laws.[3] There
was no real appeal from their decisions " unless they set out
any matter illegal on the face of the conviction; "[4] and in the
exercise of their extensive jurisdiction at quarter sessions they
were equally irresponsible.[5] It was true that the justices were
not directly paid; but they were sometimes paid indirectly
by fees, and by jobs which resulted in scamped work or even
in corruption :

Not only may the magistrate himself receive compensation in money's
worth; he may receive it in hard money by his servants. The fees of a
justice's clerk amount to a little income, often to many times a man's
wages. I have heard of a reverend justice in the country, having a clerk
whose emoluments he wished to increase, and therefore he had him
appointed surveyor of weights and measures, with a salary of a guinea
and a half a week. This person appointed a deputy, to whom he gave
five shillings and sixpence, and who did all the duty. These circumstances
came under the consideration of his brother justices; when, after a
strenuous opposition, and among others, on the part of the gentleman who
communicates the occurrence in a letter now lying before me, it was
decided, not only not to remove the first appointed person, who it was
proved was doing nothing, but to swear in the other as his assistant !
My friend is not entirely without suspicion that this functionary, having
so small a remuneration as five shillings and sixpence a week, can only
have undertaken the duty with a view of increasing it by some understanding with the people whose weights and measures it is his duty to
superintend.[6]

Justices were too ready to commit accused persons to prison
—even mere children; and those committed " do not come out
of gaol as they went in." [7] Every care is taken in selecting the
judges : very little care is taken in selecting the justices.[8] More
care should be taken to appoint fit justices; for it is through
them " more than through any other agency—except, indeed,
that of the tax-gatherer—that the people are brought directly
into contact with the Government of the country." [9]

[1] Speeches 368-369 ; Brougham's remarks were unfair to the clerical justices,
some of whom, notably Richard Burn, had done excellent work both on the bench
and as contributors to the literature of the subject, vol. x 145 ; xii 332-334.
[2] Ibid 369-372 ; for the history of this part of their work see vol. x
183-187.
[3] " There is not a worse constituted tribunal on the face of the earth, not even
that of the Turkish Cadi, than that at which summary convictions on the game
laws constantly take place; I mean a bench or brace of sporting justices,"
Speeches 373.
[4] Ibid 373.
[5] Ibid 373-374 ; I think that Brougham unduly minimized the various forms
of control exercized by the courts of common law, see vol. x 244-254.
[6] Ibid 375.   [7] Ibid 376.   [8] Ibid 378.   [9] Ibid 377.

With respect to the administration of civil, as distinct from criminal justice, what was most needed was a system of effective county courts which would relieve the central courts of smaller cases, and provide cheap redress.[1]

I made the Prothonotary, four years ago, at Lancaster, give me a list of fifty verdicts obtained at the Lent Assizes ; the average was under fourteen pounds, including, however, two or three actions brought to try rights, where the damages were of course nominal. But if the money recovered amounted in all to less than nine hundred pounds, the costs incurred certainly exceeded five thousand pounds.[2]

Efficient county courts, and the provision of better facilities for arbitration,[3] would do much to cheapen justice.

Procedure

Some of the most obvious defects in the law of procedure were the following :

(1) The Crown's privileges in litigation.[4] The Crown could, as a rule, only be sued by petition of right, and no petition of right could be brought without the fiat of the attorney-general. In other words, it is " in the discretion of your adversary's counsel to let you bring your action or not as he pleases " ;[5] and that discretion was sometimes abused.[6] Then too the Crown had numerous privileges in the law of pleading, as to the place of trial, as to the conduct of the trial, and as to costs.[7]

(2) Too many opportunities were given to rich and litigious suitors.[8] Proceedings should be made shorter and less expensive ; and "no party should be sent to two courts where one is able to afford him his whole remedy."[9] If a plaintiff could show a good *prima facie* case he should be able to get judgment on notice given to the defendant, unless the defendant could show cause and give security to defend the action.[10] In all cases in which it might be feared that future actions might be brought to question a title it should be possible to get a declaratory judgment which would settle the case once for all.[11]

(3) All obsolete modes of procedure, such as wager of law,[12] should be abolished. Why insist on the personal appearance of a defendant, and make use of the clumsy, unjust, and ineffective process of outlawry to secure his appearance ?[13]

---

[1] Speeches 406-407 ; and see Brougham's speech of April 29, 1830 on Local Courts, Speeches 489-529.

[2] Ibid 407-408.   [3] Ibid 408-409.

[4] For this subject see vol. ix 7-8, 23 ; x 342-347.

[5] Speeches 384.   [6] Ibid 384-385.   [7] Ibid 385-390.

[8] Ibid 390.   [9] Ibid.   [10] Ibid 391.

[11] Ibid 391-392 ; Brougham pointed out that such an action was allowed in Scotland.

[12] Ibid 392-393 ; for wager of law see vol. i 305-308.

[13] Ibid 412-413 ; see vol. ix 254-255.

(4) Arrest on mesne process, which operated hardly on poor men and put a weapon into the hands of unscrupulous or malicious persons, should be abolished;[1] and the law as to execution after judgment needed to be radically reformed. No property should be exempt, all debts should be payable out of a deceased debtor's estate, and imprisonment of the debtor should be resorted to only in cases of wilful concealment of property, or in case of criminal or grossly imprudent conduct in contracting the debt. Every one of these principles was broken by the rules of English law. Land was differentiated from chattels, choses in action could not be taken in execution,[2] simple contract debts were not payable out of a deceased person's realty unless he was a trader, in all cases the creditor could elect to imprison his debtor instead of proceeding against his property.[3]

(5) The whole subject of appeal from judgments recovered, and proceedings in error needed to be overhauled. Law and equity in this matter proceeded on wholly different principles ; and the practice of granting a stay of execution pending an appeal invited the loser to prosecute groundless appeals.[4]

(6) The fact that a successful litigant could not recover full costs against his adversary amounted almost to a denial of justice. The difference between the costs recoverable from the defeated party and the full costs were so large that

a man shall in vain expect me to recommend him either to bring forward a rightful claim, or to resist an unjust demand for any such sum as twenty, or even thirty pounds—at least upon a calculation of his interest. I should presently declare to him, he had much better say nothing in the one case, and pay the money a second time in the other, even if he had a stamped receipt in his pocket, provided his adversary were a rich and oppressive man, resolved to take all the advantages the law gives him.[5]

Brougham admitted that in the then state of the law this evil was to some extent inevitable. If all the costs incurred were recoverable by a successful litigant, practitioners would run up very heavy charges in a clear case.[6] But when the law had been amended so that practitioners could no longer indulge in these practices, a larger allowance of costs should be made to a successful litigant.[7]

(7) It would materially shorten the proceedings if sworn shorthand writers were assigned to all the *nisi prius* courts. An incorrect note led to an incorrect decision, and an incorrect report of a case when a motion for a new trial was made ; and

---

[1] Speeches 409-411 ; above 264, 265.
[2] This was the real reason why the creditor was able to resist attempts to limit his power to arrest his debtor—by arresting him, he was able to put pressure on him to part voluntarily with his property, see vol. xi 524, 600.
[3] Speeches 468-473.   [4] Ibid 474-475.
[5] Ibid 475-476.   [6] Ibid 476.   [7] Ibid.

a judge could give better consideration to a case if he were relieved of the mechanical task of note taking.[1]

Pleading

In the law of pleading Brougham pointed out six major defects :

(1) The pleadings gave no information as to the matters in dispute. The declaration "conveys no precise knowledge of the plaintiff's demand."[2] For instance, the declaration in an action of *indebitatus assumpsit* could be used for any one of seven, and the declaration in an action of *trover* could be used for any one of eight, different causes of action.[3] As little information was conveyed by the defendant's plea. Under a plea of *non assumpsit* eight different defences could be set up.[4]

(2) The rules of pleading were not consistent. For instance, some defences must be specially pleaded, others could be given in evidence under the general issue ; but there was no general principle which governed these rules.[5]

(3) Many kinds of repugnant counts and pleas were allowed.

When there are ten different ways of stating a defence, and all of them are employed, it is hardly possible that any three of them can be true ; at the same time their variety tends to prevent both the opposite party and the court from knowing the real question to be tried. Yet this practice is generally resorted to, because neither party knows accurately what course his opponent may take ; each, therefore, throws his drag net over the whole ground, in hopes to avail himself of everything which cannot escape through its meshes. Take the case of Debt on a bond. The first plea in such an action, almost as a matter of course, is the general issue, *non est factum*, whereby the defendant denies that it is his deed ; the second as usually is, *solvit ad diem*—he paid it on the day mentioned in the bond, a circumstance not very likely to happen, if it be not his deed ; the third is *solvit post diem*—he paid it after the day ; a thing equally unlikely to happen if it be not his bond, or if he paid it when due ; and the fourth, often is a general release. What can a plaintiff learn from a statement in which the defendant first asserts that he never executed the deed, and next that he not only executed it, but has moreover paid it off ?[6]

Any number of consistent pleas, but no repugnant pleas should be allowed.[7]

(4) Though the statute of Anne allowed defendants to plead double with leave of the court, which was never refused, the plaintiff was not allowed a double replication. The reason was by no means obvious.[8]

---

[1] Speeches 465-466. [2] Ibid 416. [3] Ibid 417-418.
[4] Ibid 421. [5] Ibid 423 ; vol. ix 323-324.
[6] Ibid 423-424 ; see vol. ix 305-306 for the practice of using several distinct counts and pleas.
[7] Ibid 424. [8] Ibid 425-427 ; vol. ix 316-317.

(5) The rule that a demurrer admitted all the facts stated by the opposite party was not reasonable. In fact it was inconsistent with the rule which allowed a defendant a double plea :

Why should a party be allowed to say, " In point of fact I deny the promise—but if I made it, six years have elapsed—or I made it under age," and be prohibited from saying—" In point of fact, I deny the promise ; but if I made it there was nothing binding in point of law.[1]

In law, as in equity, the court should first determine the question of law, and then try the issue of fact.[2]

(6) It should be possible to amend all formal errors, even at the last stage of the case. No one should lose his case on account of a mere verbal error.[3]

There is no doubt that Brougham was quite right when he said that in the law of pleading " subtlety has superseded sense," and that " ingenuity was exhausted in devising pretexts for prolixity and means of stratagem."[4] There is no doubt also that he was right when he said that, in producing this state of the law, the courts and the Legislature had been " too ready accomplices." [5]

Evidence

Many doctrines of the law of evidence were unreasonable and inconsistent. For fear of encouraging perjury, the parties were not allowed to give evidence in a trial at common law, but they were allowed to give evidence in the court of Chancery and the ecclesiastical courts, and also in the matters decided on affidavit by the common law judges.[6] But in all cases, affidavit evidence should be limited, for, the swearer not being liable to cross-examination, it was a far greater encouragement to perjury than the admission of the parties to give evidence could ever be.[7] All disqualifications on the ground of interest should be abolished, for interest should affect not competence but credit.[8] Written evidence should be encouraged. What was wanted was a new and enlarged Statute of Frauds.[9] The rule which laid down the conditions under which the account books of a deceased person were admitted as evidence was criticized ;[10] and also the rule that, in a prosecution for libel, the truth of the matter published was not allowed to be proved,[11] and the rule that if a witness denies that he is guilty of a crime,

[1] Speeches 428.   [2] Ibid.   [3] Ibid 428-430.
[4] Ibid 415 ; vol. ix 311-315, 324-327.   [5] Ibid 415.
[6] Ibid 438-441 ; see vol. ix 193-196 for the history of this rule.
[7] Ibid 441.   [8] Ibid 442.
[9] Ibid 444-445.   [10] Ibid 445-446.   [11] Ibid 447-448.

no evidence other than conviction of the crime could be adduced.[1] The rules which make witnesses incompetent on account of their religious beliefs should be abolished.[2] The rules as to the admission of extrinsic evidence to explain a latent but not a patent ambiguity were not reasonable ;[3] and the rule that, though the weight of parol evidence was left to the jury, the court alone was competent to construe written documents put in as evidence, was not logical.[4] Some of the rules of construction which the courts had invented tended to defeat the intentions of testators and settlors.[5] In fact, " it is hardly to be conceived how much, as matters at present stand, a man who makes his will is in the dark as to its final operation."[6] The law should provide formulæ for testators, by the use of which they could be certain of effecting their intentions.[7] The different methods of trying issues of fact at common law, in equity, and in the ecclesiastical courts should be abolished. All issues of fact should be tried by a jury.[8]

Some rules of substantive law

Many parts of the law of real property stood in need of reform. Such customs as Gavelkind and Borough English, and the manifold customs which regulated copyholds in different places, hindered both the free alienation and the improvement of landed estates.[9] The law affecting real property should be the same all over England. The whole apparatus of fines and recoveries should be swept away, without destroying the substance of the law as to the barring of entails ;[10] and trustees to preserve contingent remainders should likewise be abolished.[11] Uses upon uses should be recognized as legal estates,[12] and the distinction between leases and agreements for a lease, which equity recognizes and law does not, should be abolished.[13] Legatees ought to be allowed to sue the executor at law for their legacies,[14] and mortgagors ought to be allowed to enforce their rights at law.[15] In an action of ejectment a man ought to be able not only to establish his title, but also to enforce his claim

---

[1] Speeches 448-449. [2] Ibid 449.
[3] Ibid 451 ; see vol ix 221-222. [4] Ibid 451.
[5] Ibid 452-453 ; Brougham seems to have regarded the rule in Shelley's case as a rule of construction—which it was not, vol. iii 108-111.
[6] Ibid 453. [7] Ibid 457.
[8] Ibid 458. [9] Ibid 379-382. [10] Ibid 393-395, 398.
[11] Ibid 397. [12] Ibid 398-399.
[13] Ibid 399-400 ; this was a reform which Lord Mansfield tried to effect, vol. xii 589.
[14] Ibid 400; this also was a reform which Lord Mansfield tried to effect, vol. viii 28, 30 ; ibid xii 588-589.
[15] Ibid 400 ; this also was a reform which Lord Mansfield tried to effect, vol. xii 588.

to mesne profits.[1] The procedure on a writ of right, which required a tenant to prove his title, was grossly unfair.[2] The law as to future interests, and especially the rules which distinguished between executory interests and contingent remainders were very unreasonable.[3]

The statute of limitations was defective in that it did not apply to specialty debts, so that no period of limitation was fixed for them.[4] When the statute of limitations did apply, the courts had found so many means of evading it that it was wholly uncertain in its operation. Even the " simplest expression " was taken by the courts as an acknowledgment which would take the case out of the statute. In fact Lord Erskine once said that " the only safe course a defendant could take when his adversary sent a fishing witness was to knock him down ; for though he might be proceeded against for the assault, he retained the benefit of the statute." [5] The different periods of limitation fixed for different real actions were unreasonable, and even more unreasonable was the fact that no period of limitation existed for certain rights of the Church.[6]

As Brougham said at the beginning of his speech, he did not touch the topic of commercial law. But at the end of it he made two exceptions—the law of partnership and the law of bankruptcy. He said,

A man can hardly tell whether he is a partner or not : being a partner, the extent of his liability is scarcely less difficult to ascertain. . . . The distribution of estates under the bankrupt law is likewise capable of very great improvement. After all that was lately done in arranging and simplifying this code, it remains full of contradictions, and the source of innumerable frauds and endless litigation.[7]

Brougham concluded his great speech with an eloquent peroration in which he adjured the House to put its hand to the work of law reform. Here are some sentences from it :

The course is clear before us ; the race is glorious to run. You have the power of sending your name down through all times, illustrated by deeds of higher fame, and more useful import, than ever were done within these walls. You saw the greatest warrior of the age—conqueror of Italy—humbler of Germany—terror of the North—saw him account all his matchless victories poor, compared with the triumph you are now in a condition to win—saw him condemn the fickleness of Fortune, while, in despite of her, he could pronounce his memorable boast, " I shall go down to posterity with the Code in my hand. . . . " It was the boast of Augustus . . . that he found Rome of brick and left it of marble. . . .

---

[1] Speeches 402 ; see vol. vii 15 for the reason why it was necessary to bring a separate action for mesne profits.

[2] Ibid 466-467.   [3] Ibid 456-457.   [4] Ibid 459.

[5] Ibid 460 ; Lord Tenterden's Act of 1829 cured this defect.

[6] Ibid 461-463.   [7] Ibid 478.

But how much nobler will be the Sovereign's boast, when he shall have it to say, that he found law dear and left it cheap ; found it a sealed book —left it a living letter ; found it the patrimony of the rich—left it the inheritance of the poor ; found it the two edged sword of craft and oppression—left it the staff of honesty and the shield of innocence.[1]

Brougham very appropriately introduced at the end of his speech an allusion to the proposals for many far-reaching reforms in the law which had been made during the period of the Commonwealth[2]—very appropriately because the far-reaching extent of the reforms which he advocated were fairly comparable only to those proposals. But, as I have pointed out,[3] though the period of the Commonwealth was not a period when the principles and rules of English law were in a state to be extensively recast and restated, the end of the eighteenth and the beginning of the nineteenth centuries were emphatically such a period. Brougham was right when, after his account of the projected reforms of the Commonwealth period, he said : " After a long interval of various fortune, and filled with vast events, but marked from age to age by a steady course of improvement, we are again called to the grand labour of surveying and amending the laws. "[4]   In fact, we have seen that, before Brougham's speech, much had been done and more had been proposed in the way of recasting and restatement,[5] and the way had been prepared for more extensive reforms by the reports of royal commissions and the reports from committees of both Houses of Parliament.[6] But there is no doubt that his speech was the most learned and thorough criticism of the many defects of the common law that had ever been made since the Commonwealth period ; and there is no doubt that the two commissions, issued as the result of it to some of the ablest lawyers of the day,[7] to enquire into the practice and procedure of the courts of common law and into the law of real property, effected more for law reform than any of the commissions previously appointed.

The first of these commissions issued six reports between 1829 and 1834 of which four were issued before the passing of the Reform Act. The second of these commissions issued

---

[1] Speeches 484-485.

[2] For these reforms see vol. vi 412-423 ; at p. 481 Brougham cites Shepherd's book, England's Balme, in which see ibid vi 421-422.

[3] Ibid 429-430.   [4] Ibid 483-484.

[5] Above 260-270.   [6] Above 270-274.

[7] The members of the commission to enquire into the practice and procedure of the courts of common law were Bosanquet, Parke, Alderson, Stephen ; and on the first three of these being raised to the bench, they were replaced by Pollock, Starkie, Evans, and Wightman. The members of the commission to enquire into the law of real property were Campbell, Tinney, Sanders, Duval, Hodgson, Duckworth, Brodie, Tyrrell.

four reports of which all but the last were issued before the passing of the Reform Act. Brougham in 1829[1] and 1831[2] gave
well deserved praise to the thoroughness with which the commissioners had done and were doing their work; and in 1830,
Peel, while deprecating partial reforms till the commissioners
had finished their labours,[3] outlined some of the reforms which
the government contemplated as the result of the reports of
the commissioners already published. He agreed that all those
patent offices, which had so long stood in the way of the reform
of the central and local courts ought to be abolished as soon as
possible,[4] that the separate Welsh judicature should be abolished,
and that the places of the Welsh judges should be taken by
appointing additional judges of the common law courts.[5] Both
he and Brougham agreed that small debt courts ought to be
created.[6]

The fact that both parties in the state were agreed that
large reforms in the law were necessary is illustrated by Lyndhurst's speech in March, 1830, in which he sketched the progression
of reforms in the procedure of the courts of law and equity
and the ecclesiastical courts which the government were con-
templating.[7] That programme included the reforms later
embodied in the Uniformity of Process Act, 1832,[8] reforms
in the law of pleading, reforms in the distribution of business
as between the three common law courts, the abolition of the
separate system of Welsh courts, reforms in the law of real
property, reforms in the ecclesiastical courts, and extensive
reforms in the court of Chancery. The last-mentioned reforms
included measures to get rid of the arrears of business in the
court of Chancery, reforms in the Masters' offices, the abolition
of the system of payment by fees in the office of the court of
Chancery which was " the great barrier to improvements "
in that court, and improvements in the lunacy and bankruptcy
jurisdictions of the court. In fact, the era of law reform had

---

[1] " As far as the report went, he could not conceive anything more complete.
It united great firmness and moderation. It showed a determination not to
shrink from reform, from the apprehension that they might be thought by some
to go too far; and on the other hand, it manifested every disposition to consult
even the most groundless scruples, and the most ill-founded prejudices, of those
who were opposed to any change," Hansard (2nd Series) xxi 1040.

[2] Ibid xxiv 243-244.

[3] " The whole subject of the law, the subjects of enquiry before each commission, were so intimately connected and interwoven together that until we
were in possession of the entire views of the commissioners in relation to them, it
would be desirable to postpone partial reforms in the law, and wait till we had the
whole question fairly before us," Hansard (2nd Series) xxii 653.

[4] Ibid 654-656; above 189.

[5] Ibid xxii 656-659.

[6] Ibid 656; ibid xxiv 243-259, 262-274, 279-283; above 263.

[7] Ibid xxiii 674-693.

[8] 2 and 3 William IV c. 39; vol. i 222, 240.

begun more than ten years before the passing of the Reform Act of 1832 ; and it was fortunate for English law that it had begun before the great change made by that Act ; for it ensured a continuity in legal development between the pre- and the post-Reform Act eras, which was no small help in ensuring the stability of the state in the new constitutional conditions which the Reform Act introduced. Though it is true that the pace of law reform was considerably accelerated after the Act, we have seen that before the Act a considerable number of reforms had been effected in public law,[1] and all parties agreed that reforms in many other branches of the law were needed. We shall now see that a number of reforms had been made in other branches of English law.

IV

THE ENACTED LAWS

I shall deal with this topic under the following heads : Public Law ; Industry and Commerce ; Criminal Law and Procedure ; the Common Law ; Equity ; Admiralty and Prize Law ; Ecclesiastical Law.

Public Law

I have already given some account of the most important developments in English public law ; and in the next chapter I shall deal with the development in law relating to our colonies and India. All that remains is to give some account of the law relating to local government.

During this period there are no great changes in the machinery of local government or in the principles of local government law, which I have described in the first chapter of this book. A few rules and principles were elaborated, a few were modified, and one or two archaic rules were removed. I shall deal with this subject under the following heads : Machinery ; Poor Law ; Rating ; Highways and Bridges ; Prisons and Lunatic Asylums ; Liquor Licensing ; Miscellaneous.

Machinery

I shall deal with this subject under the two heads of (i) the machinery of local government ; and (ii) the police.

(i) The machinery of local government. We have seen that the machinery of local government centred round the cities

---

[1] Above 234 seqq.

and boroughs, the justices of the peace, and the vestries.[1] We must wait till the following period for any extensive overhaul of the constitutions of the cities and boroughs. But there are a number of small changes, mainly of a procedural character, in the organization of the justices of the peace. There are statutes as to the time of holding the Michaelmas quarter sessions[2] as to the fees to be taken by the clerks of the peace ;[3] as to the power of quarter sessions to sit in two divisions to order to expedite business ;[4] as to the appeals to the county quarter sessions from small corporations and franchizes ;[5] as to the power of justices not of the quorum to act in places when the number of justices was small ;[6] as to the settlement by the justices of the boundaries of the divisions of counties ;[7] as to the manner in which fines imposed by the justices should be levied and accounted for.[8] Similarly there are a number of small changes in the organization of the vestries. There are statutes as to the time at which overseers were to be appointed ;[9] as to the notices to be given of vestry meetings, the right to vote at vestry meetings, and the preservation of vestry records ;[10] as to the abolition of the presentments made by parish constables to petty sessions.[11] A statute of 1818 regulated the election of coroners by the county court.[12]

At the end of this period it was becoming apparent that, in the growing urban districts, both the organization of vestries and their powers needed to be supplemented. We have seen that in some towns and in some urban parishes the need had been met by local or private Acts which appointed special commissioners or trustees to perform such duties as paving, lighting, or watching.[13] But the fact that there was need for some more general regulations in urban districts is illustrated by two Acts of 1830 and 1831. Since this need was not felt in the rural districts these Acts were not to apply to the whole country, but only to such vestries as chose to adopt them.

The Act of 1830[14] was an Act to provide for the lighting and watching of parishes in England and Wales. It could be

[1] Vol. x 128-133.　　　　　　　[2] 54 George III c. 84.
[3] 57 George III c. 91—they were to be settled by the justices and approved by the judges of assize ; for the clerk of the peace see vol. x 129, 230.
[4] 59 George III c. 28.
[5] 1 George IV c. 36, amending 27 George II c. 38.
[6] 4 George IV c. 27.　　　　　　[7] 9 George IV c. 43.
[8] 41 George III c. 85.　　　　　　[9] 54 George III c. 91.
[10] 58 George III c. 69, amended by 59 George III c. 85 ; inhabitants whose assessments were under £50 had one vote ; and those whose assessments were over that sum had one extra vote for each £25 up to six votes, § 3.
[11] 7, 8 George IV c. 38 ; see vol. x 150 for these presentments.
[12] 58 George III c. 95 ; for the history of the coroner see vol. i 82-87.
[13] Vol. x 188-195, 214-219.
[14] 11 George IV and 1 William IV c. 27.

adopted by a vestry meeting of the inhabitants.[1] If adopted,
not less than three or more than eleven inspectors were to be
elected to carry out the provisions of the Act,[2] and the inhabitants
at the meeting adopting the Act were to fix the highest amount
of rate which the inspectors could demand to carry out the
provisions of the Act.[3] The inspectors could appoint a salaried
staff,[4] and they could sue and be sued in the name of one of them.[5]
They must keep records of their proceedings, and accounts
of money received and spent.[6] They must appoint paid watchmen,[7] and provide fire engines and street lighting.[8] Provisions
were made as to their powers in relation to gas pipes and gas
lighting, and the prevention of the contamination of water
by gas.[9] They could contract for any works which they had
power to do under the Act,[10] buy or lease land or houses needed
for the exercise of their powers,[11] and unite with inspectors
of adjoining parishes in exercising them.[12] The Act of 1831,[13]
which could be adopted by any parish which contained over
800 ratepayers,[14] provided for the annual election (by ballot
if required by five ratepayers) of vestrymen and auditors.[15] A
person was qualified to be a vestryman or auditor if he held
a tenement rated at not less than £10.[16] The number of vestrymen to be elected depended on the number of ratepayers—not
less than twelve or more than one hundred and twenty.[17] They
were to hold office for three years—one third retiring annually.[18]
The rector and churchwardens were to be *ex officio* members.[19]
The vestry must elect a chairman.[20] It must keep a record
of its proceedings open to inspection,[21] and accounts also open
to inspection after an audit,[22] which was to be conducted twice
a year by annually elected auditors.[23] The vestry must make
and publish a list of their estates (if any), and of charitable
foundations and bequests belonging to the parish.[24]

Both these Acts, and more especially the Act of 1831, illustrate the growing influence of Bentham's ideas—the reliance
on popular election, the value of publicity, the use of the ballot.
Both foreshadow changes in the machinery of local government

---

[1] §§ 1-5 ; if it was decided not to adopt the Act no proposal to adopt could
be made for one year, § 8.

[2] § 6 ; §§ 9-14 deal with the mode of their election, their tenure of office,
and their meetings.

[3] § 7.   [4] § 15.   [5] § 20.   [6] §§ 21-23.
[7] §§ 29-31.   [8] §§ 32 and 33.   [9] §§ 34-42.   [10] §§ 45 and 46.
[11] § 47.   [12] § 49.   [13] 1, 2 William IV c. 60.   [14] § 43.
[15] §§ 1-11 ; it was provided (§ 9) that if it was decided not to adopt the Act
no proposal to adopt could be made for three years.

[16] §§ 26 and 33 ; the qualification was £40 in London or in places where
there were more than 3000 resident householders.

[17] § 23.   [18] § 25.   [19] § 23.   [20] § 30.
[21] § 31.   [22] §§ 32 and 37. [23] §§ 33-38.   [24] §§ 39.

which will be made in the following period.[1] We shall now see
that the legislation on the two connected subjects of the stipendiary magistrates and the police shows that some of the changes
needed to adapt the eighteenth century machinery of local
government to the needs of the new conditions which the industrial revolution was creating, were already taking place.

(ii) The police. We have seen that the unpaid[2] constables
who were supposed to keep the peace were wholly ineffective
in times of disorder and in large towns.[3]

In times of disorder it was necessary to make arrangements
for the enrolment of special constables. In 1812 disturbances
at Nottingham were the occasion of an Act which gave the
custos rotulorum, the sheriff, or any five justices, power, in any
county in which disturbances had taken place or were apprehended,
to call a special meeting of the general sessions, and enrol as
special constables so many ratepayers between the age of
seventeen and fifty as they saw fit.[4] At the expense of the
parish, they were to provide themselves with the necessary
arms and equipment,[5] and they were to be allowed such pay
as the justices might direct.[6] This Act was continued in 1818,[7]
and was amended in 1820;[8] and another Act of 1820[9] made
it clear that persons could be compelled to act as special constables not only in cases of actual, but also in cases of apprehended,
disturbance.

We have seen that in large towns or urban districts provision
was sometimes made for a paid police force by local or private
Acts.[10] We have seen that London got a paid police force in
1829; but it is not till the following period that the whole country,
boroughs as well as the country districts, got a paid police
force.

The Poor Law

The progress of the industrial revolution had made the
problem of the pauper an increasingly pressing problem all
through this period. We have seen that the Legislature in the
eighteenth century had made many attempts to solve this

---

[1] Vol. x 219.

[2] In certain cases defined by statute payment of expenses incurred was made
to the constables, see e.g. 27 George II c. 3, and 41 George III c. 88—expenses
of conveying prisoners to gaol, of executing warrants, and of extraordinary
payments in cases of riot.

[3] Vol. x 144-145.

[4] 52 George III c. 17 §§ 1, 4, 15; but those over fifty who occupied land of
the yearly value of £20 were liable, § 15; but all those liable to serve could
provide a substitute, § 16.

[5] § 17.   [6] § 26.   [7] 58 George III c.52.

[8] 1 George IV c. 24.   [9] Ibid 37.

[10] Vol. x 188-192, 214-219.

problem. The chief expedients adopted were the provision of workhouses provided and managed by the parish and the parish officials or by a union of parishes,[1] or managed by a contractor with the parish ;[2] or the creation of statutory corporations to administer the poor law ;[3] or the granting of out relief.[4] We have seen, too, that it was a prevalent but mistaken opinion, which was shared by Bentham,[5] that it was possible to run an institution for the relief of the poor which, by means of the work done by the paupers, should be self-supporting.[6] But we have seen that most of these workhouses[7] or other institutions, whether run by parishes or unions of parishes or by statutory corporations, failed to fulfil their purpose, mainly because no intelligent supervision was undertaken by the central government to ensure honesty and efficiency in their management.[8] Since, therefore, it became impossible to insist on a rigid workhouse test, the parish authorities fell back on a system of outdoor relief, which, in accordance with the resolution of the Berkshire justices made at Speenhamland in 1795, was graduated in amount according to the price of bread and the size of the applicant's family.[9] A clause in Gilbert's Act of 1782, which contemplated the supplementing of wages by the rates, had prepared the way for the adoption of this policy ;[10] and as earlier statutes had encouraged, later statutes sanctioned it.[11] One effect of the adoption of this policy was to stop the building of new workhouses : another effect was to change the character of the existing workhouses. They ceased, as a rule, to provide work for the able bodied, and became " merely poorhouses and infirmaries."[12]

Many circumstances combined to increase the cost of the poor law in the first two decades of the nineteenth century. As Dr. Clapham says :[13]

---

[1] Vol. x 174-175, 176.

[2] Ibid 177 ; 45 George III c. 54 laid down some conditions for the validity of these contracts—they must be made with a resident in the parish, and two householders must guarantee its performance.

[3] Vol. x 211-214; for the number of all these institutions, statutory or otherwise see Clapham, An Economic History of Modern Britain i 352-357.

[4] Ibid 175-176.

[5] Above 101.

[6] Vol. x 176, 257 n. 4, 275, n. 7.

[7] For some exceptional cases see Clapham, op. cit. i 357-358, 358-359, 360.

[8] Vol. x 176, 214.

[9] Ibid 176 ; Webb, The Old Poor Law 177-180.

[10] 22 George III c. 83 § 32 ; Clapham, op. cit. i 357.

[11] 36 George III c. 23 §§ 1-3 ; 55 George III c. 137 § 3.

[12] Clapham, op. cit. i 357.

[13] Ibid 362 ; it is significant that 36 George III c. 10, 39 ; 40 George III c. 40; and 52 George III c. 73 gave power to incorporated bodies of guardians to increase the amount of the assessments limited by their incorporating Acts ; in 1817 the government were authorized to advance money to parishes and other bodies in order to give employment to the poor, 57 George III c. 34.

With workhouse and poorhouse accommodation stationary or declining, a population growing fast, Irish immigration spreading to rural districts, rural wages held down in many places by the way the poor law was worked, and the price of bread—which regulated much of the relief— abnormally high, the growing drain on the poor rates, during the first twenty years of the nineteenth century, for allowances in aid of wages and other forms of outdoor relief, is comprehensible enough. In the towns there were special drains set up by decaying trades . . . by the demobi- lized men in 1815-16, and by those thrown out of work by the severe commercial depressions in 1816 and 1825.

At the end of the second decade the good harvests, which lowered food prices, afforded some relief ;[1] and the burden of the poor rate varied considerably in different places.[2] It was most crushing in the agricultural districts of the south of England.[3] But there is no doubt that the alarm felt at its growing cost was justifiable ; and this alarm gave rise to many different expedients to diminish it, some of which got the sanction of the Legislature and were regulated by it. It was with these various expedients for dealing with the problem of pauperism that the Legislature of this period was mainly occupied. In this, as in other branches of public law, no thoroughgoing reform was attempted till after 1832.

In 1795 the section of the Act of 1722, which prevented the overseers from giving out relief in parishes where there was a workhouse, was repealed ; the overseers, with the assent of the parishioners or of a justice, were empowered to order such relief ; and a justice was empowered to order it for a period not exceeding one month.[4] In 1816 provisions limiting the power to give out relief in local Acts, and other provisions of those Acts giving powers to the masters of the workhouses, were repealed.[5] Another method of dealing with pauper children was apprenticeship.[6] Large numbers of children were apprenticed to the owners of cotton mills or other factories.[7] But the abuses of this system led, not only to the passing of the first factory Act in 1802,[8] but also to the passing of an Act in 1816 to regulate the apprenticeship of pauper children.[9] The justices were to

---

[1] Clapham, op. cit. i 363.   [2] Ibid 364-365.

[3] " The single county of Sussex spent nearly as much as Wales, and nearly twice as much per head as the average for the whole country," ibid 364-365.

[4] 36 George III c. 23 ; vol. x 174 n. 5 ; such relief had previously been given, though its legality was doubtful, ibid 175 n. 4 ; the powers of the justices to give this relief were increased by 55 George III c. 137 § 3 ; this Act also provided for the punishment of paupers who embezzled property provided for their use, or who misbehaved in workhouses, §§ 1, 2, 4.

[5] 56 George III c. 129 ; e.g. power to compel the pauper to remain in the workhouse till the charge for his maintenance had been paid for by his labour, power to apprentice a pauper child to the master of the workhouse ; power to hire out the labour of poor persons.

[6] Webb, The Old Poor Law 196-261.   [7] Ibid 201-203.

[8] Above 39, 213.   [9] 56 George III c. 139.

enquire into the matter, examine the parents, and to decide whether, having regard to the distance of the proposed master's residence from that of the child, any proposed apprenticeship was proper in the circumstances ;[1] and the indentures of apprenticeship were to be allowed by two justices.[2] No child under nine could be bound as apprentice ;[3] and the assignment or dismissal of apprentices was put under the control of the justices,[4] No settlement was to be gained by any apprentice unless these provisions were complied with.[5] This Act diminished the use of this expedient, and led overseers to make use of their powers to compel persons to take charge of these children or pay the statutory penalty of £10.[6]

The last mentioned device was somewhat similar to two other devices used by overseers in the case of adults. The first was the system of "roundsmen." The unemployed were assigned to particular farmers who gave them work, maintenance, and any starvation wage they chose, which was supplemented by the allowance made by the parish according to the size of his family.[7] The second device was the labour rate. This system is described by the Webbs as follows :[8]

What the parish had to ensure was that none of its settled labourers should be without employment. Therefore the total amount of the wages for the year of all the wage earners belonging to the parish was computed. . . . The total thus estimated was divided among all the rate payers, with or without the exemption of special classes, sometimes according to rateable value, sometimes according to acreage. Each ratepayer undertook to pay in wages to " settled labourers " during the year—credit being given only for the prices adopted in computing the labour rate—an amount at least equal to that at which he had been assessed to this labour rate. Any deficiency in his labour bill had to be compensated for by an equivalent payment to the overseer, in order to enable the parish to find maintenance for the surplus labourers. The employer thus retained his full authority over his labourers, and they their full inducement to keep in private employment in preference to being thrown on the parish for a pittance of outdoor relief.

An Act of 1831 legalized this or any other arrangement made by any rural parishes when the rates exceeded 5s. in the £.[9] The Act expressly prohibited the levy of a rate directly in aid

---

[1] § 1.
[2] § 2 ; if the master lived in a different county two justices of that county must also approve.
[3] § 7. [4] § 9. [5] § 5.
[6] Webb, The Old Poor Law 207-209 ; 8, 9 William III c. 30 § 5 ; Webb says, op. cit. 209, " We hear of cases in which a boy could in this way ' earn ' for the parish £30, or even £50, before a master could be found to accept him. The vestry of Leeds had a revenue from these fines amounting to more than £1000 a year."
[7] Webb, The Old Poor Law 189-193.
[8] Ibid 194. [9] 2, 3 William IV c. 96.

of wages[1]—though it is obvious that all these devices involved the indirect use of the rates to make up wages in money or in kind to an amount on which the labourer could live.

Another expedient sanctioned by the Legislature was the provision of land by the poor law authorities on which the poor could be employed. They were given power to take land on lease or to inclose land for this purpose, and to employ the poor upon it, or to let it to inhabitants of the parish.[2] In 1832 they were given power to let both this land, and land allotted to the poor under inclosure Acts, to inhabitants of the parish or neighbouring parishes, and to employ the rent in the purchase of winter fuel for the poor.[3]

Two other expedients made use of by the Legislature to deal with the problem were attempts to improve the machinery for relief, and a modification of the law of settlement.

An Act of 1819[4] gave power to establish select vestries for the relief of the poor.[5] Parishes could appoint paid assistant overseers,[6] and larger powers were given to build workhouses, to buy land on which to employ the poor, to raise money on loan, to give relief on loan, to remove Scotch and Irish vagrants without first imprisoning or whipping them,[7] and other powers.[8] We have seen that the law of settlement gave rise to all sorts of abuses ;[9] and that, because it placed hindrances on the mobility of labour, it was denounced by the economists.[10] An Act of 1795 modified the law by enacting that no one should be removed to his parish of settlement unless and until he became a charge upon the rates ;[11] and various attempts at further reforms were made from 1819 to 1832.[12] No reform was in fact made because, as we have seen, some law of settlement was the necessary consequence of the view that poor relief was a local and not a national service.[13]

The law as to vagrancy is closely connected with the poor law. Of the main principles of that law I have given some account.[14] The law was modified by a statute of 1821 which did away with the system of passing vagrants to their place of settlement except in certain cases defined by the Act, and with the giving of rewards for their apprehension.[15, 16] We have seen that the law was consolidated by Acts of 1822 and 1824.

---

[1] § 4.
[2] 59 George III c. 12 §§ 12 and 13 ; 1, 2 William IV c.c. 42 and 59.
[3] 2 William IV c. 42.   [4] 59 George III c. 12.   [5] § 1.
[6] § 7.   [7] §§ 8, 12, 15, 29, 34.   [8] Vol. x 272.
[9] Ibid 257-269.   [10] Ibid 268 ; above 212, 213.
[11] 35 George III c. 101 § 1 ; justices were given power to suspend the removal of sick persons, § 2 ; vol. x 266.
[12] Webb, The Old Poor Law 346-347.   [13] Vol. x 269.
[14] Ibid 177-180.   [15] 1, 2 George IV c. 64 §§ 1, 2, 7, 8.
[16] 3 George IV c. 40 ; 5 George IV c. 83 ; vol. x 178-179.

Rating

We have seen that the main principles of this branch of the law are the product of judicial decision.[1] The statutes of this, as of the preceding period, merely effect small changes in the machinery of assessment and collection.[2] A statute of 1797 gave the justices for Middlesex at their quarter or general sessions power to make a county rate in accordance with the returns of the rentals in each parish, which returns were to be annually furnished by the church wardens;[3] and this power was given to the justices of other counties by a statute of 1815.[4] This statute was amended in 1816 by an Act which gave the justices power to fix the county boundaries and the boundaries of parts of counties for the purpose of rating, and for that purpose only.[5] An Act of 1801 made some changes in the procedure for the amendment by quarter sessions of errors in the assessment of poor rates, and in the procedure in appeal to quarter sessions. A rate could be amended without being quashed and notice of appeal was not to prevent a distress for its recovery.[6]

Highways and Bridges

In the case of highways and bridges, as in the case of rating, the main principles of the law were evolved by the courts,[7] against a background of statutes which dealt mainly with the persons or bodies liable to repair, the powers given to them to enable them to perform this duty, and the means by which they could be compelled to perform it.[8] In 1792 a statute defined the duties of persons owning property and others to perform labour on the roads, and the amounts which they were liable to pay in commutation of this duty.[9] The justices were given power to exempt poor persons,[10] and, in places where the cost of hiring labour or teams of horses was high, to compel those liable to perform this duty to perform it in person or to send teams of horses.[11] In 1794 two justices were empowered to settle what parts of a highway lying in two parishes were to be repaired by each.[12] We have seen that in 1815 the procedure for stopping and diverting highways was simplified.[13] In 1803,[14] 1814,[15] and 1815[16] the powers of the surveyors of county and

---

[1] Vol. x 276-299.
[2] Ibid 170.
[3] 37 George III c. 65.
[4] 55 George III c. 51.
[5] 56 George III c. 49.
[6] 41 George III c. 23 §§ 1 and 2.
[7] Vol. x 299-332.
[8] Ibid 171-172.
[9] 34 George III c. 74 §§ 1-4, amended by 44 George III c. 52; for this statute labour see vol. x 154-155; for its unsatisfactory character and the manner in which it was constantly evaded see Webb, The Story of the King's Highway 28-32.
[10] 34 George III c. 74 § 5.
[11] § 6.
[12] 34 George III c. 64.
[13] 55 George III c. 68; vol. x 321.
[14] 43 George III c. 59.
[15] 54 George III c. 90.
[16] 55 George III c. 143.

other bridges to get material for the repair of bridges, to remove obstructions, and to purchase land were enlarged. Quarter sessions were empowered to alter the situation of county bridges ;[1] and no bridges erected by private persons were to be repairable by the county unless they were erected to the satisfaction of the county surveyor.[2] We have seen that in 1812 the justices were given power to spend a sum not exceeding £20 on the repair of a bridge without waiting for the presentment of a jury.[3] They were also empowered to contract with turnpike trustees or other persons for the repair of bridges.[4]

Prisons and Lunatic Asylums

The attention of the Legislature had been called to the disgraceful state of the prisons by Howard and Blackstone in the preceding period,[5] and by Bentham in this period.[6] During this period it made serious attempts at reform. In the first place, it provided for the erection of a prison for London and Middlesex which was controlled by the central government. In the second place it gave increased powers to the county justices and the justices of some of the larger boroughs to build prisons, and it laid down rules for the management of these county prisons.

(1) We have seen that in 1794 the Legislature encouraged Bentham to proceed with his scheme of building a prison on the panopticon principle,[7] but that in 1812 it wisely determined to abandon this scheme.[8] Instead, it compensated Bentham for his expenditure of money on, and his services to, the abandoned scheme,[9] and it made provision for the erection at Millbank of a prison to accommodate three hundred male and three hundred female prisoners convicted of transportable offences.[10] The prison was primarily a prison for persons convicted of these offences in London and Middlesex ;[11] but we can see the beginnings of an idea that the provision of a prison for those convicted of serious crimes should be a national and not a local service, in the control which the central government, through the Home Secretary, was to exercise over it,[12] and in the power given to the Crown to remove to it persons convicted in other parts of England and Wales.[13] The erection of the prison was entrusted to three supervisors appointed by the Crown.[14] When it was erected the Crown was to appoint a committee of superintendence[15]

---

[1] 43 George III c. 59 § 2.   [2] § 5 ; vol. x 329.
[3] Ibid 148 ; 52 George III c. 110 § 1.   [4] § 5.   [5] Vol. x 182-183.
[6] Above 54, 55, 101.   [7] Above 54 ; 34 George III c. 84.
[8] Above 55 ; 52 George III c. 44 ; Webb, English Prisons under Local Government 49-50.
[9] 52 George III c. 44 § 4.   [10] § 5.   [11] § 1.
[12] §§ 36-38.   [13] § 46.   [14] § 5.   [15] § 6.

who were to make rules, which were to be approved by the chief justice of the King's Bench,[1] and appoint officers.[2] The powers and duties of these officers were defined.[3] Rules were laid down for the food, lodging, and treatment of the convicts,[4] who were to be divided into two classes. During the first part of the sentence the convict was to fall into the first class, and during the second part of the sentence into the second class. The confinement of those in the first class was to be more, and those in the second class less, strict.[5] The governor must keep a register of prisoners, and reports must be made at the beginning of each session to Parliament and the King in Council.[6] This Act was amended in 1816 and 1819. In 1816 provision was made for the enlargement of the prison, and the rules for the appointment of the committee and their powers, and the powers and duties of the prison officials, were revised.[7] In 1819 the prison was again enlarged, and several amendments were made in the Act of 1816.[8]

(2) The experience which had been got from the management of the Millbank prison was used by the Legislature when, a few years later, it attempted to reform the county prisons and the prisons of some of the larger boroughs. An Act of 1823 enabled the justices to borrow money from the Exchequer for building and repairing gaols.[9] Another Act of the same year consolidated and fundamentally reformed the law as to gaols and houses of correction[10]—"the first measure of general prison reform to be framed and enacted on the responsibility of the national executive."[11] It repealed twenty-two Acts or parts of Acts ranging from 1327 to 1818,[12] and provided that in each county in the cities of London and Westminster, and in seventeen towns there should be one common gaol and one house of correction.[13] The justices were to execute the Act, and, subject to the provisions of the Act, were to determine what classes of prisoners were to be sent to the gaol and what to the house of correction[14]—rogues and vagabonds were to be sent to the house of correction;[15] and prisoners for debt were to be separated from other prisoners.[16] The Act then laid down a set of rules as to the duties of the officers and as to the management of the gaols.[17] *Inter alia* it was provided that no prisoner should be put in irons except in case of necessity,[18] and that food and bedding

---

[1] § 7.
[2] § 9.
[3] §§ 12, 29, 31.
[4] §§ 18-22.
[5] § 23.
[6] §§ 36 and 37.
[7] 56 George III c. 63.
[8] 59 George III c. 136.
[9] 4 George IV c. 63.
[10] Ibid 64.
[11] Webb, op. cit. 73.
[12] 4 George IV c. 64 § 1.
[13] §§ 2 and Schedule A; for houses of correction see vol. x 180-181.
[14] § 4.
[15] § 7.
[16] § 5.
[17] §§ 10, 28-33.
[18] § 10 rule 12.

must be provided for the prisoners who had no means of providing it for themselves.[1]   Gaols must be periodically lime
washed, and cleansed once a week; soap, towels and comb
must be provided, [2] no " Tap " and no gaming was to be allowed;
and no " garnish " permitted.[3] Further rules and regulations
for these gaols could be made by quarter sessions, and submitted for approval to the judges.[4] Visiting justices were to
be appointed who must report to quarter sessions;[5] and a general
report, after approval by quarter sessions, must be sent to the
Secretary of State to be laid before Parliament.[6] Returns
of prisoners convicted at the sessions or assizes must be sent
to the Secretary of State.[7] A list must be made of charitable
gifts for the relief of poor prisoners and displayed in the gaol.[8]
Moderate sums of money were to be paid to discharged prisoners
to enable them to return home.[9] Quarter sessions were given
power to rebuild or enlarge gaols when necessary;[10] and it was
provided that

in the altering, enlarging, repairing, building, or rebuilding of any
gaol or house of correction under this Act, the justices shall adopt such
plans as shall afford the most effectual means for the security, classification, health, inspection, employment, and religious and moral
inspection of the prisoners.[11]

For these purposes the justices could borrow on the security
of the county rates;[12] and could compel persons to sell to them
any land which they required.[13]

    This Act was amended in 1824,[14] by an Act which provided
for a report to be made to the Secretary of State as to the establishment of officers and servants kept in prisons,[15] and for a
better classification of prisoners—five classes of male and three
of female prisoners were defined both for gaols and houses of
correction.[16] No prisoners were to be put on the treadmill before
conviction; and those committed for trial must be supplied
with food without being obliged to work.[17] Travelling allowances
were to be given to discharged prisoners.[18]

---

[1] § 10 rule 13.   [2] § 10 rule 19.

[3] § 10 rules 21-23; for the " Tap "—where beer and spirits could be bought
see Holdsworth, Charles Dickens as a Legal Historian 139; for " garnish "
—a sum demanded of a new prisoner by the old prisoners—see Webb, English
Prisons 25, 65, 193.

[4] 4 George IV c. 64 § 12.   [5] §§ 16 and 23.   [6] § 24.

[7] § 20.   [8] § 36.   [9] § 39.

[10] §§ 45 and 46.   [11] § 49.   [12] §§ 54 and 55.

[13] § 58.   [14] 5 George IV c. 85.   [15] § 8.

[16] § 10; the five classes of male prisoners were first, prisoners for debt; second
and third, convicted prisoners who could be put into either of these classes by the
visiting justices according to the character of the prisoner and the nature of his
offence; fourth and fifth, prisoners committed for trial who could also be put into
either of these classes by the visiting justices.

[17] §§ 16 and 17; see Webb, English Prisons 81-82 for the reason for the enactment of these §§.   [18] §§ 22-26.

These Acts did not apply to all prisons. They did nothing to reform either the three great debtors' prisons in London, or the one hundred and fifty or so gaols and bridewells in the franchises and minor municipalities, which were at this date the " filthiest and most abominable in the Kingdom."[1] Nor were these Acts very effective. The central government had not got any effective machinery for supervision.[2] But they are historically important because they show that the Legislature had begun to realize the necessity of laying down rules for the management and conduct of prisons. This realization was a condition precedent for the reforms which were made in the following period, which were more effectual because an effective machinery for seeing that they were carried out was provided.

We can see a similar development in the statutes which provided for pauper and criminal lunatics. We have seen that the Legislature had provided for the supervision of private lunatic asylums ;[3] but it is not till this period that any provision was made for the erection and maintenance of these asylums by the public authorities. An Act of 1800 had provided for the custody during his Majesty's pleasure of insane persons indicted for crimes ;[4] but there was no direction as to where they were to be detained ; and we have seen that some had been detained in gaols.[5]

In 1806 Sir George Paul, the prison reformer of Gloucestershire, addressed a memorial to the government on the dreadful condition of these lunatics. Its result was an Act of 1808, the title of which is " An Act for the better care and maintenance of lunatics, being paupers and criminals." [6] The need for making this provision in the case of pauper lunatics is set out in the preamble to the Act, which recites that

the practice of confining such lunatics and other insane persons as are chargeable to their respective parishes in gaols, houses of correction, poor houses, and houses of industry, is highly dangerous and inconvenient.

It then empowers the quarter sessions to provide lunatic asylums, and to unite with the justices of adjoining counties to make such provision,[7] and with the directors of asylums supported by

[1] Webb, English Prisons 75.
[2] See ibid and n. 1 for Sydney Smith's objection to the appointment of government inspectors—he thought that they would take their salary and do nothing.
[3] Vol. x 179.
[4] Above 192 ; 39, 40 George III c. 94, amended 56 George III c. 117.
[5] Above 192.
[6] 48 George III c. 96.   [7] §§ 1 and 3.

voluntary contributions.[1] Regulations were made as to the situation and construction of those asylums.[2] Lunatics found wandering abroad could be committed to one of them ;[3] and lunatics directed to be detained during his Majesty's pleasure by virtue of the Act of 1800 could be detained in these asylums, and the justices could make orders for their maintenance.[4] Visiting justices were to be appointed to supervise them.[5]

The Act was amended in 1811,[6] 1815,[7] and 1824 ;[8] and in 1819 it was provided that a pauper was not to be removed to an asylum without the order of two justices assisted by a medical practitioner.[9] These statutes were repealed by an Act of 1828 " for the erection and regulation of county lunatic asylums, and more effectually to provide for the care and maintenance of pauper and criminal lunatics." [10] The justices were empowered to erect and enlarge asylums,[11] to unite with the subscribers to existing asylums maintained by voluntary contributions,[12] to appoint committees to manage the asylum,[13] to acquire land or houses,[14] to make a county rate for this purpose,[15] and to borrow money to build.[16] They were to appoint visitors,[17] to appoint officers, and to make rules for the management of these asylums.[18] Visitors must make a yearly report of the patients in each asylum and send it to the Secretary of State.[19] Convicts becoming insane could be sent to one of these asylums by the Secretary of State,[20] who was given a right to inspect them. At the same time the need for better regulations for the control of private asylums had become obvious.[21] This control was provided by another Act of 1828.[22] Of asylums in London the government took direct control through a board of fifteen commissioners appointed by the Home Secretary, of whom five at least must be physicians.[23] In the country the control was to be exercised through the justices and visitors appointed by the justices.[24] The commissioners or justices were to grant licences to keep asylums,[25] and the commissioners or visitors were to inspect asylums licensed.[26] No person could be confined in an asylum without a certificate signed by two medical practitioners.[27] This Act was amended in 1829,[28] and both Acts were repealed and the law was consolidated in 1832.[29]

---

[1] § 22.   [2] § 16.   [3] § 19.   [4] § 27.
[5] §§ 2, 6, 24, 25.   [6] 51 George III c. 79.   [7] 55 George III c. 46.
[8] 5 George IV c. 71.   [9] 59 George III c. 127.   [10] 9 George IV c. 40.
[11] §§ 1 and 51.   [12] §§ 4 and 5.   [13] § 8.
[14] §§ 17-27.   [15] § 12.   [16] §§ 13-16.
[17] §§ 8-10.   [18] § 30.   [19] § 56.   [20] § 55.
[21] For some of the abuses which prevailed see Hansard (N.S.) xviii 575-583.
[22] 9 George IV c. 41.   [23] § 2.   [24] §§ 10 and 11.
[25] §§ 2 and 10.   [26] § 20.   [27] § 30.
[28] 10 George IV c. 18.   [29] 2, 3 William IV c. 107.

Liquor Licensing

There are one or two statutes of this period which amended the existing laws[1] on this subject. An Act of 1795 made an alteration in the penalties for selling beer or spirits without a licence,[2] and required licensees to give notice of the place where they had stored their beer.[3] In 1822 there was legislation as to the recognizances to be entered into by licensees,[4] the certificates of good conduct which they must produce,[5] and the penalties for breach of the law;[6] and in 1828 the existing law was consolidated by an Act[7] which repealed twenty-one Acts or parts of Acts.[8] Two years afterwards the Act of 1830[9] in effect introduced free trade in beer. Only an excise licence, which cost only two guineas, was required,[10] the powers of the justices were confined to closing a house where a riot was taking place,[11] and the only discipline to which the beer-house keeper was submitted were penalties for permitting drunkenness on the premises,[12] and for infringing the rules as to closing hours.[13] It was the fanatical believers in free trade who procured the passing of the Act,[14] and, in spite of its disastrous results,[15] long resisted any attempt to reimpose efficient control.[16] In this as in other matters the free traders were deaf to the teachings of history, for, as the Webbs say,[17]

The student of contemporary accounts of the nineteenth century free trade in beer will find it easy to parallel, almost line for line and word for word, contemporary descriptions of the previous experiment of the eighteenth century free trade in gin.

Miscellaneous

It only remains to give one or two illustrations of some of the miscellaneous powers which were given by the Legislature to particular local authorites or to the justices of the peace throughout the country. An Act of 1794 gave power to the Mayor and Aldermen of the City of London to regulate the watermen on the Thames.[18] The watermen's company could submit objections to

---

[1] See vol. x 183-187 for these laws.   [2] 35 George III c. 113 § 1.
[3] § 7.   [4] 3 George IV c. 77 § 1.   [5] § 2.
[6] § 9.   [7] 9 George IV c. 61.   [8] § 35.
[9] 11 George IV and 1 William IV c. 64; Webb, History of Liquor Licensing chap. iv; vol. x 187.
[10] 11 George IV and 1 William IV c. 64 § 2.   [11] § 11.   [12] § 13.
[13] § 14; they were 4 a.m. to 10 p.m. on weekdays, and on Sundays the house must be closed between 10 and 1 and 3 and 5.
[14] Webb, op. cit. 114; in fact they followed very literally the mistaken views of Adam Smith on this topic, see Wealth of Nations (Cannan's ed.) i 458 cited vol. xi 517.
[15] Webb, op. cit. 116-126.   [16] Ibid 127-132.
[17] Ibid 126; for the results of the free trade in gin see ibid 20-24; vol. x 184.
[18] 34 George III c. 65; their rules must be approved by the chief justices of the common law courts and the Lord Chancellor or one of them, § 2.

these rules,[1] and their jurisdiction to decide disputes between watermen, and to adjudicate upon their offences was saved.[2] In 1800 the fares to be charged by hackney coaches in London were regulated;[3] and the commissioners for licensing these coaches were given power to increase these fares when and if the price of corn rose,[4] and also to appoint inspectors of these coaches and their horses.[5] The law on this subject was revised in 1808.[6] In 1810 new rules were made as to the running of stage coaches[7]— rules as to the number of passengers,[8] amount and size of luggage, which could be carried,[9] the conduct of drivers.[10] In 1809 the justices were given power to adjudicate upon prosecutions for penalties for breach of the customs laws.[11]

Though this legislation as to local government does not cover much ground we see in some of these statutes, for instance the statutes as to the machinery of local government, and as to prisons and lunatic asylums, signs of developments which will become important in the following period. There is no doubt that much of the machinery of local government (like much of the machinery of central government) required to be overhauled. The problems set by the new industrial age required extensive reforms in the constitution of its units, more especially in the units reponsible for the government of the towns and urban districts, in their powers, and in their relation to the central government. It was becoming clear that the central government must exercise more control, and that it must be given the powers necessary to make that control effective. That these reforms in local government, and the corresponding reforms in central government, were becoming increasingly necessary, as the result of the progress of the industrial revolution, will be clear when we have examined the changes which were taking place in the laws which regulated industry and commerce.

Industry and Commerce

We have seen that the economic theories of Adam Smith had begun to influence legislation upon industry and commerce in the preceding period;[12] and that the development of his doctrines by the school of the classical economists had tended to emphasize his insistence on the merits of the policy of *laissez faire*, and to throw into the background some of the qualifications which he

---

[1] § 3.
[2] § 9; their jurisdiction and that of the Mayor and that of the Aldermen was concurrent.
[3] 39, 40 George III c. 47 § 1.   [4] § 2.   [5] § 4.
[6] 48 George III c. 87.   [7] 50 George III c. 48.
[8] § 2.   [9] §§ 3 and 5.   [10] §§ 10-12, 15.
[11] 49 George III c. 65.   [12] Vol. xi 392-394, 503-507, 513-518.

made to that policy.[1] Though some of the conclusions of this school of economists were controverted,[2] though the Legislature refused to give to either industry[3] or commerce[4] all the freedom which the economists demanded, these conclusions tended to exercise an increasing influence on it throughout this and the following period. During this period this influence was strongest in those departments of the law which dealt with the regulation of native industries. In the preceding period the growth of the capitalist organization of industry had already begun to render obsolete the old statutes as to prices,[5] wages,[6] apprenticeship,[7] and the old common law rules as to forestalling and regrating,[8] and to cause the repeal of some of them. In this period the same cause led to the repeal of many more of the old laws.[9] Masters, and, to some extent, men got greater freedom to dispose of their capital and labour as they pleased, and a greater freedom to combine.[10] Towards the end of this period the growth of the manufacturing industries, and the consequent need for cheap food for a growing population, was causing a demand for a freer trade in corn.[11] At the same time the industrial lead amongst the nations of Europe which Great Britain had secured, was making unnecessary many of those protective tariffs under the shelter of which British industries had grown up,[12] and was giving rise to a demand for their revision in the direction of greater freedom of trade.[13] The same causes which had led Pitt to make his commercial treaty with France in 1786[14] were demanding an extension of that policy. They were demanding the conclusion of similar commercial treaties with other nations ; and, in order to effect them, a revision both of the tariff and of the Navigation Acts.[15] In fact the three sets of laws which were the pillars of the mercantile system—the corn laws, the protection of native industry, and the Navigation Acts[16]—all needed to be revised.

Nevertheless, even in the laws which regulated native industries some of the old regulations remained in some trades, and some new regulations were made. The edge of the Truck Acts was sharpened,[17] the series of Factory Acts begun ;[18] and the Legislature tried to encourage thrift by their continual encouragement of Friendly Societies[19] and the institution of savings banks.[20] Unfortunately the influence of the classical economists prevented the state from doing anything effective to secure a living

---

[1] Above 29, 30, 110.   [2] Above 36, 140.   [3] Below 328, 329.
[4] Below 357, 358.   [5] Vol. xi 466, 469-470 ; below 329, 330.
[6] Vol. xi 467-472, 474-475 ; below 327, 328, 335 seqq.   [7] Vol. xi 419-421, 473.
[8] Ibid 468-472.   [9] Below 326-330.   [10] Below 346 seqq.
[11] Above 34, 35 ; below 356, 358.   [12] Vol. xi 442-444, 449-551, 502-503.
[13] Ibid 393, 394, 503.   [14] Ibid 393, 502.   [15] Below 360-362.
[16] Vol. xi 390.   [17] Below 335, 336.
[18] Above 213, 223, 313 ; below 335 seqq.
[19] Below 333, 334.   [20] Below 334, 335.

wage for the workers.[1] Their principal recourse in times of depressed trade or famine years, or at all times when their wages had been depressed below a subsistence level, was a recourse to the poor law ;[2] and so the cost of giving a living wage, instead of falling, as it ought to have fallen, wholly on the employer, fell partly on the ratepayers, with the result that many of the workers were partially pauperized. It is true that the Combination Act of 1800[3] was repealed, and that workmen were given a right to combine to secure better wages.[4] But the unlimited right to combine, which doctrinaire free traders secured, was so disastrous that it was withdrawn after a year's trial ;[5] and the law allowing a limited right to combine, which took its place, wholly failed to introduce any workable way of settling peaceably wage disputes, because it failed to legalize completely, and therefore did not attempt to define or control, the lawful sphere of the activities and the resulting rights and liabilities of combinations of masters and men.[6] To a very large extent therefore the disputes between masters and men were withdrawn from the arbitrament of the law—with the evil results of which I have said something in an earlier volume.[7] If the Legislature had enacted a well considered law which had defined the position of trade unions ; and if the manufacturers had used the power which the industrial lead secured by Great Britain gave them, to secure prices which would have enabled them to pay their workmen a living wage, much of the misery suffered by the workmen would have been avoided, and disputes between capital and labour would have been both better regulated and less bitter.[8]

In the spheres of agriculture and commerce the Legislature never lost sight of the fact, which from an early period had always been present to its mind, that it must, in the interests of national defence, safeguard the food and the shipping of the nation.[9] Both the corn laws and the Navigation Acts were modified, but neither were repealed ;[10] and some protective duties remained,[11] and some of the preferences given to colonial goods.[12] In these spheres the doctrines of the classical economists did not in this period exercise so great an influence as they came to exercise in the following period.[13] For this fact there were several causes. In the first place, England was not quite so thoroughly industrialized as it came to be in the following period. In the second place, the agricultural interest was better represented in the unreformed

[1] Vol. xi. 472, 496 ; above 34 ; below 337, 338.
[2] Above 311-315.   [3] Vol. xi 496-498.   [4] Below 346.
[5] Below 349.   [6] Below 350, 351.   [7] Vol. xi 498-500.
[8] Cunningham, Growth of English Industry and Commerce iii 619-620.
[9] Ibid 395-411, 451-462 ; below 358, 359 seqq.
[10] Below 359, 360-362.   [11] Below 363.
[12] Vol. xi 434-438 ; below 362.   [13] Below 363, 364.

than in the reformed Parliament. In the reformed Parliament the urban middle classes exercised an ever increasing influence as the country became more thoroughly industrialized.[1] In the third place, the simple and intelligible dogmas of the free traders appealed with greater force to the less educated electorate which the Reform Act had created. The more diversified electorate of the unreformed Parliament, because it represented many diverse interests, and because it had a more intimate knowledge of the working and needs of many branches of industry and commerce, was more capable of seeing that the practical consequences of subscribing to those simple and intelligible dogmas might in some cases be disastrous.

For all these reasons the legislation of this period on the subjects of industry and commerce, though it is much influenced by the theories of the classical economists, is not dominated by them. It is the legislation of a transition period. But, since the industrialization of England and the capitalistic organization of industry and commerce were proceeding apace, there were consequential changes in the organization of industry and in finance which attracted the attention of the Legislature— notably in the spheres of joint stock enterprise[2] and banking ;[3] and some of these developments will, in the following period, give rise to important changes in, and additions to, the enacted law, and, consequently, to equally important developments in legal doctrine. There were also developments in the enacted law as to several topics of commercial law—notably bankruptcy,[4] insurance,[5] shipping,[6] and a few others.[7] I shall deal with these various developments of the law during this period under the following heads : (1) The Regulation of Industry; (2) The Agricultural Industry; (3) The Regulation of Foreign and Colonial Trade ; and (4) The Organization of Trade and Finance and the Development of Certain Topics of Commercial Law.

(1) *The regulation of industry*

I shall deal with this topic under the following two heads : (i) The New Organization of Industry ; and (ii) Industrial Combinations.

(i) *The new organization of industry.*

The new organization of industry involved, first, the relaxation of some of the old restrictions upon the conduct of various industries and upon the relations of employers and workmen ;

---

[1] Above 257.
[2] Below 366 seqq.
[3] Below 371 seqq.
[4] Below 376-378.
[5] Below 378.
[6] Below 379.
[7] Below 379 seqq.

secondly, the retention of some of these old restrictions ; and, thirdly, the evolution of new methods of controlling industry, the further regulation of devices for the encouragement of thrift amongst the workmen, and the imposition of new statutory restrictions upon the relations of employers and workmen.

First, the relaxation of the old restrictions upon the conduct of industry, which had already begun in the preceding period,[1] made rapid progress. This fact will be clear if we look at some of the statutes passed with reference to the wool, leather, and cotton manufactures. In 1803 an Act was passed to suspend prosecutions under twelve statutes relating to the woollen manufacture which ranged from 13 Richard II to 13 George I ;[2] in 1809 thirty-two statutes which ranged from 2 Edward III to 1 George I were wholly repealed, and six others were partially repealed ;[3] and in 1810 four more statutes were repealed.[4] In 1814 restrictions on the carriage or storage of wool designed to prevent its illicit export were removed ;[5] and in the same year Acts of Charles II's reign which required persons to be buried in wool were repealed.[6] In 1800 two Acts of James I's and Anne's reigns relating to the manufacture of leather were repealed, and provision was made for the appointment of inspectors to secure the quality of the hides used by the manufacturers.[7] In 1808 six Acts which dealt with tanners, curriers, shoemakers and other artificers in leather were repealed ; but tanners were still prohibited from carrying on the business of shoemakers and certain other trades in leather.[8] In 1811 two Acts of George III's reign which regulated the manufacture of calico were repealed.[9]

Similarly, more of the old Acts which regulated the relations of employers and workmen were repealed. In 1795 the Acts which prohibited artificers and workmen employed in the iron and steel manufacturers from going abroad were made perpetual ;[10] but in 1824 all these Acts were repealed.[11] In 1814 the apprenticeship statutes of Elizabeth's reign were repealed.[12] In 1813 the Acts of Elizabeth and James I which empowered magistrates to fix wages were repealed.[13] They appeared foolish to economists who were blinded by their theories, and quite ignorant of some of the practical advantages of the retention of this power to rate wages which Fielding had pointed out.[14] This repeal did not affect the special Acts which had given the justices power to rate wages in

[1] Vol. xi 466-469.
[2] 43 George III c. 136.
[3] 49 George III c. 139.
[4] 50 George III c. 83.
[5] 54 George III c. 78.
[6] Ibid 108 ; vol. vi 329.
[7] 39, 40 George III c. 66, amended by 41 George III c. 53.
[8] 48 George III c. 60.
[9] 51 George III c. 33.
[10] 35 George III c. 38 ; vol. xi 432-433.
[11] 5 George IV c. 97.
[12] 54 George III c. 96 ; vol. iv 341-342 ; vol. xi 419-421.
[13] 53 George III c. 40 ; vol. iv 382 ; vol. xi 467.
[14] Vol. xi 474-475 ; below 338, 339.

particular trades ;[1] and as late as 1811 the Acts which gave the
justices power to fix the wages of the Spitalfields' silk weavers
were extended.[2] But though these Acts worked well and secured
a living wage to the Spitalfield workers, they were anathema to
Ricardo and his school of economists,[3] and so they easily succumbed to the attacks of the London manufacturers, who complained that they were unable to compete with the cheaper labour
which manufacturers in other places were able to get.[4] In spite
of the protests of the Spitalfields' weavers, these Acts were
repealed in 1824.[5] In 1824[6] the Combination Act of 1800[7] was
repealed ; but the effects of this repeal were so disastrous that it
was found necessary in the following year to reimpose some
restrictions upon industrial combinations.[8] Of the provisions of
these two Acts and their effects,[9] and of the effects of the repeal
of the Acts which gave power to settle rates of wages,[10] I shall
have something more to say later.

But, secondly, though very many of the old restrictions upon
the conduct of industry and upon the relations of employers and
workmen had disappeared, some still remained ; for, in the
interests of the state, some regulations were needed to guard
against frauds and other abuses injurious to the state, to industry
and trade, and to individuals. Many of the statutes passed with
this object in the preceding period[11] remained on the statute book ;
and other statutes were passed in this period with similar objects.
Thus statutes were passed to regulate the trade of millers ;[12] to
prevent frauds in the manufacture of buttons ;[13] to regulate the
cutlery trade ;[14] to establish a proof house at Birmingham for
firearms, similar to that established in London by the gunmakers'
company, at which all small arms must be tested ;[15] to provide for
the accuracy of weights and measures, and to punish the use of
false weights and measures.[16] Other statutes provided punishments
for workmen who spoilt or embezzled or otherwise injured their
employers' property. We have seen that in 1777 extensive powers
were given to the manufacturers of wool and worsted in York,
Lancaster, and Chester, and to the justices of those places
to regulate their industry and to punish frauds ;[17] and these

---

[1] Vol. xi 471-472.   [2] 51 George III c. 7 ; vol. xi 472.
[3] Above 34.   [4] Hammond, The Skilled Labourer 210-220.
[5] 5 George IV c. 66.   [6] Ibid c. 95.
[7] 39, 40 George III c. 106 ; vol. xi 497-498.   [8] 6 George IV c. 129.
[9] Below 346-350.   [10] Below 338, 339.   [11] Vol. xi 421-424, 469-474.
[12] 36 George III c. 85.   [13] Ibid 60.   [14] 59 George III c. 7.
[15] 53 George III c. 115 ; small arms were defined as " any gun, fowling-piece,
blunderbuss, pistol, or other description of firearms " ; amended by 55 George III
c. 59.
[16] 35 George III c. 102 ; 55 George III c. 43 ; 5 George IV c. 74 ; a consolidating Act which repealed fifty seven statutes wholly or partially ; 6 George IV
c. 12 ; for the history of the law on this subject see vol. x 403-407.
[17] Vol. xi 423-424 ; 17 George III c. 11.

provisions were applied soon after to other areas.[1] In 1800 an Act was passed to penalize various kinds of sabotage committed by miners in collieries.[2] Other statutes were passed to regulate particular trades. There was a statute of 1795 which regulated hawkers' licences,[3] and a comprehensive statute of 1800 which regulated the trade of pawn broking.[4] We have seen that the statutes which freed the leather industry from many restrictions provided also machinery for its regulation.[5]

We have seen that the old regulations as to the prices, quality, and mode of manufacture lasted longest in the case of bread and fuel.[6] During this period the law as to the manufacture and sale of bread was very complicated. The rules in force in London differed from those in force elsewhere ; and the rules in force in other parts of the country were not uniform.[7] In London statutes of 1797 and 1805 abolished the power of the justices to set the assize of bread and allowed the baker a sum of 13s. for turning a sack of flour into bread.[8] These statutes were repealed in 1815,[9] so that bakers were left free to manufacture and sell as they pleased ; but they were still subject to penalties for adulteration,[10] and rules were laid down as to the weights of loaves.[11] Similar but not identical provisions were made for places outside London in 1819 ;[12] but in some places the assize of bread continued to be set in the old way, and, where it was set, prices were still regulated.[13] Even if it was not set the justices had power, under an Act of 1773, to force bakers in times of scarcity to make and sell only one kind of bread—the standard wheaten loaf.[14] We have seen that it was not till 1822 that the assize of bread and the other bread regulations were abolished for London, and that it was not till 1836 that they were abolished for the rest of the country.[15] This series of the laws which regulated the bread trade at different periods has by far the longest history of all the laws which have regulated different branches of industry. But, besides the trade in bread, the Legislature found it necessary to regulate the trade in other foodstuffs or materials for food or drink. Thus Acts of 1796 regulated the trade in hay and straw in London, and the fish trade at Billingsgate ;[16] and in 1800 there was legislation to prevent frauds in the buying and selling of hops.[17] We have seen that the statutes which regulated the price of fuel and the coal

[1] Vol. xi 424; cp. Clapham, An Economic History of Modern Britain i 342-344.
[2] 39, 40 George III c. 77. [3] 35 George III c. 91.
[4] 39, 40 George III c. 99. [5] Above 327. [6] Vol. xi 469-470.
[7] For a good summary see Clapham, An Economic History of Modern Britain i 344-346.
[8] Ibid 345 ; 37 George III c. 98 ; 45 George III c. xxiii.
[9] 55 George III c. xcix. [10] §§ 3 and 4. [11] § 9.
[12] 59 George III c. 36. [13] Clapham, op. cit. i 345.
[14] Ibid ; 13 George III c. 62 § 8. [15] Vol. xi 470.
[16] 36 George III c.c. 88 and 118. [17] 39, 40 George III c. 81.

trade in London long remained on the statute book;[1] and in 1807 a very elaborate Act, which contained 156 sections, was passed to regulate the London coal trade.[2]

One set of laws which regulated trades survived during this period the attacks both of Bentham and the economists. They were the usury laws.[3] A committee of the House of Commons in 1818 recommended their repeal; and bills to repeal them were lost in 1821, 1824, and 1825.[4] One reason why these bills were lost was the fact that the market rate of interest had dropped below 5 per cent., the amount allowed by law. Therefore the landowners, who were all-powerful in the unreformed Parliament, could raise money on mortgage on easy terms; and, as Dr. Clapham has said, "they disliked money lenders and that damning word usury." [5] Another reason was the fact that these laws did serve some useful purposes—as was seen when, in the following period, they were repealed in obedience to the dictates of the economists and Bentham. No doubt these laws needed modification; and it would have been wise to have exempted many commercial transactions from their operation. But their total repeal gave opportunites to such iniquitous practices on the part of some classes of money lenders that, less than half a century after their repeal, the Legislature was obliged to intervene.[6]

Thirdly, in addition to these older restrictions upon the freedom of industry, the expansion of industry, and the changing conditions in which it was carried on gave rise to new kinds of regulations for industry as a whole or for particular industries—statutory or otherwise. We find (a) that new methods of controlling certain industries were being evolved; (b) that statutes were passed to encourage thrift amongst workmen; and (c) that statutes were passed to regulate the relations of employers and workmen.

(a) New methods of controlling certain industries were being evolved

Though most of the older companies in which different trades were organized, and to which powers were entrusted to supervise the conduct of these trades, were decadent at the end of the eighteenth century; and though their place was beginning to be taken by statutes which made provision for the conduct of particular trades by means of specially appointed inspectors; some few of these older companies still exercised powers of

---

[1] Vol. xi 470; cp. 45 George III c. ii.   [2] 47 George III c. lxviii.

[3] For the history of these laws see vol. viii 100-102; for Bentham's tract see above 43, 49, 110; for the debates in Parliament on these laws see above 212 n. 4.

[4] Clapham, An Economic History of Modern Britain i 348-349.

[5] Ibid 349.   [6] Vol. viii 100-101, 112.

supervision and control.[1] In certain cases also a control, similar to that formerly exercised by these companies, was exercised by voluntary associations of persons engaged in a particular trade. These associations, like the Society of the Gentlemen Practisers in the Courts of Law and Equity,[2] gave an organization to particular industries or trades, and, like it, they were able to maintain amongst their members high standards of honour. Instances of such voluntary associations are Lloyd's, the Stock Exchange, and certain groups of traders in corn and in coal.

Edward Lloyd's coffee house was established in Tower Street in the City of London as early as 1688.[3] Its situation near the Tower and on the Thames ensured that it should be resorted to by persons connected with shipping.[4] In 1691 or 1692 Lloyd moved his coffee house to Lombard Street,[5] and in 1696 he established a paper called *Lloyd's News*, which appeared three times a week and ran from September 1696 to February 1697, and supplied shipping news from British and foreign ports.[6] It was succeeded by another paper in 1726 which still flourishes as *Lloyd's List*.[7] By that time Lloyd's coffee house was the recognized resort of marine insurance brokers and underwriters. Shortly after the middle of the eighteenth century these marine insurance brokers and underwriters decided to form themselves into a society, and to admit only persons of good repute.[8] In 1770 the society left its premises in Lombard Street, and eventually acquired new premises in the Royal Exchange.[9] In 1779 the society fixed the form of the policy of marine insurance.[10] During the wars of the end of the eighteenth and the beginning of the nineteenth centuries the business of its members increased enormously ; and the evidence given to a Parliamentary committee on marine insurance in 1810 showed that, though at the beginning of the war " Lloyd's had been weak, the association had quickly gained strength, becoming before the century had run to an end a most powerful body, able to meet enormous financial engagements, and always ready and anxious to discharge them in the promptest manner."[11] It served the state well by the information as to shipping acquired through its agents which it was able to give to the government ;[12] it played

---

[1] Vol. xi 422-424 ; below 332, 364, 365.

[2] See vol. xii 63-75 for the history of this Society and for its work in organizing and disciplining the attornies and solicitors.

[3] F. Martin, The History of Lloyd's 59.

[4] Ibid 60-61.   [5] Ibid 62-63.

[6] See ibid 67-74 for an analysis of the contents of nos. 8-76 ; the first seven nos. are not extant.

[7] Ibid 107 seqq. ; Martin says that the year 1726 " must form an epoch in the history of Lloyd's, as being the visible starting point of the great institution bound up indissolubly with *Lloyd's List* and the system it represents of collecting and distributing news relating to ships and shipping."

[8] Ibid 119, 157.   [9] Ibid 145-156.   [10] Ibid 157-160.

[11] Ibid 179.   [12] Ibid 210.

a considerable part in the institution of life boats ;[1] and it started
in 1803 the Patriotic Fund to grant relief to the wounded and the
dependents of those killed in the war, and to give rewards for
valiant deeds.[2] The constitution of Lloyd's was reformed in 1811 ;[3]
and in 1871 it was incorporated by Act of Parliament which
created the constitution under which its members now carry on
their business.[4]

Lloyd's, as Dr. Clapham has said,[5] was a type of commercial
association which sprang up in other trades, notably in the trade
of stockbrokers and stock jobbers. They had become a distinct
body of traders in the second half of the eighteenth century. The
stockbrokers had asserted their right to be free from the control
which the City of London exercized over brokers ; and stock
jobbers had been very slightly affected by Sir John Barnard's
Act which had been passed to put down " the infamous practice
of stock jobbing." [6] In 1762 those dealers in stocks, who were
accustomed to meet at Jonathan's coffee house in Change Alley,
formed themselves into a club, which in 1773 acquired its own
Stock Exchange—" though it was still something of a coffee
house " ; and in 1802 it moved to larger premises. By the beginning of the nineteenth century this self governing club had
become the centre of the financial transactions of Europe.[7] It
had organized the industry and exercized discipline over its
members. Other instances of similar organizations were the
traders of the London corn and coal exchanges. The former was
a purely voluntary association of the principal dealers in corn :
the latter was a body of a different kind. The coal traders of
London were organized in a coal exchange, the premises of which
were vested in the mayor and aldermen of the City of London, to
whom large powers of controlling the trade were given by an
Act of 1807.[8] All coal arriving at London must be sold at this
exchange, so that, as Dr. Clapham has said, the Act had made the
coal exchange " a national or at least a municipal institution." [9]
It was thus an organization which had some resemblance to the
older companies which controlled different trades, and some
resemblance to the newer statutory bodies set up to control a
particular trade. Other similar organizations were the Chambers
of Commerce which sprang up in Scottish and English towns from
1783 onwards.[10]

[1] F. Martin, The History of Lloyd's 211-216.
[2] Ibid 217-224.   [3] Ibid 273 seqq.
[4] Ibid 355-365; 34, 35 Victoria c. xxi.
[5] An Economic History of Modern Britain i 300.
[6] 7 George II c. 8 ; for this Act see vol. xi 449.
[7] Clapham, op. cit. i 301-303.
[8] 47 George III c. lxviii ; above 330.   [9] Op. cit. i 305.
[10] Clapham, op. cit. i 307-310 ; the name was borrowed from the French by the
Scots, and in England at first different names were used, ibid 307, 309.

(b) Statutes were passed to encourage thrift amongst workmen

The statutes passed to encourage thrift amongst workmen were the statutes which regulated friendly societies and savings banks.

The reason why, in the preceding period and all through this period, friendly societies were encouraged by the Legislature, are summed up in the preamble to a statute of 1819.[1] It runs as follows :

Whereas the habitual reliance of poor persons upon parochial relief, rather than upon their own industry, tends to the moral deterioration of the people, and to the accumulation of heavy burthens on parishes ; and it is desirable, with a view as well to the reduction of assessments made for the relief of the poor, as to the improvements of the habits of the people, that encouragement should be afforded to persons desirous of making provision for themselves or their families out of the fruits of their own industry : and whereas by the contribution of the savings of many persons to one common fund, the most effectual provision may be made for the casualties affecting all the contributors.

The Legislature therefore proceeds to make new and better provisions for the formation of these societies, and for their protection against fraud and miscalculation.

We have seen that an elaborate statute had been passed to regulate friendly societies in 1793.[2] This statute was amended in 1795[3] and 1809 ;[4] and in 1819[5] changes were made in the methods by which these societies were for the future to be formed. Those intending to form such a society must apply by memorial to quarter sessions for a confirmation of the rules of the society, and of the tables of payment which it proposed to make.[6] The rules and tables as approved must be enrolled.[7] Quarter sessions were given power to make general rules for the formation and government of those societies.[8] The statute laid down rules as to the appointment of trustees,[9] as to the procedure to be adopted for the alteration of the society's rules,[10] as to its dissolution,[11] and as to the powers and duties and liabilities of its trustees.[12] Trustees of these societies were liable to make good any deficiency in their funds if in writing they undertook to be liable ; and, in such writing they could limit their liability to a fixed sum[13]— an early and perhaps the first appearance in the statute book of the principle of limited liability. The justices were given power to adjudicate upon the complaints of widows and children of deceased members.[14]

In 1829[15] the law on this subject was consolidated and amended.

---

[1] 59 George III c. 128.   [2] Vol. xi 493-494.
[3] 35 George III c. 111.   [4] 49 George III c. 125.
[5] 59 George III c. 128.   [6] § 2.   [7] Ibid.   [8] § 3.   [9] § 4.
[10] § 5.   [11] § 8.   [12] §§ 7, 12-14.   [13] § 13.
[14] § 15.   [15] 10 George IV c. 56.

Any number of persons, including minors, could form such a society and make and alter rules for its management.[1] These rules must be submitted to the barrister appointed to certify the rules as to savings banks, and he must certify that they were in accordance with the law.[2] They must then be confirmed by quarter sessions.[3] Only a general meeting could alter a rule so confirmed.[4] The society could appoint officers and committees,[5] and rules were made as to the duties to account of treasurers and trustees.[6] The property of the society was vested in the treasurers or trustees for the time being who could sue or be sued in its name.[7] The liability of the trustees to make good deficiencies was the same as under the Act of 1819.[8] Rules were made as to the punishment of frauds by the justices,[9] as to the dissolution of these societies,[10] as to the settlement of any disputes between members by arbitration,[11] and as to investment of funds.[12] There must be an annual audit ;[13] and, in order to help the government to construct more accurate tables of the duration of sickness, and the probabilities of the duration of human life for the guidance of those societies, they must make returns as to the " rate of sickness and mortality experienced " by them within periods of five years.[14]

Savings banks were closely connected with friendly societies. The principal Parliamentary advocate both of friendly societies and savings banks was George Rose.[15] He said that the idea of founding savings banks originated with the Society for bettering the Conditions of the Poor.[16] But it is fairly certain that the idea originated with Bentham's plan of Frugality Banks.[17] By 1816 nearly eighty such banks had been founded ;[18] and in 1817 the first Act regulating them was passed.[19] Their close connection with friendly societies is illustrated by a clause in the Act which allowed friendly societies to become depositors.[20] In 1828 a consolidating Act was passed.[21] This Act regulated the formation of these banks—their formation must have the approval of quarter sessions and the national debt commissioners ;[22] and their rules were to be submitted to a barrister appointed by the commissioners for the reduction of the national debt, who was to certify that they conformed to the law ; and they must be approved by quarter sessions.[23] The money deposited and other

---

[1] §§ 2 and 32.   [2] § 4.   [3] §§ 4, 6 and 7.   [4] § 9.   [5] §§ 11 and 12.
[6] §§ 13 and 14 ; in case of neglect or refusal to account application was to be made to the court of the Exchequer.
[7] § 21.   [8] § 22 ; above 333.   [9] § 25.   [10] § 26.
[11] § 27.   [12] §§ 30 and 31.   [13] § 33.   [14] § 34.
[15] Clapham, An Economic History of Modern Britain i 294.
[16] Ibid 295.   [17] Ibid ; above 101.
[18] Clapham, op. cit. i 299.   [19] 57 George III c. 130.
[20] § 6 ; this clause was repeated in the Act of 1828, 8 George IV c. 92 § 27.
[21] 9 George IV c. 92.   [22] § 2.   [23] § 4.

effects were vested in trustees who must give security,[1] and could not make any profit from their office.[2] Each trustee was only to be liable for his own wilful neglect or default.[3] The trustees could pay the money deposited only into the Bank of England in the names of the commissioners for the reduction of the national debt, and the trustees of existing banks could invest any sum of £50 or over with these commissioners.[4] The money so invested was to carry interest at the rate of two pence half-penny per cent. per day,[5] and interest payable to depositors of £1 or over was not to exceed the rate of two pence farthing per cent. per day.[6] No depositor could deposit more than £30 in a year or more than £150 in the whole ; and when the interest and deposit amounted to £200 payment of interest was to cease.[7] Disputes with depositors were to be settled by arbitration, and if the arbitrators did not agree by the barrister appointed by the national debt commissioners.[8] The trustees of these banks must make up their accounts annually and submit them to the commissioners for the reduction of the national debt.[9]

This legislative encouragement was favourable to the growth of these savings banks. In 1833 " there were 408 savings banks in England and Wales with 425,000 depositors and £14,334,000 of deposits."[10] Dr. Clapham says :

The relatively high average deposit, very nearly £34, suggests extensive patronage of the banks by small tradesmen and others not entirely dependent on wages or the work of their hands for a living. But in any event, machinery had been created, during a most trying period in the social history of the nation, which brought opportunities for saving with security and a modest interest, well within the reach of all who had any saveable surplus.[11]

(c) Statutes were passed to regulate the relations of employers and workmen

The three sets of statutes of which at this point I must say something are the Factory Acts, the Truck Acts, and the Acts which provided a machinery of arbitration for industrial disputes.

Of the first of these sets of Acts I have already said something. They applied to workers in cotton mills and factories, and laid down rules as to the hours of work of persons of different ages, prohibited the employment of children under nine, prescribed certain sanitary measures, and prescribed the hours and length of time which were to be set apart for meals.[12] I have also said

---

[1] §§ 7 and 8.   [2] § 6.   [3] § 9.   [4] § 11.
[5] § 16.   [6] § 24.   [7] § 35.   [8] § 45.   [9] § 46.
[10] Clapham, op. cit. i 299-300.   [11] Ibid 300.
[12] The first Act was passed in 1802, 42 George III c. 73 and applied to apprentices, above 39, 213 ; it was followed by 59 George III c. 66 which applied to all workers below a certain age ; 60 George III c. 5 ; 6 George IV c. 63 ; 10 George IV c.c. 51 and 63 ; all these Acts were consolidated by 1, 2 William IV c. 39.

something of the second of these sets of Acts.[1] The law on this subject was consolidated by two Acts of 1831. The first of these Acts repealed eighteen Acts from 4 Edward IV c. 1 to 58 George III c. 51, which had been passed to prohibit the payment of wages in other than current coin of the realm.[2] The second stated the law.[3] First, the Act applied to the following manufactures or trades: iron and steel; mining and quarrying; salt, brick, and tile manufactures; the manufacture of iron and steel articles and articles made from other metals; wool, cloth, fur, flax, hemp, silk, or cotton industries; the glass, china, or earthenware industries; the lace industry.[4] It did not apply to domestic service or to service in husbandry.[5] Secondly, it was provided that all contracts for the hiring of workers must be made in current coin of the realm,[6] and must not contain any stipulation as to how the wages were to be expended.[7] All wages must be paid in current coin.[8] No employer could sue a workman for goods supplied in lieu of wages.[9] Penalties were imposed on employers for the infringement of these provisions.[10] Thirdly, there were certain modifications of, and exceptions to, the generality of these provisions. Employers could in certain cases supply medicine, or tools, or feed for a horse, or a house at a rent, or meals prepared by the employers, and deduct the cost from the wages of the worker; [11] and employers could advance money to a worker for certain purposes e.g. to make a contribution to a friendly society or savings bank, or for relief in sickness, or to educate his children, and deduct money from wages in payment of the advance.[12] In both these excepted cases the contract for such deduction must be in writing and signed by the worker.[13]

The Acts which provided a machinery for the arbitration of industrial disputes, many of which applied to the cotton trade, were consolidated in 1824, and made applicable to any trade or manufacture.[14] In fact the passing of this Act followed a precedent set in 1800. The Combination Act of 1800 had contained an elaborate clause which provided for the settlement by arbitration of certain industrial disputes in any manufacture.[15] The

---

[1] Above 213, 324.
[2] 1, 2 William IV c. 36; an earlier consolidation Act 1 George IV c. 93 remained unrepealed till the Statute Law Revision Act 1873.
[3] 1, 2 William IV c. 37.   [4] § 19.   [5] § 20.   [6] § 1.
[7] § 2.   [8] § 3.   [9] § 6.   [10] § 9.
[11] § 23; for a recent case on the interpretation of this section see Pratt v. Cook Son & Co. [1940] A.C. 437, which led to an amending Act of 1940 (3 and 4 George VI c. 38).   [12] § 24.   [13] §§ 23 and 24.
[14] 5 George IV c. 96; the Act repealed wholly or in part seven earlier Acts from 3 George II to 53 George III c. 75; it was amended, 7 William IV and 1 Victoria c. 67, and 8, 9 Victoria c.c. 77 and 128; for a very able account of the history of this subject see Lord Amulree, Industrial Arbitration.
[15] 39, 40 George III c. 106 § 18; vol. xi 498; unlike the Act for arbitration in the cotton industry 39, 40 George III c. 90, it did not provide for arbitration on

Act of 1824 was an elaboration of that clause, so that it may be regarded as a supplement to the Act of the same year which repealed the Combination Act of 1800.[1] The Act began by enumerating the causes of dispute which could be referred to arbitration. They included such matters as wages, hours of work, quality and quantity of the work done ; but nothing in the Act was to give the justices the power to rate wages except with the consent of both master and workman.[2] If the parties agreed in writing the dispute could be heard by a justice : if they did not agree, the justice must summon the complainant, and, on proof that the complaint had not been settled, summon the parties ; and then, at the request of either of the parties who appeared, nominate not less than four or more than six arbitrators, half from manufacturers and half from workmen. From these the manufacturer was to choose one and the workman one.[3] If an arbitrator refused or delayed to act a second arbitrator was to be appointed by the justice—the expense of such second appointment being borne by the defaulting party.[4] Provision was made for the place where the arbitration was to take place,[5] the attendance of the parties,[6] and the method of conducting the arbitration ;[7] and power was given to commit refractory witnesses.[8] If the arbitrators could not agree, and did not give a decision within three days of their appointment, the justice must determine the question within two days.[9] The parties could, if they liked, agree upon a different mode of arbitration.[10] No manufacturer could act as a justice.[11] Awards could be enforced by distress, and failing that, by the imprisonment of the party in default.[12] The arbitrators, and if they could not agree, the justice, were given power to settle which of the parties was to pay the costs of the proceedings.[13]

None of these statutes succeeded in putting the relations of employers and workmen on a satisfactory footing. We have seen that the Factory Acts were ineffective[14]—" in six years only two convictions were obtained under the Act of 1819." [15] Similarly the Truck Acts were often disregarded or evaded.[16] In 1832 it was

prices to be paid for work done *or to be done*, but only for work done ; as Lord Amulree says, op. cit. 29, this difference is important—" the workman was to be protected against the unscrupulous master who broke his terms of contract. But it did not assist the workman in driving a better bargain with the employer in respect to work he was about to undertake. In other words, there was to be no interference with individual bargaining between employers and workers " ; in fact, this change in the wording of the Act was due to amendments made by those who believed in having fairer principles, ibid 27-28.

[1] Below 346-348.   [2] § 2.   [3] § 3.   [4] § 4.
[5] §§ 5 and 6.   [6] § 7.   [7] § 8.   [8] § 9.
[9] § 10 ;   § 21 gave a power to extend the time with the consent of the parties.
[10] § 13.   [11] § 12.   [12] § 24.   [13] § 31.
[14] Above 213.   [15] Clapham, op. cit. i 376.
[16] Hammond, The Town Labourer 67-71.

acknowledged that the prevalence of the truck system was one of
the causes of the trouble in the South Wales coal mining districts ;
and it is said that it lingered on in some mining districts as late as
1842.[1] One reason for this failure was the executive weakness of
the government—local and central. No machinery was provided
for enforcing these Acts. But the main reason was the hostility
of the dominant school of classical economists. They were
opposed to such Acts as Factory Acts and Truck Acts because
they imposed restraints on that free working of economic forces
which they considered must produce the best results.[2] The
employers were not slow to assimilate doctrines which increased
their profits ; the country gentry were naturally influenced by
the employers in questions connected with trade and manufacture ;
and so very many of those who, as justices, ought to have enforced
those Acts were biased against them. It may be that the
average legislator had " not much dogmatic objections to interference " [3]—we shall see that in relation to the corn laws and in
the regulation of foreign trade he was not prepared to abandon all
control ;[4] and it may be that the repeal of the apprenticeship
Acts and the Acts which provided for wage control were due to
the fact that the existing laws worked badly.[5] But, because no
one was prepared with an alternative method of regulation, and
because the economists had a creed which taught that any
alternative plan would do more harm than good, their views
prevailed.

Nor were the Acts which attempted to set up a machinery for
the settlement by arbitration of industrial disputes any more
successful. The abandonment by the Legislature of all attempts
to secure a living wage to the workmen,[6] and its prohibition of all
combinations to secure such a wage,[7] the fluctuations of trade
conditions which led in bad times to reductions in wages and
wholesale dismissals—all tended to introduce a bitterness into the
relations of employers and workmen which was fatal to any
attempt to make use of the machinery of arbitration. The employers had evaded the earlier Acts ;[8] and the justices refused to
apply them when a large body of workmen wished for an

---

[1] Hammond, The Town Labourer 71.
[2] Clapham, op. cit. i 377, citing a speech of Phillips on the Factory Bill of 1825 ;
" Hume, in spite of Adam Smith, condemned legislation to forbid paying wages in
truck as an outrage on free trade, and Place said of the Ten Hours Bill, ' all
legislative interference must be pernicious. Men must be left to themselves to make
their own bargains,' " Hammond, The Town Labourer 206.
[3] Clapham, op. cit. i 335.   [4] Below 358.   [5] Clapham, op. cit. i 336.
[6] Above 325.   [7] Vol. xi 497-498 ; below 339 seqq.
[8] The Cotton Arbitration Act of 1800, 39, 40 George III c. 90, obliged the masters
to appoint an arbitrator but did not compel the arbitrator to act ; the masters
appointed an arbitrator who had no intention of acting, Hammond, The Skilled
Labourer 63 ; the amending Act of 1803, 44 George III c. 86, which cured this
defect, was " practically inoperative," ibid 68.

arbitration on the proposal of an employer to reduce their wages on the ground that this was an attempt to get them to fix wages.[1] As Lord Amulree says,[2]

The fact was that, forbidden to combine to present a case in concert, the workman could profit but little by any system of arbitration . . . the notion of giving arbitration as a set off against the combination laws was like giving a man a bicycle to make up for the loss of his legs.

Nor was the Arbitration Act of 1824 any more successful. We shall see that the workers objected to magistrates as arbitrators— there was a suggestion of criminality about appearances before magistrates ; and that the manner in which the magistrates applied the Combination Acts of 1825 made them suspicious of men who were too closely connected with the employers.[3] Naturally the workmen lost all confidence in the method provided by the Legislature for the settlement of industrial disputes. We shall now see that it was this failure of the Legislature to regulate fairly the relations between employers and workmen and to provide a workable machinery for disputes between them which is the cause for the very remarkable and very unfortunate development during this period of the law relating to industrial combinations.

(ii) *Industrial Combinations*

After the passing of the Acts of 1799 and 1800[4] industrial combinations were illegal both by statute and by the common law. We have seen that all these combinations whether of employers or workmen were made illegal by the Combination Act of 1800 ; and we have seen that at common law all combinations for illegal purposes, and all combinations which interfered with the freedom of trade, were indictable conspiracies.[5] Though the common law principle that combinations which interfered with the freedom of trade as regulated by the law were indictable conspiracies originated at, and was adapted to, a period when the state undertook so to regulate trade that fair wages, fair prices, and good quality in manufactured articles were secured ; and though it was ill adapted to a period when the attempt to secure these objects had, to a large extent, been abandoned ;[6] it still survived, and was used, in conjunction with the Combination Act, to suppress these combinations.[7] Though neither the Act nor the common law succeeded in suppressing these combinations,[8] both the Act and the common law worked very unfairly. In practice employers who combined, though their actions were

---

[1] 44 George III c. 63-64 ; Amulree, op. cit. 30-33.
[2] Op. cit. 44.
[3] Vol. xiv.
[4] Vol. xi 496-498.
[5] Ibid 477-484.
[6] Ibid 484-485.
[7] Below 342 seqq.
[8] Below 342.

illegal, were never prosecuted,[1] but the law was frequently set in motion to suppress combinations of men[2]—with the result that, so far as the law could do, the men were prevented from using the only weapon left to them to secure a fair wage. The injustice which resulted from the law, and from the way in which it was administered, naturally attracted the attention of the law reformers of Bentham's school, and of the economists. It was obvious that it could not be justified on Bentham's principles, and still less on the *laissez faire* principles of the economists.

According to Bentham's principles, all laws which fettered a person's freedom of action produced some evil, and could only be justified if they made for the greater happiness of the greater number of citizens. The evil which accompanied all restraint must be weighed against the good resulting from that restraint.[3] Tried by this test it was clear that the Combination Act and the common law as to conspiracy were unjust laws, because, in practice, they prevented the workmen— the greater number—from taking the only effective means at their disposal for securing a fair wage ; and it was an additional objection to the law of conspiracy that its vagueness gave the judges power to punish anyone for acts which they disliked.[4] Nor could these laws be justified on the principles of the economists. If the principle of *laissez faire*, upon which the abandonment of many of the old restrictions on industry was justified, was the right principle, it was clearly illogical and unjust to place obstacles in the way of employers and workmen who wished to combine to take measures to protect their interests. Therefore both upon the principle of utility as applied by Bentham to test the justice of a law, and upon the principles of the economists, both the Combination Act and the common law of conspiracy stood condemned.

But in fact this problem did not admit of so simple a solution. Both Bentham and the economists regarded it from a too purely individualistic point of view. Bentham regarded the good and evil flowing from any given act solely from the point of view of its effects upon a specific individual or upon a definite or indefinite number of individuals who might be affected by the act ; and, according to the results of his calculus of pains and pleasures, he pronounced as to the need for legislation, and, if legislation were necessary, what its contents should be.[5] He denied the existence of any difference between acts done by a single individual and a number of individuals acting in concert,[6] and therefore ignored

---

[1] Below 342.   [2] Below 343.   [3] Above 32.
[4] Bentham, Works ii 126.   [5] Above 68, 69.
[6] " In regard to any act that has been dealt with as criminal, the *species* of the act is one thing : *the number of the persons* co-operating in the performance of it, is another and widely different thing. Manifestly, not to any one species of act

the fact that the latter class of Acts might be far more dangerous to the community than the former. The economists were equally oblivious of this difference.

A statement somewhere to be found in Bagehot's works, that every treatise on political economy which he had read in his youth began with the supposition that two men were cast on an uninhabited island, means, in reality, that economical doctrines were the inferences drawn from the way in which the supposed " economical man " would act, if he and others were left each of them free to pursue his own interests. Economics were based on individualism.[1]

Both Bentham and the economists therefore forgot or were ignorant of the truth stated by Burke that " liberty when men act in bodies is power " [2]—a truth which forms the rationale of the crime of conspiracy.[3] They were therefore unable to see the real nature of the problem, which is raised by the question of combinations—industrial or otherwise. That problem is clearly stated by Dicey as follows :[4]

In almost every country some forms of association force upon public attention the practical difficulty of so regulating the right of association that its exercise may neither trench upon each citizen's individual freedom nor shake the supreme authority of the State. The problem to be solved, either as a matter of theory or as a matter of practical necessity, is at bottom always and everywhere the same. How can the right of combined action be curtailed without depriving individual liberty of half its value ; how can it be left unrestricted without destroying either the liberty of individual citizens, or the power of the Government ?

It was the failure both of Bentham and the economists, and of their opponents, to realize the true nature of the problem involved, which accounts for the very unsatisfactory character of the legislation on this topic during this period, and for the confused state of the law which resulted from it for nearly fifty years after.

We shall see that, under the influence of Bentham and the economists, both the Combination Act and the common law rules as to conspiracies, so far as they applied to the formation and legal activities of industrial combinations, were repealed in 1824.[5] Therefore a large liberty to combine was allowed. But the results of this liberty to combine were so disastrous that, in the following year, the Act of 1824 was repealed by an Act which gave a very restricted right of combination, and restored the unsatisfactory common law rules as to conspiracy.[6] The result was that, though

exclusively, but to every species of act whatsoever, is the circumstance of *number*, in this way applicable. . . What can be more inconsistent with clear conception— what can be more amply productive of confusion—than the manufacturing a name for a particular species of offence, out of a circumstance equally apt to have place in every species of offence," Bentham, Works v 248.

[1] Dicey, Law and Opinion 410. [2] French Revolution 9.
[3] Vol. viii 382-383. [4] Law and Opinion 465-466.
[5] Below 346. [6] Below 348.

combinations of employers and workmen got a limited right to combine, and though their members were no longer criminally liable so long as their acts came within the permission given by the Act of 1825, trade unions were technically " at best non-lawful "[1] societies because their objects were in restraint of trade.[2] The law, therefore, instead of recognizing and defining the legal position of these Unions, left them in a most unsatisfactory position. Their legality was not recognized ; and they were given no certain guide as to what acts were and what were not legal ; for, as we have seen, the common law of conspiracy, which had grown up in an age when industrial conditions and industrial policy was wholly different from the conditions prevailing in the nineteenth century, was incapable of settling satisfactorily the difficult question of the conditions upon which it was expedient for the state to permit the existence of these industrial combinations, and the limitations which it ought to impose on their activities.[3]

I shall deal with the history of this topic under the following two heads : (a) the effects of the Combination Act of 1800 and the common law of conspiracy ; and (b) the legislation of 1824 and 1825 and its effects.

(a) The effects of the Combination Act of 1800 and the common law of conspiracy

The Act of 1800 did not succeed in suppressing combinations either of employers or workmen.[4] In the salt trade and amongst the London brewers there were committees of employers to fix prices.[5] There were shipowners' societies amongst the Thames owners and at Newcastle ;[6] and at Newcastle there was the association for the limitation of the vend i.e. the mining and sale of coal from the Tyne and Wear.[7] There were also combinations amongst the iron masters.[8] Similarly, the combinations of men in the older trades continued to exist. There were unions amongst the engineers, the paper makers, the tailors, the carpenters, the plumbers, and the hatters.[9] In some cases friendly societies and other associations could be utilized for trade union activities[10]— in 1794 Place reorganized the breeches makers trade club as a Tontine Sick Club to circumvent the law.[11] There were strong unions amongst the sawyers and shipwrights, and amongst

---

[1] Dicey, Law and Opinion 194.   [2] Vol. xi 481-482 ; below 350.
[3] Vol. xi 485 ; below 350.
[4] Webb, History of Trade Unionism 64, 74-77 ; Clapham, An Economic History of Great Britain i 205.
[5] Clapham, op. cit. i 200-201.   [6] Ibid 201-202.
[7] Ibid 202-203 ; vol. xi 487.   [8] Ibid 204.
[9] Ibid 207-209.   [10] Ibid 210-212.
[11] Graham Wallas, Life of Francis Place 19.

the London coopers.[1] And against these associations the government hesitated to take action. Dr. Clapham says :[2]

A single episode illuminates the realities of the situation. One of the strongest, most widespread, and it would seem most high-handed of the eighteenth century trade clubs was that of the journeymen wool combers. It had been illegal since the reign of George II. In 1812—just mid-way in the life of the Combination Acts—the Home Office was informed that the wool combers' union meant to hold a congress at Coventry. The Law Officers of the Crown were asked to advise as to a prosecution. They replied : " These combinations are mischievous and dangerous, but it is very difficult to know how to deal with them." And so nothing was done, even though the combers were said to be mostly dissenters suspected of republicanism.

On the other hand the Act was so used that it helped to prevent the growth of unions in the new textile industries. Two instances given by the Webbs show the harsh and even illegal use which was made of the Act, and of the law of conspiracy.

In 1818 certain Bolton mill owners suggested to the operative weavers that they should concert together to leave the employment of those who paid below the current rate. Acting on this hint a meeting of forty delegates took place, at which it was resolved to ask for the advance agreed to by the good employers. A fortnight later the president and the two secretaries were arrested, convicted of conspiracy, and imprisoned for one and two years respectively, although their employers gave evidence on the prisoners' behalf to the effect that they had themselves requested the men to attend the meeting, and had approved the resolutions passed. In the following year fifteen cotton spinners of Manchester, who had met " to receive contributions to bury their dead," under " Articles " sanctioned by Quarter Sessions in 1795, were seized in the committee room by the police, and committed to trial for conspiracy, bail being refused. After three or four months imprisonment, they were brought to trial. . . . The enrolment of their club as a friendly society availed little. It was urged in court that " all societies, whether benefit societies or otherwise, were only cloaks for the people of England to conspire against the State," and most of the defendants were sentenced to varying terms of imprisonment.[3]

In fact the workers in these new industries were too poor and too oppressed to combine. " Without a common standard, a common tradition, or mutual confidence, the workers in the new mills were helpless against their masters " ;[4] and because they had no unions or associations which could keep up an organized resistance to the masters' demands, we get " the alternation of outbursts of machine breaking and outrages, with intervals of abject submission and reckless competition with each other for employment." [5] What organizations there were were driven underground

---

[1] Clapham, op. cit. i 212-213.   [2] Ibid 205.
[3] History of Trade Unionism 81-82.   [4] Ibid 87.   [5] Ibid.

and often indulged in seditious and criminal activities—as in the case of the Luddite riots of 1811-12.[1]

But, in spite of the difficulties caused by the Combination Act and other legislation of this period, there is evidence of a " growing sense of solidarity " [2] amongst the workers. Since the Legislature had refused to intervene to secure a living wage, the workmen were obliged to take measures to protect themselves ; and naturally the fact that they were engaged in a common struggle for a common object became more and more apparent. In spite of the law against corresponding societies,[3] the workers in a particular trade all over England were sometimes affiliated, and were thus able to take concerted action.[4] One instance is the action of the Liverpool rope-makers in 1823.

When a certain firm attempted to put labourers to the work, the local society of rope-spinners informed it that this was " contrary to the regulations of the trade," and withdrew all their members. The employers, failing to get men in Liverpool, sent to Hull and Newcastle, but found that the Rope-spinners' Society had already apprised the local trade clubs at those towns. The firm then imported blacklegs from Glasgow, who were met on arrival by the local unionists, inveigled to a " trade club house," and alternately threatened or cajoled out of their engagements. Finally the head of the firm went to London to purchase yarn ; but the London workmen, finding that the yarn was for a " struck shop," refused to complete the order. The last resource of the employers was an indictment at the Sessions for combination, but a Liverpool jury, in the teeth of the evidence and the judge's summing up, gave a verdict of acquittal.[5]

And different trades sometimes supported one another in resistance to the employers. " The Home Secretary was informed in 1823 that a combination of cotton spinners at Bolton, whose books had been seized, had received donations, not only from twenty-eight cotton spinners' committees in as many Lancashire towns, but also from fourteen other trades, from coal miners to butchers." [6]

The economic depression which followed the close of the war was marked by a cut-throat competition amongst employers, and constant reductions in wages, which were reduced so low that it was necessary to supplement them from the poor rates.[7] The

[1] For these riots, see above 192, 193.
[2] Webb, History of Trade Unionism 90.   [3] Above 165-167.
[4] " The various federal organizations of Curriers, Hatters, Calico-printers, Woolcombers, Woolstaplers, and other handicraftsmen kept up constant correspondence on trade matters, and raised money for common trade purposes. In some cases there existed an elaborate national organization with geographical districts and annual delegate meetings, like that of the Calico-printers who were arrested by the Bolton constables in 1818," Webb, op. cit. 90.
[5] Ibid 91.   [6] Ibid 91-92.
[7] Ibid 94 ; Clapham, op. cit. i 362 ; but much less was spent in this way than on the agricultural labourers, ibid 364-365.

result was strikes, and a political agitation which was suppressed by the Six Acts.[1] A few years before this period the movement for the repeal of the Combination Act had begun. Francis Place, a former journeyman who had become a master tailor, had seen at close quarters the manner in which the existing law oppressed the workers. Though he had become an employer, " he never forgot what he had suffered as a black listed and starving journeyman breeches maker, or while in constant danger of arrest as the underpaid secretary of the carpenters and plumbers trade clubs." [2] As a disciple of Bentham and James Mill he was a radical, an individualist, and an economist of the *laissez faire* school, so that he easily came to the conclusion that the best way to end this oppression was to work for a repeal of the Combination Act.

In 1810 Place had helped to defeat a proposal, which the master tailors had made to Parliament, to strengthen the Combination Act of 1800.[3] But he found no support for his views that the Act ought to be repealed, even amongst the workmen ; for they regarded it as a utopian scheme.[4] In 1814, he tells us, he set to work to alter this state of mind. He carefully studied the details of all trade disputes, in some cases he intervened as a mediator, and he instructed the public by articles in the papers. In 1818 he made use of a weekly paper—*The Gorgon*—which he and Bentham subsidised, to forward the cause.[5] In these ways Place made converts to his views. His most important convert was Joseph Hume, the hardworking leader of the radical party whom Disraeli admired,[6] who became his Parliamentary mouthpiece. Another convert who was almost as important was the economist McCulloch who in 1823 published an article in the *Edinburgh Review*, which converted many to Place's views.

In 1819 Place thought the matter would come before Parliament in the next session.[7] But it was not till 1824, and after many difficulties had been surmounted, that Hume got Huskisson to consent to appoint a committee, of which Hume was chairman, to consider the laws against the emigration of artisans and the export of machinery, and the combination laws.[8] Though Place was not allowed to attend the committee as Hume's assistant, he in effect managed the proceedings through Hume, prepared the evidence against the combination laws, coached the witnesses, and wrote

---

[1] Above 207-211.   [2] Graham Wallas, Life of Francis Place 199.
[3] Ibid 201-202.   [4] Ibid 203.   [5] Ibid 203-205.
[6] " Future Parliaments will do justice to the eminent services of this remarkable man, still the most hardworking member of the House, of which he is now the father. His labours on public committees will often be referred to hereafter, and then perhaps it will be remembered that, during a career of forty years, and often under circumstances of great provocation, he never once lost his temper," Life of Bentinck 9.
[7] Graham Wallas, op. cit. 205.   [8] Ibid 207-212.

comments on the evidence.[1] He persuaded Hume to induce the committee not to present a regular report, but to assent to resolutions which it laid before the House. Then he and Hume revised the bills drawn by a barrister employed by the attorney-general to give effect to the resolutions.[2] The supporters of the bills were persuaded not to speak on them, with the result that " they passed the House of Commons almost without the notice of members within or newspapers without." [3] Similar tactics were used when the bills came before the Lords.[4] The result was that three bills —the first to repeal the combination laws, the second to consolidate and amend the laws relating to the settlement of industrial disputes by arbitration, and the third to repeal the laws preventing the emigration of artisans[5]—passed almost in silence. With the second and third of these statutes I have already dealt.[6] We must now consider the provisions of the first.

(b) The legislation of 1824 and 1825 and its effects

The Act of 1824[7] began by repealing in whole or in part thirty-five Acts, from 33 Edward I St. 1 to 57 George III c. 122, and all other laws, statutes, and enactments relative to combinations to obtain increases or decreases in wages or decreases or increases in hours of labour, or relative to the regulation or control of the management of business, or relative " to obliging workmen not hired to enter into work." [8] It then provided that workmen or other persons

who shall enter into any combination to obtain an advance, or to fix the rate of wages, or to lessen or alter the hours or duration of the time of working or to decrease the quantity of work or to induce another to depart from his service before the end of the time or term for which he is hired, or to quit or return his work before the same shall be finished, or not being hired, to refuse to enter into any work or employment, or to regulate the mode of carrying on any manufacture, trade, or business, or the management thereof, shall not therefore be subject or liable to any indictment or prosecution for conspiracy, or to any other criminal information or punishment whatever, under the common or statute law.[9]

Masters were given a similar liberty to combine.[10] But if any person by violence or threats of violence to person or property wilfully or maliciously attempted to effect the objects for which a combination was allowed, he was to be liable to imprisonment with hard labour for any time not exceeding two months ;[11] and the same punishment was provided for those who combined to use

---

[1] Graham Wallas, op. cit. 212-214.   [2] Ibid 214-216.
[3] Ibid 216.   [4] Ibid.   [5] 5 George IV cc. 95-97.
[6] Above 227, 327, 336.   [7] 5 George IV c. 95.   [8] § 1.
[9] § 2.   [10] § 3.   [11] § 5.

violence and threats to effect these objects.[1] No appeal was allowed against a conviction.[2] Justices who were masters, or the father or son of a master in any trade or manufacture, were not to try offences under the Act.[3] Offenders could be compelled to give evidence, but, if so compelled, they could not be prosecuted.[4]

The extraordinarily large number of the purposes to effect which persons could combine and the character of some of those purposes is remarkable. They could even combine to commit what is now recognized as a tort, inducement to break a contract.[5] And since the common rules as to conspiracy were repealed with respect to these combinations, a combination for this purpose was not indictable as a conspiracy.[6] It was only if an individual or a combination of individuals used violence or threats or intimidation that they were punishable. These provisions embody the view held by Bentham and the economists that to restrict the right of combination is an unjustifiable infringement of individual liberty.[7] But both Bentham and the economists had a very limited knowledge of human nature. Bentham envisaged a set of middle class intelligent persons who judicially weighed the consequences of their actions, and the effect of laws, in terms of pains and pleasures. The economists envisaged the workings of the mind of a set of economic men. They did not remember that an unrestricted right to combine might be fatal to individual liberty and might even menace the authority of the state.[8] It was only to be expected that Place, whose intellectual outlook was dominated by Bentham and the economists, should have been wholly mistaken as to the effects of the Act of 1824. In 1825 he wrote :[9]

Combinations will soon cease to exist. Men have been kept together for long periods only by the oppression of the laws ; these being repealed, combinations will lose the matter which cements them into masses, and they will fall to pieces. All will be as orderly as even a Quaker could desire. He knows nothing of the working people who can suppose that, when left at liberty to act for themselves, without being driven into permanent associations by the oppression of the laws, they will continue to contribute money for distant and doubtful experiments. . . . If let alone combinations, excepting now and then, and for particular purposes, under peculiar circumstances, will cease to exist.

In fact the effect of the repeal of the combination laws had a precisely contrary effect. As was said by Nassau Senior in 1831,

---

[1] § 6 ; they were also to be liable for any specific offences committed in carrying out their object, but a conviction under this section was to exempt them from prosecution under any other law or statute, ibid.

[2] § 12. [3] § 8. [4] § 10.

[5] It was not till the decision in Lumley v. Gye (1853) 2 E and B 216 that this tort clearly emerged, vol iv 384-385.

[6] Vol. xi 481-482. [7] Above 32, 340. [8] Above 341.

[9] Graham Wallas, Life of Francis Place 217-218.

the repeal seemed to the workmen to concede their moral right
to combine ; [1] and, in spite of the warnings of Place, they
made haste to exercise their right. There was an epidemic of
strikes, with the result that the employers lost no time in
petitioning Parliament for the repeal of the Act of 1824,[2] and
the enactment of still more drastic legislation to put a stop to
all combinations of workmen. They wished, Place says, for an
Act to prevent workmen subscribing for any purpose whatever
without the consent of a local magistrate, who was to be treasurer
of the fund.[3]

On March 29 Huskisson moved for a committee to enquire into
the working of the Act of 1824.[4] The committee was appointed,
and again Place set to work through Hume, who was on the
committee, to present the case against a repeal of the Act of 1824
and the enactment of the legislation wished for by the employers.[5]
In spite of difficulties thrown in his way by the committee, Place
brought up his witnesses, and Hume insisted on at least some of
them being heard.[6] Place says :[7]

My time was wholly occupied from the day Mr. Huskisson made his
speech till some time after the passing of the Act. I examined a vast
number of persons ; made digests and briefs for Mr. Hume ; wrote
petitions to the House and to the Committee ; many letters to Mr.
Wallace, the chairman ; and to many other persons, all as the agent
of the men, and for their adoption. No one thing that could be done was
omitted, every possible advantage was taken of even the most minute
circumstance, and it was by these and Mr. Hume's extraordinary
exertions that the intentions of Mr. Huskisson and Mr. Peel were at
length so completely defeated, and the bill called Mr. Wallace's bill was
passed.

That bill was the Act of 1825.[8] Both in the House and in
committee its provisions were acrimoniously debated,[9] and, says
Place, " Mr. Denman and Mr. John Williams, whose great legal
knowledge was respected, did good service in showing that the
repeal of the common law was proper " [10]—though, as we shall
see, they failed to persuade the House to agree to this proposition.[11]
In the House of Lords Place got Lord Rosslyn [12] to propose several

[1] Cited by Graham Wallas, op. cit. 218.
[2] Ibid 218-224.
[3] Graham Wallas, op. cit. 223 ; Place says that he convinced Copley, the
attorney-general, of the impossibility of such an enactment, ibid 229.
[4] Ibid 224.   [5] Ibid 227-228.
[6] Ibid 230-232.   [7] Ibid 232-233.
[8] 6 George IV c. 129.
[9] Graham Wallas, op. cit. 235-238
[10] Ibid 235-236 ; for John Williams see above 290-292 ; for Denman see
above 209, 219, 220 ; below 427, 450, 524, 616, 617, 652.
[11] Below 349, 350.
[12] Better known as Lord Loughborough, vol. xii 569-576 ; below 578, 579, 580.

amendments, one of which gave convicted persons the right of appeal to quarter sessions.[1]

The main provisions of the Act of 1825 were[2] as follows: After repealing the Act of 1824 and the series of Acts relating to combinations repealed by that Act and all other Acts relating to combinations,[3] it penalized the use of violence, threats or intimidation to compel a workman to depart from his work; or to prevent a workman from getting employment; or to force him to join a club or association, to contribute to its funds, or to pay any fines; or to force any manufacturer to alter the mode of conducting his business. Anyone found guilty of these offences could be imprisoned with hard labour for a period not exceeding three months.[4] Then, in the form of proviso, the following limited right of combination was given to the men:[5]

Provided always . . . that this Act shall not extend to subject any persons to punishment, who shall meet together for the sole purpose of consulting upon and determining the rate of wages or prices, which the persons present at such meeting or any of them, shall require or demand for his or their work, or the hours or time for which he or they shall work in any manufacture, trade, or business, or who shall enter into any agreement, verbal or written, among themselves, for the purpose of fixing the rate of wages or prices which the parties entering into such agreement, or any of them, shall require or demand for his or their work, or the hours of time for which he or they will work, in any manufacture, trade, or business; and that persons so meeting for the purposes aforesaid or entering into any such agreement as aforesaid, shall not be liable to any prosecution or penalty for so doing; any law or statute to the contrary notwithstanding.

There was a similar proviso for combinations of masters.[6] There was the same provision as in the Act of 1824 as to the compulsion of offenders to give evidence;[7] and justices who were masters in the trade in which it was alleged that an offence had been committed were disabled from hearing these cases.[8] But a convicted person was allowed to appeal to quarter sessions whose decision was to be final.[9]

Place says that the Act of 1825 differed little from the Act of 1824.[10] This is not true. Though the two Acts have some common features, they are in many important respects very different. The

---

[1] Graham Wallas, op. cit. 239; Place says that Rosslyn objected to the retention of the common law of conspiracy in relation to combinations, and that Eldon said that "such proceedings were not contemplated by the Act, and would not be permitted," ibid; the first of these propositions was clearly untrue, below 350, and the second was a prophecy which proved to be false, below 350, 351.

[2] 6 George IV c. 129.   [3] §§ 1 and 2.   [4] § 3.

[5] § 4.   [6] § 5.   [7] § 6.

[8] § 13; this was a somewhat more limited disability than that imposed in the Act of 1824, above 347.   [9] § 12.

[10] Graham Wallas, op. cit. 238; for a clear analysis of the resemblances of and the differences between the two Acts see Dicey, Law and Opinion 190-194.

earlier Act represents the view of the Benthamites and economists which advocated a complete freedom to combine : the later Act represented the views of those who saw that a complete freedom to combine was a menace both to the freedom of the individual and to the peace of the state.[1]

The Acts have two common features. Both repealed all the former statutes directed against combinations ; and both penalized violence, threats, and intimidation. But the features in which they differed are much more important. In the earlier Act the right to combine was given in very wide terms : in the later Act it was a carefully restricted right.[2] In the earlier Act the common law of conspiracy was repealed with respect to the combinations permitted by it : in the later Act it was retained.[3] The result, as Dicey says,[4] was that " any trade combination was a conspiracy unless it fell within the limited right of combination given by the Act of 1825." It followed from this that

A strike, though not necessarily a conspiracy, certainly might be so, and a trade union, as being a combination in restraint of trade, was at best a non-lawful society, i.e. a society which, though membership in it was not a crime, yet could not claim the protection of the law.[5]

The mistake made by the Legislature—a mistake which was perhaps natural in the condition of industrial unrest which had been caused by the Act of 1824—was in not recognizing and defining the legal position of combinations, and in not laying down clear rules as to the conditions in which they could be formed and as to the sphere of their activities. If there had been legislation on these lines it would have been much easier to control these combinations, and to protect both individuals and the state from the dangers inherent in them. Instead, the Legislature adopted the policy of giving a very limited right to combine, of refusing to give a legal status to these combinations, and of leaving their members exposed to the penalties provided by the Act and to the unsatisfactory law of conspiracy, if they overstepped the boundaries of the very limited right of combination given by the Act. By taking this course the Legislature precluded itself from taking a broad view as to conditions in which a right of combination should be allowed, and, on these lines, of settling the legal position of these combinations and the legitimate sphere of their activities.

Place said of the old combination laws that

they induced workmen to break and disregard the laws. . . . They made them hate their employers with a rancour which nothing else could have

---

[1] Dicey, Law and Opinion 194-200. [2] Above 349.
[3] Above 349. [4] Law and Opinion 194.
[5] Ibid ; see Hilton v. Eckersley (1855) 6 E. and B. 47, and vol. xi 481-482 ; Hornby v. Close (1867) L.R. 2 Q.B. 153 ; Farrer v. Close (1869) L.R. 4 Q.B. 602.

produced. And they made them hate those of their own class who refused to join them, to such an extent as cordially to seek to do them mischief.[1]

We shall see in the following chapter that the later history of these industrial combinations shows that the failure of the Legislature to solve on the right lines the problems raised by their existence helped to perpetuate many of the evils which had flowed from the old combination laws.[2] Not much use was made of the machinery provided in 1824 for the settlement by arbitration of industrial disputes.[3] Both parties preferred to organize themselves in unions and to fight out their battles by means of strikes and lockouts. It may be said therefore, that contrary to Place's view, the Act of 1825 did hardly anything to stop those industrial disputes which the new economic ideas and the new organization of industry had made inevitable.

(2) *The agricultural industry*

The large number of statutes passed to regulate different aspects of the agricultural industry show that, all through this period, the policy pursued by the state was substantially similar to the policy which it had pursued in the preceding periods.[4] Since the industry was tending more and more to be organized on a capitalistic basis, the small farmer tended more and more to disappear ;[5] and this process was helped by the continued progress of inclosure.[6] The policy of the corn laws, which was directed to ensuring an adequate supply of home grown food by protecting the farmer, was continued—though the means taken to accomplish this result were varied from time to time.[7] But in times of scarcity special measures were taken which sometimes took the form of a prohibition of the use of wheat for certain purposes, e.g. the distillation of spirits or the making of starch,[8] and sometimes of powers given to the Crown to adopt measures varying or dispensing with the corn laws and other statutes.[9]

In the case of the agricultural, as in the case of other branches of industry, the new conditions brought about by the progress of the industrial revolution demanded a revision of the main feature of this policy—the corn laws. Though that policy was adhered to all through this period, and though the need

---

[1] Graham Wallas, op. cit. 239.   [2] Below, vol. xiv.
[3] 5 George IV c. 96 ; above 227, 336, 346.
[4] For this policy see vol. vi 342-346 ; vol. xi 451-452.
[5] Below 353.   [6] Below 352.   [7] Below 354 seqq.
[8] See e.g. 39, 40 George III c.c. 21 and 25.
[9] See e.g. 39 George III c. 87 ; for similar measures in the eighteenth and earlier centuries see vol. xi 451 n. 4.

for ensuring an adequate supply of home grown food prevented even the economists from advocating as a practical measure,[1] and the Legislature from adopting, a completely free trade in corn,[2] the movement towards a freer trade in corn which would lower food prices, and even for a completely free trade, was gathering weight; and there were some signs that the manufacturers were willing to sacrifice some of the protection given to them in order to secure this freer trade.[3] This movement for a freer trade in corn, and the accompanying movement for a freer trade in other things, were the result of the growth of the large new industrial population which must have cheap food if industrial expansion was to continue, and of the consciousness of the manufacturers that this expansion was enabling them to dispense with the protection which they had formerly considered to be necessary. These movements were also entirely in accord with the theories of the economists, who therefore supplied it with a theoretical backing, which made it appear to be not so much of a policy which, in the new industrial conditions, it was wise to pursue, as an application of a set of eternally true economic principles. We can see, therefore, in the controversies which, at the latter part of this period, centred round the corn laws,[4] the beginnings of a movement in favour of free trade which, in the following period, will have large effects on the economic policy pursued by the Legislature.[5]

In relating the history of the legislation as to the agricultural industry I shall say something first of the progress of inclosure, and, secondly, of the corn laws and the growth of the opposition to them.

(i) *The progress of inclosure* [6]

The best evidence of the progress of inclosure is the Inclosure Clauses Act of 1801[7] which, in order to facilitate inclosures, set out provisions usually inserted in Inclosure Acts. It should be observed that section 13 of the Act made some attempt to remedy one of the injustices inflicted on small holders by some of these Acts. We have seen that the shares allotted to some of the smaller holders were so minute, and that the expenses of getting an Act passed and of fencing the shares allotted were so

---

[1] Below 358. [2] Below 358. [3] Below 358.
[4] Below 355 seqq. [5] Below, vol. xiv.
[6] For the inclosure movement in the eighteenth century see vol. xi 453-457.
[7] 41 George III c. 109; what may be called an emergency inclosure Act was passed in the same year, 41 George III c. 30; it provided that an inclosure could be made by an agreement of a majority of shareholders in the common fields, and in default of agreement, that any occupier could enclose his strips in order to grow potatoes, subject to his making compensation to his fellow shareholders.

large, that the shares were valueless.[1] To obviate this objection it was provided that the commissioners could, on the application of the parties interested, order that these small properties could be laid together in a ring fence, and be stocked and held in common, subject to such orders for their enjoyment as the commissioners might make. The progress of inclosure went on throughout the nineteenth century. In 1835 an Act was passed to facilitate the exchange of lands in the common fields;[2] and in 1836 it was provided that such lands should be enclosed if two-thirds in the number and value of the persons having an interest in these lands consented,[3] but lands within a certain distance of London and other large towns could not be enclosed under the Act.[4] We have seen that in 1845 an elaborate Act[5] was passed under which, and its amending Acts,[6] most of the remaining common fields were enclosed, and rights of common which prevented the profitable use of the land were got rid of.

These Inclosure Acts did not eliminate the small holders,[7] but they did materially diminish their number.[8] We shall now see that both this fact, and the fact that the industrial population was increasing by leaps and bounds, had an important effect upon the manner in which the policy of protecting the agricultural interest by means of the corn laws was regarded by the nation. As Professor Barnes has said,[9]

during the greater part of the eighteenth century the landed gentry in Parliament could at least pose as the representatives of the great mass of the English population, the agrarian class; but after 1815 this was no longer possible. . . . Agricultural society was now divided into three main classes : the landlord, the large farmer, and the agricultural labourer who was subsisting in part on poor rates. Many tenant farmers, cottagers, and squatters, when they were not among the fortunate few who became large farmers, or started factories in the north, were reduced to the position of Speenhamland agricultural labourers, or helped to swell the ranks of the proletariat in the new industrial cities.

[1] Vol. xi 455-457.
[2] 4, 5 William IV c. 30 ; for the common field system of cultivation see vol. ii 56-58.
[3] 6, 7 William IV c. 115 ; amended by 3, 4 Victoria c. 31.   [4] § 55.
[5] 8, 9 Victoria c. 118 ; vol. ii 61 ; in 1851 the powers of the enclosure commissioners appointed under this Act as well as those of copyhold and tithe commissioners appointed under certain other Acts, were transferred to commissioners to be appointed under 14, 15 Victoria c. 53.
[6] 9, 10 Victoria c. 74 ; 10, 11 Victoria c. 111 ; 11, 12 Victoria c. 99 ; 12, 13 Victoria c. 83 ; 20, 21 Victoria c. 31 ; 22, 23 Victoria c. 43.
[7] Clapham, An Economic History of Modern Britain i 113-118.
[8] D. G. Barnes, A History of the English Corn Laws chap. vi. I have derived much assistance from this very illuminating work.   I do not wholly agree with Professor Barnes when he says that in 1791 to some extent, and later to a large extent, the landlords and farmers used their political power merely to keep up prices in their own interest ; I think that he has given too little weight to the consideration, which weighed most with Parliament, that it was necessary to give the farmer such a price as would ensure an adequate supply of home grown food, below 358.
[9] Op. cit. 113-114.

For these reasons the landlords and large farmers who profited by the corn laws came to be a small minority of the nation. And so although the landlords and large farmers had done good service to the nation by increasing the production of food, and so enabling it to stand the stress and strain of the Napoleonic wars, and although it was as obviously good policy now as in the past to ensure an adequate supply of home grown food, they were represented as a heartless minority who, in the interests of their own pockets, were starving the nation by the manner in which they kept up the price of food by means of the corn laws. We shall now see that, though these results of inclosure did not secure the repeal of the corn laws during this period, the new industrial conditions were making it clear that some modifications were needed; and that, if they were not modified, an agitation for their repeal was sooner or later inevitable.

(ii) *The corn laws and the growth of the opposition to them*

The Act of 1791[1] was in force at the beginning of this period, but the fact that the following years were years of war and bad harvests prevented its normal operation. The Legislature was concerned mainly with special Acts to deal with the scarcity of foodstuffs, or in giving the Crown power to make provisions to deal with it.[2] But in the first years of the nineteenth century there were a series of good harvests, prices dropped, and the farmers demanded more protection. An Act passed in 1804 gave increased protection, but otherwise adhered to the policy of the 1791 Act.[3] It was justified on the ground that this increased protection was necessary to ensure the farmer a reasonable price, and so to ensure the nation's food supply. As in 1791, so in 1804, it was said that the rise in prices justified this increased protection.[4] The years after 1804 were years of scarcity; and measures similar to those taken in the last decade of the eighteenth century were taken by the government.[5] But in 1813 the tide turned; there was a very large harvest; and prices fell.

From 1792 to 1813 the corn laws had been to a large extent inoperative. Prices had remained so high that import was in effect free. Therefore there was no considerable agitation against them. But the large harvest of 1813 caused, first a demand for a new corn law which would give increased protection, and secondly an agitation against a law which, by giving

---

[1] 31 George III c. 30, amended by 33 George III c. 65, 44 George III c. 109, 45 George III c. 86; for its provisions see vol. xi 458; § 16 of the Act provided that lower duties should be payable on the import of corn from Ireland and the American colonies—a preference which was maintained in all the later Acts, below 358.

[2] Above 351.
[4] Ibid 88.

[3] 44 George III c. 109; Barnes, op. cit. 88-89.
[5] Above 351 nn. 8, 9.

increased protection, would keep up the price of foodstuffs. In 1814 the free export of grain and flour was allowed ;[1] but attempts to give greater protection to the landlords and farmers were defeated.[2] In 1815 the whole matter was considered by a committee of the House of Commons. The report of that committee pointed out that much additional capital had been applied to land, and that much land had been reclaimed and enclosed ; that the expenses of cultivation and rent had doubled in the last twenty years ; and, consequently, in order to ensure an adequate return to the farmer, he must be ensured a price of 80/- a quarter.[3] To effect this object a new corn law was recommended which departed considerably from the former laws. The provisions of the Act[4] based on these recommendations are thus summarized by Professor Barnes :[5]

Foreign corn could be imported and warehoused at all times duty free, and taken out for home consumption when the average prices of the various kinds of grain reached the level at which imports were permitted. Foreign corn then could be imported or taken out of the warehouses without paying any duty whatsoever when the prices were at or above the following : wheat 80/- ; rye peas and beans 53/- ; barley, beer or bigg 40/- ; and oats 27/-. . . . The same conditions of admission were to apply to corn from the British North American colonies, except that the average prices were reduced.

Thus this Act and the Act of 1814 which allowed free export, substituted a new set of provisions for those which had been in force since 1670 and 1689.[6] The Act of 1814 had abolished all duties and bounties on export. The Act of 1815 prohibited all importation up to a certain price ; and, after that price had been reached, it allowed free importation—there were no graded scales of duties as under the older laws. The permission to import grain duty free at any time and deposit it in bonded warehouses was meant to ensure that so soon as corn rose to the price fixed by the Act, an immediate supply would be available.

The Act was carried in spite of bitter opposition both in and out of Parliament, and it caused riots in London.[7] It was supported by some pamphleteers—notably Malthus,[8] and attacked by others—notably Ricardo.[9] Its strongest opponents were the labouring classes and the manufacturers—the former

---

[1] 54 George III c. 69.
[2] Barnes, op. cit. 118-129.
[3] Ibid 130.
[4] 55 George III c. 26.
[5] Op. cit. 139.
[6] Vol. vi 342-343 ; vol. xi 451 n. 3.
[7] Barnes, op. cit. 135-138.
[8] The Grounds of an Opinion on the Policy of Restricting the Importation of Foreign Corn, ibid 130-132.
[9] An Essay on the Influence of a low Price of Corn on the Profits of Stock ; showing the Inexpediency of Restrictions on Importation, ibid 132-133.

because it made bread dear, and the latter because it made labour dear. Their wrath was concentrated on the landlords who, it was alleged, grew rich at the expense of their fellows. But as yet the manufacturers were not in a position to attack the policy of the corn law as bitterly as they attacked it in later years. Many of their manufactures were protected; and the importation of about a hundred and fifty foreign articles was prohibited in order to promote native manufacture.[1] It has been argued that the right policy for the Legislature to pursue was to allow a wholly free trade in corn.[2] This is very questionable. If a native grown food supply was to be ensured, if, as Adam Smith said, "defence was of more importance than opulence,"[3] some protection was needed. But, seeing that the increase in population clearly demanded an increased food supply at cheaper rates, it is arguable that the protection given was excessive. Less protection might have ruined some farmers, it would have put less fertile lands out of cultivation, and it would have diminished rents. But farming would, as the result, have become a less speculative business. The larger supply of cheaper food needed in the new industrial conditions would have been assured, and the less amount of protection given would have been some security that a considerable quantity of the nation's food was home grown.[4]

In 1822 the complaints of the farmers and landlords produced another Act.[5] Its provisions and its effect on the Act of 1815 are thus summarized by Professor Barnes :[6]

Foreign wheat was to be entirely excluded till the price reached 70/-. But at this point importation was not admitted duty free, as it was under the Act of 1815 ; for when the price was between 70/- and 80/-, a duty of 12/- was levied ; when between 80/- and 85/- one of 5/- ; and when above 85/- only 1/-. Corresponding scales of duties were fixed for other kinds of grain. The colonial preference was retained. . . . However this scale of duties did not go into operation till the price of wheat reached 80/-, because that part of the Act of 1815 which forbade the opening of the ports until that price was reached was not repealed by the new law. . . . Still another obstacle was an additional duty of 5/- during the first three months that the ports were open. Thus the duty on wheat for these three months was not 12/- but 17/-.

The farmers and landlords had retained their protection ; but they had failed to increase it ; and the result of the working of the Acts of 1815 and 1822 was to show that, even with such protection as the Legislature was inclined to give, prices and rents could not be permanently kept up to their pre-war levels.[7]

---

[1] Barnes, op. cit. 146-147 ; below 359-362.   [2] Barnes, op. cit. 150.
[3] Wealth of Nations (Cannan's ed.) i 429.
[4] See Cunningham, Growth of English Industry and Commerce iii 729-731.
[5] 3 George IV c. 60.   [6] Op. cit. 174.
[7] Barnes, op. cit. 178-179.

In the years which followed 1822 the growth of the feeling in favour of a freer trade in corn was promoted by the abolition or diminution of a large number of the protective duties on manufactured articles.[1] Both in and out of Parliament there was an agitation for the abolition or lowering of the duties on corn ; and the Petition of the Merchants presented to the House of Commons in 1820 states the case for the full free trade programme—in corn and in all other commodities.[2] " Freedom from restraint," it ran, " is calculated to give the utmost extension to foreign trade, and the best direction to the capital and industry of the country." Duties imposed for revenue purposes there must be ;

but it is against every restrictive regulation of trade not essential to the revenue—against all duties merely protective from foreign competition— and against the excess of such duties as are partly for the purpose of revenue, and partly for that of protection—that the prayer of the present petition is respectfully submitted to the wisdom of Parliament.

Neither in the case of corn nor in the case of other commodities was this free trade programme realized in this period. But it points the way to the programme realized in the following period ; and some landlords were wise enough to advocate, as a concession to the new industrial needs, a smaller fixed duty on corn.[3] One reason which induced some of the more far-seeing landowners to take this attitude was the fact that evidence was accumulating that, in the present conditions of Europe and the colonies, and having regard to present facilities for and the cost of transport, a freer importation of foreign grain was not likely seriously to affect the British farmer.[4]

In these circumstances a downward revision of the tariff was inevitable. Canning's and Huskisson's plan—the plan which Liverpool had worked out before he had been disabled by a stroke of apoplexy—was in some respects a return to the older scheme, in that it proposed a scale of duties varying inversely with the price of corn. Canning proposed a 20/- import duty when corn was at 60/- a quarter. For each shilling the price advanced beyond 60/- there was to be a reduction of 2/- in the duty.[5] This proposal aroused great opposition both in the Commons and the Lords ; and the acceptance by the Lords of the Duke of Wellington's amendment to substitute 66/- for 60/- was fatal to the bill.[6] The loss of the bill necessitated

[1] Below 358, 363, 364.

[2] For the text of this petition see Barnes, op. cit. 182-184.

[3] Barnes, op. cit. 214-215.

[4] Ibid 208-210, based on the reports of William Jacob whom the government had sent on a tour of northern Europe to investigate the possibility of getting supply of grain from thence.

[5] Barnes, op. cit. 193-194.   [6] Ibid 197.

a temporary measure in 1827.[1] After Canning's death a new bill on the same lines was introduced which was passed in 1828.[2] It was supported by Huskisson—though he preferred the earlier bill.[3] The Act repealed the Acts of 1815, 1822, and 1827. When the price of wheat was 62/- a quarter and under 63/- the duty payable was 24/8. As the price rose there was a sliding scale of diminishing duties, and at 73/- a quarter the duty was 1/-. Conversely with each shilling's diminution in the price there was an increase of 1/- in the duty. There were other rates for other cereals ; and preferential rates for colonial produce.

The corn laws thus continued all through this period. Parliament was not shaken in its belief that to ensure a sufficient supply of home grown food some protection was necessary. Even Ricardo did not deny this proposition ;[4] and Huskisson who, as we shall see was a pioneer in the work of persuading Parliament to accept a freer trade in many articles imported and exported,[5] supported the Act of 1828. But the needs of the new industrial population in the new industrial conditions had made it clear that the amount of that protection must be diminished. At the same time the movement in favour of a freer if not of an absolutely free trade was favoured by the economists ; and the industrial expansion of England, and the industrial lead which England was securing over other nations, were causing it to find favour with the manufacturers. Since both the economic theorists and the merchants and manufacturers were beginning to favour it, it was becoming clear that this policy was likely to prevail in the not very distant future. But just as the older view of the need for some protection for the farmer still held its ground, so, as we shall now see, the older views as to the need for some protection for various branches of British trade and industry still prevailed—but with very considerable modifications in the direction of a freer trade.

(3) *The regulation of foreign and colonial trade*

In this, as in earlier periods, the needs of national defence were a paramount consideration with the Legislature. During the greater part of this period Great Britain was at war ; and, when the war was over, the needs of national defence were not forgotten and were not sacrificed to purely economic considerations. But the new groupings of European powers, the new position of the United States, and the new position in the world of trade and commerce which Great Britain was taking as the

---

[1] 7, 8 George IV c. 57. [2] 9 George IV c. 60.
[3] Barnes, op. cit. 200.
[4] Clapham, An Economic History of Modern Britain i 335 ; Barnes, op. cit. 175.
[5] Below 363, 364.

result of the industrial revolution, were the cause of considerable modification in the policy pursued both with regard to colonial and to foreign trade. Though the Navigation Acts were still retained they were in some respects modified ; a large preference was given to colonial goods ; and protective tariffs, though they were still retained, were lowered and simplified. There was an abandonment of the policy of encouraging the export or import of goods by bounties, and the exclusive trading privileges of the commercial companies were abolished. Let us look at the manner in which these movements and tendencies are reflected in the statutes of this period which regulate foreign and colonial trade. I shall consider them under the following heads : (i) national defence ; (ii) the Navigation Acts ; (iii) colonial trade ; (iv) foreign trade ; (v) bounties and the trading privileges of commercial companies.

(i) *National defence*

First, the import of material useful in war was encouraged. Thus in 1806 the importation of masts, yards, bowsprits, and timber fit for naval purposes was admitted duty free from the American colonies ;[1] and in order to get raw material for munitions the restrictions imposed by the Navigation Acts were from time to time relaxed.[2] Secondly, as in the previous period, the fishing industry was encouraged because it furnished a supply of seamen. Thus salt used for curing mackerel or herrings could be imported duty free, and a bounty was given on the export of cured mackerel and herrings ;[3] and Dutch fishermen residing in England were given the same privileges as English fishermen.[4] In 1786 a society had been incorporated for extending the fisheries and improving the sea coasts of Great Britain ;[5] and in 1799 further powers were given to it to give premiums to expert fishermen, and to grant loans for the purchase of vessels.[6] Though the practice of encouraging export by bounties was being given up,[7] the bounty on the export of cured fish lasted till nearly the end of this period.[8] The whale fishery was encouraged in several ways. Premiums were given to a certain number of ships engaged in the southern whale fisheries ;[9] and bounties

---

[1] 44 George III c. 117.
[2] E.g. 43 George III c.c. 64, 153 ; 46 George III c. 74.
[3] 35 George III c. 54 ; 48 George III c. 110; for earlier Acts see vol. xi 404 n. 6.
[4] 35 George III c. 56. [5] 26 George III c. 106.
[6] 39 George III c. 100. [7] Below 364, 365.
[8] 5 George IV c. 64 ; 7 George IV c. 34 ; Clapham, An Economic History of Modern Britain i 327.
[9] 35 George III c. 92 ; 38 George III c. 57 ; 48 George III c. 124 ; 51 George III c. 34 ; 59 George III c. 113.

were granted to encourage the Greenland whale fisheries[1] and the Newfoundland[2] fisheries. Persons employed in the fishing industry were, under certain conditions, not to be liable to be impressed for the navy.[3]

Measures to further the cause of national defence less directly connected with trade, are those which gave power to the justices to impress idle and able-bodied persons for the navy;[4] and those which, to encourage volunteers for the navy, gave bounties and prize money for enemy ships taken or destroyed.[5] In 1823, in order to keep up the number of qualified seamen, ship-owners were required to take a number of apprentices pro-portioned to the tonnage of their ships.[6] Though Ricardo and the straiter economists objected to the law, they found few supporters.[7] As Dr. Clapham says, " the shipowners, for whom Huskisson had retained most of what they valued in the navi-gation code, were thus still saddled—not unwillingly, it is true —with a compensating liability to the state."[8] Several Acts gave the Crown power to take particular pieces of land for defence purposes;[9] and other Acts gave it power to take any land required for such purposes,[10] or for the erection of signal and telegraph stations.[11] They were the precursors of the more general Defence of the Realm Act passed in 1842.[12]

(ii) *The Navigation Acts*

In an earlier volume I have given some account of the pro-visions, objects, and effects of these Acts.[13] They were from time to time slightly amended to meet the needs of traders or the exigencies of war.[14] But it was not till 1797 that any substantial modification in them was made. In that year, in pursuance of a treaty with the United States, it was made lawful to import into Great Britain from the United States in ships built there and owned by United States citizens.[15] A series of Acts drawn by Thomas Wallace in 1822 effected further modifications,[16] which were reproduced in 1825 in a consolidated and restated Navigation Act,[17] which was one of the series of Acts which restated the customs code of Great Britain.[18]

[1] 42 George III c. 22.   [2] 46 George III c. 103.
[3] 50 George III c. 108.   [4] 35 George III c. 34.
[5] 43 George III c. 140 ; 45 George III c. 72.
[6] 4 George IV c. 25.   [7] Clapham, op. cit. i 337.
[8] Ibid.   [9] 34 George III c. 76 ; 56 George III c. 74.
[10] 43 George III c. 55 ; 44 George III c. 95.
[11] 55 George III c. 128.   [12] 5, 6 Victoria c. 94.
[13] Vol. xi 84-88, 407-411.
[14] 33 George III c. 50 ; 59 George III c. 55 ; above 175, 188, 226, 227.
[15] 37 George III c. 97 § 1.
[16] 3 George IV cc. 41-45 ; Clapham, An Economic History of Modern Britain i 331.
    [17] 6 George IV c. 109.   [18] Above 262.

The principal modifications of the older law contained in the Act of 1825 were as follows : Certain enumerated goods, the produce of Europe, could be imported not only in British ships and in ships of the country where the goods were produced, but also in ships of the country from which they were imported ; and the prohibition on import into Great Britain was only in respect of goods which were to be " used therein."[1]

What once had been illegal goods might now be warehoused in Great Britain to be re-exported, for the benefit of her entrepôt trade, and the attempt . . . to determine whether the goods which a foreign ship brought from one of its own home ports were really the produce of that country was abandoned, for Europe.[2]

In the case of non-European goods, they must be imported into Great Britain to be used " therein," either in British ships or in ships of the country where the goods were produced *and* from which they were imported.[3] This clause benefited chiefly the United States, for, as Dr. Clapham has said,[4] " China tea was not likely to come in junks, nor ivory in Zanzibar dhows." With certain exceptions, the prohibition of importing these non-European goods from European ports was retained,[5] in order " to give to the British ship the long instead of the short voyage."[6] The coasting trade and the carrying trade were still reserved for British ships.[7] On the other hand, the colonies were given a greater freedom to export their own commodities to any country they pleased—the list of enumerated products[8] which they could not export except to another colony or to Great Britain was dropped. We shall see, however, that some restrictions were still imposed by the Acts of 1825[9] which was passed to regulate the trade of British possessions abroad ; and that Great Britain secured the greater part of the produce of the colonies, and, conversely, the colonies were induced to buy manufactured goods from Great Britain, by means of preferential tariffs.[10]

The Acts which gave the Crown power to make reciprocity treaties with foreign states[11] were not intended to interfere with the operation of the Navigation Acts. These treaties merely gave the same treatment, in respect of customs duties, to goods legally shipped in foreign bottoms as was accorded to those shipped in British bottoms.[12] Thus it may be said that, during the whole of this period, the principles underlying the Navigation Acts remained. It was still remembered that defence

---

[1] § 2.   [2] Clapham, op. cit. i 331.   [3] § 4.
[4] Clapham, op. cit. i 331.   [5] § 3.   [6] Clapham, op. cit. i 331.
[7] §§ 5-10.   [8] Vol. xi. 85-86.
[9] 6 George IV c. 114 ; below 362.   [10] Below 362.
[11] 4 George IV c. 77 ; 5 George IV c. 1.   [12] Clapham, op. cit. i 333-334.

was of more importance than opulence. We shall now see that the same thing can be said of the laws regulating colonial trade, and, to a less degree, of the laws regulating foreign trade.

(iii) *Colonial trade*

Those parts of the Navigation Acts which regulated colonial trade—the Acts of Trade—attempted as we have seen, to regulate that trade in such a way that it was beneficial both to Great Britain and the colonies.[1] Though the foreign trade of the colonies was subjected by these Acts to restrictions, though they could only export certain of their products to Great Britain,[2] though their manufactures were discouraged or prohibited,[3] yet there were countervailing advantages. Bounties were given on the import of some of their products;[4] their ships had the privileges given to British ships by the Navigation Acts;[5] and their products as a general rule paid a smaller import duty.[6] During this period this mode of organizing colonial trade was retained in its broad outlines, but it was modified by the legislation of the second decade of the nineteenth century.

Thus very many colonial products still paid a smaller import duty than the same foreign products—corn,[7] tea, coffee, sugar, timber, hides, and textile raw materials were " the outstanding instances of preference ";[8] and there were preferences given on a very large number of other things exported by the colonies.[9] In return the colonies were required to impose preferential duties on the manufactures of the United Kingdom, so that the United Kingdom still in practice retained its monopoly of supplying the colonies.[10] Certain duties were levied upon the import of certain foreign goods into the colonies by the Act of 1825;[11] but there was an abatement of duty if they were imported through the United Kingdom, having first been warehoused there; and if they had paid duty on import into the United Kingdom, they paid no duty on import into the colony.[12] On the other hand, the export from and import into the British possessions in America were confined to a long list of free ports, with proviso that the Crown could add to the list;[13] and there were still a certain number of restrictions and prohibitions upon the import of certain commodities—e.g. gunpowder and

---

[1] Vol. xi 84-88, 434-438.   [2] Ibid 85-86.   [3] Ibid 86.
[4] Ibid 87.   [5] Ibid 88.   [6] Ibid 87.
[7] Above 356, 357.   [8] Clapham, op. cit. i 328.
[9] Ibid.   [10] Ibid 329.
[11] 6 George IV c. 114 § 9 ; these duties were paid by the collector of customs to the treasurers of the colony in which they were levied, § 13.
[12] 6 George IV c. 114 § 9.   [13] §§ 2 and 3.

munitions of war could not be imported except from the United Kingdom or some other British possession.[1]

(iv) Foreign Trade

Here again the old system[2] was still maintained with modifications. During the war import duties imposed by Pitt's Act of 1787[3] had been largely increased in 1797, 1798, and 1803.

In 1809 the duty on merchandise of a kind not specified particularly elsewhere, and wholly or partially manufactured, had been raised to $37\frac{1}{2}$ per cent. with a special war duty in addition, amounting to a third of the permanent duties. In 1813 the permanent duties were increased by a quarter on all imports ; by two thirds, while the war should last, on all goods coming from France or countries under French supremacy. Iron paid a duty of £7 18s. 4d. a ton, tin a duty of £114. The duty on earthenware exceeded 79 per cent., on cotton goods it amounted to 85 per cent., on cloth to 90 per cent., and on glass to 114 per cent. The importation of silk was absolutely prohibited.[4]

Customs duties were lowered, simplified, and consolidated by the legislation of 1825 ;[5] but the system of protective duties was by no means abandoned. The manufacturers had learned that less protection was sufficient ; but neither they nor the government proposed to abandon all protection. Just as in the case of the corn trade the needs of defence demanded that some protection should be given to the farmer,[6] so in other branches of foreign trade, the retention of some duties was valuable, if for no other reason, because their remission could be used to induce foreign states to make similar remissions. The position at the end of this period is thus summed up by Dr. Clapham :[7]

The changes in the tariff of 1824-5, generally credited to Huskisson, had not altered the system in any essential. Instead of being prohibited, French silks paid 30 per cent. *ad valorem* ; but in spite of prophesyings to the contrary, that proved enough to keep most of them out. . . . A consolidation of all duties on cotton manufactures at a uniform 10 per cent. *ad valorem* had not affected the imports perceptibly. . . . A reduction of the woollen duties from 50 per cent. and upwards to 15 per cent. worked in much the same way ; some more woollens came, but not enough to matter. So it was with glass and china and gloves and linen and lace and the rest. The final *omnibus* clause of the budget of 1825, which fixed the duty on all manufactures not specially dealt with at 20 per cent. shows the essential conservatism of the reforms. In view of

---

[1] § 7.   [2] See vol. xi 442-444.   [3] Vol. x 120-121.
[4] Halévy, History of the English People (Penguin ed.) ii 163-164 ; see 7 George III c. 15, 38 George III c. 76, 43 George III c. 68, 49 George III c. 98, 53 George III c. 33, there cited.
[5] 6 George IV c.c. 107 and 111.   [6] Above 356.
[7] Op. cit. i 326.

Britain's industrial leadership a general 20 per cent. was more than enough to close her ports to most foreign manufactures. " Little or no change," said Parnell, " was really made by the alteration of the protecting duties and prohibitions in 1825. If free trade is the right policy, the work of introducing it still remains to be done."

We have seen that the need for a cheaper and more abundant supply of food which was caused by the industrial revolution had caused the demand for a free trade in corn.[1] As Great Britain's industrial lead became more pronounced, the need to protect British industries consequently grew less. Huskisson's policy was in effect a return to the policy of Pitt.[2] Like Pitt, he advocated a freer trade because the conditions of commerce and industry demanded it ;[3] for he was a practical statesman who never allowed his vision to be blinded by the *a priori* reasonings of the economists.[4] But though the cry for free trade, which had always been preached as an ideal by the economists, became more insistent, it was not till the following period that this revolution in the commercial policy of the state was able to prevail, and to cause drastic changes in the law on very many topics connected with colonial and foreign trade.[5]

(v) *Bounties and the trading privileges of commercial companies*

We have seen that in the eighteenth century both the export and the import trade was encouraged by bounties.[6] This policy was continued during the greater part of this period. We have seen that till 1814 it was an integral part of the corn laws ;[7] and in 1825[8] the bounties given on the export of goods were consolidated and enumerated. The enumerated goods were only cordage, linen, sail cloth and sugar ; and the shortness of this list shows that, by the end of this period, the bounties both on export and import were in course of disappearance.[9] In fact during the second decade of the nineteenth century they had survived " only as a very subordinate part of the general system of preferential treatment for produce raised within the Empire."[10]

We have seen that the control exercised by the commercial companies was decaying in the preceding period.[11] It is only

---

[1] Above 351, 352, 358.   [2] Vol. x 120-121.   [3] Vol. xi 394.
[4] Huskisson " combined profound knowledge of practical affairs with an antipathy to doctrinaire theory," David Cecil, The Young Melbourne 208.
[5] Below, vol. xiv.   [6] Vol. xi 398, 404, 415, 416, 417.
[7] Above 355.   [8] 6 George IV c. 113.
[9] " To the parliamentary political economists, there was the objection of principle that some tax burdensome to producers or consumers had to be maintained in order that bounties might be paid ; and this applied to bounties of every kind," Clapham, op. cit. i 328.
[10] Ibid.   [11] Vol. xi 439-442.

very occasionally that a company was created to exercise control over an industry.[1] The East India Company's monopoly of trade with India disappeared in 1813, and its monopoly of the China trade in 1833.[2] The South Sea Company lost its exclusive trading privileges in 1815,[3] the Sierra Leone company was dissolved as from 1814,[4] the African company was dissolved in 1821,[5] and the Levant company in 1825.[6] On the other hand what were in effect purely trading companies were incorporated to develop waste land in New South Wales,[7] in Van Diemen's Land,[8] and in Canada.[9] We have seen that those of the older companies which still existed had become merely survivals of a past phase in the history of the regulation of foreign trade.[10]

Both these developments—the decay of the bounty system, and the elimination of the commercial companies—show that the old organization of foreign trade was being modified under the stress of the new trading conditions which the industrial revolution was bringing about. More freedom was left to the individual trader. He was as yet controlled in the interests of trade and the interests of the state. But the nature of that control and the reasons for its existence were being modified.

(4) The organization of trade and finance and the development of certain topics of commercial law

The expansion of trade, foreign and domestic, and the necessity of financing that trade, led to many developments in mercantile practice which were the cause of important developments of mercantile law. With these developments of mercantile law I shall deal in detail in the second part of this book. At this point I must give a brief account of the principal statutes which were occasioned by these developments. These statutes deal mainly with the following topics : (i) corporations and other commercial associations ; (ii) banking ; (iii) bankruptcy and insolvency ; (iv) insurance ; (v) shipping ; (vi) factors ; (vii) carriers ; (viii) negotiable instruments.

(i) Corporations and other commercial associations

We have seen that the Bubble Act of 1720[11] prevented the formation of unincorporated associations with a transferable

---

[1] One instance is the creation in 1793 of a company to incorporate the company of free fishers and dredgers of Whitstable, and for the better ordering and government of the fishery, 33 George III c. 42.　　　　　[2] Vol. xi 214.
[3] 55 George III c. 57.　　　　　[4] 47 George III Sess. 2 c. 44 § 21.
[5] 1, 2 George IV c. 28.　　　　　[6] 6 George IV c. 33.
[7] 5 George IV c. 86 ; 11 George IV and 1 William IV c. 24.
[8] 6 George IV c. 39.　　　　　[9] 6 George IV c. 75 ; 9 George IV c. 51.
[10] Vol. xi 441 ; cp. Clapham, op. cit. i 251-254.
[11] 6 George I c. 18 §§ 18-22.

stock. An association which wished to carry on business on a joint stock basis with a transferable stock must get itself incorporated either by Act of Parliament or by royal charter.[1] A few associations formed exclusively for trading purposes sometimes applied to Parliament for incorporation. Thus, the two companies which carried on the business of marine insurance—the London Assurance Corporation and the Royal Exchange Assurance Corporation—were incorporated by statute ;[2] and in 1799 an Act was passed to enable the Crown to incorporate the Globe Fire and Life Insurance Company.[3] More often these statutory corporations were formed for trading purposes of a semi-public character. Thus in 1799 an elaborate Act of seventy-five sections incorporated a company to construct a tunnel under the Thames from Gravesend to Tilbury ;[4] and between 1799 and 1820 several elaborate Acts were passed to incorporate dock companies in the port of London.[5] In 1825 a joint stock company was incorporated to erect buildings and machinery for the purpose of promoting manufactures in Ireland.[6] Other corporations were formed for purely public purposes, e.g. the commissioners to erect lighthouses in the northern parts of Great Britain,[7] and the company of watermen, wherrymen, and lightermen of the river Thames.[8]

An unincorporated association could only carry on business as a partnership ; and the fundamental principles of the law of partnership, being very ill adapted to the needs of a large commercial association, gave rise to very great difficulties. These difficulties are clearly explained by Mr. Formoy :[9]

The essential elements of a partnership which gave rise to these difficulties were (1) the interest of the partners in their stock and effects was a modified joint tenancy, that is, modified in the respect that there was no right of accrual to the survivors. (2) The partners had no action against each other in respect of partnership property, not even the common law action of account. (3) Each partner had power singly to dispose of the whole partnership effects, to receive or release debts, and, except in contracting by deed, to bind his co-partners by contract. (4) Each partner was liable for the partnership debts ; and (5) where no provision was made for the continuance of the partnership, the death of one partner dissolved the partnership.

---

[1] Vol. viii 220-221.   [2] 6 George I c. 18 § 1 ; below 378.

[3] 39 George III c. lxxxiii ; but it would seem that the grant of incorporation was not made, see 47 George III, Sess. 1 c. xxx ; for the reason why it was advisable to give statutory powers to the Crown to incorporate see below 370.

[4] 39 George III c. lxxiii.

[5] 39 George III c. lxix §§ 38-82—West India Docks ; 39, 49 George III c. xlviii and 44 George III c. 100—London Docks ; 50 George III c. ccvii and 57 George III c. lxii—Commercial and Surrey Docks.

[6] 6 George IV c. cxli, amended by 7 George IV c. cxxiii.

[7] 38 George III c. lvii.   [8] 7, 8 George IV c. lxxv § 4.

[9] Historical Foundations of Company Law 32-33.

It is true that equity gave some relief. One partner could force another to account, and in certain cases could get an order for the dissolution of the partnership. But to start proceedings in Chancery was, at that period, a remedy almost worse than the disease.[1] Still greater difficulties arose if the partnership wished to sue a debtor, or if a creditor of the partnership wished to sue it. All the partners, who might be some hundreds of persons, must be joined as plaintiffs or defendants ; and if an action was brought by or against the partners for debts incurred at different times, it was a matter of considerable difficulty to know who must be joined ; for at each of those times there might have been changes in the firm.[2] There were also great difficulties in levying execution against the firm. If the amount recovered could not be levied against the property of the company

the plaintiff could take the bodies of the defendants, and was obliged to keep them all in prison until his judgment was fully satisfied, because the discharge of one defendant upon payment of his aliquot share would be a discharge of them all.[3]

Conversely, for a separate debt of a partner the sheriff could take the partnership property and sell the debtor's share to a purchaser who thereafter became tenant in common with the other partners.[4]

These difficulties were partially surmounted by two expedients. The first of these expedients was a private Act of Parliament. Companies got private Acts to enable them to sue and be sued in the name of their officers.[5] But these Acts gave rise to many difficulties, some of which were surmounted by clauses which were from time to time introduced into these Acts. Lord Eldon explained the development of the provisions of these Acts in the case of *Van Sandau v. Moore*.[6] He said that it was soon found that a provision that a company could sue and be sued in the names of their officers did not meet all difficulties.

The secretary on behalf of the company sued a man of opulence ; and, if he succeeded, he recovered not only judgment but payment of the demand. On the other hand, when the secretary was sued, the person suing found that, though he had gotten an individual with whom he could go into a court of law or equity in order to enforce a claim against him as defendant, yet after he had gone thither, he frequently found that it would have been better for him not to have stirred ; for though the secretary, when he was plaintiff, got the money for which he sued, he was often unable when made defendant, to pay what the plaintiff recovered.[7]

[1] Vol. ix 339-375.
[2] Formoy, op. cit. 33-35.
[3] Ibid 35-36.
[4] Ibid 36.
[5] There are a large number of these Acts see e.g. 47 George III Sess. 1 cc. xxx-xxxiv ; 53 George III, c.c. ccvi, ccvii, ccxii, ccxv, ccxvi.
[6] (1826) 1 Russ. 441.
[7] At pp. 458-459.

To remedy this difficulty clauses were inserted in these Acts making the members of the company liable as well as the officers. But these clauses were not effective because it was difficult to find out who the members were. To meet this difficulty the company was required to keep a register of its members. But since the members were always changing, and since these changes were not registered, the difficulty remained.[1]

A further alteration was then made ; the effect of which was, that those who had been members, should continue liable although they had transferred their interest, and that those who became members, should also be liable ; an enrolment of the names both of the one and the other being required. This had a very considerable operation ; and it was wonderful to observe, how much, after it was adopted, the passion for becoming members of these companies diminished.[2]

The latest improvement was to insert a clause which allowed one or more members of these companies to sue the others— a clause which, Lord Eldon said, first made its appearance in an Act of 1825 which regulated Irish banks, and was in 1826 applied to English banks.[3]

The second expedient was an application to these companies of the law of trusts. A large partnership was constituted by a deed of settlement, under which a few of the partners nominated in the deed carried on the business of the association, in accordance with the provisions of the deed, in trust for the other partners. As to matters not contained in the deed

the general law of partnership prevailed, and as regards third parties, the shareholders stood upon the same footing as an ordinary partnership ; for instance, every shareholder was liable for the whole of the company's debts, notwithstanding a stipulation in the deed that he should be liable to no greater extent than the amount of his shares, for such a provision applied only between the shareholders themselves.[4]

This device, though it did not get over the difficulties arising from some of the fundamental principles of partnership law, did get over the difficulties in the way of suing and being sued. In the case of *Metcalf v. Bruin*[5] a bond was given to the trustees of the Globe Insurance Company to secure the faithful service to the company of a clerk. It was held that the trustees could sue on the bond if the clerk had not faithfully served the company. Lord Ellenborough, C.J. said : [6]

We could not, indeed, invert the rules of law to enable persons to sue as a body or company who are not a corporation ; but here the bond has been given to trustees, who are under no difficulty in suing upon it in their own

---

[1] At p. 459.   [2] At. pp. 459-460.
[3] At pp. 460-461 ; 6 George IV c. 42 § 10 ; 7 George IV c. 46 § 9 ; below 378.
[4] Formoy, Historical Foundations of Company Law 41 ; cp. Lord Eldon's remarks in Kinder v. Taylor (1825). L.J. Ch. at p. 80.
[5] (1810) 12 East 400.   [6] At p. 405.

names ; and the only question is as to the description of persons meant to be designated under the term company. . . . It meant a fluctuating or successive body of persons who should from time to time be carrying on the business of insurance under the name of the Globe Insurance Company. Now suppose a bond given to a trustee to secure the performance of certain services to the commoners of such a common, would there be any difficulty in applying it to the use of the commoners for the time being, whoever they might happen to be, during the period for which the services were to be performed ?

In fact a large number of these unincorporated associations or companies were formed.[1] For instance, clothiers in the early years of the nineteenth century set up what were called company mills. "From ten to forty would put up some £50 each ; would buy land, build on it, mortgage it, get the machinery on credit, and put in a manager."[2] But such associations were not recognized by the law ; and it might easily happen that some of their activities brought them within the provisions of the Bubble Act, so that they were illegal societies and their members incurred the penalties of the Act. The decisions on the question what sort of activities would come within these provisions were conflicting,[3] though it would seem that the better opinion was that, if such an association attempted to make its shares transferable, it came within the Act.[4] But Lord Eldon's hesitating judgment in the case of *Kinder v. Taylor*[5] shows that the law was very uncertain what sort of conduct would bring the members of an association within the Bubble Act, and in particular what interpretation was to be put on the provision which penalized persons who acted as a corporation ;[6] and that it was also uncertain how far such conduct was an offence against the common law as well as against the Act.[7]

Since the law was in this confused state, and since the new industrial conditions made it certain that these commercial associations or companies would continue to be formed, a change in the law was, as Lord Eldon said,[8] necessary. But during this period very little was done to put the law on a satisfactory footing. Apart from the legislation as to banks,[9] savings banks,[10] and friendly societies,[11] all that Parliament did was

---

[1] "There are in this metropolis, and throughout the country, a great many partnerships consisting of a vast number of persons," Van Sandau v. Moore (1826) 1 Russ. at pp. 470-471 *per* Lord Eldon.

[2] Clapham, An Economic History of Modern Britain i 195.

[3] For these decisions see Formoy, op. cit. 49-57 ; the principal cases are The King v. Dodd (1808) 9 East 516 ; the King v. Webb (1811) 14 East 406 ; Pratt v. Hutchinson (1812) 14 East 511 ; Brown v. Holt (1812) 4 Taunt. 587.

[4] Buck v. Buck (1808) 1 Camp. 547 ; R. v. Stratton (1809) ibid 549 n. ; Josephs v. Pebrer (1825) 3 B. and c. 639.

[5] (1825) 3 L.J. Ch. 68.

[6] At pp. 78-79, 82.

[7] At. p. 81.

[8] Above 367, 368.

[9] Below 371, 373, 375, 376.

[10] Above 213, 226, 334, 335.

[11] Above 333, 334.

to repeal the Bubble Act,[1] and to provide that, in any charter of incorporation, the Crown might provide that the members of the corporation should be individually liable for the debts of the corporation " to such extent, and subject to such regulations and restrictions as his Majesty may deem fit and proper, and as shall be declared and limited in and by such charter."[2] This clause was needed because, at common law, the Crown could not by its charter of incorporation alter the powers and capacities incident to corporate personality.[3] If therefore an individual liability was to be imposed by the charter on the members of the corporation for the corporate debts a statutory power to impose it must be given. But it should be observed that the breadth of the power also enabled the Crown to limit this liability to any extent that it chose.

We have seen that the repeal of the Bubble Act still left open the question how far and to what extent the offences created by the Act were also offences at common law, and were therefore still existent notwithstanding the repeal of the Act.[4] It is also clear that the Act did nothing to define the legal position of these associations or companies, or to prevent the frauds which were facilitated by the uncertain state of the law. This task was not undertaken by the Legislature till the following period.[5] In this period the Legislature, instead of dealing comprehensively with this difficult subject merely tinkered with it. It is true that it defined the constitution and powers of two sorts of societies—friendly societies and savings banks,[6] and that it made some regulations for private and joint stock banks.[7] But it did practically nothing to define the legal position of those large commercial associations or companies which, in the new commercial and industrial conditions, were being formed in ever increasing numbers. They were left, as Lord Eldon said, to manage their affairs " by a mutual understanding and a kind of moral rule." He added that he believed that " in that way they manage their affairs very well."[8] That might be true of many of these companies ; but it was certainly not true of all ; and it was against the risks of careless or fraudulent management that the law ought to have made provision. We have seen that both he and others had said in Parliament that what was wanted was a law which defined the legal status of these companies and gave them directions as to their powers, rights, and duties.[9]

---

[1] 6 George IV c. 91 § 1. [A wrong reference to this Act is given in vol viii 221 n. 2]. [2] § 2. [3] Vol. ix 54-56.

[4] Vol. viii 221 ; in Van Sandau v. Moore (1826) 1 Russ. at p. 472 Lord Eldon suggested that the impossibility of suing these associations or companies with effect " was a very strong argument to prove that such a constitution of a body could not be legal."

[5] Below, vol. xiv. [6] Above 333-335. [7] Below 373 seqq.

[8] Van Sandau v. Moore (1826) 1 Russ. at p. 471. [9] Above 369.

(ii) *Banking*

We have seen that at the end of the seventeenth century the practice of banking was established in England.[1] Some of the goldsmiths had begun to act as private bankers in the latter half of the century ;[2] and in 1694 a public bank—the Bank of England—had been established.[3] During the last quarter of the eighteenth century and in the first thirty years of the nineteenth century there was a great increase in the number of private banks ;[4] throughout the eighteenth century and all through this period the Bank of England was gaining a unique position in the banking world;[5] and at the end of this period a new kind of bank—the joint stock bank—had made its appearance.[6] By the end of this period the banking system of England had begun to be organized in its modern form ; and, as concomitants of that organization, two of its appendages had made their appearance—the bill brokers and the clearing house.[7]

A large part of the law relating to banks and banking was, like other parts of commercial law, made by the courts, assisted by the writers of text books. But some part of this law is statutory ; and it is with this part of the law that I must now deal. It is hardly possible, however, to understand these statutes without some knowledge of the form which the banking system was assuming during this period. I shall therefore, in the first place, describe briefly the organization of the English banking system, and, in the second place, give some account of the statute law relating to it.

The organization of the banking system. The Bank of England was the head and centre of the system. It had attained this position partly by reason of the privileges given to it by statute and charter in return for services rendered to the government, and partly by reason of the relation in which it stood, as a result of this position, to the private banks. These privileges can be summarized as follows : First, ever since 1708[8] it was the only chartered joint stock company, i.e. the only corporation, which could engage in the business of banking ; for by an Act of that year and subsequent Acts only individuals or partnerships of not more than six persons could engage in this business, which, by an Act of 1742, was defined to be the borrowing of money on their bills or notes.[9] This meant in effect that it was " the sole *joint stock company* permitted to issue bank notes

---

[1] Vol. viii 183-189.
[2] Ibid 185-186.
[3] Ibid 188-189.
[4] Below 372, 373.
[5] Below 372, 373, 374, 375.
[6] Below 373.
[7] Below 374.
[8] 7 Anne c. 7 § 61.
[9] 15 George II c. 13 § 5.

in England "; [1] and it was long erroneously supposed that these
statutes also prevented any other joint stock company from
doing business as a bank of deposit. [2] Secondly, because it was
a chartered corporation the liability of its members was limited.
" In a private copartnery " said Adam Smith, [3] " each partner
is bound for the debts contracted by the company to the whole
extent of his fortune. In a joint stock company, on the contrary,
each partner is bound only to the extent of his share." It was
therefore the only bank which could carry on its trade with
the important privilege of limited liability. Thirdly, it was
the banker of the state. In its early days the bank supported
the credit of the government : " Afterwards it derived credit
from the government." [4] As Adam Smith said, [5]

The stability of the Bank of England is equal to that of the British
Government. All that it has advanced to the public must be lost before
its creditors can sustain any loss. . . . It acts, not only as an ordinary
bank, but as a great engine of state. It receives and pays the greatest part
of the annuities which are due to the creditors of the public, it circulates
exchequer bills, and it advances to government the annual amount of the
land and malt taxes, which are frequently not paid up till some years
thereafter.

Fourthly, the London bankers kept their reserves with the
Bank of England, [6] just as the country bankers deposited their
reserves and kept their securities with the London bankers
who acted as their agents. [7] Thus, as Dr. Clapham has said, [8]
the Bank of England had not only " a monopoly by joint stock
banking and a monopoly of the banking business of the state,"
but also " the care of the ultimate reserves of all other metropolitan banks, and the only serious gold reserve in the country."

The private banks had grown up gradually and, except in one
or two matters, were almost wholly unregulated by the state.
They had long ceased to be identified with the goldsmiths.

A merchant, a manufacturer, or a shop keeper would begin by merely
dabbling in finance, accepting deposits and discounting bills of exchange.
His sole stipulation was that he need not return deposits immediately.
In the meanwhile he used them to discount bills. Very soon he would
discover that this class of business demanded too much time to be compatible with other occupations, and he would then become a banker
pure and simple—a specialist in the art of making payments and recovering debts on behalf of manufacturers and merchants. . . . Here as in all
other departments of English commerce, individualism reigned supreme. [9]

[1] Bagehot, Lombard Street 99.   [2] Ibid 101.
[3] Wealth of Nations (Cannan's ed.) ii 232.
[4] Bagehot, Lombard Street 97.
[5] Wealth of Nations (Cannan's ed.) i 303.
[6] Clapham, Economic History of Modern Britain i 279-280.
[7] Halévy, History of the English People (Penguin ed.) ii 187.
[8] Op. cit. i 263-264.
[9] Halévy, History of the English People (Penguin ed.) ii 181-182.

Adam Smith noticed the increase in the number of these private bankers;[1] and in the last quarter of the eighteenth and the first two decades of the nineteenth century they had greatly increased in number. As was only to be expected, many of them were not conducted wisely, and some not honestly. " There was never a year from 1815 to 1830 in which at least three banks did not break, and the total of bankers' bankruptcies for the fifteen years was 206."[2]

These banks used their clients' money to finance trade. They used the money deposited with them to discount traders' bills, and to make them advances; and they further extended the scope of their operations by discounting bills not only with the money deposited with them, but in their own notes.[3] " It was estimated that between the years 1810-1815 the private banks of the provinces issued notes to the value of some £20,000,000."[4]

The London bankers occupied a position somewhat different from that of a country banker. Besides doing the ordinary business of banking, they acted as agents, and bankers to the country bankers; and, consequently, as contrasted with the country bankers, their deposit business was larger. A London banker, Gilbart said in 1827, "takes care of his customers' money, but a country banker has chiefly to advance money to his customers."[5] Moreover, unlike the country bankers, they did not issue their own notes. " They had found that the Bank of England notes and cheques served all their needs."[6] For all these reasons the London bankers held a position somewhat different from, and often a status somewhat higher than, that of a country private banker.[7]

In 1826 the Legislature made it possible for joint stock companies to engage in the business of banking.[8] But for the Bank of England's monopoly, it is probable that England, like Scotland, would have had joint stock banks before this date; for banking was a business for which Adam Smith thought that a joint stock company was " extremely well fitted."[9] In 1826 and later the truth of this dictum of Adam Smith's was doubted. But the doubts were founded on a set of conditions which, in the course of the nineteenth century, were passing

---

[1] Wealth of Nations (Cannan's ed.) i 312. [2] Clapham, op. cit. i 266.
[3] Adam Smith, Wealth of Nations (Cannan's ed.) i 281.
[4] Halévy, op. cit. ii 184.
[5] Cited Clapham, op. cit. i 266. [6] Ibid 264-265.
[7] Bagehot, Lombard Street 270 says, " the name ' London Bankers ' had especially a charmed value. He was supposed to represent, and often did represent, a certain union of pecuniary sagacity and educated refinement which was scarcely to be found in any other part of society."
[8] 7 George IV c. 46; below 375, 376.
[9] Wealth of Nations (Cannan's ed.) ii 246.

away.[1] Private banks were adapted to the needs of small towns whose inhabitants were personally known to the bankers ; and no doubt for that sort of business the private bank was better adapted than the joint stock bank. But in 1873, when Bagehot was writing, the joint stock banks, being better adapted to the needs of large towns and a greatly growing trade, were superseding the private banks, and they have now almost entirely superseded them.

By the end of this period two appendages to this banking system had made their appearance—the bill brokers and the clearing house.

We have seen that, to a large extent, the bankers used the money which was deposited with them to discount bills of exchange.[2] The reason why they thus used this money is thus explained by Gilbart :[3]

As they (bills of exchange) have only a short time to run before they fall due, the capital advanced soon returns ; and being transferable, they can, if necessary, be re-discounted. Hence they are admirably adapted for the purposes of the bankers : for, as the advances of bankers are made with other people's money, and that money may at any time be withdrawn, it becomes necessary that the securities on which these advances are made should rapidly revolve and be at all times convertible.

Largely for this reason a set of persons called bill brokers emerged who specialized in dealings in bills of exchange, and advised the bankers as to what bills it was safe to accept. On the one hand, they borrowed from the bankers and deposited their bills as securities for the advance : on the other hand, they procured bills for the bankers to discount, i.e. to advance money on.[4] " Thomas Richardson, of Richardson, Overend and Co., the biggest bill broker and money agent in London, turned over about twenty millions annually, sometimes more, in 1820-3."[5]

The clearing house was established in 1775 by the London bankers,[6] and in 1827 it included the principal firms.[7] " Each bank had its drawer into which the clerks from every other bank, coming twice a day, dropped bills and cheques payable by the owner of the drawer. Debits and credits were totted up and checked by two salaried inspectors, and balances due were paid over."[8]

The statute law relating to the banking system. These statutes do not cover very much ground. First, there are a number of statutes which gave the Bank of England its privileged position and regulated its relations to the state. Some of these, as we have seen,

---

[1] Bagehot, Lombard Street 252-254, 271-280.   [2] Above 373.
[3] Principles and Practice of Banking (ed. 1873) 109.
[4] Bagehot, Lombard Street chap. xi ; Clapham, op. cit. i 254-262.
[5] Ibid 260.   [6] Gilbart, op. cit. 72.
[7] Clapham, op. cit. i 283.   [8] Ibid.

gave it a monopoly of trading as a joint stock company.[1] Others restricted its power to lend money to the government. In 1694 it had been prevented from lending to the government on the security of the revenues, unless it was permitted to lend by the Act which granted the revenue.[2] This Act was sometimes suspended;[3] and in 1819 it was provided that the bank was not to make advances to the government without the authority of Parliament,[4] but that they could purchase Exchequer or Treasury bills, or lend on the security of those bills, to make good a deficiency of the consolidated fund at any of the quarter days.[5] But the bank must lay before Parliament an account of the Exchequer or Treasury bills purchased.[6]

Secondly, the most numerous class of Acts are those which regulate the issue of notes by the Bank of England and the private banks. It was provided in 1797 that the Bank of England was not to pay cash for its notes.[7] Cash payments were resumed in 1820,[8] and the Bank was ordered to make a weekly return to the Privy Council of the average amounts of their notes in circulation.[9] In 1775 all banks were forbidden to issue notes for less than 20/-,[10] and in 1777 for less than £5:[11] in 1796 they were allowed to issue notes for under £5;[12] but in 1826 it was enacted that no notes for a less sum than £5 were to be issued after April 5, 1829.[13] In 1828 English bankers, except within the City of London and within three miles thereof, were allowed, with the licence of the commissioner of stamps to issue unstamped notes and bills payable to bearer on demand for sums of £5 and upwards.[14] In 1833 an Act giving certain privileges to the Bank of England provided that no banking company exceeding six persons should issue notes payable on demand in London or within twenty-five miles thereof.[15] In 1844 it was enacted that bankers other than the Bank of England were not for the future to issue notes. Those who were already issuing them could continue to do so, but if they ceased to issue them they could not resume their issue.[16]

Thirdly, in 1826 the Bank of England monopoly of joint stock banking was terminated.[17] Corporations and partnerships of any number of persons were allowed to carry on the business of banking at any place beyond sixty-five miles from London.[18] But

---

[1] Above 373.
[2] 5, 6 William and Mary c. 20 § 30.
[3] 33 George III c. 32.
[4] 59 George III c. 76 § 1.   [5] § 3.
[6] § 5.   [7] 37 George III c. 45 § 2; Bagehot, Lombard Street 112.
[8] 59 George III c. 49 §§ 1-8.   [9] § 9.
[10] 15 George III c. 51.   [11] 17 George III c. 30.
[12] 37 George III c.c. 28 and 32; 3 George IV c. 70.
[13] 7 George IV c. 6 § 3.
[14] 9 George IV c. 23 §§ 1 and 2; by an Act of 1833 they must make periodical returns of their notes in circulation, 3, 4 William IV c. 83.
[15] 3, 4 William IV c. 98 § 2.   [16] 7, 8 Victoria c. 32 §§ 11 and 12.
[17] 7 George IV c. 46; amended 1, 2 Victoria c. 96; 3, 4 Victoria c. 117; and 5, 6 Victoria c. 85.   [18] 11 § 1.

every member of such corporation or partnership was to be personally liable for all bills and notes issued by the bank and for all money borrowed by it.[1] Partnerships were to sue and be sued in the names of their public officers.[2] As a compensation to the Bank of England for the loss of its monopoly it was allowed to set up branch banks.[3] The private country banks protested in vain against the concession to the Bank of England—though in a few years some of the leading bankers became reconciled to it.[4]

(iii) *Bankruptcy and insolvency*

We have seen that the principal Act relating to the law of bankruptcy was the Act of 1732, which had been several times amended.[5] The growth of Britain's trade and the periodical crises which affected that trade brought the law of bankruptcy into great prominence. It is not surprising therefore that several statutes made amendments in the law, and that at the end of this period it was further amended and consolidated.

The following were the principal amendments in the law: In 1796 it was provided that a bankrupt could be compelled to transfer stock belonging to him.[6] In 1806[7] an Act, for which Romilly was responsible,[8] provided that *bona fide* dealings with bankrupts taking place two months before the issue of the commission should be valid,[9] and that debts *bona fide* contracted before the issue of the commission should be provable, though a prior act of bankruptcy had been committed.[10] There were provisions for set off where mutual credit had been given,[11] and for the discharge of debts provable under the commission.[12] Commissions were not to be avoided by an act of bankruptcy committed prior to the petitioning creditor's debt.[13] In 1809 another Act for which Romilly was responsible[14] made further amendments. In 1822[15] it was provided that the assignees could execute powers vested in a bankrupt, which he might exercise for his own benefit, and that a bankrupt could be ordered to execute conveyances ;[16] and rules were made as to the issue of joint commissions against bankrupt firms.[17]

The law was amended and consolidated by an Act of 1824,[18]

---

[1] § 1. [2] § 9. [3] § 15.
[4] Clapham, op. cit. i 276-278. [5] Vol. xi 446-447.
[6] 36 George III c. 90 § 2. [7] 46 George III c. 135.
[8] Memoirs (ed. 1842) ii 20, 22-23 ; above 265, 266. [9] § 1.
[10] § 2. [11] § 3. [12] § 4. [13] § 5.
[14] 49 George III c. 121 ; *inter alia* the Act made provision for sureties for bankrupts § 8, and for the proof of future debts § 9 ; and the consent of three parts of the number and value of the creditors was to be sufficient for a discharge § 18 ; Romilly, Memoirs ii 102, 114-115, 123-124.
[15] 3 George IV c. 81 § 3. [16] § 4.
[17] §§ 8-12. [18] 5 George IV c. 98.

which was superseded by the Consolidation Act of 1825.[1] That Act defined the classes of persons who could be made bankrupt, and the acts which were acts of bankruptcy. It defined the powers of the commissioners, and the procedure to be followed by a petitioning creditor. It gave the commissioners power to appoint assignees of the bankrupt's property to be chosen by the creditors. Six months' wages to clerks or servants of the bankrupt were to be paid in preference to other claims, and there were provisions for the set off of mutual debts and credits, and for the proof of future and contingent debts. Proof of a debt under the commission was to bar an action for the same debt. Voluntary conveyances by a person in fact insolvent were to be set aside ; but *bona fide* payments made by or to a bankrupt without notice of a prior act of bankruptcy were to be valid. Rules were made as to the distribution of dividends from the bankrupt's estate to creditors, as to the discharge of the bankrupt, and as to the effect of the certificate of discharge. It was provided that nine-tenths, in number and value, of the creditors could accept a composition which would bind the others. If a bankrupt did not surrender and submit to examination, or failed to make discovery of his property, or did not deliver up his books, or removed or embezzled property to the value of £10, he was guilty of felony and punishable by transportation. This Act was, as I have said,[2] the foundation of the modern law of bankruptcy. We have seen that in 1831 a court of Bankruptcy was established staffed by a Chief Judge, three other judges, and six commissioners. Appeals were taken to a Court of Review consisting of the judges of the court or any three of them. From them an appeal lay to the Chancellor or the House of Lords.[3]

The fact that the Bankruptcy Acts applied only to traders, and the fact that it was open to any creditor to imprison his judgment debtor and keep him in prison till his debt was paid, had, as we have seen, led to the enactment of a series of Acts which provided a machinery by which prisoners could get their release, and measures to alleviate the lot of these imprisoned debtors.[4] Most of these Acts were temporary Acts, and the series of these Acts continued till the passing of the first permanent Acts in 1813[5] and 1814.[6] The provisions of these temporary Acts were from time to time varied—e.g. in 1793 the Act was only to apply to

---

[1] 6 George IV c. 16.   [2] Vol. xi 447 n. 4.
[3] Vol. i 443 ; 1, 2 William IV c. 56 §§ 1-3 ; § 37 provided that either the Chancellor or the Court of Review, provided in the latter case that the parties consented, could direct an appeal to the House of Lords, instead of an appeal to the Chancellor or Court of Review; for its personnel, and for the names of the six commissioners appointed under the Act see 8 Bing. 140.
[4] Vol. xi 597-600.   [5] 53 George III c. 102 ; vol. xi 598 n. 2.
[6] 54 George III c. 28.

debts not exceeding £300,[1] but in 1819 it was to apply to debts under £3000 if the debtor had been five years in custody ;[2] and in 1819 the Act was to apply to persons imprisoned for contempt of the Court of Chancery.[3] Other Acts gave authority to Quarter Sessions to discharge these prisoners on certain conditions,[4] and regulated the weekly allowance which creditors must make to them.[5] In 1813 a permanent court for hearing of these cases was set up,[6] and in 1814 a permanent Act for their relief was passed.[7] On the expiration of the Act of 1813, an Act of 1820[8] set up a new court, which was established a few years later in a court house which was built in Portugal Street under a section of an Act of 1822.[9] The jurisdiction of Quarter Sessions to deal with these cases was taken away in 1824. They were to be heard instead by commissioners of the insolvent court at the various assize towns in England.[10] In 1826 a consolidation Act containing eighty-nine sections settled the constitution of the court and its jurisdiction.[11]

(iv) Insurance

The only important Act dealing with this subject is an Act of 1824[12] which abolished the monopoly in marine insurance business given to the Royal Exchange Assurance and the London Assurance Companies by the Act of 1720.[13] Other corporate bodies could now undertake this business ; but the Act was not to interfere with any other privileges given to these two corporations.[14] The continual existence of such a monopoly was quite contrary to the prevailing economic ideas, and its abolition had been recommended by a committee of the House of Commons in 1810 ;[15] but the House rejected this recommendation—Lloyd's did not wish for the repeal of the Act of 1720, since it did not wish to face the competition of other marine insurance companies.[16] But in 1824 a bill, which was promoted by Nathan Rothschild, got the support of the government, and was passed—in spite of the dislike of Lords Eldon and Redesdale to the measure.[17]

---

[1] 33 George III c. 5 § 1, made perpetual 39 George III c. 50.
[2] 49 George III c. 115 § 5.   [3] Ibid c. 6.
[4] 41 George III c. 70 ; 44 George III c. 108 ; 46 George III c. 108 ; 52 George III c. 165, amended 53 George III c. 6.
[5] 37 George III c. 85.   [6] 53 George III c. 102.
[7] 54 George III c. 28.   [8] 1 George IV c. 119.
[9] 3 George IV c. 123 § 21 ; see vol. xi 598 n. 4.
[10] 5 George IV c. 61 § 1.   [11] 7 George IV c. 57.
[12] 5 George IV c. 114.
[13] 6 George I c. 18 § 1 ; vol. xi 447-448 ; Martin, History of Lloyd's chap vi.
[14] 5 George IV c. 114 § 2.   [15] Martin, op. cit. 250-251.
[16] " The monopoly of the two chartered companies being avowedly maintained only as a protection of the interest of the associated private underwriters," ibid 273.
[17] Ibid chap xvi.

(v) Shipping

In 1813 the Acts of 1734 and 1786, which limited the liability of ship owners for losses of merchandize incurred without their default to the value of the ship and freight,[1] were amended.[2] Several losses incurred on the same voyage were not to expose the owner to any further liability.[3] If the master or mariners were also owners the Act was not to diminish their liability in their former capacity.[4] Provisions were made for the case where the value of the ship and freight was not sufficient to satisfy the loss to all the claimants. The owners could exhibit a bill in equity for the apportionment of the value.[5] The law relating to the execution of letters of attorney and the wills of seamen in the Navy, and to their prize money and other allowances, was consolidated in 1815,[6] and again in 1830.[7] In 1825 a consolidation of the laws regulating the carriage of passengers by sea was a part of the series of the customs consolidation Acts.[8] No more than one person for every five tons burthen were to be carried by any ship sailing without a licence to foreign parts, and no licence was to be granted if the ship carried more than one person for each two tons burthen.[9] Lists of persons on board were to be delivered to the collector of customs at the port of departure;[10] and the amount of water and provisions to be carried was regulated.[11] Every ship carrying fifty persons or more must be provided with a surgeon and medicine chest.[12]

(vi) Factors

The lawyers had come to regard ownership as an absolute right, which can only be created or transferred by the methods prescribed by the law.[13] And not only must the forms prescribed by the law for the transfer of ownership be complied with, but the transferor must be the owner. No transfer of possession will give the transferee ownership unless the transferor is owner; for a possessor may have acquired possession without the consent of the owner e.g. by force or fraud, or, even if he had acquired it with his consent, he may be merely a bailee, and so be unable to transfer anything but the possession which he in fact has. Not having ownership, he cannot transfer it; for *nemo dat quod non habet*. It follows that a transferee must take precautions to see that his transferor has the ownership which he is purporting to convey; for otherwise not only will he acquire no ownership, but he may also find that he is exposed to liability at the suit of the true

---

[1] 7 George II c. 15; 26 George III c. 86; vol. xi 448-449.
[2] 53 George III c. 159.   [3] § 3.   [4] § 4.   [5] § 7.
[6] 55 George III c. 60.   [7] 11 George IV and 1 William IV c. 20.
[8] 6 George IV c. 116; above 262.   [9] Ibid c. 116 § 2.
[10] § 5.   [11] § 7.   [12] §§ 12 and 13.   [13] Vol. vii 62-64, 424-430.

owner. He must therefore guard against the consequences of taking a conveyance from a transferor who, whether fraudulently or not, purports to convey an ownership which he has not got. The merchants, on the other hand, approach this question from a different angle. A quick circulation of property is the life of trade for, if property is not quickly circulated, there will be a stagnation of trade, and a consequent risk of insolvency. To make an examination into the title of a transferor whenever property is transferred would invite this risk. It follows that merchants must risk the taking of a defective title through fraud or otherwise, and assume that a possessor who is apparently the owner is in fact the owner.[1] Therefore they would like to see embodied in the law a very different principle, which is summed up in the maxim *en fait de meubles possession vaut titre.*

The expansion of trade made a conflict between these two principles inevitable. In the rules as to negotiability[2] and as to sales in market overt[3] which the common law took over from the law merchant, concessions were made to mercantile needs ; and those needs were also recognized in some of the applications of the doctrine of estoppel.[4] In all other cases the common law adhered firmly to its principles. But since, with the growth of foreign and domestic trade, the number and magnitude of mercantile dealings were growing, and since these dealings were conducted more and more on a credit basis which precluded the possibility of an examination into the title to the goods dealt with, it is not surprising that, in the early years of the nineteenth century, there was a demand that the common law should make further concessions to mercantile needs.

In 1823 a select committee of the House of Commons was appointed " to enquire into the state of the law relating to goods, wares and merchandize entrusted to merchants, agents and factors, and the effect of the law upon the interests of commerce."[5] The committee began by enquiring into the state of the law relating to advances made in the regular course of trade, to agents or factors on the security of merchandize, by persons who were ignorant of the fact that these agents or factors were not the owners of the property ; and into the state of the law relating to purchases from these agents or factors who had in fact no power to sell, although the absence of that power was not known

---

[1] " The practice of merchants . . . is not based on the supposition of possible frauds. The object of mercantile usages is to prevent the risk of insolvency, not of fraud. . . . Credit, not distrust, is the basis of commercial dealings; mercantile genius consists principally in knowing whom to trust and with whom to deal, and commercial intercourse and communication is no more based on the supposition of fraud than it is on the supposition of forgery," Sanders v. Maclean (1883) 11 Q.B.D. at p. 343 *per* Bowen L.J.

[2] Vol. viii 144, 165-167.　　　　[3] Vol. iv. 522 ; vol. v 104-105.
[4] Vol. ix 146, 161-162.　　　　[5] Parlt. Papers, 1823 vol. iv 267.

to the purchaser. The committee found that under the existing law persons thus advancing money were often deprived of their securities, and that purchasers often got no title to the goods and were obliged to pay a second time.[1] It found also that these rules of English law were contrary to the rules of law prevailing in continental states; and it therefore recommended an "immediate alteration of law for the protection of commerce," and an assimilation of English to continental law.[2]

The reasons why this alteration of the law was necessary introduced the second matter into which the committee was asked to enquire—the effect of this state of the law upon the machinery used by the merchants to carry on and develop their trade. That machinery, the committee pointed out, depended upon facilities for obtaining credit at many stages in the process of purchase and sale. It said:[3]

Advances upon the security of merchandize are not irregular or unusual transactions, which ought to excite suspicion and caution in the mind of the person to whom application is made for advances; and so far from that being the case, by far the greater part of our commerce is aided by means of advances at some period between the shipment and the sale; and in many instances there is, first an advance by the foreign shipper or consignor to the foreign proprietor, then an advance by the consignee to the consignor, who is himself a factor, and subsequently an advance by some capitalist to the factor, in consequence of the difficulty of finding a ready and advantageous sale. Such advances are of the utmost importance to the success of commercial operations.

But it is quite clear that these operations precluded the possibility of an examination into the title of these various persons to pledge or sell the goods. The result of a law which prescribed such an examination was disastrous to trade. Capitalists were alarmed, consignees refused to make advances on consignments, and "bankers, corn-factors, and brokers who are accustomed to make advances to the merchants will not continue to do so, owing to the extreme difficulty of ascertaining what legal title to goods exists in the party requiring such advances."[4] Unless the law was changed, and it was made possible for merchants to deal as freely with factors as if they were principals,[5] capital would be withdrawn from trade.[6]

On this report the Legislature took action; and so in this matter of dealings by factors and other agents the modification of the principles of the common law was made by statute, and not, as in other branches of the law merchant, by the decisions of the courts. In fact the principles of the common law on this matter had become too firmly established to be thus modified. It might

---

[1] Parlt. Papers, 1823 vol. iv. 267.　　　　[2] Ibid 268.
[3] Ibid 271-272.　　　　[4] Ibid 274.　　　　[5] Ibid 275.　　　　[6] Ibid 272.

perhaps have made for a more rapid adaptation of the law to the
needs of commerce if this development could have been made by
the courts. Both Lord Ellenborough, C.J.[1] and Le Blanc, J.[2]
regretted that the courts had no power to modify the common law
rule that a pledge by a factor gave no title to the pledgee ; and
in 1868 Willes, J. said,[3]

I might desire that it was in the power of the judges to amend the law
from time to time with reference to mercantile convenience. And, if
there were a large preponderance of opinion amongst mercantile men
that there ought to be a free power of transfer of goods by persons having
the apparent ownership, I might feel disposed to exercise that power, if it
had existed in favour of the opinion of such majority.

But though in the past this power had been recognized to exist
and had been largely used,[4] and though in some departments of
mercantile law it still exists,[5] in this matter the judges had, as
Lord Ellenborough, C.J., Le Blanc, J. and Willes, J. admitted, no
such power. The Legislature, therefore, took charge of this branch
of the law ; and it is only in so far as it has modified the common
law rules as to the effect of the dispositions made by factors or
other mercantile agents that the rules of the common law have
been changed.

This modification began with the two earliest of the Factors
Acts which were passed in 1823[6] and 1825.[7] The first of these
Acts applied only to factors in whose names goods were shipped :
the second applied also to factors entrusted with the possession
of certain documents of title to goods. Neither of the Acts is very
clearly expressed ; but the following summary, which was given
by Lord Tenterden in the fifth edition of his book on *Merchant
Shipping*, was approved by Blackburn J. :[8]

The person in whose name goods are shipped is to be deemed the true
owner thereof, so as to entitle the consignee to a lien thereon in respect of
any money or negotiable security advanced by him to such person,
or received by such person to his use, if he has not notice by the bill of

---

[1] " Perhaps it would have been as well if it had originally been decided that
where it was equivocal whether a person was authorized to act as principal or factor
a pledge made by such a person free from any circumstances of fraud was valid.
But it is idle now to speculate upon this subject since a long series of cases has
decided that a factor cannot pledge," Martini v. Coles (1813) 1 M. and S. at pp.
146-147 ; the long series of cases began with Paterson v. Tash (1743) 2 Str. 1178.

[2] " Whether it might not originally have better answered the purposes of commerce to have considered a person, in the situation of Vos, having the apparent
symbol of property, as the true owner in respect of that person who deals with him
under an ignorance of his real character, is a question upon which it is now too late
to speculate," 1 M. and S. at p. 148.

[3] Fuentes v. Montis (1868) L.R. 3 C.P. at p. 282.   [4] Above 380.

[5] The custom of the merchants may make an instrument negotiable, Bechuanaland Exploration Co. v. London Trading Bank [1898] 2 Q.B. 658 ; Edelstein v.
Schuler [1902] 2 K.B. 144.

[6] 4 George IV c. 84.   [7] 6 George IV c. 94.

[8] Cole v. North Western Bank (1875) L.R. 10 C.P. at pp. 361-362.

lading or otherwise, at or before the advance or receipt, that such person is not the actual and *bona fide* owner of the goods ; and such person shall be taken for the purposes of the Act to have been intrusted with the goods for the purpose of consignment or of sale, unless the contrary be made to appear.[1]

So also a person entrusted with and in possession of a bill of lading, or any of the warrants, certificates, or orders mentioned in the Act, is to be deemed the true owner of the goods described therein, so as to give validity to any contract or agreement made by him from the date or disposition of the goods or the deposit or pledge thereof, if the buyer, disposer, or partner has not notice, by the document or otherwise, that such person is not the actual and *bona fide* owner of the goods.[2] But if such person deposit or pledge the goods as security for a pre-existing debt or demand, he who so takes the deposit or pledge without notice shall acquire such right, title, or interest, and no further or other, than was possessed by the person making the deposit or pledge.[3] And, further, any person may contract for the purchase of goods with any agent intrusted with the goods, or to whom they may be consigned, and receive and pay for the same to the agent, notwithstanding he shall have notice that the party, with whom he contracts is an agent, if such contract and payment be made in the ordinary and usual course of business, and he has not at the time of the contract or payment notice that the agent is not authorized to sell or to receive the price.[4] Also, any person may accept any goods, or any such document aforesaid, notwithstanding he shall have notice that the party is a factor or agent ; but, in such case, he shall acquire such right, title, or interest, and no further or other than was possessed by the factor or agent at the time of the deposit or pledge.[5] It is, however, provided that the Act shall not prevent the true owner of the goods from recovering them from his factor or agent before a sale, deposit, or pledge, or from the assignee of such factor or agent, in the event of his bankruptcy ; nor from the buyer the price of the goods, subject to any right of set-off on the part of the buyer against the factor or agent ; nor from recovering the goods deposited or pledged upon repayment of the money or restoration of the negotiable instrument advanced on the security thereof to the factor or agent ; and upon payment of such further money or restoration of such other negotiable instrument (if any) as may have been advanced by the factor or agent to the owner, or on payment of money equal to the amount of such instrument ; nor from recovering from any person any balance remaining in his hands as the produce of a sale of the goods after deducting the money on negotiable instruments advanced on the security thereof. And, in case of the bankruptcy of the factor or agent, the owner of the goods so pledged and redeemed shall be held to have discharged *pro tanto* his debt to the estate of the bankrupt.[6]

These Acts, as both Lord Tenterden and Blackburn, J. said, partly confirmed and partly altered the common law.[7] For instance, the principle that " if the owner of goods had so acted as to clothe the seller or pledgor with apparent authority to sell or pledge, he was precluded, as against those who were induced *bona fide* to act on the faith of the apparent authority, from denying

---

[1] 6 George IV c. 94 § 1.   [2] Ibid § 2.   [3] § 3.
[4] 6 George IV c. 94 § 4.   [5] § 5.   [6] § 6.
[7] Cole v. North Western Bank (1875) L.R. 10 C.P. at p. 362.

that he had given such authority "—was recognized by the common law.[1] But the common law denied that a factor had power to pledge,[2] so that a pledge by a factor gave no title to the pledgee. In this matter the law was changed where goods were shipped in the factor's name. An advance of money by the consignee to the factor and a pledge made by a consignee were, by the Act of 1823, to be valid.[3] A further change was made in 1825 when it was enacted that the possession by a person of certain documents of title entrusted to him enabled him to give a good title to a *bona fide* purchaser or pledgee, who had no notice that he was not the owner.[4] But notwithstanding the apparently general terms in which these Acts were expressed, the extent to which they were held to have altered the common law was very limited. In effect they applied only to dealings by mercantile agents, entrusted with goods as agents, for the purpose of sale in the course of mercantile transactions.[5] It is for this reason that, in the following period, these two Acts were amended and enlarged, in order to give fuller effect to the views of the merchants as to the effect which ought to be given to the dispositions by factors or other agents entrusted with the possession of goods or documents of title to goods.[6]

(vii) Carriers

The growth of trade increased the number and variety of goods requiring to be transported. For this reason the carriers of these goods complained of a hardship arising from the strict liability imposed upon them by the common law.[7] This hardship is explained in the preamble to the Act of 1830[8] which was passed to mitigate it. It runs as follows :

Whereas by reason of the frequent practice of bankers and others of sending by the public mails, stage coaches, waggons, vans, and other public conveyances, by land for hire, parcels and packages containing money, bills, notes, jewellery and other articles of great value in small compass, much valuable property is rendered liable to depredation, and the responsibility of mail contractors, stage coach proprietors, and common carriers for hire is greatly increased.

It was therefore enacted that such carriers should not be liable for the loss of certain goods specified in the Act when their value exceeded £10, unless, at the time of their delivery to the carrier, their value was declared, and an increased charge was paid.[9]

---

[1] Cole v. North Western Bank (1875) L.R. 10 C.P. at p. 363.   [2] Above 382.
[3] Cole v. North Western Bank (1875) L.R. 10 C.P. at pp. 366-367.
[4] Ibid at p. 367.
[5] Fuentes v. Montis (1868) L.R. 3 C.P. at pp. 278-279.   [6] Below, vol. xiv.
[7] For this liability see vol. viii 452-453 ; vol. xii 519.
[8] 11 George IV and 1 William IV c. 68.   [9] § 1.

Notice of the amount of this increased charge and a receipt for it must be given by the carrier ;[1] but the common law liability of the carrier for the safe carriage of these and other articles could not be otherwise varied by public notice.[2] Such liability could only be varied by a special contract to that effect.[3] Carriers were still to be liable for loss arising from the felonious acts of their servants, and these servants were still to be liable for their own negligence or misconduct.[4] Carriers were to be liable only for the proved value of the goods if this was less than the declared value.[5]

(viii) Negotiable instruments

The principles and rules of the law as to negotiable instruments were developed by the courts.[6] But just as, at an earlier period, the reluctance of Abbott, C.J. to give effect to the general usage of the merchants, which attached the quality of negotiability to promissory notes, made it necessary for the Legislature to intervene,[7] so in this period two of the decisions of the courts made the same intervention necessary. In 1811, in the case of *Glyn v. Baker*,[8] the court of King's Bench had held that the bonds of the East India Company were not negotiable, mainly because they were contracts under seal.[9] This decision was remedied by an Act passed in the same year which made these bonds transferable on delivery.[10] In 1820, in the case of *Rowe v. Young*,[11] there was a division of judicial opinion on the question whether, if a bill were accepted payable at a banker's, this was a general or a qualified acceptance. The House of Lords held that it was a qualified acceptance, with the result that in an action on the bill the plaintiff must prove that he had presented it for payment at the banker's. This decision was criticized in a long, learned, and lucid analysis of the case by G. J. Halcomb, which was appended to the second volume of Broderick and Bingham's reports.[12] Halcomb pointed out[13] that there was much authority for the combined opinions of Abbott, C.J.[14] and Holroyd, J.[15] that such acceptance was, by the general usage of the merchants, general. This view was taken by the Legislature. In 1821, an Act was passed[16] which, after reciting this general usage, enacted that an acceptance made payable at a banker's was to be a general acceptance.

[1] §§ 2 and 3.   [2] § 4.   [3] § 6.   [4] § 8.   [5] § 9.
[6] For the early history see vol. viii 146-177 ; for Lord Mansfield's decisions see vol. xii 529-531 ; the later history will be dealt with in Part II of this book.
[7] Vol. viii 172-176.   [8] (1811) 13 East 509.
[9] See Crouch v. Crédit Foncier (1873) L.R. 8, Q.B. at p. 386.
[10] 57 George III c. 64, 94.   [11] (1820) 2 Brod. and B. 165.
[12] At pp. 6 and 7 he gives in tabular form the various opinions of the judges.
[13] At pp. 16-20.   [14] 2 Brod. and B. at pp. 274-283.
[15] Ibid at pp. 208-222.   [16] 1, 2 George IV c. 78 § 1.

The other statutes on this topic deal only with a few minor points. A statute of 1818[1] remedied a hardship caused by the usury laws. A negotiable instrument given for a usurious consideration was void, and therefore even a *bona fide* holder for value was unable to sue upon it. This statute enabled such a holder to sue if he had had no notice of the usurious consideration. The statute of 1821, already mentioned, enacted that for the future, the acceptance of an inland bill must be in writing and on the bill.[2] Acts of 1800 and 1827 were passed to settle the law as to negotiable instruments which became payable on Good Friday and Christmas Day, and on days proclaimed to be fast or thanksgiving days ;[3] and an Act of 1832 was passed to fix the place at which bills of exchange were to be protested for non-payment, when the drawee refused to accept. The place was to be the place of payment, though that place was not the residence of the drawee.[4]

This series of statutes is a striking proof of the growth of the importance of commercial law. They are more numerous and more important than the corresponding series of statutes in the preceding period.[5] Though they do not cover so much ground as is covered by the decisions of the courts, they show that the Legislature is prepared to take, and will in future take, a hand in the development of this branch of the law, and will not leave it, as in earlier periods, to be developed almost entirely by the courts ; and some of these statutes indicate what will be the chief field of the Legislature's activity. They are the statutes, such as the Factors Acts, which introduce new principles into the law. We shall see that in the following period that it is mainly through the Legislature that important new principles are introduced into commercial and industrial law.[6] In this period the statutes on the topic of commercial law, like the statutes which deal with the regulation of industry, of agriculture, and of colonial and foreign trade, bear witness to the transition stage through which all branches of industry and commerce were passing.

Criminal Law and Procedure

I have already given some account of some of the statutes which altered or added to the criminal law. Those relating to the law of treason,[7] to unlawful assemblies and riots[8] and to

---

[1] 58 George III c. 93. [2] § 2.
[3] 39, 40 George III c. 42 ; 7 and 8 George IV c. 15.
[4] 2, 3 William IV c. 98. [5] For these statutes see vol. xi 444-449.
[6] Below, vol. xiv. [7] Vol. viii 307-322.
[8] Ibid 324-331 ; vol. x 701-705.

libel,[1] those relating to the game laws,[2] those relating to foreign enlistment,[3] and those relating to punishment,[4] have been sufficiently dealt with either in this or in preceding chapters. Similarly, in dealing with local government and with commerce and industry, I have necessarily dealt with many statutes which created criminal offences. As in the preceding period, there are many statutes relating to such topics as the poor law,[5] the highways,[6] vagrancy,[7] liquor licensing,[8] which have made large additions to the criminal law; and the same proposition is true of such topics as smuggling[9] and other offences against the revenue laws, and the combination laws.[10] At this point I must say something, first, of some of the other statutes which added to or altered the law relating to particular crimes: secondly, of the statutes relating to criminal procedure; thirdly, of statutes which relate to subjects connected with the criminal law; and, lastly, of the new variety of statutes which emerges in this period —the statutes which consolidated large parts of the criminal law.

(1) *The statutes which add to or alter the law relating to particular crimes*

I shall deal with these statutes under the following heads: (i) wrongs to property; (ii) wrongs to the person; (iii) coinage offences; (iv) lotteries; (v) miscellaneous.

(i) *Wrongs to property*

As in an earlier chapter I shall deal with these wrongs under the two heads of misappropriation, and the destruction of or injury to property.

Misappropriation. We have seen that the crime of embezzlement had been created in 1799.[11] In 1800 there was legislation as to the embezzlement of naval stores,[12] and in 1810 as to the embezzlement of public money by persons to whom it had been issued.[13] The making of false statements by such persons as to money entrusted to them or collected by them was made punishable by fine and imprisonment.[14] Just as *Bazeley's Case* in 1799 had led to the creation of the crime of embezzlement,[15] so the case of *R. v. Walsh*[16] led in 1812 to the creation

---

[1] Vol. viii 337-345; for the controversy as to the right of the jury to return a general verdict in prosecutions for libel see vol x 672-695.
[2] Vol. xi 543-545.   [3] Above 216, 217.   [4] Vol. xi 556-579; above 217, 218.
[5] Above 311-315.   [6] Vol. x 209, 321.
[7] Ibid 178-179; above 315.   [8] Vol. x 187.
[9] See e.g. the Smuggling Consolidation Act 1825, 6 George IV c. 108 §§ 56-59.
[10] Above 339 seqq.   [11] 39 George III c. 85; vol. xi 534.
[12] 39, 40 George III c. 89.   [13] 50 George III c. 59.
[14] § 2.   [15] Leach 835; vol. xi 534.   [16] (1812) 4 Trans. 258.

of an analogous crime. The short facts of that case was as follows : Walsh was a stockbroker. Sir Thomas Plumer gave him a cheque for £22,200 and directed him to invest the money in Exchequer bills. Walsh paid the cheque into his bank, drew out the proceeds in bank notes, and applied part of them to his own use. His crime was not embezzlement since he was neither a clerk nor a servant. He was therefore indicted for larceny. There was an elaborate argument as to whether this conduct amounted to larceny. No judgment was given, for Walsh was released, no doubt, as Stephen says,[1] " on the ground that the property in the specified bank notes received by Walsh never came to Sir T. Plumer, but passed to Walsh, subject to a contract to invest them in Exchequer bills for his employer."

Immediately afterwards a statute, introduced by Drummond the banker,[2] was passed to make it a misdemeanour if bankers, merchants, brokers, attorneys or other agents sold, or applied to their own use, securities deposited with them for safe custody or for special purposes ; or if they applied to their own use the money for security deposited with them, with an order in writing signed by the depositor to invest the money in any particular way, or to apply it to any particular purpose.[3]

In the same year (1812) the offence of obtaining money or goods by false pretences was extended to the obtaining by false pretences of a large number of choses in action ;[4] and the offences of sending letters threatening to accuse of an infamous crime in order to extort money or property, was extended to such letters sent to extort choses in action.[5] Those who had sent these letters were to be punished as if they had obtained these choses in action by false pretences.[6] In 1822 those who received certain classes of stolen choses in action, knowing them to be stolen, were to be punished in the same way as those who had knowingly received stolen goods.[7] I have already said something of the statutes which took away the punishment of death in certain cases of misappropriation.[8] We shall see

[1] H.C.L. iii 154.

[2] Ibid 155, citing the speech of the attorney-general, Sir R. Bethell, 145 Hansard 680 ; he pointed out that § 6 of the Act provided that it was not to apply to trustees or mortgagees ; this chapter in the law was not remedied till, by the Act proposed by Bethell, fraudulent breach of trust was made a crime, 20, 21 Victoria c. 54.

[3] 52 George III c. 63 §§ 1 and 2.

[4] Vol. xi 532 ; 52 George III c. 64.

[5] Ibid.

[6] Ibid ; the law as to sending threatening letters, vol. xi 532, was restated in 1823, 4 George IV c. 54 § 3, and amended by 6 George IV c. 19 which defined the meaning of the term " infamous crime."

[7] 3 George IV c. 24.

[8] Above 279 ; 48 George III c. 129 ; 51 George III c. 41 ; 4 George IV cc. 53 and 54.

that the statute law on this subject was consolidated, restated, and amended in 1827.[1]

Additions were made to the series of statutes which made the fabrication of particular kinds of documents forgery.[2] In 1797 forging the names of witnesses to letters of attorney for the transfer of stock,[3] and in 1803 the forgery of foreign bills of exchange and promissory notes,[4] were made felonies. In 1830 the law was consolidated and the different kinds of forgeries were grouped into classes according to the punishment awarded.[5] Certain forgeries were treasonable and capitally punished, e.g. forgery of the great seal or the sign manual.[6] Others were felonious and capitally punished, e.g. the forgery of exchequer bills or bank notes.[7] Others were felonies which were punished by transportation for various terms of years, e.g. forging a deed or bond,[8] or personating the owner of stock,[9] or knowingly receiving forged bank notes,[10] or inserting a false entry or forging an entry in a register of baptisms, marriages, or burials.[11] No forgery was to be punishable with death unless made so punishable by the Act.[12] Similarly, additions were made to the series of statutes which punished offences akin to forgery,[13] such as possessing or using any instrument for the making of banknote paper;[14] or engraving on any plate the impression of a bank note, or using or possessing such a plate.[15] These statutes were also consolidated in 1830.[16]

The destruction of or injury to property

Additions were made to the statutes which made it a criminal offence to injure timber and crops of different kinds;[17] and in 1820 trespassing on, or damaging, wilfully and maliciously, buildings, fences, hedges, gates, stiles, guide posts, mile stones, trees and other crops, and other real and personal property, was made an offence punishable summarily by a justice of the peace, who was empowered to award compensation for the damage up to the sum of £5.[18] In 1803 there was further legislation directed against those who cast away or destroyed ships

---

[1] Below 396-400. [2] Vol. xi 534.
[3] 37 George III c. 122. [4] 43 George III c. 139.
[5] 11 George IV, 1 William IV c. 66; it repealed wholly or partially twenty-seven statutes.
[6] § 2. [7] § 3. [8] § 10. [9] § 7.
[10] § 12. [11] § 20. [12] § 1. [13] Vol. xi 535.
[14] 41 George III c. 39; in 1803 engraving plates purporting to be bills or notes of any foreign prince or state or foreign persons or corporations was made an offence punishable by imprisonment, 43 George III c. 139 § 2.
[15] 52 George III c. 138 § 5; 1 George IV c. 92.
[16] 11 George IV and William IV c. 66 §§ 13-19.
[17] Vol. xi 536; 13 George III c. 32; 42 George III c. 67.
[18] 1 George IV c. 56, § 1.

to the prejudice of the owners or insurers.[1] The industrial disturbances of the second decade of the nineteenth century[2] were the occasion of statutes which strengthened the existing statutes directed against those who destroyed buildings or machinery used for the purpose of carrying on any trade or manufacture,[3] and provided for the punishment of those who destroyed stocking or lace frames or any articles in the frames.[4] We shall see that in 1827 the statute law on the subject of malicious injury to property was consolidated and amended.[5]

(ii) *Wrongs to the person*

We have seen that the first general Act which dealt with wrongs to the person not resulting in death was the Act of 1803 generally known as Lord Ellenborough's Act.[6] By that Act it was made a felony punishable with death to shoot, stab, or cut a person with intent to kill, rob, maim, or prevent an arrest ; or to administer or cause to be administered poison with intent to murder or to cause a miscarriage, or to set fire to a house or other building with intent to injure the owner. But if a person was indicted for shooting, cutting, or stabbing, and if death had ensued the offence would not have been murder, he was to be acquitted.[7] It was also made a felony to administer drugs with intent to procure abortion.[8] The concealment of the birth of a bastard was made punishable by imprisonment.[9] In 1795 the punishment for bigamy was increased ;[10] in 1814 child stealing was in effect made punishable by transportation ;[11] in 1820 drivers of coaches and public carriages who injured persons by furious driving or racing were to be guilty of a misdemeanour ;[12] and in 1827 persons who set man traps or spring guns or who permitted them to be set were also to be guilty of a misdemeanour.[13] We shall see that the statute law on this subject was consolidated in 1828.[14]

(iii) *Coinage offences*

Additions were made to this series of statutes.[15] In 1797 the counterfeiting of copper coin, and of foreign gold and silver

---

[1] Vol. xi 535 ; 43 George III c. 113 § 2.   [2] Above 180, 192, 193.
[3] 52 George III c. 130.   [4] Ibid 16 ; 54 George III c. 42.
[5] Below 399, 400.   [6] Vol. xi 537 ; 43 George III c. 58.
[7] § 1.   [8] § 2.
[9] § 4 ; § 3 repealed 21 James I c. 27, vol. iv 501, which made a mother who concealed the birth of her bastard child liable to the punishment for murder ; she was only to be liable to be so punished if in fact she had murdered the child.
[10] 35 George III c. 67.   [11] 54 George III c. 101.
[12] 1 George IV c. 4.
[13] 7, 8 George IV c. 18 ; the Act did not apply to man traps or spring guns set in a house from sunrise to sunrise for its protection, § 4 ; above 267.
[14] Below 605.   [15] Vol. xi 538-539.

coin, and the bringing of such foreign coin into the realm, were made offences.[1] In 1811 it was made an offence to counterfeit silver pieces denominated tokens intended to be issued by the Bank of England or to bring such counterfeits into the kingdom;[2] and in 1812 an Act was passed to prevent the circulation of gold or silver tokens other than those issued by the Bank of England or Ireland.[3] We shall see that the statute on this topic was consolidated in 1832.[4]

(iv) *Gaming and lotteries*

The struggle against the gambler continued.[5] An Act of 1802[6] recited that

> evil disposed persons do frequently resort to public houses and other places, to set up certain mischievous games or lotteries called *Little Goes*, and to induce servants, children, and unwary persons to play at the said games; and thereby most fraudulently obtain great sums of money from servants, children, and unwary persons, to the great impoverishment and utter ruin of many families.

It enacted that persons keeping an office or place for the holding of any lottery not authorized by Parliament were to be deemed rogues and vagabonds, and were to be punished as such. Persons who agreed to pay any sum or confer any benefit on any event or contingency connected with the drawing of lottery tickets were to forfeit £100.

(v) *Miscellaneous*

We have seen that in 1800 the Legislature had provided for the custody of insane criminals;[7] and we have seen that it abolished the doctrine of corruption of blood as a consequence of a conviction for felony, but not as a consequence of a conviction for high or petty treason, or murder, or counselling or procuring the same.[8] In 1802 the legislation which provided for the trial in England of governors of colonies,[9] and persons accused of committing crimes in India,[10] was extended to all persons in public employment abroad.[11] Other statutes

---

[1] 37 George III c. 126; 43 George III c. 139 § 3.
[2] 51 George III c. 110; amended by 52 George III c. 138.
[3] Ibid 157.　　　　[4] Below 402, 403.
[5] For the eighteenth century legislation see vol. xi 539-543.
[6] 42 George III c. 119.
[7] Above 320; 39, 40 George III c. 94; 56 George III c. 117.
[8] 54 George III c. 145; above 281; for this doctrine, which Blackstone criticized, see vol. iii 69, 70; vol. xi 558-559; vol. xii 723, 728; the whole doctrine was abolished in 1834, 3, 4 William IV c. 106 § 10.
[9] 11, 12 William III c. 12; vol. vi 402; vol. xi 254.
[10] 13 George III c. 63 §§ 39 and 40; 24 George III Sess. 2 c. 25 §§ 44, 53 and 54; vol. xi 168, 207, 208.　　　　[11] 42 George III c. 85.

provided for the mitigation of punishment. Persons convicted of high treason were to be hanged by the neck till they were dead;[1] females were not to be whipped;[2] and the pillory was abolished as a punishment except in cases of perjury.[3] We have seen that in very many cases transportation or imprisonment had been substituted for the death penalty.[4] In 1821 the penalties for rescuing prisoners charged with felony, and for assaulting constables in order to prevent their arrest, were increased.[5] In 1822 the first of the statutes for the prevention of cruelty to animals was passed. Ill treatment of horses or cattle was made punishable by a fine, or, in default of payment, imprisonment.[6] But if the justice thought that the complaint was vexatious he could order compensation up to the amount of 20/- to be paid to the accused.[7] In 1794 the Sunday Observance Acts[8] were modified in their application to bakers. They were allowed to carry on their trade on Sundays between 9 and 1.[9] The legislation against cursing and swearing[10] was retained; but the provisions of the Act which required it to be read in the churches four times a year were repealed.[11] In 1820 it was provided that in cases of crimes committed at sea, which fell within the jurisdiction of the Admiralty, benefit of clergy could be pleaded; and that the jurisdiction of the Admiralty extended not only to murder and manslaughter, but also to other crimes defined by Lord Ellenborough's Act of 1803.[12]

(2) *Statutes relating to criminal procedure*

These statutes do not cover much ground. We shall see that it is not till 1826 and 1827 that any considerable improvements were made, and any considerable number of archaisms were weeded out of this branch of the law.[13]

As in the preceding period,[14] difficulties caused by the rules as to the venue gave rise to a number of statutes. Two statutes of 1798 and 1811[15] provided for the trial of cases, both civil and criminal, which arose in cities and towns which were counties. The trial of these cases could take place, if the court so directed, in the county next adjoining, and the prisoner could be removed to the custody of the sheriff of that county. In 1802 it was enacted that persons indicted for robbing the mail could be tried either in the county where the offence was committed or in the

---

[1] 54 George III c. 146.
[2] 57 George III c. 75; 1 George IV c. 51.
[3] 56 George III c. 138.
[4] Above 284, 285.
[5] 1, 2 George IV c. 88.
[6] 3 George IV c. 7, § 1; above 266.
[7] § 5.
[8] Vol. vi 404; vol. xi 547.
[9] 34 George III c. 61.
[10] Vol. vi 404; vol. xi 547.
[11] 4 George IV c. 31.
[12] 1 George IV c. 90; above 390.
[13] Below 396, 397.
[14] Vol. xi 550.
[15] 38 George III c. 52; 51 George III c. 100.

county where the thief was arrested ;[1] and in 1819 it was enacted
that felonies committed on coaches, carriages, and waggons
could be tried in any county through which the vehicle had passed
and that felonies committed within five hundred yards of the
boundaries of two counties could be tried in either county.[2]
A similar provision was made for felonies committed on ships
in rivers and canals.[3] On the trial of public servants for offences
committed abroad the venue could be laid in Middlesex.[4]

There was some legislation as to the trial of offences on
the high seas. An Act of Henry VIII had enacted that " treasons,
felonies, robberies, murders, and confederacies " committed
on the high seas could be tried in any county.[5] In 1799 this rule
was extended to all other crimes.[6] In 1806 it was enacted
that an Act of 1698-9,[7] by which piracies, felonies, and robberies
within the Admiralty jurisdiction could be tried either at sea
or in any colony or factory beyond the sea appointed by the Crown,
should be extended to the trial of other offences ;[8] and in 1819[9] the
provisions of this Act were extended to offences created by a statute
passed to enforce the Act for the abolition of the slave trade.[10]

A useful set of Acts was passed to deal with persons who
committed criminal offences in England, Scotland, or Ireland,
and escaped from that part of the United Kingdom where the
offence had been committed to another part. An Act of 1773[11]
had provided that, if a criminal escaped to Scotland, the English
warrant for his arrest could be endorsed by the appropriate
Scotch authority, and that that endorsement should be authority
for his arrest in Scotland ;[12] and a similar provision was made
for the converse case.[13] It was also provided that a thief in England, who was arrested with the stolen property on him in
Scotland, could be tried in Scotland or vice versa ;[14] and receivers
of stolen property could be indicted where they received the
property as if the property had been stolen there.[15] Similar
provisions were made for Ireland in 1804.[16] Both these Acts
were amended in 1805 ;[17] and provision was made for the service
of writs of subpoena and other process in Scotland and Ireland.[18]

Two statutes were passed to expedite the trial of misdemeanours. The first was a statute of 1808,[19] introduced by

---

[1] 42 George III c. 81 § 3.
[2] 59 George III c. 96.
[3] Ibid 27.
[4] 42 George III c. 85 § 1 ; above 391.
[5] 28 Henry VIII c. 15 ; vol. i 550 ; vol. iv 523.
[6] 39 George III c. 37 ; it was provided, § 2, that a person convicted of manslaughter should be entitled to the benefit of clergy when tried under this statute.
[7] 11 William III c. 7 ; vol. vi 400-401, 426 and n. 13.
[8] 46 George III c. 54.
[9] 59 George III c. 97.
[10] 51 George III c. 23.
[11] 13 George III c. 31.
[12] § 1.
[13] § 2.
[14] § 4.
[15] § 5.
[16] 44 George III c. 92.
[17] 45 George III c. 92.
[18] § 3.
[19] 48 George III c. 58.

Vicary Gibbs,[1] which applied to the trial of misdemeanours a procedure which had been devised for revenue cases.[2] If a person was charged with a misdemeanour for which he could be prosecuted by indictment or information in the King's Bench, a judge could issue a warrant to arrest the accused. He must then either give bail or be committed. If a person so committed did not plead within eight days after a copy of the indictment or information and a notice had been delivered by the prosecutor, the prosecutor could enter a plea of not guilty, and the trial could proceed.[3] The provisions of this statute were, says Foss,[4] so obnoxious that they were never put into force. The second was a statute of 1819.[5] Delays caused by imparlances were abolished, and the accused must plead within four days of his appearance,[6] unless the court allowed a longer time.[7] Persons held to bail or in custody twenty days before the sessions of the peace or of oyer and terminer must plead forthwith;[8] but if held to bail or in custody for less than twenty days before the sessions they must plead at the next sessions.[9] In both cases the court could allow a longer time in which to plead.[10] The attorney-general must give a copy of the information to the accused *gratis*;[11] and if, on a prosecution by the attorney-general, the case was not brought to trial within twelve months of the entry of a plea of not guilty, the court could order that the trial should be forthwith held.[12]

We shall see that the consolidation Acts of 1826 and 1827 dealing with criminal procedure made more extensive changes in the law.[13]

(3) *The statutes relating to topics connected with the criminal law*

This is a small group of statutes which does not fall under either of the two preceding heads. The gaol fees charged by gaolers on commitments or discharges from prison, and the fees payable to clerks of assize, clerks of the peace, and other clerks on an aquittal or other discharge from an indictment were an old established abuse. They were abolished in 1815, and compensation was provided for the gaolers and clerks out of the county rates.[14] Similarly, persons in prison for debt were no longer to be liable on their discharge to pay a fee to the sheriff

---

[1] Foss, Judges viii 290; for Vicary Gibbs see below 535-543.

[2] 26 George III c. 77 § 18; 35 George III c. 96.

[3] 48 George III c. 58 § 1; § 2 provided for the application to this procedure of the statutes, 13 George III c. 31 and 45 George III c. 92.

[4] Judges viii 290.   [5] 60 George III c. 4.

[6] § 1.   [7] § 2.   [8] § 3.   [9] § 5.

[10] § 7.   [11] § 8.   [12] § 9.   [13] Below 396-397.

[14] 55 George III c. 50; amended 56 George III c. 116; extended 8, 9 Victoria c. 114; vol. x 181.

or under-sheriff. In 1818 all fees for pardons under the great seal were abolished ;[1] and in 1825 it was enacted that a warrant under the sign manual for a pardon should have the same effect as a pardon under the great seal.[2] We have seen that several statutes had promised rewards to those who assisted in the discovery, apprehension, or conviction of criminals.[3] In 1818 the Legislature came to the conclusion that this expedient was inefficacious, and even encouraged the commission of crimes.[4] It therefore repealed all but one of the statutes which promised these rewards.[5] It also empowered the Court to order the payment of the expenses of the prosecutor of a felon and the prosecutor's witnesses, or of other persons who had assisted to apprehend the felon.[6] In 1823 the rule that the body of a suicide was to be buried in the highway with a stake driven through his body was repealed. A suicide was to be buried in the churchyard, but without any religious ceremony.[7]

(4) *The consolidating statutes*

We have seen that, under the influence of Bentham's criticisms of the statute book, his advocacy of codification, and his denunciation of useless and archaic technicalities, an attempt was made between the years 1826 and 1830 to consolidate and amend the criminal law.[8] These statutes were designed to do for the criminal law what the customs code of 1825 had done for the laws which regulated the customs and subjects cognate thereto.[9] We have seen that a statute of 1827 cleared the ground for the other legislation of that year by repealing wholly or in part 137 statutes ;[10] that statutes of 1826 and 1827 dealt with procedure ; that other statutes of 1827 dealt with larceny and cognate offences, with malicious injuries to property, and with remedies against the hundred ; that a statute of 1828 dealt with offences against the person ; that a statute of 1830 dealt with forgery ;[11] and that a statute of 1832 dealt with coinage offences.[12] These statutes mark an important epoch in the history

[1] 58 George III c. 29.
[2] 6 George IV c. 25 ; Blackstone tells us, Comm. iv 400, that, at common law, " a warrant under the privy seal or sign manual, though it may be sufficient authority to admit the party to bail, in order to plead the king's pardon when obtained in proper form, yet is not of itself a complete irrevocable pardon."
[3] Vol. vi 405-406 ; vol. xi 552.   [4] 58 George III c. 70 preamble.
[5] The only statute left unrepealed was 10, 11 William III c. 23 which dealt with burglary and robberies in shops, warehouses, and stables, and the stealing of horses ; it was repealed by 7, 8 George IV c. 27.
[6] § 4.   [7] 4 George IV c. 52.
[8] Above 260, 262, 263.   [9] Above 261, 262.
[10] 7, 8 George IV c. 27 ; above 262 ; but the repeal was not to affect Acts relating to the post office, or the revenue, or (with two exceptions) to the public stores, or to the Bank of England or the South Sea Company, § 2.
[11] Above 226, 263, 389.   [12] Above 391.

of the criminal law, and therefore it is necessary at this point to say something of their contents.

Procedure

The Act of 1826[1] dealt with the rules to be observed by the justices as to the admission to bail of persons accused of felony, their duties when a person was accused of a misdemeanour, and the duties of coroners when a person was indicted for murder or manslaughter.[2] These sections reproduced the statutes of Philip and Mary dealing with these subjects.[3] Then followed some sections dealing with the intricacies of the law as to benefit of clergy,[4] and as to the trial of accessories before and after the fact;[5] and with the law as to offences committed on the boundaries of counties,[6] and those committed on a journey by land or on a voyage on a river or canal.[7] Then came a series of sections which stated the law as to how the ownership of property should be laid when it belonged to partners or joint owners, counties, poor law or highway authorities, turnpike trustees, or commissioners of sewers.[8] Indictments were not to abate for misnomer,[9] and certain defects were set out which were not to vitiate an indictment after verdict or outlawry, and other defects were set out which were to be insufficient to stay or reverse a judgment after verdict.[10] The Acts which allowed the payment of expenses to prosecutors or others were restated.[11] The Act ended by repealing wholly or partially thirty-one statutes from 3 Edward 1, c. 15 to 6 George IV, c. 56.[12]

The Act of 1827[13]—" an Act for further improving the administration of justice in criminal cases "—made a larger number of reforms. A plea of not guilty was to involve, as a necessary consequence, that the accused consented to be tried by jury.[14] If he refused to plead the court was to enter a plea of not guilty.[15] Other pleading reforms relate to challenges and pleas of attainder of another crime.[16] The enquiry as to lands and tenements and whether the person fled,[17] and benefit of clergy[18] were abolished, but no offence was to be capitally punished unless previously excluded from clergy.[19] The punishment for non-capital felonies was defined; and if a prisoner was convicted of two felonies

[1] 7 George IV c. 64. [2] §§ 1, 3, 4.
[3] 1, 2 Philip and Mary c. 13; 2, 3 Philip and Mary c. 10; vol. i 294-296; vol. v 527-530. [4] §§ 7 and 8.
[5] §§ 9-11. [6] § 12. [7] § 13. [8] §§ 14-18.
[9] § 19; see vol. iii 617. [10] §§ 20 and 21; see vol. iii 618.
[11] §§ 22-30; above 395. [12] § 32.
[13] 7, 8 George IV c. 28. [14] § 1.
[15] § 2; for the old law see vol. i 326-327.
[16] §§ 3 and 4; vol. i 336-337; vol. iii 614.
[17] § 5; for the old law see vol. iii 312.
[18] § 6; for benefit of clergy see vol. iii 294-302. [19] § 7.

a sentence of imprisonment or transportation for the second
felony could be passed to begin after the expiration of the first
sentence.[1] Second and subsequent offences were to be more
severely punished.[2] The punishment for offences committed
within the jurisdiction of the Admiralty was to be the same as
that for offences committed on land.[3] The effect of free or
conditional pardons was defined.[4]

Larceny and cognate offences

The statute relating to this topic is entitled "an Act for consolidating and amending the law relative to larceny and other
offences connected therewith."[5] It begins by abolishing
the distinction between grand and petit larceny. All larcenies
are to be treated as grand larceny;[6] and, if no other provision
for punishment was made, they were to be simple larcenies
and punishable with transportation for seven years, or imprisonment up to two years with or without whipping.[7] The theft
of various securities and choses in action set out in the Act
was to be punishable as the theft of chattels.[8] Stealing from
the person, assaults with intent to rob, the demanding of property
with menaces, the obtaining of money by a threat to accuse
of an infamous crime, and the sending of threatening letters,
were then dealt with.[9] Then came three crimes which were to
be punished by death—sacrilege, burglary, and house-breaking.[10]
But robbery in a building not part of a dwelling house, and robbery
in a shop or warehouse were not to be capitally punished.[11]
After that follows a large number of sections which reproduce
older statutes passed at different periods to punish thefts of
many different classes of property, or in many different sets
of circumstances—stealing from a ship in a port or river, plundering a wrecked ship, stealing the records of courts of justice,
wills, title deeds, cattle, deer, taking or killing hares or rabbits
in a warren at night, stealing dogs, birds or beasts kept in
confinement, pigeons, fish in a private fishery, oysters, coal or
ore from mines, trees and shrubs, fences, posts or rails, fruit or
vegetables, fixtures from buildings.[12] There followed a clause
dealing with the theft by lodgers or tenants of property in
the house or apartments let to them;[13] and after that, by a
natural transition, the crime of embezzlement was dealt with,[14]
and the pledging by a factor for his own benefit of his principal's

---

[1] §§ 9 and 10. [2] § 11. [3] § 12.
[4] § 13; above 394, 395. [5] 7, 8 George IV c. 29.
[6] § 2; for this distinction see vol. ii 359; vol. iii 366-367.
[7] § 3. [8] § 5. [9] §§ 6-9. [10] §§ 10-13.
[11] § 14. [12] §§ 16-44. [13] § 45.
[14] §§ 47-50; see vol. xi 533-534.

property.[1] Then came a section as to obtaining money or property by false pretences.[2]

The statute then went on to deal with receivers of stolen
property. If the original offence was a felony the receiver could
be indicted either as an accessory after the fact or for a substantive felony : if it was a misdemeanour, for a misdemeanour.[3]
They could be tried either where the principal was tried, or where
the property was found in their possession, or where the receiving
took place.[4] They could be punished by transportation of from
seven to fourteen years or by imprisonment up to three years
if the original offence was a felony, and by transportation for
seven years or imprisonment up to two years if it was a misdemeanour.[5] With some exceptions, the owner of stolen property
prosecuting to conviction was entitled to get a writ for its restitution.[6] Taking a reward for restoring the stolen property
without bringing the thief to trial, and advertising a reward
for the return of stolen property with a promise to ask no questions
—were offences punishable in the first case by transportation
or imprisonment, and in the second case by a fine.[7] Accessories
before the fact and principals in the second degree, and those
who aided or abetted a misdemeanour, were to be punished
in the same way as those who had committed the crime.[8] Accessories after the fact (other than receivers of stolen goods) were
to be punishable by imprisonment up to two years.[9] There were
clauses as to arrests without a warrant, as to the power to issue
a search warrant,[10] and as to the procedure to be followed by
the justices when the offence could be dealt with summarily.[11]
The Act applied only to England ; but if a person stole in one
part of the United Kingdom, and was arrested with the property
on him in another part, he could be tried where he was arrested.
Similarly, a person who received property stolen in another
part of the United Kingdom, could be tried in that part of the
United Kingdom where he received it.[12]

Though the Act is not a model of arrangement, though
it bears upon it the marks of the haphazard way in which the
law had been constructed by many different statutes passed
at different periods, it did effect a simplification. The substance
of the law was stated in clearer and terser language, it was collected
together, and a considerable number of antiquated technicalities
were removed. It was the basis of the later consolidations of
the law in 1861 [13] and 1916.[14]

---

[1] §§ 51 and 52.   [2] § 53 ; vol. xi 532-533.
[3] §§ 54 and 55.   [4] § 56.   [5] §§ 54 and 55.
[6] § 57 ; see vol. ii 361 ; vol. iv 522, 523.   [7] §§ 58 and 59.
[8] § 61.   [9] Ibid.   [10] § 63.
[11] §§ 64-74.   [12] § 76 ; above 393.
[13] 24, 25 Victoria c. 96.   [14] 6, 7 George V c. 50.

Malicious injuries to property

The chief part of this Act[1] consists of a large number of sections which reproduce the numerous statutes which had, from time to time, been passed to punish with various degrees of severity injuries to different kinds of property. Injuries to some of these different kinds of property were felonies, punishable sometimes with death, and sometimes with transportation or imprisonment. Instances of injuries punishable by death are setting fire to churches[2] or coal mines,[3] demolishing churches, various kinds of buildings or machinery,[4] destroying ships,[5] wrecking by false lights.[6] Instances of injuries punishable by transportation or imprisonment are destroying silk, wool, linen, or cotton goods in the loom, and machinery connected with their manufacture,[7] destroying threshing machines and machines employed in manufactures,[8] damaging ships, and sea, canal or river banks, and bridges.[9] Injuries to other kinds of property were misdemeanours, e.g. destroying toll gates[10] or the dam of a fishpond.[11] Other minor injuries were offences punishable on summary conviction by fines or short terms of imprisonment, e.g. damaging trees or shrubs or vegetables, or destroying fences, walls or gates.[12] In many of these cases the offence was defined as a *malicious* injury to a person's property. To clear up doubts as to the meaning of this phrase, it was provided that the offence was to be deemed to have been committed, " whether the offence shall be committed from malice conceived against the owner of the property or otherwise "—that is, " maliciously " really meant " wilfully."[13] Principals in the second degree and accessories before the fact were punishable in the same way as principals in the first degrees ; accessories after the fact were punishable by imprisonment up to two years ; and those who abetted a misdemeanour, or an offence punishable on summary conviction, were punishable in the same way as those who had committed the crime.[14] It was provided that persons caught in the act of committing these offences could be arrested without warrant ;[15] and rules were laid down as to points connected with the procedure in the case of offences punishable on summary conviction.[16]

This statute is one of the least successful of this series of consolidating Acts. No attempt was made to classify on any intelligible principle different varieties of the offence. By far the greater part of the statute is a mere enumeration of specific injuries which, if inflicted on different kinds of property, were to be punishable in different ways. In other words, it merely puts

---

[1] 7, 8 George IV c. 30. [2] § 2. [3] § 5. [4] § 8.
[5] § 9. [6] § 11. [7] § 3. [8] § 4.
[9] §§ 10, 12, 13. [10] § 14. [11] § 15. [12] §§ 19-23.
[13] § 25. [14] § 26. [15] § 28. [16] §§ 29-40.

together a large number of separate statutes, and makes no attempt to extract from them any general principles or rules. From this point of view the Act which consolidated this branch of the law in 1861 is more satisfactory.[1]

Remedies against the hundred

We have seen that, during the eighteenth century, the procedure by which a person who had been robbed of his property, or whose property had been injured, by criminals who had not been brought to justice, could get compensation from the hundred, had been reformed;[2] and other statutes passed during this period had made additions to and changes in the law.[3] All these statutes which imposed this liability on the hundred had been repealed in 1827;[4] and the new Act of 1827[5] defined its liability anew and confined it to damage to certain kinds of property inflicted by rioters. The kinds of property set out in the Act were churches or chapels, houses or other buildings used to carry on any trade or manufacture, machinery employed in any manufacture, engines, bridges, or waggon ways used in the working of mines.[6] Plaintiffs must within seven days go before a justice of the peace residing near to the place where the riot had taken place, and state on oath the circumstances of the case, and the action must be begun within three months of the commission of the offence.[7] If the damage did not exceed £30 the claim was to be settled by petty sessions.[8] Actions were to be brought against the high constable,[9] and the treasurer of the county must pay any damages awarded.[10]

Offence against the person

The Act of 1828[11] which consolidated the law on this subject began by repealing in whole or in part fifty-seven statutes from 9 Henry III c. 26 to 3 George IV c. 114.[12] It abolished the crime of petty or petit treason, which was, for the future, to be treated as murder.[13] It then dealt with murder and its punishment, and principals and accessories to murder.[14] Murder and manslaughter by British subjects, though committed abroad, could be tried in England.[15] For the future, no forfeiture or punishment was to be

---

[1] 24, 25 Victoria c. 97.   [2] Vol. xi 551-552.
[3] See 41 George III c. 24; 52 George III c. 130 § 2; 56 George III c. 125; 57 George III c. 19; 3 George IV c. 33.   [4] 7, 8 George IV c. 27.
[5] 7, 8 George IV c. 31 cp. Halsbury, Laws of England (2nd ed.) ix 89 n. (e).
[6] § 2; to which in 1832 threshing machines were added, 2, 3 William IV c. 72.
[7] § 3.   [8] § 8.   [9] § 4.   [10] § 6.
[11] 9 George IV c. 31.   [12] § 1.
[13] § 2; for petty or petit treason see vol. ii 450; vol. iii 288, 291.
[14] §§ 3-6.   [15] § 7.

inflicted for homicide which was not felonious.[1] Attempts to murder, and wounding with intent to maim were then dealt with.[2] Then came the offence of procuring a miscarriage and concealment of birth, sodomy, rape, carnal knowledge of girls under ten and between ten and twelve years of age, abduction of an heiress, abduction of a girl under sixteen from her parents, child stealing, and bigamy.[3] Arrest of a clergyman on civil process while performing divine service, or going to or returning therefrom, was to be a misdemeanour.[4] Then various sorts of assaults were dealt with—assaults on officers endeavouring to save shipwrecked property, on peace or revenue officers, on persons attempting to effect a lawful arrest; assaults in pursuance of a conspiracy to raise wages, or on seamen to prevent them from working; assaults with intent to obstruct the buying or selling or the free passage of grain, and common assaults.[5] Lastly, it was provided that the master of a ship abroad, who forced a seaman to go ashore and refused to bring him home, was to be guilty of a misdemeanour punishable by imprisonment.[6] Offences against the Act committed at sea were to be punished in the same way as offences committed on land.[7] Accessories before the fact were to be punished by transportation or imprisonment, and those who aided or abetted a misdemeanour punishable under the Act were to be punished as principals.[8] Certain rules were laid down as to offences punishable on summary conviction;[9] and it was provided that the Act was not to affect the law as to high treason, the Acts dealing with the revenue or smuggling, or the Combination Act of 1825.[10]

Forgery

This Act[11] is entitled " an Act for reducing into one Act all such forgeries as shall henceforth be punished with death and for otherwise amending the laws relative to forgery."[12] It begins by enacting that no forgeries and certain other offences akin thereto, such as personation, were to be capital offences, unless they were made capital offences by this Act.[13] Forgeries not made capital offences by this Act were to be punished by transportation.[14] The Act then gives a list of the forgeries which were to be punished with death. They include the forgery of the great and privy seal, and the sign manual, which was treason,[15] the forgery of exchequer bills, bank notes, bills of exchange, promissory notes,

---

[1] § 10 ; for the reason for this clause see vol. iii 312.   [2] §§ 11 and 12.
[3] §§ 13-22.   [4] § 23.   [5] §§ 24-27.   [6] § 30.
[7] § 32.   [8] § 31.   [9] §§ 27-29, 33, 36.   [10] § 37; above 341-351.
[11] 11 George IV and 1 William IV c. 66.
[12] The Act was not to apply to coinage offences, § 1.
[13] § 1.   [14] Ibid.   [15] § 2.

wills ;[1] the making of false entries in the books in which the accounts of the stock transferable at the Bank of England were kept ;[2] the forgery of transfers of such stock and powers of attorney to transfer it or to receive dividends on it, and the personation of the owner of such stock or dividends upon it.[3] The Act then goes on to give a list of the forgeries and kindred offences which are to be punished by transportation for various terms of years. They include attempts to defraud by personating the owners of stock,[4] and forging the attestation of a power of attorney for its transfer ;[5] issuing incorrect dividend warrants with intent to defraud ;[6] the forgery of deeds, bonds, or receipts ;[7] knowingly purchasing, receiving or possessing forged bank notes.[8] A group of sections deals with offences connected with the forgery of bank notes or bills of exchange, e.g. having materials for making bank note paper or engraving on any plate any words or numbers resembling any part of a bank note.[9] Lastly come the sections dealing with the inserting of false entries or otherwise tampering with registers of baptisms, marriages, or burials.[10] The phrase " having a document in a person's possession " was to mean either having it in his personal custody or knowingly or wilfully having it in any house or building ; and if the phrase " intent to defraud any person " was used, person was to include bodies corporate or unincorporate bodies.[11] The Act was to apply to the forging or uttering in England of documents made or purporting to be made out of England, and to the forgery in England of documents purporting to be payable out of England.[12] The Act ended by repealing wholly or partially twenty-seven statutes from 25 Edward I St. 5, c. 2 to 4 George IV c. 26.[13]

Coinage offences

The Act[14] makes the majority of coinage offences felonies, thus getting rid of the law which made certain of these offences treason.[15] It begins with sections as to the counterfeiting of gold or silver coins, or colouring coin so as to make it pass for gold or silver coin, or altering genuine coin so as to make it pass for coin of a higher value.[16] Then it deals with diminishing or lightening of gold or silver coin, and the putting off or importation or uttering of counterfeit gold or silver coin.[17] Then come sections penalizing the possession of tools for coining, and taking coining tools from

---

[1] §§ 3 and 4. [2] § 5. [3] § 6. [4] § 7.
[5] § 8. [6] § 9. [7] § 10. [8] § 12.
[9] §§ 13-19. [10] §§ 20-22.
[11] § 28 ; in the case of unincorporate bodies it was to be sufficient to have one member only of them in the indictment.
[12] § 30. [13] § 31. [14] 2, 3 William IV c. 34.
[15] Stephen, H. C. L. iii 179 ; vol. iii 289.
[16] §§ 3 and 4. [17] §§ 5-8.

the mint.[1] Then come sections as to similar offences in relation to copper coins.[2] Lastly there are sections as to the right of persons to whom counterfeit or clipped coin is tendered to deface it, and as to powers of seizure of counterfeit coin or tools for coining, and as to powers of searching for such coin or tools.[3]

This group of statutes illustrates the influence of the new ideas as to law reform, as clearly as some of the statutes relating to local government and to commerce and industry illustrate the influence of the new problems set by the industrial revolution and the new ideas of the economists.

The Common Law

It was chiefly in the criminal branch of the common law that the Legislature enacted important consolidating and amending statutes. In the civil branch there are, it is true, numerous statutes ; but they cover very little ground. Though the work of royal commissions was preparing the way for reforms in many different departments of this branch of the common law,[4] and though in one or two cases their recommendations had resulted in legislation,[5] it is not till the following period that the influence of their work upon legislation becomes marked.[6] I shall give some account of the legislation of this period, very little of which is of first rate importance, under the following heads : the courts ; procedure ; evidence ; property ; contract ; and miscellaneous.

The courts

In the second decade of the century the press of business in the *Court of King's Bench* was so great[7] that various provisions were made from time to time for authorizing its sittings out of term at Serjeants' Inn or some other convenient place.[8] We shall see that this legislation was superseded by an Act of 1830, which made considerable changes in the judicial machinery.[9] The survival of archaisms which had lost their meaning is a characteristic feature of the judicial machinery. In the Middle Ages the King's Bench superseded other courts in the place where, and during the time that, it was sitting.[10] At the beginning of the nineteenth century

<hr/>

[1] §§ 10 and 11. [2] § 12. [3] §§ 13 and 14.
[4] Above 306-308. [5] Vol. i 131, 222, 262 ; above 307, 308 ; below 406.
[6] Below, vol. xiv. [7] Vol. xii 448, 503 ; above 306, 307.
[8] 1 George IV c. 21 ; 1, 2 George II c. 16 ; 3 George IV c. 102.
[9] Below 404, 405.
[10] Putnam, Proceedings before the Justices of the Peace in the 14th and 15th Centuries (Ames Foundation) lxi, lxiii-lxvii, lxxii, lxxvi ; Miss Putnam has shown that the court often moved about the country in the reigns of Edward III and Richard II, that it was generally fixed at Westminster in Henry IV's reign, that it was occasionally migratory in Henry V's reign, and that it did not move from Westminster after Henry V's reign, ibid lviii.

it had long been stationary at Westminster. But it was by reason of this old rule that it was necessary in 1828 to pass a statute to provide that the sessions of the peace could be held at Westminster although the King's Bench was sitting at Westminster or at some other place in Middlesex.[1] Two statutes made some reforms in the *Court of Exchequer*. A statute of 1820[2] improved the equity side of the court by making better provision for the care of the suitor's money. An accountant-general of the court was appointed, and accounts were to be kept as they were kept in the court of Chancery.[3] Two masters were to be appointed to deal with matters of account and other matters, of whom the accountant-general was to be one. A statute of 1832 effected considerable reforms in the official staff of the common law side of the court.[4] Two small reforms were made in the system of the *Itinerant Justices*. The statutes which prevented a judge of assize from acting in a county where he was born or resident were repealed in 1809 ;[5] and it was provided in 1822 that the commission need not be opened on the day appointed for holding the assize.[6] I have already said something of the statutes which increased the salaries of the judges, and made provision for retiring allowances.[7]

The most comprehensive statute relating to the courts is the statute of 1830 "for the more effectual administration of justice in England and Wales,"[8] which made some of the reforms suggested by Brougham in his great speech on law reform.[9] This statute, which was drawn by Scarlett, the future Lord Abinger,[10] made provision for the appointment of an additional puisne judge to each of the courts of common law ; and it enacted that not more than three judges were to sit in banc, so as to leave the other judges free to attend to other business.[11] It regulated the length of the terms and length of the sittings of the courts out of term.[12] It provided that the attornies of the King's Bench and Common Pleas could practise in the Exchequer ; so that no clerk in court need be employed.[13] It gave the judges the power

---

[1] 9 George IV c. 9.   [2] 1 George IV c. 35.

[3] For the similar reforms made in the court of Chancery see vol. i 440; vol. xii 213.

[4] 2, 3 William IV c. 110.   [5] 49 George III c. 91 ; vol. i 283 n. 5.

[6] 3 George IV c. 10 ; the difficulties which arose in 1818 because Garrow did not arrive at Gloucester in time to open the commission are described by Campbell, Life i 352-354 ; the result was that no business could be done and the Lord Chancellor decided that all the commissions for the city and county of Gloucester must be reviewed.

[7] Vol. i 254.   [8] 11 George IV and 1 William IV c. 70.

[9] Above 296-300.   [10] Foss, Judges IX 260; below, vol. xiv.   [11] § 1.

[12] §§ 6 and 7; not more than twenty-four days after the Hilary, Trinity and Michaelmas terms, and not more than six days after the Easter term were to be appropriated to sittings out of term, § 7 ; for the relief which this gave the judges and counsel see a letter of Pollock, C.B. cited by Hanworth, Life of Lord Chief Baron Pollock 166.

[13] § 10 ; in this matter the Court of Exchequer had followed the Chancery practice, vol. ix 370 ; above 296.

(which in fact they had long exercised) of making rules of practice.[1]
It abolished the separate judicial system of Wales, and extended
the jurisdiction of the common law courts to Chester and Wales.[2]
It regulated the dates for the holding of quarter sessions.[3] It
made some changes in the procedure on writs of error and in
actions of ejectment.[4]

Procedure

For the most part the statutes on this topic made a number
of small reforms which removed archaic rules or attempted
to redress abuses. We have seen that trial by battle was abolished
in 1819[5] and compurgation in 1833.[6] In 1803, 1811 and 1827
further reforms were made in the law as to arrest on mesne
process.[7] A deposit of the sum endorsed on the writ and £10
for costs was to secure release without the need to give bail,
and defendants were to get costs if the plaintiff did not recover
the sum claimed.[8] No person was to be held to special bail
if the sum at stake was under £15, and the power of the plaintiff
to enter an appearance for a defendant who failed to appear
was extended.[9] Other small reforms in this branch of the law
were made in 1827.[10] To stop frauds on creditors by the giving
of secret cognovits to enter judgment, it was enacted they
must be registered within twenty-one days.[11] In 1831 improvements were made in the procedure for obtaining writs of mandamus and prohibition.[12] In 1816 the law as to the distraint
of farming stock was amended. No straw, chaff or turnips
were to be carried off, or any other produce when it would be
contrary to covenants in the lease to take it off the land.[13] Persons
distraining for rent not exceeding £20 were only to charge for
costs the sum specified in the Act.[14] Further attempts were
made to stop frivolous proceedings in the courts.[15] If in actions
in local courts for assault and battery or slander less than 40s.
damages were recovered, the plaintiff could recover only as much
costs as the damages given,[16] and, to put a stop to frivolous

---

[1] § 11.   [2] §§ 13-34; vol. i 131-132.   [3] § 35.
[4] §§ 8, 36-38.   [5] Vol. i 310.   [6] Ibid 308.
[7] For the mesne process and its abuses and for the earlier legislation see vol.
xi 595-597; for the reason why these arrests were so long permitted see ibid 524,
600.   [8] 43 George III c. 46.
[9] 51 George III c. 124.   [10] 7, 8 George IV c. 71.
[11] 3 George IV c. 39, amended 6, 7 Victoria c. 66.
[12] 1 William IV c. 21; for earlier legislation on this subject see vol. xi 602.
[13] 56 George III c. 50; for earlier legislation as to distress for rent see vol.
xi 588-589.
[14] 57 George III c. 93; extended to distresses for rates, taxes and tithes by 7, 8
George IV c. 17.
[15] For earlier legislation see vol. iv 539; vol. vi 409; vol. xi 601.
[16] 58 George III c. 30.

writs of error, it was enacted that execution was not to be delayed by such a writ without the special order of the court.[1] In 1822 improvements were made in the procedure of the courts of justices of the peace. A common form of conviction was provided, and convictions were not to be set aside for defects of form.[2]

The three most important statutes on this topic were statutes relating to the jury, a statute relating to interpleader, and the Uniformity of Process Act.

In 1825 the law relating to juries was consolidated.[3] The Act dealt *inter alia* with the qualifications of jurors, exemptions from jury service, the preparation of jury lists, the summoning of juries, challenges, special juries, the praying of a tales,[4] juries *de medietate linguae*, coroners juries, penalties for non-attendance, and for embracery or corruption; and it abolished the writ of attaint.[5] Till 1831 interpleader proceedings could only be taken by a separate suit in equity. A statute of that year enabled the common law courts to entertain such proceedings.[6] On the application of a defendant in an action of assumpsit, debt, detinue, or trover, stating that he has no interest in the subject matter of the action, but that the right to the subject matter in dispute is in some third person, and that he is ready to deal with the subject matter as the court shall direct, the court was given power to summon the third party, hear his case, and, after staying proceedings in the original action, to order that he be made a party. The court could then finally dispose of the question at issue between the plaintiff and the third party.[7] If the third party did not appear, any claim he might have against the original defendant was barred.[8] We have seen that in 1832 the Uniformity of Process Act,[9] passed in consequence of the recommendations of the common law procedure commissioners, substituted for the various and devious ways by which personal actions were begun in the common law courts a uniform writ of summons.[10] The statute regulated the mode of appearance to the writ,[11] and the modes in which appearance could be enforced.[12] Writs issued under the Act could be served in term or vacation, and all proceedings to judgment and execution could be taken at the expiration of eight days from the service of the writ; but no declaration or pleading could be delivered

---

[1] 6 George IV c. 96. [2] 3 George IV c. 23.
[3] 6 George IV c. 50; for earlier statutes see vol. xi 603.
[4] For this process see vol. i 332 n. 8.
[5] § 60; see vol. i 337-342 for the history of this writ.
[6] 1, 2 William IV c. 58. [7] § 1. [8] § 3. [9] 2, 3 William IV c. 39.
[10] § 1; vol. i 222, 240; vol. ix 249-250. [11] § 2.
[12] §§ 3-9; writs were to be in force for four months, but could be continued by writs of alias and pluries, § 10.

between August 10 and October 24.[1] The Act gave the judges power to make rules for the enforcement of the Act.[2]

Evidence

A statute of 1804 made provision for the issue by the judges of the common law courts of writs of *habeas corpus ad testificandum* to bring before any court of record or a jury, persons in prison whom it was desired to examine as witnesses.[3] In 1806 it was enacted that a witness could not refuse to answer a relevant question because the answer might expose him to a civil liability.[4] The statute was passed to settle a doubtful point of law. A statute of 1828,[5] which shows that the influence of Bentham's views was making itself felt, amended the law of evidence in the following ways: quakers could affirm in all cases civil or criminal;[6] in prosecutions for forgery the person whose name was forged was to be a competent witness;[7] felons who had served their sentence were to be competent witnesses;[8] and a conviction for a misdemeanour, except a conviction for perjury, was not to make the convict incompetent as a witness after the sentence had been served.[9] A statute of 1831[10] extended the provisions of a statute of 1773, which provided for the examination of witnesses in India,[11] to the colonies and to all actions in the common law courts.[12] If a witness was within the jurisdiction of the English court he was to be examined by an officer of the court: if out of the jurisdiction a commission was to issue for his examination.[13] No deposition taken under the Act was to be read without the consent of the party against whom it was offered, unless the deponent was out of the jurisdiction, dead, or unable by reason of sickness to attend the trial.[14]

Property

The legislation on the subject of real and personal property, other than the legislation on topics of commercial law,[15] covers little ground. The Thellusson Act, passed in consequence of Peter Thellusson's will, of which I have already given an account, is the most important of these statutes.[16] For the rest, there are statutes as to suffering recoveries in the case of land held by copyhold tenure[17] or in ancient demesne,[18] as to wills

---

[1] § 11.   [2] §§ 14 and 18.   [3] 44 George III c. 102.
[4] 46 George III c. 37.   [5] 9 George IV c. 32.   [6] § 1.
[7] § 2.   [8] § 3.   [9] § 4.   [10] 1 William IV c. 22.
[11] 13 George III c. 63 §§ 40 and 44; Stephen, Digest of the Law of Evidence (4th ed.) 140 n. 2; vol. xi 168; for a proposal in 1705-1706 to effect some of the reforms made by this Act see ibid 522-523.
[12] § 1.   [13] § 4.   [14] § 10.
[15] Above 378-386.   [16] 39, 40 George III c. 98; vol. vii 228-231.
[17] 47 George III Sess. 2 c. 8.   [18] 59 George III c. 80.

of copyhold,[1] and as to the remedies of landlords to recover
their rent,[2] or to regain possession if a tenant held over.[3]   In
1830 the statutes of Fraudulent Devises[4] were repealed and replaced by a more effective statute.[5]   If a testator had bound
himself and his heirs by deed to pay a creditor and devised
his land away from his creditor, the devise was to be deemed
fraudulent as against the creditor.[6]   Both the heir and the devisee
could be sued.[7]   The heir was liable, although he had alienated
the land, to the extent of its value.[8]   The Land Act made the
land of traders equitable assets in the paying of their simple
contract debts.[9]   If it was necessary to sell the land to pay the
debt, the life tenant was to have the option to sell or mortgage
the fee simple.[10]   The Act of 1777 as to the registration of
annuities[11] was replaced by a similar Act in 1813.[12]

On the subject of copyright there was legislation of some
importance.   The Act of 1709[13] did two things : first it gave to
authors of books the sole right of printing for a term of fourteen
years ; and, if at the end of that term the author was alive,
it gave that right for a further term of fourteen years.[14]   The
books must be registered at Stationers' Hall to get this privilege.[15]
Secondly, it put publishers under the obligation of supplying
nine copies of each book to nine libraries.[16]   In 1775 it was provided in effect that failure to fulfil this obligation was to entail
loss of copyright.[17]   By Acts of 1735 and 1767 copyright was
given to the makers of prints and engravings for a term of
twenty-eight years ;[18] and in 1798 it was given to persons who
made models and casts of busts and statues for fourteen years.[19]
In 1802 changes were made in the law as to both the topics
dealt with by the Act of 1709.   First, authors of books, whether
published or not, were to have copyright for the term of fourteen
years throughout the British dominions, and for a further term
of fourteen years if they were living at the end of the first term ;[20]
and the importation of copyright books printed abroad was

---

[1] 55 George III c. 192.
[2] 57 George III c. 52 ; for the earlier legislation on this subject see vol. xi 589.
[3] 1 George IV c. 87.   [4] For these statutes see vol. vi 397-398.
[5] 11 George IV and 1 William IV c. 47.
[6] § 2.   [7] § 3.   [8] § 6.   [9] § 9.
[10] § 12 ; 2, 3 Victoria c. 60 ; this provision was applied to the heir or co-heirs
of a debtor subject to an executory division in favour of a non-existing person,
11, 12 Victoria c. 87.   [11] Vol. xi 604-606.
[12] 53 George III c. 141, amended by 3 George IV c. 92.
[13] 8 Anne c. 19 ; vol. vi 377-378 ; Bl. Comm. ii 407.
[14] §§ 1 and 11.   [15] § 2.
[16] § 5 ; the royal library, the libraries of Oxford and Cambridge, of the four
Scottish Universities, of Sion College, and of the faculty of advocates at Edinburgh.
[17] 15 George III c. § 6.   [18] 8 George II c. 13 ; 7 George III c. 38.
[19] 38 George III c. 71, amended by 54 George III c. 56 which gave an additional
term of fourteen years if the artist was alive at the end of the first term.
[20] 41 George III c. 107 § 1.

penalized.[1] As before, the books must be entered at Stationers'
Hall.[2] Secondly, since the copyright law was extended to Ireland,
publishers were put under the obligation of supplying two more
copies for two Irish libraries,[3] so that they were now obliged
to supply eleven free copies. The publishers were much aggrieved
by this obligation ; and after considerable agitation[4] a new copyright statute was passed in 1814.[5] The obligation to supply
eleven copies was retained,[6] but they were not obliged to supply
copies of later editions unless these editions contained additional
matter.[7] But the term of copyright was extended to twenty-
eight years, and, if the author was alive at the end of that term,
for the rest of his life.[8]

Contract

With the exception of those statutes relating to contracts
which fall under the head of commercial law,[9] the only statute
of importance on the subject of contract is Lord Tenterden's
Act of 1828.[10] We have seen that the courts had been so ready
to find in the words or conduct of a person liable under a contract
an acknowledgment which would take the case out of the statute
of limitations, that that statute had been deprived of its proper
effect.[11] This evil was remedied by requiring either an acknowledgment in writing signed by the person or persons liable,
or a part payment of principal or interest.[12] An indorsement
of payment upon a bill, note, or other writing by the payee
was to be a sufficient proof of payment to take the case out of
the statute.[13] A promise made by a person after he attained
full age to pay a debt contracted during infancy, or a ratification
of such a debt, was made unenforceable, unless in writing and
signed by the party to be charged ;[14] and writing was also required
to charge any person upon a representation as to credit on the
faith of which money or goods had been obtained.[15] Lastly,
section 17 of the Statute of Frauds was extended to executory
contracts of sale.[16]

Miscellaneous

Two statutes dealt with anomalies connected with legislation. The first of these statutes was passed to prevent the

[1] § 7.   [2] § 4.
[3] § 6 ; the libraries were those of Trinity College, Dublin, and the King's
Inns, Dublin.
[4] For an account of this agitation see R. C. B. Partridge, History of the Legal
Deposit of Books, chap. v.   [5] 54 George III c. 156.
[6] § 2.   [7] § 3.   [8] § 4.
[9] Above 378-386.   [10] 9 George IV c. 14.   [11] Above 305.
[12] § 1.   [13] § 3.   [14] § 5.   [15] § 6.
[16] § 7 ; for this section of the Statute of Frauds see vol. vi 386.

injustice which resulted from the rule that a statute took effect from the first day of the session on which it was passed. The result was that acts, lawful when done, were retrospectively penalized. For the future, statutes were to take effect from the day upon which they received the royal assent, unless another date was fixed by the statute.[1] The second of these statutes dealt with the question of Acts which continued Acts which were about to expire. To prevent their expiry before the continuing Act received the royal assent, the continuing Act was to take effect from the date of the expiry of the expiring Act; but this enactment was not to subject any persons to the penalties provided by the expiring Act between its expiry and the date when the continuing Act received the royal assent.[2]

It was during this period that provision was made by the Legislature for a periodical census. A bill for the taking of an annual census had been introduced into the House of Commons in 1753;[3] but, though it passed the House of Commons, it was rejected by the House of Lords. It was thought that it might give useful information to foreign enemies, that its machinery was inquisitorial and "subversive of the last remains of English liberty", and that it would involve too great an expense.[4] It was not till 1801 that an Act for this purpose was passed.[5] By that time the speculations of Malthus,[6] and the need felt by the economists for accurate information as to the growth, distribution, and employments of the population, had converted Parliament to the need for providing this information. The census was to be taken by the local authorities of the parish; and the returns were to be made to and examined by the justices, transmitted to the secretary of state, and laid before Parliament.[7] Ministers of religion were to make and transmit to the bishop returns as to the number of baptisms and burials in the parish in each decade between 1700 and 1780 and in each year from .1780 to the end of 1800; and as to the number of marriages in each year from 1754-1800. Acts on similar lines provided for the holding of a census in 1811, 1821, and 1831;[8] but the questions

---

[1] 33 George III c. 13.   [2] 48 George III c. 106.

[3] Its title was " A bill for taking and registering an annual account of the total number of people and of the total number of marriages, births and deaths; and also of the total number of poor receiving alms from every parish and extra-parochial place in Great Britain," Parlt. Hist. xiv 1318.

[4] Ibid 1319-22; it appears, too, that a superstitious dread of numbering the people made it unpopular, ibid 1336.

[5] 41 George III c. 15.   [6] For Malthus see above 32, 34.

[7] The questions to be answered were: (1) the number of inhabited houses in the parish, the number of families occupying them, and the number of uninhabited houses. (2) The number of males and females in the parish exclusive of seamen and soldiers serving in the army or militia. (3) The number of persons employed in agriculture, in trade or manufacture, and of persons not so employed.

[8] 51 George III c. 6; 1 George IV c. 94; 11 George IV and 1 William IV c. 30.

to be answered varied in these three periods and more information was asked for. The collection of accurate information as to baptisms, marriages, and burials was helped by an Act of 1812 which provided for the better keeping of these registers by the clergy, and the transmission annually of copies to the registrar of the diocese.[1]

One or two statutes were passed to regulate the legal profession. We have seen that two statutes of 1799 were passed to enable a barrister who was to be made a judge to become a serjeant-at-law in the vacation.[2] One or two Acts were passed to regulate the attornies—*inter alia* the period of articles for graduates of Oxford, Cambridge, and Dublin was shortened to three years.[3] In 1801 an Act was passed to regulate the profession of the notaries.[4] To become a notary a person must serve as an apprentice to a practising notary for seven years. No person could be admitted as a notary by the court of the faculties without an affidavit that he had served such an apprenticeship. The old connection of the notaries with the Scriveners' Company[5] was preserved by a clause in the Act which compelled all notaries practising in the City of London or within three miles of the City, to take up their freedom with the Company.[6] The Company thus retained a connection with the notaries which they had failed to retain with the conveyancers.[7]

The crimes of the " resurrection men " who robbed churchyards of bodies and sold them to schools of anatomy, and the fact that hundreds were committed for the purpose of making money of the sale of the bodies of the victims, was the occasion of an Act sponsored by Sir John Campbell to regulate the supply of bodies to persons licensed to practice anatomy.[8]

Equity

During this period the ground covered by the statutes relating to equity is smaller than even the small amount of ground covered by the statutes relating to the common law. The largest group of these statutes relate to conveyancing difficulties caused by the absence or disability of trustees or beneficial owners of property; there are one or two statutes which deal with

---

[1] 52 George III c. 146.

[2] Vol. xii 6 ; 39 George III c. 67 (barons of the Exchequer), c. 113 (judges of the common law courts) ; for the serjeants-at-law see vol. ii 485-493 ; for the rule that only a serjeant could be made a judge, see ibid 486 ; vol. iv 340-341.

[3] 1, 2 George IV c. 48; 3 George IV c. 16; 7 George IV c. 44; for the earlier history of the attornies and solicitors see vol. ii 331-412, 504-505 ; vol. vi 432-457 ; vol. xii 51-75.

[4] 41 George III c. 79 ; for the notaries see vol. v 78-79, 114-115.

[5] For this Company see vol. xii 70.

[6] § 13.   [7] Vol. xii 70-72.

[8] 2, 3 William IV c. 75 ; Campbell, Lives of the Chief Justices iii 323-324.

points of equitable procedure ; and towards the end of this period
there are one or two reforms of equitable doctrine.

A statute of 1796 gave the court power, when a trustee or
a personal representative was absent, out of the jurisdiction,
a bankrupt, or a lunatic, to order a transfer of stocks transferable
at the Bank of England.[1]   In 1731[2] and 1821[3] power was given
to order a conveyance of estates in land belonging to lunatics,
whether so found or not.   In 1803 power was given to the Lord
Chancellor to order the sale or mortgage of a lunatic's estate
for the payment of his debts, and to exercise powers of leasing
vested in the lunatic.[4]   In 1825 the law relating to the transfers
of property vested in trustees or mortgagees who were infants
or of unsound mind or who refused to act was consolidated.[5]
In 1812 power was given to the court to order that the dividends
of stock, to which infants were entitled, should be paid to their
guardians for their maintenance, education or benefit.[6]

In 1809 the Acts which enabled prisoners for debt to get
their discharge if they made full disclosure of their property,
and handed it over to their creditors, were extended to persons
imprisoned by the court of Chancery for non-payment of money
or costs which they had been ordered to pay.[7]   In 1830 an Act
for which Sugden was responsible made new rules as to persons
committed for contempt.   The warden of the Fleet must report
four times a year the names of all such prisoners and the causes
of their commitment.   Every quarter a Master was to examine
these prisoners and report whether or not the costs of the contempt should be paid out of the suitors' fund, and to assign
a counsel for defending the prisoners selected by him *in forma
pauperis*.   The procedure to be followed in various cases in which
a prisoner was committed for contempt was set out in detail,
and the court was given a general power to order a discharge
on such terms as it saw fit.   The Act also provided for the case
of persons who did not appear to the writ of subpoena or other
process, and for the cases when bills could be taken *pro confesso*.[8]
In 1832 it was enacted that the process of the court of Chancery
in suits concerning land in England could be served in other
parts of the United Kingdom.[9]   In 1807[10] and 1830[11] the process
of the court against members of Parliament, who could not be
imprisoned for failure to answer, was improved.   In 1825 changes

[1] 36 George III c. 90, amended 39, 40 George III c. 36.
[2] 4 George II c. 10.   [3] 1, 2 George IV c. 94.
[4] 43 George III c. 75.
[5] 6 George IV c. 74 ; repealed and re-enacted with large amendments 11 George
IV and 1 William IV c. 60.
[6] 52 George III c. 32.   [7] 49 George III c. 6 ; vol. xi 599.
[8] 11 George IV ; 1 William IV c. 36.   [9] 2, 3 William IV c. 33.
[10] 47 George III Sess. 2 c. 40.
[11] 11 George IV 1 William IV c. 36 § 13.

were made in the procedure for traversing an inquisition finding
a person to be of unsound mind.[1]

In 1800 provision was made for the case where land charged
with trusts passed by escheat or otherwise to the Crown. To
settle the doubt whether the Crown could, in that case, order
the trust to be performed, it was enacted that it should have
this power, and that it could make grants of such land for this
purpose.[2] In the same year a change was made in the law
as to the rights of persons entitled to money directed to be laid
out in the purchase of land and settled in tail. If all those entitled were under no disability they could take the money.
It was no longer to be necessary to buy the land before the estate
tail could be barred.[3] Evidence brought before Parliament
of the misuse of public charitable trusts led to some legislation
on this topic. In 1812 a more speedy remedy for breaches
of these trusts was provided.[4] In 1818 the statutory commission
to enquire into educational charities, which 'Brougham had
proposed,[5] was brought into effect ; and the powers, procedure,
and pay of the commissioners were defined.[6] In 1819 it was
provided that the commissioners could set the attorney-general
in motion to remedy breaches of trust, or to deal with any other
cause of complaint, for which orders or direction of the court
of Chancery were necessary.[7] It was also provided that charity
trustees could apply to the court for the amendment of their
statutes or regulations when these were insufficient.[8] In 1821
the Legislature provided a somewhat cumbrous procedure
by means of which charity trustees could exchange their lands
for others more beneficial to the charity.[9] We have seen that
in 1832 the Roman Catholics were put on the same footing
as Protestant dissenters in respect of schools, churches, education,
and charities.[10]

Some changes were made at the end of this period in the law

[1] 6 George IV c. 53.

[2] 39, 40 George III c. 88 § 12, amended 47 George III Sess. 2 c. 24, and 59
George III c. 94 ; the doubt was occasioned by the provisions of 1 Anne Stat. 1
c. 7 § 5, and 34 George III c. 75 which imposed restrictions on the power of the
Crown to make grants of land, see vol. x 348.

[3] 39, 40 George III c. 56, repealed and re-enacted with amendments 7 George
IV c. 45.

[4] 52 George III c. 101.   [5] Above 214.

[6] 58 George III c. 91 ; this Act was amended and the powers of the commission
were extended in the following year, 59 George III c. 81.

[7] 59 George III c. 91, continued and amended by 2, 3 William IV c. 57.

[8] § 5.

[9] 1, 2 George IV c. 92 ; application was to be made to the bishop of the diocese
where the lands were situate ; he issued a commission to enquire ; after laying the
findings of the commission before counsel he could either approve them or order
a new commission ; deeds of conveyance were to be enrolled and a transcript
entered in the diocesan registry.

[10] 2, 3 William IV c. 115 ; vol. viii 412.

as to the administration of assets. In 1807 real estate was made equitable assets for the payment of the simple contract as well as the specialty debts of traders.[1] In 1830 the statutes of fraudulent devises[2] were consolidated and amended.[3] The provisions of these statutes were re-enacted;[4] the Act of 1807 was also re-enacted;[5] the demurrer of the parol was abolished;[6] infant heirs or devisees could be compelled to convey land to satisfy their ancestor's or devisor's liability for debts;[7] and if lands liable to pay debts had been settled, the limited owner was given power to convey when the court ordered a sale.[8] In 1830 the presumption of equity that executors were entitled to the undisposed-of residue, unless the testator had shown an intention to the contrary, was reversed as against the next of kin. They were to take as trustees for the next of kin unless the testator showed an intention that they should take beneficially.[9] But as against the Crown the old presumption was retained.[10]

In 1814 a small change was made in the law as to the formalities required for the attestation of instruments exercising or revoking powers of appointment;[11] and in 1830 the equitable doctrine that illusory appointments were invalid in equity— a doctrine which had been much criticized by the judges[12]— was abolished by an Act[13] which was proposed by Sugden, the future Lord St. Leonards.[14]

Admiralty and Prize Law

There are a few statutes which deal with the Court of Admiralty and matters falling within its jurisdiction, or connected with shipping. But since, during the greater part of this period, Great Britain was at war, the statutes which deal with prize law and topics connected therewith are more numerous. I shall say something first of the statutes which deal with the Court of Admiralty and shipping, and, secondly, with those which deal with prize law and topics connected therewith.

(1) The Court of Admiralty and shipping

There are two statutes which regulate the machinery of the court. In 1810 the offices of registrar of the Court of Admiralty

---

[1] 47 George III Sess. 2 c. 74 ; above 265, 276.
[2] For these statutes see vol. vi 397-398.
[3] 11 George IV and 1 William IV c. 47.   [4] §§ 2-4, 6-8.   [5] § 9.
[6] § 10 ; for this doctrine see vol. iii 513-516.   [7] § 11.   [8] § 12.
[9] 11 George IV and 1 William IV c. 40.
[10] § 2.   [11] 54 George III c. 168.
[12] " No rule has ever given me so much pain as that ; and every judge has felt difficulties arising from it," Spencer v. Spencer (1800) 5 Ves. at p. 365, per Arden, M.R.

[13] 11 George IV and 1 William IV c. 46 ; for this equitable doctrine see vol. vii 174-175.   [14] Sugden, Powers (8th ed.) 449.

and the Prize Court ceased to be patent offices paid by fees. After the expiry of the existing vested interests, the fees were to be applied first in the payment of expenses, and then one-third was to go to the registrar and an assistant-registrar, whom the registrar, if necessary, was to appoint, and the remaining two-thirds were to go to the consolidated fund.[1] In 1813 arrangements were made for the deposit in the bank by the registrar of the Admiralty and Prize Courts of the suitors' money and securities, and for the payment out or transfer of the money or securities to those entitled to it or them.[2]

There are one or two statutes which regulate the criminal jurisdiction of the Admiralty.

To provide for the more speedy trial of offences committed on the high seas, sessions were to be held twice a year at the Old Bailey, or at other times and places in England appointed by the Lords of the Admiralty.[3] Commissioners of oyer and terminer and justices of the peace were given power to take information as to offences, and bind over witnesses to appear;[4] and this power was extended to commissioners appointed to try offences committed at sea.[5]

There was legislation in 1808 to prevent frauds on merchants, shipowners, and underwriters committed by boatmen and others within the jurisdiction of the Cinque Ports.[6] These persons took anchors, cables and other property which had been lost, and made exorbitant demands for the assistance which they gave to ships.[7] To remedy the first of these grievances, it was provided that anchors, cables, ship's stores, and property from wrecked ships found within the jurisdiction must be deposited with the Lord Warden's officers. The retention, sale or receiving of this property, the removal of buoys or buoy ropes, and acts done to destroy a ship in fraud of the owners, were made criminal offences;[8] and, in order to prevent the commission of some of them, regulations were made for the conduct of the business of dealers in ship's stores.[9] To remedy the second of these grievances, the Lord Warden was empowered to appoint commissioners to settle speedily disputes as to salvage and as to charges for assistance.[10] Rules laid down by a statute of 1713[11] were to settle the amount of salvage payable if the services were rendered

---

[1] 50 George III c. 98; by § 4 the judge could, if he thought it necessary, direct the registrar to appoint an assistant; below 674.

[2] 53 George III c. 151.   [3] 45 George III c. 72 § 114.

[4] §§ 115 and 116.   [5] 7 George IV c. 38; above 393.

[6] 48 George III c. 130; the boundaries of the jurisdiction of the Cinque Ports were defined by § 20.

[7] Preamble.   [8] §§ 6-12.   [9] §§ 13 and 14.

[10] §§ 1, 3, 4; a right of appeal from the commissioners was given to the Court of Admiralty, § 5.

[11] 12 Anne St. 2 c. 18.

at the request of the captain or an officer of the ship.[1] If they were rendered without such request the justices of the peace were to settle the amount.[2] In 1809 a similar Act was passed for the rest of England.[3]

These two Acts were continued and amended in 1813.[4] Lords of manors entitled to wreck flotsam, jetsam, and lagan[5] must not appropriate it till it had been reported to a vice-admiral;[6] but with the consent of a justice of the peace perishable goods could be sold.[7] In case of a wreck those engaged in salvage work were to have a right of way over private property to get to and from the shore.[8] A dispute between the common law courts and the Admiralty was settled by a section enacting that all questions as to salvage services done between high and low water marks were to be within the jurisdiction of the Admiralty.[9] If damage was done in a harbour by a foreign ship the ship could be arrested till security was given for the costs and damages which might be recoverable.[10]

Perhaps the most important Act as to shipping was a consolidation Act of 1823 " the registering of vessels."[11] It dealt with the conditions for the registration of ships which were to have the privileges of British ships, and the form of the certificate of registration.[12] With certain exceptions aliens could not be registered as the owners of British ships.[13] Before registration the ship must be surveyed,[14] and the mode of ascertaining the tonnage was prescribed.[15] The name of the registered ship must not be changed;[16] and ships so altered that they ceased to correspond with the certificate of registration must be re-registered.[17] Rules were laid down as to the transfer of a ship by a bill of sale ;[18] and it was enacted that priorities of purchasers and mortgagees should depend on the date of entry in the registry.[19] If the ship was owned by more than one owner, it must be divided into sixty-four parts and the number of shares belonging to each owner must be entered in the registry.[20] No more than thirty-two owners could be registered as the legal owners, but this was not to affect the title of equitable owners.[21] Rules were made as to the rights of mortgagors and mortgagees.[22]

[1] § 21.   [2] § 22.
[3] 49 George III c. 122.   [4] 53 George III c. 87.
[5] For the definition of these terms see vol. i 560 n. 3.
[6] § 2.   [7] § 3.   [8] §§ 4 and 5.
[9] § 6.   [10] § 7.   [11] 4 George IV c. 41.
[12] §§ 2-6, 8-10, 12, 13, 19-21, 23 ; §§ 24 and 25 dealt with the loss or the unlawful detention of a certificate of registration.
[13] § 11.   [14] § 14.   [15] §§ 15-18.
[16] § 22.   [17] § 26.   [18] §§ 29, 35, 36, 38-40.
[19] § 37.   [20] § 30.
[21] § 31.   [22] §§ 43 and 44.

(2) *Prize law and topics connected therewith*

Some of these statutes regulated the Vice-Admiralty Courts in the colonies, and laid down rules for their jurisdiction and procedure.[1] Acts of 1803[2] and 1805[3] made regulations for a variety of topics connected with Prize law. They regulated the distribution of prize money and bounties payable for enemy ships captured or destroyed.[4] British ships recaptured were to be restored on payment of salvage.[5] The conditions for the issue and revocation of letters of marque were prescribed.[6] Ransom contracts were, as in earlier statutes, declared to be void.[7] Ships collusively restored by captains of privateers without adjudication were to be adjudged prizes of the Crown ;[8] but ships retaken before they had been brought to an enemy's port were allowed to continue their voyage.[9] Provision was made for the maintenance of discipline on privateers.[10] Naval stores on foreign ships brought into British ports could be purchased for the navy.[11] The Court of Admiralty and Vice-Admiralty Courts must obey and enforce any instructions given by the Crown for the adjudication and condemnation of prizes ;[12] and we have seen that rules for the procedure of the court were made sometimes by the Crown and sometimes by the court.[13] Judges and officers of, and practitioners in, these courts must not be interested in any ship to which letters of marque were issued, nor could officers of these courts act as advocates or proctors.[14] Rules were laid down for the speedy hearing of prize cases,[15] for appeals from their decisions,[16] for appraisements of captured ships or cargoes by prize agents,[17] and for the payment by them of prize money and bounties.[18] Undistributed balances were paid to the treasurer of Greenwich hospital who made the final distribution.[19] To prevent frauds on sailors the form of letters of attorney for receiving prize money, and the form of bills for payment, were prescribed.[20]

In 1803 it was enacted that merchants ships must sail under convoy ;[21] and several statutes regulated the rules which convoyed ships must observe.[22] Captured British ships bought by

---

[1] 41 George III c. 96 (the West Indies and Halifax) ; 43 George III c. 160 § 20, and 45 George III c. 72 §§ 33-35 (Malta, Bahama, and the Bermudas).

[2] 43 George III c. 160.

[3] 45 George III c. 72 which repealed the Act of 1803.

[4] §§ 2-6.   [5] § 7.

[6] §§ 9-15 ; other statutes authorizing the issue of letters of marque are 33 George III c. 66 and 41 George III c. 76 ; ships condemned for smuggling could be sold by the commissioners of customs to privateers, 33 George III c. 70 § 6.

[7] 45 George III c. 72 §§ 16-19 ; for these contracts and the earlier statutes see vol. xii 534-535.   [8] § 20.   [9] § 21.

[10] § 26.   [11] § 28.   [12] §§ 32 and 37.

[13] Vol. xii 683.   [14] § 40.   [15] §§ 43-48.

[16] §§ 49-52.   [17] § 53.   [18] §§ 60-79.

[19] §§ 80-91.   [20] §§ 92 and 97.   [21] 43 George III c. 57 § 1.

[22] 43 George III c. 57 ; 45 George III c. 72 §§ 23-25 ; 55 George III c. 173.

British subjects were not to be registered as British ships, since the permission so to register them made them more valuable to the enemy.[1] Provision was made for the landing in Great Britain and warehousing of prize goods, and for the duties payable on them.[2] If they were not cleared within three years they were to be sold.[3]

These statutes were the foundation on which the system of prize law, which Leoline Jenkins and his successors had begun to build up,[4] was completed by Lord Stowell during the Napoleonic wars.[5]

Ecclesiastical Law

The legislation upon the various topics which fall under this head is considerable. There is much legislation as to the clergy ; there is some legislation as to the marriage laws, and a statute dealing with Probate ; and there is some legislation as to the Ecclesiastical Courts and their procedure.

(1) Legislation as to the clergy

An Act of 1817 repealed and consolidated with amendments twelve statutes, from 21 Henry VIII c. 1 to 53 George III c. 149, on three topics—(a) farming or trading by the clergy, (b) residence, and (c) the appointment and pay of curates.[6] (a) No clergyman could take more than eighty acres of land for the purpose of farming it without the consent of the bishop,[7] nor could he " engage in or carry on any trade or dealing for gain or profit."[8] But this did not apply to the purchase or sale of things needed for his house, or for any school which he might be keeping, or for the farming of his glebe.[9] (b) As a general rule a beneficed clergyman must not, without permission of the bishop, absent himself from his benefice for more than three months in the year ;[10] and a list of the cases in which a bishop could grant this permission was set out.[11] There was a long list of statutory exceptions to this rule ;[12] deans and canons who held benefices could count their residence at the cathedral as residence in their benefices ;[13] and bishops and archbishops could hold a benefice without any obligation to reside.[14] Moreover the Crown could always dispense with this obligation to reside.[15] The conditions in which the bishop could, in cases other than those enumerated in the Act, grant licences for non-residence were set out ; and it was provided that a return of these licences,

[1] 48 George III c. 70.　　　[2] 43 George III c. 134.
[3] 51 George III c. 74.　　　[4] Vol. xii 654-656.
[5] Below 679, 680.　　　[6] 57 George III c. 99.
[7] § 2.　　　[8] § 3.　　　[9] § 4.　　　[10] § 5.　　　[11] § 15.
[12] § 1　　　[13] § 11.　　　[14] § 82.　　　[15] § 80.

with the reasons for granting them, must be sent annually to the archbishop, who must approve them, and send them to the Privy Council who could revoke the licence.[1] If a beneficed clergyman was non-resident without licence, the bishop could, in the last resort, sequester the profits of the benefice,[2] and if the benefice remained sequestered for two years, or suffered three sequestrations within that period, it was to become void.[3] Contracts to let houses in which a clergyman was required by the bishop to reside were to be void.[4] A series of other statutes were passed to promote residence by giving facilities for the sale, exchange, or purchase of houses as residences for the clergy.[5] Beneficed clergy must keep their residences in repair.[6] (c) Non-resident clergy who did not perform their functions in the parish, must appoint a curate, and, in default, a curate could be appointed by the bishop.[7] In other cases where, by reason of the circumstances of the parish or neglect of the beneficed clergyman, a curate was needed, the bishop could order that a curate be appointed, and, in default, appoint.[8] The bishop could appoint what stipends were to be paid to curates, and determine disputes as to the stipends payable.[9] The scale of salaries was set out in the Act ;[10] and it was provided that, as a rule, no clergyman was to serve more than two churches in one day.[11] In certain cases the rectory or vicarage house could be allotted by the bishop as the curate's residence.[12] Without the bishop's licence, curates must not leave their cures without giving three months' notice to the holder of the benefice and the bishop.[13]

In 1831 a statute of 1677,[14] which provided for the augmentation of livings, was extended so as to facilitate this object.[15] The powers given by the Act applied to benefices of less than £300 a year, and no benefice could be augmented to more than £350 a year.[16] Powers were given to rectors and vicars to charge the revenues of their benefices for the benefit of chapels of ease in their parishes,[17] and tithes arising from a place not within a rector's or vicar's parish could be annexed by the rector or vicar to churches in that place.[18] Some slight remissions of taxation were given to the poorer rectors, vicars, and curates—if their income was so small that they paid no income tax they could keep a horse without paying the duty on it ;[19] and arrangements were made for exonerating livings of less than £150 a year from

[1] §§ 16-22.   [2] §§ 26-30.   [3] § 31.   [4] § 32.
[5] 43 George III c. 107 ; 55 George III c. 147 § 12 ; 56 George III c. 52 ; 1 George IV c. 6 ; 6 George IV c. 8 ; 7 George IV c. 66.
[6] 57 George III c. 99 § 14.   [7] §§ 48 and 49.
[8] § 50.   [9] § 53.   [10] §§ 54-58, 60-65.
[11] § 59.   [12] §§ 64, 66, 67.   [13] § 68.
[14] 29 Charles II c. 99 ; vol. vi 410.   [15] 1, 2 William IV c. 45.
[16] § 16.   [17] § 21.   [18] § 20.
[19] 41 George III c. 40.

the land tax.[1] In 1832 the procedure in actions for tithes was improved by an Act which shortened to thirty years and sixty years the periods required to establish a prescriptive right to a *modus decimandi* or to exemption from liability to pay tithe.[2] The conditions under which these two periods gave rise to a prescriptive right were substantially similar to those laid down by the Act of the same year in the case of easements and profits.[3]

There was a little legislation on the subject of pluralities ; but the problem was not tackled directly or thoroughly. A statute of Henry VIII's reign had forbidden a clergyman to have more than one benefice ;[4] but many exceptions to this rule were made in this statute, and the statute could be dispensed with. In 1801 this statute was suspended,[5] so that it was still easier for a fortunate cleric to hold several benefices. The provisions of the Act of 1817, which dealt with non-residence and the appointment of curates, were meant to mitigate the evils which resulted from this state of affairs.[6] But it was only a mitigation. In fact the law on this subject remained in a very unsatisfactory state till 1838, when a statute was passed which begins the modern history of this branch of ecclesiastical law.[7]

The curious history of the law as to the validity of resignation bonds, i.e., bonds given by a person presented to a living promising to resign his living in certain events, gave rise to legislation. During the greater part of the eighteenth century the validity of these bonds had been recognized and upheld by the courts of law[8] and equity.[9] But in 1783, in the case of *Bishop of London v. Ffytche* [10] the House of Lords by a majority of one [11] reversed the decision of the courts of Common Pleas and King's Bench, and held that a bond conditioned to resign in a certain event was void because it was a simoniacal contract forbidden by a statute of 1589 ;[12] and in 1827, in the case of *Fletcher v. Lord Sondes*,[13] it was held that a bond conditioned to resign a benefice, not generally, but in favour of a particular person, was void

---

[1] 57 George III c. 100.   [2] 2, 3 William IV c. 100.

[3] 2, 3 William IV c. 71 ; vol. vii 300-352 ; both these Acts were drawn by Lord Tenterden, Campbell, Lives of the Chief Justices iii 325-328 ; for Lord Tenterden see below 516 seqq.

[4] 21 Henry VIII c. 13 ; vol. iv 489.

[5] 41 George III c. 102 ; 42 George III c. 86 ; a statute of 1819 dealt with the construction to be put on dispensations which permitted the holding of more than one benefice, 59 George III c. 40.

[6] 57 George III c. 99; above 418, 419.   [7] 1, 2 Victoria c. 106 ; below, vol. xiv.

[8] Peele v. Earl of Carlisle (1720) 1 Stra. 227.

[9] Peele v. Capel (1723) 1 Stra. 534 ; Grey v. Hesketh (1755) Amb. 268.

[10] 2 Bro. P.C. 211.

[11] All the bishops were on the one side and all the lawyers except Lord Thurlow on the other, see vol. i 376 n. 5 ; L.Q.R. xvii 367-368.

[12] 31 Elizabeth c. 6 ; vol. iv 489.   [13] 3 Bing. 501.

for the same reason. These decisions created considerable hardship. As the archbishop of Canterbury said, their result was that "a large number both of patrons and incumbents had exposed themselves to severe penalties."[1] To remedy this grievance an Act was passed in 1828 which provided that no bond to resign in favour of a particular person should be void, nor should persons entering into such bonds be liable to penalties if they were entered into before April 9, 1827.[2] If the person named in the bond was not presented within six months the resignation was to be void.[3] In 1828 resignation bonds were made valid if made in favour of certain prescribed persons related by blood or marriage to the patron.[4]

A statute of 1804 enacted that persons should not be ordained deacons before the age of twenty-three, or priests before the age of twenty-four;[5] and a statute of 1819 provided for the ordination of persons for the colonies "although such persons may not be provided with the title required by the canon of the Church of England."[6] Persons so ordained were not to be capable of holding a living in Great Britain without the consent of the bishop of the diocese.[7]

We have seen that in 1705 there had been legislation on the subject of briefs for the collection of money for charitable purposes.[8] The issue of these briefs was abolished in 1828. Undisposed-of money collected by briefs, which was in the hands of the Undertaker of Briefs, was to be turned over to the Church Building Society, which was incorporated and regulated by the Act. All sums collected under royal letters for the building or repairing of churches were to be applied by the Society.[9]

(2) Legislation as to marriage and probate

At the beginning of this period Lord Hardwicke's marriage Act[10] was the principal Act relating to marriage. The section of the Act[11] which made the marriage of minors void if they were celebrated without the consent of their parents or guardians had occasioned some hardship,[12] and was repealed in 1822. Marriages already solemnized by licence without this consent were made voidable, and could not be avoided after the death

[1] Bing. 600.
[2] 7, 8 George IV c. 25 §§ 1 and 2.
[3] § 4.
[4] 9 George IV c. 94.
[5] 44 George III c. 43.
[6] 59 George III c. 60 § 1.
[7] § 2; there was a similar proviso with regard to persons ordained by colonial or Indian bishops § 3; and those ordained by a colonial bishop who had no diocese could hold no ecclesiastical preferment in His Majesty's dominions § 4; for the earlier legislation on this subject see vol. xi 611-612, and 26 George III c. 84.
[8] Vol. xi 612-613.
[9] 9 George IV c. 42.
[10] 26 George II c. 33; vol. x 82; vol xi 609-610.
[11] § 11.
[12] Horner v. Horner (1799) i 337; Priestley v. Hughes (1809) 1; below 514.

of one of the parties or after the passing of this Act.[1] The result
was that thereafter these marriages were valid. The Act also
laid down rules as to conditions in which licences could be
obtained[2] or banns published,[3] and the form of the consent
of parents or guardians.[4]

These rules were repealed in 1823 ;[5] and a later Act of the
same year repealed the earlier Act of 1823 and Lord Hardwicke's
Act, except in so far as they repealed former Acts, but not the
clauses of the Act of 1822 which made the marriage of minors
without the consent of parents or guardians valid.[6] The Act then
laid down new rules as to the formalities required for a valid
marriage. It regulated the publication and republication of
banns, and made provision for keeping a register of banns published.[7] Ministers were not to be liable for marrying minors
without the consent of parents or guardians unless they had
notice of their dissent.[8] Licences to marry were only to be given
to celebrate a marriage in the parish church when one of the
parties had resided for fifteen days before its grant.[9] Before
a licence was granted one of the parties must swear to the absence
of any impediment, and, if either party were a minor, to the
consent of the parent, guardian,[10] or other person whose consent
was required by the Act.[11] Marriages must be solemnized between
the hours of 8 a.m. and 12 noon.[12] Penalties were provided for
solemnizing a marriage contrary to the rules laid down in the
Act ;[13] and if a minor were married without consent, the party who
swore falsely that such consent had been obtained, forfeited
all property which accrued from the marriage, and any settlements
made previous to such marriages were to be void.[14] All marriages
must be solemnized in the presence of two witnesses, and a register
of marriages must be kept.[15] The right of the archbishop of
Canterbury to issue a special licence to marry at any time or
place was preserved.[16] The clause in Lord Hardwicke's Act,[17]
which abolished suits to compel a celebration of marriage by
reason of a contract to marry, was re-enacted.[18]

In 1820 an Act was passed to enable the examination of
witnesses to be taken in India in support of bills for divorce
on account of adultery committed in India ; and it was provided
that in such cases the bill should not be discontinued by a prorogation or dissolution of Parliament.[19]

---

[1] 3 George IV c. 75 §§ 1 and 2 ; for Eldon and Stowell's opposition to the
retrospective effect of the Act, see Twiss, Life of Eldon ii 458-461 ; Eldon's objection was that it would unsettle rights of property.
[2] §§ 8, 10-14.   [3] §§ 16-20.   [4] § 9.   [5] 4 George IV c. 17.
[6] 4 George IV c. 76 ; slightly amended by 5 George IV c. 32.
[7] §§ 2-7, 9.   [8] § 8.   [9] §§ 10-15.
[10] § 14.   [11] §§ 16 and 17.   [12] § 21.
[13] §§ 21 and 22.   [14] §§ 23 and 24.   [15] § 28.
[16] § 20.   [17] 26 George II c. 33 § 13 ; vol. ii 685-686.
[18] 4 George IV c. 76 § 27.   [19] 1 George IV c. 101.

A statute was passed in 1798 to provide for the case where an executor or executors, to whom probate had been granted, were resident out of the kingdom.[1] In such a case a grant of administration could be made limited to the right to become a party to a suit in equity against the estate ;[2] and the court of Chancery could appoint persons to collect debts due to the estate.[3] If an infant were appointed sole executor, administration with the will annexed was to be granted to the guardian till the infant attained his majority.[4] The administrator was to have the same powers as an administrator *durante minore aetate*.[5]

(3) *Legislation as to the ecclesiastical courts and their procedure*

We have seen that in 1813 excommunication was abolished as part of the mesne process of the Ecclesiastical Courts and as a punishment for contempt.[6] As had been suggested as long ago as 1584,[7] the writ *de contumace capiendo* was substituted for the writ *de excommunicato capiendo*.[8] Excommunication remained only as a punishment for ecclesiastical offences,[9] and for the future it was to involve no other civil penalty or incapacity than imprisonment for a period not exceeding six months.[10] The same Act made some improvement in the procedure for the recovery of small tithes, and in the procedure against Quakers for the recovery of tithes and church rates.[11] Proceedings for the recovery of church rates, when the validity of the rate was not questioned, could be taken before the justices.[12] We have seen that the Act also dealt with persons who acted as proctors without qualification.[13] In 1832 provision was made for enforcing in Ireland writs *de contumace capiendo* issued by an English court and *vice versa*, and for enforcing obedience to such writs by sequestration of property when, as in the case of peers or members of Parliament, they could not be enforced by imprisonment.[14]

To carry out the recommendations of reports made in 1823 by the commission appointed to enquire into the officials of the courts of justice,[15] an Act of 1829[16] regulated the duties and salaries of the officers of the Prerogative court and the court of Peculiars of the archbishop of Canterbury,[17] and the Consistory and Commissary courts of the bishop of London.[18] The fees payable were to be settled and published, and powers to alter fees and make rules for the officials were given to the judges of these courts,

---

[1] 38 George III c. 87. [2] §§ 1-3. [3] § 4. [4] § 6.
[5] § 7. [6] 53 George III c. 127 ; vol. i 632.
[7] Ibid. [8] § 1. [9] § 2. [10] § 3.
[11] §§ 4 and 5 ; for earlier legislation on this subject see vol. xi 612.
[12] § 7. [13] §§ 8 and 9 ; vol. xii 75-76.
[14] 2, 3 William IV c. 93. [15] Above 263, 272, 273.
[16] 10 George IV c. 53. [17] For these courts see vol. i 602.
[18] For these courts see ibid 599.

subject to the approval of the archbishop or bishop.[1] They were also given power to appoint additional court days, to make rules to expedite the hearing of cases, and to curtail the number of holidays kept in the office of the Prerogative Court.[2] With the same object it was enacted that the courts should sit during a vacancy of the sees of London and Canterbury, and that the officers of the courts should continue to act during the vacancy of the office of judge.[3] We have seen that in 1832 the High Court of Delegates was abolished and its jurisdiction turned over to the Privy Council.[4]

This survey of the enacted law shows that the Legislature had begun to adapt the rules of English law to the needs of an age in which men's ideas upon matters political, religious, social, industrial, and economic were undergoing many fundamental changes. It shows that the new ideas which were coming to the front on all these matters had begun to influence the statute book. More especially it shows that Bentham's principles, and many of his concrete suggestions for reform, had begun to influence the minds both of statesmen and lawyers. Just as the influence of the new political ideas can be seen in the Reform Act of 1832, just as the influence of the new economic ideas can be seen in much of the legislation upon commerce and industry, so, in much of the legislation upon English law, criminal and civil, the influence of Bentham is apparent. In this period the age of reform had begun ; but it had only just begun. We shall see that in the course of the next period, from 1832 to the Judicature Acts, reform proceeded very rapidly ; and that in that period many more of Bentham's ideas were translated into practical rules, and pieced on to the fabric of English law. But at this point we must turn from the history of the enacted law to the history of the professional development of the law, and examine the extent to which, and manner in which, the lawyers were adapting its rules to the needs of this new age.

V

THE REPORTS

We have seen that by the end of the eighteenth century both the modern conditions in which contemporaneous or nearly contemporaneous reports of decided cases were published, and the modern style in which these cases were reported, had been reached.[5] No doubt there are differences in the way in

---

[1] 10 George IV c. 53 §§ 1-6. [2] §§ 9 and 10.
[3] §§ 12 and 13. [4] 2, 3 William IV c. 92 ; vol. i 518, 605.
[5] Vol. xii 110-117.

which different reporters constructed their reports. Some, like Campbell,[1] were very concise ; and most of the nisi prius reports are short. Others, more especially the "authorized" reporters,[2] were a great deal more elaborate ; and they give us, more especially when they were making reports of cases heard in banc or in the Exchequer Chamber, full reports of pleadings, arguments, and judgments. Then too, the differences in character between the procedure of the Court of Chancery or the Ecclesiastical Courts and the Court of Admiralty on the one hand, and the procedure of the Common Law Courts on the other, caused differences in the style of the reports of cases heard in these different courts.[3] But though there are differences between the reports, it is clear that the main principle of law-reporting as laid down by Burrow, Cowper, and Douglas had been accepted, with the result that law reporting had been to a large extent standardized. The result was a great improvement in the average quality of the reports. In 1860 the writer of a learned article on Wallace's *Reporters* could truthfully say,[4]

With respect to the question of the general accuracy of the English law reports published during the last half century—a period which comprises not only the greatest amount of matter, but the resolution of the most complicated questions that have been dealt with by our courts, perhaps during any equal period of history—the result of enquiry, we think, will prove on the whole satisfactory. No doubt the only available test is the comparison of contemporary reports of given cases. The general result will be, we believe, to produce a sentiment of warm admiration in the examiner, who goes into the task with due qualifications in respect of learning and understanding, and a candid recollection of the various difficulties that environ the task, and the arduous and incessant watchfulness and labour which it demands.

This is pre-eminently the period of what are known as the "authorized" reports. These reports during this period enjoyed the privilege of exclusive citation.[5] The reporters were known to and approved by the judges, who allowed them free access to any papers needed for the preparation of the report, and often revised the reports of their judgments.[6] When it became necessary to change a reporter, the old reporter and the judges

---

[1] Below 437.
[2] For the authorized reports see vol. xii 117 ; below 427, 428.
[3] Vol. xii 114-115 ; Addams, in the Preface to his reports of cases in the Ecclesiastical Courts explains that, since the Court of Delegates simply gave a judgment allowing or dismissing an appeal without reasons, it was necessary to make a fuller report of the facts and the argument.
[4] Law Magazine and Review (1st Series) ix 340-341.
[5] W. T. S. Daniel, The History of the Law Reports 102, 266.
[6] W. T. S. Daniel, op. cit. 66, 102.

approved the successor.[1] Usually there were two reporters in each court, and the report, though made by one, was checked by the other.[2] For a time this system seems to have worked well. There was a large sale for these authorized reports—it was said that in 1824-30 " before competition had displaced monopoly, the regular circulation of the Queen's Bench reports was 4000, occasionally more, and that of the Chancery reports 2000,"[3] The reporters were well paid, and therefore able lawyers were induced to undertake the work.[4] It is not surprising therefore, that their authors and publishers were able to maintain a successful fight against rivals who attempted to compete with them. " In the King's Bench, Dowling and Ryland[5] struggled in vain for years to establish themselves as a co-equal authority with Barnewall and Cresswell ; and at a later period the attempt of Tamlyn at the Rolls to compete with Russell and Mylne was a signal failure."[6]

But, towards the end of this period, the practical monopoly enjoyed by the authorized reports began to give rise to certain disadvantages. They were expensive.[7] They were published at irregular intervals and often long after the cases had been decided.[8] There were sometimes breaks in the continuity of the reports.[9] As Daniel says,[10]

Exclusive citation, originally a necessity, had grown up into a right which was maintained by authority; what followed was costliness in the price, delay and irregularity in the publication. . . . A commercial monopoly having been established, the interests and convenience of the individuals, whether as reporters or publishers, were allowed to predominate over all considerations for the public and the profession.

It is not surprising, therefore, that rival and unauthorized reports should appear in order to remedy these defects. The earliest, and the only one of these rivals which still survives, is the series of Law Journal Reports.[11] The Law Journal was

---

[1] W. T. S. Daniel, op. cit. 106 ; when Alderson's practice made it necessary for him to give up reporting he wrote to the Chief Justice resigning his position ; C. Alderson, Selection from the Charges and other detached papers of Baron Alderson, with an introductory notice of his life, 27.

[2] W. T. S. Daniel, op. cit. 166.   [3] Ibid 188.

[4] It was said that the Chancery reporters were paid £800 a year, ibid 268.

[5] For these reporters see below 429.

[6] W. T. S. Daniel, op. cit. 265-266 ; but Tamlyn fills a gap between Russell's reports and those of Russell and Hughes ; J. C. Fox, A Handbook of English Law Reports 57.

[7] To take in and bind the authorized reports cost about £30 a year ; Hanworth, Life of Chief Baron Pollock 22.

[8] Thus Swanston reports cases of the years 1818-19, but the three volumes of his reports were not published till 1821-27 ; Jacob's reports of the years 1821-22 were not published till 1828.

[9] W. T. S. Daniel, op. cit. 66, 192-193.   [10] Ibid 268.

[11] These Reports came to an end in 1949. Eds.

founded in 1822. It contained, amongst other matter, some reports of cases ; and some of the reports of cases in the King's Bench between 1803 and 1806 were separately published by J. P. Smith.[1] But it was not until 1822 that the regular weekly publication of the Law Journal Reports began. In the Preface to the first volume it was explained that it was intended to publish reports of cases in the Courts of Equity, the Courts of King's Bench and Common Pleas, some reports of cases heard at nisi prius, some cases in the Ecclesiastical and Admiralty Courts, a supplement to Burn's *Justices* which would contain some magistrates' cases, an annual Digest of reports of cases decided in all the courts, and a summary of the statutes. The publishers were careful to say that they had no thought of competing with the authorized reports. They pointed out that the different style adopted in these reports made it impossible to suppose that any opposition to these reports was intended. In the authorized reports, they said, there was given

A copy of the pleadings—a full statement of all the facts—the arguments of counsel at length—and almost every word uttered by the several judges in pronouncing their opinions. In the present publication only so much of the pleadings and facts will be given as will illustrate the judgment : and no more of the arguments of the counsel will be stated, than what may be necessary to connect the facts with the decision of the Court, which will be compressed into one statement. Each method of reporting has, it is conceived, its respective merits. The former is necessary for reports which are to prevent the necessity for inspecting the record, and to be authority in the Courts, and the latter is sufficient for the purposes of practice.[2]

The needs of practice and the defects of the authorized reports encouraged the growth of unauthorized reports even when the authorized reports had the privilege of exclusive citation. When Denman became Chief Justice of the King's Bench in 1832 he took away this privilege, and the other courts gradually followed the lead of the King's Bench.[3] Naturally there was a great increase in the numbers of the series of unauthorized reports. The new series of the Law Journal Reports started in 1832 ; the Legal Observer was started in 1830 ;[4] and, even before these dates it was becoming obvious that these reports were directly competing with the authorized reports. We shall see in the next chapter that other rival series of reports were started shortly afterwards.[5] At the same time the authorized reports still retained some of their other privileges and their prestige, though, as the competition became more severe, their circulation

---

[1] Wallace, The Reporters 531 n. 1.　　　　[2] Preface p. 2.
[3] W. T. S. Daniel, op. cit. 266.　　　[4] Ibid 38.　　　[5] Below, vol. xiv.

was constantly diminishing.[1] We shall see that this state of free trade in, and free competition amongst, reports produced an intolerable state of affairs, which, after much discussion, led to the termination of the authorized reports and the establishment of the quasi-official Law Reports. But the history of this movement and its effects belongs to the following period.[2]

At this point I shall, in the first place, give a list of the reports of this period, together with some notes upon some of them; and, in the second place, an account of some of the more notable reporters.

(1) A list of the Reports of this period [3]
House of Lords

	Brown[4]	..	..	..	..	1702-1800.
(a)	Dow[5]	..	..	..	..	1812-1818.
(a)	Bligh[6]	..	..	..	..	1819-1821.
(a)	Bligh (New Series)[7]		..	..	..	1827-1837.
(a)	Dow and Clark	..	..	..	..	1827-1831-2.
(a)	Clark and Finelly	..	.	..	..	1831-1846.

Privy Council

(a)	Acton[8]	..	..	..	..	1809-1811.
(a)	Knapp[9]	..	..	..	..	1829-1836.

The Common Law and courts connected therewith
King's Bench

	Durnford and East [10] (Term Reports)				1785-1800.
(a)	East [11]	..	..	..	1801-1812.
(a)	Maule [12] and Selwyn [13]		..	..	1813-1817.
(a)	Barnewall [14] and Alderson [15]			..	1817-1822.
(a)	Barnewall and Cresswell[16]			..	1822-1830.
(a)	Barnewall and Adolphus[17]			..	1830-1834.

[1] In 1863 Sir Roundell Palmer said that their circulation must be reckoned not by thousands but by hundreds, W. T. S. Daniel, op. cit. 188.
[2] Below, vol. xiv.
[3] The reporters marked with the letter (a) are the authorized reporters; the list is compiled mainly from the list given in Wallace, The Reporters 525-546.
[4] Vol. xii 104.   [5] Ibid 104-105.   [6] Below 434, 455.
[7] The report of the last case reported—Garland v. Carlisle—is unfinished; it breaks off in the middle of a sentence; the case is fully reported in 4 Cl. and Fin. 693; the part missing in Bligh begins at p. 760. The gap between the first and second series of Bligh is pieced by Lord St. Leonards' book on the Law of Property as administered in the House of Lords, published in 1849, see J. C. Fox, op. cit. 12n., 13; for Lord St. Leonards and his books, see vol. xiv.
[8] Vol. xii 106.   [9] Ibid.   [10] Ibid 116.
[11] Ibid 116-117.   [12] Below 434, 435, 551, 574, 645.
[13] Below 437, 438, 460, 574.   [14] Below 435, 436, 438.
[15] Below 430, 435, 436, 438.   [16] Below 433, 434, 436, 437.
[17] Below 438.

Dowling[1] and Ryland	.. ..	1821-1827.
Manning[2] and Ryland	.. ..	1827-1830.
Nevile and Manning	.. ..	1831-1836.

Common Pleas

(a)	Blackstone (Henry)[3]	.. ..	1788-1796.
(a)	Bosanquet and Puller[4]	..	1796-1804.
(a)	Bosanquet and Puller, N.R.	..	1804-1807.
(a)	Taunton[5]	.. ..	1807-1819.
(a)	Broderip[6] and Bingham[7] ..	..	1819-1822.
(a)	Bingham	..	1822-1834.
	Marshall	..	1814-1816.
	Moore (J. B.) ..	..	1817-1827.
	Moore and Payne ..	..	1828-1831.
	Moore and Scott ..	..	1831-1834.

Exchequer (common law and equity)

(a)	Anstruther[8]		1792-1797.
(a)	Forrest[9]		1800-1801.
(a)	Wightwick		1810-1811.
(a)	Price[10]		1814-1824.
(a)	M'Cleland		1824.
(a)	M'Cleland and Younge		1825.
(a)	Younge and Jervis		1826-1830.
(a)	Crompton and Jervis		1830-1832.
	Tyrwhitt		1830-1835.

[1] Dowling was born in 1787, and was called to the bar by the Middle Temple in 1815; in 1827 he became a judge of the court of New South Wales, and Chief Justice in 1837; he died in 1844, D.N.B.; in their Preface the authors call their work "The New Term Reports".

[2] Below 430, 438, 455, 553.

[3] Vol. xii 122, 140.

[4] Ibid 123, 135; to the end of vol. i from pp. 471-659 there is appended reports of the Easter term 1796, which fill the gap between the end of H. Blackstone's reports and the beginning of this series; they were compiled from the notes of A. Moore by Bosanquet and Puller, 1 B. and P. 471.

[5] The eighth volume of these reports was said by Parke, B. to be "an apocryphal authority", made up from Taunton J.'s notes and not revised by him, Hadley v. Baxendale (1854) 23 L.J. Ex. at p. 180; the compiler of the reports was not the judge, but William Pyle Taunton (?) his son.

[6] He was born in 1789 and called to the bar by Lincoln's Inn in 1817; from 1822 to 1837 he was a magistrate at the Thames police court; he was treasurer of Gray's Inn in 1851, and was eminent as a naturalist as well as a lawyer, D.N.B.

[7] Below 438, 439, 490.

[8] Vol. xii 114-115, 117, 122, 138.

[9] The author laments in his preface the absence of regular reports of Exchequer cases.

[10] Price was the author of a book on the Exchequer, below and his reports contain long and learned notes on some of the decisions in revenue cases, see e.g. 8 Price 374, 11 Price 41, 12 Price 7, 573, 13 Price 819.

Exchequer (equity)

(a)	Wilson	..	..	..	..	1817.
(a)	Daniell	..	..	..	..	1817-1820.
(a)	Younge	..	..	..	..	1830-1832.

Crown Cases

Russell and Ryan[1]	..	..	..	1799-1823.
Lewin[2]	..	..	..	1822-1838.
Moody[3]	..	..	..	1824-1844.

Nisi Prius Cases

Peake[4]	..	..	..	1790-1794.
Peake's Additional Cases	..	..	1795-1812.
Espinasse[5]	..	..	..	1793-1807.
Campbell[6]	..	..	..	1808-1816.
Holt[7]	..	..	..	1815-1817.
Starkie[8]	..	..	..	1815-1822.
Gow	..	..	..	1818-1820.
Dowling and Ryland	..	..	1822-1823.
Ryan and Moody	..	..	..	1823-1826.
Carrington and Payne	..	..	1823-1841.
Moody and Malkin	..	..	1827-1830.
Moody and Robinson	..	..	1831-1844.

Magistrates' Cases

Dowling and Ryland	..	..	1822-1827.
Manning and Ryland	..	..	1827-1829.
Nevile and Manning	..	..	1832-1836.

Settlement Cases

Bott[9]	..	..	..	..	1761-1827.

[1] For Russell and Ryan see below 437 ; these are reports of crown cases reserved : the editors were allowed to use the note book of Bayley J. which they used to supply the greater part of the head notes.

[2] Lewin was said by Blackburn J. to be an inaccurate reporter, R. v. Francis (1874) 43 L.J. N.S. M.C. at p. 100, cited Wallace, The Reporters 537 n. 2 ; he is one of the parties to the dialogue in " Circuiteers," vol. ix 415 ; the first vol. of the reports is dedicated to Alderson J., the second to Hallam, the historian.

[3] The earlier part of the volume was edited jointly with Ryan ; the editors used in compiling their reports the note books of Bayley and Gaselee J.J., Preface.

[4] Vol. xii 109-110, 122.

[5] Ibid 110, 123.

[6] Below 437, 481, 488, 489.

[7] For Holt see below 481, 488, 489 ; he adds useful notes on the points of law involved in the cases.

[8] For Starkie see below 439, 465, 488 ; there are short notes on some of the cases by the reporters in this and other series of these nisi prius reports ; the notes to vol. i of Carrington and Payne's reports are by Carrington.

[9] Vol. vii 108, 121.

Bail Court and cases in practice and pleading

| | Chitty (Joseph)[1] | .. | .. | .. | 1810-1820. |
| | Dowling | .. | .. | .. | 1830-1840. |

Chancery

The High Court of Chancery

	Brown[2]	..	..	..	..	1778-1794.
	Cox[3]	..	..	..	..	1783-1796.
(a)	Vesey Junior[4]	..	..	..	1789-1816.
(a)	Vesey and Beames[5]	..	..	1812-1814.
(a)	Cooper (G.)[6]	..	..	..	1815.
(a)	Merivale[7]	..	..	..	..	1815-1817.
(a)	Swanston[8]	..	..	..	1818-1819.
(a)	Wilson	..	..	..	..	1818-1819.
(a)	Jacob and Walker	..	..	..	1819-1821.
(a)	Jacob[9]	..	..	..	..	1821-1822.

[1] The first volume is entitled " Reports of Cases principally on Practice and Pleading determined in the Court of King's Bench in Hilary, Easter-Trinity and Michaelmas Terms, 1819, with copious notes of other important decisions " ; the second volume is entitled " Reports of Cases principally on Practice and Pleading and relating to the office of magistrates determined in the Court of King's Bench. Also reports of cases temp. Lord Mansfield in the years 1782, etc. from the MSS. of Mr. Justice Ashhurst; with notes "; for Joseph Chitty see below 443, 458, 459.

[2] Vol. xii 125 ; J. C. Fox, A Handbook of English Law Reports 32-34.

[3] Ibid 125, 144 ; J. C. Fox, op. cit. 35-36.

[4] Ibid 125, 143-144; J. C. Fox, op. cit. 36-38 ; in 1827 J. E. Hovenden published a supplement to these reports ; it consists of notes on the cases, and some cases of the time of Hardwicke and King from the MSS. of Forrester which had come into the hands of the publisher, see vol. xii 142-143 ; Hovenden explains in his preface that the fact that it was necessary for Vesey to publish his reports promptly left him no time to examine authorities relevant to the cases ; and that his object was both to examine these authorities and to give cross references to the cases in Vesey's nineteen volumes ; to some extent Hovenden's work was anticipated by Vesey's notes to his second edition which was also published in 1827 ; in 1833 Vesey published a twentieth volume which contained a digest of his nineteen volumes and an index ; in the preface thereto he attempts to answer some of the criticisms of Miller, below, vol. xiv, on the condition of English Law. Campbell, Chancellors vi 237 n., says that he knew Vesey well ; he was, he says, good-natured, honest, and painstaking, but dull ; he wrote his notes in shorthand " which will never produce good reporting " and succeeded better in reporting the judgments of Grant M.R. than those of Eldon, because the judgments of the former were " perfect in charges and expression ", while those of the latter were very discursive.

[5] Beames (1781-1853) was a King's Counsel, a member of the Charge Commission of 1824, a commissioner of lunatics, or a commissioner in bankruptcy, J. C. Fox, op. cit. 38.

[6] He became chief justice of Madras in 1817, ibid 39.

[7] Merivale's reports are a continuation of Cooper's ; both Cooper and Merivale were encouraged by Vesey to publish their reports—in fact Vesey seems to have regarded first Cooper, and then, when Cooper went to India, Merivale, as his successors, see the Prefaces to Cooper and Merivale's reports ; for Merivale see below 439, 440.

[8] Undertaken at the suggestion of Merivale as a continuation of his and Cooper's reports, Prefaces to 2 Mer. and 1 Swanst. ; for Swanston's reports see below 440, 441.   [9] Below 440.

(a) Turner[1] and Russell[2]   ..   ..   1822-1824.
(a) Russell   ..   ..   1826-1829.
(a) Russell and Mylne ..   ..   ..   1829-1831.

The Court of the Master of the Rolls

Tamlyn [3]   ..   ..   1829-1830.

The Vice-Chancellor's Courts

(a) Maddock[4]   ..   ..   1815-1822.
(a) Simons[5] and Stuart [6]   ..   ..   1822-1826.
(a) Simons   ..   ..   1826-1849.

The Court of Admiralty

Robinson, Sir Christopher[7]   ..   1799-1808.
Edwards [8]   ..   ..   1808-1810.
Dodson [9]   ..   ..   1811-1822.
Haggard [10]   ..   ..   1822-1838.

The Ecclesiastical Courts

Haggard (Consistory)[11]   ..   ..   1789-1821.
Phillimore[12] ..   ..   1809-1821.
Addams   ..   ..   1822-1826.
Haggard (Ecclesiastical)   ..   ..   1827-1833.

Reports of cases on special topics
Bankruptcy

Rose[13]   ..   ..   1810-1816.
Buck[14]   ..   ..   1816-1820.
Glyn and Jameson ..   ..   ..   1821-1828.
Montagu[15] and Macarthur   ..   1828-1830.
Montagu   ..   ..   1830-1832.

[1] Below 439, 629.   [2] Below 437, 440, 464.
[3] Below 477.   [4] Below 439, 497, 577, 578, 628.
[5] Simons (1788-1870) was an equity craftsman and conveyancer and became registrar of the Manchester Bankruptcy court, J. C. Fox, op. cit. 62.
[6] Below 439, 679.
[7] Vol. xii 105, 126, 145; below 689, 690, 691; Lord Glenville said in 1801 that his reports were " calculated to prove to the world that Great Britain administers the Gothic law of nations with the same distinguished ability and unblemished purity which has so long been the glory of her courts of municipal judicature," 1 Hass 235.
[8] (1775?-1848), a fellow of Trinity Hall, Cambridge, and advocate of Doctors' Commons, D.N.B.   [9] Below 441, 679.
[10] (1794-1856) a fellow of Trinity Hall, Cambridge, and advocate of Doctors' Commons, chancellor of Lincoln, Winchester, and Manchester dioceses, D.N.B.
[11] Vol. xii 106, 126, 145.   [12] Below 441, 677.   [13] Below 441, 442.
[14] Called to the bar by Lincoln's Inn 1813, D.N.B.
[15] Below 441, 442, 480, 485, 491.

Insolvency

  Cresswell (R.N.) .. ..   ..   1827-1829.

Mercantile Law

  Danson and Lloyd[1]   ..   ..   1828-1829.
  Lloyd and Welsby[2]   ..   ..   1829-1830.

Election cases

  Peckwell[3] ..   ..   1802-1806.
  Corbett and Daniell   ..   ..   1819.

Patent cases

  Carpmael[4] ..   ..   1802-1840.
  Webster[5] ..   ..   1802-1855.
  Davies[6] ..   ..   1785-1816.

Tithe cases

  Gwillim[7] ..   ..   —
  Eagle and Young[8] ..   ..   ..   —

Cases on Outlawry [9]

  Conroy   ..   ..   17th and 18th
                      centuries.

[1] The title of these reports is " Reports of Cases relating to Commerce, Manufactures, etc., etc., determined in the Courts of Common Law at nisi prius and in banc, with practical notes " ; the design of the book was to present " in a simple and compendious form", decisions on topics " which, both in number and importance, now occupy the chief place in the business of the courts."   [2] Below 441, 442.

[3] To these reports there is appended an introduction which gives an account of the practice on election petitions.

[4] The author had been called to the bar, but he was a civil engineer with an extensive practice, and had advised on questions of patent law ; the reports are intended not only for lawyers, but also for patentees, manufacturers and inventors, Preface.   [5] Below 441, 442, 443.

[6] An official in the Rolls Chapel which was one of the offices where specifications were enrolled ; it is prefaced by an historical introduction to patent law.

[7] The full title of the book is, " A Collection of Acts and Records of Parliament with Reports of Cases argued and determined in the Courts of Law and Equity respecting Tithes " ; the book is in four volumes ; the first 103 pp. of vol. i consists of records and statutes, the rest of the work consists of the reports of cases ; the author had been a judge of the supreme court of Madras ; in his Preface he tells us that he had intended to prefix a tract on tithes, but this seems not to have been completed.

[8] This is a book in five volumes which sets out all the authorities in chronological order—statutes, cases, and records ; the first entry is from the patent roll of 6 John ; sometimes several reports are given of a single case.

[9] The full title of the book is, " Custodiam Reports, or a Collection of Cases relative to outlawries and grants thereon, as argued and determined on the revenue sides of the courts of Exchequer both in England and Ireland. To which is prefixed an Introduction consisting of two chapters, the first containing a short account of outlawry and the process thereon, the second the manner of obtaining the grant in custodiam, the mode of accounting thereon, and how the same is dissolved, likewise an Appendix of precedents " ; the book was published in 1795, and the cases are taken from the printed reports.

Reports in all the courts

The Law Journal[1] .. .. .. 1822.

The Legal Observer[2] .. .. 1830-1856.

(2) *Some notable reporters*

Of most of the reporters of the House of Lords and Privy Council cases I have already said something.[3] The only reporter of whom I need here say anything is Bligh. Bligh (1780-1838)[4] was the son of Captain, afterwards Admiral, Bligh of the Bounty. He was educated at Westminster School and Trinity College, Cambridge, was called to the bar by the Inner Temple, and practised at the Chancery Bar.[5] He tells us that he had spent twelve years taking notes of House of Lords decisions before he published his first series of House of Lords reports. But though these reports won praise they hardly paid the expense of publication. This was the reason for the delay in the publication of the second series. The second series was written on the same plan as the first, except that the appeals from the Scottish courts were relegated to the appendix. Besides reporting cases in the House of Lords, Bligh collaborated with Basil Montague[6] in a set of reports of bankruptcy cases ;[7] he wrote a digest of bankruptcy law ; and a book on the report of the poor law commission and poor law bill of 1834.

The reporters in the common law courts and the courts connected therewith include several famous lawyers, some of whom attained judicial rank. I shall first say something of those who attained judicial rank, and then of some of the others.

(i) *Reporters who attained judicial rank*

Maule (1788-1858)[8] was a distinguished mathematician and classical scholar—senior wrangler in 1810, and fellow of Trinity, Cambridge, in 1811. For a year or two after his election as fellow he took mathematical pupils at Cambridge, amongst whom was Cresswell.[9] He became a student at Lincoln's Inn in 1810 [10] and was called to the bar in 1814.[11] It was in his early days as a special pleader and student that he combined with Selwyn to compile the reports which bear their names. Though his progress at the bar was slow, his merits as a lawyer and an advocate ensured his success. He made his name as a commercial lawyer, and in 1833

---

[1] Above 426, 427.   [2] Above 427.

[3] Vol. xii 104-105, 106.

[4] D.N.B. ; Pref. to the two series of his reports.

[5] He was admitted *ad eundem* by Lincoln's Inn in 1826, Registers ii 121.

[6] Below 442.   [7] Above 432.

[8] Foss, Lives of the Judges ix 223-226 ; E. Manson, The Builders of our Law during the reign of Queen Victoria (2nd ed.) 66-72 ; D.N.B.

[9] Below 436.   [10] Lincoln's Inn Admission Register ii 41.

[11] Black Books iv 246.

he took silk, became a bencher of Lincoln's Inn,[1] and was appointed counsel to the bank of England in succession to Scarlett.[2] In 1837 he represented the borough of Carlow in the House of Commons, and in 1839 he was appointed a baron of the Exchequer, from which court he moved a few months later to the Court of Common Pleas. He remained a judge of that court till ill-health forced him to resign in 1855. He was then made a member of the judicial committee of the Privy Council, and was an effective member of it till his death in 1858. He was an excellent judge— combining great common sense and a dry and somewhat cynical humour with a profound knowledge of the law. " No one," says Veeder, " ever had a finer sense of the anomalies and incongruities of English law . . . his subtle mind was balanced by good sense and entire freedom from technicality." [3] His conversational powers were so great that he was said to have been the only man whom Brougham feared.[4] Mr. Justice Hawkins said of him that he was a man of great wit, good sense, a curious humour and a keen apprehension with little love of mediocrities.[5] The memory of his dry humour is perpetuated by many tales, the best known of which is his address to a poor man convicted of bigamy after the elopement of his wife, which was a preface to a nominal sentence of one day's imprisonment.[6]

Alderson[7] (1787-1857) was the son of a recorder of Norwich, Ipswich, and Yarmouth. He was educated at Caius College, Cambridge, where he took the highest honours both in classics and mathematics. He was called to the bar by the Inner Temple in 1811, and from 1817 to 1822 he was the reporter, with Barnewall, in the King's Bench. He soon acquired a leading practice at Westminster and on the northern circuit ; and in 1828 he was appointed one of the commissioners to enquire into the practice and procedure of the courts of common law.[8] We have seen that an Act of 1830 had created additional judges in the common law

[1] Black Books iv 186.   [2] For Scarlett see below, vol. xiv.
[3] A century of English Judicature, Essays A.A.L.H. i 745 ; Sir F. Pollock, L.Q.R. xxiv 96, says of this essay that " it shows a critical appreciation of modern English judges which, if it were not before our eyes, we should not have thought attainable even by a good lawyer and a diligent reader of the reports without intimate personal knowledge " ; I endorse this verdict, for I have found the essay most useful and instructive.
[4] E. Manson, The Builders of our Law (2nd ed.) 66.
[5] Reminiscences 42.
[6] Vol. i 623-624 ; for others see Manson, op. cit. ; one story is that before the hearing of a heavy appeal in the House of Lords he had a heavy lunch of stout and steak ; Follett his leader, who had lunched off sherry and biscuits, asked why he was lunching so plentifully. " To reduce myself to the intellectual level of the Judges," said Maule.
[7] Foss, Judges ix 130-133 ; Alderson, Selection from the Charges and other detailed papers of Baron Alderson, with an introductory notice of his life ; Manson, op. cit. 91-99 ; D.N.B.
[8] Above 306.

courts.[1] Alderson, though still only a junior counsel, was, on the suggestion of Pollock (the future Chief Baron),[2] appointed the additional judge of the Common Pleas under this Act. In 1834, in pursuance of an agreement made with Lyndhurst when he was raised to the bench, he removed to the Exchequer where he took charge of the equity side of the court. He remained a judge of the court till his death. He was a learned, vigorous, and efficient judge, and particularly good as a criminal lawyer.[3] His one fault was a tendency to come to too rapid a decision at the opening of a case. But he was, says Foss, a popular judge with juries, " and while sitting in Banco he had much influence in the decisions of the court." He had a sense of humour, and never lost his love of literature. Some of his poetical pieces have been printed by his son.[4]

Cresswell[5] (1794-1863) was educated at Emmanuel College, Cambridge. He was called to the bar by the Inner Temple in 1819, and from 1822 to 1830 he, with Barnewall, was the reporter in the King's Bench. He soon acquired a leading practice on the northern circuit. In 1830 he became recorder of Hull, and took silk in 1834. He was elected member of Parliament for Liverpool in the conservative interest in 1841. In 1842 Peel made him a judge of the Common Pleas. There he remained till 1858. In that year he was made the first judge of the new probate and divorce court. His work there did much to ensure the success of the court. " He reformed," said Lord Sumner, " the old ecclesiastical rules of evidence in matrimonial causes, and did for this branch of the law what Mansfield did for mercantile law."[6] At the opening of the court after his death Sir Robert Phillimore, the Queen's advocate, said of him that,

he possessed many and rare qualifications for the judicial office. To a memory of extraordinary swiftness and tenacity, to habits of most careful and accurate thinking, to great quickness of perception, to considerable logical power, to a ready command of apt and proper language, aiding and adorning a capacity seldom surpassed for clear and luminous statement, he added a profound knowledge of the common law of this country, and an industry so conscientious and indefatigable that it enabled him during the time that he sat upon that bench thoroughly to master the principles and precedents of a jurisprudence with which he had not previously been familiar.

[1] Above 404, 405.   [2] Hanworth, Lord Chief Baron Pollock 47.
[3] Veeder, Essays A.A.L.H. i 748 ; " A Complete Mastery of the Law," Selborne, Memorials, Family and Personal i 373.
[4] Translations from Horace, Sophocles, and other classical authors, and Latin versions of English poems, C. Alderson, op. cit. 246-265.
[5] Foss, Judges ix 184-187 ; D.N.B.—article by J. A. Hamilton, later Lord Sumner.
[6] Veeder, Essays A.A.L.H. i 799-800 agrees with Lord Sumner ; he says, " the reports of Swabey and Tristram, which contain his clear and concise opinions and charges to juries, are monuments of learning and common sense ; and so skilfully, and with such foresight, were the modern foundations of this jurisdiction laid that his judgment is said to have been only once reversed."

The large amount of work with which his court was filled undermined his constitution, and a road accident, which broke his kneecap, gave him a shock which soon after led to his death from heart disease.

Crompton[1] (1797-1865) was called to the bar by the Inner Temple in 1821. As first tubman and then postman in the Court of Exchequer,[2] and as counsel for the board of stamps and taxes, he was well fitted to be the reporter of the decisions of that court. In 1851 he was appointed one of the commissioners to enquire into the practice of the Court of Chancery. He became a judge of the King's Bench in 1852. On the bench he proved himself to be a very sound lawyer and a good judge.

The most eminent of the nisi prius reporters who attained judicial rank is Lord Campbell, Chief Justice, Lord Chancellor, and author of the *Lives of the Chancellors* and the *Lives of the Chief Justices*.[3] We have seen that he deliberately refused to report cases which seemed to him to lay down bad law.[4] The accuracy of his reports was praised by Blackburn, J. ;[5] but they were said by Maule, J. to err on the side of brevity, more especially in their statement of the facts of the cases.[6]

Other reporters, like Puller and East,[7] attained judicial rank in India. Russell, who reported Crown Cases, became chief justice of Bengal ; and, before he attained this rank, he had written a classic treatise on the criminal law.[8] Ryan, his co-editor of the reports of Crown Cases, also became chief justice of Bengal, and, after he resigned that office, a member of the Judicial Committee of the Privy Council. Later he gave up the membership of the Judicial Committee, and became the president of the civil service commission. Holt, who reported nisi prius cases, was the writer of legal text books, and of several plays ; and he became Vice-Chancellor of the county palatine of Lancaster.

(ii) *Some of the other reporters*

Of the other reporters the most noteworthy are the following : Selwyn (1775-1855),[9] the father of Lord Justice Selwyn,[10] was educated at Eton and Trinity College, Cambridge. He was a distinguished classical scholar and something of a mathematician. He was called to the bar by Lincoln's Inn in 1807,[11] took silk in 1827, and became Treasurer in 1840.[12] Soon after Queen Victoria's

---

[1] Foss, Judges ix 187-188 ; D.N.B.
[2] Held by the senior barristers on the equity and the common law sides of the court, vol. i 234 n. 4.
[3] See vol. xiv for an account of his career.
[4] Vol. xii 158 n. 1 ; Lives of the Chancellors iv 458.
[5] Readhead v. Midland Rly. Co. (1867) L.R. 2 Q.B. at p. 438.
[6] Wallace, The Reporters 542, n. 1.   [7] Vol. xii, 135.
[8] Below 464.   [9] D.N.B.   [10] Below, vol. xiv.
[11] Black Books iv 244.   [12] Ibid 173, 202.

marriage he was chosen to help Prince Albert in his legal studies. Besides his reports, he published in 1806-8 an *Abridgement of the Law of Nisi Prius* which reached a thirteenth edition in 1869. Barnewall[1] (1780-1842) was called to the bar by the Inner Temple in 1806. He reported in the Court of King's Bench from 1817 to 1834. Testimony to his excellence as a reporter was given by both bench and bar when he retired, the former presenting him with a silver vase and the latter with an address. His partner in the first part of the first volume of his and Alderson's reports was not Alderson, but Selwyn.[2] Adolphus[3] (1795-1862) was the son of a distinguished criminal lawyer and historian. He was educated at Merchant Taylors' and St. John's College, Oxford. Like his father, he combined law with literature. He was the first to detect the real author of the Waverley novels, and his book laid the foundation of a friendship with Sir Walter Scott. Of his wit the Eclogue entitled "the Circuiteers," printed in an earlier volume of this History,[4] is the best illustration. He was a bencher of the Inner Temple, and in 1852 was appointed judge of the Marylebone county court. Besides his reports, he wrote other non-legal books, and at the time of his death he was completing his father's history of England under George III.

Serjeant Manning[5] (1781-1866) was a learned black-letter lawyer. He helped Brougham and Denman in their defence of Queen Caroline, and was recorder of Sudbury, Banbury and Oxford. From 1847 to 1883 he was judge of the Whitechapel county court. Besides his reports, he was the author of two learned works on the practice of the plea and revenue side of the court of Exchequer,[6] and a report of the proceedings arising from Brougham's attempt to suppress the privileges of the Serjeants, which is entitled *Serviens ad Legem*.[7] The extent of his learning is also illustrated by the numerous notes which he attached to his reports of cases in the Court of Common Pleas which, in conjunction with T. C. Granger, he published between 1840 and 1844.[8] These notes show that he was as well acquainted with the Year Books and the mediæval sources of the law as with the modern reports and the modern literature of the law. Bingham[9] (1788-1864) was called to the bar by the Middle Temple in 1818, and was for a number of years police magistrate at Great Marlborough Street. He was of the school of the philosophical radicals,[10] and had charge of the literary and artistic department of the *Westminster Review*, to the first number of which he contributed

---

[1] D.N.B.
[3] D.N.B.; vol. ix 413-414.
[5] D.N.B.
[7] Atlay, The Victorian Chancellors i 433-436; below 455.
[8] Below, vol. xiv.   [9] D.N.B.

[2] Wallace, The Reporters, 530 n. 2.
[4] Ibid 415-417.
[6] Below 443, 454, 455.
[10] Above 65, 66.

five articles.[1] Besides his reports, he edited Bentham's *Book of Fallacies*,[2] and wrote books on a number of other legal topics.[3] Starkie, the reporter of *nisi prius* cases, was the writer of several valuable text books,[4] a member of the commission on the practice and procedure of the courts of common law which was appointed in 1828,[5] and Downing Professor of the Laws of England at Cambridge. Of Chitty who wrote useful books on many branches of law I shall speak later.[6]

Of the Chancery reporters two were raised to the bench—George Turner and John Stuart.

Turner[7] (1798-1867) was educated at Charterhouse and Pembroke College, Cambridge. He was called to the bar by Lincoln's Inn in 1821 ; and between 1822 and 1824 he, with Russell, compiled a volume of Chancery reports. He took silk in 1840, entered Parliament in 1847, and was made a Vice-Chancellor in 1851. He was a leading member of the Chancery commission of 1852, the recommendations of which were the basis of the most important and far reaching reforms of Chancery procedure which the Legislature had as yet made.[8] In 1853 he became a Lord Justice of Appeal, where he sat with Knight-Bruce, L. J. Mr. E. F. Turner says,[9]

" The marked contrast in their habits of thought and mode of expression —the vivacity and dry humour of Knight-Bruce, and the steadiness and gravity of Turner—blended admirably in result, and their joint judgments have stood the test of time. Turner was on all occasions jealous to repel any attempt to narrow the limits of the jurisdiction of the court, and courageous in expanding its remedial powers to meet modern developments."

Stuart[10] was called to the bar by Lincoln's Inn in 1819, and, with Simons reported cases in the Vice-Chancellor's Court between 1822 and 1826. He took silk in 1839, and entered Parliament in 1846. He was made Vice-Chancellor in 1852. But he was not a strong judge, and his decisions were often reversed.[11]

Of the other Chancery reporters one of the more notable is Maddock, who wrote the earliest first-rate text-book on modern equity.[12] Of him and his book I shall speak later. Merivale [13] (1779-1844) was a member of the Chancery commission of 1824, and favoured more radical reforms than those recommended by

---

[1] Mill, Autobiography 95.   [2] Above 65.   [3] Below 490.
[4] Below 465, 488.   [5] Above 306.   [6] Below 458, 459.
[7] D.N.B. ; Foss, Judges ix 287-288.
[8] Vol. i 444-445 ; vol. ix 375-376, 406-407 ; below, vol. xiv.
[9] D.N.B. ; Rolt says, Memoirs of Sir John Rolt 173, that he was " much loved and valued by the whole legal profession as a lawyer and as a man."
[10] Foss, Judges ix 267.
[11] " A witty barrister once placed an appeal from his decision on the calendar of motions of course," Veeder, A Century of Judicature, Essays, A.A.L.H. i 797.
[12] Below 497, 577, 578, 628.   [13] D.N.B. ; J. C. Fox, op. cit. 39-40.

the commission. Besides being a learned lawyer, he was a classical scholar, a poet, and a man of letters, a friend of Byron, and a frequent contributor to the *Quarterly* and other reviews. Russell[1] (1790-1861) was called to the bar by the Inner Temple in 1822, and in the same year began his career as a law reporter. He acquired a large junior practice, took silk in 1841, and became the leader in Vice-Chancellor Knight-Bruce's court. But though he was an effective leader in that court, because Knight-Bruce knew and understood him, he was an ineffective speaker and hardly fitted to be a leader in a court where he was not known.[2] He contributed to the *Quarterly*, and was for some years the editor of the *Annual Register*. Jacob (1796-1841) was a senior wrangler and fellow of Caius College, Cambridge. He was called to the bar by Lincoln's Inn in 1819, and took silk in 1834. He would have been made a judge if his health had not failed.[3] Rolt says of him that he had never seen the advocate " the value of whose advice or opinion in the conduct of a cause could for one moment be compared with that of Jacob, and his advocacy, tho' it may have been equalled, was second to none." [4]

The best and the most learned of all these Chancery reports are Swanston's. Swanston (1783-1863)[5] tells us that his aim was to set out the facts clearly and fully, to summarize the pleadings, to state briefly the substance of the arguments with all the authorities cited, and to " represent exactly " the reasoning by which the court reached its conclusion.[6] That aim he succeeded in attaining ; and, in addition, he gives references to the entry of the case in the Registrar's books, and, if it seemed to be necessary, an extract of the order made by the court.[7] But his reports are remarkable not only for their excellence as reports, but also for the learned notes which are appended to some of the cases. In a former volume of this History I have made much use of the cases which Swanston printed from Lord Nottingham's MSS.[8] By printing these extracts he made a notable contribution to the history of equity. Many of his notes give a clear and comprehensive account of various bodies of equitable doctrine. For instance to the case of *Dillon v. Parker*[9] is appended a valuable note on the doctrine of election ; [10] to the case of *Crawshay v.*

[1] D.N.B.; J. C. Fox, op. cit. 43, 44 ; Wallace, op. cit. 527.

[2] " His knowledge of law and his judgment and tact in the management of a cause in Chambers were first-rate, and his services in court before any judge who knew him were equally valuable, but his thick and confused utterance, his hesitating manner, his repetition, and the repetition of the beginning of sentences were most painful to strangers or to those who seldom heard him," Memoirs of Sir John Rolt 104.

[3] Memoirs of Sir John Rolt 62 n. 2, 73 ; J. C. Fox, op. cit. 42.

[4] Memoirs of Sir John Rolt 64.   [5] Preface.   [6] Ibid.

[7] Ibid.   [8] Vol. vi 542-548.

[9] (1818) 1 Swanst. 359.   [10] Ibid 394-409.

Maule,[1] a note on the dissolution of partnership ;[2] to the case of *Davis v. Duke of Marlborough,*[3] notes on dealings with expectant heirs,[4] and on waste ;[5] and to the case of *Drewry v. Thacker* [6] some valuable precedents from Lord Nottingham's MSS. and the Registrar's book.[7] These notes were the more valuable when they were written because, as we shall see, at that date, Maddock's book, the only good up to date text-book on equity, had only been very recently published. They show that Swanston was one of the few equity lawyers of his day who possessed both the learning and the literary ability needed for the composition of a first-rate book on the principles of equity.

Of the reporters in the Court of Admiralty and the Ecclesiastical Courts, the most notable are Phillimore and Dodson.

Joseph Phillimore [8] (1775-1855) was the progenitor of a famous legal family. He was educated at Westminster and Christ Church, Oxford, where he distinguished himself as a classical scholar. He became a member of Doctors' Commons in 1804, and soon got a considerable practice in the Admiralty and the Ecclesiastical Courts. In 1809 he became Regius Professor of Civil Law at Oxford, Chancellor of the diocese of Oxford and judge of the Admiralty court of the cinque ports. From 1817 to 1830 he was a member of the House of Commons. There he advocated the cause of Catholic emancipation, and gained a considerable reputation for his knowledge of international law. He was also chancellor of the dioceses of Worcester and Bristol, commissary of the dean of St. Paul's, and judge of the consistory court of Gloucester. " At Oxford he was long remembered for the golden latinity and distinguished manner in which he discharged the duty incident to his chair of presenting strangers for degrees at commemoration." [9] Sir John Dodson [10] (1780-1858) was educated at Merchant Taylors' school and Oriel College, Oxford. He became an advocate of Doctors' Commons in 1808. From 1819 to 1823 he represented Rye in Parliament. He was appointed advocate to the Admiralty in 1829. In 1834 he was called to the bar by the Middle Temple and elected a bencher. He was made master of the faculties in 1841, and vicar-general to the archbishop of Canterbury in 1849. He was judge of the Prerogative Court from 1852 to the abolition of that jurisdiction in 1857.

Of the reporters on special topics the four most notable are Rose, Montagu, Welsby, and Webster.

Sir George Rose[11] (1782-1873) was called to the bar by the Inner Temple in 1809, and practised in the common law courts

---

[1] (1818) Swanst. 495. [2] Ibid 509-518. [3] Ibid 108.
[4] Ibid 139-143. [5] Ibid 145-152, 170-173.
[6] (1818) 3 Swanst. 529. [7] Ibid 529-536. [8] D.N.B.
[9] Ibid. [10] Ibid. [11] Ibid.

and on the northern circuit. He took silk in 1827, and in the same year was made a bencher of his Inn, of which he became Treasurer in 1835. His father's bankruptcy turned his attention to the law of bankruptcy, and led to the compilation of his bankruptcy reports. In 1831 he was made a member of the court of review of bankruptcy cases, and in 1840 a master in Chancery—a post which he held till the office was abolished in 1852. He had a reputation for wit—one of the best known of his efforts are the verses on a day in the Court of Chancery in Lord Eldon's time which are cited in the first volume of this History.[1] Basil Montagu[2] (1770-1852)—best known as the editor of the complete edition of Bacon's Works which Macaulay made the text of his essay on Bacon—was a famous lawyer and literary man of his day. He was a friend of Coleridge, Wordsworth, Godwin, and for some time of Carlyle—till Carlyle took offence at his offer to him of a clerkship at £200 a year. He was called to the bar in 1798, and took silk in 1835. His practice was mainly bankruptcy. He wrote several books on the law of bankruptcy,[3] and also on topics connected with equity.[4] In 1841 he was made accountant-general in bankruptcy. Besides his legal works, he wrote many philosophical works and miscellaneous literary works. He was all his life an advocate for legal and other reforms. He advocated reforms in the law of bankruptcy and insolvency, he denounced the infliction of the death penalty, and he advocated the emancipation of the Jews. His long experience in the working of the bankruptcy laws makes his series of reports of these cases the best of this series of reports. Welsby (1802-1864) is best known as the editor, with Meeson, of the Exchequer reports. He was called to the bar in 1826, and became recorder of Chester and junior counsel to the Treasury. He was a good scholar as well as a good lawyer. In addition to his reports of commercial cases he edited the second edition of Chitty's Statutes, the twenty-first edition of the fourth volume of Blackstone's Commentaries, and editions of many other law books. He also edited the *Lives of Sixteen English Judges of the seventeenth and eighteenth Centuries*, to which he had contributed nine of the lives. Thomas Webster[5] (1810-1875) —the father of Lord Alverstone, C.J.—was secretary to the Institution of Civil Engineers from 1837-1841. In 1841 he was called to the bar by Lincoln's Inn and joined the northern circuit. Since he had studied engineering and other branches of natural science, he soon acquired a large practice in patent cases, and also a considerable Parliamentary practice. His *Reports and Notes of Cases on Letters Patent* became a standard work on this branch of the law. The Preface to the first volume, and the earlier cases

---

[1] Vol. i 438 n. 1 : for other instances see Memoirs of Sir John Rolt 82-84.
[2] D.N.B.   [3] Below 480.   [4] Below 485, 491, 492.   [5] D.N.B.

and statutes there printed, give a short historical introduction to
the law. He took a large part in getting the law as to the granting
of patents reformed in 1852,[1] and in organizing the great exhibition
of 1857.

No new abridgements of the law were published during this
period. We have seen that successive editions of Bacon's Abridgement continued to be issued,[2] that a new edition of Viner's
Abridgement was issued between 1791 and 1795, and that a
supplement to it was issued between 1799 and 1806.[3] But
there were several digests of case law. We have seen that R.W.
Bridgeman published in 1798 and 1800 an unfinished digest of
equity cases.[4] In 1804 he published a digest of English and Irish
equity cases, and of House of Lords cases, which reached a third
edition in 1822.[5] Between 1798 and 1803 T. W. Williams published an abridgement of cases decided in George III's reign.[6]
In 1813 Serjeant Manning published a digest of *nisi prius* reports,
which reached a second edition in 1820.[7] In 1819 Hammond
published a digest of Term and other reports of George III and
George IV's reigns ; and in 1827 Thomas Coventry and Samuel
Hughes published a digest of the common law reports from the
time of Henry III to the beginning of the reign of George III,
which was intended as a supplement to Hammond.[8] In 1821
Hammond published a digest of the later reports in equity, and in
1831 Edward Chitty, the third son of Joseph Chitty,[9] published
a digest of the English and Irish equity cases, and cases in the
Privy Council and the House of Lords, which reached a fourth
edition in 1883. In 1841 the same author, with F. Forster, published a digest of conveyancing and bankruptcy cases.

Several law dictionaries were published during this period.
William Marriot published a dictionary in 1798,[10] and T. W.
Williams published another in 1816. In 1829 James Wishaw
published a short concise dictionary which was intended to be
useful both to lawyers and laymen, and no doubt was useful, since

[1] Below, vol. xiv.
[2] Vol. xii 170-171 ; Cowley, A Bibliography of Abridgements (S.S.) 151, 154,
159.
[3] Vol. xii 167 ; Cowley, op. cit. 148.
[4] Vol. xii 172 ; Bridgeman was an attorney, and one of the clerks to the Grocers'
Company, D.N.B.
[5] Practice and Pleading cases were omitted, but cases questioned, doubted, or
denied were noted.
[6] Cowley, op. cit. 156.
[7] " A Digest of Nisi Prius Reports with notes and references, and some original
cases, chiefly collected on the Western Circuit " ; it was originally designed as a
supplement to Comyns's Digest, and it is arranged on a somewhat similar plan ;
references are given to cases other than those heard at *nisi prius* and to text-books.
[8] Matter contained in the notes to the reports was included, and references were
given to relevant statutes and equity cases.
[9] Below 458, 459.
[10] Cowley, op cit. 155 ; for the older dictionaries see vol. xii 176-177.

the definitions given are short and clear.[1] In 1819 Thomas Taylor of Clement's Inn published a useful glossary of Latin, French, and Greek law terms and phrases, which reached a second edition in 1823.[2] In 1822 Charles Petersdorff published an index to the precedents in civil and criminal pleading taken from the books of precedents and the cases.[3]

VI

The Common Law

With the history of the legal profession during this period—its ranks, organization and discipline, and education—I have dealt in the last chapter. In this section I shall deal first with the literature of the common law, and, secondly, with the chief justices and other lawyers.

The Literature of the Common Law

I shall deal with this literature under the following heads : (i) Public Law ; (ii) Civil procedure and pleading ; (iii) Criminal law and procedure ; (iv) Evidence ; (v) Conveyancing and Land Law ; (vi) Commercial and Maritime Law ; (vii) Special topics ; (viii) Legal history.

The literature on this topic falls into two divisions—central government and local government.

Public Law

Central government

There are no books of first rate importance. But books of some merit were written on the theory of the constitution, on the prerogative, and on Parliament.

The book on the theory of the constitution is a book by Professor J. J. Park [4] and is entitled *The Dogmas of the Constitution*. It consists of four lectures taken from his course of lectures on the theory of the constitution.[5] Considering that the book was published in 1832, at the height of the Reform Bill controversies, it is remarkable how successful the author is in steering clear of them.

---

[1] A New Law Dictionary, containing a concise exposition of the main terms of art and such obsolete words as occur in old legal, historical and antiquarian writers.

[2] A Law Glossary of Latin, Greek, Norman-French and other Languages interspersed in the Commentaries by Sir William Blackstone, Knt., and various law treatises upon each branch of the Profession. Translated into English and alphabetically arranged.

[3] There are 320 pages of precedents in civil cases, and 122 pages of precedent in criminal cases ; for Petersdorff's Abridgement see vol. xii, 171.

[4] Above 295.

[5] They are the fourth, tenth, eleventh, and thirteenth lectures.

The book is at times somewhat verbose, and the historical and foolish pedantical disquisitions inserted in it sometimes obscure the argument. But it is in some respects almost a historic work. In the first place the author anticipates Bagehot in his criticism of the theory that the powers of government are divided, and that its excellence consists in a system of checks and balances. He insists that the real power resides in the House of Commons, and that in the House of Commons the government of the day has the greatest power in shaping policy and initiating legislation. But he fails to bring out the fact, so clearly emphasized by Bagehot, that the most impressive feature of the constitution is the system of Cabinet government. Considering the date at which it was written, it is not surprising that he regarded the system of legislation rather than the Cabinet as the means by which the efficient working of the constitution was secured.[1] In the second place he exposes the fallacy of going back to Anglo-Saxon times, or even earlier, to discover the principles of the constitution. He points out that the constitution, as it existed in his day, was the product, not of ancient history, but of the developments which had taken place in the preceding century and a half.

There are three notable books on the prerogative—an historical book by Allen, a practical law book by Chitty, and a book on the Ceremonial of a Coronation by Taylor.

Taylor's book [2] was the first to describe systematically and to explain the ceremonies of a coronation—the regalia, the persons who assisted at it, and the political, ecclesiastical, and feudal elements inherent in the ceremonies. There is also an account of the coronation of the English kings from that of Egbert of Mercia in 785 to that of Elizabeth. It is an interesting and learned book on this subject.

The principal books written on Parliament were written by T. N. B. Oldfield (1755-1822),[3] who was a keen advocate of Parliamentary reform. They were all historical books intended to illustrate the evil effects of the unreformed representation system, and to prove the right of all freemen to a vote. His two earlier books—a History of the Boroughs of Great Britain, published in 1792,[4] and a History of the Original Constitution-of Parliaments,[5] published in 1797—were embodied in his six-volume History of the

---

[1] See vol. x 631-635.
[2] The Glory of Regality. An Historical Treatise of the anointing and crowning of the Kings and Queens of England (1820).   [3] D.N.B.
[4] An Entire and Complete History, Political and Personal of the Boroughs of Great Britain, together with the Cinque Ports; to which is prefaced an Original Sketch of Constitutional Rights from the earliest Period until the present time; there was a second ed. in 1794.
[5] History of the Original Constitution of Parliament from the Time of the Britons to the present day; to which is added the present state of the Representation.

House of Commons, published in 1816 [1]   The first two volumes deal
with the history of the House of Commons from the time of the
Britons to the year 1812.   The last four volumes describe in detail
the state of the representation in each of the counties and boroughs
of Great Britain and Ireland.   It is a learned work, but the earlier
history contained in the first volumes is worthless both because it is,
like Coke's incursions into early history, [2] written to advocate a
thesis and because the author had no more appreciation of the
fundamental difference between the ancient Briton, the Saxon, and
the Norman and Angevin periods than had the author of the Mirror
of Justices. [3]   The later history contained in volumes one and two
is nothing more than a summary of the leading events in the history
of the House of Commons.   The detailed account of the representation in the counties and boroughs of Great Britain and Ireland
contained in the last four volumes is a large collection of facts and
rulings of House of Commons committees, which illustrate their
representation history.   These volumes are an industrious compilation designed to advocate the cause of Parliamentary reform;
but they are not of much value for any other purpose.

For the rest there are books on special subjects.   There are
books on the law as to elections, which digested the statutes, the
resolutions of the House of Commons, and the decisions of election
committees. [4]   There is a short digest of the laws affecting protestant dissenters. [5]   It deals with law as to laymen and clergy,
school masters, places of worship, and trusts for dissenters.   Lastly,
the growing elaboration of military law produced two books on this
subject.

Local government

No very important books on this topic were published during
this period.   The most authoritative and complete book continued
to be Burn's *Justices of the Peace*.   But several books were published
which gave useful, generally accurate and sometimes learned
statements of various sides of local government laws.   A brief
glance at a few of these books, arranged like many of the books
themselves in alphabetical order, will suffice.

A short, clearly written book on *Constables* was published in

[1] The Representative History of Great Britain and Ireland: Being a History
of the House of Commons, and of the Counties, Cities, and Boroughs of the United
Kingdom, from the earliest period.
[2] Vol. v 472-473.
[3] For this book see vol. ii 327-333.
[4] S. Heywood, A Digest of the Law respecting County Electors (1790, 2nd ed.
1812); S. Heywood, A Digest of so much of the Law respecting Borough Elections
as concerns Cities and Boroughs in general (1797); R. Orme, A Practical Digest
of the Election Laws (1796).
[5] J. Beldam, A Summary of the Laws peculiarly affecting Protestant Dissenters
(1827).

1827 by J. W. Willcock.[1] Its object was to give to constables information as to their powers, duties and liabilities. It gives a clear straight-forward account of these matters, with references to the principal authorities. Though in theory all were liable to serve as constables if appointed the list of exemptions was remarkably long. A very good book on *Coroners* was published in 1829 by John Jervis,[2] the future Chief Justice of the Common Pleas,[3] and author of the Acts which regulated the powers and the procedure to be followed by the justices and of quarter sessions.[4] It reached a seventh edition in 1927. Jervis points out that the importance of the office had declined since the mediæval period and that it had in modern times too often fallen into the hands of persons " incompetent to the discharge of even their present limited authority." The book is divided into three parts. Part I deals with the different kinds of coroners, the nature of the office, their powers, rights and duties, and the manner of their election. Part II contains a very clear and able account of the different sorts of homicide, of the coroner's inquisition, and of the subsequent proceedings. Part III gives an account of the procedure on the inquisition. There is also a large collection of forms and precedents. It is a clearly written book by a good lawyer who was well acquainted with and knew how to use all the authorities on the subject mediæval as well as modern. The law is tersely and accurately stated, and there are good discussions on doubtful points of law, e.g. as to whether the coroner can exclude the public from his court—a question which, as he points out, had been settled two years before he wrote, by the case of *Garnett v. Ferrand*.[5]

A book on *Municipal Corporations* was published in 1827 by J. W. Willcock, the author of the book on *Constables*.[6] He pointed out that it was thirty years since Kyd's book [7] was published, and that the law had developed considerably since he wrote ; and that his subject was more limited than that of Kyd since it dealt only with municipal corporations, and did not deal with corporate property. After a very slight historical introduction, a careful but rather pedestrian account is given of the main principles and rules of this branch of the law. But some parts of the law were not very certain, and here the author is apt to be obscure. A notable instance is his treatment of the effect of the successful bringing of a writ of

---

[1] The Office of Constable : comprising the Laws relating to High, Petty, and Special Constables, head-boroughs tithing-men, bondholders, and watchmen, with an account of their institution and appointment.
[2] A Practical Treatise on the Office and Duties of Coroners, with Forms and Precedents.   [3] Below, vol. xiv.
[4] Above 309.   [5] (1827) 6 B. and C. 611.
[6] The Law of Municipal Corporations, together with a brief sketch of their history and a treatise on Mandamus and Quo Warranto.
[7] Vol. xii 400.

Quo Warranto on the existence of a corporation.[1] He was a liberal in politics. He pointed out in his concluding remarks that the elaborate constitutions of these corporations were kept up mainly because it was through them that members of Parliament were elected and other corporate officials derived most of their powers to govern their corporation from the fact that they were justices of the peace.[2] He looked forward to the time when the whole of England would be divided into municipal districts governed by councils elected by the inhabitants who would also elect members of Parliament. These councils should be quite distinct from the justices who should be confined to judicial functions. This was a somewhat remarkable anticipation of some of the main features of the Municipal Corporations Act of 1835, and of the way in which English local government was " municipalized " in 1888.

A short book on *Highways* was published by John Egremont in 1830.[3] It is not a good book—the cases and statutes are very roughly strung together.

By far the largest number of books on this topic deal with the *Poor Law*. The most considerable of these books was by Michael Nolan.[4] It was a successful book since the first edition was published in 1805, and it reached a fourth edition in 1825. It set out, the author tells us, to explain the underlying principles of the law, and to illustrate their application in practice. In its forty chapters it gives a good straight-forward account of the law with full references to the authorities. Collections of the decisions of the King's Bench and of statutes relating to the poor law were made by Edmund Bow and were continued by Francis, Court Librarian, 1771 and 1833. Smaller books are a compendium published by William Robinson in 1827 designed mainly for working justices. The law is grouped under eleven alphabetical heads, and in 2061 paragraphs.[5]

A small book on the poor law was published by J. S. Caldwell in 1821.[6] The information is grouped under twenty-nine alphabetical heads which run from Appeal to Workhouse. Each head is divided into sections. The longest head is Settlement. The main principles and rules are stated clearly but it is too short to be exhaustive

There are two books on *Session Law*. One is a *Magistrate's*

---

[1] At pp. 334-336.   [2] See vol. x 228.
[3] The law relating to Highways, Turnpike Roads, Public Bridges, and Navigable Rivers ; with precedents of indictments, presentments, etc. ; for nuisance to the same; and the forms directed to be used under the highways and turnpike Acts ; also the powers and duties of Surveyors of Highways.
[4] A Treatise of the Laws for the Relief and Betterment of the Poor.
[5] Lex Parochialis, or a compendium of the laws relating to the Poor, with the adjudged claims in Parochial Sittings.
[6] A Digest of the Laws relating to the Poor.

Pocket Book by William Robertson published in 1825[1] which deals very shortly with the principal topics under alphabetical heads. The other is a longer book by the Rev. Samuel Clapham which was published in 1818. He was a justice of the peace for Hertfordshire [2] and his book is, he says, designed to help his fellow magistrates, to supply the clergy with professional information, and to enable vestries to transact the business of their parishes. The book is in effect a glorified index, which sets out under the alphabetical heads into which the book is divided the references to the main authorities. At the end of his book he has some sensible remarks on the need to control the hours during which workmen waste their wages and listen to seditious talk, on the evil of paying wages out of the poor rates, on the law of settlement, and the laws as to vagrancy.

Lastly, I must notice a book which deals with one of those local courts of request which, as we have seen, were instituted in many places in the eighteenth century. It is an interesting and sometimes amusing book on the Birmingham court of requests which was published in 1787 by W. Hutton, one of the commissioners of the Birmingham court.[3] The judges of the court were seventy-two unpaid commissioners chosen from householders having £20 a year or £500 in personalty. Only about six of them ever attended,[4] but Hutton says that he had been a commissioner for fifteen years and in some years had never missed a day's attendance.[5] There were two clerks of the court and a beadle appointed by the lord of the manor who was paid by fees.[6] It was a busy court, hearing some 130 cases a week.[7] The book consists of two parts. The first and shorter part describes the court's process. The second part is an account of ninety-nine of the cases, some of them humorous, which had come before the court.[8] The book ends with some wise maxims which commissioners should bear in mind.[9] Hutton himself was not a professional laywer. But he seems to have picked up a considerable amount of useful legal information during his

---

[1] The Magistrate's Pocket Book ; or an epitome of the Duties and Practice of a Justice of Peace and of Session alphabetically arranged.

[2] A Collection of the several points of Session Law, alphabetically arranged, contained in Burn and Williams on the office of a justice, Blackstone's Commentaries, East and Hawkins on Common Law, Addington's Penal Statutes and Courts, and Notes on the Poor Laws.

[3] Courts of Requests : their nature, ability, and powers described, with a variety of cases determined in that of Birmingham ; for these courts see vol. i 190-191.

[4] Op. cit. 72-75.   [5] Op. cit. Preface.

[6] Op. cit. 75-76 ; an account is given of an astute but drunken beadle who took the fees and paid the two clerks.

[7] Op. cit. 11.

[8] Some of the titles given to the cases are—The man deceived by himself, the pleasures of matrimony, watch a knave, the lovers, the living outwitted by the dead, the stumbling wife, a trip to Lichfield races.

[9] Op. cit. 423-425.

tenure of office ; and he criticizes justly the state of the prisons where those unable to satisfy judgment were confined.

Civil procedure and pleading

As in the preceding period there are a large number of books on these topics. I shall say something first of the books on procedure, secondly of the books on pleading, thirdly of books on law and practice and *nisi prius*, and lastly, of a book entitled the *Pleader's Guide* which satirized in verse some of the leading characteristics of these branches of the law.

(a) Books on procedure

The most famous and the most comprehensive book on procedure is Tidd's *Practice of the Courts of King's Bench and Common Pleas.*

It is clear that Holdsworth must have intended to deal at length with so important a work, but we have been unable to find any manuscript on the subject. We have, accordingly, ourselves written the following account, which appears within square brackets. (Eds.)

[William Tidd (1760-1847) was the second son of Julius Tidd, a small merchant of Holborn. He was admitted to the Honourable Society of the Inner Temple in 1782, but he was not called to the bar until 1813 as he practised as a special pleader " under the bar " for more than thirty years. The best description of Tidd's office and work can be found in the autobiography of John, Lord Campbell,[1] who became his pupil in 1804 and remained with him for nearly three years. In a letter to his father he wrote : [2] " Tidd is by far the first man in this line. He has constantly from ten to fifteen pupils. ' He is in Tidd's office '— it has a prodigious fine sound." At one time four of his former pupils—Lord Lyndhurst, Lord Cottenham, Lord Campbell, and Lord Denman—sat together in the House of Lords. The three former had held the office of Lord Chancellor, and the latter had been Lord Chief Justice of the Court of Queen's Bench.

In describing Tidd's office Campbell said : [3] " His office, however, for a man really desirous and determined to improve himself, is in my mind by far the best in London. You see here such a quantity and such a variety of business that you may learn more in six months than by reading or hearing lectures for seven years." Of Tidd himself he said : [4] " He is a man at

---

[1] *Life of John, Lord Campbell*, edited by his daughter, the Hon. Mrs. Hardcastle, 1881.

[2] Ibid 133.   [3] Ibid 148.   [4] Ibid 159.

once of the greatest good temper and of the strictest honour. Notwithstanding his legal knowledge and his eminence in the profession, he is quite unassuming. He places himself not only on a level with you, but below you. He never speaks to his clerk even without a smile."

Campbell was less enthusiastic about the science of special pleading which he learned in Tidd's office. Soon after he became a pupil he wrote to his father : [1] " Nothing but the irresistible motives which spur me on could enable me to combat the disgust inspired by special pleading. It is founded upon reason, but rude, rude is the superstructure. This, however, is now a necessary *post* in carrying on your professional *advances*. The four judges who preside in the Court of King's Bench all practised as special pleaders."

In a letter to his brother, Campbell gave the following lucid description of the science of special pleading : [2]

You desire me to give you some notion of *special pleading*. It is the business of the special pleader to draw all the written proceedings in a suit at law. First, the declaration, which contains a statement of the cause of action, or the injury of which the plaintiff complains : that the defendant has seduced his wife ; has trespassed upon his land ; has given him a beating ; has sold him an unsound horse, etc. Next comes the plea, setting forth the defendant's answer, who says that he is not guilty, or that the land is his own, or that the plaintiff made the first assault, or that he did not warrant the horse as sound, etc. The *replication*, the *rejoinder*, etc., contain what each party has to allege, till at last they take issue upon some point of fact and the cause is submitted to a jury. If it is thought that what is stated in the *declaration*, though true, would not be sufficient in law to sustain an action, or in the *plea* to establish a defence, then there is a demurrer, and the cause is decided by the judges. There is the most scrupulous nicety required in these proceedings. For instance, there are different kinds of actions, as assumpsit, detinue, trespass, case, etc. The difficulty is to know which of these to bring, for it seldom happens that more than one of them will lie. There is still more difficulty in the defence, to know what is a good justification and how it ought to be pleaded, to be sure that you always suit the nature of the defence to the nature of the action, and to take advantage of any defect on the opposite side. Special pleaders in general are not at the bar. One or two who remain pleaders permanently are considered as something between attorneys and barristers, but the common way is for a young man to plead a few years *under the bar*, as they call it, before being called. It is easier to get this kind of business than briefs in the court, and you thus gradually form and extend your connections. This is a very bad plan for the profession ; in the first place, the special pleaders take much lower fees than if they were at the bar, and thus carry away a great deal of business ; and in the next place, by continuing in this low illiberal drudgery so long, their minds are contracted and they are mere quibblers all their lives after."

[1] Op. cit. 138.   [2] Ibid 147-148.

The special pleaders have long since disappeared from the law, but the popular phrase " special pleading " remains as a monument to their work.

Although Tidd was the most distinguished of all the special pleaders, his fame rests on his book *The Practice Of The Court Of King's Bench In Personal Actions With References To Cases Of Practice In The Court of Common Pleas.*[1] The first part, which was published in 1790, contained the whole of the proceedings in personal actions in the Court of King's Bench previous to the plea, together with all that was peculiar to the proceedings by and against attornies and officers of the court, against peers of the realm, and members of the House of Commons, upon the writ of habeas corpus, and against prisoners in the actual custody of the sheriff or marshal. In the second part, which was published in 1794, the proceedings at large were continued from the demand of plea, to final judgment and execution. The third part, which treated of the proceedings in *scire facias* and *error*, was published in 1798. The success of this work was instantaneous, and for nearly fifty years it was almost the sole authority for common-law practice. It has achieved a permanent place in literature because in *David Copperfield*[2] Charles Dickens describes Copperfield as saying :

I found Uriah reading a great fat book, with such demonstrative attention, that his lank forefinger followed up every line as he read, and made clammy tracks along the page (or as I fully believed) like a snail.
. . .
' I am not doing office work, Master Copperfield,' said Uriah.
' What work, then ? ' I asked.
' I am improving my legal knowledge, Master Copperfield,' said Uriah. ' I am going through Tidd's *Practice*. Oh, what a writer Mr. Tidd is, Master Copperfield.'

Dickens probably gained his knowledge of Tidd's *Practice* when he was in the office of Mr. Edward Blackmore, attorney, of Gray's Inn, in 1828. By 1850, when *David Copperfield* was published, Tidd was out-of-date, the 9th and last edition having been published in 1828, although consolidated supplements were issued in 1837. Apparently the publishers thought that the alterations in practice and procedure introduced in this period were so radical as to make a revision of the book impractical after the death of the author in 1847. It is interesting to note, however, that an edition was published in the United States as late as 1856 by Asa I. Fish.

[1] The title of the 9th edition, 1828, reads : The Practice Of The Courts of King's Bench And Common Pleas In Personal Actions, and Ejectment : To Which Are Added, The Law And Practice Of Extents ; And The Rules Of Court, And Modern Decisions, In The Exchequer Of Pleas, in 2 Vols.
[2] Ch. xvi.

In spite of Uriah Heep's tribute to Tidd as an author, the book can hardly have been easy reading even in 1824 for it is written in a harsh and unattractive style. It is obviously intended for practitioners rather than for students. The various technical rules are set forth in detail, but only occasionally is any reference made to their history or to the reasons on which they were based. There are no criticisms of any of the rules and no suggestions for any amendments in them, although it was at that time that Bentham and his disciples were arguing that only by sweeping away the mass of technicalities could the law be adequately reformed.

As a bare statement of the law of procedure the book is, however, unequalled. It is conveniently arranged, and the presentation of the rules is as lucid as the subject-matter permits. There are many things in it which are still of interest both to historians and to lawyers. The detailed list in the first chapter of the officers of the Court of King's Bench, such as the pro-thonotary, the clerk of the common bails, posteas and estreats, the filacers, exigenter, and clerk of the outlawries, all of whom held their places for life when the book was first published and most of whom had deputies, shows how much justification there was for Bentham's criticism. The method of commencing an action by arresting a defendant and holding him to bail must have given rise to much injustice and hardship in those cases in which the defendant was not a man of property. Of equal interest is the chapter dealing with the process of out-lawry and its consequences. The harshness of the law inevitably led to the most technical rules which are set out in great detail. Although subject to much criticism, the rules of strict pleading undoubtedly succeeded in simplifying the issue to be tried and in clarifying the law. Here again, their extreme technicality led to their eventual abolition, although, as Maitland has said : " The forms of action we have buried, but they still rule us from their graves." [1] Finally, in the longest chapter in the book, Tidd deals with the writ of error, the forerunner of the modern system of appeals.

In 1799 Tidd published his book of *Practical Forms and Entries of Proceedings in the Courts of King's Bench, Common Pleas, and Exchequer of Pleas* which was a companion volume to his *Practice*. It is necessary to read the two together, be-cause the *Practice* can hardly be understood without continual reference to the *Forms*. The 8th edition was published in 1840. Other less important books by Tidd were *Law of Costs in Civil Actions*, 1792, much of this material being later

[1] Forms of Action at Common Law 2.

incorporated in his *Practice, Forms of Proceedings in Replevin and Ejectment*, 1804, and *The Act for Uniformity of Process in Personal Actions*, 1833.]

J. F. Archbold published a book on the proceedings in the court of King's Bench in 1819, which in later editions, edited by Thomas Chitty, was expanded to include an account of the procedure of the other two common law courts.[1] Its merits are shown by the fact that it reached a fourteenth edition in 1885.

A useful general book on procedure was a Dictionary of the practice of the King's Bench and Common Pleas in civil actions by Thomas Lee.[2] It was first published in 1811-12 and reached a second edition in 1825. The object which the author had in view was, he says, to produce a book of ready reference for office use. He achieved this object. Under each title the nature and origin of the subject matter is explained with references to the leading decisions, then directions as to the practice are given, and lastly the appropriate forms. The author acknowledges his debt to earlier writers, and more especially to Tidd, whose book he regards as a classic comparable to Blackstone's *Commentaries*. He approves generally of the system of practice, but admits the need for reform in several matters.

In addition to these more general books on procedure there are a number of books on special topics in this branch of the law. Here is a selection of them arranged alphabetically. J. F. Archbold published in 1826 a book on the law and practice of bankruptcy under the statute of 1826, which reached a second edition in 1827.[3] It sets out the statute, then the substantive law, and then the procedure. Like Archbold's other books it is clearly written and arranged. In 1792 John Hullock published a book on *Courts*. It was a useful book on a complex branch of the law. The law was complex because there were divergent rules for the different forms of action, because the practice of the courts was sometimes uncertain, and because the rules of practice applied to the different common law courts were not the same. Also there was a certain amount of statute law applicable in certain cases. It is a useful summary of the law in thirteen chapters.

In 1819 James Manning published a book on the practice of the

---

[1] The Practice of the Court of King's Bench in Personal Actions and Ejectments including the practice of the Courts of Common Pleas and Exchequer ; Archbold strongly objected to Chitty's editing his book ; but he could do nothing as he had sold the copyright and the publishers employed Chitty, who did his work very well.

[2] A Dictionary of the Practice in Civil Actions in the Courts of King's Bench and Common Pleas with Practical Directions and Forms, arranged under each title. With a brief summary prefixed of the civil actions on process at law and its incidents in K.B. and C.P.

[3] " The Law and Practice in Bankruptcy as founded on the recent Statute, with Forms."

common law side of the Court of Exchequer and a summary of the law of extents.[1] Manning (1781-1866) [2] was for many years leader of the western circuit. He was not a great advocate, but was a very learned black letter lawyer. He became serjeant at law in 1840, Queen's serjeant in 1846 and a county court judge in 1847. He took some part in the trial of Queen Caroline, and wrote his *Serviens ad Legem* to vindicate the privileges of his order which Brougham tried to abolish.[3] The first volume is a very complete and learned work in four Books on the practice of the court.[4] The second volume contains the law as to extents with an Appendix of forms, rules of court, and returns as to the offices of the Exchequer made to a select committee of the House of Commons on finance in 1798. The author tells us that on many matters the rules of practice were uncertain—no doubt his book did something to cure the uncertainty. He tells us also that he had intended to preface his book by an historical introduction on the origin, constitution, and jurisdiction of the Exchequer ; but that, as his conclusion on these matters differed from those of other learned writers, he had postponed publication till he had made further researches.

Manning published in 1826 a book on the revenue side of the courts of Exchequer which dealt with extents, *scire facias*, and revenue information.[5] A book on the practice of the Exchequer in equity was published in 1795 by D. B. Fowler, one of the six clerks of the court.[6] It was a further treatise which also gave some information as to the substantive rules of equity and as to points of difference between the Exchequer and the Chancery equity practice. It gives clear and practical information arranged according to the order of steps in the action. Another book on the law of extents by Edward West was published in 1817.[7] It was compiled both from printed and MS. reports, and states the law clearly.

Two books were published on *The Practice in Appeals to the House of Lords*. The first by W. R. Sydney was published in 1824.[8] He was helped by Bligh, the House of Lords reporter. It is clear

---

[1] The Practice of the Officer of Pleas, and the Court of Exchequer in the Exchequer at Westminster, with a summary of the Law of Extents.
[2] D.N.B.
[3] Vol. vi 477 n. 7 ; below 551.
[4] Book I, The Commencement of actions in the Exchequer (24 chaps.) ; Book II, Prosecution of actions in the Exchequer (44 chaps.) ; Book III, Termination of actions in the Exchequer (9 chaps.) ; Book IV, account of proceedings in the Exchequer (5 chaps.)
[5] The Practice of the Courts of Exchequer Part I containing the Law and Practice of Extents, Scire Facias, and Revenue Information in the Office of the King's Remembrancer; this is said to be a second edition probably because extents had been dealt with in the earlier book.
[6] The Practice of the Court of Exchequer upon proceedings in Equity.
[7] A Treatise on the Law and Practice of Extents in Chief and in Aid, with an appendix of Forms.
[8] A Treatise on the Jurisdiction and Modern Practice in Appeals to the House of Lords, and in Proceedings on Claims to Dormant Peerages.

from what is said in the preface to both books that the practice was not certain with the result that the hearing was delayed by the imperfect manner in which the cases were brought before the House. This book dealt with the jurisdiction of the House, the practice in appeals from the courts of Chancery in England and Ireland, and the practice in hearing cases. It is interesting to note that the author thought that the House was not bound by its own decisions, though it generally adhered to them.[1] The second of these books by John Palmer, for fifty years a Parliamentary solicitor and agent,[2] is a fuller and more complete book than Sydney's since it deals both with the matters dealt with in Sydney's book and also with the practice on writs of error and on Scotch appeals. It contains much useful information both historical and practical—Tidd praised it in a letter which the author inserted in his book.

A book on the procedure in relation to juries was published in 1826 by James Kennedy.[3] It is a useful little book with a good historical introduction. The author rightly rejects the claim that the jury is Saxon in origin, and he gives a good summary of the many rules as to the different kinds of juries. A book on the practice of the Crown side of the court of King's Bench was published by R. Gude in 1828.[4] The author had served many years in the crown office, but having been passed over for the place of clerk in court, he retired. It is a very complete account of the organization, machinery and practice of the crown side with a large apparatus of forms and precedents. It gives away a good deal of esoteric information of which the clerks in court used to make some profit,[5] and it gives many illustrations of the survival of those mediæval rules which permeated the offices of the courts. Thus to each clerk in court, one of the circuits of the judges was allotted which gave him the right to certain fees. This "circuit" was the clerk's freehold which paid land tax and gave him a vote for the county of Middlesex.[6]

In 1826 W. J. Impey published a useful book on the law as to the writ of *mandamus*.[7] It deals with the origin of the writ, when

---

[1] " It is not like other courts, confined to precedents, orders, or rules ; it does not, however, depart from, relax, or dispense with them, but on particular and necessary occasions."

[2] The Practice of the House of Lords on appeals, writs of error, and claims of peerage with a compendious account of dignities, to which is prefixed an introductory historical essay on the appellate jurisdiction ; in the preface he tells us that he had heard Mansfield, Camden, Thurlow and Wedderburn speak and argue.

[3] A Treatise on the Law and Practice of Juries as amended by the Statute 6 George IV c. 50, including the Coroner's Inquest, etc.

[4] The Practice of the Crown Side of the Court of King's Bench, and the Practice of the Sessions ; the General Rules of Court from the reign of James I to the present time ; and the Statutes relating to the Practice ; together with a Table of Fees and Bills of Costs. Also an Appendix of Forms and Precedents.

[5] Preface.　　　　　　　　　　　[6] Vol. i 37.

[7] A Treatise on the Law and Practice of the Writ of Mandamus.

it will be granted and when not, how it is obtained, the contents of the writ and of the return to it, proceedings against the person to whom it is directed and costs.

In 1825 Henry Roscoe published a book on the the law of actions relating to *Real Property*, of which I will speak later.[1]

The last of these books on special topics in the law of procedure is a little book by W. Hands, an attorney of the court of King's Bench, which contains the forms of various rules which could be got by the parties to personal actions in the court of King's Bench, with notes thereon.[2] It was, he says, based on his thirteen years' experience as an attorney of the court, and was meant to assist the junior attorneys.

All these books deal with procedure in the central court or quarter sessions. Very few books deal with procedure in the local courts.

Hutton's book on courts of request tells us something of the procedure of the Birmingham court of request,[3] and there are two books on the procedure of two London courts. In 1819, H. Ashley, who held a post in the office of the Lord Mayor's court, published a book on the doctrine and practice of attachment in that court.[4] He claimed that the practice of foreign attachment as used in that court was the most prompt, efficacious, and cheapest remedy for the recovery of debts known to English law.[5] This was not generally known since the practice in the court was monopolized by four attornies who bought their places, and four pleaders. It is interesting to note first that the rolls of the court still passed between the opposing attorneys for the entry of their pleas,[6] as the rolls of the common law courts had to pass in mediæval days ;[7] and the mayor's court had a supplementary equitable jurisdiction.[8] The second of these books is a book on the Marshalsea and Palace courts by W. Buckley, which was published in 1827.[9] After a clear and interesting historical introduction the author deals with the jurisdiction and procedure of these courts and with costs. It is clear from his introduction that excessive fees charged by its officials, who had paid large sums for their places, was as recognized an abuse of the courts in 1827 as it was when Thackeray in his *Ballads* wrote his melancholy tale of "Jacob Omnium's Hoss."[10]

---

[1] Below 474.

[2] A Selection of Rules occurring in the Prosecution and Defence of Personal Actions in the Court of King's Bench; with notes on each Rule illustrative of the Practice of the Court.   [3] Above 449, 450.

[4] The Doctrine and Practice of Attachment in the Mayor's Court, London ; with various corrections and editions ; this is a second edition ; the first edition seems to have disappeared—no copy of it is in the British Museum.

[5] Preface.   [6] As p. 66.   [7] Vol. iii 643-644.   [8] Chap. ix.

[9] The Jurisdiction and Practice of the Marshalsea and Palace Courts, with Tables of Costs and Charges and an Appendix containing Statutes, letters patent, rules of court, etc. ; for this court and its history see vol. i 208-209.

[10] Vol. i 209.

(b) *Books on pleading*

What Tidd's book was to the law of procedure, Stephen's book was to the law of pleading.

Three books on special topics on the law of pleading may be noticed. In 1812, Thomas Lee, who wrote the *Dictionary of Practice*,[1] published a collection of pleadings in assumpsit in actions upon bills of exchange, promissory notes and cheques, with short notes.[2] The author in his preface criticizes the way in which the time of students was wasted in copying precedents and laments disuse of mooting and the absence of any further teaching of law.

In 1828 G. B. Mansel published a book on demurrers.[3] The first part of the book gives a slight account of the law of pleading from the beginning of an action to the writ of *audita auerela*, the defendant's last resource in English law.[4] The second part gives an account of the methods of taking advantage of defects in pleadings up to final judgment and the manner in which pleadings can be amended at common law or by statute. The book states dryly the relevant rules. There is no attempt to explain or discuss underlying principles.

A useful supplement to the books on pleading and the collections of the precedents of pleading was Petersdorff's[5] *Index*[6] which was published in 1822. Where necessary references were added to decisions on the pleadings and the references to common form pleadings were taken from modern books in general use.

The only other books on procedure and pleading which call for notice are two works on these subjects by Joseph Chitty.[7]

Chitty was an eminent pleader, the author of a large number of practitioners' books, and the founder of a famous legal family. His eldest son Joseph was also a pleader and wrote some long-lived books on contract,[8] and, as we have seen, on the prerogative.[9] His

---

[1] Above 454.

[2] Precedents of Declaration in Assumpsit, fully adapted to most cases occurring on Promissory Notes, or Bills of Exchange, inland or foreign ; and also on Bankers' Checks, with explanatory notes.

[3] A Treatise on the Law and Practice of Demurrer to Pleadings and Evidence of Bills of Exceptions ; Wagers of Law ; Issue and Trial of the Record ; Motions in Arrest of Judgment ; Judgments *non obstante veredicto ;* Re-pleader ; and award of *venire facias de novo* in personal actions, with an introduction as to the nature and forms of pleading, to which is added a selection of precedents.

[4] See vol. I, 224 ; Bl. Comm. III, 405.

[5] Petersdorff (1800-1886) was one of the counsel to the Admiralty ; as such he compiled for the Admiralty a collection of statutes relating to the navy, shipping, ports and harbours ; he became a serjeant-at-law in 1858, and a county court judge in 1863, D.N.B. ; for his abridgments see vol. xii 171.

[6] A General Index to the Precedents in Civil and Criminal Pleading applicable to the present practice in every ancient and modern collection : including also the Precedents in the Books of Reports, from the earliest period to Easter Term, 3 George IV ; most of the material was collected by the author for his own use.

[7] D.N.B.   [8] Below 483, 484.   [9] Above 445.

second son, Thomas, was as eminent a pleader as his father, and trained many famous lawyers—among them were Cairns, Willes, Herschell, and A. L. Smith ; Thomas's second son was Lord Justice Chitty ; and his grandson was Thomas Willes Chitty who edited his grandfather's book on *Forms of Practical Proceedings at the King's Bench* and other text books.[1]

Joseph Chitty wrote books on commercial law,[2] international law, criminal law,[3] medical jurisprudence,[4] and an edition of Beawes *Lex Mercatoria* and of Blackstone's *Commentaries*. He edited some reports, and he produced an edition of the *Statutes of Practical Utility* which still flourishes.[5] His longest book on practice [6] is something much more than a book on that subject. The first volume contains an account of the substantive rules of law and equity arranged on the plan of Blackstone's *Commentaries*, and designed to be a practical continuation of that work.[7] The second volume gives some account of the legal profession, of retainers, of arbitration, and of summary proceedings before the magistrates. The third volume gives a full account of the practice of the courts of common law, and the concluding chapter describes the practice of the ecclesiastical courts. It is a full and learned book ; and that it was appreciated by the students and practitioners for whom it was written can be seen from the fact that between 1833 and 1837 the first two volumes passed through three editions.[8]

Besides this book Chitty published shorter books on the practice of the King's Bench, Common Pleas and Exchequer. The first volume of his book on Pleading[9] contains an account of the necessary parties to an action ; of the forms of action ; of the principles and rules of pleading; of the rules applicable to the declaration in general and in different classes of actions, to various kinds of pleas, to replications and subsequent pleadings ; and of the rules as to defects in pleading. The second and third volumes contain precedents of pleadings and short notes thereon. Like his book on practice it is a large book, clearly arranged and expressed. That it was a successful book is shown by the fact that it was first published in 1808, and reached a seventh edition in 1844. But though it gave the practitioner and the student the information he wanted, it did not explain, as Stephen's classic work explained, the rational and underlying

---

[1] D.N.B.   [2] Below 479, 481, 482, 486.   [3] Below 464.   [4] Below 492.
[5] A list of twenty-one books is given in the D.N.B. ; for some of these books see vol. xii 386-387 ; below 442, 459.
[6] The Practice of the Law in all its Principal Departments ; with a view of Rights, Injuries and Remedies ; and comprising the practice in arbitrations before Justices, in courts of common law, equity, ecclesiastical and spiritual, admiralty, bankruptcy, insolvency, and courts of error and appeal. With new Practical Forms.
[7] Preface to the first edition.
[8] The third edition of vol. iii was published in 1842.
[9] Treatise on Pleading and Parties to Actions, with second and third volumes containing Modern Precedents of Pleading, and Practical Notes.

principles of the detailed rules contained in the cases. It is mainly occupied in classifying and explaining these detailed rules.

(c) *Books on the law and practice at nisi prius*

We have seen that the first of the books on this topic had been written by Henry Bathhurst, afterwards Lord Chancellor, and that later editions were edited by his nephew Buller who later became a judge.[1] It was succeeded by a similar work of the reporter, Espinasse, which went through four editions. Both were superseded by William Selwyn ; *Abridgment of the Law of Nisi Prius* which was first published in 1806-8 and reached a thirteenth edition in 1869. Selwyn (1775-1855)[2] was called to the bar by Lincoln's Inn in 1807 and became Treasurer in 1840. He was recorder of Portsmouth, 1819-1829, and after Victoria's marriage was chosen to help the Prince Consort in his legal studies. To him the tenth edition of this book is dedicated. It is a clear, able, and well-arranged summary of the law and practice relating to the principal topics of private law arranged under forty-two alphabetical heads from Accounts to Wagers. Practitioners could find there the law on most of the topics which arose in trials at *nisi prius*, so that it is not surprising that it became in this and the following period the standard book on this topic. A book by Archbold[3] on the same subject which was published in 1803, did not get beyond a second edition in 1845.

(d) *The Pleader's Guide*

In an earlier volume I remarked upon the fact that the law of procedure and pleading had given rise to a certain amount of humorous and satirical literature, and gave some specimens of it.[4] At this point I must notice a witty poem entitled *The Pleader's Guide*[5] from which I have quoted one or two extracts in an earlier volume, to illustrate my account of the history of civil procedure and pleading.[6] Its author was John Anstey, a barrister of Lincoln's Inn and a commissioner of public accounts. The first part was published in 1796, and the second in 1804. It satirizes with con-

---

[1] Vol. xii 354.   [2] D.N.B.

[3] The Law of *Nisi Prius:* comprising the Declaration and other pleadings in Personal Actions and the evidence necessary to support them ; it did not include actions on negotiable instruments or on insurance policies, or all actions on the case ; it deals with the actions of *assumpsit*, account, debt, covenant, detinues, trespass, case, trover, replevin ; a great deal of law is compressed into a small space.

[4] Vol. ix 413-443.

[5] The Pleader's Guide, A Didactic Poem in Two Books, containing the conduct of a Suit at Law, with the arguments of Counsellor Bother'em and Counsellor Bore'em in an action betwixt John-a-Gull, and John-a-Gudgeon, for Assault and Battery at a late-contested election. By the late John Garchilton, Esq., special pleader and barrister-at-law.

[6] Vol. ix 250-251, 253, 254.

siderable wit both the common lawyers and their procedure and the civilians and their procedure. Here are a few illustrations :

Part I of the poem begins as follows :

> Of legal fictions, Quirks and Glosses,
> Attorney's gains and Client's losses,
> Or suits created, lost and won,
> How to undo and be undone,
> Whether of *Common Law* or *Civil*
> A man goes sooner to the Devil,
> Things which few mortals can disclose,
> In verse, or comprehend in Prose,
> I sing.

Here is an account of the training of the law student in a special pleader's chambers :

> Who for three hundred guineas paid
> To some great master of the trade,
> Have at his rooms by *special* favour,
> His leave to use their best endeavour
> By drawing Pleas, from nine till four,
> To earn him twice three hundred more,
> And, after dinner, may repair
> To, *foresaid* rooms and *then* and *there*,
> Have, *foresaid* leave, from five till ten,
> To draw th' *aforesaid* Pleas again.

He tells how the civilians were turned out of Westminster Hall, but allowed to practice at Doctors' Commons, but under the strict supervision of the common law :

> They set up shop at Westminster ;
> But of their practice were debarred,
> And fairly kicked from Palace Yard,
> Till thinking they had no intent
> To hurt th' established Government,
> O'er-rule the Laws and ride the Land
> With Romish edicts contraband,
> The Nation proud of the submission
> Of men of birth and erudition,
> Gave them a lodging, and in pity
> Sent them to settle in the City,
> Begg'd them to gather up their alls,
> And vend their drugs behind St. Pauls—
> *Provided always* that if e'er
> Said Quack or Quacks should interfere,
> Or any Quack, in word or deed
> presume his province to exceed,
> Or take upon him as a Scholar,
> *Prohibitory writ* should follow :
> Blest writ ! by which their fees are stay'd
> And briefs into our bags conveyed.

He touches upon " the secrets of the Pleading arts " and other cognate topics :

> The practice of *Attaching*,
> *Distraining*, hunting down and catching,
> In *Trespass* how to spread his net,
> In *Case*, in *Trover*, or in *Debt*,
> And not to spread alone, but draw
> Assignments, and demur in Law.

The processes of the three common law courts are described : [1]

> If haply *John-a-Stile* provoke
> The legal bill 'gainst *John-a-Noke*
> The *Latitat* the foe besieges
> And baffles him in *Banco Regis*,
> Skilled with *Ac-Etiams* to perplex
> And foil with *Bills of Middlesex*,
> *Quo minus* guides the wordy war
> And *mates* him at Th' Exchequer bar,
> While *Capias* is rejoiced to seize
> And plunder him at Common Pleas.

This part of the poem ends with an invocation to John Doe and Richard Roe : [2]

> Good men and true who never fail
> The needy and distressed to bail,
> Direct unseen the dire dispute,
> And pledge their names in ev'ry suit.

An invocation which awakes a response from the ghosts of old pleaders :

> Levinz and Lutwyche, Pleaders old,
> With Writs and Entries round him spread,
> See Plodding Saunders rears his head,
> Lo ! *Ventris* wakes ! before mine eyes
> *Brown*, *Lilly*, and *Bohun* arise.
> Each in his parchment shroud appears,
> Some with their Quills behind their ears,
> Flourish their velvet caps on high,
> Some wave their grizzel wigs and cry
> Hail happy Pair ! the Glory and the Boast,
> The Strength and Bulwark of the legal Host.

The second part of the book which deals more especially with pleading, the conduct of cases in court, and the action for assault between John-a-Gull and John-a-Gudgeon, is not so amusing as the first part.   But the verbosity of the pleadings in a common law action is pleasantly satirized in the following passage in which the pleadings are opened :

[1] Vol. i 200, 219-222, 240 ; vol. ix 249-251.
[2] See vol. ix 432-433.

The Pleadings state that *John-a-Gull*
With envy, wrath, and malice full,
With swords, knives, sticks, fist and bludgeon,
Beat, bruised and wounded *John-a-Gudgeon*,
First counts " *for that* " with divers jugs,
To wit twelve pots, twelve cups, twelve mugs,
Of certain vulgar drink called toddy
Said Gull did sluice said Gudgeon's body ;
The *second counts*, for other toddy,
Cast, flung or hurl'd on Gudgeon's body
To wit, his gold-lac'd hat and hair on
And clothes which he had then and there on ;
To wit, twelve jackets, twelve surtouts,
Twelve pantaloons, twelve pairs of boots,
Which did thereof much discompose
Said *Gudgeon's* mouth, eyes, ears and nose,
Back, belly, neck, thighs, feet and toes ;
By which, and other wrongs unheard of,
His clothes were spoil'd, and life despaired of
To all these counts the plea I find
Is *son assaut*, and issues join'd.

The defendant's counsel thus deals with the cases which the plaintiff's counsel had cited against him :

My Lord these cases I have noted ;
Loose law, my Lord, quite out of use—
My learned friend is fond of citing
Old cases, which he's seldom right in ;
Settling the Law, as some great men do,
On points reported *arguendo*.

In the end—

Both lovingly agreed at once to draw
A special Case, and save the point in Law,
That so the Battle, *neither lost nor won,*
Continued, ended, and again begun,
Might still survive, and other suits succeed,
For future Heroes of the Gown to lead,
And future Bards in loftier vein to *Plead*.

Criminal law and procedure

In 1814, W. Paley published a book on *Summary Convictions*. It consists of a short historical introduction and four Parts. Part I deals with matters antecedent to conviction ; Part II with convictions ; Part III with proceedings subsequent to convictions ; and Part IV with the responsibility and indemnity of the justices and their officers, and with the effect of convictions in collateral proceedings. It is a complete and clear summary, in small compass. Its merits are shown by the fact that it reached a ninth edition in 1926.

A large treatise on the criminal law substantive and adjective and on the law of evidence in criminal cases was published by Joseph Chitty in 1816. The first volume deals with the principles, rules, and practice which regulate criminal prosecutions, the second and third with the law relating to particular offences, and the rules of practice which regulated their prosecution; the fourth with precedents of pleadings and forms for magistrates. It is clearly written, well arranged, and covers the ground very completely. But it is no improvement on the treatises of Hale, Hawkins, and East. It appeared first before great reforms were made in criminal law and procedure, so that parts of it, e.g. the complex law which centred round benefit of clergy, soon became obsolete. Since it never reached a second edition there was no opportunity to remedy this defect. It was superseded by two books which were published shortly afterwards, and have survived till to-day.

The first of these books was W. O. Russell's *Treatise on Felonies and Misdemeanours*, which was first published in 1819 and reached a tenth edition in 1951. Russell (1785-1833) [1] was a student of Christ Church, and was called to the bar by Lincoln's Inn in 1809. He became a serjeant at law in 1827 and Chief Justice of Bengal in 1832. His treatise, said by Samuel Warren to be the best general treatise on the criminal law,[2] deals very fully with the whole of the criminal law except the law of treason.[3] The first edition was divided into five Books : I. Persons capable of committing crimes, principals and accessories, and indictable offences. II. Offences affecting the government, the public peace or public rights. III. Offences against the person. IV. Offences against property. V. Offences affecting persons or property. To the second edition a sixth Book dealing with evidence was added. Its merits are proved by its continued life, and also by the fact that seven American editions appeared between 1824 and 1853.

The second of these books is J. F. Archbold's book on criminal procedure.

Archbold was a voluminous writer on all aspects of criminal law and criminal procedure and pleading, on civil procedure and pleading in the courts of common law and the county courts, on magistrates' law, on the poor law, on other aspects of local government law, and on several topics of private law. But by far the most important and successful of his books is his *Pleading and Evidence in Criminal Cases* [4] which was first published in 1822, and reached a twenty-eighth edition in 1931. In the preface to his first edition

---

[1] D.N.B. [2] The Law Student (2nd ed.) 620, cited D.N.B.

[3] It was said in the Preface that it was omitted partly because of the additional space which would be required to deal adequately with it, and partly because of its rarity.

[4] Pleading and Evidence in criminal cases with the Statutes, Precedents, Indictments, etc., and the Evidence necessary to support them.

the author tells us that in 1812 he had entered upon an intensive study of all the authorities on the criminal law from Bracton onwards, in order to write a digest of the criminal law. At that time, he says, works on that subject were scarce and dear. He published one volume, but, as other works on this subject appeared, he abandoned it for a work on pleading and evidence in criminal cases. Its contents and arrangement are thus explained by the author :

The work consists of two books—the First Book, which treats of Pleading and Evidence in criminal cases generally, is divided into two parts : the first treating of Pleading generally, namely of indictments, informations, special pleas, demurrers, etc. ; the second, treating of Evidence generally, namely, of evidence of records, of matters *quasi* of record, of private written instruments, and of parol evidence, the competency and credit of witnesses, etc., etc.   The Second Book, which treats of Pleading and Evidence in particular cases, is divided into four parts : the first treats of offences against the property and persons of individuals ; the second treats of offences of a public nature, namely, offences against the King and his government, offences against public justice, offences against the public peace. Offences against public trade, and offences against public political economy ; the third treats of conspiracies, and the fourth of principals and accessories.

It is a severely practical book.   But it is clear, well arranged, terse and complete.   It has fallen into the hands of a series of very competent editors, so that its continued life and success are not surprising.

Two other books by Archbold on criminal law and procedure are *The Practice of Quarter Sessions*[1] which was first published in 1836 and reached a sixth edition in 1908, and a book on the practice of the Crown Office which was published in 1844.   Both books are marked by the same qualities as the book on Pleading and Evidence in Criminal Cases, but they did not attain the same success.

In 1814 Thomas Starkie,[2] the author of books on evidence and defamation,[3] published a book on criminal pleading.[4]   The questions answered by the book are those described by the author [5] :

The legal definition of an offence being proposed, as well as the circumstances of a particular case falling within that definition, how is the charge to be described against the offender on the face of the record ? With what certainty of legal terms and language ?   With what enunciation and detail of circumstances ?

The first seventeen chapters deal with indictments, the eighteenth with arraignments, the nineteenth with pleas, and

---

[1] The Practice of the Court of Quarter Sessions, and its original, appellate, and criminal jurisdiction ; with forms of indictments, notices of appeal, etc.
[2] Above 306, 430, 439.   [3] Below 488.
[4] A Treatise on Criminal Pleading with Precedents of Indictments, Special Pleas, etc.   [5] Preface.

the last three with verdict, judgment, and the avoiding of judgment by plea or writ of error. It is a very good summary of the law.

In 1826 F. A. Carrington, the reporter,[1] published a useful supplement to the treatises on the criminal law which summarized the alterations made by recent statutes and gave some information as to points of surgery and chemistry which were material in criminal cases.[2] It goes through the principal heads, first of criminal procedure and pleading, and then of the substantive law, and points out how the law had been modified by recent legislation and judicial decisions. The many changes in the law made by Peel's Act and other legislation [3] made it so useful a book to practitioners that it reached a third edition in 1828.

A summary of the law as to treason and cognate offences was published by a barrister in 1793.[4] It is a jejune account of the law probably written in view of the impending trials for treason of Hardy and others.

I have already said something of Anthony Hammond's code and digest of the criminal law which he compiled as a preparation to the consolidation of a large part of the criminal law by Peel's Act.[5]

Evidence

An important contribution to the literature of the law of evidence was made by W. D. Evans. Evans (1767-1821) [6] began life as an attorney, but became a student at Gray's Inn, and was called to the bar in 1794. He practised first at Liverpool and then at Manchester, became the first stipendiary magistrate for Manchester in 1813, and Vice-Chancellor of the county palatine of Lancashire in 1815. In 1819 he went to India as recorder of Bombay where he died. Evans was a good English lawyer who had studied other systems of law. He was an advocate of the study of jurisprudence and comparative law ; of reforms in the law of bankruptcy, and of Catholic emancipation. The cosmopolitan character of Lord Mansfield's learning attracted him, and he produced a collection of his decisions which was not a great success.[7] His translation of Pothier's work on *Obligations*, which was published in 1806, was

---

[1] Above 430.
[2] A Supplement to all the Treatises on the Criminal Law : containing the alterations by Statutes—and the cases—with an Appendix of Statutes, and also of those points in surgery and chemistry which are material in criminal cases.
[3] Above 285-287, 386-392, 394.
[4] A Treatise upon the Law and Proceedings in cases of High Treason, etc.
[5] Above 286, 287.   [6] D.N.B.
[7] He said in his translation of Pothier on Obligations i Introd. 99 that the book had " remained three years almost entirely unnoticed " ; he says that he thought that it would be a useful book for the student who had read Blackstone—" facilitating the passage from the elementary to the more technical study of law."

more successful.   To it he added an Appendix on several topics of
English law, and arranged these topics as a disquisition on the law
of evidence.[1]   It is an able discussion of fifteen topics in the law of
evidence—the *onus probandi*, the best evidence rule, public evidence
such as records, deeds, the evidence of handwriting, writings
inferior to deeds, the Statute of Frauds, the explanation of written
evidence by parol, the examination of witnesses, plurality of witnesses, hearsay, the competence of witnesses, confessions, presumptions, the authority of *res judicata*.   And it is not only an
able discussion, but it is also a critical discussion.   Thus he criticizes
the rules as to the competence of witnesses, and some of the rules
relating to confessions.   As he says,[2] the object of his book is
different from that of Peake's.   Peake's book was meant to be a
book of reference for the practitioner : his book takes a more
" scientific view " of the subject, and criticizes and suggests amendments of the law.   In fact Evans was a pioneer student of comparative law.   No doubt his work on Lord Mansfield's decisions
had helped to broaden his knowledge and confirm his views as to the
value of this study ; and his work on the law of evidence, though
considerable, was only one aspect of his work on Pothier.   He
helped to make English lawyers acquainted with Pothier's work,
and, by so doing, did considerable service to the development of
the English law of contract during this period.[3]

An attempt to state the law of evidence in the form of a code
was made by S. B. Harrison in 1825.[4]   The main principles of the
law are digested into thirty-four sections.   Considering that this was
a new venture in legal literature, it has considerable merits.   The
propositions into which the law is digested are clear, terse, and
accurate.   But it is not detailed enough to be of much use to the
practitioner.

A little book on the principles of the law of evidence was
published by Richard Garde in 1830.[5]   It set out to give students
instruction in the main principles of the law, which, he rightly
pointed out, should be mastered before they were immersed in the
technicalities of practice by which those principles were often
obscured.   It is a good clear summary, illustrated by cases, of the
main principles and rules in four short chapters.

Another small book of a severely practical kind by J. W. Willis
set out the main rules as to interrogatories in equity and in law.[6]

---

[1] Vol. ii 141-360.   [2] Vol. i Introd. 97.

[3] Pothier's work is referred to by Fry, Specific Performance (6th ed.) 103, 352.

[4] Evidence Forming a title of the Code of Legal Proceedings according to the
plan proposed by Crofton Uniacke, Esq.

[5] A Practical Treatise of the General Principles and Elementary Rules of the
Law of Evidence.

[6] A Digest of the Rules and Practice as to Interrogations for the Examination
of Witnesses in Courts of English Common Law, with Precedents.

The rules are stated shortly, and the greater part of the book consists of a collection of forms and precedents.[1]

A book which combined the law of evidence with the law of pleading in civil actions was published by J. S. Saunders in 1828. It is an abridgment of the law upon those topics arranged alphabetically. It is terse and clear, the titles are well arranged, and it covers much ground. As the author says in his preface, it contains not only the general principles of the law of pleading and evidence, but also the law as to the different forms of action, the pleadings and the evidence necessary for the support of every ground of action and of every defence, together with precedents of pleading in all those actions. But it is a practitioner's book and nothing else. Principles and rules are stated, but they are not explained or discussed. The book contains a great deal of information given in a very concise form.[2]

Conveyancing and Land Law

There are several books—some short, some long and elaborate—which explain the principles of conveyancing, which give collections of precedents, which combine both these matters, which deal with other matters cognate thereto.

Charles Barton[3] (1768-1843), a barrister of the Inner Temple, a conveyancer, and the author of *An Historical Treatise of a Suit in Equity*,[4] produced two considerable books on these topics. The first was a book in five volumes on the principles of conveyancing.[5] It was first published 1802-05, and originated, the author tells us, in lectures which he read to his pupils. It deals with the nature and incidents of estates in realty, and the effect and operation of assurances. There are some remarks on the study of conveyancing, advice to the student as to his reading, and as to his conduct as a conveyancer and as a lawyer. It is divided into five Books. Book I deals with the different kinds of real property; Book II (which takes up two volumes) with estates and interests; Book III with conveyancing, original, derivative, those deriving their operation from the Statute of Uses, and Assurances by matter of record (fines recoveries); Books IV and V, which take up the last volume, with devises and inheritance. There was a second and enlarged edition which was published between the years 1810 and

---

[1] Only thirty pages out of 317 are devoted to the rules.
[2] The Law of Pleading and Evidence in Civil Actions, arranged alphabetically with Practical Forms : and the Pleading and Evidence to support them.
[3] D.N.B.   [4] Vol. xii 181-182.
[5] Elements of Conveyancing with cursory remarks upon the study of that Science. Including a list of books for the use of students and practitioners. And also observations and directions relative to the practice of conveyancing, particularly with respect to the perusal of abstracts of titles and preparing of deeds and assurances of real and personal property—this is the title page of the second ed.

1822. The book deserved to succeed. It is well arranged, and it contains clear statements of principles and rules.

The second of Barton's books is a collection of precedents in conveyancing, first published in five volumes between 1807 and 1810.[1] In the preface to the first edition it is said that the book was intended to be a collection of ordinary precedents for the use mainly of students and solicitors. The simple precedents are given first, and then those which deal with more complex needs. But all are adapted to the circumstances which most usually occur in practice, and all are made as concise as possible. To the precedents notes are appended explaining the clauses referring to the relevant cases, and showing how the precedent ought to be varied to meet different contingencies. The precedents are grouped under nine heads : purchase deeds, liens, mortgages, annuity deeds, deeds between debtors and creditors, deeds of copartnership, marriage settlements, wills, miscellaneous. It was a successful book. There was a second edition in six volumes, 1811-14, and a third in seven volumes between 1821 and 1824.

Another considerable book " analytically and synthetically arranged " was published in two volumes by James Stewart in 1827 and 1829.[2] The first volume gives precedents under twelve heads of the principal parts of deeds, and then it gives precedents of eight classes of deeds. The second volume gives precedents of agreements, bonds, and wills. The author published a third volume in 1831 which dealt in thirty-two chapters with the precedents of conveyancing. The first twenty-one chapters deal with the preparation and examination of different varieties of abstracts of title. Chapters xxii-xxxii deal with the rules of evidence applicable to the titles to real and personal property. All three volumes are clearly written, and show that the author was able and learned. There was a second edition in 1832-40, and a third edition of Volume I in 1846-7.

Watkins, whose main work consisted of learned books on copyholds and the law of inheritance, wrote an elementary book on conveyancing for students,[3] which between 1800 and 1845 went through nine editions. It is divided into three Books, dealing with Estates, Conveyances as they relate to Estates, and Conveyances with respect to Parties. Preston, who edited the third edition, tells us that he used it as a text book for his students. The comments which he made on it in his lectures to them had

---

[1] Original Precedents in Conveyancing ; the later editions were entitled Modern Precedents in Conveyancing.

[2] The Practice of Conveyancing : comprising every usual deed analytically and synthetically arranged.

[3] Principles of Conveyancing designed for the use of Students. With an Introduction on the Study of that Branch of Law.

been circulated in MSS. and he embodied them in this edition. It is accompanied by an Introduction which gives students valuable advice as to their course of reading.

The most considerable book of precedents, with dissertations on the practice of conveyancing, comes from the end of this period.[1] Its authors were W. M. Bythwood and Thomas Jarman, the author of the standard treatise on wills,[2] and it was published in ten volumes between 1821 and 1834. The first third was by Bythwood, the remaining two thirds by Jarman. The precedents were taken from manuscript drafts of actual conveyances, most of them drawn by eminent counsel. The book is arranged under alphabetical heads from " Abstracts " to " Wills." To each title is prefixed a dissertation on the law relating to the conveyancing contained in it. It remained a standard book through this and the following period and beyond. The fourth and last edition, edited by L. G. G. Robbins, was published between 1884 and 1890.

A much smaller book of precedents of settlements was published by J. B. Bird in 1800.[3] The author said in his preface that of recent years there had been many improvements in the art of conveyancing which had been effected by such distinguished lawyers as Fearne, Hargrave, and Butler. Conveyances, he said, had become less verbose and more perspicuous ; and he proposed to produce a collection of precedents which embodied these improvements. But he exaggerated the extent to which verbosity had been pruned. The real cure for this defect was not found till later in the century when conveyances ceased to be paid by length.[4] Two other short books dealt with the cognate subject of fines and recoveries. The first was by W. Hands, an attorney of the Common Pleas, and was published in 1800.[5] It was " intended for clerks and attornies " and dealt only with the formal steps needed to levy a fine or suffer a recovery. It is very short—the greater part consists of an appendix of forms,[6] but it gives a clear account of the many formalities required by the law, and of the fees payable at various stages of these processes. The second was by Francis Bayley, a barrister of Lincoln's Inn,

---

[1] A Selection of Precedents in Conveyancing taken from modern manuscript collections and drafts of actual practice with Dissertations and Practical Notes.
[2] Vol. xiv.
[3] Original Precedents of Settlements, drawn by the most distinguished conveyancers of the present day, and now first published under the direction and inspection of James Barry Bird. Bird also produced a supplement to Barton's Precedents, and a collection in two volumes of precedents in conveyancing relating to Agreements with preliminary observations on the precedents, Sweet and Maxwell, Legal Bibliography iii 21. [4] Vol. xiv.
[5] The Modern Practice of Levying Fines and Suffering Recoveries in the Court of Common Pleas at Westminster, with an Appendix of select precedents.
[6] The book itself takes thirty-nine pages and nineteen pages of introduction : the precedents 112 pages.

and was published in 1825. In twenty-six short chapters he gives a clear but pedestrian statement of the main rules. It is purely a practice book; but it states sufficiently fully as much of the underlying theory as was needed to make the rules of practice intelligible.

A book on a very special but very important topic connected with conveyancing was written by Thomas Coventry. It is entitled *Observations on the Title to Lands through Inclosure Acts*.[1] It is interesting because it sheds light on the not very intelligent way in which these Acts were carried out, and the consequent conveyancing difficulties which were sometimes caused. It also illustrates the unjudicial conduct of which the commissioners appointed to carry out these Acts were sometimes guilty. The author tells us that conveyancing difficulties were caused by the way in which the commissioners refused to listen to the representations of counsel or solicitors, and " excluded from their considerations all subjects not immediately connected with roads, rates and acres."[2] The lands allotted were held on the same title as the lands in respect of which they were allotted. Hence if the latter were held by five different titles, and it was not stated in respect of which of the five the land was allotted, a purchaser of the allotted land might have to investigate five different titles. It was said that a case had occurred in which 200 abstracts of title were needed to show the state of the title.[3] Moreover it was difficult to draw up claims to common and other rights apportioned to land; and this difficulty was aggravated by the fact that individual commissioners were apt to regard themselves as agents for the parties by whom they had been nominated.[4]

The subject of conveyancing is a somewhat arid subject, and precedents in conveyancing are not very exciting reading. But just as another somewhat arid subject—pleading—gave birth to some humorous literature,[5] so did conveyancing. *The Conveyancer's Guide* is a humorous poem somewhat on the lines of Anstey's *Pleader's Guide*.[6] It describes itself accurately as " a burlesque poem, showing the origin of property and of uses and trusts; how uses are distinguished from trusts; the reason of the Statute of Uses; how uses are executed by the Statute; with an explanation of the deeds of feoffment, bargains

---

[1] For these Acts which were very numerous in the late eighteenth century and the first half of the nineteenth century, see vol. ii 60-61; vol. vi 344-345; Vol. xi 453-457, 625, 627.

[2] The advice of counsel they not only never take, but uniformly reject when submitted to them, the remarks of solicitors too are usually treated in a way to prevent repetition. The Commissioners read the Act as excluding from their considerations all subjects not immediately connected with roads, rates and acres. Pp. 1-2.

[3] Pp. 4-5.

[5] Vol. ix 413-433.

[4] Pp. 138-140.

[6] For this work see above 460, 461.

at sales and lease and release ; and advice to students designed
for the bar."   Its author was S. G. B. Grant, " an apprentice of
the law ."   It was published in 1820, and there was a second
edition in 1832.   Here are the opening lines :

> Oh ! Ockham, Britton, Glanville, Bracton, Brooke,
> St. Germain, West, Booth, Littleton, and Coke,
> Lilly and Horsman, Duane, Booth,[1], and Fearne,
> Bridgman and Blackstone, Butler, Hargrave, Hearne,
> Hill, Preston, Sugden, Sanders, Rowe and Cruise,
> Names now immortalized, assist my Muse ;
> Whilst thus she soars on high with venturous wing,
> The science of conveyancing to sing :
> A noble theme which Coke himself supposes
> To be at least as old as Lawyer Moses.

Special topics in the land law

Some of these were topics which long ago had been treated
separately, and round which some literature had already gathered.
Most, however, were topics which had not as yet been treated
separately, but which, by reason of the growing elaboration of the
law, it was desirable to treat of in this way.   The following is an
account of the principal books arranged in the alphabetical order
of topics :

There was already a considerable literature on the subject of
Copyhold and the topics cognate thereto.   The standard book on
this subject was published by Serjeant John Scriven in 1816.[2]
There was a second edition, 1821-3, and a seventh edition was
published in 1896.   It is a very learned, well-arranged book
which deals not only with copyhold, but with lands held by the
tenure of Ancient Demesne and with customary freeholds and
with the manorial courts and courts leet.   The titles of its twenty-
two chapters indicate the completeness with which copyhold and
the topics related to it are treated.   They are as follows :

1. The nature and properties of a manor.   2. The ambiguity
of copyhold estate—and its incidental and collateral qualities.
3. The lord of the manor.   4. Surrender.   5. Devise.   6. Admittance.   7. Fine.   8. Service.   9. The Steward's fees.   10.
Guardianship.   11. Trust estates.   12. Trees and mines.   13.
Forfeiture.   14. Ejectment.   15. Customary plaints.   16. Evidence, pleading, prescription, waste and common.   17. Mandamus

[1] There were two Booths well-known as real property lawyers, George Booth
who published one book on real action in 1734, vol. xii 367-368, and James Booth
to whom Fearne dedicated the third ed. of his Contingent Remainders, ibid 372, n. 7.

[2] A Treatise on Copyholds, Customary Freeholds, and Ancient Demesne Tenure,
with the jurisdiction of Courts Baron and Courts Leet ; also an Appendix containing
rules for holding customary courts, courts baron, and courts leet, forms of court rolls,
deputations, and copyhold assurances, and extracts from the relative Acts of Parliament.

and equitable remedies. 18. Extinguishment and enfranchize-
ment. 19. Customary freeholds. 20. Ancient Demesne. 21.
The jurisdiction of courts baron, the fruits of tenure, and
seignorial franchizes. 22. Courts Leet and their jurisdiction.

The adequate treatment of these topics demanded a knowledge
of legal rules substantive and adjective which covers all periods
of our legal history. The author shows that he is as well read
in the early mediæval as in the eighteenth and nineteenth
century authorities.

A book on *Covenants* by Thomas Platt, which was published
in 1829 broke new ground.[1] It is a very complete treatise. It is
clearly expressed, and it contains intelligent discussions of the
cases. Its treatment of covenants running with the land and the
reversion is clear and good. In 1829 the concept of restrictive
covenants running with the land in equity had not yet emerged.
The only restrictive covenants with which the author deals are
those as between landlord and tenant, which, as Jessel, M. R.
once said, were one of the roots of the equitable doctrines on this
subject.[2] The book is divided into the following six Parts :
1. The nature and kinds of covenants and the parties thereto.
2. The general rules for the construction of covenants. 3.
Particular express covenants. 4. The liabilities and rights
arising from covenants at common law and by virtue of the
Statute 32 Hen. VIII chap. 34. 5. The remedies and relief
incidental to covenants. 6. Covenants void in their creation ;
and of the means by which covenants originally valid may be
discharged or suspended.

In 1847 Platt published a learned work on Leases, but its discussions of the cases and its statements of the law were somewhat lengthy, and for that reason it could not compete against
Woodfall's work[3] which had by that time come to be the standard
treatise on this subject.

A *Treatise on the law of Descent* was published in 1825 by that
prolific legal authority Joseph Chitty. It was clearly written and
more complete than Watkins' book—though occasionally, e.g.
in his descriptions of incorporeal hereditaments, he gives us
information which has little to do with the subject. The titles
of the twenty chapters into which the book is divided are as
follows :
1. Descent. 2. Who may be heirs. 3.-10. The canons
of descent. 11. Estates tail. 12. Descent by custom.

---

[1] A Practical Treatise on the Law of Covenants.
[2] " The doctrine of that case [Tulk v. Moxhay (1848), 2 Ph. 74], rightly considered,
appears to me to be either an extension in equity of the doctrine of *Spencer's Case*
to another line of cases, or else an extension in equity of the doctrine of negative
easements." L.S.W.R. v. Gomm (1882) 20 C.D. at p. 583.
[3] Below 476.

13. Incorporeal hereditaments. 14. Remainders and reversions.
15. Conditions, powers, rights, possibilities. 16. Heirlooms.
17. The Crown. 18. Estates in equity. 19. Posthumous
heirs. 20. How descent is affected by devise, fine or recovery,
dower, curtesy, debts, ouster, attainder.

A book on the law of *Dower*, mainly from the point of view of
the conveyancer, was published by J. J. Park in 1819.[1] It is a
good and complete treatise on a topic which involved a knowledge
of mediæval law, modern law, and equitable modifications of the
law. The author appears to have a first hand acquaintance with
the authorities from the sixteenth century onwards. The Year
Books he cites mainly from the Abridgments and Coke. In his
preface he argues for the utility of text books on special topics—
scattered cases are reconciled and reduced to first principles.
But he admits that the reasoning of the writers of these books is
sometimes far-fetched—so that " the law speaks one language in
the books[2] and another in the treatises."

A good book on the *Action of Ejectment* was published by John
Adams in 1812.[3] There was a second edition in 1818, and a fourth
in 1846. Adams points out that the action was not firmly fixed
on its modern basis till the time of Lord Mansfield ;[4] that he
attempted to give effect to equitable rights by means of it ;[5] but
later this attempt was frustrated by Lord Kenyon, who, says
Adams, united the equitable fictions of the action with the general
principles of the law, and so " preserved unbroken the great
boundaries of our legal jurisprudence." The book is good, clear
and succinct—for instance, there is a very clear account of the
rule that the plaintiff must prove his title so that a *jus tertii*
could be pleaded in answer to his claim.[6] A more ambitious and
less successful book was published in 1825 by Henry Roscoe, the
son of the historian attorney and banker William Roscoe.[7]
Henry Roscoe[8] was called to the bar by the Inner Temple in
1826 and became assessor to the Mayor's Court at Liverpool.
During his short life (1800-36) he published many law books, the
most successful of which were his books on evidence in trials at
nisi prius and in criminal cases.[9] This book is comprehensive,
learned, and clearly written. But the whole of the first volume
is devoted to the real actions which in 1825 were on their last legs ;

---

[1] A Treatise of the Law of Dower ; particularly with a view to the modern practice
of conveyancing ; for Park see above 295, 444. [2] I.e. the cases.
[3] A Treatise on the Principles and Practices of the Action of Ejectment, and
the resulting action for mesne profits. [4] See vol. vii 10-19.
[5] Ibid 19-20 ; vol. xii 588-589. [6] At pp. 32-33.
[7] A Treatise of the Law of Actions relating to Real Property.
[8] D.N.B.
[9] Other books were Lives of Eminent British Lawyers for Lardner's Encyclopaedia ; an edition of the Lives of the Norths ; a Digest of the Law of bills
of exchange ; a Digest of the law as to offences against the coinage.

and, though there is something in his view that the law which centred round them elucidated the principles of the law of real property, the practitioner must have regarded the space allotted them as disproportionate to their practical importance. The second volume describes fifteen actions connected with real property.[1] The principles and rules are well stated, and to the more important actions a larger space is given—the action of ejectment, for instance, occupies 139 pages out of 356 pages of the volume. But probably the practitioner preferred to consult the regular books which dealt with procedure in practice, or books which dealt specially with some of these actions.

A pioneer treatise on the law of *Fixtures* was published by A. Amos and J. Ferrand in 1827, and reached a third edition in 1883.[2] It is an able book on a topic which needed systematic treatment. As the authors point out, the difficulties of the subject were increased by the division of the law of property into realty and personalty, and by the paucity of decided cases— many disputes on this matter were regularly referred by the judges to arbitration. Moreover the manner in which the law had grown up had made it difficult to see in it any general principles, for it " rests on a series of judicial decisions in contra-vention of an ancient rule in favour of the freehold. And as these decisions arose out of particular emergencies, and were pro-nounced at different periods of time, it is extremely difficult to reduce them into a uniform system, or to extract from them any principles of general application." [3]

They pointed out, for instance, that it is often said that there are differences in the law applicable to different classes of persons as between whom disputes as to fixtures arise, as between, for instance, the heir and executors, the executors of the tenant for life or in tail and the remainderman or reversioner, and landlord and tenant.[4] But these differences, they point out, are nowhere clearly stated.[5] Our law on this topic, they said, was not so clear as French Law, Roman Law, or Scots Law. It would be better if it were based, not on a series of modifications of the rule

---

[1] Actions on the case for nuisance and disturbance   actions on the case in the nature of waste ; actions on the case for dilapidations ; actions on the case for slander of title ; assumpsit on the sale of real property ; assumpsit for use and occupation ; covenant ; debt for rent ; debt for use and occupation ; debt for double value ; debt for double rent ; ejectment ; replevin ; trespass quare clausum fregit : trespass for mesne profits.

[2] A Treatise on the Law of Fixtures, and other property partaking both of a real and personal nature ; comprising the law relating to annexations to the freehold in general ; as also emoluments, charters, heirlooms, etc., with an Appendix containing practical rules and directions respecting the removal, purchase, valuation, etc. of fixtures between landlord and tenant, and between outgoing and incoming tenants.   [3] Preface.

[4] See Elwes v. Maw (1802) 3 East at p. 51 per Lord Ellenborough C.J., cited vol. vii 284.   [5] Introduction.

which favoured the freehold, but on the principle of French Law, *nemo detrimento alterius locupletior fieri potest*. A right to remove fixtures should be the rule, not the exception.[1] The book consists of the introduction, from which I have quoted, and two parts. The first part deals in six chapters with the right of property in fixtures, and the second with the remedies by action, etc. in respect of fixtures. The appendix contains a summary of practical rules and directions relating to fixtures as between landlord and tenant.

A useful summary of the law as to *Leases and Terms of Years*, based on the article on that topic in Bacon's *Abridgment*, was published in 1819 by C. H. Chambers. It consists of an introduction, which is mainly historical, and three chapters—leases for years considered as contracts ; leases considered with reference to persons who are not parties to the contracts ; and leasehold property in terms of years. It is a good outline, but only an outline. Principles are well stated and the cases are clearly summarized and distinguished. It was, no doubt, a useful book to students as well as to practitioners.

William Woodfall's book on *Landlord and Tenant* [2] has been a standard book on this subject from its first publication in 1802 to its twenty-third edition published in 1934. Naturally it has been enlarged and altered in the course of its career. In its original form it consisted of twenty-one chapters. Chapters I and II dealt with leases and agreements for leases ; chapters III and IV with the parties to leases ; chapter V with the subject matter of leases ; chapters VI and VII with the terms for which they could be made ; chapters VIII-X with their general incidents ; chapter XI with assignments and under-leases ; chapter XII with the effect of bankruptcy, marriage, or death, on covenants running with the land or the reversion ; chapters XIII-XV with remedies for and against landlord and tenant ; chapter XVI with remedies for waste ; chapter XVII with the landlord's remedies against third person ; chapters XVIII-XX with the tenants' remedies against landlords ; and chapter XXI with the tenant's remedies against third persons. In 1830 it was remodelled and enlarged by S. B. Harrison, in order to make it useful both to lawyers and to landowners.

A book on the law of *Mortmain and Charitable Uses* was published by Anthony Highman in 1789 and reached a second edition in 1809.[3] There is a good historical introduction and an

---

[1] Introduction.   [2] Above 473.

[3] A succinct View of the History of Mortmain and the Statutes relative to Charitable Uses ; with a full imposition of the Land Statute of Mortmain 9 Geo. II c. 36 and its subsequent alterations : Comprising the law as it now stands relative to devises, bequests, visitations, leases, taxes and other incidents to the establishment of Public Charities.

interesting account of the passage through Parliament of the Charitable Uses Act in 1736.[1] It is a comprehensive work. Its main fault is that it too often states the cases at length without a sufficient indication of the principals to be deduced from them. R. H. Coote published his standard work on the law of *Mortgage* in 1821-3. Its merits are shown by the fact that it reached a ninth edition in 1927.

A learned book on certain special topics relating to terms of years was published in 1825 by J. Tamlyn, the reporter of Chancery cases.[2] It deals mainly with points relating to executory interests in terms of years.

The standard work on *Powers* [3] was published in 1808 by that very learned equity and real property lawyer, Sugden, afterwards Lord St. Leonards.[4] The subject, as Sugden said, embraced a large part of the law of real property. As we have seen it had already been made the subject of a book by Powell, which Sugden criticized.[5] Sugden's book is a complete treatise which gives an independent and original view of the subject. Many of the cases cited had been compared with the registrar's books, and cases not in print had been sought out. It is the best authority both for the present law and for its history. The author had a genuine enthusiasm for his subject, and a real reverence for all the most technical doctrines of real property law. As we have seen he had some very pronounced views on the doctrine of *scintilla juris*.[6] It was long the only complete treatise on the subject, and it has been a standard book ever since its first publication. It reached an eighth edition in 1861, and it had no rival till the publication of Farwell's book on the same subject in 1874.

Sugden was also the author of what was long the standard book on *Vendors and Purchasers*.[7] It is a severely practical book which covers the ground very completely. The topics dealt with are : Different kinds of Sale—sale by auction, by private agreement, and by the authority of courts of equity ; Parol Agreements and Evidence ; Effect of the Contract ; Considerations ; Defects in the quantity or quality of the Vendor's Estate ; Title ; Time for Completion ; Abstract of Title and Conveyance ; Interests and Costs ; Purchaser's obligation to see to the application of the purchase money ; Vendor's Lien ; Covenants for

[1] Vol. xi 590-593.
[2] A Treatise on Terms of Years and other Chattels, including a dissertation on Executory Interests and Trusts ; and an enquiry into the point whether Terms of Years merge in each other. [3] A Practical Treatise of Powers.
[4] For Sugden, see below 538, 607, 640, 646, 647.
[5] Vol. xii 382. [6] Vol. vii 140 ; below 647.
[7] A Practical Treatise on the Law of Vendors and Purchasers of Estates ; it was first published in 1805, and by 1862 it had gone through fourteen editions, and had expanded from one to three volumes.

Title ; Persons incapable of purchasing ; Joint Purchases and Purchases with Trust Money ; Protection given to Purchasers by Statutes and rules of Equity : Notice ; Plea of Purchase for value without notice.

Perpetuities and Accumulations was the subject of an essay by H. Randall in 1822.[1] It had an historical introduction on the alienation of property which is fairly well done. The main part of the essay is slighter ; and the author is guilty of error when he lays it down that the rule that after a limitation to an unborn person for life, a contingent remainder cannot be limited to that unborn person's child, is the application of the rule against perpetuities to contingent remainders.[2]

The distinguished conveyancer W. Hayes, who had given evidence before the real property commission, published in 1831 a little book designed to show what would be the effects of introducing the register of titles recommended by the commissioners.[3] In order to make these intelligible he prefaced them with a short but clear account of some of the leading principles of the land law. He agreed with the commissioners as to the expediency of establishing a register ; because under the present system the holders neither of legal nor of equitable estates were perfectly safe.[4] He did not approve of compulsory registration, but he agreed with the commissioners that registered conveyances should prevail over unregistered,[5] and, after a long discussion, that a notice should not violate a preference gained by registration.[6] Then he pointed out that if the register were a perfect register the result of eliminating notice would be to give so great an advantage to equitable estates that in time all estates might become equitable. This he thought might pave the way to the elimination of the distinction between legal and equitable estates, a step towards which would be a return to the intention of the framers of the Statute of Uses by the elimination of many passive trusts.

J. J. Park, the professor of law at King's College, London,[7] discussed the question of registration in an introductory lecture to a course of lectures on conveyancing delivered in 1833.[8] It is an interesting lecture, and some instructive comparisons are made with foreign law. As he said, the perfect register (like the register of stock) is designed to protect the purchaser :

---

[1] An Essay on the Law of Perpetuity and on Trusts of Accumulation, with an Introduction containing the History of Alienation.

[2] See vol. vii 209-214, 234-237.

[3] A Popular View of the Law of Real Property with an application of its principles to the important measure of a General Register, showing what changes in the system a Register is calculated to produce ; for Hayes' other and more important works, see vol. xiv.

[4] Op. cit. 74-75. [5] Ibid 85-86. [6] Ibid 89-121.
[7] Above 295, 444, 445. [8] System of Registration and Conveyancing.

the English system of conveyancing is designed to protect the rightful owner.

The disadvantage of the English system was that it tended to make titles uncertain.   Its advantage was the great freedom of disposition which it gave to landowners.   He, like others, hoped that the suggestions of the real property commissioners would provide a workable system of registration.   But, like others, he did not see that, till the substance of the law was radically reformed, the provision of such a system was impossible.

In another lecture [1] he discussed the original meaning of the term equity, and contrasts it with the technical meaning which it has come to have in the English legal system.   Equity had, he says, become in effect a separate system of law.   It differed from the common law in that it was administered in different courts and with a different system of procedure ; and whereas the common law was " resolutory and retributive," it was " administrative, declaratory, and protective."

Commercial and Maritime Law

With the exception of Joseph Chitty's belated book on *The Laws of Commerce and Manufactures* [2] the books on this topic have assumed their modern form.

A general book on commercial law was published by H. W. Woolrych in 1819.[3]   Woolrych (1795-1871) was a serjeant-at-law who wrote many law books.   This book is divided into four parts: the law of shipping, which includes an account of the Navigation Acts and the law of blockade ; commercial contracts, which includes some account of the law of contract, the contract of sale of goods, suretyship, partnership, and agency, and of aliens, auctioneers, brokers, bankers, and carriers ; bills of exchange and promissory notes ; and bankruptcy and insolvency.   It is a useful compendium which states the main principles of the law on these various topics.

Many books on different parts of the subject were published. Most were competent pieces of work which lived on into the next period, and one or two became standard books which have lasted till our own days.

The great fluctuations in trade—the alternate periods of prosperity and depression—which marked this period,[4] were partly the reason why in this period, as in the last,[5] much was written on the law of *Bankruptcy*.   Partly also new books on this subject were called for by the changes made in it by the Legislature.[6]

---

[1] A Lecture delivered at King's College, London, on April 6, 1832.
[2] Vol. xii 386-387.
[3] A Practical Treatise on the Commercial and Mercantile Law of England.
[4] Above 354-358.   [5] Vol. xii 387-388.   [6] Above 265, 266, 376-378.

Moreover, it was a topic which touched or might touch on most
topics of commercial law, for all merchant contracts might be
investigated by the bankruptcy courts ; so that there was some
justification for Christian's claim that " the system of the bankrupt law now forms the most extensive and important branch of
the mercantile law of the United Kingdom."[1] The best book
on this topic was a book by E. E. Deacon which was first published in 1827 and reached a third edition in 1864.[2] Deacon
said that former books had been written by equity lawyers, and
that his was the first book by a common lawyer. He sets out
the law in the twenty-three chapters of his first volume. In
his second volume he prints the Act of 1826, and gives a
collection of forms and proceedings. It gives a full and clear
account of the law and the practices. Basil Montagu,[3] a commissioner in bankruptcy, a practitioner in the court of Chancery
and the author of the edition of *Bacon* which Macaulay made the
text of his famous essay, published a digest of the law in 1803
which reached a second edition in 1819.[4] The first volume
contains the digest, and the second notes to the text of the first
volume and a collection of statutes and forms. It is a lengthy
work, but the subject matter is not very well arranged. Under
his longest heading—procedure—he discusses much that belonged
properly to the substantive law. He states the rules, but there
is very little explanation or discussion of the cases or the leading
principles. A short, but well-arranged, summary was published
by J. P. Archbold in 1825 and reached an eleventh edition in
1856.[5]

Edward Christian[6] published two books on this subject. He
was, as we have seen,[7] the first Downing Professor of the Laws
of England at Cambridge and the author of a very good edition
of Blackstone's *Commentaries*. He was also the younger brother
of Fletcher Christian, the *Bounty* Mutineer. He had a distinguished career at Cambridge, being third Wrangler, Chancellor's Medallist, and fellow of St. John's. He was called to the
bar by Gray's Inn in 1786, but did not succeed in getting a
practice. He became Downing Professor, professor of law at the

---

[1] The Origin, Progress and present Practice of the Bankrupt Law, preface.
[2] The Law and Practice of Bankruptcy as altered by the new act (6 Geo. 4 c. 16)
with a collection of forms and precedents in Bankruptcy and Practical Notes.
[3] (1770-1851) ; Montagu was a well-known man of letters in his day—a friend
of Coleridge and Wordsworth, and Carlyle, the last of whom he offended by offering
him a clerkship at £200 a year : he wrote many books suggesting reforms in the
bankruptcy law, and in the law of copyright, advocating the emancipation of the
Jews, and denouncing capital punishment ; he also edited several series of bankruptcy reports (above 442), and wrote several other law books, and books on philosophical subjects, D.N.B. [4] A Digest of Bankrupt Laws.
[5] The Law and Practice in Bankruptcy as founded on the recent Statute with
Forms.
[6] D.N.B. [7] Vol. xii 715.

East India Company's college, a commissioner of bankrupts, Chief Justice of the Isle of Ely, and a bencher and treasurer of his Inn. His contemporaries thought poorly of his abilities.[1] But he had a good knowledge of old law and legal history, and there is no doubt that his edition of Blackstone is good and that some of his notes are learned and useful. But his works on the law of bankruptcy show that he was not so successful when he wrote an independent book. The first of his books, published 1812-14,[2] is an annotated edition of all the bankruptcy statutes beginning with the Statute of 34, 35 Henry VIII c. 4, and ending with 52 George III c. 144. Interspersed amongst the statutes are disquisitions on points in the law of bankruptcy, general orders of the Lord Chancellor, and an account of the jurisdiction of the courts of law and of the Lord Chancellor. There is a great deal of information in the book, and some good discussions of cases, but the subject matter is scattered and not very intelligently arranged. His other book, published in 1816,[3] sets out to give information as to the mode of serving out and prosecuting a commission of bankruptcy, together with a collection of forms. It is a purely practical book, and its main idea is to give correct precedents, for he says that those given in the books are so faulty that their use had caused miscarriages of justice. That it was found to be useful is shown by the fact that it reached a second edition in 1820.

A book on shipping, which is not without merits, was published by F. L. Holt in 1820.[4] Holt (1780-1844),[5] was the author of other law books [6] and a good lawyer who tried his hand at play-writing, and rose to the position of Vice-Chancellor of the county palatine of Lancaster. The book deals with the Navigation Acts and the ship registry Acts, with merchant shipping and seamen, and with maritime contracts. It is comprehensive and well-written, but, though it reached a second edition in 1824, it could not compete with the more authoritative work of Abbott.

Two important books were published on *Bills of Exchange.* The first is by that prolific writer of law books, Joseph Chitty.[7] It was first published in 1812, and reached an eleventh edition in

---

[1] There is a well known tale that Ellenborough, when a ruling of the Chief Justice of Ely was cited to him, said that he was not fit to rule a copybook ; and at his death it was said that he died in " the full vigour of his incapacity."

[2] The Origin, Progress and Present Practice of the Bankrupt Law both in England and Ireland.

[3] Practical Instructions for serving out and prosecuting a commission of Bankruptcy with the best modern precedents and a digest of supplementary cases.

[4] A system of the Shipping and Navigation Laws of Great Britain and of the Laws relative to Merchant Ships and Seamen and Maritime Contracts.

[5] D.N.B. [6] Below 488, 489.

[7] For Joseph Chitty see above 458, 459 ; its full title is A Practical Treatise on Bills of Exchange, Checks on Bankers, Promissory Notes, Bankers' Cash Notes, and Bank Notes."

1878. It is divided into two parts, the first of which deals with the substantive law and the second with procedure. Byles, in the preface to his book on bills of exchange, said that it was

a laborious and full collection of almost all the cases by an eminent counsel, the extent of whose legal acquirements, and the readiness of his application can only be appreciated by those who have been in the habit of personal intercourse with him. But the size of the book is an objection with many, and a cloud of authorities will sometimes obscure the most luminous arrangement.

The latter part of this criticism is not quite fair. The book is not unduly long ; it is well arranged ; and the law is clearly stated. The fact that it reached an eleventh edition is the best proof of its merit.

The second of these books was published by John Barnard Byles (1801-1884), which became the standard work on this subject, and reached a twentieth edition in 1939.[1] Byles was called to the bar by the Inner Temple in 1831.[2] He became a serjeant in 1834, and Queen's serjeant in 1857. He was a conservative in politics, and a tract on the Sophisms of Free Trade, which he published in 1849, shows that he saw through the fallacies of the free traders. He never sat in Parliament, though he once unsuccessfully contested Aylesbury. His legal reputation was so high that, in spite of his politics, Lord Cranworth made him a judge of the Common Pleas in 1858, a post which he held till his retirement in 1873. During his tenure of office he helped to make that court a very strong commercial court. In London and in the country Byles on his white horse, which for obvious reasons his friends christened " Bills," was a familiar figure. His book on *Bills* was at once accepted, as it deserved to be, as a work of great authority. He appreciated the work of his predecessors Bayley [3] and Joseph Chitty.[4] But his work is undoubtedly superior to theirs. It is not merely a practitioners' handbook like the larger book of Chitty, in which the cases are noted, with the result that it is difficult to grasp the underlying principles. The history of, and the reasons for, the rise and growth of bills of exchange are very briefly but accurately touched on in the preface. The body of the book is in twenty-eight chapters, in which principles are stated, the most important cases are discussed, and the bearing of other branches of law upon the law of bills of exchange, such as the Statutes of Limitation, set-off, pleading, evidence, and bankruptcy, is

---

[1] A Treatise on the Laws of Bills of Exchange, Promissory Notes, Bank Notes, and Cheques.

[2] D.N.B. Foss, Judges ix 154-155.

[3] Vol. xii 389-390.   [4] Above 481, 482.

explained. Besides his book on bills and his tract on free trade, he published a book on the *Usury Laws*.

A good summary of the law as to *Charterparties and Bills of Lading* was published by Edward Lawes in 1813 [1]—the first book to be devoted exclusively to these subjects. It deals with these two topics and with the law of stoppage in *transitu*, and it discusses the law as applied in the prize court as well as in the court of Admiralty. The law is clearly stated and the cases are intelligently discussed.

There were two books on the law of contract published during this period. The first, by S. Comyn, was published in 1807 and reached a second edition in 1824.[2] It was a treatise on the law of simple contracts " as settled in the action of assumpsit." The topics dealt with are somewhat heterogeneous. In Part I, after a short introduction in which the nature of a contract and the doctrine of consideration are discussed, the following topics are dealt with : the construction of written contracts and penalty and liquidated damages ; cancellation, rescission and performance ; the stamps required on written contracts ; illegality ; the statute of limitations. Part II deals with particular contracts ; and Part III with contracts between particular persons such as partners, brokers, factors, carriers, infants, married women. One of the chapters in Part II, which deals at considerable length with the cases in which the action of *indebitatus assumpsit* lies, is in effect an account of the law of quasi-contracts which is not without merit. In fact the book throughout gives a good summary of the cases on the topics selected. But its somewhat haphazard arrangement shows that the law of contract is as yet somewhat amorphous—there is as yet no agreement as to what such a book should contain, or as to the logical connection between its parts. A better arranged work on somewhat similar lines was published by Joseph Chitty Junior [3] in 1826.[4] That it has attained the rank of a standard work on this subject can be seen from the fact that it reached its twentieth edition in 1948—much enlarged and almost entirely rewritten. Chitty tells us that his objects were, first to write a complete book on the substantive law of simple contract, and that with that object he had studied both English and foreign text books on the subject ; and secondly to write a book which would be useful to the *nisi prius* practitioner.[5] He succeeded in his object. The

---

[1] A Practical Treatise on Charter Parties of Affreightment, Bills of Lading, and Stoppage in Transition ; with an Appendix of Precedents.

[2] The Law of Contracts and Promises upon various subjects and with particular persons as settled in the Action of Assumpsit.

[3] Above 458.

[4] A Practical Treatise on the Law of Contracts not under seal, and upon the usual defences to actions thereon. [5] Preface.

book is well arranged, and the law is clearly explained.[1] The cases are explained, reconciled and criticized.

The only other book published on this subject is an unfinished book by H. T. Colebrook on *Obligations and Contracts*.[2] It is an attempt, which is not wholly unsuccessful, to deal with the law of contract from a jurisprudential point of view. The topics discussed are the definition of an obligation and a contract, validity, interpretations and effects, and dissolution. The discussions are based on Roman Law, foreign law, Scots law, and English law.

A good book on the law of *Insurance*[3] was published by Serjeant Samuel Marshall in 1802 which reached a fifth edition in 1865. The book was designed for both merchants and lawyers. Merchants, said the author, ought to have a sufficient knowledge of law to transact ordinary business without professional help, for though " a man who purchases an estate may act with caution, a merchant in many cases must decide at once, and act upon his own judgment."[4] But it is essentially a lawyer's book. The outlines of the history of the different kinds of insurances are correctly related. The cases are stated carefully and there is some acute criticism of the reasoning in some of them. According to the author, the main difficulty of the subject lay not so much in the underlying principles of the law as in their application to complicated sets of facts. The book is divided into four parts—marine insurance, bottomry and respondentia, insurance upon lives, insurance against fire. Marine insurance is still by far the most important form of insurance. In the second edition it takes up 732 out of the 813 pages in the book. A short book on this subject intended for merchants as well as lawyers was published by J. J. Burns in 1801.[5] It is little more than a summary of Park's book,[6] and, as authorities are sparingly cited, it was more useful to merchants than to lawyers.

Three books were published on the law of *Partnership*. The earliest, by W. Watson, was first published in 1794.[7] It deals with the subject in sixteen short chapters, in a manner which shows that the law on this subject is as yet scanty. The author states shortly and often vaguely general principles, which he

---

[1] Chap. I deals with the classification of contracts, consideration, forms, and stamping ; chap. II with contracts with particular persons, e.g. infants and agents ; chap. III with various kinds of contracts, e.g. sales of realty and personalty, work and labour, money had and received ; chap. IV with illegal contracts chap. V with defences ; and chap. VI with damages.

[2] A Treatise on Obligations and Contracts (1818).

[3] A Treatise on the Law of Insurance in four Books.

[4] Preface.

[5] A Practical Treatise or Compendium of the Law of Marine Insurance.

[6] For Park's book, see vol. xii 390-391 ; this book is dedicated to Park.

[7] A Treatise on the Law of Partnership.

sometimes illustrates from Roman Law, and he takes up a large space by citing verbatim the arguments and decisions in a number of cases decided by the courts of law and equity. It is not a well constructed book. The second edition, which was prepared by the future Lord Campbell,[1] and to which he contributed an introduction, is an improvement. It is fuller, the new cases are inserted in appropriate places, and their effect is clearly stated.

The second and best of the three books is by John Collyer.[2] It was first published in 1832 and reached a second edition in 1840. The preface to the second edition tells us that it was thought so well of that an American edition of it had been published, and that that had led the author to cite some American cases. It is divided into five books—the constitution of the contract of partnership ; the rights of partners *inter se*, the relative rights of the partners and third persons, the bankruptcy of partners, particular partnerships. Under the last head joint stock companies, mining partnerships, and the part ownership of ships are discussed. It was not till the following period that statutory changes separated company law from the law of partnership. Lindley's book on partnership, when it was first published in 1860, dealt with both partnerships and companies. It was not till 1888 that these two topics were divided and made the subject of separate treatises.

The third book is Basil Montagu's [3] *Digest of the Law of Partnership* in two volumes, published in 1815 ; [4] the first volume contains the digest, and the second the cases on which it is founded. The first volume is divided into two Books. The first deals with the formation of partnership, its legal consequences, and dissolution ; the second with particular problems in the law of partnership such as dormant partners, infant partners, illegal partnerships, admission of new members. It is a well arranged book, and there is an attempt to state the principles of the law ; but, unlike Pollock's *Digest*,[5] which was throughout a statement of principles illustrated by the cases, it is too often merely a summary of decisions.

A pioneer book on the law of *Principal and Agent* was published by W. Paley in 1811, and reached a third edition in 1833.[6] It is

---

[1] Life of Lord Campbell, 205. An account of Lord Campbell's career will appear in vol. xiv.

[2] A Practical Treatise on the Law of Partnership with an Appendix of Forms.

[3] Above 442, 480.

[4] There was an earlier book on this subject by W. Watson entitled A Treatise of the Law of Partnership (1st ed. 1794, 2nd ed. 1807) ; in the introduction there are one or two comparisons of English with French and Roman law, but the book itself is for the most part a summary of cases set out at considerable length.

[5] It was the ground work of the bill drafted by Pollock which became the Partnership Act of 1890.

[6] A Treatise of the Law of Principal and Agent : chiefly with reference to Mercantile Transactions.

well written and well arranged.   The author pointed out that
there were not many cases to be found on this topic in the older
reports, and that many of the modern cases heard at *nisi prius*
were not reported, but that with the growth of trade it was a
subject of rapidly growing importance.   The book is concerned
mainly with mercantile agency, but the foundations of the law
had been laid in the law of master and servant, and the author
admitted that it was not always possible to separate the two.[1]
It was in fact an original idea to treat mercantile as a separate
topic of commercial law.

Another pioneer treatise on the law of *Sale of Goods* was
published by G. Ross in 1811 and reached a second edition in 1826.[2]
It is a clearly written book on a topic which was rapidly developing,
but was still in a somewhat rudimentary state.   For instance,
hardly any of the implied conditions and warranties which are so
marked a feature of the modern law were then recognized.[3]   One
of the very few of the implied conditions recognized was the
condition that on a sale by sample the bulk must correspond with
the sample.

A curious little book on *Maritime Law* was published by F. M.
Van Heythuysen in 1819.[4]   It was meant to give practitioners
sufficient nautical information to enable them to examine
nautical witnesses and conduct cases, such as collision cases, in
which this evidence was essential.   The author disclaimed any
intention of writing a book about shipping laws, but gives some
information on elementary points which he thought would be
useful to shipowners.

Special topics

The number of books on special topics naturally increase in
number as the law gets more elaborate.   I have selected a few
specimens of this considerable mass of literature.   Some of them
became standard works, the life of which has been prolonged by
successive editors even to our own days.   I describe them in the
alphabetical order of the topics dealt with by them.

A book on apprentices, journeymen, and the restrictions on
exercising trades was published by J. Chitty in 1812.[5]   It was

---

[1] For an explanation of this fact, see vol. viii 227.
[2] The Law of Vendors and Purchasers of Personal Property.
[3] See pp. 334-354.
[4] An Essay upon Marine Evidence with Courts of Law and Equity in which is
considered the competency of a marine witness, the legal title to British Ships, the
proof and construction of a Ship's Policy, and the Evidence necessary to establish a
variety of nautical subjects to which is added a glossary of sea terms which frequently occur in nautical pleadings.
[5] A Practical Treatise on the Law relative to Apprentices and Journeymen and to
exercising trades.

caused by events which arose out of the industrial revolution—
there had been numerous prosecutions against persons for exercising trades without having served as apprentices, and against
journeymen for combinations to raise wages.   It gives a good
account of the Elizabethan statute as to apprentices,[1] the law as
binding apprentices, the rights and liabilities of masters and
apprentices, and the position of corporate towns as to setting up
trades therein.[2]   It is a good summary of the law, and illustrates
the fact that it was getting more and more out of touch with the
new economic and industrial conditions of the day.

A book on the law of *Arbitration* was published by J. S.
Caldwell in 1817.[3]   The author pointed out that there was a need
for such a book because Kyd's work [4] was out of date.   It contains a good summary of the law and a large number of precedents
are given.

Two books appeared on the law relating to *Attornies*.   The
first of these books was written by Robert Maugham and was
published in 1825.[5]   The preface contains a lament that attornies
had " neither college, hall, library nor society."   The lament was
slightly exaggerated because the Society of Gentlemen Practisers
did provide a fairly efficient organization,[6] and in 1825 it was
raising the money to build a hall in Chancery Lane.[7]   But
Maugham was always an enthusiastic advocate for the improvement in the education and organization of his branch of the
profession ; and twenty years later he proposed that the revenues
of the Inns of Chancery should be applied to the education of
attornies and solicitors.[8]   His book is a pioneer treatise.   It
gives a clear summary of the statute and common law and rules
of practice.   The second of these books, published by J. Merrifield in 1830, is larger and more elaborate ; and it takes in also
the law as to costs.[9]   It is a comprehensive book which deals with
its subjects systematically and clearly.

Rights of Common formed the subject of a book by H. W.
Woolrych in 1824.   The author tells us that no book on this
topic had been published for more than a century.   It is a good
and clear summary of the law.

---

[1] 5 Elizabeth c. 4 ; vol. iv 341-342 ; vol. xi 419-421.
[2] Vol. i 568 ; vol. vi 337 ; vol. xi 419.
[3] A Treatise on the Law of Arbitration with an Appendix of Precedents.
[4] For this book, see vol. xii 393.
[5] A Treatise on the Law of Attornies, Solicitors, and Agents with Notes and
Disquisitions.
[6] For this Society, see vol. xii 63-75.
[7] Ibid 66.   [8] Ibid 44.
[9] The Law of Attornies, with Practical Directions in Actions and Proceedings
by and against them, and for the taxation and recovery of Costs.   Also the Law of
Costs at common law, in equity, in bankruptcy, and in criminal proceedings and
penal actions.

A good book on *Copyright* was published in 1828 [1] by R.
Maugham, the secretary of the Law Institution. It is a well
written book which is something more than a law book. There
is a good account of the law, a good discussion of the general
question of copyright at common law, [2] and a good survey of the
principles which underlie or should underlie this branch of the
law.

There are as yet no books on the law of *Tort* as a whole. But,
as in the preceding period, the importance of the law of libel is
shown by the fact that three books were published on this topic.
The most important was Starkie's [3] work, first published in 1813,
which dealt with the law of libel, both criminal and civil, the
law of slander, malicious persecution, and contempt of court. [4]
To it was prefixed a valuable commentary on the law of slander
and libel which discussed the history of the law, the reasons why
the law must deal with these abuses of the right to speak and
write, some comparison of the rules of English law with those of
Roman law, Scots law, and the foreign civilians. Starkie's
chief criticism of the law was the rule, got rid of by the Slander of
Women Act, 1891, [5] that a woman could get no damages for oral
imputations upon her chastity unless she could prove pecuniary
damage. In other respects he considered that the law was
founded on just and equitable principles. But not every one
would agree with this verdict. In particular the difference
between oral and written imputation, though it might justify
in some cases a difference in the measures of damages recoverable,
hardly justifies their differentiation into two different kinds of
tort. [6] Starkie's work was the ablest and most complete book on
this topic which had yet been published. There was a second
edition in 1830, and later editions in 1869, 1876, 1891, 1897, and
1908. The other two books are of much less importance.
Neither of these gives a satisfactory account of the law. The
author of one of them was J. George who published his book in
1812. [7] It is verbose and neither accurate nor complete. A large
part of it is taken up by a disquisition on political discussion. The
author of the other was F. L. Holt, who published the first edition

---

[1] A Treatise on the Laws of Literary Property, comprising the Statutes and
Cases relating to books, manuscripts, lectures, dramatic and musical compositions ;
engravings, sculpture, maps, etc. Including the piracy and transfer of copyright ;
with an Historical View, and disquisitions on the principles and effects of the Law.

[2] See vol. vi 378-379 ; vol. xii 559.

[3] For Starkie, see above 306, 430, 439, 465.

[4] A Treatise on the Law of Slander and Libel : including the Pleading and
Evidence, civil and commercial, with Forms and Precedents : also Malicious
Prosecutions, Contempt of Court, etc.

[5] 54, 55 Victoria c. 51.   [6] See vol. viii 366-367.

[7] A Treatise on the Offence of Libel : with a Disquisition on the right, benefit and
proper boundaries of Political Discussion.

of his book in 1812 and the second in 1816.[1] The author begins
by telling us something of the law of libel in classical times, and
follows this up with a somewhat inaccurate historical sketch of
the English law. Then he deals with libels against different
kinds of persons and bodies—the government, Christianity,
morals, international law, Parliament, the courts, private persons,
and the law as to *scandalum magnatum*,[2] the last part of the book
deals with procedure and criminal and civil cases. The account
of the law on all these matters is superficial. There is nothing
about privilege.

An able book on the law of Executors and Administrators was
published by Sir Samuel Toller, the advocate general of Madras in
1800. He pointed out that there had been no book on this
subject since Wentworth's, first published in 1641 ; [3] and that
though attempts had been made to bring it up to date the later
editors, the latest of whom was Serjeant Wilson in 1774, merely
added an undigested collection of cases. Since Wentworth's
book did not deal with administrators, and since the decisions of
the court of Chancery at the end of the eighteenth century in
effect " constituted a new system," a new book on this system
was wanted. That Toller was right, and that he had succeeded
in supplying this want by his well arranged and clear summary
of the law is shown by the fact that it reached a seventh edition
in 1838.

A somewhat verbose, but useful collection of cases on the
Statute of Frauds was published by W. Roberts in 1851.[4] Though
it was a good guide to the cases, and though its discussion of the
admissibility of parol evidence is useful, it never got beyond a
first edition.

Joseph Chitty published a comprehensive work on the *Game
Laws* and on *Fisheries* in 1812, and a supplement to it consisting
mainly of precedents in 1816. That it was a successful book is
shown by the fact that there was a second edition in 1826. In
1817, Christian, Blackstone's editor, published a book on the
Game Laws which set out to disprove Blackstone's theory that
the property of game was vested in the Crown.[5] The book is an

---

[1] The Law of Libel : in which is contained a general history of this law in the
ancient codex, and of its introduction and successive alterations in the Law of
England. Comprehending a Digest of all the leading cases upon Libels from the
earliest to the present time.

[2] For this offence, see vol iii 409-410. [3] For this book, see vol. v 15.

[4] A Treatise on the Statute of Frauds, as it regards Declarations in Trust,
Contracts, Surrenders, Conveyances, and the execution and proof of wills and
codicils. To which is prefixed a systematic discussion upon the admissibility of
parol and extrinsic Evidence to explain and control written instruments.

[5] A Treatise on the Game Laws : in which it is fully proved that except in
particular cases Game is now and always has been by the law of England the property
of the occupier of the land upon which it is found or taken. With alterations
suggested for the improvement of the system.

expansion of the author's note to this passage in the *Commentaries*.[1] He maintains that game is the property of the occupier of the land on which it is found. Whether that was so in all cases when he wrote is perhaps doubtful. There is authority that occupiers for limited interests were not in all cases entitled.[2] But the thesis for which Christian contended became law as a result of the Game Act 1831, subject to any contract to the contrary between the landlord and the tenant.[3]

A book on the law as to *Gaming and Wagers* was published by John Disney in 1806.[4] It deals with the distinction between legal and illegal wagers, stakeholders, wagers on horse-races, money lent to game with, securities for money so lent, public gaming houses, rules and precedents of pleading as applied to actions on wagers. The book gives a clear summary of the law.

Two books were published on the law of *Husband and Wife*. The first was published by James Clancy in 1814. It is divided into five books. The first deals with the interests of husband and wife in one another's personalty and realty. The husband's liability for the wife's debts is also dealt with in the first book. The third book deals with property held to the wife's separate use : the fourth with pin money, separation, and separation maintenance ; and the fifth with the wife's and husband's equities in respect of the wife's property. It is a clear and comprehensive statement of the law which reached a third edition in 1827. The second of these books was published by R. S. O. Roper in 1820.

A book on the status of infants and married women by P. Bingham was published in 1816.[5] It is a good summary of what was then a difficult and very technical branch of the law, parts of which were by no means well settled. The most important cases, old and new, are discussed.

A little book which deals with the law of *Inns, Hotels and Alehouses* was published by J. W. Willcock in 1828.[6] It gives a good short summary of the law, useful to lawyers and laymen.

The fact that other forms of *Insurance* besides marine insurance were becoming important is shown by the publication in 1823 and 1832 of books on fire and life insurances. The first of these books was by G. Farrar, a solicitor, who was a director of a big

[1] Comm. ii 419, n. 10.
[2] Vol. vii 493, n. 11.
[3] 1, 2 William IV c. 32, 97 ; Halsbury, Laws of England 2nd ed. xv 418, n. (b).
[4] The Laws of Gaming, Wagers, Horse Racing, and Gaming Houses.
[5] The Law of Infancy and Coverture.
[6] The Laws relating to Inns, Hotels, Alehouses and Places of Public Entertainment : to which is added an abstract of the Statute for the regulation of Post Horses.

insurance company.[1]   It is a short book with a long appendix of cases.

It discusses the different kinds of life insurance companies—proprietory and mutual, the legality of these companies having regard to the provisions of the Bubble Act,[2] and the method of calculating premiums.   It is a book on various problems connected with life insurance rather than a book on the law of life insurance.   The second of these books by Charles Ellis on fire and life insurance is distinctly a law book.[3]   These two forms of insurance had recently, the author tells us, become much more important ;   and as he was connected with two insurance companies he presumably knew what he was talking about.   The book gives a good summary of the law on these two topics, and also on a subject connected with life insurance annuities.   Another book on life annuities, published in 1817, deals with annuities granted to secure loans of money.[4]   It explains their nature, the powers and remedies of the annuitants, the statute law and the way in which they were regarded by the courts.   The greater part of the book is concerned with the Annuity Acts of 1777 and 1813.[5]

The law of *Legacies* was explained in a lengthy book by R. S. O. Roper which was published in 1799.   It is a very complete book but it would have been improved by a little compression—there is a tendency to discuss the cases at undue length.   But that it was found useful by practitioners is shown by the fact that it reached a fourth edition in 1847.

A good clear account of the law as to *Liens* and *Stoppage in Transitu* was published by R. Whitaker in 1812.[6]   The nature of different kinds of lien is discussed, as also acquisition and loss of particular and general liens.   The last chapter contains an account of the solicitors' and attorneys' lien, and the liens recognized in seventeen other trades.   The nature and origin of the right of stoppage *in transitu* is described, and how and when the right can be exercised or divested is discussed.

Another book on liens was published by Basil Montagu[7] in 1821 :[8] and another on *Set Off*, first published in 1801,[9]

---

[1] A Treatise on Life Assurance in which the systems and practice of the leading life institutions are stated and explained, and the statutes and judicial determinations affecting such institutions brought under review.   With an Appendix of Cases, including arguments particularly relating to the formation of Trading Joint Stock Companies.

[2] For this Act, see vol. viii 220-221.

[3] The Law of Fire and Life Insurance and Annuities with practical observations.

[4] A Practical Treatise on Life Annuities by Frederick Blayney.

[5] Vol. xi 604-606 ;   17 George III c. 26 ;   53 George III c. 141 ;   above 408.

[6] A Treatise of the Law relative to the Rights of Lien and Stoppage in Transitu.

[7] For Montagu, see above 441, 442, 480, 485.

[8] A Summary of the Law of Lien.

[9] A Summary of the Law of Set-off with an Appendix of Cases ;   there was a second edition in 1828.

broke new ground. They were both short books with a long appendix of cases. The law is stated in short propositions based on the cases, and there is no attempt to state or discuss principles. They are well arranged.

A book on the *Statutes of Limitations* was published by W. Blanshard in 1825. It deals in ten chapters with the application of these statutes to real and personal actions at law and in equity ; information in the nature of a *quo warranto* ; penal actions ; actions against justices of the peace and against the hundreds ; actions for which periods of limitation had been provided by special statutes. It is a useful summary of a complex branch of law on which there was no complete treatise.

A good short book on *Lunacy* was published by H. Highman in 1807.[1] It deals with commissions of lunacy, the disabilities of lunatics, criminal insanity, and mad houses and their regulation by statute.

Joseph Chitty projected a great work on medical jurisprudence in 1834.[2] The first part contained mainly medical information, the second was to contain mainly pathological and surgical information, and the third part was to connect up this information with the law as to public health, the criminal law, and medical jurisprudence, together with some account of insurance on lives and property. Only the first part appears to have been published, so that as it stands it is not a law book.

Joseph Chitty published, a useful book on the *Stamp Laws* in 1829 which reached a third edition in 1850.[3] He wrote it, he tells us, because the law was so complex that the parties to actions frequently failed by reason of the fact that the documents on which they relied were not sufficiently stamped. These duties, he says, were invented by the Dutch, adopted by the French, and introduced into this country by Statutes of 1694 and 1695.[4] A good short account is given of the law, and there is a useful appendix of annotated statistics.

A book of considerable learning and authority on *The Statutes* was published by Sir Fortunatus Dwarris [5] in 1830-1. Dwarris [6]

[1] A Treatise on the Law of Idiocy and Lunacy, to which is subjoined an Appendix containing the practice of the Court of Chancery on this subject, and some useful practical forms.

[2] A Practical Treatise on Medical Jurisprudence, with as much of Anatomy, Physiology, Pathology and the practice of Medicine and Surgery as are essential to be known by Members of Parliament, Lawyers, Coroners, Magistrates, Officers in the Army and Navy, and private gentlemen ; and all the laws relating to medical practitioners, with explanatory plates.

[3] A Practical Treatise on the Stamp Laws with an Appendix of Statistical Notes thereon.

[4] 6 William and Mary c. 21 ; 6, 7 William and Mary c. 12.

[5] A General Treatise on Statutes : their Rules of Construction, and the Proper Boundaries of Legislation and of Judicial Interpretation. Including a Summary of the Practice of Parliament, and the ancient and modern method of proceeding in passing bills of every kind. [6] D.N.B.

was born in Jamaica, but he came to England in his childhood, and was educated at Rugby and University College, Oxford. He was called to the bar by the Middle Temple in 1811. For his services on the commission to enquire into the state of the law in the West Indies he was knighted in 1838. He served on the Municipal Corporations commission, was a master at the court of Queen's Bench, and was the recorder of Newcastle-under-Lyme. He became a bencher of his Inn in 1850, and treasurer in 1859. That his intellectual interests were varied is shown by the fact that he was a fellow of the Royal Society, and a fellow of the Society of Antiquaries. He wrote several essays and papers on legal subjects ; [1] but it is his book on the Statutes which is his one solid contribution to legal learning. It had a considerable success. The author, with the help of his son-in-law Amyot, produced a second edition in 1848, and an American edition was edited by a judge of the Supreme Court of the State of New York in 1871. The book is in two parts. The first part is called by the author " Constitutional and Parliamentary." It deals with the early history of the Statutes, and the substitution of the modern method of introducing them by bill for the older method of introducing them by petition. It goes on to describe Parliament—its constitutional elements, how it is summoned, and the forms observed at its opening. Privilege of Parliament is then dealt with. Then comes an account of the business done and the opening of a session, qualifications and disqualifications for sitting and voting, rules as to motions, debates and divisions, adjournments, prorogation and dissolution. The last two chapters are devoted to a full account of the procedure on bills public and private. The subject matter of this part of the book is somewhat similar to the subject matter of Anson's *Parliament.* The second part of the book is called by the author " Legal " ; and it is this part which has proved to be of permanent importance and value. It deals with the classification of statutes, their form, certain rules and maxims applicable to statute law, how they are recited and pleaded, how far they bind the King, to what territory they apply, the effect of non-user and repeal. The next two chapters on the construction of statutes are two of the most important in the book. The first of them deals with the general rules of construction, and the second with particular rules applicable to distinct parts of statutes. The next chapter discusses the problem of the proper sphere of the judicial interpretation of statutes, and gives a long historical account of statutory alterations of the law at different periods. The last chapter deals with the mode of making laws in Scotland and

[1] He wrote for the British Archæological Association papers on the local law courts and customs of Derbyshire, on the forest laws, and on Sanctuary.

Ireland, and gives some information as to legislation in India and in the colonies. The book is very comprehensive. It not only surveys all the English authorities, but also makes instructive comparisons with foreign systems of law. It discusses the distinction between personal, penal, and mixed statutes drawn by foreign jurists ; the rules of private international law on the binding force of statutes ; and foreign views as to the scope allowed to judicial interpretation. It is not surprising that so comprehensive and so learned a book should have retained its importance down to our own days.

The law of *Suretyship* was the subject of a book by W. W. Fell in 1811, which reached a second edition in 1820.[1] The author explains that the large extension of the custom of giving credit in mercantile transactions had brought into prominence the question of the securities to be given by those to whom credit was given, so that the law of suretyship had become of much greater importance. Section 4 of the Statute of Frauds is discussed at some length ; and it appears that the case of *Wain v. Warlters*,[2] which decided that a note or memorandum of a promise to answer for the debt or default of another was defective if it did not include the consideration for the promise, had overturned some generally held views as to the conditions which a note or memorandum in writing of a contract of suretyship must satisfy.[3] Some information is also given of the fidelity guarantees given by clerks and their construction.

A book on the law of *Usury* was published by R. B. Comyn in 1817.[4] It is a good clear summary of the law, and it contains useful discussions and explanations of the decisions upon the contracts to which the statutes of usury applied. It is in three parts. Part I gives an account of usury as defined by the statutes and the courts. Part II deals with the avoidance of and ruling against usurious contracts and securities given for the performance of such contracts. Part III deals with the punishment of usury.

A short tract on the *Usury Laws*, supporting the need for some such laws as against Bentham and the economists,[5] was published by Robert Maugham in 1824.[6] Maugham puts up a good argument. He very truly said that though the repeal of these laws would not hurt a first rate merchant, it might expose " inferior classes of traders and manufacturers " to

---

[1] A Treatise of the Law of Mercantile Guarantees and of Principal and Surety in General. [2] (1804) 5 East 10.

[3] The decision in Wain v. Warlters was disapproved by Lord Eldon in ex parte Minet (1807) 14 Ves. at p. 190, and ex parte Gardom (1808) 15 Ves. at p. 288.

[4] A Treatise on the Law of Usury. [5] Above 29, 30, 110, 330.

[6] A Treatise on the Principles of the Usury Laws ; with Disquisitions on the Arguments adduced against them by Mr. Bentham and other Writers, and a Review of the Authorities in their favour.

extortion, and that borrowers with no marketable securities would be thrown on the mercy of the money-lenders. We have seen that the truth of these views was proved by the passing of the Money-lenders Act, 1900.[1]

A book on the law of *Wills and Executors* was published by W. Roberts in 1809, and reached a third edition in 1826.[2] It deals fully and well with the making, the operation, the construction, the revocation, and the republication of wills. The concluding part which deals with the law relating to executors and administrators is scanty.

A Comprehensive book on *Water Rights* in the sea, on rivers and canals, and other cognate topics was published by H. W. Woolrych in 1830.[3] It is a learned work which covers much ground. Clear explanations are given of many branches of law which are sometimes very complex—a good illustration is the author's treatment of the law as to fisheries, several and in common.

Another book dealing with a part of this subject is an essay on the rights of the Crown and privileges of the subjects on the *Seashore*, published by R. G. Hall in 1830.[4] It is a learned essay which is founded on Hale's *De Jure Maris*.[5] It sums up and discusses all the authorities mediæval and modern. A second edition brought up to date with reference to Scottish, Irish and American decisions, was published by R. J. Loveland in 1875. In it is printed as an appendix the whole of Hale's tract.

W. H. Woolrych published a little book on the law of *Window Lights* in 1833.[6] It summarizes the law as to ancient lights, dealing with their acquisition, obstruction, and extinguishment.

A student's book which is little more than an abstract of Blackstone's *Commentaries* was published by F. M. Van Heythusen in 1812, which reached a second edition in 1826.[7]

A writer of Bentham's school—one G. Ensor—published a book on the defects of English law in 1812.[8] The author knows some

---

[1] 63, 64 Victoria c. 51 ; vol. viii 100-101, 112.

[2] A Treatise on the Laws of Wills and Codicils including the construction of Devises and the Office and Duties of Executors and Administrators with an Appendix of Precedents.

[3] A Treatise of the Law of Waters, and of Sewers ; including the law relating to rights in the sea, and rights in rivers, canals, dock companies, fisheries, mills, water-courses, etc.

[4] An Essay on the Rights of the Crown and the Privileges of the Subject in the Sea Shores of the Realm.

[5] For this tract, see vol. vi 585.

[6] A Practical Treatise on the Law of Window Lights with various other matters relating to the subject.

[7] Rudiments of the Laws of England ; Designed as a Preparatory Study for persons entering the profession, as a compendium to strengthen the memory of those who have studied the law, and to convey a general idea of jurisprudence to all classes of persons.

[8] Defects of the English Laws and Tribunals.

law, and has read fairly widely. He seizes upon the obvious
defects, but he is very verbose, he has no historical sense, and
he makes no constructive proposals for reform. He is especially
severe on ecclesiastical law which he regards as more obnoxious
than common law, equity, or the law of the constitution. One of
his more absurd statements is to the effect that the unwritten
common law " bears the same relation to written law as a
legendary tale does to authentic history." [1]

Legal History

There is no outstanding book on legal history as a whole. The
only book is Crabb's *History of English Law*, which was published in 1829.[2] It relates the history of the law in thirty-four
short chapters, from the period of the Anglo-Saxons to the
reign of George IV. The earlier periods are the most fully
dealt with—the period from James II to George IV is all included in one last chapter. Unlike Reeves' book,[3] in which the
history of legal doctrine is fully dealt with, it deals very sparingly
with this topic. It deals more fully with the external history of
the law—with the statutes, the reporters, and the legal authors.
Though it is defective in the later periods, it is a praiseworthy
attempt to describe the outstanding events in, and features of,
English legal history, and its sources and literature.

A learned book on the origins of the laws and institutions of
England and Modern Europe was published by George Spence in
1826.[4] Spence (1787-1850) [5] was a practitioner in the court of
Chancery and between 1829 and 1832 a member of Parliament.
He was interested in Chancery reform, on which subject he wrote
several pamphlets, and in legal education, and he was an original
member of the Society for Promoting the Amendment of the Law
which was founded in 1844.[6] He was a student of Roman Law
and had translated the Code Napoleon. It was because he had
these wide legal and historical interests that he wrote this book
of comparative legal history. Book I deals with the condition
of England and Europe under Roman sway; Book II with the
laws of the Germanic tribes and their intercourse with the Romans;
and Book III with the settlements of these tribes, and the institutions and codes of law established by them. The book
concludes with an account of the effects of the Norman Conquest
on England and English law. Spence realized that effective

---

[1] At p. 59.

[2] A History of English Law; and an attempt to trace the rise, progress and
successive changes of the Common Law from the earliest period to the present
times.　　　　　　　　　　　　　　　[3] For this book, see vol. xii 413-415.

[4] An Enquiry into the Origin of the Laws and Political Institutions of Modern
Europe, particularly those of England.

[5] D.N.B.　　　　　　　　　　　　　　[6] Below 645, 652.

legal history involves, as Maitland said, comparison. Though he is inclined to exaggerate the effects of the Roman occupation and Roman law on English law, it is an able attempt to sketch the history of the origins of English law. It gives a clear account of the sources and influences which shaped Anglo-Saxon law based on the best authorities then available.[1] But it is defective in its account of the law from the Conquest to Henry III in that it fails to take account of the fundamental differences between the new law of the *Curia Regis* which was described by Glanvil, and the Anglo-Saxon law and its restatements in such compilations as the *Leges Henrici Primi*.

Spence, having lost a good deal of his practice when he took silk, found time to write a much more important historical book—the first volume of his *Equitable Jurisdiction of the Court of Chancery*, which was published in 1846.[2] The object of the book, its author tells us,[3] was " to trace the history of the Laws of England so far as they relate to property, and to set forth in a short compass their leading principles." He wished, he said, " to explain how it has arisen that those laws are administered by distinct tribunals, the Courts of Common Law and the Court of Chancery ; and to point out, as far as it can be done, the boundary lines between their respective jurisdictions." The first Part of the book deals with the Roman conquest of England, the Anglo-Saxon period, the Norman conquest and its effects, the law and legal institutions down to the reign of Edward I, the history of the law of real and personal property, the origins of the bankruptcy law, procedure and pleading in Roman and English law, actions on the case, limitations of actions and prescription, the origins of Parliament. Though the topics dealt with may seem to be heterogeneous, this first Part of the book gives a large amount of valuable information upon the history both of legal institutions and legal doctrine from the earliest times. It covers in part the same ground as that covered by Reeves' history,[4] but the treatment of these topics is not so overburdened with technical minutiae, their history is at some points carried down to modern times, and the book is written in a much more interesting

---

[1] Since it was written before Allen's book on the Prerogatives, above 445, it does not make the mistake of defining folk land as land of the folk or common land ; he defines it correctly (p. 391) as land held, not by a written title, but by folk-rights ; but in his book on the history of equity, i 8, he subscribes to Allen's theory.

[2] The Equitable Jurisdiction of the Court of Chancery. Comprising the rise, progress, and final establishment of the modern jurisdiction of the Court of Chancery. To which is prefixed a concise summary of the Leading Principles of the Common Law, so far as regards Property, Real and Personal, and a short account of the Judicial Institutions of England ; vol. ii of the book, which was published in 1849, is a treatise on equity with special reference to equitable estates and interests, which, as the title page says, incorporates Maddock's treatise ; for this treatise, see below 577, 578.

[3] Preface.   [4] Vol. xii 413-415.

style. This Part is preparatory to the second Part which deals ably, systematically, and fully with the history of the equitable jurisdiction of the court of Chancery, with the original principles on which that equitable jurisdiction was based, with the various heads of the modern equitable jurisdiction, and with the obsolete jurisdiction of the court. This Part of Spence's book covers the ground so completely that it is still a standard authority upon the history of equity. Both Parts were a notable addition to the scanty literature on the history of English law ; for Spence had read and mastered all the principal authorities upon his subject—Roman, Anglo-Saxon, mediæval and modern.

Besides these books of Crabb and Spence there are a few books on special topics. C. P. Cooper,[1] the secretary of the second Record Commission, wrote an interesting account of some of the most important public records, of the Harleian and Cottonian collections, of the Year Books, and of early legal treatises ; and in his preface he called attention to the need for providing more ready access to the records, for their preservation, and for a school, like the Ecole des Chartes, for training young men in the use of records.[2] There is an interesting and learned collection of essays on topics in legal history by Ludon.[3] There is a history of the Inns of Court and Chancery by W. Herbert,[4] based upon Dugdale's *Origines Juridiciales*,[5] to which is prefixed a short historical sketch of the origins of the common law, the judges and lawyers, the local and central courts of common law, the different modes of trial, punishment, the law terms, and fines. The book concludes with an account of the Serjeants' Inns, and of the status of the serjeants.

There is a history of the Jews in England down to their expulsion in Edward I's reign, and from their re-entry in the seventeenth century, which contained an enquiry into their existing civil disabilities and an argument for their removal.[6]

---

[1] Above 260, 289, 290.

[2] An Account of the most important Public Records of Great Britain and the Publications of the Record Commissions, together with other miscellaneous, historical and antiquarian information. Compiled from various printed books and manuscripts ; for later books on this subject, see vol. ii 599-402.

[3] Tracts on various subjects in the Law and History of England (1810) ; the subjects of these tracts are constructive treason, the judgment in high treason, the right of succession to the Crown in the reign of Elizabeth, the constitution of Parliament in the reign of Henry III, *non obstante*, the use of French in our ancient laws and acts of state, the history of the law of Oleron.

[4] Antiquities of the Inns of Court and Chancery ; containing historical and descriptive sketches relative to their original foundation, customs, ceremonies, buildings, government, etc. With a concise History of the English Law (1804).

[5] Vol. vi 596.

[6] A History of the Establishment and Residence of the Jews in England with an Enquiry into their Civil Disabilities by J. E. Blunt (1830); for some accoun of the Jews, see vol. i 45-46.

The Chief Justices and other Lawyers

The list of the Chief Justices of the courts of King's Bench and Common Pleas, and of the Chief Barons of the Exchequer during this period will be found at the foot of this page.[1] Of the careers of some of them, and of some of the other lawyers of this period I shall say something ; and then I shall briefly sum up the effect of their work upon the development of the common law.

The two Chief Justices of the King's Bench during this period were Edward Law, Lord Ellenborough, who succeeded Lord Kenyon in 1802, and Charles Abbott, Lord Tenterden, who succeeded Lord Ellenborough in 1818.

Edward Law,[2] the fourth son of Edmund Law, bishop of Carlisle, was born at Salkeld November 16, 1750. He was educated at Charterhouse, and at Peterhouse, Cambridge, of which college his father was master. Even at this early period he showed the characteristics which distinguished him in later life—great intellectual powers, coupled with a power of vigorous expression and a love of sarcasm which gave great offence ; but, at the same time, an honesty of intention, which procured him many friends and admirers,[3] amongst whom were some of his future rivals at the bar and associates on the bench.[4] His talents and industry gave him the position of third wrangler and first gold medallist in classics in 1771, and in 1773 he was elected fellow of his college. In 1769 he had become a student at Lincoln's Inn. Following the advice and example of Buller, J.,[5] he began his legal apprenticeship with the study of the art of special pleading.

[1] *King's Bench*	*Common Pleas*	*Exchequer*
Lord Ellenborough	James Eyre	Archibald Macdonald
1802-1818	1793-1799	1793-1813
Lord Tenterden	Lord Eldon	Vicary Gibbs
1818-1832	1799-1801	1813
	Lord Alvanley	Alexander Thomson
	1801-1804	1813-1817
	James Mansfield	Richard Richards
	1804-1814	1817-1824
	Vicary Gibbs	William Alexander
	1814-1818	1824-1831
	Robert Dallas	Lord Lyndhurst
	1818-1824	1831-1834
	Lord Gifford	
	1824	
	William Best	
	1824-1829	
	Nicolas Tindal	
	1829-1846	

[2] Foss, Judges viii 317-324 ; Campbell, Lives of the Chief Justices iii 94-247 ; Brougham, Historical Sketches ii 174-194 ; D.N.B.

[3] See the account by Coxe, the future historian and archdeacon—his friend and contemporary—cited Campbell, op. cit. 97.

[4] Gibbs, Le Blanc, and Lawrence.

[5] For Buller see vol. xii 488-492.

From 1773 to 1775 he was a pupil of George Wood.[1] During those two years he made himself a master of this subject ; and between 1775 and 1780 he acquired a large practice as a special pleader. In 1780 he was called to the bar and at once got into a good practice in London and on the northern circuit. He took silk in 1787, and in the same year he held a junior brief for the Crown on the trial of Lord George Gordon and others for seditious libel.[2] He made his name as one of the best lawyers and advocates at the bar by his defence of Warren Hastings. He led for the defence and with him were two future judges—Dallas and Plumer.

It is probable that he owed this piece of good fortune to his brother-in-law Rumbold, who had held office in India. Hastings had wished Erskine to defend him. But the impeachment had become a party question, and Erskine belonged to the party whose leaders supported the impeachment. Erskine, therefore, could not be secured. In these circumstances, no better man than Law could have been chosen. He was an expert special pleader and therefore well fitted to expose the wordy and declamatory style in which the articles of the impeachment were drawn up.[3] He was an expert *nisi prius* lawyer and therefore well fitted to insist upon a due observance of the rules of evidence. He won his first victory when he resisted the unfair proposal of the managers to take each charge separately and pursue it to judgment. As he pointed out, in answering one charge the accused would be compelled to disclose to his adversaries the line of defence which he proposed to adopt in answering others. Throughout the impeachment there were many controversies as to the admission of evidence, largely because the managers claimed that the Lords ought not, in the trial of an impeachment, to be bound either by the ordinary rules of evidence or by the rules of pleading. In twenty out of twenty-three cases in which these points were referred to the judges the ruling was in Law's favour.[4] His opening speech for the defence disappointed Miss Burney. Law for once was nervous.[5] But she admitted that on the second day

---

[1] Created a Baron of the Exchequer in 1807, and the author of a book on Tithes, below 517, 581 ; Foss, Judges ix 53-54.

[2] 22 S.T. 175.

[3] See vol. vi 201-203.

[4] Townsend, op. cit. i 314.

[5] " Mr. Law was terrified exceedingly, and his timidity induced him so frequently to beg quarter from his antagonists, both for any blunders and any deficiencies, that I feel angry even with modest egoism. We (Windham and I) spoke of Mr. Law, and I expressed some dissatisfaction that such attackers should not have had able and more equal opponents. ' But do you not think Mr. Law spoke well,' cried Windham, ' clear, forcible ? ' ' Not forcible,' cried I—' I would not say *not clear*.' ' He was frightened,' said Windham, ' he might not do himself justice. I have heard him elsewhere, and been very well satisfied with him ; but he looked pale and alarmed, and his voice trembled '," Diary, cited Campbell, Chief Justices iii 124.

he made up for his deficiencies on the first day.[1] On the other hand, Scarlett says that " it had very great merit," [2] and though some authorities thought that Dallas's and Plumer's speeches were better,[3] there is no doubt that it was Law's conduct of the case which was mainly instrumental in securing the acquittal of Hastings.

His work as Hastings' counsel put him by the side of Erskine as one of the two leaders of the bar. Erskine was the better orator and advocate : Law was the better lawyer ; and was constantly retained in heavy mercantile cases.[4] And, in addition, he was no mean advocate. His somewhat rotund eloquence reminded men of Johnson, and his rough bluff manner in the courts and in the House of Commons were reminiscent of Thurlow. But, unlike Thurlow, he was a man of high moral and political principle, and took great pains to master his cases both at the bar and on the bench, and so he made himself a better lawyer than Thurlow ever was.[5]

Though he had become a leader at the bar promotion was slow. He had been given a silk gown in 1787, and had been made attorney-general of the county palatine of Lancaster in 1792. He had deserted the Whig party with Burke in 1791, and had held briefs in important state trials—the trial of Walker,[6] of Yorke,[7] and of the Earl of Thanet and others.[8] But no opportunity for further promotion arose till the resignation of Pitt in 1801. In that year Mitford,[9] the attorney-general, was made Lord Chancellor of Ireland, and Grant,[10] the solicitor-general, was made Master of the Rolls. Addington made Law attorney-general, and a seat was found for him in Parliament. As a member of Parliament he made his mark as a vigorous defender of the government. As attorney, his most notable prosecution was that of Governor Wall,[11] who was convicted and executed for the murder of a soldier whom, twenty years previously, he had irregularly sentenced to be flogged for mutiny, as the result of which flogging he had died. The feeling against Wall was so strong that the government dared not mitigate the sentence. But Campbell has given good reasons for doubting its justice.[12] However that may be, it cannot be said that Law pressed the case unfairly against the accused ; for he

---

[1] " In his second oration Mr. Law was far more animated and less frightened, and acquitted himself so as almost to merit as much commendation as, in my opinion, he had merited censure at the opening," Diary, cited Campbell, Chief Justices iii 124.

[2] Memoir of Lord Abinger 83.

[3] Campbell, Chief Justices iii 131.

[4] Townsend, op. cit. i 318-320.

[5] For Thurlow see vol. xii 314-327.

[6] (1794) 23 S.T. 1055 ; above 161.

[7] (1795) 25 S.T. 1003.

[8] (1799) 27 S.T. 822.

[9] Below 575, 576, 614.

[10] Below 578, 656-662.

[11] (1802) 28 S.T. 51.

[12] Chief Justices iii 149-152.

admitted that if the charge of mutiny was made out Wall's acts might be justified.[1]

Law only held the office of attorney-general for fourteen months. Kenyon,[2] the chief justice of the King's Bench, died in April 1802, and Law succeeded him. On his appointment to this office he was made a peer and took the title of Lord Ellenborough.

As a peer Ellenborough took a prominent part in the debates of the House of Lords. But his rough sarcastic manner, and his irascible temper, were not wholly pleasing to his brother peers. " His arguments were enforced with extraordinary power, and seemed to be urged without preparation ; but his temper being too easily ruffled he was apt to use expressions the violence of which rather astonished than convinced that august assembly; and their coarseness and intemperance frequently called down upon him deserved castigation."[3] On one occasion on which he had violently attacked Lord Holland he was answered by him in a tone of polite and cutting sarcasm which delighted his hearers. " Lord Holland," said Mackintosh, " spoke with the calm dignity of a magistrate, and Lord Ellenborough with the coarse violence of a demagogue."[4]

In 1806, on Pitt's death, the ministry of " all the talents " was formed.[5] Addington, now Lord Sidmouth, joined the ministry, and it was stipulated that he should bring in one of his friends. He wanted to bring in Ellenborough as Chancellor ; but Ellenborough (like Mansfield before him[6]) wisely declined this honour. Though he could not persuade Ellenborough to come in as Chancellor, he insisted upon his being given a seat in the cabinet ; and Ellenborough, remembering perhaps the precedent of Mansfield,[7] saw no harm in accepting that position. His view was that there was no more harm in a judge being a member of the Cabinet than of being a member of the Privy Council.[8] But it is obvious that this view rested upon an antiquated and quite unreal view of the modern position and functions of these two bodies. By 1806 the Cabinet had definitely emerged as the body through which the executive government of the state was conducted. It was clearly undesirable that a man who had, as cabinet minister, advised or concurred in a decision to take action in the courts,

---

[1] 28 S.T. at pp. 63-64. [2] For Kenyon see vol. xii 576-583.
[3] Foss, Judges viii 321. [4] Townsend, op. cit. i 331-333.
[5] Above 176. [6] Vol. xii 473 and n. 1. [7] Ibid 473.
[8] He wrote to his brother on the occasion of the motion of censure against him in both Houses of Parliament : " If any vote of the kind intended should be carried it is my determination to resign my situation as a Privy Councillor ; with the duties of which I shall consider the vote (if it has any meaning at all) as pronouncing my judicial function as incompatible. The vote, if it comes at all, must be under an entire ignorance or misunderstanding of the history of the country and the precedents respecting the situation I fill, its proper and usual duties, and the political duties which the Legislature and the Sovereign have from time to time in the most anxious and important periods connected therewith," cited Campbell, Chief Justices iii 185-186.

should sit as judge in the proceedings taken as a result of that decision.[1] Ellenborough was surprised at the storm aroused by his acceptance of a seat in the Cabinet. The government defeated the motions of censure, but the experiment was never again tried ; and, later, it is said that Ellenborough himself saw that it was hardly defensible.[2]

This episode illustrates Ellenborough's main defect as a statesman—his conviction—as deeply rooted as Eldon's[3]—that in a changing age it was possible to stand obstinately on the ancient ways, and his opposition to all the changes in the law which new ideas and new conditions were making necessary. It is true that one Act stands to his credit—the Act which made a much needed addition to the criminal law as to offences against the person.[4] Its severity has been criticized ; but having regard to the prevailing views as to the best means of suppressing crime, with which Ellenborough fully agreed, this defect was inevitable, and some of its provisions are not wholly indefensible.[5] We have seen that he was the strongest opponent of all Romilly's attempts to mitigate the severity of the penal code.[6] Other necessary changes in the law were also opposed by him, often on very flimsy grounds. Instances are his opposition to Catholic emancipation,[7] to the bills to make real property liable for the simple contract debts of a deceased person,[8] and the insolvent debtors' Acts.[9] We have seen that the vested interests which officials paid by fees had in resisting reforms was one of the most serious obstacles to reform.[10] Ellenborough, Romilly tells us, " was extremely averse to every alteration in the fees of the officers of the courts, and very much alive to everything that had a tendency to such kind of reforms." [11] It followed that he was

---

[1] Above 176.　　　　　　　　　　　　　　[2] Campbell, Chief Justices iii 188-189.
[3] Above 181, 189, 222 ;　below 605, 607, 608, 610.
[4] 43 George III c. 58 ;　above 390.
[5] " It can scarcely be contended with success, that the criminal who has evidenced his murderous intent by the use of deadly weapons, but whose malice has been defeated by the providence of God, ought not to suffer the heaviest penalty which the law can impose on persons convicted of such a guilty purpose. In no case could a prisoner be convicted under this Act, where the death, if death had ensued, would not have amounted to the crime of murder," Townsend, op. cit. i 337-338.
[6] Above 279-281 ; Romilly, Memoirs (ed. 1842) ii 151-152, 201 ; for his controversy with Romilly as to the effect of Madan's book in producing a greater severity in the administration of criminal law, see vol. xi 564.
[7] Campbell, Chief Justices iii 193-194 ;　Townsend, op. cit. i 336.
[8] Romilly, Memoirs ii 376 ; but at one time he was not so decidedly opposed to it, see ibid 38-39.　　　　　　　　[9] Ibid 316-317, 323-324 ; above 261, 377, 378.
[10] Above 307 ; Campbell, Chief Justices iii 156.
[11] Romilly, Memoirs ii 123 ; cp. Campbell, op. cit. iii 156 n. for an instance of this aversion ; the question was whether money paid into court was liable to poundage ; " I was counsel in the cause," says Campbell, " and threw him into a furious passion by strenuously resisting the demand. The poundage was to go into his own pocket—being payable to the chief clerk—an office held in trust for him " ; but Campbell adds, " if he was in any degree influenced by this consideration, I make no doubt he was wholly unconscious of it.''

prepared to resist very many of the most necessary procedural reforms on this wholly inadequate ground.

At the same time it is well to remember that his opposition to legislative change sprang from an honest, though mistaken belief in its inexpediency. He was a man of strong convictions and never hesitated to express and act on those convictions even though they ran counter to the policy of his party. He voted for the conviction of Melville.[1] He supported the abolition of the slave trade.[2] He tried to stop a bill to give further compensation to the family of the Duke of Atholl for the cesser of their rights in the Isle of Man, because he regarded it as a " gross job." [3] It was because he was a man of strong and honest convictions, opposed to anything that savoured in the least of dishonesty or chicanery, and because he was both a learned lawyer and a skilled practitioner in all sides of a barrister's practice, from the drawing of pleadings to the conduct as leader of the heaviest cases, that his achievement as a Chief Justice was as great as his achievement as a statesman was small.

These qualities made Ellenborough a real chief in his court. Lord Campbell, who practised before him, who feared him,[4] and who was sometimes oppressed by him,[5] says :[6]

Not only had he the incorruptibilitynow common to all English judges, but he was inspired by a strong passion for justice, and he could undergo any degree of labour in performing what he considered his duty. He possessed a strong voice, an energetic manner, and all physical requisites for fixing attention and making an impression upon the minds of others. I must likewise state as a great merit that he could cope with and gain an ascendancy over all the counsel who addressed him, and that he never had a favourite—dealing out with much impartiality his rebuffs and sarcasms. The defects in his judicial aptitude were a bad temper, an arrogance of nature, too great a desire to gain a reputation by despatch, and an excessive leaning to punishment.

[1] " The sentence of the Lords in Melville's case may yet be deferred for some time. Ellenborough and Eldon are battling it most furiously. The former said on Thursday night that something laid down as law by the latter was ' neither law nor common sense '," Life of Campbell i 183.

[2] Campbell, Chief Justices iii 189-192 ; and on this matter he had another sharp altercation with Eldon.

[3] Townsend, op. cit. i 329-331.

[4] " I *funk* before Ellenborough as much as ever. I almost despair of ever acquiring a sufficient degree of confidence before him to put me in proper possession of my faculties," Life of Lord Campbell i 295.

[5] " He still has particular pleasure in discharging my rule or in making one absolute against me," ibid 315—though he admits that his manner to others was much the same, ibid ; see ibid 310 for an account of an occasion when he managed to score off the Chief Justice.

[6] Lives of the Chief Justices iii 154 ; Scarlett says that he carried his love of sarcasm too far on the bench, Memoirs of Lord Abinger 83 ; but, he says, the best policy when arguing a case before him was to let him discover its strongest points for himself ; for he opposed the argument as it proceeded, but if the evidence disclosed facts not put forward at counsel's opening, his sagacity in discovering what had escaped the counsel achieved a triumph which flattered his vanity and gave him something like the interest of a parent in the cause," ibid.

This estimate of Ellenborough's merits and defects as a judge agrees substantially with that of Brougham, who said that he was apt to make up his mind without a full hearing of the case, so that it was said that whilst the defect of the Chancery was *oyer sans terminer*, the defect of the King's Bench was *terminer sans oyer*.[1] This defect, as Brougham pointed out, was not so apparent in banc, where Ellenborough was assisted by such able puisnes as Lawrence, Bayley, Le Blanc, Abbott, Dampier, and Holroyd.[2] But it was apparent at *nisi prius* where he sat alone :

There a false step is easily made, and it may not be easily retraced. If the judge's powers have prevented a moderately experienced practitioner from taking an objection in due time, or from urging it with sufficient directness, his client may often be told that he is too late when he seeks to be relieved against the consequences of this mishap. So where a verdict has been obtained against the justice of the case, and the judge through the impatience of his nature, has not disapproved it, the injury is remediless, because a new trial will in most instances be refused, or if granted, can only be obtained on the payment of all costs.[3]

Ellenborough's striking personality, his voice, his manner, his tempers, his power of sarcasm, coupled with his great legal knowledge, made him as formidable to brother lawyers out of court as he was in court. " I remember," says Brougham,[4]

being told by a learned serjeant, that at the table of Serjeants' Inn, where the judges meet their brethren of the coif to dine, the etiquette was, in those days, never to say a word after the Chief Justice, nor ever begin any topic of conversation ; he was treated with fully more than the obsequious deference shown at court to the sovereign himself.

Ellenborough's too great tendency to severity, his stern code of morals which led him to abominate anything that savoured of fraud, and his strong political prepossessions, sometimes made him an unsatisfactory judge in criminal cases. In some of the many prosecutions for libel instituted by Vicary Gibbs the attorney-general,[5] his summing up was in effect a speech for the prosecution—one notorious instance was the case of Leigh Hunt[6] in which Brougham distinguished himself by securing an acquittal,[7] and another was the case of William Hone in 1817, one of the last cases which he tried, in which again his efforts to get a

---

[1] Historical Sketches ii 184-185.   [2] Ibid 185.

[3] Brougham, Historical Sketches ii 185.

[4] Ibid 187 ; here again we are reminded of the awe with which Thurlow was regarded by his contemporaries, vol. xii 318, 321.

[5] Below 536, 537, 538.   [6] (1811) 31 S.T. 367 at pp. 408-414.

[7] Campbell said, " Brougham acquired great *éclat* to-day by his defence of the Hunts. His speech was the best that has been made in the King's Bench these seven years, and from the extraordinary luck of getting a verdict against the Attorney-General and the Chief Justice in a case of libel he is a made man," Life i 226-227.

conviction failed.[1]   In the case of Lord Cochrane in 1814,[2]
Campbell says that his hatred of fraud led him unconsciously to
lean against the accused,[3] but Atlay has proved that his criticism
is not justified.[4] It is certain, however, that the severity of the
sentence was generally condemned[5]—it was, says Brougham,[6] a
sentence " which at once secured Lord Cochrane's re-election for
Westminster when the Commons expelled him upon his conviction, and abolished for ever the punishment of the pillory, in
all but one excepted case—perjury." But Brougham, though he
admitted that Ellenborough sometimes allowed " the strength
of his political feelings to break forth, and to influence the tone
and temper of his observations," said that he never " knowingly
deviated one hair's breadth from justice in the discharge of his
office." [7] His summing up in the case of Perry, the editor of *The
Morning Chronicle*, is a model of impartiality, and secured an
acquittal.[8]

In the trial of civil cases Ellenborough's intellectual defects
were not so apparent, and the strong points of his intellectual
qualities were more apparent. The Napoleonic wars and the
repercussion of the Berlin and Milan decrees on the one side,
and of the orders in Council on the other, enormously increased
the commercial business of the court of King's Bench. The result
was that, as Campbell says,[9] " more new questions arose between
underwriters and merchants, between shipowners and shippers
of goods, between foreign consignors and English factors, in
a single year than in a century of peace or regular warfare."
At the same time the suspension of cash payments, the fluctuations in the value of money, and the speculative trading which
these fluctuations encouraged, gave rise to many bankruptcies,
and much consequent litigation. A large part of this business
was dealt with by Ellenborough in the sittings of the court
at the Guildhall after the end of term.   That business was,

---

[1] Campbell, Chief Justices iii 223-225.

[2] There was a motion for a new trial by Lord Cochrane which was refused on
the technical ground that the other persons convicted with him had not attended
(1814) 3 M. and S. 10 note ; and also a motion in arrest of judgment which was
also refused, R. V. De Berenger, ibid 67.

[3] Campbell, Chief Justices iii 218-220.

[4] The Victorian Chancellors ii (1888-1891) and his book on the trial of Cochrane
there cited.

[5] Romilly, Memoirs ii 342.   [6] Historical Sketches ii 194.

[7] Historical Sketches ii 192 ; Brougham was counsel for Cochrane, and he says,
" none of us entertained any doubt that he had acted impartially, according to his
conscience, and had tried it as he would have tried any other cause in which neither
political nor personal feelings could have interfered. Our only complaint was his
Lordship's refusal to adjourn after the prosecutor's case closed, and his requiring
us to enter upon our defence at so late an hour, past nine o'clock, that the adjourn-
ment took place at midnight, and before we called our witnesses," ibid 193.

[8] (1810) 31 S.T. at pp. 363-368 ; cp. Campbell, Chief Justices iii 196-201.

[9] Life i 214.

Campbell says, "ten times greater than when Lord Mansfield was Chief Justice."[1] Ellenborough, helped by a very able bar, speedily disposed of these cases ;[2] and Campbell, who reported many of them and who takes credit to himself for suppressing reports of obviously wrong decisions,[3] says :[4]

Probably no other judge than Lord Ellenborough could have supported such a burden as was now cast upon him . . . . He was not only laborious and indefatigable, but he was acute, rapid, bold, decisive, ratiocinative, and eloquent. He never shirked any point that was raised before him, decided it without copiously and pointedly giving his reasons. He had some barbarisms of pronunciation which were supposed to have been brought from Cumberland and which he never attempted to correct, and he sometimes became quaint in trying to be forcible ; but generally speaking his diction was forcible, nervous and classical. He had likewise a rich fund of humour and an uncommon power of sarcasm, which often flavoured his judgments, and gave life and animation to the proceedings of the court in which he presided.

The decisions of these commercial cases, and the decisions of himself and his very able colleagues on the many cases, commercial and otherwise, which came before them in *banc* or at *nisi prius*, made a very considerable contribution to many branches of the common law—civil and criminal. No doubt some of the credit is due to his colleagues ; but to him must be given the largest share of that credit. As I have said, he was a real chief and generally gave the leading and most important judgment. Let us look at one or two of these judgments which illustrate Ellenborough's qualities as a lawyer, and the contribution which he made to the development of the law.

Several of Ellenborough's decisions on matters of *public law* are important, and some have taken rank as leading cases.

---

[1] Life i 214.

[2] " The state of the bar, and the distribution of business in Lord Ellenborough's time made it much easier for him to give the despatch. . . . In his time the whole City business was in the hands of Gibbs, Garrow, and Park ; with occasionally, as in the case of the Baltic risk, the intervention of Topping ; and it was a main object with them all to facilitate the despatch of business. This they effected by at once giving up all but the arguable points of law, on which they immediately took the judge's opinion ; and the maintainable questions of fact, on which they went to jury. Fifteen or twenty important causes were thus disposed of in a morning, more to the satisfaction of the court and the benefit of counsel than to the contentment of the parties or their attorneys," Brougham, Historical Sketches ii 185-186 ; Brougham testifies to Topping's honourable character, ibid 186 n. 1, and Campbell tells a story of how he stood up to Gibbs, but he adds, that drink led to his early death—" his custom always in the afternoon was to drink a bottle of port wine, and sometimes more. I recollect a great City attorney saying to me : ' A very remarkable thing happened to me last night ; I found Mr. Topping at consultation quite sober '," Life i 219-220.

[3] Ibid 215 ; vol. xii 158 n. 1.

[4] Life i 215 ; Scarlett said that on " the very last day he sat at the Guildhall, when he was labouring under great infirmity and weakness, he tried seventeen defended cases, whereas during the week before the three puisne judges who sat for him alternately in the same place Bailey tried seven, Abbott five, and Holroyd three a day," Memoirs of Lord Abinger 85.

One of the most important is *Burdett v. Abbott*[1] in which the right of the House of Commons to commit for contempt was upheld after a most elaborate argument. Ellenborough showed that this right was sanctioned by precedent ; that it was necessary to vindicate the dignity of Parliament ; that it would be absurd to suppose that a power which belongs to the superior courts of law should not belong to the High Court of Parliament ; and that it included a power to break outer doors to effect an arrest. At the same time he admitted that the courts might have jurisdiction to enquire into a committal for a cause which was not in fact a contempt and was contrary to law.[2] It was not till the cases of *Stockdale v. Hansard*[3] and *The Sheriff of Middlesex*[4] that this sort of case came before the courts, and that an opportunity was given to them to distinguish between the circumstances in which the House of Commons could, and in which it could not, withdraw a case from their jurisdiction on the ground of privilege.[5] The case of *Nicholson. v. Mouncey*[6] applied the principle of *Lane v. Cotton*[7] to the captain of a ship of war. He could not, like the master of a merchant ship, be made liable for the negligence of a subordinate officer. Both the captain and the subordinate officer were servants of the Crown, so that the relation of employer and employee did not exist between them.

The case of *Viveash v. Becker*[8] decides that as a consul is not entitled to the diplomatic privileges of an ambassador and his staff, he could therefore be arrested on mesne process. Ellenborough came to this conclusion after a survey of the relevant authorities both in English and in international law, and of the resulting inconveniences if the law were otherwise. He said :[9]

I cannot help thinking that the Act of Parliament [10] which mentions only " ambassadors and public ministers " and which was passed at a time when it was an object studiously to comprehend all kinds of public ministers entitled to these privileges, must be considered as declaratory

---

[1] (1811) 14 East 1 at pp. 136-158.

[2] " If a commitment appeared to be for a contempt of the House of Commons generally, I would neither in a case in that Court, nor of any other of the Superior Courts, inquire further ; but if it did not profess to commit for contempt, but for some matter appearing on the return, which could by no reasonable intendment be considered as a contempt of the Court committing, but a ground of commitment palpably and evidently arbitrary, unjust, and contrary to every principle of positive law, or national justice ; I say that in the case of such a commitment . . . we must look at it and act upon it as justice may require from whatever Court it may profess to have proceeded," 14 East at pp. 150-151.

[3] (1839) 1 Ad. and E. 1.   [4] (1840) 11 Ad. and E. 273.

[5] Vol. vi 271-272 ; cp. vol. i 393-394.   [6] (1812) 15 East 384.

[7] (1701) 1 Ld. Raym. 646 ; cp. Whitfield v. Lord le Despencer (1778) 2 Cowp. 754 ; vol. vi 267-268 ; vol. x 655.

[8] (1814) 3 M. and S. 284.   [9] At p. 298.

[10] 7 Anne c. 12 ; vol. x 370-371.

not only of what the law of nations is, but of the extent to which that law is to be carried. It appears to me that a different construction would lead to enormous inconveniences, for there is a power of creating vice-consuls; and they too must have similar privileges. Thus a consul might appoint a vice-consul in every port to be armed with the same immunities, and be the means of creating an exemption from arrest indirectly which the Crown could not grant directly. The mischief of this would be enormous.

He said nevertheless that " if we saw clearly that the law of nations was in favour of the privilege, it would be afforded to the defendant and it would be our duty rather to extend than to narrow it "[1]—thus recognizing the principle stated by Mansfield that international law must be regarded as part of the law of England.[2] But since this immunity was not accorded by international law to consuls, and since there was no reason to think it was accorded by English law, it could not be allowed. In the case of *R. v. Creevey*[3] Ellenborough followed the case of *R. v. Lord Abingdon,*[4] and held that a member of Parliament who publishes in a newspaper a libellous speech spoken in Parliament can be convicted of libel. The correctness of this decision has been questioned, on the ground that a speech, published as this was, without malice and only to give information to the member's constituents ought to be privileged.[5] Whether or not the courts would take this view of the law is uncertain. But it is clear that to allow such a privilege might be dangerous, because such a speech is an *ex parte* statement, and is therefore very different from the report of a debate which states both sides of the case. For that reason it does not fall within the *ratio decidendi* of *Wason v. Walter,*[6] in which it was held that fair reports by newspapers of debates in Parliament and fair comments thereon were privileged. In the cases of *O'Mealey v. Wilson*[7] and *Alciator v. Smith*[8] the doctrine as to what facts would give a person an enemy " character " was elucidated.[9]

It would be impossible to set out in detail the many rules of *commercial law* which were created, elucidated, or elaborated in the hundreds of judgments which Ellenborough gave on this topic. All that can be done is to give one or two illustrations. In the case of *Bennett v. Farnell*[10] he held that a bill of exchange made payable to a fictitious person or order was void, and was

---

[1] 2 M. and S. at p. 298. [2] Vol. x 372-373.
[3] (1813) 1 M. and S. 273. [4] (1794) 1 Esp. 226; vol. xii 581.
[5] Davison v. Duncan (1857) 7 El. and Bl. 229, 233 *per* Lord Campbell, C.J.; cp. Campbell, Lives of the Chief Justices iii 167-168; with this criticism Cockburn, C.J. agreed, Wason v. Walter (1868) L.R. 4 Q.B. at p. 95.
[6] (1868) L.R. 4 Q.B. 73. [7] (1808) 1 Camp. 482.
[8] (1812) 3 Camp. 245.
[9] For the history of the law as to enemy character see vol. ix 99-104.
[10] (1807) 1 Camp. 130, 180.

therefore not payable either to the order of the drawer or to the bearer, unless the fact that the payee was fictitious was known to the acceptor. That was the law till it was altered by the Bills of Exchange Act, 1882.[1] The case of *Feise v. Wray*[2] decides that an agent who buys goods for his principal in his own name, and who consigns them to his principal, can stop *in transitu* as against his principal, on the principal's bankruptcy. The rule that in such a case the agent has this and also the other rights of an owner has been followed in subsequent cases.[3] In the case of *Wilkinson v. King*[4] Ellenborough held that a wharfinger in Southwark who, without authority, sold goods entrusted to him, could pass no property to a purchaser. A wharfinger as such has no authority to sell, nor could such a sale be considered to be a sale in market overt within the custom of London. On the other hand in the case of *Pickering v. Busk*,[5] he held that where a purchaser had put goods stored in a wharf into the name of a broker, a sale by the broker passed a good title to a purchaser, because a broker, whose ordinary business it is to sell, has an implied authority to sell.

Not all Ellenborough's decisions on points of commercial law have been followed. His decision in the case of *Godsall v. Boldero*[6] that a contract of life insurance is, like a contract of marine or fire insurance, a contract of indemnity, so that, if no loss is suffered by the death, the insured cannot recover, was never acquiesced in by insurers,[7] and was overruled in the case of *Dalby v. India and London Life Assurance Co.*[8] That case established the proposition that a contract of life insurance is not a contract of indemnity, but as Parke B. said,[9] " a contract to pay a certain sum of money on the death of a person, in consideration of the due payment of a certain annuity for his life." In the case of *Conway v. Gray*[10] and other cases Ellenborough held that a foreigner, who insures in this country, is not entitled to abandon when an embargo is laid on the property by his own government, because his assent is implied to the act of his government, so that the embargo is his act. This

---

[1] 45, 46 Victoria c. 61 § 7 subsect. 3; Bank of England v. Vagliano [1891]. A.C. at p. 160 *per* Lord Macnaghten.

[2] (1802) 3 East 93.

[3] Falk v. Fletcher (1865) 18 C.B.N.S. 403, at pp. 412-413; cp. the remarks of Martin B. in Ireland v. Livingston (1870) L.R. 5 Q.B. at p. 535, and of Brett, M.R. in Cassaboglou v. Gibb (1883) 11 Q.B.D. at pp. 803-804.

[4] (1809) 2 Camp. 335.

[5] (1812) 15 East 38 at p. 42; cp. the remarks of Blackburn, J. in Cole v. North Western Bank (1875) L.R. 10 C.P. at pp. 364-365.

[6] (1807) 9 East 72; the insurance in this case was by a creditor of Pitt; his debts were paid by the nation, and it was held that the creditor could not recover on his policy.

[7] 15 C.B. at p. 392 *per* Parke, B.

[8] (1854) 15 C.B. 265.

[9] At p. 387.

[10] (1809) 10 East 536.

is a very shadowy reason; and it was questioned in later cases,[1] and not followed by the Supreme Court of the United States.[2] As Erle, C.J. said in the case of *Aubert v. Gray* in which the doctrine was overruled,[3]

The assertion that the act of the government is the act of each subject of that government, is never really true. In representative governments it may have a partial semblance of truth, but in despotic governments it is without that semblance.

Lord Ellenborough decided several important cases in the *law of contract*. The cases of *Wain v. Warlters*[4] and *Boydell v. Drummond*[5] are leading cases on the interpretation of S.4 of the Statute of Frauds. In the case of *Dry v. Boswell*[6] he distinguished between an agreement to share profits which constitutes a partnership and an agreement to share gross returns which does not. In the case of *Adams v. Lindsell*[7] he held, in effect, that when a contract is made by post, acceptance is complete when the letter of acceptance is posted. That was a case where the letter making the offer was delayed because the offeror had misdirected it. But the main principle of the case, that the posting of a letter of acceptance makes the contract,[8] has been approved and applied to the case of a lost letter.[9] In the case of *Squires v. Whisken*[10] Ellenborough refused to hear an action on a wager on a cock-fight. His judgment illustrates the shifts to which the judges were driven to discountenance such actions before all wagers were made void by the Gaming Act of 1845.[11] He said:[12]

Cock-fighting must be considered a barbarous diversion, which ought not to be encouraged or sanctioned in a court of justice. I believe that cruelty to these animals, in throwing at them, forms part of the dehortatory charge of judges to grand juries and it makes little difference

[1] See the cases cited in argument in Aubert v. Gray (1862) 3 B. and S. at pp. 176-177; as it is there pointed out Lord Ellenborough's own decision in Simeon v. Bazett (1813) 2 M. and S. 94 is hardly consistent with his decision in Conway v. Gray, and still less with the decision of the Exchequer Chamber in the same case *sub. nom* Bazett v. Meyer (1814) 5 Taunt. at p. 829.

[2] See Aubert v. Gray (3 B. and S.), 163, 177, where counsel cite Francis v. Ocean Insurance Co. (6 Cowen, 404; 2 Wend, 64); see also Kent's Commentaries, Vol. III, 292.

[3] Ibid at p. 182; the principle of this decision was approved by the House of Lords, Janson v. Driefontein Consolidated Mines [1902] A.C. 484.

[4] (1804) 5 East 10.   [5] (1809) 11 East 142.

[6] (1808) 1 Camp. 329.   [7] (1818) 1 B. and Ald. 681.

[8] It was argued that the offeror ought not to be bound till the letter of acceptance was received; to that the court said, "if that were so no contract could ever be completed by post. For if the defendants were not bound by their offer when accepted by the plaintiffs till the answer was received, then the plaintiffs ought not to be bound till after they had received the notification that the defendants had received their answer and assented to it. And so it might go on *ad infinitum*," ibid at p. 683.

[9] Household Fire Insurance Co. v. Grant (1879) 4 Ex. Div. 216 at pp. 219-220.

[10] (1811) 3 Camp. 140.   [11] 8, 9, Victoria c. 109 § 18.   [12] At p. 141.

whether they are lacerated by sticks and stones, or by the bills of each other. There is likewise another principle on which, I think, an action on such wagers cannot be maintained. They tend to the degradation of courts of justice. It is impossible to be engaged in ludicrous enquiries of this sort, consistently with that dignity which it is essential to the public welfare that a court of justice should always preserve.

Some of Ellenborough's decisions on the *law of Tort* are equally important—though the correctness of many of his dicta has been questioned. In the case of *Carr v. Hood*[1] he stated the basic principle which, in an action for libel, underlies the defence of fair comment. He said :[2]

Every man who publishes a book commits himself to the judgment of the public, and anyone may comment on his performance. If the commentator does not step aside from the work, or introduce fiction for the purpose of condemnation, he exercises a fair and legitimate right.

In the case of *Crockford v. Winter*[3] Ellenborough emphasized the purely common law character of the action to recover back money obtained by fraud, and resisted the invitation of counsel to regard it as an equitable action designed to give effect to the actual rights of the parties.[4] In the case of *Pickering v. Rudd*[5] he denied that trespass lay for interference " with the column of air superincumbent on a close,"[6] so that it would not lie for fixing a board which projected over the close or for the passage of a balloon. In 1865 Blackburn, J. doubted the correctness of this statement,[7] and his view is approved by Pollock[8]—" unless indeed it can be said that the scope of possible trespass is limited by that of possible effective possession, which might be the most reasonable rule, and is in effect embodied in the Air Navigation Act, 1920." On the other hand, so far as the case decided that a person has a right to cut away branches overhanging his land,[9] it has been followed.[10] His decision in the case of *Carrington v. Taylor*,[11] in which he perhaps extended the principle laid down by Holt, C.J. in the case *Keeble v. Hickergill*,[12] has been criticized and perhaps overruled,[13]—though on the facts it is quite possible that the acts of the defendant amounted to a nuisance.[14] His ruling in the case of *Vicars v.*

---

[1] (1808) 1 Camp. 355.   [2] At p. 358.   [3] (1807) 1 Camp. 124.
[4] At p. 128 ; cp. Sinclair v. Brougham [1914] A.C. at p. 455 *per* Lord Sumner.
[5] (1815) 4 Camp. 219.
[6] At p. 220 ; but case might lie if damage were proved, ibid 221.
[7] Kenyon v. Hart (1865) 6 B. and S. at p. 252.
[8] Torts (14th ed.) 278.
[9] Pickering v. Rudd (1815) 1 Stark. 56.
[10] Lemmon v. Webb (1894) 3 Ch. at pp. 12-13; [1895] A.C. 1.
[11] (1809) 2 Camp. 259 ; 11 East 571.
[12] (1707) 11 Mod. 74, 130, 11 East 574 note ; vol. viii 426.
[13] Allen v. Flood [1898] A.C. at pp. 103, 135-136.
[14] Pollock, Torts (14th ed.) 268 n. (*z*).

Wilcock[1] that the damage recoverable for a tort must be both the legal and the natural consequence of the act has, as we have seen, been disapproved.[2] We have seen too that his ill-considered dictum in the case of *Baker v. Bolton* [3] that " in a civil court the death of a human being could not be complained of as an injury " has been a source of much difficulty and some very dubious law.[4] Similarly his statement in the case of *Bilbie v. Lumley* [5] in which, following a statement of Buller, J. in *Lowery v. Bourdieu,*[6] he said that " every man must be cognizant of the law," [7] has caused considerable difficulties. It was acutely criticized soon after it was made by W. D. Evans ; [8] and with this criticism Lord Wright is in wholehearted agreement. He says :

whatever force may be given to it in criminal law it clearly is not true as a general proposition. It is not only against principle and early authority but also against common sense, and has been consistently disavowed by great judges, though often repeated by some who should have known better. The result has been great confusion in the law relating to transfers by mistake of law, so that the actual position in England would be difficult precisely to define.[9]

I have already said something of one of the modifications made by equity to the generality of the principle as stated by Buller and Ellenborough.[10]

Ellenborough had never been a conveyancer or made a special study of *The Land Law.* It is said that on one occasion Preston, the famous conveyancer, was briefed to argue a case on the construction of a will, which involved points of real property law. Preston, says Campbell,[11]

having not yet exhausted the Year Books, when the shades of evening were closing in upon him, applied to know when it would *be their Lordships' pleasure* to hear the remainder of his argument. Lord Ellenborough replied—Mr. Preston, we are bound to hear you out, and I hope we shall do so on Friday—but alas ! pleasure has been long out of the question.

But his judgments show that he was a competent real property lawyer. For instance his elaborate judgment in the case of *Roe v. Archbishop of York,*[12] which turned on the effect of the surrender of a lease, is a decision which showed a good knowledge of the authorities, and a power of interpreting them in such

---

[1] (1806) 8 East 1. [2] Vol. viii 358.
[3] (1808) 1 Camp. 493. [4] Vol. iii 330, 333-336, 676-677.
[5] (1802) 2 East 469. [6] (1780) 2 Dougl. at pp. 451, 454.
[7] 2 East at p. 472.
[8] Pothier on obligations ii App. No. xviii ; Essay on Mistakes in Law.
[9] Legal Essays and Addresses 43 ; and with this view Professor Winfield agrees, L.Q.R. liv 536.
[10] Vol. xii 546. [11] Lives of the Chief Justices iii 238.
[12] (1805) 6 East 85.

a way that effect was given to the intentions of the parties. On the other hand, we have seen that his decision in the case of *Elwes v. Maw*,[1] as to what could be regarded as tenants' fixtures in the case of agricultural tenants, worked substantial injustice which has called for the intervention of the Legislature.[2]

Ellenborough decided one or two important points in the law of *husband and wife*. In the case of *Rodney v. Chambers*[3] he held with some reluctance that a covenant by a husband to pay to trustees an annuity as a maintenance for his wife in case they separated, was valid. He said :[4]

If it were now a new question, whether any contract could by law be made which tended to facilitate the separation of husband and wife, I should have thought that it would have fallen in better with the general policy of the law to have prohibited any such contract : but they are now become inveterate in the laws.

Lord Ellenborough's doubts were confirmed in 1819 by the case of *Durant v. Titley*[5] in which the Exchequer Chamber, reversing a decision of the court of Exchequer, held that an agreement for future separation was void. But there is no doubt that the older cases,[6] which upheld the validity of an agreement for an immediate separation then contemplated by the parties, are correct.[7] On the other hand, he held in a subsequent case arising out of the same separation,[8] that since under the deed of separation there were provisos which recognized the marital relation as still existing, it did not debar the husband from bringing an action for criminal conversation against a man who had committed adultery with his wife. He distinguished this case from the case where there was a separation which showed that the husband had abandoned all claims to the *consortium* of his wife, and was therefore debarred from bringing this action.[9] We have seen that his strict construction of a section of Lord Hardwicke's Marriage Act, which in effect rendered the marriage of an illegitimate minor impossible, was the cause of a modification of the law.[10]

Many of Ellenborough's rulings on the *law of evidence* helped to develop the law. This development was, as Professor Wigmore

---

[1] (1802) 3 East 38.　　　　[2] Vol. vii 286.
[3] (1802) 2 East 283.　　　　[4] At p. 293.
[5] (1819) 7 Price 577 ; cp. Westmeath v. Westmeath (1830) 1 Dow. and Cl. 519.
[6] Vol. vi 646.
[7] Wilson v. Wilson (1848) 1 H.L.C. 538 (1854) 5 H.L.C. 40.
[8] Chambers v. Caulfield (1805) 6 East 244.
[9] Weedon v. Timbrell (1793) 5 T.R. 357.
[10] Priestley v. Hughes (1809) 11 East 1 ; above 421.

has pointed out, the result of the practice of reporting *nisi prius* decisions. He says :[1]

In the *nisi prius* reports of Peake, Espinasse, and Campbell, centering round the quarter century from 1790 to 1815, there are probably more rulings upon evidence than in all the prior reports of two centuries. In this development the dominant influence is plain ; it was the increase of printed reports of *Nisi Prius* rulings. This was at first the cause, and afterwards the self-multiplying effect, of the detailed development of the rules. Hitherto, upon countless details, the practice had varied greatly on the different circuits ; moreover, it had rested largely in the memory of the experienced leaders of the trial bar and in the momentary discretion of the judges. In both respects it therefore lacked fixity, and was not amenable to tangible authority. These qualities it now rapidly gained. As soon as *Nisi Prius* reports multiplied and became available to all, the circuits must be reconciled, the rulings once made and recorded must be followed, and these precedents must be open to the entire profession to be invoked. There was, so to speak, a sudden precipitation of all that had hitherto been suspended in solution.

As we have seen,[2] and as Professor Wigmore points out,[3] the result was the appearance of new books on evidence in which the results of these cases were summarized. Ellenborough gave many such rulings of which I will give two illustrations. In the case of *Doe v. Thomas*[4] he decided the question when evidence of reputation was admissible, which, says the reporter, " has been *vexata questio* for many years in Westminster Hall ;"[5] and in the case of *R. v. Johnson*[6] there was a ruling as to the admissibility of certain letters in the handwriting of the defendant to prove that he was accessory to the publication of a libel in Cobbett's *Weekly Register*.

Ellenborough gave several important decisions on points of law arising in *criminal cases*. In the case of *Earle v. Rowcroft*[7] he repeated Lord Mansfield's definition of barratry[8] as a fraudulent breach of duty on the part of the master or mariners which caused loss to the owners ; and his restatement was approved by the House of Lords in 1883.[9] In the case of *R. v. Johnson*[10] the defendant, an Irish judge, was indicted for publishing a libel in Middlesex. He pleaded that the court of King's Bench had no jurisdiction to hear the case on the ground that he was a native of, and domiciled in, Ireland. Ellenborough held that this plea to the jurisdiction was bad because it did not state, as all such pleas should state, what other court, if any, had jurisdiction.[11] If this plea were good

---

[1] Survey of the History of the Rules of Evidence, Essays A.A.L.H. ii 696.
[2] Above 466-468. [3] Wigmore, op. cit. ii 696.
[4] (1811) 14 East 323. [5] Ibid 327 n. [6] (1800) 7 East 65.
[7] (1806) 8 East 126 at p. 134. [8] Vol. xii 533.
[9] Cory v. Burr (1883) 8 A.C. at p. 339 *per* Lord Blackburn.
[10] (1805) 6 East 583. [11] At pp. 597-601.

it would follow that the publication of a libel in Middlesex by a person in the position of the defendant would be no crime in this country. But if this was what was meant by the plea it ought to have been, not a plea to the jurisdiction, but a plea in bar ; for " it is at most an argumentative plea of not guilty," which could be taken advantage of by pleading not guilty and giving the special matter in evidence.[1] In the famous case of *Ashford v. Thornton,*[2] after hearing a most exhaustive argument Ellenborough said,[3] " the general law of the land is in favour of the wager of battel, and it is our duty to pronounce the law as it is, and not as we may wish it to be." In the case of *R. v. Peltier*[4]—a case in which Peltier was prosecuted for a libel on Napoleon contained in a paper which could be taken to be an incitement to assassinate him—Ellenborough laid it down that

any publication which tends to degrade, revile, and defame persons in considerable situations of power and dignity in foreign countries may be taken to be and treated as a libel, and particularly where it has a tendency to interrupt the pacific relations between the two countries. If the publication contains a plain and manifest incitement and persuasion addressed to others to assassinate and destroy the persons of such magistrates, as the tendency of such a publication is to interrupt the harmony subsisting between two countries, the libel assumes a still more criminal complexion.[5]

These few illustrations are sufficient to show that Ellenborough played a considerable part in developing very many branches of English law.

Charles Abbott[6] succeeded Ellenborough in 1818. He was the second son of a hairdresser in Canterbury, and was born October 7, 1762. He was educated at the King's School, Canterbury, and there showed such ability and industry that, with the help of subscriptions from those who knew his reputation as a scholar, and an exhibition from the school, he was able to go to Corpus Christi College, Oxford, at which college he was elected to a classical scholarship. At Oxford he won the Chancellor's medals for Latin and English composition, and became a fellow and tutor of his college. He had intended to take orders ; but the accident of his becoming tutor to the son of Buller, J. changed his career. Buller saw that Abbott would make a good lawyer and persuaded him to adopt the profession of the law. Acting on Buller's advice, he entered the office of Sandys

---

[1] At pp. 601-602.   [2] (1818) 1 B. and Ald. 405.   [3] At p. 460.
[4] (1803) 28 S.T. 529 ; Peltier was found guilty, but, since the war with France was soon afterwards renewed, he was never called up for judgment, ibid 619.
[5] At p. 617.
[6] Campbell, Lives of the Chief Justices iii 248-348 ; Townsend, Lives of Twelve Eminent Judges ii 234-278 ; Foss, Judges ix 68-73 ; D.N.B.

& Co., a firm of attornies, and remained there for a few months before entering the chambers of the eminent special pleader George Wood,[1] in whose chambers Ellenborough had begun his study of the law. He also followed Ellenborough's example by beginning to practise as a special pleader before he was called to the bar. He continued to practise as a special pleader for seven years; and he acquired so great a reputation as a sound lawyer that, when he was called to the bar by the Inner Temple in 1796, he at once acquired a good practice. " He was employed as junior counsel for the Crown in all the numerous state prosecutions for the next ten years,"[2] and in 1801 he was made recorder of Oxford.

It was by the advice of Lord Eldon that he published in 1802 his book on *Merchant Ships and Seamen*, of the merits of which I have spoken;[3] and to Eldon the book was dedicated. It gave him so large a practice in commercial and maritime cases that in 1807 he was earning over £8,000 a year, and in 1808 he refused the offer of a seat on the bench. He never took silk, because he was conscious that he had not got the gifts required for a leader; but his practice as a junior continued to be so large that in 1816 his health made some relief necessary. He accepted the offer of a seat on the bench of the Court of Common Pleas in that year, but, three months later, at the request of Ellenborough, he moved to the King's Bench. He was made chief justice of that court on Ellenborough's resignation in 1818, and was raised to the peerage as Lord Tenterden in 1827. Abbott had always been a Tory, and, as Lord Tenterden, he opposed the Catholic Emancipation Act. In fact, he was a true prophet as to some of its effects.[4] The Reform Bill, in his opinion, presaged the ruin of his country; and, in his last speech in opposition to it, he said that, when it had passed, he would never again enter a House which as its result would become " the phantom of its departed greatness."[5] He kept his word for the few remaining months of his life. But he continued to act as chief justice till the end. He presided on October 25, 1832, at the opening of the trial of the mayor of Bristol[6] for neglecting his duty at the time of the Reform Bill riots. But after two days he was obliged to return to bed from which he never rose again. He died November 4, 1832.

Tenterden was a great contrast to his predecessor. He had none of Ellenborough's vigorous self-confident personality,

---

[1] Above 500 n. 1.   [2] Foss, Judges ix 70.   [3] Above 382, 481.
[4] He said "nothing could follow from it but a delusive and temporary calm . . . Parliament would in future have to struggle against a combination of physical and political power," cited Townsend, Twelve Eminent Judges ii 270-271.
[5] Cited Campbell, Lives of the Chief Justices iii 332.
[6] R. v. Pinney 3 S.T.N.S. 17.

and none of his gifts as an advocate. On the contrary, he had the mind and temperament of a somewhat retiring academic lawyer. He was a master of legal principles, which he could expound in lucid language, and an accomplished special pleader. But he had neither the physical nor the mental qualities of a leader—as we have seen, he never took silk because he was conscious of this fact. Campbell, who practised before him, says :[1]

I believe that he never addressed a jury in London in the whole course of his life. On the circuit he was now and then forced into the lead in spite of himself, from all the silk gowns being retained on the other side—and on these occasions he did show the most marvellous inaptitude for the functions of an advocate, and almost always lost the verdict. This partly arose from his power of discrimination and soundness of understanding, which, enabling him to see the real merits of the cause on both sides, afterwards fitted him so well for being a judge. . . . Abbott could not struggle with facts which were decisive against him, and if a well-founded objection was taken, recollecting the authorities on which it rested, he betrayed to the presiding judge a consciousness that it was fatal. His physical defects were considerable, for he had a husky voice, a leaden eye, and an unmeaning countenance. Nor did he ever make us think only of intellectual powers by any flight of imagination, or ebullition of humour, or stroke of sarcasm. But that to which I chiefly ascribed his failure was a want of boldness, arising from the recollection of his origin and early occupations. " He showed his blood " . . . I remember once when he began by making an abject apology for the liberty he was taking in contending that Lord Ellenborough had laid down some bad law at nisi prius, he was thus contemptuously reprimanded :—" Proceed, Mr. Abbott, proceed ; it is your duty to argue that I misdirected the jury if you think so."

A man with a mind and a temperament of this kind does not easily adapt himself to a new environment. Though he had an eminently judicial temperament, great learning, and an almost instinctive appreciation for the correct solution of legal problems, he did not immediately adapt himself to his new position when he was raised to the bench.

Never having led at nisi prius, and having been accustomed to attend to detached points as they arose, rather than to take a broad and comprehensive view of the merits of a cause, he at first occasioned considerable disappointment among those who were prepared to admire him ; but he gradually and steadily improved, and before the expiration of the second year he gave decided proof of the highest judicial excellence.[2]

And so, when Ellenborough resigned and there was no other obvious successor, Abbott was appointed chief justice. Here again it took a little time for him to acquire " the ascendancy and the prestige " which a Chief Justice should have.[3] But

---

[1] Lives of the Chief Justices iii 276-277 ; with this view Scarlett agrees, Memoirs of Lord Abinger 84.

[2] Campbell, Lives of the Chief Justices iii 287-288.   [3] Ibid 291.

he acquired it ; he became a real chief ;[1] and, with the assistance of his very learned puisnes Bayley, Littledale, and Holroyd,[2]
he made the court of King's Bench a model court. Campbell
says :[3]

Before such men there was no pretence for being lengthy or importunate.
Every point made by counsel was understood in a moment, the application of every authority was discovered at a glance, the counsel saw
when he might sit down, his case being safe, and when he might sit
down, all chance of success for his client being at an end. I have practised at the bar when no case was secure, no case was desperate, and
when, good points being overruled, for the sake of justice it was necessary
that bad points should be taken ; but during that golden age law and
reason prevailed—the result was confidently anticipated by the knowing
before the argument began—and the judgment was approved by all
who heard it pronounced—including the vanquished party. Before such
a tribunal the advocate becomes dearer to himself by preserving his
own esteem, and feels himself to be a minister of justice, instead of a
declaimer, a trickster, or a bully. I do not believe that so much important
business was ever done so rapidly and so well before any other court that
ever sat in any age or country.

But Tenterden had his defects. In the first place, he was
apt to be too impatient with counsel who made long speeches
to the jury. He seemed to think, Brougham said, "that an address
to the jury could be framed on the model of a special plea or
the counts in a declaration."[4] He often failed to see the need
for a long cross-examination.[5] These failings were probably
due to the fact that he had never been a leading advocate, and
therefore failed to grasp some of the elementary principles
of the art of advocacy. Though it is fair to say that these defects
were caused partly by the immense press of business in his
court.[6] In the second place, and for the same reason, he was
not very ready in meeting objections raised by counsel.
Brougham tells us that

during the interlocutory discussions with the counsel, whether on
motions in banc, or on objections taken before him at nisi prius, he was
uneasy, impatient, and indeed irascible, at nothing so much as at cases
put by way of trying what the court had flung out. Being wholly devoid

[1] Campbell, Lives of the Chief Justices iii 292.   [2] Below 566, 567.
[3] Campbell, op. cit. iii 292.   [4] Historical Sketches ii 188.
[5] " It was chiefly in obstructing cross-examination, which he wholly under-
valued, from his utter incapacity of performing his part in it, that his pleader-like
habits broke out. . . . His constant course was to stop the counsel by reminding
him that the witness had already said so, or had already sworn to the contrary, and
this before the question was answered ; to which it was natural, and indeed became
usual, for the counsel to make answer, that this was the very reason why the question
had been asked ; the object being either to try the witness's memory, or to test his
honesty," ibid 188-189.
[6] " It was a subject of astonishment when Lord Ellenborough had a list laid
before him at the Guildhall of 588 causes entered for trial. Under the aching sight
of his successor there sprung up the vast array of 850," Townsend, op. cit. ii 260.

of imagination to supply cases in reply, and even without much quickness to sight the application of those put, he often lost his temper, and always treated the topic as an offence.[1]

In the third place, it is said that he had favourites at the bar. Scarlett's tact made him a chief favourite—so much so that when, on one occasion, Scarlett said, " there is a difference between the practice here and at the Old Bailey," Adolphus replied, " I know there is. There the judge rules the advocate : here the advocate rules the judge."[2]

In spite of these defects there is no doubt that he was a great judge. Though during the hearing of a case his manners to counsel were so ferocious that they kept even Brougham in order,[3] there was no trace of ruffled temper in his directions to the juries and his judgments. " It was," says Brougham,[4] " an edifying sight to observe Lord Tenterden, whose temper had been visibly affected during the trial . . . addressing himself to the points of the cause, with the same perfect calmness and indifference, with which a mathematician pursues the investigation of an abstract truth." His judgments were neatly and correctly phrased, and, as might be expected from an expert special pleader, with great accuracy. He always tried to make his decisions accord with reason and substantial justice, and to prevent the technical rules of procedure and pleading from doing injustice. As he once pointed out, these rules were necessary, but it was only a profound knowledge of them which would enable a judge so to apply them that he could make them serve the cause of justice. He said :[5]

The preservation of forms, however unpopular, is of the essence of all establishments—of the judicial in particular—for if judges disregard them, they become authors and not expounders of laws. The great art of a lawyer is to understand them. If a judge does not understand them, he will violate the law in a few instances by breaking them ; and if of a cautious temper, do injustice in many by a mistaken adherence to their

[1] Historical Sketches ii 188 ; Scarlett said that he would have been more effective if he had had more confidence in his own judgment—" he had not vigour to resist the pertinacity of the bar, nor to rescue the jury from an eloquent and forcible reply which sometimes carried the day against the justice of the case," Memoirs of Lord Abinger 86.

[2] Townsend, op. cit. ii 263.

[3] See Thesiger's account of his " rough and uncourteous manners " cited from the Chelmsford MS. by Abbey ; Victorian Chancellors ii 84-85.

[4] Historical Sketches, cited Townsend, op. cit. ii 249.

[5] Letter to Sir Egerton Brydges, cited Campbell, Chief Justices iii 297 ; a good illustration is his answer to an objection to the declaration in Keyworth v. Hill (1820) 3 B. and Ald. 685 ; it was an action of trover against husband and wife, and the declaration said that they had converted the property to their use ; it was objected after the verdict that it was bad because the wife could own no property ; Abbott replied that a conversion of property to *their* use did not necessarily imply the acquisition of property, for a conversion might consist in the destruction of the property, and after verdict the court must so presume.

supposed effect : the latter has been the most common error. The less a judge knows of special pleading, the more non-suits take place under his direction. Buller told me so many years ago, and experience has shown the truth of his assertion.

Lord Tenterden's contribution to the development of the law was two-fold. In the first place, at the end of his life he drew several statutes for the reform of different branches of the law. In the second place, his more important contribution was the series of cases which he decided during the fourteen years tenure of his office as Chief Justice.

(1) Brougham in his great speech on law reform in 1828, and the commissions appointed as the result of it,[1] had advocated several reforms in the law. Tenterden, though in politics he was a high Tory,[2] and though he was not prepared to adopt all the reformer's proposals,[3] was prepared to adopt some of them ; and so he set to work to draft bills to give effect to them.[4] The Act, generally known as Lord Tenterden's Act, which amended James I's statute of limitations and made other changes in the law of contract,[5] the Uniformity of Process Act,[6] and a short Act to prevent failures of justice by reason of variances between writings produced in evidence and their recital on the record,[7] are his most successful efforts in drafting. He also drafted two Acts to amend the law of prescription in claims for tithes,[8] and in claims to easements and profits.[9] But though he was a very competent real property lawyer, he was not so learned in this branch of the law as in commercial and other branches of the common law.[10] It is not surprising, therefore, that these two Acts, and more especially the second, did not succeed in simplifying the law.

(2) Lord Tenterden's decisions cover the whole field of the common law. Many of them have taken rank as leading cases. All of them illustrate the fact that the unenacted, like the enacted, law was being expanded and adapted to the new needs and new ideas of the time.

---

[1] Above 306, 307. [2] Above 517.

[3] Thus in 1830 he opposed the bill, which was ultimately passed, to abolish the death penalty in certain cases of forgery, Hansard (N.S.) xxv 854-855 ; above 401, 402.

[4] In 1830 he wrote to Sir Egerton Brydges, " the reports contain recommendations and proposals for many alterations, some of which I think useful and practicable. . . . I have employed myself since the circuit in preparing no fewer than five bills, intended to give some further powers to the common law courts, and make some alteration in the practice, but without infringing any important principle, adopting some of the recommendations, with some alterations from the proposals," cited Campbell, Lives of the Chief Justices iii 324-325.

[5] 9 George IV c. 14 ; above 409.

[6] 2, 3 William IV c. 39 ; above 307, 406.

[7] 9 George IV c. 15. [8] 2, 3 William IV. c. 100 ; above 420.

[9] 2, 3 William IV c. 71 ; vol. vii 350-352 ; above 420. [10] Below 524 seqq.

In the sphere of *public or semi-public law* there are several important cases. In the leading case of *Blundell v. Catterall*[1] it was held by the whole court, Best, J. dissenting, that the public had no common law right to bathe in the sea, and therefore no right to cross the sea-shore to the sea in bathing machines or on foot. The most learned of the judgments was delivered by Holroyd, J.[2] who cited Bracton, The Year Books, and Hale. Tenterden showed that the supposed right could not be supported as a general custom since the practice of sea bathing was modern ; that a general right of passage over the shores would prevent any use being made of the shore by the building of embankments or harbours ; and that no usage or practice so to use the shore could be shown. Acquiescence by the owner of the soil in this user of the shore, where it did no harm to the owner, was no proof of the right so to use it. Such acquiescence was usual in the case of waste or common land. " Yet no one ever thought that any right existed in favour of this enjoyment, or that any justification could be pleaded to an action at the suit of the owner of the soil."[3] This decision has been universally approved and followed.[4] In the case of *Lumley v. Battine*[5] there was a discussion as to what servants of the King's household were privileged from arrest on mesne process ; and, in the case of *Novello v. Toogood*,[6] a discussion as to the extent of the privilege of an ambassador's servant. Tenterden held that though by international law, which was part of the common law,[7] an ambassador's servant and his house were privileged, yet if, as in this case, he kept a house, part of which he let as lodgings, he could not claim exemption from the duty to pay rates on the house. In *R. v. Waddington*[8] he followed the older cases,[9] and held that " Christianity was a part of the law of the land." We have seen that in *Thomas v. Acklam*[10] he held that persons born in the United States after the recognition of their independence were aliens ; but that the children of parents who, after that event, adhered to the British government, came within the statute of 1730,[11] and were therefore British subjects.[12] In the case of *R. v. Davison*[13] Tenterden upheld the power of a judge sitting at nisi prius, and indeed of a judge of any court to fine for contempt ; in the case of *R. v. Mary Carlile*[14] he upheld the power of the court to stop the report of

---

[1] (1821) 5 B. and Ald. 268.   [2] At pp. 288-304.   [3] At p. 315.
[4] See Llandudno Urban Council v. Woods [1899] 2 Ch. 705 ; Brinkman v. Matley [1904] 2 Ch. 313.
[5] (1818) 2 B. and Ald. 238 ; vol. x 353-354.   [6] (1823) 1 B. and C. 534.
[7] At. p. 562 ; see vol. x 371-373.   [8] (1822) 1 B. and C. 26.
[9] Vol. iii 408-410, 413.   [10] (1824) 2 B. and C. 779 ; vol. ix 87.
[11] 4 George II c. 21 ; vol. ix 88.
[12] Auchmutz v. Mulcaster (1826) 5 B. and C. 771.
[13] (1821) 4 B. and Ald. 329 at p. 334.   [14] (1819) 3 B. and Ald. 168.

indecent or defamatory matter read in the course of a trial; and in the case of *Garnett v. Ferrand*[1] he held that no action would lie against a coroner for excluding a person from an inquest held by him, because this was an act done by him in the exercise of his judicial functions.

Some of Tenterden's decisions in the sphere of *the law of contract and commercial law* are very important.

The case of *Street v. Blay*[2] is a leading case as to the rights of a purchaser in cases where the vendor has been guilty of a breach of a condition or a warranty—though the term warranty is used in a somewhat confusing way to cover both condition and warranty. The case of *Montague v. Benedict*[3] is a leading case as to the conditions in which a husband can be made liable for his wife's debts. Tenterden said that he hoped that the decision that a husband was not liable for goods which were not necessaries, supplied to the wife under a contract which he had neither authorized nor ratified, would be a warning to tradesmen.[4] The case of *Baxter v. Earl of Portsmouth*[5] lays down the modern rule as to contracts with an insane person not known by the other contracting party to be insane. The case of *Robson and Sharp v. Drummond*[6] is a leading authority for the principle that a promisor cannot assign his liabilities under a contract. But the rule is subject to modifications; and it is possible that if the same case now came before the courts, they would hold that, since no special personal qualifications were needed for its performance, it could be performed vicariously.[7] In the case of *Good v. Cheesman*[8] a composition with creditors was upheld, and Lord Tenterden ingeniously, if not very logically, evaded the difficulty arising from the apparent absence of consideration for such an agreement.[9] The case of *Withers v. Reynolds*[10] lays it down that in a contract of sale payment and delivery are concurrent conditions, so that a refusal to pay for any one delivery entitles the vendor to repudiate the contract.[11]

---

[1] (1827) 6 B. and C. 611.
[2] (1831) 2 B. and Ad. 456.
[3] (1825) 3 B. and C. 631; see vol. iii 528-530.
[4] At pp. 638-639.
[5] (1826) 5 B. and C. 170; see Moulton v. Camroux (1849) 4 Ex. 17; Imperial Loan Co. v. Stone [1892] Q.B. 599.
[6] (1831) 2 B. and Ad. 303.
[7] In the case of the British Waggon Co. v. Lea (1880) 5 Q.B.D. 149 Cockburn C. J. said at p. 153, " we cannot but think that, in applying the principle, the Court of Queen's Bench in Robson v. Drummond went to the utmost length to which it can be carried, as it is difficult to see how in repairing a carriage when necessary, or painting it once a year, preference would be given to one coach-maker over another."
[8] (1831) 2 B. and Ad. 328.
[9] He said at pp. 333-334 that each creditor was bound " in consequence of the agreement of the rest "—" the consideration to each creditor being the engagement of the others not to press their individual claims "; but how does this contract between the creditors bind the debtor who is not on this theory a party to it? see vol. viii 85 n. 2.
[10] (1831) 2 B. and Ad. 882.
[11] See Lord Blackburn's summary of the result of the case in Mersey Steel and Iron Co. v. Naylor (1884) 9 A.C. at pp. 442-443.

The case of *Thomson v. Davenport*[1] is a leading case, much discussed and distinguished,[2] on the rights of a person who has contracted with an agent who has not disclosed the name of his principal.

The following are a few illustrations of Lord Tenterden's many decisions on points of commercial law : In the case of *Baring v. Corrie*[3] he distinguished between the functions of a broker and a factor. The former, unlike the latter, has generally no possession of the goods and is not authorized to sell in his own name. Therefore, if a broker sells in his own name the purchaser cannot set off against the price a debt due from the broker to himself. In the case of *Hall v. Fuller*[4] he held that if the words and figures on a cheque are altered by a holder, in such a way that the alteration was not apparent by an inspection of the cheque, and the banker pays the holder the altered amount, he could only charge his customer for the sum for which the cheque was originally drawn. This problem of the effect of fraudulent alterations in bills or cheques has been discussed in later cases, and has been submitted to a considerably closer analysis than was applied to it in this case. In particular the duty of the acceptor of a bill in accepting a bill so carelessly drawn that fraud is facilitated,[5] and the duty of the drawer of a cheque,[6] have been distinguished. In the former case the acceptor cannot be made liable to pay the altered amount : in the latter case the drawer can be made liable. In two cases Lord Tenterden in substance laid down the rule, which has prevailed, that a general custom of the merchants to treat instruments as negotiable must be given effect to by the courts.[7] But his ruling in the case of *Gill v. Cubitt*[8] that a holder in due course could not sue on a bill, if he acquired it in circumstances which would have excited the suspicions of a prudent man, has been overruled both by the court of King's Bench[9] and by the House of Lords.[10] As Lord Campbell has said,[11] this rule,

---

[1] (1829) 9 B. and C. 78.

[2] See Heald v. Kenworthy (1855) 10 Ex. at pp. 745-746 ; Armstrong v. Stokes (1872) L.R. 7 Q.B. at pp. 607-610 ; Irvine v. Watson (1880) 5 Q.B.D. at pp. 418-419.

[3] (1818) 2 B. and Ald. 137.   [4] (1826) 5 B. and C. 750.

[5] Schofield v. Londesborough [1896] A.C. 514.

[6] London Joint Stock Bank v. Macmillan [1918] A.C. 777 ; below 547.

[7] Wookey v. Pole (1820) 4 B. and Ald. 1 ; Georgier v. Mieville (1824) 3 B. and C. 45 ; cp. Goodwin v. Robarts (1876) 1 A.C. 476 at p. 490 ; vol. xii 528 and n. 3.

[8] (1824) 3 B. and C. 466.

[9] " We are of opinion that gross negligence only would not be a sufficient answer, when the party has given consideration for the bill. Gross negligence may be evidence of *mala fides*, but is not the same thing. We have shaken off the last remnant of the contrary doctrine," Goodman v. Harvey (1836) 4 Ad. and E. at p. 876 *per* Lord Denman C.J.

[10] London Joint Stock Bank v. Simmons [1892] A.C. 201 at p. 219.

[11] Lives of the Chief Justices iii 311.

which was contrary to the rule laid down by Lord Kenyon,[1] and inconsistent with the principle of negotiability, which demands that the title of a holder in due course is impeachable only for fraud, " died with its author."

Almost equally important are some of Lord Tenterden's decisions on points arising in the *criminal law and the law of tort*. In the case of *R. v. Carlile*[2] he laid it down that " where there is a misdemeanour at common law, a statute providing a particular punishment for it does not repeal the common law," so that a prosecutor may proceed either at common law or under the statute. In *R. v. Burdett*[3] he ruled that the composition of an unpublished treasonable paper was an overt act of high treason, just as an unpublished defamatory paper might amount to the crime of libel. But this ruling is questionable.[4] In the case of *R. v. Thistlewood*[5] he laid down clearly two leading characteristics of the most important of the varieties of the crime of treason—the fact that the crime consists in the intent to kill the King, but that the intent must be manifested by an overt act. We have seen that his decisions in the cases of *R. v. Harvey*[6] and *Bromage v. Prosser*[7] finally disposed of the idea that malice was an essential ingredient of the crime and tort of libel.[8] In the case of *R. v. Moore*[9] he laid it down that a person " who collects together a crowd of persons to the annoyance of his neighbours " could be prosecuted for a nuisance ; and later cases show that the same acts will also amount to the tort of nuisance.[10] In the case of *R. v. Somerton*[11] he gave practical effect to Hale's view[12] that it was a disgrace to the law to allow criminals to escape " by nice and captious objections of form."[13]

We have seen that the decision of Tenterden and Littledale in *Laughter v. Pointer*[14] helped to establish the modern rule that a master, though liable for the acts of his servant, is not as a general rule liable for the acts of an independent contractor. Tenterden's decision in the case of *Polhill v. Walter*[15] laid down the rule that if a false statement is in fact made to a person with the intent that it should be acted on by him, and it is acted

---

[1] Lawson v. Weston (1801) 4 Esp. 56.

[2] (1819) 3 B. and Ald. at p. 163.

[3] (1820) 4 B. and Ald. at p. 159.

[4] Halsbury's Laws of England (2nd ed.) ix 305 n. (e).

[5] (1820) 33 S.T. at p. 920 ; vol. viii 309, 311.

[6] (1823) 2 B. and C. 257. [7] (1825) 4 B. and C. 247.

[8] Vol. viii 374-375. [9] (1832) 3 B. and Ad. 184.

[10] Bellamy v. Wells (1890) 63 L.T. 635 in which the reasoning of R. v. Moore was followed ; cp. Winfield, Law of Tort, 5th ed., 490.

[11] (1827) 7 B. and C. 463. [12] P.C. ii 193, cited vol. iii 619.

[13] 7 B. and C. at pp. 466-467.

[14] (1826) 5 B. and C. 547 : vol. viii 480 ; from this decision Bayley and Holroyd J.J. dissented.

[15] (1832) 3 B. and Ad. 114.

on to his damage, an action of deceit lies, although there was
"no corrupt motive of gain to the defendant or wicked motive
of injury to the plaintiff."[1] In the case of *Ilott v. Wilkes*[2] he held
that a trespasser in a wood, who knew that there were spring
guns set, could not sue for an injury received from one of them.
The decision was attacked by Sydney Smith,[3] and we have seen
that it led to a change in the law ;[4] but, Pollock says,[5] "it has
not been doubted in subsequent authorities that on the law as
it stood, and the facts as they came before the court, it was
well decided."[6] In the case of *Hannam v. Mocket*[7] it was held
that the firing of guns near the plaintiff's close, with the result
that the rooks were driven away, so that the plaintiff was prevented from shooting them and taking their young, gave the
plaintiff no cause of action, because the rooks were *ferae naturae*
so that the plaintiff had no property in them. The authority
of this case has been questioned ;[8] and it is doubtful if it would
be held to be good law at the present day. Probably it would
be held that the plaintiff would be liable for creating a nuisance
on his land.[9]

One of the most important decisions of Lord Tenterden's
in the law of *personal property* is *Irons v. Smallpiece*,[10] in which
he held that to perfect a gift of chattels there must be either
delivery or a deed—a decision which was followed by the court
of Appeal in *Cochrane v. Moore*.[11] In the case of *Townson v.*

---

[1] At p. 123.   [2] (1820) 3 B. and Ald. 304.
[3] Works 365-373.   [4] Above 267, 390.
[5] Torts (14th ed.) 128 ; cp. Winfield, Law of Tort, 5th ed., 52.
[6] Dr. Stallybrass, Salmond, Law of Tort, 10th ed., 489 criticizes the decision ;
he thinks that an injury so inflicted is equivalent to the intentional shooting of the
trespasser ; but there is an obvious distinction between the injury inflicted by
mechanical means, of the presence of which the trespasser had notice, and an
intentional shooting ; it is clear that in the first case the trespasser knew of and
faced the danger, but that in the second case he did not ; moreover, as Gibbs C.J.
pointed out in Deane v. Clayton (1817) 7 Taunt. 489 at pp. 534-535 in the one case
a direct attack is made which is unjustifiable if the trespasser can be removed by
less violent means : in the other a guard is set up against all trespassers—the
primary object of the guard being protection to property, not the infliction of injury
to others—" a spiked gate will inflict wounds on men or animals who endeavour to
break over them, which if the owner of a field or garden found them therein, he
would not be justified in inflicting." Mr. Hart, L.Q.R. xlvii 102-103 draws a
distinction between a deterrent danger created by the owner of property which is
lawful, and a retributive danger which is not ; but there is little or no authority
for this distinction, and it would be difficult to draw in practice ; suppose one trespasser fell on barbed wire which pierced his hand, and suppose the hand of another
trespasser were pierced by a bullet from a spring gun—apart from the legislation
against spring guns, the two injuries would be much the same, but on Mr. Hart's
theory he could recover in the second case and not in the first.
[7] (1824) 2 B. and C. 934.
[8] Read v. Edwards (1864) 17 C.B.N.S. at p. 258.
[9] Allen v. Flood [1898] A.C. at p. 101 ; Hollywood Silver Fox Farm v. Emmett
[1936] 2 K.B. 468.
[10] (1819) 2 B. and Ald. 551.
[11] (1890) 25 Q.B.D. 60 ; vol. iii 354 ; vol. vii 505-509.

Tickell [1] he laid down the principle that a devisee may disclaim a gift by deed. In the case of *Cannan v. Bryce* [2] he held that an assignment of property made in pursuance of an illegal transaction is void so that the trustee in bankruptcy of the assignor can recover it from the assignee.

The case of *R. v. Lord Yarborough* [3] is the leading case in English law on title to land by that species of *accessio* known as *alluvio*. Of the many other cases connected with the land law, which came before the court on reference from the court of Chancery and otherwise, perhaps the most famous is *Birt-whistle v. Vardill*, [4] which held, in accordance with the Statute of Merton, [5] that the heir to English land must be born of married parents, so that a child legitimated according to the law of the parents' domicil by subsequent marriage cannot inherit. The case of *Moore v. Rawson* [6] is a leading case as to when an easement will be lost by non-user. But the correctness of two of his decisions on questions of real property law in the cases of *Doe v. Hilder* [7] and *Partridge v. Bere* [8]—have been questioned. [9]

So eminent a special pleader as Lord Tenterden was likely to have acquired some just ideas as to the reasons for, and justification of, the system of special pleading, and also as to its weaknesses. [10] Those reasons, that justification, and those weaknesses were clearly explained in the following passage from his judgment in the case of *Selby v. Bardons* : [11]

I consider the system of special pleading, which prevails in the law of England, to be founded upon and adapted to the peculiar mode of trial established in this country, the trial by the jury ; and that its object is to bring the case, before trial, to a simple, and, as far as practicable, a single question of fact, whereby not only the duties of the jury may be more easily and conveniently discharged, but the expense to be incurred by the suitors may be rendered as small as possible. . . . I am sensible that this principle has not always been kept in view by the Courts, and that there have been, in practice, many instances of departure from it founded upon very nice and subtle distinctions.

and just as some of the pleading rules were arbitrary and worked injustice because they were founded on archaic rules which had lost their meaning, [12] so many of the rules of practice suffered from the same defect. Just as it fell to Ellenborough to try

---

[1] (1819) 3 B. and Ald. 31 ; at the present day not even a deed is necessary, see Lindley L.J.'s summary of the history of the law on this point in In re Birchall (1889) 4 C.D. at p. 439.

[2] (1819) 3 B. and Ald. 179.   [3] (1824) 3 B. and C. 91 ; vol. ii 286 n. 1.

[4] (1826) 5 B. and C. 438.   [5] Vol. ii 220-221, 231 ; vol. ix 151.

[6] (1824) 3 B. and C. 332 ; cp. Cheshire, Real Property (6th ed.) 246.

[7] (1819) 2 B. and Ald. 782—presumption of the surrender of a term.

[8] (1822) 5 B. and Ald. 604—relation of mortgagor and mortgagee.

[9] Townsend, Twelve Eminent Judges ii 259.

[10] Vol. ix 308-315.   [11] (1832) 3 B. and Ad. at pp. 16-17.

[12] Vol. ix 313-314.

the last case in which the defendant demanded trial by battle,[1] so it fell to Tenterden to try the last case in which the defendant waged his law.[2]

Lastly, some of Tenterden's decisions elucidate points connected with the legal profession. In the case of *R. v. Benchers of Lincoln's Inn*[3] he held that a mandamus could not be granted to compel an Inn of Court to admit a student or to call a student to the bar, but that in the latter case a student could appeal to the judges against such a refusal. In the case of *Collier v. Hicks*[4] he held that any court could decide whether it would allow barristers or attornies to appear before it as advocates for the parties, and that therefore the justice could lawfully eject the plaintiff, who was an attorney, when he persisted, contrary to their orders, in attempting to act as advocate for a defendant. In the case of *Bramwell v. Lucas*[5] he gave a somewhat too restricted definition of what communications between a solicitor and client are privileged from disclosure.[6]

The Chief Justices of the court of Common Pleas did not during this period make so considerable a contribution to the development of the law as the two Chief Justices of the King's Bench. This was due partly to the fact that they held office for shorter terms than the two Chief Justices of the King's Bench, partly to the fact that the jurisdiction of their court was less extensive than that of the court of King's Bench, but chiefly to the fact that, between the years 1823 and 1827, more than three times as many civil actions, over which the court of Common Pleas had a concurrent jurisdiction, were brought in the court of King's Bench than were brought in the court of Common Pleas.[7] It was not till the reforms in procedure, which were made at the end of this period,[8] that the court of Common Pleas was able to compete on more equal terms with the court of King's Bench. It was not till the end of this period that the court got in Tindal, C.J.[9] a Chief Justice who, both by reason of his abilities and the length of time during which he held his office, made as great a contribution to the development of the law as that made by Ellenborough or Tenterden.

Of the first of the Chief Justices of the Common Pleas during this period—James Eyre—I have already given some account.[10]

---

[1] Above 217, 405.   [2] King v. Williams (1824) 2 B. and C. 538 vol. i 308.

[3] (1825) 4 B. and C. 855 ; vol. ii 497 n. 5.

[4] (1831) 2 B. and Ad. 663 ; Campbell tells a story in his Life i 283-285 of the indignation of the attorneys at the Monmouth sessions when the justices ordered that the barristers were to have the exclusive right of audience.

[5] (1824) 2 B. and C. 745.

[6] Townsend, Twelve Eminent Judges ii 259.

[7] Vol. i 200 n. 8 ; above 296, 403 ; for a similar estimate made by Lord Lyndhurst in 1830 see below 555.

[8] Above 405, 406.   [9] Below 549-555.   [10] Vol. xii 565-568.

His successor was John Scott, Lord Eldon. Since his tenure of office as Chief Justice only lasted for two years (1799-1801), and since he is famous as one of the greatest of our Lord Chancellors I shall give an account of his career in the following section.[1] During his short tenure of office as Chief Justice he showed that he was a very sound common lawyer. In the case of *Browning v. Wright*[2] he gave a careful explanation of the nature and interpretation of covenants for title. In the case of *Beard v. Webb*[3] he proved in a learned judgment that a married woman carrying on a trade in the City of London, though she could sue and be sued in the city courts, could not sue or be sued in the common law courts ; and in the case of *Marsh v. Hutchinson*[4] he held that the fact that a woman's husband was abroad did not make her liable to be sued on her contracts as a feme sole. His decision in the case of *Astley v. Weldon*[5] begins the modern line of cases which determine when a sum fixed by the parties to be paid on the breach of a contract is to be regarded as a penalty, and when it is to be regarded as liquidated damages.[6] In the case of *Lord Petre v. Lord Auckland*,[7] after an elaborate account of the history of the privilege then possessed by members of both Houses of Parliament of franking letters, he held that a Roman Catholic peer, who was unable to sit as a Lord of Parliament, had not got this privilege. His decision in the case of *Morris v. Langdale*,[8] that to say of a stock jobber that he was a " lame duck "—meaning that he did not fulfil his contracts, was not an actionable slander, is, to say the least, questionable ; and he showed his ignorance of the course of business on the Stock Exchange when he said,[9] " my brother Heath has removed from my mind the impression which it had at first received, viz. that a jobber or dealer in the funds was always to be considered as a culpable person, by showing the necessity of such persons for the accommodation of the market." He was in fact more learned in matters of real property law than in matters of mercantile law. The cases in which, contrary to the older practice, he gave reasons for the opinion of the court on cases submitted by the court of Chancery, show his learning in the former branch of the law ; and in the latter branch of the law at least one of his decisions has been overruled.[10] The fact that while he was

---

[1] Below 595-638.   [2] (1799) 2 B. and P. 13.
[3] (1800) 2 B. and P. 93.   [4] Ibid 226.   [5] (1801) 2 B. and P. 346.
[6] Eldon's statement, ibid at p. 350, that " where a doubt is stated whether the sum inserted be intended as a penalty or not, if a certain damage less than that sum is made payable upon the face of the same instrument in case the act intended to be prohibited be done, that sum shall be construed to be a penalty," was cited with approval by Jessel M.R. in Walters v. Smith (1882) 21 C.D. at p. 259.
[7] (1800) 2 B. and P. 139.   [8] Ibid 284.   [9] At p. 288.
[10] Page v. Fry (1800) 2 B. and P. 240, not followed in Cohen v. Hannam (1813) 5 Taunt. 101, and held to be overruled in Ebsworth v. Alliance Marine Insurance Co. (1873) L.R. 8 C.P. 644.

Chief Justice there were no such complaints of delay in the giving of his decisions, as there were when he was Chancellor, shows that these delays were partly, though not wholly, due to the vicious system of equity procedure,[1] and to the fact that he had no assistants. On the other hand his effectiveness as Chief Justice was diminished by some of those intellectual characteristics which distinguished him as Chancellor. Scarlett says :[2]

When he was Chief Justice of the Common Pleas he investigated every case to the bottom, considered every argument advanced by counsel, and every other topic besides, that the cause suggested : laid the whole of them before the jury in an elaborate and full summing up which presented more points and more subtle distinctions and more ingenious hypotheses than men [un]accustomed to such discussions were able to deal with, and finally after an admirable lecture for a student at law, puzzled and confounded the jury, and made it often uncertain on what ground they pronounced their verdict.

Of his successor, Richard Pepper Arden, Lord Alvanley, I have already given some account.[3] We have seen that, as Master of the Rolls, he had shown that he was a learned equity lawyer. As Chief Justice of the Common Pleas (1801-1804) he soon showed that he was as learned a common lawyer. His judgments show a mastery of legal principles, together with a power of clear exposition both of the facts of the cases which came before him and the law applicable thereto. The following are a few examples of some of his important decisions : In the case of *McConnell v. Hector* [4] he gave a clear exposition of the effects of an enemy commercial domicil upon the right of a British subject to sue in an English court ; and we have seen that in the case of *Furtado v. Rogers* [5] he affirmed the principle which in Lord Mansfield's time had been doubtful, that the insurance of an enemy ship is an illegal contract. In the case of *Touteng v. Hubbard* [6] the effect of an embargo, laid by the British government upon Swedish ships, upon the rights and duties of persons who had chartered a Swedish ship, was discussed ; and in the course of his judgment he laid down the principle that

if a party contract to do anything he shall be bound to the performance of his contract, if from the nature of that contract it is capable of being performed, and legally may be performed. But where the policy of the state intervenes and prevents the performance of the contract, the party will be excused.[7]

---

[1] See vol. ix 373-374.   [2] Memoirs of Lord Abinger 89.
[3] Vol. xii 328-329.   [4] (1802) 3 B. and P. 113.
[5] (1802) 3 B. and P. 191 ; vol. xii 539-540.
[6] (1802) 3 B. and P. 291 ; see the remarks of Blackburn J. upon this case in Geipel v. Smith (1872) L.R. 7 Q.B. at pp. 412-413.   [7] At. p. 301.

The case of *Hodgkinson v. Robinson*[1] is a leading case upon the question as to the events which will make underwriters liable, when they have insured a ship against capture and restraint of princes. His decision in the case of *Tappenden v. Randall*[2] that a party to a void contract (in this case a wager), can recover back his money if nothing has been done in pursuance of the contract, has been approved.[3] On the other hand, his view as to what will amount to an acceptance within the meaning of § 17 of the Statute of Frauds[4] has not been followed.[5] In the case of *Johnson v. Johnson*[6] he showed that he was opposed to Lord Mansfield's attempt to give effect to equitable rights in a court of law—" no man," he said,[7] " is more disposed to be cautious in admitting equitable matters to be agitated in a court of law than myself." In the case of *Tapp v. Lee*[8] he held that no action would lie for a false representation unless it was made with intent to deceive. His decisions on questions relating to the land law show that he was a learned real property lawyer.[9] One—a writ of false judgment from the judgment of a manor court on a writ of right[10]—was something of an anti-quarian curiosity.[11] The case illustrates the need for that meticulous accuracy in the pleadings on such a writ which is character-istic of an early period in the history of law,[12] and was one of the causes of the disuse of the real actions.[13] His decision in the case of *Monroe v. Twisleton*[14] that a divorced wife is a competent witness to prove facts arising after the divorce as against her late husband, but not those arising before the divorce, has been followed in later cases.[15]

---

[1] (1803) 3 B. and P. 388; cp. Mercantile Steamship Co. v. Tyser (1881) 7 Q. B.D. at p. 76 where the principle of this case was followed.

[2] (1801) 2 B. and P. 467.

[3] Hermann v. Charlesworth [1905] 2 K.B. at p. 132.

[4] Now § 4 of the Sale of Goods Act 1893, 56, 57 Victoria c. 71.

[5] Kent v. Huskinson (1802) 3 B. and P. 233; see Page v. Morgan (1885) 15 Q.B.D. 228; Halsbury, Laws of England (2nd ed.) xxix 30 n. (*b*).

[6] (1802) 3 B. and P. 162.

[7] At p. 169; for Lord Mansfield's views see vol. xii 588-589; for their rejection see ibid 595-601.　　　　　　　　　[8] (1803) 3 B. and P. 367.

[9] See e.g. the case of Seale v. Barter (1801) 2 B. and P. 485—a case sent by the Lord Chancellor for the opinion of the court.

[10] Slade v. Dowland (1801) 2 B. and P. 570.　　　　[11] Vol. i 59 n. 2.

[12] " We are of opinion that this being a real action, though originating in a manor court, all the forms of proceeding must be as strictly observed as if it had been a writ of right originally commenced in this court, and that the tenant has a right to avail himself of any inaccuracy which the demandant may have committed in the course of the proceedings," 2 B. and P. at p. 578; for the reluctance of the court to make any amendment to the pleadings in a writ of right see Tooth v. Boddington (1823) 1 Bing. 208; Worley v. Blunt (1833) 9 Bing. 635; see ibid at p. 637 for Tindal C.J.'s explanation of this reluctance. See vol. iii 7-8; for the old maxim *qui cadit a syllaba cadit a tota causa* see vol. i 301.

[13] Vol. iii 8; vol. vii 5-6.　　　　　　[14] (1802) Peake, Add. Cases 219.

[15] Doker v. Hasler (1824) Ry. and Moo. 198; O'Connor v. Majoribanks (1842) 4 M. and Gr. 435; cp. Shenton v. Tyler [1939] Ch. at pp. 630-633 for some remarks on these cases by Lord Greene.

Lord Alvanley's successor was Sir James Mansfield who held office from 1804 to 1814.

James Mansfield (1733-1821)[1] (whose name was originally Manfield) was educated at Eton and King's College, Cambridge, and was called to the bar by the Middle Temple in 1758. He took silk in 1772, and was appointed counsel to Cambridge University and elected as one of its members in 1774. He was one of the counsel for the Duchess of Kingston[2] in 1776, and appeared for the Crown on the trial of Hill for setting on fire the rope house at Portsmouth,[3] and on the trial of Stratton and others for deposing Lord Piggott, the governor of Madras.[4] In 1780 he was appointed solicitor-general—a post which he held till the fall of Lord North's government in 1782. He was appointed to his old office by the coalition ministry of Fox and North, but lost it when the coalition was dismissed, and Pitt took office. In the election to the new Parliament in 1784 he lost his seat for Cambridge. He never again sat in Parliament, where he had never been a success, and he was out of office till 1799, when he was made chief justice of Chester. He was a competent, though not a brilliant advocate. The one neat retort which he is recorded as having made was in the case of *Ex pte. Wrangham.*[5] Wrangham was appealing to the Lord Chancellor, as visitor to his college of Trinity Hall, Cambridge, against their refusal to elect him to a fellowship. He contended that as a B.A. of the college and *idoneus moribus et ingenio* he was entitled to be elected, since his morals were unimpeachable. The college replied that *mores* did not mean only morals but manners and character, and, in reply to the classical quotations produced by Wrangham's counsel, Mansfield cited a line of Ovid in which Ovid, speaking of his two mistresses, says,

Haec specie melior *moribus* illa fuit.[6]

Wrangham lost his case. In 1797 Mansfield was one of the counsel for the plaintiffs in the great case of *Thellusson v. Woodford.*[7] In 1804 he was made Chief Justice of the Common Pleas. When he took the degree of serjeant-at-law preparatory to his appointment as Chief Justice, he took as the motto on his rings *Serus in coelum redeas*, thus humorously alluding to his long exclusion from office. In 1806 he, like Ellenborough,[8] wisely declined the great seal. His health gave way in 1814; he was absent from his court during the Hilary term,[9] and resigned his office

---

[1] Foss, Judges viii 332-335 ; D.N.B.
[2] 20 S.T. 355.
[3] (1777) 20 S.T. 1318.
[4] (1779-80) 21 S.T. 1045.
[5] (1795) 2 Ves. 609.
[6] At. p. 619.
[7] 4 Ves. 227, 11 Ves. 112 ; vol. vii 228-231.
[8] Above 502.
[9] 5 Taunt. 302.

in the Hilary vacation of 1814. But he survived for nearly eight years. He died November 23, 1821.

Foss sums up his character as follows :

Though a good average lawyer his promotion occurred rather too late in life ; and though anxious to dispense justice in the cases that came before him, he was too apt to give way to the irritation of the moment. Of this deficiency of temper the serjeants were not backward in taking advantage ; and towards the end of his career they worried him to such a degree that he could not always refrain from venting in audible whispers curses against his tormentors.

The reports show that he was a very competent lawyer. His decisions are clearly expressed, and occasionally learned. But more often they are short, and express a conclusion which has generally been approved, without much parade of authority. Among them there are no decisions of first-rate importance, but there are some of considerable interest.

In the sphere of *public law* the following cases are interesting : in the case of *Warden v. Bailey*[1] Mansfield held, contrary to the dicta of Lords Mansfield and Loughborough in the case of *Sutton v. Johnstone,*[2] that an inferior officer could sue his superior officer for imprisoning him for disobedience to an order which he had no authority to give. That decision was reversed by the court of King's Bench,[3] because on the facts, it was held that the imprisonment was justifiable. We have seen that though this decision has not been followed by the court of Queen's Bench,[4] it was approved by Cockburn, C.J. in a very learned dissenting judgment.[5] Mansfield's judgment in the court of Exchequer Chamber, affirming the decision of the court of King's Bench in the case of *Burdett v. Abbot,*[6] is a clear and concise statement of the facts and of the law applicable thereto. The case of *King v. Foster*[7] affirmed the privilege of the King's servant of freedom from arrest on mesne process. In the sphere of *criminal law* he heard the argument in the case of *R. v. Depardo,*[8] from which it would appear that an enemy alien cannot be tried for a crime committed by him by the ordinary courts.[9] We

[1] (1811) 4 Taunt. 67.
[2] (1785-86) 1 T.R. 510 ; vol. x 384-385 ; above 508.
[3] Bailey v. Warden (1815) 4 M. and S. 400.
[4] Dawkins v. Lord Paulet (1869) L.R. 5.Q.B. 94.
[5] At pp. 105-107 ; see vol. x 384-386.
[6] (1812) 4 Taunt. at pp. 444-450 ; (1811) 14 East 1 ; above 508.
[7] (1809) 2 Taunt. 167 ; vol. x 352-353 ; above 508, 509.
[8] (1807) 1 Taunt. 26 ; no judgment was given, but the prisoner was released.
[9] In effect the principle laid down in Perkin Warbeck's Case, cited in Calvin's Case (1609) 7 Co. Rep. at f. 6 b., for treason committed by an alien enemy was logically applied to other crimes ; of course this does not apply to an enemy alien allowed to reside in this country who, like an alien friend, owes a temporary allegiance to the King, vol. ix 96 n. 798.

have seen that the case of *R. v. Walsh* [1] was the cause of an Act which filled a gap in the law as to larceny, which had enabled a fraudulent stockbroker to escape punishment. [2]

In the law of *contract* we have seen that in two cases Mansfield adhered to the view that a moral obligation was a valid consideration. [3] His decision that a contract made on a Sunday, if not in the exercise of the ordinary calling of the vendor, was not invalidated by the common law or by the statute of 1677, [4] was not approved by his successors. [5] It would seem from his judgment in the case of *Hill v. Smith* [6] that sales by sample were very new phenomena. In fact he denied that they were sales—" it is a contract to sell a quantity of goods answering to the sample, but not any specific goods." [7] He helped to advise the House of Lords in the case of *Lucena v. Craufurd,* [8] in which the question of the circumstances in which such persons as consignees, agents, or trustees had an insurable interest in a ship or cargo was discussed. In the case of *Harris v. Packwood* [9] he followed reluctantly the cases which had held that a carrier could limit his common law liability by a public notice—a state of the law to some extent remedied by the Carriers Act, 1830 which required a special contract to relieve the carrier of his liability. [10] His decision in *Addison v. Gandassequi* [11] is one of the chain of cases which have settled the law as to the rights and liabilities of an undisclosed principal. These are all cases which relate to modern problems in the law of contract. But this branch of the law, like other branches of English law, had in it archaic elements, as a plaintiff found when he tried to bring an action of debt against the administrator of a deceased person. Much against his will Mansfield was obliged to rule that no such action would lie. [12]

In the law of *tort* his decision in the case of *Sutton v. Buck* [13] that mere possession is sufficient to enable a person to maintain

---

[1] (1812) 4 Taunt. 258 ; above 387.   [2] Above 387-389.

[3] Barnes v. Hedley (1809) 2 Taunt. 184 ; Lee v. Muggeridge (1813) 5 Taunt. 36 ; vol. viii 30-33.

[4] Drury v. Defontaine (1808) 1 Taunt. 131 ; 29 Charles II c. 7 ; vol. vi 404.

[5] Smith v. Sparrow (1827) 4 Bing. at p. 88.

[6] (1812) 4 Taunt. 520—the question was, could a toll be levied on the sale of goods by sample in a market, which goods were later brought into the city ? The answer given was no.   [7] At p. 532.

[8] (1807) 2 B. and P. N.R. 269 ; a clear account of this important case is given by Bovill C.J. in Ebsworth v. Alliance Marine Insurance Co. (1873) L.R. 8 C.P. at pp. 617-623.   [9] (1810) 3 Taunt. 264 at p. 271.

[10] 11 George IV and 1 William IV c. 68 §§ 4 and 6 ; above 384, 385 ; see Shaw v. G.W.R. (1894) 1 Q.B. at pp. 380-381 *per* Wright J.

[11] (1812) 4 Taunt. 574.

[12] " The distinction between actions of debt and assumpsit, as applicable to the case of executors, is not founded in good sense ; but still that distinction has always been recognized in law," Barry v. Robinson (1805) 1 B. and P. N.R. at p. 297 ; for this rule see vol. iii 423, 578.   [13] (1810) 2 (Taunt.) 302.

trover against a wrongdoer, was cited by the court in the case of *The Winkfield*,[1] which finally established the truth of this proposition. We have seen that, with some regret, he helped, in the case of *Thorley v. Kerry*, to establish finally the distinction between the torts of libel and slander.[2]

In the *land law* he decided many cases turning on intricate points referred to his court by the court of Chancery, as well as many actions brought in his court. In the cases of *Gibson v. Wells*[3] and *Herne v. Benbow*[4] he held that an action on the case could not be brought by a landlord against his tenant for permissive waste;[5] and these decisions were followed by Kay, J. in 1889.[6] In the case of *Pitcher v. Donovan*[7] his decision that, on the letting of a house from year to year, with liberty to quit at a quarter's notice, the notice must expire at the end of the year of tenancy, has also been followed.[8]

In the case of *Owen v. Warburton*[9] he settled a doubtful point in the law of evidence, by refusing to accept the affidavit of a juryman that the jury had arrived at their verdict by casting lots. The decision was based on grounds of public policy. He said :

> It is singular indeed that almost the only evidence of which the case admits should be shut out ; but, considering the arts which might be used if a contrary rule were to prevail, we think it necessary to exclude such evidence. If it were understood to be the law that a juryman might set aside a verdict by such evidence, it might sometimes happen that a juryman, being a friend to one of the parties, and not being able to bring over his companions to his opinion, might propose a decision by lot, with a view afterwards to set aside the verdict by his own affidavit, if the decision should be against him.[10]

The case of *White v. Howard* is a good illustration of the traps which an ingenious pleader could lay for an unwary opponent. But, though the court refused to quash a very tricky plea, it foiled the pleader by requiring him to amend it.[11]

Mansfield's successor was Vicary Gibbs.[12] Gibbs was born in 1751. He was educated at Eton and King's College, Cambridge, became a distinguished classical scholar, and was elected a fellow of his college in 1772. He had become a member of Lincoln's

---

[1] [1902] P. 42 at p. 57 ; vol. iii 345-347 ; vol. vii 454-455.
[2] (1812) 4 Taunt. 355 at pp. 363-366 ; vol. viii 365, 366.
[3] (1805) 1 B. and P. N.R. 290.
[4] (1813) 4 Taunt. 764.   [5] Vol. vii 276, 277.
[6] Re Cartwright 41 C.D. 532.   [7] (1809) 1 Taunt. 555.
[8] Dixon v. Bradford Railway Servants Coal Supply [1904] 1 K.B. 444. This doctrine has been applied to monthly and weekly tenancies ; the notice will be invalid unless it expires at the end of a current period of the tenancy : Queen's Club Gardens Estates Ltd. v. Bignell [1924] 1 K.B. 117 : Lemon v. Lardeur [1946] K.B. 613.   [9] (1805) 1 B. and P. N.R. 326.
[10] At pp. 329-330.   [11] (1810) 3 Taunt. 339.
[12] Foss, Judges viii 287-294 ; Townsend, Twelve Eminent Judges i 239-298 ; Brougham, Historical Sketches, (1st ed.) i 124-134 ; D.N.B.

Inn in 1769. Like Ellenborough and Tenterden, he made himself an accomplished pleader, and acquired a large practice in that capacity before he was called to the bar in 1783. He made his name at the bar by his share in the defence of Hardy and Horne Tooke in 1794.[1] It is said that he was chosen as counsel on the recommendation of Horne Tooke, because he had been impressed by his defence of Winterbotham, when he was indicted for preaching sedition in two sermons which he delivered at Plymouth.[2] He was an admirable second to Erskine, supplementing Erskine's eloquence by his clear exposition of the law and his keen dissection and criticism of the evidence against the accused. His speech won high praise from Sir John Scott, the attorney-general.[3] Earlier in 1794 he had been made recorder of Bristol. In the same year he took silk, and in 1795 and 1799 he became successively solicitor- and attorney-general to the Prince of Wales. In 1804 he was made chief justice of Chester and entered Parliament. In 1805 he became solicitor-general, but ceased to hold that office when the ministry of " all the talents " took office on Pitt's death. On the fall of that ministry in 1807 he became attorney-general and was elected member for Cambridge.

As a member of the House of Commons he was a failure—he was too much the lawyer and the pleader, his manner was too caustic, and his conceit too great.[4] As attorney-general he made himself most unpopular by his campaign against the press. We have seen that he carried an Act which allowed any person against whom an information had been filed to be arrested and held to bail, but that it was generally regarded as too severe and was never put into force.[5] The number of informations which he filed against newspaper proprietors and others caused attacks to be made on him in both Houses of Parliament.[6] These attacks,

---

[1] Above 162. [2] (1793) 22 ST. 823.

[3] At the end of the trials he passed the following note to Gibbs : " I say from my heart you did yourself great credit as a good man, and great credit as an excellent citizen, not sacrificing any valuable public principle ; I say from my judgment that no lawyer ever did himself more credit or his client more service ; so help me God ! " cited Foss, Judges viii 289.

[4] Brougham says, op. cit. 133, " there he really had no place at all ; and feeling his nullity, there was no place to which he was with more visible reluctance dragged by the power that office gives the government over its lawyers. He could only obtain a hearing upon legal questions, and those he handled not with such felicity or force as repaid the attention of the listener. He seldom attempted more than to go through the references from one Act of Parliament to another ; and though he was doing only a mechanical work, he gave out each sentence as if he had been consulted and gifted like an oracle, and looked and spoke as if when citing a section he was making a discovery."

[5] 48 George III c. 58 ; above 393.

[6] Scarlett said in the House of Commons that he had been present in the King's Bench when twenty persons had been brought up for judgment no one of whom was morally guilty. Among them were several women who had annuities charged on the newspapers, so that their names were registered as required by statute as joint proprietors of the papers. They were all fined £20, Townsend, op. cit. i 256.

the publicity given to them by the press, and more especially the acquittals of Perry and Lambert,[1] and John and Leigh Hunt [2] caused a cessation in these prosecutions. In defence of Gibbs it can be said that the press was licentious, that the government favoured the prosecutions, and that the bench was inclined to second the government's wish to stop seditious libels. But as Foss says,[3]

it might well be a question whether the attorney-general's power was not too freely exercised, when by a return made to the House of Commons it appears that from 1808 to 1810 no less than forty-two informations had been filed, while only fourteen had been filed during the preceding seven years. The wisdom of these proceedings becomes still more doubtful, when out of these forty-two informations no less than twenty-five were not prosecuted, but the subjects of them were left in a state of suspense and anxiety.

In fact Gibbs was a Tory of the Eldon school. His politics, and their results as seen in his conduct as attorney-general—not only in these informations for libel but in the way in which he pressed the case against the accused—made him very unpopular amongst the growing number of persons who saw that reforms were necessary.

Gibbs made himself equally unpopular with the members of his own profession by his conceit and his absence of common politeness. Scarlett said of him that " there was an asperity in his countenance and manner that was very repulsive," and that " nothing but his sterling knowledge of the law and his acute reasoning could have raised him to any eminence." [4] Another contemporary lawyer said of him :[5]

My intercourse with him in the profession was frequent, and in business time I was in the daily habit of seeing him, [but] I do not recollect ever to have observed a ray of pleasantry pass across his countenance. He stooped occasionally to be what he thought gracious, but he wished to have it considered as condescension. This made his civility disgusting, as it was accompanied with an air of assuming superiority ; it seemed to be a reluctant homage which he paid to the settled rules of decent civility, not the offering of good nature, good feeling, or good manners. This majesty of bearing was displayed upon all occasions, but chiefly at consultations. After stating his own view of the case, he went through the ceremony of asking the opinions of the other counsel in the case who attended him. He received their answers with a simper of affected acquiescence ; but it was evident that he paid no attention to their suggestions or opinions, and had made up his mind to act wholly on his own. The exercise of this prerogative of absolute judgment was not confined to those who were his juniors and without rank ; silk gowns and coifs came in for an equal share of it. In one instance only do I recollect to have observed him relax his unbending superiority ; it was at a

---

[1] (1810) 31 S.T. 335 ; above 506.   [2] (1811) 31 S.T. 367 ; above 196, 505.
[3] Judges viii 291.   [4] Memoir of Lord Abinger 87.
[5] Townsend, Twelve Eminent Judges i 275-276.

consultation at which Mr. (now Sir Edward) Sugden attended him as one
of the counsel in the cause. It would be unjust to deny that on that
occasion he violated his second nature, and treated Mr. Sugden with
civility, and his opinion with respect. It was on a question of real
property, in which he condescended to think that Mr. Sugden might be
as well informed as himself.

On one occasion Topping[1] at a trial at the Guildhall administered
a well merited rebuke. Townsend says :[2]

He observed on the assuming tone and manner adopted by Sir Vicary
Gibbs in the most pointed and indignant language, and concluded with
the emphatic delivery of the lines from the speech of Cassius in Julius
Caesar :—

> He doth bestride the narrow world
> Like a Colossus, and we petty men
> Walk under his huge legs and peep about
> To find ourselves dishonourable graves.

This was accompanied by an angry look of ineffable contempt ; and the
figure and manner of Topping, contrasted with the meanness of Sir
Vicary's appearance, gave force to the reproof, and all the bar present
joined in the opinion of the justness of it.

In 1812 Gibbs accepted a seat on the bench as puisne judge of
the court of Common Pleas. It was so unusual for a law officer
of the Crown to accept a puisne judgeship that some thought that,
knowing his unpopularity, he was frightened by the assassination
of Perceval. However that may be, he was promoted eighteen
months later and became chief baron of the Exchequer. He held
that post for less than three months, and in 1814 became Chief
Justice of the Common Pleas. In 1817 his health began to fail—
he was absent from his court on account of ill-health for the whole
of the Hilary term.[3] On November 5, 1818 he resigned. He died
February 8, 1820.

According to Brougham, when he became a judge he treated
his brethren on the bench in much the same way as he had treated
his fellow barristers. Brougham says :[4]

When he came among the heads of the law, whether in his own court or at
occasional meetings of the twelve, even while junior puisne judge, he
arrogated the place and deference due to the chief of the whole ; and
when he was made first Chief Baron, and afterwards Chief Justice, there
were no bounds to his contempt for all the opinions of his brethren.

It is not surprising that his conduct on the bench was not a
model of judicial behaviour. Though he was a good and not too
severe a judge in criminal cases, yet, says Brougham,[5]

---

[1] For Topping see above 507.   [2] Op. cit. 277.   [3] 7 Taunt. 257.
[4] Historical Sketches (1st ed.) i 132.   [5] Ibid.

in trials at *Nisi Prius* he was distinguished for the little and peevish temper which predominated in him, often to the seeming injury of his judgment, almost always to the detriment of his judicial powers ; and so absolutely was he persuaded of his own universal capacity, and the universal unfitness of others, that it was no uncommon thing for him to ask, somewhat roughly, for a counsel's brief, that he might see what was intended to be stated ; then lecture the attorney who had prepared it ; soon after the witnesses ; and down to the officers of the court, whose functions of keeping silence and order he would occasionally himself undertake to perform. So that it was not an uncommon remark that the learned Chief Justice was performing at once in his own person, the offices of judge and jury, counsel for both parties, attorneys for both, witnesses on both sides, and crier of the court.

He had few intimate friends, and, as attorney-general and judge, he has been accused of unduly favouring some of those few.[1] Among them were Gifford and Dampier who owed him much. Foss, also, who seems to have known him professionally,[2] insists that his character of severity and harshness was undeserved —though he is obliged to admit that his manner justified his reputation.[3]

And yet there is no doubt that all these defects were redeemed by his abilities as an advocate and a judge. Brougham—no partial judge as we have seen—says of his arguments[4] that

they were much to be admired. He did not go by steps, and move on from point to point, garnishing each head with two observations, as many citations, and twice as many cases ; so that the whole argument should be without breadth or relief, and each single portion seem as much as any other, the pivot upon which the conclusion turned—but he brought out his governing principle roundly and broadly ; he put forward his leading idea by which the rest were to be marshalled and ruled ; he used his master key at once, and used it throughout. . . . It might be said of him, as he said himself of Sir James Mansfield, that " he declared the law," while he argued his cases; and while others left only the impression on the hearer that many authorities had been cited, and much reading displayed, his argument penetrated into the mind.

Throughout his career as an advocate he showed the same gifts as he had shown in his defence of Hardy and Horne Tooke[5]— a power of so dealing with the evidence that, without any appeal to the feelings or passions of the jury, he was able to impress them with the justice of his case.[6] All admitted that his eminence as a

---

[1] Townsend, op. cit. i 297 ; but Foss, Judges viii 293 says that he had " many familiar friends " ; and that in his own domestic circle and among these friends he was a pleasant companion.

[2] " The author of these pages well remembers the surprise he felt during his pupilage at the number of patents which he saw on the shelves of the then eminent barrister," Judges viii 289.

[3] Ibid 291-292.   [4] Op. cit. i 128-129.   [5] Above 162, 536.

[6] " He could present to the jury the facts of his case boldly and in high relief ; though he was wholly unable to declaim, and never dreamt of addressing the feelings or the passions, any more than if he were speaking to mummies " ; and, as a judge, " he could deliver himself with considerable emphasis, though without any fluency,

lawyer qualified him for his promotion to the office of Chief
Justice; and this opinion is borne out by his conduct of arguments
on points of law, and by the clarity and grasp of principle which
characterize his decisions.[1] The following cases afford a few
illustrations of his capacity as a judge.

The best known of these cases is the case of *Deane v. Clayton*.[2]
In that case the plaintiff's dog trespassed on to the defendant's
land in pursuit of a hare, and was killed by a dog spear placed on a
track made by hares, and designed to kill foxes or dogs which
chased the hares. Gibbs, C.J. and Dallas, J., Park and Burrough,
J.J. dissenting, held that the plaintiff had no cause of action. Gibbs'
statement of the law has been generally approved.[3] He said:[4]

The defendant's act in laying the dog spears was harmless till the
plaintiff's dog wrongfully intruded upon him. The hurt which he received
is therefore to be referred to his own wrongful intrusion, which was the
immediate cause of it. If the dog had no right to be there, as he certainly
had not, his owner cannot complain that he was injured by the defences
set up against all dogs in general.

As we have seen, he distinguished between the case of the
deliberate killing of a dog by the owner of the land and the
erection of defences, like a spiked gate, which might injure those
who tried to break through them.[5] His decision in the case of
Sutton v. Clarke,[6] that if a body of persons, acting under statutory
authority with due care, injures another, no action lies, has been
followed by the House of Lords.[7] In the case of *Soares v. Thornton*[8]
he discussed the conditions in which the owner of a ship might be
guilty of barratry.

In the case of *Simpson v. Bloss*[9] the extent to which obligations
arising out of an illegal bet will be enforced—a problem which has
frequently come before the courts—was discussed. Gibbs held
that any claim which could only be substantiated by a proof of an
illegal transaction was unenforceable on the ground of illegality;

and could effect the purpose of impressing the facts upon the jury's mind, by the
same strong and even choice phrases . . . which we have remarked among the
characteristics of his arguments to the Court upon the law," Brougham, op. cit.
129.

[1] " He would sometimes, in giving judgment, suggest a case in point which had
wholly escaped the notice of counsel, and often interposed in the course of their
arguments with pertinent questions, not put unseasonably, or in a manner that
would distract the attention, but with an appositeness that tended to save time by
bringing discussion to a point," Townsend, op. cit. i 293; for an instance in which
he cited a case in his judgment which had escaped the notice of counsel see Crump
v. Norwood (1815) 7 Taunt. at p. 372.

[2] (1817) 7 Taunt. 489.

[3] Jordin v. Crump (1841) 8 M. and W. at p. 788; Ponting v. Noakes [1894]
2 Q.B. at p. 286; cp. Lowery v. Walker [1910] 1 K.B. at pp. 185, 192.

[4] At p. 529.   [5] At. pp. 534-535; above 526, n. 6.

[6] (1815) 6 Taunt. 29 at pp. 42-44.

[7] Mersey Docks Trustees v. Gibbs (1866) L.R. 1 H. of L. at p. 112.

[8] (1817) 7 Taunt. 627.   [9] (1816) 7 Taunt. 246.

and this decision has been frequently followed.[1] In the case of
Bosanquet v. Wray[2] he affirmed the principle that one firm cannot
sue another if a member of one of the firms is also a member of the
other, and that therefore, if the common member died, his
representative could not sue. The only remedy, Gibbs pointed
out, was in the court of Chancery.[3] In *in re Webb*[4] he held that
carriers who gratuitously warehouse goods on arrival till called
for, cease to be liable as carriers, and therefore are not liable if
the goods are accidentally destroyed. It followed that a member
of a firm of carriers who had paid for the damage could not
recover from his partners. In a time of war the question of the
enforceability of contracts with alien enemies naturally emerged.
Gibbs stated the general principles applicable to such contracts
in the case of *Antoine v. Morshead.*[5] He held that, though on a
contract with an alien enemy, originally valid because made before
the outbreak of war, an alien enemy could not sue during the war,
nevertheless, if the debt had not been recovered by the Crown[6]
during the war, the alien enemy could sue on it and recover after
the war. But, in the case of *Willison v. Patteson,*[7] he held that if
the contract was originally void, because made with the alien
enemy after the outbreak of war, he could not sue on it after the
war.

Dealing with a question of maritime law—the question what
could be considered to be a general average loss—Gibbs said :
" nothing in foreign jurists ought to govern our judgment on
these points, unless they have been sanctioned by received
principles, decided cases, or the general usage of merchants." [8]
This statement shows that English lawyers were conscious that
English law had acquired a body of principles applicable to
commercial and maritime law which enabled it to stand on its own
feet. But it is difficult to see how it could have acquired them if
Lord Mansfield had literally followed this dictum. In fact this
attitude tended to make some of the judges give too little weight
to the effect of the general usage of merchants. We have seen
that in two cases it was necessary for the Legislature to intervene
to correct decisions upon the law as to negotiable instruments
which disregarded this usage.[9] It is clear that Gibbs inclined to
the view, held by the judges in the case of *Glyn v. Baker,*[10] that an

---

[1] Begbie v. Phosphate Sewage Co. (1857) L.R. 10 Q.B. at pp. 499-500 ; Scott
v. Brown [1892] 2 Q.B. at pp. 731-732 ; Hyams v. Stuart King [1908] 2 K.B. at
pp. 707-708.

[2] (1815) 6 Taunt. 597. [3] At p. 605.

[4] (1818) 8 Taunt. 443 ; followed in Chapman v. G.W.R. (1880) 5 Q.B.D. 278.

[5] (1815) 6 Taunt. 237.

[6] As to the rights of the Crown to take the property of alien enemies see vol.
ix 98. [7] (1817) 7 Taunt. 439.

[8] Taylor v. Curtis (1816) 6 Taunt. at p. 624. [9] Above 385.

[10] (1811) 13 East at p. 514 ; Crouch v. Crédit Foncier (1873) L.R. 8 Q.B. at
p. 383.

instrument under seal could not be a negotiable instrument.[1]
That view is no longer tenable because it is now recognized that a
general custom of the merchants can attach the quality of
negotiability to an instrument, even though it is under seal.[2]
In the case of *Smith v. Mercer*[3] Gibbs discussed the position of a
banker who paid a bill apparently accepted by a customer, when
it afterwards turned out that he had not accepted it because his
signature was forged. He held that the bankers could not recover
from a *bona fide* holder of the bill because they ought to have
detected the forgery of their customer's signature. But later
cases have shown that the question whether or not the bankers
can recover turns upon somewhat different considerations.[4]
Gibb's ruling at *nisi prius* that a sale induced by fraud does not
pass the property in the goods, is obviously wrong.[5]

In the case of *Taylor v. Waters*[6] Gibbs gave a clear exposition
of the difference between an interest in land and a licence to do
something on the land ;[7] and in the case of *Bunn v. Markham*[8]
he emphasized the rule that a genuine delivery of the property is
needed for a valid *donatio mortis causa*. His decision in the case
of *Rose v. Hart*,[9] which turned on the mutual credit clause of the
bankruptcy Act then in force, has been much discussed,[10] and one
of the reasons given for that decision has been shown not to be
correct.[11] The case of *Morish v. Foote*[12] illustrates the inconvenience of the rule that a person interested in the result of the
action was an incompetent witness. It was held that in an action
against a mail coach proprietor for the negligent driving of the
coachman, the coachman was not a competent witness, because
his liability to his master, if he were proved to be negligent,
made him a person interested in the result of the action.

Gibbs was succeeded by Robert Dallas.[13] Dallas was born in
1756, became a student at Lincoln's Inn in 1772, and was called
to the bar in 1782. Being both a good lawyer and an accomplished
speaker, he soon got a good practice. He greatly distinguished

---

[1] Slack v. Highgate Archway Co. (1814) 5 Taunt. 792.
[2] Goodwin v. Robarts (1875) L.R. 10 Ex. 337 ; Bechuanaland Exploration Co.
v. London Trading Bank [1898] 2 Q.B. 658.
[3] (1815) 6 Taunt. 76.
[4] London and River Plate Bank v. Bank of Liverpool [1896] 1 Q.B. at p. 11
where the principle was stated to be this : " If the mistake is discovered at once,
it may be that the money may be recovered back ; but if it be not, and the money
is paid in good faith, and is received in good faith, and there is an interval of time
in which the position of the holder may be altered, the principle seems to apply that
money once paid cannot be recovered back."
[5] Noble v. Adams (1816) 7 Taunt. at p. 60 ; see Vilmont v. Bentley (1886) 18
Q.B.D. at p. 328 *per* Esher, M.R.
[6] (1816) 7 Taunt. 374.   [7] At pp. 383-384 ; vol. vii 326-328.
[8] (1816) 7 Taunt. 224.   [9] (1818) 8 Taunt. 499.
[10] See In re Daintrey [1900] 1 Q.B. at pp. 557-558.
[11] Gibson v. Bell (1835) 1 Bing. N.C. at pp. 754-755 *per* Tindal C.J.
[12] (1818) 8 Taunt. 454.   [13] Foss, Judges ix 15-17 ; D.N.B.

himself as one of the counsel for Warren Hastings, and, at the conclusion of his trial in 1795, he took silk. He became a member of Parliament in 1802. There he was an effective but not a frequent speaker on the side of the government. In 1804 he was made chief justice of Chester, and in 1813 solicitor-general. Later in the same year he became a judge of the Common Pleas. He acted on the special commission for the trial of the Luddites in 1817, and in the following year succeeded Vicary Gibbs as Chief Justice. Shortly afterwards he was made a Privy Councillor. As Chief Justice he presided at the trial of the Cato Street conspirators. Failing health compelled him to resign in 1823. He died December 25, 1824.

Dallas was a very good lawyer. His judgments are tersely and clearly expressed. They show a remarkable grasp of legal principle, and a power of stating clearly the essential facts of a case. The following are a few of his more important decisions.

Several of his decisions on questions of *public law* are interesting. We have seen that in the case of *Gidley v. Lord Palmerston*[1] he laid down the principle that an aggrieved person cannot bring an action against a servant of the Crown for any act, not amounting to a tort, done by such servant in the course of his official duty. In the case of *Butt v. Conant*[2] he gave a learned and elaborate judgment on the question of the power of the magistrates to arrest a person charged with the publication of a libel. In the case of *Home v. Bentinck*[3] he held that the report of a commission of enquiry into the conduct of an officer, held by the direction of the commander-in-chief, was a privileged communication, so that it could not be given in evidence in an action for libel brought by the officer against the president of the commission. It was, he said, one of those cases in which " for reasons of state and policy information is not permitted to be disclosed."[4] It is a decision which has been frequently cited and approved.[5] In the case of the *Duke of Newcastle v. Clark*[6] he gave an interesting account of the powers and legal position of the commissioners of sewers.[7]

Of his many decisions on the *law of contract and commercial law* the following may be noted :

In the case of *Leigh v. Paterson*[8] Dallas held that if there is a

---

[1] (1822) 3 Brod. and B. 275 ; vol. x 654-655.
[2] (1820) 1 Brod. and B. 548.   [3] (1820) 2 Brod. and B. 130.
[4] At. p. 162.
[5] Hennessy v. Wright (1888) 21 Q.B.D. 509 ; Chatterton v. Secretary of State for India [1895] 2 Q.B. 189.
[6] (1818) 8 Taunt. 602 at pp. 620-626.
[7] For the history of these Commissioners see vol. x 199-206.
[8] (1818) 8 Taunt. 540.

contract to sell goods at a future date, and if a vendor repudiates the contract before that date, and the purchaser does not acquiesce in that repudiation, the measure of damage is the difference between the contract price and the price on the date when they ought to have been delivered.[1] Later cases have established the rule that the other contracting party may acquiesce in the repudiation of the contract and sue at once for damages ;[2] but in the case of a contract for the sale of goods the measure of damages is the same as if he had not acquiesced at once in the repudiation.[3] In the case of *Idle v. Royal Exchange Assurance Co.*[4] he reviewed in a very elaborate judgment the law as to when the captain of a ship may abandon a voyage and sell the ship ; and in the case of *Davidson v. Case*[5] he settled a doubtful point in the law of insurance by holding that if a ship is abandoned to the underwriters, they are entitled to the freight subsequently earned, just as an assignee of the ship would be entitled to it. This decision has always been accepted as correct.[6] In the case of *Rowe and Young*[7] he took the view that an acceptance of a bill of exchange payable at a banker's was a qualified and not a general acceptance—a view which, as we have seen, commended itself to the House of Lords but not to the Legislature.[8]

Two of Dallas's decisions illustrate the rule that where the facts show both a breach of contract and a tort, the plaintiff may elect to sue either in contract or tort.[9] His best known decision in the *law of tort* is in the case of *Wakeman v. Robinson* in which, as we have seen, he ruled that an action will not lie for a purely accidental trespass.[10] In the case of *Turner v. Meymott* [11]

---

[1] The rule is now statutory, Sale of Goods Act 1893, 56, 57 Victoria c. 71 § 51 (3).

[2] Hochster v. De la Tour (1853) 2 El. and Bl. 678 ; Frost v. Knight (1872) L.R. 7 Ex. 111.

[3] 56, 57 Victoria c. 71 § 51 (3).

[4] (1819) 8 Taunt. 755 ; a new trial was ordered by the King's Bench on the ground that the verdict of the jury did not find that the sale was necessary, 3 Brod. and B. 151 n.

[5] (1820) 2 Brod. and B. 379 ; the ship had been captured and abandoned ; then it was recaptured and earned freight ; the contest was between the underwriter of the ship and the underwriters of the freight.

[6] Keith v. Burrows (1877) 2 A.C. at p. 656 *per* Lord Blackburn.

[7] (1820) 2 Brod. and B. 165 at pp. 260-283.   [8] Above 385.

[9] Knights v. Quarles (1820) 2 Brod. and B. 102—action of assumpsit against an attorney for negligence in investigating a title—held to be an action for breach of contract so that the maxim *actio personalis etc.* did not apply ; Bretherton v. Wood (1821) 3 Brod. and B. 54—action on the case against ten defendants as owners of a coach for injuries sustained by negligent driving ; the jury having found a verdict against eight of them, it was observed that the action being one of contract and therefore the liability being joint, judgment could not be given against eight only ; but it was held that the action was in tort, that the liability was therefore several, so that judgment could be given against eight.

[10] (1823) 1 Bing. at p. 215 ; vol. viii 456.

[11] (1823) 1 Bing. 158 ; see Hemmings v. Stoke Poges Golf Club (1920) 1 K.B. 720 ; Pollock, Torts (14th ed.) 307.

he held that trespass did not lie against a landlord who had entered upon a house after the tenant's lease had expired. If he used force he could be indicted, but he could not be sued in an action of trespass if he used no more force than was necessary.

Dallas was a good real property lawyer. Among his many judgments on this topic the following may be noted : If a lessee lets land for the whole term of his lease, he cannot distrain for a rent reserved, because this letting amounts to an assignment, and there is no tenure between him and his assignee.[1] We have seen that in the case of *Williams v. Bosanquet* [2] he agreed with most other common lawyers that Lord Mansfield's decision in the case of *Eaton v. Jacques* [3] could not be supported. In the case of *Nind v. Marshall* [4] he explained the manner in which a lessor's covenant for quiet enjoyment and other covenants for title had been interpreted in different cases ; and in the case of *Buckland v. Butterfield* [5] he surveyed the development of the law as to fixtures. His remarks in the latter case have been approved by Coleridge, J.[6] and by Stirling, L.J.[7] In the case of *Gray v. Bond* [8] he held that twenty years' user of an easement raised a presumption that a grant had been made ; but that it was merely a rebuttable presumption of law.[9]

In the case of *Cromack v. Heathcote* [10] he extended unduly the privilege of an attorney to refuse to testify as to communications between him and his client ; for in that case the rule that privilege does not extend to communications made for the purpose of perpetrating a fraud was disregarded.[11]

Dallas was succeeded by Robert Gifford ; but Gifford, after holding the office of Chief Justice only three months, was made Master of the Rolls. I shall give some account of him when I deal with the holders of that office during this period.[12]

Gifford was succeeded in 1824 by William Draper Best.[13] Best was born in 1767 and was educated at Wadham College, Oxford, which college he left without taking a degree. He was called to the bar by the Middle Temple in 1789, and early in his

---

[1] Parmenter v. Webber (1818) 8 Taunt. 593 ; see Lewis v. Baker [1905] 1 Ch. at p. 50.
[2] (1819) 1 Brod. and B. at p. 263.
[3] (1780) 2 Dougl. 455 ; vol. xii 588.
[4] (1819) 1 Brod. and B. at pp. 345-349.
[5] (1820) 2 Brod. and B. at p. 58.
[6] Bishop v. Elliott (1855) 11 Ex. at p. 120.
[7] In re De Falbe [1901] 1 Ch. at p. 539.
[8] (1821) 2 Brod. and B. at pp. 670-671.
[9] For the history of the law on this topic see vol. vii 345-349.
[10] (1820) 2 Brod. and B. 4.
[11] R. v. Cox and Railton (1884) 14 Q.B.D. 153.
[12] Below 578, 664-665.   [13] Foss, Judges ix 9-12 ; D.N.B.

career had the good fortune to be complimented by Lord Kenyon for his conduct of a case.[1] He soon acquired a leading practice. He became a serjeant-at-law in 1799, and a member of Parliament in 1802. In 1804 he acted as one of the managers of Lord Melville's impeachment. He became a great favourite with the Prince Regent, to whom, it was said, he owed his further promotions.[2] He was made successively solicitor- and attorney-general to the Prince, chief justice of Chester, and in 1818 a judge of the King's Bench. In 1824 he became Chief Justice of the Common Pleas. Ill-health compelled him to retire in 1829,[3] and, the royal favour continuing, he was raised to the peerage as Baron Wynford, and appointed deputy-speaker of the House of Lords. In the House of Lords he took part in the hearing of appeals, and, since he had become a stout Tory, it is not surprising that he had several altercations with Brougham.[4] On one occasion Brougham actually tried to reverse by Act of Parliament one of his decisions on a Scotch appeal in the House of Lords, which was right in principle.[5] He died on March 3, 1845.

Best was an effective advocate, pressing his clients' causes with zeal and acuteness. Throughout his life he never lost the temperament of an advocate ; and so, in Campbell's opinion, he made a bad judge[6]—"amiable and eloquent but not very logical." [7] It is said that he sometimes allowed his political bias to appear in his utterances from the bench,[8] that his temper was irritable,[9] and that he was apt, in his summings up, to show so much partiality that he was nicknamed the " judge advocate." [10] These were the opinions of contemporaries. No doubt they are good evidence as to Best's manners on the bench ; but I think that the reports show that they do not do justice to his dislike of technical objections which prevented substantial justice from

[1] Shakespear v. Peppin (1796) 6 T.R. 741.
[2] Campbell, Chief Justices iii 291 ; Campbell, Chancellors viii 418 ; Foss, Judges ix 11.
[3] He was absent from Court during the Michaelmas term 1827 through illness, 4 Bing. 387.   [4] Campbell, Chancellors viii 418-419.
[5] Ibid 400-402 ; Wynford had ordered a new trial and had directed that it should be before a special jury and that the parties should be examined—but special juries were not known in Scotland, and both parties were dead ; the House corrected the judgment on these points, as it had power to do.
[6] " I remember a serjeant-at-law having brilliant success at the bar from always sincerely believing that his client was entitled to succeed, although, when a Chief Justice, he proved without any exception, and beyond all comparison, the most indifferent judge who has appeared in Westminster Hall in my time," Campbell, Chief Justices iii 276.   [7] Ibid 291.
[8] See e.g. his remarks on the corn laws in Woodley v. Brown (1825) 2 Bing. at p. 530, which, though sensible, were inappropriate.
[9] An illustration of his display of temper is seen in his conduct in fining a defendant three times for words used by him in his argument, R. v. Davison (1821) 4 B. and Ald. at p. 330 ; but as Campbell said, being good natured though a passionate man, he remitted the fines before the court rose, Chief Justices iii 294 n.
[10] Foss, Judges ix 12.

being done,[1] to his grasp of legal principles, and to his capacity to state those principles clearly.

Several of his decisions on the *law of contract and commercial law* are important. The case of *Routledge v. Grant*[2] is the foundation of the line of cases which establishes the rule that a promise to keep an offer open for a fixed time is a unilateral promise which, being made without consideration, can be withdrawn at any time before acceptance. The case of *Young v. Grote*[3] settled that if a person drew a cheque so carelessly that fraud was facilitated, and fraud was committed, the drawer, not the bank, must bear the loss. That case, after having been so commented on and discussed that it appeared to be almost overruled, was finally resuscitated and restored to life by the decision of the House of Lords in the case of *London Joint Stock Bank v. Macmillan*.[4] In the case of *East London Waterworks v. Bailey* Best's remarks as to what contracts of a corporation need not be under seal[5] have been approved,[6] though it has been held that in that case those rules were wrongly applied.[7] His decision in the case of *Homer v. Ashford*,[8] and his remarks upon the question what contracts in restraint of trade are invalid and what are valid,[9] are sound and sensible. His decision in the case of *Jones v. Bright*[10] laid down the broad principle, which has been frequently approved[11] and is now embodied in the Sale of Goods Act 1893,[12] that " if a man sells an article he thereby warrants that it is merchantable—that is, fit for some purpose . . . If he sells it for a particular purpose, he thereby warrants it fit for that purpose ; and no case has decided otherwise, although there are, doubtless, some dicta to the contrary."[13] The reasons which he gave for his

---

[1] In Ditcham v. Chivas (1828) 4 Bing. at p. 709 he said, " I have no objection that it should be said of me that I always entertained a strong impression against deciding on the ground of variance " [i.e. variance between the allegation in the declaration and the proof] ; in Strother v. Barr (1828) 5 Bing. at p. 153 he said, " Lord Mansfield, speaking many years ago against subtilties and refinements being introduced into our law, said they were encroachments upon common sense, and mankind would not fail to regret them. . . . Our jurisprudence should be bottomed on plain broad principles, such as, not only judges can without difficulty apply to the cases that occur, but as those whose rights are to be decided upon by them can understand. If our rules are to be encumbered with all the exceptions which ingenious minds can imagine, there is no certain principle to direct us, and it were better to apply the principles of justice to every case, and not to proceed to more fixed rules."

[2] (1828) 4 Bing. 653 ; see Bryne v. Van Tienhoven (1880) 5 C.P.D. at p. 347 ; Stevenson v. McLean (1880) 5 Q.B.D. at p. 351 ; Bristol Aerated Bread Co. v. Maggs (1890) 44 C.D. at p. 625.   [3] (1827) 4 Bing. 253.
[4] [1918] A.C. 777 ; above 524.   [5] (1827) 4 Bing. at pp. 287-288.
[6] Wells v. Mayor of Kingston-upon-Hull (1875) L.R. 10 C.P. at pp. 411-412.
[7] South of Ireland Colliery Co. v. Waddle (1868) L.R. 3. C.P. at p. 475.
[8] (1825) 3 Bing. 322.   [9] At pp. 326-327.   [10] (1829) 5 Bing. 533.
[11] See e.g. Drummond v. Van Ingen (1887) 12 A.C. at pp. 290-291 *per* Lord Herschell ; Jones v. Padgett (1890) 24 Q.B.D. at pp. 652-653 *per* Lord Coleridge, C.J.
[12] 56, 57 Victoria c. 71 § 14 (1).   [13] 5 Bing. at p. 544.

decision in the case of *Davis v. Bank of England*[1] as to the
liabilities of the bank when it transfers stock under a forged power
of attorney have been approved.[2]   In the case of *Williams v.
Barton*[3] he made some just criticisms upon a defect in the common
law, which has been partially remedied by the Factors Acts[4] and
by a clause in the Sale of Goods Act 1893.[5] He said,[6]

> had I authority to alter the law as the mode of carrying on commerce
> has altered, I would say that, when the owner of property conceals
> himself, whoever can prove a good title under the person whom the
> concealed owner permits to hold it, should retain that property against
> the owner—but this is not yet the law of England. Possession is not
> proof of property.

Best's judgments in the case of *Garland v. Jekyll*[7] on the
lord's rights to heriots, and in the case of *Rennell v. Bishop of
Lincoln*[8] on the right to present to a living, show that he was a
learned real property lawyer. His opinion, and the opinions of the
other judges, which he delivered to the House of Lords in the case
of *Gifford v. Lord Yarborough*[9] states the law as to the acquisition
of property by *alluvio*. Those opinions show that English law
had taken over *via* Bracton the Roman rules on this topic.[10]
We have seen that his opinion as to the validity of resignation
bonds in the case of *Fletcher v. Lord Sondes*,[11] though contrary to a
decision of the House of Lords and therefore bad law, was probably
the better opinion ; and that the House of Lords agreed that the
law there laid down must be amended by the Legislature.[12]
Several of his decisions in the *law of tort* are important. In the
case of *Bird v. Holbrook*[13] Best defended himself successfully from
the strictures passed upon his judgment in *Ilott v. Wilkes*,[14] and
held that if, as in the former case, no notice of the existence of
spring guns were given to a trespasser, and he was injured by them,
he could recover. In the case of *Dunne v. Anderson*[15] he stated the
basic principle upon which the defence of fair comment rests.
His decision in the case of *Adamson v. Jarvis*,[16] that the rule
that there could be no contribution between joint tortfeasors
must be limited to the case where the person seeking contribution

---

[1] (1824) 2 Bing. 393 ; the decision was reversed, but on a point of pleading
only (1826) 5 B. and C. 185.
[2] Bank of England v. Cutler [1908] 2 K.B. at pp. 234-235 *per* Farwell L. J.
[3] (1825) 3 Bing. 139.   [4] Above 382-384.
[5] 56, 57 Victoria c. 71 § 25.   [6] 3 Bing. at p. 145.
[7] (1824) 2 Bing. 273 ; for heriots see vol. ii 75 ; vol. iii 57, 200 ; vol. vii 307.
[8] (1825) 3 Bing 223.
[9] (1828) 5 Bing. 163 ; above 527 ; the name of the attorney-general is substituted
for that of the King as plaintiff in this report.
[10] Vol. ii 289 n. 6.   [11] (1826) 3 Bing. 501, at pp. 567-596.
[12] Above 420, 421.   [13] (1828) 4 Bing. 628.
[14] (1820) 3 B. and Ald. 304 ; above 526.
[15] (1825) 3 Bing. at p. 97.   [16] (1827) 4 Bing. 66

knew that he was doing an unlawful act,[1] has been generally approved.[2] On the other hand, some of the reasons which he gave for his decision in the case of *Hall v. Smith*[3] as to the non-liability of public authorities for the torts of their employees have not been approved.[4] Some of his decisions which turn upon the limits of the jurisdiction of inferior courts show a very accurate knowledge of the law upon this intricate and technical subject.[5] His decision in the case of *Douglas v. Forrest*[6] is an authority on the right to sue on a foreign judgment, and for the proposition that, until an executor has either accepted office or proved the will, there is no one against whom an action can be effectively brought, so that till the happening of those events the operation of the statute of limitations is suspended.[7]

Best's successor, Nicolas Conyngham Tindal, was the most eminent of all the Chief Justices of the Common Pleas appointed during this period ; and since, as the result of the Uniformity of Process Act,[8] the court of Common Pleas was able to compete on more equal terms with the court of King's Bench, he and his court were able to make a more considerable contribution to the development of the common law than his predecessors.

Tindal[9] was born at Coval Hall near Chelmsford December 12, 1776. He came of a literary and legal stock. Matthew Tindal, the deist and civilian,[10] and the Whig opponent of Jacobites and high churchmen, was one of his ancestors ; and Nicolas Tindal the historian, who was Matthew's nephew, was his great-grandfather. He was educated at Chelmsford Grammar School and Trinity College, Cambridge. At Cambridge he graduated as eighth wrangler in 1799, won the Chancellor's gold medal in the same year, and in 1801 was elected a fellow of Trinity. He entered Lincoln's Inn in 1802, and learned the art of pleading in the chambers of John Richardson,[11] afterwards a judge of the court of Common Pleas. Like many other lawyers, he acquired a good practice as a pleader before he was called to the bar in 1809. He soon made his name as a very learned lawyer, who was capable of presenting to the court lucid and logical arguments on the most abstruse points of law.

---

[1] (1827) 4 Bing. at p. 73. [2] Pollock, Torts (14th ed.) 160.
[3] (1824) 2 Bing. 156.
[4] Mersey Docks Trustees v. Gibbs (1866) L.R. 1 H. of L. at pp. 115-116.
[5] See Briscoe v. Stephens (1824) 2 Bing. 213, approved, Mayor of London v. Cox (1867) L.R. 2 H. of L. at p. 263 ; Wickes v. Clutterbuck (1825) 2 Bing. 483 ; Scott v. Bye (1824) 2 Bing. 344 ; Tingle v. Roston (1825) ibid 463.
[6] (1828) 4 Bing. 686 ; but the dictum at p. 703 that the fact that the defendant had property in the foreign country gives the foreign court jurisdiction has not been approved, Halsbury, Laws of England (2nd ed.) vi 332 n. (v).
[7] See Mohamidu Mohideen Hadjiar v. Pitchey [1894] A.C. at pp. 442-443.
[8] 2 and 3 William IV c. 39 ; vol. i 222.
[9] Foss, Judges ix 281-286 ; E. Manson, The Builders of our Law (2nd ed.) 18-25 ; D.N.B.
[10] Vol. xii 664. [11] Foss, Judges ix 37-39.

In 1818 he showed his knowledge of old law by his argument in the case of *Ashford v. Thornton*, which persuaded the court of King's Bench that it must order a trial by battle.[1] Amongst his pupils were Brougham and Parke ; and it was through Brougham that he was retained as one of the counsel for Queen Caroline. He became a member of Parliament in 1824, and in 1827 he was elected as a member for Cambridge University. The year before, though he had not yet taken silk, he was made solicitor-general. He waived his claims to the attorney-generalship in 1827 when Scarlett succeeded Wetherell, and in 1828 when Wetherell was reappointed. In 1829 he was made Chief Justice of the Common Pleas. He held that post till his death on July 6, 1846.

Tindal had all the qualities of a great judge. He was learned in all branches of the common law new and old, so that it is not surprising that many of his judgments show a considerable knowledge of legal history, medieval[2] and modern.[3] His learning, coupled with his lucid and logical mind, gave him the power of disengaging and stating clearly the essential facts of the case, and of explaining clearly and succinctly the legal principles and rules applicable to those facts. His grave dignity inspired respect, and his urbane manners and the kindliness of his disposition made him popular with the bar, in spite, in his later years, of a tendency to procrastinate. He had a pretty wit of a professional kind of which many specimens are remembered. Here are one or two examples : One of the serjeants, coming in late for dinner at Serjeants Inn Hall, found no place left for him. " How now, brother," said Tindal, " you look like an outstanding term that's unsatisfied." Being asked whether another serjeant, whose oratory was of the serjeant Buzfuz type, was a sound lawyer, he replied, " Well, sir, you raise a doubtful point, whether roaring is unsoundness." Towards the end of his career he was joined, while riding in the park, by John Campbell, who, it was said, wished for his chief justiceship. Campbell congratulated him on the sure-footedness of his horse. He is getting old, said Tindal. All the better for that, said Campbell, I advise you on no account to part with him. I thought over this advice, said Tindal, and sold him next day to someone I knew would take good care of him.

Tindal tried several *causes célèbres*—the action for criminal conversation brought by Norton against Lord Melbourne ;[4]

---

[1] 1 B. and Ald. at pp. 440-453.

[2] See for instance, the opinion which he gave to the House of Lords in Birtwhistle v. Vardill (1840) 6 Bing. N.C. at pp. 386-399, and the historical account of writs of quo warranto and informations in the nature of quo warranto which he gave to the House of Lords in Darley v. Reg. (1846) 12 Cl. and Fin. at pp. 536-542.

[3] See, for instance, the history which he gave of the statutes regulating the Bank of England in the Bank of England v. Anderson (1837) 3 Bing. N.C. at pp. 650-662.

[4] See Life of Lord Campbell ii 82-85—Campbell, then attorney-general, was Lord Melbourne's counsel.

the trial of Courvoisier for the murder of Lord William Russell;[1] and the trial of M'Naghten,[2] after which the House of Lords took the opinion of the judges,[3] which Tindal delivered, as to the effect of insanity upon criminal liability. It was while he was Chief Justice that Brougham procured the issue to himself of a royal warrant under the sign manual depriving the serjeants of their right of exclusive audience in the court of Common Pleas.[4] This mandate was sent by Brougham to the Chief Justice, and it was for a short time obeyed;[5] but, after hearing arguments for and against its validity, Tindal decided that it was ultra vires the prerogative and therefore invalid.[6] But Tindal's main contribution to the development of the common law was made in the hundreds of civil cases which he decided in his court of Common Pleas. The following are a very few of the most notable of these cases :

Many of Tindal's decisions in the sphere of the *law of contract and commercial law* are very important. The case of *Kemble v. Farren*[7] is a leading case on the distinction between penalty and liquidated damages. The case of *Horner v. Graves*[8] is the most important decision on contracts in restraint of trade since the case of *Mitchell v. Reynolds*.[9] This and other decisions of Tindal on this subject deservedly won high praise from Lord Macnaghten,[10] for they lay down for the first time the modern principle which the House of Lords has approved—the principle that the test of the validity of such contracts is reasonableness both from the point of view of the parties to them and from the point of view of the public.[11] His decision in the case of *Planche v. Colburn*[12] is a leading case on the conditions on which a party to a contract can sue on a

---

[1] Kenny, Outlines of Criminal Law (ed. Turner), 374.

[2] (1843) 10 Cl. and Fin. 200.

[3] Except Maule J. who gave a separate opinion.

[4] For the order see 10 Bing. 571-572 ; above 438, 455 ; below n. 6 (this page).

[5] See Power v. Izod (1834) 1 Bing. N.C. at p. 305.

[6] (1839) 1 Bing. N.C. 187-196, 232-239 ; the serjeants created after this episode engraved on their rings the motto, " *honos nomenque manebunt* " ; the validity of the order was also argued before the Privy Council, see vol. ii 311 n. 3 ; above 438, 455. [7] (1829) 6 Bing. 141.

[8] (1831) 7 Bing. 735.

[9] (1711) 1 P. Wms. 181 ; for an account of this case and its historical importance see vol. viii 60-62.

[10] " There is no higher authority on this subject in modern times than Tindal, C.J. He had more to do with moulding the law on this head and bringing it into harmony with common sense than all the judges since Lord Macclesfield's time put together. You will hardly find any judgment in reference to restraint of trade delivered by any court in England or America during the last sixty years in which some passage is not cited from some judgment of Tindal, C.J.," Nordenfelt v. Maxim Nordenfelt Co. [1894] A.C. at pp. 569-570.

[11] "The greater question is whether this is a reasonable restraint of trade. And we do not see how a better test can be applied to the question, whether reasonable or not, than by considering whether the restraint is such only as to afford a fair protection to the interests of the party in favour of whom it is given, and not so large as to interfere with the interests of the public," Horner v. Graves (1831) 7 Bing. at p. 743. [12] (1831) 8 Bing. 14.

quantum meruit for its breach. The case of *Flight v. Booth*[1] for the first time laid down the broad principle that on a contract to sell leasehold premises, a material misdescription will make the contract voidable, and that a vendor is under a duty to disclose facts relating to the title of which he had, and the purchaser could not have, any knowledge.

In the case of *Yates v. Why:*[2] he laid down a principle which has been approved by the House of Lords,[3] that where the underwriters have paid for the damage suffered by a ship, the wrongdoer, who has caused the damage, cannot deduct from the damages payable by him the amount of the insurance.[4] His decision in the case of *Brandao v. Barnett*,[5] in which he upheld the mercantile custom which gave bankers a lien on their customers' securities deposited with them, was upheld by the House of Lords.[6] In the case of *Brown v. Edgington*[7] he laid down the principle that if a chattel is supplied by a dealer in such chattels for a particular purpose disclosed to the dealer, there is an implied warranty that it is fit for that purpose ; and in the case of *Shepherd v. Pybus*[8] he laid down the principle that on the sale of a chattel there is an implied warranty that it is reasonably fit for use. His statement of one of the essential conditions for the ratification by a person of an act done on his behalf without authority—the condition that it must be done on behalf of that person[9]—has been approved by the House of Lords.[10]

Many of Tindal's decisions in the *law of tort* lay down basic principles. In the case of *Saunders v. Mills*[11] he laid down the principle that a fair and accurate report of the proceedings in the courts is privileged ; and in the case of *Ward v. Weeks*[12] he laid it down that a person who utters a slander is not responsible for damage caused by its unauthorized repetition—a decision which, though criticized,[13] has been recognized as authoritative by the court of appeal[14] and the House of Lords.[15] His judgment in the

---

[1] (1834) 1 Bing. N.C. 370. [2] (1838) 4 Bing. N.C. 272.

[3] Simpson v. Thomson (1877) 3 A.C. 279 at p. 285.

[4] " If the plaintiff cannot recover, the wrongdoer pays nothing, and takes all the benefit of a policy of insurance without paying the premium," 4 Bing. N.C. at p. 283. [5] (1840) 1 Man. and Gr. at p. 936.

[6] (1846) 12 Cl. and Fin. 787—restoring the judgment of the Common Pleas which had been reversed by the Exchequer Chamber (1843) 6 Man. and Gr. 630.

[7] (1841) 2 M. and Gr. 279 ; approved in Jones v. Just (1868) L.R. 3 Q.B. at p. 203 ; approved and applied in Randall v. Newson (1877) 2 Q.B.D. 102.

[8] (1842) 3 M. and Gr. 868 ; approved in Jones v. Just (1868) L.R. 3 Q.B. at p. 203.

[9] Wilson v. Tumman (1843) 6 M. and Gr. at pp. 242-243.

[10] Keighley Maxted & Co. v. Durant [1901] A.C. at pp. 246-247.

[11] (1829) 6 Bing. at p. 218, cited with approval in Kimber v. Press Association [1893] 1 Q.B. at p. 76. [12] (1830) 7 Bing. 211.

[13] Riding v. Smith (1876) 1 Ex. Div. at p. 94 *per* Kelly, C.B.

[14] Ratcliffe v. Evans [1892] 2 Q.B. at p. 530.

[15] Weld-Blundell v. Stephens [1920] A.C. 956.

case of *Coxhead v. Richards*,[1] from which two of his brethren
dissented, as to the occasions on which privilege can be pleaded
to an action for libel, has been approved by Lindley, L.J.[2]
The case of *Foster v. Charles*[3] lays down the principle that a
statement, false to the knowledge of its maker, is not the less an
actionable deceit because the maker's motive in making it was not
a bad motive. His definition of champerty, in the case of *Stanley
v. Jones*,[4] has been cited with approval ;[5] and his statement, in the
case of *Anthony v. Haney*,[6] of the circumstances in which an owner
can enter on land to retake his goods, has also been approved.[7]
On the other hand, his decision that the true owner of land who
makes a forcible entry is liable to be sued in tort, has not been
upheld.[8] We have seen that his decision in the case of *Leake v.
Loveday* settled the question when the defence of a jus tertii could
be pleaded to an action of trover ;[9] and that his decision in
Vaughan v. Menlove settled that the degree of care required by the
law was to be fixed by an objective standard—the standard of the
ordinary prudent man.[10] His decision in the case of *Dobree v.
Napier*[11] is an authority for the proposition that an act done by a
British subject in a foreign country, with the authority of that
country's sovereign, is an act of state which gives no right of action
in an English court. His dicta and those of the other judges in the
case of *Gregory v. Duke of Brunswick*[12] have been frequently cited
in cases upon the tort of conspiracy.[13] His decision in the case of
Grinnell v. Wells[14] called forth the often cited criticism of Manning,
the reporter, upon the shortcomings of the action for seduction.[15]

Tindal gave many notable decisions on *the law of property
real and personal*. His decision in the case of *Liggins v. Inge*[16] as to
the rights and duties of a licensee who has acted under the licence
has been approved by the Judicial Committee of the Privy
Council[17]—though some of the dicta in that case as to the rights
of the public in water flowing in a stream have been questioned.[18]
His decision as to what amounts to user as of right within the

---

[1] (1846) 2 C.B. 569.   [2] Stuart v. Bell [1891] 2 Q.B. at pp. 346-347.
[3] (1830) 6 Bing. 396 ; cp. Derry v. Peek (1889) 14 A.C. at p. 365 *per* Lord
Herschell.   [4] (1831) 7 Bing. at p. 377.
[5] Guy v. Churchill (1888) 40 C.D. at pp. 488-489.
[6] (1832) 8 Bing. at pp. 192-193.
[7] Salmond, Torts (9th ed.) 199 n. (*p*).
[8] Newton v. Harland (1840) 1 Man. and Gr. 644 ; Hemmings v. Stoke Poges
Golf Club [1920] 1 K.B. 720.
[9] (1842) 4 M. and Gr. 972 ; vol. vii 429.
[10] (1837) 3 Bing. N.C. 468 at p. 475 ; vol. viii 450.
[11] (1836) 2 Bing. N.C. 781 ; see Carr v. Fracis Times and Co. [1902] A.C.
at pp. 179-180.   [12] (1844) 6 M. and Gr. 953.
[13] Pollock, Torts (14th ed.) 254-255.   [14] (1844) 7 M. and Gr. 1033.
[15] Ibid at p. 1044 n., cited vol. viii 429.   [16] (1831) 7 Bing. 682.
[17] Plimmer v. Mayor of Wellington (1884) 9 A.C. at p. 714.
[18] Ormerod v. Todmorden Mill Co. (1883) 11 Q.B.D. at pp. 159-161 *per* Cave, J.

meaning of the Prescription Act 1832 has been approved ;[1] his decision in *Harrison v. Harrison* [2] settled a doubtful point as to the scope of the rule in *Shelley's Case* ;[3] and his decision in *Adams v. Gibney* [4] is an authority as to the extent of the covenant implied by the use of the word " demise ". We have seen that in the case of *Reeves v. Capper* he recognized the rule that a verbal gift of chattels without delivery passes no property to the donee.[5]

Some of Tindal's opinions and decisions in the law of evidence are important. His opinion given to the House of Lords in the case of *Wright v. Tatham,* [6] that letters written to a testator, upon which there was no evidence that he took any action, were not admissible evidence of his sanity, was adopted by the House of Lords. The case of *Miller v. Travers* [7] is an illustration of the rule that no parol evidence of the intention of a testator is admissible to interpret his will. Tindal's judgment gives a very clear exposition of the cases where parol evidence is admissible in order to interpret a written document and when it is not. In the case of *O'Connor v. Marjoribanks*[8] he discussed and explained the scope of the rule that a wife is not a competent witness for or against her husband, and held that she was an incompetent witness and that her evidence was inadmissible even though the marriage had been dissolved by death.

Several of his decisions touch on points of *private international law.* The case of *Trimbey v. Vignier,*[9] though it comes to a right conclusion, does not accurately state the modern rule as to what is the " proper law " to be applied to contracts made abroad.[10] On the other hand, the distinction which, following Story, he drew between a foreign statute which extinguishes an obligation, and a foreign statute which only bars the right of action, is accepted.[11] His opinion and that of the other judges given to the House of Lords in the case of *Birtwhistle v. Vardill,*[12] that an heir to an estate of inheritance must

---

[1] Beasley v. Clarke (1836) 2 Bing. N.C. 705 ; cp. Gardner v. Hodgeson's Kingston Brewery Co. [1903] A.C. 229 ; Hyman v. Van den Bergh [1907] 2 Ch. at p. 531.

[2] (1844) 7 M. and Gr. 938.

[3] Van Grutten v. Foxwell [1897] A.C. at p. 668 *per* Lord Macnaghten.

[4] (1830) 6 Bing. 656 ; see vol. vii 252-253, 255.

[5] (1838) 5 Bing. N.C. at p. 139 ; vol. vii 509.

[6] 1838 4 Bing. N.C. 489 at pp. 566-571 ; but he thought that one letter ought to be admitted, because, contrary to the view of six judges and the House of Lords, he held there was evidence that the testator had acted on it.

[7] (1832) 8 Bing. 244.

[8] (1842) 4 M. and Gr. 435 at pp. 442-442 ; for a discussion of this case see Shenton v. Tyler [1939] Ch. 620 at pp. 632-633 ; see 56 L.Q.R. 137.

[9] (1834) 1 Bing. N.C. 151.

[10] Cheshire, Private International Law (3rd ed.) 305.

[11] Huber v. Steiner (1835) 2 Bing. N.C. 202 at pp. 211-212 ; Cheshire, Private International Law (3rd ed.) 75, 834.

[12] (1840) 6 Bing. N.C. 385 ; above 527, 550.

be born of parents who at the time of his birth were married, though undoubtedly the law of England, is an anomaly from the point of view of private international law, but an anomaly which, since the legislation of 1925, is of little practical importance.[1] In the case of *Smith v. Nicolls* [2] he laid down the rule that by a foreign judgment the original cause of action is not merged, as it is by judgment of an English court of record, so that the successful party can sue either on the judgment or on the original cause of action. His decision in the case of *Pisani v. Lawson*,[3] that an alien resident abroad could sue in England for a libel upon him published in England, was founded on authorities which went back to the sixteenth century.[4]

Some other of his rulings in miscellaneous matters are interesting. In the case of *Whitaker v. Tatham*, which turned on an executor's right to undisposed of residue, he, in effect, admitted that law had followed equity.[5] In the case of *Mellish v. Richardson*[6] he stated the rule which prevailed down to the Judicature Acts, that "the practice of the courts is a matter which belongs by law to the exclusive discretion of the court itself." He and the other judges, though bound to answer questions put to them by the House of Lords as to the interpretation of Acts of Parliament and other points of law, held that they were not bound to answer a question as to the construction of a bill which was being considered by the House.[7] The case of *Tucker v. Inman* [8] illustrates the working arrangement between the courts of common law, the court of Chancery, and the ecclesiastical courts as to matters relating to the administration of the estates of deceased persons, which, as we have seen, had been reached in the eighteenth century.[9]

We have seen that the court of King's Bench between the years 1823 and 1827 heard more than three times as many actions as the court of Common Pleas.[10] During the same period the court of Common Pleas heard slightly more than double as many

---

[1] Cheshire, op. cit. 528.

[2] (1839) 5 Bing. N.C. 208 ; Cheshire, op. cit. 768 ; Dr. Cheshire regards the doctrine as anomalous ; it is, I think, the logical consequence of the view that a merger can only take place by the judgment of a court of record ; for the history of the very technical and not wholly rational concept of a court of record see vol. v 157-160.

[3] (1839) 6 Bing. N.C. 90.

[4] Vol. ix 97.

[5] (1831) 7 Bing. at p. 636.

[6] (1832) 9 Bing. at p. 126 ; under the Judicature Acts the judges have a statutory power to make rules of practice, vol. i 646.

[7] In re London and Westminster Bank (1834) 1 Bing. N.C. 197.

[8] (1842) 4 M. and Gr. 1049.

[9] Vol. vii 697-701.

[10] Above 296, 297, 403, 404.

actions as the court of Exchequer.[1] As Brougham said in 1828,[2] and as the Common Law Procedure Commissioners pointed out in 1829,[3] the time of the judges of that court was not fully occupied. Therefore the contribution made by the court of Exchequer to the development of the common law was considerably less than that of the other two common law courts. In fact the great days of the court as a court of common law did not begin till the following period, when the effect of the Uniformity of Process Act[4] and other procedural changes, coupled with an improvement in the equity of the judges of the court,[5] enabled it to compete upon more equal terms with the other two common law courts. But the common law jurisdiction of the court, like its equitable jurisdiction,[6] was not its principal and proper jurisdiction. It was originally and primarily a court for revenue cases, and it exercised a supervisory jurisdiction over the officers of the Exchequer and other revenue officials.[7] These revenue cases and its equitable jurisdiction in cases of tithes [8] occupy the largest space in the Exchequer reports. And so, although the judges of the court were less fully occupied than the judges of the other two common law courts, the variety in the jurisdiction of their court demanded from them a larger range of legal knowledge than that demanded from the other common law judges. At this point I shall give a short account of the careers of the chief barons of the Exchequer, and then say something of their contribution to the development of the different branches of the law administered in their court.

The first of the chief barons during this period was Archibald Macdonald, who succeeded James Eyre[9] in 1793. Macdonald[10] was born at Armidale Castle in the Isle of Skye on July 13, 1747. He was educated at Westminster School, and Christ Church, Oxford, and was called to the bar by Lincoln's Inn in 1770. He soon gained a reputation as a sound lawyer—his argument in the case of *Campbell v. Hall* was praised by Lord Mansfield.[11] His further advancement was due partly to his own abilities legal and social, and more especially to his marriage to the daughter of the Earl of Gower. In 1778 he

[1] Vol. i 200 n. 8 ; the figure 27,197 is a mistake for 37,197 ; in 1830 Lyndhurst in a speech in the House of Lords said that the number of cases brought to trial during the preceding five years were in the King's Bench 11,000, in the Common Pleas 3,000, and in the Exchequer 500, and that in the City of London not a single special jury case was set down for trial in the Exchequer, Hansard (2nd Ser.) xxiii 678. [2] Above 296, 297.

[3] Parlt. Papers 1829 ix 17. [4] 2 and 3 William IV c. 39 ; vol. i 222, 240.

[5] Greville, Memoirs iii 73 says that Lyndhurst had so increased the popularity of the court that in 1833 48,000 actions were begun there, and only 39,000 from the King's Bench ; Atlay, the Victorian Chancellors i 82-83.

[6] Vol. i 240-242 ; below 565, 566. [7] Vol. i 238-239 ; below 558-560.

[8] Below 565, 566. [9] Vol. xii 565-568.

[10] Foss, Judges viii 329-332 ; D.N.B. [11] (1774) 20 S.T. at p. 306.

took silk and became a member of the House of Commons. It was his consistent support of Pitt that gained for him the position of solicitor-general in 1784, and attorney-general in 1788. As attorney-general he prosecuted Stockdale for a libel in the House of Commons, and Paine for the seditious libels contained in his *Rights of Man*. In that capacity he always used his powers, as Burke said in the House of Commons,[1] with judgment, prudence, and humanity. He was made chief baron of the Exchequer in 1793, and filled that post till he retired in 1813. He died May 18, 1826. As chief baron he was one of the judges on the trial of Hardy,[2] and he presided at the trial of Governor Wall.[3] His decisions show that he was a competent, but not a very distinguished judge. His successor was Vicary Gibbs of whom I have given an account.[4] Gibbs held the post of chief baron for less than three months, and was succeeded by Alexander Thomson.[5] Thomson, before he was raised to the bench, had practised in the court of Chancery, and had been successively a master in, and accountant-general of, that court. He was made a baron of the Exchequer in 1787, and succeeded Gibbs as chief baron in 1814. He died in 1817. Foss says of him :[6]

His reputation as a lawyer and as a judge was of the highest order, his acquirements in scholastic literature were very great, and his disposition as a man was eminently social and kind. To his deep learning and comprehensive understanding was united a great love of jocularity. On being asked how the business proceeded in his court, when sitting between Chief Baron Macdonald and Baron Graham, he is reported as saying, " What between snuff-box on one side and chatter-box on the other, we get on pretty well."

Thomson's successor was Richard Richards.[7] He was born at Dolgelly on November 5, 1752, and was educated at Ruthin Grammar School, and at Jesus and Wadham Colleges, Oxford. He was called to the bar by the Inner Temple in 1780 and practised in the court of Chancery. In 1813 he became chief justice of Chester and in 1814 a baron of the Exchequer. He became chief baron in 1817. In 1819 he was appointed deputy speaker of the House of Lords while Eldon was ill. He died in 1823, respected as a sound though not a brilliant lawyer. He was succeeded by William Alexander.[8] He had had a large equity practice, and was made a master in Chancery in 1809 by Lord Eldon. It was Eldon's favour which procured him the position of chief baron of the Exchequer in 1824—to the surprise, it

[1] Parlt. Hist. xxix 512.
[2] Above 160, 162.
[3] Above 501, 502.
[4] Above 535-542.
[5] Foss, Judges viii 373-374.
[6] Ibid 374.
[7] Ibid ix 36-37 : D.N.B.
[8] Foss, Judges ix 74-75.

was said, of the legal profession. But he proved himself to be an able judge—more especially on the equity side of the court. He resigned in 1831 to make way for Lord Lyndhurst, and died in 1842. Of Lord Lyndhurst, Lord Chancellor for a few years in this period, and twice Lord Chancellor in the following period, I shall speak in the next chapter.

The proper and original jurisdiction of the court was its jurisdiction in revenue cases.[1] This was a very special and a very intricate subject. In the first place, it demanded a knowledge of the many procedural advantages which were part of the King's prerogative, and of the peculiar procedural processes by which in revenue cases effect was given to that prerogative.[2] Much of the law on this topic, enacted and unenacted, was mediæval, much depended upon cases and statutes of the sixteenth, seventeenth, and eighteenth centuries, and the scope of many of its rules was obscure. In the second place, it demanded a knowledge of the lengthy and complicated revenue statutes of the eighteenth and nineteenth centuries; and the interpretation of those statutes then, as in earlier and later periods in our legal history, often involved a consideration of many different legal and equitable principles and rules. In the third place, since it gave to the court the right of survey and control over Exchequer and revenue officials, it sometimes involved the consideration of nice questions as to their rights and duties and their conduct. Lastly, it involved the delicate task of holding the balance between the maintenance and assertion of the King's prerogative rights on the one hand, and, on the other hand, the maintenance and protection of the liberties of the subject against over-zealous revenue officials. Let us look at this part of the jurisdiction of the court from these different points of view.

First, the fact that the law applicable to revenue cases involved the knowledge of much mediæval law as to the procedural prerogatives of the Crown, and of much law enacted and unenacted from all centuries in English legal history, can be illustrated from many classes of cases. One of these classes of cases raised the question of the conditions in which, by means of an extent in aid,[3] the Crown could get hold of the property of the debtor of its debtor. We shall see that many of these cases involved a consideration of the conflicting claims of the Crown and the subject.[4] At this point we should note that to adjust these claims, the court was often obliged to consider much old law. Thus, to determine the question whether, when the Crown seized and sold the lands of its simple contract debtor

---

[1] Vol. i 238-239.
[2] Vol. iii 459; ix 7-8; x 342-347.
[3] For these extents in aid see vol. x 344-345.
[4] Below 562-564.

which were subject to an equitable mortgage, it was bound to satisfy the equitable mortgagee out of the proceeds of the sale,[1] counsel for the mortgagee found it necessary to trace the whole history of the prerogative rights of the Crown upon this point from Henry III's reign downwards, citing Madox, statutes of Henry III, Henry VIII, Elizabeth, and James I, and a case from Plowden as well as modern cases.[2] One of the court's decisions on the question as to the evidence which the Crown must adduce to prove the debts on which extents issued, was considered by the reporter to be wrong, because it over- turned a long established practice.[3] To prove his point he appealed to the *cursus scaccarii*, to Plowden, and to a statute of Henry VIII's reign.[4] The question whether goods seized by the sheriff by virtue of a writ of fi. fa. could be attached by the Crown while they were in the sheriff's hands, was answered in different ways by the court of Exchequer, and the courts of King's Bench and Common Pleas,[5] and, in his observations on this case,[6] the reporter cited Magna Carta, Coke, Gilbert's treatise on the Exchequer, and appealed to the form of Ex- chequer writs from Henry III to the present day. In 1816 the extent of a grant of forest rights in the forest of Windsor was considered ; and this question involved an interpretation of Crown grants from Henry III's to Charles I's reigns.[7] The claims of lords of liberties to a share of certain fines was raised by the dean and chapter of Westminster,[8] but " was not further pursued on account of the expense of proceeding more formally to establish the rights of the liberty."[9] In 1825, on the question whether a wharfinger's lien prevailed against an extent against the owner of the goods,[10] the court considered in detail a case

---

[1] Casberd v. The Attorney-General (1819) 6 Price 411.

[2] " They [counsel for the plaintiffs] then proceed to trace from its origin the history of that branch of the law which gives, in some instances, to the Crown a preference in recovering its debts for the benefit of the public. For that purpose they brought under the consideration of the Court the several statutes and all the decided cases in any way bearing on this particular question ; and they minutely investigated and commented on the character, situation, and liabilities of persons connected with the Crown, in quality of accountant or debtor, and the prerogative course of proceeding in the case of such debtors or accountants making default (referring to Madox's History of the Exchequer chap. 23, sec. 22) with a view to showing that both from the nature and purpose of the prerogative or common law right of the Crown, and from the legislative recognition and extension of it, that no right had ever existed in fact on the part of the Crown to seize the lands of its simplest contract debtor," ibid 419-420.

[3] The King v. Hornblower (1822) 11 Price 29.   [4] Ibid at pp. 41-56.

[5] Giles v. Grover (1823) 12 Price at p. 6 ; the House of Lords upheld the view of the court of Exchequer that the Crown had this right (1832) 9 Bing. 128.

[6] Ibid at pp. 7-50.

[7] Attorney-General v. Marquis of Downshire (1816) 5 Price 269.

[8] In re Dean and Chapter of Westminster (1823) 12 Price 174.

[9] Ibid at p. 182.

[10] The King v. Humphrey (1825) M'Cle. and Yo. 173.

reported in the Year Book of 35 Henry VI.[1] In 1827 the application of cap. 8 of Magna Carta (1225),[2] and Cokes' commentary
thereon[3] was considered.

Secondly, many cases turn upon the lengthy and complicated
revenue statutes of the eighteenth and nineteenth centuries.
Many cases turned on the interpretation of statutes imposing
legacy duty, e.g. how it should be computed upon a residuary
bequest,[4] and how far foreigners were liable to pay it.[5] Other
cases turned upon the persons liable to make a return to income
tax.[6] Another case turned on the powers of the commissioners
for auditing the public accounts to summon the executors of
a deceased accountant to the Crown.[7] In many of these cases,
though they were concerned primarily with the interpretation
of a revenue act or with the statutory rights of the Crown to
a forfeiture, the court found it necessary to consider the meaning
and ambit of legal principles and rules applicable to many
different branches of law, in order to arrive at the interpretation
of the statute.   Thus in the case of *Attorney-General v. Jones*[8]
the question what instruments were testamentary in character,
so that benefits given by them were liable to legacy duty, divided
the court of Exchequer; and in the case of *The King v. Capper*[9]
the question whether government stock passed under a grant
of *bona et catalla felonum* raised the question what was the nature
of such stock.[10] It was held that it was a chose in action, like
a debt, which never passed under such a grant.[11] In the case
of *Attorney-General v. Norstedt*[12] the effect of a sale of a ship
by order of the court of Admiralty, on the Crown's rights to
seize the ship for a breach of the revenue laws, involved a consideration of the effect of the judgment of the court of Admiralty
ordering a sale.   In fact, at all periods of our legal history the
interpretation of revenue Acts and the interpretation of the
extent of the fiscal rights of the Crown, have involved a consideration of many different branches of the law, because these Acts
and these rights affect many social and economic relations.
The right understanding of the early history of the land law
depends on an appreciation of the nature of those fiscal resources
of the King which are known as the incidents of tenure, and of

[1] At pp. 192-193 ; Y.B. 35 Hy. VI Mich. pl. 33.
[2] Attorney-General v. Atkinson (1827) 1 Yo. and J. 207.
[3] Second Instit. 18-20.
[4] Attorney-General v. Cavendish (1810) Wight. 82.
[5] In re Bruce (1832) 2 Cr. and J. 436.
[6] Attorney-General v. Borrodaile (1814) 1 Price 148.
[7] The King v. Incledon (1810) Wight. 369.
[8] (1817) 3 Price 368 ; a similar question was discussed in In the goods of Robinson (1867) L.R. 1 P. and D. 384.
[9] (1817) 5 Price 217.   [10] Ibid at p. 262.
[11] Ibid at pp. 263-264.   [12] (1816) 3 Price 97.

the devices used by the landowners to evade them;[1] the Statute of Uses, which shaped the development of the modern land law, was the product of the fiscal needs of Henry VIII;[2] the first real attempt in a reported case to analyse the nature of an agreement was made in a revenue case;[3] and in 1916 the construction of a revenue Act involved a consideration of the difference between legal and equitable assets and the doctrine of reconversion.[4] As Lord Greene has said, and as these cases show, " the questions which fall to be decided in the Revenue Court demand a very deep knowledge of legal principle and a sound instinct for the science of the law."[5]

Thirdly, the court had the right of survey and control over Exchequer and revenue officials. Thus in 1794 the court held that the Treasurer's Remembrancer could only appoint to clerkships in his office those who had been articled to a sworn clerk and had served their clerkship.[6] In 1796 Macdonald, C.B. said that the court had " a general jurisdiction over every part of the public revenue," and " complete power in the taking of the public accounts in every stage of their process," so that it could control the conduct of the commissioners for auditing the public accounts.[7] Similarly the court exercised control over contractors with the government.[8] In 1828 a dispute as to the appointment of a deputy by one of the Exchequer officials caused the court to order an account to be given of the duties of some of the Exchequer officials.[9] The court had power to respite process or fines set by the judges of assize.[10]

Lastly, the court, in the exercise of this jurisdiction, had the delicate task of holding the balance between the maintenance of the King's prerogative rights and the rights and liberties of the subject. In 1790[11] and 1793[12] it was held that cases affecting the revenue and officers of the revenue could be removed into the court of Exchequer. This power was said by Eyre, C.B.

---

[1] Holdsworth, Historical Introduction to the Land Law 35-36.

[2] Vol. iv 450-461.

[3] R. M. Jackson, L.Q.R. liii 526, citing Reniger v. Fogossa (1550) Plowden at pp. 5, 8b-9a, 17a.   [4] O'Grady v. Wilmot (1916) 2 A.C. 231.

[5] Journal of the Society of Public Teachers of Law, 1936, 15.

[6] Ex Pte. Deverell (1794) 2 Anst. 483.

[7] Ex Pte. Durrand (1796) 3 Anst. at p. 746; cp. Colebrooke v. Attorney-General (1819) 7 Price 146.

[8] Attorney-General v. Cochrane (1810) Wight. 10; Attorney-General v. Lindegren (1819) 6 Price 287.

[9] They were the foreign apposer, the clerk of the estreats, the comptroller of the pipe, and the surveyor of green wax. In the matter of the Foreign Apposer (1828) 2 Yo. and J. 564.

[10] In the matter of a Fine set upon the Inhabitants of the City of Norwich (1823) 11 Price 766.

[11] Cawthorne v. Campbell (1790) 1 Anst. 205 n.; for a modern example of this proceeding see Stanley v. Wild (1900) 1 Q.B. 256.

[12] Anon. (1793) 1 Anst. 205.

to be "an injunction to stay proceedings in the other court qualified and softened by a liberty given to sue here";[1] and in the case of *The King v. Pickman*[2] the court laid it down that the King by his prerogative had the right to have all questions relating to his fiscal rights decided by the court of Exchequer. In 1811 it was held that the Prince of Wales, like the King, could proceed by information in respect of land which was part of the duchy of Cornwall.[3] On the other hand, the court was ready to protect the subject from excessive claims by over-zealous revenue officials. Thus Macdonald, C.B., in a very learned judgment in which the Books of Assizes were cited, held that the fact that money had been received from the Crown to its use, and was therefore owed to the Crown as on a simple contract, created no lien on the debtor's land, which would bind a *bona fide* purchaser of such land.[4] If, he said, it were the law that the lands of any private person who had got the King's money into his hands was bound, "there must be a universal suspicion of all titles because it will be impossible to discover who are the persons that may have privately got the King's money into their hands."[5] The court refused to allow one indebted to the Crown in respect of taxes to use the process of an extent in aid against his own debtor.[6] "If this were permitted," said Thomson, C.B.[7]

almost any person whatever who should be in any matter indebted to the Crown (as almost every individual is at all time for taxes of some description) and that to the smallest amount, would be entitled to the benefit of this extraordinary proceeding, and in cases of insolvency would gain a priority over the other creditors of the debtor.

Similarly, though the statute of limitations could not be pleaded by the Crown's debtor to a claim by the Crown, it could be pleaded as against the Crown by a debtor of the Crown's debtor, because the Crown when it seizes such a debt "stands precisely in the same situation as its debtor."[8]

These cases show that the court succeeded in the difficult task of holding the balance fairly between the Crown and the taxpayer, by so interpreting the prerogatives of the Crown, procedural and otherwise, that whenever possible, injustice was avoided. It was a difficult task because the interpretation of these prerogatives often involved the consideration of mediæval authorities which spoke with an uncertain voice, and of statutes

---

[1] Anon. (1793) 1 Anst. at p. 208.   [2] (1797) 3 Anst. 852.
[3] Attorney-General to the Prince of Wales v. St. Aubyn (1811) Wight. 167.
[4] The King v. Smith (1810) Wight. 34.   [5] Ibid at pp. 47-48.
[6] The King v. Wilton (1816) 2 Price 368.
[7] At. p. 377 ; for the statutory limitation of the issue of these extants in aid by an Act of 1817 (57 George III c. 117) see vol. x 344 n. 11.
[8] The King v. Morrall (1818) 6 Price 24 at p. 28.

which came from all periods in the history of the law. That it was successfully performed was due largely to the fact that in the sixteenth century the court of Exchequer had ceased to be staffed by officials and had come to be staffed by lawyers.[1] Just as, in the sphere of the criminal law, the fairness of the English as contrasted with the continental criminal procedure was due to the fact that it was accusatory, i.e., a judicial process like the process in an ordinary action, and not inquisitorial i.e., an enquiry into the guilt or innocence of an accused person by Crown officials;[2] so, in the sphere of revenue law, undue oppression of the taxpayer, and of officials and others who were accountants to the Crown, was prevented by the fact that the law was administered by a court which applied to the rights and duties of the Crown and its subjects the same standards as it applied to the trial of ordinary actions. Thus the rule of law, and therefore the preservation of those standards of fairness and justice which the law demands, were preserved. The fact that this fundamental principle of English public law demanded that the administration of the revenue law should be thus super-intended by such a court, was very ably demonstrated in an argument in the case of *Colebrooke v. Attorney-General*.[3] In that case the plaintiffs had filed a bill against the attorney-general claiming certain allowances which had been disallowed by a decision of the commissioners for auditing the public accounts. The attorney-general had demurred to the bill on the ground that the court had no jurisdiction to give this relief. The court overruled this demurrer—thus acceding to the arguments of the plaintiffs. The plaintiffs' counsel in the course of their argument said:[4]

It was glaringly incompatible with the system and constitution of British jurisprudence, and every principle of the law of England, that a tribunal (if indeed the Board of Commissioners for auditing the public accounts could be so called) . . . being nominated and appointed by the Crown should be subject to no sort of appeal. The particular duties entrusted to them were no less than the adjudication and determination of counter-claims, involving rights and interests often of immense pecuniary amount and great legal difficulty between the Crown and the subject accountant—the individuals being in no way connected with the law—and who, however well chosen they might be in point of integrity and all other respects, for their office, were deficient in a most essential and indispensable qualification for so important a charge in that they were persons who were not possessed of any legal knowledge or fitness, and could not therefore be properly invested with any judicial character or authority, without which they could not be considered competent to the ultimate discharge of such extensive powers. Yet such were the persons who were contended to be authorized to decide finally, and

---

[1] Vol. i 236-237.   [2] Vol. v 176.
[3] (1806) 7 Price 146.   [4] Ibid at pp. 165-166.

determine conclusively, on all questions pending between the Crown and the subject, regarding the allowance of the articles of discharge in an accountant's accounts, without appeal or being subject to the revision or superintendence of any Court of Law, erected for the due administration of justice in the kingdom.

It is on these very sufficient grounds that in spite of the many powers of a judicial and legislative kind which, in modern times, have been given to officials by the Legislature, the ultimate power to adjudicate upon the fiscal claims of the state has been jealously preserved for the courts.

Besides its revenue jurisdiction the court had both a common law and an equitable jurisdiction.

There are no very leading decisions in the common law cases heard by the court during this period. There are several decisions on the *land law*. Instances are cases as to the liability of a tenant to pay rent when the premises had been destroyed by fire ;[1] as to the validity of a lease made under a power of appointment[2]—an Exchequer Chamber case which went to the House of Lords and there evoked a valuable statement by Lord Eldon as to the weight to be given to the practice of conveyancers ;[3] as to obligations of a lessor to show a title to grant the lease ;[4] as to the right to light as between two purchasers who bought from the same vendor on the same day[5]— a decision approved by the House of Lords ;[6] and as to what covenants will run with the land.[7] In the sphere of *contract* there is a decision as to the right to sue for money had and received when a contract of sale has been rescinded ;[8] and in another case the principle that the defendant in such an action must have assented to hold the money for the plaintiff was asserted.[9] It was held that a person who had deposited his money with a stakeholder to abide the result of a bet on a foot race could recover it in such an action.[10] In the sphere of *tort* there are decisions as to the evidence admissible in an action for libel as to the plaintiff's reputation ;[11] and as to what agreements were not void because they did not amount to champerty.[12] In the case of *Attorney-General v. Siddon*[13] a master was held

---

[1] Hare v. Groves (1796) 3 Anst. 687.
[2] Smith v. Doe (1821) 7 Price 379.
[3] Ibid at pl. 509-511.
[4] Purvis v. Rayer (1821) 9 Price 488.
[5] Compton v. Richards (1814) 1 Price 27.
[6] Russell v. Watts (1885) 10 A.C. at p. 603.
[7] Easterby v. Sampson (1830) 1 Cr. and J. 105.
[8] Reed v. Blandford (1828) 2 Yo. and J. 278.
[9] Wedlake v. Hurley (1830) 1 Cr. and J. 83.
[10] Bate v. Cartwright (1819) 7 Price 540.
[11] Jones v. Stevens (1822) 11 Price 235.
[12] Williams v. Protheroe (1829) 3 Yo. and J. 129.
[13] (1830) 1 Cr. and J. 220.

criminally liable where his servant, in the conduct of his business, had concealed smuggled goods, not on the principle of employer's liability, which does not apply to criminal liability, but on the ground that the master must be presumed to have authorized the servant so to act.[1] In the case of *In re Clement*[2] the court, following a decision of the court of King's Bench,[3] upheld the legality of a fine for contempt, imposed by the justices of gaol delivery for disobedience to an order not to publish an account of the Cato Street conspirators till all the trials had been finished.

In the exercise of its equitable jurisdiction the court held that it could not interfere in a case which was before the court of Chancery.[4] On the other hand, it held that it had jurisdiction in a case in which the parties resided within the jurisdiction of the Chancery court of the county palatine of Lancaster.[5] The cases which came before the court were similar to those which came before the court of Chancery. There are cases turning on the doctrines of performance,[6] satisfaction,[7] and election.[8] There is an interesting case of a precatory trust, in which the court (Graham, B. dissenting) laid down the conditions with which such a trust must comply in accordance rather with the conditions imposed in the modern cases, than with those which, before the decision of *Lambe v. Eames*,[9] prevailed in the court of Chancery.[10] Where a father covenanted on his daughter's marriage to leave her at his death a share of his personalty equal to that of his son, and he made a gift of all his stock in the funds to his son, reserving to himself the dividends, the court held that there had been no breach of the covenant[11]—a decision which was very properly reversed by the House of Lords.[12] There are cases as to the administration of assets,[13] as to the interpretation of the Charitable Uses Act of George II's reign,[14] as to the effect of a mistake, as to the existence of an estate contracted for,[15] as to fraudulent conduct by trustees,[16] as to undue influence.[17] Tithe cases were the one class of case which were almost invariably brought before

---

[1] See Newman v. Jones (1886) 17 Q.B.D. at p. 137.
[2] (1822) 11 Price 68.   [3] R. v. Clement (1821) 4 B. and Ald. 218.
[4] Pitcher v. Rigby (1821) 9 Price 79.
[5] Cheetham v. Crook (1825) M'Cle. and Yo. 307.
[6] Roper v. Bartholomew (1824) 12 Price 797.
[7] Golding v. Haverfield (1824) 13 Price 593.
[8] Tucker v. Sanger (1824) 13 Price 607.   [9] (1871) L.R. 6 Ch. 597.
[10] Heneage v. Viscount Andover (1822) 10 Price 230 ; for a discussion of this case see In re Williams [1897] 2 Ch. at pp. 33-35 *per* Rigby, L.J.
[11] Jones v. Martin (1797) 3 Anst. 882.   [12] (1798) 6 Bro. P.C. 437.
[13] Noel v. Lord Henley (1819) 7 Price 241.
[14] Kirkbank v. Hudson (1819) 7 Price 212 ; for this statute see vol. xi 590-593.
[15] Hitchcock v. Giddings (1817) 4 Price 135.
[16] Oliver v. Court (1820) 8 Price 127.
[17] Goddard v. Carlisle (1821) 9 Price 169.

this court, and not before the court of Chancery. These cases were more numerous than any of the other class of equity case heard by the court. They concerned the rights of rectors and vicars and lay impropriators, and the validity of moduses ; and they often involved the consideration of complicated questions of tithe and much mediæval and modern law. In fact most of the law on this topic, before its reform in the following period, was made by the court of Exchequer.

The fact that the court had both an equitable and a common law jurisdiction, enabled it to take account of both the legal and the equitable rights of the parties, in cases where the question arose whether an injunction against suing at law should be granted or continued,[1] or in cases where it was argued that, because the legal remedies sufficed, there was no ground for equitable interference with the law.[2]

This account of the Chief Justices, and the account which I have given of the lawyers who have contributed to the literature of the law either by their books or reports, leave only a few of the leading lawyers unaccounted for. These few fall into three classes : first, some of the puisne judges, secondly, some of the law officers, and thirdly, two lawyers who are interesting not for professional but for literary reasons.

First, it would be impossible and in fact unnecessary to say something of all the puisne judges of the common law courts. But it is useful to recall a few of the human traits and characteristics of some of them, which can be culled from the accounts left to us by their contemporaries. Campbell, speaking of the court of King's Bench when he was a leader in the court,[3] has told us something of some of the puisne judges before whom he practised. Littledale, he tells us, was " one of the most acute, learned, and simple-minded of men." He was an eminent special pleader ; and it is said that in drawing an indictment for murder, which had been committed with a double-barrelled pistol, he spent many hours endeavouring to invent some form of words by which to cover the possibility of the fact of the ball having issued from either barrel.[4] He presided at the trial of Pinney, the Lord Mayor of Bristol,[5] for neglect of duty in connection with the Bristol riots of 1831, and, in his summing up, he gave a lucid and accurate explanation of the duties of a magistrate called upon to suppress a riot.[6] Of Bayley, who had written what was

---

[1] Solly v. Moore (1820) 8 Price 631.
[2] Cupit v. Jackson (1824) 13 Price 721.
[3] Lives of the Chief Justices iii 291-292.
[4] E. Manson, The Builders of our Law (2nd ed.) 142.
[5] (1832) 3 S.T. N.S. 1.
[6] Ibid at pp. 510-512—" he is bound to hit the exact line between an excess and doing what is sufficient."

long the standard book on bills of exchange and promissory notes,[1] Campbell says :

He did not talk very wisely on literature, or on the affairs of life, but the whole of the common law of this realm he carried in his head, and in seven little red books. These accompanied him day and night ; and in them every reported case was regularly posted, and in them, by a sort of magic, he could at all times turn up the authorities required.

Of Holroyd, the friend and fellow student of Romilly,[2] he said that he was " born with a genius for law," and that he

was not only acquainted with all that had ever been said or written on the subject, but reasoned most scientifically and beautifully upon every point of law which he touched, and, notwithstanding his husky voice and sodden features, as often as he spoke he delighted all who were capable of appreciating his rare excellence.

Secondly, most of the law officers of the Crown became the chiefs of one of the three common law courts, and sometimes Lord Chancellors, Masters of the Rolls, or Vice-Chancellors. But there are one or two who, for one reason or another, did not rise so high. Spencer Perceval[3] was one of the few lawyers who was as successful in the House of Commons as he was in the courts. " He was," Scarlett said, " capable of adorning any station in the profession of the law."[4] Addington made him solicitor-general in 1801 and he became attorney-general in 1802. In 1804 he refused the Chief Justiceship of the Common Pleas, and kept his post as attorney-general till 1806. Under the Portland administration he abandoned law for politics, became Chancellor of the Exchequer, and succeeded Portland as prime minister. In 1811 the Regent retained him in office, and he remained prime minister till his assassination in 1812.[5] Arthur Piggott,[6] who had been solicitor-general to the Prince of Wales and a leading practitioner in the court of Chancery, was attorney-general in 1805-7 during the ministry of " all the talents ". During his period of office he conducted very ably the impeachment of Melville. After his resignation in 1807 he never held any office. He was a competent lawyer, but a dull and lengthy speaker.[7] Samuel Shepherd,[8] though he was a very sound lawyer, never attained high judicial office. He was solicitor-general in 1813 and attorney-general in 1817, and he could have become Chief Justice either of the King's Bench or Common Pleas in 1818. But partly on account of his deafness, and partly because he disliked criminal work, he refused to take either office. In 1819 he became chief baron of the Exchequer

---

[1] Vol. xii 389-390.   [2] Memoirs i 49, cited vol. vi 497 n. 5.
[3] D.N.B.   [4] Memoirs of Lord Abinger 88.
[5] Above 180.   [6] D.N.B.   [7] Ibid.   [8] Ibid.

in Scotland. Horne,[1] who was solicitor-general in 1830, and attorney-general in 1832, never held judicial office because he objected to passing sentence of death. He became a master in Chancery in 1839. Charles Wetherell[2] was the least intellectually eminent of the law officers of this period. He practised in the court of Chancery, where he owed something to the favour of Lord Eldon, for his father was master of University College, Oxford—Eldon's college ; and he was a whole-hearted supporter of Eldon's political views. In Parliament he defended all the abuses of the court of Chancery, and was opposed both to Catholic emancipation and Parliamentary reform. But he was not a success in the House of Commons—his style of oratory made him somewhat ridiculous. He became solicitor-general in 1824, and attorney-general in 1826, but he refused to join Canning's ministry, and resigned in the same year. The Duke of Wellington reinstated him in the office of attorney-general, but he lost office when he refused to support Catholic emancipation. His opposition to the reform bill was so bitter that his arrival at Bristol in 1831 to carry out his duties as recorder was the signal for the Bristol riots. Garrow,[3] who had been solicitor-general in 1812, and attorney-general 1813-17, became a puisne judge of the court of Exchequer. Though a skilful and powerful advocate, a very effective cross-examiner, and a competent judge in criminal cases, he was a poor lawyer. Scarlett called him " an eloquent scolder with a fine voice," with " a high reputation with the public, but none in the profession." [4] He knew nothing of the law of real property,[5] and his judgments in the courts of Exchequer show that he had not mastered the principal branches of the law which the court administered.

Thirdly, there are two lawyers who are interesting not for professional but for literary reasons. Gaselee, J. appears in the *Pickwick Papers* as the judge who tried the case of *Bardell v. Pickwick* under the thin disguise of Stareleigh, J. Foss says of him that he was " a painstaking and upright judge,"[6] and though, as a rule, his judgments are short, he was not wholly incompetent. One at least of his opinions given to the House

---

[1] D.N.B.   [2] Ibid.
[3] Foss, Judges ix 86-90 ; D.N.B.   [4] Memoirs of Lord Abinger 87.
[5] Romilly, Memoirs ii 428 gives two instances of cases before the House of Lords in which he read an argument prepared by Hobhouse, one of the solicitors to the Treasury ; he adds that two days after the hearing of one of these cases he had to argue in the court of Chancery that a theatrical manager could not discharge his duties without personal attendance, and said " that it would be as difficult as for a counsel to do his duty in that court by writing arguments, and sending them to some person to read them for him. The Lord Chancellor interrupted me by saying, ' In this Court or in any other ? ' And after the Court rose, he said to me, ' You knew, I suppose, what I alluded to ? It was Garrow's written argument in the House of Lords.' "
[6] Judges ix 91.

of Lords is full and learned.[1] It is said that in his younger days he had no illusions as to his professional prospects, for he betted a friend 100 to 1 in guineas that he would not reach the bench—which he duly paid to the son of his deceased friend when he became a judge.[2] The figure he cuts in the *Pickwick Papers* is not creditable, for he displays the qualities of deafness, irritability, and inability to produce an adequate summing up. It is a curious coincidence that he resigned in the Hilary term 1837—shortly after the appearance of the trial scene in *Pickwick*. The second of these lawyers is William St. Julien Arabin, who became a serjeant-at-law in 1825,[3] and was appointed one of the commissioners of the central criminal court and judge of the sheriff's court in London in 1827. He held these posts till his death in 1841, and he served for a short time as judge advocate-general.[4] He is noted for a little book of his recorded dicta and charges to juries called *Arabiniana*, collected by H.B.C.[5] from his own and his friends' recollections, and privately printed with a witty preface in 1843.[6] Pollock describes it as follows :[7]

Here is a group of judicial remarks on the morals of the home counties. In the original the cases are duly identified by name and date, and one indication is peculiar to this volume of reports. "The student will observe," says the Preface, "that A.P. signifies *Ante Prandium*; and P.P. *Post Prandium.*" From this we may learn that in the reign of King William IV the Court still sat after dinner (the luncheon interval not having been at that time introduced) ; but at least one student has diligently perused *Arabiniana* without finding any manner of difference between the ante-prandial and post-prandial utterances of the Court.

To my mind the best dictum in the book is the last :[8]

Of beer.

R. v. Higgins. February 1839, P.P.
The prisoner was convicted.
The Court, to prisoner. I have no doubt of your guilt ; you go into a public house, and break bulk, and drink beer ; and that's what in law is called embezzlement.

The two following are nearly as good :

Of looking at several things.[9]

R. v. Mary Sauter. April 1832, P.P.
The Court, in charge. I cannot suggest a doubt : she goes into a shop, and looks at several things, and purchases nothing : that always indicates some guilt.

---

[1] Giles v. Grover (1832) 9 Bing. at pp. 210-231.
[2] Theobald Mathew, Bardell v. Pickwick L.Q.R. xxxiv, citing the Gentleman's Magazine.
[3] Foss, Judges ix 7.
[4] Pollock, Essays in the Law 287-288.
[5] H. Blencowe Churchill.
[6] Pollock, Essays in the Law 289-290.
[7] Op. cit. 290.
[8] At p. 16.
[9] At p. 7.

Of Apollo. [1]

R. v.—

Jew had given prisoner a good character.

The Court, in charge. Now gentlemen, you have heard the case ; and the Jew says that the prisoner has borne a good character ; and that he, the Jew, never heard anything against him. All that I shall say to that is, *Credat Judaeus Apollo.* If he does, I don't, and I daresay you won't, gentlemen.

I must now try to sum up briefly the effect of the work of the lawyers of this period upon the development of the common law.

The reports show as clearly as the statute law and the literature of the common law that this period is a transition period. Just as the Legislature was adapting the law to modern needs under the influence of changing political and economic conditions and of Bentham's ideas as to law reform ; just as the literature of the common law shows that the books upon the older branches of the law—the land law, many branches of public law, the law of pleading and procedure—were becoming more and more elaborate and technical, while at the same time separate books upon newer branches of the law, such as the law as to insurance, negotiable instruments, shipping, partnership, and evidence, were making their appearance ; so in the professional development of the law we get the same mixture of old and new. The illustrations which I have given of the work done by the Chief Justices and the chief barons show that new problems in the law of contract and tort were emerging, and that the law as to many topics of mercantile and maritime law were being elaborated. At the same time the Acts, public or private, which incorporated important commercial companies and the Acts which gave powers to special bodies to perform some of the functions of local government, were giving rise to a considerable body of case law. Political events—the Berlin decrees and the Orders in Council, and the legislation as to the convoying of British ships—gave rise to other series of cases. A certain number of patent cases illustrate the progress of the industrial revolution. All these bodies of law were relatively modern ; and the courts were showing their skill in creating and developing these modern bodies of law to meet the needs of the day. At the same time older branches of the law were being developed in great detail. The law of real property was being developed by the practice of conveyancers like Preston and Butler, by the books which some of them wrote, and by cases decided by the courts of common law and the court of Chancery, and more especially by the solution of the problems

[1] At p. 5.

in the land law set by the court of Chancery to the common law courts ; and many cases were elaborating the law of landlord and tenant. Through the actions of trespass and conversion the law as to the possession and ownership of chattels was being applied to solve some of the problems of commercial law ; and through points of law reserved for discussion by the judges doubtful questions in the criminal law were being decided.[1] In cases on public law like *Burdett v. Abbott*[2] much old law was considered, explained, applied, and thereby rendered more precise ; and this process was applied to problems not only of the central, but also of local government, e.g. the case of *Harding v. Pollock*,[3] which raised the question of the right of the custos rotulorum to appoint the clerk of the peace, was decided after much research into the law as to judicial appointments, as to justices of the peace, and as to the custos rotulorum and his clerks, from the reign of Edward I onwards.

All these different branches of the common law new and old were developed under the technical conditions fixed by two of the oldest parts of the common law—the law of procedure and the law of pleading. Representative books on these topics, such as Tidd's *Practice*[4] and Stephen's book on *Pleading*,[5] illustrate the elaboration, the complexity, and the consequent rigidity of these two branches of the law ; and they illustrate both the manner in which the law of procedure and pleading determined the manner in which the substantive law was adapted to the new conditions, and the limits within which this adaptation was possible. The development of the law under these conditions had certain good results. The fact that that development took place by means and under the guidance of decisions as to the scope and application of the different forms of action made for the logical interdependence of its principles and rules.[6] The fact that those decisions were given under the conditions fixed by the rules of pleading ensured great accuracy in the statement of those principles and rules and great precision in their application to the facts of concrete cases.[7] But the development of the law under these conditions had also bad results ; and since the increasing complexity and rigidity of the old rules of procedure and pleading were making them less fit to control the development of some of the newer branches of the law which were emerging in response to the problems

---

[1] In these cases the arguments, but no formal judgment, are given, but it is stated whether the prisoner was reprieved or pardoned, or whether the sentence was carried out, so that it is possible to see in the successful argument the reasons which the court accepted ; see e.g. R. v. Fauntleroy (1824) 2 Bing. 413.

[2] (1811) 14 East 1 ; above 508, 533.

[3] (1829) 6 Bing. 25 ; for the clerk of the peace see vol. x 129, 230.

[4] Above 450, 452, 453, 454.   [5] Above 458, 459.

[6] Vol. ix 222-334.   [7] Ibid 331-332.

of this new age, these bad results tended more and more to predominate over the good.[1] Let us look at one or two illustrations of the bad results of this dependence of the law on the rules of procedure and pleading.

In the law of procedure all sorts of semi-obsolete institutions and rules survived. They occasionally emerged, and their discussion took up the time and energy of the courts which could have been more usefully employed. We have seen that both trial by battle[2] and trial by compurgation[3] gave rise to cases during this period. In 1822 it was held by the Exchequer Chamber that where, in an action for libel, the jury had not assessed the damages, a writ of enquiry to assess them could not be issued, because the defendant would thereby lose his right to sue out his writ of attaint if the damages were excessive.[4] Though in 1757 Lord Mansfield had said that this writ was " a mere sound,"[5] in 1822 Dallas, C.J. said :[6]

We cannot treat it [the writ of attaint] as obsolete, the remedy is still available to parties, although in modern times not resorted to. Certainly the courts are not to deprive the party of his remedy, by so moulding their course of proceeding on the part of a plaintiff as to have that effect. Whenever a jury may be subjected to attaint, their liability must be preserved to the party injured, however remote the probability of recurring to the remedy. It is therefore an objection to the mode of proceeding by writ of inquiry.

Writs of right afforded the opportunity for the resurrection of much obsolete law. The manner of choosing the four knights needed for the grand assize, and the procedure to be followed if one were too ill to attend ;[7] and the question whether the persons summoned were in fact knights ;[8] furnished material for two reported cases. The case of *Davies v. Lowndes*[9]—the last case of a writ of right—came repeatedly before the courts on different technical points of procedure,[10] including the question whether the proceedings could be continued by a writ of *Journey's Accounts* against the heir of the deceased tenant, after the writ of right had been abolished by the statute of 1833.[11] The return

---

[1] Vol. ix 308-314.   [2] Above 528, 550.   [3] Above 405.
[4] Clement v. Lewis (1822) 10 Price 181.
[5] Bright v. Eynon 1 Burr. at p. 393 cited vol. i 342.
[6] 10 Price at pp. 195-196.   [7] Tooth v. Bagwell (1826) 3 Bing. 373.
[8] Augell v. Augell (1826) 3 Bing. 393.   [9] (1838) 5 Bing. N.C. 161.
[10] (1835) 1 Bing. N.C. 597 ; (1838) 4 Bing. N.C. 478, 711 ; (1840) 1 M. and Gr. 473 ; (1843) 6 M. and Gr. 471.
[11] (1844) 7 M. and Gr. 762 ; the writ is thus explained in the Termes de la Ley (ed. 1721) [for this book see vol. v 401] : " Journies accounts (Dietae computatae) is a term in the law which is understood thus : if a writ be abated without the default of the plaintiff or demandant, he may purchase a new writ, which if it be purchased by Journies accounts (that is within as little time as he possibly can after the abatement of the first writ) then this second writ shall be as a continuance to the first, and so shall oust the tenant or defendant of . . . any plea which arises upon matter happening after the date of the first writ."

to a writ of pone was set aside because the sheriff attempted to traverse the formal cause assigned for its issue.[1] On the facts the proceedings taken for this purpose were, as the plaintiffs' counsel said, " disgraceful to the administration of justice." But the court said :[2]

That is an observation for the legislature. We cannot alter the practice of centuries. The allegation of cause for a writ of pone is a mere matter of form ; as much so as the allegation of latitancy upon mesne process, of the affection of John Doe for the tenant in possession.

These bad effects of the retention of obsolete forms were aggravated by the strictness with which the courts applied the rules of procedure to all actions which came before them, and the opportunities which they gave to the parties of enforcing these rules. We have seen that the choice of a wrong writ might mean that a plaintiff failed even after he had got a verdict or a judgment.[3] The difficulties of a plaintiff were further aggravated by the strictness of the rules of pleading, which had, as we have seen, become a very rigid, and a very technical body of law, developed with great logical precision from premises which, though sometimes sensible, were often archaic survivals.[4] Lord Campbell, speaking of the state of the common law at the time of Lord Ellenborough, very truly says :[5]

The writ of latitat was as much venerated as the writ of habeas corpus, and all the arbitrary and fantastic rules respecting declarations, pleas, replications, rejoinders, surrejoinders, rebutters, and surrebutters, which had arisen from accident or had been devised to multiply fees, or had been properly framed for a very different state of society, were still considered to be the result of unerring wisdom, and eternally essential to the due administration of justice.

That under these handicaps the common law succeeded partially in keeping abreast of the needs of the age is a testimony both to the soundness of its principles and to the abilities of the judges. As I have pointed out, though the system of special pleading had many defects and caused much injustice, especially in its latter days, it cannot be denied that its discipline trained accomplished lawyers, who were not only masters of technical principles, but also capable of moulding those principles to meet the needs of a changing society.[6] Even in this period their efforts to adapt these principles to their needs were, as we have seen, to some extent assisted by the Legislature. But it was not till the following period that the gradual removal of these handicaps by the Legislature enabled the courts both

---

[1] Talbot v. Binns (1831) 8 Bing. 71.
[2] At p. 74.
[3] Vol. ix 248.
[4] Ibid 313-314.
[5] Lives of the Chief Justices iii 155.
[6] Vol. ix 334.

to develop more freely the substantive principles of the common law in such a way that they met modern needs, and, under the guidance of the Legislature, to introduce new ideas into the law and to develop and settle new branches of that law.   Just as, in the middle years of the seventeenth century, Hale pointed out that the legislation of the sixteenth century had rendered obsolete much mediæval law,[1] so, in the middle years of the nine-teenth century, Lord Campbell pointed out that the legislation of that century had rendered equally obsolete much of the law which he had learned and applied in his youth.   He says :[2]

In looking over the bulky volumes of East and of Maule and Selwyn. it is wonderful to observe how many of the decisions which they record may already be considered obsolete. A vast majority of them are upon rules of practice and pleading, since remodelled under the authority of the legislature—upon Sessions law respecting settlements, rating, and bastardy, which has been entirely altered by successive statutes—upon the old Quo Warranto law, swept away by the Parliamentary Reform Act and the Municipal Corporations' Amendment Act—upon the law of Tithes, abolished by the Tithe Commutation Act—and upon concerted commissions of bankruptcy and the validity of petitioning creditors' debts, which have become immaterial by new Bankrupt and Insolvent Codes.

With the history of this transformation of the common law by the joint efforts of the Legislature and the courts I shall deal in the following chapter.

VII

EQUITY

The rules of equity were not so closely connected with the political, economic, and social developments of this period as the rules of the common law, so that they do not reflect the transitional character of this period to anything like the same extent as the rules of the common law.   It is true that those rules, and more especially the rules of procedure, attracted the criticism of Bentham, who, having been a practitioner in the court of Chancery, was able to direct against them criticisms which were especially detailed and deadly ;[3] and it is true that lawyers who agreed with these criticisms, used them to advocate their proposals for reform.[4]   But, during this period, though much evidence was accumulated as to the need for reform by debates in Parliament and by the commission which reported in 1826,[5] though many proposals for reform were made, very few reforms were effected.[6]   The result is that the main characteristics

---

[1] Preface to Rolle's Abridgement, cited vol. vi 625-626.
[2] Lives of the Chief Justices iii 157.   [3] Above 99, 100.
[4] Above 226, 260, 287-295.   [5] Above 288, 289, 290, 291.   [6] Above 295, 296.

of the development of equity are the steady progress of that process of settlement and systematization which had been going on all through the eighteenth century, and the settlement of its relation to the common law and to the branches of law administered by the civilians.[1] Just as in the eighteenth century this process of settlement and systematization was due largely to Hardwicke,[2] so, in this period, its completion was due mainly to Eldon.[3] During the quarter of a century in which he held the office of Chancellor he and his colleagues settled the scope and contents of most of its leading principles and many of its detailed rules, and, with the help of the common lawyers and the civilians, their relation to the common law and the branches of law administered by the civilians. This achievement was possible because, for some part of this period, equity still showed some of that capacity for expansion which had been its characteristic during the eighteenth century.[4] But the result of Eldon's work and the work of his immediate predecessors was a marked diminution of this capacity for expansion. When Eldon resigned his office in 1827 the sphere of equity had become as fixed as the sphere of the common law,[5] so that it had ceased to show any superiority to the common law in this respect. It would not, indeed, be true to say that either the rules of equity or the rules of the common law were incapable of further expansion. In the following period both common law and equity, with the help and under the guidance of the Legislature, showed an equal capacity for expansion and development to meet new conditions and new needs.

These characteristics of the development of the rules of equity during this period are apparent both in the literature of equity, and in the work of the Chancellors, the Masters of the Rolls, and the Vice-Chancellors. I shall deal with their development under these two heads.

The Literature of Equity

This literature falls into three groups. First, there are a considerable number of books on practice and pleading. Secondly, there are books on special topics in equity. Thirdly, there are two text books on equity.

(1) At the beginning of this period the standard book on equity pleading was Mitford's book of which I have already given some account.[6] During this period a number of books both on pleading and practice were published. That there was a demand for them is shown by the fact that some of

---

[1] Vol. xii 601-602, 697-701.   [2] Ibid 296-297.
[3] Below 627.   [4] Vol. xii 260, 463.
[5] Vol. i 468-469 ; below 627.   [6] Vol. xii 183-185.

them went through several editions. The earliest successor to Mitford's book was a work on pleading which was published by G. Cooper in 1809.[1] It was a book on the lines of Mitford's book, but brought up to date, rearranged, and in some respects expanded. It is a clearly written and well-arranged book. A clear account of the practice of the court was given by J. Newland in a book which was first published in 1813 and reached a third edition in 1830.[2] It gives an account of all the stages of a suit on equity from the filing of the bill to its conclusion. A book which attempted to compile the reason for the rules of equity pleading was published by Barnes in 1818.[3] It deals mainly with the pleas which could be used by a defendant, and comparisons are drawn between the rules of the common law and equity on this subject. A more considerable book by the same author was an annotated collection of the General Orders of the Courts from Francis Bacon's Orders of 1618 to the date of publication.[4] No collection of orders had been published, the author points out, since 1739, and this collection was incomplete. Nor was this surprising. There was no official collection of orders and by no means all of them were entered in the Registrar's book,[5] so that it was difficult to find them. In fact, the court was sometimes ignorant of their existence, with the result that the practice established by the court sometimes contradicted an order. As the author said, what was needed was a revision of the orders and their publication in an official form. It was an original and meritorious piece of work. There were other more purely practical books written by s olicitors for young students, dealing mainly with pleadings and procedural forms and with costs.[6] The standard work on the forms of decrees, orders, and judgments, with notes explaining them was published in 1830 by Henry Seton, who became a judge of the High Court of Calcutta.[7] It reached a seventh edition in 1912, and expanded from one to three volumes. The one volume of the first edition contained 478 pages : the first volume of the seventh edition contains 846 pages.

[1] A Treatise of Pleading on the Equity Side of the High Court of Chancery.
[2] The Practice of the High Court of Chancery, with forms of pleading and proceeding.
[3] The Elements of Pleas in Equity, with Precedents of such Pleas.
[4] The General Orders of the High Court of Chancery, from the year 1600 to the present time, collated with the Registrar's Book . . . To which are added practical notes.
[5] Apparently many more orders were made than were entered ; see vol. v 265-266.
[6] Such as The Solicitor's Assistant in the Court of Chancery by W. Hands 1809).
[7] Forms of Decrees in Equity and of Orders connected therewith, with Practical Notes ; the first edition had a short introduction by Beames on the form of the early decrees.

(2) In 1806 J. Newland, the author of a book on equity practice,[1] wrote *A Treatise on Contracts within the Jurisdiction of the Courts of Equity*. It covers the ground in thirty-six short chapters. It is a good summary of the cases, but it is a pedestrian performance. The law as to portions and provisions for children was the subject of a small and clearly written little book which was published in 1829.[2] A little book, intended mainly for laymen, states clearly some of the leading principles of the law of trustees.[3]

The fact that equity had taken over the most important part of the jurisdiction over the administration of the estates of deceased persons is illustrated by the literature on this subject. The important books on wills, legacies, and executors and administrators were written not by the civilians, but by equity barristers ; the greater part of the law expounded in them is either common law or equity ; and equity is the more important of the two.

(3) At the beginning of this period the only text book on equity was Foblanque's edition of Ballow's Treatise, of which I have already given an account.[4] During this period two more satisfactory books appeared. The more important is Maddock's book.[5]

[Maddock's treatise,[6] the substance of which was incorporated by Spence into his great work on Equitable Jurisdiction,[7] was published in 1820. It was the first general treatise on the principles and practice of modern equity.[8] It was an original book, based on the equity reports ancient and modern, and it was the first book adequately to sum up the work of the great Chancellors of the eighteenth century. It reached a third edition in 1837. He dedicated the work to Lord Eldon, of whom he thought highly, though he inferentially condemns his habit of procrastination [9] by his suggestion that English law might be benefited by the importation of the rule of Spanish Law, that twenty days only should be allowed to all judges for the purpose of pronouncing sentence, when the proceedings are in such a situation as to be definitive. He is a great advocate for the study of principles before that of cases. The book avoids, as far as possible, doctrines of pure common law, but a small part, which is placed at the very beginning of the first volume,

---

[1] Above 576.
[2] A Treatise on the Law of Portions and Provisions for children in the nature of portions, by J. H. Mathews.
[3] Advice to Trustees and to those who appoint to that office, by H. Grant.
[4] Vol. xii 192-193.
[5] It is clear from the state of the MSS. that Holdsworth intended to deal at some length with this book, but no material can be found. We have accordingly written the following account, which appears within square brackets. (Eds.)
[6] A Treatise on the Principles and Practice of the High Court of Chancery.
[7] Above 497. [8] Holdsworth, Sources and Literature of English Law, 190.
[9] Vol. i 437.

is necessarily devoted to a study of the Chancellor's common law jurisdiction.[1] The rest of the first volume is divided into the six heads of (i) accident and mistake, (ii) account, (iii) fraud (under this head we find injunctions), (iv) reports, (v) specific performance, (vi) trusts ; all of these receive very comprehensive treatment. The subject-matter of the second volume would appear, from the standpoint of a modern writer, to be rather loosely arranged, under the wide umbrella of legacies, for the volume contains much valuable information about the doctrines of conversion, election, satisfaction and ademption (whose spheres are not clearly demarcated), and many points concerning implied and resulting trusts, which had already been touched on, in different connections, in the first volume. The work ends with a lengthy account of Chancery practice.]

The second is a useful book by G. Jeremy which was published in 1828.[2] After an historical introduction, it deals in three Books with the exclusive, the assistant, and the concurrent jurisdiction of the court of Chancery. The first Book deals with trusts, mortgages, married women, idiots and lunatics, infants, charities, receiving and the payment of money into court ; the second with discovery and other matters relating to evidence ; and the third with equitable remedies. It is an ably written book which must have been of considerable use both to practitioners and students.

The Chancellors, Masters of the Rolls, and the Vice-Chancellors

A list of the Chancellors, Commissioners appointed during a vacancy of the office of Chancellor, the Masters of the Rolls, and the Vice-Chancellors will be found at the foot of this page.[3]

The Chancellors

With the career and character of the first of the Chancellors —Alexander Wedderburn, Lord Loughborough and Earl of Rosslyn—and with his work as Chief Justice of the Common Pleas, I have already dealt.[4] It is only necessary, therefore, to say something of his work as Chancellor.

---

[1] Vol. i 398-399, 449-453.
[2] A Treatise on the Equity Jurisdiction of the High Court of Chancery.

[3]

Chancellors		Masters of the Rolls	Vice-Chancellors
Eyre	Commis-	Pepper Arden, 1788-1801	Plumer, 1813-1818
Ashhurst	sioners,	(vol. xii 328-329)	Leach, 1818-1827
Wilson	1792-1793	Grant, 1801-1818	Hart, 1827
Loughborough, 1793-1801		Plumer, 1818-1824	Shadwell-1827-1850
Eldon, 1801-1806		Gifford, 1824-1826	
Erskine, 1806-1807		Lyndhurst, 1826-1827	
Eldon, 1807-1827		Leach, 1827-1834	
Lyndhurst, 1827-1830			
Brougham, 1830-1834			

[4] Vol. xii 569-576.

As Chancellor he exhibited the same qualities as he had shown as Chief Justice. He was courteous to the bar, attentive to the arguments, and soon made himself familiar with the leading principles of equity and with the practice of his court. His capacity to grasp quickly the facts of a case, and to state his conclusions in clear and often elegant language, was conspicuous. No one could accuse him of incompetence or want of attention to his duties.[1] But Butler's verdict that he showed "a want of real taste for legal learning"[2] is as true of him as Chancellor as it is of him as Chief Justice. As Campbell says:[3]

He would not submit to the labour and drudgery necessary for acquiring permanent reputation as a magistrate. When out of court, instead of dedicating his time to the consideration of the cases pending before him, or in reviving and extending his juridical knowledge, he was absorbed in politics, or he mixed in fashionable society, or he frequented the theatre.

Several of his decisions were reversed,[4] and many of his judgments can only be described as thin.[5] Occasionally he exerted himself to give a full and learned judgment;[6] but a study of his decisions confirms the truth of Campbell's verdict that the best judgments during these years were given by Pepper Arden (afterwards Lord Alvanley), the Master of the Rolls.[7]

Though none of his decisions show any striking developments in the principles and rules of equity, they do illustrate the growing fixity and precision of those rules and principles. The principle that the sphere of the equitable, and the spheres of the common law and ecclesiastical jurisdictions ought not to be disturbed is illustrated by a case in which Loughborough was asked to supersede a writ of *de excommunicato capiendo*.[8] He refused to do so, saying that, if he did, it would destroy the jurisdiction of the ecclesiastical courts, and that "by parity of reason they might apply to me to stop an action on a bond."[9] There are decisions on the subject of secret trusts,[10] precatory trusts,[11] charitable trusts,[12] and the effect of George II's statute

---

[1] Campbell, Chancellors vi 236-237.
[2] Cited vol. xii 575.
[3] Lives of the Chancellors vi 236.
[4] Instances are Abel v. Heathcote (1793) 2 Ves. 98; Stuart v. Earl of Bute (1796) 3 Ves. at p. 220; Strode v. Blackburn (1796) ibid at p. 227; Franco v. Bolton (1797) ibid at p. 371 *note*; Dench v. Bampton (1799) 4 Ves. 700, 708; Main v. Melbourn (1799) ibid 720, 724.
[5] A conspicuous instance is his judgment in the great case of Thellusson v. Woodford (1798-1799) 4 Ves. at pp. 340-343.
[6] E.g. Brydges v. Chandos (1794) 2 Ves. at pp. 426-437.
[7] For Pepper Arden see vol. xii 328-329.
[8] The King v. Blatch (1799) 5 Ves. 113.
[9] At p. 117.
[10] Mordaunt v. Hussey (1798) 4 Ves. 117.
[11] Malim v. Keighley (1795) 2 Ves. 529.
[12] Attorney-General v. Bower (1798) 3 Ves. 714.

of Charitable Uses on these trusts.[1]   In the case of *Fells v. Read* [2]
he held that the court could order the delivery up of a chattel
of peculiar rarity in the custody of the defendant, and more
especially when, as in this case, he held it upon a special trust.
The case of *Tate v. Hilbert* [3] illustrates the difference between
a gift *inter vivos* and a *donatio mortis causa*, and the effect of the
death of a donor of a cheque and a promissory note on the donee's
rights.   In the case of *Walpole v. Orford* [4] the effect of an agreement
to make mutual wills was discussed.   The case of *Matthews
v. Warner*,[5] which was an application for a commission to review a decision of the Court of Delegates, illustrates, as Loughborough said, the need for a Wills Act to prescribe the form
in which wills must be drawn up.[6]   The case of *Bemfide v.
Johnstone* [7] establishes the principle that the personal property
of an intestate must be distributed according to the law of his
domicil, and discusses the question as to how domicil is determined.
The case of *Tait v. Northwick*[8] illustrates the rule that personalty
is the primary fund for the payment of debts, and that a mere
charge of debts upon realty is not sufficient to exempt it.   The
case of *Elibank v. Montolieu*[9] is a leading case upon a wife's equity
to a settlement.   That the nature of good-will was imperfectly
understood is shown by the case of *Hammond v. Douglas* [10] which
decided that, on the death of a partner, it survives.   Eldon had
doubts whether this was right,[11] and later cases have justified his
doubts.[12]

Loughborough was succeeded by Eldon.   His two periods of
office, 1801-1806 and 1807-1827, are almost as important an epoch
in the history of equity as the chancellorship of Hardwicke.   But
before I deal with Eldon and his importance in the history of
equity I must say something of Erskine who held office from
February 1806 to April 1807.

Erskine[13] was not a great Chancellor, but he is none the less
one of the great figures in our legal history because he was the
greatest advocate who has ever practised at the English bar.   He
was born at Edinburgh on January 21, 1750.   His father was the
Earl of Buchan, an impoverished Scottish peer ;   and, since

---

[1] Blandford v. Thackerall (1793) 2 Ves. 238 ; 9 George II c. 36 ; for this
statute see vol. xi 590-593.
[2] (1796) 3 Ves. 70 ; for some remarks of Eldon on this case see Nutbrown v.
Thornton (1804) 10 Ves. at p. 163.
[3] (1793) 2 Ves. 111.   [4] (1797) 3 Ves. 402.
[5] (1798) 4 Ves. 186.   [6] At p. 210.
[7] (1796) 3 Ves. 198.   [8] (1799) 4 Ves. 816 at pp. 823-824.
[9] (1810) 5 Ves. 737.   [10] (1800) 5 Ves. 539.
[11] Crawshay v. Collins (1801) 15 Ves. at p. 227.
[12] In re David and Mathews [1899] 1 Ch. at p. 382.
[13] Townsend, Twelve Eminent Judges i 398-474, ii 1-144 ; Foss, Judges viii
268-282 ; Campbell, Lives of the Chancellors vi 367-709 ; Brougham, Historical
Sketches of Statesmen of the Time of George III 236-245 ; D.N.B.

Erskine was the youngest of three sons, there was little money to spare for his education. For a short time he was at the university of St. Andrews, but in 1764 he went to sea as a midshipman. In 1768 he abandoned the navy, entered the army, and became a lieutenant in 1773. He employed his leisure while on garrison duty in Minorca in the study of English literature ; and, on his return to England in 1772, his aristocratic birth, his intelligence, and his charm of manner gave him the *entrée* both to aristocratic and to literary circles. Boswell tells us that on April 6, 1772, he had met Erskine at dinner at the house of Sir Alexander Macdonald, and that he had " talked with vivacity, fluency, and precision so uncommon that he attracted particular attention." That he possessed also considerable literary capacity is shown by a tract on abuses in the army, which was published anonymously and had a large circulation. It attracted the attention of Bentham who said that it was " characterized by something different from common writing ";[1] and after the publication of Bentham's *Fragment* in 1776 Erskine made his acquaintance.[2]

But in the army promotion was slow. In 1773 Erskine had only risen to the rank of lieutenant, he had no money to buy further advances, and the expenses of his growing family were increasing. His resolve to leave the army is said to have been due to a chance meeting with Lord Mansfield, under the command of whose nephew he had sailed when he was a midshipman. Lord Mansfield, whilst he was on circuit, saw him in court, and, learning who he was, invited him to sit on the bench with him, and explained to him the case which was being tried. It occurred to Erskine that he might do quite as well as the eminent barristers who were appearing in the case, and he took the resolution of going to the bar. Neither Lord Mansfield nor his own relations discouraged this idea. Money was provided by the sale of his commission, and he became a student at Lincoln's Inn on April 26, 1775, and a gentleman commoner of Trinity College, Cambridge, on January 13, 1776. While at Cambridge he studied law in the chambers of Buller,[3] and afterwards of Wood—both of whom afterwards became judges. During these years he was very poor. Bentham, who sometimes met him at Dr. Burton's, said that " he was so shabbily dressed as to be quite remarkable."[4] On July 3 he was called to the bàr by Lincoln's Inn. In the following term, by a series of happy accidents, he got his chance of making his name at the bar which he took so effectually that he at once obtained a large practice.

This series of happy accidents began with a chance meeting

---

[1] Works x 564.
[2] Ibid.
[3] For Buller see vol. xii 488-492.
[4] Works x 565.

at dinner with Captain Baillie, who was the lieutenant-governor of Greenwich Hospital. Baillie had discovered gross abuses in the management of the hospital, and failing to get them redressed by the governors or the Lords of the Admiralty, he had published a pamphlet describing the abuses and reflecting on Lord Sandwich, the First Lord, who had, for electioneering purposes, given places in the hospital to unqualified persons. For the publication of this pamphlet Baillie was suspended. Sandwich thought it best to keep in the background, but some of his accomplices, who had also been reflected on, got a rule to show cause why a criminal information for libel should not be filed against Baillie. Erskine says :[1]

I had met during the long vacation this Captain Baillie at a friend's table, and after dinner I expressed myself with some warmth, probably with some eloquence, on the corruption of Lord Sandwich as First Lord of the Admiralty, and then adverted to the scandalous practices imputed to him with regard to Greenwich Hospital. Baillie nudged the person who sat next to him and asked who I was. Being told that I had just been called to the bar, and had been formerly in the navy, Baillie exclaimed with an oath, " then I'll have him for my counsel."

It is said that the four counsel briefed with Erskine suggested a compromise. But Erskine, supported by his client, refused to consent to take this course, and the case came on.[2] Erskine says :[3]

I trudged down to Westminster Hall when I got the brief, and being the junior of five, who would be heard before me, never dreamt that the court would hear me at all. Dunning, Bearcroft, Bower, Hargrave, were all heard at considerable length, and I was to follow. Hargrave was long winded and tired the court. It was a bad omen ; but, as my good fortune would have it, he was afflicted with strangury, and was obliged to retire once or twice in the course of his argument. This protracted the cause so long, that, when he had finished, Lord Mansfield said that the remaining counsel should be heard the next morning. This was exactly what I wished. I had the whole night to arrange in my chambers what I had to say the next morning, and I took the court with their faculties awake and freshened, succeeded quite to my own satisfaction . . . and, as I marched along the Hall after the rising of the judges, the attorneys flocked around me with their retainers. I have since flourished, but I have always blessed God for the providential strangury of poor Hargrave.

In fact Erskine's speech was a wonderful display of advocacy, which astonished not only the bar and the onlookers, but the judges themselves. Joseph Jekyll, coming by chance into the court, said that he found the whole court, judges and all, " in a trance of amazement."[4] What impressed all was not only the

---

[1] Cited by Townsend, Twelve Eminent Judges i 405-406.
[2] Campbell, Chancellors i 392 ; the case is reported 21 S.T. 1.
[3] Cited Townsend, op. cit. i 406.   [4] D.N.B.

skill with which the facts and the law relevant to the publication of the alleged libel were stated, and the wonderful eloquence
with which the statement was made, but also the boldness with
which interruptions by the court were dealt with and turned to
account. Here is the famous passage in which he dealt with an
interruption by Lord Mansfield :[1]

Such, my lords, is the case. The defendant, not a disappointed malicious
informer, prying into official abuses because without office himself, but
himself a man in office ; not troublesomely inquisitive into other men's
departments, but conscientiously correcting his own ; doing it pursuant
to the rules of law, and, what heightens the character, doing it at the
risk of his office, from which the effrontery of power has already suspended him without proof of his guilt ; a conduct not only unjust and
illiberal, but highly disrespectful to this Court, whose judges sit in the
double capacity of ministers of the law, and governors of this sacred and
abused institution. Indeed, Lord Sandwich has, in my mind, acted such a
part.
   *Here Lord Mansfield, observing the Counsel heated with his subject, and
growing personal on the First Lord of the Admiralty, told him that Lord
Sandwich was not before the Court.*
   I know that he is not formally before the Court, but, for that very
reason, *I will bring him before the Court* : he has placed these men in the
front of the battle in hopes to escape under their shelter, but I will not
join in battle with them ; *their* vices, though screwed up to the highest
pitch of human depravity, are not of dignity enough to vindicate the
combat with *me*. I will drag him to light who is the dark mover behind
this scene of iniquity. I assert that the Earl of Sandwich has but one road
to escape out of this business without pollution and disgrace : and *that* is,
by publicly disavowing the acts of the prosecutors, and restoring Captain
Baillie to his command. If he does this then his offence will be no more
than the too common one of having suffered his own *personal* interest to
prevail over his *public* duty, in placing his voters in the Hospital. But if,
on the contrary, he continues to protect the prosecutors, in spite of the
evidence of their guilt, which has excited the abhorrence of the numerous
audience that crowd this Court ; if he keeps this injured man suspended,
or dares to turn that suspension into a removal, I shall then not scruple
to declare him an accomplice in their guilt, a shameless oppressor, a
disgrace to his rank, and a traitor to his trust.[2]

The quiet and effective peroration with which Erskine ended his
speech showed that he had an instinct and a genius for impressing upon his audience, and leaving them impressed by,
exactly the effect which he wished to produce. It is the measure
of his supreme mastery of the art of advocacy. It runs as follows :[3]

And now, my lord, I have done ; but not without thanking your lordship
for the very indulgent attention I have received, though in so late a stage
of this business, and notwithstanding my great incapacity and in-
experience. I resign my client into your hands, and I resign him with a

[1] 21 S.T. at pp. 43-44.
[2] It is said that, having been asked how he had got the courage thus to stand
up to Lord Mansfield, he replied that he thought that his children were plucking at
his robe, and saying " Now, father, is the time to get us bread," Campbell, op. cit.
397.   [3] 21 S.T. at p. 45.

well-founded confidence and hope ; because that torrent of corruption, which has unhappily overwhelmed every other part of the constitution, is, by the blessing of Providence, stopped *here* by the sacred independence of the judges. I know that your lordships will determine *according to law* ; and, therefore, if an information should be suffered to be filed, I shall bow to the sentence, and shall consider this meritorious publication to be indeed an offence against the laws of this country ; but then I shall not scruple to say, that it is high time for every honest man to remove himself from a country in which he can no longer do his duty to his country with safety ; where cruelty and inhumanity are suffered to impeach virtue, and where vice passes through a court of justice unpunished and un-reproved.[1]

Considering all the circumstances—the fact that Erskine had only just been called, and the fact that he spoke after four eminent counsel—Lord Campbell, no mean judge of forensic oratory, is justified in saying that it was " the most wonderful forensic effort of which we have any account in our annals."[2]

Erskine at once got into large practice ; and his reputation was enhanced by his defence of Admiral Keppel, who was tried by a court martial for negligence and incapacity in 1779, and by his defence of Lord George Gordon on his trial for treason in 1781. By that time his business both at the Parliamentary and the common law bar had so increased that he found it necessary to refuse junior briefs. But that meant that no one could be em-ployed with him unless he had been called after him—with the result that many senior barristers suffered. The only remedy was to give him silk, and so he got his silk gown in May 1783—before he had been five years at the bar.

Erskine was a lifelong Whig and a supporter of Fox. In 1783 the Whigs procured his election for Portsmouth, and he made his first speech in support of Fox's India bill. But as a Parlia-mentary speaker he was a comparative failure.[3] He was over-awed by Pitt, and, though he occasionally made a successful speech, he never seems to have become acclimatized to the atmosphere of the House, or to have been able to adopt the style of oratory suited to it. As Brougham says,[4]

he never gave his whole mind to the practice of debating ; he had a very scanty provision of political information ; and his time was always occupied with the laborious pursuits of his profession ; he came into the

---

[1] The rule for the information was discharged. There was an enquiry into the mismanagement of Greenwich Hospital by the House of Lords in 1779, as a result of which Lord Sandwich was ultimately whitewashed by the government votes, 21 S.T. 72-484.   [2] Chancellors vi 396.

[3] Scarlett says, " Though I admit that Erskine's success in the House of Commons was not equal to his reputation at the bar . . . I am far from conceding that he had not very great success. . . . I have heard him several times when he spoke second only to Pitt and Fox, and commanded the profoundest attention," P. C. Scarlett, Memoir of Lord Abinger 68.

[4] Historical Sketches i 236-237 ; Scarlett takes the same view, Memoir of Lord Abinger 66-67.

House of Commons, where he stood among several equals, and behind some superiors, from a stage where he shone alone, and without a rival ; above all he was accustomed to address a select and friendly audience, bound to lend him their patient attention, and to address them by the compulsion of his retainer, not as a volunteer coming forward in his own person ; a position from which the transition is violent and extreme, to that of having to gain and keep a promiscuous and, in great part, hostile audience, not under any obligation to listen beyond the time during which the speaker can flatter, or interest, or amuse them.

When the coalition ministry of Fox and North was dismissed and when Pitt triumphed in the general election of 1784, Erskine was one of Fox's Martyrs. But though he ceased to be a member of the House of Commons he continued to win triumphs in the courts. In 1783 he made his famous speech in the *Dean of St. Asaph's Case*[1] in support of a rule to arrest judgment. That speech shows that he was nearly as great a lawyer as he was an advocate ; and that he could present to the court an argument upon a point of law with the same eloquence and charm as he was able to present to a jury an argument upon the facts and upon the conduct of the parties. I have analysed this speech in a preceding volume.[2] We have seen that, though it advocated what is most probably an erroneous view upon a doubtful point of law,[3] it stated the case for that view with consummate skill ; and that whether or not Erskine's views on the point of law were correct, a reform of the law, so as to bring it into conformity with this view, was absolutely necessary.[4] His defence of Stockdale,[5] who was prosecuted by order of the House of Commons for publishing Logan's reflections upon the managers of the impeachment of Warren Hastings and upon the House, shows that his capacity to appeal to a jury was as great as, if not greater than, his capacity to appeal to the court. Campbell said that he had been told by Scarlett, his father-in-law, who was present in court, that its " effect upon the audience was wholly unexampled." [6] Erskine again entered Parliament in 1790, and in 1791 he seconded Fox's motion for leave to bring in the bill which became Fox's Libel Act.[7] We have seen that that Act declared that the view of the law for which Erskine had unsuccessfully argued in the *Dean of St. Asaph's Case* was correct.[8]

When the French Revolution caused the split between the old and the new Whigs [9] Erskine adhered to the new Whigs. He supported Grey's motion for the reform of Parliament in 1792,[10] and opposed the war with France and the measures taken to suppress seditious writings.[11] At the cost of offending the Prince

[1] 21 S.T. 971-1023.
[2] Vol. x 681-688.
[3] Ibid 674-680.
[4] Ibid 688-690.
[5] (1789) 22 S.T. 237 at pp. 252-284.
[6] Chancellors vi 450.
[7] 32 George III c. 60.
[8] Vol. x 689-692.
[9] Above 157.   [10] Above 157, 160.
[11] Above 160 seqq.

of Wales, and the consequent loss of his position as his attorney-general, he undertook the defence of Paine ;[1] and we have seen that it was in his speech in his defence that he stated most clearly the reason why the liberty of the press was a condition precedent to the existence of constitutional government,[2] and the kind of limitations which such a government is justified in placing upon it.[3]

In these circumstances it was inevitable that he should be briefed to defend Hardy, Horne Tooke, Thelwall, and the nine other persons who were indicted for high treason in 1794.[4] His defence of Hardy was not only a marvellous feat of advocacy but also a wonderful effort of physical endurance. During the eight days that the trial lasted the court sat from 8 a.m. till midnight, and Erskine was ever on the watch to take any points favourable to his client. Then, after the court rose, he spent a large part of the night in preparation for the proceedings of the following day. At the end of the case for the prosecution, having with difficulty extorted from the court a permission to begin the proceedings at noon,[5] he made a speech of seven hours duration which Horne Tooke said would last for ever. For ten minutes before its close he could only whisper to the jury, but so deep was the silence that every word was heard. We have seen that Hardy's acquittal was the signal for an outburst of enthusiasm from the spectators and the crowds which thronged the streets, and that the streets could not be cleared till Erskine went out and addressed the crowd and asked them to depart peaceably.[6] His success in thus stopping the attempt of the government to use the doctrine of constructive treason to fetter unduly freedom of speech, coupled with his efforts to prevent the law of libel from being used for the same purpose, almost justify Brougham's verdict upon his achievement :[7]

if there be yet amongst us the power of freely discussing the acts of our rulers ; if there be yet the privilege of meeting for the promotion of needful reforms ; if he who desires wholesome changes in our Constitution be still recognized as a patriot, and not doomed to die the death of a traitor ; let us acknowledge with gratitude that to this great man, under Heaven, we owe this felicity of the times.

Hardy's acquittal was perhaps the greatest triumph in Erskine's career. His defence of Hadfield,[8] indicted for shooting at George III in Drury Lane Theatre, is remarkable, not only as a feat of advocacy, but as a skilful exposition of the conditions in

---

[1] (1792) 22 S.T. at pp. 410-472.
[2] (1792) 22 S.T. at p. 437, cited vol. x 673.
[3] Ibid at pp. 414-415, cited vol. x 694.   [4] Above 162, 163.
[5] 24 S.T. at pp. 864-865.   [6] Above 162.
[7] Historical Sketches i 243.   [8] (1800) 27 S.T. at pp. 1307-1330.

which the defence of insanity is operative. It was so successful that Lord Kenyon stopped the case and directed an acquittal on this ground. It is not surprising to learn that in these years Erskine's practice was enormous. In 1791 he was said to have made £10,000—£1600 more than any other counsel had ever made, and his clerk was said to have saved £20,000.[1] It was wholly a common law practice. He never appeared in the House of Lords or the Privy Council or in the court of Chancery, and only occasionally, when he was out of Parliament, before a committee of the House of Commons. But his liberal opinions, and his consistent support of Fox, prevented him from getting any official appointment. Moreover he had published a pamphlet, of which thirty-seven editions were called for, on the war with France, which attacked Pitt. On Pitt's resignation there were some thoughts of appointing him attorney-general. But the Prince of Wales dissuaded him, and shortly afterwards made him chancellor of the Duchy of Cornwall.

In 1803, when it was thought that Napoleon was about to invade England, volunteers were enrolled, and Erskine took command of the volunteers from the Temple, who were generally known as " The Devil's Own." Lord Campbell says that he remembers seeing him drilling his men in the Temple gardens— " he gave the word of command from a paper which he held before him, and in which I conjectured that his ' instructions ' were written out as in a *Brief*." [2] When the scare was over the question arose whether a volunteer could resign at his pleasure. The law officers gave it as their opinion that they could not, and that they were bound to serve for the duration of the war.[3] Erskine gave a contrary opinion,[4] which was upheld by the court of King's Bench ;[5] and he secured the withdrawal of a clause in a bill introduced in 1804 to overrule this decision.[6]

It was not till Pitt's death that Erskine at length gained office. It was most unfortunate that it was impossible to appoint him to the Chief Justiceship of the court of King's Bench or Common Pleas. But both Ellenborough and Taunton refused the offer of the Chancellorship, and so it was offered to and accepted by Erskine, who had never in his life conducted a case in the court of Chancery. Naturally there were great forebodings amongst the members of the Chancery bar. Its leader Romilly wrote in his diary,[7]

Although the new administration has been formed in general of the public men of the greatest talents and highest character of any in the country, yet there are some few appointments which have been received

---

[1] Life of Lord Campbell i 193.
[2] Chancellors vi 548 n.
[3] Ibid 548.
[4] Ibid.
[5] R. v. Dowley (1804) 4 East 512.
[6] Campbell, Chancellors vi 549-550.
[7] Life of Romilly (ed. 1842) ii 2.

by the public with much dissatisfaction, and none with more than that of Erskine to be Lord Chancellor. The truth undoubtedly is, that he is totally unfit for the situation. His practice has never led him into courts of equity ; and the doctrines which prevail in them are to him almost like the law of a foreign country. It is true that he has a great deal of quickness, and is capable of much application ; but, at his time of life, with the continual occupation which the duties of his office will give him, and the immense arrear of business left him by his tardy and doubting predecessor, it is quite impossible that he should find the means of making himself master of that extensive and complicated system of law which he will have to administer. He acts, indeed, very ingenuously on the subject ; he feels his unfitness for his office, and seems almost overcome with the idea of the difficulties which he foresees that he will have to encounter. He called on me a few days ago. and told me he should stand in great need of my assistance, that I must tell him what to read, and how best to fit himself for his situation. " You must "—these were the very words he used to me—" You must make me a Chancellor now, that I may afterwards make you one."

Though it was said that Erskine in later life said that " the most discreditable passage in his life was sitting in the court of Chancery," [1] the appointment turned out better than might have been expected. [2] But there is no doubt that if Erskine had been made a chief justice of one of the common law courts he would have had a position for which he was eminently well fitted, and would consequently have made his name not only as a great advocate, but as a great lawyer and judge. Moreover it would have been a life-appointment, so that he would have spent his days employed in the pursuits for which he was most fitted.

When, in little over a year, the fall of the government deprived Erskine of his office, he was wholly unemployed. He could not return to the bar, and he took little part in the business of the House of Lords. He made an eloquent speech against the proposal to prohibit the export of Jesuits bark as a war measure against the French, and against Gibbs's bill giving the Crown power to arrest persons against whom information for libel had been filed. [3] He proposed bills to prevent cruelty to animals in 1809 and 1810. Naturally he opposed the restrictions placed on the Regent's powers by the Act of 1810, for which the Regent rewarded him by making him a Knight of the Thistle. But the Regent deserted his friends, and so Erskine lost all chance of further official employment. He became a social figure, and amused himself with literature—he wrote a romance entitled *Armata*, modelled on *Utopia* and *Gulliver's Travels*—farming, and the entertainment of his friends. He took even less part than before in either the legislative or the judicial business of the

[1] Lord Kingsdown's Recollections cited Ed. Rev. cxxix 46.
[2] Below 594.   [3] Above 393, 394, 536.

House of Lords.[1] He emerged from his retirement to oppose the Six Acts, and he revived some of his old popularity by his opposition to the bill against Queen Caroline. His last speech in the House of Lords was a speech of rejoicing that the bill had been abandoned. The rule of law, he said, had been thereby vindicated, and he closed his speech with the quotation of Hooker's well-known panegyric upon law. It was after his efforts on behalf of the Queen that he was invited to a public dinner in Edinburgh, and revisited his native land for the first time since he had left it as a midshipman.

During his last days he suffered from pecuniary embarrassment. He lost money by investing in American securities, and bought an estate in Sussex which turned out to be worth very little. He was obliged to sell his house at Hampstead and his other estates. But he was still lively and gay in society, and he wrote occasional pamphlets—one to support the cause of the Greeks in 1822, and one on agricultural distress in 1823. In the latter year he determined to revisit Scotland, but he was taken ill on the voyage, and was put ashore at Scarborough. He was taken to the house of his sister-in-law at Almondell where he died on November 23. His admirers erected a statue by Westmacott to his memory. It now stands in the library of Lincoln's Inn, and, in Lord Campbell's opinion, it gives a better impression of the man than any of his other portraits or busts.

Erskine had his faults—faults which, as Scarlett, who knew him well, said, were due to "imprudence and ill-regulated passions." [2] But his happy disposition and social gifts procured him the affection of his friends, and even an absence of all jealousy on the part of his professional rivals at his sudden rise to leadership at the bar. Scarlett says : [3]

His manners were courteous and obliging. His conversation full of spirit and gaiety. His imagination had something fantastic about it, that made him a constant source of amusement. His good temper was imperturbable. His spirits were lively, his disposition for frolic and fun in private society so extraordinary that to those who were strangers to him it was impossible to believe that he was the celebrated Mr. Erskine or anything else but a schoolboy broken loose for the holidays.

And these characteristics he showed throughout his life. " When I entered Westminster Hall," says Lord Campbell,[4] " it rang with

---

[1] In June 1814 Romilly complained of his inattention to business—"Lord Erskine told me on Saturday that he should certainly bring on my bills, which he has taken charge of on this day. He had not, however, given any notice of his intention, or required that the Lords should be summoned ; and though he formerly presided in the House as Chancellor for above a year, he was ignorant till he learned from me with surprise and evident mortification, that a previous notice was, according to constant usage, necessary before he could move the second reading of any Bill," Life of Romilly ii 340.

[2] P. C. Scarlett, Memoir of Lord Abinger 64.

[3] Ibid.   [4] Chancellors vi 695.

Erskine's jokes—some of them very good "; and the story is told of how one morning at the beginning of the Trinity term, after he had ceased to be Chancellor, he came into the barristers' robing room at Westminster Hall, jumped on to a table, and exclaimed, " Well, here am I again, the first day of term, and not a single brief in my bag." [1] To the end he was an adept in writing witty epigrams in verse. The failing most often alleged against him was that he was vain and egotistical—a failing which Canning satirized in the Anti-Jacobin.[2] The best answer to this and other criticisms was given by Lord Kenyon to one who had been criticizing Erskine. He said :[3]

Young man, what you have mentioned is most probably unfounded, but these things, even if they were true, are only spots in the sun. As for his egotism, which they are so fond of laying to his charge, they would talk of themselves as much as Mr. Erskine does of himself, if they had the same right to do so. His nonsense would set up half-a-dozen of such men as run him down.

But though Erskine might be accused of vanity and egotism in his social life, no such charge can be brought against him in his professional capacity. " Through life," says Lord Campbell,[4] " he was often ridiculed for vanity and egotism, but not for any-thing he ever said or did in conducting a cause in a court of justice. There, from the moment the jury were sworn, he thought of nothing but the verdict, till it was recorded in his favour."

This whole-hearted devotion to his clients' interest was one, but only one, of the causes which made him the greatest advocate that the English bar has ever seen. His greatness as an advocate was due to a combination of qualities which have never been united before or since in such perfect harmony in one individual.

In the first place, his powers as a forensic orator were far greater than, and different from, anything that had hitherto been seen or heard in the courts. His voice and his action combined with his intellectual and literary powers to produce an over-whelming effect.[5] He had a combination of intellectual powers which enabled him to appeal both to the feelings and passions of his audience, and to their reason. " He knew every avenue to the heart ;"[6] and he knew how to argue clearly and closely ; for he had " a nice discernment of the relative importance and weight of different arguments, and the faculty of assigning each to its proper place, so as to bring forward the main body of the

---

[1] Townsend, Twelve Eminent Judges ii 88.

[2] See the passage cited by Campbell, Chancellors vi 691-693.

[3] Cited by Townsend, Twelve Eminent Judges i 426 ; and Scarlett was of the same opinion, P. C. Scarlett, Memoir of Lord Abinger 64.

[4] Chancellors vi 680.

[5] P. C. Scarlett, Memoir of Lord Abinger 65-66 ; Brougham, Historical Sketches i 237-238.   [6] Ibid 238.

reasoning in bold relief." [1] In his very first case he showed his remarkable power of introducing his authorities and arguments on points of law and using them to enforce the conclusions which he wished to draw from the facts. [2] His literary powers enabled him to use with effect a bold imagination, for his taste was always correct, and his execution felicitous. [3] And " to his parts as an orator he added those of a consummate actor." [4]

In the second place, he was a perfect legal tactician. Brougham says : [5]

His memory was accurate and retentive in an extraordinary degree ; nor did he ever, during the trial of a cause, forget any matter, how trifling soever, that belonged to it. His presence of mind was perfect in action, that is, before the jury, when a line is to be taken upon the instant, and a question risked to a witness, or a topic chosen with the tribunal, on which the whole fate of the cause may turn. No man made fewer mistakes ; none left so few advantages unimproved ; before none was it so dangerous for an adversary to slumber and be off his guard ; for he was ever broad awake himself, and was as adventurous as he was skilful ; and as apt to take advantage of any the least opening, as he was cautious to leave none in his own battle.

He was a skilled examiner and cross-examiner ; [6] and, though capable of holding his own against his opponent or the court, he was always courteous to both. [7]

In the third place, all these qualities predisposed both the jury and the court in his favour. " Juries have declared that they felt it impossible to remove their looks from him when he had riveted and, as it were, fascinated them by his first glance." [8] On the trial of Hardy it was the interposition of the jury which procured for him the extra hour which he asked for to prepare his speech for the defence. [9] We have seen that that stern moralist Lord Kenyon so loved him that he referred to some of his lapses as " spots in the sun." [10] Scarlett tells us that Mr. Justice Chambers used to say that Erskine could make a day at *nisi prius* entertaining by his wit and imagination ; and he adds that

---

[1] Brougham, Historical Sketches, i 238.
[2] Above 583-584.   [3] Brougham, op. cit. 239.
[4] P. C. Scarlett, op. cit. 66 ; Campbell, Chancellors vi 681-682 says that when he went down into the country on special retainers, " he examined the Court the night before the trial, in order to select the most advantageous place for addressing the jury. On the cause being called, the crowded audience were perhaps kept waiting a few minutes before the celebrated stranger made his appearance ; and when, at length, he gratified their impatient curiosity, a particularly nice wig and a pair of nice new yellow gloves distinguished and embellished his person beyond the ordinary costume of the barristers of the circuit."
[5] Historical Sketches i 238-239 ; with this verdict Scarlett agrees, P. C. Scarlett, Memoir of Lord Abinger 64-65.
[6] Brougham, op. cit. i 240-241.
[7] Campbell, Chancellors vi 682—speaking from personal observation ; P. C. Scarlett, Memoir of Lord Abinger 65.
[8] Brougham, op. cit. i 237.   [9] Above 586.   [10] Above 590.

he was the favourite of every jury and judge before whom he practised.[1]

These were the qualities which made Erskine a great advocate. Was he also a great lawyer ? He himself once said that " no man can be a great advocate who is no lawyer." [2] I think that the evidence shows that Erskine had the qualities of a great lawyer, and that if he had had the chance of displaying them as chief justice of one of the common law courts, this fact would have been very evident. Lord Campbell, it is true, says of him that he was only " a clever *nisi prius* pleader," " only familiar with the rules of evidence, and the points likely to occur in the conduct of a case before a jury, or in the common routine of a King's Bench leader in banco." [3] But Lord Campbell contradicts himself ; for he admits that he successfully conducted a practice which included every kind of civil action which came before the court of King's Bench,[4] and it is difficult to see how such a practice could be conducted without a considerable knowledge of law. He admits also the masterly character of his argument in the *Dean of St. Asaph's Case*,[5] and his masterly treatment of the law of treason both in Lord George Gordon's and in Hardy's cases.[6] Then, too, when he was Chancellor he presided over Melville's impeachment so ably that Lord Campbell says that to him " belongs the merit of proving that it (an impeachment) may still be so conducted as to prove an efficient safeguard of the Constitution." [7] For these reasons I think that it may be affirmed that Erskine had the qualities of a great lawyer, and that Scarlett was right when he said that he would " unquestionably have presided with great applause " over the court of King's Bench.[8]

This conclusion is, I think, confirmed by the manner in which Erskine acquitted himself in the court of Chancery.

In spite of Romilly's apprehensions, the business of the court of Chancery proceeded smoothly. Erskine made no changes in the official staff of the court. He was helped by the bar, and he enlisted (as Thurlow had done)[9] the services of the learned Hargrave, to whom he gave a silk gown.[10] On occasion he referred to Lord Eldon for information on points of practice ;[11] and the very learned and experienced Sir William Grant, the Master of the Rolls,[12] was always at hand to give further help. At the end of his term of office he was able to boast that there had been only

---

[1] P. C. Scarlett, Memoir of Lord Abinger 65.

[2] Cited Townsend, Twelve Eminent Judges ii 70 ; the letter cited was written in 1819 to an impudent person, who, having made a bet on the number of Erskine's decrees which had been reversed, wrote to him for information on the subject.

[3] Chancellors vi 553.

[4] Ibid vi 527.

[5] Ibid vi 433-434.

[6] Ibid vi 408, 478-479.

[7] Ibid vi 577.

[8] P. C. Scarlett, Memoir of Lord Abinger 68.

[9] Vol. xii 323.

[10] Campbell, Chancellors vi 560.

[11] Fisher v. Bayley (1806) 12 Ves. at p. 20.

[12] Below 656-662.

one appeal against his decisions, and that that appeal had been dismissed.[1] But though this fact stands to his credit, it is well to remember that he only held office for a short time ; that some of his decisions have not been followed ;[2] and that many of his judgments are, as might be expected, somewhat thin. On the other hand, Scarlett said that " on the woolsack the profession were struck by his great facility," [3] and the reports show that he was beginning to acquire so sound a knowledge of equitable doctrines that he was able to state them shortly and clearly, and occasionally to criticize them. Thus in the case of *Hillary v. Waller* [4] there is a clear account of the presumptions as to title which long possession or enjoyment of property afford, and of the principle upon which those presumptions rest. In the case of *Grant v. Grant* [5] there is a good account of the principles upon which equity can make a decree for specific performance with compensation. In one of the cases in which Thellusson's will came before the courts he gave a good and clear account of the doctrine of election.[6] In the case of *Holmes v. Coghill*[7] he gave a critical account of the rules as to when, in favour of creditors, equity would aid the defective execution of a power—though it refused to intervene in case of its non-execution. He said : [8]

It is much to be regretted that the right of creditors to receive satisfaction out of the estate of their debtor should depend upon either artificial modes of conveyancing or artificial rules of law, clashing with each other, and not to be reconciled with clear principles of law or equity. I confess I am not able to reconcile what a Court of Equity has been in the constant habit of doing, and what it has refused to do.

And then, after saying that authority prevented him from aiding the non-execution of a power, he said,[9]

I lament that these difficulties and inconsistencies are to be found upon this subject. They are for the consideration of the legislature ; who may declare, that, where a power is given to dispose of property by a certain act, if the party dies without doing that act, still it shall be assets.

In cases in which the question of the relations of law and equity were raised, or in cases which involved the consideration of rules of law, some of his judgments are good and clear. In the case of *Corporation of Carlisle v. Wilson* [10] he gave a good account of the reasons why equity had come to exercise a concurrent jurisdiction with the courts of common law in matters of account.

---

[1] See a letter of Erskine, above 592 n. 2, cited Townsend op. cit. ii 70.
[2] 12 Ves. 464 n. 1 ; 13 Ves. 62.   [3] Memoir of Lord Abinger 68.
[4] (1806) 12 Ves. 239 at pp. 265-266.   [5] (1806) 13 Ves. 73 at pp. 76-79.
[6] Thellusson v. Woodford (1806) 13 Ves. 209 at pp. 220-224 ; for Thellusson and the case arising from his will see vol. vii 228-231.
[7] (1806) 12 Ves. 206 at pp. 212-216. [8] At p. 212. [9] At p. 216.
[10] (1807) 13 Ves. 276 at pp. 278-279.

In the case of *White v. Hall* [1] he stressed the essential similarity of the treatment of fraud by courts of law and equity; and in the case of *Clifford v. Brooke* [2] he answered Lord Eldon's criticisms [3] upon the decision of the courts of King's Bench in the case of *Pasley v. Freeman,* [4] that an action in tort lay for a fraud. In the case of *Crosbie v. M'Dowal* [5] he pointed out that in equity as well as at law a contract made without consideration was *nudum pactum.* In the case of *Griffiths v. Hamilton* [6] he discussed the different points of view of law and equity as to the title of the executor to undisposed of residue. In the case of *ex parte Bulmer* [7] he discussed the thorny subject of what transactions connected with, or collateral to, an illegal transaction are so affected by the illegality that a plaintiff cannot enforce them. On the question whether copyright could exist in such works as a directory or a map he could speak with some authority since he had argued such cases in the common law courts. [8]

Though Erskine cannot be said to have had any influence on the development of the doctrines of equity, I think his decisions show that he was rapidly acquiring a knowledge of the system; that, if he had had a longer term of office, his grasp of common law principles would have enabled him to assimilate and master the closely allied principles of equity; and that his capacity for clear thinking and clear exposition, might have enabled him to leave some mark upon the development of equitable doctrine. Romilly, it is true, thought differently. [9] But he was not a wholly impartial judge. We have seen that he took a very unfavourable view of his appointment; [10] and he had been irritated by what he considered an injustice to one of his clients, [11] by Erskine's appointment of his son-in-law to a mastership in Chancery two days before he quitted office, [12] and by his failure to support one of his bills in the House of Lords. [13] However that may be, I think

---

[1] (1806) 12 Ves. 321 at p. 324.
[2] (1806) 13 Ves. 131 at pp. 133-134.
[3] For these criticisms see vol. xii 597.
[4] (1789) 3 T.R. 51.
[5] (1806) Ves. 148 at pp. 157-158.
[6] (1806) 12 Ves. 298 at pp. 308-309.
[7] (1807) 13 Ves. 313 at pp. 315-320.
[8] Matthewson v. Stockdale (1806) 12 Ves. at p. 274.
[9] He wrote in 1807: " The present Ministry can hardly, considering what the crisis is to which public affairs are hastening, be very long in power; and if those whom they have supplanted should recover their authority, the Great Seal can scarcely again be entrusted to the hands of Lord Erskine; with all his talents (and very great they undoubtedly are) his incapacity for the office was too forcibly and too generally felt for him to be again placed in it," Life of Romilly ii 533-544.
[10] Above 587, 588.
[11] In the case of Purcell v. M'Namara, Life of Romilly ii 30-35.
[12] Ibid ii 49; the complaint was not that he appointed his son-in-law, but that he did so two days before he went out of office; it must be remembered that these offices were in the gift of the Chancellor—Lord Eldon made one such an appointment to gratify the Regent, below 616, and in another case he appointed a connection by marriage, below 617; Erskine had had few chances to exercise this patronage since he had confirmed the existing officers in their posts, above 592.
[13] Above 589 n. 1.

it is clear that his short term of office as Chancellor shows that though he was greater as an advocate than as a lawyer, yet he had such considerable talents as a lawyer, and such ability to preside over a court, that he would have made an admirable Chief Justice of one of the common law courts.

Erskine's predecessor and successor was one of the greatest of our Chancellors—John Scott, Lord Eldon.[1] I shall describe first his career, secondly his character as a man and as Chancellor, and thirdly his achievement as Chancellor.

Eldon's Career

John Scott was born at Newcastle on June 4, 1751. He was the youngest son of a coal fitter[2] and member of the Hoastman's Company of Newcastle. Besides his business as a coal fitter, he conducted a trade in malt, sugar and grindstones, did some underwriting business, and was a considerable landowner. " At his death," Eldon said,[3] " there were few persons in Newcastle town of substance equal." John Scott, like his elder brother William, was educated at the Royal Grammar School at Newcastle. Hugh Moises, the headmaster, was a very efficient teacher, and throughout their lives both John and William Scott were grateful to him. As soon as John became Chancellor he made him one of his chaplains, and later offered him preferment in the church. His father had intended that John should go into his business. But William, who had become a fellow and tutor of University College, Oxford, persuaded his father to send John to the University, so that it was due to his brother that the first step was taken which made his career possible.

Scott became a member of University College, Oxford, and was matriculated in May 1766. At University College his tutors were his brother and Chambers, afterwards Vinerian Professor and a judge at Calcutta. In 1767 the influence of his brother secured his election to a fellowship at his college. He took his degree in 1770, and in 1771 he gained the university prize for an English essay. At this period it seems to have been taken for granted that he would enter the church and in due course take a college living. But in 1772 the whole course of his life was changed by what was the most romantic episode in it—his elopement with

[1] H. Twiss, The Life of Lord Chancellor Eldon ; Campbell, The Lives of the Chancellors, vol. vii ; Foss, Judges ix 39-52 ; Townsend, The Lives of Twelve Eminent Judges ii 366-520 ; Brougham, Historical Sketches, ii 54-72 ; W. E. Surtees, The Lives of Lord Eldon and Lord Stowell ; D.N.B. ; Bentham, Works, v 348-382 ; Edinburgh Rev. xxxviii 281-314, xxxix 246-260, lxxxi 131-180 ; Quart. Rev. lxxiv 71-123, lxxv 32-54.
[2] " The coal fitter is the factor who conducts the sales between the owner and the shipper, taking the shipper's order for the commodity, supplying the cargo to him, and receiving from him the price of it for the owner," Twiss, op. cit. i 25.
[3] Ibid i 102, citing a memorandum of Eldon.

Elizabeth, the daughter of Aubone Surtees, a Newcastle banker, and his marriage at Blackshiels near Edinburgh. Both his brother William and his old master Moises deplored his folly.[1] But in fact it was the wisest step he ever took. It was the beginning of a happy union which lasted till his wife's death in 1831, for Scott acted up to his dictum that " the only reparation that one man can make to another for running away with his daughter is to be exemplary in his conduct to her ";[2] and, since it entailed the loss of his fellowship, it put an end to his idea of entering the church, and caused him to enter the profession of the law. George III told him, when he became Chancellor, that he wished to be remembered to his wife because, said the King, " I know that you would have made yourself a country curate and that she has made you my Lord Chancellor." [3]

Both the parents—first Scott and a little later Surtees—forgave their children and made a small settlement upon them. Scott, in order that he might have, as he said, two strings to his bow, became a student at the Middle Temple in 1773 and started to study law. But his college statutes allowed him to keep his fellowship for a year after his marriage, and, if any college living had fallen vacant during that year, he would have accepted it. The church, he said, was " his first mistress," and the law " had much less of his affection and respect." [4] Fortunately no living fell vacant. Scott read law steadily, and followed his maxim that a lawyer who wishes to succeed must " live like a hermit and work like a horse." [5] His brother gave him some pecuniary help, he took some pupils, and Chambers, the Vinerian Professor of Law and the Principal of New Inn Hall, who had been allowed to keep his chair for three years notwithstanding his appointment to an Indian judgeship, appointed him his deputy and allowed him to live in his lodgings at New Inn Hall. Of his first lecture as Chambers' deputy he told the following anecdote :[6]

Immediately after I was married, I was appointed Deputy Professor of Law at Oxford, and the law professor sent me the first lecture, which I had to read *immediately* to the students, and which I began without knowing a single word that was in it. It was upon the statute of young men running away with maidens (4, 5 Philip and Mary c. 8). Fancy me reading, with about one hundred and forty boys and young men all giggling at the professor. Such a tittering audience no one ever had.

Some months before his call to the bar he went to London and took a small house in Cursitor Street.[7] Duane, the well known

[1] Campbell, Chancellors vii 28.   [2] Twiss, op. cit. iii 189-190.
[3] Ibid i 374.   [4] Ibid i 83.   [5] Ibid i 374.   [6] Ibid i 91.
[7] " In his later life, as he was one day passing through Cursitor Street with Mr. Pensam his secretary of bankrupts, he pointed to a house in that street, and said,' there was my first perch. Many a time have I run down from Cursitor Street to Fleet Market (then occupying the site which is now called Farringdon Street) to get sixpennyworth of sprats for supper '," Twiss, op. cit. i 96.

Roman Catholic conveyancer, who did much conveyancing business for Northumberland landowners, took him into his chambers without a fee. It was the experience gained in these chambers, coupled with the manner in which he had mastered Coke upon Littleton, the reports, and other authorities, that laid the foundations of his extensive knowledge of conveyancing and the law of real property. He could not afford the fee needed to admit him to the chambers of a special pleader or equity drafts-man. " I mastered these arts," he said in later life, " by copying everything I could lay my hand upon." [1] His study of the reports was so intensive that it was said he knew the page of the report where each case was to be found, and could state pre-cisely the way in which it agreed or differed from other cases. By these means " he entered on his profession with a stock of learning that would not have disgraced the bench." [2]

Scott was called to the bar on February 9, 1776. For the first three or four years progress in London was slow. In later life he said : [3]

When I was called to the bar, Bessy and I thought all our troubles were over : business was to pour in, and we were to be almost rich immediately. So I made a bargain with her, that during the following year, all the money I should receive in the first eleven months should be mine, and whatever I should get in the twelfth month should be hers. What a stingy dog I must have been to make such a bargain ! I would not have done so afterwards. But, however, so it was ; *that* was our agreement : and how do you think it turned out ? In the twelfth month I received half a guinea ; eighteen pence went for fees, and Bessy got nine shillings : in the other eleven months I got not one shilling.

But he got work on the northern circuit, in the year that he was called to the bar. [4] In the year after, the Duke of Northumberland, out of compliment to his father-in-law Surtees, gave him a brief in a House of Lords case, and Surtees got him a general retainer for the corporation of Newcastle. In 1777 and 1780 he was briefed by Bowes, the candidate for Newcastle, to appear for him in election petitions. [5] In London he used his leisure to study law so hard that he nearly had a breakdown. He devoted himself mainly to the court of Chancery because, he tells us, he imagined that Lord Mansfield favoured Westminster and Christ Church men. A better reason was the fact that, though he was a good common lawyer and able to hold his own at *nisi prius*, his learning and talents were better suited to the equity than the common law bar. His name first appears in the Chancery reports in 1779. [6]

---

[1] Twiss, op. cit. i 98.   [2] Townsend, op. cit. ii 379.
[3] Twiss, op. cit. i 100.
[4] Surtees, op. cit. 32 citing a letter from William Scott to his brother Henry in which he says " my brother Jack seems highly pleased with his circuit success."
[5] Ibid 54-56, 58.   [6] Green v. Howard 1 Bro. C.C. 31.

But his progress had been so slow, that in 1777 he had taken a house at Newcastle. Though he assigned the lease of this house to his brother Henry, he was still seriously considering the project of returning to Newcastle, and setting up as a provincial counsel ;[1] and there was a suggestion that he should be a candidate for the recordership of Newcastle.[2] But this plan did not materialize ;[3] and two cases, in which he scored two great successes, led him to abandon all thought of returning to Newcastle.

The first was the case of *Ackroyd v. Smithson.*[4] Scott's argument in that case on behalf of the heir-at-law as to the effect of the failure of a trust for conversion, revolutionized the opinion previously held on this topic, and went far to settle the rules applicable to this equitable doctrine. The fact that it revolutionized the opinion previously held is shown by the history of his connection with the case. He had been given a guinea brief to consent on the part of the heir-at-law ; but his study of the cases convinced him that the heir-at-law was entitled. His argument, though it was praised by Sewell, M. R., failed to convince him. The case came on appeal to Lord Thurlow, and Scott was again given a guinea brief to consent on behalf of the heir-at-law. Here is the rest of the story as told by Eldon at the end of his life :[5]

You see the lucky thing was, there being *two* other parties, and the disappointed one not being content, there was an appeal to Lord Thurlow. In the meanwhile, they had written to Mr. Johnston, Recorder of York, guardian to the young heir-at-law, and a clever man, but his answer, was " Do not send good money after bad : let Mr. Scott have a guinea to give consent, and if he will argue it, why let him do so, but give him no more. " So I went into Court, and when Lord Thurlow asked who was to appear for the heir-at-law, I rose and said modestly, that I was, and as I could not but think (with much deference to the Master of the Rolls, for I might be wrong) that my client had the right to the property, if his Lordship would give me leave, I would argue it. It was rather arduous for me to rise against all the eminent counsel. I do not say that their *opinions* were against me, but they were *employed* against me. However, I argued that the testator had ordered this fifteenth share of the property to be converted into personal property, for the benefit of one particular individual, and that therefore he never contemplated its coming into possession of either the next of kin, or the residuary legatee ; but being land at the death of the individual, it came to the heir-at-law. Well, Thurlow took three days to consider, and then delivered his judgment in accordance with my speech, and that speech is in print, and has decided all similar questions ever since. As I left the Hall, a respectable solicitor, of the name of Forster, came up and touched me on the shoulder, and said, " Young man, your bread and butter is cut for life."

---

[1] Surtees, op. cit. 37-44.   [2] Ibid 42 n.   [3] Ibid.
[4] (1780) 1 Bro. C.C. 503 ; Scott's argument is reported at pp. 505-514.
[5] Twiss, op. cit. i 118-119.

The effect of his argument on contemporary legal opinion is illustrated by the sequel to the story told by Eldon at the same period :

In the Chancellor's Court of Lancaster, where Dunning (Lord Ashburton) was Chancellor, a brief was given me in a cause in which the interest of my client would oblige me to support, by argument, the reverse of that which had been decided by the decree in Ackroyd v. Smithson. When I had stated to the court the point I was going to argue, Dunning said, " Sit down, young man." As I did not immediately comply, he repeated, " Sit down, Sir, I won't hear you." I then sat down. Dunning said, " I believe your name is Scott, Sir." I said it was. Upon which Dunning went on : " Mr. Scott, did not you argue that case of Ackroyd v. Smithson ? " I said that I did argue it. Dunning then said, " Mr. Scott, I have read your argument in that case of Ackroyd v. Smithson, and I defy you or any man in England to answer it. I won't hear you." [1]

Even after this success Scott was still thinking of going back to Newcastle. But in March of the following year (1781) he was asked about 6 a.m. to supply the place of counsel briefed in the Clitheroe election petition, which was to come on at 10 a.m. Probably he was chosen on account of his successful conduct of the Bowes election petitions in 1777 and 1780. The result of his conduct of the Clitheroe case was that both the leading counsel in the case—Mansfield and Wilson—strongly advised him to stay in London. He took their advice, and, as they had predicted, business flowed in both in London and on circuits in an increasing volume ; [2] for he showed himself to be not only a learned lawyer, but a very able advocate. His speaking was of that subtle, correct, and deliberate kind that has more the appearance of written than of oral eloquence ; his arguments were well arranged ; and he showed great readiness in reply. Frequently, it was said,

he will take up the concluding argument of his opponent ; or at other times seize upon some observation which has fallen in the middle of the adverse speech. Here he will begin his attack ; and proceeding by his usual clear and deliberate method, pursue one regular chain of reasoning till he has confuted, or at least replied to, every proposition advanced against him. [3]

In 1783 he took silk ; and in the same year Lord Weymouth, through Lord Thurlow, offered him a seat in the House of Commons for Weobly. He showed his independence by stipulating that he should be free to vote as he thought right. Lord Weymouth assented, and he was elected.

[1] Twiss, op. cit. i 119-120.
[2] " His name occurs (in the reports) rarely, and at distant intervals, in 1779—occasionally in the beginning of 1780, more frequently in the latter end of that year—still more frequently, and often as leader, in 1781 and 1782—and perpetually in 1782," Townsend, op. cit. ii 382-383 ; for his circuit business see Twiss, op. cit. i 124-133.
[3] Townsend, op. cit. ii 382, citing a contemporary work entitled Strictures on the Lives of Eminent Lawyers.

Scott attached himself to Pitt's party, and, to the end of his life, he never wavered in his allegiance to Pitt's post-revolution political creed. But he had none of that streak of liberalism which Pitt never wholly lost. He was not a success as a debater in the House of Commons, but his eminence as a lawyer always insured him a respectful hearing on points of law; and this respect was merited by the fact that he did not allow his party allegiance to prevent him from opposing a course of conduct which he considered to be illegal. On a question connected with the Westminster scrutiny he voted against his party, and his opposition was one of the reasons which induced Pitt to assent to Fox's proposal to an Act to limit the duration of polls and scrutinies.[1] In 1787 Lord Thurlow's brother, the bishop of Durham, gave him the Chancellorship of the county palatine of Durham. In the following year he was made solicitor-general. In that capacity he took a principal part in supporting, as against Fox, Pitt's proposals for dealing with the question of a regency on account of the King's madness.[2] In fact there is reason to think that these very legalistic proposals originated with him.[3] The King recovered; and Scott's action on this occasion earned for him the King's lasting friendship. John Surtees, his brother-in-law, said that his sister, Lady Eldon, had told him that

George III, after his first malady, sent a message to Lord Eldon, then Solicitor-General, to call upon him, I believe, at Windsor. The call was of course obeyed. The King told him that he had no other business with him than to thank him for the affectionate fidelity with which he adhered to him when so many had deserted him in his malady.[4]

In 1790 Scott, Macdonald the attorney-general, Pepper Arden the Master of the Rolls, and Erskine all differed from their leaders on both sides of the House on the question whether an impeachment was ended by a dissolution of Parliament. They held that an impeachment was ended by a dissolution, and, as a matter of law, they were probably right. But the House voted that it was not ended.[5] In fact throughout his career as a law officer Scott showed both honesty and independence. Wilberforce, who saw much of him at this period, said that

When he was Solicitor- and Attorney-General under Pitt, he never fawned and flattered as some did, but always assumed the tone and station of a man who was conscious that he must show he respects himself, if he wishes to be respected by others.[6]

---

[1] 25 George III c. 84; Twiss, op. cit. i 171.
[2] Vol. x 439-445.
[3] Ibid 443; Twiss, op. cit. i 192.
[4] Ibid i 196.   [5] Ibid i 205-206.
[6] Twiss, op. cit. i 314, citing Life of Wilberforce v 214.

In 1792 his loyalty to his friend and patron Thurlow nearly ended his official career. On learning from Pitt that Thurlow had been dismissed, he at once tendered his resignation. Pitt with some difficulty induced him to consult Thurlow before taking this step. Thurlow told him not to do anything so foolish, and said that sooner or later he must get the Great Seal.[1] Scott took this advice, and, in the following year, he was made attorney-general in succession to Macdonald.

As attorney-general it fell to him to draft the Traitorous Correspondence Act of 1793,[2] to prosecute Hardy, Horne Tooke, Thelwall and others for high treason in 1794,[3] and to draft the legislation which, after their acquittals, amended the law of treason and suppressed seditious societies.[4] His action in prosecuting Hardy and others for high treason and not for sedition has often been justly criticized. His argument that it was necessary to prosecute for high treason in order that all the evidence might be produced, and that the country might be thereby awakened to its danger,[5] carries little weight, since the same evidence would have been produced on a trial for sedition. In fact the evidence produced to the Privy Council and before the committees of the two Houses convinced Scott, as it convinced many others, that a rebellion was imminent.[6] In the heated political atmosphere of the day this conclusion was almost inevitable, and, as Scott said, he did not think himself at liberty, " as attorney-general and public prosecutor to let down the character of the offence." [7] He did not realize the strength of the popular feeling against the doctrine of constructive treason upon which his case rested, the great difficulty of applying that doctrine to the complicated facts of these cases, the strength of the evidence for the defence, or the effect of Erskine's inspired advocacy.[8] But whatever we may think of the political wisdom of the prosecutions, there is no doubt that Scott, in spite of much provocation to act otherwise, conducted them with humanity and fairness. We have seen that he congratulated Gibbs on his able defence ;[9] and Horne Tooke, meeting Scott in Westminster Hall shortly after his trial, thanked him for his " humane and considerate conduct." [10] In spite of these and other prosecutions

---

[1] Thurlow said, " Scott, if there could be anything that could make me regret what has taken place (and I do not repent it), it would be that you should do so foolish a thing. . . . I did not think that the King would have parted from me so easily. As to that other man, he has done to me just what I should have done to him, if I could. . . . It is very possible that Mr. Pitt from party and political motives, *at this moment* may overlook your pretensions ; but sooner or later you *must* hold the Great Seal. I know of no man but yourself qualified for its duties," Twiss, op. cit. i 213-214.

[2] Above 156.
[3] Above 162.
[4] Above 165.
[5] Twiss, op. cit. i 282-284.
[6] Above 163, 164.
[7] Twiss, op. cit. i 283.
[8] Above 162, 586, 592.
[9] Above 536.
[10] Twiss, op. cit. i 282.

for high treason, in which he generally failed to get a conviction, and in spite of his many prosecutions for libel, his honesty and fairness were generally recognized. As Townsend truly says :[1]

No laboured eulogy can carry further the effect of Sir John Scott's personal demeanour and the general homage paid to his integrity and candour, then the simple fact that for six years of active official and extra-official duty, during which he screwed the pressure of his power more tightly than any Attorney-General before or since, with the single exception of Sir Vicary Gibbs, he should still have retained a large share of personal goodwill, and should have been the favourite alike of the bar, of suitors, and the public.

In 1799 Eyre the Chief Justice of the Common Pleas died, and Scott claimed the vacant post. Pitt was reluctant to lose his attorney-general, but he consented on the condition that he should take a peerage so that he would still have his services in Parliament, and the King consented on condition that he would not refuse the Great Seal if it were offered to him. He was raised to the peerage, and took his title—Eldon—from an estate in the county of Durham which he had purchased in 1792.[2] He was not sorry to leave the House of Commons ; for he was too much of the lawyer ever to shine as a debater. He was far more at home in the dignified atmosphere of the House of Lords, where he exercized an influence which tended to increase during the greater part of his tenure of his two periods of office as Chancellor.[3] We have seen that though, in Scarlett's opinion, the subtlety of his reasoning in his summing up to juries sometimes puzzled them,[4] he was a very able judge. Kenyon from the bench congratulated the legal profession on the appointment of a man who, he said, would be found to be " the most consummate judge that ever sat in judgment."[5] Pitt's resignation in 1801, in consequence of the King's refusal to couple a measure of Catholic emancipation with the Act of Union with Ireland, and the accession of Addington, was the cause of Eldon's promotion to the Chancellorship. Since he and Addington agreed with the King in opposing any such measure it is not surprising that the King should have taken the opportunity to call upon Eldon to redeem his promise. Eldon considered it his duty to keep that promise. He said :[6]

I was the King's Lord Chancellor, not the Minister's. When I was made Chief Justice of the Common Pleas, the King insisted upon my giving him my promise that whenever he called upon me to fulfil the office of Chancellor, I would do so. He did call upon me when Addington succeeded Pitt, and I could not do otherwise than fulfil my promise.

[1] The Lives of Twelve Eminent Judges ii 401.

[2] " The property conveyed was the manor of Eldon, and upwards of 1300 acres of land, arable, meadow and pasture in the parish of St. Andrew Auckland, in the Darlington Ward of the County Palatine of Durham," Twiss, op. cit. i 216.

[3] He was very angry when the House rejected his proposed amendment to the Marriage Act of 1822, above 421, 422, see Twiss, op. cit. ii 461.

[4] Above 530.   [5] Twiss, op. cit. i 331.   [6] Ibid i 367.

In fact he was genuinely sorry to leave the court of Common Pleas. In 1801 he wrote to one of his friends :[1]

I left the Common Pleas with inexpressible regret. I there sat in an honourable, independent, and reasonably profitable situation for life, with employment for life, probably neither too much nor too little. Of politics I had had more than enough before I got there. No man, there-fore, said " Nolo episcopari " with more sincerity than I did.

In the same year he was made steward of Oxford University.[2] In 1809 he would have been elected Chancellor of the University if the votes for his party had not been split by the candidature of the Duke of Beaufort.[3]

During Eldon's first Chancellorship the mental condition of the King in 1801 and 1804 threw upon him the burden of deciding whether the King was in a fit state to sign the commission for giving assent to bills and other state papers. On both occasions he took the responsibility of deciding that he was fit ; and his action on these occasions was unfairly used by Lord Grey in 1811, when the King finally became mad, as the basis of a groundless charge that Eldon had knowingly certified the King to be com-petent when in fact he was incompetent. He had a share in negotiating the change-over from Addington to Pitt in 1804 ; but there is no reason to think that he was in any way disloyal to Addington.[4] On Pitt's death in 1805 the ministry of " all the talents " was formed, and Erskine replaced Scott as Chancellor in 1806. While he was out of office he was much consulted by the Princess of Wales whose conduct was, as we have seen, under inquiry. The character of the Princess was cleared of the graver charges, and her readmission into the royal circle enabled Eldon to prevent the publication of a book in which her grievances were set forth. There is no reason to think that Eldon professed a friend-ship for the Princess and used her grievances (as Brougham later did[5]) as a means to embarrass the government. Nor is there any reason to think that Eldon advised the King to get rid of his ministers on account of their differences on the Catholic question. The ministry was dismissed in 1807 and Eldon entered on his second and longer term of office.

Throughout the Napoleonic wars Eldon was one of the most important members of the government. He smoothed over the difficulties which arose from the dispute between Canning and Castlereagh,[6] he had a large share in the formation of Perceval's administration ; and, when Perceval was assassinated in 1812,[7]

[1] Twiss, op. cit. i 388.   [2] Ibid i 394.
[3] Ibid ii 107-115.   [4] Quart. Rev. lxxiv 93-94 ; D.N.B.
[5] Above 199.   [6] Above 177, 178.
[7] Eldon always thought that the assassin intended to kill him, see Twiss, op. cit. ii 203-204.

in the reconstruction of the ministry under Lord Liverpool. The King had finally gone mad in 1811, and the Prince of Wales had become Regent. It was generally supposed that this event would mean the dismissal of the King's ministers and the advent of the Prince's friends to power. But the Prince determined to keep his father's ministers in power ; and, though he had formerly disliked Eldon cordially because he thought that he had tried to keep him at a distance from his father, he changed his mind when he looked through his father's papers. He told me, says Eldon, that " he was convinced that I had always endeavoured to do the direct contrary of what was imputed to me . . . and from that time he treated me with uniform friendliness." [1] He became an honoured member of the Prince's circle, who invented for him the nickname of ' Old Bags,' because his inseparable companion was the bag in which he carried the Great Seal. That friendliness secured Eldon in office during the whole period of Liverpool's ministry ; and during the greater part of that period he wielded an immense influence both in the Cabinet and in the House of Lords.

In so far as that influence was directed to the support of all measures needed to bring the war to a successful end it was wisely exercised. He defended the seizure of the Danish fleet, the Orders in Council, and the Peninsular campaigns. His great defect as a stateman was his failure to see that after 1815 a large number of legislative reforms were overdue, to adapt the constitution and law of the country to the new intellectual, social and economic conditions. When in 1834 he attended the Encaenia at Oxford a man in the crowd shouted, " there is old Eldon—cheer him, for he never ratted." [2] He never ratted because his political opinions had always been static, " an attack on Church and State was to him the same thing as a violation of his paternal roof or an insult to a domestic affection," [3] and he was far too honourable to profess opinions which he did not feel. As Townsend says, [4]

His mind seems to have been moulded between 1788 and 1798, and to have subsequently undergone no material alteration—mistrusting the most specious improvement, considering any organic change as synonymous with confusion, and satisfied that audacity in reform was the principle of revolution.

Thus, as attorney-general, he helped to draft and to carry the legislation which suspended the Habeas Corpus Act, suppressed

[1] Twiss, op. cit. ii 198.
[2] Ibid iii 231 ; in 1826 he wrote to Peel : " As to my political conduct, it has been either all right or all wrong, for in the forty-three years in which I have been in Parliament there has been no change, I think, in the character of that conduct or the principles by which it has been regulated," cited Campbell, Chancellors vii 444 ; see also a letter to his grandson cited ibid 470.
[3] Quart. Rev. lxxv 42.   [4] The Lives of Twelve Eminent Judges ii 457.

the Corresponding Societies, and dealt with the situation created by the mutiny at the Nore ;[1] and as Chancellor he approved legislation, like the Six Acts,[2] which was designed to suppress industrial unrest and agitation for reforms. It is true that he sometimes admitted the need for reforms. He said from the bench that the law of bankruptcy was a disgrace,[3] and that the charitable funds given on trust for schools were grossly mis-managed ;[4] and he said from his place in Parliament that there was urgent need to legislate on the subject of joint stock com-panies.[5] On the last named subject he even gave notice of his intention to introduce a bill,[6] but he abandoned that intention on the flimsy pretext that he was hearing a case which concerned one of these companies, " and he did not think it right to be declaring the law in that House, while he had to give judgment in another place." [7]

In spite of these admissions, he never introduced any adequate measures of reform, and opposed the proposals made by others. The measures which he introduced or approved were trifling. In 1805 he proposed a bill to encourage the cultivation of church and college lands, and he approved of the Act of 1803 which was passed to promote the building of churches and the provision of residences and endowments for the clergy.[8] He supported the Act of 1813 which created a Vice-Chancellor,[9] and he introduced the bill (of very questionable utility) which provided for trial by jury in civil cases in Scotland.[10] He promoted a consolidation of the bankruptcy laws ; [11] and he supported the abolition of appeals of felony and trial by battle, [12] the Act making the setting of spring guns illegal,[13] and the Act allowing the Chancellor to make serjeants-at-law during the vacation.[14] In 1825 he supported a bill to prohibit the sale of places in the courts, and to compensate the judges by giving them higher salaries ;[15] and, after his retire-ment, he introduced a bill to settle the law in cases where a divorce was sought in Scotland of an English marriage.[16] All large measures of law reform he opposed. We have seen that he opposed Romilly's and Mackintosh's proposals for the reform of

[1] The Lives of Twelve Eminent Judges ii 460 ; above 167.
[2] Above 208.　　　　　　　　　　　　[3] (1801) 6 Ves. 1.
[4] Townsend, op. cit. ii 459.　　　　　[5] Above 269.
[6] Hansard (2nd Series) xii 31, 127-128.　　[7] Ibid 1196.
[8] Townsend, op. cit. ii 460 ; 43 George III c. 108.
[9] 53 George III c. 24 ; above 190, 288.
[10] 55 George III c. 42 ; Twiss, op. cit. ii 259 ; at first he had been sceptical of the utility of this measure, ibid 75, and Campbell, Chancellors vii 323, gives reasons why this scepticism was justified.
[11] Townsend, op. cit. ii 461 ; above 265.
[12] 59 George III c. 46 ; Twiss, op. cit. ii 336 ; vol. i 310.
[13] 7, 8 George IV c. 18 ; above 267, 390.
[14] 39 George III c. 113 ; vol. xii 6 n. 2.
[15] Hansard (2nd Ser.) xiii 1284.　　　　[16] Townsend, op. cit. ii 461.

the criminal law ;[1] and, though he was not inhumane, as his careful consideration of the Recorder's report on prisoners sentenced to death shows,[2] he resisted all attempts to take away the death penalty for trifling offences.[3] He opposed all attempts to reform his court, and especially the proposal to lighten his labours by separating the bankruptcy from the equitable juris-diction.[4] It was not till after the report of the Chancery com-mission that he supported a bill to make some reforms in the practice of his court[5] in accordance with the very inadequate recommendations of that commission.[6] He opposed the Act which abolished the slave trade,[7] and he was convinced that the smallest reform in the representative system, and the smallest concession to religious non-conformity would shake the foundations of the constitution. He opposed the disfranchizement of Grampound for corruption,[8] and the only relaxation in the laws against noncomformity which he did not oppose was the Act which allowed the Roman Catholic Duke of Norfolk to act as Earl Marshal.[9] He held that all the exclusive privileges of the established church must be maintained if the state was to con-tinue to be religious. They existed, according to his famous phrase " not for the purpose of making the church political, but for the purpose of making the state religious " ; for unless it was religious " the state can have no solid peace." [10] Bagehot described his intellectual attitude with substantial truth when he said :[11]

He believed in everything which it is impossible to believe in—the danger of Parliamentary Reform, the danger of Catholic Emancipation, the danger of altering the Court of Chancery, the danger of altering the Courts of Law, the danger of abolishing capital punishment for trivial thefts, the danger of making landowners pay their debts, the danger of making anything more, the danger of making anything less.

In his opposition to reform he appealed successfully both to the prejudice in favour of things established felt by ordinary men in an age of revolutions, and to the scepticism felt by more

---

[1] Above 282.

[2] Peel wrote : " It had fallen to his lot to send to the Chancellor at the rising of his court to inform him that on the ensuing morning his Majesty would receive the Recorder's report, containing, probably, forty or fifty cases. On proceeding from the Court of Chancery the noble lord would . . . apply himself to the reading of each individual case and abstract notes from all of them, and he had known more than one instance in which Lord Eldon had commenced this labour in the evening, and had been found pursuing it at the rising of the sun," cited Townsend, op. cit. ii 468.   [3] Above 280.

[4] Above 290 ; cp. Campbell, Chancellors vii 538-539.

[5] Twiss, op. cit. ii 586.   [6] Vol. i 442-443 ; vol. ix 375.

[7] Twiss, op. cit. ii 21-22.   [8] Ibid ii 418-419.

[9] 5 George IV c. 109 ; for Eldon's support of the bill, and the King's dislike of it ; see Twiss, op. cit. ii 521-523.

[10] Ibid ii 538, citing a letter of Feb. 1825.

[11] Literary Studies i 6-7.

enlightened men of the efficacy of any suggested change, and their feeling that the smallest change might be the beginning of a series of undesirable reforms.[1] As Bagehot says,[2]

We read occasionally in conservative literature alternations of sentences, the first an appeal to the coarsest prejudice—the next a subtle hint to a craving and insatiable scepticism. We may trace this even in Vesey junior. Lord Eldon never read Hume or Montaigne, but sometimes, in the interstices of cumbrous law, you may find sentences with their meaning, if not in their manner: "Dumpor's case always struck me as extraordinary; but if you depart from Dumpor's case, what is there to prevent a departure in every direction?"

And this scepticism as to the expediency of reforming the law was reinforced by his belief that drastic reforms would destroy the existence of law as a logical system of connected rules and principles, and therefore the existence of a race of learned lawyers. In 1826 he wrote to Sugden :[3]

Great alterations in our system of law, I confess, I do not think are likely to improve either our law or our lawyers. The history and progress of our legal system will be unknown by our lawyers, and they will, therefore, be ignorant. King William told Maynard that he was almost the only lawyer left. Maynard told him that if he, said William, had not come, there would have been no law left.[4] Indulge the appetite for alteration in the law, which we hear so much of now-a-days, and in a reign or two more we shall not have a lawyer—a well grounded lawyer—left.

In conducting this opposition to reform he used to the full his legal subtlety and his skill as a draftsman to pick holes in bills sent up to or proposed in the House of Lords. It is true that this kind of criticism to which he delighted to subject both public and private bills was often useful ;

He exercised a sort of royal veto on the crude schemes and ambitious theories of those dilettante legislators, who, neither lawyers nor states-men, would yet fain have exercised the functions of both. Nothing delighted the experienced old judge more than to point out the futility of some particular clause, or in his own phrase, to drive a coach and six through some heavy bill as it plodded in committee.[5]

But this sort of criticism was not usefully employed when it was made an argument for rejecting or delaying or emasculating a bill

[1] Thus in 1810 in his speech opposing the bill to prevent the granting offices in reversion he warned the House against yielding to popular clamour, and said that " everyone who recollected what had passed during the last sixteen or twenty years must be impressed with a sense of what he owed to the general welfare of the state, after seeing the great and awful events that had occurred," Hansard (1st Series) xvi 1069.

[2] Literary Studies i 11-12.   [3] Twiss, op. cit. iii 438.

[4] The tale is slightly altered by Eldon to make it fit the moral he was drawing, see vol. vi 512.

[5] Townsend, op. cit. ii 461-462.

which proposed sensible reforms.[1] Moreover, he, like many others, was always afraid of disturbing vested interests in those offices which had come to be regarded as a species of property.[2] He objected to a bill abolishing the grant of offices in reversion because he objected to legislating without inquiry, and no inquiry, he thought, could justify this bill.[3] When Brougham's bankruptcy bill was before the House of Lords he wrote to Brougham insisting, upon public grounds, that liberal compensation ought to be paid to the holders of offices abolished, and that such compensation should be paid to a member of Lord Thurlow's family who held an office which was about to be abolished.[4]

In the business of the Queen's trial which occupied the opening years of George IV's reign, Eldon played a considerable part. Even when in 1806-7 he had been on friendly terms with the Princess and her adviser, he had formed a low opinion of her character ;[5] and the discoveries of the Milan commission and the subsequent trial convinced him of her guilt. It was for that reason that he disapproved of the abandonment of the bill.[6] But there is no doubt that he presided over the trial with dignity, impartiality, and courtesy. He tells us that he had determined that the proceedings on the bill should be a properly conducted trial, and not, as so many impeachments and proceedings on similar bills had been, a trial only in name ; and that, with that end in view, he had resolved to admit no evidence which would have been rejected in Westminster Hall.[7] On the many points in the law of evidence which arose during the trial he summoned the judges to advise the House, and always accepted their opinion. He framed the questions submitted to them with great skill and fairness " without the slightest regard to the manner in which their answer might operate." [8] On the occasion of the King's coronation he was promoted to an earldom. That promotion had been previously offered to him by George III and George IV and declined ; but on this occasion the King would take no refusal, saying " if you will not make out your own patent, I will get

---

[1] Romilly tells us that in 1807 Eldon wishes to add clauses to the bill making traders' land assets for the payment of their simple costs and debts which Romilly found very obscure, and persuaded Eldon to drop, Life of Romilly ii 72 ; see ibid 345 n. for Eldon's doubts and difficulties as to the bill altering the punishment for high treason ; in 1813 he denounced the sinecure offices bill as a crude project, and pointed out that it proposed to abolish *inter alia* the offices of the deputy registrars of the court of Chancery without which the court could not function, Hansard (1st Ser.) xxvi 222-223 ; in 1814 he said that most of the measures of reform proposed in Parliament were repugnant to common sense, ibid xxviii 634.

[2] Above 189.

[3] Twiss, op. cit. ii 116-117 ; Hansard (1st Ser.) xv 598-599, xvi 1069 ; above 189 n. 3.

[4] Twiss, op. cit. iii 137-139.

[5] In 1813 he said to Lord Grey that in 1807, " my opinion is, and always was, that, though she was not with child, she supposed herself to be with child," Life of Romilly ii 311.

[6] Twiss, op. cit. ii 398.

[7] Ibid 402-403.

[8] Campbell, Chancellors vii 369.

someone else to do it, and when I send it to you, I will see if you dare to return it." [1]

In the third decade of the nineteenth century the need for reform was becoming more and more apparent, and Eldon's influence upon the policy of the government began to decline. Liverpool admitted Canning and Huskisson to office in 1823 without consulting him ; [2] and he several times complained that he was not adequately defended in the House of Commons against the attacks of Michael Angelo Taylor, Williams, and others. [3] To one of these letters of complaint in 1825 Liverpool replied that no adequate reply could be given till the Chancery commission had reported. [4] When in 1827 Canning became Prime Minister Eldon and Peel resigned because they were opposed to Canning's views in favour of Catholic emancipation, and their example was followed by the Duke of Wellington and four other members of Liverpool's government. So ended Eldon's long tenure of office. His two Chancellorships had lasted for twenty-four years, ten months and twenty-three days—a period longer than that for which any of his predecessors had held the office.

Eldon did not imagine that his resignation meant a final retirement from office. He was disappointed that the Duke of Wellington did not include him in his government, and did not realize that his politics were growing more and more out of date. He vigorously opposed the repeal of the Test and Corporation Acts, and shrewdly surmised that this concession to the Protestant Dissenters would be followed by a like concession to the Roman Catholics. [5] He led the opposition to the Act of 1829 which emancipated the Roman Catholics ; and it was to commemorate his services " to the Protestant constitution of his country " [6] that the Eldon Law Scholarship was founded in 1830, which has assisted many deserving Oxford men to meet the expenses of a call to the bar.

Eldon realized the effect which the Revolution in France was having upon English politics. In August 1830 he wrote : [7]

To get a thorough insight into the effect of the French Revolution here, you have only to read the proceedings at meetings in London, and all that is stated in them. It will require a master-head, such as Pitt had and nobody now has in this country, to allay what is brewing, a storm for changes here, especially for Reform in Parliament. Everybody here seems to think that the borough members of Parliament can scarcely be preserved until another Parliament.

[1] Twiss, op. cit. ii 422.
[2] See his letter to his brother on the admission of Huskisson to the Cabinet, Twiss, op. cit. ii 468.
[3] Twiss, op. cit. ii 228 (1812), 561-564 (1825).
[4] Ibid ii 564-565.   [5] Ibid iii 38.
[6] Ibid iii 92.   [7] Ibid iii 115.

He opposed the Reform bill to the end, and also the other measures of the Whig government—more especially the Irish Church Temporalities bill,[1] and the bills for reforming the law of real property,[2] for reforming the procedure of the court of Chancery,[3] for establishing a Judicial Committee of the Privy Council,[4] and for establishing county courts.[5] The last time that he spoke in the House of Lords was on July 25, 1834, in opposition to a Great Western Railway bill.[6] He sat for the last time on the Judicial Committee of the Privy Council in 1833,[7] and heard his last appeal in the House of Lords in 1835.[8] By that time he had become an almost legendary personage. His past opposition to reform was forgotten, and his services to the law and his stout defence of the Church were remembered. When in 1833 he appeared at a grand night at the Middle Temple his health was drunk and he was cheered by the students. When the Duke of Wellington held his first encaenia at Oxford at which Eldon attended as Steward of the University, and when at that encaenia his grandson Viscount Encombe was presented for an honorary degree, the mention of Eldon's name in the presentation speech was the signal for repeated cheers. He wrote to his daughter :[9]

It is quite overpowering to have met with the congratulations of multitudes, great multitudes, here, upon the reception of my name in the Theatre yesterday over and over again. When Encombe had his degree, the manner in which the Duke of Wellington received and handed him up to me, the people calling out " Eldon," was affecting beyond any thing I ever met.

Eldon had in the course of his long life suffered many bereavements. He had lost his eldest son in 1805, who died just after his wife had given birth to a son who ultimately succeeded to the title and estates. In 1831 he had lost his wife, and that was a loss from which he never quite recovered. On one of his visits to his Eldon estates in Durham he was asked by a friend from Newcastle why he had never revisited his birth place. He replied, " Aye, I know my fellow-townsmen complain of my not coming to see them ; but how can I pass that bridge ? " The bridge looked upon the Sandhill, the site of the house where his wife had lived before their marriage. His eyes filled with tears at these recollections, and, after a short pause, he exclaimed, " Poor Bessy ! if ever there was an angel on earth, she was." [10]

---

[1] Twiss, op. cit. iii 195.   [2] Townsend, op. cit. ii 462-463.
[3] Twiss, op. cit. iii 187.   [4] Ibid iii 196-197.   [5] Ibid iii 197.
[6] Hansard (3rd Ser.) xxv 463, Twiss op. cit. iii 234 ; Campbell, Chancellors vii 584.
[7] Twiss, op. cit. iii 200 ; the case was Drax v. Grosvenor.
[8] Twiss, op. cit. iii 243 ; the case was White v. Baugh ; it is reported 9 Bligh N.S. 181, and 3 Cl. and Fin. 44, but Eldon's presence is not mentioned.
[9] Twiss, op. cit. iii 231.   [10] Ibid iii 189.

In 1832 he lost his son William Henry, and in 1836 his brother Lord Stowell.

He spent his remaining years partly in London where he had a house at Hamilton Place, partly in visiting his estate at Eldon, but mainly at his place at Encombe. He died of old age at Hamilton Place on January 13, 1838, and was buried by the side of his wife and son in his family vault in the burial ground of Kingston chapel near Encombe.

Eldon's character as a man and as Chancellor

Eldon as a man

The success of Eldon's career was due not only to his great legal abilities, and not only to the consistency with which he adhered and acted up to his political and religious principles, but also to his cheerful and happy disposition and his great social gifts. These social gifts were displayed not only in his family circle and amongst his familiar friends, with whom he loved to crack a bottle or bottles of old port,[1] but also in the courts, in Parliament, and in the royal circle.

When a young man he entered into all the fun of the Northern circuit.

In the Grand Courts held for the trial of mock offences " against the peace of our Lord the Junior " he acted a distinguished part, in so much that in 1780 he was appointed Solicitor-General, and in 1781 Attorney-General, of the circuit.[2]

In his own court he was courteous to all—to the officers, to the counsel—from the leaders to the newly called junior, to the solicitors, and to the suitors who appeared in person.[3] A Mr. Hall, who was a learned but somewhat superannuated barrister, had made a speech in which he had praised the old times, and ended up by saying, " but *now*, my Lord, I find that I know no law." Eldon said :[4]

" Mr. Hall, if you now know no law, I can say of my own knowledge that you have forgot a great deal since I sat in those rows in which you now sit." Old Hall's broad face spread wider and wider, and his eyes became full of morning dew : and attempting to say something in reply, he abruptly sat down without being able to finish the sentence.

[1] " Though never pushing hilarity to excess, Lord Eldon, like his brother Lord Stowell, loved to crack a bottle, at least, of old port. When the Chancellor, Admiralty Judge, and Master of the Rolls, Sir William Grant, met together, there were few good Tories and loyal subjects who could, according to the royal pun, *comport* themselves better, if so well," Townsend, op. cit. ii 506.

[2] Campbell, Chancellors vii 62.

[3] " Upon these unhappy persons, the afflicted in mind, body, or estate, who sometimes broke through the trammels of Chancery etiquette to make their grievances known in person, his singular kindness of manner acted with the force of a spell," Twiss, op. cit. iii 474.　　　　　　　　[4] Twiss, op. cit. iii 472.

Brougham said that in amiability and courtesy of manner Eldon " surpassed every other judge, from the highest to the lowest, that he had ever seen." [1] No difference in political opinion, no attacks upon him by barristers in Parliament, made any difference to his uniform courtesy[2]—even John Williams, from whom he had suffered much,[3] said, after appearing before him, " Your Chancellor is an abundantly agreeable judge." [4] At the same time he kept perfect order in his court. There is a story that on one occasion he gave judgment in a case which had been so long in the paper that every one had forgotten its facts :

When the Chancellor had finished giving judgment, " I know I was in this case," said Mr. Heald ; " but whether judgment is for me or against me, I have not at this distance of time the most remote conception." " I have a glimmering notion that it is for me," answered Mr. Horne. Their chief instantly stopped further discussion, by desiring, in a tone of grave rebuke, that counsel would not make him the subject of their observations.[5]

He showed the same social gifts in Parliament and in the royal circle.

He was a favourite guest at Pitt's select suppers, to which only a chosen few from the House of Commons were invited at the close of the debate. Lord Eldon used to revert with much pleasure to these symposia ; and described their host to have been in the habit of taking off the speeches and manner of the different members who had spoken in the course of the evening, and with perfect impartiality.[6]

He was a favourite with the Princess of Wales in the days when he acted as her adviser, and with George III ; and we have seen that he overcame all the hostility once felt for him by the Prince of Wales, and became and remained his trusted friend during his life.[7] He had great powers of conversation—a fund of anecdotes which he introduced appositely and told extremely well, wit, and capacity for repartee.[8]

To these social gifts he added the quality of supreme tact. This quality was shown in the manner in which he helped to make and keep together the Cabinets in which he served in the first decade of the nineteenth century, and in the manner in which he mediated between George III and the Prince of Wales without

---

[1] Twiss, op. cit. iii 472, citing a speech of June 7 1825.
[2] Townsend, op. cit. ii 495. [3] Above 289, 290, 291.
[4] Twiss, op. cit. ii 555. [5] Ibid iii 475.
[6] Townsend, op. cit. ii 506. [7] Above 604.
[8] Twiss, op. cit. iii 485, says, " his great forte lay in telling a story ; which he did in a rich low tone, with a demure smile, a quiet gleam of his eye, and a seductive humour that no gravity could resist ; " Brougham, Historical Sketches ii 72 says that in " relating anecdotes he excelled most men," that the " mingled grace and dignity of his demeanour added no small charm to his whole commerce with society," and that " it was usual to observe that, except Sir W. Scott, no man was so agreeable as Lord Eldon."

losing the respect of either.[1] And to the quality of tact he added the quality of political courage. Brougham contrasted his political courage in an emergency with his doubts and hesitations when all was plain sailing. He says :[2]

When common matters occurred in Parliament, no kind of importance could be attached to the adoption of one course rather than another, bless us! what inexhaustible suggestions of difficulty, what endless effusion of conflicting views, what a rich mine of mock diamonds, all glittering and worthless, in the shape of reasons on all sides of some question never worth the trouble of asking, and which none but this great magician would stop to resolve! . . . But let there come any real embarrassment, any substantial peril which required a bold and vigorous act to ward it off—let there be but occasion for nerves to work through a crisis which it asked no common boldness to face at all . . . and no man that ever sat at a Council board more quickly made up his mind, or more gallantly performed his part. . . . He did in the twinkling of an eye the act which unexpectedly discomforted his adversaries, and secured his own power for ever.

He had also a large share of physical courage. During the Gordon riots, at considerable risk of life and limb, he took his wife through the crowds to a place of safety in the Temple.[3] At the trial of Hardy a threatening mob was collected outside the court, but saying that " the King's Attorney-General must not show a white feather," he took his way home. " The mob," he said,

kept thickening round me, till I came to Fleet Street, one of the worst parts of London that I had to pass through, and the cries began to be rather threatening, " Down with him "—" Now is the time lads "—" Do for him "—and various others horrible enough. So I stood up, and spoke as loud as I could—" You may do for me if you like, but remember there will be another Attorney-General before eight o'clock to-morrow morning ; the King will not allow the trials to be stopped." Upon this one man shouted out, " Say you so ? You are right to tell us. Let's give him three cheers lads." And they actually cheered me, and I got safe to my own door.[4]

When rioters had broken into his house at Bedford Square during the corn law riots in 1815 he collared a rioter who had broken into his room, and told him that if he did not mind what he was about he would be hanged. The man replied " perhaps so, old chap, but I think it looks now as if you'll be hanged first " ; and Eldon added, when he told the story " I had my misgivings that he was right." [5]

He was charitable in a very unostentatious way—to poor prisoners, to decayed members of the legal profession, to men of education who had seen better days,[6] to deserving students of the

[1] Twiss, op. cit. i 483.
[2] Historical Sketches i 59.
[3] Twiss, op. cit. i 115.
[4] Ibid i 269-270.
[5] Townsend, op. cit. ii 512.
[6] Ibid ii 501-502.

law, like Belt, the publication of whose notes to Vesey Senior's reports he subsidized.[1] He was willing that his salary should be diminished for public objects. He consented to contribute £2500 a year to the Vice-Chancellor's salary, and at his own expense he increased the salaries of the clerks in the Bankrupt Office when he made reforms which involved a diminution of their perquisites and a lengthening of their hours of work.[2] These traits in his character show first that he was a man who felt for the misfortunes of others, and, secondly, that he had a keen sense of public duty. In fact he had high ideals, and their strength was the cause of a vein of sentimentality in his character which not only led him to give liberally to the unfortunate, but also made him very sensitive both to the loss of friends and to any imputation upon his acts or motives. It was an age in which men showed their feelings more openly than they do now.[3] When he came into court after Romilly's death and saw his empty place " his eyes filled with tears. I cannot stay here, he exclaimed ; and rising in great agitation, broke up his court." [4] In his speech in reply on the trial of Horne Tooke, he began by protesting his conscientious belief in the need for the prosecution, and his desire to leave a reputation for probity as an inheritance to his children.[5] He was so affected by this sentiment that he shed tears.

To the surprise of the court Mr. Solicitor-General was seen to weep in sympathy with the emotion of his friend. Just look at Mitford was the remark of a neighbour to Horne Tooke : what on earth is he crying for ? At the thought of the little inheritance, retorted Horne Tooke, that poor Scott is likely to leave his children.[6]

His opponents often mocked at his appeals to his conscience, and Brougham said (unjustly) that no man spoke more of conscientious scruples, and no man felt them less.[7]

It was inevitable that Eldon's sentimentality should sometimes expose him to ridicule. Another characteristic which was often commented on was the meanness of his menage, and his failure to hold those levees and entertainments which were expected from a Chancellor.

The wicked wits of the law used to satirize his house-keeping; and even the stern Romilly had his jest which he put into a professional form. At a time when there was a great complaint of delay in the Chancellor's Court, Sir Thomas Plumer, the Master of the Rolls, gave a series of dinners. " Very right," said Romilly, " he is clearing away the Chancellor's arrears." [8]

---

[1] Twiss, op. cit. iii 483, cited vol. xii 145-146.   [2] Ibid iii 481-482.
[3] " Once at Bowood, when Tom Moore was singing, one by one the audience slipped away in sobs : finally the poet himself broke down and bolted, and the old Marquis was left alone. We are in an age when, if brides sometimes swooned at the altar, Ministers sometimes wept at the Table," G. M. Young, Victorian England 14.
[4] Twiss, op. cit. ii 324.   [5] Ibid i 279-280.   [6] Ibid i 280.
[7] Historical Sketches ii 58.   [8] Twiss, op. cit. iii 479.

But this apparent meanness was due to another aspect of his sentimentality—to the strength of his affection for his wife.[1] In the days of their youth she had had to exercize a rigid economy, with the result that she had contracted a dislike for society. Her whole life was centred in her home and her husband, and he was always willing to indulge her slightest wish. After her death his house-keeping was conducted on a more liberal scale.[2]

Eldon's enemies, and they were many at the latter part of his period of office, made the most of any peculiarities which they could use to hold him up to ridicule. None of them could deny his great social charm. But even this virtue they tried to turn to account by insinuating that it was used for unworthy motives. We have seen that Brougham insinuated that he used his charm of manner to mislead the Chancery commission.[3] Bentham in his bitter attack upon him said that his courtesy was his armour, offensive and defensive, which kept everyone in good humour and provided the cement which kept cabinets together.[4]

There is some truth in Bentham's remarks—vulgar and unjust though they are. But the truth in them is not exactly that which Bentham meant to convey. The truth is this : Eldon's great social gifts, and his high sense of honour and devotion to duty enhanced very considerably the effectiveness of his work as a statesman and, as we shall now see, as a Chancellor.

Eldon as a Chancellor

The Lord Chancellor played and still plays many parts.[5] As a great officer of state and a member of the cabinet he must play the statesman's part. As the legal member of the cabinet he was and is the head of the legal profession, and, as such, he was and is responsible for appointments to the bench, to the higher ranks of the legal profession, and to the ranks of the justices of the peace. At this period he also appointed the officers of his court. As the judge of the court of Chancery he and the Master of the Rolls were, until the appointment of a Vice-Chancellor in 1813, solely responsible for the administration of equity. With Eldon's activities as a statesman I have already dealt. I must now say

---

[1] Above 595, 596, 610.   [2] Twiss, op. cit. iii 479-480.   [3] Above 292 n. 9.
[4] " That which beauty, according to Anacreon, is to woman, *courtesy*, according to everybody, is to Lord Eldon ; to armour of all sorts—offensive as well as defensive —a matchless and most advantageous substitute. With the exception of those, whom, while doubting, he is ruining, and without knowing anything of the matter, plundering—this it is that keeps everybody in good humour : everybody—from my lord duke, down to the barrister's servant-clerk. Useful here, useful there, useful everywhere—of all places, it is in the cabinet that it does knight's service. It is the court *sticking plaster*, which, even if it fails to heal, keeps covered all solutions of continuity ; it is the *grand imperial* cement which keeps political corruption from dissolving in its own filth," Indications respecting Lord Eldon, Works v 372.   [5] Vol. i 397.

something, in the first place, of the way in which he performed his duties as head of the legal profession : and, in the second place, of the way in which he performed what is, from the point of view of legal history, his most important duty as the principal legal member of the House of Lords and as the judge of the court of Chancery.

(1) The way in which Eldon performed his duties as head of the legal profession is open to serious criticism. Whether we look at the way in which he constantly blocked much needed reforms in the law, and in the organization, jurisdiction, and procedure of his court ; or at the way in which he exercised his patronage— it is impossible to deny the existence of serious short-comings. Of the first of these topics enough has already been said. At this point I must say something of the second topic.

Eldon was jealous of his right as Chancellor to appoint the judges of the common law courts, and he was quick to protest when the Prime Minister tried to encroach upon it.[1] There is no doubt that in this matter he used his powers wisely. We have seen that during his Chancellorship the benches of the common law courts were staffed by able judges.[2] Some of his appointments of Chancery judges were criticized. Romilly criticized bitterly his appointment of Plumer as the first Vice-Chancellor, and said that he heard cases even more slowly than the Lord Chancellor.[3] His criticism on Plumer's appointment as Master of the Rolls was equally bitter.[4] But we shall see that there is reason to think that this criticism is not justified.[5] His appointment of Leach to succeed Plumer as Vice-Chancellor is, as we shall see,[6] more open to criticism. Romilly thought that, of all the lawyers he had known, Leach was " the worst qualified for any judicial situation."[7] His promotion was largely due to the fact that he was a personal friend of the Prince of Wales.[8] But it is only fair to Eldon to say that at this period the influence of the Crown was a far more potent influence, and far more difficult to resist, than it became after the Reform Act.

It was partly this influence, and partly the increasing difficulty which he felt in making up his mind, which accounts for his neglect to give silk to men like Brougham, Scarlett, Wetherell, Denman, and Williams, who were obviously among the most distinguished counsel of the day.[9] In the case of Brougham and

---

[1] Twiss, op. cit. iii 467.   [2] Above 505.
[3] Life of Romilly ii 310, 374 ; it is said that the place had practically been promised to Richards, ibid 310 ; Twiss, op. cit. ii 242-243 ; for Richards see above 449, 557 ; for Plumer see below 663.
[4] Life of Romilly ii 481.   [5] Below 663-664.   [6] Below 665-667.
[7] Life of Romilly ii 397—though later, ibid 481, he said that the fact that he would decide quickly would make him a useful judge.
[8] Below 665.   [9] Twiss, op. cit. iii 468-469.

Denman, Eldon said that, contrary to his advice, the King refused to appoint them King's Counsel;[1] but he probably did not press his advice very strongly, because it would seem from a letter which he wrote to his daughter that he more than sympathised with the King's objections. Alluding to an attack made on him by Brougham in 1825 he said,

no young lady was ever so unforgiving for being refused a silk gown, when silk gowns adorned female forms, as Brougham is with me, because, having insulted my master, the insulted don't like to clothe him with distinction and honour, and silk.[2]

There were no such objections to Scarlett or Wetherell, so that the delay in their case was due to what he himself called his " cunctative habit." [3]

Not all his appointments to masterships in his court can be defended. The personal pressure of the Prince Regent was the cause for his appointment of Jekyll.[4] After considerable hesitation he gave a mastership to Farrer who had married his eldest son's widow—largely it would seem because he was grateful for benefits which Farrer's uncle and father, who like Farrer were solicitors, had conferred upon him when he was a young and struggling barrister.[5] The appointment of a militia officer named Cross was due to his wife—Cross had helped her to escape from an anti-corn law mob. That was the only appointment to which any real exception could be taken ; and Eldon himself admitted that it was open to criticism.[6] But there is something to be said in his defence. No doubt, according to modern ideas, it is not right, in appointing to offices, to give way to pressure, or to prefer friends and relations. But that was not quite the view of Eldon's day. Offices both in the courts and in the departments of the state were, if not exactly property, benefits which those entitled to appoint to them could use in their own interests, or in that of their friends, or relations, or in that of their political party.[7] To appoint a relative, not obviously incompetent, to a valuable office like a mastership was so ordinary and natural a step to take that it caused no remark. We have seen that when Erskine appointed his son-in-law to a mastership Romilly objected, not because he appointed his son-in-law, but because he made the appointment after the dismissal of the ministry and only two days before his resignation.[8] Eldon, unfortunately for himself, lived at a time when this view of the obligations and duties of those invested with patronage was beginning to be questioned, and at a time when such old established institutions as saleable offices and sinecures were being

[1] Twiss, op. cit. iii 2-3.
[2] Ibid ii 537.
[3] Ibid iii 469.
[4] Ibid ii 268-269.
[5] Ibid ii 502 ; W. E. Surtees, op. cit. 153.
[6] Ibid 150.
[7] Vol. i 246-251 ; vol. v 353-354 ; vol. x 509-511.
[8] Above 594.

attacked. It is, I think, arguable that the attacks made upon Eldon by the Benthamite radicals are not wholly fair, because they applied to his actions a standard which was not then accepted and did not gain acceptance till many years later.

No serious fault can be found with Eldon's appointments of the justices of the peace. He acted in the usual way on the recommendations of the Lords-Lieutenant ;[1] but he insisted that it was only the Chancellor who could remove a justice from the commission of the peace ;[2] and his reluctance to remove justices from the commission is more open to criticism. He thought that before any such step was taken the justice ought to have been heard in his own defence, with the result that, as Brougham said in 1828,[3] he made it an inflexible rule that

however unfit a magistrate might be for his office, either from private misconduct or party feeling, he would never strike that magistrate off the list until he had been convicted of some offence by the verdict of a court of Record.

There is no doubt that Brougham was right when he said that this practice " opened the door to very serious mischief and injustice." [4]

It must be admitted, therefore, that the manner in which Eldon performed his duties as the head of the legal profession cannot be wholly approved. His failure to initiate any measures of reform, and his sturdy opposition to the proposals for reform made by others is the greatest blot upon his reputation. The manner in which he exercized his patronage in his appointments to the bench is for the most part unexceptionable ; but in other respects the exercize of his patronage is open to some criticism— particularly his neglect or refusal to appoint to the rank of King's Counsel ; and some of his other appointments were due to favour rather than to merit. But, having regard to the manner in which the duties and obligations of an appointor were then regarded, they are for the most part capable of explanation, if not of complete defence. However that may be, it is not upon Eldon's action as the head of the legal profession that his reputation rests. His reputation rests upon his work as the most important legal member of the House of Lords and as the judge of the court of Chancery. To the consideration of his intellectual qualifications for this work, and more especially for his work as the judge of the court of Chancery, we must now turn.

(2) Eldon was the most learned and capable lawyer of his day. That he was an excellent common lawyer his career as Chief Justice of the Common Pleas shows.[5] His large practice in the

---

[1] Vol. i 291.
[2] Twiss, op. cit. iii 122.
[3] Hansard (2nd Ser.) xviii 162.
[4] Ibid 162-163.
[5] Above 529.

court of Chancery had made him a complete master of equity. He was a first-rate real property lawyer and conveyancer. His practice as a junior in the common law courts and in the court of Chancery had made him a competent pleader and equity draftsman ; and his practice at *nisi prius* shows that he was an able advocate in a common law court. But there is no doubt that it was as an advocate in the court of Chancery, when the argument turned upon the application of a principle or rule of equity, that he most excelled—his powers in this department of the law can best be appreciated by a study of his argument in the case of *Ackroyd v. Smithson*.[1] From the first, however, it is clear that he had the judge's rather than the advocate's mind. He tells us that early in his career he ceased to be asked to give many opinions, partly because he insisted upon so thorough a study of the authorities bearing on the question that it led to delay, and to corrections of an opinion first given, which did not please the solicitors ; and partly because, not content with the facts stated in the case, he went on to consider what the answer would be if facts had been suppressed or other facts emerged. Naturally the solicitors said that " They did not want opinions that had so many ' ifs ' in them." [2]

When he was at the bar he had tried to avoid taking briefs to appear in Scottish appeals. Thurlow had warned him not to take this course, and when he became Chancellor, he realized the wisdom of this advice. He found, he tells us, that " the duty of deciding such cases was most extremely painful, and required infinite labour." [3] But he applied himself to the task of mastering Scots law with such success that in 1823 Brougham said in the House of Commons[4] that

The noble Lord decided on the cases which came before him with a degree of skill and penetration—and in appeal causes from Scotland and Ireland with a degree of wisdom—which was most extraordinary, considering that to the law of the latter countries, and especially Scotland, the noble and learned Lord was in some sort a foreigner. *Their law, however, he had reformed ; inveterate abuses he had corrected ;* and the Scotch lawyers, however averse they at first were to the suggested reformations, soon perceived their value, acknowledged their expediency, and ultimately adopted them.

But it is Eldon's contribution to the development of equity that is his chief title to fame. It was to equity that, both as an advocate and a judge, his time and his talents were mainly devoted. The result was that he was so intimately acquainted with all the authorities bearing upon any point of equity argued

---

[1] (1780) 1 Bro. C.C. at pp. 505-514 ; above 598, 599.
[2] Twiss, op. cit. i 136-139.   [3] Ibid iii 432-433.
[4] Cited ibid iii 431-432. [The italicized words refer to his speech in 1815 in moving the Scottish Juries Bill. Eds.]

before him that he knew them better than most of the counsel who were arguing the case, and could appreciate their bearing upon the case more accurately than they did. And to these authorities, if they were clear and to the point he always deferred, although he might himself have come to a different conclusion. Thus in the case of *Sheddon v. Goodrich*[1] he said,

After the doctrine has been so long settled (though with Lord Kenyon I think the distinction such as the mind cannot well fasten upon) it is better the law should be certain than that every judge should speculate upon improvements in it.

And in the oft cited case of *Gee v. Pritchard*[2] he said,

But it is my duty to submit my judgment to the authority of those who have gone before me ; and it will not be easy to remove the weight of the decisions of Lord Hardwicke and Lord Apsley. The doctrines of this court ought to be as well settled and made as uniform almost as those of the common law, laying down fixed principles, but taking care that they are to be applied according to the circumstances of each case.

But if the authorities spoke, as they often did, with an uncertain voice, he always insisted that a guiding principle must be discovered according to which the case must be decided. In the *Case of the Queensberry Leases*[3] he said :

All law ought to stand upon principle, and unless decision has removed out of the way all argument and all principle so as to make it impossible to apply them to the case before you, you must find out what is the principle upon which it must be decided.

Since he had a very subtle and ingenious mind, and since the authorities were often conflicting, it was not difficult for him to distinguish the cases, and lay down rules which were so satisfactory to himself, to the parties, and to the profession that they settled the law for the future. In 1826, in his last year of office, he said that in great and important cases he had[4]

endeavoured to sift all the principles and rules of law to the bottom, for the purpose of laying down . . . something in the first place, which may satisfy all who are concerned as parties that I have taken pains to do my duty ; something, in the second place, which may inform those, who, as counsel, are to take care of the interests of their clients, what the reasons are upon which I have proceeded, and may enable them to examine whether justice has been done ; and, further, something which may contribute towards laying down a rule, so as to save those who may succeed to me in this great situation much of that labour which I have had to undergo by reason of cases having been not so determined, and by reason of a due exposition of the grounds of judgment not having been so stated.

[1] (1803) 8 Ves. at p. 497.   [2] (1818) 2 Swanst. at p. 414.
[3] (1819) 1 Bligh at pp. 486-487.
[4] Attorney-General v. The Skinners Co. (1826) 2 Russ. at p. 437.

This respect for authority, and this desire to base the rules of equity upon fixed and ascertainable principles, led him, as they had led many other great lawyers, to think that no expenditure of time and labour was too great to reach an absolutely right decision. The truth insisted upon both by Fortescue and Coke, that the law " will more readily suffer a delay than an inconvenience," [1] was fully accepted by Eldon. And we have seen that, like those other great lawyers, [2] he attached so much importance to the maintenance of the law of England as a logical system of connected rules and principles that he feared and suspected any radical alteration of those rules. [3] He had also an almost morbid fear that any decision of his should do injustice to the parties, with the result that he spared neither time nor labour to avoid such a catastrophe. " It will be a consolation to me," he once said in the House of Lords, [4]

knowing that it has been said that I have been dilatory in decision, that I have, by looking at the original instruments, saved the right owner many a landed estate, which would otherwise, probably, have been given to his adversary.

He had also an earnest desire that his decisions should, as he said on another occasion " not only set that particular question at rest," but that it should have " the effect of preventing other parties from wasting time and incurring expense by bringing forward claims of a similar description." [5] Naturally he was delighted when he read in Butler's *Reminiscences* the very similar sentiments of D'Aguesseau. [6] He referred to them in his letter to Butler in which he thanked him for his appreciation of his work, [7] and in other letters. [8]

It was this desire to settle the principle of equity upon absolutely right principles, and this desire to do complete justice to the parties which led him to spare no pains to master completely the facts of every case. The result was that he was

---

[1] See vol. ii 593 and n. 3.
[2] Thus Coke lamented the disuse of the real actions because it produced " want of true judgment in the Profession of the Law and gross ignorance in Clerkes of the right Entries and Proceedings in those cases," 8 Co. Rep. Pref. xxviii cited vol. v 479 n. 2.
[3] Above 180, 293. [4] Ruscombe v. Hare (1817-1818) 6 Dow. at p. 16.
[5] Twiss, op. cit. iii 358.
[6] D'Aguesseau said to his son who had told him that complaint was made of his slowness in decision : " My child, when you shall have read what I have read, seen what I have seen, and heard what I have heard, you will feel, that if, on any subject, you know much, there may be also much that you do not know ; and that something even of what you know may not, at the moment, be in your recollection ; you will then, too, be sensible of the mischievous and often ruinous consequences of even a small error in a decision ; and conscience, I trust, will then make you as doubtful, as timid, and consequently as dilatory, as I am accused of being," Butler, Reminiscences i 279.
[7] Twiss, op. cit. iii 411-415. [8] Ibid iii 355.

sometimes able to discover decisive facts which had been over-
looked by all the counsel. Basil Montague told the Chancery
Commission that he had once argued a case before him two or
three times, that he was satisfied that he was right, and that he
had pressed for a decision in his favour :

> At last the Lord Chancellor stated that he had been deliberating upon
> the case for many hours during the night, and that there was one point
> which had escaped me in my argument, to which he wished to direct
> my attention ; and he was pleased to direct my attention to it, and to
> desire it to be reargued : and upon rearguing it, I was satisfied that he
> was right, and I was wrong ; and whatever may have been the cause
> of the delay, the consequence has been that he has prevented the in-
> justice which I should have persuaded him to have committed.[1]

Brougham relates that an appeal to the House of Lords on a writ
of error was once decided on a point of pleading discovered by
Eldon, which had escaped the notice of all the common law judges
before whom the case had come.[2] Lord Abergavenny told Eldon
that he had compromised a suit because

> his attorney had told him there was in his case a weak point, which,
> though the opposing parties were not aware of it, *that old fellow* would
> be sure to find out if the case came before him.[3]

It was this combination of qualities which made Eldon's
influence upon the development of equity both large and beneficial. All the Chancellors since Nottingham had agreed that the
principles of equity ought to be ascertained and sufficiently
fixed to be able to be readily applied by members of the legal
profession to solve the problems set to them by their clients.[4]
At the same time all were agreed that in the administration of
equitable rule there must be an element of discretion ; for, since
equity acts in personam, its rules must be so applied that justice
is done in each individual case.[5] It is difficult, if not impossible,
wholly to reconcile these two ideals. But Eldon's great knowledge
of the common law, and of the principles and rules of equity, and
his great care to sift to the bottom all the facts of the cases which
came before him, enabled him to come very near to realizing it.
This is a large claim to make, but that it can be made is, I think,
clear from the testimony of some of the most eminent of his contemporaries who were best qualified to judge. Let us look first
at the testimony of his two successors in the office of Chancellor—
Lyndhurst and Brougham, secondly, at the testimony of Romilly
who had during many years a leading practice in his court, and,

---

[1] Twiss, op. cit. iii 353, citing the evidence given to the Chancery Commissioners at pp. 411-412.

[2] Historical Sketches ii 65.

[3] Twiss, op. cit. iii 353, cited vol. xii 294 n. 8.

[4] Vol. i 468 ; 337-338 ; vol. vi 546-547 ; vol. xii 227-228, 261-262.

[5] Vol. xii 262-263.

thirdly, at the testimony of the most eminent of the real property lawyers of the day—Charles Butler.

In 1829, Lyndhurst said, in a speech supporting a bill to give the Crown power to appoint an additional equity judge that,

no man sitting on the same bench which he so long filled and considering the nature of his decisions, can refrain from admiring his profound sagacity, his great erudition, and his extraordinary attainments. It has often been said in the profession, that no one ever doubted his decrees, except the noble and learned Lord himself. I am sure, from the short opportunity which I have had of judging them, that none of his predecessors ever had a more complete command of the whole complicated system of equity, than that noble and learned personage. I therefore feel bound to say that I do not ascribe the delays which have taken place in the court of Chancery to the noble Earl, but to the system established in that court.[1]

In 1839 Brougham's critical sketch of Eldon contains the following appreciation of his character as a lawyer :[2]

That he had all the natural qualities, and all the acquired accomplishments, which go to form the greatest legal character, is undeniable. To extraordinary acuteness and quickness of apprehension, he added a degree of patient industry which no labour could weary, a love of investigation which no harshness in the most uninteresting subject could repulse. His ingenuity was nimble in a singular degree, and it was inexhaustible ; subtlety was at all times the most distinguishing feature of his understanding ; and after all other men's resources had been spent, he would at once discover matters which, though often too far refined for use, yet seemed so natural to the ground which his predecessors had laboured, and left apparently bare, that no one could deem them exotic and far-fetched, or even forced. When, with such powers of apprehending and of inventing, he possessed a memory almost unparalleled, and alike capable of storing up and readily producing both the most general principles and the most minute details, it is needless to add that he became one of the most thoroughly learned lawyers who ever appeared in Westminster Hall, if not the most learned ; for, when it is recollected that the science had been more than doubled in bulk, and in variety of subjects has been increased fourfold since the time of Lord Coke, it is hardly possible to question his superiority to that great light of English jurisprudence, the only man in our legal history with whom this comparison can be instituted.[3]

In 1811 Romilly, after saying that he could not consent to any motion which reflected upon Eldon, praised his conduct to the bar, his learning, and his anxiety to do justice to the suitors :

His general attention to the bar, his conciliatory demeanour, and his strict love of justice had endeared him to all the gentlemen who practised in that court. A man more eminently qualified, in point of talents and learning, for all parts of his profession, he knew not ; and he most firmly believed that he never had his equal in point of anxiety to do justice to the suitors of the court. If he had any defect it was over anxiety in that respect.[4]

[1] Cited Twiss iii 89-90.   [2] Historical Sketches ii 64-65.
[3] Above 621.   [4] Cited Twiss, op. cit. ii 169.

In 1822 Charles Butler, in his *Reminiscences*, wrote :[1]

In profound extensive and accurate knowledge of the principles of his court, and the rules of practice by which its proceedings are regulated, in complete recollection and just appreciation of former decisions, in discerning the just inferences to be drawn from them, in the power of instantaneously applying this immense theoretical and practical knowledge to the business immediately before the court, in perceiving, almost with intuitive readiness, on the first opening of a case, its real state, and the ultimate conclusion of equity upon it, yet investigating it with the most conscientious, most minute, and most edifying industry. In all, or in any of these requisites, for a due discharge of his high office, Lord Eldon, if he has been equalled, has assuredly never been surpassed by any of his predecessors. He throws a lustre on the whole profession to which he belongs ; they gratefully acknowledge it, and will feel its loss.

But Eldon had necessarily the defects of some of the great qualities which are emphasized in these appreciations. These defects can be summarized as follows :

First, Eldon was nothing but a lawyer. Law was the sole subject of his study. He had no literary skill, no literary taste, no idea of literary style. Hence his judgments, which he never took the trouble to write, are formless things. Facts and law are mixed together, and it is often difficult to extract the guiding principle from the detailed consideration of the particular facts which accompanies its statement. No doubt they were more effective as spoken than as written compositions. Campbell says :[2]

It was interesting to hear him deliver a judgment ; for his voice was clear, and notwithstanding his Newcastle burr, very sweet ; his manner was earnest and impressive ; he helped out the involution of his sentences by change of emphasis, and the varying expression of a most benevolent and intellectual countenance.

But there is no doubt that Eldon's indifference to the literary form in which he expressed his judgments is a serious defect which, if it has not impaired their usefulness, has created a difficulty in using them. And this indifference to literary form is aggravated by the subtlety of his mind which enabled him to draw superfine distinctions. As Brougham said his subtlety was " so nimble that it materially impaired the strength of his other qualities, by lending his ingenuity an edge sometimes too fine for use." [3]

Secondly, by far the greatest of his defects was his habit of delaying judgment till he had satisfied his scrupulous mind that he had fully mastered all the facts of the case and all the law applicable to those facts. Of this defect I have already said

[1] C. Butler, Reminiscences i 135-136.
[2] Chancellors vii 636.   [3] Historical Sketches ii 58.

something.[1] At this point I will give only one illustration. On March 8, 1811, Romilly wrote in his diary :[2]

What has passed to-day in the Court of Chancery affords a strong exemplification of my assertion of yesterday, that the Lord Chancellor was over anxious to decide properly. He has for a long time had a great number of cases which have been argued before him, waiting for judgment to be pronounced—some original causes, and many more motions and petitions. The distress which is occasioned to many parties by this is hardly to be conceived. On this day three cases were, by his order, put into his paper, for him to deliver his judgment. Of two of them he merely directed that they should stand over till the following Monday, without giving any reason. The third was a case of *Foster v. Bellamy*. It was a Bill filed by a pauper to redeem a very old mortgage, the plaintiff alleging that he was heir-at-law to the mortgagor. The defendant disputed the fact of his being heir, and the plaintiff had gone into evidence to prove his title ; but the evidence was so unsatisfactory, that all that I, who was counsel for the plaintiff, could do, was to ask that an issue might be directed to try the fact of his being heir. Of this case, which had been argued before the long vacation, the Lord Chancellor said to-day, that he had read all the evidence over three several times, and that he did not think that there was sufficient proved to warrant his directing an issue, but that, as it was a case of a pauper, he would go over all the evidence once more ; and for that purpose he directed the cause to stand over generally, without appointing any time for his final determination. He thus condemns all the other impatient suitors to continue waiting in anxious expectation of having their causes decided, till he shall have made himself quite sure, by another perusal of the depositions, that he has not already been three times mistaken.

Romilly was so irritated by Eldon's doubts that, though he had said in Parliament that the delays were due rather to the system of procedure than to the Chancellor,[3] he tried in his diary to explain away his statement in Parliament, and said that it was Eldon's procrastination which was their principal cause ;[4] and that one cure would be for the Chancellor to stay away from his court for a couple of terms, because then his place could be supplied by Grant, the Master of the Rolls, who had shown, on an occasion when Eldon had been absent through illness, how quickly he could clear off the arrears.[5]

Thirdly, this habit of personally examining all the papers in the case in order to be quite sure that he was doing justice led him to be inattentive to the arguments of counsel. He did not follow Hardwicke's practice of relying on their diligence, attending to their arguments, and then giving judgment on the materials

---

[1] Above 291, 292, 293, 577, 621 ; vol. i 437-438.
[2] Life of Romilly (ed. 1842) ii 187-188.　　　　[3] Above 289.
[4] " My opinion is that the Chancellor's hesitation and delays, and habits of procrastination are the principal, if not the only causes of the evil ; but it is impossible for me, who am constantly attending his court as counsel, with decency to state this to the House," Life of Romilly ii 185.
[5] Ibid. ii 224-225.

put before him.[1] He preferred to find out everything for himself. This defect was aggravated by the fact that his courtesy led him to be reluctant to interfere to suppress irrelevance or to shorten an argument,[2] and to tolerate the practice of hearing a large number of counsel on each side, and sometimes to allow a case to be argued two or three times.[3]

Fourthly, like Hardwicke, and with less justification than Hardwicke, he seems to have thought that his refusal to take measures to reform the procedure of his court could be compensated by devoting all the time that he could spare to the working of the existing system.[4] A tale told by Wilberforce illustrates this mistaken belief. Wilberforce says :[5]

I remember coming to speak with Romilly in court, and seeing him look fagged, and with an immense pile of papers before him. This was at a time when Lord Eldon, having been reproached for having left business undischarged, had declared that he would get through all arrears by sitting on till the business was done. As I went up to Romilly, Lord Eldon saw me, and beckoned to me with as much cheerfulness and gaiety as possible. When I was alone with Romilly, and asked him how he was, he answered, " I am worn to death, here we have been sitting on in the vacation from nine in the morning till four, and when I leave this place I have to read through all my papers to be ready for to-morrow morning ; but the most extraordinary part of all this is that Eldon, who has not only mine but all the other business to go through, is just as cheerful and untired as ever."

It was a thoroughly mistaken belief, partly because no human being could compensate for the inherent defects in the system of equity procedure, and partly because his other duties prevented him from applying himself continuously to the work of his court.

These were the outstanding defects of Eldon as the judge of the court of Chancery. Some of them were summarized in 1823 in a bitter criticism in the *Edinburgh Review*, which is supposed to have been written by John Williams.[6] His decisions, the author said, raised more doubts and difficulties than they cleared away, and they established no general principles. He was blind to the vices in the constitution and administration of his court. His judgments were so involved, so verbose, and so encumbered with limitations and qualifications, that little profit could be derived from their study. No doubt they settled satisfactorily the rights of the parties. But they did nothing to settle or to elucidate the principles of equity. They were " the exclusion of all conclusion," and could be useful only

[1] Vol. xii 294-295.
[2] He used to say that " when the defendants had failed in satisfying him that the plaintiff was wrong, the plaintiff's counsel often succeeded in doing so in his reply," Lord Kingsdown, Recollections, cited Ed. Rev. cxxix 48.
[3] Campbell, Chancellors vii 621-622.   [4] Vol. xii 294, 295-296.
[5] Townsend, op. cit. ii 417-418.   [6] Vol. xxxix 249-251.

when the Platonic year, in its revolution, shall have brought round not merely the same precise state of facts, but the very same plaintiff and defendant, the same learned gentleman to contest and defend their mutual interests, and (to crown all) the self-same Chancellor to decide.

That there is some truth in this criticism cannot, as we have seen, be denied. But that there is far less truth in it than in the contemporary appreciations of Eldon's great qualities as a lawyer and a Chancellor which I have cited, will be clear when we have examined his achievement as Chancellor.

Eldon's achievement as Chancellor

Eldon is the third of the three great Chancellors who have created our modern system of equity. Nottingham is its father ;[1] Hardwicke settled its leading principles and many of its subordinate rules ;[2] Eldon worked out in detail the scope and application of those principles and rules, harmonized conflicting interpretations of them, and thus completed the task of making it almost as systematic as the common law. Townsend has said :[3]

Lords Nottingham and Hardwicke may be considered the fountains of equity law ; it was reserved for Lord Eldon to illustrate them both, as Coke illustrated Littleton, by the admirable commentaries he has pronounced on the decisions of his predecessors.

This comparison of Eldon to Coke is particularly happy. Just as Coke fixed the relation of the common law to its rivals,[4] so Eldon fixed the relations of law and equity. Just as Coke fixed the sphere of the common law in the English legal system, so Eldon fixed the sphere of equity.[5] Just as Coke deduced some of the leading principles of the modern common law from scattered and often conflicting dicta which he found in the Year Books and other mediæval authorities,[6] so Eldon deduced from the decisions of his predecessors and stated in their final form many of the principles and rules of modern equity. Let us look at his work from these three points of view.

(1) Of his work in settling the relations of law and equity I have already spoken. We have seen that he and Kenyon played the principal part in securing the rejection of Mansfield's project of fusing the rules of law and equity, and the acceptance of the idea that they must be kept separate but must work in partnership with one another.[7] He said :[8]

---

[1] Vol. vi 539-548.   [2] Vol. xii 237-297.
[3] The Lives of Twelve Eminent Judges ii 418.
[4] Vol. v 428-432, 438-439, 470-471.
[5] Ibid 492.   [6] Ibid 489-490.
[7] Vol. xii 596-598.   [8] Booth v. Jackson (1801) 6 Ves. at p. 39.

I have had occasion while sitting in the court of Common Pleas to think the character of the law of this country, dividing itself into distinct courts of law and equity, has suffered more by the circumstances of courts of law acting upon what they conceive to be the rules of equity than by any other circumstance. If you address yourself to the question, how courts of law are to execute the equitable jurisdiction upon this question,[1] it is absolutely impossible that they can execute it.

The common law judges must settle what the law was, and the Chancellor, if in doubt as to what it was, must send them a case for their opinion. Only by taking this course could the Chancellor be sure that, in his equitable modification of common law rules, he was not starting from false premises.[2] It follows from this that the Chancellor must accept the statements as to the law made by the common law judges. This was the logical principle. It was not, it is true, accepted by Eldon ;[3] but this was not the view of Hardwicke ;[4] and Eldon's view is justly criticized by Maddock.[5]

(2) We have seen that Eldon several times laid it down that the fact that the common law courts had decided to apply a principle which had once fallen within the exclusive sphere of equity, did not affect the sphere of equity's jurisdiction.[6] In his last year of office he said :[7]

There are some cases in which the court entertains jurisdiction, though there would be a good defence at law; but that is because in those cases the matter was of such a kind that there was an original juris-diction belonging to this court ; and this court will not allow itself to be ousted of any part of its original jurisdiction, because a court of law happens to have fallen in love with the same or a similar juris-diction, and has attempted (the attempt for the most part is not very successful) to administer such relief as originally was to be had here and here only.

[1] The doctrine of part performance.
[2] Vol. xii 599-601.
[3] " Although it is highly useful in legal questions to resort to the assistance of courts of law, yet it must be well known to those experienced in the practice of the courts of equity, that they are not bound to adopt the opinion of the courts of law to which they send for advice. It has occurred to me to send the same case successively to the Courts of King's Bench and Common Pleas, and not to adopt the opinion (though highly to be respected) of either of these courts," Lansdowne v. Lansdowne (1820) 2 Bligh at p. 66.
[4] " I shall not send it again to law ; and however much I might have doubted, if I had sat in the King's Bench, on the argument in point of law, yet I shall not depart from the opinion of those learned judges," Ekins v. Macklish (1753) Amb. at p. 185 ; Chesterfield v. Janssen (1750-1751) 2 Ves. Sen. at p. 153.
[5] A Treatise on the Principles and Practice of the High Court of Chancery (3rd ed.) xxvi n. (d).
[6] Vol. xii 596-597 ; in Kemp v. Pryor (1802) 7 Ves. at p. 250 he said, " I cannot hold that the jurisdiction is gone, merely because the courts of law have exercised an equitable jurisdiction, more especially in the action for money had and received " ; in Jackman v. Mitchell (1807) 13 Ves. at p. 586 he said, " it is well settled that the jurisdiction of Courts of Equity is not gone by the resolution of Courts of Law to adopt the principle of Equity."
[7] Eyre v. Everett (1826) 2 Russ. at p. 382.

We have seen that at earlier periods in the history of equity this principle was not recognized—changes in common law rules directly affected the sphere of the equitable jurisdiction.[1] But Eldon laid down the law for the future. In 1861 Turner, L.J. said :[2]

It is new to me that the creation of jurisdiction in courts of law can oust the jurisdiction of this court in matters originally within its cognizance.

Prevention of mischief by injunction is a head of equity of which instances few and far between are to be found before his time. Lord Thurlow would hardly grant an injunction when the parties had a remedy at law. Before his time there are not more than half a dozen instances of each species of injunction, and in these relief was as often denied as granted. Now injunction is, it is well known, the right arm of the Court, pervading the workshop of the artisan, the studio of the artist, entering alike the miner's shaft, and the merchant's counting house. Almost all the principles upon which this relief is granted or refused, the terms and conditions upon which it is dissolved, revived, continued, extended, or made perpetual, are to be found in Lord Eldon's judgments alone.

(3) Of Eldon's work in settling and systematizing very many of the principles and rules of equity I shall have more to say in the second Part of this Book in which I describe the history of some of the leading principles of equity. At this point I can (i) only give one or two illustrations of some of his important decisions, (ii) indicate one or two matters upon which equitable doctrine has developed since his time, and (iii) say a few words of some of his decisions which have been the subject of legitimate criticism.

(i) We have seen that Eldon had shown as Chief Justice of the Common Pleas that he was learned in the common law of *real property and chattels real*.[3] As Chancellor he showed that he was equally learned in the equitable modifications of this branch of the law. In two cases he held that it was only the fraud of a trustee in dealing with the title deeds, or such gross negligence as amounted to fraud, that would postpone the holder of the legal estate to a subsequent incumbrancer.[4] In two other cases he lamented that it should ever have been held that " a mere deposit of deeds should be considered as evidence of an agreement to make a mortgage."[5] In the case of *Townley v. Bedwell*[6] he defined the rights of the heir and the personal representative of a testator who had given his tenant an option to purchase property, which

---

[1] Vol. xii 595 n. 3.
[2] Jenner v. Morris (1861) 3 De G.F. and J. at p. 56. [3] Above 529, 619.
[4] Evans v. Bicknell (1801) 6 Ves. 174 at p. 191 ; Martinez v. Cooper (1826) 2 Russ. at p. 217 ; cp. Northern Counties Fire Insurance v. Whipp (1884) 26 C.D. at pp. 488-491 ; Oliver v. Hinton (1899) 2 Ch. 264.
[5] Ex pte. Haigh (1805) 11 Ves. 403 ; Ex pte. Coombe (1810) 17 Ves. 370-371.
[6] (1808) 14 Ves. 591.

option had been exercized after the testator's death. Till the exercize of the option the rent belonged to the heir : after its exercize the purchase money belonged to the personal representative. In the case of *Church v. Brown*[1] he discussed elaborately what are the "usual" covenants in a lease. He upheld the unsatisfactory doctrine that the court would interfere to prevent an illusory appointment,[2] in spite of the powerful argument (which the Legislature later indorsed)[3] of Grant, M.R.[4] and he reversed another decision of Grant, M.R. in which he had held that a general power of appointment could not be vested in the tenant in fee simple.[5]

Many of Eldon's decisions make important additions to the *law of trusts*. The case of *Brown v. Higgs*[6] is a leading case upon the distinction between a trust, a power, and a power in the nature of a trust. In many of his decisions the vexed question of what is a valid charitable trust is discussed. In one case he held that a trust for objects of benevolence and liberality to be selected by the trustee was not a good charitable trust. The objects were too indefinite to make it possible for the court to superintend the execution of the trust, and they did not necessarily fall within the technical definition of the word charity.[7] In two other cases he held that a trust for charity would not fail by reason of the fact that the particular objects were not specified.[8] The earlier of these cases contains an elaborate history of the development of the principle applied in such a case, and lays down the rule that if an indefinite charitable purpose is expressed and no trustees are appointed, the King must direct its execution under the sign manual, but if trustees are appointed it is for the court to direct a scheme. In the case of *Muckleston v. Brown*[9] he discussed questions arising out of a secret trust ; and in several cases the question of what words would create a precatory trust was considered. Though Eldon laid down accurately the modern rules which govern the creation of these trusts,[10] some of the cases show a tendency too readily to construe a trust from precatory words.[11] In other cases the duties,[12] rights,[13] and liabilities[14] of trustees are

---

[1] (1808) 15 Ves. 258.   [2] Bax v. Whitehead (1809) 16 Ves. 15.
[3] Vol. vii 175 ; above 414.
[4] Butcher v. Butcher (1804) 9 Ves. at pp. 393-395 ; below 660.
[5] Maundrell v. Maundrell (1805) 10 Ves. at pp. 264-269.
[6] (1803) 8 Ves. at pp. 570-574.
[7] Morice v. Bishop of Durham (1805), 10 Ves. 522.
[8] Moggridge v. Thackwell (1802) 7 Ves. 36 ; Mills v. Farmer (1815) 19 Ves. 483.
[9] (1801) 6 Ves. 52.
[10] Wright v. Atkyns (1823) Turn. and Russ. at p. 157.
[11] Wright v. Atkyns (1815) 19 Ves. 299 ; Tibbits v. Tibbits (1821) Jac. 317.
[12] Walker v. Symonds (1818) 3 Swanst. at pp. 62-64.
[13] Worrall v. Harford (1802) 8 Ves. at p. 8 (right of indemnity).
[14] Walker v. Symonds (1818) 3 Swanst. at p. 76 (the liability of several trustees is joint and several).

explained, and also the circumstances in which a trustee is liable for the acts of his co-trustee.[1] In *ex parte Lacey*[2] the rule prohibiting trustees from purchasing the trust property from their *cestuis que trusts* is discussed.

There are many important decisions upon various points in the *law of partnership*. There are decisions as to the rights of the representatives of a deceased partner or the trustee of a bankrupt partner to a share in the profits, when the capital of the deceased or the bankrupt is used in the business by the surviving partners;[3] as to the power of a partner to borrow money for partnership purposes;[4] and as to when real property becomes partnership property and is thereby converted into personalty.[5] There are several decisions as to the application of the rule that in the case of the bankruptcy of a partner or partners the joint estate must be applied first in paying the joint debts, and the separate estate of each partner in paying his separate debts,[6] and on the exceptions to this rule.[7] The rule, Eldon thought, was based rather " upon principles of convenience " than upon " legal reasoning."[8] But some of the principles of this branch of the law were not fixed in their final form. Eldon thought that profit sharing must always connote partnership;[9] and thought the right of the vendor of a good will to set up a new business in competition with the purchaser was established.[10] Eldon's definition of good will was incomplete,[11] in that it only referred to one of several elements which go to make up its value.[12]

Eldon settled many important principles in the law relating to *the administration of assets*. The case of *Harmood v. Oglander*[13] is a leading case as to the order in which different kinds of assets are liable to the payment of a deceased person's debts; and the case of *Aldrich v. Cooper*[14] is a leading case as to the right of a simple contract creditor to stand in the place of a mortgagee against the realty, when the mortgagee has exhausted the personalty in the payment of his debt. " The principle is," said Eldon, " that it

---

[1] Chambers v. Minchin (1802) 7 Ves. at pp. 197-198; Shipbrook v. Hinchinbrook (1805) 11 Ves. 252; Brice v. Stokes (1805) ibid 319.

[2] (1802) 6 Ves. 625.

[3] Crawshay v. Collins (1808) 15 Ves. 218.

[4] Ex parte Bonbonus (1803) 8 Ves. 540.

[5] Ripley v. Waterworth (1802) 7 Ves. 425.

[6] Gray v. Chiswell (1803) 9 Ves. 118; Dutton v. Morrison (1810) 17 Ves. 193; vol. viii 242-243.

[7] Ex pte. Ruffin (1801) 6 Ves. 119; Ex pte. Harris (1813) 2 V. and B. 210.

[8] Dutton v. Morrison (1810) 17 Ves. at p. 211.

[9] Ex pte. Hamper (1811) 17 Ves. at p. 412; Ex pte. Langdale (1811) 18 Ves. at p. 301.

[10] Shackle v. Baker (1808) 14 Ves. at p. 469; Cruttwell v. Lye (1810) 17 Ves. 335.

[11] "Nothing more than the probability that the old customers will resort to the old place," ibid at p. 346.

[12] Cp. Lord Macnaghten's description in Trego v. Hunt [1896] A.C. at pp. 23-24.

[13] (1803) 8 Ves. at pp. 124-125.　　　　[14] (1803) 8 Ves. 382.

shall not depend upon the will of one creditor to disappoint another." [1] The case of *Bootle v. Blundell* [2] defines the circumstances in which the personalty will be exonerated from its primary liability to the payment of debts. The case of *M'Leod v. Drummond* [3] discusses the powers of executors to deal with the assets and the limitations upon those powers. The famous case of *Howe v. Lord Dartmouth* [4] decides that when residuary personalty of a wasting or a reversionary character has been left to a person for life and then over, it is the duty of executors to sell the property and convert it into a form in which it can be enjoyed by all the beneficiaries as and when their interests take effect. The case of *ex pte. Garland* [5] lays down the basic principles governing the rights and liabilities of an executor who has been directed to carry on his testator's trade, and the rights of the creditors of the testator and the creditors of the executor. It is the foundation of Lord Macnaghten's exposition of the law on this subject in the case of *Dowse v. Gorton.* [6]

Questions arising out of *the doctrines of satisfaction and election* were discussed by Eldon in several cases. [7] In *ex pte. Pye* [8] he lamented the existence of the equitable presumption that a legacy by a parent to a child was satisfied by a portion, though the portion was of less amount than the legacy, because it bore hardly upon legitimate children as compared with illegitimate children, in whose case no such presumption was made. He seems for some time to have been doubtful whether election to take against an instrument meant forfeiture of the benefit given or only created a liability to compensate. [9] But the authorities in favour of the principle of compensation predominated, and that principle has been generally accepted since the decision of Plumer, M.R. and the case of *Gretton v. Haward.* [10] These equitable doctrines are closely related to family law since they arise out of dispositions of property made by settlement or will. Another topic of family law—the law of guardianship—is illustrated by two famous cases decided by Eldon—the cases of *Shelley v. Westbrooke* [11] and *Wellesley v. Duke of Beaufort* [12] in which he asserted the jurisdiction of the court to control the legal rights of a father over his children on the ground of his irreligious or immoral conduct. Though these decisions were criticized at the time when they were

---

[1] At p. 389.
[2] (1815) 19 Ves. 494 at pl. 518-534.
[3] (1810) 17 Ves. 152 at pp. 160-172.
[4] (1802) 7 Ves. 137 at p. 148.
[5] (1804) 10 Ves. 110 at pp. 119-122.
[6] [1891] A.C. at pp. 201-201.
[7] Pole v. Somers (1801) 6 Ves. 309 ; Druce v. Denison (1801) ibid 385.
[8] (1811) 18 Ves. at pp. 151-153.
[9] Tibbits v. Tibbits (1816) 19 Ves. 656 ; Green v. Green (1816) ibid 665 ; but he seems to have finally decided in favour of the principle of compensation; see Rancliffe v. Parkyns (1818) 6 Dow. at p. 179 ; Ker v. Wauchope (1819) 1 Bligh at p. 25-26.
[10] (1819) 1 Swanst. 409.   [11] (1811) Jac. 266.   [12] (1827) 2 Russ. 1.

given, the latter was upheld by the House of Lords,[1] and both are recognized as authoritative.

There is no doubt that many of Eldon's decisions enlarged and improved the scope of *equitable remedies*. He made important contributions to the topic of specific performance ; and he enlarged the scope of the special injunctions. On this matter a writer in the *Law Review*[2] said :

Prevention of mischief by injunction is a head of equity upon which instances few and far between are to be found before his time. Lord Thurlow would hardly grant an injunction where the parties had a remedy at law. Before his time, there are not more than half a dozen instances of each species of injunction, and on these relief was as often denied as granted. Now injunction is, it is well known, the right arm of the court, pervading the workshop of the artisan, the studio of the artist, entering alike the miner's shaft and the merchant's counting-house. Almost all the principles upon which this relief is granted or refused, the terms and conditions upon which it is dissolved, revived, continued, extended or made perpetual are to be found in Lord Eldon's fragments alone.

The same writer pointed out that " the reference of title to the master, when nothing but title is in dispute, is an invention of Lord Eldon's, by which an infinite number of suits have been stopped *in limine* " ;[3] and that he perfected the rules as to the payment of money into court and as to the appointment of receivers.[4] He relaxed the strict rule that all interested persons must be made parties, " and in spite of his horror of joint stock companies he allowed a bill to be filed by several persons on behalf of themselves and all others the proprietors of an unincorporated institution." [5]

The fact that the range of Eldon's legal knowledge extended over the whole field of English law, and was by no means limited to the law of property and equity, is illustrated by *Crowley's Case*,[6] in which the history of the very intricate law, from the Year Books onwards, as to the power of the Chancellor to issue a writ of habeas corpus in a civil case was discussed. Only two of his decisions were reversed ; and those decisions did not involve any important principles.[7] On the other hand, he did not hesitate, if he thought that he had gone wrong, to refuse to follow his own decision.[8]

---

[1] (1828) 2 Bligh (N.S.) 124.
[2] Law Review No. iv 282, cited Campbell, Chancellors vii 645-646.
[3] Campbell, Chancellors vii. 645.   [4] Ibid 646.
[5] Ibid 647 ; Cockburn v. Thompson (1809) 16 Ves. 321.
[6] (1818) 2 Swanst. 1 ; see vol. ix 112-122 for the history of this subject.
[7] Stuart v. Marquis of Bute (1806) 11 Ves. 657 (1813) 1 Dow. 73 ; Innes v. Jackson (1809) 16 Ves. 356, (1819) 1 Bligh 104—both cases are cited by Campbell, Chancellors vii 651-652.
[8] Ex. pte. Note (1828) 2 Gl. and J. 295, 307, cited Campbell, Chancellors vii 650.

(ii) These specimens of Eldon's decisions illustrate the extent of his achievement in settling the principles of equity. His decisions cover almost the whole field of equity—but not quite all. As Jessel, M.R. said, the doctrines of equity are, as compared with the doctrines of the common law, modern.[1] There are some equitable doctrines which have emerged, or have assumed their modern form, since the time of Eldon. One instance is the right to follow trust property as expounded by Jessel, M.R. in *Re Hallett's Estate*,[2] and another is the development of the rules as to covenants running in equity with the land, which started with the case of *Tulk v. Moxhay*.[3] Eldon did not recognize the modern doctrine as to the following of trust property. It is true that he was prepared to issue an injunction to prevent a person holding money in a fiduciary capacity, which he had invested in his own name, from disposing of it.[4] But that he did not recognize the modern doctrine is clear from the fact that he could say generally that

it would certainly be a matter of some novelty to say that if a man has sold stock in breach of trust, and afterwards buys other stock of the like description, any part of the stock so purchased can be considered as specifically the property of the *cestui que trust*.[5]

Neither Eldon nor Brougham seem to have recognized that covenants, though they might not run with the land at law, might, if negative in character, run with the land in equity. In the case of *Collins v. Plumb*[6] Eldon thought that it was doubtful whether a covenant not to sell water from a well to the prejudice of the covenantee ran with the land at law, and that it was too uncertain to be enforced by injunction. There is no hint that a negative covenant may run in equity with the land, though it does not run at law. In the case of *Duke of Bedford v. Trustees of the British Museum*[7] he doubted but refused to decide whether a covenant by a purchaser not to build could run with the land at law,[8] and there is no hint that, whether or not it ran at law with the land, it might so run in equity. He decided the case on the ground that the character of the property had so changed that it would be inequitable to enforce it by injunction[9]—a principle which has been recently recognized

---

[1] In re Hallett's Estate (1879) 13 C.D. at p. 710, cited vol. i 465-466.
[2] (1879) 13 C.D. at pp. 707-721.   [3] (1848) 2 Ph. 774.
[4] Chedworth v. Edwards (1802) 8 Ves. 46.
[5] Vulliamy. v. Noble (1817) 3 Mer. at p. 616; this might be true if the sale and the purchase were made in such circumstances that it was clear that the money produced by the sale was not used for the purchase : it is not true if the money produced by the sale was used for the purchase, see Re Hallett's Estate (1879) 13 C.D. at p. 709.
[6] (1810) 16 Ves. 454.   [7] (1822) 2 My. and K. 552.
[8] At p. 562.   [9] At pp. 568-569, 573-574.

and extended by the Legislature.[1] Similarly, in Brougham's very learned and able judgment in the case of *Keppel v. Bailey*,[2] the proposition that a covenant, which does not run at law with the land, may run in equity, if the land is taken with notice of the covenant, is categorically denied.[3]

(iii) Some of Eldon's decisions have been made the subject of legitimate criticism. These decisions can be divided into four classes.

First, we have seen that Eldon was not a commercial lawyer.[4] He had little knowledge of the manner in which a new mechanism and new ideas as to trade were superseding the old mechanism and the old ideas. Remembering the old common law principle that trade ought to be free from all restraints not imposed by law,[5] he regarded all combinations which threatened this freedom as illegal. It is for this reason that in the case of *Cousins v. Smith*[6] he held that a combination of wholesale grocers, called " The Fruit Club," which was formed to buy all imported fruit and to sell it to the trade, was illegal. " This " said Eldon,[7]

is not according to the legal definition of the term forestalling, much less regrating ; still less monopolizing : but in the consideration of a Court of Equity it contains the mischief of all three. First, there is a conspiracy against the vendors ; next, a conspiracy against the world at large ; enabling those persons to buy at any price that they may think proper ; and then, it is true, they can, if they please, sell at a lower price than a fair competition in the market would produce : but it must also be recollected, that they can sell upon their own terms ; and the manner in which that discretion will probably be exercised, is obvious.

From the strictly legal point of view there is more to be said for Eldon's ruling than a hard-shelled free trader like Campbell imagined.[8] None the less it is true that the modern mechanism and modern ideas as to the activities lawful to traders were moving in the direction of getting rid of old restraints which the law once deemed necessary to safeguard the individual's freedom of trade.[9] It is because Eldon was ignorant of the trend of economic thought that he failed to see that legal doctrine on these matters must be modified. But in fairness to him it

---

[1] Law of Property Act 1925, 15 George V c. 20 § 84 ; Ashburner, Equity 2nd ed.) 371 ; Hanbury, Modern Equity (5th ed.) 482.

[2] (1834) 3 My. and K. 517 ; below 650.

[3] " If such would be its construction at law, does the notice which the purchaser had of its existence alter the case in this Court upon an application for an injunction ? . . . Certainly not. The knowledge by an assignee of an estate, that his assignor had assumed to bind others than the law authorizes him to affect by his contracts . . . cannot bind such assignee by affecting his conscience. . . . That of which the assignees have had notice, was their assignor's covenant, affecting to bind the land on which by law it could not operate," ibid at pp. 546-547.

[4] Above 529. [5] Vol. xi 477-480.

[6] (1807) 13 Ves. 542. [7] At p. 545.

[8] Chancellors vii 653-654. [9] Vol. xi 391-394 ; above 179, 183, 357.

must be remembered that economic thought was not as yet prepared to sweep away all the old restraints.[1] It was not till 1889, when freedom of trade had become a dogma which was accepted without reflection, that it could be said by Bowen, L. J. that Eldon's decision in the case of *Cousins v. Smith* was " not very intelligible,"[2] and that " peaceable and honest combinations of capital for purposes of trade competition " were not " under the ban of the common law ;"[3] and even then the older ideas found a champion in Lord Esher, M.R.[4]

Secondly, Eldon held that " when a school is instituted as a free grammar school, without more, it is a school to teach the elements of the learned languages,"[1] so that the Latin and Greek classics must always be the principal subjects taught. Coleridge said that Eldon's view was founded " on an insufficient view of the history and literature of the sixteenth century ";[5] and there is some truth in Campbell's criticism that his decisions " have had the effect of preventing these institutions in country towns from being adapted to the wants of society."[6]

Thirdly, Eldon has been accused of religious intolerance because he held that, after the repeal of so much of the Blasphemy Act of 1698 as related to the denial of the doctrine of the Trinity, such denial was still an offence at common law, so that a trust to propagate Unitarian opinions could not be enforced.[7] We have seen that this view was overruled by the House of Lords in a later case.[8] Eldon's view was grounded upon the then recognized principle that Christianity was so integral a part of the law that no disposition of property designed to propagate anti-Christian views was legal.[9] Given his premise, for which there was much authority,[10] his conclusion was logical. It was upon the same principle that he held in another case that Jews were not entitled to participate in the Bedford Charity.[11] A

---

[1] Above 328, 329, 357, 358.
[2] Mogul Steamship Co. v. McGregor (1889) 23 Q.B.D. at p. 619.
[3] Ibid at p. 620.   [4] Ibid at pp. 601-611.
[5] Attorney-General v. Hartley (1820) 2 Jac. and W. at p. 378; see also Attorney-General v. Earl of Mansfield (1827) 2 Russ. at pp. 520-521.
[6] Chancellors vii 654 ; Campbell also rightly criticizes the theory which Eldon put forward in Attorney-General v. Earl of Mansfield (1827) 2 Russ. at pp. 521-522 that these schools were all founded by Edward VI or Elizabeth to promote the Reformation.
[7] Attorney-General v. Pearson (1817) 3 Mer. at p. 399 ; vol. viii 411.
[8] Vol. viii 412 ; Shore v. Wilson (1842) 9 Cl. and Fin. 355.
[9] Vol. viii 410.   [10] Ibid 407-410.
[11] " I apprehend that it is the duty of every judge presiding in an English Court of Justice, when he is told that there is no difference between worshipping the Supreme Being in chapel, church, or synagogue, to recollect that Christianity is part of the Law of England ; that in giving construction to the charter and acts of parliament, he is not to proceed on the principle further than just construction requires ; but to the extent of just construction of that charter and those acts, he is not at liberty to forget that Christianity is part of the law of the land," in re Bedford Charity (1819) 2 Swanst. at p. 528.

technical case can be made for Eldon's views on religious matters, just as a technical case can be made for his views on economic matters ; but only a technical case. On both these matters he was wholly out of touch with the prevailing trend of thought on these matters.

Fourthly, it was Eldon's decisions in certain copyright cases which aroused the fiercest and, from the point of view both of technical correctness and public policy, the most justifiable criticism. *Walcot v. Walker*[1] is the first of these cases. An injunction had been got by Dr. Walcot, an author better known as Peter Pindar, to restrain the defendants, until an answer was filed, from publishing two editions of his books in contravention of a contract between himself and the defendants. The defendants by their answer submitted to the injunction in respect of one of these editions. But, in spite of this submission, Eldon made an order to dissolve the injunction, unless within a week the book was produced for his examination, upon the ground that it was possibly libellous, and was therefore not entitled to be protected by an injunction. This case was followed by others in which he laid down the same principle.[2] The most extraordinary is the case of *Lawrence v. Smith*,[3] in which he dissolved an injunction obtained *ex parte* to protect the copyright in the plaintiff's book entitled ' Lectures on Physiology, Zoology, and the Natural History of man,' on the ground that it tended to cast doubts on the immortality of the soul.

These decisions have been justified on the ground that it is a well-established principle that no action will lie at law or in equity in respect of an illegal transaction.[4] The principle is no doubt well established. But when the illegality alleged is the fact that a publication is libellous the Chancellor ought to walk more warily than Eldon walked. In a criminal case the question whether or not a publication is libellous is a question for the jury ; and in a civil case, if the question is left to the jury, it is for them to decide it as between plaintiff and defendant. It follows that if there is the smallest doubt the Chancellor ought not to prejudice the question by refusing an injunction to a plaintiff *prima facie* entitled to copyright. That was the practice of Eldon's predecessors ;[5] and he admitted that in case of doubt the question ought to be sent to a court of law

---

[1] (1802) 7 Ves. 1.

[2] Southey v. Sherwood (1817) 2 Mer. 435—Southey's poem Wat Tyler ; Murray v. Benbow (1822) Jac. 474 *note*—Byron's poem Cain.

[3] (1822) Jac. 471.

[4] See Ashburner, Equity (2nd ed.) 465 ; Halsbury, Laws of England (2nd ed.) xiii 88 n. (*o*).

[5] Campbell, Chancellors vii 656 ; Ed. Rev. xxxviii 290-296.

for decision.[1] It follows that till the question had been decided
adversely to an author, he ought to have the benefit of the presumption in favour of innocence, and get at any rate a provisional
protection against the piracy of a copyright of which he is in
possession, and to which, if the book turns out not to be libellous
he may have a good title. Moreover to allow a pirate to resist
an injunction on this ground is tantamount to allowing him
to defend himself by pleading his own illegal act in publishing
a libellous book, and to increase, at any rate temporarily, its
circulation.[2] As Campbell very truly says :[3]

Let us always recollect, that if the injunction is refused, a meritorious
writer may be ruined by the "doubt" of a Lord Chancellor, and that
if the injunction is granted, no injury can possibly be done to the defendant or to the public. The consideration that, by permitting the
piracy of a work, which is really improper, it is rendered much more
mischievous to society, ought not in strictness to weigh with equity
judges ; but on other occasions they are wonderfully astute and ingenious
in accommodating their jurisdiction to their own notions of the public
good. . . . There can be no practical danger of the author of any grossly
immoral or seditious work applying for an injunction, for, on his own
affidavit, he might immediately be prosecuted and sentenced to an
infamous punishment ; while the permission to object to the character
of the pirated work not only renders all literary property insecure,
but holds out the strongest temptation to spoliation and fraud.

But these decisions are a minute part of the mass of the
hundreds of sound decisions which settled the main principles
and rules of modern equity. Greville was right when he said
that Eldon " had lived to see his name venerated and his decisions received with profound respect, with the proud assurance
that he has left to his country a mighty legacy of law and secured
to himself an imperishable fame."[4]

Of Eldon's successor, John Singleton Copley, Lord Lyndhurst,
I shall speak in the next chapter, since he was Chancellor not

[1] " I will not act upon the submission in the answer. If upon inspection the
work appears innocent, I will act upon that submission : if criminal I will not act
at all ; and, if doubtful, I will send the question to law," Walcot v. Walker (1802)
7 Ves. at p. 2.

[2] Eldon admitted this ; he said, " it is very true that in some cases it may operate
so as to multiply copies of mischievous publications by the refusal of the Court to
interfere by restraining them ; but to this my answer is, that, sitting here as a
Judge upon a mere question of property, I have nothing to do with the nature of
the property nor with the conduct of the parties except as it relates to their civil
interests ; and if the publication be mischievous, either on the part of the author or
the bookseller, it is not my business to interfere with it," Southey v. Sherwood
(1817) 2 Mer. at pp. 439-440 ; logically this reasoning supplies a good reason
against Eldon's action ; if he had nothing to do with " the nature of the
property " or the " conduct of the parties," what right had he to refuse an
author a remedy on account of the contents of his book ? For some pertinent
remarks on the consequences of this view see Ed. Rev. xxxviii 306-307.

[3] Chancellors vii 663-664.   [4] Memoirs ii 338.

only between 1827 and 1830, but also in 1834-5 and from 1841 to 1846. His successor, and the last of the Chancellors who held office during this period, was Henry Brougham.[1]

Of Brougham's earlier career and character I have already spoken.[2] At this point I must, in the first place, say something of his short career as Chancellor and his contributions to the law in that capacity, and, in the second place, sketch briefly his later career.

(1) We have seen that Grey had solved the problem of finding for Brougham a place in the ministry by offering him the post of Chancellor ; and that he accepted it in spite of his mother's advice, and in spite of his declaration when elected member for Yorkshire that nothing on earth would induce him to accept office.[3] His motives for accepting it were probably, in the first place, the knowledge that unless he did accept a Whig government could not be formed, so that the reform of Parliament and the many reforms in the law which he wished to effect would either not be undertaken at all, or undertaken in an ineffective way ; and, secondly, the fact that his acceptance of the Chancellorship would give him the best vantage-ground for proposing reforms in the law.[4] With all his faults, Brougham was faithful to certain causes—the abolition of slavery, education, supervision of the administration of charitable trusts, and above all law reform.[5] But having attained high office all his characteristic failings, his want of loyalty and occasional acts of downright treachery to his colleagues, his liking for tortuous courses of conduct which engendered suspicion, his excitable temperament which at times deprived him of all discretion, his vanity, and his affectation of omniscience,[6] soon appeared in an exaggerated form.

As speaker of the House of Lords he treated his peers " with the same contempt for their susceptibilities that he had displayed when pleading the cause of Caroline of Brunswick at their lordships' bar." He made full use of his powers of invective and sarcasm with the result that " he found himself the veritable

---

[1] Atlay, The Victorian Chancellors i 168-378—much the best account; Campbell, Lives of the Chancellors viii 213-596—a posthumous publication, not very accurate and sometimes unfair ; Foss, Judges ix 78-86 ; D.N.B.

[2] Above 195-200.　　　　　　　[3] Above 241.

[4] It has been suggested that another motive may have been his hostility to radicalism, see above 198 and the consciousness that his position in the House of Commons could only be maintained by concessions to democratic feeling, Ed. Rev. 587.

[5] In 1839 The Times said of him that he was an " advocate and nothing more," who could " as rarely win the sympathy of jurors as he could the sober sanction of the judge," cited Campbell, op. cit. viii 508 ; this was true of Brougham as a barrister, and to some extent as a politician ; but it was not wholly true, because there were certain causes he had at heart, and for which he accomplished much, above 197, 273, 296-306, 501 ; below 644.　　　　　[6] Above 198.

Ishmael of the Peerage, and in these frequent encounters the honours of war did not always rest with the master of flouts and jeers."[1] On the other hand, his great social and intellectual gifts which had helped him out of many scrapes in the past,[2] were less able to atone for the more serious consequences which followed from such failings when they appeared in a Lord Chancellor. They did, however, help to mitigate some of the bitter feelings which his failings aroused. They were admitted by *The Times* in one of the most bitter articles which its editor ever wrote about his career;[3] and it is worthy of note that most of the men with whom he quarrelled—Grey (though not Grey's family),[4] Durham,[5] Melbourne (who made him his executor),[6] Croker,[7] Sugden,[8] Queen Adelaide (who made him her executor),[9] —were all sooner or later reconciled to him; and after his exclusion from office he and Lyndhurst for the remainder of their long lives became the firmest of friends.

When, in November, 1833, at a meeting of the Whig chiefs at Lansdowne House, it was resolved to offer the Chancellorship to Brougham, Lord Holland said, " I suppose it must be so, but this is the last time we shall meet in peace within these walls ";[10] and, when he was at the height of his fame, Macaulay prophesied truly that he would soon place himself in a false position before the public, that his popularity would go down, and that he would find himself alone.[11] These prophecies were fulfilled. But, until the Reform Act was passed, all went well. Brougham took a large, perhaps the largest, part in securing its passage, with the result that " among the newly enfranchized electorate he monopolized the popularity and authority of the government. It was believed, and not unjustly, that to him, more than to any single individual, was due the victory of the people over the Crown, the territorial magnates, and the owners of the rotten boroughs."[12] But it was not long after the Act was passed that the difficulties in which the government found itself, and Brougham's conduct in the face of these difficulties, antagonized his colleagues, and dissipated his popularity.

---

[1] Atlay, op. cit. i 297. [2] Above 197-200.
[3] " In society, as one of the most agreeable, amusing, kindly, and convivial of associates, there is no individual capable of filling the space which would have been left void by Lord Brougham's untimely exit. There are a multitude of friends who loved him for what he was and is, as there are of observers who have admired him for what he might have been," cited Campbell, op. cit. viii 508 ; cp. Greville, Memoirs iii 346 (1836)—though Greville adds a note that in 1850 much of what he had written had ceased to be true ; ibid iv 69.
[4] Atlay, op. cit. i 359. [5] Greville, Memoirs iv 156.
[6] Campbell, op. cit. viii 549-550. [7] Ibid 379 n.
[8] Sugden, Misrepresentation in Campbell's Lives of Lyndhurst and Brougham 27-36.
[9] Atlay, op. cit. i 359. [10] Ibid 326.
[11] Trevelyan, Life of Macaulay i 187-188. [12] Atlay, op. cit. i 313.

One of the earliest of these difficulties was occasioned by Ireland. In 1833 the government had infuriated O'Connell by passing a Coercion Act for one year. In 1834, when the question of its renewal arose, it was proposed to drop the court-martial clauses ; but Wellesley, the viceroy, told the government that unless those clauses were retained he would not be responsible for the government of the country. Littleton, the chief secretary and son-in-law of the viceroy, had been told by the viceroy to consult Brougham if he found himself in difficulties. He did so, and he and Brougham concocted a scheme by which O'Connell's opposition to the Whig candidate at Wexford was to be bought off by dropping the clauses in the Coercion Act which prohibited public meetings. The viceroy agreed, but when Althorp was told of this deal he intimated his doubts as to whether the cabinet would consent. In spite of this intimation Littleton told O'Connell that the clauses would be dropped, and O'Connell performed his part of the bargain. When the story of these negotiations came out at a meeting of the cabinet Grey was indignant at the part played by Brougham, who had meddled in business with which he had no concern ; and Brougham in spite of the bargain with O'Connell which he had helped to make, voted in the cabinet for renewing the Coercion Act in its entirety. O'Connell was naturally furious, and told the House of Commons the whole story. The result was the resignation of Littleton, Althorp, and Grey. The two first withdrew their resignations and the government was reconstituted under Melbourne. But Althorp in a letter to Brougham summed up succinctly the case against him ;[1] and many thought (unjustly) that his actions were deliberately designed to drive Grey from office.[2]

Meanwhile Brougham, who had played a large part in the reconstitution of the government, thought, for that reason, that he was its most influential member. He thought also, quite untruly, that the King regarded him with special favour.

He regarded himself as practically the head of the Administration. He patronized Melbourne, and though he fought the Government Bills in the House of Lords with all his energy and pertinacity, and was ready as ever to meet all comers in debate, he took delight in trampling upon the susceptibilities of his colleagues. He thought nothing of volunteering to give evidence before a committee of the Commons in direct contradiction to the views of the Government. . . . Finally,

---

[1] " Without communication with one of your colleagues, with the view I know of facilitating business in Parliament, you desired Littleton to write Lord Wellesley, and you wrote to him yourself, to press him to express an opinion that the first three clauses of the Bill might be omitted. . . . Having originally produced the difficulty by writing to Lord Wellesley, you gave your decision directly against what you had advised Lord Wellesley to do," Melbourne Papers 257, cited Atlay, op. cit. i 331. [2] Ibid 332.

he expounded in the House of Lords, as a Government measure, a Bill to amend the appellate jurisdiction of their Lordships, without having submitted a single line of it to the Cabinet.[1]

In the long vacation of 1834 Brougham set off on his famous tour of Scotland.[2] There his escapades and adventures threw discredit on the government; and his speeches, which sometimes favoured the radicals and sometimes the Whigs, annoyed his colleagues, and increased the indignation of the King who was very angry at his taking the great seal over the border. Meanwhile Brougham imagined that he was in high favour with the King and sent him a continuous series of letters reporting upon his tour. One of his last escapades was to butt in on a banquet given in Edinburgh in honour of Lord Grey—though he was well aware of the hostile feelings with which the Grey family regarded him. Here his social gifts stood him in good stead. Campbell, who had helped to organize the dinner, says:[3]

Never did I so much admire Brougham's boldness of heart and loftiness of manner. He was fully aware of the feelings of all the Greys towards him, and if he had been before ignorant he must now have been informed by their averted eyes, cold looks and shunning demeanour. But he accosted them and continued to behave to them as if he had believed they regarded him with unmixed benevolence—only that his approaches were more than usually respectful, and his caresses more than usually tender. He conquered, and to my utter amazement has since been in confidential correspondence with Lord Grey and invited to Howick.

Brougham's tour probably strengthened the King's resolution to get rid of his ministers as soon as he could. The removal of Althorp to the House of Lords by the death of his father gave the King his chance. Melbourne left it to the King to decide whether he would continue to act with his present ministers, the King decided that they could not satisfactorily carry on the government, and so Melbourne's ministry was dismissed on November 13.[4] Brougham had heard the news on that day. Though, as a cabinet minister, he was bound to secrecy till the meeting of the cabinet, he communicated the intelligence to *The Times* that night.[5] The paragraph in *The Times* ran:

The King has taken the opportunity of Lord Spencer's death to turn out the Ministry. There is every reason to believe that the Duke of Wellington has been sent for. The Queen has done it all.

---

[1] Op. cit. i 333-334.

[2] Ibid 334-335; Campbell, op. cit. viii 447-457: Aspinall, Lord Brougham and the Whig Party 206.

[3] Life of Lord Campbell ii 51.

[4] For a full account of this episode see Sir Ivor Jennings, Cabinet Government 299-302.

[5] Atlay, op. cit. i 337-338.

The King naturally supposed that Melbourne had inspired this paragraph, and the ministers were dismissed with scant courtesy. Then on top of it all Brougham proposed that he should be made Chief Baron in succession to Lyndhurst, who had succeeded him as Chancellor, without any other emolument than his retiring pension. This proposal

was regarded as a violation of the rules of the profession, as a shabby attempt to deprive Scarlett of his due, and as an act of political desertion. H.B. drew a cartoon of "the Vaux and the grapes," and the incident extinguished finally and for ever Brougham's popularity with the masses of his countrymen. In Gladstone's judgment "no man had ever fallen so fast and so far."[1]

It is not surprising that Melbourne "spoke in no measured terms of his former colleague,"[2] and that when, after a short interval he returned to power, he resolved that under no circumstances could he tolerate Brougham as Chancellor. When Brougham wrote to him demanding an explanation of the criticisms which he had passed upon him, he wrote a long reply in the course of which he said:

I must plainly state that your conduct was one of the principal causes of the dismissal of the late Ministry, and that it forms the most popular justification of that step[3] . . . When I wrote that your conduct had been amongst the causes which led to the late change of government . . . I intended to state strongly and shortly my conviction that, during the four years you had been Chancellor, you had committed errors and imprudences of such magnitude as greatly to impair the vast and almost unparalleled powers which you possess of rendering service to your country[4] . . . You domineered too much, you interfered too much with other departments, you encroached upon the province of the Prime Minister, you worked, I believe, with the press in a manner unbecoming the dignity of your station, and you formed political views of your own and pursued them by means which were unfair towards your colleagues.[5]

Brougham's career in office was closed for good. For a few months the seal was put in commission, and Brougham was led to believe that it was the hostility of the King which was a bar to his reinstatement as Chancellor. He was thereby led to hope that he might yet be again made Chancellor. Buoyed up by this belief, he supported the government and piloted the Municipal Reform Act through a hostile House of Lords. But in January, 1836, Pepys was appointed Chancellor with the title of Lord Cottenham. It was said that Melbourne must feel very much like a man who had parted with a brilliant capricious mistress and married his housekeeper.[6] Brougham learned of

[1] Atlay, op. cit. i 339.   [2] Ibid i 340.
[3] Melbourne Papers 257.   [4] Ibid 259-260.   [5] Ibid 261.
[6] Lord Kingsdown's Recollections 112, cited Ed. Rev. cxxix 60.

Cottenham's appointment from the newspapers. Though Melbourne had suffered from Brougham's treachery, his lack of common courtesy on this occasion cannot be justified. As Atlay has said: [1]

One cannot help contrasting the care which was taken to manage Brougham at the moment when the formation of the Cabinet was in the balance, and when his hostility might have been fatal, with the callous disregard for his susceptibilities when the Ministry had safely weathered their first Session.

I must now say something of Brougham's contribution to the development of the law during the time when he was Chancellor.

It was as the author or supporter of legislative reforms, rather than as a judge of the court of Chancery, that he made his greatest contribution. We have seen that his great speech on law reform in 1828 had resulted in the appointment of royal commissions, the recommendations of which were the basis of large and salutary reforms in the law of real property and in the practice and procedure of the courts of common law.[2] Within a few weeks after he had become Chancellor he proposed a bill to establish local courts, and was considering schemes to reform the practice of the court of Chancery, and its lunacy and bankruptcy jurisdiction.[3] He proposed a local courts bill in 1833 which, owing to the opposition of Lyndhurst who voiced the opinion of the common law bar and the London attorneys, was lost in the Lords.[4] It was not till 1846 that Brougham's object was achieved, and by that time Lyndhurst was a convert to his views.[5] He established a court of review in bankruptcy, and so helped to relieve the court of Chancery of some of its bankruptcy work.[6] He abolished the sinecure court of Exchequer in Scotland,[7] the court of Delegates,[8] and a number of sinecure offices in the court of Chancery.[9] He regulated the procedure of the Masters' and other offices in the court of Chancery.[10] He passed an Act to reform the lunacy jurisdiction,[11] and he supported the Truck Act.[12] One of his best pieces of legislation was the Act which established the Judicial Committee of the Privy Council [13]—for which he was heartily abused by Greville, the Clerk to the Council.[14] He supported the Uniformity of Process

---

[1] Op. cit. i 346.
[2] Above 260, 273, 296 seqq.
[3] Atlay, op. cit i 300-301.
[4] Ibid 102-107.
[5] Ibid 106; vol. i 191.
[6] 1, 2 William IV c. 56; vol. i 443.
[7] 2, 3 William IV c. 103; vol. xi 9 n. 1.
[8] Ibid c. 92; vol. i 518, 605.
[9] Ibid c, 111.
[10] 3, 4 William IV c. 94; Vol. i 444.
[11] Ibid c. 36.
[12] 1, 2 William IV c. 37; above 336.
[13] 3, 4 William IV c. 41; vol. i 518-519.
[14] Memoirs ii 350-351, 352-353.

Act,[1] the Acts which reformed the law of real property,[2] the Act which created the Central Criminal Court,[3] the Act which reformed the Poor Law,[4] the Municipal Corporations Act,[5] the Act which abolished slavery[6] and the Irish Church Temporalities Act.[7]

To the end of his days he never lost his interest in law reform. It is true that, as Atlay says, " he had neither the mind of the codifier nor the patient skill of the conveyancer."[8] But it is true that he gave a great impetus to the cause of law reform. It is true that the claims made by Eardley Wilmot in a book which he published in 1857, entitled *Lord Brougham and Law Reform*, exaggerates Brougham's claims to the authorship of many of the law reforms of the nineteenth century.[9] But it is true that by his proposals for legislation, and by his establishment of the Law Amendment Society in 1844[10] he kept the subject of law reform before the public. His advocacy of, or opposition to, particular projects of law reform may not always have been either discriminating or enlightened—he was the advocate of an impossible scheme for setting up courts of reconciliation before which the parties must appear in person before they started an action;[11] he thought that the Common Law Procedure Act of 1854[12] did not go far enough, and he would have liked to see the informal procedure of the county courts applied in all actions in the superior courts.[13] He advocated a very crude bill for codifying the criminal law, which was condemned, and in Campbell's opinion rightly condemned, by a select committee of the House of Lords and the judges.[14] But there is no doubt that he inaugurated and helped to forward and maintain that movement for the statutory reform of the law which is the distinguishing characteristic of the succeeding period in the history of English law. What has been said of his contributions to literature and science is true also of his contributions to the cause of law reform—" They must be taken in the block, and not judged individually of by the piece . . . the real aim of the essay

---

[1] 2 and 3 William IV c. 39 ; vol. i 222, 240.

[2] Two of the most important of these Acts were the Real Property Limitation Act, 3, 4 William IV c. 27, vol. vii 22-23, 78, 114 ; and the Fines and Recoveries Act, 3, 4 William IV c. 74, vol. vii 78, 114.

[3] 4, 5 William IV c. 36 ; vol. i 285.   [4] Ibid c. 76.

[5] 5, 6 William IV c. 76.   [6] 3, 4 William IV c. 73.

[7] Ibid c. 37.   [8] The Victorian Chancellors i 365.

[9] Ibid 366.   [10] Ibid ; below 652.

[11] Campbell, Chancellors viii 579 ; he borrowed the idea from Bentham, above 99-101.

[12] Ibid ; below, vol. xiv.   [13] Hansard (3rd Ser.) cxix 343-344.

[14] Chancellors viii 579-580 ; as Campbell said, Brougham was a poor draftsman, and this fact "justified the answer given by Maule, J. to the question whether the attempt to codify the criminal law could now be safely made—' I think the attempt would now be particularly dangerous, for the scheme is impracticable, and there are some who believe that they could easily accomplish it.' "

or article was attained by the inquiry it stimulated or the example it set. He led the way and others followed, who without him would not have moved at all."[1] It was this kind of service to the development of the law which is his greatest title to fame as a Chancellor.

As a judge of the court of Chancery his reputation amongst the laymen was for a time high because it was thought that he had done much to clear off arrears and to reform the court. But these claims were soon found to be exaggerated; and amongst the lawyers his ignorance, at the beginning of his Chancellorship, of the principles of equity and of the practice of his court, which was aggravated by a sublime unconsciousness of this deficiency, caused his abilities as a lawyer to be unduly depreciated.

There is a story that Lord Grey and Brougham were crossing a ford at Alnmouth at a time when the state of the tide rendered the crossing none too safe. " Half-way over Grey turned in his saddle and shouted back ' Brougham, can you swim ?' ' I never have swum,' was the self-confident answer, ' but I have no doubt I could if I tried.' "[2] It was in this spirit that he approached his duties in the court of Chancery. He had never practised in that court so that he was very ignorant of its practice and procedure ; and, though he was a good common lawyer, he had never studied the principles of equity. And yet he was reported to have said that his office was " a mere plaything, that there was nothing to do, and that when he had cleared off the arrears, which he should do forthwith, he really did not know how he should get rid of his time."[3] Nor was his judicial behaviour a model. He wrote letters, read newspapers, or corrected proof sheets while he was supposed to be listening to the arguments—a practice which once involved him in an altercation with Sugden,[4] who hated him because he had held him up to ridicule in the House of Commons,[5] and because

---

[1] Quart. Rev. cxxvi 60 ; Campbell agrees—he says, Chancellors viii 360, " without his exertions the optimism of our legal procedure might have long continued to be preached up, and *Fines and Recoveries* might still have been regarded with veneration."

[2] Trevelyan, Lord Grey of the Reform Bill 191.

[3] Greville, Memoirs ii 131.

[4] Atlay, op. cit. i 295 ; Campbell, op. cit. viii 386 ; Sugden, Misrepresentation in the lives of Lyndhurst and Brougham 5-9 ; for a speech by Brougham in the House of Lords in which he abused Sugden, to which Sugden replied, see Greville, Memoirs ii 319-321 ; Sugden, op. cit. 19-24.

[5] It was said that in a debate Sugden had said that he had no great respect for the authority of Charles James Fox—" on which Brougham merely said, loud enough to be heard all over the House, and in that peculiar tone which strikes like a dagger, ' Poor Fox.' The words, the tone were electrical, everybody burst into roars of laughter, Sugden was so overwhelmed that he said afterwards it was with difficulty he could go on, and he vowed that he would never forgive this sarcasm," Greville iii 23—however, he did forgive Brougham, above 640.

he thought that Brougham treated legal learning with a levity which seemed almost blasphemous to a man who took that learning very seriously, and treated legal doctrines with a respect proportioned to their mystery.[1]

At the outset of his career the public were disposed to take him at his own valuation. He sat for long hours in term and vacation, and " on two occasions at least he had to adjourn because there was no business to transact."[2] This achievement gave him a momentary popularity. But there is no doubt that these results were sometimes achieved by methods which amounted to a gross dereliction of duty. Two illustrations given by Atlay prove this :[3]

Once at the close of the hearing of a heavy cause, he desired that the account books, on which everything hinged, might be handed to him to be consulted at leisure. When judgment had been given the solicitor applied to the registrar for the half dozen bulky packets which had been entrusted to his Lordship, and it was found that not a single tape or string had been untied. Again in *Townley v. Bedwell*, tried when he had occupied his high position for over three years, he was only saved by accident from perpetrating a gross injustice. Two cross petitions of considerable magnitude were in his list, and assuming that they were appeals and that the decision of the Vice-Chancellor was probably right, he did not even open the papers, but marked them ' Petitions dismissed ; orders affirmed with costs.' The first glance showed the registrar that they were original petitions, that there were no orders to affirm or disaffirm, and that a hearing was absolutely necessary. Had Brougham's supposition been correct, the whole costs of the appeal would have been thrown away ; and it was commonly believed in Lincoln's Inn that his much vaunted despatch was only feasible by these methods.

Lord Kingsdown in his *Recollections* gives an instance in which Brougham and Wynford dismissed an appeal to the House of Lords which involved new and difficult points of law, without paying any adequate attention to the arguments, and without reading all the papers.[4] When, towards the end of his career as Chancellor, *The Times* had turned against him, complaints began again to be heard of arrears in his court. In 1834 he instructed Campbell, the attorney-general, to move for returns of cases heard in his court, and to state that there were no arrears either in the court of Chancery or the House of Lords. This was at once contradicted ;[5] and Shadwell, V.C. told Greville[6] that

---

[1] Campbell, Life i 113 says that his earliest messmate at Lincoln's Inn was Sugden who " introduced himself to me by asking me *what I thought of the scintilla juris* "—the boy was father of the man, for when Chancellor he carried an Act to settle in the way he approved the controversy as to the scintilla juris, vol. vii 140.

[2] Atlay, op. cit. i 295.   [3] Op. cit. i 318.

[4] Ed. Rev. cxxix 51-53, citing Recollections 61-65.

[5] Atlay, op. cit. i 318-319.   [6] Memoirs iii 78.

he had taken the trouble to examine the returns of hearings, decrees, and orders, and he found there was scarcely a shade of difference between what had been done severally by Eldon, Lyndhurst, and Brougham in equal spaces of time.

That this verdict is correct is the more probable when we remember that the cause for the arrears in Chancery was the system of procedure and pleading, and that as yet nothing effective had been done to reform it.

The legal profession had a low opinion of his knowledge of equity. Greville, writing in 1834, says:[1]

It is quite ludicrous to talk to any lawyer about the Chancellor; the ridicule and aversion he has excited are universal. They think he has degraded the profession, and his tricks are so palpable, numerous and mean, that political partiality can neither screen nor defend them. As to the separation of the judicial from the ministerial duties of his office, it is in great measure accomplished without any legislative act, for nobody ever thinks of bringing an original cause into his Court. He has nothing to hear but appeals, which *must* come before him, and lunacy and other matters, over which he has sole jurisdiction.

But Greville wisely opined that " though the general opinion of the Bar seems to condemn him as a bad Chancellor, he is probably not near so bad as they endeavour to make him out."[2] This was the opinion of Campbell;[3] and it is borne out by the evidence of his secretary Le Marchant, who told Greville that Brougham, " by severe and constant application had made himself very tolerably acquainted with equity law, and very extensively with cases."[4] It is true that he may have made mistakes on points of practice which excited ridicule,[5] and it is true that to some of the cases which came before him he did not give the attention which he ought to have given.[6] But if we look at some of his decisions, it is clear that he had a considerable mastery of the principles of law and equity, the power to state them clearly, and a capacity to grasp quickly the essential facts of the cases which came before him.

Brougham had always been interested in the problem of securing the proper administration of charitable trusts—we have seen that he had been chairman of a committee to enquire into the administration of trusts for education,[7] and that he had supported the enactment of a statute to improve the law as to the enforcement of these trusts.[8] Two cases decided by him illustrate important principles in the law relating to charitable trusts. In the case of *Attorney-General v. Smythies* [9]

[1] Memoirs iii 73. [2] Ibid 74.
[3] Chancellors viii 381, 385. [4] Memoirs iii 22-23.
[5] Some of these cases were collected in a paper in the Law Magazine xiii 280 and a few are cited from that paper by Atlay, op. cit. i 317-318.
[6] Above 646. [7] Above 639. [8] Above 214, 215.
[9] (1831) 2 Russ. and My. 717, Coop. Cases t. Brough. 5.

he held that a profit made by a person entrusted with the administration of land held on trust for a charity must be held on trust for the charity; and the question of the application of the increased revenue from the charity land was discussed. The answer to this question, he held, must depend on the interpretation of the trust instrument, but in coming to a conclusion on this question " contemporaneous usage and long acquiescence " must be taken into account.[1] The case of *Attorney-General v. Ironmongers Co.*[2] is a leading decision on the doctrine of the application of charitable funds *cyprès*; but the view taken by Brougham that application must necessarily be amongst the other objects of the charity if any, is not now followed if the various objects are distinct from one another.[3] In the case of *Garrard v. Lauderdale*[4] he held that a trust for creditors, to which the creditors were not parties, was not a trust which the creditors could enforce, but " an arrangement made by a debtor for his own personal convenience and accommodation . . . over which he retains power and control."[5] This is accepted as the presumptive rule. But later cases have elaborated the circumstances in which this presumption is rebutted.[6]

In the case of *King v. Hamlet*[7] there is an able discussion of the principles upon which equity relieves expectant heirs from bargains to sell or mortgage their reversionary interests. But his view that whenever the father or person in possession of the property knew of the bargain, no protection could be given to the expectant heir, has been questioned on the ground that it lays down the law too widely—it might apply if the father assisted the heir to complete the transaction, not if he merely knew of it.[8] The case of *Walburn v. Ingilby*[9] is interesting for the statement by Brougham that large unincorporated companies were not unlawful at common law, and that such companies could not limit the liability of their shareholders to third persons. Brougham's decision in *McCarthy v. Decaix*[10] in which, following *Lolley's Case*,[11] he held that a foreign court could never dissolve a marriage celebrated in England, has been overruled.[12] In the case of *St. George v. Wake*[13] the semi-obsolete doctrine that

[1] Coop. Cases t. Brough. at p. 18.　　　　[2] (1833) 2 My. and K. 576.

[3] Ironmongers Co. v. Attorney-General (1844) 10 Cl. and Fin. at pp. 928-929 *per* Lord Campbell.

[4] (1831) 2 Russ. and My. 451.　　　　[5] At. p. 455.

[6] Underhill, Law relating to Private Trusts (10th ed.) 43.

[7] (1834) 2 My. and K. 456.

[8] Talbot v. Staniforth (1861) 1 J. and H. at pp. 502-503 *per* Page Wood, V.C.

[9] (1833) 1 My. and K. 61 at p. 76; vol. viii 221; above 369, 370.

[10] (1831) 2 Russ. and My. 614.　　　　[11] (1812) Russ. and Ry. 237.

[12] Harvey v. Farnie (1882) 8 A.C. 43. See Dicey, Conflict of Laws, 6th ed., 346.

[13] (1833) 1 My. and K. 610; for this doctrine see vol. v. 312, 313; vol. vi 644-645; vol. xii 324-325; for a case of 1826 in which effect was given to it by Gifford, M.R. see below 665.

a settlement made by a wife before marriage could be set aside by her husband on the ground that it was a fraud on his marital rights, was discussed with considerable learning. It is clear that the doctrine was not favoured by the court.[1] As Brougham said, the principle that a settlement could be avoided on this ground had been very rarely acted on—" in almost all the cases where the principle is recognized there were circumstances which the court laid hold of to escape from the application of the rule." In the case of *Casamajor v. Strode*[2] he considered the question when a purchaser of several lots of land can, and when he cannot, repudiate the whole contract, because the title to one lot is defective. This decision that the purchaser can repudiate the whole contract if he can prove that the purchases of the several lots were substantially one transaction is recognized as laying down the right principle.[3]

The case of *Keppel v. Bailey*[4] is the best known of Brougham's decisions. One aspect of that case I have already mentioned.[5] The other questions there discussed were : First, whether the rule against perpetuities could apply to a covenant. Brougham held that it no more applied to a covenant than to an easement or a rent.[6] Secondly, whether the burden of a covenant runs at law with the land as between vendor and purchaser of an estate in fee simple. Brougham held that it did not run.[7] Thirdly, it was in the course of the discussion of this principle that Brougham laid down the rule that " incidents of a novel type " cannot " be devised and attached to property at the fancy or caprice of any owner."[8] Though a person can make what contracts he pleases, and bind himself to pay damages if he breaks them, it is quite another matter to allow him to attach any obligation or burden upon property which will bind successive owners of that property.

Every close, every messuage, might thus be held in a several fashion ; and it would hardly be possible to know what rights the acquisition of any parcel conferred, or what obligations it imposed.

This principle has been approved,[9] but approved with this limitation, that new species of easement may be validly created

---

[1] 1 My. and K. at p. 620.
[2] (1833) 2 My. and K. 706, at pp. 724-731.
[3] Fry, Specific Performance (6th ed.) 385.
[4] (1834) 2 My. and K. 517.
[5] Above 635.
[6] 2 My. and K. at pp. 527-529 ; cp. Worthing Corporation v. Heather [1906] 2 Ch. 532 ; South Eastern Rly. v. Associated Portland Cement [1910] 1 Ch. 12.
[7] 2 My. and K. at pp. 533-555 ; cf. Austerberry v. Oldham (1885) 29 C.D. 750 ; vol. iii 163-165.
[8] 2 My. and K. at pp. 535-536.
[9] Hill v. Tupper (1863) 2 H. and C. 121 ; vol. vii 333.

provided that they comply with the conditions which the law imposes on the creation of all easements.[1]

So keen a critic of the law as Brougham could not resist the temptation to point out occasionally either the evil results of rules of law which ought to be changed, or the advantage of adopting means to avoid some of the inconveniences in the existing law. Thus in the case of *Sherratt v. Sherratt* [2] he pointed out that the unjust immunity of a deceased person's land from liability for his simple contract debts was the reason why the courts had tried to discover in wills an intention not to take advantage of this immunity, with the result that they put very strained constructions on the words used by testators, and thereby rendered the law very uncertain. As he rightly said, these consequences necessarily follow when " the judge endeavours to supply the defects of the legislator." In the case of *Guy v. Sharp*[3] he animadverted upon the difficulties occasioned by the use of inapt words in bills and other instruments, and made the suggestion, which has to some extent been followed, that the Legislature should

provide that certain formulas should have in law certain prescribed significations, receive a certain judicial construction, and produce a certain legal effect ; not of course preventing parties from using whatever other forms of expression they might choose ; but ensuring them at least thus far, that they shall be able without the chance of failure to accomplish certain things by employing certain expressions.

No doubt Brougham might have made a much better judge of the court of Chancery if he had devoted more time to the study of the principles of equity and the practice and procedure of his court, and if he had heard his cases with more care and attention. But a study of his decisions shows that he had acquired no small knowledge of the principles and practice of equity. I think therefore that Atlay is right when he says :[4]

Intricacies which would have baffled men of weaker calibre yielded up their secrets to him in an incredibly short time. He had a remarkable faculty of analysing and appreciating the authorities cited to him, and of applying their principles to the case in hand, and he was quick at unravelling a web of technicalities or exposing a sophistry.

(2) The shock and disappointment at the appointment of Cottenham as Chancellor in January 1836 came at a moment when Brougham was ill. That appointment caused a complete breakdown in his health, which lasted throughout the year. But in 1837 he was back in Parliament. In 1838 he attacked

[1] Cheshire, Real Property (6th ed.) 223 ; vol. vii 331-333.
[2] (1833) Coop. Cases t. Brough. at p. 44.   [3] Ibid p. 90.
[4] Op. cit. i 294 ; cf. Campbell, Chancellors viii 385.

some of the actions of Lord Durham, the governor-general of Canada, and reduced the government to the necessity of disallowing them. During the remainder of the term of Melbourne's government, he joined with the Tories in attacking it.[1] He supported Peel's government, but sometimes in a manner which caused that government some embarrassment—" he had little hesitation in making himself spokesman for the government and explaining their measures for them."[2] He had always advocated free trade, and so, though he disliked Cobden and his anti-corn law league, he supported Peel's Act to abolish the duties on corn. He took some part in the Parliament of 1847-1852. Though he approved of free trade, he was not a fanatic like Cobden and his followers, and so he was wise enough to oppose the total repeal of the Navigation Acts. His main interest was the proposal and advocacy of bills for the amendment of the law. He had founded a Law Amendment Society in 1844 with a journal of its own called the *Law Review*, and he introduced the measures which it proposed in the House of Lords. On one evening he produced no less than nine bills to reform various branches of the law ; and

year after year he published a sort of encyclical addressed now to Lord Denman, now to Lord Lyndhurst, in which the sessional work on law reform was passed in review, and the cases which cried most urgently for immediate action were indicated.[3]

This was the last Parliament in which Brougham played a prominent part. In his latter days he was more in sympathy with the conservatives than with the liberals. We have seen that he opposed the repeal of the Navigation Acts, and at the end of his life he was opposed to an extension of the franchize[4] —even in the great days of the Reform Bill he had never been a democrat.[5] He and Lyndhurst had long been close friends, and they delighted to chaff that seriously minded Scot, Sir John Campbell, in a manner which amused the public. Campbell imagined that he would vindicate himself by his lives of Lyndhurst and Brougham in his posthumous volume of *The Chancellors*. But the faults of that volume are so many that it has operated rather to depress his own reputation, than that of men whose biographies he wrote. Lyndhurst and Brougham were greater men than John Campbell, and they appreciated one anothers' very different qualities. As Atlay says,[6] Brougham was never quite the same man after Lyndhurst's death in 1863.

---

[1] For some account of his antics in the House of Lords at this period see Life of Lord Campbell ii 174.

[2] Atlay, op. cit. i 361.　　　　　[3] Ibid 366.

[4] Campbell, Chancellors viii 590.

[5] Above 243, 245, 247, 252.　　　[6] Op. cit. i 374.

Every afternoon Brougham would drive round to the house in George Street where his senior lay crippled with gout, and cheer him with gossip and *bavaderie* ; and in the dark days after Lyndhurst's death, when his own mental powers were fast fading, he would still rouse himself to be driven there, and it was with pain and difficulty that the hopeless nature of his quest could be explained to him.

For some years after 1835 Brougham had hoped that he might get, if not the Chancellorship, at least some office. But the same failings which had led to his downfall prevented either of the political parties from taking so great a risk. He was still guilty of eccentricities which ruled him out as a serious statesman.[1] In 1839 the report of his death in a carriage accident for which, in spite of his denials, there is little doubt he was responsible ; and his foolish attempt in 1848 to get himself naturalized in France with a view of becoming a deputy in the French Chamber, while retaining his British nationality in England—exposed him to much ridicule. His attempt in 1844 to induce the Legislature to appoint a permanent president of the Judicial Committee, who should take rank after the Lord Privy Seal, was a transparent device to get an official position for himself.[2] His affectation of omniscience was illustrated by his publication of a translation of Demosthenes on *The Crown*, the defects of which were thoroughly exposed by *The Times*. All these happenings ruled him out as a serious statesman.

His chief work for the State in these years was his work on the Judicial Committee and in hearing appeals in the House of Lords. In the Judicial Committee he gave important judgments on the effect of marriage induced by misrepresentation ;[3] on the extent to which the rules of English law are introduced into a conquered country ;[4] on the liability of a colonial governor to be sued in the courts of his colony ;[5] on the effect of partial insanity upon testamentary capacity, on the question of what constitutes a lucid interval, and on the burden of proving such an interval.[6] In the House of Lords he took part in many famous

[1] Greville, Memoirs v 153-155, 240-241.

[2] Atlay, op. cit. i 362 ; he denied in the House of Lords that this was his object and said that the post had been offered to him and refused, but no one believed this ; Greville said, Memoirs v 240, " no other man would have dared to get up, and, in the presence of at least half a dozen men who knew the whole truth, deliberately and vehemently tell a parcel of impudent lies."

[3] Swift v. Kelly (1835) 3 Knapp 257.

[4] Mayor of Lyons v. E. India Co. (1836) 1 Moo. 175.

[5] Hill v. Bigge (1841) 3 Moo. 465, in which Lord Mansfield's dictum to the contrary in Fabrigas v. Mostyn (1773) 20 S.T. at p. 229 was overruled, and the Irish decisions as to the non-liability of the viceroy of Ireland were questioned, vol. xi 257-260.

[6] Waring v. Waring (1848) 6 Moo. 34 ; but Brougham's denial that such a thing as partial insanity could exist is not now followed, Banks v. Goodfellow (1870) L.R. 5 Q.B. 549, at pp. 559-572.

cases of which the following are illustrations : *Wright v. Tatham* [1]
—admissibility of evidence to prove testamentary capacity ;
Birtwhistle v. Vardill [2]—the refusal to recognize legitimation
per subsequens matrimonium as sufficient to qualify a person
to take as heir to English land ; *R. v. Millis* ;[3] *O'Connell v.
R.,*[4] in which many points relating to the law of criminal procedure and to the law of conspiracy were decided ; *Hammersley
v. De Biel* [5]—a contract to leave property by will ; *Duke of
Brunswick v. King of Hanover* [6]—the immunity from action
of a foreign sovereign, even though he was a British subject, for
acts done by him in the country in which he was sovereign ;
Egerton v. Earl Brownlow [7]—the leading case upon the question
as to what transactions are void on the ground that they are
contrary to public policy ; and *Jeffereys v. Boosey,*[8] in which
Brougham, in a very learned judgment, discussed the question
whether copyright existed at common law.[9]

But though some of Brougham's decisions in the House of
Lords and Privy Council, just as some of his decisions in the
court of Chancery, illustrate his capacity as a lawyer, he showed
the same faults as he had shown when he was Chancellor. He
was often inattentive to the arguments of counsel,[10] with the
result that some of his judgments are short and superficial.
He sat for the last time in the Privy Council in 1850 ; but he
continued to sit in the House of Lords till nearly the end of
his life. When, in 1850, after Cottenham's death, he, assisted
only by two lay lords, alone did the appellate work in the House
of Lords, the results aroused unfavourable, though in Campbell's
opinion unjust, comment both amongst the bar and the public.
He tried to induce the House to treat one of these attacks upon

---

[1] (1838) 5 Cl. and Fin. 670.   [2] (1839-1840) 7 Cl. and Fin. 895.
[3] (1843-1844) 10 Cl. and Fin. 534 ;   for this case see vol. i 622 ;   below 689 ;
the House was equally divided—three against three, so that a decision in the court
below stood ;   Brougham was one of the three who were for reversing the judgment,
and, historically, this is the better opinion, P. and M. ii 370.
[4] (1844) 11 Cl. and Fin. 155 ;   Campbell, Chancellors viii 143-146 ; ibid at pp.
530-531 Campbell said that he acted as a partizan, delivered his judgment " with
unjudicial asperity," and when the judgment was reversed, contrary to his view, said
that it was a decision which had " gone forth without authority and would return
without respect " ;   for the importance of the decision in that case, that only Law
Lords should vote on appeals see vol. i 377.
[5] (1845) 12 Cl. and Fin. 45 ;   for the supposed equitable doctrine of making
representation good, based on this case, see Pollock, Principles of the Law of
Contract (10th ed.) App. Note i 696-703.
[6] (1848) 2 H.L.C. 1.
[7] (1853) 4 H.L.C. 1 ;   vol. viii 54-55 ;   Pollock, Principles of the Law of Contract
(13th ed.) 293.
[8] (1854) 4 H.L.C. 815.   [9] At pp. 960-976 ;   see vol. vi 379.
[10] " He sits every day at the Judicial Committee, but pays very little attention
to the proceedings ;   he is incessantly in and out of the room, giving audience to one
odd-looking man or another, and while in court more occupied with preparing
articles for the ' Edinburgh Review' or his Parliamentary tirades than with the
cases he is by way of hearing," Greville Memoirs, iv 62.

him in the newspapers as a breach of privilege. But he was pacified, and no " steps were taken to detect and punish the libeller."[1] For the rest, he spent some part of his winters at Cannes at his villa which he called Chateau Eleanor Louise, after his daughter whom he had lost in 1839. When in France he sometimes attended the Institut or wrote papers which he communicated to it. Of one of these papers, which he read to it, it was said " C'est bien, très bien, mais il n'y a rien d'original là-dedans."[2] And the same thing might have been said of the many papers and tracts and books which he wrote during his life. At the end of the collected edition of his works there is a bibliographical list of one hundred and thirteen publications ;[3] and he wrote a philosophical novel, of which his daughter was the heroine, which was suppressed.[4] In 1863 he began, too late, to compose his autobiography. Its arrangement is faulty, and its accuracy is dubious.[5] At the end of his life he was the moving spirit in the formation of the National Association for the Promotion of Social Science. He was the president at its opening meeting in 1857, and for some years attended its annual meetings. He attended its meeting at Manchester for the last time in 1866, and in the same year he wrote what he called his legacy to his countrymen—a letter protesting against electoral corruption. It was these numerous and miscellaneous activities—literary and otherwise—and the memory of his past achievements which kept his fame alive in the country long after it had waned in London. An Edinburgh reviewer, writing in 1869 said :[6]

Long after Londoners had ceased to speak of Brougham otherwise than in tones of impatience or amusement, we have seen parties of provincial visitors, especially of that staunch old Lancashire dissenting interest . . . whose first object in the metropolis seemed to be to learn his proceedings and to follow his movements ; men who mentioned him with a kind of awe as a superior being, and whose faces merely expressed the most unfeigned incredulity and surprise, when he was spoken of by others as anything less than the great apostle of progress and champion of reform.

---

[1] Campbell, Chancellors viii 566-570. [2] Atlay, op. cit. i 372.
[3] " Many of them are purely ephemeral pamphlets ; but they include in addition to (his Historical Sketches of Statesmen and Philosophers in the time of George III and his Speeches) two series of Lives of Men of Letters and Science in the reign of George III ; a discourse on natural theology prefixed to an edition of Paley ; tracts mathematical and physical ; and a History of England and France under the House of Lancaster," ibid 357 ; at the end of his life he published, with E. J. Routh, an Analytical View of Newton's *Principia*, ibid 373 ; his best book is the Historical Sketches, where they deal with the men he had known, or of whom he had heard at first hand, ibid 356.
[4] Ibid 357-358.
[5] Its chief value is a correspondence with Lord Grey and letters which passed between him and William IV which are included in it, ibid 375.
[6] Vol. cxxix 600.

His years were beginning at last to tell upon him : Pollock, who met him in 1861, said, though he spoke little, he seemed very fresh, and "looking like a shadow of the past."[1] Almost his last public appearance was at the dinner in the Middle Temple given by the English bar to M. Berryer, the doyen of the French bar in 1864. In his speech he said, as he had said in his speech on behalf of Queen Caroline, that it was the duty of an advocate "to reckon *everything* subordinate to the interests of his client." This was not the view generally held by the bar, and Cockburn in his speech pointed out that the arms which the advocate wields were those of the warrior not of the assassin, and that he must uphold his client's interests *per fas*, but not *per nefas*. Coleridge said that Cockburn had made some capital " out of a slip of poor old Brougham whom he might have spared." Atlay's comment justly sums up the situation :[2]

Poor Old Brougham ! That was the light in which the budding Solicitor-General regarded the man who rescued a Queen of England from the very jaws of destruction, who struck the fetters from the slave, who carried the Reform Bill in the teeth of King and Peers. He had indeed lived too long, he had lagged superfluous on the stage, a living monument of the vanity of human wishes, of the instability of human fame.

His mental powers began to decay in 1867, and he died at Cannes on May 7, 1868, in his ninetieth year.

The Masters of the Rolls, and the Vice-Chancellors

At the beginning of this period Pepper Arden, afterwards Lord Alvanley, was Master of the Rolls.[3] He was succeeded in 1801 by Sir William Grant[4]—a very great English lawyer, a very great jurist, and one of the best judges who have ever sat in a court of equity.

Grant was born in Morayshire in 1755. He was educated at Aberdeen University, and then, following an old custom amongst Scottish lawyers, he went to Leyden[5] to complete his study of Roman law. In January 1769 he became a student of Lincoln's Inn, and was called to the bar in February 1774.[6] In 1775 he went to Quebec. There he helped to repel an American invasion ; and, in the following year, he was appointed attorney-general of Canada. We have seen that the government of Canada had by the Quebec Act of 1774 been entrusted to a Governor and Council, that the French law in civil matters

[1] Personal Reminiscences of Sir F. Pollock ii 99.
[2] Op. cit. i 375-376.   [3] Vol. xii 328-329 ; above 530-532.
[4] Townsend, Twelve Eminent Judges ii 191-233 ; Brougham, Historical Sketches i 135-141 ; Foss, Judges viii 295-300 ; D.N.B.
[5] See Lord Macmillan, Law and Other Things 104-105, 106-108 ; vol. xi 15.
[6] Lincoln's Inn Admissions i 462 ; Black Books iii 419.

was maintained, but that in criminal matters English had been substituted for French law.[1] A large part of the difficult task of working the government and administering the law of Canada under this Act fell on Grant's shoulders. The knowledge and experience which he thus gained determined the whole course of his subsequent career.

He returned to England in 1787. After three briefless, or almost briefless, years at the bar the turn of the tide came in 1790. Pitt was preparing his bill for the government of Canada. He consulted Grant, and was so impressed by his ability that he got him a seat in the House of Commons for the borough of Shaftesbury. Grant took his seat in November 1790, and in 1791 he was able to support the government's Quebec Government Bill, and give the House valuable information as to the commercial law prevailing in Canada.[2] His education in Roman law, his experience in Canada of the working of a mixed system of English and Canadian law, and the knowledge which he had acquired of English law as a student at the Inns of Court and as a barrister, gave him a range of legal knowledge far wider than that of the ordinary English lawyer. At the same time his logical mind, and powers of clear and terse exposition, put him amongst that very small band of lawyers who have been as eminent in the House of Commons as in the courts ; and, unlike most English lawyers who got a seat in the House of Commons because they had succeeded in the courts, it was his success in the House of Commons which gave him a leading practice at the bar. He specialized in Scotch appeals to the House of Lords, and, in accordance with Thurlow's advice, in equity practice. In 1793 he was appointed a Welsh judge and was given a patent of precedence.[3] In 1794 he was appointed solicitor-general to the Queen, in 1798 chief justice of Chester, and in 1799 solicitor-general. In 1801 he became Master of the Rolls. He held that office for nearly seventeen years ; and both as a judge of a court of equity, and as a member of the Privy Council in the exercise of its appellate jurisdiction in Prize and Colonial appeals, he showed himself to be a consummate lawyer and a judge of exceptional merit. Though his health and his faculties were unimpaired, he resigned his Mastership of the Rolls in December 1817 at the early age of sixty-three. For some years after his retirement he occasionally heard appeals to the Privy Council ; but he gradually withdrew from public life and died in May 1832.

[1] 14 George III c. 83 ; vol. xi 65-66.
[2] Parlt. Hist. xxix 407-409 ; for the bill which became the Act of 1791 see vol. xi 66.
[3] In the same year he was elected a bencher of Lincoln's Inn, Black Books iv 56.

In Parliament he was a tower of strength to the government on questions of foreign policy, and more especially on questions which involved points of international law. As solicitor-general he powerfully defended the rights of visit and search,[1] and when Master of the Rolls he equally powerfully defended the Orders in Council. His argument in their defence, based upon the impolicy of adhering closely to the rules of international law, when fighting an enemy which breaks all these rules, has a truth which smacks of the same quality of universality as the timid error which it combats. In 1808 in defence of these Orders he said:[2]

Persons entertained strange notions of the law of nations, when they supposed that a nation could not perform an act of vigour for its own preservation, without violating the rule of its conduct. But this could not be a violation of the rule, for the case was out of the rule. When the enemy abandoned the rule, it was our duty not to be bound by it, but to inflict that injury upon him which he intended for us, until we forced him to peace. . . . He would not suffer his country to perish, merely because the measures which were necessary for its preservation might press upon neutral commerce, which Buonaparte had before violated. There was no contract without a reciprocal obligation, and if neutrals did not oblige the other party to adhere to the law of nations, they could not complain of us for not adhering to it.

His reputation in Parliament was won, not by oratory or by wit, but by sheer force of reasoning. Brougham says:[3]

His style was peculiar; it was that of the closest and severest reasoning ever heard in any popular assembly. . . . It was from the first to the last throughout, pure reason and the triumph of pure reason. All was sterling, all was perfectly plain; there was no point in the diction, no illustration in the topics, no ornament of fancy in the accompaniments. The language was choice—perfectly clear, abundantly correct, quite concise, admirably suited to the matter which the words clothed and conveyed. In so far it was felicitous, no farther; nor did it ever leave behind it any impression of the diction, but only of the things said; the words were forgotten, for they had never drawn off the attention for a moment from the things; those things were alone remembered. No speaker was more easily listened to; none so difficult to answer. Once Mr. Fox, when he was hearing him with a view to making that attempt was irritated in a way very unwonted to his sweet temper by the conversation of some near him, even to the show of some crossness, and (after an exclamation) sharply said, " Do you think it so very pleasant a thing to have to answer a speech like that."

As a judge both in the Privy Council and as Master of the Rolls he showed the same qualities.

---

[1] Parl. Hist. xxxv 921-931. [2] Cobbett, Parl. Debates x 336.
[3] Historical Sketches i 138-139; his style of speaking made the same impression upon Horner, see the passage from his diary cited by Townsend, op. cit. ii 206-207 and in the D.N.B.

In the Privy Council the reported decisions on Prize appeals are generally his. They are very brief, but "in spite of their brevity they must be considered as placing Sir William Grant as second only to Lord Stowell as a master of English prize law."[1] In fact when Stowell was sitting in the Prize court,[2] and Grant was sitting in the Privy Council to hear appeals from him, no nation can at any time have had two lawyers so supremely competent to deal with these cases.

It is with his work as a judge in a court of equity with which we are here concerned; and it is this work which has made his name as a very great lawyer.

During the hearing of the case he listened silently but attentively. At the same time the respect which he inspired deterred counsel from irrelevancy or the attempt to advance obviously unsound arguments.[3] Then came the judgment. Of these judgments Butler has said:[4]

The most perfect model of judicial eloquence which has come under the knowledge of the reminiscent is that of Sir William Grant. In hearing him, it was impossible not to think of the character given of Menelaus by Homer, or rather by Pope, "He spoke no more than just the thing he ought." But Sir William did much more; in decompounding and analyzing an immense mass of confused and contradictory matter, and forming clear and unquestionable results, the sight of his mind was infinite. His exposition of acts, and of the consequences deducible from them, his discussion of former decisions, and showing their legitimate weight and authority, and their real bearings upon the point in question, were above praise, but the whole was done with such admirable ease and simplicity, that, while real judges felt its supreme excellence, the herd of hearers believed that they could have done the same. Never was the merit of Dr. Johnson's definition of a perfect style, "proper words in proper places," more sensibly felt than it was by those who listened to Sir William Grant.

And with this verdict of Butler's, Brougham,[5] and Grant's successor Plumer,[6] were in substantial agreement. We have seen that he succeeded so well in despatching the business of his court that Romilly said that, if the Lord Chancellor would stay away for a few terms and hand over his business to Grant, the arrears would disappear.[7] This testimony is the more valuable because Grant was almost as high a Tory as Eldon, and opposed some of Romilly's proposals to reform the law.[8]

[1] E. S. Roscoe, Studies in the History of the Admiralty and Prize Courts 75.
[2] For Stowell see below 668-689.
[3] Brougham, Historical Sketches i 136-137.
[4] See Townsend, Lives of Twelve Eminent Judges ii 213.
[5] Historical Sketches i 137-138.
[6] Cholmondeley v. Clinton (1820) 2 Jac. and W. at p. 67.
[7] Above 625.
[8] Townsend, op. cit. ii 207-210; but he supported his bill to take away the punishment of death for privately stealing from the person, ibid 211; above 279.

Grant may not have been so well versed in equity practice and procedure as Eldon. But he had as firm a grasp of the principles of equity, and a power of lucidly expounding and of logically arranging his judgments which Eldon did not possess. It was very seldom that his judgments were reversed. One illustration is the case of *Mills v. Farmer*,[1] where Eldon differed from Grant on the question whether, in a case where a charitable intention had been expressed, the gift could be held void for uncertainty. Eldon held that it could not. Another case is as we have seen, Grant's treatment of the very unsatisfactory doctrine of illusory appointments.[2] If an appointment had been made, Grant refused to go into the question of whether a sufficient amount had been appointed. He gave some very good reasons for his refusal, and proved that the contrary doctrine was very illogical.[3] We have seen that the Legislature subsequently changed the law in a manner which accorded with his views.[4]

As we might expect, so distinguished a judge has left a considerable mark upon the development of equitable doctrine. The following are a few illustrations of some of the branches of that doctrine which have been illuminated by his judgments. One of the most complicated set of cases which came before him were those which arose out of the bankruptcy of the banking firm of Devaynes Noble and Co.[5] One of these cases was the well-known *Clayton's Case*[6] in which, in a learned judgment in which relevant texts of the Digest were cited, he laid down the general rule that, when a person draws on his banking account, the draft must be presumed to be satisfied out of the sum first paid into that account—" there is no room for any other appropriation than that which arises from the order in which the receipts and payments take place, and are carried into the account. Presumably it is the sum first paid in which is first drawn out."[7] Other points connected with the dissolution of partnership were settled in the case of *Featherstonhaugh v. Fenwick*.[8] In the law of trusts several of his decisions are important—one drew a distinction between " charitable " and " benevolent " purposes ;[9] another emphasized the principles that there is no equity to perfect an imperfect gift, and that a failure to make a perfect gift cannot be cured by construing it as a declaration of trust.[10] On the other hand it has been held that all the reasons

---

[1] (1815) 1 Mer. 55.
[2] Butcher v. Butcher (1804) 9 Ves. 382 ; for Eldon's view see Bax v. Whitehead (1809) 16 Ves. 15 ; above 630 ; for another case where he reversed one of Grant's decisions see ibid *note*.
[3] At pp. 393-395.   [4] Above 414, 630.   [5] (1816) 1 Mer. 529.
[6] At p. 572.   [7] At p. 608.   [8] (1810) 17 Ves. 298.
[9] Morice v. Bishop Durham (1804) 9 Ves. at pp. 405-406.
[10] Antrobus v. Smith (1805) 12 Ves. 39.

given for his decisions in the case of *Burrowes v. Lock*[1] as to the liability of a trustee who gives false information to his *cestui que trust* as to the state of the trust fund, or to a stranger about to deal with the *c.q. trust*, are not accurate.[2] Many equitable doctrines are explained and settled by his decisions—the wife's equity to a settlement and the right of her children to enforce it after her death;[3] the equitable modifications of the maxim *in pari delicto potior est conditio defendentis*;[4] the question which of the beneficiaries under a marriage settlement are within the marriage consideration;[5] the doctrine of dependent relative revocation.[6] All these decisions are remarkable not only for their soundness in substance, but also for the clarity of the form in which they are expressed. Of this characteristic I will give one illustration taken from the case of *Hill v. Simpson*,[7] in which Grant discussed the question of an executor's power to deal with the assets of his testator, and the extent to which he could be considered to be a trustee. He said:[8]

It is true that executors are in equity mere trustees for the performance of the will; yet in many respects and for many purposes third persons are entitled to consider them absolute owners. The mere circumstance that they are executors will not vitiate any transaction with them; for the power of disposition is generally incident; being frequently necessary; and a stranger shall not be put to examine whether in that particular instance that power has been discreetly exercized. But from the proposition that a third person is not bound to look to the trust in every respect and for every purpose, does it follow that, dealing with the executor for the assets, he may equally look upon him as absolute owner, and wholly overlook his character as trustee, when he knows that the executor is applying the assets to a purpose wholly foreign to his trust? No decision necessarily leads to such a conclusion.

Grant's logical mind made him an effective critic of some of the doctrines of equity. We have seen that he criticized the doctrine of illusory appointments.[9] He also criticized the rule that if money was left on a charitable trust which was illegal, e.g. because it was to educate children in the Roman Catholic religion, the property did not result to the next of

---

[1] (1805) 10 Ves. 470.
[2] Low v. Bouverie [1891] 3 Ch. 82; but it was pointed out that the decision in Burrowes v. Lock could be justified on the ground of estoppel, ibid at p. 101. Note that the remarks in Low v. Bouverie on Burrowes v. Lock are based on the decision in Derry v. Peek [1889] 14 A.C. 337; *quaere* whether the inferences drawn from Derry v. Peek are correct since the case of Nocton v. Lord Ashburton [1914] A.C. 932.
[3] Murray v. Lord Elibank (1806) 13 Ves. 1.
[4] Osborne v. Williams (1811) 18 Ves. 379.
[5] Sutton v. Chetwynd (1817) 3 Mer. 249.
[6] *Ex parte* Ilchester (1803) 7 Ves. 348 at pp. 379-380.
[7] (1801) 7 Ves. 152.   [8] At p. 166.   [9] Above 630, 660.

kin, but must be applied to a legal charity, because the testator
had shown a general charitable intention. He said :[1]

Whenever a testator is disposed to be charitable in his own way, and
upon his own principles, we are not to content ourselves with disappoint-
ing his intention if disapproved by us ; but we are to make him charitable
in our way and upon our principles. If once we discover in him any
charitable intention, that is supposed to be so liberal as to take in objects,
not only within his intention, but wholly adverse to it. It is not for
me to attempt to overturn the settled law and practice ; according to
which charitable bequests void as to one object may be appropriated
to another.

In the case of *Holmes v. Coghill*[2] he drew a clear distinction
between a power and a right of property, and criticized the
doctrine that, in favour of creditors, equity would aid the defective execution of a power. In the case of *Pratt v. Sladden*[3]
he pointed out that the manner in which equity had dealt with
the legal right of an executor to undisposed of residue had
given, and must continue to give, rise to much litigation ; for
different judges took different views as to what evidence of
intention was sufficient to bar that legal right and give the
property to the next of kin. The difficulty was partially met
by an Act of 1830 ;[4] but it was not till 1925 that the legal right
of the executor was wholly got rid of,[5] and with it the difficulties
created by the equitable modification of the legal rule.

These few illustrations of Grant's decisions make it clear
that he was one of the series of great Masters of the Rolls—
in the same class as men like Julius Caesar in the seventeenth,[6]
Jekyll and Kenyon in the eighteenth,[7] and Jessel in the nineteenth centuries.

Grant's successor was Sir Thomas Plumer.[8] He was born
in 1753 and was educated at Eton and University College,
Oxford. At Oxford he distinguished himself as a classical scholar,
and became a Vinerian scholar and a fellow of his college. He
was called to the bar by Lincoln's Inn in 1778, and went on the
Oxford and Welsh circuits. His first important case was the
defence of Rumbold in 1783, against whom a bill of pains and
penalties had been introduced in the House of Commons for
his conduct as governor of Madras. His success in that case
caused him to be selected as one of the counsel for Warren
Hastings. He spoke for three days in his defence on the first
article of the impeachment in February 1792, and for four days
in summing up the evidence for the defence on the second article

[1] Cary v. Abbot (1802) 7 Ves. at p. 494.
[2] (1802) 7 Ves. at pp. 506-507.
[3] (1807) 14 Ves. at p. 197. [4] 1 William IV c. 40.
[5] Administration of Estates Act 1925. 15 George V c. 23 § 49b.
[6] Vol. v 6, 261. [7] Vol. xii 219-222, 328.
[8] Foss, Judges ix 32-36 ; D.N.B.

in April 1793. He took silk in 1793, and at the end of the eighteenth and beginning of the nineteenth centuries he appeared in a number of state trials—he defended Reeves, O'Connor, and Melville, and he was counsel for the prosecution in the trials of Wall and Despard. "He had a great reputation as a tithe lawyer and had much employment before election committees."[1] In 1807 he became solicitor-general, and in 1812 attorney-general. In 1813 he was made the first Vice-Chancellor of England, and in 1818 he succeeded Grant as Master of the Rolls. He died in 1824.

There is no doubt that Plumer was an able lawyer. Romilly, it is true, said that no worse appointment to the position of Vice-Chancellor could have been made, that he was ignorant of equity[2] and even slower than Eldon in hearing cases,[3] and that he was quite incapable of discharging the duties of Master of the Rolls.[4] In his opinion Richards ought to have been made Vice-Chancellor, and it is said that Eldon admitted it, and had almost promised him the post.[5] But Romilly had a grudge against Plumer because he had opposed some of his bills for the reform of the criminal law.[6] There is no doubt that Campbell is right when he said that Plumer's defects were exaggerated by Romilly.[7] Scarlett said of him that he was not a good speaker, but admitted that he had considerable merit.[8] After all, he had served as a law officer, and therefore had a claim to the position of Vice-Chancellor. At any rate his decisions show that, though he was apt to be prolix, he was a sound lawyer. He assisted Eldon to decide the case of *Duke of Bedford v. Trustees of the British Museum*,[9] and his judgment states clearly the principle upon which the decision was given.[10] His decision in the case of *Gretton v. Haward*[11] is an able survey of the doctrine of election, and it establishes the proposition that an election to take against the instrument entails, not forfeiture of the benefit given, but a duty to compensate. His most famous decision is that in *Dearle v. Hall*.[12] Though that decision cannot be supported on all the grounds upon which Plumer based it, his view that the assignee of a reversionary interest in personalty, by giving notice to the trustee, completes his title, because the notice makes the trustee a trustee for him, and is thus the equivalent of taking possession,[13]

---

[1] Foss, Judges ix 34. [2] Life of Romilly (ed. 1842) ii 310.
[3] Ibid 374. [4] Ibid 481.
[5] Ibid 310 *note* ; Twiss, Life of Eldon ii 242-243.
[6] Life of Romilly ii 89 ; D.N.B.
[7] Chancellors vii 303-304. [8] P. C. Scarlett, Memoir of Lord Abinger 90.
[9] (1882) 2 My. and K. 552 ; above 634. [10] At pp. 570-575.
[11] (1819) 1 Swanst. 409. [12] (1823) 3 Russ. 1.
[13] At pp. 12-13.

has been sanctioned by the House of Lords;[1] and, notwithstanding the dislike of Lord Macnaghten for the rule,[2] it is in fact so reasonable that its scope has been extended by the Legislature.[3]

Plumer's successor, Robert Gifford,[4] was born at Exeter in 1779. Foss says:

The commencement of his life bore a striking similarity to that of Lord King[5] . . . The father of both carried on the same general business of grocer and linen-draper, residing in the same city, and some say in the same house; and though Robert Gifford was not doomed like Peter King to pursue for some time his father's business he had to go through the drudgery of an attorney's office for many years.

His success in that office encouraged him to try his fortunes at the bar. He became a member of the Middle Temple in 1800, and, having made himself a proficient special pleader, he practised in that capacity till his call to the bar in 1808. He soon got a large practice on the Western circuit and in London; and in 1817 he was made solicitor-general, and entered Parliament. In that capacity he prosecuted Watson for treason, and conducted the prosecutions of the Luddite rioters. In 1819 he became attorney-general, and in that capacity prosecuted Thistlewood and his associates, and opened the case against Queen Caroline. His opening speech was not a success, but his reply was an able summing up of the evidence against her. He had practised in the court of Chancery after he had become solicitor-general, and, after the death of Romilly, had acquired a leading practice in that court, and also a considerable practice in Scotch appeals to the House of Lords. In January 1824 he became Chief Justice of the Common Pleas and a peer. As a peer he was made deputy speaker of the House of Lords, and assisted in the hearing of Scotch appeals—a duty he fulfilled to the great satisfaction of the Scottish lawyers. In less than three months he resigned his Chief-Justiceship and became Master of the Rolls. He died prematurely in 1826. If he had survived he would probably have been Eldon's successor with Eldon's approval.[6]

There is no doubt that Gifford was an able lawyer. Tenterden[7]

---

[1] Foster v. Cockerell (1835) 3 Cl. and Fin. 456; cf. Loveredge v. Cooper (1828) 3 Russ. at pp. 57-57 per Lord Lyndhurst; Stephens v. Green [1895] 2 Ch. at p. 158 per Lindley, L.J. and at p. 164 per Kay, L.J.

[2] Ward v. Duncombe [1893] A.C. at pp. 392-394.

[3] Law of Property Act 1925, 15 George V § 137.

[4] Foss, Judges ix 17-22; D.N.B.

[5] For Lord King see vol. xii 210-214.   [6] Twiss, Life of Eldon ii 571.

[7] Tenterden in a letter to his friend Brydges written in Oct. 1813 says of Gifford, " he will probably be his (Eldon's) successor: he is a good lawyer and a sound headed man; warm rather than vigorous, and without dignity of person or manner. Yet I think he is the fittest person to succeed one for whom a successor must soon be found—though perhaps an equal never will be," cited Campbell, Chief Justices iii 296.

and Eldon[1] had a high opinion of his abilities; and his decisions as Master of the Rolls are a sufficient refutation of Twiss's view,[2] founded perhaps on contemporary opinion,[3] that his knowledge of equity was insufficient. They show that he had a logical mind, a power of clear exposition, and a considerable mastery of the principles of equity. In the case of *Purdew v. Jackson*[4] he gave a very able survey of the wife's right to take by survivorship her choses in action not reduced to possession by her husband, of what property is a chose in action for the purpose of this rule, and what is a reduction into possession. In the case of *Smith v. Attersoll*[5] he expounded the law as to secret trusts; in the case of *Franklin v. Bank of England*[6] he held in a clearly reasoned judgment that an executor can transfer stock, though it had been specifically bequeathed; and, in the case of *Goddard v. Snow*,[7] in giving effect to the rule that a settlement in fraud of marital rights is void, he gave a lucid statement of the principles underlying that rule.

Of Lyndhurst, Gifford's successor as Master of the Rolls, I shall speak in the next chapter. He held that office only for eight months, and was succeeded by Sir John Leach.

Leach[8] was born at Bedford in 1760, and was educated at Bedford Grammar School. He entered the Middle Temple in 1785, and was called to the bar in 1790. He soon got a good practice on the Home circuit and the Surrey sessions. In 1800 he left the circuit and the sessions and began to practise in the court of Chancery. He succeeded so well that he was called within the bar with a patent of precedence in 1807. In 1806 he had been elected to Parliament as a member for Seaford. In Parliament he won the favour of the Prince of Wales by defending the Duke of York against the attacks of Col. Wardle in 1809, and by supporting the regency bill of 1811. He was rewarded by the Chancellorship of the Duchy of Cornwall in 1816; and in 1817 he was made chief justice of Chester. Though he had opposed the Act of 1813 which created a Vice-Chancellor, he was appointed to that office in 1818 in succession to Plumer. He was an eager supporter of the Prince's project to get a divorce, managed the Milan commission which was sent out to get evidence against the Princess,[9] and hinted that the Prince was not properly supported in this project by his ministers.[10] He succeeded Gifford

---

[1] Letter to Peel cited Campbell, Chancellors vii 448.
[2] Life of Eldon ii 507.
[3] Eldon alludes to this opinion which he thought was mistaken, Campbell, Chancellors vii 448.
[4] (1842) 1 Russ. 1.
[5] (1826) 1 Russ. 266.
[6] Ibid 575.
[7] Ibid 485.
[8] Foss, Judges ix 92-95; D.N.B.
[9] Campbell, Chancellors vii 330.
[10] Wilberforce, Diary v. 54, cited ibid 329 n.

as Master of the Rolls in 1827. His hopes that he might be appointed Chancellor in 1830[1] were frustrated by the appointment of Brougham. He died in 1834.

Leach was a good advocate, since he was a clear and forcible speaker with a practitioner's knowledge of law.[2] But as a judge he was a failure. Romilly had, justifiably, a poor opinion of his qualities as a lawyer and a judge.[3] It is true that he decided quickly,[4] but he decided before he had fully heard the case. Terminer sans oyer was his fault, it was said, just as oyer sans terminer was Eldon's fault;[5] and Romilly, though he deplored Eldon's slowness, was forced to admit that he was " better pleased with the tardy justice of the principal than with the swift injustice of the deputy."[6] His irritable temper made him so unpopular with the bar " that a deputation of the most distinguished counsel practising in his court waited upon him with a formal remonstrance upon his intemperate and dictatorial deportment towards the profession."[7] In fact he despised his brother lawyers. On the strength of his friendship with the Prince and other aristocratic personages, he tried to pose as a man of fashion,[8] and assumed an affected manner which he considered to be appropriate to that character.[9] The Prince was much amused by this foible, as the following story related by Eldon shows :[10]

[1] Greville, Memoirs ii 70.   [2] Life of Romilly ii 397.

[3] " He is of all the persons almost I have known in the profession, the worst qualified for any judicial situation. He is extremely deficient in knowledge as a lawyer. All that he knows he has acquired, not by any previous study which would have enabled him to understand the general system of our law, and the grounds and reasons of its particular provisions, but by his daily practice. In judgment he is more deficient than any man possessed of so clear an understanding that I ever met with," Life of Romilly ii 397.

[4] Ibid 481.

[5] Foss, op cit. 94-95 ; the contrast between the two inspired the following lines :

> In Equity's high court there are
> Two sad extremes, 'tis clear ;
> Excessive slowness strikes us there,
> Excessive quickness here.

> Their source, 'twixt good and evil, brings
> A difficulty nice ;
> The first from Eldon's *virtue* springs,
> The latter from his *Vice*.

[6] Townsend, Twelve Eminent Judges ii 439.   [7] Foss, op. cit. 94.

[8] Romilly, Life ii 397, spoke of his ambition " to unite the character of a fine gentleman to that of a great lawyer. Constant attendance at the opera and at the gayest assemblies appears, in his opinion, to be as necessary to the support of his reputation as his presence in Westminster Hall ; and he prides himself upon hastening every night from the dull atmosphere of the Rolls and Lincoln's Inn to the brilliant circles of high birth and fashion."

[9] Twiss, Life of Eldon ii 301-302.   [10] Ibid 302.

It has long been the habit to give the Chancellor carrying his purse the nick-name of Bags. When Sir John Leach was Chancellor to the Prince, he also had a purse ; and the Prince said, as Sir John was not so rough in his manners as a King's Chancellor usually was, but a much more polite person, he should call him " Reticule."

In fact Leach, though an effective advocate, was a poor lawyer because he was not really interested in the law, and a very bad judge because, in addition to his inadequate knowledge of law, his impatience and bad temper made him incapable of giving an adequate hearing to the cases which came before him.

Leach's successor as Vice-Chancellor was Anthony Hart,[1] who had been an equity practitioner for forty-six years. But he only held that office from May to October 1827, since in November 1827 he was made Lord Chancellor of Ireland. In that capacity he proved himself to be so able a judge that none of his judgments were reversed. His successor—Lancelot Shadwell[2]—was the last who held the title of Vice-Chancellor of England, given to the single Vice-Chancellor provided for by the Act of 1813.[3] Shadwell, who was the son of a distinguished real property lawyer, was born in 1779 and was educated at Eton and St. John's College, Cambridge, of which college he became a fellow in 1800. He was a considerable athlete as well as a distinguished mathematical and classical scholar.[4] It is said that he once walked from Cambridge to London in one day at the rate of four miles an hour throughout the journey ; and in later days he was so fond of the water that he bathed in the river all the year round, and once in the long vacation was said to have granted an injunction while so occupied. He was called to the bar by Lincoln's Inn in 1803, and took silk in 1821. He confined his practice to the Lord Chancellor's court because he did not think it possible to do justice to his clients if he took briefs in other courts. In 1826 he entered Parliament, and in 1827 he proposed bills for the limitation of the period for bringing a writ of right and for reform of the law of dower, which failed to become law. In 1827 he succeeded Hart as Vice-Chancellor. He held that post till his death in 1850. He was a weak judge. " The tyranny," says Selborne,[5] " which successive leaders exercised over Shadwell would be inconceivable to those who did not witness it." His earliest favourite was Snyder, then it was Knight Bruce and then

[1] Foss, Judges ix 23-24 ; D.N.B.
[2] Foss, Judges ix 261-264 ; D.N.B.
[3] 53 George III c. 24 ; above 190, 605.
[4] He was seventh wrangler and a Chancellor's medallist.
[5] Memorials, Family and Personal i 374-376 ; see also Memoirs of Sir John Rolt 63-64.

Bethell—the future Lord Westbury.[1] But he was not without ability as a lawyer, and he was a patient and courteous judge.[2]

During this period the development of equity, even more than the development of the common law, was hampered by a vicious system of procedure and pleading. With the reform of that system I shall deal in the next chapter. Because its development was less affected by the new political, economic, and social developments of this and the following period, the attention of the Legislature was concentrated upon these reforms in procedure and pleading rather than upon reforms in its substantive rules. We shall see that down to the Judicature Acts only minor reforms were made in its substantive rules. For the most part these rules were developed and elaborated by the courts ; and the increase in the number of the courts of equity by the creation of additional Vice-Chancellors and of the court of appeal in Chancery[3] made this development and elaboration more speedy than it had been in the preceding period. But equity follows the law, so that it could not be wholly unaffected by some of the important changes in, and additions to, the law made by the Legislature. Changes in the law of bankruptcy, for instance, and the rise of the limited company, resulted in new applications of equitable principles and additions to equitable doctrines. With the history of the development and elaboration of equitable principles, and with the repercussion of changes in the statute law upon them, I shall deal in the second Part of this Book.

VIII

SOME EMINENT CIVILIANS

The greatest of all the civilians in the whole history of English law is William Scott, Lord Stowell. I shall, in the first place, give some account of his career and of his place in our legal history, and then say something of some of the more notable of the other civilians.

William Scott, Lord Stowell[4] was the elder brother of John Scott, Lord Eldon. There are some remarkable resemblances between the careers and characters of the two men and one remarkable contrast. Both were fellows of University College, Oxford. Both were knighted within two months of one another,

---

[1] Why is Shadwell like King Jeroboam ? Because he has set up an idol in Bethell, Nash, Life of Westbury i 95.
[2] Memoirs of Sir John Rolt 65.   [3] Vol i 334-335.
[4] Townsend, Twelve Eminent Judges ii 279-365 ; E. S. Roscoe, Lord Stowell ; W. E. Surtees, Lords Stowell and Eldon ; Brougham, Historical Sketches ii 73-80 ; N. Bentwick f. 9, Lord Stowell (Great Jurists of the World) 517-531 ; D.N.B. ; Lord Sankey, Lord Stowell, L.Q.R. lii 327-344.

and they attended their first levée together, William as advocate-general and John as solicitor-general. They were both made Privy Councillors on the same day, and William became judge of the court of Admiralty less than a year before John became Chief Justice of the Common Pleas. William resigned his position as judge of the court of Admiralty the year after John resigned his position as Lord Chancellor. Just as John completed the development of the modern system of equity, so William settled many fundamental principles of Admiralty and ecclesiastical law, and created the system of Prize law which governs both England and the United States. Both had great social charm. This parallelism between the careers and characters of the two brothers was once, it is said, alluded to by George III in the hunting field. " Being in at the death of a stag, which had given the field a very bad run, while a stag of the same herd had afforded excellent sport the day before, ' Ah !' exclaimed the King, ' there are not often two Scotts to be found in the same family.' "[1] The great contrast between the two brothers is the form in which their contributions to English law is expressed. We have seen that there is no spark of literature in Eldon's judgments,[2] but all Stowell's judgments have a markedly literary flavour and some are great literature.

I shall deal first with Stowell's life and character ; secondly, with the reasons why his work has had so large an influence on English law ; and thirdly, with some of his decisions in the various spheres of the practice of the civilians.

Stowell's Life and Character

Stowell was born on October 8, 1745. The approach of the Young Pretender to Newcastle was expected, and on that account Mrs. Scott was removed to Heworth on the south side of the Tyne in the County of Durham. There William Scott was born ; and it was this accident of birth in the county of Durham which influenced directly his own career, and directly that of his brother John, because it made him eligible for a Durham scholarship at Corpus College, Oxford, and for a fellowship at University College, Oxford. If he had not been born in the county of Durham he might not have gone to Oxford ; and if he had not gone to Oxford, both he and his brother John would probably have remained at Newcastle, and neither would have entered the legal profession. So momentous in its effects upon our legal history was this accident of birth.

William Scott was elected a scholar of Corpus on February 24, 1761, and a fellow of University College on December 13,

---

[1] Townsend, op. cit. ii 306.   [2] Above 624.

1764. At University College he succeeded the celebrated orientalist and Indian judge Sir William Jones[1] as a tutor of the college ; and he was a very successful tutor, for in four out of five years (1768-1772) the Chancellor's prize for English prose was gained by members of University College.[2] He was appointed Camden reader in ancient history in 1774. His lectures were as successful as Blackstone's [3]—in fact Gibbon mentions Scott's work as a tutor and reader and Blackstone's lectures as evidence that the state of the University had improved since he knew it as an undergraduate.[4] Like Blackstone he gave both his time and his money to help the Bodleian. His lectures as Camden reader, like Blackstone's lectures as Vinerian professor,[5] spread his fame outside Oxford. Dr. Parr said of them :[6]

To these discourses, which . . . captivated the young and interested the old—which are argumentative without formality, and brilliant without gaudiness—and in which the happiest selection of topics was united with the most luminous arrangement of matter—it cannot be unsafe for me to pay the tribute of my praise, because every hearer was an admirer, and every admirer will be a witness.

The lectures were not published by Scott, and he left instructions that they never should be published. But Gibbon thought that they ought to be published,[7] and Dean Milman, who saw the MS. said that, though then out of date, they were remarkable for their literary qualities. Chambers,[8] one of his colleagues at University College and later Vinerian Professor and an Indian judge, had introduced him to Dr. Johnson. His friendship with Johnson, whose intellectual powers he admired and respected[9] his literary ability, and his social charm, secured his election to Johnson's famous club in 1778—the year after he migrated from Oxford to London. Throughout Johnson's life he was one

[1] Vol. xi 220-221 ; vol. xii 393-394.
[2] Twiss, Life of Eldon i 58 n.   [3] Vol. xii 720-721.
[4] " Many students have been attracted by the merit and reputation of Sir William Scott, then a tutor in University College, and now conspicuous in the profession of the Civil law : my personal acquaintance with that gentleman has inspired me with a just esteem for his abilities and knowledge ; and I am assured that his lectures on history would compose, were they given to the public, a most valuable treatise," The Autobiography of Edward Gibbon, Memoir F., pp. 93-94 ; for Gibbon's appreciation of Blackstone's lectures and Commentaries see vol. xii App. IV pp. 750-754.
[5] Vol. xii 706.   [6] Quart. Rev. lxxv 33.
[7] Above n. 4 (this page).   [8] Above 595, 596.
[9] " William Scott informed me that on the death of the late Lord Lichfield, who was Chancellor of the University of Oxford, he said to Johnson, ' What a pity it is, Sir, that you did not follow the profession of the law. You might have been Lord Chancellor of Great Britain, and attained to the dignity of a peerage ; and now that the title of Lichfield, your native city is extinct, you might have had it.' Johnson, upon this, seemed much agitated ; and, in an angry tone, exclaimed, ' Why will you vex me by suggesting this, when it is too late ? ' " Boswell, Life of Johnson, April 17, 1778.

of his closest friends, and Johnson made him one of his executors and left him the Dictionnaire de Commerce and Lectius's edition of the Greek poets—books which were suitable both to his professional and his classical studies.

It would seem that soon after Scott went to Oxford he had resolved to enter the legal profession, for he had become a student of the Middle Temple in 1762. But his success as a tutor and then as Camden reader caused him temporarily to abandon this project. It revived after his father's death in 1776, as the result of which he became possessed of an independent income.[1] He resigned his tutorship at University College in that year, and, in the following year, he took chambers in the Middle Temple. In 1779 he took the degree of D.C.L. and became a fellow of Doctors' Commons. In 1780 he was called to the bar. His connection with educational work at Oxford came to an end when he resigned his Camden readership in 1785.

Scott acted very wisely when he resolved to practise as a civilian, and not at the common law or equity bars. He was not a ready speaker or debater—in fact when he first began to practise he read his speeches from a MS.[2] He had an academic mind, capable of surveying and explaining the facts of a complex case and the legal principles applicable to those facts ; but his mind was not well fitted for the cut and thrust of the common law bar, or sufficiently rapid in its operations to make him a successful examiner or cross examiner of witnesses. Brougham correctly diagnosed the character of his intellect when he said,[3]

Confining himself to the comparatively narrow and sequestered walks of the consistorial tribunals, he . . . had never acquired the habits which forensic strife is found to form—the preternatural power of suddenly producing all the mind's resources at the call of the moment and shifting their application nimbly from point to point, as that exigency varies in its purpose or its direction. But . . . if the retired and almost solitary habits of the comparatively secluded walk in which he moved, had given him little relish for the strenuous and vehement warfare of rapid argumentation and the logic of unprepared debate, his vast superiority was apparent when, as from an eminence, he was called to survey the whole field of dispute, and to marshall the variegated facts, disentangle the intricate mazes, and array the conflicting reasons which were calculated to distract or suspend men's judgment. If ever the praise of being luminous could be justly bestowed upon human compositions it was upon his judgments.

In fact there is a close parallel between the character of the minds and the quality of the achievements of Blackstone and

---

[1] Surtees, op. cit. 21-22.

[2] " Those professionally opposed to him objected to this innovation in their routine ; but he persisted for some months as he had begun, till he had acquired greater confidence, or more accuracy and elegance," Townsend, op. cit. ii 294.

[3] Historical Sketches ii 73-74.

Scott. Both combined legal learning and university learning. Both had great literary gifts which enabled them to give a unique literary form to their writings upon legal subjects. Both had orderly and systematic minds. Both combined academic learning in the law with practical experience of its working.[1]

Besides these intellectual characteristics which fitted him to shine as a civilian, there were other reasons why he was better fitted for the business of a civilian than for the business of a common law or equity barrister. His classical training and his knowledge of ancient history enabled him to understand and assimilate the authorities, English and foreign, on the Roman civil law, upon which the procedure of the courts which administered law at Doctors' Commons was based, and also the authorities, English and foreign, on those questions of international law which fell within the sphere of the civilian practice. That same training and knowledge and his long residence at Oxford gave him " an insight into the questions involving the rights and interests, the difficulties and dangers, of the Church of England in his own day, equal to that, which his studies, as professor of ancient history would supply him with respecting the church catholic of primitive times."[2] He had a practical knowledge of maritime affairs. His father's business was concerned with shipping, and after his father's death he had for a short time carried on that business.[3] His brother Henry had been concerned in a privateering venture, and he had consulted William as to difficulties which had arisen out of the misconduct of the master and crew.[4] He had necessarily studied those branches of English law which were related to the practice of the civilians. He combined with his academic learning and literary gifts the shrewd business-like outlook of a man of the world, which was strengthened and informed when his success as an advocate brought him into closer contact with the many different problems which arose in the course of the variegated practice of the civilians.

It is not surprising that his success at Doctors' Commons was very rapid. In 1782, the first year after his " year of silence"[5] had expired, he wrote saying that he was " exceedingly oppressed with business ";[6] and in the same year he was appointed advocate to the Lord High Admiral. In January 1783 John Scott wrote that he had been given a sinecure place by the Archbishop of Canterbury which was worth over £400 a year. " His success is wonderful," wrote John, " and he has been fortunate beyond example."[7] The sinecure place was the post of registrar of the

[1] For Blackstone's intellectual characteristics see vol. xii 717-720.
[2,5] Surtees, op. cit. 63.   [3] Ibid.   [4] Ibid 64-65.
For the year of silence imposed upon advocates when admitted to Doctors' Commons see vol. xii 47.   [6] Surtees, op. cit. 66.   [7] Ibid 67.

court of faculties ; and other more important places soon followed. In 1788 he was appointed judge of the consistory court of London, King's advocate, vicar-general of the province of Canterbury, commissary of the city and diocese of Canterbury, and chancellor of the diocese of London. In 1790 he was appointed master of the faculties, and in 1798 judge of the court of Admiralty.

Only one untoward incident marked his career as a judge. As the judge of the Bishop of London's consistorial court he had ordered one Beaurain to appear as guardian *ad litem* for his son, and, on his refusing so to do, he had excommunicated him. The sentence had been upheld as regular by Sir John Nicholl, the Dean of the Arches, and the excommunication had issued and had been published. The result was that Beaurain who was an attorney, had lost his business. Scott had given him £150 to relieve his necessities but refused to give more, Beaurain then petitioned Parliament and brought an action on the case against Scott on the grounds that the court had no authority to order him to become guardian *ad litem* to his son, and that no regular citation or monition had been served upon him.[1] Whether or not the excommunication was regular was a doubtful point of law.[2] Sir John Nicholl[3] gave evidence that it was regular. Lord Ellenborough, C. J. treated this question of the practice of the ecclesiastical courts as a question of fact, and left the case to the jury. They found a verdict for the plaintiff with 40/- damages, saying, however, that " they did not mean to throw the slightest reflection upon the highly respectable character of Sir William Scott."[4]

Scott's success as an advocate led him to aspire to a seat in Parliament. The death of Sir Roger Newdigate in 1780 left the representation of Oxford University vacant. Scott and Sir William Jones were both candidates. Dr. Johnson rightly opined that neither would succeed ;[5] and though Jones, whose politics were too liberal for the University, resigned in favour of Scott, he was beaten by Sir William Dolben. In 1784 he was elected for Downton, but was unseated on petition. It was not till 1790 that he was again returned for Downton. He represented that place till 1801 when he became member for Oxford University, which he represented till he was raised to the peerage in 1821. His politics were as conservative as those of his brother. But he was not an active member of Parliament. He himself said that " it was always with great reluctance

---

[1] Beaurain v. Scott (1813) 3 Camp. 388.

[2] Lord Eldon doubted whether the court could order a person to be guardian *ad litem* to his son in these circumstances, see Boraine's Case (1809) 16 Ves. at p. 348.

[3] For Nicholl see below 691-696.   [4] 3 Camp. at p. 391.

[5] Townsend, op. cit. ii 307, citing a letter to Mrs. Thrale.

and not infrequently with some degree of personal pain that he obtruded himself on the notice of the House."[1] It was mainly on bills which dealt with ecclesiastical or Admiralty matters that he intervened. At the instigation of Romilly[2] he brought in the bill which became the Act of 1813,[3] by which, *inter alia*, the process of the ecclesiastical courts was reformed. He also introduced the bill which became the Act of 1817, by which farming and trading by the clergy, residence and appointment and pay of curates were regulated.[4] He was opposed to all extensive reforms. He successfully opposed Curwen's tithe bills, he beat the government on a proposal to exempt dissenters' chapels from the payment of rates, and he opposed a bill which provided temporal penalties for the offence of adultery.[5] He opposed Horne Tooke's contention that a priest in orders was eligible for a seat in the House of Commons. He defended his own court of Admiralty when attacked in the House of Commons,[6] and, though he had at first opposed,[7] he later supported the bill to reform the office of registrar of the court of Admiralty[8]—though, to Romilly's disgust, he succeeded in amending it in such a way that its original supporters voted against its third reading.[9] When he did intervene in debate his speeches were carefully prepared, and show the same literary qualities as his judgments.

In 1821 he resigned his position as judge of the consistory court of the bishop of London, and in the same year he was raised to the peerage and took the title of Lord Stowell. His only speech in the House of Lords was on the Marriage Act of 1822.[10] Age and infirmity compelled him to resign his position as judge of the court of Admiralty on December 27, 1827. In the following year Sir Walter Scott, after dining with him, entered in his diary " I met my old and much esteemed friend Lord Stowell, looking very frail and even comatose. *Quantum mutatus*. He was one of the pleasantest men I ever knew."[11] His faculties gradually failed and during the last two years of his life his reason failed. He never knew of the death of his son in 1835. He died January 29, 1836.

Stowell was married twice. By his first marriage he had, besides two other children who died in infancy, a son who

---

[1] Townsend, op. cit. ii 308.
[2] Life of Romilly ii 233-234, 263, 318-319.
[3] 53 George III c. 127 ; above 190, 269, 423.   [4] Above 418.
[5] Townsend, op. cit. ii 311-312 ; Life of Romilly ii 461-462, 484-485, 487-488.
[6] Townsend, op. cit. ii 309.
[7] Life of Romilly ii 262.   [8] Ibid 320.
[9] Ibid ; the bill by implication sanctioned the practice, during the life of the present holder, of allowing the registrar to keep the interest on the suitors' money in court ; Romilly's object was to put a stop to this abuse.
[10] For this Act see above 421, 422.   [11] Cited Surtees, op. cit. 136.

pre-deceased him, and a daughter who married Lord Sidmouth. His second marriage, which had a curious history, was the one great mistake he made in his life. It was brought about in this wise : [1] In 1812 the Marquis of Sligo was indicted at the Admiralty sessions of the Old Bailey for inducing two seamen to desert the navy and take service on his ship. For this he was sentenced to a fine and a short term of imprisonment. The marquis's mother had been impressed by Stowell's manner, and shortly after the two became acquainted and within four months, much to the amusement of London society, they married. It was not a happy marriage. Stowell was then aged sixty-eight and his wife forty-five. The disposition and habits of both were set, and were quite incompatible. "The wife was generous, the husband parsimonious ; the wife liked her evenings at home, the husband preferred the society of the Club and of his legal friends." [2] Naturally they became estranged. Fortunately for Stowell she died in 1817 "during a visit to Paris and Amsterdam while Stowell was making a tour in Switzerland." [3] He continued to travel in Switzerland for some weeks after he had heard of his wife's death. [4]

Stowell had his faults. He was too parsimonious for a man of his wealth, and was careless of his personal appearance. [5] He was a great eater and a great drinker of port [6]—Eldon said of him that "he would answer for it his brother never had fewer than 365 dinners in one year, but how many more he would not take upon himself to affirm." [7] But his virtues greatly predominated. He had strong family affections. He delighted in simple pleasures—he would always stop to look at a Punch and Judy show ; [8] and "it was at all times a current observation that the person who first saw any sight exhibited in London, be it the production of nature or of art or artifice . . . was Sir William Scott." [9] His social gifts were recognized by all. All agreed that he was a delightful companion, a witty conversationalist, ever ready with an apt story, or an appropriate quotation or retort. [10] Many were the stories which circulated of his sayings. They convey but a slight impression of his powers, for, as Brougham said, [11] "it is of the nature of the refined essence

---

[1] Surtees, op. cit. 128-135.   [2] Roscoe, Lord Stowell 25-26.
[3] Ibid.   [4] Surtees, op. cit. 135.
[5] Ibid 137-138, 140.   [6] Ibid 139.
[7] Townsend, op. cit. ii 360.   [8] Ibid ii 358.
[9] Brougham, Historical Sketches ii 77 ; cp. Surtees, op. cit. 140-141.
[10] Here is an example : "When a late celebrated duchess bantered the consistory judge, and enquired 'how his court would manage if he himself should be guilty of a faux pas,' he answered . . . 'that the idea of such an embarrassing situation had only occurred to him since he had become acquainted with her Grace,'" Townsend, op. cit. ii 363 n.
[11] Historical Sketches ii 78.

in which the spirit of the best society consists, not to keep."
But, as Townsend says,[1]

to a lawyer the greatest of all conversational treats was to meet Lord
Eldon and Lord Stowell together in a friendly dinner party of lawyers.
Here, sure of deference and appreciation, each brother would playfully
unbend after the labours of the day ; talk one against the other ; and
narrate, alternately, professional anecdotes. In playful banter they
would not spare each other. A neighbour having asked Lord Stowell
aside, the conversation being on feats of sportsmanship, if his brother
killed much : " Nothing," he quietly answered, " he kills nothing but
time." The maligned sportsman had his revenge. When asked whether
Lord Stowell took much exercize, " None," he said, " but the exercize
of eating and drinking." On another occasion a remark being hazarded
that Lord Stowell seemed more abstemious at his own table than at
a friend's, the Chancellor remarked archly, " he will take any *given*
quantity of wine."

Such then, was the man. We must now examine the reasons
why he was able to exercise so large an influence on English
law.

The reasons for Stowell's influence on English law

There were four main reasons for Stowell's great influence
on English law.

In the first place, Stowell had a remarkable combination
of intellectual qualities. He had, as Brougham said, a clear
logical mind which enabled him to grasp rapidly the essential
issues in the case which he was trying, to come to the right
conclusions upon the facts, and to state and explain the principles which must be applied in the light of these facts to determine these issues.[2] He had a full mind—a mind well stored with
classical and modern learning and literature, and with the
technical rules both of the civil law and of English law. He
had the synthetic mind of an historian which enabled him to
appreciate the manner in which rules of law had developed
in the past, and the form which their future development ought
in consequence to take. He had, in addition, that measure
of legal statesmanship which is the mark of the greatest of our
lawyers. That quality was more especially needed by a judge
of a Prize court ; and it is because Stowell possessed it that
he was able to create our system of prize law. Lastly, he had,
as I have said, a power of literary expression which gave to his
judgments a form which enhanced the effect of his grasp of
principle, his mastery of the authorities, and his statesmanlike
solutions of difficult problems.

The literary form which he gave to his judgments was not

[1] Op. cit. ii 364.   [2] Above 671.

attained without effort. " He is said to have had the press stopped for the correction of a single line, and to have been anxious even in the marshalling of his colons "; and Phillimore testifies to the repeated revisions and corrections of his manuscripts and proofs.[1] An anthology of striking passages could be selected from his judgments. One of the best known is the passage from his judgment in *The Indian Chief*,[2] in which he explains why an American residing at Calcutta must be deemed to have a British commercial domicil, and was therefore amenable to the law against trading with the enemy. It had been argued that, being resident at Calcutta, he was a subject, not of the King of Great Britain, but of the Mogul, so that not being a British subject, he was liable to no penalty for trading with Great Britain's enemies. That argument Stowell answered as follows :[3]

Taking it that such a paramount sovereignty, on the part of the Mogul princes, really and solidly exists, and that Great Britain cannot be deemed to possess a sovereign right there; still it is to be remembered that wherever a mere factory is founded in the Eastern parts of the world, European persons, trading under the shelter and protection of those establishments, are conceived to take their national character from that association under which they live and carry on their commerce.

Traders in the East, unlike those in European countries, do not normally mix with the natives of the countries in which they are resident, and so [4]

Not trading under any recognized authority of their own original country, they have been held to derive their present character from that of the association or factory, under whose protection they live and carry on their trade.

Another good example is his elaborate judgment in the case of *Evans v. Evans*[5] in which Mrs Evans sued her husband for a separation on the ground of cruelty. At the opening of his judgment he explained the reasons why the law refused to allow a separation unless cogent reasons, such as cruelty clearly proved, existed. It is not only a good example of Stowell's judicial style, but it also states clearly the reasons for the views as to the need for maintaining the permanence of the marriage tie which were then generally accepted, and later were at the back of the minds of the Legislature when it reformed the law of divorce. Here is the passage.[6]

---

[1] Townsend, op. cit. ii 320.   [2] (1801) 3 C. Rob. 12, 22.
[3] Ibid at pp. 28-29.
[4] This sentence is a condensation of Lord Stowell's intervening remarks : it is not clear, from the MS., how much of the judgment the learned author intended to reproduce. (Eds.)
[5] (1790) 1 Hagg. Con. 35.   [6] At pp. 35-37.

The humanity of the court has been loudly and repeatedly invoked. Humanity is the second virtue of courts, but undoubtedly the first is justice. If it were a question of humanity simply, and of humanity which confined its views merely to the happiness of the present parties, it would be a question easily decided upon first impressions. Everybody must feel a wish to sever those who wish to live separate from each other, who cannot live together with any degree of harmony, and consequently with any degree of happiness ; but my situation does not allow me to indulge the feelings, much less the *first* feelings of an individual. The law has said that married persons shall not be *legally* separated upon the mere disinclination of one or both to cohabit together. The disinclination must be founded upon reasons, which the law approves, and it is my duty to see whether those reasons exist in the present case. To vindicate the policy of the law is no necessary part of the office of a judge ; but if it were, it would not be difficult to show that the law in this respect has acted with its usual wisdom and humanity, with that true wisdom, and that real humanity, that regards the general interests of mankind. For though in particular cases the repugnance of the law to dissolve the obligations of matrimonial cohabitation may operate with great severity upon individuals ; yet it must be carefully remembered, that the general happiness of the married life is secured by its indissolubility. When people understand that they *must* live together, except for a very few reasons known to the law, they learn to soften by mutual accommodation that yoke which they know they cannot shake off ; they become good husbands and good wives, from the necessity of remaining husbands and wives ; for necessity is a powerful master in teaching the duties which it imposes. If it were once understood, that upon mutual disgust married persons might be legally separated, many couples who now pass through the world with mutual comfort, with attention to their common offspring and to the moral order of civil society, might have been at this moment living in a state of mutual unkindness—in a state of estrangement from their common offspring—and in a state of the most licentious and unreserved immorality. In this case, as in many others, the happiness of some individuals must be sacrificed to the greater and more general good.

In the second place, Stowell's influence was due to the stage of development which ecclesiastical, maritime, and prize law had reached when he became a judge. We have seen that it was not till he became the judge of the court of Admiralty that we begin to get a regular series of the reports of cases decided in that court,[1] and it was not till 1822, when Haggard published his reports of cases decided in the consistory court of London from 1789-1821, that regular reports of cases decided in the ecclesiastical courts began to appear.[2] As Stowell himself recognized,[3] this scarcity of authority gave his genius much freer play than it would otherwise have had. It therefore enabled him to harmonize and systematize all these bodies of law.

---

[1] Vol. xii 105. 　　　　　　　　　　　[2] Ibid 106.

[3] " This dearth of direct authority . . . drives us necessarily to the consideration of what is the most reasonable rule in principle, and the most useful and beneficial in practice ; aided as it may be by the prevailing practice of other maritime states," The Neptune (1824) 1 Hagg. Ad. at p. 235.

" For a generation," Lord Sumner has said,[1] " he was rather a law giver than a judge in the ordinary sense of the term. Upon many maritime points his judgments are still the only law." When they were given they were not popular with the Americans who, both as neutrals and later as belligerents, suffered by them. But such is their soundness that the Americans eventually accepted them. Judge Story, in a letter to Stowell acknowledging the present of a copy of some of his judgments, said :[2]

In the excitement caused by the hostilities then raging between our countries, I frequently impugned your judgments and considered them as severe and partial, but on a calm review of your decisions after a lapse of years, I am bound to confess my entire conviction both of their accuracy and equity. I have taken care that they shall form the basis of the maritime law of the United States, and I have no hesitation in saying that they ought to do so in that of every civilized country in the world.

At the same time the fact that he was well reported by Christopher Robinson, Edwards, Dodson, and Haggard made it possible for his judgments to become the original authority for very many principles and rules. It was a happy accident that the first appearance of regular reports should coincide with the judicial career of the greatest civilian which this country has ever produced.

In the third place, the long duration of the Napoleonic wars gave Stowell the chance of settling permanently the prize law of Great Britain.[3] In prize cases prohibitions were not issued after Coke's fall in 1616,[4] so that the court of Admiralty had a free hand in the development of prize law. During the course of the eighteenth century it was recognized that the prize jurisdiction of the court was quite distinct from its instance jurisdiction,[5] and that it administered not municipal, but international law.[6] Here was Stowell's opportunity ; for the ecclesiastical and maritime jurisdiction of the courts over which he presided was very small as compared with the mass of prize cases which the Napoleonic war brought to his court.

He used his opportunity so well that he created a system of prize law which was not, like the prize law of some continental states " an unsystematic and indefinite collection of administrative decrees, decisions, and academic opinions,"[7] but a definite body of principles and rules. This definite body of principles and rules, which depend on Lord Stowell's decisions, is the international law administered by the Prize court ; and it

---

[1] D.N.B.   [2] Cited Townsend, op. cit. ii 335.
[3] For the history of the prize jurisdiction see vol. i 561-568.
[4] Marsden, Law and Custom of the Sea i 359 ; vol. i 564.
[5] Lindo v. Rodney (1781) 2 Dougl. at p. 614, cited vol. i 564-565.
[6] Ibid at p. 616 ; below 680 ; vol. i 565-566.
[7] Roscoe, Lord Stowell 51.

is safe to say that it is more definite and better obeyed than any other part of international law. The reason for these characteristics of British prize law is the fact that its development by decided cases has given it the precision of a body of municipal law. The best illustration of this fact is the decision of the Privy Council in the case of *The Zamora*,[1] which, as we have seen, overrules a dictum of Lord Stowell, and lays it down that an Order in Council can no more alter an established rule of the international law administered by the Prize court than it can alter an established rule of English law.[2]

In the fourth place, his industry was as great as his talents. In the year 1806 he gave 2206 decrees and judgments. In addition he was often called on to advise the Lords of the Admiralty, and he had his work in the ecclesiastical courts of which he was judge.[3]

These were the reasons for Stowell's great influence upon English law. We must now look at some of his decisions which are the foundation of important principles of our modern law.

Stowell's decisions

Stowell's greatest work was done in the Prize courts. Therefore it is the effect of some of his decisions in that court that we must first consider.

We have seen that Stowell, like Mansfield,[4] emphasized the fact that a Prize court administers international law;[5] and that foreigners had the right to insist that that law, and that law alone, should be applied to determine their rights and duties. British subjects on the other hand, must regard it as a court which administers their own municipal law as well as international law, so that they may be subject to rules which do not apply to the foreigner.[6] It follows from this premise that the court, though locally situate in Great Britain, must apply the rules of international law impartially as between neutrals and belligerents. Stowell said[7] that he sat in his court,

not to deliver occasional and shifting opinions to serve present purposes of particular national interest, but to administer with indifference that justice which the law of nations holds out without distinction to independent states, some happening to be neutral and some belligerent. The seat of judicial authority is, indeed, locally *here*, in the belligerent country, according to the known law and practice of nations; but the law itself has no locality.

---

[1] [1916] 2 A.C. 77.   [2] Vol. i 567, n. 1.
[3] N. Bentwich, Great Jurists of the World 520.
[4] Lindo v. Rodney (1783) 2 Dougl. at p. 616, cited vol. i 565.
[5] The Recovery (1807) 6 C. Rob. at pp. 348-349, cited vol. i 565-566.
[6] The Recovery at p. 349.
[7] The Maria (1799) 1 C. Rob. at pp. 349-350.

And to all states alike, whether great or small or strong or weak, the same impartial justice was due ; for " the perfect equality and entire independence of all distinct states " is a fundamental principle of international law.[1] Any advantage taken of a weak state, because it is weak, is " mere usurpation."[2]

Stowell was always anxious to give effect to the rights both of neutrals and belligerents. He laid it down that a captor must, as a general rule, bring in for adjudication all ships captured " that it may be ascertained whether it be enemy's property ; and that mistakes may not be committed by captors, in the eager pursuit of gain, by which injustice may be done to neutral subjects, and national quarrels produced with the foreign states to which they belong."[3] Enemy's property which it is impossible to bring in for adjudication could be destroyed ; but if it is doubtful whether it is enemy's property, and it is impossible to bring it in, " the safe and proper course is to dismiss."[4] When the property is neutral

the act of destruction cannot be justified to the neutral owner, by the gravest importance of such an act to the public service of the captor's own state. To the neutral it can only be justified, under any such circumstances, by a full restitution in value.[5]

On the other hand, in considering the manner in which belligerent rights should be exercised it was legitimate to take into consideration the nature and character of the war. He cited Puffendorf for the proposition that " the nature and purpose of a war was not entirely to be omitted in the consideration of the warrantable exercise of (a belligerent's) rights relatively to neutral states."[6] He added :[7]

The nature of the present war does give this country the rights of war, relatively to neutral states, in as large a measure as they have been regularly and legally exercised, at any period of modern and civilized times. Whether I estimate the nature of the war justly, I leave to the judgment of Europe, when I declare that I consider this as a war in which neutral states themselves have an interest much more direct and substantial than they have in the ordinary, limited, and private quarrels, if I may so call them, of Great Britain and its great public enemy.

But the fact that such circumstances as these could be taken into consideration did not mean that they would justify breaches of international law. Stowell made it clear that no motive, however laudable, such as the suppression of the slave trade, could justify such breaches. He said :[8]

---

[1] The Le Louis (1817) 2 Dods. at p. 243. [2] Ibid.
[3] The Felicity (1819) 2 Dods. at p. 385. [4] Ibid at p. 386. [5] Ibid.
[6] The Maria (1799) 1 C. Rob. at p. 352. [7] At p. 350.
[8] The Le Louis (1817) 2 Dods. at p. 257.

To press forward to a great principle by breaking through every other great principle that stands in the way of its establishment ; to force the way to the liberation of Africa by trampling on the independence of other states in Europe, in short, to procure an eminent good by means that are unlawful ; is as little consonant to private morality as to public justice. Obtain the concurrence of other nations, if you can, by application, by remonstrance, by example, by every peaceable instrument that man can employ to attract the consent of men. But a nation is not justified in assuming rights that do not belong to her merely because she means to apply them to a laudable purpose ; nor in setting out upon a moral crusade of converting other nations by acts of unlawful force.

This, then, was Stowell's conception of the law which a Prize court administered, and the duty of the judge of such a court. Let us look at one or two illustrations of the way in which he applied that law to the enforcement of the rights and duties of neutrals and belligerents.

In the case of *The Maria*[1] Stowell stated the basic principles of the doctrine of *continuous voyage* in these words :

It is an inherent and settled principle in all cases . . . that the mere *touching* at any port without importing the cargo into the common stock of the country, will not alter the nature of the voyage, which continues the same in all respects, and must be considered as a voyage to the country to which the vessel is actually going for the purpose of delivering her cargo at the ultimate port.

In several cases he defined the conditions in which *a blockade* existed. In the case of *the Vrouw Judith*[2] he defined a blockade as

a sort of circumvallation round a place, by which all foreign connexion and correspondence is, as far as human force can effect it, to be entirely cut off. It is intended to suspend the entire commerce of that place ; and a neutral is no more at liberty to assist the traffic of exportation than of importation.

In the case of *The Betsey*[3] he laid it down that to prove a valid seizure for the breach of a blockade three things must be proved —its existence, the knowledge of the person accused of breaking it, and some act of violation by ingress or egress. In the case of *The Maria*[4] he stated the rights of a belligerent *to visit and search* a neutral ship, and held that the fact that the ship so visited and searched was under convoy did not prejudice that right. The right, he said, was the logical consequence of the right of maritime capture, " because if you are not at liberty to ascertain by sufficient enquiry whether there is property that can be legally captured, it is impossible to capture."[5] The fact that the neutral was convoyed by a warship of its own country

---

[1] (1805) 5 C. Rob. at p. 368.
[2] (1799) 1 C. Rob. at p. 151 ; cp. The Frederick Moltke (1798) ibid 86.
[3] (1798) ibid 92. [4] (1799) 1 C. Rob. 340. [5] At pp. 359-360.

could not prejudice the right, and if the warship obstructed the right it would amount to " the opposition of illegal violence to legal right."[1] Moreover all international lawyers were agreed that resistance to the right entailed confiscation of the cargo.[2] In other cases there were discussions on the questions when goods *ancipitis usus* could be deemed contraband;[3] when a captor could demand freight on goods carried to their destination;[4] when a neutral acquired an enemy commercial domicil;[5] the purchase by a neutral of an enemy ship in time of war.[6] The case of *The Hoop* explains, in a classical passage,[7] why, on grounds of public policy, all trading with the enemy without the licence of the Crown is illegal, and why on procedural grounds it is impossible to enforce such a contract because an alien enemy, both by English and international law, cannot sue in the courts of the enemy country—he is not " in the language of the civilians a *persona standi in judicio*."

So well and truly did Stowell construct the English system of prize law that, in spite of changes in mercantile conditions, and in spite of changes in the procedure of the court, it was found adequate in the war of 1914-18. The principles which he laid down were found to be capable of adaptation to changed conditions, so that, as Mr. Roscoe has said, they remain " fixed more firmly than ever as the corner stone of one branch of British jurisprudence."[8]

Though, as we have seen, the instance jurisdiction of the Admiralty had been reduced to small dimensions by the common law courts, it still retained some jurisdiction;[9] and in two classes of cases Stowell's decisions have elucidated important principles of maritime law. In his elaborate judgment in the case of *The Gratitudine*[10] he examined the question whether, in a case of necessity, the master could hypothecate the cargo and freight for the repairs needed by the ship in order to enable her to complete her voyage. Stowell explained why, and proved that, the master must have such a power in order to enable him to fulfil his primary duty under his contract[11]—" the safe conveyance of the property entrusted to his care in that same vehicle which he had contracted to furnish."[12] He showed that both the English and the foreign authorities, though scanty, favoured the view that the master had such a power;[13] and that it was sanctioned by

---

[1] At p. 361. [2] At pp. 363-369.
[3] The Jonge Margaretha (1799) 1 C. Rob. 188.
[4] The Emmanuel (1799) ibid 296 ; The Vrow Anna Catharina (1806) 6 C. Rob. 269.
[5] The Harmony (1800) 2 C. Rob. 322.
[6] The Bernon (1798) 1 C. Rob. 102.
[7] (1799) 1 C. Rob. at pp. 199-202. [8] Life of Lord Stowell 91.
[9] Vol. i 557-558 ; vol. xii 692. [10] (1801) 3 C. Rob. 240.
[11] At pp. 257-266. [12] At. p. 261. [13] At pp. 266-267.

mercantile practice, which, as he said, "goes a great way to constitute that *lex mercatoria*, which all tribunals are bound to respect, wherever that practice does not cross upon any known principle of law, justice, or national policy."[1] In the case of *The Aquila*[2] the principles underlying the law of salvage were explained. He pointed out that by English maritime law salvors did not acquire the property in a derelict ship by occupancy. If no owner appeared they were a droit of the Admiralty. But the finder was entitled to be rewarded for his services. He was not entitled, as some thought, to half the value of the thing salved in all cases ; but the reward must be proportioned to the service, and, if there were more than one set of salvors, in proportion to the value of the services of each set. Those engaged in salvage work have, he said, in the case of *The Blenden Hall*,[3] "a legal interest."[4] If able to complete the work a third person is not entitled to interfere and claim as a salvor. Such interference can only be justified by necessity. To permit it in any other circumstances would diminish the reward of the original salvors and increase the expense to the owners.[5] In the case of *The Neptune*[6] the meaning and scope of the maxim " freight is the mother of wages " was examined. It was shown that it was not wholly accurate, that the law of other states admitted many exceptions, and, in particular, that that law generally allowed that wages were due if any part of the ship survived. In the absence of authority to the contrary, Stowell held that this must be taken to be the law of England. Otherwise the mariner would have no claim, for he could claim neither as a salvor nor on a *quantum meruit*. The passage in which he demonstrated the justice of this rule illustrates at once the scant justice with which maritime law treated seamen, and the clarity and felicity with which Stowell could explain its rules. He said :[7]

Upon all these grounds of the general practice of maritime states, upon the just policy of the rule, its simplicity and convenience, upon the legal nature and duration of the original contract, and upon the understanding of the law which has generally, though silently prevailed, I adhere to the spirit, I nearly said the letter, of what I am reminded of having said in a former case not exactly upon this question, " that a seaman had the right to cling to the last plank of his ship in satisfaction of his wages or part of them." Be it remembered that by the general and first policy of all maritime states, the total loss of the ship occasioned solely by the act of God visiting the deep with storms and tempest, brings with it the loss of all the earned wages (except advances), although the general rule of law is, that the act of God prejudices no man ; and although the mariner has contributed nothing to the mischance

[1] At pp. 270-271.   [2] (1798) 1 C. Rob. 37.
[3] (1814) Dods. 414.   [4] At p. 416.
[5] The Maria (1809) Edw. at p. 177.
[6] (1824) Hagg. Adm. 227.   [7] At p. 239.

but exerted his utmost endeavours to prevent it ; and although he is prohibited by law from protecting himself from loss by insurance, as his owner is empowered to do for his, it is surely a moderate compensation for these disadvantages, that he shall be entitled upon the parts saved, as far as they will go, in satisfaction of his wages already earned by past services and perils.

As judge of the consistory court of London, Stowell gave some decisions of great importance on the law of marriage and divorce, and on various topics of ecclesiastical law.

In the case of *Lindo v. Belisario*[1] Stowell defined the legal conception of marriage. He said :[2]

The opinions which have divided the world, or writers at least, on this subject are generally two. It is held by some persons that marriage is a contract merely civil, by others that it is a sacred, religious, and spiritual contract, and only so to be considered. The jurisdiction of the Ecclesiastical Court was founded on ideas of this last described nature ; but in a more correct view of the subject, I conceive that neither of these opinions is perfectly accurate. According to juster notions of the nature of the marriage contract, it is not merely either a civil or a religious contract ; and at the present time it is not to be considered as originally and simply one or the other. It is a contract according to the law of nature, antecedent to civil institution, and which may take place to all intents and purposes, wherever two persons of different sexes engage, by mutual contracts, to live together. . . . It cannot be a mere casual and temporary commerce, but must be a contract at least extending to . . . purposes of a more permanent nature, in the intention of the parties. The contract thus formed in the state of nature, is adopted as a contract of the greatest importance in civil institutions, and it is charged with a vast variety of obligations merely civil. Rights of property are attached to it on very different principles in different countries . . . In most countries it is also cloaked with religious rites, even in rude societies, as well as in those which are more distinguished for their civil and religious institutions. Yet in many of those societies . . . marriages may be irregular, informal, and discountenanced on that account, yet not invalidated. Scotch marriages have been mentioned. The rule prevailed in all times, as the rule of the canon law, which existed in this country and in Scotland, till other civil regulations interfered in this country.

The view that in England, as in other countries governed by the canon law, consent was the essence of a valid marriage, Stowell proved in his very learned judgment in the case of *Dalrymple v. Dalrymple*.[3] The correctness of that view equally divided the House of Lords in 1843-44.[4] It was overruled because the judgment appealed from had dissented from it, and, when the House is equally divided, *praesumitur pro negante*.[5]

---

[1] (1795) Hagg. Con. 216.   [2] At pp. 231-232.
[3] (1811) 2 Hagg. Con. 54 at pp. 69-70.
[4] R. v. Millis (1844) 10 Cl. and Fin. 534.
[5] In fact the court below was equally divided, but one judge withdrew his judgment so that an appeal might be taken to the House of Lords.

Some of his other decisions lay down important principles of the law of divorce on such questions as the nature of the cruelty which will justify a judicial separation,[1] the evidence by which adultery can be proved,[2] the defence of recrimination.[2] The literary art with which Stowell discusses the evidence in some of these cases was well described by a *Quarterly* reviewer. He says :[3]

The embroidery of each case is so equally woven, the effect so much depends upon harmony of colour and exact proportion ; the sly humour is so nicely, and almost imperceptibly, mingled with the worldly wisdom, that it would be unjust to tear any fragments and exhibit them as specimens . . . Although the refinement of expression is almost undisturbed, the sense is always manly—nothing affected, sickly or sentimental—but common sense arrayed in the garb of fancy. The vivid exhibition of scenes in domestic life ; the opposition of motives and passions ; all invested with a certain air from the rank in society (for the poor rarely indulge in the luxuries of the Consistory Court) remind us . . . of the style of comedy which was fading from the stage before Sir William Scott retired from the bench. . . . The curtain seems lifted on an elegant drama of manners ; husbands and wives quarrel and recriminate in dialogue almost as graceful as Sheridan's ; youths of fortune become the prey of rustic lasses in spite of obdurate fathers ; and good moral better enforced than most stage conclusions, dismisses the parties and charms the audience. . . . He once said he could furnish a series of stories from the annals of Doctors' Commons which should rival the Waverley Novels in interest.

Stowell gave many judgments on various topics of ecclesiastical law—on tithe questions,[4] on the elections of churchwardens,[5] on the respective functions and authority of the churchwarden and the parson,[6] on the need to get a faculty to erect a monument in a church,[7] on legal points arising in causes of defamation.[8] Two cases of criminal proceedings under a statute of Edward VI[9] for brawling in church—one by a parson against a churchwarden,[10] and the other by a lady against a parson who had rebuked her by name from the pulpit[11]—resemble the causes of defamation in that they give us a glimpse of the human beings and the human passions which some of the rules of ecclesiastical law attempted to regulate.

---

[1] Evans v. Evans (1790) 1 Hagg. Con. 35.

[2] Loveden v. Loveden (1810) 2 Hagg. Con. 1.

[3] Quart. Rev. lxxv 48-49.

[4] See e.g. Filewood v. Marsh (1797) 1 Hagg. Con. 478 ; Filewood v. Kemp (1805) ibid 487 ; (1807) ibid 494.

[5] Anthony v. Seger (1789) 1 Hagg. Con. 9.

[6] Hutchins v. Deniloe (1792) 1 Hagg. Con. 170.

[7] Maidman v. Malpas (1794) 1 Hagg. Con. 205.

[8] Crompton v. Butler (1790) 1 Hagg. Con. 460 ; Smith v. Watkins (1792) ibid 467.

[9] 5, 6 Edward VI c. 4.

[10] Hutchins v. Denzilow (1792) 1 Hagg. Con. 181.

[11] Cox v. Goodday (1810) 2 Hagg. Con. 138.

One of the most curious of these cases on ecclesiastical law was the case of *Gilbert v. Buzzard* [1] in which the question was raised whether the churchwardens could prevent the use of an iron coffin. Stowell's judgment on this somewhat unpromising topic is an interesting historical essay upon the methods of disposing of the bodies of the dead, in which he refers to the Old Testament, the practice of the Greeks and Romans, Sir Thomas Browne's book on urn burial, Christian and Mahomedan practice, and Spelman *De Sepultura*. He held that the churchwardens could not prevent the use of these coffins, but that they were entitled to charge an extra fee because their use was likely to block up the available space for burial for a longer period, and so occasion a greater expense to the parish; for, he said: [2]

The common cemetery is not *res unius aetatis*, the property of one generation now departed, but is likewise the common property of the living, and of generations yet unborn, and is subject only to temporary appropriations. There exists in the whole a right of succession, which can be lawfully obstructed only in a portion of it, by public authority, that of the ecclesiastical magistrate who gives occasionally an exclusive title in such portion to the succession of some family, or to an individual who has a fair claim to be favoured by such a distinction ; and this, not without a just consideration of its expedience, and a due attention to the objections of those who oppose such an alienation from the common property. . . . If this view of the matter be just, all contrivances that, whether intentionally or not, prolong the time of dissolution beyond the period at which the common local understanding and usage have fixed it, is an act of injustice unless compensated in some way or other.

Some of Stowell's decisions touch upon the problems of the as yet very rudimentary topic of Private International Law. In the case of *Dalrymple v. Dalrymple* [3] he laid down the basic principle that the question whether a right exists must be determined by the law of the place where that right originated. In that case the question was whether Dalrymple had married Miss Gordon in Scotland. He said : [4]

The cause being entertained in an English court, it must be adjudicated according to the principles of English law applicable to such a case. But the only principle applicable to such a case by the law of England is, that the validity of Miss Gordon's marriage rights must be tried by reference to the law of the country, where, if they exist at all, they had their origin. Having furnished this principle, the law of England withdraws altogether and leaves the legal question to the exclusive judgment of the law of Scotland.

[1] (1821) 2 Hagg. Con. 333.   [2] At. p. 353.
[3] (1811) 2 Hagg. Con. 54.
[4] At pp. 58-59 ; Cheshire, Private International Law (3rd ed.) 47.

In the case of *Lindo v. Belisario*[1] the question was whether an alleged marriage between two Jews was a valid marriage. The answer turned upon the question whether by Jewish law the ceremonies which passed between the parties constituted a valid marriage ; and Stowell, after considering the evidence of experts in Jewish law, held that they did not. In the case of *Ruding v. Smith*[2] he held that though it was true that a foreign marriage valid according to the law of the place where it was celebrated was valid everywhere, the converse was not always true.[3] There might be cases where the marriages of British subjects not celebrated in accordance with the *lex loci* were valid. If, for instance, an officer of the British army of occupation in France married a French lady the law of France would not apply;[4] and so in this case a marriage between British subjects at the Cape of Good Hope celebrated the year after its capture, which was not valid by the law of Holland, was held to be valid. In the case of *The Slave Grace*[5] he held that since slavery was a recognized legal status in Antigua, a slave who returned from England to Antigua with her master, though free while in England, reverted on her return to her original status. The law of England, it is true, did not recognize the status of slavery, but the law of Antigua did recognize it ; and the law of England recognized the existence of that status in Antigua.[6] Therefore the fact that the slave was free while in England and subject to English law, could not affect her former status when she left England and returned to a place which was governed by the law of Antigua. The decision was much criticized ; but the principle upon which it is based is sound, and was approved by that great American judge and professor—Mr. Justice Story.[7]

Very few of Lord Stowell's decisions have been questioned by his successors, and, where they have been dissented from, the dissent has not met with universal approbation. Many people consider that his dicta in the case of *The Fox*[8] are preferable to the decision of the Privy Council in the case of *The Zamora*.[9] His views as to the necessary conditions of a valid

---

[1] (1795) 1 Hagg. Con. 216.   [2] (1821) 2 Hagg. Con. 371.
[3] At p. 381.   [4] At pp. 387-388.   [5] (1827) 2 Hagg. Adm. 94.
[6] " It has been said that the law of England discourages slavery, and so it certainly does within the limits of these islands ; but the law uses a very different language and enters a very different force when it looks to her Colonies ; for to this trade in those colonies it gives an almost unbounded protection. . . . Even since slavery has become odious in England, it has been fully supported by the authority of many statutes for the purpose of carrying it into full effect in the colonies," at pp. 128-129.
[7] See 2 S.T. N.S. 303 n. (*a*).   [8] (1811) Edw. at pp. 312-313.
[9] [1916] 2 A.C. 77 ; see vol. i 566-568 ; Holdsworth, Some Makers of English Law 219 n. 1 ; L.Q.R. xxxii 153-159, 167 ; it should be noted that 45 George III c. 72 § 37 (above) recognizes the right of the Crown to make rules and give directions to the court of Admiralty for the adjudication and condemnation of prizes ; and

marriage, which he expounded in the case of *Dalrymple v. Dalrymple*,[1] were dissented from by three of the Lords who decided the case of *R. v. Millis*;[2] but three others agreed with him, and, as we have seen, the case was only settled in accordance with the opinion of the first three lords because their opinion agreed with the opinion of the court below. But as Pollock and Maitland say, " It is the vanquished cause that will please the historian of the Middle Ages."[3] In other words, Stowell's opinion was better history and sounder law.

It is, I think, true to say that what Hardwicke and Eldon did for equity and what Mansfield did for the common law, Stowell did for all those branches of law which fell within the sphere of the civilian's practice. Their achievement was possible not only because they were all very great lawyers, but also because they held their offices for sufficiently long periods to make their influence felt, and because they all came at periods when English law especially needed this kind of guidance. Consequently they all succeeded in creating large parts of the law which governs us to-day.

Stowell was succeeded both as judge of the consistory court and as judge of the court of Admiralty by Christopher Robinson.

Robinson[4] was born in 1766 and educated at University and Magdalen Colleges, Oxford. He took the degree of D.C.L. in 1796, and was admitted a member of Doctors' Commons in the same year. We have seen that in 1798 he started the earliest regular series of reports in the court of Admiralty;[5] and, in addition he translated two chapters of the *Consolato del Mare*[6] relating to prize law, and edited a collection of public instruments on prize law. His reports show that he was a good lawyer. He soon got a practice, and in 1809 he was appointed King's advocate. In that capacity he had a very large practice in Prize. In 1821 he succeeded Stowell as judge of the consistory court and chancellor of the diocese of London, and in 1828 he succeeded him as judge of the court of Admiralty. For several years before Stowell's resignation he had read his decisions for him. He acted as judge of the court of Admiralty till his death in 1833.

---

that the Naval Prize Act 1864, 27, 28 Victoria c. 25 § 37 provides in effect that captors must obey Orders in Council or Proclamations relating to Prize, and that § 55 (a) provides that nothing in the Act is to abridge any of the Crown's prerogatives ; no doubt there was some authority for the decision in *The Zamora*, but for the reasons given in the authorities cited I think that there is more authority in favour of the contrary view.

[1] (188) 2 Hagg. Con. 54.
[2] (1843-44) 10 Cl. and Fin. 534 ; above 654 n 3.
[3] H.E.L. (1st ed.) ii 370.   [4] D.N.B. ; vol. xii 145.
[5] Ibid 106 ; above 432.   [6] For this treatise see vol. v 70-71.

Amongst the small number of his judgments as judge of the consistory court there is nothing very remarkable. As judge of the court of Admiralty his sphere of action was limited as compared with that of Stowell; for there was no Prize court; and the instance jurisdiction of his court was still small. It was not till after he had ceased to be judge that it was enlarged by the Legislature.[1] He was an industrious and painstaking judge, and he showed his grasp of principles by the clarity with which he explained them; but he had none of Stowell's legal and literary genius.

In the case of *The Margaret*[2] the question of the law to be applied where the owners of the shares in a ship differed as to the employment of the ship, was discussed.[3] Robinson pointed out that the court of Admiralty had been prevented by the courts of common law from adopting the law in force in some other countries, and compelling a sale; and that the expedient had been adopted of allowing the majority to sail the ship, provided they gave a bond to the minority for her safe return. In the case of *The Cognac*[4] it was settled that, though the usury laws did not apply to loans on bottomry, the court had jurisdiction to moderate the interest on a bottomry bond. It was pointed out that the court of Chancery would not help the obligee of such a bond if it carried an unreasonable interest, and that foreign systems of law allowed the interference of the court to prevent fraud or extortion. Therefore he held that the court of Admiralty could revise rates of interest both on English and foreign bonds. In the case of *The General Palmer*[5] the rights and duties of pilots were discussed. In two cases important points as to the rights of seamen to their wages were settled. The condemnation of a ship for illegal trading, to which the seamen were not privy, did not deprive them of their wages —it was a recognized exception to the rule that freight was the mother of wages.[6] An unnecessary deviation, to which the seamen had not assented, was a breach of contract, and entitled them to their wages earned and to their discharge.[7] Other interesting judgments were given as to the territorial limits of the Admiralty's jurisdiction;[8] and as to the claims of the Admiralty and officers of the King's ships to reward for operations by which bullion contained in a wrecked ship was salved.[9] It should be noted that the Acts which abolished the slave trade made additions to the jurisdiction of the Vice-Admiralty

---

[1] Vol. i, 558-559.
[2] (1829) 2 Hagg. Adm. 275.
[3] Vol. viii 247-248.
[4] (1832) 2 Hagg. Adm. 377, 387-389.
[5] (1828) 2 Hagg. Adm. 176.
[6] The Malta (1828) 2 Hagg. Adm. at p. 163.
[7] The Cambridge (1829) 2 Hagg. Adm. 243.
[8] The Public Opinion (1823) 2 Hagg. Adm. 398.
[9] H.M.S. Thetis (1833) 3 Hagg. Adm. 14.

courts and the court of Admiralty, which gave rise to a number of legal problems.[1]

Of the civilians who gave their names to the reports of Admiralty and Ecclesiastical cases I have already spoken.[2] Of the other civilians notable names are Nicholl, French Laurence, and Lushington.

John Nicholl[3] was born in 1759, and was educated at St. John's College, Oxford, of which College he became a fellow. He was admitted to Doctors' Commons in 1785, and succeeded Stowell as King's advocate in 1798. In Parliament, of which he was a member from 1802 until 1832, he defended the Orders in Council, and opposed Catholic emancipation and Parliamentary reform. He introduced the Act of 1829[4] which effected valuable reforms in the staff and procedure of the ecclesiastical courts. He was one of the founders of King's College, London, which was established by members of the Church of England to counteract the influence of the radical and utilitarian University College. In 1809 he became Dean of the Arches and judge of the prerogative court. He held that post till 1834 when he became vicar general to the Archbishop of Canterbury. In 1833 he succeeded Robinson as the judge of the court of Admiralty. He died in 1838. His decisions, both in the ecclesiastical courts and in the court of Admiralty merit very high praise. They show an intimate knowledge of the authorities, a capacity to state clearly the facts of a case, and an equal capacity to deduce from the authorities and apply to the facts the relevant principles and rules of law. The only untoward incident in his career as judge of the prerogative court was a complaint made against him by a disappointed suitor, who presented a petition to the House of Commons which was backed by Joseph Hume. The burden of the complaint was the expense of the suit, the inadequate machinery for the taxation of the costs, and the refusal of Nicholl to hear objections to the established procedure on such taxation. Nicholl was ably defended by Lushington, and the House refused to receive the petition.[5]

As Dean of the Arches Nicholl heard appeals from the diocesan courts, and had a limited original jurisdiction in ecclesiastical cases.[6] The usual class of cases came before him in this capacity—grants of faculties,[7] suits against peccant clergymen,[8] the right to pews and the duties of churchwardens in

---

[1] See e.g. The Slave, Fanny Ford (1829) 2 Hagg. Adm. 271 ; Two Slaves (1828) ibid 273 ; Three Slaves (1832) ibid 412.

[2] Above 441.   [3] D.N.B.   [4] 10 George IV c. 53.

[5] Hansard (2nd ser.) xix 1749-1762. The Petition disclosed a case of some hardship, but the fault was with the law and not with the judge.

[6] Vol. i 601.   [7] E.g. Butt v. Jones (1829) 2 Hagg. Eccl. 417.

[8] E.g. Burgoyne v. Free (1825) 2 Add. 414 (1829) 2 Hagg. Eccl. at pp. 483-495.

respect to their allocation,[1] matrimonial cases on appeal from the diocesan courts.[2] From the point of view of the development of legal doctrine his decisions as judge of the prerogative court are more important. As judge of that court he was the principal judge in probate cases in the southern province. These cases gave rise to some very difficult problems since, before the Wills Act of 1837,[3] the proof of the making or revocation of a will was, in the then state of the law, a very difficult matter. It involved the careful weighing of often conflicting evidence both as to the acts and as to the intentions of testators, as well as a knowledge of the relevant rules of law. Nicholl showed himself to be an acute analyst of evidence with a capacity for stating clearly the conclusions to be drawn from it,[4] and a very learned civilian. Some of his judgments upon the law as to the making and revocation of wills were rendered obsolete by the Wills Act of 1837;[5] but many of them upon other problems which came before his court lay down principles which were accepted by its successors, the court of Probate and the Probate Division of the High Court. Let us look at a few illustrations of both these classes of cases.

He held in one case that, in considering whether an instrument should be admitted to probate as a will, the court must look at the substance and not at the form, so that a deed of gift, if so intended, could operate as a will;[6] and, in another case, that if a will is destroyed without the consent of the testator, its contents, if proved, can be admitted to probate.[7] Nuncupative wills were still possible. But Nicholl insisted upon the necessity for the clearest proof of their making. He said:[8]

The factum of a nuncupative will requires to be proved by evidence more strict and stringent than that of a written one, in every single particular. This is requisite in consideration of the facilities with which frauds in setting up nuncupative wills are obviously attended—facilities which absolutely require to be counteracted by the courts insisting on the strictest proof as to the " facta " of such alleged wills.

[1] Fuller v. Lane (1825) 2 Add. 414.
[2] E.g. Greg v. Greg (1824) 2 Add. 276; Durant v. Durant (1826) 1 Hagg. Eccl. 528.
[3] 1 Victoria c. 26.
[4] Illustrations of the manner in which Nicholl analysed the evidence in complicated cases will be found in Sapp v. Atkinson (1822) 1 Add. 162, and Dew v. Clark (1826) 3 Add. 79.
[5] 7 Will. IV. and 1 Vict. C. 26.
[6] Trevelyan v. Trevelyan (1810) 1 Phill. 149; cf. Sugden v. Lord St. Leonards (1876) 1 P.D. 154.
[7] The footnote was missing from the MS. and we have been unable to trace the decision which the learned author intended to cite, but Nicholl's view of the law on this point may be illustrated by his judgment in Lillie v. Lillie (1829), 3 Hagg, Ecc. 184, where he was satisfied that the destruction was done by the testator, or with his consent. (Eds.).
[8] Lemann v. Bonsall (1823) 1 Add. at pp. 389-390.

There are decisions as to the effect of a codicil in reviving a revoked will, and in revoking a will made subsequently to the revoked and revived will ;[1] and as to the legal effect of a mutual or conjoint will.[2] There are decisions upon the question where a will is revoked by marriage or by marriage and the birth of children[3]—a difficult question before the Wills Act 1837,[4] since the presumption that the testator intended to revoke could be rebutted by his declarations or by other circumstances, e.g. by the way in which his estate was settled ; and there is a decision upon the doctrine of dependent relative revocation.[5] In the case of *Dew v. Clarke*,[6] which came several times before the court, the question of the effect of partial insanity upon testamentary capacity was very elaborately discussed ; and in the case of *Ingram v. Wyatt*[7] the question of the meaning of the influence which is sufficiently undue to invalidate a will was considered. In *Paske v. Ollat*[8] he laid down the principle that if a legatee draws the will under which he benefits, very strict proof is required that the testator knew and approved its contents. The proceedings which were taken by an alleged beneficiary under George III's will provided the occasion for a judgment which discussed the subject of royal wills, in which he held that, as the proceedings were in substance against the King, and as the process of the court could not issue against the King, they could not be entertained.[9] He also stated the rule that the court " prefers *ceteris paribus* a sole to a joint administrator."[10]

On the subject of *marriage* he laid it down that " if a marriage has been solemnized the law strongly presumes that all the legal requisites have been complied with," so that in the case of the marriage of a minor the consent of the father may be presumed from the circumstances.[11] He held that a marriage which is voidable, by reason of affinity, cannot be avoided after the death of one of the parties to it ;[12] but that an incestuous marriage

---

[1] Rogers v. Pittis (1822) 1 Add. 30.

[2] Hobson v. Blackburn (1822) 1 Add. 274.

[3] Johnston v. Johnston (1817) 1 Phill. 447 ; Gibbens v. Cross (1825) 2 Add. 455 ; Talbot v. Talbot (1828) 1 Hagg. Eccl. 705.

[4] 7 Will. IV. and 1 Vict. c. 26.

[5] In the goods of Appelbee (1828) 1 Hagg. Eccl. 143.

[6] (1822) 1 Add. 279 (1824) 2 Add. 102 (1826) 3 Add. 79 ; it is in the latest report that the law is fully discussed.

[7] (1828) Hagg. Eccl. 384 ; the decision was reversed on the facts (1831) 3 Hagg. Eccl. 466 ; the correctness of the law as stated by Nicholl was not questioned.

[8] (1815) 2 Phill. 325 ; approved by the judicial committee in Donnelly v. Broughton [1891] A.C. 435, 442.

[9] In the goods of George III (1822) 1 Add. 255.

[10] Warwick, Earl of v. Greville (1809) 1 Phill. 123, 126.

[11] Smith v. Huson (1811) 1 Phill. 287.

[12] Elliott and Sugden v. Gurr (1812) 2 Phill. 16, the husband was the sister's son of the woman's former husband.

is void, and the parties to it can be ordered to do penance.[1] Many of his decisions deal with *other topics of ecclesiastical law.* In one of his decisions he held that a clergyman could be proceeded against for irregularities in the conduct of service, and for chiding and brawling in church ;[2] in another he considered the question whether a church rate was validly imposed ;[3] and in another he held that the incumbent has the right to preside at a meeting of the vestry.[4] The most famous of his decisions was in the case of *Kemp v. Wickes*[5] in which it was held that a clergyman could not refuse to bury the child of a dissenter baptized according to the rites of the dissenting church. The case raised the question of the validity of lay baptism which Nicholl in a most elaborate judgment held to be valid. The question was again raised in the case of *Escott v. Mastin,*[6] and decided in the same way by the then Dean of the Arches, C. Jenner-Fust, and of the Privy Council.

It is clear from the cases of *Telford v. Morison*[7] and *Grignion v. Grignion*[8] that all the questions as to the exact boundaries between the jurisdiction of the common law courts and the courts of equity on the one side, and that of the ecclesiastical courts on the other, were not completely settled. But it is clear from the latter case that the relations between these rival courts had ceased to be hostile.[9] In that case the question was whether the ecclesiastical court had jurisdiction to compel the executor to pay a legacy. The court admitted that if any question as to the enforcement of a trust arose, it was a matter for a court of equity, but it denied the exclusive jurisdiction of equity when no trust was involved. Nicholl said :[10]

In the present case, in my view, the simple duty of the executor remains to pay the legacy. There is no longer any trust but that which belongs to all executorships. I have considerable doubts whether any courts of equity would enjoin, and perhaps have reason to think that they would not. Times are changed—a more liberal and enlightened view of questions of jurisdiction is taken : on the one hand these courts have no disposition to encroach—*ampliare jurisdictionem ;* on the other hand, temporal courts have no jealousy—no wish to resort to fictions and to technicalities : they look (when not bound by former decisions directly in point) to the real substance and sound sense of the question —to that which is really most beneficial to the suitors—the public— and subjects of the country. There is quite as much business in all courts, as, under the increase of wealth and population, the institutions are able to discharge.

[1] Blackmore and Thorp v. Brider (1816) 2 Phill. 389.
[2] Newbery v. Godwin (1811) 1 Phill. 282.
[3] Chetton v. Cherry (1816) 2 Phill. 373.
[4] Wilson v. M'Math (1819) 3 Phill. 67.
[5] (1809), 3 Phill. 264.   [6] (1842), 4 Moo. P.C. 104.
[7] (1809) 3 Phill. 264.   [8] (1841) 2 Cart. 692 ; (1842) 4 Moo. P.C. 104.
[9] See vol. xii 695-701 for the way in which these relations had been settled.
[10] (1828) 1 Hagg. Eccl. at p. 545.

This passage shows that Nicholl had a firm grasp of principle which was based upon a knowledge of the history of the courts in which he administered justice, and of the law which they applied. We can see the same qualities in some of his decisions as the judge of the court of Admiralty.

Nicholl's decisions as a judge of the court of Admiralty are considerably fewer in number, both because the jurisdiction of the court was limited and because he only held office for a short time. But some of his decisions show that he was a master of the principles of maritime law and of all the branches of law which fell within the jurisdiction of the Admiralty. In the case of *H.M.S. Thetis*[1] the effect of the legislation as to prize money is reviewed. In the case of *The Clifton*,[2] Nicholl explained the consideration of which the court must take account to determine the value of a salvage service. In the case of *The Hersey*[3] he reviewed the conditions in which the master of a ship could borrow money on bottomry. In the cases of *The Neptune*[4] and *The Girolans*[5] he made some very valuable remarks on the nature of the law which the court must administer. In *The Neptune*,[6] which raised the question whether material men had a lien on the proceeds of the sale of a ship,[7] he explained the law which the court applied as follows :[8]

Generally the court of Admiralty is governed by the civil law, the law marine, and law merchant, unless when those laws are controlled by the statute law of the realm, or by the authority of the municipal courts, which unquestionably possess a superintending power, and might restrain the court should it overstep the just limits of its jurisdiction . . . Thenceforward the civil and maritime law so controlled becomes the law governing the decisions of this court.

In *The Girolamo*,[9] which raised the question of the liability of a foreign ship in charge of a pilot, for damages caused by a collision to a British ship called *The Edward*, he pointed out that municipal laws applicable to British ships, which exempted the owners from liability when under compulsory pilotage, did not necessarily apply to a proceeding *in rem* against a foreign ship. He said :[10]

---

[1] (1834) 3 Hagg. Adm. 129.   [2] (1835) 3 Hagg. Adm. 288.
[3] (1837) 3 Hagg. Adm. 404 ; vol. vii 261.
[4] (1834) 3 Hagg. Adm. 129.   [5] Ibid 169.   [6] Ibid 129.
[7] Nicholl held that though by the law of England, which differs from the civil law on this matter, material men had no lien, other than a possessory lien on the ship, they had a lien on the proceeds of sale ; this decision was reversed by the Privy Council (1835) 3 Knapp 94.
[8] 3 Hagg. Adm. at. p. 136.
[9] The Girolamo (1834) 3 Hagg. Adm. 169.
[10] At pp. 185-189.

This defence is set up by a foreign owner, in behalf of a foreign ship, in a court governed by the principles of international law ; and a question arises whether a foreigner can, in a suit in this court, set up as a defence a municipal law made to regulate municipal courts only, and contrary to those general rules of law which prevail amongst commercial nations. Reciprocity or mutuality has always been considered as one of the leading principles of justice on questions arising between nation and nation. . . . But does this principle of reciprocity apply to cases of collision ? . . . Before the enactment of the municipal law by 52 Geo. III and 6 Geo. IV, the general rule of international law, by which this court was governed in cases of collision, was that a vessel doing damage to another was liable to make full compensation. This rule was recognized by Lord Stowell in the case of *The Nostra Signora de Los Dolores* (1 Dods. 290), when he decided that foreigners when suing British subjects were not bound by the municipal law . . . Foreign vessels and foreign persons are indeed liable to the municipal laws for acts done within the local jurisdiction of the municipal courts . . . But it does not follow that, having commenced a voyage, and doing damage, they are entitled to make the same defence that British subjects might make *inter se*. If the owners of *The Edward* had . . . brought an action at law against the foreign master, the statute would probably have been a good defence to such a proceeding, but it is a defence which cannot be set up in a court proceeding *in rem*, and governed by the rules of international law.

But we have seen that later cases, though they admit that the law administered by the court is derived from foreign sources, emphasize its essentially English character.[1]

One of his most learned decisions is *The King v. Forty-nine Casks of Brandy*,[2] in which he gave an elaborate historical survey of the law as to flotsam, jetsam, and *wreccum maris*,[3] as to the rights of the Admiralty to these droits, and as to the rights of lords of manors to whom these franchizes had been granted. The decision of this case involved a knowledge of Admiralty law from the Middle Ages to modern times. But some of the cases which came before Nicholl involved very modern problems. In the case of *The Perth*[4] he laid down the rule that steamships were obliged to take the utmost care not to damage sailing ships. He said :[5]

Respecting steamers generally, they are a new species of vessel, and call forth new rules and considerations ; they are of vast power, liable to inflict great injury and particularly dangerous to coasters—if not most carefully managed ; yet they may, at the same time, with due vigilance easily avoid doing damage, for they are much under command, both by altering the helm, and by stopping the engines . . . The owners of sailing vessels have, I think, a right to expect that steamers will take every possible precaution.

---

[1] Vol. i 559. [2] (1836) 3 Hagg. Adm. 257.
[3] For the meaning of these terms see vol. i 560 n. 3, and for Admiralty droits and the history of the title to them see ibid 559-561.
[4] (1838) 3 Hagg. Adm. 414. [5] At pp. 415-416.

French Laurence[1] (1757-1809) was educated at Winchester School, and Corpus Christi College, Oxford. He was admitted a member of Doctors' Commons in 1788. He was a great admirer of Burke, who made him his literary executor ; and, having helped him in preparing the case against Warren Hastings, he was retained as one of the counsel for the managers of the impeachment. He soon acquired a leading practice as a civilian, and in 1796 he was appointed regius professor of civil law at Oxford. In the same year he became a member of Parliament. He opposed the Act of Union with Ireland, and helped to frame the articles of impeachment against Melville. Laurence was a very learned and industrious lawyer and a recognized authority on international law. He had also some literary ability and was not without wit—as his contributions to *The Rolliad* show.[2] But though his learning ensured his success as an advocate, he lacked the power of using it effectively in the House of Commons. A speech made by him, said Brougham,[3] was

> sure to contain materials not for one, but for half a dozen speeches ; and a person might with great advantage listen to it, in order to use those materials, in part, afterwards, as indeed many did both in Parliament and at the bar. . . . But whoever did so, was sure to hear a vast deal that was useless, and could serve no purpose, but to perplex and fatigue ; and he was equally sure to hear the immaterial points treated with as much vehemence, and as minutely dwelt upon, as the great and commanding branch of the subject.

These defects which would have been fatal to his success at the common law bar, were not felt in the courts at Doctors' Commons. There his learning, his industry, and his power of combating his opponents' arguments ensured his success ; and, as Brougham said, these qualities enabled him to assist his political associates in Parliament.[4]

Stephen Lushington[5] (1782-1873) had made his name as one of the leading civilians before the end of this period. He had distinguished himself as one of the counsel for Queen Caroline, who appointed him as one of her executors, and in 1828 he had succeeded Robinson as judge of the consistory court of London. In Parliament he supported all liberal measures. But his career as a lawyer and a judge belongs to the following period, and I shall deal with it in the next chapter.

The law administered by the civilians in their courts at Doctors' Commons was as yet but little affected by the new social,

[1] D.N.B. ; Brougham, Historical Sketches ii 81-87.
[2] Brougham, op. cit. 81, that he " united the indefatigable labour of a Dutch commentator with the alternative playfulness and sharpness of a Parisian wit,"
[3] Ibid 82-83.   [4] Ibid 84-86.   [5] D.N.B.

political and economic ideas. The principal change as compared with the preceding period, is the greater precision and elaboration of its rules, which followed upon the new practice of reporting the decisions of the Ecclesiastical and Admiralty courts.[1] But otherwise, with one great exception, it was developed smoothly and continuously along the old lines. The one great exception was the creation of the system of prize law by Stowell.[2] But both the legislation of this period on matters falling within the sphere of the civilian's practice,[3] and still more the proposal made for further reforms,[4] foreshadowed considerable changes. The fact that the relations between the court of Admiralty and the ecclesiastical courts on the one hand, and the courts of law and equity had been settled, with the result that the old jealousy and hostility between them had ceased to exist,[5] created conditions which made statutory reforms in these relations possible. A settlement on more logical and convenient lines of the relation of the jurisdiction of the court of Admiralty to the common law courts became possible ; and that settlement was affected in the following period. We have seen that much of the literature on matters falling within the sphere of the jurisdiction of the ecclesiastical courts, and some of the literature dealing with other branches of the civilians' practice, emanated, not from the civilians, but from English lawyers ;[6] that proposals for statutory changes in the law as to marriage and divorce had been made ;[7] that the law as to the making of wills was in urgent need of reform ;[8] and that the criminal jurisdiction of the ecclesiastical courts was both ineffective and unpopular.[9] These facts foreshadow changes in the law which will diminish drastically the jurisdiction of the ecclesiastical courts, and the sphere of the civilian's practice, and add that jurisdiction to the sphere of the English lawyers. "The enormous profession of the common lawyers," to use Gibbon's phrase,[10] showed signs of entirely overwhelming the civilians. We shall see in the next chapter that this development took place in the following period.

By the year 1832 the age of reform had begun. The new conditions brought about by the industrial revolution had given birth to many changes in political, social, and economic ideas, and to a demand for changes in the law to adapt it to these new conditions and ideas. A considerable number of statutes had already been passed to effect these necessary changes ; and the manner in which the lawyers were assimilating them

---

[1] Vol. xii 105-107.   [2] Above 678-680.   [3] Above 417, 418, 421-423.
[4] Above 268, 269, 297, 298, 304, 307.   [5] Vol. xii 695-701 ; above 555.
[6] Above 433, 490.   [7] Above 268-269, 421-423.   [8] Above 580.
[9] Vol. i 620-621 ; above 269.
[10] See the passage from Gibbon's Autobiography cited vol. xii 605.

into the body of the English legal system showed that they possessed a capacity to adapt old principles and rules to new conditions, which will be vitally important to that system in the following period of still more extensive statutory changes in, and additions to, the law. In fact the possession of this capacity was of the first importance both to English law and to the English state. To the law, because it meant that its continuity as a logical system of interconnected principles and rules will be preserved. To the state, because it meant that this system, by reason of its retention of these characteristics of continuity and logic, will be able to exert a steadying influence which will enable necessary reforms to be carried out without the risk of disturbances to its peace, and thus enable the constitution to function regularly in the new political conditions created by the Reform Act. The changes made in the law from 1832 to the passing of the Judicature Act in 1875, and the development of the principles of English law by the lawyers in this period of reform, is the subject of the next chapter.

LIST OF BOOKS AND PERIODICALS

ADAMS, JOHN
A Treatise on the Principles and Practices of the Action of Ejectment, and the resulting action for mesne profits (1812), p. 474.

ADDAMS
Reports of cases in the ecclesiastical courts with his Preface, p. 425.

ADDINGTON
Penal Statutes and Courts and Notes on the Poor Laws, p. 449.

ADOLPHUS
The Eclogue entitled " the Circuiteer ", p. 438.

ALDERSON, C.
Selection from the Charges and other detached papers of Baron Alderson, with an introductory notice of his life, pp. 426, 435, 436.

ALLEN
The Royal Prerogative in England, pp. 445, 497.

ALLEN, C. K.
The Young Bentham, L.Q.R., xliv, 506, p. 63.

AMOS, A. and FERRAND, J.
A Treatise on the Law of Fixtures, and other property partaking both of a real and personal nature (1827), p. 475.

AMULREE, Lord
Industrial Arbitration, pp. 336, 337, 339.

ANNUAL REGISTER, p. 440.

ANSON, Sir W.
The Crown (4th ed.), p. 216.
Statutes, p. 493.

ANSTEY, JOHN
The Pleader's Guide, A Didactic Poem in Two Books, containing the conduct of a Suit at Law, with the arguments of Councellor Bore'em in an action betwixt John-a-Gull and John-a-Gudgeon, for Assault and Battery at a late-contested election. By the late John Garchilton, Esq., special pleader and barrister-at-law (1796, 2nd ed. 1804), pp. 450, 460, 471.

ANTI-JACOBIN (anon.), p..166

ARABIN, ST. JULIEN, WILLIAM
Arabiniana, collected by H. B. C. (H. Blencowe Churchill), pp. 569, 570.

ARCHBOLD, J. F.
The Law of Nisi Prius : comprising the Declaration and other pleadings in Personal Actions and the evidence necessary to support them (1803), p. 460.
The Law and Practice in Bankruptcy as founded on the recent Statute, with Forms (1826), p. 454.
Pleading and Evidence in criminal cases with the Statutes, Precedents, Indictments, etc., and the Evidence necessary to support them (1822, 28th ed. 1931), p. 464.
The Practice of the Court of King's Bench in Personal Actions and Ejectments, including the practice of the Courts of Common Pleas and Exchequer (1891) (later editions by Chitty), p. 454.
The Practice of the Court of Quarter Sessions, and its original appellate, and criminal jurisdiction (1836, 6th ed. 1908), p. 465.
The Practice of the Crown Office (1844), p. 465.

ARNDT
Bentham on Administrative Jurisdiction, Journal of Comparative Legislation, xxi, 198-204, p. 92.

ASHBURNER
Equity (2nd ed.), pp. 635, 637.

ASHLEY, H.
The Doctrine and Practice of Attachment in the Mayor's Court, London
(1819), p. 457.
ASPINALL, A.
Lord Brougham and the Whig Party, pp. 184, 195, 198, 642.
Letters of George IV, with Webster's Introduction, pp. 218, 220, 222.
ATKINSON, C. M.
Jeremy Bentham, pp. 43, 51, 54, 56.
ATLAY
The Victorian Chancellors, pp. 195, 196, 197, 214, 215, 218, 219, 220, 226,
232, 241, 245, 438, 546, 639, 640, 641, 642, 643, 644, 646, 647, 648, 651,
652, 653, 655, 656.
BACON, FRANCIS, Lord VERULAM
Works, Spedding's ed., p. 96.
Abridgement, pp. 443, 474, 476.
BAGEHOT, W.
Biographical Studies, pp. 128, 195, 197, 198, 199, 223, 225.
Essay on Parlamentary Reform, pp. 256, 258.
Literary Studies (Silver Library ed.), pp. 36, 128, 138, 143, 606, 607.
Lombard Street, pp. 372, 373, 374, 375.
BALLOW, H.
A Treatise of Equity, Foblanque's ed.   Pub. 1737, p. 577.
BARNES, D. G.
A History of the English Corn Laws, pp. 353, 354, 355, 356, 357, 358.
BARNES, R.
The General Orders of the High Court of Chancery, from the year 1600 to
the present time, collated with the Registrar's Book, p. 576.
The Elements of Pleas in Equity, with Precedents of such Pleas (1818), p. 576.
An Enquiry into Equity Practice and the Law of Real Property with a view
to Legislative Revision (1823), p. 295.
BARTON, C.
A Historical Treatise of a Suit in Equity, p. 468.
Elements of Conveyancing with cursory remarks upon the study of that
Science, p. 468.
Original Precedents in Conveyancing, p. 469.
BEAWES
Lex Mercatoria, p. 459.
BEER, M.
History of British Socialism, pp. 28, 40.
BELDAM, J.
A Summary of the Laws peculiarly affecting Protestant Dissenters (1827),
p. 446.
BENTHAM, JEREMY
The Analysis of the Influence of Natural Religion on the Temporal Happiness
of Mankind, p. 117.
Anarchical Fallacies ; being an examination of the Declaration of Rights
issued during the French Revolution.   Works ii 488-534, pp. 22, 56, 68,
69.
Auto-Icon, or farther uses of the Dead to the Living, pp. 61, 67.
Book of Fallacies.   (Edited by Bingham with the help of James Mill and
Place.)   Works ii 375-487, pp. 65, 68, 69, 124, 439.
Catechism of Parliamentary Reform, p. 58.
Chrestomathia.   Edited by Southwood Smith.   Works viii 1-191, pp. 58,
66, 113, 114.
Church of Englandism and its Catechism examined (1818), pp. 50, 116.
Codification Proposal (1822).   Works iv 535-594, pp. 52, 107.
Collected Works—The Works of Jeremy Bentham, xi vols.   Published
under Superintendence of his Executor, John Bowring, with Introduction
of J. H. Burton, pp. 67, 114, 595, 615.
A Comment on the Commentaries, being a critical examination of the
Introduction to Sir William Blackstone's Commentaries on the Laws of
England (ed. by C. W. Everett with his Introduction. Pub. Oxford, 1928),
pp. 43, 46, 47, 59.

Commentary on Mr. Humphrey's Real Property Code. Works v 387-416, pp. 59, 81, 295.

Constitutional Code (ed. by R. Doane). Works ix 1-662, pp. 58, 88-95, 101, 106.

Daemon of Chicane. Works vii 219 n., p. 45.

Defence of Usury (London, 1787), pp. 29, 43, 49, 110.

De l'Organization judiciaire et de la Codification. Dumont's ed., pub. 1828, p. 64.

Deontology. See Works, Burton's Introd., 19 n., p. 67.

Draught of a New Code for the Organization of Judicial Establishment in France. Works iv 285-406, pp. 51, 105, 106.

The Elements of the Art of Packing as applied to special Juries, particularly in case of Libel Law (1810). Works v 61-186, pp. 50, 58, 99.

Emancipate your Colonies, tract Bentham addressed in 1793 to the French National Convention. Works iv 407-418, pp. 29, 106.

Equity Dispatch Court Bill. Works iii 319-431, p. 99.

Equity Dispatch Court Proposal. Works iii 297-317, pp. 58, 99.

Essay on Language. Works viii 294-338, p. 115.

Essay on Logic. Works viii 213-293, pp. 58, 114, 115.

Essay on Political Tactics. Works ii 299-373, pp. 51, 56, 94, 105.

Essay on Promulgation of Laws, p. 97.

A Fragment on Government (edited by F. C. Montague with his Introduction, Oxford Clarendon Press, 1891). Works i 221-295, pp. 43, 48, 50, 59, 66, 68, 79, 581.

A Fragment of Ontology. Works viii 192-211, p. 115.

Fragment on Universal Grammar. Works viii 339-357, p. 115.

A General View of a Complete Code of Laws. Works iii 155-210, pp. 59, 68, 72, 73, 96, 97.

The Influence of Time and Place in Matters of Legislation. Works i 171-194, pp. 52, 53, 64, 68, 76, 77.

Introduction to the Principles of Morals and Legislation. Works i 1 ff., pp. 49, 64, 68, 73.

An Introductory view of the Rationale of Evidence (ed. by James Mill). Works vi 1-187, pp. 66, 83, 84, 102.

Jeremy Bentham to his Fellow Citizens of France on Houses of Peers and Senates. Works iv 419-450, p. 107.

Justice and Codification Petitions. Works v 436-548, p. 83.

Leading Principles of a Constitutional Code for any State. Works ii 267-274, p. 95.

The Levelling System, appendix to Bentham's Civil Code. Works i 358-364, pp. 74, 81, 104.

The Limits of Jurisprudence Defined (ed. by C. W. Everett, 1945), p. 68.

Lord Brougham Displayed. Works v 549-610, p. 103.

Manual of Political Economy. Works iii 31-84, pp. 29, 34, 36, 111.

MSS. of Bentham (in custody of University College, London ; reported, catalogued and indexed by Thomas Whittaker, see p. 66), pp. 46, 51, 56, 62, 63, 64, 65, 66, 67, 115, 116.

Nomography or the Art of Inditing Laws. Works iii 231-283, p. 97.

Not Paul but Jesus (put together by F. Place in 1817, ed. 1823), pp. 66, 116.

Observations on the Poor Bill. Works viii 440-461, p. 101.

Observations on the Restrictive and Prohibiting Commercial System. Works iii 85-103, p. 112.

Official Aptitude Maximized ; Expense Minimized. Works v 263-386, p. 95.

Outline of a Plan of a General Register of Real Property. Works i 417-435, p. 82.

Pannomial Fragments. Works iii 211-230, pp. 35, 96, 97.

A Plan for saving all trouble and expense in the transfer of stock and for enabling the proprietors to receive their dividends without powers of attorney, or attendance at the Bank of England by the conversion of stock into note annuities. Works iii 105-153, p. 112.

Panopticon Correspondence. Works ii 1-188, p. 54.

BLANSHARD, W.
Statutes of Limitations (1825), p. 492.
BLAYNEY, F.
A Practical Treatise on Life Annuities (1817), p. 491.
BLUNT, J. E.
A History of the Establishment and Residence of the Jews in England with
an Enquiry into their Civil Disabilities (1830), p. 498.
BOSWELL, J.
Life of Samuel Johnson, p. 670.
BOWRING, Sir JOHN
The Collected Works of Jeremy Bentham published under the superinten-
dence of his executor, J. Bowring, 11 vols., 1938-43, Edinburgh, p. 67.
Life of Jeremy Bentham in vols. x and xi of Bentham's Works, pp. 43, 67.
BRIDGEMAN, R. W.
Digest (1798 and 1803), p. 443.
BRODERICK and BINGHAM
Reports, p. 385.
BROUGHAM, HENRY, Lord
Works, 11 vols., London 1855-1861 (at the end of this collected edition of
Brougham's Works there is a list of 113 of his publications), p. 655.
Colonial Policy of the European Powers, p. 195.
Historical Sketches of Statesmen and Philosophers in the time of George
III, pp. 274, 449, 505, 506, 507, 519, 520, 535, 536, 538, 539, 540, 584,
586, 590, 591, 595, 612, 613, 614, 622, 623, 624, 655, 658, 659, 668, 671,
675, 697.
Speeches of Lord Brougham with Historical Introductions (1838), pp. 42,
128, 277, 283, 296, 297, 298, 299, 300, 301, 302, 303, 304, 305, 306.
Brougham's translation of Demosthenes on The Crown, p. 653.
BROWNE, Sir THOMAS
Hydriotaphia : Urn Burial, 1658, p. 687.
BRYCE, Lord
Modern Democracies, p. 24.
BUCKLE, H. T.
History of Civilization of England, p. 125.
BUCKLE, MONYPENNY and BUCKLE
Life of Disraeli (rev. ed.), p. 147.
BUCKLEY, W.
The Jurisdiction and Practice of the Marshalsea and Palace Courts, with
Tables of Costs and Charges and an Appendix containing Statutes, letters
patent, rules of court, etc. (1827), p. 457.
BURKE, E.
Appeal from the New to the Old Whigs (Bohn's ed.), p. 258.
Reflections on the Revolution in France, pp. 7, 13, 14, 23, 156, 341.
Works, Bohn's ed., p. 118.
BURN
Justices of the Peace, pp. 427, 446.
BURNEY, FANNY
Diary, pp. 500, 501.
BURNS, J. J.
A Practical Treatise or Compendium of the Law of Marine Insurance (1801),
p. 484.
BURTON, JOHN HILL
General Preface and Introduction to the study of Bentham's Works
(Bowring's ed, 1843), pp. 67, 114, 132.
BUTLER, C.
Reminiscences, pp. 621, 624.
BUTLER, J. R. M.
The Passing of the Great Reform Bill, pp. 240, 241, 242, 243, 244, 245, 246,
249, 250.
BYLES, J. B.
Tract on the Sophisms of Free Trade (1849), p. 482.
A Treatise on the Laws of Bills of Exchange, Promissory Notes, Bank
Notes, and Cheques (20th ed., 1939), p. 482.
Usury Laws, p. 483.

A Treatise on the Game Laws and on Fisheries, 1812, p. 489.

Treatise on Pleading and Parties to Actions, with second and third volumes containing Modern Precedents of Pleading, and Practical Notes, 1808 (7th ed., 1844), p. 459.

Statutes of Practical Utility, pp. 442, 459.

CHITTY, JOSEPH, Junior

A Practical Treatise on the Law of Contracts not under seal, and upon the usual defences to actions thereon, 1826 (20th ed., 1948), pp. 483, 484.

On the Prerogative, pp. 445, 458.

CHRISTIAN, E.

The Origin, Progress and Present Practice of the Bankrupt Law both in England and Ireland (1812-14), pp. 480, 481.

Practical Instruction for serving out and prosecuting a commission of Bankruptcy with the best modern precedents and a Digest of supplementary cases, 1816 (2nd ed., 1820), p. 481.

A Treatise on the Game Laws : . . ., 1817, pp. 489, 490.

CHURCH, P. W.

The Oxford Movement, p. 147.

CLANCY, J.

Husband and Wife, 1814 (3rd ed., 1827), p. 490.

CLAPHAM, Dr.

An Economic History of Modern Britain, pp. 27, 38, 90, 312, 313, 329, 330, 332, 334, 335, 337, 338, 342, 343, 344, 353, 358, 359, 360, 361, 362, 364, 372, 373, 374, 376.

CLAPHAM, Rev. SAMUEL

A Collection of the several points of Session Law, alphabetically arranged, contained in Burn and Williams on the office of a justice, Blackstone's Commentaries, East and Hawkins on Common Law, Addington's Penal Statutes and Courts and Notes on the Poor Laws (1818), p. 449.

CLOKIE, H. M. and ROBINSON, J. W.

On Royal Commissions of Inquiry, pp. 270, 271, 272, 273.

COBBETT

Parliamentary Debates, pp. 176, 178, 179, 180, 187, 189, 190, 191, 192, 658.

COKE, Sir E.

Institutes of the Laws of England, p. 560.

Reports, p. 621.

COLEBROOK, H. T.

A Treatise on Obligations and Contracts (1818), p. 284.

COLERIDGE, S. T.

Table Talk, pp. 123, 153, 164, 172, 227, 256.

COLLYER, J.

A Practical Treatise on the Law of Partnership with an Appendix of Forms, 1832 (2nd ed., 1840), p. 485.

COMYN, R. B.

A Treatise on the Law of Usury (1817), p. 494.

COMYN, S.

The Law of Contracts and Promises upon various subjects and with particular persons as settled in the Action of Assumption, 1807 (2nd ed., 1824), p. 384.

COMYNS

Digest, p. 443.

CONROY

Custodiam Reports, or a Collection of Cases relative to outlawries . . . pub. 1795, p. 433.

CONWAY

Life of Paine, pp. 24, 25.

COOPER, C. P.

An Account of the most important Public Records of Great Britain and the Publications of the Record Commissions, together with other miscellaneous, historical and antiquarian information. Compiled from various printed books and manuscripts (1828), pp. 490, 498.

A Brief Account of some of the most important proceedings in Parliament relative to the defects in the administration of justice in the Court of

HANDS, W.
The Modern Practice of Levying Fines and Suffering Recoveries in the Court of Common Pleas at Westminster with an Appendix of select precedents (1800), p. 470.
A Selection of Rules occurring in the Prosecution and Defence of Personal Actions in the Court of King's Bench ; with notes on each Rule illustrative of the Practice of the Court, p. 457.
The Solicitor's Assistant in the Court of Chancery, 1809, p. 576.

HANSARD
Parliamentary History of England, pp. 34, 35, 36, 156, 157, 161, 162, 163, 167, 169, 172, 173, 230, 232, 236, 237, 238, 244, 247, 250, 251, 253, 254, 255, 256, 257, 258, 260, 264, 265, 266, 267, 268, 269, 277, 279, 281, 283, 248, 285, 286, 288, 291, 307, 321, 410, 556, 557, 605, 607, 608, 610, 618, 645, 657, 658, 691.

HANWORTH
Life of Chief Baron Pollock, pp. 198, 404, 426, 436.

HARRISON, S. B.
Evidence Forming a title of the Code of Legal Proceedings according to the plan proposed by Crofton Uniacke, Esq. (1825), p. 467.

HAWKINS
Reminiscences, p. 435.

HAWKINS, EAST and HAWKINS
Common Law, p. 449.

HAYES, W.
A Popular View of the Law of Real Property with an application of its principles to the important measure of a General Register, showing what changes in the system a Register is calculated to produce (1831), p. 478.

HELVETIUS
De l'Esprit, pp. 41, 42.

HERBERT, W.
Antiquities of the Inns of Court of Chancery ; containing historical and descriptive sketches relative to their original foundation, customs, ceremonies, buildings, government, etc. With a concise History of the English Law (1804), p. 498.

HEYTHUSEN, Van, F. M.
An Essay upon Marine Evidence with Courts of Law and Equity . . . (1819), p. 486.
Rudiments of the Laws of England ; . . ., 1812 (2nd ed., 1826), p. 495.

HEYWOOD, S.
A Digest of the Law respecting County Electors (1790, 2nd ed., 1812), p. 446.
A Digest of so much of the Law respecting Borough Elections as concerns Cities and Boroughs in general (1797), p. 446.

HIGHMAN, A.
A succinct View of the History of Mortmain and Statutes relative to Charitable Uses ; . . . (1789, 2nd ed. 1809), pp. 476, 477.

HIGHMAN H.
A Treatise on the Law of Idiocy and Lunacy, to which is subjoined an Appendix containing the practice of the Court of Chancery on this subject, and some useful practical forms (1807), p. 492.

HOLDSWORTH, Sir W. S.
Charles Dickens as a Legal Historian, pp. 270, 319.
Historical Introduction to the Land Law, p. 561.
Some Makers of English Law, p. 688.
Sources and Literature of English Law, p. 577.

HOLLAND, Lord
Memoirs of the Whig Party, p. 195.

HOLLAND, Sir R. E.
Essay on Bentham in the Encyclopædia Britannica, p. 62.

HOLT, F. L.
The Law of Libel : in which is contained a general history of this law in the ancient codex and successive alterations in the Law of England. Comprehending a Digest of all the leading cases upon Libels from the earliest to the present time, pp. 481, 488, 489.

MANSEL, G. B.
A Treatise on the Law and Practice of Demurrer to Pleadings and Evidence of Bills of Exceptions ; . . . (1828), p. 458.

MANSON, E.
The Builders of our Law (2nd ed.), pp. 434, 435, 549, 566.

MARRIOT, W.
Law Dictionary, pub. 1798, p. 443.

MARSDEN
Law and Custom of the Sea, p. 679.

MARSHALL, S.
A Treatise on the Law of Insurance in four Books (pub. 1802, 5th ed. 1865), p. 484.

MARTIN, F.
History of Lloyd's, pp. 331, 332, 378.

MARTINEAU
History of the Peace, pp. 201, 205.

MATHEW, T.
Bardell v. Pickwick, L.Q.R., xxxiv, p. 569.

MATHEWS, J. H.
A Treatise on the Law of Portions and Provisions for children in the nature of portions (1829), p. 577.
A Treatise on the Law of Arbitration with an Appendix of Precedents, (1825).
A Treatise on the Laws of Literary Property, comprising the Statutes and Cases relating to books, manuscripts, lectures, dramatic and musical compositions ; engravings, sculpture, maps, etc. Including the piracy and transfer of copyright ; with an Historical View, and disquisitions on the principles and effects of the Law (1828), p. 488.
A Treatise on the Principles of the Usury Laws ; with Disquisitions on the Arguments adduced against them by Mr. Bentham and other Writers, and a Review of the Authorities in their favour (1824), pp. 494, 495.

MAXWELL, SWEET and MAXWELL, see Sweet.

MAY, Sir T. Erskine
Constitutional History of England, p. 248.

MERRIFIELD, J.
The Law of Attornies, with Practical Directions in Actions and Proceedings by and against them, and for the taxation and recovery of Costs . . . (1824), p. 487.

MELBOURNE, Lord
Melbourne Papers, pp. 641, 642, 643.

MILL, JAMES
Analysis of the Phenomena of the Human Mind, p. 141.
Commerce Defended (1807), p. 179.
An Essay on Government (Barker's ed.), pp. 35, 105, 138, 139, 142.
Elements of Political Economy, p. 140.
History of India, pp. 135, 136.

MILL, J. S.
Autobiography, pp. 36, 65, 117, 135, 136, 137, 138, 142, 143, 144, 258, 439, Dissertations and Discussions, pp. 61, 63, 67, 115, 119, 120, 122, 123, 126, 127, 129, 130, 131, 143, 148, 154.
Representative Government, p. 258.

MILLER, J.
The Civil Law of England, p. 292.
An Enquiry into the present State of the Statute and Criminal Law, p. 284.

MIRROR OF JUSTICES, p. 44.

MITFORD
A Treatise of Pleading on the Equity Side of the High Court of Chancery (published by G. Cooper in 1809), pp. 575, 576.

MITCHELL, A. A.
Essay on Bentham in Jurid. Rev. xxix, p. 43.

MONYPENNY and BUCKLE
Life of Disraeli (Rev. ed.), p. 147.

PALEY, W.
Summary Convictions (1814), p. 463.
A Treatise of the Law of Principal and Agent ; . . . (1811, 3rd ed., 1833), pp. 485, 486.

PALEY, WILLIAM
Moral and Political Philosophy, p. 49.

PALMER, J.
The Practice of the House of Lords on appeals, writs of error, and claims of peerage with a compendious account of dignities, to which is prefixed an introductory historical essay on the appellate jurisdiction, p. 456.

PARK, J. J.
A Contra-Project to the Humphreysian Code, and to the projects of re-action by Messrs. Hammond, Uniacke and Twiss (1828), p. 295.
The Dogmas of the Constitution (1832), p. 444.
A Lecture delivered at King's College, London, on April 6, 1832, p. 478.
System of Registration and Conveyancing, p. 478.
A Treatise of the Law of Dower ; particularly with a view to the modern practice of conveyancing, pp. 295, 474.

PARKER, C. S.
Sir Robert Peel, pp. 192, 203, 228, 230, 232.

PARKES, J.
A History of the Court of Chancery ; with Practical Remarks on the recent Commission, report and evidence and on the means of improving the administration of justice in the English courts of equity (1828), p. 293.

PARLIAMENTARY PAPERS, pp. 272, 273, 380, 381, 556.

PARTRIDGE, R. C. B.
History of the Legal Deposit of Books, p. 409.

PHILANTHROPIST, p. 135.

PLATT, T.
A Practical Treatise on the Law of Covenants (1829), p. 473.

PLOWDEN, E.
Commentaries, p. 561.

PETERSDORFF, C.
A Practical and Elementary Abridgment of the Cases argued and determined in the Courts of King's Bench, Common Pleas, Exchequer and at Nisi Prius ; and of the Rules of Court from 1660 (1825, London), p. 444.

POLITICAL REGISTER, pp. 180, 201, 240.

POLITICAL SCIENCE QUARTERLY, pp. 43, 44, 48, 53.

POLLOCK, Sir F.
Digest of the Law of Partnership, p. 485.
Essays in the Law, p. 569.
History of the Science of Politics, p. 131.
Personal Remembrances, pp. 291, 656.
Principles of the Law of Contract (13th ed.), p. 654.
Torts (14th ed.), pp. 512, 526, 544, 549, 553.

POLLOCK, Sir F. and MAITLAND, F. W.
The History of English Law before the Time of Edward I (1898), p. 689.

PORRITT
The Unreformed House of Commons, p. 256.

POTHIER
A Treatise of the Obligations or Contracts Translation from the French by W. D. Evans (1806), pp. 466, 467, 513.

PRICE, R.
The Love of our Country. Sermon at the Meeting House, Old Jewry, preached by R. Price, p. 13.

POUND, R.
Bentham's The Limits of Jurisprudence Defined ; reviewed by Roscoe Pound. Texas Law Review, June 1945, p. 68.

PUTNAM, B. H.
Proceedings before the Justices of the Peace in the fourteenth and fifteenth centuries (Ames Foundation), pp. 238, 403.

Rousseau, J. J.
Contrat Social, p. 12.
Russell, W. O.
Treatise on Felonies and Misdemeanours (1819, 10th ed., 1951), p. 464.
Russell and Hughes
Reports, p. 426.
Ryland, *see* Dowling and Ryland.
Salmond
Law of Torts (10th ed., edited by Dr. Stallybrass), pp. 526, 553.
Sankey, Viscount
Lord Stowell, p. 668.
Saunders, J. S.
The Law of Pleading and Evidence in Civil Actions, arranged alphabetically with Practical Forms : and the Pleading and Evidence to support them (1828), p. 468.
Say, J. B.
Traité d'Economie Politique (1803), p. 30.
Scarlett, P. C. (Lord Abinger)
Memoirs of the Life of Lord Abinger, pp. 50, 158, 256, 275, 278, 501, 504, 507, 518, 520, 530, 537, 567, 568, 584, 589, 590, 591, 592, 593, 663.
Scott, Sir Walter
Waverley Novels, pp. 438, 686.
Scriven, J.
A Treatise on Copyholds, Customary Freeholds and Ancient Demesne Tenure, with the jurisdiction of Courts Baron and Courts Leet (1816, 2nd ed., 1821-23, 7th ed., 1896), pp. 472, 473.
Selborne, Lord
Memorials Family and Personal, pp. 67, 436, 667.
Selwyn
Abridgment of the Laws of Nisi Prius, p. 438.
Seton, H.
Forms of Decrees in Equity and of Orders connected therewith with Practical Notes (1830, 7th ed., 1912), p. 576.
Shepherd,
England's Balme, p. 306.
Smith, A.
The Wealth of Nations (Cannan's ed.), pp. 4, 28, 29, 37, 322, 356, 372, 373.
Smith, S.
Noodle's Oration, pp. 69, 124.
Works (ed. 1869), pp. 69, 526.
Southey
Colloquies on Society, p. 145.
Wat Tyler, p. 637.
Spedding
Letters and Life of Bacon, p. 150.
Spelman
De Sepultura, p. 687.
Spence, G.
An Enquiry into the Origin of the Laws and Political Institutions of Modern Europe, particularly those of England (1826), pp. 496, 497.
The Equitable Jurisdiction of the Court of Chancery (1849), pp. 497, 498.
Spence, T.
The Real Rights of Man (1775), p. 37.
Starkie, T.
A Treatise on Criminal Pleading with Precedents of Indictments, Special Pleas, etc. (1814), p. 465.
A Treatise on the Law of Slander and Libel : including the Pleading and Evidence, civil and commercial, with Forms and Precedents : also Malicious Prosecutions, Contempt of Court, etc. (1813, 2nd ed., 1830 and later editions in 1869, 1876, 1897, 1908), p. 488.

THURSFIELD, J. R.
Peel, pp. 223, 224, 225, 227, 229.

TIDD, W.
The Act of Uniformity of Process in Personal Actions (1833), p. 454.
Law of Costs in Civil Actions (1792), p. 453.
Practical Forms and Entries of Proceedings in the Courts of King's Bench, Common Pleas, and Exchequer of Pleas (1799), p. 453.
Practice, Forms of Proceedings in Replevin and Ejectment (1804), pp. 453, 454, 571.
The Practice of The Court of King's Bench in Personal Actions with References to Cases of Practice in the Court of Common Pleas (pub. 1790-1794-1798, 9th ed., 1828), pp. 450, 452, 453, 454, 571.

TIMES, THE, pp. 99, 199, 293, 640, 642, 647, 653.

TOLLER, Sir S.
The Law of Executors and Administrators (1800), p. 489.

TOWNSEND
Lives of Twelve Eminent Judges, pp. 500, 501, 502, 503, 504, 516, 517, 519, 520, 527, 528, 535, 536, 537, 538, 539, 540, 580, 582, 590, 592, 593, 595, 597, 599, 602, 604, 605, 606, 607, 611, 612, 613, 626, 627, 656, 658, 659, 666, 668, 669, 671, 673, 675, 676, 677, 679.

TREATISE UPON THE LAW AND PROCEEDINGS IN CASES OF HIGH TREASON, etc. (ed., 1793) (anonymous), p. 466.

TREVELYAN
Life and Letters of Macaulay, pp. 195, 235.
Lord Grey of the Reform Bill, pp. 156, 160, 165, 167, 177, 186, 187, 196, 220, 228, 233, 241, 242, 244, 245, 246, 247, 250, 253, 646.

TWISS
Life of Eldon, pp. 102, 422, 595, 596, 597, 598, 599, 600, 601, 602, 603, 604, 605, 606, 607, 608, 609, 610, 611, 612, 613, 614, 615, 616, 617, 618, 619, 621, 622, 623, 663, 664, 665, 666.

UNDERHILL
Law relating to Private Trusts (10th ed.), p. 649.

VEEDER, Van VECHTEN
A century of English Judicature (in " Select Essays in Anglo-American Legal History "), pp. 435, 436, 439.

VEITCH
The Genesis of Parliamentary Reform, pp. 159, 160, 161, 162, 163, 172, 187.

VINER, C.
A General Abridgment of Law and Equity, alphabetically digested under Proper Titles, with Notes and References to the Whole. Second edition, 24 vols., 1791-1794, London, p. 443.
Supplement in 6 vols. by various authors entitled An Abridgement of the Modern Determinations in the Courts of Law and Equity (1799-1806), p. 443.

VINOGRADOFF, Sir P.
Outlines of Historical Jurisprudence (2 vols., Oxford, 1920-1922), p. 145.

WALLACE, J. W.
The Reporters, pp. 425, 427, 428, 430, 437, 438, 440.

WALLAS, G.
Life of Francis Place, pp. 7, 66, 112, 158, 180, 181, 187, 198, 205, 209, 211, 212, 345, 347, 346, 348, 349, 351.

WALPOLE, H.
Letters of Horace Walpole (Toynbee ed.), pp. 12, 119.

WALPOLE, S.
History of England, p. 264.

WARREN, S.
The Law Student (2nd ed.), p. 464.

WATKINS
Principles of Conveyancing, designed for the use of Students. With an Introduction on the Study of that Branch of Law (1800, 9th ed., 1845), pp. 469, 473.

WOOLER
Black Dwarf, p. 201.

WOOLRYCH, H. W.
Rights of Common (1824), p. 487.
A Practical Treatise on the Commercial and Mercantile Law of England (1819), p. 479.
A Treatise of the Law of Waters, and of Sewers ; including the law relating to rights in the sea, and rights in rivers, canals, dock companies, fisheries, mills, water courses, etc. (1830), p. 495.
A Practical Treatise on the Law of Window Lights with various other matters relating to the subject (1833), p. 495.

WRIGHT, Lord
Essay on Mistakes in Law, p. 513.

YOUNG, G. M.
Victorian England, pp. 25, 121, 138, 184, 185, 614.

INDEX OF NAMES

NAME INDEX

APPENDICES

APPENDIX I

BENTHAM, JEREMY

abuses in English Law, views and writings on, 45, 46, 47, 48, 58, 98-103, 131, and see, common law.
America, relations with and views on, 3, 4, 5, 6, 8, 12, 15, 21, 23, 24, 29, 32, 35, 36, 41, 42, 53, 107.
apprenticeship, criticism of the old laws of, 75.
" average man," Bentham's idea of, 76, 77, 123, 124.
Bar,
call to, 44.
Lincoln's Inn, keeping terms at, 44.
bencher of, 60.
no serious attempt to practise, 44, 45.
Benthamism, 5.
Benthamites, 135, 146, 294, 350.
Blackstone, attitude to, 59, 103.
attended his lectures, 44.
criticism of, 44, 47, 48, 59, 60.
Brougham, relations with, 42, 53, 60, 103, 128.
case law, see common law.
cat, Sir John Langborn, Bentham's cat, 62.
champerty, 110.
Chancery, the Court of,
practice at, 44, 45, 99, 574.
reform of, views on, 99, 100, 103, 574.
character of Bentham, 61, 62.
charity,
plan of a national charity company, 101.
chicanery in law,
early inspiration of his ideas as to, 45.
childhood, 43.
Chrestomatic School, plans of, and papers on, 58, 59, 66, 113, 114, 136.
Christianity, views on, 58, 113, 116, 117.·
Church of England, 58, 113, 116.
civil law, 73, 81.
classical authors and languages, view of, 113.
codes of law,
civil code, 73.
connection of, with the penal code, 73.
codification and drafting of statutes, 96, 97, 110, 131.
" Complete Code of Law "—Bentham's work on, 59, 68, 72, 73, 96, 97.
constitutional code, 88-94.

735

Eldon, Lord, Bentham's views on, 102, 103, 124, 165.
end of law, 35, 73, 74, 75.
   and see, law.
English law, criticism of, 45, 46, 47, 48, 58, 60, 79, 80, 82, 86, 87, 98-103, 119, 126-128, 131.
   exaggeration in his criticism, 126, 127.
   influence of Bentham on the development of, 4, 120, 121, 124, 155.
equality and inequality, views on, 23, 35.
equity, views on, 90, 100.
evidence, works on, 65, 66, 83-86.
family of Bentham, 43.
foreign contracts, various, 52, 53, 108-110.
foreign politics, writings on, 105-110.
France, connections with, 22, 50, 51, 52, 56-57, 105, 106.
French Revolution, 56, 57.
frugality banks, plans of, 101, 334.
   saving banks and, 334.
general characteristics of, as thinker and legal reformer, 117-130.
Gorgon, weekly paper subsidized by, 345.
government, views and works relative to problems of, 35, 48, 49, 56, 57, 59, 66, 79, 80, 88-95, 118, 125, 126.
governmental action, views on the proper sphere of, 29, 93, 111, 121.
guardian and ward, 75.
happiness, the greatest happiness principle, 35, 41, 57, 68, 69, 70, 71, 73, 78, 89, 91.
health minister, plan as to, 90.
Helvetius and Bentham, 46.
Historical School of Savigny, criticism of, 107, 118, 145.
history, views on, 80, 97, 118, 125.
House of Commons, views on, and plans as to, 93, 94.
   and see, constitution, constitutional reform.
House of Lords, views on, and plans as to, 89, 102, 125.
   and see, constitution, constitutional reform.
Indigence relief, minister, plans of, 90.
industrial combination, views on, 340, 341, 347, 350.
international law, views and works on,
   end of, 95.
   term " international law " invented by Bentham, 63, 96.
   works on, 95, 96.
   intolerance of Bentham, as to opinions of others, 102, 103.
judicature, views and works relative to, 51, 58, 64, 65, 66, 98-102.
   English system of, its criticism, 106.
   " Judge & Co."—Bentham's attack against, 116, 126.
   reform of, plans as to, 90, 91.
   and see, courts.
jury system,
   criticism of, 90, 91, 99, 134.
   quasi-jury, plans of, 91, 134.
justice, minister of, plans as to, 89, 93.
King, views on, 125.
laissez-faire, attitude to the doctrine of, 29, 32, 34, 110, 111, 122.
language, international, 117.
law and legislation, Bentham's theory of,
   civil law, 72, 73.
   code of law, scientific, based on the principle of utility, 52, 53, 58, 59, 76, 93, 96, 104, 124, 125, 131, 141.
   criminal law, 70, 71, 73, 82, 83.
   divine law, 80.
   division of law, 49.
   ends of law, 35, 73, 74, 75.
      objects of law, 52, 53, 73, 74.
   influence of time and place on law, 52, 53, 64, 76, 77, 110.
      physical and social environment of law, 52, 77.

APPENDIX II

BROUGHAM, HENRY, LORD,

APPENDIX III

ELDON, EARL OF (JOHN SCOTT)

APPENDIX VI

APPENDIX VII

STOWELL, LORD (SIR WILLIAM SCOTT)

APPENDIX VIII

TENTERDEN, LORD (CHARLES ABBOTT),

SUBJECT INDEX

ecclesiastical courts,
commissions on,
commission of 1815, on officials of the courts of justice, 272.
reports of, 1823, 1824, on official of ecclesiastical courts, 272, 273.
commission of 1830, to enquire into ecclesiastical courts, 273.
Consistory and Commissary Courts of the bishop of London, 423.
criminal jurisdiction of, 269, 423, 674, 698.
ineffective and unpopular, 269, 698.
Romilly's actions against, 269, 674.
defamation, abuses of actions for, in ecclesiastical courts, 269.
diocesan courts,
jurisdiction of, 691, 692.
divorce to be dealt with by ecclesiastical courts,
Phillimore's proposition as to, 268, 269.
excommunication abolished as part of the process of, 190, 269, 423, 674.
High Court of Delegates, abolished, 424.
inferior ecclesiastical courts, debate on, 1812, 269.
jurisdiction of, and of the common law and equity courts, 694.
boundaries between, and of the courts of law and equity, 694.
legislation on, 423, 424.
Peculiar, Court of, of the Archbishop of Canterbury, 423.
Prerogative court, 423.
process and procedure in, reforms of, 190, 269, 307, 423, 424.
methods of trying issues of fact, 304.
tithes, procedure in actions for, 269, 420, 423, 521.
reports of cases in, 432, 441, 678.
writ, *de excommunicato capiendo* superseded by the writ of *de contumace
capiendo*, 423.
ecclesiastical law, 418-424.
clergy, legislation as to, 418-421, 674.
judicial decisions on topics related to, 691, 692, 694.
livings, augmentation of, 419.
marriage and probate, legislation on, 421-423.
matrimonial causes, evidence in, 436.
pluralities, 420.
resignation bonds, validity of, 420, 421, 548.
judicial decisions relative to, 420, 421, 548.
legislation on, 421, 548.
simoniacal contracts, 420.
Stowell's judicial decisions, 685-687.
economic ideas,
classical political economy, 30, 33, 36, 107, 148, 212, 323-326, 364.
Adam Smith and his influence, 4, 8, 12, 15, 21, 28-36, 110, 111, 323.
criticism of, by Coleridge, 152, 153.
development of, after Adam Smith, 29, 30, 139, 323, 324, 325, 326, 338.
difficulties it encountered, 31, 32.
industry and commerce, influence of classical economic theories on the
law of, 226, 227, 239, 323, 324, 325, 326, 340, 347, 358.
Malthus' doctrine, 31, 32.
Mill's essay on political economy, 137.
Ricardo's doctrine, 30, 31, 33, 134.
interference, governmental, opposed by economists, and by philosophic
radicals, 33, 34, 140, 324, 325, 338, 339, 340, 341, 347, 352, 358.
philosophic radicals, economic views of, 139, 140.
physiocrats, 30.
Political Economy Club, 136.
" Saints," economic views of, 184.
socialistic ideas, 38, 39, 40, 99, 144.
and see, *laissez faire*, the doctrine of.
Edinburgh University, 135, 136, 195.
education,
all classes, education of, 112, 113.
Bell and Lancaster's educational methods, 112, 113, 136.

government,
   abolishment of, planned by Godwin and Hodgskin, 40.
   economic conditions, interference in, 33-35, 111, 118, 140, 324, 325, 338.
      Adam Smith's views on, 30, 31.
   Paine's views on, 19-21.
   reduction of the powers of, suggested by Mackintosh, 15.
   statutes relative to small reforms in, 215, 216.
   and see, constitution, local government, parliament, parliamentary reform.
graduates of Oxford, Cambridge and Dublin, see, legal profession.
Gray's Inn, 274.
Gresham College, 173.

Habeas Corpus, 161.
   common law courts judges authorized to issue writs of Habeas Corpus ad
      testificandum, 407.
   extension of the Habeas Corpus Act of 1679 in 1816, 217.
   Lord Chancellor's power to issue a writ of Habeas Corpus in a civil case, 633.
   suspension of the rights to a writ of Habeas Corpus, statutes as to, 162, 172,
      175, 203, 204, 604.
      Act of 1794, 162, 203.
         expiration of, 1801, 172.
      Act of 1817, 203, 204.
hackney coaches, legislation as to, 323.
Hampden Club, 187, 201.
happiness, the greatest happiness principle,
   Beccaria on, 41.
   Priestley on, 46.
   and see, Bentham, in Name Index.
hawkers, legislation on, 329.
hay trade, 329.
Heep, Uriah (Dickens, " David Copperfield "), 452, 453.
heriots, lord's rights to, 548.
high treason, see, treason.
highways and bridges,
   Egremont's book on, 448.
   legislation on, 316, 317, 448.
historical and romantic ideas after the French Revolution, 145 seqq.
historical school of Savigny, 107, 118, 145.
   J. J. Park and, 295.
history,
   Coleridge's views on, 149.
   and see, Bentham in Name Index.
history, legal, see, legal history.
Holland House, 185, 195, 282.
Holy Alliance, 52, 221.
Home Secretary, control of, over police appointments, 236, 237.
hops, law as to commerce in, 329.
House of Commons,
   history of, 445, 446.
   landed gentry, its influence on, 258.
   reforms, small, as to, 191.
   role of,
      changed by the Reform Act, 258.
      Park's views on, 445.
      " poise " or centre of the constitution, 258.
   sale of seats in, Curwen's Act, 191, 192.
   speaker of, legislation on, 237.
House of Lords,
   appeals to and jurisdiction of, literature on, 455, 456.
   arrears of appeals in, Eldon's move for a committee on, 1811, 263, 288
   criminal law, reform of, and the House of Lords, 279.
   decrease in the powers of, after 1875, 133.
   destruction of, feared by Tories, 1831, 7.